For all the
family, from G'Ma Betty
7-21-04

WEBSTER'S
SPANISH–ENGLISH
ENGLISH–SPANISH
DICTIONARY &
PHRASEBOOK

Other reference works from Random House Value Publishing:

WEBSTER'S NEW CENTURY DICTIONARY

WEBSTER'S COMPACT DICTIONARY

WEBSTER'S COMPACT THESAURUS

WEBSTER'S CONCISE ENCYCLOPEDIA

WEBSTER'S
SPANISH–ENGLISH
ENGLISH–SPANISH
DICTIONARY &
PHRASEBOOK

GRAMERCY BOOKS
NEW YORK

This 2002 edition is published by Gramercy Books™, an imprint of
Random House Value Publishing, Inc., 280 Park Avenue, New York, NY 10017,
by arrangement with Geddes & Grosset, Scotland, UK.

Gramercy Books™ and design are trademarks of Random House Value Publishing, Inc.

Printed and bound in Great Britain.

Random House
New York . Toronto . London . Sydney . Auckland
http://www.randomhouse.com/

A CIP catalog record for this title is available from the Library of Congress.

WEBSTER'S SPANISH–ENGLISH/ENGLISH–SPANISH DICTIONARY & PHRASEBOOK
ISBN: 0-517-21991-3

9 8 7 6 5 4 3 2 1

Contents

Spanish Verbs and English Irregular Verbs   481

List of Abbreviations

The following abbreviations are used throughout the dictionary.

	Abbreviation	Abreviaturas
abbrev	abbreviation	abreviatura
adj	adjective	adjectivo
adv	adverb	adverbio
art	article	artículo
auto	automobile	automóvil
aux	auxiliary	auxiliar
bot	botany	botánica
chem	chemistry	química
col	colloquial term	lengua familiar
com	commerce	comercio
compd	in compounds	usada en palabras compuestas
comput	computers	informática
conj	conjunction	conjunctión
excl	exclamation	exclamación
f	feminine noun	sustantrivo femenino
fig	figurative use	uso figurado
gr	grammar	gramática
interj	interjection	interjección
invar	invariable	invariable
law	law term	jurisprudencia
ling	linguistics	lingüística

	Abbreviation	**Abreviaturas**
m	masculine noun	sustantivo masculino
math	mathematics	matemáticas
med	medicine	medicina
mil	military term	lo militar
mus	music	música
n	noun	sustantivo
pej	pejorative	peyorativo
pl	plural	plural
pn	pronoun	pronombre
poet	poetical term	vocablo poético
pref	prefix	prefijo
prep	preposition	preposición
rad	radio	radio
rail	railway	ferrocarilero
theat	theater	teatro
tec	technology	téchnica, tecnologia
TV	television	televisión
vi	intransitive verb	verbo intransitivo
vr	reflexive verb	verbo reflexivo
vt	transitive verb	verbo transitivo

WEBSTER'S
SPANISH–ENGLISH
DICTIONARY

A

a *prep* to; in; at; according to; on; by; for; of.
abacería *f* grocery.
abacero *m* grocer.
ábaco *m* abacus.
abad *m* abbot.
abadejo *m* cod.
abadesa *f* abbess.
abadía *f* abbey.
abajo *adv* under; underneath; below; ~ **de** *prep* under, below.
abalanzarse *vr* to rush forward.
abalorio *m* glass bead.
abanderado *m* (*mil*) ensign; standard bearer.
abandonado/da *adj* derelict; abandoned; neglected.
abandonar *vt* to abandon; to leave; ~**se** *vr* ~ **a** to give oneself up to.
abandono *m* desertion; neglect; retirement.
abanicar *vt* to fan.
abanico *m* fan.
abaratar *vt* to lower the price of.
abarca *f* sandal.
abarcar *vt* to include.
abarrancarse *vr* to get into difficulties.
abarrotado/da *adj* packed.
abarrotar *vt* to tie down.
abastecedor/ra *m/f* supplier, purveyor.
abastecer *vt* to supply, provide.
abastecimiento *m* supplying; provisions.
abasto *m* supply of provisions.
abate *m* French abbot.
abatido/da *adj* dejected, low-spirited
abatimiento *m* low spirits *pl*; depression.
abatir *vt* to knock down; to humble.
abdicación *f* abdication.
abdicar *vt* to abdicate.
abdomen *m* abdomen.
abdominal *adj* abdominal.
abecé *m* alphabet.
abecedario *m* alphabet; spelling book, primer.
abedul *m* birch tree.
abeja *f* bee; ~ **reina** queen bee.
abejar *m* beehive.
abejarrón *m* bumblebee.
abejón *m* drone; hornet.
abejorro *m* bumblebee.
aberración *f* aberration.
abertura *f* aperture, chink, opening.
abeto *m* fir tree.
abetunado/da *adj* dark-skinned.
abierto/ta *adj* open; sincere; frank.
abigarrado/da *adj* multicolored.

abintestato *adj* intestate.
abismal *adj* abysmal.
abismo *m* abyss; gulf; hell.
abjuración *f* abjuration.
abjurar *vt* to abjure, to recant; * *vi*: ~ **de** to abjure, to recant.
ablandamiento *m* softening.
ablandar *vt*, *vi* to soften.
ablativo *m* (*gr*) ablative.
ablución *f* ablution.
abnegación *f* self-denial.
abnegado/da *adj* selfless.
abnegar *vt* to renounce.
abobado/da *adj* silly.
abobamiento *m* stupefaction.
abobar *vt* to stupefy.
abocado/da *adj* light (wine).
abocar *vt* to seize with the mouth; ~**se** *vr* to meet by agreement.
abochornar *vt* to swelter; ~**se** *vr* to shame.
abofetear *vt* to slap.
abogacía *f* legal profession.
abogado/a *m/f* attorney-at-law, counsel.
abogar *vi* to intercede; ~ **por** to advocate.
abolengo *m* ancestry; inheritance from ancestors.
abolición *f* abolition, abrogation.
abolir *vt* to abolish.
abolladura *f* dent.
abollar *vt* to dent.
abominable *adj* abominable, cursed.
abominación *f* abomination.
abominar *vt* to detest.
abonado/da *adj* ready; prepared; * *m/f* subscriber; season ticket holder.
abonar *vt* to settle; to fertilize; to endorse; ~**se** *vr* to subscribe; * *vi* to clear up.
abono *m* payment; subscription; dung, manure.
abordaje *m* boarding.
abordar *vt* (*mar*) to board; to broach.
aborigen *m* aborigine.
aborrecer *vt* to hate, to abhor.
aborrecible *adj* hateful, detestable.
aborrecimiento *m* abhorrence, hatred.
abortar *vi* to miscarry; to have an abortion.
abortivo/va *adj* abortive.
aborto *m* miscarriage; abortion; monster.
abortón *m* abortion (in animals).
abotagado/da *adj* swollen.
abotinado/da *adj* tied up.
abotonar *vt* to button.
abovedado/da *adj* vaulted.
abrasar *vt* to burn; to parch; ~**se** *vr* to burn oneself.

abrazadera f bracket; clasp.
abrazar vt to embrace; to surround.
abrazo m embrace.
abrebotellas m invar bottle opener.
abrecartas m invar letter opener.
abrelatas m invar can opener.
abrevadero m watering place.
abrevar vt to water (cattle).
abreviación f abbreviation, abridgement; shortening.
abreviar vt to abridge, to cut short.
abreviatura f abbreviation.
abridor m opener.
abrigar vt to shelter; to protect; ~se vr to take shelter.
abrigo m coat; shelter; protection; aid.
abril m April.
abrillantar vt to polish.
abrir vt to open; to unlock; ~se vr to open up; to clear the way; to be open.
abrochador m buttonhook.
abrochar vt to button; to do up.
abrogar vt to abrogate.
abrumador/ra adj overwhelming; annoying.
abrumar vt to overwhelm.
abrupto/ta adj abrupt; steep.
absceso m abscess.
absentismo m absenteeism.
absolución f forgiveness, absolution.
absoluto/ta adj absolute.
absolutorio/a adj absolutely.
absolver vt to absolve.
absorbente adj absorbent.
absorber vt to absorb.
absorción f absorption; takeover.
absorto adj engrossed.
abstemio adj teetotal.
abstención f abstention.
abstenerse vr to abstain.
abstinencia f abstinence.
abstinente adj abstinent, abstemious.
abstracción f abstraction.
abstracto/ta adj abstract.
abstraer vt to abstract; ~se vr to be absorbed.
abstraído adj absent-minded.
absuelto/ta adj absolved.
absurdidad f , **absurdo** m absurdity.
absurdo adj absurd.
abuela f grandmother.
abuelo m grandfather.
abulia f lethargy.
abultado/da adj bulky, large, massive.
abultar vt to increase, to enlarge; * vi to be bulky.
abundancia f abundance.
abundante adj abundant, copious.
abundar vi to abound.
aburrido/da adj boring, dull.
aburridor/ra adj Lat Am boring, dull.

aburrimiento m boredom.
aburrir vt to bore.
abusador/ra adj Lat Am greedy.
abusar vt to abuse.
abusivo/va adj abusive.
abuso m abuse.
abyección f abjectness.
abyecto/ta adj abject, wretched.
acá adv here.
acabado/da adj perfect, accomplished.
acabar vt to finish, to complete; to achieve; ~se vr to finish; to be over; to run out; * vi to finish; to die, to expire.
acabose m: el ~ the last straw.
acacia f acacia.
academia f academy.
académico/ca m/f academician; * adj academic.
acaecer vi to happen.
acallar vt to quiet, to hush; to soften, to appease.
acalorado/da adj heated.
acalorarse vr to become heated.
acampar vt to camp.
acanalado/da adj grooved; fluted.
acanalar vt to corrugate.
acanto m acanthus.
acantonamiento m cantonment.
acantonar vt to billet.
acaparar vt to monopolize; to hoard.
acápite m Lat Am paragraph.
acariciar vt to fondle, to caress.
acarrear vt to transport; to occasion.
acarreo m carriage, transportation.
acaso m chance; * adv perhaps.
acatarrarse vr to catch (a) cold.
acaudalado/da adj rich, wealthy.
acaudalar vt to hoard.
acaudillar vt to command.
acceder vi to agree; ~ a to have access to.
accesible adj attainable; accessible.
acceso m access; fit.
accesorio/ria adj, m accessory.
accidentado/da adj uneven; hilly; eventful.
accidental adj accidental; casual.
accidentarse vr to have an accident.
accidente m accident.
acción f action, operation; share.
accionar vt to work; Lat Am to bring a suit against.
accionista m shareholder.
acebo m holly tree.
acebuche m wild olive tree.
acechador/ra m/f spy, observer.
acechar vt to lie in wait for; to spy on, observe.
acecho m spying, watching; ambush.
aceitar vt to oil.
aceite m oil.
aceitera f oilcan.
aceitoso/sa adj oily.

aceituna f olive.
aceitunado/da adj olive-green.
aceitunero m olive seller.
aceituno m olive tree.
aceleración f acceleration.
acelerada f Lat Am acceleration.
aceleradamente adv swiftly, hastily.
acelerador m gas pedal.
acelerar vt to accelerate; to hurry.
acelga f (bot) chard (a variety of beet).
acento m accent.
acentuación f accentuation.
acentuar vt to accentuate.
aceña f water mill.
acepción f acceptation.
aceptable adj acceptable.
aceptación f acceptance; approval.
aceptar vt to accept, to admit.
acequia f canal, channel; drain.
acera f sidewalk.
acerado/da adj steel compd, made of steel; sharp; steely.
acerbo/ba adj rigorous, harsh; cruel.
acerca prep about, relating to.
acercar vt to move nearer; ~**se** vr ~ **a** to approach.
acerico m pincushion.
acero m steel.
acérrimo/ma adj staunch; bitter.
acertado/da adj correct, proper; prudent.
acertar vt to hit; to guess right; * vi to get it right; to turn out true.
acertijo m riddle.
acervo m heap, pile.
acetato m (chem) acetate.
achacar vt to impute.
achacoso/sa adj sickly, unhealthy.
achantar vt (col) to scare; ~**se** vr to back down.
achaparrado/da adj stunted; stocky.
achaque m ailment; excuse; subject, matter.
achicar vt to diminish; to humiliate; to bale (out).
achicharrar vt to scorch; to overheat.
achicoria f (bot) chicory.
achiquitar vt Lat Am to make smaller.
achisparse vr to get tipsy.
aciago/ga adj unlucky; ominous.
acíbar m aloes; (fig) bitterness; displeasure.
acicalar vt to polish; ~**se** vr to dress in style.
acicate m spur.
acidez f acidity.
ácido m acid; * ~/**da** adj acid, sour.
acierto m success; solution; dexterity.
aclamación f acclamation.
aclamar vt to applaud, to acclaim.
aclaración f clarification.
aclarar vt to clear; to brighten; to explain; to clarify; ~**se** vr to understand; * vi to clear up.

aclimatar vt to acclimatize; ~**se** vr to become acclimatized.
acne m acne.
acobardar vt to intimidate.
acodarse vr to lean.
acogedor/ra adj welcoming.
acoger vt to receive; to welcome; to harbor; ~**se** vr to take refuge.
acogida f reception; asylum.
acolchar vt to quilt; to cushion.
acólito m acolyte; assistant.
acometer vt to attack; to undertake.
acometida f attack, assault.
acomodadizo adj accommodating.
acomodado/da adj suitable, convenient, fit; wealthy.
acomodador/ra m/f usher, usherette.
acomodar vt to accommodate, to arrange; ~**se** vr to comply.
acomodaticio/cia adj accommodating; pliable.
acompañamiento m (mus) accompaniment.
acompañar vt to accompany; to join; (mus) to accompany.
acompasado/da adj measured; well-proportioned.
acondicionado/da adj conditioned.
acondicionar vt to arrange; to condition.
acongojar vt to distress.
aconsejable adj advisable.
aconsejar vt to advise; ~**se** vr to take advice.
acontecer vi to happen.
acontecimiento m event, incident.
acopio m gathering, storing.
acopiar vt to gather, to store up.
acoplamiento m coupling.
acoplar vt to couple; to fit; to connect.
acorazado/da adj armored; * m battleship.
acordado/da adj agreed.
acordar vt to agree; to remind; Lat Am to award; ~**se** vr to agree; to remember.
acorde adj harmonious; * m chord.
acordeón m accordion.
acordonado/da adj cordoned-off.
acordonar vt to tie up; to cordon off.
acorralar vt to round up, corral; corner.
acortar vt to abridge, to shorten; ~**se** vr to become shorter.
acosar vt to pursue closely; to pester.
acostado/da adj in bed; lying down.
acostar vt to put to bed; to lay down; ~**se** vr to go to bed; to lie down.
acostumbrado/da adj usual.
acostumbrar vi to be used to; ~**se** vr ~ **a** to get used to; * vt to accustom.
acotación f boundary mark; quotation in the margin; stage direction.
acotar vt to set bounds to; to annotate.
ácrata m/f anarchist.
acre adj acid; sharp; * m acre.

A

acrecentamiento m increase.
acrecentar vt to increase, to augment.
acreditar vt to guarantee; to assure, to affirm; to authorize; to credit; ~**se** vr to become famous.
acreedor m creditor.
acribillar vt to riddle with bullets; to molest, to torment.
acriminar vt to incriminate; to accuse.
acrimonia f acrimony.
acriollado/da adj Lat Am integrated.
acrisolar vt to refine, to purify.
acritud f acrimony.
acróbata m/f acrobat.
acta f act; ~**s** fpl records pl.
actitud f attitude; posture.
activar vt to activate; to speed up.
actividad f activity; liveliness.
activo/va adj active; diligent.
acto m act, action; act of a play; ceremony.
actor m actor; plaintiff.
actriz f actress.
actuación f action; behavior; proceedings pl.
actual adj actual, present.
actualidad f present time; ~**es** fpl current events pl.
actualizar vt to update.
actualmente adv at present.
actuar vt to work; to operate; * vi to work; to act.
acuarela f watercolor.
acuariano/na adj Lat Am Aquarian (zodiac sign).
acuario m tank.
Acuario m Aquarius (zodiac sign).
acuartelamiento m quartering of troops.
acuartelar vt (mil) to quarter (troops).
acuático/ca adj aquatic.
acuchillar vt to cut; to plane.
acuciar vt to urge on.
acuclillarse vr to crouch.
acudir vi to go to; to attend; to assist.
acueducto m aqueduct.
acuerdo m agreement; **de** ~ (col) OK, all right.
acumular vt to accumulate, to collect.
acuñación f coining.
acuñar vt to coin, to mint; to wedge in.
acuoso/sa adj watery.
acupuntura f acupuncture.
acurrucarse vr to squat; to huddle up.
acusación f accusation.
acusador/ra m/f accuser; * adj accusing.
acusar vt to accuse; to reveal; to denounce; ~**se** vr to confess.
acusativo m (gr) accusative.
acuse m: ~ **de recibo** acknowledgement of receipt.
acústica f acoustics pl.
acústico/ca adj acoustic.
adagio m adage, proverb; (mus) adagio.

adalid m chief, commander.
adamascado/da adj damask.
adaptable adj adaptable.
adaptación f adaptation.
adaptador m adapter.
adaptar vt to adapt.
adecuado/da adj adequate, fit; appropriate.
adecuar vt to fit, to accommodate, to proportion.
adefesio m folly, nonsense.
adelantado/da adj advanced; fast.
adelantamiento m progress, improvement, advancement; overtaking.
adelantar vt, vi to advance, to accelerate; to pass; to ameliorate, to improve; ~**se** vr to advance; to outdo.
adelante adv forward(s); **de hoy en** ~ from now on; **más** ~ later on; further on; ~ **de** Lat Am in front of; * excl come in!
adelanto m advance; progress; improvement.
adelfa f (bot) rosebay.
adelgazar vt to make thin/slender; * vi to lose weight.
ademán m gesture; attitude.
además adv moreover, besides; ~ **de** besides.
adentrarse vr to get inside; to penetrate.
adentro adv in; inside; ~ **de** Lat Am inside.
adepto/ta m/f supporter.
aderezar vt to dress, to adorn; to prepare; to season.
aderezo m adorning; seasoning; arrangement.
adeudado adj in debt.
adeudar vt to owe; ~**se** vr to run into debt.
adherencia f adhesion, cohesion; alliance.
adherente adj adhering to, cohesive.
adherir vi: ~ **a** to adhere to; to espouse.
adhesión f adhesion; cohesion.
adición f addition.
adicionar vt to add.
adicto/ta adj: ~ **a** addicted to; devoted to; * m supporter; addict.
adiestrar vt to guide; to teach, to instruct; ~**se** vr to practice.
adinerado/da adj wealthy, rich.
adiós excl goodbye; hello.
aditivo m additive.
adivinanza f enigma; riddle.
adivinar vt to foretell; to guess.
adivino/na m/f fortune-teller.
adjetivo m adjective.
adjudicación f adjudication.
adjudicar vt to adjudge; ~**se** vr to appropriate.
adjuntar vt to endorse.
adjunto/ta adj united, joined, annexed; * m/f assistant.
administración f administration.
administrador/a m/f administrator.
administrar vt to administer.
administrativo/va adj administrative.

admirable *adj* admirable, marvelous.
admiración *f* admiratión; wonder; (*gr*) exclamation mark.
admirar *vt* to admire; to surprise; ~**se** *vr* to be surprised.
admisible *adj* admissible.
admisión *f* admission, acceptance.
admitir *vt* to admit; to let in; to concede; to permit.
admonición *f* warning.
adobado *m* pickled pork.
adobar *vt* to dress; to season.
adobe *m* adobe, sun-dried brick.
adobo *m* dressing; pickle sauce.
adoctrinar *vt* to indoctrinate; to teach.
adolecer *vi* to suffer from.
adolescencia *f* adolescence.
adolescente *adj, m/f* adolescent.
adonde *adv* (to) where.
adónde *adv* where.
adopción *f* adoption.
adoptar *vt* to adopt.
adoptivo/va *adj* adoptive; adopted.
adoquín *m* paving stone.
adoración *f* adoration, worship.
adorar *vt* to adore; to love.
adormecer *vt* to put to sleep; ~**se** *vr* to fall asleep.
adormidera *f* (*bot*) poppy.
adornar *vt* to embellish, to adorn.
adorno *m* adornment; ornament, decoration.
adosado/da *adj* semidetached, joined to another building by a common wall.
adquirir *vt* to acquire.
adquisición *f* acquisition.
adrede *adv* on purpose.
adscribir *vt* to appoint.
aduana *f* customs *pl.*
aduanero *m* customs officer; ~/**ra** *adj* customs *compd.*
aducir *vt* to adduce.
adueñarse *vr:* ~ **de** to take possession of.
adulación *f* adulation.
adulador/ra *m/f* flatterer.
adular *vt* to flatter.
adulterar *vt* to adulterate; * *vi* to commit adultery.
adulterio *m* adultery.
adúltero/ra *m/f* adulterer, adulteress.
adulto/ta *adj, m/f* adult, grown-up.
adusto/ta *adj* gloomy; stern.
advenedizo *m* upstart.
advenimiento *m* arrival; accession.
adverbio *m* adverb.
adversario *m* adversary; antagonist.
adversidad *f* adversity; setback.
adverso/sa *adj* adverse.
advertencia *f* warning, foreword.
advertido/da *adj* sharp.

advertir *vt* to notice; to warn.
Adviento *m* Advent.
adyacente *adj* adjacent.
aéreo/rea *adj* aerial.
aerobic *m* aerobics *pl.*
aerobismo *m Lat Am* aerobics *pl.*
aerodeslizador *m* hovercraft.
aerodeslizante *m* hovercraft.
aerogenerador *m* wind turbine.
aeromozo/za *m/f Lat Am* air steward/ess).
aeronauta *m* aeronaut.
aeronáutica *f* aeronautics.
aeronave *f* spaceship.
aeroplano *m* airplane.
aeropuerto *m* airport.
aerosol *m* aerosol.
aerostática *f* aerostatics.
afabilidad *f* affability.
afable *adj* affable.
afán *m* hard work; desire.
afanar *vt* to harass; (*col*) to pinch; ~**se** *vr* to strive.
afanoso/sa *adj* hard, industrious.
afear *vt* to deform, to misshape.
afección *f* affection; fondness, attachment; disease.
afectación *f* affectation.
afectadamente *adv* affectedly.
afectado/da *adj* affected.
afectar *vt* to affect, to feign.
afectísimo/ma *adj* affectionate; ~ **suyo** yours truly.
afectivo/va *adj* fond, tender.
afecto *m* affection; passion; ~/**ta** *adj* affectionate; disposed; reserved.
afectuoso/sa *adj* affectionate; moving; tender.
afeitada *f Lat Am* shave.
afeitar *vt,* ~**se** *vr* to shave.
afeite *m* make-up, rouge.
afeminado/da *adj* effeminate.
afeminar *vt* to make effeminate.
aferrado/da *adj* stubborn.
aferrar *vt* to grapple, to grasp, to seize.
afianzamiento *m* strengthening.
afianzar *vt* to strengthen; to prop up; ~**se** *vr* to become established.
afiche *m Lat Am* poster.
afición *f* affection; hobby; fans *pl.*
aficionado/da *adj* keen; * *m/f* lover, fan; amateur.
aficionar *vt* to inspire affection; ~**se** *vr* ~ **a** to grow fond of.
afiebrado/da *adj Lat Am* feverish.
afiladera *f* grindstone.
afilado *adj* sharp.
afilar *vt* to sharpen, to grind.
afín *m* related; similar.
afinar *vt* to tune; to refine.
afincarse *vr* to settle.

afinidad *f* affinity; analogy; relationship.
afirmación *f* affirmation.
afirmado *m* road surface.
afirmar *vt* to secure, to fasten; to affirm, to assure.
afirmativo/va *adj* affirmative.
aflicción *f* affliction, grief.
aflictivo/va *adj* distressing.
afligir *vt* to afflict, to torment.
aflojar *vt* to loosen, to slacken, to relax; * *vi* to grow weak; to abate; to relent; ~**se** *vr* to relax.
aflorar *vi* to emerge.
afluente *adj* flowing; * *m* tributary.
afluir *vi* to flow.
afónico/ca *adj* hoarse; voiceless.
aforismo *m* aphorism.
afortunado/da *adj* fortunate, lucky.
afrancesado/da *adj* Frenchified.
afrenta *f* outrage; insult.
afrentar *vt* to affront; to insult.
afroamericano/na *adj, m/f* African-American.
afrontar *vt* to confront; to bring face to face.
afuera *adv* out, outside; ~ **de** *Lat Am* outside.
afueras *fpl* outskirts *pl*.
agacharse *vr* to stoop, to squat.
agalla *f* gill; ~**s** *pl* pluck, guts; tonsils *pl*; tonsillitis.
agarradera *f Lat Am* handle.
agarradero *m* handle.
agarrado/da *adj* miserly, stingy.
agarrar *vt* to grasp, to seize; ~**se** *vr* to hold on tightly.
agarrón *m Lat Am* fight.
agarrotar *vt* to tie down; to squeeze tightly; to garrote.
agasajar *vt* to receive and treat kindly; to regale.
agasajo *m* graceful reception; kindness.
ágata *f* agate.
agazaparse *vr* to crouch.
agencia *f* agency.
agenciarse *vr* to obtain.
agenda *f* diary.
agente *m* agent; police officer.
ágil *adj* agile.
agilidad *f* agility, nimbleness.
agitación *f* shaking; stirring; agitation.
agitanado/da *adj* Gypsy-like.
agitar *vt* to wave; to move; ~**se** *vr* to become excited; to become worried.
aglomeración *f* crowd; ~ **de tráfico** traffic jam.
aglomerar *vt*, ~**se** *vr* to crowd together.
agnóstico/ca *adj, m/f* agnostic.
agobiar *vt* to weigh down; to oppress; to burden.
agolparse *vr* to assemble in crowds.
agonía *f* death throes *pl*.
agonizante *adj* dying.
agonizar *vi* to be dying.
agorar *vt* to predict.
agostar *vt* to parch.

agosto *m* August.
agotado/da *adj* exhausted; finished; sold out.
agotador/ra *adj* exhausting.
agotamiento *m* exhaustion.
agotar *vt* to exhaust; to drain; to misspend.
agraciado/da *adj* attractive; lucky.
agraciar *vt* to pardon; to reward.
agradable *adj* pleasant; lovely.
agradar *vt* to please, to gratify.
agradecer *vt* to be grateful for; to thank.
agradecido/da *adj* thankful.
agradecimiento *m* gratitude, gratefulness, thanks *pl*.
agrado *m* agreeableness, courteousness; will, pleasure; liking.
agrandar *vt* to enlarge; to exaggerate; to aggrandize; ~**se** *vr* to get bigger.
agrario/ria *adj* agrarian; agricultural.
agravante *f* further difficulty.
agravar *vt* to oppress; to aggrieve; to aggravate; to exaggerate; ~**se** *vr* to get worse.
agraviar *vt* to wrong; to offend; ~**se** *vr* to be aggrieved; to be piqued.
agravio *m* offence; grievance.
agredir *vt* to attack.
agregado *m* aggregate; attaché.
agregar *vt* to aggregate, to heap together; to collate; to appoint.
agremiado/da *adj Lat Am* unionized.
agresión *f* aggression, attack.
agresivo/va *adj* aggressive.
agresor *m* aggressor, assaulter.
agreste *adj* rustic, rural.
agriar *vt* to sour; to exasperate.
agrícola *adj* farming *compd*.
agricultor/ra *m/f* farmer.
agricultura *f* agriculture; ~ **biológica** organic farming.
agridulce *adj* sweet and sour.
agrietarse *vr* to crack.
agrimensor *m* surveyor.
agrimensura *f* surveying.
agrio *adj* sour, acrid; rough, sharp, rude, unpleasant.
agronomía *f* agronomy.
agropecuario/ria *adj* farming *compd*.
agrupación *f* group(ing).
agrupar *vt* to group, to cluster; to crowd.
agua *f* water; slope of a roof; ~ **fuerte** etching; ~ **bendita** holy water; ~**s** *fpl* waters *pl*.
aguacate *m* avocado pear.
aguacero *m* short, heavy shower of rain.
aguachento/ta *adj Lat Am* watery.
aguachirle *f* slops *pl*.
aguado/da *adj* watery; *Lat Am* weak.
aguador *m* water carrier.
aguafuerte *m* etching.
aguamarina *f* aquamarine (precious stone).
aguanieve *f* sleet.

aguantador/ra *adj Lat Am* patient.
aguantar *vt* to bear, to suffer; to hold up.
aguante *m* firmness; patience.
aguar *vt* to water down.
aguardar *vt* to wait for.
aguardiente *m* brandy.
aguarrás *f* turpentine.
aguatero/ra *m/f Lat Am* water seller.
agudeza *f* keenness, sharpness; acuteness; acidity; smartness.
agudizar *vt* to make worse; ~**se** *vr* to get worse.
agudo/da *adj* sharp; keen-edged; smart; fine; acute; witty; brisk.
aguero *m*: **buen/mal** ~ good/bad omen.
aguijar *vt* to prick, to spur, to goad; to stimulate.
aguijón *m* sting of a bee, wasp etc; stimulation.
aguijonear *vt* to prick; to spur; to stimulate.
águila *f* eagle; genius.
aguileño/ña *adj* aquiline; sharp-featured.
aguilucho *m* eaglet.
aguinaldo *m* Christmas box, New Year gift, tip.
aguja *f* needle; spire; hand; magnetic needle; (*rail*) points *pl*.
agujerear *vt* to pierce, to bore.
agujero *m* hole.
agujetas *fpl* stitch; stiffness; pains *pl* from fatigue.
agustino *m* monk of the order of St Augustine.
aguzar *vt* to whet, to sharpen; to stimulate.
ahí *adv* there.
ahijada *f* goddaughter.
ahijado *m* godson.
ahijar *vt* to adopt (as one's own child).
ahínco *m* earnestness; eagerness.
ahogar *vt* to smother; to drown; to suffocate; to oppress; to quench; ~**se** *vr* to drown; to suffocate.
ahogo *m* breathlessness; financial difficulty.
ahondar *vt* to deepen; to study deeply; * *vi*: ~ **en** to penetrate into.
ahora *adv* now, at present; just now.
ahorcar *vt* to hang; ~**se** *vr* to hang oneself.
ahorrar *vt* to save; to avoid.
ahorrativo/va *adj* thrifty, careful with money.
ahorro *m* saving; thrift.
ahuecar *vt* to hollow, to scoop out; ~**se** *vr* to get pig-headed.
ahumar *vt* to smoke, to cure (in smoke); ~**se** *vr* to fill with smoke.
ahuyentar *vt* to drive off; to dispel.
airado/da *adj* angry.
airarse *vr* to get angry.
airbag *m* airbag.
aire *m* air; wind; aspect; musical composition.
airearse *vr* to take the air.
airoso/sa *adj* airy; windy; graceful; successful.
aislado/da *adj* insulated; isolated.
aislar *vt* to insulate; to isolate.
ajar *vt* to spoil; to abuse.

ajardinado/da *adj* landscaped.
ajedrez *m* chess.
ajedrezado/da *adj* checkered.
ajenjo *m* wormwood, absinth.
ajeno/na *adj* someone else's; foreign; ignorant; improper.
ajetrearse *vr* to exert oneself; to bustle; to toil; to fidget.
ajetreo *m* activity; bustling.
ají *m* red pepper.
ajo *m* garlic.
ajorca *f* bracelet.
ajuar *m* household furniture; trousseau.
ajustado/da *adj* tight; right; close.
ajustar *vt* to regulate, to adjust; to settle (a balance); to fit; to agree on; * *vi* to fit.
ajuste *m* agreement; accommodation; settlement; fitting.
ajusticiar *vt* to execute.
al = a el.
ala *f* wing; aisle; row, file; brim; winger.
alabanza *f* praise; applause.
alabar *vt* to praise; to applaud.
alabastro *m* alabaster.
alacena *f* cupboard, closet.
alacrán *m* scorpion.
alado/da *adj* winged.
alambique *m* still.
alambrada *f* wire fence; wire netting.
alambrado *m Lat Am* wire fence; wire netting.
alambre *m* wire.
alambrista *m/f* tightrope walker.
alameda *f* avenue; poplar grove.
álamo *m* poplar.
alano *m* mastiff.
alarde *m* show.
alargador *m* extension lead.
alargar *vt* to lengthen; to extend; to hasten; to stretch out; to spin out; ~**se** *vr* to get longer; to drag on.
alarido *m* outcry, shout; **dar** ~**s** to howl.
alarma *f* alarm.
alarmante *adj* alarming.
alarmar *vt* to alarm.
alarmista *m* alarmist.
alazán *m* sorrel.
alba *f* dawn.
albacea *m* executor.
albahaca *f* (*bot*) basil.
albañil *m* bricklayer.
albañilería *f* bricklaying.
albarán *m* invoice.
albarda *f* saddle.
albaricoque *m* apricot.
albedrío *m* free will.
alberca *f* reservoir; swimming pool.
albergar *vt* to lodge, to harbor; ~**se** *vr* to shelter.
albergue *m* shelter; ~ **de juventud** youth hostel.

albóndiga f meatball.
albor m dawn; whiteness.
alborada f dawn; reveille.
alborear vi to dawn.
albornoz m dressing gown.
alborotado/da adj restless, turbulent.
alborotar vi to make a row; * vt to stir up; ~**se** vr to get excited; to get rough.
alboroto m noise; disturbance, riot.
alborozar vt to exhilarate; ~**se** vr to rejoice.
alborozo m joy.
albricias fpl good news pl.
albufera f lagoon.
álbum m album.
albumen m egg white.
alcachofa f artichoke.
alcahuete/ta m/f pimp, bawd.
alcalde m mayor.
alcaldesa f mayoress.
alcaldía f office and jurisdiction of a mayor; mayor's office.
alcalino/na adj alkaline.
alcance m reach; bad balance.
alcancía f Lat Am money box.
alcanfor m camphor.
alcantarilla m sewer; gutter.
alcanzar vt to reach; to get, to obtain; to hit; * vi to suffice; to reach.
alcaparra f caper.
alcatraz m gannet.
alcayata f hook.
alcázar m castle, fortress.
alcoba f bedroom.
alcohol m alcohol.
alcohólico/ca adj, m/f alcoholic.
alcoholismo m alcoholism.
alcornoque m cork tree.
aldaba f knocker.
aldea f village.
aldeano/na m/f villager; * adj rustic.
ale excl come on!
aleación f alloy.
aleatorio/ria adj random.
aleccionar vt to instruct; to train.
alegación f allegation.
alegar vt to allege; to quote; * vi Lat Am to argue; to complain.
alegato m allegation; argument.
alegoria f allegory.
alegórico/ca adj allegorical.
alegrar vt to cheer; to poke; to liven up; ~**se** vr to get merry.
alegre adj happy; merry, joyful; content.
alegría f happiness; merriment.
alegrón m sudden joy; flicker.
alejamiento m remoteness; removal.
alejar vt to remove; to estrange; ~**se** vr to go away.

aleluya f hallelujah.
alemán/ana adj, m/f German; * m German language.
alentador/ra adj encouraging.
alentar vt to encourage.
alergia f allergy.
alero m gable-end; eaves pl.
alerta adj, f alert.
alertar vt to alert.
aleta f fin; wing; flipper; fender.
aletargarse vr to get drowsy.
aletazo m flap.
aletear vi to flutter.
aleteo m fluttering.
alevosía f treachery.
alevoso/sa adj treacherous.
alfabéticamente adv alphabetically.
alfabético/ca adj alphabetical.
alfabeto m alphabet.
alfalfa f (bot) lucerne.
alfarería f pottery.
alfarero m potter.
alféizar m window sill.
alférez m second lieutenant; (US navy) ensign.
alfil m bishop (at chess).
alfiler m pin; clip; clothes peg.
alfiletero m pincushion.
alfombra f carpet; rug.
alfombrar vt to carpet.
alfombrilla f mouse mat.
alforja f saddlebag; knapsack.
alga f (bot) seaweed.
algarabia f gabble, gibberish.
algarroba f (bot) carob.
algarrobo m (bot) carob tree.
algazara f din.
álgebra f algebra.
álgido/da adj chilly; crucial.
algo pn something; anything; * adv somewhat.
algodón m cotton; cotton plant; cotton wool; ~ azucarado m cotton candy.
algodonero m cotton plant; dealer in cotton.
alguacil m bailiff; mounted official.
alguien pn someone, somebody; anyone, anybody.
alguno/na adj some; any; no; * pn someone, somebody.
alhaja f jewel.
alhajera f Lat Am jewelry box.
alhelí m wallflower.
aliado/da adj allied.
alianza f alliance, league; wedding ring.
aliar vt to ally; ~**se** vr to form an alliance.
alias adv alias.
alicaído/da adj weak; downcast.
alicates mpl pincers pl, nippers pl.
aliciente m attraction; incitement.
alienación f alienation.

aliento *m* breath; respiration.
aligerar *vt* to lighten; to alleviate; to hasten; to ease.
alijo *m* lightening of a ship; alleviation; cache.
alimaña *f* pest.
alimentación *f* nourishment; food; grocery.
alimentar *vt* to feed, to nourish; ~**se** *vr* to feed.
alimenticio/cia *adj* food *compd*; nutritious.
alimento *m* food; ~**s** *mpl* alimony.
alineación *m* alignment; line-up.
alinear *vt* to arrange in line; ~**se** *vr* to line up.
aliñar *vt* to adorn; to season.
aliño *m* dressing; ornament, decoration.
alisar *vt* to plane; to polish; to smooth.
alistarse *vr* to enlist, to enroll; *Lat Am* to get ready.
aliviar *vt* to lighten; to ease; to relieve, to mollify.
alivio *m* alleviation; mitigation; relief; comfort.
aljibe *m* cistern.
allá *adv* there; over there; then.
allanamiento *m*: ~ **de morada** burglary.
allanar *vt* to level, to flatten; to overcome difficulties; to pacify; to subdue; to burgle; *Lat Am* to raid; ~**se** *vr* to submit; to tumble down.
allegado/da *adj* near; * *m/f* follower.
allí *adv* there, in that place.
alma *f* soul; human being.
almacén *m* warehouse, store; magazine.
almacenaje *m* storage.
almacenar *vt* to store (up).
almanaque *m* almanac.
almeja *f* clam.
almena *f* battlement.
almendra *f* almond.
almendrado/da *adj* almond-shaped; * *m* macaroon.
almendro *m* almond tree.
almiar *m* haystack.
almíbar *m* syrup.
almidón *m* starch.
almidonado/da *adj* starched; affected; spruce.
almidonar *vt* to starch.
almirantazgo *m* admiralty.
almirante *m* admiral.
almirez *m* mortar.
almizcle *m* musk.
almohada *f* pillow; cushion.
almohadilla *f* small pillow; pad; pincushion.
almohadón *m* large cushion.
almorranas *fpl* hemorrhoids *pl*.
almorzar *vt* to have for lunch; * *vi* to have lunch.
almuerzo *m* lunch.
alocado/da *adj* crazy; foolish; inconsiderate.
alocución *f* allocution.
áloe *m* (*bot*) aloes.
alojamiento *m* lodging; housing.
alojar *vt* to lodge; ~**se** *vr* to stay.
alondra *f* lark.

alpargata *f* rope-soled shoe.
alpinismo *m* mountaineering.
alpinista *m/f* mountaineer.
alpiste *m* canary seed.
alquería *f* farmhouse.
alquilar *vt* to let, to rent; to hire.
alquiler *m* renting, letting; hiring; rent; hire.
alquimia *f* alchemy.
alquimista *m* alchemist.
alquitrán *m* tar, liquid pitch.
alquitranado/da *adj* tarred.
alrededor *adv* around.
alrededores *mpl* surroundings *pl*.
alta *f* discharge from hospital.
altanería *f* haughtiness.
altanero/ra *adj* haughty, arrogant, vain, proud.
altar *m* altar; ~ **mayor** high altar.
altavoz *m* loudspeaker.
alterable *adj* changeable.
alteración *f* alteration; disturbance, tumult.
alterar *vt* to alter, to change; to disturb; ~**se** *vr* to get upset.
altercado *m* altercation, controversy; quarrel.
alternar *vt*, *vi* to alternate.
alternativa *f* alternative.
alternativo/va *adj* alternate.
alterno/na *adj* alternate; alternating.
Alteza *f* Highness (title).
altibajos *mpl* ups and downs *pl*.
altillo *m* hillock.
altiplanicie *f* high plateau.
altísimo/ma *adj* extremely high, most high; * *m* **el A~** the Most High, God.
altisonante, **altísono/na** *adj* high-sounding, pompous.
altitud *f* height; altitude.
altivez *f* haughtiness.
altivo/va *adj* haughty, proud, high-flown.
alto/ta *adj* high; elevated; tall; sharp; arduous, difficult; eminent; enormous; * *m* height; story; highland; (*mil*) halt; (*mus*) alto; **¡~!, ¡~ ahí!** *interj* stop!
altoparlante *m* *Lat Am* loudspeaker.
altramuz *m* (*bot*) lupin.
altura *f* height; depth; mountain summit; altitude; ~**s** *pl*: **las ~s** the heavens.
alubia *f* bean.
alucinación *f* hallucination.
alucinar *vt* to blind, to deceive; * *vi* to hallucinate; ~**se** *vr* to deceive oneself, to labor under a delusion.
aludir *vi* to allude.
alumbrado *m* lighting; illumination.
alumbramiento *m* lighting; illumination; childbirth.
alumbrar *vt* to light; * *vi* to give birth.
aluminio *m* aluminum.
alumno/na *m/f* student, pupil.

alunizar *vi* to land on the moon.
alusión *f* allusion; hint.
alusivo/va *adj* allusive.
aluvión *f* alluvium; flood.
alvéolo *m* socket; cell of a honeycomb.
alza *f* rise; sight.
alzacuello *m* dog collar.
alzada *f* height; appeal.
alzamiento *m* rise; elevation; higher bid; uprising.
alzar *vt* to raise, to lift up; to construct, to build; to gather (in); ~**se** *vr* to get up; to rise in rebellion; ~**se** *vr*: ~ **con algo** to make off with something.
ama *f* mistress, owner; housewife; foster mother; ~ **de llaves** housekeeper; ~ **de leche** nurse.
amabilidad *f* kindness, niceness.
amable *adj* kind, nice.
amaestrado/da *adj* performing.
amaestrar *vt* to teach; to instruct; to train.
amagar *vt* to threaten; to shake one's fist at; * *vi* to feint.
amago *m* threat; indication; symptom.
amalgama *f* amalgam.
amalgamar *vt* to amalgamate.
amamantar *vt* to suckle.
amanecer *vi* to dawn; **al** ~ at daybreak.
amanerado/da *adj* affected.
amansar *vt* to tame; to soften; to subdue; ~**se** *vr* to calm down.
amante *m/f* lover.
amanuense *m* amanuensis, clerk, copyist.
amapola *f* (*bot*) poppy.
amar *vt* to love.
amargar *vt* to make bitter; to exasperate, ~**se** *vr* to be bitter.
amargo/ga *adj* bitter, acrid; painful; * *m* bitterness.
amargor *m* bitterness; sorrow, distress.
amargura *f* bitterness; sorrow.
amarillear *vi* to turn yellow.
amarillento/ta *adj* yellowish.
amarillo/lla *adj* yellow; * *m* yellow.
amarra *f* mooring rope.
amarrar *vt* to moor; to tie, to fasten.
amartelar *vt* to court, to woo; ~**se** *vr* to fall in love with.
amartillar *vt* to hammer; to cock (a gun/pistol).
amasar *vt* to knead; (*fig*) to arrange, to settle; to prepare.
amasijo *m* dough; mixed mortar; medley.
amateur *m/f* amateur.
amatista *f* amethyst.
amatorio/ria *adj* relating to love.
amazona *f* amazon; masculine woman.
ambages *mpl*: **sin** ~ in plain language.
ámbar *m* amber.
ambición *f* ambition.

ambicionar *vt* to crave, to covet.
ambicioso/sa *adj* ambitious.
ambidextro/tra *adj* ambidextrous.
ambientación *f* setting; sound effects *pl*.
ambiente *m* atmosphere; environment.
ambigüedad *f* ambiguity.
ambiguo/gua *adj* ambiguous; doubtful, equivocal.
ámbito *m* circuit, circumference; field; scope.
ambos/bas *adj, pn* both.
ambrosía *f* ambrosia.
ambulancia *f* ambulance.
ambulante *adj* traveling.
ambulatorio *m* state-run clinic.
ameba *f* ameba.
amedrentar *vt* to frighten, to terrify; to intimidate.
amén *f* amen; so be it; ~ **de** besides; except.
amenaza *f* threat.
amenazar *vt* to threaten.
amenizar *vt* to make pleasant.
ameno/na *adj* pleasant; delicious; flowery (of language).
América *f* America; ~ **del Norte/del Sur** North/South America.
americano/na *adj, m/f* (Latin) American.
ameritar *vt Lat Am* to deserve.
ametralladora *m* machine gun.
amianto *m* asbestos.
amiga *f* (female) friend.
amigable *adj* amicable, friendly; suitable.
amigo *m* friend; comrade; lover; ~/**ga** *adj* friendly.
amilanar *vt* to frighten, to terrify; ~**se** *vr* to get scared.
aminorar *vt* to diminish; to reduce.
amistad *f* friendship.
amistoso/sa *adj* friendly, cordial.
amnesia *f* amnesia.
amnistía *f* amnesty.
amo *m* owner; boss.
amoblar *vt Lat Am* to furnish.
amodorrarse *vr* to grow sleepy.
amohinar *vt* to annoy; ~**se** *vr* to sulk.
amoldar *vt* to mold; to adapt; ~**se** *vr* to adapt oneself.
amonestación *f* advice; admonition; ~**ones** *fpl* publication of marriage banns.
amonestar *vt* to advise; to admonish; to publish banns of marriage of.
amoníaco *m* ammoniac.
amor *m* love; fancy; lover; ~ **mío** my love; **por** ~ **de Dios** for God's sake; ~ **propio** self-love.
amoratado *adj* livid.
amordazar *vt* to muzzle; to gag.
amorfo/fa *adj* shapeless.
amorío *m* love affair.
amoroso/sa *adj* affectionate, loving; lovely.
amortajar *vt* to shroud.

amortiguador *m* shock absorber.
amortiguadores *mpl* suspension.
amortiguar *vt* to mortify; to deaden; to temper; to muffle.
amortización *f* repayment; redemption.
amortizar *vt* to entail (an estate), to render inalienable; to pay, to liquidate, to discharge (a debt).
amotinamiento *m* mutiny.
amotinar *vt* to incite rebellion; ~**se** *vr* to mutiny.
amparar *vt* to shelter, to protect; to favor; ~**se** *vr* to claim protection.
amparo *m* protection, support; help; refuge, asylum.
amperio *m* amp.
ampliación *f* amplification, enlargement.
ampliar *vt* to amplify, to enlarge; to extend; to expand.
amplificación *f* enlargement.
amplificador *m* amplifier.
amplificar *vt* to amplify.
amplio/lia *adj* ample, extensive.
amplitud *f* amplitude, extension, largeness.
ampolla *f* blister; ampoule.
ampuloso/sa *adj* pompous.
amputación *f* amputation.
amputar *vt* to amputate.
amueblar *vt* to furnish.
amuleto *m* amulet.
amurallar *vt* to surround with walls.
anacoreta *m* anchorite, hermit.
anacronismo *m* anachronism.
ánade *m/f* duck.
anadear *vi* to waddle.
anagrama *f* anagram.
anales *mpl* annals *pl*.
analfabetismo *m* illiteracy.
analfabeto/ta *adj* illiterate.
analgésico *m* painkiller.
análisis *m* analysis.
analista *m/f* analyst.
analítico/ca *adj* analytical.
analizar *vt* to analyze.
analogía *f* analogy.
analógico/ca, análogo/ga *adj* analogous.
ananá *m* pineapple.
anaquel *m* shelf (in a bookcase).
anaranjado/da *adj* orange-colored.
anarquía *f* anarchy.
anárquico/ca *adj* anarchic, chaotic.
anarquismo *m* anarchism.
anarquista *m/f* anarchist.
anatema *f* anathema.
anatomía *f* anatomy.
anatómico/ca *adj* anatomical.
anca *f* rump.
ancho/cha *adj* broad, wide, large; * *m* breadth, width.
anchoa *f* anchovy.

anchura *f* width, breadth.
anciano/na *adj* old; * *m/f* old man/woman.
ancla *f* anchor.
ancladero *m* anchorage.
anclaje *m* anchorage.
anclar *vi* to anchor.
andaderas *fpl* baby walker.
andadura *f* walk; pace; amble.
andamio *m* scaffold.
andamiaje *m* scaffolding.
andanada *f* (*mar*) broadside.
andar *vi* to go, to walk; to fare; to act, to proceed, to work; to behave; to elapse; to move; * *vt* to go, to travel; * *m* walk, pace.
andariego/ga *adj* wandering.
andarín *m* fast walker.
andas *fpl* stretcher.
andén *m* sidewalk; (*rail*) platform; quayside.
andinismo *m* Lat Am mountaineering.
andinista *m/f* Lat Am mountaineer.
andrajo *m* rag.
andrajoso/sa *adj* ragged.
andurriales *mpl* byways *pl*.
anécdota *f* anecdote.
anegar *vt* to inundate, to submerge; ~**se** *vr* to drown; to sink.
anejo/ja *adj* attached.
anemia *f* anemia.
anestésico *m* anesthetic.
anexar *vt* to annex; to join.
anexión *f* annexation.
anexionamiento *m* annexation.
anexo/xa *adj* annexed.
anfibio/bia *adj* amphibious.
anfiteatro *m* amphitheater.
anfitrión/ona *m/f* host/ess.
ángel *m* angel.
angelical *adj* angelic, heaven-born.
angélico/ca *adj* angelic.
angina *f* angina.
anglicano/na *adj*, *m/f* Anglican.
anglicismo *m* Anglicanism.
angosto/ta *adj* narrow, close.
anguila *f* eel.
angula *f* elver.
angular *adj* angular; **piedra** ~ *f* cornerstone.
ángulo *m* angle, corner.
anguloso/sa *adj* angled, cornered.
angurria *f* Lat Am hunger; greed.
angurriento/ta *adj* Lat Am hungry; greedy.
angustia *f* anguish; heartache.
angustiar *vt* to cause anguish.
anhelante *adj* eager; longing.
anhelar *vi* to gasp; * *vt* to long for.
anhelo *m* desire, longing.
anidar *vi* to nestle, to make a nest; to dwell, to inhabit.
anillo *m* ring.

ánima f soul.

animación f liveliness; activity.

animado/da adj lively.

animador/ora m/f host(ess).

animadversión f ill-will.

animal adj, m animal.

animar vt to animate, to liven up; to comfort; to revive; ~se vr to cheer up.

ánimo m soul; courage; mind; intention, meaning; will; thought; * excl come on!

animosidad f valor, courage; boldness.

animoso/sa adj courageous, spirited.

aniñarse vr to act in a childish manner.

aniquilar vt to annihilate, to destroy; ~se vr to decline, to decay.

anís m aniseed; anisette.

aniversario/ria adj annual; * m anniversary.

ano m anus.

anoche adv last night.

anochecer vi to grow dark; * m nightfall.

anodino/na adj (med) anodyne.

anomalia f anomaly.

anómalo/la adj anomalous.

anonadar vt to annihilate; to lessen; ~se vr to humble oneself.

anonimato m anonymity.

anónimo/ma adj anonymous.

anormal adj abnormal.

anotación f annotation, note.

anotar vt to comment, to note.

anquilosamiento m paralysis.

ánsar m goose.

ansia f anxiety, eagerness, hankering.

ansiar vt to desire.

ansiedad f anxiety.

ansioso/sa adj anxious, eager.

antagónico/ca adj antagonistic; opposed.

antagonista m antagonist.

antaño adv formerly.

antártico/ca adj Antarctic; * m: el A~ the Antarctic.

ante m suede; * prep before; in the presence of; faced with.

anteanoche adv the night before last.

anteayer adv the day before yesterday.

antebrazo m forearm.

antecámara f antechamber.

antecedente adj, m antecedent.

anteceder vt to precede.

antecesor/ra m/f predecessor; * m forefather.

antedicho/cha adj aforesaid.

antelación f: con ~ in advance.

antemano adv: de ~ beforehand.

antena f feeler, antenna; aerial; ~ parabólica satellite dish.

antenoche adv Lat Am the night before last.

anteojo m eyeglass; ~ de larga vista telescope; ~s mpl Lat Am glasses pl.

antepasado/da adj passed, elapsed; ~s mpl ancestors pl.

antepecho m (mil) parapet; ledge.

anteponer vt to place in front; to prefer.

anteproyecto m sketch; blueprint.

anterior adj preceding; former.

anterioridad f priority; preference.

antes prep, adv before; * conj before.

antesala f antechamber.

antiaéreo/rea adj anti-aircraft.

antibalas adj bullet-proof.

antibiótico m antibiotic.

anticiclón m anticyclone.

anticipación f anticipation.

anticipado/da adj advance.

anticipar vt to anticipate; to forestall; to advance.

anticipo m advance.

anticonceptivo m contraceptive.

anticongelante m antifreeze.

anticuado/da adj antiquated.

anticuario m antiquary, antiquarian.

anticuerpo m antibody.

antídoto m antidote.

antífona f antiphony; anthem.

antiestético/ca adj unsightly.

antifaz m mask.

antigualla f monument of antiquity; antique.

antiguamente adv in ancient times, of old.

antigüedad f antiquity, oldness.

antiguo/gua adj antique, old, ancient; * m senior; ~s mpl: los ~s the ancients.

antílope m antelope.

antinatural adj unnatural.

antimonio m antimony.

antipatía f antipathy.

antipático/ca adj unpleasant.

antipasto m Lat Am antipasto.

antípodas mpl antipodes.

antirrobo adj anti-theft.

antisemita adj anti-Semitic.

antiséptico/ca adj antiseptic.

antítesis f (gr) antithesis.

antojadizo/za adj capricious, fanciful.

antojarse vr to long, to desire; to itch.

antojo m whim, fancy; longing.

antología f anthology.

antorcha f torch; taper.

antro m (poet) cavern, den, grotto.

antropófago m cannibal.

antropología f anthropology.

antropólogo/ga m/f anthropologist.

anual adj annual.

anualidad f annuity.

anublar vt to cloud, to obscure; ~se vr to become clouded.

anudar vt to knot; to join; ~se vr to get into knots.

anulación f annulment; cancellation.

anular vt to annul; to revoke; to cancel; * adj annular.

anunciación f announcement.

anunciante m/f advertiser.

anunciar vt to announce; to advertise.

anuncio m advertisement.

anverso m obverse.

anzuelo m hook; allurement.

añadidura f addition.

añadir vt to add.

añejo/ja adj old; stale, musty.

añicos mpl bits pl, small pieces pl; **hacer** ~ to shatter.

añil m indigo plant; indigo.

año m year.

añojo m yearling calf.

añoranza f longing.

aorta f aorta.

aovar vi to lay eggs.

apabullar vt to squash.

apacentar vt to graze.

apacible adj affable; gentle; placid, quiet.

apaciguar vt to appease; to pacify, to calm.

apadrinar vt to support, to favor; to be godfather to.

apagado/da adj dull; quiet; muted; listless.

apagar vt to put out; to turn off; to quench, to extinguish; to damp; to destroy; to soften.

apagón m power cut, outage.

apalabrar vt to agree to; to engage.

apalancar vt to lever.

apalear vt to cane, to drub; to winnow.

apañado/da adj skillful; suitable.

apañar vt to grasp; to pick up; to patch; ~se vr to manage.

aparador m sideboard; shop/store window.

aparato m apparatus; machine; ostentation, show.

aparatoso/sa adj showy; spectacular.

aparcamiento m parking lot.

aparcar vt, vi to park.

aparcería f partnership in a farm/other business.

aparcero/ra m/f partner; associate.

aparecer vi to appear; ~se vr to appear.

aparecido/da m/f ghost.

aparejar vt to prepare; to harness (horses); to rig (a ship).

aparejo m preparation; harness, gear; (mar) tackle, rigging; ~s mpl tools pl, implements pl.

aparentar vt to look; to pretend; to deceive.

aparente adj apparent; convenient.

aparición f apparition; appearance.

apariencia f outward appearance.

apartadero m (rail) siding.

apartado m paragraph; ~ **de correos/postal** PO Box.

apartamento m apartment.

apartamiento m isolation; separation; apartment.

apartar vt to separate, to divide; to remove; to sort; ~se vr to go away; to be divorced; to desist.

aparte m aside; new paragraph; * adv apart, separately; besides; aside.

apasionado/da adj passionate; devoted; fond; biased.

apasionar vt to excite; ~se vr to get excited.

apatía f apathy.

apático/ca adj apathetic, indifferent.

apeadero m halt, stopping place; station.

apearse vr to dismount; to get down/out/off.

apechugar vt to face up to.

apedrear vt to stone; * vi to hail.

apegarse vr: ~ **a** to become fond of.

apego m attachment, fondness.

apelación f (law) appeal.

apelar vi (law) to appeal; ~ **a** to have recourse to.

apelativo adj (gr): **nombre** ~ m generic name.

apellidar vt to call by name; to proclaim; ~se vr to be called.

apellido m surname; family name; epithet.

apelmazar vt to compress.

apenar vt to grieve; to embarrass; ~se vr to grieve; to be embarrassed.

apenas adv scarcely, hardly; * conj as soon as.

apéndice m appendix, supplement.

apendicitis f appendicitis.

apercibido/da adj provided; ready.

apercibirse vr to notice.

aperitivo m aperitif; appetizer.

apero m agricultural implement.

apertura f aperture, opening, chink; cleft.

apesadumbrar vt to sadden.

apestar vt to infect; * vi: ~ **a** to stink of.

apetecer vt to fancy.

apetecible adj desirable; appetizing.

apetito m appetite.

apetitoso/sa adj pleasing to the taste, appetizing; tempting.

apiadarse vr to take pity.

apiario m Lat Am apiary.

ápice m summit, point; smallest part of a thing.

apilar vt to pile up; ~se vr to pile up.

apiñado/da adj crowded; pyramidal; pine-shaped.

apiñarse vr to clog, to crowd.

apio m (bot) celery.

apisonadora f steamroller, roadroller.

apisonar vt to ram down.

aplacar vt to appease, to pacify; ~se vr to calm down.

aplanadora f Lat Am roadroller, steamroller.

aplanar vt to level, to flatten.

aplastar vt to flatten, to crush.

aplatanarse vr to get weary.

aplaudir vt to applaud; to extoll.

aplauso m applause; approbation, praise.

aplazamiento m postponement.

aplazar vt to postpone.

aplicable adj applicable.

aplicación f application; effort.
aplicado/da adj studious; industrious.
aplicar vt to apply; to clasp; to attribute; ~**se** vr: ~ **a** to devote oneself to.
aplique m wall light.
aplomo m self-assurance.
apocado/da adj timid.
Apocalipsis m Apocalypse.
apocamiento m timidity; depression.
apocar vt to lessen, to diminish; to contract; ~**se** vr to feel humiliated.
apócrifo/fa adj apocryphal; fabulous.
apodar vt to nickname.
apoderado/da m/f proxy, attorney; agent.
apoderar vt to authorize; to give the power of attorney to; ~**se** vr: ~ **de** to take possession of.
apodo m nickname, sobriquet.
apogeo m peak.
apolillar vt to gnaw/eat (clothes); ~**se** vr to be moth-eaten.
apología f eulogy; defense.
apoltronarse vr to grow lazy; to loiter.
apoplejía f apoplexy.
apoplético/ca adj apoplectic.
apoquinar vt (col) to fork out.
aporrear vt to beat up.
aportar vi to arrive at a port; to arrive; * vt to contribute.
aposentar vt to harbor; to put up.
aposento m room.
aposición f (gr) apposition.
apósito m (med) external dressing.
aposta adv on purpose.
apostar vt to bet, to wager; to post soldiers; * vi to bet.
apostasia f apostasy.
apóstata m apostate.
apostatar vi to apostatize.
apostilla f marginal note; postscript.
apóstol m apostle.
apostolado m apostleship.
apostólico/ca adj apostolic(al).
apostrofar vt to apostrophize.
apóstrofe m apostrophe.
apóstrofo m (gr) apostrophe.
apostura f neatness.
apoteosis f apotheosis.
apoyar vt to rest; to favor, to patronize, to support; ~**se** vr to lean.
apoyo m support; protection.
apreciable adj appreciable; valuable; respectable.
apreciar vt to appreciate; to estimate, to value.
aprecio m appreciation; esteem.
aprehender vt to apprehend, to seize.
aprehensión f apprehension, seizure.
apremiante adj urgent.
apremiar vt to press; to compel.
apremio m pressure, constriction; judicial compulsion.

aprender vt to learn; ~ **de memoria** to learn by heart.
aprendiz/za m/f apprentice.
aprendizaje m apprenticeship.
aprensión f apprehension.
aprensivo/va adj apprehensive.
apresar vt to seize, to grasp.
apresurado/da adj hasty.
apresuramiento m hurry.
apresurar vt to accelerate, to hasten, to expedite; ~**se** vr to hurry.
apretado/da adj tight; cramped;, difficult.
apretar vt to compress, to tighten; to constrain; to distress; to urge earnestly; * vi to be too tight.
apretón m squeeze.
apretura f squeeze.
aprieto m conflict; tight spot.
aprisa adv quickly, swiftly; promptly.
aprisco m sheepfold.
aprisionar vt to imprison.
aprobación f approbation, approval.
aprobar vt to approve; to pass; * vi to pass.
apropiación f appropriation, assumption.
apropiado/da adj appropriate.
apropiarse vr to appropriate.
aprovechable adj profitable.
aprovechado/da adj industrious; thrifty; selfish.
aprovechamiento m use; exploitation.
aprovechar vt to use; to exploit; to profit from; to take advantage of; * vi to be useful; to progress; ~**se** vr: ~ **de** to use; to take advantage of.
aproximación f approximation; closeness.
aproximado/da adj approximate.
aproximar vt to approach; ~**se** vr to approach.
aptitud f aptitude, fitness, ability.
apto/ta adj apt; fit, able; clever.
apuesta f bet, wager.
apuesto/ta adj neat.
apuntado/da adj pointed.
apuntador m prompter.
apuntalar vt to prop up.
apuntar vt to aim; to level, to point at; to mark; * vi to begin to appear/show itself; to prompt (theater); ~**se** vr to score; to enroll.
apunte m annotation; prompting (theater).
apuñalar vt to stab.
apurado/da adj poor, destitute of means; exhausted; hurried.
apurar vt to purify; to clear up, to verify; to exhaust; to tease and perplex; ~**se** vr to worry; to hurry.
apuro m want; pain, affliction; haste; jam.
aquejado/da adj afflicted.
aquel/~la adj that; ~**los/~las** pl those.
aquél/~ la; pn that (one); ~ **los/~ las** pl those (ones).

aquello *pn* that.
aquí *adv* here; now.
aquietar *vt* to quiet, to appease.
aquilino *adj* aquiline.
aquilón *m* north wind.
ara *f* altar.
árabe *adj*, *m/f* , *m* (*ling*) Arabic.
arabesco *m* arabesque.
arado *m* plow.
arancel *m* tariff.
arándano *m* bilberry; blueberry.
arandela *f* washer.
araña *f* spider; chandelier.
arañar *vt* to scratch; to scrape; to corrode.
arar *vt* to plow.
arbitraje *m* arbitration.
arbitrar *vt*, *vi* to arbitrate; to referee.
arbitrariedad *f* arbitrariness.
arbitrario/ria *adj* arbitrary.
arbitrativo/va *adj* arbitrary.
arbitrio *m* free will; arbitration.
árbitro *m* arbitrator; referee; umpire.
árbol *m* tree; (*mar*) mast; shaft.
arbolado/da *adj* forested; wooded; * *m* woodland.
arboladura *f* rigging; masts *pl*.
arbolar *vt* to hoist, to set upright.
arboleda *f* grove.
arbusto *m* shrub.
arca *f* chest, wooden box.
arcada *f* arch; arcade; ~s *fpl* retching.
arcaico/ca *adj* archaic.
arcaísmo *m* archaism.
arcángel *m* archangel.
arce *m* maple tree.
archipiélago *m* archipelago.
archivador *m* filing cabinet.
archivar *vt* to file.
archivero, **archivista** *m* keeper of records, archivist.
archivo *m* file(s) (*pl*); archives *pl*.
arcilla *f* clay.
arcilloso/sa *adj* clayey.
arcipreste *m* archpriest.
arco *m* arc; arch; fiddle bow; hoop; *Lat Am* goalmouth; ~ **iris** rainbow.
arder *vi* to burn, to blaze.
ardid *m* stratagem, artifice; cunning.
ardiente *adj* burning; ardent, passionate; active; fiery.
ardilla *f* squirrel.
ardor *m* heat; valor; vivacity; fieriness, fervor.
ardoroso/sa *adj* fiery; restless.
arduo/dua *adj* arduous, difficult; high.
área *f* area.
arena *f* sand; grit; arena.
arenal *m* sandy ground.
arenga *f* harangue; speech.
arengar *vi* to harangue.

arenisca *f* sandstone; grit.
arenoso/sa *adj* sandy.
arenque *m* herring; ~ **ahumado** smoked herring, kipper.
argamasa *f* mortar.
argamasar *vi* to mix mortar.
argolla *f* large ring.
argot *m* slang.
argucia *f* subtlety.
argüir *vi* to argue, to dispute; * *vt* to deduce; to argue; to imply.
argumentación *f* argumentation.
argumentar *vt*, *vi* to argue, to dispute; to conclude.
argumento *m* argument.
aria *f* (*mus*) aria; tune, air.
ariano/na *adj Lat Am* Arien (zodiac sign).
aridez *f* drought, want of rain.
árido/da *adj* dry; barren.
Aries *m* Aries (sign of the zodiac).
ariete *m* battering ram.
ario/a *adj* Aryan.
arisco/ca *adj* fierce; rude; intractable.
aristocracia *f* aristocracy.
aristócrata *m* aristocrat.
aristocrático/ca *adj* aristocratic.
aritmética *f* arithmetic.
arlequín *m* harlequin, buffoon.
arma *f* weapon, arm.
armada *f* fleet, armada.
armadillo *m* armadillo.
armado/da *adj* armed; reinforced.
armador *m* ship owner; privateer; jacket, jerkin.
armadura *f* armor; framework; skeleton; armature.
armamento *m* armament.
armar *vt* to man; to arm; to fit; ~**la** to kick up a fuss.
armario *m* wardrobe; cupboard.
armatoste *m* hulk; contraption.
armazón *f* chassis; skeleton; frame.
armería *f* arsenal; heraldry; gunsmith's (premises).
armero *m* gunsmith.
armiño *m* ermine.
armisticio *m* armistice.
armonía *f* harmony.
armonioso/sa *adj* harmonious.
armonizar *vt* to harmonize; to reconcile.
arnés *m* harness; ~**eses** *mpl* gear, trappings *pl*.
aro *m* ring; earring.
aroma *m* aroma, fragrance.
aromaterapia *f* aromatherapy.
aromático/ca *adj* aromatic.
arpa *f* harp.
arpegio *m* (*mus*) arpeggio.
arpía *f* (*poet*) shrew.
arpillera *f* sackcloth.

arpón *m* harpoon.
arqueado/da *adj* arched, vaulted.
arquear *vt* to arch; to bend.
arqueo *m* arching; tonnage, capacity (of a ship).
arqueología *f* archeology.
arqueólogo/ga *m/f* archeologist.
arquero *m* archer; *Lat Am* goalkeeper.
arqueta *f* small trunk.
arquetipo *m* archetype.
arquitecto *m* architect.
arquitectónico/ca *adj* architectural.
arquitectura *f* architecture.
arrabal *m* suburb; slum.
arrabalero *m* suburbanite.
arraigado *adj* deep-rooted; established.
arraigar *vi* to root; to establish; * *vt* to establish; ~**se** *vr* to take root; to settle.
arrancar *vt* to pull up by the roots; to pull out; to wrest; to extract; * *vi* to start; to move.
arranque *m* sudden start; start; outburst.
arras *fpl* security.
arrasar *vt* to demolish, to destroy.
arrastrado/da *adj* miserable; painstaking; servile.
arrastrar *vt* to drag; * *vi* to creep, to crawl; to lead a trump at cards; ~**se** *vr* to crawl; to grovel.
arrastre *m* dragging.
¡arre! *excl* gee!, go on!
arrear *vt* to drive on; * *vi* to hurry along.
arrebañar *vt* to scrape together; to pick up.
arrebatado/da *adj* rapid; violent, impetuous; rash, inconsiderate.
arrebatar *vt* to carry off, to snatch; to enrapture.
arrebato *m* fury; rapture.
arrebol *m* rouge.
arrebujar *vt* to crumple; to wrap up.
arrecife *m* reef.
arrecirse *vr* to grow stiff with cold.
arreglado *adj* neat; regular, moderate.
arreglar *vt* to regulate; to tidy; to adjust; ~**se** *vr* to come to an understanding.
arreglo *m* rule, order; agreement; arrangement.
arrellanarse *vr* to sit at ease; to make oneself comfortable.
arremangar *vt* to roll up; ~**se** *vr* to roll up one's sleeves.
arremeter *vi* to attack; to seize suddenly.
arremetida *f* attack, assault.
arrendador *m* landlord.
arrendamiento *m* leasing; hire; lease.
arrendar *vt* to rent, to let out, to lease.
arrendatario/ria *m/f* tenant.
arreo *m* dress, ornament; ~**s** *mpl* harness.
arrepentido/da *adj* repentant.
arrepentimiento *m* repentance, penitence.
arrepentirse *vr* to repent.
arrestar *vt* to arrest; to imprison.
arresto *m* boldness; prison; arrest.

arriada *f* flood, overflowing.
arriar *vt* (*mar*) to lower, to strike; to pay out.
arriate *m* bed; causeway.
arriba *adv* above, over, up; high, on high, overhead; aloft; ~ **de** *Lat Am* above.
arribada *f* (*mar*) arrival (of a vessel) in port.
arribar *vi* (*mar*) to put into harbor.
arribeño/ña *m/f Lat Am* highlander.
arribista *m/f* upstart.
arriendo *m* lease; farm rent.
arriero *m* muleteer.
arriesgado/da *adj* risky; daring.
arriesgar *vt* to risk, to hazard; to expose to danger; ~**se** *vr* to take a chance.
arrimar *vt* to approach, to draw near; (*mar*) to stow (cargo); ~**se** *vr* to side up; to lean.
arrinconar *vt* to put in a corner; to lay aside.
arrobado/da *adj* enchanted.
arrobamiento *m* rapture; amazement.
arrobarse *vr* to be totally amazed; to be out of one's senses.
arrocero/ra *adj* rice-producing.
arrodillarse *vr* to kneel down.
arrogancia *f* arrogance, haughtiness.
arrogante *adj* arrogant; haughty, proud; stout.
arrojadizo/za *adj* easily thrown.
arrojar *vt* to throw, to fling; to dash; to emit; to shoot, to sprout; ~**se** *vr* to hurl oneself.
arrojo *m* boldness, fearlessness.
arrollador/ra *adj* overwhelming.
arrollar *vt* to run over; to defeat heavily.
arropar *vt* to clothe, to dress; ~**se** *vr* to wrap up.
arrostrar *vt* to face (up to).
arroyo *m* stream; gutter.
arroz *m* rice.
arrozal *m* paddy, paddy field, rice field.
arruga *f* wrinkle; rumple.
arrugar *vt* to wrinkle; to rumple; to fold; ~ **la frente** to frown; ~**se** *vr* to shrivel.
arruinar *vt* to demolish; to ruin; ~**se** *vr* to go bankrupt.
arrullador/ra *adj* flattering, cajoling.
arrullar *vt* to lull; * *vi* to coo.
arrullo *m* cooing (of pigeons); lullaby.
arrumaco *m* caress.
arsenal *m* arsenal; dockyard.
arsénico *m* arsenic.
arte *m/f* art; skill; artfulness.
artefacto *m* appliance.
arteria *f* artery.
artero/ra *adj* dexterous, cunning, artful.
artesa *f* trough; kneading trough.
artesanía *f* craftsmanship.
artesano *m* artisan, workman.
ártico/ca *adj* arctic; * *m*: **el A~** the Arctic.
articulación *f* articulation; joint.
articulado/da *adj* articulated; jointed.
articular *vt* to articulate; to joint.

artículo *m* article; clause; point; (*gr*) article; condition.

artífice *m* artisan; artist.

artificial *adj* artificial.

artificio *m* workmanship, craft; artifice, cunning trick.

artificioso/sa *adj* skillful, ingenious; artful, cunning.

artillería *f* gunnery; artillery.

artillero *m* artillery man.

artimaña *f* trap; cunning.

artista *m* artist; craftsman.

artístico/ca *adj* artistic.

artritis *f* arthritis.

arzobispado *m* archbishopric.

arzobispo *m* archbishop.

as *m* ace.

asa *f* handle; lever.

asado *m* roast meat; barbecue.

asador *m* spit.

asadura *f* offal.

asalariado/da *adj* salaried.

asaltador/a *m/f* assailant.

asaltante *m/f* assailant.

asaltar *vt* to assault; to storm (a position); to assail.

asalto *m* assault, attack; stick-up.

asamblea *f* assembly, meeting.

asar *vt* to roast.

asbesto *m* asbestos.

ascendencia *f* ascendancy; ancestry.

ascendente *adj* ascending; (*rail*) **tren** ~ *m* up train.

ascender *vi* to be promoted; to rise; * *vt* to promote.

ascendiente *m* forefather; influence.

Ascensión *f* feast of the Ascension.

ascenso *m* promotion; ascent.

ascensor *m* elevator.

asceta *m* ascetic.

ascético/ca *adj* ascetic.

asco *m* nausea; loathing.

ascua *f* red-hot coal.

aseado/da *adj* clean; elegant; neat.

asear *vt* to clean; to tidy.

asediar *vt* to besiege; to chase.

asedio *m* siege.

asegurado/da *adj* insured.

asegurador *m* insurer.

asegurar *vt* to secure; to insure; to affirm; to bail; ~**se** *vr* to make sure.

asemejarse *vr* to be like, to resemble.

asentado/da *adj* established.

asentar *vt* to sit down; to affirm, to assure; to note; * *vi* to suit.

asentir *vi* to acquiesce, to concede.

aseo *m* cleanliness; neatness; ~**s** *mpl* bathroom facilities *pl*.

aséptico/ca *adj* germ-free.

asequible *adj* attainable; obtainable.

aserción *f* assertion, affirmation.

aserradero *m* sawmill.

aserrar *vt* to saw.

aserrín *m* sawdust.

asertivo/va *adj* affirmative.

asesinar *vt* to assassinate; to murder.

asesinato *m* assassination; murder.

asesino *m* assassin; murderer.

asesor *m* counselor, adviser, consultant.

asesorar *vt* to advise; to act as consultant to; ~**se** *vr* to consult.

asestar *vt* to aim, to point; to strike.

aseverar *vt* to affirm.

asfalto *m* asphalt.

asfixia *f* suffocation.

asfixiar *vt* to suffocate; ~**se** *vr* to suffocate.

así *adv* so, thus, in this manner; like this; therefore; so that; also; ~ **que** so that; therefore; **así, así** so-so; middling.

asidero *m* handle.

asiduidad *f* assiduousness.

asiduo/dua *adj* assiduous.

asiento *m* chair; bench, stool; seat; contract; entry; residence.

asignación *f* assignation; destination.

asignar *vt* to assign, to attribute.

asignatario/a *m/f Lat Am* heir.

asignatura *f* subject; course.

asilado/da *m/f* inmate; refugee.

asilo *m* asylum, refuge; ~ **político** political asylum.

asimilación *f* assimilation.

asimilar *vt* to assimilate.

asimismo *adv* similarly, in the same manner.

asir *vt* to grasp, to seize; to hold, to grip; * *vi* to take root.

asistencia *f* audience; presence; assistance, help.

asistente *m* assistant, helper.

asistir *vi* to be present; to assist; * *vt* to help.

asma *f* asthma.

asmático/ca *adj* asthmatic.

asno *m* ass.

asociación *f* association; partnership.

asociado *m* associate.

asociar *vt* to associate; ~**se** *vr* to associate.

asolar *vt* to destroy; to devastate.

asolear *vt* to expose to the sun; ~**se** *vr* to sunbathe.

asomar *vi* to appear; ~**se** *vr* to appear, to show up.

asombrar *vt* to amaze; to astonish; ~**se** *vr* to be amazed; to get a fright.

asombro *m* dread, terror; astonishment.

asombroso/sa *adj* astonishing, marvelous.

asomo *m* mark, token, indication; conjecture.

asonancia *f* assonance; harmony.

aspa *f* cross; sail.

aspaviento m astonishment; fuss.
aspecto m appearance; aspect.
aspereza f roughness; surliness.
áspero/ra adj rough, rugged; craggy, knotty; horrid; harsh, hard; severe, austere; gruff.
asperón m grindstone.
aspersión f sprinkling; aspersion.
áspid m asp.
aspiración f breath; pause.
aspirante m aspirant, aspirer.
aspirar vt to breathe; to aspire; (gr) to aspirate.
aspirina f aspirin.
asquear vt to sicken; * vi to be sickening; ~se vr to feel disgusted.
asqueroso/sa adj disgusting.
asta f lance; horn; handle.
astado/da adj horned.
asterisco m asterisk.
astilla f chip (of wood), splinter.
astillero m dockyard.
astral adj astral.
astringente adj astringent.
astro m star.
astrología f astrology.
astrológico/ca adj astrological.
astrólogo/ga m/f astrologer.
astronauta m/f astronaut.
astronave f spaceship.
astronomía f astronomy.
astronómico/ca adj astronomical.
astrónomo/ma m/f astronomer.
astucia f cunning, slyness.
astuto/ta adj cunning, sly; astute.
asueto m time off; vacation, holiday.
asumir vt to assume.
Asunción f Assumption.
asunto m subject, matter; affair, business.
asustar vt to frighten; ~se vr to be frightened.
atacar vt to attack.
atajada f Lat Am (sport) save.
atajo m short cut.
atalaya f watchtower.
atañer vi: ~ a to concern.
ataque m attack.
atar vt to tie; to fasten.
atardecer vi to get dark; * m dusk; evening.
atareado/da adj busy.
atascar vt to jam; to hinder; ~se vr to become bogged down.
atasco m traffic jam.
ataúd m coffin.
ataviar vt to dress up, to trim, to adorn.
atavío m dress; ornament; ~s mpl finery.
ateísmo m atheism.
atemorizar vt to frighten; ~se vr to get scared.
atenazar vt to grip; to torment.
atención f attention, heedfulness; civility; observance, consideration.

atender vi to be attentive; * vt to attend to; to heed, to expect, to wait for; to look at.
atenerse vr: ~ a to adhere to.
atentado m terrorist attack; transgression, offence.
atentamente adv observantly; **le saluda** ~ yours faithfully.
atentar vt to attempt; to commit.
atento/ta adj attentive; heedful; observing; mindful; polite, courteous, mannerly.
atenuante adj extenuating.
atenuar vt to diminish; to lessen.
ateo/a adj, m/f atheist.
aterciopelado/da adj velvety.
aterido/da adj frozen stiff.
aterirse vr to grow stiff with cold.
aterrador/a adj frightening.
aterrar vt to terrify; ~se vr to be terrified.
aterrizaje m landing.
aterrizar vi to land.
aterrorizar vt to frighten, to terrify.
atesorar vt to treasure/hoard up (riches).
atestación f testimony, evidence.
atestado/da adj packed; * m affidavit.
atestar vt to cram, to stuff; to attest, to witness.
atestiguar vt to witness, to attest.
atiborrar vt to stuff; ~se vr to stuff oneself.
ático m attic.
atildar vt to punctuate with a tilde; to censure.
atinado/da adj wise; correct.
atisbar vt to pry into; to examine closely.
atizar vt to stir (the fire) with a poker; to stir up.
atlántico/ca adj Atlantic; * m: **el A**~ the Atlantic.
atlas m atlas.
atleta m/f athlete.
atlético/ca adj athletic.
atletismo m athletics.
atmósfera f atmosphere.
atmosférico/ca adj atmospheric.
atolladero m bog; obstacle; impediment.
atollar vi to stick; ~se vr to get stuck.
atolondramiento m stupefaction, consternation.
atolondrar vt to stun, to stupefy; ~se vr to be stupefied.
atómico/ca adj atomic.
atomizador m spray.
átomo m atom.
atónito/ta adj astonished, amazed.
atontado/da adj stunned; silly.
atontar vt to stun, to stupefy; ~se to grow stupid.
atormentar vt to torture; to harass; to torment.
atornillar vt to screw on; to screw down.
atosigar vt to poison; to harass; to oppress.
atracadero m landing-place.
atracador/a m/f robber.
atracar vt to moor; to rob; ~se vr: ~ (de) to stuff oneself (with).

atracción f attraction.

atraco m stick-up, robbery.

atractivo/va adj attractive; magnetic; * m charm.

atraer vt to attract, to allure.

atragantarse vr to stick in the throat, to choke.

atrancar vt to bar (a door).

atrapar vt to trap; to nab; to deceive.

atrás adv backward(s); behind; previously, **hacia ~** backward(s); **~ de** Lat Am behind.

atrasado/da adj slow; backward; in arrears.

atrasar vi to be slow; * vt to postpone; **~ el reloj** to put back a watch; **~se** vr to stay behind; to be late.

atraso m backwardness; slowness; delay.

atravesado/da adj oblique; cross; perverse; mongrel; degenerate.

atravesar vt to cross; to pass over; to pierce; to go through; **~se** vr to get in the way; to meddle.

atrayente adj attractive.

atreverse vr to dare, to venture.

atrevido/da adj bold, audacious, daring.

atrevimiento m boldness, audacity.

atribución f attribution, imputation.

atribuir vt to attribute, to ascribe; to impute.

atribular vt to vex, to afflict.

atributivo/va adj attributive.

atributo m attribute.

atrición f attrition.

atril m lectern; music stand.

atrio m porch; portico.

atrocidad f atrocity.

atrochar vi to take a short cut.

atropellado/da adj hasty, precipitate.

atropellar vt to trample; to run down; to hurry; to insult; **~se** vr to hurry.

atropello m accident; push; outrage.

atuendo m attire.

atroz adj atrocious, heinous; cruel.

atufar vt to vex, to plague; **~se** vr turn sour; to get mad.

atún m tuna.

aturdido/da adj hare-brained.

aturdimiento m stupefaction; astonishment; dullness.

aturdir vt to stun, to confuse; to stupefy.

atusar vt to smooth.

audacia f audacity, boldness.

audaz adj audacious, bold.

audible adj audible.

audiencia f audience.

audífonos mpl Lat Am headphones.

auditivo/va adj auditory.

auditor m auditor.

auditoría f audit.

auditorio m audience; auditorium.

auge m boom; climax.

augurar vt to predict.

augurio m omen.

aula f lecture room.

aullar vi to howl.

aullido/aullo m howling.

aumentar vt to augment, to increase; to magnify; to put up; * vi to increase; to grow larger.

aumento m increase; promotion, advancement.

aún adv even; **~ así** even so.

aun adv still; yet.

aunar vt to unite, to assemble.

aunque adv though, although.

¡aúpa! excl come on!

aura f Lat Am turkey vulture/buzzard.

áureo/rea adj golden, gilt compd.

aureola f glory; nimbus.

auricular m receiver; **~es** mpl headphones pl.

aurora f dawn.

auscultar vt to sound.

ausencia f absence.

ausentarse vr to go out.

ausente adj absent.

auspicio m auspice; prediction; protection.

austeridad f austerity.

austero/ra adj austere, severe.

austral adj southern.

autenticar vt to authenticate.

autenticidad f authenticity.

auténtico/ca adj authentic.

autillo m brown owl.

auto m judicial sentence; car; edict, ordinance; **~ de fe** auto-da-fé.

autoadhesivo/va adj self-adhesive.

autobiografía f autobiography.

autobús m bus.

autocar m bus.

autocracia f autocracy.

autócrata m autocrat.

autóctono/na adj native.

autodefensa f self-defense.

autodeterminación f self-determination.

autoedición f desktop publishing.

autoescuela f driving school.

autoestop, autostop f hitchhiking; **hacer ~** to hitchhike.

autoestopista, autostopista m/f hitchhiker.

autógrafo m autograph.

autómata m automaton.

automático/ca adj automatic.

automatización f automation.

automedicación f self-medication.

automotor m diesel train.

automóvil m automobile.

automovilismo m motoring; motor racing.

automovilista m/f motorist, driver.

automovilístico/ca adj car compd.

autonomía f autonomy.

autónomo/ma adj autonomous.

autonómico/ca adj autonomous.

autopista f highway, superhighway, expressway; ~ **de la información** information superhighway; ~ **de peaje** turnpike.

autopsía f post mortem, autopsy.

autor/ra m/f author; maker; writer.

autoridad f authority.

autorización f authorization.

autorizar vt to authorize.

autorradio m car radio.

autorretrato m self-portrait.

autoservicio m self-service store; self-service restaurant.

autosuficiencia f self-sufficiency.

autovía f state highway.

auxiliar vt to aid, to help, to assist; to attend; * adj auxiliary.

auxilio m aid, help, assistance.

aval m guarantee; guarantor.

avalancha f avalanche.

avaluar vt I at Am to value.

avance m advance; attack; trailer (for a film).

avanzada f (mil) vanguard.

avanzar vt, vi to advance.

avaricia f avarice.

avaricioso/sa adj avaricious, covetous.

avaro/ra adj miserly; * m/f miser.

avasallar vt to subdue; to enslave.

ave f bird; fowl.

avecinarse vr to be on the way.

avellana f hazelnut.

avellano m hazelnut tree.

ave maría f Hail Mary.

avena f oats pl.

avenencia f agreement, bargain; union.

avenida f avenue.

avenido/da adj agreed.

avenir vt to reconcile; ~**se** vr to reach a compromise.

aventajado/da adj advantageous, profitable; beautiful; excellent.

aventajar vt to surpass, to excel.

aventar vt to fan; to expel.

aventura f adventure; event, incident.

aventurado/da adj risky.

aventurar vt to venture, to risk.

aventurero/ra adj adventurous.

avergonzar vt to shame, to abash; ~**se** vr to be ashamed.

avería f breakdown.

averiado/da adj broken down; out of order.

averiarse vr to break down.

averiguación f discovery; investigation.

averiguar vt to inquire into; to investigate, to explore.

aversión f aversion, dislike; abhorrence.

avestruz m ostrich.

aviación f aviation; air force.

aviador/a m/f aviator.

avicultura f poultry farming.

avidez f covetousness.

ávido/da adj (poet) greedy, covetous.

avieso/sa adj irregular, out of the way; mischievous, perverse.

avinagrado/da adj sour.

avinagrarse vr to go sour.

avío m preparation, provision.

avión m airplane.

avioneta f light aircraft.

avisado/da adj prudent, cautious; **mal** ~ ill-advised.

avisar vt to inform; to warn; to advise.

aviso m notice; warning; hint; Lat Am advertisement.

avispa f wasp.

avispado/da adj lively, brisk; vivacious.

avisparse vr to worry.

avispero m wasp's nest.

avispón m hornet.

avistar vt to sight.

avituallar vt (mil) to supply (with food).

avivar vt to quicken, to enliven; to encourage.

avutarda f bustard.

axioma m axiom, maxim.

¡ay! excl ouch!; ow! **¡** ~ **de mí!** alas!, poor me!

aya f governess, instructress.

ayer adv yesterday.

ayuda f help, aid; support; * m deputy, assistant.

ayudante m (mil) adjutant; assistant.

ayudar vt to help, to assist; to further.

ayunar vi to fast, to abstain from food.

ayuno m fasting, abstinence from food.

ayuntamiento m town/city hall.

azabache m jet.

azada f spade; hoe.

azafata f air stewardess.

azafrán m saffron.

azahar m orange/lemon blossom.

azar m unforeseen disaster; unexpected accident; fate; **por** ~ by chance; **al** ~ at random.

azaroso/sa adj unlucky, ominous; risky.

azogue m mercury.

azor m goshawk.

azorar vt to frighten, to terrify.

azotaina f drubbing, sound flogging.

azotar vt to whip, to lash.

azote m whip.

azotea f flat roof of a house.

azteca m/f Aztec.

azúcar m/f sugar.

azucarado/da adj sugared; sugary.

azucarar vt to sugar, to sweeten.

azucarero m sugar bowl.

azucena f white lily.

azufre m sulfur, brimstone.

azul adj blue; ~ **celeste** sky blue.

azulado/da adj azure, bluish.

azulejo m tile.

azuzar vt to irritate, to stir up.

B

baba *f* dribble, spittle.
babear *vi* to dribble, to drool.
babel *m* bedlam.
babero *m* bib.
babia *f:* **estar en ~** to be absent-minded/
  dreaming.
baboso/sa *adj* dribbling, drooling.
babucha *f* slipper.
baca *f* (*auto*) roof rack.
bacalao *m* cod.
bache *m* pothole.
bachillerato *m* baccalaureate; a sermon delivered
  to a graduating class.
báculo *m* stick.
bagaje *m* baggage.
bagatela *f* trinket, trifle.
bahía *f* bay.
bailador/ra *m/f* dancer.
bailar *vi* to dance.
bailarín/ina *m/f* dancer.
baile *m* dance, ball; **~ de disfraces** fancy-dress
  ball; **~ de gala** prom.
baja *f* fall; casualty.
bajada *f* descent; inclination; slope; ebb.
bajamar *f* low water, low tide.
bajar *vt* to lower, to let down; to lessen; to humble;
  to go/come down; to bend downward(s); * *vi*
  to descend; to go/come down; to grow less; **~se**
  vr to crouch; to lessen.
bajeza *f* meanness; lowliness.
bajío *m* shoal, sandbank; lowlands *pl*.
bajo/ja *adj* low; abject, despicable; common; dull
  (of colors); deep; humble; * *prep* under,
  underneath, below; * *adv* softly; quietly; * *m*
  (*mus*) bass; low place.
bajón *m* fall.
bakalao *m* (*col*) rave music.
bala *f* bullet; **lanzamiento de ~** *Lat Am* shot put.
balacear *vt* *Lat Am* to shoot.
balacera *f* *Lat Am* shootout.
baladronada *f* boast, brag; bravado.
balance *m* hesitation; balance sheet; balance;
  rocking chair; rolling (of a ship).
balancear *vt*, *vi* to balance; to roll; to waver;
  ~se *vr* to swing.
balancín *m* balance beam; seesaw; balancing
  pole.
balanza *f* scale; balance.
balar *vi* to bleat.
balaustrada *f* balustrade, banister.
balazo *m* shot.
balbucear *vt*, *vi* to stutter.

balbuciente *adj* stammering, stuttering.
balcón *m* balcony.
baldar *vt* to cripple, to disable.
balde *m* bucket; **de ~** *adv* gratis, for
  nothing; **en ~** in vain.
baldío/día *adj* waste; uncultivated.
baldosa *f* floor; tile; paving stone, flagstone.
balear *vt* *Lat Am* to shoot.
baleo *m* *Lat Am* shootout.
balido *m* bleating, bleat.
balín *m* buckshot.
balística *f* ballistics *pl*.
ballena *f* whale; whalebone.
ballenato *m* calf of a whale.
ballenero *m* (*mar*) whaler.
ballesta *f* crossbow; **a tiro de ~** at a great
  distance.
ballestero *m* archer; crossbow-maker.
ballet *m* ballet.
balneario *m* spa; *Lat Am* seaside resort.
balón *m* ball.
baloncesto *m* basketball.
balonmano *m* handball.
balonvolea *m* volleyball.
balsa¹ *f* balsa wood; raft, float.
balsa² *f* pool, pond.
bálsamo *m* balsam, balm.
baluarte *m* bastion; bulwark.
bamba *f* fat; (*bot*) swelling; flabbiness.
bambolear *vi* to reel; **~se** *vr* to sway.
bamboleo *m* reeling, staggering.
bambú *m* bamboo.
banana *f* banana; plantain.
banano *m* banana tree.
banasta *f* large basket.
banca *f* bench; banking; **~ electrónica** electronic
  banking.
bancario/ria *adj* bank(ing) *compd*.
bancarrota *f* bankruptcy.
banco *m* bench; work bench; bank.
banda *f* band; sash; ribbon; troop; party; gang;
  touchline.
bandada *f* flock; shoal.
bandearse *vr* to move to and fro.
bandeja *f* tray, salver.
bandera *f* banner, standard; flag.
banderilla *f* small decorated dart used at a
  bullfight.
banderillear *vt* to plant banderillas in a bull's
  neck/shoulder.
banderillero *m* thrower of banderillas.
banderín *m* small flag, pennant.

bandido *m* bandit, outlaw.
bando *m* faction, party; edict.
bandolera *f* bandoleer.
bandolero *m* bandit.
bandurria *f* bandore (musical instrument resembling a lute).
banquero/ra *m/f* banker.
banqueta *f* three-legged stool; sidewalk.
banquete *m* banquet; formal dinner.
banquillo *m* dock; bench.
bañador *m* swimsuit.
bañar *vt* to bathe; to dip; to coat (with varnish); ~**se** *vr* to bathe; to swim; *Lat Am* to have a shower.
bañera *f* bath(tub).
bañero *m* lifeguard.
bañista *m/f* bather.
baño *m* bath; *Lat Am* shower; dip; bathtub; varnish; coating.
baptista *m/f* Baptist.
bar *m* bar.
baraja *f* pack of cards.
barajar *vt* to shuffle (cards); to jumble up.
baranda *f* rail.
barandilla *f* small balustrade, small railing.
baratijas *fpl* trifles *pl*; toys *pl*; trash, junk.
baratillo *m* secondhand goods *pl*; secondhand shop; bargain sale.
barato/ta *adj* cheap; **de** ~ gratis; * *m* cheapness; bargain sale; money extracted from winning gamblers.
baraúnda *f* noise, hurly-burly.
barba *f* chin; beard; ~ **a** ~ face to face; * *m* actor who impersonates old men.
barbacoa *f* barbecue.
barbaridad *f* barbarity, barbarism; outrage.
barbarie *f* barbarism; savagery.
barbarismo *m* barbarism (form of speech).
bárbaro/ra *adj* barbarous; cruel; rude; rough.
barbecho *m* first plowing, fallow land.
barbería *f* barber shop.
barbero *m* barber.
barbilampiño/ña *adj* clean-shaven; (*fig*) inexperienced.
barbilla *f* (tip of the) chin.
barbo *m* barbel.
barbudo/da *adj* bearded.
barca *f* boat.
barco *m* boat; ship.
barítono *m* (*mus*) baritone.
barman *m* barman.
barniz *m* varnish; glaze.
barnizar *vt* to varnish.
barómetro *m* barometer.
barón *m* baron.
baronesa *f* baroness.
barquero *m* boatman.
barquilla *f* (*mar*) log; basket (of an air balloon).
barquillo *m* wafer; cornet, cone.

barra *m* bar; rod; lever; French loaf; sandbank; **de** ~ **a** ~ from place to place.
barrabasada *f* trick, plot.
barraca *f* hut.
barranco *m* gully, ravine; (*fig*) great difficulty.
barranquismo *m* (*sport*) canyoning.
barrena *f* drill, bit, auger.
barrenar *vt* to drill, to bore; (*fig*) to frustrate.
barrendero *m* sweeper.
barreno *m* large drill; borehole.
barreño *m* tub.
barrer *vt* to sweep; to overwhelm.
barrera *f* barrier; turnpike, claypit.
barriada *f* suburb, area of a city; *Lat Am* shanty town.
barricada *f* barricade.
barrido *m* sweep.
barriga *f* abdomen; belly.
barrigudo/da *adj* pot-bellied.
barril *m* barrel; cask.
barrio *m* area, district.
barrizal *m* claypit.
barro *m* clay, mud.
barroco/ca *adj* baroque.
barrote *m* ironwork (of doors, windows, tables); crosspiece.
barruntar *vt* to guess; to foresee; to conjecture.
barrunto *m* conjecture.
bártulos *mpl* gear, belongings *pl*.
barullo *m* uproar.
basamento *m* base.
basalto *m* basalt.
basar *vt* to base; ~**se** *vr*: ~ **en** to be based on.
basca *f* squeamishness, nausea.
báscula *f* scales *pl*.
base *f* base, basis.
básico/ca *adj* basic.
basílica *f* basilica.
basilisco *m* basilisk.
básquetbol *m* *Lat Am* basketball.
basquetbolista *m/f* *Lat Am* basketball player.
bastante *adj* sufficient, enough; * *adv* quite.
bastar *vi* to be sufficient, to be enough.
bastardo/da *adj*, *m/f* bastard.
bastidor *m* embroidery frame; ~**es** *mpl* scenery (on stage).
bastión *m* bastion.
basto/ta *adj* coarse, rude, unpolished.
bastón *m* cane, stick; truncheon; (*fig*) command.
bastonazo *m* beating.
bastos *mpl* clubs *pl* (in cards).
basura *f* garbage, trash, refuse; dung.
basurero *m* garbageman, refuse collector; dunghill.
bata *f* dressing gown; coveralls; laboratory coat.
batacazo *m* noise of a fall.
batalla *f* battle, combat; fight.
batallador/a *adj* battling.

batallar *vi* to battle, to fight; to fence with foils; to waver.

batallón *m* (*mil*) battalion.

batata *f* sweet potato.

bate *m* bat.

batería *m* battery; percussion.

bateristo/sta *m/f Lat Am* drummer.

batida *f* beating (of woodland/moorland); search; chase.

batido/da *adj* shot (of silk); well-trodden (of roads); * *m* batter; ~ **de leche** milk shake.

batidora *f* food mixer; whisk.

batir *vt* to beat; to whisk; to dash; to demolish; to defeat.

batista *f* fine cotton cloth, cambric.

batuta *f* baton.

baúl *m* trunk(of a car), trunk (luggage); (*col*) belly.

bautismal *adj* baptismal.

bautismo *m* baptism.

bautizar *vt* to baptize, to christen.

bautizo *m* baptism.

baya *f* berry.

bayeta *f* cloth.

bayo/ya *adj* bay (color of a horse).

bayoneta *f* bayonet.

bayonetazo *m* thrust with a bayonet.

baza *f* card trick.

bazar *m* bazaar.

bazo *m* spleen.

bazofia *f* refuse; hogwash.

be *m* baa (of sheep).

beatificación *f* beatification.

beatificar *vt* to beatify; to hallow, to sanctify, to make blessed.

beato/ta *adj* happy; blessed; devout; * *m* lay brother; *m/f* pious person; beatified person.

bebé *m/f* baby.

bebedero *m* drinking trough.

bebedizo *m* (love) potion.

bebedor/ra *m/f* (hard) drinker.

beber *vt* (*vi*) to drink.

bebida *f* drink, beverage.

beca *f* fellowship; grant, bursary, scholarship; sash; hood.

becada *f* woodcock.

becerro *m* yearling calf.

bedel *m* janitor; uniformed employee.

befa *f* jeer, taunt.

befarse *vr*: ~ **de** to mock, to ridicule.

beldad *f* beauty.

belén *m* nativity scene.

bélico/ca *adj* warlike, martial.

belicoso/sa *adj* warlike; aggressive.

beligerante *adj* belligerent.

bellaco/ca *adj* artful; cunning.

belladona *f* (*bot*) deadly nightshade.

belleza *f* beauty.

bello/lla *adj* beautiful; handsome; lovely; fine.

bellota *f* acorn; Adam's apple; pomander.

bemol *m* (*mus*) flat.

bencina *f* benzine.

bendecir *vt* to bless; to consecrate; to praise.

bendición *f* blessing, benediction.

bendito/ta *adj* saintly; blessed; simple; happy.

benedictino/na, benito/ta *adj*, *m/f* Benedictine.

beneficiado *m* incumbent; beneficiary.

beneficiar *vt* to benefit; to be of benefit to.

beneficiario/ra *m/f* beneficiary.

beneficio *m* benefit, advantage; profit; benefit night.

beneficioso/sa *adj* beneficial.

benéfico/ca *adj* beneficent, kind.

benemérito/ta *adj* worthy, meritorious.

beneplácito *m* consent, approbation.

benevolencia *f* benevolence.

benévolo/la *adj* benevolent, kind-hearted.

benigno/na *adj* benign; kind; mild.

beodo/da *adj* drunk, drunken.

berberecho *m* cockle.

berenjena *f* eggplant.

bergantín *m* (*mar*) brig.

bermejo/ja *adj* red.

berrear *vi* to low, to bellow.

berrido *m* bellowing (of calf).

berrinche *m* anger, rage, tantrum (applied to children).

berro *m* watercress.

berza *f* cabbage.

besamanos *m invar* levee; royal audience.

besamel *f* white sauce.

besar *vt* to kiss; to graze; ~**se** *vr* to kiss.

beso *m* kiss; collision of persons/things.

bestia *f* beast, animal; idiot.

bestial *adj* bestial; (*col*) marvelous, great.

bestialidad *f* bestiality.

besugo *m* sea bream.

besuquear *vt* to cover with kisses.

besuqueo *m* repeated kisses *pl*.

betún *m* shoe polish.

bezo *m* thick lip; (*med*) swollen tissue in a wound.

biberón *m* feeding bottle.

Biblia *f* Bible.

bíblico/ca *adj* biblical.

bibliófilo/la *m/f* book-lover, bookworm.

bibliografía *f* bibliography.

bibliográfico/ca *adj* bibliographical.

bibliógrafo/fa *m/f* bibliographer.

biblioteca *f* library.

bibliotecario/ria *m/f* librarian.

bicarbonato *m* bicarbonate.

bicho *m* small animal; bug; **mal** ~ villain.

bici *f* (*col*) bike.

bicicleta *f* bicycle; ~ **de montaña** mountain bike.

bidé *m* bidet.
bielda *f* pitchfork.
bien *m* good, benefit; profit; ~**es** *mpl* goods *pl*, property; wealth; ~**es raíces** *mpl* real estate; * *adv* well, right; very; willingly; easily; ~ **que** *conj* although; **está** ~ he is well.
bienal *adj* biennial.
bienaventuranza *f* blessedness; bliss; happiness; prosperity; ~**s** *fpl* the Beatitudes.
bienestar *m* wellbeing.
bienhablado/da *adj* well-spoken.
bienhecho/cha *adj* well-shaped.
bienhechor/ra *m/f* benefactor.
bienio *m* space of two years.
bienvenida *f* welcome.
bifurcación *f* fork.
bigamia *f* bigamy.
bígamo/ma *m/f* bigamist.
bigote *m* mustache; whiskers *pl*.
bigotudo/da *adj* with a big mustache.
bikini *m* bikini.
bilingüe *adj* bilingual.
bilioso/sa *adj* bilious.
bilis *f* bile.
billar *m* billiards *pl*.
billete *m* note, banknote, greenback; ticket; (*rail*) ticket; ~ **sencillo** single ticket; ~ **de ida y vuelta** return ticket.
billetero *m* billfold, wallet.
billón *m* trillion.
bimensual *adj* twice-monthly.
bimotor *m* twin-engined plane.
binario *m* binary.
binoculares *mpl* binoculars *pl*; opera glasses *pl*.
binóculos *mpl* Lat Am binoculars.
biodegradable *adj* biodegradable.
biodiversity *f* biodiversity.
biografía *f* biography.
biógrafo/fa *m/f* biographer.
biología *f* biology.
biológico/ca *adj* biological.
biólogo/ga *m/f* biologist.
biombo *m* screen.
biopsia *f* biopsy.
bípedo *m* biped.
birlar *vt* to knock down at one blow; (*col*) to pinch.
birreta *f* biretta.
bis *excl* encore.
bisabuela *f* great-grandmother.
bisabuelo *m* great-grandfather.
bisagra *f* hinge.
bisexual *adj* bisexual.
bisexualidad *f* bisexuality.
bisiesto *adj*: **año** ~ leap year.
bisnieto/ta *m/f* great-grandson/daughter.
bisoño/na *adj* raw, inexperienced; novice.
bisonte *m* American bison, buffalo.

bistec *m* steak.
bisturí *m* scalpel.
bisutería *f* costume jewelry.
bizarro/rra *adj* brave, gallant; generous.
bizco/ca *adj* cross-eyed.
bizcocho *m* sponge cake; biscuit; ship's biscuit.
bizquear *vi* to squint.
blanco/ca *adj* white; blank; * *m* whiteness; White person; blank, blank space; target (to shoot at).
blancura *f* whiteness.
blandir *vt* to brandish a sword; ~**se** *vr* to swing.
blando/da *adj* soft, smooth; mild, gentle; (*col*) cowardly.
blanducho/cha *adj* flabby.
blandura *f* softness; gentleness, mildness.
blanquear *vt* to bleach; to whitewash; to launder (money); * *vi* to show white.
blanquecino/na *adj* whitish.
blanqueo *m* laundering (of money).
blasfemador/ra *m/f* blasphemer.
blasfemar *vi* to blaspheme.
blasfemia *f* blasphemy; verbal insult.
blasfemo/ma *adj* blasphemous; * *m* blasphemer.
blasón *m* heraldry, honor, glory.
blasonar *vt* to emblazon; to praise highly.
bledo *m*: **me importa un** ~ (*col*) I don't give a damn.
blindado/da *adj* armor-plated; bullet-proof.
bloc *m* writing pad.
bloque *m* block.
bloquear *vt* to block; to blockade.
bloqueo *m* blockade.
blusa *f* blouse.
boato *m* ostentation, pompous show.
bobada *f* folly, foolishness.
bobear *vt* to act/talk in a stupid manner.
bobería *f* silliness, foolishness.
bobina *f* bobbin.
bobo/ba *m/f* idiot, fool; clown, funny man; * *adj* stupid, silly.
boca *f* mouth; entrance, opening; mouth of a river; ~ **en** ~ *adv* by word of mouth; **a pedir de** ~ to one's heart's content.
bocacalle *f* entrance to a street.
bocadillo *m* sandwich, roll.
bocado *m* mouthful.
bocal *m* pitcher; mouthpiece of a trumpet.
bocamanga *f* cuff, wristband.
bocanada *f* mouthful (of liquor); gust.
bocazas *m/f invar* loudmouth.
boceto *m* sketch.
bochinche *m* Lat Am (*col*) racket.
bochorno *m* sultry weather, scorching heat; blush.
bochornoso/sa *adj* sultry; shameful.
bocina *f* trumpet; megaphone; car horn.
bocón/ona *m/f Lat Am* (*col*) big mouth.

boda f wedding.
bodega f wine cellar; warehouse; bar.
bodegón m cheap restaurant, diner; still life (in art).
bodoque m pellet; lump; (col) idiot.
bodorrio m quiet wedding.
bofes mpl lungs; lights.
bofetada f slap (in the face).
bofetón m hard slap.
boga f fashion; (rail) bogie/bogy; rower; rowing; **estar en ~** to be fashionable.
bogar vi to row, to paddle.
bohemio m/f Bohemian.
boicot m boycott.
boicotear vt to boycott.
boina f beret.
boj m box; boxwood; box tree.
bola f ball; marble; globe; slam (in cards); shoe polish; (col) lie, fib.
bolazo m blow with a ball.
bolchevique adj Bolshevik.
bolear vi to knock balls about (billiards); * vt to throw (a ball).
bolera f bowling alley.
bolero m bolero jacket; bolero dance.
boleta f entrance ticket; pass, permit.
boletería f Lat Am ticket office.
boletín m bulletin; journal, review.
boleto m Lat Am ticket.
boli m (col) (ballpoint) pen.
boliche m jack (at bowls); bowls, bowling alley; dragnet.
bolígrafo m (ballpoint) pen.
bolillo m bobbin.
bollo m bread roll; lump.
bolo m ninepin; (large) pill.
bolsa f purse, handbag; bag; pocket; sac; stock exchange; **~ de dormir** Lat Am sleeping bag.
bolsillo m pocket; purse.
bolsista m/f stockbroker.
bolso m purse.
bomba f pump; bomb; surprise; **dar a la ~** to pump; **~ de gasolina** gas pump.
bombardear vt to bombard.
bombardeo m bombardment.
bombardero m bomber.
bombazo m explosion; bombshell.
bombero m firefighter, fireman
bombilla f light bulb.
bombín m derby.
bombo m large drum.
bombón m candy; chocolate.
bonachón/ona adj good-natured.
bonanza f fair weather (at sea); prosperity; bonanza.
bondad f goodness, kindness; courtesy.
bondadoso/sa adj good, kind.
bonete m clerical hat; college cap.

bonito adj pretty, nice-looking; pretty good, passable; * m tuna (fish).
bono m bond (financial).
boñiga f cow pat.
bonsái m bonsai.
boqueada f act of opening the mouth; **la última ~** the last gasp.
boquear vi to gape;, to gasp; to breathe one's last; * vt to pronounce, to utter (a word).
boquerón m anchovy; large hole.
boquete m gap, narrow entrance.
boquiabierto/ta adj open-mouthed; gaping.
boquilla f mouthpiece of a musical instrument; nozzle.
borbollón, borbotón m bubbling; **salir a borbollones** to gush forth.
borda f (mar) gunwale/gunnel; hut.
bordado m embroidery.
bordadora f embroiderer.
bordar vt to embroider; to do anything very well.
borde m border; margin; (mar) board.
bordear vi (mar) to tack; * vt to go along the edge of; to flank.
bordillo m curb.
bordo m (mar) board; **a ~** on board (a ship).
boreal adj boreal, northern.
borgoña m burgundy wine.
borla f tassel; tuft.
borona f maize; corn; corn bread.
borrachera f drunkenness; hard drinking; spree.
borracho/cha adj drunk, intoxicated; blind with passion; * m/f drunk, drunkard.
borrador m first draft; scribbling pad; eraser.
borraja f (bot) borage.
borrar vt to erase, to rub out; to blur; to obscure.
borrasca f storm; violent squall of wind; hazard; danger.
borrascoso/sa adj stormy.
borrego/ga m/f yearling lamb; simpleton, blockhead.
borrico/ca m/f donkey, ass; blockhead.
borrón m blot, blur; rough draft of a writing; first sketch of a painting; stain, blemish.
borronear vt to sketch.
boscaje m grove, small wood; landscape (in painting).
bosque m forest; wood.
bosquejar vt to make a sketch of (a painting); to make a rough model of (a figure).
bosquejo m sketch (of a painting); unfinished work.
bostezar vi to yawn; to gape.
bostezo m yawn; yawning.
bota f leather wine-bag; boot.
botánica f botany.
botánico/ca adj botanic; * m/f botanist.
botanista m/f botanist.

B

botar vt to cast, to fling; to launch.
bote m bounce; thrust; tin, can; boat.
botella f bottle.
botica f drugstore.
boticario/ria m/f pharmacist.
botijo m earthenware jug.
botín m high boot, half-boot; gaiter; booty.
botiquín m medicine chest.
botón m button; knob (of a radio etc); (bot) bud.
botonadura f set of buttons.
botones m invar bellhop, bellboy.
bóveda f arch; vault, crypt.
box m Lat Am boxing.
boxeador m boxer.
boxeo m boxing.
boya f (mar) buoy.
boyante adj buoyant, floating; (fig) fortunate, successful.
bozal m muzzle.
bozo m down (on the upper lip/chin); headstall, head collar (of a horse).
braceada f violent movement of the arms.
bracear vi to swing the arms.
bracero m day-laborer; farmhand.
braga f sling, rope; diaper; ~s fpl pants pl.
bragazas m invar henpecked husband.
braguero m truss.
bragueta f fly, flies pl (of trousers).
braille m Braille.
bramante m twine, string.
bramar vi to roar, to bellow; to storm, to bluster.
bramido m roar, bellow, howl.
brasa f live coal; **estar hecho una ~** to be very flushed.
brasero m brazier.
bravamente adv bravely, gallantly; fiercely; roughly; extremely well.
bravío/vía adj ferocious, savage, wild; coarse; * m fierceness, savageness.
bravo/va adj brave, valiant; bullying; savage, fierce; rough; sumptuous; excellent, fine; * excl well done!
bravura f ferocity; courage.
braza f fathom.
brazada f extension of the arms; armful.
brazado m armful.
brazal m armband; irrigation channel.
brazalete m bracelet.
brazo m arm; branch (of a tree); enterprise; courage; **luchar a ~ partido** to fight hand to hand.
brea f pitch; tar.
brear vt to pitch; to tar; to abuse, to ill-treat; to play a joke on.
brebaje m potion.
brecha f (mil) breach; gap, opening; **batir en ~** (mil) to make a breach.

bregar vi to struggle; to quarrel; to slog away.
breva f early fig; early large acorn.
breve m papal brief; * f (mus) breve; * adj brief, short; **en ~** shortly.
brevedad f brevity, shortness, conciseness.
breviario m breviary; (fig) daily reading.
brezo m (bot) heather.
bribón/ona adj dishonest, rascally.
bribonear vi to be idle; to play dirty tricks.
bricolaje m home improvement.
brida f bridle; clamp, flange.
bridge m bridge (card game).
brigada f brigade; squad, gang.
brigadier m brigadier.
brillante adj brilliant; bright, shining; * m diamond.
brillar vi to shine; to sparkle, to glisten; to shine, to be outstanding.
brillo m brilliance, brightness.
brincar vi to skip; to leap, to jump; to gambol; to fly into a passion.
brinco m leap, jump; bounce.
brindar vi: **~ a la salud de/~ por** to drink the health of, to toast; * vt to offer, to present.
brindis m invar toast.
brío m spirit, dash.
briosamente adv spiritedly, dashingly.
brioso/sa adj dashing, full of spirit; lively.
brisa f breeze.
brisca f card game.
broca f reel; drill; shoemaker's tack (nail).
brocado m gold/silver brocade; ~/**da** adj embroidered; like brocade.
brocal m rim, mouth; curb.
brocha f large brush; **~ de afeitar** shaving brush.
brochada f brushstroke.
broche m clasp; brooch; cufflink.
broma f joke.
bromear vi to joke.
bromista m/f joker.
bronca f row.
bronce m bronze.
bronceado/da adj tanned; * m bronzing, suntan.
broncearse vr to get a suntan.
bronco/ca adj rough, coarse; rude; harsh.
bronquitis f bronchitis.
broquel m shield.
brotar vi (bot) to bud, to germinate; to gush, to rush out; (med) to break out.
brote m (bot) shoot; (med) outbreak.
bruces adv: **de ~** face downward(s).
bruja f witch.
brujería f witchcraft.
brujo m sorcerer, magician, wizard.
brújula f compass.
bruma f mist; (mar) sea mist.
brumoso/sa adj misty.
bruñido m polish.

bruñir vt to polish; to put rouge on.
brusco/ca adj rude; sudden; brusque.
brutal adj brutal, brutish.
brutalidad f brutality; brutal action.
bruto m brute, beast; ~/ta adj stupid; gross; brutish.
buba f tumor.
bucal adj oral.
bucear vi to dive.
buceo m diving.
bucle m curl.
bucólica f pastoral poetry; (col) food.
buche m craw, maw; (col) guts pl; mouthful; crease (in clothes).
budismo m Buddhism.
buen adj (before m nouns) good.
buenamente adv easily; willingly.
buenaventura f fortune, good luck.
bueno/na adj good, perfect; fair; fit, proper; good-looking; ¡buenos días! good morning!; ¡buenas tardes! good afternoon; ¡buenas noches! good night!; ¡~! right!
buey m ox, bullock.
bufa f joke, mock.
búfalo m buffalo.
bufanda f scarf.
bufar vi to choke with anger; to snort.
bufete m desk, writing-table; lawyer's office.
bufido m snorting (of an animal).
bufo/fa adj comic; ópera ~a f comic opera.
bufón m buffoon; jester; ~/ona adj funny, comical.
bufonada f buffoonery; joke.
buhardilla f attic.
búho m owl; unsociable person.
buhonero m hawker, peddler.
buitre m vulture.
bujía f candle; spark plug.
bula f papal bull.
bulbo m (bot) bulb.
bulboso/sa adj bulbous.
bulevar m boulevard.

bulla f confused noise, clatter; crowd; **meter ~** to make a noise.
bullicio m bustle; uproar.
bullicioso/sa adj lively, restless, noisy, busy; turbulent; boisterous.
bulto m bulk; tumor, swelling; bust; baggage.
buñuelo m donut/doughnut; fritter.
buque m vessel, ship, tonnage, capacity(of a ship); hull (of a ship).
burbuja f bubble.
burbujear vi to bubble.
burdel m brothel.
burdo/da adj coarse, rough.
burgués/esa adj bourgeois.
burguesía f bourgeoisie.
buril m engraver's chisel.
burla f trick; gibe; joke; **de ~s** in fun.
burlar vt to hoax; to defeat; to play tricks on, to deceive; to frustrate; ~**se** vr to joke, to laugh at.
burlesco/ca adj burlesque; comical, funny.
burlón/ona m/f joker.
burocracia f bureaucracy.
burócrata m/f bureaucrat.
burrada f drove of asses; stupid action.
burro m ass, donkey; idiot; saw-horse.
bursátil adj stock exchange compd.
bus m bus.
busca f search, hunt; bleeper.
buscapiés m invar jumping jack (fireworks).
buscar vt to seek, to search for; to look for; to hunt after; * vi to look, to search, to seek
buscavidas m prying person, busybody.
buscón m petty thief, small-time crook.
búsqueda f search.
busto m bust.
butaca f armchair; seat.
butano m butane.
butifarra f Catalan sausage.
buzo m diver.
buzón m mailbox; conduit, canal; cover of a jar.

B

C

cabal adj just, exact; right; complete; accomplished.
cábalas fpl intrigue.
cabalgada f cavalcade; (mil) cavalry raid.
cabalgadura f mount, horse; beast of burden.
cabalgar vi to ride, to go riding.
cabalgata f procession.
cabalístico/ca adj cabalistic.
caballa f mackerel.
caballar adj equine.
caballería f mount, steed; cavalry; cavalry horse; chivalry; knighthood.
caballeriza f stable; stud; stablemen, stableboys pl.
caballerizo m groom.
caballero m knight; gentleman; rider, horseman; horse soldier; ~ **andante** knight errant.
caballerosidad f chivalry.
caballeroso/sa adj noble; gentlemanlike.
caballete m ridge of a roof; painter's easel; trestle; bridge (of the nose).
caballo m horse; ~ **de carreras** racehorse; knight (at chess); queen (in cards); **a** ~ on horseback.
cabaña f hut, cabin; hovel; livestock; balk (in billiards).
cabaré m cabaret.
cabecear vi to nod (with sleep); to shake one's head; (mar) to pitch.
cabeceo m nod; shaking (of the head).
cabecera f headboard; head; far end; pillow; headline; vignette.
cabecilla m ringleader.
cabellera f head of hair; wig; tail of a comet.
cabello m hair.
cabelludo/da adj hairy, shaggy.
caber vi to fit.
cabestrillo m sling.
cabestro m halter; leading/bell ox.
cabeza f head; chief, leader; main town, chief center.
cabezada f butt; nod/shake of the head.
cabezal m pillow; compress.
cabezón m collar (of a shirt); opening in a garment for the head.
cabezudo/da adj big-headed; pig-headed.
cabida f room, capacity; **tener** ~ **con una persona** to have influence with someone.
cabildo m chapter (of a church); meeting of a chapter; corporation of a town.
cabina f cabin; telephone booth.
cabizbajo/ja, cabizcaído/da adj crestfallen; pensive, thoughtful.
cable m cable, lead, wire.
cabo m end, extremity; cape, headland; (mar) cable, rope.
cabra f goat.

cabrero m goatherd.
cabrío/a adj goatish.
cabriola f caper; gambol.
cabritilla f kidskin.
cabrito m kid.
cabrón m cuckold; ¡~! (col) bastard!
cacahuete m peanut.
cacao m (bot) cacao tree; cocoa.
cacarear vi to crow; to brag, to boast.
cacareo m crowing of a cock, cackling of a hen; boast, brag.
cacería f hunting-party.
cacerola f pan, saucepan; casserole.
cachalote m sperm whale.
cacharro m pot; piece of junk.
cachear vt to frisk.
cachemir m cashmere.
cacheo m frisking.
cachete m cheek; slap in the face.
cachimbo m Lat Am pipe.
cachiporra f club, truncheon.
cachivache m pot; piece of junk.
cacho m crumb, bit, small slice, piece; horn (of an animal).
cachondeo m (col) farce.
cachondo/da adj randy; funny.
cachorro/ra m/f puppy; cub (of any animal).
cacique m chief; local party boss.
caco m pickpocket; coward.
cacofonía f cacophony.
cacto/cactus m cactus.
cada adj invar each; every.
cadalso m scaffold.
cadáver m corpse, cadaver.
cadavérico/ca adj cadaverous.
cadena f chain; series, link; radio/TV network.
cadencia f cadence.
cadente adj harmonious.
cadera f hip.
cadete m (mil) cadet.
caducar vi to become senile; to expire, to lapse; to deteriorate.
caducidad f expiry.
caduco/ca adj worn out; decrepit; perishable; expired, lapsed.
caer vi to fall; to tumble down; to lapse; to happen; to die; ~**se** vr to fall down.
café m coffee; coffee bar/shop.
cafetera f coffee pot.
cafetería f coffee shop/bar; small restaurant.
cafetero/ra m/f coffee merchant; coffee bar/shop owner.

cafre *adj* savage, inhuman; rude.
cagar *vi* (*col*) to have a shit.
caída *f* fall, falling; slope, descent.
caimán *m* cayman/caiman, alligator.
caja *f* box, case; casket; cashbox; cash desk; check-out, till; ~ **de ahorros** savings bank; ~ **de cambios** gearbox; ~ **negra** black box.
cajero/ra *m/f* cashier, teller.
cajero automático *m* cash dispenser, cash machine, cash point, automated teller machine (ATM).
cajetilla *f* packet.
cajón *m* chest of drawers; locker.
cal *f* lime; ~ **viva** quick lime.
cala *f* creek, small bay; small piece of melon etc; (*mar*) hold; dipstick.
calabacín *m* small marrow, courgette.
calabaza *f* pumpkin, squash.
calabozo *m* prison; cell.
calada *f* soaking; lowering of nets; puff, drag; swoop.
calado *m* openwork in metal/wood/linen.
calafatear *vt* (*mar*) to caulk.
calamar *m* squid.
calambre *m* cramp.
calamidad *f* calamity, disaster.
calamitoso/sa *adj* calamitous.
calaña *f* model; pattern.
calandria *f* lark.
calar *vt* to soak, to drench; to penetrate, to pierce; to see through; to lower; ~**se** *vr* to stall (of a car).
calavera *f* skull; madcap.
calaverada *f* ridiculous/foolish action.
calcañar *m* heel.
calcar *vt* to trace, to copy.
calcáreo/rea *adj* chalky, calcareous.
calceta *f* (knee-length) stocking.
calcetín *m* sock.
calcio *m* calcium.
calco *m* tracing.
calcomanía *f* transfer.
calculable *adj* calculable.
calculadora *f* calculator.
calcular *vt* to calculate, to reckon; to compute.
cálculo *m* calculation, estimate; calculus; (*med*) gallstone.
caldear *vt* to weld; to warm, to heat up.
caldera *f* kettle, boiler; **las** ~**s de Pero Botero** (*col*) hell.
calderada *f* stew.
calderilla *f* holy-water vessel; small change.
caldero *m* small boiler.
caldo *m* stock; broth.
caldoso/sa *adj* having too much broth/gravy.
calefacción *f* heating.
calendario *m* calendar.
calentador *m* heater.

calentamiento global *m* global warming.
calentar *vt* to warm up, to heat up; ~**se** *vr* to grow hot; to dispute.
calentura *f* fever.
calenturiento/ta *adj* feverish.
calesa *f* buggy, chaise.
calibre *m* caliber; (*fig*) caliber.
calidad *f* grade, quality, condition; kind.
cálido/da *adj* hot; (*fig*) warm.
caliente *adj* hot; fiery; **en** ~ in the heat of the moment.
califa *m* caliph.
califato *m* caliphate.
calificación *f* qualification; grade.
calificar *vt* to qualify; to assess, to mark; ~**se** *vr* to register as a voter.
caligrafía *f* calligraphy.
cáliz *m* chalice.
caliza *f* limestone.
calizo/za *adj* limy (of ground).
callado/da *adj* silent, quiet.
callandico *adv* softly, silently.
callar *vi*, ~**se** *vr* to be silent, to keep quiet.
calle *f* street; road.
calleja *f* lane, narrow passage.
callejear *vi* to loiter about the streets.
callejero/ra *adj* loitering.
callejón *m* alley.
callejuela *f* lane, narrow passage; subterfuge.
callista *m/f* chiropodist, podiatrist.
callo *m* corn; callus; ~**s** *mpl* tripe.
callosidad *f* hard patch, callosity.
calloso/sa *adj* callous; horny.
calma *f* calm, calmness.
calmante *m* (*med*) sedative.
calmar *vt* to calm, to quiet, to pacify; * *vi* to become calm.
calmoso/sa *adj* calm; tranquil.
calor *m* heat, warmth; ardor, passion.
caloría *f* calorie.
calumnia *f* calumny, slander.
calumniar *vt* to slander.
calumnioso/sa *adj* slanderous.
caluroso/sa *adj* warm; hot; lively.
calva *f* bald patch.
calvario *m* Calvary; (*fig*) debts *pl*.
calvicie *f* baldness.
calvinismo *m* Calvinism.
calvinista *m/f* Calvinist.
calvo/va *adj* bald; bare, barren.
calza *f* wedge.
calzado *m* footwear.
calzador *m* shoehorn.
calzar *vt* to put on (shoes); to wear (shoes); to stop (a wheel); ~**se** *vr* to put on one's shoes.
calzón *m* shorts *pl*; pants *pl*; panties *pl*.
calzonazos *m invar* stupid guy; **es un** ~ he is a weak-willed guy.

calzoncillos *mpl* underpants *pl*, shorts *pl*.
calzonudo *m Lat Am* stupid guy; **es un ~** he is a weak-willed guy.
cama *f* bed; **hacer la ~** to make the bed.
camada *f* litter (of animals); **~ de ladrones** gang of thieves.
camafeo *m* cameo.
camaleón *m* chameleon.
camalote *m Lat Am* water hyacinth.
camandulero/ra *adj* prudish; hypocritical; sly, tricky.
cámara *f* hall; chamber; room; camera; cine camera.
camarada *m/f* comrade, companion.
camarera *f* waitress; maid; *Lat Am* air stewardess.
camarero *m* waiter; *Lat Am* air steward.
camarilla *f* clique; lobby.
camarín *m* dressing room; elevator car.
camarón *m* shrimp, prawn.
camarote *m* berth, cabin.
cambalache *m* exchange, swap.
cambalachear *vt* to exchange, to swap.
cambiable *adj* changeable, variable; interchangeable.
cambiar *vt* to exchange; to change; * *vi* to change, to alter; **~se** *vr* to move house.
cambio *m* change, exchange; rate of exchange; bureau de change.
cambista *m/f* exchange broker.
camelar *vt* to flirt with.
camello *m* camel.
camilla *f* couch; cot; stretcher.
caminante *m/f* traveler; walker.
caminar *vi* to travel; to walk, to go.
caminata *f* long walk; hike.
camino *m* road; trail, way.
camión *m* truck.
camioneta *f* light truck, van.
camisa *f* shirt; chemise.
camiseta *f* T-shirt; undershirt.
camisón *m* nightgown.
camorra *f* quarrel, dispute.
camorrista *m/f* quarrelsome person.
campamento *m* (*mil*) encampment, camp.
campana *f* bell.
campaña *f* countryside; level country, plain; (*mil*) campaign.
campanada *f* peal of a bell; (*fig*) scandal.
campanario *m* belfry.
campaneo *m* bellringing, chime.
campanero *m* bell founder; bellringer.
campanilla *f* handbell; (*med*) uvula.
campante *adj* outstanding; smug.
campánula *f* bellflower.
campear *vi* to go out to pasture; to work in the fields.
campechano/na *adj* open.
campeón/ona *m/f* champion.
campeonato *m* championship.

campesino/na, campestre *adj* rural.
campiña *f* flat tract of cultivated farmland.
camping *m* camping, campsite.
campista *m/f* camper.
campo *m* country; countryside; field; camp; ground; pitch; scope, range; **~ de refugiados** refugee camp; **~ abierto** range, open countryside.
campus *m invar* campus.
camuflaje *m* camouflage.
caña *f* cane, reed; stalk; shinbone; glass of beer; **~ dulce** sugar cane.
canal *m* channel; canal.
canalla *f* mob, rabble.
canalón *m* large gutter.
cáñamo *m* hemp.
cañamón *m* hemp seed.
canana *f* cartridge belt.
canapé *m* couch, sofa.
canario *m* canary.
canas *fpl* gray hair; **peinar ~** to grow old.
canasta *f* basket, hamper.
canastilla *f* small basket.
canasto *m* large basket.
cañaveral *m* reedbed.
cancel *m* storm door.
cancelación *f* cancellation.
cancelar *vt* to cancel; to write off.
Cáncer *m* Cancer (zodiac sign).
cáncer *m* cancer.
canceriano/na *adj Lat Am* Cancerian.
cancerígeno/na *adj* carcinogenic.
canceroso/sa *adj* cancerous.
cancha *f* (*sport*) court, *Lat Am* course, *Lat Am* pitch.
canciller *m* chancellor; foreign minister.
canción *f* song.
cancionero *m* songbook.
candado *m* padlock.
candela *f* candle.
candelabro *m* candlestick.
candente *adj* red-hot.
candidato/ta *m/f* candidate.
cándido/da *adj* simple, naive; white, snowy.
candil *m* oil lamp.
candilejas *fpl* footlights *pl*.
candor *m* candor; innocence.
canela *f* cinnamon.
canelón *m* icicle.
cañería *f* water conduit, water pipe.
cangrejo *m* crab; crawfish.
canguro *m* kangaroo; * *f* baby-sitter.
caníbal *m/f* cannibal, man-eater.
canica *f* marble.
canícula *f* dog days *pl*.
canijo/ja *adj* weak, sickly.
canilla *f* shinbone; arm-bone; tap of a cask; spool.
canillera *f Lat Am* (*sport*) shin pad.
canino/na *adj* canine; **hambre ~a** *f* ravenous hunger.

canje *m* exchange.
canjear *vt* to exchange.
caño *m* tube, pipe; sewer.
cano/na *adj* gray-haired; white-haired.
canoa *f* canoe.
canon *m* canon; tax; royalty; rent.
cañón *m* tube, pipe; barrel; gun; canyon.
cañonazo *m* gunshot; (*fig*) bombshell.
cañonear *vt* to shell, to bombard.
cañoneo *m* shelling, gunfire.
cañonera *f* gunboat.
canónico/ca *adj* canonical.
canónigo *m* canon, prebendary.
canonización *f* canonization.
canonizar *vt* to canonize.
canoso/sa *adj* gray-haired; white-haired.
cansado/da *adj* weary, tired; tedious, tiresome.
cansancio *m* tiredness, fatigue.
cansar *vt* to tire, to tire out; to bore; **~se** *vr* to get tired, to grow weary.
cantable *adj* suitable for singing.
cantante *m/f* singer.
cantar *m* song; * *vt* to sing; to chant; * *vi* to sing; to chirp.
cántara *f* large jug, pitcher.
cantarín/ina *m/f* someone who sings a lot.
cántaro *m* pitcher; jug; **llover a ~s** to rain heavily, to pour.
cantera *f* quarry.
cantero *m* quarryman.
cántico *m* canticle.
cantidad *f* quantity, amount; number.
cantimplora *f* water bottle; hip flask.
cantina *f* (*rail*) restaurant car; canteen; wine cellar.
cantinela *f* ballad, song.
canto *m* stone; singing; song; edge.
cantón *m* corner; canton.
cantonear *vi* to loaf around.
cantor/ra *m/f* singer.
canuto *m* (*col*) joint, marijuana cigarette.
caoba *f* mahogany.
caos *m* chaos; confusion.
capa *f* cloak; cape; layer, stratum; cover; pretext; **~ de ozono** ozone layer.
capacho *m* hamper; big basket.
capacidad *f* capacity; extent; talent.
capar *vt* to geld; to castrate; (*fig*) to curtail.
caparazón *m* caparison.
capataz *m* foreman, overseer.
capaz *adj* capable; capacious, spacious, roomy.
capazo *m* large basket; carrycot.
capcionar *vt* to seize, to arrest.
capcioso/sa *adj* wily, deceitful.
capear *vt* to flourish (one's cloak in front of a bull); * *vi* (*mar*) to ride out/weather (a storm).
capellán *m* chaplain.
capeo *m* challenging of a bull with a cloak.
caperuza *f* hood.

capilar *adj* capillary.
capilla *f* hood, cowl; chapel.
capirote *m* hood.
capital *m* capital; capital sum; * *f* capital, capital city; * *adj* capital; principal.
capitalismo *m* capitalism.
capitalista *m/f* capitalist.
capitalizar *vt* to capitalize.
capitán *m* captain.
capitana *f* flagship; (*sport*) female captain.
capitanear *vt* to captain; to command.
capitanía *f* captaincy.
capitel *m* capital (of a column).
capitolio *m* capitol; imposing building.
capitulación *f* capitulation; agreement; **~ones** *fpl* marriage contract.
capitular *vi* to come to terms, to make an agreement.
capítulo *m* chapter (of a cathedral); chapter (of a book).
capó *m* (*auto*) hood.
capón *m* capon.
caporal *m* chief, ringleader.
capota *f* hat, bonnet; (*auto*) hood.
capote *m* greatcoat; bullfighter's cloak.
capricho *m* caprice, whim, fancy.
caprichoso/sa *adj* capricious, whimsical; obstinate.
capricorniano/na *adj* Lat Am Capricornean (zodiac sign).
Capricornio *m* Capricorn (zodiac sign).
cápsula *f* capsule.
captar *vt* to captivate; to understand; (*rad*) to tune in to, to receive.
captura *f* capture, arrest.
capturar *vt* to capture.
capucha *f* circumflex (accent); cap, cowl, hood of a cloak.
capuchino *m* Capuchin monk; (**café**) ~ cappuccino (coffee).
capullo *m* cocoon of a silkworm; rosebud; coarse cloth made of spun silk.
caqui *adj*, *m* khaki.
cara *f* face; appearance; **~ a** ~ face to face.
carabina *f* carbine, rifle.
carabinero *m* carabineer.
caracol *m* snail; seashell; spiral.
caracola *f* shell.
caracolear *vi* to prance about (of a horse).
carácter *m* character; quality; condition; handwriting.
característico/ca *adj* characteristic.
caracterizar *vt* to characterize.
caradura *m/f*: **es un** ~ he's got a nerve.
caramba *excl* well!
carámbano *m* icicle.
carambola *f* cannon (at billiards); trick.
caramelo *m* caramel (candy).

caramente *adv* dearly.

caramillo *m* small flute; piece of gossip.

carantoña *f* hideous mask; dressed-up old woman; ~s *fpl* caresses *pl*.

carátula *f* pasteboard mask; **la** ~ the stage.

caravana *f* group of wagons/camels/pack mules etc traveling in single file ; tailback (of traffic); trailer.

caray *excl* well!

carbón *m* coal; carbon; carbon paper.

carbonada *f* grill; kind of pancake.

carboncillo *m* charcoal.

carbonera *f* coal tip; coal mine.

carbonería *f* coalyard.

carbonero *m* someone who sells coal; (*mar*) coal ship.

carbónico/ca *adj* carbonic.

carbonilla *f* coaldust.

carbonizar *vt* to carbonize.

carbono *m* (*chem*) carbon.

carbunclo, carbunco *m* carbuncle.

carburador *m* carburetor.

carcaj *m* quiver.

carcajada *f* (loud) laugh.

carcamal *m* nickname for an old person.

cárcel *f* prison; jail.

carcelero *m* warder, jailer.

carcoma *f* deathwatch beetle; woodworm; anxious concern.

carcomer *vt* to gnaw, to corrode; ~se *vr* to get worm-eaten.

carcomido/da *adj* worm-eaten.

cardar *vt* to card (wool).

cardenal *m* cardinal; cardinal bird; (*med*) bruise, weal.

cardenalicio/cia *adj* belonging to a cardinal.

cárdeno/na *adj* purple; livid.

cardíaco/ca, cardiaco/ca *adj* cardiac; * heart *compd*.

cardinal *adj* cardinal, principal.

cardo *m* thistle.

carear *vt* to bring face to face; to compare; ~se *vr* to come face to face.

carecer *vi*: ~ **de** to want, to lack.

carencia *f* lack.

careo *m* confrontation.

carero/ra *adj* pricey.

carestía *f* scarcity, want; famine.

careta *f* pasteboard mask.

carga *f* load; freight, cargo; (*mil*) charge; duty, obligation; tax.

cargadero *m* loading place.

cargado/da *adj* loaded; live (electricity).

cargador *m* loader; carrier; longshoreman.

cargamento *m* cargo.

cargar *vt* to load, to burden; to charge; * *vi* to charge; to load (up); to lean.

cargo *m* burden, loading; employment, post; office; charge, care; obligation; accusation.

carguero *m* freighter.

cariarse *vr* to decay.

caricato *m* Lat Am caricature.

caricatura *f* caricature.

caricia *f* caress.

caridad *f* charity.

caries *f* (*med*) tooth decay, caries.

carilargo/ga *adj* long-faced.

carilla *f* side (of paper); beekeeper's mask.

cariño *m* fondness, tenderness; love.

cariñoso/sa *adj* affectionate; loving.

caritativo/va *adj* charitable.

cariz *m* look.

carmelita *adj*, *m/f* Carmelite.

carmesí *adj*, *m* crimson.

carmín *m* carmine; rouge; lipstick.

carnada *f* bait, lure.

carnal *adj* carnal, of the flesh; **primo** ~ first cousin.

carnaval *m* carnival.

carn *f* flesh; meat; pulp (of fruit).

carné, carnet *m* driving license; ~ **de identidad** identity card.

carnero *m* sheep; mutton.

carnicería *f* butcher's shop; carnage, slaughter.

carnicero/ra *m/f* butcher; * *adj* carnivorous.

carnívoro/ra *adj* carnivorous.

carnoso/sa, carnudo *adj* beefy, fat; fleshy.

caro/ra *adj* dear; affectionate; dear, expensive; * *adv* dearly.

carótida *f* carotid artery.

carpa *f* carp (fish); Lat Am tent.

carpeta *f* table cover; folder, file, portfolio.

carpintería *f* carpentry; carpenter's premises.

carpintero *m* carpenter.

carraca *f* carrack (ship); rattle.

carrasca *f* kermes oak tree.

carraspera *f* hoarseness.

carrera *f* career; course; race; run, running; route; journey; **a** ~ **abierta** at full speed.

carreta *f* long narrow cart.

carrete *m* reel, spool, bobbin.

carretera *f* road; ~ **de circunvalación** belt, beltway, ring road.

carretero *m* carter, cartwright.

carretilla *f* carter; truck; trolley; go-cart; squib, cracker; wheelbarrow.

carretón *m* small cart.

carril *m* lane (of highway); furrow; ~ **bus** bus lane.

carrillo *m* cheek; pulley.

carro *m* cart; car.

carrocería *f* bodywork, coachwork.

carromato *m* covered wagon, Gypsy caravan.

carroña *f* carrion.

carroza *f* state coach; (*mar*) awning.

carruaje *m* carriage; vehicle.

carrusel *m* merry-go-round.

carta f letter; map; document; playing card; menu; ~ **blanca** carte blanche; ~ **bomba** letter-bomb; ~ **credencial/de creencia** credentials pl; ~ **certificada** registered letter; ~ **postal** Lat Am postcard; ~ **verde** green card.

cartabón m square (tool).

cartapacio m notebook; folder.

cártel m cartel.

cartel m placard; poster; wall chart; cartel.

cartera f satchel; billfold; handbag; briefcase; postwoman.

carterista m/f pickpocket.

cartero m postman.

cartilaginoso/sa adj cartilaginous.

cartílago m cartilage.

cartilla f first reading book, primer.

cartón m cardboard, pasteboard; cartoon.

cartuchera f (mil) cartridge belt.

cartucho m (mil) cartridge.

cartuja f Carthusian order.

cartujo m Carthusian monk.

cartulina f card, pass; thin cardboard.

casa f house; home; firm, company; ~ **de campo** country house; ~ **de moneda** mint; ~ **de huéspedes** boarding house.

casaca f coat.

casación f abrogation.

casadero/ra adj marriageable.

casado/da adj married.

casamentero/ra m/f marriage-maker, matchmaker.

casamiento m marriage, wedding.

casar vt to marry; to couple; to abrogate; to annul; ~**se** vr to marry, to get married.

cascabel m small bell; rattlesnake.

cascada f cascade, waterfall.

cascanueces m invar nutcracker.

cascar vt to crack, to break into pieces; (col) to beat; ~**se** vr to be broken open.

cáscara f rind, peel; husk, shell; bark.

cascarón m eggshell.

casco m skull; helmet; fragment; shard; hulk (of a ship); crown (of a hat); hoof; empty bottle, returnable bottle; ~**s azules** blue berets (soldiers of a UN peacekeeping force).

cascote m rubble, fragment of material used in building.

casera f landlady.

caserío m country house; small village.

casero m landlord; janitor; * ~/**ra**, adj domestic; household compd; home-made.

cassette/casette m cassette; * f cassette-player.

casi adv almost, nearly; ~ **nada** next to nothing; ~ **nunca** hardly ever, almost never.

casilla f hut, cabin; box office; square (on a chess board); pigeonhole, compartment.

casillero m pigeonholes (set of) pl; baggage locker.

casino m club, social club.

caso m case; occurrence, event; happening, casualty; occasion; (gr) case; **en ese** ~ in that case; **en todo** ~ in any case; ~ **que** in case.

casorio m unwise marriage.

caspa f dandruff.

casquete m helmet.

casquillo m bottle top; tip, cap; point.

casta f caste; race; lineage; breed; kind, quality.

castaña f chestnut; demijohn.

castañar m chestnut grove.

castañetear vi to play the castanets.

castaño m chestnut tree; ~/**na** adj chestnut-colored, brown.

castañuela f castanet.

castellano m Castilian, Spanish.

castidad f chastity.

castigar vt to castigate, to punish; to afflict.

castigo m punishment; correction; penalty.

castillo m castle.

castizo/za adj pure, thoroughbred.

casto/ta adj pure, chaste.

castor m beaver.

castrar vt to geld, to castrate; to prune; to cut the honeycombs out of (beehives).

casual adj casual, accidental.

casualidad f chance, accident.

casucha f hovel; slum.

casulla f chasuble.

cata f tasting.

catacumbas fpl catacombs pl.

catador/ra m/f wine tester.

catadura f looks pl, face.

catalejo m telescope.

catalizador m catalyst; catalytic converter.

catálogo m catalog.

catamarán m catamaran.

cataplasma f poultice.

catapulta f catapult.

catar vt to taste; to inspect, to examine; to look at; to esteem.

catarata f (med) cataract; waterfall.

catarro m catarrh.

catarroso/sa adj catarrhal.

catástrofe f catastrophe.

catavino m small cup for tasting wine; ~**s** m/f invar wine-taster; tippler.

catecismo m catechism.

cátedra f professorship, chair (university).

catedral f cathedral.

catedrático/ca m/f professor (of a university).

categoría f category; rank.

categórico/ca adj categorical, decisive.

catequismo m catechism.

caterva f mob.

catolicismo m Catholicism.

católico/ca adj, m/f catholic.

catorce adj, m fourteen.

catre m cot.

cauce m riverbed; (fig) channel.

C

caucho *m* rubber; tire.

caución *f* caution; (*law*) security; bail.

caucionar *vt* to prevent, to guard against; (*law*) to bail.

caudal *m* volume, flow; property, wealth; plenty.

caudaloso/sa *adj* carrying much water (of rivers); wealthy, rich.

caudillo *m* leader.

causa *f* cause; motive, reason; lawsuit; **a ~ de** considering, because of.

causal *adj* causal.

causante *m/f* originator; * *adj* causing, originating.

causar *vt* to cause; to produce; to occasion.

cáustico *m* caustic; **~/ca** *adj* caustic.

cautela *f* caution, cautiousness.

cauteloso/sa *adj* cautious, wary.

cauterizar *vt* (*med*) to cauterize; to apply a drastic remedy to.

cautivar *vt* to take prisoner in war; to captivate, to charm.

cautiverio *m* captivity.

cautividad *f* captivity.

cautivo/va *adj*, *m/f* captive.

cauto/ta *adj* cautious, wary.

cava *f* digging and earthing of vines; wine cellar; sparkling wine.

cavar *vt* to dig up, to excavate; * *vi* to dig, to delve; to think profoundly.

caverna *f* cavern, cave.

cavernoso/sa *adj* cavernous.

cavidad *f* cavity, hollow.

cavilación *f* deep thought.

cavilar *vt* to ponder, to consider carefully.

caviloso/sa *adj* obsessed; suspicious.

cayado/da *m/f* shepherd's crook.

caza *f* hunting; shooting; chase; game; * *m* fighter-plane.

cazador/ra *m/f* hunter; *m* huntsman; **~ furtivo** poacher.

cazamoscas *m invar* flycatcher (bird).

cazar *vt* to chase, to hunt; to catch.

cazo *m* saucepan; ladle.

cazuela *f* casserole; pan.

cazurro/rra *adj* silent, taciturn.

cebada *f* barley.

cebar *vt* to feed (animals), to fatten.

cebo *m* feed, food; bait, lure; priming.

cebolla *f* onion; bulb.

cebolleta *f* spring onion, scallion.

cebollino *m* onion seed; chive.

cebón *m* fattened hog/pig.

cebra *f* zebra.

cecear *vt* to pronounce **s** the same as **c**; to lisp.

cecina *f* dried meat; salt beef.

cedazo *m* sieve, strainer.

ceder *vt* to hand over; to transfer, to make over; to yield, to give up; * *vi* to submit, to comply, to give in; to diminish, to grow less.

cederrón *m* CD-ROM.

cedro *m* cedar.

cédula *f* certificate; document; slip of paper; bill; **~ de cambio** bill of exchange; **~ de identidad** *Lat Am* identity card.

cegar *vi* to grow blind; * *vt* to blind; to block up.

cegato/ta *adj* short-sighted.

ceguera *f* blindness.

ceja *f* eyebrow; edging of clothes; (*mus*) bridge of a stringed instrument; brow of a hill.

cejar *vi* to go backward(s); to slacken, to give in.

celada *f* helmet; ambush; trick.

celador *m* guard, watchman; maintenance man; linesman.

celda *f* cell.

celdilla *f* cell; cavity.

celebración *f* celebration; praise.

celebrar *vt* to celebrate; to praise; **~ misa** to say mass.

célebre *adj* famous, renowned; witty, funny.

celebridad *f* celebrity, fame.

celeridad *f* speed, velocity.

celeste *adj* heavenly; sky-blue.

celestial *adj* heavenly; delightful.

celibato *m* celibacy.

célibe *m/f* bachelor, spinster.

celo *m* zeal; rut (in animals); Sellotape™; **~s** *mpl* jealousy.

celofán *m* Cellophane™.

celosía *f* lattice (of a window).

celoso/sa *adj* zealous; jealous.

célula *f* cell.

celular *adj* cellular; * *m Lat Am* cellular phone, mobile phone.

celulitis *f* cellulitis.

celuloide *m* celluloid.

cementerio *m* graveyard.

cemento *m* cement; *Lat Am* glue.

cena *f* dinner, supper.

cenador *m* arbor.

cenagoso/sa *adj* miry, marshy.

cenagal *m* quagmire.

cenar *vt* to have for dinner; * *vi* to have supper, to have dinner.

cencerro *m* jangle, clatter.

cenicero *m* ashtray.

ceniciento/ta *adj* ash-colored.

ceñido/da *adj* tight-fitting; sparing, frugal.

ceñir *vt* to surround, to circle; to abbreviate, to abridge; to fit tightly.

cenit *m* zenith.

ceniza *f* ashes *pl*; **miércoles de ~** Ash Wednesday.

ceño *m* frown.

censo *m* census; tax; ground rent; **~ electoral** electoral roll.

censor/ra *m/f* censor; reviewer, critic.

censura *f* censorship; review; censure, blame.

censurar *vt* to review, to criticize; to censure, to blame.

centella f lightning; spark.
centellear vi to sparkle.
centena f hundred.
centenadas adv: a ~ by hundreds.
centenar m hundred.
centenario/ia adj centenary; * m centenary.
centeno m rye.
centésimo/ma adj hundredth; * m hundredth.
centígrado m centigrade.
centímetro m centimeter.
céntimo m cent.
centinela f sentry, guard; lookout.
central adj central; * f head office, headquarters; (telephone) exchange; ~ **nuclear** nuclear power station.
centralización m centralization.
centralizar vt to centralize.
céntrico adj central.
centrífugo/ga adj centrifugal.
centrista adj centrist.
centro m center; ~ **comercial** shopping center.
centuplicar vt to increase a hundredfold.
céntuplo/pla adj one hundredfold.
ceñudo/da adj frowning, grim.
cepa f stock (of a vine); origin (of a family).
cepillar vt to brush.
cepillo m brush; plane (tool).
cepo m branch, bough; trap; snare; poor box.
cera f wax; ~s fpl honeycomb.
cerámica f pottery.
cerca f enclosure; fence; ~s mpl objects pl in the foreground of a painting; * adv near, at hand, close by; ~ **de** close, near.
cercanías fpl outskirts.
cercano/na adj near, close by; neighboring, adjoining.
cercar vt to enclose, to circle; to fence in.
cerciorar vt to assure, to ascertain, to affirm; ~se vr to find out.
cerco m enclosure; Lat Am fence; (mil) siege.
cerdo m pig, hog.
cereal m cereal.
cerebelo m cerebellum.
cerebro m brain.
ceremonia f ceremony.
ceremonial adj, m ceremonial.
ceremonioso/sa adj ceremonious.
cereza f cherry; Lat Am coffee bean.
cerezo m cherry tree.
cerilla f wax taper; ear wax; match, safety match.
cerner vt to sift; * vi to bud, to blossom; to drizzle; ~se vr to hover; to swagger.
cernido m sifting.
cero m nothing, zero.
cerquita adv close by.
cerrado/da adj closed, shut; locked; overcast, cloudy; broad (of accent).
cerradura f locking-up; lock.

cerrajería f trade of a locksmith; locksmith's (premises).
cerrajero m locksmith.
cerrar vt to close, to shut; to block up; to lock; ~ **una cuenta** to close an account; ~se vr to close; to heal; to cloud over; vi to close, to shut; to lock.
cerril adj mountainous; rough, wild, untamed.
cerro m hill; neck (of an animal); backbone; combed flax/hemp; **en** ~ bareback.
cerrojo m bolt (of a door).
certamen m competition, contest.
certero adj accurate; well-aimed.
certeza, certidumbre f certainty.
certificación f certificate.
certificado m certificate; ~/**da** adj registered (of a letter).
certificar vt to certify, to affirm.
cervato m fawn.
cervecería f bar; brewery.
cervecero m brewer.
cerveza m beer.
cerviz f nape of the neck; cervix.
cesación f cessation, stoppage.
cesar vt to cease, to stop; to fire (col); to remove from office; * vi to cease, to stop; to retire.
cese m suspension; dismissal; ~ **del fuego** Lat Am ceasefire.
cesión f cession; transfer.
césped m grass; lawn.
cesta f basket, pannier.
cestería f shop that specializes in baskets; basketwork.
cesto m (large) basket.
cetrino/na adj greenish-yellow; sallow; jaundiced, melancholic.
cetro m scepter.
chabacano/na adj coarse, vulgar; shoddy.
chabola f shack.
cháchara f chitchat, chatter, idle talk.
chacolí m light white wine with a sharp taste.
chafar vt to crush; to ruin.
chal m shawl.
chalado/da adj crazy.
chale(t) m detached house.
chaleco m vest.
chalupa f (mar) boat, launch.
chamarra f sheepskin jacket.
champán m champagne.
champiñón m mushroom.
champú m shampoo.
chamuscar vt to singe, to scorch.
chamusquina f scorching; (fig) row, quarrel.
chance m/f Lat Am chance.
chancho m Lat Am pig, hog.
chanchullo m (col) fix, fiddle.
chanciller m chancellor.
chancleta f slipper.

chanclo m clog; galosh.
chándal m tracksuit.
chanfaina f cheap stew.
chantaje m blackmail.
chanza f joke, jest; ~s fpl fun.
chapa f metal plate; panel; (auto) license plate.
chaparrón m heavy rain shower.
chapotear vt to wet with a sponge; * vi to paddle (in water).
chapucear vt to botch, to bungle.
chapucero m bungler; ~/ra adj clumsy, crude.
chapurrar vt to speak (a language) badly; to mix (drinks).
chapuza f badly done job.
chapuzarse vr to duck; to dive.
chaqueta f jacket, coat; ~ **deportiva** sports coat, sports jacket.
charca f pool.
charco m pool, puddle.
charcutería f shop selling pork meat products.
charla f chat, talk.
charlar vi to chat.
charlatán/ana m/f chatterbox.
charlatanería f talkativeness.
charol m varnish; patent leather.
charrada f coarse thing; bad breeding; bad taste.
charretera f shoulder pad.
charro m coarse individual; ~/rra adj coarse; gaudy.
charter m charter flight.
chasco m disappointment; joke, jest.
chasis m invar (auto) chassis.
chasquear vt to crack (a whip); to disappoint.
chasquido m crack; click.
chatarra f scrap.
chato/ta adj flat, flattish; snub-nosed.
chaval/la m/f lad/lass.
cheque m check.
chequeo m check-up; service.
chequera f checkbook.
chicano/na adj Chicano.
chicha f corn liquor.
chicharra f harvest fly.
chicharrón m pork crackling.
chichón m lump, bump.
chichonera f helmet.
chicle m chewing gum.
chico/ca adj little, small; * m/f boy/girl.
chicote m Lat Am whip.
chifla f whistle; hiss.
chiflado/da adj crazy.
chiflar vt to boo.
chile m chili pepper.
chillar vi to scream, to shriek; to howl; to creak.
chillido m squeak; shriek, howl.
chillón/ona adj loud, noisy; gaudy; * m/f whiner, moaner.
chimenea f chimney; fireplace.

china f pebble; porcelain, chinaware; China silk.
chinche f bug; Lat Am thumbtack; * m nuisance.
chincheta f thumbtack.
chinela f slipper.
chinita f Lat Am maid.
chino/na adj, m/f Chinese; * m Chinese language.
chiquero m pigpen.
chiripa f fluke.
chirla f mussel.
chirriar vi to hiss; to creak; to chirp.
chirrido m chirping (of birds); squeaking.
chis excl sh!
chisgarabís m (col) meddler.
chisme m tale, thing.
chismear vi to tell tales.
chismoso/sa adj gossiping; * m/f gossip.
chispa f spark; sparkle; wit; drop (of rain); drunkenness.
chispazo m spark.
chispeante adj sparkling.
chispear vi to sparkle; to drizzle.
chisporrotear vi to crackle; to sparkle; to hiss (of liquids).
chistar vi to speak.
chiste m funny story, joke.
chistoso/sa adj witty; amusing, funny.
chivato m kid; child.
chivo/va m/f billy/nanny goat.
chocante adj startling; odd.
chocar vi to strike, to knock; to crash; * vt to shock.
chochear vi to dodder, to be senile; to dote.
chocho adj doddering; doting.
chocolate m chocolate.
chocolatero/ra adj fond of chocolate.
chófer m driver.
chollo m bargain.
chopo m black poplar tree.
choque m shock; crash, collision; clash, conflict.
chorizo m pork sausage.
chorlito m plover (bird).
chorrear vi to spout, to gush; to drip.
chorrera f channel; frill.
chorro m gush; jet; stream; a ~s abundantly.
choto m kid; calf.
choza f hut, shack.
chubasco m squall.
chuchería f trinket.
chucho m mongrel.
chufleta f joke; taunt, jeer.
chulada f funny speech/action.
chulear vi to brag.
chuleta f chop.
chulo m rascal; pimp.
chunga f fun, joke; **estar de** ~ to be in good humor.
chunguearse vr to be in good humor.

chupado/da *adj* skinny; easy.
chupaflor *m Lat Am* hummingbird.
chupar *vt* to suck; to absorb.
chupete *m* pacifier.
chupetear *vi* to suck gently.
chupón/ona *m/f* (*col*) swindler, sponger.
churro *m* fritter.
churruscarse *vr* to scorch.
churrusco *m* burnt toast.
chusco/ca *adj* pleasant; funny.
chusma *f* rabble, mob.
chuzo *m* little spear/spike; **llover a ~s** to pour (with rain) heavily.
cianuro *m* cyanide.
ciática *f* sciatica.
ciático/ca *adj* sciatic.
cibercafé *m* Internet café.
ciberespacio *m* cyberspace.
cicatear *vi* to be mean.
cicatriz *f* scar.
cicatrizar *vt* to heal.
ciclismo *m* cycling.
ciclista *m/f* cyclist.
ciclo *m* cycle.
ciclón *m* cyclone.
cicloturismo *m* bicycle tourism.
cicuta *f* (*bot*) hemlock.
ciegamente *adv* blindly.
ciego/ga *adj* blind.
cielo *m* sky; heaven; atmosphere; climate.
cien *adj*, *m* a hundred.
ciénaga *f* swamp.
ciencia *f* science.
cieno *m* mud; mire.
cienpiés *m invar* centipede.
científico/ca *adj* scientific.
ciento *adj*, *m* a hundred.
cierne *m*: **en ~** in blossom; **estar en ~** to be in its infancy.
cierre *m* zipper.
cierto/ta *adj* certain, sure; right, correct; **por ~** certainly.
cierva *f* hind.
ciervo *m* deer, stag; **~ volante** stag beetle.
cierzo *m* cold northerly wind.
cifra *f* number, numeral; quantity; cipher; abbreviation.
cifrar *vt* to write in code; to abridge.
cigala *f* langoustine.
cigarra *f* cicada.
cigarrera *m* cigar case.
cigarrería *f Lat Am* tobacconist's (shop).
cigarrillo *m* cigarette.
cigarro *m* cigar; cigarette.
cigüeña *f* stork; crank, handle; winch.
cilicio *m* hair shirt; spiked belt.
cilíndrico/ca *adj* cylindrical.
cilindro *m* cylinder.

cima *f* summit; peak; top.
címbalo *m* cymbal.
cimbor(r)io *m* cupola, dome.
cimbr(e)ar *vt* to shake, to swish, to swing; **~ a uno** to give one a clout (with a stick); **~se** *vr* to sway.
cimbronazo *m Lat Am* shock wave.
cimentado *m* refinement of gold.
cimentar *vt* to lay the foundation of (a building); to found; to refine (metals); to strengthen, to cement.
cimiento *m* foundation, groundwork; basis, origin.
cinc *m* zinc.
cincel *m* chisel.
cincelar *vt* to chisel, to engrave.
cincha *f* girth.
cinchar *vt* to fasten a girth (on a horse).
cinco *adj*, *m* five.
cincuenta *adj*, *m* fifty.
cine *m* movie theater, movie house.
cineasta *m/f* film maker.
cinematográfico/ca *adj* cinematographic.
cínico/ca *adj* cynical.
cinismo *m* cynicism.
cinta *f* band, ribbon; reel.
cinto *m* belt.
cintura *f* waist.
cinturón *m* belt, girdle; (*fig*) zone; **~ de seguridad** seatbelt.
ciprés *m* cypress tree.
circo *m* circus.
circuito *m* circuit; circumference.
circulación *f* circulation; traffic.
circular *adj* circular; circulatory; * *vt* to circulate; * *vi* (*auto*) to drive.
círculo *m* circle; (*fig*) scope, compass.
circuncidar *vt* to circumcise.
circuncisión *f* circumcision.
circundar *vt* to surround, to encircle.
circunferencia *f* circumference.
circunflejo/ja *adj*: **acento ~** *m* circumflex.
circunscribir *vt* to circumscribe.
circunscripción *f* division; electoral district.
circunspección *f* circumspection.
circunspecto/ta *adj* circumspect, cautious.
circunstancia *f* circumstance.
circunstante *m/f* bystander.
circunvalación *f*: **carretera de ~** beltway, bypass.
cirio *m* wax candle.
ciruela *f* plum; **~ pasa** prune.
ciruelo *m* plum tree.
cirugía *f* surgery.
cirujano *m* surgeon.
cisco *m* coaldust.
cisma *m* schism; discord.
cismático/ca *adj* schismatic.
cisne *m* swan.

C

cisterna f cistern.
cisura f incision.
cita f quotation; appointment, meeting.
citación f quotation; (law) summons.
citar vt to make an appointment with; to quote; (law) to summon.
cítrico/ca adj citric; ~s mpl citric fruits pl.
ciudad f city; town.
ciudadanía f citizenship.
ciudadano/na m/f citizen; * adj civic.
ciudadela f citadel.
cívico/ca adj civic.
civil adj civil; polite, courteous; * m Civil Guard; civilian.
civilización f civilization.
civilizar vt to civilize.
civismo m public spirit; patriotism.
cizaña f discord.
clamar vt to clamor for.
clamor m clamor, outcry; peal of bells.
clamoroso/sa adj noisy, loud.
clandestino/na adj clandestine, secret, concealed.
clara f egg-white.
claraboya f skylight.
clarear vi to dawn; ~se vr to be transparent.
clarete adj, m claret.
claridad f brightness, clearness.
clarificar vt to brighten; to clarify.
clarín m bugle; bugler.
clarinete m clarinet; * m/f clarinetist.
claro/ra adj clear, bright; evident, manifest; * m opening; clearing (in a wood); skylight.
claroscuro m chiaroscuro (in painting).
clase f class; rank; order.
clásico/ca adj classical.
clasificación f classification.
clasificado m Lat Am classified ad/advertisement.
clasificar vt to classify.
claudicar vi to limp; to act deceitfully; to back down.
claustro m cloister; faculty (of a university); womb, uterus.
cláusula f clause.
clausura f closure, closing.
clavado/da adj tight-fitting; nailed.
clavar vt to nail; to fasten in, to force in; to drive in; (col) to cheat, to deceive; ~se vr to penetrate.
clave f key; (mus) clef; * m harpsichord.
clavel m (bot) carnation.
clavetear vt to decorate with studs.
clavicordio m clavichord.
clavícula f clavicle, collar bone.
clavija f pin, peg.
clavo m nail; corn (on the feet); clove.
claxon m horn.
clemencia f clemency.
clemente adj clement, merciful.

cleptómano/na m/f kleptomaniac.
clerecía f clergy.
clerical adj clerical.
clérigo m priest; clergyman.
clero m clergy.
clic, click m click.
cliché m cliché; negative (of a photo).
cliente m/f client.
clientela f clientele.
clima m climate.
climatizado/da adj air-conditioned.
clínica f clinic; private hospital.
clínico/ca adj clinical.
clip m paperclip.
cloaca f sewer.
cloquear vi to cluck.
clon m clone.
clonación f cloning.
clonar vt to clone.
clónico/ca adj cloned.
clóset m Lat Am fitted cupboard.
club m club.
clueca f broody hen.
coacción f coercion, compulsion.
coactivo/va adj coercive.
coadjutor/ra m/f coadjutor.
coagular vt, ~se vr to coagulate; to curdle.
coágulo m: ~ sanguíneo blood clot.
coalición f coalition.
coartada f (law) alibi.
coartar vt to limit, to restrict, to restrain.
cobalto m cobalt.
cobarde adj cowardly, timid.
cobardía f cowardice.
cobayo/ya m/f guinea pig.
cobertizo m small shed; shelter.
cobertura f cover; coverage; bedspread.
cobija f Lat Am blanket.
cobijar vt to cover; to shelter.
cobra f cobra.
cobrador/ra m/f conductor/conductress; collector.
cobrar vt to recover; ~se vr (med) to come to.
cobre m copper; kitchen utensils pl; (mus) brass.
cobrizo/za adj coppery.
cobro m payment; recovery.
cocaína f cocaine.
cocción f cooking.
cocear vt to kick; (fig) to resist.
cocer vt to boil; to bake (bricks); * vi to boil; to ferment; ~se vr to suffer intense pain.
cochambre m dirty, stinking object.
cochambroso/sa adj nasty; filthy, stinking.
coche m car; coach, carriage; baby carriage; ~ bomba car bomb; (rail) ~ cama sleeping car/carriage; (rail) ~ restaurante restaurant car/carriage.
cochera f garage, carport, depot.
cochero m coachman.

cochinilla f woodlouse; cochineal.
cochino/na adj dirty, filthy; nasty; * m hog, pig.
cochiquera f pigpen.
cocido/da adj boiled; (fig) skilled, experienced;
  * m stew.
cocina f kitchen; cooker; cookery.
cocinero/ra m/f cook.
coco m coconut; bogeyman.
cocodrilo m crocodile.
codazo m blow given with the elbow.
codear vt, vi to elbow; ~**se** vr: ~**se con** to rub
  shoulders with.
códice m codex, old manuscript.
codicia m covetousness, greediness.
codiciable adj covetable.
codiciar vt to covet, to desire.
codicilo m (law) codicil.
codicioso/sa adj greedy, covetous.
código m law; set of rules; code; ~ **postal** post
  code.
codillo m knee (animal); (bot) stump; (tec)
  elbow (joint), bend; angle iron.
codo m elbow.
codorniz f quail.
coerción f coercion; restraint.
coercitivo/va adj coercive.
coetáneo/nea adj contemporary.
coexistencia f coexistence.
coexistente adj coexistent.
coexistir vi to coexist.
cofia f (nurse's) cap.
cofrade m member (of a brotherhood).
cofradía f brotherhood, fraternity.
cofre m chest; case; trunk.
cogedor m shovel; dustpan.
coger vt to catch, to take hold of; to occupy, to
  take up; ~**se** vr to catch.
cognitivo/va adj cognitive.
cogollo m heart of a lettuce/cabbage; shoot of a
  plant.
cogote m back of the neck.
cohabitar vi to cohabit, to live together.
cohechar vt to bribe, to suborn.
cohecho m bribery.
coherencia f coherence.
coherente adj coherent.
cohete m rocket.
cohibido/da adj shy.
cohibir vt to prohibit; to restrain.
cohorte m cohort.
coincidencia f coincidence.
coincidente adj coincidental.
coincidir vi to coincide.
coito m intercourse, coitus.
cojear vi to limp, to hobble; (fig) to go astray.
cojera f lameness; limp.
cojín m cushion.
cojo/ja adj lame, crippled.

col f cabbage.
cola¹ f tail; queue; last place; Lat Am (col) bum.
cola² f glue.
colaborador/ra m/f collaborator; contributor.
colaborar vi to collaborate.
colación f comparison; light meal, snack; buffet
  meal.
colada f wash, washing; (chem) bleach; sheep
  run.
coladera f Lat Am colander, strainer.
coladero m colander, strainer.
colador m sieve.
colapso m collapse.
colar vt to strain, to filter; * vi to ooze;
  ~**se** vr: ~ **en** to get into without paying.
colateral adj collateral.
colcha f bedspread, counterpane.
colchón m mattress.
colchoneta f mattress.
coleada f wagging (of an animal's tail).
colear vi to wag the tail.
colección f collection.
coleccionar vt to collect.
coleccionista m/f collector.
colecta f collection (for charity).
colectar vt to collect (taxes).
colectivo/va adj collective.
colector m collector; sewer.
colega m/f colleague.
colegial m schoolboy.
colegiala f schoolgirl.
colegiata f collegiate church.
colegio m college; school.
colegir vt to collect; to deduce, to infer.
cólera f bile; anger; fury, rage.
coléricamente adv in a rage.
colérico/ca adj angry; furious; bad-tempered.
colesterol m cholesterol.
coleta f pigtail.
colgadero m hook, hanger, peg.
colgadura f tapestry; hangings pl, drapery.
colgajo m tatter, rag.
colgante adj hanging; * m pendant.
colgar vt to hang; to suspend; to decorate with
  tapestry; * vi to be suspended.
colibrí m hummingbird.
cólico m colic.
coliflor m cauliflower.
colilla f end/butt of a cigarette.
colina f hill.
colindante adj neighboring.
colindar vi to adjoin.
coliseo m coliseum; opera house; theater.
colisión f collision; friction.
collar m necklace; (dog) collar.
colmar vt to heap up; * vi to fulfill, to realize.
colmena f hive, beehive.
colmenar m apiary.

C

colmillo *m* eyetooth; tusk.

colmo *m* height, summit; extreme; **a ~** plentifully.

colocación *f* employment; placing; situation.

colocar *vt* to arrange; to place; to provide with a job; **~se** *vr* to get a job.

colon *m* (*med*) colon.

colonia *f* colony; silk ribbon.

colonial *adj* colonial.

colonización *f* colonization.

colonizador/a *m/f* settler; * *adj* colonizing.

colonizar *vt* to colonize.

colono *m* colonist; farmer.

coloquio *m* conversation; conference.

color *m* color, hue; dye; rouge; suit (in cards).

coloración *f* coloring, coloration.

colorado/da *adj* ruddy; red.

colorar *vt* to color; to dye.

colorear *vt* to color; to excuse.

colorete *m* rouge.

colorido *m* coloring.

colosal *adj* colossal.

columna *f* column.

columnata *f* colonnade.

columpiar *vt*, **~se** *vr* to swing to and fro.

columpio *m* swing, seesaw.

colusión *f* collusion.

colza *f* (*bot*) rape; rape seed.

coma *f* (*gr*) comma; * *m* (*med*) coma.

comadre *f* midwife; godmother; neighbor.

comadreja *f* weasel.

comadrón/ona *m/f* midwife.

comandancia *f* command.

comandante *m* commander.

comandar *vt* to command.

comarca *f* territory, district.

comba *f* curve; warp (of lumber); skipping rope.

combar *vt* to bend; **~se** *vr* to warp.

combate *m* combat, conflict; fighting.

combatiente *m* combatant.

combatir *vt* to combat, to fight; to attack; * *vi* to fight.

combi *f* Lat Am minibus.

combinación *f* combination; (*chem*) compound; cocktail; scheme.

combinar *vi* to combine.

combustible *adj* combustible; * *m* fuel.

combustión *f* combustion.

comedero *m* dining room; trough.

comedia *f* comedy; play, drama.

comediante *m/f* player, actor/actress.

comedido/da *adj* moderate, restrained.

comedirse *vr* to restrain oneself.

comedor/ra *m/f* glutton; * *m* dining room.

comendatorio/ria *adj* introductory (of letters).

comensal *m/f* fellow diner.

comentar *vt* to comment on, to expound.

comentario *m* comment, remark; commentary.

comentarista *m/f* commentator.

comenzar *vi* to commence, to begin.

comer *vt* to eat; to take (a piece at chess); * *vi* to have lunch.

comercial *adj* commercial; * *m* Lat Am commercial.

comerciante *m/f* trader, merchant, dealer.

comerciar *vi* to trade, to do business.

comercio *m* trade, commerce; business; **~ electrónico** e-commerce; **~ justo** fair trade.

comestible *adj* eatable;* *mpl* **~s** food, foodstuffs *pl*.

cometa *m* comet; * *f* kite.

cometer *vt* to commit, to charge; to entrust.

cometido *m* task.

comezón *f* itch; itching.

comicios *mpl* elections *pl*.

cómico/ca *adj* comic, comical.

comida *f* food; eating; meal; lunch; **~ basura** junk food.

comienzo *m* beginning.

comillas *fpl* quotation marks *pl*.

comilón/ona *m/f* great eater, glutton; * *f* blow-out.

comino *m* cumin (plant/seed).

comisaría *f* police station; commissariat.

comisario/-a *m/f* commissioner.

comisión *f* commission; committee.

comisionado/da *m/f* commissioner; committee member.

comisionar *vt* to commission.

comité *m* committee.

comitiva *f* suite, retinue, followers *pl*.

como *adv* as; like; such as.

cómo *adv* how?; why? * *excl* what?

cómoda *f* chest of drawers.

comodidad *f* comfort; convenience; **~es** *fpl* wealth, comforts *pl*.

comodín *m* joker.

cómodo/da *adj* convenient; comfortable; cozy.

compact disc *m* compact disc.

compacto/ta *adj* compact; close, dense.

compadecer *vt* to pity; **~se** *vr* to agree with each other.

compadre *m* godfather; friend.

compaginar *vt* to arrange, to put in order; **~se** *vr* to tally.

compañero/ra *m/f* companion, friend; comrade; partner.

compañia *f* company.

comparación *f* comparison.

comparar *vt* to compare.

comparativo/va *adj* comparative.

comparecer *vi* to appear in court.

comparsa *m/f* extra (in the theater/movies).

compartimento *m* compartment.

compartir *vt* to divide into equal parts.

compás *m* compass; pair of compasses; (*mus*) measure, beat.

compasión *f* compassion, commiseration.

compasivo/va *adj* compassionate.

compatibilidad *f* compatibility.

compatible *adj*: ~ **con** compatible with, consistent with.

compatriota *m/f* countryman; countrywoman; fellow citizen.

compeler *vt* to compel, to constrain.

compendiar *vt* to abridge.

compendio *m* abridgment; summary.

compensación *f* compensation; recompense.

compensar *vt* to compensate; to recompense.

competencia *f* competition, rivalry; competence.

competente *adj* competent; adequate.

competer *vi* to be one's responsibility.

competición *f* competition.

competidor/ra *m/f* competitor, contestant; rival.

competir *vi* to vie; ~ **con** to compete with, to rival.

compilación *f* compilation.

compilador *m* compiler.

compilar *vt* to compile.

compinche *m* (*col*) pal, buddy.

complacencia *f* pleasure; indulgence.

complacer *vt* to please; ~**se** *vr* to be pleased with.

complaciente *adj* pleasing.

complejo *m* complex; ~/**ja** *adj* complex.

complementario/ria *adj* complementary.

complemento *m* complement.

completar *vt* to complete.

completo/ta *adj* complete; perfect.

complexión *f* constitution, temperament; build.

complicado/da *adj* complicated.

complicar *vt* to complicate.

cómplice *m/f* accomplice.

complicidad *f* complicity.

complot *m* plot.

componer *vt* to compose; to constitute; to mend, to repair; to strengthen, to restore; to adorn; to adjust; to reconcile; to compose, to calm; ~**se** *vr*: ~ **de** to consist of.

comportamiento *m* behavior.

comportarse *vr* to behave.

composición *f* composition; composure, agreement; settlement.

compositor/ra *m/f* composer; compositor.

compostura *f* composition, composure; mending, repairing; discretion; modesty, demureness.

compota *f* sauce.

compra *f* purchase; ~ **a plazos** installment plan.

comprador/ra *m/f* buyer; customer, shopper.

comprar *vt* to buy, to purchase.

comprender *vt* to include, to contain; to comprehend, to understand.

comprensible *adj* comprehensible.

comprensión *f* comprehension, understanding.

comprensivo/va *adj* comprehensive.

compresa *f* sanitary napkin.

compresión *f* compression.

comprimido *m* pill.

comprimir *vt* to compress; to repress, to restrain.

comprobante *m* receipt; voucher.

comprobar *vt* to verify, to confirm; to prove.

comprometer *vt* to compromise; to embarrass; to implicate; to put in danger; ~**se** *vr* to compromise oneself.

compromiso *m* compromise.

compuerta *f* hatch; sluice.

compuesto *m* compound; ~/**ta** *adj* composed; made up of.

compulsar *vt* to collate, to compare; to make an authentic copy.

compulsivo/va *adj* compulsive.

compunción *f* compunction, regret.

compungirse *vr* to feel remorseful.

computación *f Lat Am* computing.

computador/dora *m/f* computer.

computar *vt* to calculate; to compute.

cómputo *m* computation; calculation.

comulgar *vt* to administer communion to; * *vi* to receive communion.

común *adj* common, usual, general; * *m* community; public; **en** ~ in common.

comunal *adj* communal.

comunicación *f* communication; report.

comunicado *m* announcement.

comunicar *vt* to communicate; ~**se** *vr* to communicate (with each other).

comunicativo/va *adj* communicative.

comunidad *f* community; **C~ Europea** European Community.

comunión *f* communion.

comunismo *m* communism.

comunista *adj, m/f* communist.

comunitario/ria *adj* of the European Union.

con *prep* with; by; ~ **que** so then, providing that.

coñac *m* brandy, cognac.

conato *m* endeavor; effort; attempt.

concavidad *f* concavity.

cóncavo/va *adj* concave.

concebir *vt* to conceive; * *vi* to become pregnant.

conceder *vt* to give; to grant; to concede, to allow.

concejal/la *m/f* member of a council.

concejo *m* council.

concentración *f* concentration.

concentrar *vt*, ~**se** *vr* to concentrate.

concéntrico/ca *adj* concentric.

concepción *f* conception; idea.

concepto *m* conceit, thought; judgement, opinion.

concerniente *adj*: ~ **a** concerning, relating to.

concernir *v imp* to regard, to concern.

concertar *vt* to coordinate; to settle; to adjust; to agree; to arrange, to fix up; * *vi* (*mus*) to harmonize, to be in tune.

concesión *f* concession.

concesionario *m* agent.

C

concha *f* shell; tortoiseshell.
conchabar *vt* to mix, to blend; ~**se** *vr* to plot, to conspire.
conciencia *f* conscience.
concienciar *vt* to make aware; ~**se** *vr* to become aware.
concientizar *vt Lat Am* to make aware; ~**se** *vr* to become aware.
concierto *m* concert; agreement; concerto; **de** ~ in agreement, in concert.
conciliación *f* conciliation, reconciliation.
conciliar *vt* to reconcile; * *adj* of a council.
conciliatorio/ra *adj* conciliatory.
concilio *m* council.
concisión *f* conciseness.
conciso/sa *adj* concise, brief.
conciudadanía *f* joint-citizenship.
conciudadano/na *m/f* fellow citizen.
cónclave *m* conclave.
concluir *vt* to conclude, to end, to complete; to infer, to deduce; ~**se** *vr* to conclude.
conclusión *f* conclusion.
concluyente *adj* conclusive.
concordancia *f* concordance, concord; harmony.
concordar *vt* to reconcile, to make agree; * *vi* to agree, to correspond.
concordato *m* concordat.
concordia *f* conformity, agreement.
concretar *vt* to make concrete; to specify.
concreto/ta *adj* concrete; * *m Lat Am* concrete.
concubina *f* concubine.
concupiscencia *f* lust.
concurrencia *f* concurrence; coincidence; competition; crowd, gathering.
concurrido/da *adj* busy.
concurrir *vi* to meet; to contribute; to coincide; to compete.
concursante *m/f* competitor.
concurso *m* crowd; competition; help, cooperation.
concusión *f* concussion.
condado *m* county.
conde *m* earl, count.
condecoración *f* medal.
condecorar *vt* to adorn; (*mil*) to decorate.
condena *f* condemnation.
condenable *adj* culpable.
condenar *vt* to condemn; to find guilty; ~**se** *vr* to blame oneself; to confess (one's guilt).
condenatorio/ria *adj* condemnatory.
condensación *f* condensation.
condensar *vt* to condense.
condesa *f* countess.
condescendencia *f* helpfulness, willingness; acquiescence; compliance.
condescender *vi* to acquiesce, to comply.
condición *f* condition, state; quality; status; rank; stipulation.
condicionado/da *adj* conditioned.

condicional *adj* conditional.
condimentar *vt* to flavor, to season.
condimento *m* condiment, seasoning.
condiscípulo/la *m/f* fellow pupil; fellow student.
condolerse *vr* to sympathize.
condón *m* condom.
condominio *m Lat Am* condominium.
condonar *vt* to condone; to forgive.
conducción *f* conveyance; management; (*auto*) driving.
conducente *adj*: ~ **a** leading to.
conducir *vt* to convey, to conduct; to drive; to manage; * *vi* to drive; ~ (**a**) to lead (to); ~**se** *vr* to conduct oneself.
conducta *f* conduct, behavior; management.
conducto *m* conduit, pipe; drain; (*fig*) channel.
conductor/ra *m/f* conductor, guide; (*rail*) guard; driver.
conectado/da *adj* on-line.
conectar *vt* to connect.
conejera *f* warren, burrow.
conejo *m* rabbit.
conexión *f* connection; plug; relationship.
conexo/xa *adj* connected, related.
confabularse *vr* to conspire.
confección *f* preparation; clothing industry.
confeccionar *vt* to make up.
confederación *f* confederacy.
confederado/da *adj* confederate.
confederarse *vr* to confederate.
conferencia *f* conference; telephone call.
conferenciar *vi* to confer; to be in conference.
conferir *vt* to award; to compare.
confesar *vt* to confess; to admit.
confesión *f* confession.
confeso/sa *adj* (*law*) self-confessed.
confesonario *m* confessional.
confesor *m* confessor.
confeti *m* confetti.
confiable *adj Lat Am* reliable.
confiado/da *adj* trusting; confident; arrogant.
confianza *f* trust; confidence; conceit; familiarity; **en** ~ confidential.
confiar *vt* to confide, to entrust; * *vi* to trust.
confidencia *f* confidence.
confidencial *adj* confidential.
confidente *m/f* confidant/e; informer.
configurar *vt* to shape, to form.
confín *m* limit, boundary.
confinar *vt* to confine; * *vi*: ~ **con** to border upon.
confirmación *f* confirmation.
confirmar *vt* to confirm; to corroborate.
confiscación *f* confiscation.
confiscar *vt* to confiscate.
confite *m* candy.
confitería *f* , candy; candy store.

confitero/ra *m/f* confectioner.
confitura *f* preserve; jam.
conflagración *f* conflagration.
conflictivo/va *adj* controversial.
conflicto *m* conflict.
confluencia *f* confluence.
confluir *vi* to join (of rivers); to gather (of people).
conformar *vt* to shape; to adjust, to adapt; * *vi* to agree; ~**se** *vr* to conform; to resign oneself.
conforme *adj* alike, similar; agreed; * *prep* according to.
conformidad *f* similarity; agreement; resignation.
conformista *m/f* conformist.
confortable *adj* comfortable.
confortar *vt* to comfort; to strengthen; to console.
confortativo/va *adj* comforting.
confraternidad *f* fraternity.
confrontación *f* confrontation.
confrontar *vt* to confront.
confundir *vt* to confound, to jumble; to confuse; ~**se** *vr* to make a mistake.
confusamente *adv* confusedly.
confusión *f* confusion.
confuso/sa *adj* confused.
congelación *f* freezing.
congelado/da *adj* frozen; * *mpl*: ~**s** frozen food.
congelador *m* freezer.
congelar *vt* to freeze; ~**se** *vr* to congeal.
congeniar *vi* to get on well.
congestión *f* congestion.
congestionar *vt* to congest.
congoja *f* anguish, distress, grief.
congraciarse *vr* to ingratiate oneself.
congratulación *f* congratulation.
congratular *vt* to congratulate.
congregación *f* congregation, assembly.
congregar *vt*, ~**se** *vr* to assemble, to meet, to collect.
congresista *m/f* delegate.
congreso *m* congress.
cónico/ca *adj* conical.
conjetura *f* conjecture, guess.
conjeturar *vt* to conjecture, to guess.
conjugación *f* (*gr*) conjugation.
conjugar *vt* (*gr*) to conjugate; to combine.
conjunción *f* conjunction.
conjuntamente *adv* together.
conjunto/ta *adj* united, joint; * *m* whole; (*mus*) ensemble, band; team.
conjuración *f* conspiracy, plot.
conjurado/da *m/f* conspirator.
conjurar *vt* to exorcise; * *vi* to conspire, to plot.
conjuro *m* incantation, exorcism.
conmemoración *f* commemoration.
conmemorar *vt* to commemorate.
conmigo *pn* with me.

conminación *f* threat.
conminar *vt* to threaten.
conminatorio/ria *adj* threatening.
conmiseración *f* commiseration, pity, sympathy.
conmoción *f* shock; upheaval; commotion; (*med*) concussion.
conmovedor/ra *adj* touching.
conmover *vt* to move; to disturb.
conmutación *f* commutation, exchange.
conmutador *m* switch; *Lat Am* switchboard.
conmutar *vt* (*law*) to commute; to exchange.
connotar *vt* to imply.
coño *excl* (*col*) hell!, damn!
cono *m* cone.
conocedor/ra *m/f* connoisseur.
conocer *vt* to know, to understand; ~**se** *vr* to know one another.
conocido/da *m/f* acquaintance.
conocimiento *m* knowledge, understanding; (*med*) consciousness; acquaintance; (*mar*) bill of lading.
conque *m* condition.
conquista *f* conquest.
conquistador *m* conqueror; * *adj* ~/**ra** *adj* conquering.
conquistar *vt* to conquer.
consabido/da *adj* well-known; above-mentioned.
consagración *f* consecration.
consagrar *vt* to consecrate.
consanguíneo/nea *adj* related by blood.
consanguinidad *f* blood relationship.
consecución *f* acquisition; attainment.
consecuencia *f* consequence; conclusion; consistency; **por** ~ therefore.
consecuente *adj* consistent.
consecutivo/va *adj* consecutive.
conseguir *vt* to attain; to get, to obtain.
consejero/ra *m/f* adviser; councilor/councillor.
consejo *m* advice; council.
consenso *m* consensus.
consentido/da *adj* spoiled (of children).
consentimiento *m* consent.
consentir *vt* to consent to; to allow; to admit; to spoil (a child).
conserje *m/f* doorman, porter; janitor.
conservación *f* conservation.
conservante *m* preservative.
conservar *vt* to conserve; to keep; to preserve (fruit).
conservas *fpl* canned food.
conservatorio *m* (*mus*) conservatoire.
considerable *adj* considerable.
consideración *f* consideration; respect.
consideradamente *adv* considerately.
considerado/da *adj* respected; considerate.
considerar *vt* to consider.
consigna *f* (*mil*) watchword; order, instruction; (*rail*) checkroom.

C

consignación f consignment.

consignar vt to consign, to dispatch; to assign; to record, to register.

consignatario/ria m/f consignee.

consigo pn (m) with him; (f) with her; (vd) with you; (reflexivo) with oneself.

consiguiente adj consequent.

consistencia f consistence, consistency.

consistente adj consistent; firm, solid.

consistir vi: ~ en to consist of; to be due to.

consistorio m town council; town hall.

consocio/cia m/f fellow member; partner.

consola f control panel; console.

consolación f consolation.

consolador/ra adj consoling, comforting.

consolar vt to console, to comfort, to cheer.

consolidar vt to consolidate.

consomé m consommé.

consonancia f consonance.

consonante m rhyme; * f (gr) consonant; * adj consonant, harmonious.

consorcio m partnership.

consorte m/f consort, companion, partner; accomplice.

conspiración f conspiracy, plot.

conspirador/ra m/f conspirator, plotter.

conspirar vi to conspire, to plot.

constancia f constancy; steadiness.

constante adj constant; firm.

constar vi to be evident, to be certain; to be composed of, to consist of.

constatar vt to note; to check.

constelación f constellation.

consternación f consternation.

consternar vt to dismay; to shock.

constipado/da adj: estar ~ to have a cold.

constiparse vr to catch a cold.

constitución f constitution.

constitucional adj constitutional.

constituir vt to constitute; to establish; to appoint.

constitutivo/va adj constitutive; essential.

constituyente adj constituent.

constreñimiento m constraint.

constreñir vt to restrict; to force; (med) to constipate; to constrict.

constricción f constriction, contraction.

construcción f construction.

constructor/ra m/f builder.

construir vt to form; to build, to construct; to construe.

consuegro/gra m/f father-in-law/mother-in-law of one's son/daughter.

consuelo m consolation, comfort.

cónsul m consul.

consulado m consulate.

consulta f consultation.

consultar vt to consult, to ask for advice.

consultivo/va adj consultative.

consultor/ra m/f adviser, consultant.

consultorio m (med) surgery.

consumación f consummation, finishing.

consumado/da adj consummate; complete; accomplished; perfect.

consumar vt to consummate, to finish; to carry out.

consumición f consumption; drink.

consumidor/ra m/f consumer.

consumir vt to consume; to burn, to use; to waste, to exhaust; ~se vr to waste away, to be consumed.

consumismo m consumerism.

consumo m consumption.

contabilidad f accounting; bookkeeping.

contable m/f accountant.

contacto m contact; (auto) ignition.

contado/da adj: ~s scarce, few; * m: pagar al ~ to pay (in) cash.

contador m meter; counter in a cafe; ~/a m/f Lat Am accountant.

contaduría f Lat Am accountancy; accountant's office.

contagiar vt to infect; ~se vr to get infected.

contagio m contagion.

contagioso/sa adj contagious.

contaminación f contamination; pollution.

contaminar vt to contaminate; to pollute; to corrupt.

contante m cash.

contar vt to count, to reckon; to tell; * vi to count; ~ con to rely upon.

contemplación f contemplation.

contemplar vt to look at; to contemplate, to consider; to meditate.

contemplativo/va adj contemplative.

contemporáneo/nea adj contemporary.

contemporizar vi to temporize.

contencioso/sa adj contentious; quarrelsome.

contender vi to contend, to compete.

contendiente m/f competitor.

contenedor m container.

contener vt to contain, to hold; to hold back; to repress; ~se vr to control oneself.

contenido/da adj moderate, restrained; * m contents pl.

contentar vt to content, to satisfy; to please; ~se vr to be pleased/satisfied.

contento/ta adj glad; pleased; content; * m contentment; (law) release.

contestación f answer, reply.

contestador m: ~ automático answering machine.

contestar vt to answer, to reply; to prove, to corroborate.

contexto m context.

contienda f contest, dispute.

contigo pn with you.

contigüidad f contiguity.
contiguo/gua adj contiguous, close.
continencia f continence, abstinence, moderation.
continental adj continental.
continente m continent, mainland; * adj continent.
contingencia f risk; contingency.
contingente adj contingent, accidental; * m contingent.
continuación f continuation; sequel.
continuar vt, vi to continue.
continuidad f continuity.
continuo/nua adj continuous.
contonearse vr to walk affectedly.
contoneo m affected manner of walking.
contorno m environs pl; contour, outline; **en ~** round about.
contorsión f contortion.
contra prep against; contrary to; opposite.
contraataque m counter-attack.
contrabajo m (mus) double bass; bass guitar; low bass.
contrabandista m/f smuggler.
contrabando m contraband; smuggling.
contracción f contraction.
contrachapado m plywood.
contradecir vt to contradict.
contradicción f contradiction.
contradictorio/ria adj contradictory.
contraer vt to contract, to shrink; to make (a bargain); **~se** vr to shrink, to contract.
contrafuerte m buttress; foothill; heel-pad.
contragolpe m backlash.
contrahecho/cha adj deformed; hunchbacked; counterfeit, fake, false.
contralto m (mus) contralto.
contramaestre m (mar) boatswain; foreman.
contrapartida f (com) balancing entry.
contrapaso m step backwards.
contrapelo adv: **a ~** against the grain.
contrapesar vi to counterbalance.
contrapeso m counterpoise; counterweight.
contraponer vt to compare, to oppose.
contraposición f comparison; contrast.
contraproducente adj counterproductive.
contraprogramación f competitive scheduling.
contrapunto m (mus) counterpoint.
contrariar vt to contradict, to oppose; to vex.
contrariedad f opposition; setback; annoyance.
contrario/ria m/f opponent; * adj contrary, opposite; **por el ~** on the contrary.
contrarreloj f time trial.
contrarrestar vt to return a ball; (fig) to counteract.
contrarrevolución f counter-revolution.
contraseña f countersign; (mil) watchword.
contrasentido m contradiction.
contrastar vt to resist; to contradict; to assay

(metals); to verify (measures and weights); * vi to contrast.
contraste m contrast.
contrata f contract.
contratación f signing-up, hiring.
contratar vt to contract; to hire, to engage.
contratiempo m setback; accident.
contratista m contractor.
contrato m contract, agreement.
contravención f contravention.
contraveneno m antidote.
contravenir vi to contravene, to transgress; to violate.
contraventana f shutter.
contribución f contribution; tax.
contribuir vt, vi to contribute.
contribuyente m/f contributor; taxpayer.
contrincante m competitor.
contrito/ta adj contrite, penitent.
controlador/ra m/f controller.
controlar vt to control; to check.
controversia f controversy, dispute.
contumacia f obstinacy, stubbornness; (law) contempt of court.
contumaz adj obstinate, stubborn; (law) guilty of contempt of court.
contundente adj overwhelming; blunt.
contusión f bruise.
convalecencia f convalescence.
convalecer vi to recover from sickness, to convalesce.
convaleciente m/f, adj convalescent.
convalidar vt to recognize.
convencer vt to convince.
convencimiento m conviction.
convención f convention, pact.
convencional adj conventional.
conveniencia f suitability; usefulness; agreement; **~s** fpl property.
conveniente adj useful; suitable.
convenio m convention, agreement, treaty.
convenir vi to agree, to suit.
convento m convent, nunnery; monastery.
conventual adj monastic.
convergencia f convergence.
converger vi to converge.
conversa f Lat Am conversation, talk.
conversación f conversation, talk; communication.
conversar vi to talk, to converse.
conversión f conversion, change.
converso/sa m/f convert.
convertir vt, **~se** vr to convert.
convexo/xa adj convex.
convicción f conviction.
convicto/ta adj convicted (found guilty).
convidado/da m/f guest.
convidar vt to invite.
convincente adj convincing.

C

convite *m* invitation; banquet.
convivencia *f* living together.
convocar *vt* to convoke, to assemble.
convocatoria *f* summons; notice of a meeting.
convoy *m* convoy.
convulsión *f* convulsion.
convulsivo/va *adj* convulsive.
conyugal *adj* conjugal, married.
cónyuge *m/f* spouse.
cooperar *vi* to cooperate.
cooperativa *f* cooperative.
cooperativo/va *adj* cooperative.
coordinadora *f* coordinating committee.
coordinar *vt* to arrange, to coordinate.
copa *f* cup; glass; top of a tree; crown of a hat; **~s** *fpl* hearts *pl* (in cards).
copete *m* quiff; pride.
copia *f* plenty, abundance; copy, duplicate.
copiador/ra *m/f* copyist; copier.
copiar *vt* to copy; to imitate.
copioso/sa *adj* copious, abundant, plentiful.
copla *f* verse; (*mus*) popular song, folk song.
copo *m* small bundle; flake of snow.
copropietario/ria *m/f* joint owner.
cópula *f* copulation; conjunction; (*gr*) copula.
copulativo/va *adj* copulative.
coqueta *f* coquette, flirt.
coquetear *vi* to flirt.
coquetería *f* coquetry, flirtation.
coraje *m* courage; anger, passion.
coral *m* coral; choir; * *adj* choral.
coraza *f* cuirass; armor-plating.
corazón *m* heart; core; **de ~** willingly.
corazonada *f* feeling; inspiration; quick decision; presentiment.
corbata *f* tie.
corbeta *f* corvette.
corcel *m* steed, charger.
corchea *f* (*mus*) quaver.
corchete *m* clasp; hook and eye.
corcho *m* cork; float (for fishing); cork bark.
cordel *m* cord, rope; (*mar*) line.
cordero *m* lamb; lambskin; meek/gentle person.
cordial *adj* cordial, affectionate; * *m* cordial.
cordialidad *f* cordiality.
cordillera *f* range of mountains.
cordón *m* cord, string; lace; cordon.
cordura *f* prudence, good sense, wisdom.
corista *m/f* chorister.
cornada *f* thrust with a bull's horn.
cornadura *f* horns *pl*.
cornamenta *f* horns *pl* of an animal.
córnea *f* cornea.
cornear *vt* to gore.
córneo/ea *adj* horny, corneous.
corneta *f* bugle.
cornisa *f* cornice.
cornudo/da *adj* horned.

coro *m* choir; chorus.
corona *f* crown; coronet; top of the head; crown (of a tooth); tonsure; halo.
coronación *f* coronation.
coronar *vt* to crown; to complete, to perfect.
coronario/ria *adj* coronary.
coronel *m* (*mil*) colonel.
coronilla *f* crown of the head.
corpiño *m* bodice.
corporación *f* corporation.
corporal *adj* corporal.
corpóreo/rea *adj* corporeal.
corpulencia *f* corpulence.
corpulento/ta *adj* corpulent, bulky.
Corpus *m* Corpus Christi.
corral *m* yard; farmyard; corral; playpen.
correa *f* leather strap, thong; flexibility.
correaje *m* leather straps *pl*.
corrección *f* correction; reprehension; amendment.
correccional *m* reformatory.
correctivo/va *adj* corrective.
correcto/ta *adj* exact, correct.
corrector/ra *m/f* proof-reader.
corredizo/za *adj* sliding; easy to be untied.
corredor/ra *adj* running; * *m/f* broker, runner; *m* corridor.
corregir *vt* to correct, to amend; to reprehend; **~se** *vr* to reform.
correlación *f* correlation.
correo *m* post, mail; courier; postman; **~ electrónico** e-mail; **a vuelta de ~** by return of post; **~s** *mpl* post office.
correoso/sa *adj* flexible, leathery.
correr *vt* to run; to flow; to travel over; to pull (a drape); * *vi* to run, to rush; to flow; to blow (applied to the wind); **~se** *vr* to be ashamed; to slide, to move; to run (of colors).
correría *f* incursion.
correspondencia *f* correspondence; communication; agreement.
corresponder *vi* to correspond; to answer; to be suitable; to belong; to concern; **~se** *vr* to love one another.
correspondiente *adj* corresponding, suitable.
corresponsal *m/f* correspondent.
corretear *vi* to rush around; to hang about the streets.
corrida *f* run, dash; bullfight.
corrido/da *adj* expert; knowing; ashamed.
corriente *f* current; course, progression; electric current; * *adj* current; common, ordinary, general; fluent; flowing, running.
corrillo *m* circle of persons; clique.
corro *m* circle of people.
corroborar *vt* to corroborate.
corroer *vt* to corrode, to erode.
corromper *vt* to corrupt; to rot; to turn bad; to seduce; to bribe; **~se** *vr* to rot; to become corrupted; * *vi* to stink.

corrosión f corrosion.
corrosivo/va adj corrosive.
corrupción f corruption; rot, decay.
corruptible adj corruptible.
corrupto/ta adj corrupted, corrupt.
corruptor/ra m/f corrupter, perverter.
corrusco m broken bread.
corsé f corset.
cortacésped m lawn mower.
cortada f Lat Am shortcut.
cortado m coffee with a little milk; ~/da adj cut; sour; embarrassed.
cortadura f cut; cutting; incision; fissure; ~s fpl shreds pl, cuttings pl, parings pl.
cortafuegos m invar fire lane, firebreak.
cortaplumas m invar penknife.
cortar vt to cut; to cut off, to curtail; to intersect; to carve; to chop; to cut (in cards); to interrupt; ~se vr to be ashamed/embarrassed; to curdle.
cortauñas m invar nail clippers pl.
corte¹ m cutting; cut; section; length (of cloth); style.
corte² f (royal) court; capital city; Lat Am law court; **C~s** fpl Spanish Parliament.
cortedad f shortness, smallness; stupidity; bashfulness.
cortejar vt to court.
cortejo m entourage; courtship; procession; lover.
cortés/esa adj courteous, polite.
cortesana f courtesan.
cortesía f courtesy, good manners pl.
corteza f bark; peel; crust; (fig) outward appearance.
cortina f drape; ~s drapes.
cortinaje m set of drapes.
corto/ta adj short; scanty, small; stupid; bashful; **a la ~a o a la larga** sooner or later.
corvo/va adj bent, crooked.
corzo/za m/f roe deer, fallow deer.
cosa f thing; matter; affair; **¡no hay tal ~!** nothing of the sort!
cosaco m Cossack.
cosecha f harvest; harvest time; **de su ~** of one's own invention.
cosechar vt to harvest, to reap.
coser vt to sew; to join.
cosido m stitching, sewing.
cosmético/a adj, m cosmetic.
cosmopolita adj, m cosmopolitan.
cosquillas fpl tickling; (fig) agitation.
costa f cost, price; charge, expense; coast, shore; **a toda ~** at all events.
costado m side; (mil) flank; side of a ship.
costal m sack, large bag.
costalada f heavy fall.
costar vt to cost; to need.
coste m cost, expense.

costear vt to pay for.
costera f side; slope; coast.
costero/ra adj coastal; (mar) coasting.
costilla f rib; (fig) wife; cutlet; ~s fpl back, shoulders pl.
costillar m human ribs pl.
costo m cost, price; expense.
costoso/sa adj costly, dear, expensive.
costra f crust; (med) scab.
costumbre f custom, habit.
costura f sewing; seam; needlework.
costurera f seamstress.
costurero m sewing box.
cotejar vt to compare.
cotejo m comparison, collation.
cotidiano/na adj daily.
cotilla m/f gossip.
cotización f quotation.
cotizar vt to quote; ~se vr: ~ **a** to sell at; to be quoted at.
coto m enclosure; reserve; boundary stone.
cotorra f magpie; small parrot; (col) chatterbox.
covacha f small cave, grotto.
coyote m coyote.
coyuntura f joint, articulation; juncture.
coz f kick; recoil (of a gun); ebbing (of a flood); (fig) insult.
cráneo m skull.
cráter m crater.
creación f creation.
creador/ra adj creative; * m/f creator.
crear vt to create, to make; to establish.
crecer vi to grow, to increase; to rise.
creces fpl increase.
crecida f swell (of rivers).
crecido/da adj full-grown (of a person); large; (fig) vain.
creciente f crescent (moon); (mar) flood tide; * adj growing; crescent.
crecimiento m increase; growth.
credenciales fpl credentials pl.
credibilidad f credibility.
crédito m credit; belief, faith; reputation.
credo m creed.
credulidad f credulity.
crédulo/la adj credulous.
creencia f credence, belief.
creer vt, vi to believe; to think; to consider.
crema f cream; custard.
cremallera f zipper.
crepúsculo m twilight.
crespo/pa adj curled; angry, displeased.
crespón m crepe.
cresta f crest (of birds).
creyente m/f believer.
cría f breeding; young.
criada f servant, maid.
criadero m (bot) nursery; breeding place.

C

criadilla f testicle; small loaf; truffle.
criado/da m/f servant; adj reared, brought up, bred.
criador f creator; breeder.
crianza f breeding, rearing.
criar vt to create, to produce; to breed; to nurse; to breast-feed; to bring up, to raise.
criatura f creature; child.
criba f sieve.
cribar vt to sift.
crimen m crime.
criminal adj, m/f criminal.
criminalista m/f criminologist; criminal lawyer.
crin f mane; horsehair.
crío/a m/f (col) kid.
criollo/lla adj, m/f Creole.
cripta f crypt.
crisis f invar crisis.
crisma f holy oil, chrism.
crisol m crucible; melting pot.
crispar vt to set on edge; to tense up
cristal m crystal; glass; pane; lens.
cristalino/na adj crystalline.
cristalización f crystallization.
cristalizar vt to crystallize.
cristiandad f Christianity.
cristianismo m Christianity.
cristiano/na adj, m/f Christian.
Cristo m Christ.
criterio m criterion.
crítica m/f criticism.
criticar vt to criticize.
crítico/ca m/f critic; * adj critical.
croar vi to croak.
cromo m chrome.
crónica f chronicle; news report; feature.
crónico/ca adj chronic.
cronista m/f chronicler; reporter, columnist.
cronología f chronology.
cronológico/ca adj chronological.
cronómetro m stopwatch.
cruce m crossing; crossroads.
crucero m cruiser; cruise; transept; crossing; Southern Cross (constellation).
crucificar vt to crucify; to torment.
crucifijo m crucifix.
crucigrama m crossword.
crudeza f unripeness; crudeness; undigested food (in the stomach).
crudo/da adj raw; green, unripe; crude; cruel; hard to digest.
cruel adj cruel.
crueldad f cruelty.
cruento/ta adj bloody; cruel.
crujido m crack; creak; clash; crackling.
crujiente adj crunchy.
crujir vi to crackle; to rustle.
crustáceo m crustacean.

cruz f cross; tails (of a coin).
cruzada f crusade.
cruzado m crusader; ~/da adj crossed.
cruzar vt to cross; (mar) to cruise ~se vr to cross; to pass each other.
cuaderna f fourth part; rib.
cuaderno m notebook; exercise book; logbook.
cuadra f block; stable.
cuadrado/da adj, m square.
cuadragenario/ria adj forty-year-old.
cuadragésimo/ma adj, m fortieth.
cuadrangular adj quadrangular, four-cornered; * m Lat Am home run.
cuadrángulo m quadrangle.
cuadrante m quadrant; dial.
cuadrar vt, vi to square; to fit, to suit, to correspond.
cuadricular adj squared.
cuadrilátero/ra adj, m quadrilateral.
cuadrilla f party, group; gang, crew.
cuadro m square; picture, painting; window frame; scene; chart; (sport) team; executive; Lat Am slaughterhouse.
cuadrúpedo/da adj quadruped.
cuádruple adj quadruple.
cuádruplo/pla adj quadruple, fourfold.
cuajada f curd.
cuajar vt to coagulate; to thicken; to adorn; to set; ~se vr to coagulate, to curdle; to set; to fill up.
cuál pn which (one).
cual pn which; who; whom; * adv as; like; * adj such as.
cualidad f quality.
cualquier adj any.
cualquiera adj anyone, anybody; someone, somebody; whoever; whichever.
cuándo adv when; ¿de ~ acá? since when?.
cuando adv when; if; even; * conj since; de ~ en ~ from time to time; ~ más/mucho at most/at best; ~ menos at least.
cuantía f quantity, amount; importance.
cuantioso/sa adj numerous; substantial.
cuantitativo/va adj quantitative, quantitive.
cuánto adj what a lot of; how much?; ¿~s? how many?; * pn, adv how; how much; how many.
cuanto/ta adj as many as; as much as; all; whatever; * adv en ~ as soon as; en ~ a as regards; ~ más moreover, the more as.
cuarenta adj, m forty.
cuarentena f space of forty days; Lent; quarantine.
cuaresma f Lent.
cuarta f fourth; span; (mar) point (of the compass).
cuartear vt to quarter, to divide up; ~se vr to split into pieces.
cuartel m quarter, district; barracks pl.
cuarteta f (poet) quatrain.

cuartilla f fourth part; sheet of paper.

cuarto m fourth part; quarter; room, apartment; span; **~s** mpl cash, money; **~/ta** adj fourth.

cuarzo m quartz.

cuatrero m horse thief.

cuatro adj, m four.

cuatrocientos/tas adj four hundred.

cuba f cask; tub; (fig) drunkard.

cubeta f small cask.

cúbico/ca adj cubic.

cubierta f cover; deck of a ship; (auto) hood; tire; pretext.

cubierto m cover; shelter; place at table; meal at a fixed charge; **~s** mpl cutlery.

cubil m lair.

cubilete m tumbler; dice box.

cubo m cube; bucket.

cubo de la basura m ash can, trash can, garbage can.

cubrecama m bedspread.

cubrir vt to cover; to disguise; to protect; to roof a building; **~se** vr to become overcast.

cucaña f (col) soft job; bargain; cinch.

cucaracha f cockroach.

cuchara f spoon.

cucharada f spoonful; ladleful.

cucharadita f teaspoonful.

cucharita f teaspoon.

cucharón m ladle; large spoon.

cuchichear vi to whisper.

cuchicheo m whispering.

cuchilla f large kitchen knife; chopping knife; blade.

cuchillada f cut; gash; **~s** fpl wrangles, quarrels.

cuchillo m knife.

cuchitril m pigpen.

cuclillas adv: **en ~** squatting.

cuclillo m cuckoo; (fig) cuckold.

cuco m cuckoo; **~/ca** adj sharp.

cucurucho m paper cornet.

cuello m neck; collar.

cuenca m bowl, deep valley; hollow; socket of the eye.

cuenco m earthenware bowl.

cuenta f calculation; account; check (in a restaurant); count, counting; bead; importance.

cuentakilómetros m invar odometer.

cuentapropista m/f Lat Am self-employed person.

cuentarrevoluciones m invar tachometer.

cuentista m/f storyteller.

cuento m tale, story, narrative.

cuerazo m Lat Am lash.

cuerda f rope; string; spring.

cuerdo/da adj sane; prudent, judicious, canny.

cuerear vt Lat Am to lash.

cuerno m horn.

cuero m hide, skin, leather; Lat Am whip.

cuerpo m body; cadaver, corpse.

cuervo m raven.

cuesta f slope, hill; incline; **ir ~ abajo** to go downhill; **~ arriba** uphill.

cuestión f question, matter; dispute; quarrel; problem.

cuestionable adj questionable, problematic.

cuestionar vt to question, to dispute.

cuete m Lat Am rocket.

cueva f cave; cellar.

cuidado m care, worry, concern; charge.

cuidadosamente adv observantly.

cuidadoso/sa adj careful; anxious.

cuidar vt to care for; to mind, to look after.

culata f butt, breech (of a gun); hindquarters pl (of an animal); rear of a horse.

culebra f snake.

culinario/ria adj culinary.

culminación f culmination.

culo m backside, bottom; (col) ass.

culpa f fault, blame; guilt.

culpabilidad f guilt.

culpable adj culpable; guilty; * m/f culprit.

culpar vt to accuse, to blame.

cultivación f cultivation, culture.

cultivar vt to cultivate.

cultivo m cultivation; crop.

culto/ta adj cultivated, cultured; refined, civilized; * m culture; worship.

cultura f culture.

cumbre f top, summit.

cumpleaños m invar birthday.

cumplido/da adj large, plentiful; complete, perfect, courteous; * m compliment.

cumplidor/ora adj reliable.

cumplimentar vt to compliment.

cumplimiento m fulfillment; accomplishment; completion.

cumplir vt to carry out, to fulfill; to serve (a prison sentence); to carry out (death penalty); to attain, to reach (a certain age); **~se** vr to be fulfilled; to expire, to be up.

cúmulo m heap, pile.

comunicado m communiqué.

cuna f cradle.

cuña f wedge.

cuñado/da m/f brother/sister-in-law.

cundir vi to spread; to grow, to increase.

cuneta f ditch.

cuota f quota; fee; Lat Am installment.

cupé m (auto) coupé.

cupo m share.

cupón m coupon.

cúpula f cupola, dome.

cura m priest; * f cure; treatment.

curable adj curable.

curación f cure; curing; **primera ~** first aid.

curandero m quack (doctor).

curar vt to cure; to treat, to dress (a wound); to salt; to dress; to tan.

C

curativo/va *adj* curative, healing.

curia *f* ecclesiastical court.

curiosear *vt* to glance at; * *vi* to look round.

curiosidad *f* curiosity.

curioso/sa *adj* curious; * *m/f* bystander.

Curita™ *f Lat Am* Band-Aid™.

currante *m/f* (*col*) worker.

currar *vi* (*col*) to work.

currículum *m* curriculum vitae.

cursado/da *adj* skilled; versed.

cursar *vt* to frequent a place; to send, to dispatch; to study.

cursillo *m* short course of lectures (in a university).

cursivo/va *adj* italic (type).

curso *m* course, direction; year (at university); subject.

cursor *m* cursor.

curtidor *m* tanner.

curtidos *mpl* tanned leather.

curtir *vt* to tan leather; **~se** *vr* to become sunburned; to become inured.

curva *f* curve, bend.

curvatura *f* curvature.

curvilíneo/nea *adj* curvilinear.

curvo/va *adj* curved, bent.

cuscurro *m* little crust of bread.

cúspide *f* summit, peak; apex.

custodia *f* custody, safekeeping, care; monstrance.

custodio *m* guard, keeper; watchman.

cutáneo/nea *adj* cutaneous.

cutícula *f* cuticle.

cutis *m* skin.

cutre *adj* (*col*) unpleasant, nasty, mean; of poor quality.

cuyo/ya *pn* whose, of which, of whom.

D

dactilógrafo/fa *m/f* typist.
dádiva *f* gift, present; donation.
dadivoso/sa *adj* generous, open-handed.
dado *m* die; ~**s** dice.
daga *f* dagger.
dale *excl* come on!
daltónico/ca *adj* color-blind.
dama *f* lady, gentlewoman; mistress; queen; actress who performs principal parts.
damasco *m* damask (fabric); damson (plum).
damasquino/na *adj* damask.
damnificar *vt* to hurt, to injure, to damage.
danza *f* dance.
danzar *vi* to dance; to meddle.
danzarín *m* fine dancer; meddler.
dañar *vt* to hurt, to injure; to damage.
dañino/na *adj* harmful; noxious; mischievous.
daño *m* harm, damage; prejudice; loss.
dar *vt* to give; to supply, to administer, to afford; to deliver; to bestow; to strike, to beat, to knock; to communicate; ~**se** *vr* to conform (to the will of another); to give oneself up; ~**se prisa** to hurry.
dardo *m* dart.
datar *vt* to date.
dátil *m* (*bot*) date.
dativo *m* (*gr*) dative.
dato *m* fact.
de *prep* of; from; for; by; on; to; with.
deambular *vi* to stroll.
deán *m* dean.
debajo *adv* under, underneath, below.
debate *m* debate, discussion; contest; altercation.
debatir *vt* to debate, to argue, to discuss.
debe *m* (*com*) debit; ~ **y haber** debit and credit.
deber *m* obligation, duty; debt; * *vt* to owe; to be obliged to; * *vi*: **debe (de)** it must, it should.
debidamente *adv* justly, duly; exactly, perfectly.
débil *adj* feeble, weak; sickly; frail.
debilidad *f* dimness; weakness.
debilitar *vt* to debilitate, to weaken.
débito *m* debt; duty.
debutar *vi* to make one's debut.
década *f* decade.
decadencia *f* decay, decline.
decaer *vi* to decay, to molder; to decline, to fade.
decaimiento *m* decay, decline.
decálogo *m* Decalogue.
decano *m* senior; dean.
decantar *vt* to decant.
decapitación *f* decapitation, beheading.
decapitar *vt* to behead.

decena *f* ten.
decencia *f* decency.
decente *adj* decent; honest.
decepción *f* disappointment.
dechado *m*: ~ **de virtudes** model of virtue and perfection.
decidir *vt* to decide, to determine.
decimal *adj* decimal.
décimo/ma *adj*, *m* tenth.
decir *vt* to say; to tell; to speak; to name.
decisión *f* decision; determination, resolution; sentence.
decisivo/va *adj* decisive; final.
declamación *f* declamation, discourse, oration.
declamar *vi* to declaim; to harangue.
declaración *f* declaration; explanation, interpretation; (*law*) deposition.
declarar *vt* to declare; to manifest; to expound; to explain; (*law*) to decide; ~**se** *vr* to declare one's opinion; * *vi* to testify.
declinación *f* declination, descent; decline.
declinar *vi* to decline; to decay, to degenerate; * *vt* (*gr*) to decline.
declive *m* slope; decline.
decolaje *m* *Lat Am* take-off.
decolar *vi* *Lat Am* to take off.
decolorarse *vr* to become discolored.
decomiso *m* confiscation.
decoración *f* decoration.
decorado *m* scenery.
decorar *vt* to decorate, to adorn; to illustrate.
decorativo/va *adj* decorative.
decoro *m* honor, respect; circumspection; honesty; decency.
decoroso/sa *adj* decorous, decent.
decrecer *vi* to decrease.
decrépito/ta *adj* decrepit, worn out with age.
decrepitud *f* decrepitude.
decretar *vt* to decree, to determine.
decreto *m* decree; decision; judicial decree.
dedal *m* thimble; very small drinking glass.
dedicación *f* dedication; consecration.
dedicar *vt* to dedicate, to devote; to consecrate; ~**se** *vr* to apply oneself to.
dedicatoria *f* dedication.
dedo *m* finger; toe; small bit; ~ **meñique** little finger; ~ **pulgar** thumb; ~ **índice** index finger; ~ **corazón** middle finger; ~ **anular** ring finger.
deducción *f* deduction, inference; derivation.
deducir *vt* to deduce, to infer; to allege in pleading; to subtract.

defección f defection; apostasy.
defectivo/va adj defective.
defecto m defect; defectiveness.
defectuoso/sa adj defective, imperfect, faulty.
defender vt to defend, to protect; to justify, to assert, to maintain; to prohibit, to forbid; to resist, to oppose.
defensa f defense, justification, apology; guard, shelter, protection, fence.
defensiva f defensive.
defensivo m defense, safeguard; ~/**va** adj defensive.
defensor/ra m/f defender, protector; lawyer, defense counsel.
deferente adj pliant, docile, yielding.
deferir vi to defer; to yield (to another's opinion); * vt to communicate.
deficiencia f deficiency.
deficiente adj defective.
déficit m deficit.
definición f definition; decision.
definir vt to define, to describe, to explain; to decide.
definitivo/va adj definitive; positive.
deformar vt to deform; ~**se** vr to become deformed.
deforme adj deformed; ugly.
deformidad f deformity; ugliness; gross error.
defraudación f fraud; usurpation.
defraudar vt to defraud, to cheat; to usurp; to disturb.
defunción f death; funeral.
degeneración f degeneration; degeneracy.
degenerar vi to degenerate.
degollación f beheading.
degollar vt to behead; to destroy, to ruin.
degradación f degradation.
degradar vt to degrade; ~**se** vr to degrade/demean oneself.
degustar vt to taste.
dehesa f pasture, field.
deidad f deity, divinity; goddess.
dejadez f slovenliness, neglect.
dejado/da adj slovenly, idle, indolent; dejected.
dejar vt to leave, to quit; to omit; to let; to permit, to allow; to leave, to forsake; to bequeath; to pardon; ~ **de** to stop; to fail to; ~**se** vr to abandon oneself.
dejo m accent; aftertaste, tang.
del adj of the (contraction of **de** and **el**).
delantal m apron.
delante adv in front; opposite; ahead; ~ **de** in front of; before.
delantera f front, forepart (of something); advantage; forward line.
delantero/ra adj front; * m/f forward.
delatar vt to accuse; to denounce.
delator m accuser; informer, denouncer.

delegación f delegation; substitution.
delegado/da m/f delegate; deputy.
delegar vt to delegate; to substitute.
deleitar vt to delight.
deletrear vt to spell; to examine; to conjecture.
delfín m dolphin; dauphin.
delgadez f thinness.
delgado/da adj thin; delicate, fine; light; slender, lean; acute; ingenious; little, scanty.
deliberación f deliberation; resolution.
deliberadamente adv deliberately.
deliberar vi to consider, to deliberate; * vt to debate; to consult.
delicadeza f tenderness, softness; delicacy, daintiness; subtlety.
delicado/da adj delicate, tender; faint; exquisite; delicious, dainty; slender, subtle.
delicia f delight, pleasure.
delicioso/sa adj delicious; delightful.
delincuencia f delinquency.
delincuente m delinquent.
delineante m/f draftsman/woman.
delinear vt to delineate, to sketch; to describe.
delinquir vi to offend.
delirante adj delirious.
delirar vi to rave; to talk nonsense.
delirio m delirium; dotage; nonsense.
delito m offense; crime.
demacrado/da adj pale and drawn.
demagogia f demagogy.
demagogo m demagog.
demanda f demand, claim; pretension, complaint; challenge; request.
demandado/da m/f defendant.
demandante m/f claimant.
demandar vt to demand; to ask; to claim; to sue.
demarcación f demarcation; boundary line.
demarcar vt to mark out (limits).
demás adj other; remaining; * pn **los/las** ~ the others, the rest; **estar** ~ to be over and above; to be useless/superfluous; **por** ~ in vain, to no purpose.
demasía f excess; arduous enterprise; rudeness; want of respect; abundance, plenty; **en** ~ excessively.
demasiado/da adj too; excessive; * adv too, too much.
demencia f madness.
demente adj mad, insane.
democracia f democracy.
demócrata m/f democrat.
democrático/ca adj democratic.
demoler vt to demolish; to destroy.
demolición f demolition.
demonio m demon.
demora f delay; demurrage.
demorar vt to delay; ~**se** vr to be delayed; * vi to linger.

demostrable *adj* demonstrable.
demostración *f* demonstration; manifestation.
demostrar *vt* to prove, to demonstrate; to manifest.
demostrativo/va *adj* demonstrative.
denegación *f* denial; refusal.
denegar *vt* to deny; to refuse.
dengue *m* prudery.
denigración *f* defamation; stigma, disgrace.
denigrar *vt* to blacken; to insult.
denominación *f* denomination.
denominar *vt* to name; to designate.
denotar *vt* to denote; to express.
densidad *f* density; obscurity.
denso/sa *adj* dense, thick; compact.
dentado/da *adj* jagged, toothed; perforated (of stamps).
dentadura *f* set of teeth.
dentellada *f* gnashing of the teeth; nip; pinch with the teeth; **a ~s** snappishly, peevishly.
dentera *f* (*fig*) the shivers *pl*.
dentición *f* dentition, teething.
dentífrico *m* toothpaste.
dentista *m/f* dentist.
dentro *adv* within; * *pn*: **~ de** in, inside.
denuncia *f* denunciation; accusation; report.
denunciar *vt* to advise; to denounce; to report.
deparar *vt* to offer, to present.
departamento *m* department; (*rail*) compartment; apartment.
dependencia *f* dependency; relation, affinity; dependence; office; business, affair.
depender *vi*: **~ de** to depend on, to be dependent on.
dependienta *f* saleswoman.
dependiente *m* shop/store assistant; * *adj* dependent.
depilar *vt* to depilate, remove hair from.
depilatorio *m* hair remover.
deplorable *adj* deplorable, lamentable.
deplorar *vt* to deplore.
deponer *vt* to depose; to declare; to displace; to deposit.
deportación *f* deportation.
deportar *vt* to deport.
deporte *m* sport.
deportista *m/f* sportsman/woman.
deportivo/va *adj* sports *compd*.
deposición *f* deposition; assertion, affirmation; (*law*) deposition upon oath.
depositar *vt* to deposit; to confide; to put away for safekeeping.
depósito *m* deposit; warehouse; tank.
depravación *f* depravity.
depravar *vt* to deprave, to corrupt.
depreciar *vt* to depreciate.
depredador/ra *adj* predatory; * *m* predator.
depresión *f* depression.
deprimido/da *adj* depressed.

deprimir *vt* to depress; **~se** *vr* to become depressed.
deprisa *adv* quickly.
depuración *f* purification.
depuradora *f* purifier.
depurar *vt* to cleanse; to purify; to filter.
de quitapón *adj* detachable, removable.
derecha *f* right hand, right side; right.
derecho/cha *adj* right; straight; just; perfect; certain; * *m* right, justice; law; tax, duty; fee; * *adv* straight.
derivación *f* derivation; source; origin.
derivado/da *adj* derivative; * *m* derivative; by-product.
derivar *vt*, *vi* to derive; (*mar*) to drift.
dermatología *f* dermatology.
dermatólogo/ga *m/f* dermatologist.
derogar *vt* to derogate, to abolish; to reform.
derogatorio/ria *adj* derogatory.
derramamiento *m* effusion; waste; dispersion; **~ de sangre** bloodshed.
derramar *vt* to drain off (water); to spread; to spill, to scatter; to waste, to shed; **~se** *vr* to pour out.
derrame *m* spelling; overflow; discharge; leakage.
derredor *m* circumference, circuit; **al/en ~** around, about.
derrengado/da *adj* bent, crooked.
derrengar *vt* to sprain.
derretir *vt* to melt; to consume; to thaw; **~se** *vr* to melt.
derribar *vt* to demolish; to flatten.
derribo *m* demolition; ruins of a demolished building *pl*.
derrocar *vt* to pull down, to demolish.
derrochador *m* spendthrift.
derrochar *vt* to dissipate; to squander.
derroche *m* waste.
derrota *f* ship's course; road, path; defeat.
derrotar *vt* to destroy; to defeat.
derrotero *m* collection of sea charts; ship's course; (*fig*) course, way.
derruir *vt* to demolish.
derrumbar *vt* to throw down; **~se** *vr* to collapse.
desabastecer *vt* to cut off supplies from.
desabillé *m* deshabille/dishabille.
desabollar *vt* to take the bulges out of.
desabotonar *vt* to unbutton; **~se** *vr* to come undone.
desabrido/da *adj* tasteless, insipid; rude; unpleasant.
desabrigado/da *adj* uncovered; unsheltered.
desabrigar *vt* to uncover; to deprive of clothes/shelter.
desabrochar *vt* to undo; **~se** *vr* to come undone.
desacatar *vt* to treat in a disrespectful manner.

desacato *m* disrespect, incivility.

desacertado/da *adj* mistaken; unwise; inconsiderate.

desacierto *m* error, gross mistake, blunder.

desaconsejado/da *adj* inconsiderate; ill-advised.

desaconsejar *vt* to advise against.

desacorde *adj* discordant.

desacostumbrado/da *adj* unusual.

desacreditar *vt* to discredit.

desacuerdo *m* blunder; disagreement; forgetfulness.

desafiar *vt* to challenge; to defy.

desafilado/da *adj* blunt.

desafinado/da *adj* out of tune.

desafinar *vi* to be out of tune.

desafío *m* challenge; struggle; contest, combat.

desaforado/da *adj* huge; disorderly, lawless; impudent.

desafortunadamente *adv* unfortunately.

desafortunado/da *adj* unfortunate, unlucky.

desafuero *m* outrage; excess.

desagradable *adj* disagreeable, unpleasant.

desagradar *vt* to displease; to pester.

desagradecido/da *adj* ungrateful.

desagradecimiento *m* ingratitude.

desagrado *m* harshness; displeasure.

desagraviar *vt* to make amends for.

desagravio *m* amends *pl*; satisfaction.

desaguar *vt* to drain; * *vi* to drain off.

desagüe *m* channel, drain; drainpipe; drainage.

desaguisado *m* outrage.

desahogado/da *adj* comfortable; roomy.

desahogar *vt* to ease; to vent; ~se *vr* to recover; to relax; to let off steam.

desahogo *m* ease, relief; freedom.

desahuciar *vt* to cause to despair; to give up; to evict.

desahucio *m* eviction.

desairado/da *adj* disregarded; slighted.

desairar *vt* to disregard, to take no notice of.

desaire *m* disdain, disrespect; unattractiveness.

desajustar *vt* to make uneven; to unbalance; ~se *vr* to get out of order.

desajuste *m* disorder; imbalance.

desalentador/ra *adj* disheartening.

desalentar *vt* to make breathless; to discourage.

desaliento *m* dismay.

desaliño *m* slovenliness; carelessness.

desalinizadora *f* desalination plant.

desalinizar *vt* to desalinate.

desalmado/da *adj* cruel, inhuman.

desalojar *vt* to eject; to move out; * *vi* to move out.

desamarrar *vt* to cast off (a ship); to untie; to remove.

desamor *m* indifference.

desamparado/da *adj* helpless.

desamparar *vt* to forsake, to abandon; to relinquish.

desamparo *m* abandonment; helplessness; dereliction.

desamueblar *vt* to remove the furniture from.

desandar *vt* to retrace; to go back the same road.

desangrar *vt* to bleed; to drain (a pond); (*fig*) to exhaust (one's means); ~se *vr* to lose a lot of blood.

desanimado/da *adj* downhearted.

desanimar *vt* to discourage; ~se *vr* to lose heart.

desapacible *adj* disagreeable; unpleasant, harsh.

desaparecer *vi* to disappear.

desaparecido/da *adj* missing; * *mpl* ~s missing people.

desaparejar *vt* to unharness, unhitch (beasts); (*mar*) to unrig (a ship).

desaparición *f* disappearance.

desapego *m* coolness; lack of interest.

desapercibido/da *adj* unnoticed.

desaplicado/da *adj* lazy; careless, neglectful.

desapolillar *vt* to free from moths; ~se *vr* (*fig*) to get rid of the cobwebs.

desaprensivo/va *adj* unscrupulous.

desaprobación *f* disapproval.

desaprobar *vt* to disapprove; to condemn; to reject.

desaprovechado/da *adj* useless; unprofitable; backward; slack.

desaprovechar *vt* to waste, to turn to a bad use.

desarmar *vt* to disarm; to disband (troops); to dismantle; (*fig*) to pacify.

desarme *m* disarmament.

desarraigar *vt* to uproot; to root out; to extirpate.

desarraigo *m* eradication.

desarrapado/da *adj* ragged.

desarreglado/da *adj* untidy.

desarreglar *vt* to disorder, to upset.

desarreglo *m* disorder; untidiness.

desarrollar *vt* to develop; to unroll; to unfold; ~se *vr* to develop; to be unfolded; to open.

desarrollo *m* development.

desarropar *vt* to undress.

desarticular *vt* to take apart.

desasir *vt* to loosen, to disentangle; ~se *vr* to extricate oneself.

desasosegar *vt* to disquiet, to disturb.

desasosiego *m* restlessness; anxiety.

desastrado/da *adj* wretched, miserable; ragged.

desastre *m* disaster; misfortune.

desastroso/sa *adj* disastrous.

desatado/da *adj* untied; wild.

desatar *vt* to untie, to loose; to separate; to solve; ~se *vr* to come undone; to break.

desatascar *vt* to unblock; to clear.

desatender *vt* to pay no attention to; to disregard.

desatinado/da *adj* foolish; extravagant; * *m* fool, madman.

desatinar *vi* to talk nonsense; to reel, to stagger.

desatino *m* blunder; nonsense.

desatornillar *vt* to unscrew.

desatrancar *vt* to unbar; to unblock.
desautorizado/da *adj* unauthorized.
desautorizar *vt* to deprive of authority; to deny.
desavenencia *f* discord, disagreement.
desavenido/da *adj* contrary, disagreeing.
desaventajado/da *adj* disadvantageous, unprofitable.
desayunar *vt* to have for breakfast; ~**se** *vr* to breakfast; * *vi* to have breakfast;
desayuno *m* breakfast.
desazón *f* disgust; uneasiness; annoyance.
desazonado/da *adj* ill-adapted; ill-humored.
desazonar *vt* to annoy; ~**se** *vr* to be annoyed; to be anxious.
desbancar *vt* to break (the bank in gambling); (*fig*) to supplant.
desbandarse *vr* to disband; to go off in all directions.
desbarajuste *m* confusion.
desbaratar *vt* to destroy.
desbarrar *vi* to talk rubbish.
desbastar *vt* to smooth; to polish; to waste.
desbloquear *vt* to unblock.
desbocado/da *adj* open-mouthed; wild (of a horse); foul-mouthed; indecent.
desbocarse *vr* to bolt (of a horse).
desbordar *vt* to exceed; ~**se** *vr* to overflow.
descabalgar *vi* to dismount.
descabellado/da *adj* disheveled; disorderly; wild, unrestrained; disproportional; violent.
descabellar *vt* to ruffle.
descafeinado/da *adj* decaffeinated.
descalabrado/da *adj* wounded on the head; imprudent.
descalabrar *vt* to wound on the head; to smash.
descalabro *m* blow; misfortune; considerable loss.
descalificar *vt* to disqualify; to discredit.
descalzar *vt*, ~**se** *vr* to take off one's shoes.
descalzo/za *adj* barefooted; (*fig*) destitute.
descambiar *vt* to exchange.
descaminado/da *adj* (*fig*) misguided.
descaminar *vt* to misguide, to lead astray.
descamisado/da *adj* shirtless.
descampado/da *adj* disengaged; free; open; * *m* open space, open country.
descansado/da *adj* rested, refreshed; quiet.
descansar *vt* to rest; * *vi* to rest; to lie down.
descansillo *m* landing.
descanso *m* rest, repose; break; interval.
descapotable *m* convertible.
descarado/da *adj* cheeky, barefaced.
descararse *vr* to behave insolently.
descarga *f* unloading; volley, discharge.
descargar *vt* to unload, to discharge; ~**se** *vr* to unburden oneself.
descargo *m* discharge; evidence; receipt.
descarnado/da *adj* scrawny.
descarnar *vt* to strip the flesh from; to clean away the flesh from; to corrode; ~**se** *vr* to grow thin.

descarado/da *adj* cheeky.
descaro *m* nerve.
descarriar *vt* to lead astray; to misdirect; ~**se** *vr* to lose one's way; to stray; to err.
descarrilamiento *m* (*rail*) derailment.
descarrilar *vi* (*rail*) to leave/run off the rails.
descarrío *m* losing of one's way.
descartar *vt* to discard; to dismiss; to rule out; ~**se** *vr* to excuse oneself.
descascarillado/da *adj* peeling.
descastado *adj* degenerate; ungrateful.
descendencia *f* descent; offspring.
descendente *adj* descending; **tren** ~ *m* (*rail*) down train.
descender *vt* to take down; * *vi* to descend; walk down; to flow; to fall; ~ **de** to be derived from.
descendiente *adj* descending; * *m/f* descendant.
descenso *m* descent; drop; relegation.
descerrajar *vt* to force the lock (of a door etc); to discharge firearms.
descifrar *vt* to decipher; to unravel.
desclavar *vt* to draw out nails (from).
descocado/da *adj* bold, impudent.
descodificador *m* decoder (for TV).
descolgar *vt* to take down; to pick up; ~**se** *vr* to let oneself down.
descollar *vi* to excel.
descolorido/da *adj* pale, colorless.
descomedido/da *adj* impudent, insolent; huge.
descompaginar *vt* to disarrange.
descomponer *vt* to discompose, to set at odds; to disconcert; (*chem*) to decompose.
descomposición *f* disagreement; discomposure; decomposition.
descompuesto/ta *adj* decomposed; broken.
descomunal *adj* uncommon; huge.
desconcertado/da *adj* disconcerted; bewildered.
desconcertar *vt* to disturb; to confound; to disconcert; ~**se** *vr* to be bewildered; to be upset.
desconchado/da *adj* peeling.
desconchar *vt* to peel off.
desconcierto *m* disorder, confusion; uncertainty.
desconectar *vt* to disconnect.
desconfiado/da *adj* mistrustful, distrustful.
desconfianza *f* distrust; jealousy.
desconfiar *vi*: ~ **de** to mistrust, to suspect.
descongelar *vt* to defrost.
descongestionar *vt* to clear.
desconocer *vt* to disown, to disavow; to be totally ignorant of (a thing); not to know (a person); not to acknowledge (a favor received).
desconocido/da *adj* unknown; disguised; * *m/f* stranger.
desconocimiento *m* ignorance.
desconsiderado/da *adj* inconsiderate; imprudent.

D

desconsolado/da *adj* disconsolate; painful; sad.
desconsolar *vt* to distress.
desconsuelo *m* distress; trouble; despair.
descontado *adj*: **por** ~ of course; **dar por** ~ to take for granted.
descontar *vt* to discount; to deduct.
descontento *m* dissatisfaction; disgust.
descorazonar *vt* to dishearten, to discourage.
descorchar *vt* to uncork.
descorrer *vt* to draw.
descortés/esa *adj* impolite, rude.
descortesía *f* rudeness.
descoser *vt* to undo, take apart; to separate; ~**se** *vr* to come apart at the seams.
descosido/da *adj* unstitched; disjointed.
descoyuntar *vt* to dislocate; to vex, to annoy.
descrédito *m* discredit.
descreído/da *adj* incredulous.
descremado/da *adj* skimmed.
describir *vt* to describe; to draw, to delineate.
descripción *f* description; delineation; inventory.
descriptivo/va *adj* descriptive.
descuartizar *vt* to quarter; to carve.
descubierto *m* deficit; overdraft; ~/**ta** *adj* uncovered.
descubrimiento *m* discovery; revelation.
descubrir *vt* to discover, to disclose; to uncover; to reveal; to show; ~**se** *vr* to reveal oneself; to take off one's hat; to confess.
descuento *m* discount; decrease.
descuida *excl* don't worry!
descuidado/da *adj* careless, negligent.
descuidar *vt* to neglect; * *vi*, ~**se** *vr* to be careless.
descuido *m* carelessness, negligence; forgetfulness; incivility; improper action.
desde *prep* since; after; from; ~ **luego** of course; ~ **entonces** since then.
desdecirse *vr* to retract one's words.
desdén *m* disdain, scorn.
desdentado/da *adj* toothless.
desdentar *vt* to draw out (teeth).
desdeñable *adj* contemptible, despicable.
desdeñar *vt* to disdain, to scorn; ~**se** *vr* to be disdainful.
desdeñoso/sa *adj* disdainful; contemptuous.
desdicha *f* misfortune, calamity; great poverty.
desdichado/da *adj* unfortunate; wretched, miserable.
desdoblar *vt* to unfold, to spread open.
desear *vt* to desire, to wish; to require, to demand.
desecación *f* desiccation.
desecar *vt* to dry up.
desechar *vt* to depreciate; to reject; to refuse; to throw away.
desecho *m* residue; ~**s** *mpl* rubbish.
desembalar *vt* to unpack.

desembarazado/da *adj* free.
desembarazar *vt* to free; to clear; ~**se** *vr*: ~ **de** to get rid of.
desembarcadero *m* landing stage.
desembarcar *vt* to unload, to disembark; * *vi* to disembark, to land; *Lat Am* to get off.
desembarco *m* landing.
desembargo *m* (*law*) raising an embargo.
desembarque *m* landing.
desembocadura *f* mouth.
desembocar *vi*: ~ **en** to flow into.
desembolsar *vt* to pay out.
desembolso *m* expenditure.
desembragar *vi* to declutch.
desembuchar *vt* to disgorge; to tell all.
desempaquetar *vt* to unpack.
desempatar *vi* (*sport*) to hold a play-off.
desempate *m* play-off.
desempeñar *vt* to redeem; to extricate from debt; to fulfill (any duty/promise); to acquit; ~**se** *vr* to get out of debt.
desempeño *m* redeeming a pledge; occupation.
desempleado/da *adj* unemployed; * *m/f* unemployed person.
desempleo *m* unemployment.
desempolvorar *vt* to dust.
desencadenar *vt* to unchain; ~**se** *vr* to break loose; to burst.
desencajar *vt* to disjoint; to dislocate; to disconnect.
desencallar *vt* to refloat.
desencanto *m* disenchantment.
desenchufar *vt* to unplug.
desenfadado/da *adj* free; unembarrassed.
desenfado *m* ease; facility; calmness, relaxation.
desenfocado/da *adj* out of focus.
desenfrenado/da *adj* outrageous; ungovernable.
desenfreno *m* wildness; lack of self-control.
desenganchar *vt* to unhook; to uncouple.
desengañado/da *adj* disillusioned.
desengañar *vt* to disillusion; ~**se** *vr* to become disillusioned.
desengaño *m* disillusionment; disappointment.
desengrasar *vt* to take the grease off.
desenhebrar *vt* to unthread; to unravel.
desenlace *m* climax; outcome.
desenmarañar *vt* to disentangle; to unravel.
desenmascarar *vt* to unmask.
desenredar *vt* to disentangle.
desenrollar *vt* to unroll.
desenroscar *vt* to untwist; to unroll.
desentenderse *vr* to pretend not to understand; to pass by without noticing.
desenterrar *vt* to exhume; to dig up.
desentonar *vi* to be out of tune; to clash.
desentrañar *vt* to unravel.
desentumecer *vt* to stretch; to loosen up.
desenvainar *vt* to unsheathe; to show.

desenvoltura f sprightliness; cheerfulness; impudence, boldness.

desenvolver vt to unfold; to unroll; to decipher, to unravel; to develop; ~se vr to develop; to cope.

desenvuelto/ta adj forward; natural.

deseo m desire, wish.

deseoso/sa adj anxious.

desequilibrado/da adj unbalanced.

deserción f desertion; defection.

desertar vt to desert; to abandon (a cause).

desertificación f desertification.

desertor m deserter; fugitive.

desesperación f despair, desperation; anger, fury.

desesperado/da adj desperate, hopeless.

desesperar vi, ~se vr to despair; * vt to make desperate.

desestabilizar vt to destabilize.

desestatizar vt Lat Am to privatize.

desestatización f Lat Am privatization.

desestimar vt to disregard, to reject.

desfachatez f impudence.

desfalcar vt to embezzle.

desfalco m embezzlement.

desfallecer vi to get weak; to faint.

desfallecimiento m fainting.

desfasado/da adj old-fashioned.

desfase m gap.

desfavorable adj unfavorable.

desfigurar vt to disfigure, to deform; to disguise.

desfiladero m gorge.

desfilar vi (mil) to parade.

desfogarse vr to give vent to one's passion/anger.

desforestación f deforestation.

desgajar vt to tear off; to break in pieces; ~se vr to be separated; to be torn to pieces.

desgana f disgust; loss of appetite; aversion, reluctance.

desganado/da adj not hungry; half-hearted; **estar** ~ to lose all pleasure in doing a thing; to lose one's appetite.

desgano m Lat Am disgust; loss of appetite; aversion, reluctance.

desgañitarse vr to scream, to bawl.

desgarrador/a adj heartrending.

desgarrar vt to tear; to shatter.

desgarro m tear; grief; impudence.

desgarrón m large tear.

desgastar vt to waste; to corrode; ~se vr to get worn out.

desgaste m wear (and tear).

desglosar vt to break down.

desgracia f misfortune; disgrace; accident; setback.

desgraciado/da adj unfortunate; unhappy, miserable; out of favor; disagreeable.

desgreñado/da adj disheveled.

desgreñar vt to dishevel (the hair); to disorder.

desguarnecer vt to strip down; to dismantle.

deshabitado/da adj deserted, uninhabited; desolate.

deshacer vt to undo, to destroy; to cancel, to efface; to rout (an army); to solve; to melt; to break up, to divide; to dissolve in a liquid; to violate (a treaty); to diminish; to disband (troops); ~se vr to melt; to come apart.

desharrapado/da adj shabby; ragged, in tatters.

deshecho/cha adj undone, destroyed; wasted; melted; in pieces; * m Lat Am short cut.

deshelar vt to thaw; ~se vr to thaw, to melt.

desheredar vt to disinherit.

deshidratado/da adj dehydrated.

deshidratar vt to dehydrate.

deshielo m thaw.

deshilachar vt to unravel.

deshilar vt to fray.

deshinchar vt to deflate; ~se vr to go flat, to go down.

deshojar vt to strip the leaves off.

deshollinador m chimney sweep.

deshonesto/ta adj indecent.

deshonra f dishonor; shame.

deshonrar vt to affront, to insult, to defame; to dishonor.

deshonroso/sa adj dishonorable, indecent.

deshora f unseasonable time.

deshuesar vt to get rid of bones; to stone.

desidia f idleness, indolence.

desierto/ta adj deserted; solitary; * m desert; wilderness.

designación f designation.

designar vt to design; to intend; to appoint; to express, to name.

designio m design, purpose; road, course.

desigual adj unequal, unlike; uneven, craggy.

desigualdad f inequality, dissimilitude; inconstancy; roughness, unevenness.

desilusión f disappointment.

desilusionar vt to disappoint; ~se vr to become disillusioned.

desinfección f disinfection.

desinfectar vt to disinfect.

desinflar vt to deflate.

desintegración f disintegration.

desinterés m unselfishness; disinterestedness.

desinteresado/da adj disinterested; unselfish.

desistir vi to desist, to cease.

deslave m Lat Am landslide.

desleal adj disloyal; unfair.

deslealtad f disloyalty, breach of faith.

desleír vt to dilute; to dissolve.

deslenguado/da adj foul-mouthed.

desligar vt to separate; to loosen, to unbind; ~se vr to extricate oneself.

desliz m slip, sliding; lapse, weakness.

deslizadizo/za adj slippery, slippy; glib.

D

deslizar vt to slip, to slide; to let slip (a comment); **~se** vr to slip; to skid; to flow softly; to creep in.

deslucido/da adj tarnished; dull; shabby.

deslucir vt to tarnish; to damage; to discredit.

deslumbramiento m glare; confusion.

deslumbrar vt to dazzle; to puzzle.

desmán m outrage; disaster; misconduct.

desmandarse vr to behave badly.

desmantelar vt to dismantle; to abandon, to forsake.

desmaquillador m make-up remover.

desmarañar vt to disentangle.

desmayado/da adj unconscious; dismayed; appalled; weak.

desmayar vi to be dispirited; to be faint-hearted; **~se** vr to faint.

desmayo m unconsciousness; faint, swoon; dismay.

desmedido/da adj disproportionate.

desmejorar vt to impair; to weaken.

desmembrar vt to dismember; to separate.

desmemoriado/da adj forgetful.

desmentir vt to give the lie to; **~se** vr to contradict oneself.

desmenuzar vt to crumble; to chip at; to fritter away; to examine minutely.

desmerecer vt to be unworthy of; * vi to deteriorate.

desmesurado/da adj excessive; huge; immeasurable.

desmontar vt to level; to remove (a heap of rubbish); to dismantle; * vi to dismount.

desmoralización f demoralization.

desmoralizar vt to demoralize.

desmoronar vt to destroy little by little; **~se** vr to fall into disrepair.

desnatado/da adj skimmed.

desnatar vt to skim (milk); to take the choicest part of.

desnaturalizar vt to divest of naturalization rights; **~se** vr to forsake one's country.

desnivel m unevenness of the ground.

desnucar vt to break (one's neck).

desnudar vt to undress; to strip; to discover, to reveal; **~se** vr to undress.

desnudez f nakedness.

desnudo/da adj naked; bare, uncovered; ill-clothed; (fig) plain, evident.

desnutrición f malnutrition.

desnutrido/da adj undernourished.

desobedecer vt, vi to disobey.

desobediencia f disobedience; insubordination.

desobediente adj disobedient.

desocupado/da adj empty; at leisure.

desocupar vt to vacate; to empty; **~se** vr to retire from a business; to withdraw from an arrangement.

desodorante m deodorant.

desolación f destruction; affliction.

desolado/da adj desolate, disconsolate.

desolar vt to lay waste; to harass.

desollar vt to flay, to skin; (fig) to extort.

desorden m disorder, confusion.

desordenado/da adj disorderly; untidy.

desordenar vt to disorder; to untidy; **~se** vr to get out of order.

desorganización f disorganization.

desorganizar vt to disorganize.

desorientar vt to mislead; to confuse; **~se** vr to lose one's way.

desovar vi to spawn.

despabilado/da adj watchful, vigilant; wide-awake.

despabilar vt to snuff (a candle); (fig) to dispatch quickly; to sharpen; **~se** vr to wake up.

despacio adv slowly, leisurely; little by little; Lat Am quietly; ¡~! softly!, gently!

despachar vt to dispatch; to expedite; to sell; to send.

despacho m dispatch, expedition; cabinet; office; commission; warrant, patent; expedient; smart answer.

despachurrar vt to squash, to crush; to mangle.

desparejar vt to make unequal/uneven.

desparpajo m ease; savoir-faire.

desparramar vt to disseminate, to spread; to spill; to squander, to lavish; **~se** vr to be dissipated.

despavorido adj frightened.

despectivo/va adj pejorative, derogatory.

despecho m indignation; displeasure; spite; dismay, despair; deceit; derision, scorn; **a ~ de** in spite of.

despedazar vt to tear into pieces; to mangle.

despedida f farewell; sacking.

despedir vt to discharge; to dismiss (from office); to see off; **~se** vr: **~ de** to say goodbye to.

despegado/da adj cold; detached.

despegar vt to unglue; to take off; **~se** vr to come loose.

despego m detachment; coolness.

despegue m take-off.

despeinado/da adj disheveled.

despeinar vt to ruffle.

despejado/da adj sprightly, quick; clear.

despejar vt to clear away; **~se** vr to cheer up; to clear; * vi to clear.

despellejar vt to skin.

despensa f pantry, larder; provisions pl.

despeñadero m precipice.

despeñar vt to precipitate; **~se** vr to throw oneself headlong.

despepitarse vr to bawl.

desperdiciar vt to squander.

desperdicio m waste; **~s** mpl rubbish; waste.

desperdigar vt to separate; to scatter.

desperezarse vr to stretch oneself.

desperfecto *m* slight damage; flaw.

despertador *m* alarm clock.

despertar *vt* to wake up, to rouse from sleep; to excite; * *vi* to wake up; to grow lively/sprightly; **~se** *vr* to wake up.

despiadado/da *adj* heartless; merciless.

despido *m* dismissal.

despierto/ta *adj* awake; vigilant; fierce; brisk, sprightly.

despilfarrar *vt* to waste.

despilfarro *m* slovenliness; waste; mismanagement.

despintar *vt* to deface (a painting); to obscure (things); to mislead; **~se** to lose its color.

despistar *vt* to mislead; to throw off the track; **~se** *vr* to take the wrong way; to become confused.

desplante *m* bold statement; wrong stance; insolence.

desplazamiento *m* displacement.

desplazar *vt* to move; to scroll; **~se** *vr* to travel.

desplegar *vt* to unfold, to display; to explain, to elucidate; (*mar*) to unfurl; **~se** *vr* to open out; to travel.

despliegue *m* display.

desplomarse *vr* to fall to the ground; to collapse.

desplumar *vt* to fleece; to pluck.

despoblado *m* desert.

despoblar *vt* to depopulate; to desolate; **~se** *vr* to become depopulated.

despojar *vt*: **~ (de)** to strip (of); to deprive (of); **~se** *vr* to undress.

despojo *m* plunder; loot; **~s** *mpl* giblets *pl*; remains *pl*; offal.

desposado/da *adj* newlywed.

desposar *vt* to marry, to betroth; **~se** *vr* to be betrothed/married.

desposeer *vt* to dispossess.

desposeimiento *m* dispossession.

déspota *m* despot.

despótico/ca *adj* despotic.

despotismo *m* despotism.

despreciable *adj* contemptible, despicable.

despreciar *vt* to offend; to despise.

desprecio *m* scorn, contempt.

desprender *vt* to unfasten, to loosen; to separate; **~se** *vr* to give way; to fall down; to extricate oneself.

desprendimiento *m* alienation, disinterestedness.

despreocupado/da *adj* careless; unworried.

despreocuparse *vr* to be carefree.

desprestigiar *vt* to run down.

desprevenido/da *adj* unawares, unprepared.

desproporción *f* disproportion.

desproporcionado/da *adj* disproportionate.

desproporcionar *vt* to disproportion.

despropósito *m* absurdity.

desprovisto/ta *adj* unprovided.

después *adv* after, afterwards; next.

despuntar *vt* to blunt; * *vi* to sprout; to dawn; **al ~ del día** at break of day.

desquiciar *vt* to upset; to discompose; to disorder.

desquitar *vt* to retrieve (a loss); **~se** *vr* to win one's money back again; to return by giving like for like; to take revenge.

desquite *m* recovery of a loss; revenge, retaliation.

desrizar *vt* to uncurl.

destacamento *m* (*mil*) detachment; **~ de policía** *Lat Am* police station.

destacar *vt* to emphasize; (*mil*) to detach (a body of troops); **~se** *vr* to stand out.

destajo *m* piecework; **trabajar a ~** to do piecework.

destapar *vt* to uncover; to open; **~se** *vr* to be uncovered.

destartalado/da *adj* untidy.

destello *m* signal light; sparkle.

destemplado/da *adj* out of tune; badly blended (of paint); intemperate.

desteñir *vt* to discolor; **~se** *vr* to fade.

desternillarse *vr*: **~ de risa** to roar with laughter.

desterrar *vt* to banish; to expel, to drive away.

destetar *vt* to wean.

destete *m* weaning.

destierro *m* exile, banishment.

destilación *f* distillation.

destilar *vt*, *vi* to distill.

destinar *vt* to assign to; to destine for, to intend for.

destinatario/a *m/f* addressee.

destino *m* destiny; fate, doom; destination; office.

destitución *f* destitution, abandonment.

destituir *vt* to dismiss.

destornillador *m* screwdriver.

destornillar *vt* to unscrew.

destreza *f* dexterity, cleverness, cunning, expertness, skill.

destripar *vt* to disembowel; to trample.

destronar *vt* to dethrone.

destrozar *vt* to destroy, to break into pieces; (*mil*) to defeat.

destrozo *m* destruction; (*mil*) defeat, massacre.

destrucción *f* destruction, ruin.

destructivo/va *adj* destructive.

destruir *vt* to destroy.

desunir *vt* to separate, to disunite; to cause discord between.

desuso *m* disuse.

desvaído/da *adj* tall and graceless.

desvalido/da *adj* helpless; destitute.

desvalijar *vt* to rob; to burgle.

desván *m* garret.

desvanecer *vt* to dispel; **~se** *vr* to grow vapid, to become insipid; to vanish; to be affected with giddiness; to faint.

D

desvanecimiento *m* pride, haughtiness; giddiness; fainting fit.

desvariar *vi* to be delirious.

desvarío *m* delirium; giddiness; inconstancy, caprice; extravagance.

desvelar *vt* to keep awake; **~se** *vr* to stay awake.

desvelo *m* want of sleep; watchfulness.

desvencijado/da *adj* broken-down, rickety.

desvencijar *vt* to disunite, to divide; to weaken; **~se** *vr* to be ruptured; to come apart.

desventaja *f* disadvantage; damage.

desventura *f* misfortune; calamity.

desventurado/da *adj* unfortunate; calamitous.

desvergonzado/da *adj* impudent, shameless.

desvergonzarse *vr* to behave in an impudent manner.

desvergüenza *f* impudence; shamelessness.

desvestir *vt*, **~se** *vr* to undress.

desviar *vt* to divert; to dissuade; to parry (at fencing); **~se** *vr* to go off course.

desvío *m* turning away, going astray; aversion; disdain; indifference.

desvivirse *vr*: **~ por** to long for.

detallar *vt* to detail, to relate minutely.

detalle *m* detail.

detallista *m* retailer.

detención *f* detention; delay.

detener *vt* to stop, to detain; to arrest; to keep back; to reserve; to withhold; **~se** *vr* to stop; to stay.

detenidamente *adv* carefully.

detenido/da *adj* detailed; sparing, niggardly; slow, inactive.

detergente *m* detergent.

deterioración *f* deterioration; damage.

deteriorar *vt* to damage.

deterioro *m* deterioration.

determinación *f* determination, resolution; boldness.

determinado/da *adj* determined; resolute.

determinar *vt* to determine; **~se** *vr* to decide.

detestable *adj* detestable.

detestar *vt* to detest, to abhor.

detonación *f* detonation.

detonar *vi* to detonate.

detractar *vt* to denigrate, to defame, to slander.

detrás *adv* behind; at the back, in the back.

detrimento *m* detriment; damage; loss.

deuda *f* debt; fault; offense.

deudor/ra *m/f* debtor.

devaluación *f* devaluation.

devanar *vt* to reel; to wrap up.

devastación *f* devastation, desolation.

devastador/ra *adj* devastating.

devastar *vt* to devastate.

devengar *vt* to accrue.

devoción *f* devotion, piety; strong affection; ardent love.

devolución *f* return; (*law*) devolution.

devolutivo/va *adj* (*law*) transferable.

devolver *vt* to return; to send back; to refund; to throw up; * *vi* to be sick.

devorar *vt* to devour, to swallow up.

devoto/ta *adj* devout, pious; devotional; strongly attached.

día *m* day.

diablo *m* devil.

diablura *f* prank.

diabólico/ca *adj* diabolical; devilish.

diácono *m* deacon.

diadema *m/f* diadem; halo.

diafragma *m* diaphragm; midriff.

diagnosis *f invar* diagnosis.

diagnóstico *m* diagnosis.

diagonal *adj* diagonal.

diagrama *m* diagram.

dialecto *m* dialect.

diálisis *f invar* dialysis.

diálogo *m* dialog.

diamante *m* diamond.

diámetro *m* diameter.

diana *f* (*mil*) reveille; bull's-eye.

diapasón *m* (*mus*) diapason, octave.

diapositiva *f* transparency, slide.

diario *m* journal, diary; daily newspaper; daily expenses *pl*; **~/ria** *adj* daily.

diarrea *f* diarrhea.

dibujar *vt* to draw, to design.

dibujo *m* drawing; sketch, draft; description.

dicción *f* diction; style; expression.

diccionario *m* dictionary.

diciembre *m* December.

dictado *m* dictation.

dictador *m* dictator.

dictadura *f* dictatorship.

dictamen *m* opinion, notion; suggestion, insinuation; judgement.

dictar *vt* to dictate; *Lat Am* to teach.

dicha *f* happiness; good fortune; **por ~** by chance.

dicho *m* saying; sentence; declaration; promise of marriage; **~/cha** *adj* said.

dichoso/sa *adj* happy, prosperous.

diecinueve *adj*, *m* nineteen.

dieciocho *adj*, *m* eighteen.

dieciséis *adj*, *m* sixteen.

diecisiete *adj*, *m* seventeen.

diente *m* tooth; fang; tusk.

diestro/tra *adj* right; dexterous, skillful, clever; sagacious, prudent; sly, cunning; * *m* skillful fencer; halter; bridle.

diesel, diésel *adj* diesel *compd*.

dieta *f* diet, regimen; diet, assembly.

dietista *m/f* *Lat Am* dietician.

diez *adj*, *m* ten.

diezmar *vt* to decimate.

diezmo m tithe.
difamación f defamation.
difamar vt to defame, to libel.
difamatorio/ria adj defamatory, calumnious.
diferencia f difference.
diferencial adj differential.
diferenciar vt to differentiate, to distinguish; ~se vr to differ, to distinguish oneself.
diferente adj different, unlike.
diferido/da adj recorded.
diferir vt to defer, to put off; to differ.
difícil adj difficult.
dificultad f difficulty.
dificultar vt to put difficulties in the way of; to render difficult.
dificultoso/sa adj difficult; painful.
difundir vt to diffuse, to spread; to divulge; ~se vr to spread (out).
difunto/ta adj dead, deceased; late.
difusión f diffusion.
difuso/sa adj diffusive, copious; large; long-winded; circumstantial.
digerir vt to digest; to bear with patience; to adjust, to arrange; (chem) to digest.
digestión f digestion; concoction.
digestivo/va adj digestive.
digitador/a m/f Lat Am (comput) someone who keys in text by means of a keyboard.
digital adj digital.
digitalizar vt to digitize.
digitar vt Lat Am (comput) to key in.
dignarse vr to condescend; to deign.
dignidad f dignity, rank.
digno/na adj worthy; suitable.
dije m relic; trinket.
dilapidar vt to squander, to waste.
dilatación f dilation, extension; greatness of mind; calmness.
dilatado/da adj large; numerous; prolix; spacious, extensive.
dilatar vt to dilate, to expand; to spread out; to defer, to protract.
dilatorio/ria adj dilatory.
dilema m dilemma.
diligencia f diligence; affair, business; call of nature; stage coach.
diligente adj diligent, assiduous, prompt, swift.
dilucidar vt to elucidate, to explain.
diluir vt to dilute.
diluviar vi to rain in torrents.
diluvio m flood, deluge, inundation; abundance.
dimensión f dimension; extent; capacity; bulk.
diminutivo/va adj diminutive.
diminuto/ta adj defective, faulty; minute, small.
dimisión f resignation.
dimitir vt to give up, to abdicate; * vi to resign.
dinámica f dynamics.
dinámico/ca adj dynamic.

dinamita f dynamite.
dínamo, dinamo f dynamo.
dínamo, dinamo m Lat Am dynamo.
dinastía f dynasty.
dineral m large sum of money.
dinero m money.
diocesano/na adj diocesan.
diócesis f diocese.
Dios m God.
diosa f goddess.
diploma m diploma, patent.
diplomacia, diplomática f diplomacy.
diplomado/da adj qualified.
diplomático/ca adj diplomatic; * m/f diplomat.
diptongo m diphthong.
diputación f deputation.
diputado m deputy.
diputar vt to depute.
dique m dike, dam.
dirección f direction, guidance; administration; steering.
directivo/va adj governing.
directo/ta adj direct, straight; apparent, evident; live.
director/ra m/f director; conductor; president; manager; headmaster (of a private school).
dirigir vt to direct; to conduct; to regulate, to govern; ~se vr to go toward(s); to address oneself to.
discernimiento m discernment.
discernir vt to discern, to distinguish.
disciplina f discipline.
discípulo m disciple; scholar.
disco m disc; record; discus; light; face (of the sun/moon); lens (of a telescope); ~ compacto compact disc.
díscolo/la adj ungovernable; peevish.
disconforme adj differing.
discordancia f disagreement, discord.
discordante adj dissonant, discordant.
discordar vi to clash, to disagree.
discorde adj discordant; (mus) dissonant.
discordia f discord, disagreement.
discoteca m discotheque, disco.
discreción f discretion; acuteness of mind.
discrecional adj discretionary.
discrepancia f discrepancy.
discrepar vi to differ.
discreto/ta adj discreet; ingenious; witty, eloquent.
discriminación f discrimination.
disculpa f apology; excuse.
disculpar vt to exculpate, to excuse; to acquit, to absolve; ~se vr to apologize; to excuse oneself.
discurrir vi to ramble about; to run to and fro; to discourse (upon a subject); * vt to invent, to contrive; to meditate.

D

discurso m speech; conversation; dissertation; space of time.
discusión f discussion.
discutir vt, vi to discuss.
disecar vt to dissect; to stuff.
disección f dissection.
diseminar vt to scatter; to disseminate, to propagate.
disentería f dysentery.
disentir vi to dissent, to disagree.
diseñador/ra m/f designer.
diseñar vt to draw; to design.
diseño m design; draft; description; picture.
disfraz m disguise; mask.
disfrazar vt to disguise, to conceal; to cloak, to dissemble; ~**se** vr to disguise oneself as.
disfrutar vt to enjoy; ~**se** vr to enjoy oneself.
disgustar vt to disgust; to offend; ~**se** vr to be displeased; to fall out.
disgusto m disgust, aversion; quarrel; annoyance; grief, sorrow.
disidente adj dissident; * m/f dissident, dissenter.
disimular vt to hide; to tolerate.
disimulo m dissimulation; tolerance.
disipado/da adj prodigal, lavish.
disipar vt to dissipate, to disperse, to scatter; to lavish.
dislocación f dislocation.
dislocarse vr to be dislocated/out of joint.
disminución f diminution.
disminuir vt to diminish; to decrease.
disolución f dissolution; liquidation.
disolver vt to loosen, to untie; to dissolve; to disunite; to melt, to liquefy; to interrupt.
disonancia f dissonance; disagreement, discord.
disparada f Lat Am flight; stampede.
disparar vt to shoot, to discharge, to fire; to let off; to throw with violence; * vi to shoot, to fire.
disparatado/da adj inconsistent; absurd, extravagant.
disparate m nonsense, absurdity, extravagance.
disparo m shot; discharge; explosion.
dispensar vt to dispense; to excuse; to dispense with; to distribute.
displicencia f displeasure; dislike.
disponer vt to arrange, to prepare; to dispose.
disponible adj available; disposable.
disposición f disposition, order; resolution; command; power, authority.
dispositivo m device.
dispuesto/ta adj disposed; fit, ready.
disputa f dispute, controversy.
disputar vt to dispute, to controvert, to question; * vi to debate, to argue.
disquera f Lat Am record company.
disquete m floppy disk.
distancia f distance; interval; difference.
distanciarse vr to become estranged.

distante adj distant, far off.
distinción f distinction; difference; prerogative.
distinguido/da adj distinguished, conspicuous.
distinguir vt to distinguish; to discern; ~**se** vr to distinguish oneself.
distintivo m distinctive mark; particular attribute.
distinto/ta adj distinct, different; clear.
distracción f distraction, want of attention.
distraer vt to distract; ~**se** vr to be absent-minded, to be inattentive.
distraído/da adj absent-minded, inattentive.
distribución f distribution; division, separation; arrangement.
distribuidor m distributor.
distribuir vt to distribute.
distrito m district; territory.
disturbar vt to disturb, to interrupt.
disturbio m riot; disturbance, interruption.
disuadir vt to dissuade.
disuasión f dissuasion.
diurno/na adj daily.
diva f prima donna.
divagar vt to digress.
diván m divan.
divergencia f divergence.
divergente adj divergent.
diversidad f diversity; variety of things.
diversificar vt to diversify; to vary.
diversión f diversion; sport; amusement; (mil) diversion.
diverso/sa adj diverse, different; several, sundry.
divertido/da adj amused; amusing.
divertir vt to divert (the attention); to amuse, to entertain; (mil) to draw off; ~**se** vr to amuse oneself.
dividir vt to divide; to disunite; to separate; to share out.
divieso m (med) boil.
divinidad f divinity.
divino/na adj divine, heavenly; excellent.
divisa f emblem.
divisar vt to perceive.
divisible adj divisible.
división f division; partition; separation; difference.
divorciar vt to divorce; to separate; ~**se** vr to get divorced.
divorcio m divorce; separation, disunion.
divulgación f publication; dissemination.
divulgar vt to publish, to divulge.
dobladillo m hem; cuff.
dobladura f fold.
doblar vt to double; to fold; to bend; * vi to turn; to toll (bell); ~**se** vr to bend, to bow, to submit.
doble adj double; dual; deceitful; **al** ~ doubly; * m double.

doblegar vt to bend; **~se** vr to yield.
doblez m crease; fold; turn-up; * f duplicity.
doce adj, m twelve.
docena f dozen.
docente adj teaching.
dócil adj docile, tractable.
docilidad f docility, gentleness; compliance.
doctor/ra m/f doctor.
doctorado m doctorate.
doctrina f doctrine, instruction; science.
doctrinal m catechism; * adj doctrinal.
documentación f documentation.
documento m document; record.
dogma m dogma.
dólar m dollar.
dolencia f disease; affliction.
doler vi to feel pain; to ache; **~se** vr to feel for the sufferings of others; to complain.
dolor m pain; aching, ache; affliction.
doloroso/sa adj painful.
domador/ra m/f trainer; tamer.
domar vt to tame; to subdue, to master.
domesticar vt to domesticate.
domiciliarse vr to establish oneself in a residence.
domicilio m domicile; home, abode.
dominación f domination; dominion; authority, power.
dominante adj dominant; domineering.
dominar vt to dominate; to be fluent in; **~se** vr to moderate one's passions.
domingo m Sunday; (Christian) Sabbath.
dominguero/ra adj done/worn on Sunday; * m/f Sunday driver.
dominical adj Sunday.
dominio m dominion; domination; power, authority; domain.
donación f donation; gift.
donar vt to donate; to bestow.
donativo m contribution.
doncella f virgin, maiden; lady's maid.
donde adv where.
dónde adv where; ¿de ~? from where?; ¿por ~? where?
dondequiera adv anywhere.
dorado/da adj gilt compd; golden; * m gilding.
dorar vt to gild; (fig) to palliate.
dormilón/ona m/f dull, sleepy person.
dormir vi to sleep; **~se** vr to fall asleep.
dormitorio m dormitory.
dorsal adj dorsal.
dos adj, m two.
dosaje m Lat Am dose.

doscientos/tas adj pl two hundred.
dosis f invar dose.
dotado/da adj gifted.
dotar vt to endow.
dote f dowry; **~s** fpl gifts of nature pl; endowments pl.
dragón m dragon; (mil) dragoon.
drama m drama.
dramático/ca adj dramatic.
dramatizar vt to dramatize.
dramaturgo/ga m/f dramatist.
droga f drug; stratagem; artifice, deceit.
drogadicción f drug addiction.
drogadicto/ta m/f drug addict.
droguería f hardware store.
dromedario m dromedary.
dubitativo/va adj doubtful, dubious; uncertain.
ducado m duchy; ducat.
ducha f shower; (med) douche.
ducharse vr to have a shower.
ducho/cha adj skilled, experienced.
duda f doubt; suspense; hesitation.
dudar vt to doubt.
dudoso/sa adj doubtful, dubious.
duelo m grief, affliction; mourning.
duende m elf, hobgoblin.
dueño/ña m/f owner; landlord/lady; employer.
dulce adj sweet; mild, gentle, meek; soft; * m candy.
dulcificar vt to sweeten.
dulzura f sweetness; gentleness; softness.
dúo m (mus) duo, duet.
duodécimo/ma adj twelfth.
duplicación f duplication.
duplicado m duplicate.
duplicar vt to duplicate, to double; to repeat.
duplicidad f duplicity; falseness.
duplo m double.
duque m duke.
duquesa f duchess.
duración f duration.
duradero/ra adj lasting, durable.
durante adv during.
durar vi to last, to continue.
duraznero m Lat Am peach tree.
durazno m Lat Am peach; peach tree.
dureza f hardness; harshness; **~ de oído** hardness of hearing.
durmiente adj sleeping; * m (rail) sleeping car.
duro/ra adj hard; cruel; harsh, rough; * m five peseta coin; * adv hard.
duunviro m magistrate in ancient Rome.

D

E

e *conj* and (before words starting with **i** and **hi**).
ea *interj* hey!, come on!; ¡~ **pues!** well then!, let's see!
ebanista *m* cabinet-maker, carpenter.
ébano *m* ebony.
ebrio/ia *adj* drunk.
ebullición *f* boiling.
eccema *m* eczema.
echar *vt* to throw; to add; to fire; to pour out; to mail; to give off; to bud; **~se** *vr* to lie down; to rest; to stretch out.
eclesiástico/ca *adj* ecclesiastical.
eclipsar *vt* to eclipse; to outshine.
eclipse *m* eclipse.
eco *m* echo.
ecografía *f* ultrasound scan.
ecología *f* ecology.
ecologismo *m* green movement.
ecologista *m/f* ecologist, environmentalist.
economato *m* cut-rate store.
economía *f* economy.
económico/ca *adj* economic; cheap; thrifty; financial; avaricious.
economista *m/f* economist.
ecosistema *m* ecosystem.
ecotasa *f* ecotax.
ecoturismo *m* ecotourism.
ecuación *f* equation.
ecuador *m* equator.
ecuánime *adj* level-headed.
ecuestre *adj* equestrian.
ecuménico/ca *adj* ecumenical; universal.
edad *f* age.
edecán *m* (*mil*) aide-de-camp.
edición *f* edition; publication.
edicto *m* edict.
edificación *f* construction.
edificante *adj* edifying, instructive.
edificar *vt* to build, to construct; to edify.
edificio *m* building; structure.
editar *vt* to edit; to publish.
editor/ra *m/f* editor; publisher.
educación *f* education; upbringing; (good) manners *pl*.
educador/ra *m/f* teacher, educator.
educando/da *m/f* pupil.
educar *vt* to educate, to instruct; to bring up.
efectivamente *adv* exactly; really; in fact.
efectivo/va *adj* effective; true; certain.
efecto *m* effect; consequence; purpose; ~ **invernadero** greenhouse effect **~s** *mpl* effects *pl*, goods *pl*; **en ~** in fact, really.

efectuar *vt* to effect, to carry out.
efeméride *f* event (remembered on its anniversary).
efervescencia *f* effervescence, fizziness.
eficacia *f* effectiveness, efficacy.
eficaz *adj* efficient; effective.
eficiente *adj* efficient.
efigie *f* effigy, image.
efímero/ra *adj* ephemeral.
efluvio *m* outflow.
efusión *f* effusion.
efusivo/va *adj* effusive.
égloga *f* (*poet*) eclogue.
egoísmo *m* selfishness.
egoísta *m/f* self-seeker; * *adj* selfish.
egregio/gia *adj* eminent, remarkable.
egresado/da *m/f Lat Am* graduate.
egresar *vi Lat Am* to graduate.
egreso *m Lat Am* graduation.
eje *m* axle; axis.
ejecución *f* execution.
ejecutar *vt* to execute, to carry out, to perform; to put to death; (*law*) to attach, to seize.
ejecutivo/va *adj* executive; * *m/f* executive.
ejecutor/ra *m/f* executor.
ejecutoria *f* (*law*) writ of execution.
ejecutorio/ria *adj* (*law*) executory.
ejemplar *m* specimen; copy; example; * *adj* exemplary.
ejemplificar *vt* to exemplify.
ejemplo *m* example; **por ~** for example, for instance.
ejercer *vt* to exercise.
ejercicio *m* exercise.
ejercitación *f* exercise, practice.
ejercitar *vt* to exercise; **~se** *vr* to train.
ejército *m* army.
ejote *m* green bean.
el *art, m* the.
él *pn* he, it.
elaboración *f* elaboration.
elaborado/da *adj* elaborate.
elaborar *vt* to elaborate.
elasticidad *f* elasticity.
elástico/ca *adj* elastic.
elección *f* election; choice.
eleccionario/a *adj Lat Am* electoral.
elector/ra *m/f* elector.
electorado *m* electorate.
electoral *adj* electoral.
electricidad *f* electricity.
electricista *m/f* electrician.
eléctrico/ca *adj* electric, electrical.
electrización *f* electrification.

electrizar vt to electrify.
electrocardiograma m electrocardiogram.
electrocutar vt to electrocute.
electrodoméstico m (electrical) domestic appliance.
electrónico/ca adj electronic.
electrotecnia f electrical engineering.
elefante m elephant.
elegancia f elegance.
elegante adj elegant, fine.
elegía f elegy.
elegir vt to choose, to elect.
elemental adj elemental; elementary.
elemento m element; ~s mpl elements pl, rudiments pl, first principles pl.
elevación f elevation; highness; rise; haughtiness, pride; height; altitude.
elevar vt to raise; to elevate; ~se vr to rise; to be enraptured; to be conceited.
eliminar vt to eliminate, to remove.
eliminatoria f preliminary (round).
elipse f (geom) ellipse.
elipsis f (gr) ellipsis.
elite, élite f elite.
elixir m elixir.
ella pn she; it.
ello pn it.
elocución f elocution.
elocuencia f eloquence.
elocuente adj eloquent.
elogiar vt to praise, to eulogize.
elogio m eulogy, praise.
elote m corn on the cob.
elucidación f elucidation, explanation.
eludir vt to elude, to escape.
emanación f emanation.
emanar vi to emanate.
emancipación f emancipation.
emancipar vt to emancipate, to set free.
embadurnar vt to smear, to bedaub.
embajada f embassy.
embajador/ra m/f ambassador.
embalaje m packing, package.
embalar vt to bale, to pack in bales.
embaldosar vt to pave with tiles.
embalsamador m embalmer.
embalsamar vt to embalm.
embalse m reservoir.
embarazada f pregnant woman; * adj pregnant.
embarazar vt to embarrass; to make pregnant; ~se vr to become intricate.
embarazo m pregnancy; embarrassment; obstacle.
embarazoso/sa adj difficult; intricate, entangled.
embarcación f embarkation; any vessel/ship.
embarcadero m quay, wharf; port; harbor.
embarcar vt to embark; ~se vr to go on board; (fig) to get involved (in a matter).

embargar vt to lay on an embargo; to impede, to restrain.
embargo m embargo; sin ~ still, however.
embarque m embarkation.
embastar vt to stitch, to tack.
embate m breakers pl, surf, surge; sudden attack.
embaucador/ra m/f swindler; impostor.
embaucar vt to deceive; to trick.
embebecer vt to fascinate; ~se vr to be fascinated.
embebecimiento m amazement, astonishment; fascination.
embeber vt to soak; to saturate; * vi to shrink; ~se vr to be enraptured; to be absorbed.
embelesamiento m rapture.
embelesar vt to amaze, to astonish.
embeleso m amazement, enchantment.
embellecer vt to embellish, to beautify.
emberrincharse vr to have a tantrum.
embestida f assault, violent attack.
embestir vt to assault, to attack.
emblanquecer vt to whiten; ~se vr to grow white; to bleach.
emblema m emblem.
embobado/da adj amazed; fascinated.
embobamiento m astonishment; fascination.
embobar vt to amaze; to fascinate; ~se vr to be amazed; to stand gaping.
embobecer vt to make silly; ~se vr to get silly.
embobecimiento m silliness.
émbolo m plunger; piston.
embolsar vt to put money into (a purse); to pocket.
emborrachar vt to intoxicate, to inebriate; ~se vr to get drunk.
emboscada f (mil) ambush.
emboscarse vr (mil) to lie in ambush.
embotar vt to blunt; ~se vr to go numb.
embotellamiento m traffic jam.
embotellar vt to bottle (wine).
embozado/da adj covered; covert.
embozar vt to muffle up (the face); (fig) to cloak, to conceal.
embozo m part of a cloak, veil, anything with which the face is muffled; covering of one's face.
embrague m clutch.
embrear vt to cover with tar/pitch.
embriagar vt to intoxicate, to inebriate; to transport, to enrapture.
embriaguez f intoxication, drunkenness; rapture, delight.
embrión m embryo.
embrollador/ra m/f troublemaker.
embrollar vt to muddle; to entangle, to embroil.
embrollo m muddle.
embromar vt to tease; to cajole, to wheedle.
embrujar vt to bewitch.
embrutecer vt to brutalize; ~se vr to become depraved.

E

embudo *m* funnel.

embuste *m* fraud; lie, fib, story (*col*).

embustero/ra *m/f* impostor, cheat; liar; * *adj* deceitful.

embutido *m* sausage; inlay.

embutir *vt* to insert; to stuff; to inlay; to cram.

emergencia *f* emergency.

emerger *vi* to emerge, to appear.

emético/ca *adj* emetic.

emigración *f* emigration; migration.

emigrado/da *adj* emigrated; * *m/f* emigrant.

emigrante *m/f* emigrant.

emigrar *vi* to emigrate.

eminencia *f* eminence.

eminente *adj* eminent, high; excellent, conspicuous.

emisario *m* emissary.

emisión *f* emission; broadcasting; program; issue.

emisora *f* broadcasting station.

emitir *vt* to emit, to send forth; to issue; to broadcast.

emoción *f* emotion; feeling; excitement.

emocionante *adj* exciting.

emocionar *vt* to excite; to move, to touch.

emoliente *adj* emollient, softening.

emolumento *m* emolument.

emotivo/va *adj* emotional.

empacar *vt* to pack; to crate.

empachar *vt* to give indigestion; ~**se** *vr* to have indigestion.

empacho *m* (*med*) indigestion.

empachoso/sa *adj* indigestible.

empadronamiento *m* register; census.

empadronarse *vr* to register.

empalagar *vt* to sicken; to disgust.

empalago *m* disgust; boredom.

empalagoso/sa *adj* cloying; tiresome.

empalizada *f* (*mil*) palisade.

empalmadura *f* join; weld; splice.

empalmar *vt* to join.

empalme *m* (*rail*) junction; connection.

empanada *f* (meat) pie.

empanar *vt* to cover with breadcrumbs.

empantanarse *vr* to get swamped; to get bogged down.

empañar *vt* to wrap up (baby); to mist; to steam up; ~**se** *vr* to steam up; to tarnish one's reputation.

empapar *vt* to soak; to soak up; ~**se** *vr* to soak.

empapelar *vt* to paper.

empaquetar *vt* to pack, to parcel up.

emparedado *m* sandwich.

emparejar *vt* to level; to match, to fit; to equalize.

emparentar *vi* to be related by marriage.

emparrado *m* vine arbor.

empastar *vt* to paste; to fill (a tooth).

empaste *m* filling (of a tooth).

empatar *vi* to draw, tie, have a dead heat.

empate *m* draw, dead heat.

empedernido/da *adj* inveterate; heartless.

empedernir *vt* to harden; ~**se** to be inflexible.

empedrado *m* paving.

empedrador *m* paver.

empedrar *vt* to pave.

empeine *m* instep.

empellón *m* push; heavy blow.

empeñado/da *adj* determined; pawned.

empeñar *vt* to pawn, to pledge; ~**se** *vr* to pledge oneself to pay debts; to get into debt; ~**se en algo** to insist on something.

empeño *m* obligation; determination; perseverance.

empeorar *vt* to make worse; * *vi*, ~**se** *vr* to grow worse.

empequeñecer *vt* to dwarf; (*fig*) to belittle.

emperador *m* emperor.

emperatriz *f* empress.

emperifollarse *vt* to dress oneself up.

empero *conj* yet, however.

emperrarse *vr* to get stubborn; to be obstinate.

empezar *vt* to begin, to start.

empinado/da *adj* high; proud.

empinar *vt* to raise; to exalt; * *vi* to drink heavily; ~**se** *vr* to stand on tiptoe; to soar.

empírico/ca *adj* empirical.

empirismo *m* empiricism.

empizarrado *m* slate roofing.

empizarrar *vt* to slate, to roof with slate.

emplasto *m* plaster.

emplazamiento *m* summons; location.

emplazar *vt* to summon; to locate.

empleado/da *m/f* official; employee.

emplear *vt* to employ; to occupy; to commission.

empleo *m* employ, employment, occupation.

empobrecer *vt* to reduce to poverty; * *vi* to become poor.

empobrecimiento *m* impoverishment.

empollar *vt* to incubate; to hatch; (*col*) to cram.

empolvar *vt* to powder; to sprinkle powder upon.

emponzoñador/ra *m/f* poisoner.

emponzoñamiento *m* poisoning.

emponzoñar *vt* to poison, to taint, to corrupt.

emporio *m* emporium.

empotrado/da *adj* built-in.

empotrar *vt* to embed; to build in.

emprendedor/ra *m/f* entrepreneur.

emprender *vt* to embark on; to tackle; to undertake.

empresa *f* (*com*) company; enterprise, undertaking.

empresario/ria *m/f* manager.

empréstito *m* loan.

empujar *vt* to push; to press forward.

empuje *m* thrust; pressure; (*fig*) drive.

empujón *m* push; impulse; **a ~ones** in fits and starts.

empuñadura *f* hilt (of a sword).

empuñar *vt* to clench, to grip with the fist; to clutch.
emulación *f* emulation.
emular *vt* to emulate, to rival.
emulsión *f* emulsion.
en *prep* in; for; on, upon.
enaguas *fpl* petticoat.
enajenación *f* alienation; absent-mindedness.
enajenamiento *m* alienation; absent-mindedness.
enajenar *vt* to alienate; ~**se** *vr* to fall out.
enamoradamente *adv* lovingly.
enamoradizo/za *adj* inclined to fall in love.
enamorado/da *adj* in love, lovesick.
enamoramiento *m* falling in love.
enamorar *vt* to inspire love in; ~**se** *vr* to fall in love.
enano/na *adj* dwarfish; * *m* dwarf.
enarbolar *vt* to hoist, to raise high.
enardecer *vt* to fire with passion, to inflame.
enarenar *vt* to fill with sand.
encabezamiento *m* heading; foreword.
encabezar *vt* to head; to put a heading to; to lead.
encabritarse *vr* to rear (of horses).
encadenamiento *m* linking together, chaining.
encadenar *vt* to chain, to link together; to connect, to unite.
encajadura *f* insertion; socket; groove.
encajar *vt* to insert; to drive in; to encase; to intrude; ~**se** *vr* to squeeze; to gatecrash; * *vi* to fit (well).
encaje *m* encasing; joining; socket; groove; inlaid work.
encajera *f* lacemaker.
encajonamiento *m* packing into boxes etc.
encajonar *vt* to pack up in a box.
encalabrinar *vt* to make confused; ~**se** *vr* to become obstinate.
encaladura *f* whitening, whitewash.
encalar *vt* to whitewash.
encallar *vi* (*mar*) to run aground.
encallecer *vi* to get corns.
encamarse *vr* to take to one's bed.
encaminar *vt* to guide, to show the way; ~**se** *vr*: ~ **a** to take the road to.
encandilar *vt* to dazzle.
encanecer *vi* to grow gray; to grow old.
encantado/da *adj* bewitched; delighted; pleased.
encantador/ra *adj* charming; *m/f* magician.
encantamiento *m* enchantment.
encantar *vt* to enchant, to charm; (*fig*) to delight.
encanto *m* enchantment; spell, charm.
encañonar *vt* to hold up; to point a gun at; * *vi* to grow feathers.
encapotar *vt* to cover with a cloak; ~**se** *vr* to be cloudy.
encapricharse *vr* to become stubborn.
encapuchar *vt* to cover with a hood.
encaramar *vt* to raise; to extoll; *Lat Am* to make blush.

encararse *vr*: ~ **a** to come face to face with.
encarcelación *f* incarceration.
encarcelar *vt* to imprison.
encarecer *vt* to raise the price of; ~**se** *vr* to get dearer.
encarecimiento *m* price increase; **con** ~ insistently.
encargado/da *adj* in charge; * *m/f* representative; person in charge.
encargar *vt* to charge; to commission.
encargo *m* charge; commission; job; order.
encariñarse *vr*: ~ **con** to grow fond of.
encarnación *f* incarnation, embodiment.
encarnado/da *adj* incarnate; flesh-colored; * *m* flesh color.
encarnar *vt* to embody, to personify.
encarnizado/da *adj* bloodshot, inflamed; bloody, fierce.
encarrilar *vt* to put back on the rails; to put on the right track.
encasillar *vt* to pigeonhole; to typecast.
encasquetar *vt* to pull on (a hat).
encastillarse *vr* to refuse to yield.
encauzar *vt* to channel.
encebollado *m* casserole of beef/lamb and onions, seasoned with spice.
encenagado/da *adj* muddy, mud-stained.
encenagamiento *m* wallowing in mud.
encenagarse *vr* to wallow in mud.
encendedor *m* lighter, cigarette lighter.
encender *vt* to kindle, to light, to set on fire; to inflame, to incite; to switch on, to turn on; ~**se** *vr* to catch fire; to flare up.
encendido/da *adj* inflamed; high-colored; * *m* ignition (of car).
encerado *m* chalkboard; adhesive tape.
encerar *vt* to wax; to polish.
encerrar *vt* to shut up, to confine; to contain; ~**se** *vr* to withdraw from the world.
encespedar *vt* to turf.
enchapar *vt* to veneer.
encharcarse *vr* to be flooded.
enchufar *vt* to plug in; to connect.
enchufe *m* plug; socket; connection; (*col*) contact, connection.
encía *f* gum (of the teeth).
encíclica *f* encyclical.
enciclopedia *f* encyclopedia.
enciclopédico/ca *adj* encyclopedic.
encierro *m* confinement; enclosure; prison; bullpen; penning (of bulls).
encima *adv* above; over; at the top; besides; ~ **de** *prep* above; over; at the top of; besides.
encina *f* holm oak, evergreen oak.
encinar *m* holm oak wood/grove.
encinta *adj* pregnant.
enclaustrado,da *adj* cloistered; hidden away.
enclenque *adj* weak, sickly; * *m* weakling.

E

encoger vt to contract, to shorten; to shrink; to discourage; ~**se** vr to shrink; (fig) to cringe.

encogidamente adv shyly, timidly, bashfully.

encogido/da adj shy, timid, bashful.

encogimiento m contraction; shrinkage; shyness; timidness; bashfulness.

encoladura f gluing.

encolar vt to glue.

encolerizar vt to provoke, to irritate; ~**se** vr to get angry.

encomendar vt to recommend; to entrust; ~**se** vr: ~ **a** to entrust oneself to; to put one's trust in.

encomiar vt to praise.

encomienda m commission, charge; message; (mil) command; patronage, protection; Lat Am parcel post.

encomio m eulogy, praise; commendation.

enconar vt to inflame; to irritate.

encono m ill-feeling, rancor.

enconoso/sa adj hurtful, prejudicial; malevolent.

encontrado/da adj conflicting; hostile.

encontrar vt to meet, to encounter; ~**se** vr: ~**se con** to run into; * vi to assemble, to come together.

encopetado/da adj presumptuous, boastful.

encorvadura f curvature; crookedness.

encorvar vt to bend, to curve.

encrespar vt to curl, to frizzle (hair); (fig) to anger; ~**se** vr to get rough (of the sea); (fig) to get cross.

encrucijada f crossroads; junction.

encuadernación f binding.

encuadernador/ra m/f bookbinder.

encuadernar vt to bind (books).

encubiertamente adv secretly; deceitfully.

encubierto/ta adj hidden, concealed.

encubridor/ra m/f concealer, harborer; receiver of stolen goods.

encubrimiento m concealment, hiding; receiving of stolen goods.

encubrir vt to hide, to conceal.

encuentro m meeting; collision, crash; match, game.

encuesta f inquiry; opinion poll.

encumbrado/da adj high; elevated.

encumbramiento m elevation; height.

encumbrar vt to raise, to elevate; ~**se** vr to be raised; (fig) to become conceited.

encurtir vt to pickle.

endeble adj feeble, weak.

endecasílabo/ba adj consisting of eleven syllables.

endecha f dirge, lament.

endemoniado/da adj possessed with the devil; devilish.

enderezamiento m guidance, direction.

enderezar vt to straighten out; to set right; ~**se** vr to stand upright.

endeudarse vr to get into debt.

endiablado/da adj devilish, diabolical; ugly.

endiosar vt to deify; ~**se** vr to be high and mighty.

endosar vt to endorse.

endoso m endorsement.

endrina f sloe, fruit of the blackthorn.

endrino m blackthorn, sloe.

endulzar vt to sweeten; to soften.

endurecer vt to harden, to toughen; ~**se** vr to become cruel; to grow hard.

endurecidamente adv cruelly.

endurecimiento m hardness; obstinacy; hard-heartedness.

enebro m (bot) juniper.

enemigo/ga adj hostile; * m enemy.

enemistad f enmity.

enemistar vt to make an enemy; ~**se** vr to become enemies; to fall out.

energía f energy, power, drive; strength of will; ~ **nuclear** nuclear power; ~ **solar** solar energy; ~ **renovables** renewable forms of energy.

enérgico/ca adj energetic; forceful.

energúmeno/na m/f (col) madman/woman.

enero m January.

enervar vt to enervate.

enfadadizo/za adj irritable, crotchety.

enfadar vt to anger, to irritate; to trouble; ~**se** vr to become angry.

enfado m trouble; anger.

enfadoso/sa adj annoying, troublesome.

énfasis m emphasis.

enfático/ca adj emphatic.

enfermar vi to fall ill; * vt to make sick; to weaken.

enfermedad f illness.

enfermería f infirmary; sick bay.

enfermero/ra m/f nurse.

enfermizo/za adj infirm, sickly.

enfermo/ma adj sick, ill; * m/f invalid, sick person; patient.

enfervorizar vt to arouse; to inflame, to incite.

enflaquecer vt to weaken; to make thin.

enflaquecimiento m loss of weight; (fig) weakening.

enfocar vt to focus; to consider (a problem).

enfoque m focus.

enfrascarse vr to be deeply embroiled.

enfrentar vt to confront; to put face to face; ~**se** vr to face each other; to meet (two teams).

enfrente adv over against, opposite; in front.

enfriamiento m refrigeration; (med) cold, chill.

enfriar vt to cool; to refrigerate; ~**se** vr to cool down; (med) to catch a cold/chill.

enfurecer vt to madden, to enrage; ~**se** vr to get rough (of the wind and sea); to become furious/enraged.

enfurruñarse vr to get sulky; to frown.

engalanar vt to adorn, to deck.

engallarse *vr* to be arrogant.

engañabobos *m invar* trickster; trick, trap.

engañadizo/za *adj* gullible, easily deceived.

engañador/ra *adj* cheating; deceptive; * *m/f* cheat, impostor, deceiver.

engañar *vt* to deceive, to cheat; ~se *vr* to be deceived; to make a mistake.

enganchar *vt* to hook, to hang up; to hitch up; to couple, to connect; to recruit into military service; ~se *vr* (*mil*) to enlist.

engañifa *f* deceit, trick.

engaño *m* mistake; misunderstanding; deceit, fraud.

engañoso/sa *adj* deceitful, artful, false.

engarzar *vt* to thread; to link; to curl.

engastar *vt* to set, to mount.

engaste *m* setting, mount.

engatusamiento *m* deception, coaxing.

engatusar *vt* to coax.

engendrar *vt* to beget, to engender; to produce.

engendro *m* fetus, embryo; (*fig*) monstrosity; brainchild.

englobar *vt* to include.

engolfarse *vr* (*mar*) to sail out to sea; ~ **en** to be deeply involved in.

engolosinar *vt* to entice; ~se *vr* to find delight in.

engomadura *f* gluing.

engomar *vt* to glue.

engordar *vt* to fatten; * *vi* to grow fat; to put on weight.

engorro *m* nuisance, bother.

engorroso/sa *adj* troublesome, cumbersome.

engranaje *m* gear; gears, gearing.

engrandecer *vt* to augment; to magnify; to speak highly of; to exaggerate.

engrandecimiento *m* increase; aggrandizement; exaggeration.

engrapadora *f Lat Am* stapler.

engrapar *vt Lat Am* to staple.

engrasar *vt* to grease, to lubricate.

engreído/da *adj* conceited, vain.

engreimiento *m* presumption, vanity.

engreír *vt* to make proud; ~se *vr* to grow proud.

engrosar *vt* to enlarge; to increase.

engrudo *m* paste.

engullidor/ra *m/f* devourer; guzzler.

engullir *vt* to swallow; to gobble, to devour.

enharinar *vt* to cover/sprinkle with flour.

enhebrar *vt* to thread.

enhilar *vt* to thread.

enhorabuena *f* congratulations *pl*; * *interj* congratulations!

enhoramala *interj* good riddance.

enigma *m* enigma, riddle.

enigmático/ca *adj* enigmatic; dark, obscure.

enjabonar *vt* to soap; (*col*) to soft soap.

enjaezar *vt* to harness (a horse).

enjalbegar *vt* to whitewash.

enjambre *m* swarm (of bees); crowd, multitude.

enjaular *vt* to shut up in a cage; to imprison.

enjoyar *vt* to adorn with jewels.

enjuagar *vt* to rinse out; to wash out.

enjuague *m* (*med*) mouthwash; rinsing, rinse.

enjugar *vt* to dry (the tears); to wipe off.

enjuiciar *vt* to prosecute, to try; to pass judgement on, to judge.

enjuto/ta *adj* dried up; (*fig*) lean.

enlace *m* connection, link; relationship.

enladrillado *m* brick paving.

enladrillador *m* bricklayer.

enladrillar *vt* to pave with bricks.

enlazable *adj* able to be fastened together.

enlazar *vt* to join, to unite; to tie.

enlodar *vt* to cover in mud; (*fig*) to stain.

enloquecer *vt* to madden, to drive crazy; * *vi* to go mad.

enloquecimiento *m* madness.

enlosar *vt* to pave with flagstones.

enlutar *vt* to put into mourning; ~se *vr* to go into mourning.

enmaderar *vt* to roof with lumber.

enmarañar *vt* to entangle; to complicate; to confuse; ~se *vr* to become entangled; to get confused.

enmascarar *vt* to mask; ~se *vr* to go in disguise, to masquerade.

enmendar *vt* to correct; to reform; to repair, to compensate for; to amend; ~se *vr* to mend one's ways.

enmienda *f* correction, amendment.

enmohecer *vt* to make moldy; to rust; ~se *vr* to grow moldy/musty; to rust.

enmohecido/da *adj* moldy.

enmudecer *vt* to silence; ~se *vr* to grow dumb; to be silent.

ennegrecer *vt* to blacken; to darken; to obscure.

ennoblecer *vt* to ennoble.

ennoblecimiento *m* ennoblement.

enojadizo/za *adj* peevish; short-tempered, irritable.

enojar *vt* to irritate, to make angry; to annoy; to upset; to offend; ~se *vr* to get angry.

enojo *m* anger, annoyance.

enojoso/sa *adj* offensive, annoying.

enorgullecerse *vr*: ~ (**de**) to be proud (of).

enorme *adj* enormous, vast, huge; horrible.

enormidad *f* enormity; monstrousness.

enramar *vt* to cover with the branches of trees.

enranciarse *vr* to grow rancid.

enrarecer *vt* to thin, to rarefy.

enredadera *f* climbing plant; bindweed.

enredador/ra *m/f* gossip; troublemaker; busybody.

enredar *vt* to entangle, to ensnare, to confound, to perplex; to puzzle; to sow discord among; ~se *vr* to get entangled; to get complicated; to get embroiled.

enredo *m* entanglement; mischievous lie; plot of a play.

enredoso/sa *adj* complicated.

enrejado *m* trelliswork.

enrejar *vt* to fix a grating to (a window); to grate, to lattice.

enrevesado/da *adj* complicated.

enriquecer *vt* to enrich; to adorn; ~**se** *vr* to grow rich.

enristrar *vt* to string (garlic, onions); to straighten out; to go straight to.

enrobustecer *vt* to strengthen.

enrojecer *vt* to redden; * *vi* to blush.

enrolar *vt* to recruit; ~**se** *vr* (*mil*) to join up.

enrollar *vt* to roll (up).

enronquecer *vt* to make hoarse; * *vi* to grow hoarse.

enroscadura *f* twist.

enroscar *vt* to twist; ~**se** *vr* to curl/roll up.

ensalada *f* salad.

ensaladera *f* salad bowl.

ensaladilla (**rusa**) *f* Russian salad.

ensalmar *vt* to set (dislocated bones); to heal by spells.

ensalmo *m* enchantment, spell.

ensalzar *vt* to exalt, to aggrandize; to exaggerate.

ensamblador/ra *m/f* joiner.

ensamblar *vt* to assemble.

ensanchar *vt* to widen; to extend; to enlarge; ~**se** *vr* to expand; to assume an air of importance.

ensanche *m* dilation, augmentation; widening; expansion.

ensangrentar *vt* to stain with blood.

ensañar *vt* to irritate, to enrage; ~**se con** *vr* to treat brutally.

ensartar *vt* to string (beads etc).

ensayar *vt* to test; to rehearse.

ensayo *m* test, trial; rehearsal of a play; essay.

ensenada *f* creek.

enseña *f* colors *pl*, standard.

enseñanza *f* teaching, instruction; education.

enseñar *vt* to teach, to instruct; to show.

enseres *mpl* belongings *pl*.

ensillar *vt* to saddle.

ensimismarse *vr* to be/become lost in thought.

ensoberbecer *vt* to make proud; ~**se** *vr* to become proud; (*mar*) to get rough.

ensordecer *vt* to deafen; * *vi* to grow deaf.

ensordecimiento *m* deafness.

ensortijar *vt* to fix a ring in (the nose); to curl the hair.

ensuciar *vt* to stain, to soil; to defile; ~**se** *vr* to wet oneself; to dirty oneself.

ensueño *m* fantasy; daydream; illusion.

entablar *vt* to board (up); to strike up (conversation); * *vi Lat Am* to draw.

entablillar *vt* (*med*) to put in a splint.

entallar *vt* to tailor (a suit); * *vi* to fit.

ente *m* organization; entity, being; (*col*) odd character.

entendederas *fpl* understanding; brains *pl*.

entender *vt*, *vi* to understand, to comprehend; to remark, to take notice (of); to reason, to think; **a mi** ~ in my opinion; ~**se** *vr* to understand each other.

entendido/da *adj* understood; wise; learned, knowing.

entendimiento *m* understanding; knowledge; judgement.

enteramente *adv* entirely, completely.

enterar *vt* to inform; to instruct; ~**se** *vr* to find out.

entereza *f* entireness, integrity; firmness of mind.

enternecer *vt* to soften; to move (to pity); ~**se** *vr* to be moved.

enternecimiento *m* compassion, pity.

entero/ra *adj* entire, complete; perfect; honest; resolute; **por** ~ entirely, completely.

enterrador *m* gravedigger.

enterrar *vt* to inter, to bury.

entibiar *vt* to cool.

entidad *f* entity; company; body; society.

entierro *m* burial; funeral.

entoldar *vt* to cover with an awning.

entomología *f* entomology.

entonación *f* intonation; modulation; (*fig*) presumption, pride.

entonar *vt* to tune, to intone; to tone; * *vi* to be in tune; ~**se** *vr* to give oneself airs.

entonces *adv* then, at that time.

entontecer *vt* to fool; * *vi*, ~**se** *vr* to get silly.

entontecimiento *m* silliness.

entornar *vt* to half close.

entorpecer *vt* to dull; to make lethargic; to hinder; to delay.

entorpecimiento *m* numbness; lethargy.

entrada *f* entrance, entry; (*com*) receipts *pl*; entree; ticket (for movies, theater etc).

entrambos/bas *pn*, *pl* both.

entrampar *vt* to trap, to snare; to mess up; to burden with debts; ~**se** *vr* get into debt.

entrañable *adj* intimate; affectionate.

entrañas *fpl* entrails *pl*, intestines *pl*.

entrante *adj* coming, next.

entrar *vi* to enter, to go in; to commence.

entre *prep* between; among(st); in; ~ **manos** in hand.

entreabrir *vt* to half open (a door), to leave ajar.

entrecano/na *adj* gray-black, grayish.

entrecejo *m* space between the eyebrows; frown.

entrecortado/da *adj* faltering; difficult.

entredicho *m* (*law*) injunction; **estar en** ~ to be banned; **poner en** ~ to cast doubt on.

entrega *f* delivery; installment.

entregar *vt* to deliver; to hand over; ~**se** *vr* to surrender; to devote oneself.

entrelazar *vt* to interlace.

entremedias *adv* in the meantime.
entremeses *mpl* hors d'oeuvres *pl.*
entremeter *vt* to put (one thing) between (others); ~**se** *vr* to interfere, to meddle.
entremetido/da *m/f* meddler; * *adj* meddling.
entremetimiento *m* insertion; meddling.
entrenador/ra *m/f* trainer, coach.
entrenar *vt* to train; ~**se** *vr* to train.
entreoír *vt* to half hear.
entrepaño *m* panel.
entrepierna *f* crotch.
entresaca *f* thinning out (of trees).
entresacar *vt* to thin out; to sift, to separate.
entresuelo *m* mezzanine floor, entresol.
entretanto *adv* meanwhile.
entretejer *vt* to interweave.
entretela *f* interfacing, stiffening, interlining.
entretener *vt* to amuse; to entertain, to divert; to hold up; to maintain; ~**se** *vr* to amuse oneself; to linger.
entretenido/da *adj* pleasant; amusing; entertaining.
entretenimiento *m* amusement, entertainment.
entrever *vt* to have a glimpse of.
entreverado/da *adj* patchy; streaky.
entrevista *f* interview.
entrevistar *vt* to interview; ~**se** *vr* to have an interview.
entristecer *vt* to sadden.
entromoter *vt* to put (one thing) between (others); ~**se** *vr* to interfere, to meddle.
entrometido/da *m/f* meddler; * *adj* meddling.
entroncar *vi* to be related/connected.
entronización *f* enthronement.
entronizar *vt* to enthrone.
entumecer *vt* to swell; to numb; ~**se** *vr* to become numb.
entumecido/da *adj* numb, stiff.
entumecimiento *m* numbness.
enturbiar *vt* to make cloudy; to obscure, to confound; ~**se** *vr* to become cloudy; (*fig*) to get confused.
entusiasmar *vt* to excite, to fill with enthusiasm; to delight.
entusiasmo *m* enthusiasm.
entusiasta *m/f* enthusiast.
enumeración *f* enumeration.
enumerar *vt* to enumerate.
enunciación *f*, **enunciado** *m* enunciation, declaration.
enunciar *vt* to enunciate, to declare.
envainar *vt* to sheath(e).
envalentonar *vt* to give courage to; ~**se** *vr* to boast.
envanecer *vt* to make vain; to swell with pride; ~**se** *vr* to become proud.
envaramiento *m* stiffness; numbness.
envarar *vt* to numb.
envasar *vt* to pack; to bottle; to can.

envase *m* packing; bottling; canning; container; package; bottle; can.
envejecer *vt* to make old; * *vi*, ~**se** *vr* to grow old.
envenenador/ra *m/f* poisoner.
envenenar *vt* to poison; to embitter.
envenenamiento *m* poisoning.
envergadura *f* (*fig*) scope.
envés *m* wrong side (of material).
enviado/da *m/f* envoy, messenger.
enviar *vt* to send, to transmit, to convey, to dispatch.
enviciar *vt* to vitiate, to corrupt; ~**se** *vr* to get corrupted.
envidia *f* envy; jealousy.
envidiable *adj* enviable.
envidiar *vt* to envy; to grudge; to be jealous of.
envidioso/sa *adj* envious; jealous.
envilecer *vt* to vilify, to debase; ~**se** *vr* to degrade oneself.
envío *m* (*com*) dispatch, remittance of goods; consignment.
enviudar *vi* to become a widower/widow.
envoltorio *m* bundle of clothes.
envoltura *f* cover; wrapping.
envolver *vt* to involve; to wrap up.
enyesar *vt* to plaster; (*med*) to put in a plaster cast.
enzarzarse *vr* to get involved in a dispute; to get oneself into trouble.
épico/ca *adj* epic.
epicúreo/rea *adj* Epicurean.
epidemia *f* epidemic.
epidémico/ca *adj* epidemic.
epidermis *f* epidermis; cuticle.
Epifanía *f* Epiphany.
epígrafe *f* epigraph, inscription; motto; headline.
epigrama *m* epigram.
epilepsia *f* epilepsy.
epílogo *m* epilog.
episcopado *m* episcopacy; bishopric.
episcopal *adj* Episcopal.
episódico/ca *adj* episodic.
episodio *m* episode, installment.
epístola *f* epistle, letter.
epistolar *adj* epistolary.
epistolario *m* collected letters *pl.*
epitafio *m* epitaph.
epíteto *m* epithet.
epítome *m* epitome; compendium.
época *f* epoch; period, time.
epopeya *f* epic.
equidad *f* equity, honesty; impartiality, justice.
equidistar *vi* to be equidistant.
equilátero/ra *adj* equilateral.
equilibrar *vt* to balance; to poise.
equilibrio *m* balance, equilibrium.
equinoccial *adj* equinoctial.
equinoccio *m* equinox.

E

equipaje m baggage; fixings; equipment.
equipar vt to fit out, to equip, to furnish.
equipararse vr: ~ **con** to be on a level with.
equipo m equipment; team; shift.
equitación f horsemanship; riding.
equitativo/va adj equitable; just.
equivalencia f equivalence.
equivalente adj equivalent.
equivaler vi to be of equal value.
equivocación f mistake, error; misunderstanding.
equivocado/da adj mistaken, wrong.
equivocar vt to mistake; ~**se** vr to make a mistake, to be wrong.
equívoco/ca adj equivocal, ambiguous; * m equivocation; quibble.
era f era, age; threshing floor.
erario m treasury, public funds pl.
erección f foundation, establishment; erection, elevation.
erguir vt to erect, to raise up straight; ~**se** vr to straighten up.
erial m fallow land.
erigir vt to erect, to raise, to build; to establish.
erizamiento m standing on end (of hair etc).
erizarse vr to bristle; to stand on end.
erizo m hedgehog; ~ **de mar** sea urchin.
ermita f hermitage.
ermitaño m hermit.
erosionar vt to erode.
erótico/ca adj erotic.
erotismo m eroticism.
errante adj errant; stray; roving.
errar vi to be mistaken; to wander.
errata f misprint.
erre: ~ **que** ~ adv obstinately.
erróneo/nea adj erroneous.
error m error, mistake, fault.
eructar vi to belch, to burp.
eructo m belch, burp.
erudición f erudition, learning.
erudito/ta adj learned, erudite.
erupción f eruption, outbreak.
esa: f of **ese**.
ésa: f of **ése**.
esbelto/ta adj slim, slender.
esbirro m bailiff; henchman; killer.
esbozo m outline.
escabechar vt to marinate; to pickle.
escabeche m pickle; pickled fish.
escabel m footstool.
escabrosidad f unevenness, roughness; harshness.
escabroso/sa adj rough, uneven; craggy; rude, risqué.
escabullirse vr to escape, to evade; to slip through one's fingers.
escafandra f diving suit; space suit.
escala f ladder; (mus) scale; port of call; stopover.
escalador/ra m/f climber.

escalar vt to climb.
escaldado/da adj cautious, suspicious, wary.
escaldar vt to scald.
escalera f staircase; ladder.
escalfar vt to poach (eggs).
escalofríos mpl shivers pl.
escalofriante adj chilling.
escalón m step of a stair; rung.
escama f (fish) scale.
escamado/da adj wary, cautious.
escamar vt to scale, to take off the scales; ~**se** vr to flake off; to become suspicious.
escamoso/sa adj scaly.
escamotear vt to swipe; to make disappear.
escampar vi to stop raining.
escanciador m wine waiter; cupbearer.
escanciar vt to pour (wine).
escandalizar vt to scandalize; ~**se** vr to be shocked.
escándalo m scandal; uproar.
escandaloso/sa adj scandalous; shocking.
escanear vt to scan.
escáner m scanner.
escaño m bench with a back.
escapada f escape, flight.
escapar vi to escape; ~**se** vr to get away; to leak (water etc).
escaparate m shop/store front, shop/store window; wardrobe.
escapatoria f escape, flight; excuse.
escape m escape, flight; leak; exhaust (of motor); **a todo** ~ at full speed.
escapulario m scapulary.
escarabajo m beetle.
escaramuza f skirmish; dispute, quarrel.
escaramuzar vt to skirmish.
escarbadura f act and effect of scratching.
escarbar vt to scratch (the earth as hens do); to inquire into.
escarcha f white frost.
escarchar vi to be frosty.
escardador m weeding hoe.
escardillo m small weeding hoe.
escarlata adj scarlet.
escarlatina f scarlet fever.
escarmentar vi to learn one's lesson; * vt to punish severely.
escarmiento m warning, caution; punishment.
escarnecer vt to mock, to ridicule.
escarnio m gibe, ridicule.
escarola f (bot) endive.
escarpa f slope; escarpment.
escarpado/da adj sloped; craggy.
escarpín m sock; pump (shoe).
escasear vi to be scarce.
escasez f shortage; poverty.
escaso/sa adj small, short, little; sparing; scarce; scanty.

escatimar *vt* to curtail, to lessen; to be scanty with.

escena *f* stage; scene.

escenario *m* stage; set.

escepticismo *m* skepticism.

escéptico/ca *adj* skeptical.

esclarecer *vt* to lighten; to illuminate; to illustrate; to shed light on (problem etc).

esclarecido/da *adj* illustrious, noble.

esclarecimiento *m* clarification; enlightenment.

esclavina *f* short cloak/cape.

esclavitud *f* slavery, servitude.

esclavizar *vt* to enslave.

esclavo/va *m/f* slave; captive.

esclusa *f* sluice, floodgate.

escoba *f* broom, brush.

escobazo *m* blow given with a broom.

escobilla *f* brush, small broom; blade.

escobillar *vt Lat Am* to brush.

escocer *vt* to sting; to burn; ~**se** *vr* to chafe.

escoger *vt* to choose, to select.

escolar *m/f* schoolboy/girl; * *adj* scholastic.

escolástico/ca *adj* scholastic; * *m* scholar.

escollo *m* reef, rock.

escolta *f* escort.

escoltar *vt* to escort.

escombros *mpl* rubbish; debris.

esconder *vt* to hide, to conceal; ~**se** *vr* to be hidden.

escondidas: **a ~** *adv* in a secret manner.

escondite *m* hiding place; **juego del ~** hide-and-seek.

escondrijo *m* hiding place.

escopeta *f* shotgun; **a tiro de ~** within gunshot.

escopetazo *m* gunshot; gunshot wound.

escopetero *m* gunsmith.

escoplo *m* chisel.

escorbuto *m* scurvy.

escoria *f* dross; scum; dregs *pl*.

Escorpio *m* Scorpio (zodiac sign).

escorpión *m* scorpion.

escotado/da *adj* low-cut.

escotadura *f* low neck(line).

escotar *vt* to cut low in front.

escote *m* low neck (of a dress).

escotilla *f* (*mar*) hatchway.

escozor *m* smart; burning pain; sting(ing).

escriba *m* scribe (of the Hebrews).

escribanía *f* clerk's office; writing desk.

escribano *m* court clerk; lawyer's clerk.

escribiente *m* transcriber; copyist; clerk.

escribir *vt* to write; to spell; * *vi* to write.

escrito *m* document; manuscript, text.

escritor/ra *m/f* writer, author.

escritorio *m* writing desk; office, study.

escritura *f* writing; deed.

escrúpulo *m* doubt, scruple, scrupulousness.

escrupulosidad *f* scrupulousness.

escrupuloso/sa *adj* scrupulous; exact.

escrutar *vt* to examine; to count (ballot papers).

escrutinio *m* scrutiny, inquiry.

escrutiñador *m* scrutinizer, inquirer.

escuadra *f* square; squadron; squad.

escuadrar *vt* to square.

escuadrón *m* squadron.

escuálido/da *adj* skinny; squalid.

escucha *f* listening(-in); * *m* scout.

escuchar *vt* to listen to, to heed.

escudar *vt* to shield; to guard from danger; ~**se** *vr* to protect oneself.

escudero *m* squire; page.

escudilla *f* bowl.

escudo *m* shield.

escudriñamiento *m* investigation, scrutiny.

escudriñar *vt* to search, to examine; to pry into.

escuela *f* school; ~ **primaria** grade school; ~ **secundaria** secondary/high school.

escueto/ta *adj* plain; simple.

esculpir *vt* to sculpt.

escultor/ra *m/f* sculptor.

escultura *f* sculpture.

escupidera *f* cuspidor.

escupidura *f* spit.

escupir *vt* to spit.

escurreplatos *m invar* plate rack.

escurridizo/za *adj* slippery.

escurrir *vt* to drain; to drip; ~**se** *vr* to slip away; to slip, to slide; * *vi* to wring out.

ese/esa *adj* that; **esos/as** *pl* those.

ése/ésa *pn* that (one); **ésos/as** *pl* those (ones).

esencia *f* essence.

esencial *adj* essential; principal.

esfera *f* sphere; globe.

esférico/ca *adj* spherical.

esferoide *f* spheroid.

esfinge *f* sphinx.

esforzado/da *adj* strong, vigorous; valiant.

esforzarse *vr* to exert oneself, to make an effort.

esfuerzo *m* effort.

esfumarse *vr* to fade away.

esgrima *f* fencing.

esgrimidor *m* fencer.

esgrimir *vi* to fence.

esguince *m* (*med*) sprain.

eslabón *m* link of a chain; steel; shackle.

eslabonar *vt* to link; to unite.

esmaltador *m* enameler.

esmaltar *vt* to enamel.

esmalte *m* enamel.

esmerado/da *adj* careful, neat.

esmeralda *f* emerald.

esmerar *vt* to polish; ~**se** *vr* to take great care; to work hard.

esmeril *m* emery.

esmerilar *vt* to polish with emery.

esmero *m* careful attention, great care.

esnob *adj* snobbish; * *m/f* snob.

eso *pn* that.

esófago m esophagus; throat.

esos, ésos pl of **ese, ése**.

espabilar vt to wake up; ~**se** vr to wake up; (fig) to get a move on.

espacial adj space compd.

espaciar vt to spread out; to space (out).

espacio m space; (rad/TV) program.

espaciosidad f spaciousness, capacity.

espacioso/sa adj spacious, roomy.

espada f sword; ace of spades.

espadachín m bully.

espadaña f (bot) bulrush.

espadín m small short sword.

espaguetis mpl spaghetti.

espalda f back, back-part; ~**s** fpl shoulders pl.

espaldilla f shoulder blade.

espantadizo/za adj timid, easily frightened.

espantajo m scarecrow; bogeyman.

espantapájaros m invar scarecrow.

espantar vt to frighten; to chase/drive away.

espanto m fright; menace, threat; astonishment; Lat Am ghost.

espantoso/sa adj frightful, dreadful; amazing.

español/la adj Spanish; * m/f Spaniard; * m Spanish (language).

esparadrapo m adhesive tape.

esparcir vt to scatter; to divulge; ~**se** vr to amuse oneself.

espárrago m asparagus.

esparto m (bot) esparto.

espasmo m spasm.

espátula f spatula.

especia f spice.

especial adj special; particular; **en** ~ especially.

especialidad f specialty.

especie f species; kind, sort; matter.

especificación f specification.

especificar vt to specify.

específico/ca adj specific.

espectáculo m spectacle; show.

espectador/ra m/f spectator.

espectro m specter, phantom, ghost, apparition.

especulación f speculation; contemplation; venture.

especulador/ra m/f speculator.

especular vt to speculate.

especulativo/va adj speculative; thoughtful.

espejismo m mirage.

espejo m mirror.

espeluznante adj horrifying.

espera f stay, waiting; (law) respite, adjournment, delay.

esperanza f hope.

esperanzar vt to give hope to.

esperar vt to hope; to expect, to wait for.

esperma f sperm.

espesar vt to thicken; to condense; ~**se** vr to grow thick; to solidify.

espeso/sa adj thick, dense.

espesor m thickness.

espesura f thickness; density, solidity.

espía m/f spy.

espiar vt to spy.

espiga f ear (of corn).

espigón m ear of corn; sting; (mar) breakwater.

espina f thorn; fishbone.

espinaca f (bot) spinach.

espinazo m spine, backbone.

espinilla f shinbone.

espino m hawthorn.

espinoso/sa adj thorny; dangerous.

espionaje m spying, espionage.

espiral adj, f spiral.

espirar vt to exhale.

espíritu m spirit, soul; mind; intelligence; **el E~ Santo** the Holy Ghost; ~**s** pl demons pl, hobgoblins pl.

espiritual adj spiritual; ghostly.

espiritualidad f spirituality.

espiritualizar vt to spiritualize.

esplendidez f splendor.

espléndido/da adj splendid.

esplendor m splendor.

espliego m (bot) lavender.

espolear vt to spur, to instigate, to incite.

espolón m spur (of a cock); spur (of a mountain range); sea wall; jetty; (mar) buttress.

espolvorear vt to sprinkle.

espondeo m (poet) spondee.

esponja f sponge.

esponjar vt to sponge; ~**se** vr to be puffed up with pride.

esponjoso/sa adj spongy.

esponsales mpl betrothal.

espontaneidad f spontaneity.

espontáneo/nea adj spontaneous.

esposa f wife.

esposar vt to handcuff.

esposas fpl handcuffs pl.

esposo m husband.

espuela f spur; stimulus; (bot) larkspur.

espuerta f pannier, basket.

espulgar vt to delouse; to examine closely.

espuma f froth, foam.

espumadera f skimmer.

espumajear vi to foam at the mouth.

espumar vt to skim, to take the scum off.

espumarajo m foam, froth (from the mouth).

espumoso/sa adj frothy, foamy; sparkling (wine).

espurio/ria adj spurious; adulterated; illegitimate.

esputo m spit, saliva.

esqueje m cutting (of plant).

esquela f note, slip of paper.

esqueleto m skeleton.

esquema m scheme; diagram; plan.

esquí m ski; skiing.

esquiar *vi* to ski.
esquife *m* skiff, small boat.
esquilador *m* sheep-shearer.
esquilar *vt* to shear sheep.
esquina *f* corner, angle.
esquinado/da *adj* cornered, angled.
esquinar *vt* to form a corner with.
esquirol *m* blackleg.
esquivar *vt* to shun, to avoid, to evade.
esquivez *f* disdain; shyness.
esquivo/va *adj* scornful; shy, reserved.
esta: *f* of **este**.
ésta: *f* of **éste**.
estabilidad *f* stability.
estable *adj* stable.
establecer *vt* to establish.
establecimiento *m* establishment.
establo *m* stable.
estaca *f* stake; stick; post.
estacada *f* fence; fencing; stockade.
estacazo *m* blow with a stick.
estación *f* season (of the year); station; railroad station, terminus; ~ **de autobuses** bus station; ~ **de servicio** service station.
estacional *adj* seasonal.
estacionamiento *m* parking; parking lot; (*mil*) stationing.
estacionar *vt* to park; (*mil*) to station.
estacionario/ria *adj* stationary.
estadía *f* Lat Am stay.
estadio *m* phase; stadium.
estadista *m* statesman; statistician.
estadística *f* statistics *pl*.
estadístico/ca *adj* statistical.
estado *m* state, condition.
Estados Unidos *mpl* United States (of America).
estafa *f* trick, fraud.
estafador/ra *m/f* swindler, racketeer.
estafar *vt* to deceive, to defraud.
estafeta *f* post office.
estallar *vi* to crack; to burst; to break out.
estallido *m* explosion; (*fig*) outbreak.
estambre *m* stamen.
estamento *m* estate; body; layer; class.
estameña *f* serge.
estampa *f* print; engraving; appearance.
estampado/da *adj* printed; * *m* printing; print; stamping.
estampar *vt* to print.
estampida *f* stampede.
estampido *m* report (of a gun); crack.
estampilla *f* seal; Lat Am stamp.
estancar *vt* to check (a current); to monopolize; to prohibit, to suspend; ~**se** *vr* to stagnate.
estancia *f* stay; bedroom; ranch; (*poet*) stanza.
estanco *m* tobacconist's (shop); ~/**ca** *adj* watertight.
estándar *adj*, *m* standard.

estandarizar *vt* to standardize.
estandarte *m* banner, standard.
estanque *m* pond, pool; reservoir.
estanquero/ra *m/f* tobacconist.
estante *m* shelf (for books).
estantería *f* shelves *pl*, shelving.
estaño *m* tin.
estar *vi* to be; to be (in a place).
estatal *adj* state *compd*.
estática *f* statics *pl*.
estático/ca *adj* static.
estatua *f* statue.
estatura *f* stature.
estatuto *m* statute, law.
este[1] *m* east;
este/ta[2] *adj* this; **estos/tas** *pl* these.
éste *pn m* this (one); **éstos/tas** *pl* these (ones).
estera *f* mat.
estercolar *vt* to manure.
estercolero *m* dunghill.
estéreo *adj invar*, *m* stereo.
estereotipar *vt* to stereotype.
estereotipo *m* stereotype.
estéril *adj* sterile, infertile.
esterilidad *f* sterility, infertility.
esterilla *f* mat; Lat Am canework.
esterlina *adj*: **libra** ~ pound sterling.
estético/ca *adj* esthetic; * *f* esthetics.
estiércol *m* dung; manure.
estilar *vi*, ~**se** *vr* to be in fashion; to be used.
estilo *m* style; fashion; stroke (in swimming).
estima *f* esteem.
estimable *adj* estimable, worthy of esteem.
estimación *f* estimation, valuation.
estimar *vt* to estimate, to value; to esteem; to judge; to think.
estimulante *adj* stimulating; * *m* stimulant.
estimular *vt* to stimulate, to excite; to goad.
estímulo *m* stimulus.
estío *m* summer.
estipendiario *m* stipendiary.
estipulación *f* stipulation.
estipular *vt* to stipulate.
estirado/da *adj* stretched tight; (*fig*) pompous.
estirar *vt* to stretch out.
estirón *m* pulling; tugging; **dar un** ~ to grow rapidly.
estirpe *f* race, origin, stock.
estival *adj* summer *compd*.
esto *pn* this.
estocada *f* stab.
estofa *f*: **de baja** ~ poor quality.
estofado *m* stew.
estola *f* stole.
estolidez *f* stupidity.
estólido/da *adj* stupid.
estomacal *adj* stomach *compd*.
estómago *m* stomach.

E

estopa f tow.
estoque m rapier, sword.
estorbar vt to hinder; (fig) to bother; * vi to be in the way.
estorbo m obstacle, hindrance, impediment.
estornudar vi to sneeze.
estornudo m sneeze.
estos, éstos pl of **este, éste**.
estrada f highway; expressway.
estrado m drawing room; stage, platform; ~ **de los testigos** witness stand.
estrafalario/ria adj slovenly; eccentric.
estrago m ruin, destruction; havoc.
estrambótico/ca adj eccentric, odd.
estrangulador/ra m/f strangler.
estrangulamiento m bottleneck.
estrangular vt to strangle; (med) to strangulate.
estraperlo m black market.
estratagema f stratagem, trick.
estrategia f strategy.
estratégico/ca adj strategic.
estrato m stratum, layer.
estraza f rag; **papel de** ~ brown paper.
estrechar vt to tighten; to contract, to constrain; to compress; ~ **la mano** to shake hands; ~**se** vr to grow narrow; to embrace.
estrechez f strictness, narrowness; shortage of money.
estrecho m straits pl; ~/**cha** adj narrow, close; tight; intimate; rigid, austere; short (of money).
estrella f star.
estrellado/da adj starry; **huevos** ~**s** fried eggs.
estrellar vt to dash to pieces; ~**se** vr to smash; to crash; to fail.
estremecer vt to shake, to make tremble; ~**se** vr to shake, to tremble.
estremecimiento m trembling, shaking.
estrenar vt to wear for the first time; to move into (a house); to show (a film) for the first time; ~**se** vr to make one's debut.
estreñido/da adj constipated.
estreñimiento m constipation.
estrépito m noise, racket; fuss.
estrepitoso/sa adj noisy.
estribar vi: ~ **en** to be supported by; to be based on.
estribillo m chorus.
estribo m buttress; stirrup; bracket; brace; **perder los** ~**s** to fly off the handle (col).
estribor m (mar) starboard.
estrictez f Lat Am strictness.
estricto/ta adj strict; severe.
estrofa f (poet) verse, strophe.
estropajo m scourer.
estropajoso/sa adj tough, leathery; despicable; mean; stammering.
estropear vt to spoil; to damage; ~**se** vr to get damaged.
estructura f structure.

estruendo m clamor, noise; confusion, uproar; pomp, ostentation.
estrujar vt to press, to squeeze.
estrujón m pressing, squeezing.
estuario m estuary.
estuche m case (for scissors etc); sheath.
estudiante m/f student.
estudiantil adj student compd.
estudiar vt to study.
estudio m study; studio; ~**s** mpl studies pl; learning.
estudioso/sa adj studious.
estufa f heater, fire.
estufilla f muff; small stove.
estupefacción f stupefaction.
estupefaciente m narcotic.
estupefacto adj speechless; thunderstruck.
estupendo/da adj terrific, marvelous.
estupidez f stupidity.
estúpido/da adj stupid.
estupor m stupor, astonishment.
estupro m rape.
etapa f stage; stopping place; (fig) phase.
etcétera adv etcetera, and so on.
éter m ether.
etéreo/rea adj ethereal.
eternidad f eternity.
eternizar vt to eternalize, to perpetuate.
eterno/na adj eternal.
ética f ethics.
ético/ca adj ethical, moral.
etimología f etymology.
etimológico/ca adj etymological.
etiqueta f etiquette; label, tag.
Eucaristía f Eucharist.
eufemismo m euphemism.
euforia f euphoria.
euro m euro.
eurocámara f European Parliament.
eurodiputado/da m/f Euro-MP.
euroescéptico/ca m/f Euroskeptic.
Europa f Europe.
eurotúnel m Eurotunnel, Channel tunnel.
evacuación f evacuation.
evacuar vt to evacuate, to empty.
evadir vt to evade, to escape.
evaluar vt to evaluate.
evangélico/ca adj evangelical.
evangelio m gospel.
evangelista m evangelist.
evangelizar vt to evangelize.
evaporar vt to evaporate; ~**se** vr to vanish.
evasión f evasion, escape.
evasivo/va adj evasive; * f excuse.
eventual adj possible; temporary, casual (worker).
evidencia f evidence, proof.
evidente adj evident, clear.
evitable adj avoidable.
evitar vt to avoid.

evocación f evocation; invocation.
evocar vt to call out; to invoke.
evolución f evolution, development; change; (mil) maneuver.
evolucionar vi to evolve.
ex adj ex.
exacción f exaction; extortion.
exacerbar vt to exacerbate; to irritate.
exactamente adv exactly.
exactitud f exactness.
exacto/ta adj exact; punctual; accurate.
exageración f exaggeration.
exagerar vt to exaggerate.
exaltación f exaltation, elation.
exaltar vt to exalt, to elevate; to praise, to extoll; ~se vr to get excited.
examen m exam, examination, test; inquiry.
examinador m examiner.
examinar vt to examine.
exánime adj lifeless, weak.
exasperación f exasperation.
exasperar vt to exasperate, to irritate.
excavación f excavation.
excavadora f excavator.
excavar vt to excavate, to dig out.
excedente adj excessive.
exceder vt to exceed, to surpass, to excel, to outdo.
excelencia f excellence.
Excelencia f Excellency (title).
excelente adj excellent.
excelso/sa adj elevated, sublime, lofty.
excentricidad f eccentricity.
excéntrico/ca adj eccentric.
excepción f exception.
excepto adv excepting, except (for).
exceptuar vt to except, to exempt.
excesivo/va adj excessive.
exceso m excess.
excitación f excitement; excitation.
excitar vt to excite; ~se vr to get excited.
exclamación f exclamation.
exclamar vt to exclaim, to cry out.
excluir vt to exclude.
exclusión f exclusion.
exclusiva f exclusive; (com) sole right.
exclusivamente, exclusive adv exclusively.
exclusivo/va adj exclusive.
excomulgar vt to excommunicate.
excomunión f excommunication.
excremento m excrement.
excursión f excursion, trip.
excusa f excuse, apology.
excusable adj excusable.
excusado m bathroom, lavatory.
excusar vt to excuse; to avoid; ~ de to exempt from; ~se vr to apologize.
execrable adj execrable, abhorrent.
execrar vt to execrate, to curse.

exención f exemption; immunity, privilege.
exento/ta adj exempt, free.
exequias fpl funeral rites pl, obsequies pl.
exhalación f exhalation; fumes pl, vapor.
exhalar vt to exhale; to give off; to heave (a sigh).
exhausto/ta adj exhausted.
exhibición f exhibition, display.
exhibir vt to exhibit.
exhortación f exhortation.
exhortar vt to exhort.
exhumación f exhumation.
exhumar vt to disinter, to exhume.
exigencia f demand, requirement.
exigir vt to demand, to require.
exiguo/gua adj meager, small.
exiliado/da adj exiled; * m/f exile.
exilio m exile.
eximir vt to exempt, to free; to excuse.
existencia f existence, being.
existente adj existing, in existence.
existir vi to exist, to be.
éxito m outcome; success; (mus) hit; **tener** ~ to be successful.
exoneración f exoneration.
exonerar vt to exonerate.
exorbitante adj exorbitant, excessive.
exorcismo m exorcism.
exorcista m exorcist.
exorcizar vt to exorcise.
exótico/ca adj exotic.
expandir vt to expand.
expansión f expansion; extension.
expansivo/va adj expansive.
expatriarse vr to emigrate; to go into exile.
expectativa f expectation; prospect.
expectoración f expectoration.
expectorar vt to expectorate.
expedición f expedition.
expedicionario/ria adj expeditionary.
expediente m expedient; means; (law) proceedings pl; dossier, file.
expedir vt to send, to forward, to dispatch.
expeditivo/va adj expeditious.
expedito/ta adj speedy; clear, free.
expeler vt to expel.
expendio m Lat Am shop.
expensas fpl: **a** ~ **de** at the expense of.
experiencia f experience; trial.
experimentado/da adj experienced; expert.
experimental adj experimental.
experimentar vt to experience; * vi: ~ **con** to experiment with.
experimento m experiment, trial.
experto/ta adj expert; experienced.
expiación f expiation; purification.
expiar vt to atone for; to purify.
expiatorio/ria adj expiatory.
expirar vi to expire.

explanada f esplanade.

explayarse vr to speak at length.

explicación f explanation.

explicar vt to explain, to expound; **~se** vr to explain oneself.

explícito/ta adj explicit.

exploración f exploration.

explorador/ra m/f explorer.

explorar vt to explore.

explosión f explosion.

explotación f exploitation; running.

explotar vt to exploit; to run; * vi to explode.

exponente m (math) exponent.

exponer vt to expose; to explain.

exportación f export; exports pl.

exportar vt to export.

exposición f exposure; exhibition; explanation; account.

expresar vt to express.

expresión f expression.

expresivo/va adj expressive; energetic.

expreso/sa adj express, clear, specific; fast (train).

express m (rail) express train.

exprimidor m squeezer.

exprimir vt to squeeze out.

ex profeso adv on purpose.

expropriar vt to expropriate.

expuesto/ta adj exposed; on display.

expulsar vt to expel, to drive out.

expulsión f expulsion.

exquisito/ta adj exquisite; excellent.

éxtasis m ecstasy, enthusiasm.

extático/ca adj ecstatic.

extender vt to extend, to stretch out; **~se** vr to extend; to spread.

extensión f extension; extent.

extensivo/va adj extensive.

extenso/sa adj extensive.

extenuación f emaciation; debility, exhaustion.

extenuar vt to exhaust, to debilitate.

exterior adj exterior, external; * m exterior, outward appearance.

exteriormente adv externally.

exterminador m exterminator.

exterminar vt to exterminate.

exterminio m extermination.

externo/na adj external, outer; * m/f day pupil/ student.

extinción f extinction.

extinguidor m Lat Am (fire) extinguisher.

extinguir vt to wipe out; to extinguish.

extintor m (fire) extinguisher.

extirpación f extirpation, extermination.

extirpar vt to extirpate, to root out.

extorsión f extortion.

extra adj invar extra; good quality; * m/f extra; * m bonus.

extracción f extraction.

extracto m extract.

extradición f extradition.

extraditar vt to extradite.

extraer vt to extract.

extranjero/ra m/f stranger; foreigner; * adj foreign, alien.

extrañar vt to find strange; to miss; **~se** vr to be surprised; to grow apart.

extrañeza f strangeness; surprise.

extraño/ña adj foreign; rare; singular, strange, odd.

extraordinario/ria adj extraordinary, uncommon, odd.

extravagancia f extravagance.

extravagante adj extravagant.

extraviado/da adj lost, missing.

extraviar vt to mislead; **~se** vr to lose one's way.

extravío m deviation; loss.

extremado/da adj extreme; accomplished.

extremaunción f extreme unction.

extremidad f extremity; brim; tip; **~es** fpl extremities pl.

extremo/ma adj extreme, last; * m extreme, highest degree; **en ~** extremely.

extrínseco/ca adj extrinsic, external.

extrovertido/da adj, m/f extrovert.

exuberancia f exuberance; luxuriance.

F

fábrica *f* factory.

fabricación *f* manufacture, production.

fabricante *m/f* producer, manufacturer.

fabricar *vt* to build, to construct; to manufacture; (*fig*) to fabricate.

fabril *adj* manufacturing *compd*, industrial.

fábula *f* fable; fiction; rumor, common talk.

fabulista *m/f* writer of fables.

fabuloso/sa *adj* fabulous, fictitious.

facción *f* (political) faction; feature.

faccioso/sa *adj* factious, turbulent.

facha *f* appearance, look; face.

fachada *f* facade, face, front.

fácil *adj* facile, easy.

facilidad *f* facility, easiness; **con ~** *adv* cozily, easily.

facilitar *vt* to facilitate.

fácilmente *adv* easily.

facineroso *adj* wicked, criminal.

facsímil *m* facsimile, fax.

factible *adj* feasible, practicable.

factor *m* (*math*) factor; (*com*) factor, agent.

factoría *f* agency; factory.

factura *f* invoice.

facultad *f* faculty; *Lat Am* college.

facultativo/va *adj* optional; * *m/f* doctor, practitioner.

faena *f* task, job; hard work.

faisán *m* pheasant.

faja *f* band, sash; strip (of land); corset.

fajo *m* bundle; wad.

falacia *f* fallacy; fraud.

falange *f* phalanx.

falaz *adj* deceitful, fraudulent; fallacious.

falda *f* skirt; lap; flap; train; slope, hillside.

faldero/ra *adj*: **hombre ~** ladies' man; **perrito ~** lap-dog.

faldón *m* coat-tails *pl*; skirt.

falencia *f* *Lat Am* bankruptcy.

falible *adj* fallible.

falla *f* *Lat Am* mistake.

fallar *vt* (*law*) to pronounce sentence on, to judge; * *vi* to fail.

fallecer *vi* to die.

fallecimiento *m* decease, death.

fallido/da *adj* unsuccessful, frustrated.

fallo *m* judgement, sentence; failure.

falsamente *adv* falsely.

falsario/ria *adj* falsifying, forging.

falsear *vt* to falsify, to counterfeit.

falsedad *f* falsehood; untruth, lie; hypocrisy.

falsete *m* (*tec*) plug; bung; (*mus*) falsetto.

falsificación *f* falsification.

falsificador/ora *m/f* forger, counterfeiter.

falsificar *vt* to falsify, to forge, to counterfeit.

falso/sa *adj* false, untrue; deceitful; fake.

falta *f* fault, defect; want; flaw, mistake; (*sport*) foul.

faltante *m* *Lat Am* deficit.

faltar *vi* to be wanting; to fail; not to fulfill one's promise; to need; to be missing.

falto/ta *adj* wanting, deficient, lacking; miserable, wretched.

faltriquera *f* pocket.

fama *f* fame; reputation, name.

famélico/ca *adj* starving.

familia *f* family.

familiar *adj* familiar; homely, domestic; * *m/f* relative, relation.

familiaridad *f* familiarity.

familiarizarse *vr*: **~ con** to familiarize oneself with.

famoso/sa *adj* famous.

fan *m/f* fan.

fanático/ca *adj* fanatical; enthusiastic; * *m/f* fanatic; fan.

fandango *m* fandango.

fanfarrón/ona *m/f* bully, braggart.

fanfarronada *f* boast, brag.

fanfarronear *vi* to bully, to brag.

fanfarronería *f* boast, brag.

fango *m* mire, mud.

fangoso/sa *adj* muddy, miry.

fantasía *f* fancy; fantasy; caprice; presumption.

fantasma *f* phantom, ghost.

fantástico/ca *adj* fantastic, whimsical; presumptuous.

fardo *m* bale, parcel.

farfullar *vi* to talk with a stammer.

farisaico/ca *adj* pharisaical; hypocritical.

fariseo *m* Pharisee; hypocrite.

farmacéutico/ca *adj* pharmaceutical; * *m/f* druggist.

farmacia *f* drugstore.

faro *m* (*mar*) lighthouse; (*auto*) headlamp/light; floodlight.

farol *m* lantern.

farola *f* street light.

farsa *f* farce.

farsante *m/f* fraud, fake.

fascículo *m* part, installment.

fascinación *f* fascination.

fascinar *vt* to fascinate; to enchant.

fascismo *m* fascism.

fascista *adj, m/f* fascist.

fase *f* phase.

fastidiar *vt* to annoy; to offend; to spoil.

fastidio *m* annoyance; boredom; disgust.
fastidioso/sa *adj* annoying; tedious.
fatal *adj* fatal; mortal; awful.
fatalidad *f* fatality; mischance, ill-luck.
fatalismo *m* fatalism.
fatalista *m/f* fatalist.
fatiga *f* weariness, fatigue.
fatigar *vt* to fatigue, to tire; to harass.
fatigoso/sa *adj* tiresome, troublesome.
fatuidad *f* fatuity, foolishness, silliness.
fatuo/tua *adj* fatuous, stupid, foolish; conceited.
fauces *fpl* jaws *pl*; gullet.
fausto/ta *adj* happy, fortunate; * *m* splendor, pomp.
favor *m* favor; protection; good turn.
favorable *adj* favorable.
favorecer *vt* to favor, to protect.
favorecido/da *m/f Lat Am* prizewinner.
favorito/ta *adj* favorite.
fax *m* fax.
faz *f* face.
fe *f* faith, belief.
fealdad *f* ugliness.
febrero *m* February.
febril *adj* feverish.
fecha *f* date (of a letter etc).
fechar *vt* to date.
fechoría *f* misdeed; exploit.
fecundar *vt* to fertilize.
fecundidad *f* fecundity, fertility.
fecundo/da *adj* fruitful, fertile.
federación *f* federation.
felicidad *f* happiness.
felicitaciones *interj Lat Am* congratulations!
felicitar *vt* to congratulate.
feligrés/esa *m/f* parishioner.
feliz *adj* happy, fortunate.
felpa *f* plush; toweling.
felpudo *m* doormat.
femenil *adj* feminine, womanly.
femenino/na *adj* feminine; female.
feminismo *m* feminism.
feminista *adj*, *m/f* feminist.
fenómeno *m* phenomenon; (*fig*) freak, accident; * *adj* (*col*) great, marvelous.
feo/ea *adj* ugly; bad, nasty.
feracidad *f* productivity, fertility.
feraz *adj* fertile, fruitful.
féretro *m* bier, casket.
feria *f* fair, rest day; village market.
feriado *m Lat Am* public holiday.
fermentación *f* fermentation.
fermentar *vi* to ferment.
fermento *m* ferment; leaven.
ferocidad *f* ferocity, wildness; cruelty.
feroz *adj* ferocious, savage; cruel.
ferretería *f* hardware store.
ferrocarril *m* railroad.

ferroviario/ria *adj* rail *compd*.
ferry *m* ferry.
fértil *adj* fertile, fruitful.
fertilidad *f* fertility, fruitfulness.
fertilización *f* fertilization.
fertilizar *vt* to fertilize.
férula *f* ferule; (*med*) splint.
ferviente *adj* fervent; ardent.
fervor *m* fervor, zeal; ardor.
fervoroso/sa *adj* fervent, ardent, passionate.
festejar *vt* to feast; to court, to woo.
festejo *m* courtship; feast.
festín *m* feast.
festividad *f* festivity.
festivo/va *adj* festive, merry; witty; **día ~** holiday.
festón *m* garland; festoon.
festonear *vt* to decorate with garlands.
fétido/da *adj* fetid, stinking.
feto *m* fetus.
feudal *adj* feudal.
fiable *adj* trustworthy; reliable.
fiador/ra *m/f* guarantor; (*com*) backer.
fiambre *m* cold meat.
fiambrera *f* dinner pail; lunch basket.
fianza *f* (*law*) surety.
fiar *vt* to entrust, to confide; to bail; to sell on credit; to buy on credit; * *vi* to trust.
fibra *f* fiber.
fibroso/sa *adj* fibrous.
ficción *f* fiction.
ficha *f* token, counter (at games); (index) card.
ficticio/cia *adj* fictitious.
fidedigno/na *adj* reliable, trustworthy.
fideicomisario/ria *m/f* trustee.
fideicomiso *f* trust.
fidelidad *f* fidelity; loyalty.
fideos *mpl* vermicelli *pl*.
fiebre *f* fever.
fiel *adj* faithful, loyal; * *mpl* **los ~es** the faithful *pl*.
fieltro *m* felt.
fiera *f* wild beast.
fiereza *f* fierceness, ferocity; cruelty.
fiero/ra *adj* fierce, ferocious; cruel; rough, harsh.
fierrero/ra *m/f Lat Am* weightlifter.
fierro *m Lat Am* iron.
fiesta *f* party; festivity; **~s** *fpl* feast days; holidays *pl*.
figura *f* figure, shape.
figurado/da *adj* figurative.
figurar *vt* to figure; **~se** *vr* to fancy, to imagine.
figurilla *f* ridiculous little figure.
fijador *m* fixative; gel (for the hair).
fijar *vt* to fix, to fasten; **~se** *vr* to become fixed; to establish oneself; **~se en** to notice.
fijo/ja *adj* fixed, firm; settled, permanent.
fila *f* row, line; (*mil*) rank; **en ~** in a line, in a row.
filamento *m* filament.
filantropía *f* philanthropy.

filántropo/pa m/f philanthropist.
fildeador/ra m/f Lat Am fielder.
fildear vi Lat Am to field.
fildeo m Lat Am fielding.
filete m fillet; fillet steak.
filiación f lineage; personal description, personal particulars pl.
filial adj filial; * f (com) subsidiary.
filibustero m pirate.
filigrana f filigree.
filmar vt to film.
filo m edge, blade.
filología f philology.
filológico/ca adj philological.
filólogo/ga m/f philologist.
filoso/sa adj Lat Am sharp.
filosofar vt to philosophize.
filosofía f philosophy.
filosófico/ca adj philosophical.
filósofo/fa m/f philosopher.
filtración f filtration.
filtrar vt to filter, to strain.
filtro m filter.
fin m end; termination, conclusion; aim, purpose; **al ~** at last; **en ~** (fig) well then; **por ~** finally, lastly.
final adj final; * m end; termination, conclusion; * f (sport) final.
finalizar vt to finish, to conclude; * vi to be finished.
finalmente adv finally, at last.
financiar vt to finance.
financista m/f Lat Am financier.
finca f land, property, real estate; country house; farm; Lat Am plantation.
fineza f fineness, perfection; elegance; courtesy; small gift.
fingido/da adj feigned, fake, sham.
fingimiento m simulation, pretense.
fingir vt to feign, to fake; to invent; to imitate; **~se** vr to pretend to be; * vi to pretend.
finito/ta adj finite.
fino/na adj fine, pure; slender; polite; acute; dry (of sherry).
finura f fineness.
firma f signature; (com) company.
firmamento m firmament, sky, heaven.
firmar vt to sign.
firme adj firm, stable, strong, secure; constant; resolute; * m road surface.
firmeza f firmness, stability, constancy.
fiscal adj fiscal; * m/f district attorney.
fiscalía f office and business of the district attorney.
fiscalizar vt to inspect; to criticize.
fisco m treasury.
fisgar vt to pry into.
fisgón/ona m/f prying person, snooper.

física f physics.
físico/ca adj physical; * m/f physicist; * m physique.
fisonomía f physiognomy.
fisonomista m/f: **ser buen ~** to have a good memory for faces.
flaco/ca adj lean, skinny; feeble.
flagelación f flagellation.
flagrante adj flagrant.
flamante adj flaming, bright; brand-new.
flan m crème caramel.
flanco m flank.
flanquear vt (mil) to flank.
flaquear vi to flag; to weaken.
flaqueza f thinness, leanness; feebleness, weakness.
flash m flash.
flato m (med) flatulence; depression.
flatulento/ta adj flatulent.
flauta f (mus) flute.
flautista m/f flute player, flautist.
flecha f arrow.
fleco m hair cut straight across the forehead, fringe.
flema f phlegm.
flemático/ca adj phlegmatic.
flemón m ulcer in the gums.
flequillo m hair cut straight across the forehead, fringe.
fletar vt to freight (a ship).
flete m (mar) freight; charter.
flexibilidad f flexibility.
flexible adj flexible; compliant; docile.
flojedad f feebleness; laxity, laziness; negligence.
flojera f: **me da ~** I can't be bothered.
flojo/ja adj loose; flexible; lax, slack; lazy.
flor f flower.
florecer vi to blossom.
florero m vase.
floresta f wood, grove; beauty spot.
florete m fencing foil.
florido/da adj full of flowers; in bloom; choice.
florista m/f florist.
flota f fleet.
flotador m float.
flotante adj floating.
flotar vi to float.
flote m: **a ~** afloat.
flotilla f small fleet, flotilla.
fluctuación f fluctuation; uncertainty.
fluctuar vi to fluctuate; to waver.
fluidez f fluidity; fluency.
fluido/da adj fluid; (fig) fluent; * m fluid.
fluir vi to flow.
flujo m flux; flow; **~ de sangre** (med) loss of blood.
fluvial adj fluvial, river compd.
foca f seal.

F

foco *m* focus; center; source; floodlight; (light)bulb; *Lat Am* street light; *Lat Am* car headlight.

fofo/fa *adj* spongy; soft; bland.

fogata *f* blaze; bonfire.

fogón *m* stove; hearth.

fogonazo *m* flash; explosion.

fogosidad *f* dash, verve; fieriness.

fogoso/sa *adj* fiery; ardent, fervent; impetuous, boisterous.

folk *m* folk music.

follaje *m* foliage.

folletista *m/f* pamphleteer.

folleto *m* pamphlet; folder, brochure.

follón *m* (*col*) mess; fuss.

fomentar *vt* to encourage; to promote.

fomento *m* promotion.

fonda *f* hotel; inn; boarding house.

fondeadero *m* anchorage.

fondeado/da *adj Lat Am* wealthy.

fondear *vi* to drop anchor.

fondista *m/f* innkeeper.

fondo *m* bottom; back; background; space; ~s *mpl* stock, funds *pl*, capital; **a** ~ perfectly, completely.

fontanería *f* plumbing.

fontanero/ra *m/f* plumber.

footing *m* jogging.

forajido *m* outlaw.

foral *adj* belonging to the statute law of a country.

forastero/ra *adj* strange, exotic; * *m/f* stranger.

forcejear *vi* to struggle.

forense *adj* forensic; * *m/f* forensic scientist.

forjador/ra *m/f* framer; forger.

forjadura *f* forging.

forjar *vt* to forge; to frame; to invent.

forma *f* form, shape; pattern; (*med*) fitness; (*sport*) form; means, method; **de** ~ **que** in such a manner that.

formación *f* formation; form, figure; education; training.

formal *adj* formal; proper, genuine; serious, grave.

formalidad *f* formality; gravity.

formalizar *vt* (*law*) to formalize; to regularize; ~**se** *vr* to be regularized.

formar *vt* to form, to shape.

formidable *adj* formidable, dreadful; (*col*) terrific.

fórmula *f* formula.

formulario *m* formulary.

fornicación *f* fornication.

fornicador *m* fornicator.

fornicar *vi* to commit fornication, to fornicate.

fornido/da *adj* well-built.

foro *m* court of justice; forum.

forraje *m* forage.

forrajear *vt* to forage.

forrar *vt* to line; to face; to cover.

forro *m* lining; book jacket.

fortalecer *vt* to fortify, to strengthen.

fortaleza *f* courage; strength, vigor; (*mil*) fortress, stronghold.

fortificación *f* fortification.

fortificar *vt* to strengthen; to fortify (a place).

fortín *m* (*mil*) small fort.

fortuito/ta *adj* fortuitous.

fortuna *f* fortune; wealth.

forzar *vt* to force.

forzoso/sa *adj* indispensable, necessary.

forzudo/da *adj* strong, vigorous.

fosa *f* grave; pit.

fósforo *m* phosphorus; ~**s** *mpl* matches *pl*.

fósil *adj*, *m* fossil.

foso *vt* pit; moat, ditch, fosse.

foto *f* photo.

fotocopia *f* photocopy.

fotocopiar *vt* to photocopy.

fotografía *f* photography; photograph.

fotógrafo/fa *m/f* photographer.

frac *m* tails, dress coat.

fracasar *vi* to fail.

fracaso *m* failure.

fracción *f* fraction.

fractura *f* fracture.

fracturar *vt* to break (a bone).

fragancia *f* fragrance, sweetness of smell; odor.

fragante *adj* fragrant, scented.

fragata *f* (*mar*) frigate.

frágil *adj* fragile, frail.

fragilidad *f* fragility, brittleness; frailty.

fragmento *m* fragment.

fragosidad *f* roughness; denseness.

fragoso/sa *adj* craggy, rough, uneven.

fragua *f* forge.

fraguar *vt* to forge; to contrive; * *vi* to solidify, to harden.

fraile *m* friar, monk.

frambuesa *f* raspberry.

francés/sa *adj* French; * *m* French (language); * *m/f* Frenchman/woman.

franco/ca *adj* frank; candid; free, gratis.

franela *f* flannel; undershirt.

franja *f* strip, band, fringe.

franquear *vt* to clear; to overcome; to stamp (letters); ~**se** to unbosom oneself.

franqueo *m* postage.

franqueza *f* frankness.

franquicia *f* immunity from taxes.

frasco *m* flask.

frase *f* phrase.

fraternal *adj* fraternal, brotherly.

fraternidad *f* fraternity, brotherhood.

fratricida *m/f* fratricide (person).

fratricidio *m* fratricide (act).

fraude *m* fraud, deceit; cheat.

fraudulento/ta *adj* fraudulent, deceitful.
frazada *f Lat Am* blanket.
frecuencia *f* frequency.
frecuentar *vt* to frequent.
frecuente *adj* frequent.
freezer *m Lat Am* freezer.
fregadero *m* (kitchen) sink.
fregado *m* scouring, scrubbing; (*fig*) intrigue; underhand work.
fregar *vt* to scrub; to wash up.
fregona *f* kitchen maid, someone who washes dishes.
freír *vt* to fry.
frenar *vt* to brake; (*fig*) to check.
frenesí *m* frenzy.
frenético/ca *adj* frantic; frenzied, wild.
frenillo *m* speech impediment.
freno *m* bit (horse's); brake; (*fig*) check.
frente *f* front; (*mil*) front; face; ~ a ~ face to face; **en** ~ opposite; * *m* forehead.
fresa *f* strawberry.
fresal *m* strawberry plant; ground bearing strawberry plants.
fresco/ca *adj* fresh; cool; new; ruddy; * *m* fresh air; * *m/f* (*col*) shameless/impudent person.
frescura *f* freshness; frankness; cheek, nerve.
fresno *m* ash tree.
frialdad *f* coldness; indifference.
fricción *f* friction.
friega *f* rubbing; nuisance.
frígido/da *adj* frigid.
frigorífico *m* refrigerator.
frijol *m* bean.
frío/fría *adj* cold; indifferent; * *m* cold; indifference.
friolento/ta *adj Lat Am* chilly.
friolera *f* trifle
friso *m* frieze; wainscot.
fritada *f* dish of fried meat/fish.
fritar *vt Lat Am* to fry.
frito/ta *adj* fried.
frivolidad *f* frivolity.
frívolo/la *adj* frivolous.
frondosidad *f* foliage.
frondoso/sa *adj* leafy.
frontera *f* frontier.
fronterizo/za *adj* frontier *compd*; bordering.
frontón *m* (*sport*) pelota court; pelota.
frotación, frotadura *f* friction, rubbing.
frotar *vt* to rub.
fructífero/ra *adj* fruit-bearing, fruitful.
fructificar *vi* to bear fruit; to come to fruition.
fructuoso/sa *adj* fruitful.
frugal *adj* frugal, sparing.
frugalidad *f* frugality, parsimony.
fruncir *vt* to pleat; to knit; to contract; ~ **las cejas** to knit the eyebrows.
frustrar *vt* to frustrate.

fruta *f* fruit; ~ **del tiempo** seasonal fruit.
frutal *m* fruit tree.
frutera *f* fruit dish.
frutería *f* fruit shop.
frutero/ra *m/f* fruiterer, fruit seller; * *m* fruit basket.
frutilla *f* strawberry.
fruto *m* fruit; benefit, profit.
fuego *m* fire.
fuelle *m* bellows *pl*.
fuente *f* fountain; spring; source; large dish.
fuera *adv* out(side); away; ~ **de** *prep* outside; ¡~! out of the way!
fueraborda *m* outboard motor.
fuero *m* statute law of a country; jurisdiction.
fuerte *m* (*mil*) fortification, fort; forte; * *adj* vigorous, tough; strong; loud; heavy; * *adv* strongly; hard.
fuerza *f* force, strength; (electric) power; violence; **a** ~ **de** by dint of; ~**s** *mpl* troops *pl*.
fuga *f* flight, escape; leak (of gas).
fugarse *vr* to escape, to flee.
fugaz *adj* fleeting.
fugitivo/va *adj*, *m/f* fugitive.
fulano/na *m/f* so-and-so, what's-his-name/what's-her-name.
fulgurar *vi* to flash.
fullería *f* cheating.
fullero *m* cardsharp, cheat.
fulminar *vt* to fulminate; * *vi* to explode.
fumador/ra *m/f* smoker.
fumar *vt*, *vi* to smoke.
fumigación *f* fumigation.
funambulista *m/f* tightrope walker.
función *f* function; duties *pl*; show, performance.
funcionar *vi* to function; to work (of a machine).
funcionario/ria *m/f* official; civil servant.
funda *f* case, sheath; ~ **de almohada** pillowcase.
fundación *f* foundation.
fundador/ra *m/f* founder.
fundamental *adj* fundamental.
fundamentalismo *m* fundamentalism.
fundamentalista *adj*, *m/f* fundamentalist.
fundamento *m* foundation; groundwork; reason, cause.
fundar *vt* to found; to establish; to ground.
fundición *f* fusion; foundry.
fundir *vt* to fuse; to melt; to smelt; ~**se** *vr* (*com*) to merge; to bankrupt; to blow (of a fuse).
fúnebre *adj* mournful, sad; funereal.
funeral *m* funeral; ~**es** *mpl* funeral, funeral rites *pl*, obsequies *pl*.
funerario/ria *adj* funeral *compd*, funereal.
funesto/ta *adj* ill-fated, unfortunate; fatal.
furgón *m* wagon.
furgoneta *f* pick-up truck; station wagon.
furia *f* fury, rage.
furibundo/da *adj* furious; frenzied.

F

furioso/sa *adj* furious.
furor *m* fury, rage.
furtivamente *adv* furtively.
furtivo/va *adj* furtive.
furúnculo *m* (*med*) boil.
fusible *m* fuse.
fusil *m* rifle.
fusilar *vt* to shoot.
fusilero *m* rifleman.

fusión *f* fusion; (*com*) merger.
fusta *f* riding crop.
fútbol *m* football; ~ **americano** American football.
futbolista *m/f* football player, footballer.
fútil *adj* futile; trifling.
futilidad *f* futility.
futuro/ra *adj, m* future.

G

gabán m overcoat.

gabardina f raincoat.

gabarra f (mar) lighter.

gabinete m cabinet (in politics), study; office (of lawyers etc).

gaceta f gazette.

gachas fpl any soft/semi-liquid food; porridge.

gacho/cha adj curved, bent downward.

gafas fpl glasses pl, spectacles pl.

gafe m jinx.

gaita f bagpipe; flageolet.

gaitero/ra m/f bagpiper, bagpipe player.

gaje m: ~s del oficio occupational hazards pl.

gajo m segment (of orange).

gala f full dress; (fig) cream, flower; ~s fpl finery; **hacer ~ de** to display, to show off.

galán m lover; handsome young man; (theat) male lead.

galante adj gallant.

galanteador m lover, suitor.

galantear vt to court, to woo.

galanteo m gallantry, courtship.

galantería f gallantry; politeness; compliment.

galápago m tortoise.

galardón m reward, prize.

galardonar vt to reward, to recompense.

galaxia f galaxy.

galbana f laziness, idleness.

galeón m (mar) galleon.

galera f (mar) galley; wagon.

galería f gallery.

galgo m greyhound.

gallardete m (mar) pennant, streamer.

gallardía f fineness, elegance, gracefulness; dash.

gallardo/da adj graceful, elegant; brave, daring.

gallería f Lat Am cockpit.

galleta f cookie.

gallina f hen; * m/f (fig) coward; ~ ciega blindman's buff.

gallinero m henhouse, coop; poulterer; (theat) top gallery; hubbub.

gallineta f woodcock (bird).

gallo m cock.

galón m (mil) stripe; braid; galloon.

galopar vi to gallop.

galope m gallop.

galvánico/ca adj galvanic.

galvanismo m galvanism.

gallardete m (mar) pennant, streamer.

gallardía f fineness, elegance, gracefulness; dash.

gallardo, da adj graceful, elegant; brave, daring.

galleta f biscuit.

gallina f hen; * m/f (fig) coward; ~ ciega blindman's buff.

gallinero m henhouse, coop; poulterer; (theat) top gallery; hubbub.

gallineta f Lat Am woodcock (bird).

gallo m cock.

gama[1] f (mus) scale; (fig) range, gamut.

gama[2] f doe (of the fallow deer).

gamba f shrimp; prawn.

gamberro/rra m/f hooligan.

gamo m buck (of the fallow deer).

gamuza f chamois (goat antelope); chamois leather.

gana f desire, wish; appetite; will, longing; **de buena ~** with pleasure, voluntarily; **de mala ~** unwillingly, with reluctance.

ganadería f cattle raising; cattle; livestock.

ganadero m rancher; cattle dealer.

ganado m livestock, cattle pl; ~ **mayor** horses and mules pl; ~ **menor** sheep, goats and pigs pl.

ganancia f gain, profit; increase.

ganancial adj lucrative.

ganar vt to gain; to win; to earn; * vi to win.

gancho m hook; crook.

gandul adj, m/f layabout, lazy person.

ganga f bargain.

gangoso/sa adj nasal.

gangrena f gangrene.

gangrenarse vr to become gangrenous.

gangrenoso/sa adj gangrenous.

ganso/sa m/f gander; goose; (col) idiot.

garabatear vi, vt to scrawl, to scribble.

garabatos mpl scrawling letters/characters pl.

garaje m garage.

garage m Lat Am garage.

garante m/f guarantor; * adj responsible.

garantía f warranty, guarantee.

garañón m jackass, male donkey.

garapatear vi, vt to scrawl, to scribble.

garapiñar vt to freeze; to ice.

garbanzo m chickpea.

garbo m gracefulness, elegance; stylishness; generosity.

garboso/sa adj graceful; elegant, stylish; generous.

garduña f marten (animal).

gargajo m phlegm, spit.

garganta f throat, gullet; instep; neck (of a bottle); narrow pass between mountains; river gorge.

gargantilla f necklace.

gárgara f noise made by gargling.
gargarismo m gargling, gargle.
gargarizar vi to gargle.
garita f (mil) sentry box; (rail) signal box.
garra f claw; talon; paw.
garrafa f carafe; (gas) cylinder.
garrafal adj great, vast, huge.
garrapata f tick (insect).
garrocha f Lat Am vaulting pole.
garrotazo m blow with a stick/club.
garrote m stick, club, cudgel; (med) tourniquet; (law) garrote.
garrotillo m (med) croup.
garrucha f pulley.
garza f heron.
garzo/za adj blue-eyed.
gas m gas; petrol, gas.
gasa f gauze.
gaseoso/sa adj fizzy; * f lemonade.
gasfitero/ra m/f plumber.
gasoil m diesel (oil).
gasolina f gasoline.
gasolinera f service station.
gasómetro m gasometer.
gastador/ra m/f spendthrift.
gastar vt to spend; to expend; to waste; to wear away; to use up; ~se vr to wear out; to waste.
gasto m expense, expenditure; use.
gastronomía f gastronomy.
gata f she-cat; a ~s on all fours.
gatear vi to go on all fours.
gatera f catlover; (mar) cat hole.
gatillazo m click of the trigger in firing.
gatillo m trigger of a gun; (med) dental forceps.
gato m tomcat; jack, clamp, vice.
gatuno/na adj catlike, feline.
gaveta f drawer of a desk, locker.
gavilán m sparrow hawk.
gavilla f sheaf of corn.
gaviota f seagull.
gay adj invar, m (col) gay; homosexual.
gazapo m young rabbit; liar; lie.
gazmoñada, gazmoñería f prudery; hypocrisy.
gazmoñero/ra, gazmoño/ña adj hypocritical.
gaznate m gullet, wind pipe.
gazpacho m Spanish cold tomato soup.
gazuza f ravenous hunger.
gelatina f jelly; gelatin.
gemelo/la m/f twin.
gemido m groan, moan, howl.
geminiano/na adj Lat Am Geminian (zodiac sign).
Géminis m Gemini (zodiac sign).
gemir vi to groan, to moan.
genciana f (bot) gentian.
gendarme m policeman.
gendarmería f police.
genealogía f genealogy.

genealógico/ca adj genealogical.
generación f generation; progeny, race.
general m general; * adj general; en ~ generally, in general.
generalidad f generality.
generalizar vt to generalize.
generalmente adv generally.
genérico/ca adj generic.
género m genus; kind, type; gender; (com) cloth, material; ~s mpl goods pl, commodities pl.
generosidad f generosity.
generoso/sa adj noble, generous.
Génesis f Genesis.
genial adj inspired, brilliant; genial.
genio m nature, character; genius.
genital adj genital; * mpl ~es genitals pl.
genitivo m (gr) genitive case.
gente f people; nation; family.
gentil m/f pagan, heathen; * adj elegant; graceful; charming.
gentileza f grace; charm; politeness.
gentilhombre m gentleman.
gentío m crowd, throng.
genuflexión f genuflection.
genuino/na adj genuine; pure.
geografía f geography.
geográfico/ca adj geographical.
geógrafo/fa m/f geographer.
geología f geology.
geólogo/ga m/f geologist.
geometría f geometry.
geométrico/ca adj geometrical, geometric.
geranio m (bot) geranium.
gerenciar vt Lat Am to manage.
gerente m/f manager; director.
geriatría f (med) geriatrics.
germen m germ, bud; source, origin.
germinar vi to germinate, to bud.
gerundio m (gr) gerund.
gesticular vi to gesticulate.
gestión f management; negotiation.
gesto m face; grimace; gesture.
giganta f giantess.
gigante m giant; * adj gigantic.
gigantesco/ca adj gigantic, giant.
gilipollas adj invar (col) stupid; * m/f invar wimp.
gimnasia f gymnastics.
gimnasio m gymnasium.
gimnasta m/f gymnast.
gimnástico/ca adj gymnastic.
ginebra f gin.
ginecólogo/ga m/f gynecologist.
gira f trip, tour.
girar vt to turn around; to swivel; (com) to draw, to issue; * vi to go round, to revolve; (com) to do business; to draw.
giratorio/ria adj revolving.
girasol m sunflower.

giro *m* turning round; tendency; change; (*com*) draft.

gitano/na *m/f* Gypsy.

glacial *adj* icy.

glaciar *m* glacier.

glándula *f* gland.

glandular *adj* glandular.

globalización *f* globalization.

globo *m* globe; sphere; orb; balloon; ~ **aerostático** air balloon.

glóbulo *m* globule; corpuscle.

gloria *f* glory.

gloriarse *vr*: ~ **en** to glory in, to take pride in; to take delight in.

glorieta *f* bower, arbor; traffic circle.

glorificación *f* glorification; praise.

glorificar *vt* to glorify.

glorioso/sa *adj* glorious.

glosa *f* gloss; comment.

glosar *vt* to gloss; to comment on.

glotón/ona *m/f* glutton.

glotonería *f* gluttony.

gobernación *f* government.

gobernador/ra *m/f* governor.

gobernar *vt* to govern; to regulate; to direct.

gobierno *m* government.

goce *m* enjoyment.

gol *m* goal.

goleta *f* schooner.

golf *m* golf.

golfa *f* (*col*) slut.

golfito *m* Lat Am mini-golf.

golfo¹ *m* gulf, bay.

golfo² (*col*) urchin; lout.

golondrina *f* swallow.

golosina *f* delicacy, tidbit; bauble, trifle; sweet tooth.

goloso/sa *adj* sweet-toothed.

golpe *m* blow, stroke, hit; knock; clash; coup; **de** ~ suddenly.

golpear *vt* to beat, to knock; to punch.

golpiza *f* Lat Am beating.

goma *f* gum; rubber; elastic.

gomosidad *f* stickiness, viscosity.

gomoso/sa *adj* gummy, viscous.

góndola *f* gondola; (*rail*) freight car.

gondolero *m* gondolier.

gordinflón/ona *m/f* very fat person.

gordo/da *adj* fat, plump, big-bellied; first, main; (*col*) enormous.

gordura *f* grease; fatness, corpulence, obesity.

gorgojo *m* grub, weevil.

gorgorito *m* trill, warble.

gorila *m* gorilla.

gorjear *vi* to twitter, to chirp.

gorjeo *m* chirping.

gorra *f* cap; bonnet; (*mil*) bearskin.

gorrión *m* sparrow.

gorro *m* cap; bonnet.

gorrón/ona *m/f* scrounger.

gota *f* drop; (*med*) gout.

gotear *vt* to drip; to drizzle.

gotera *f* leak.

gótico/ca *adj* Gothic.

gotoso/sa *adj* gouty.

gozar *vt* to enjoy, to have, to possess; ~**se** *vr* to enjoy oneself, to rejoice.

gozne *m* hinge.

gozo *m* joy, pleasure.

gozoso/sa *adj* joyful, cheerful; content, glad, pleased.

grabación *f* recording.

grabado *m* engraving.

grabador *m* engraver.

grabadora *f* tape recorder.

grabar *vt* to engrave; to record.

gracejo *m* wit;, charm; gracefulness.

gracia *f* grace, gracefulness; wit; ¡(**muchas**) ~**s!** thanks (very much); **tener** ~ to be funny.

gracioso/sa *adj* graceful; beautiful; funny; pleasing; * *m* comic character.

grada *f* step of a staircase; tier; row; ~**s** *fpl* seats *pl* of a stadium/theater.

gradería *f* (flight of) steps *pl*; row of seats; Lat Am terraces.

grado *m* step; degree; **de buen** ~ willingly.

graduación *f* graduation; (*mil*) rank.

gradual *adj* gradual.

graduar *vt* to graduate.

gráfico/ca *adj* graphic; * *m* diagram; * *f* graph.

grajo/ja *m/f* rook.

grama *f* grass; Lat Am lawn.

gramática *f* grammar.

gramatical *adj* grammatical.

gramático/ca *m/f* grammarian.

gramo *m* gram.

gran *adj* = **grande**.

grana *f* grain; scarlet.

granada *f* (*mil*) grenade; pomegranate.

granadero *m* (*mil*) grenadier.

granadilla *f* passionflower; passion fruit.

granado *m* pomegranate tree.

granate *m* garnet (precious stone).

grande *adj* great; big; tall; grand; * *m/f* adult.

grandeza *f* greatness; grandeur; size.

grandiosidad *f* greatness; grandeur, magnificence.

grandioso/sa *adj* grand, magnificent.

granel *adv*: **a** ~ in bulk.

granero *m* granary.

granito *m* granite.

granizada *f* hail; hailstorm; shower, volley.

granizado *m* iced drink.

granizar *vi* to hail (weather).

granizo *m* hail (weather).

granja *f* farm.

granjero/ra *m/f* farmer.

G

grano *m* grain.

granuja *m* rogue; urchin.

grapa *f* staple; clamp.

grasa *f* suet, fat; grease.

grasiento/ta *adj* greasy; rusty; filthy.

grasoso/sa *adj Lat Am* greasy; rusty; filthy.

gratificación *f* gratification; recompense.

gratificar *vt* to gratify; to reward, to recompense.

gratis *adj* free; *adv* freely.

gratitud *f* gratitude, gratefulness.

grato/ta *adj* pleasant, agreeable.

gratuito/ta *adj* gratuitous; free.

gravamen *m* charge, obligation; nuisance; tax.

gravar *vt* to burden; (*com*) to tax.

grave *adj* weighty, heavy; grave, important; serious.

gravedad *f* gravity; graveness.

gravemente *adv* gravely, seriously.

gravilla *f* gravel.

gravitación *f* gravitation.

gravitar *vt* to gravitate; to weigh down on.

gravoso/sa *adj* onerous, burdensome; costly.

graznar *vi* to croak; to cackle; to quack.

graznido *m* croak; cackle; quack.

greda *f* clay.

gremial *f Lat Am* (labor) union.

gremialista *m/f Lat Am* union member.

gremio *m* union, guild; society; company, corporation.

greña *f* tangle; shock of hair.

greñudo/da *adj* disheveled.

gresca *f* clatter; outcry; confusion; wrangle, quarrel.

grieta *f* crevice, crack, chink.

grifo *m* faucet; gas station.

grilletes *mpl* shackles *pl*; fetters *pl*.

grillo *m* cricket; bud, shoot; **~s** *mpl* fetters *pl*, irons *pl*.

grima *f* disgust; annoyance.

gripe *f* flu, influenza.

gris *adj* gray.

gritar *vi* to cry out, to shout, to yell.

gritería *f* shouting, clamor, uproar.

grito *m* shout, cry, scream.

grosella *f* redcurrant; **~ negra** blackcurrant.

grosellero *m* currant bush.

grosería *f* coarseness, rudeness; vulgar comment.

grosero/ra *adj* coarse; rude, bad-mannered.

grosor *m* thickness.

grotesco/ca *adj* grotesque.

grúa *f* crane (machine); derrick.

grueso/sa *adj* thick; bulky; large; coarse; * *m* bulk.

grulla *f* crane (bird).

grumo *m* clot; curd.

grumoso/sa *adj* clotted.

gruñido *m* grunt; growl.

gruñidor/ra *m/f* grunter, mumbler; (*fig*) grumbler.

gruñir *vi* to grunt; to grumble; to creak (of hinges etc).

grupa *f* rump.

grupo *m* group.

gruta *f* grotto.

guachimán *m Lat Am* night watchman.

guadaña *f* scythe.

guagua *f* trifle, small thing.

gualdrapa *f* trappings *pl* (of a horse); tatter, rag.

guantada *f* slap.

guante *m* glove.

guapo/pa *adj* good-looking; handsome; smart.

guarda *m/f* guard, keeper; * *f* custody, keeping.

guardaagujas *m invar* (*rail*) switchman.

guardabosque *m* ranger, gamekeeper, forester.

guardacostas *m invar* coastguard vessel.

guardaespaldas *m/f invar* bodyguard.

guardafuegos *m invar* firescreen.

guardameta *m/f* goalkeeper.

guardapolvo *m* dust cover; coveralls *pl*.

guardar *vt* to keep, to preserve; to save (money); to guard; **~se** *vr* to be on one's guard; **~se de** to avoid, to abstain from.

guardarropa *f* wardrobe; cloakroom.

guardavallas *m/f invar Lat Am* goalkeeper.

guardia *f* guard; (*mar*) watch; care, custody; * *m/f* guard; policeman/woman; * *m* (*mil*) guardsman.

guardián/ana *m/f* keeper; guardian.

guardilla *f* garret, attic.

guarecer *vt* to protect; to shelter; **~se** *vr* to take refuge.

guarida *f* den, lair; shelter; hiding place.

guarismo *m* figure, numeral.

guarnecer *vt* to provide, to equip; to reinforce; to garnish, to set (in gold etc); to adorn.

guarnición *f* trimming; gold setting; sword guard; garnish; (*mil*) garrison.

guasa *f* joke.

guasón/ona *m/f* joker, jester.

gubernativo/va *adj* governmental.

guedeja *f* lock of hair.

guerra *f* war; hostility.

guerrear *vi* to fight, to wage war.

guerrero/ra *m/f* warrior; * *adj* martial, warlike.

guerrilla *f* guerrilla warfare; guerrilla group.

gueto *m* ghetto.

guía *m/f* guide; * *f* guidebook.

guiar *vt* to guide; (*auto*) to steer.

guijarral *m* stony place.

guijarro *m* pebble.

guillotina *f* guillotine.

guillotinar *vt* to guillotine.

guinda *f* cherry.

guindal *m* cherry tree.

guindilla *f* chili pepper.

guiñapo *m* tatter, rag; rogue.

guiñar *vt* to wink.

guión *m* hyphen (in writing); script (of film).

guirigay *m* gibberish, confused language.
guirnalda *f* garland, wreath.
güiro *m Lat Am* gourd.
guisado *m* stew.
guisante *m* (*bot*) pea.
guisar *vt* to cook.
guiso *m* cooked dish; stew; seasoning.
guisote *m* hash; (*col*) grub.
guitarra *f* guitar.

guitarrista *m/f* guitar player.
gula *f* gluttony.
gusano *m* maggot, worm.
gustar *vt* to taste; to sample; * *vi* to please, to be pleasing; **me gusta**... I like....
gusto *m* taste; pleasure, delight; liking.
gustosamente *adv* gladly, with pleasure.
gustoso/sa *adj* pleasant; tasty.
gutural *adj* guttural.

G

H

haba f broad bean.

haber vt to get, to lay hands on; to occur; * v imp: **hay** there is, there are; * v aux to have; ~**se** vr: **habérselas con uno** to have it out with somebody; * m income, salary; assets pl; (com) credit.

habichuela f bean.

hábil adj able, clever, skillful, dexterous, apt.

habilidad f ability, ableness, dexterity, aptitude.

habilitación f entitlement, qualification.

habilitar vt to qualify, to enable; to finance.

habitable adj habitable.

habitación f habitation, abode, lodging, dwelling, residence; room.

habitante m/f inhabitant, occupant.

habitar vt to inhabit, to live in.

hábito m dress; habit, custom.

habitual adj habitual, customary.

habituar vt to accustom; ~**se** vr to become accustomed to.

habla f speech; language; dialect.

hablador/ra m/f talkative person.

habladuría f rumor; ~**s** fpl gossip.

hablante adj speaking; * m/f speaker.

hablar vt (vi) to speak; to talk.

hacedor/ra m/f maker; author.

hacendado m property owner; landowner; rancher.

hacendoso/sa adj industrious.

hacer vt to make; to do; to put into practice; to perform; to effect; to prepare; to imagine; to force; (math) to amount to, to make; * vi to act, to behave; ~**se** vr to become.

hacha f torch; ax, hatchet.

hachazo m blow with an ax.

hacia adv toward(s); about; ~ **arriba/abajo** up(wards)/down(wards).

hacienda f property; large farm; ranch; **H~** Treasury.

hacinar vt to stack/pile up; to hoard.

hada f fairy.

hado m fate, destiny.

halagar vt to cajole, to flatter.

halago m cajolery; pleasure.

halagüeño adj attractive, flattering.

halcón m falcon.

halconero m falconer.

hálito m breath; gentle breeze.

hall m hall; (theat) foyer.

hallar vt to find; to meet with; to discover; ~**se** vr to find oneself; to be.

hallazgo m finding, discovery.

hamaca f hammock.

hambre f hunger; famine; longing.

hambreado/da adj Lat Am hungry; starved.

hambriento/ta adj hungry; starved.

hamburguesa f hamburger.

haragán/ana m/f idler, good-for-nothing.

haraganear vi to idle, to loiter.

haraganería f idleness, laziness.

harapo m rag, tatter.

haraposo adj ragged.

hardware m (comput) hardware.

harina f flour; ~ **de maíz** cornstarch.

harinoso/sa adj floury.

hartar vt to satiate; to glut; to tire, to sicken; ~**se** vr to gorge oneself (with food); to get fed up.

harto/ta adj full; fed up; * adv enough.

hartura f surfeit; plenty, abundance.

hasta prep up to; down to; until, as far as; * adv even.

hastío m loathing; disgust; boredom.

hatajo m lot, collection.

hato m clothes pl; herd of cattle, flock of sheep; provisions pl; crowd, gang, collection.

haya f beech tree.

haz m bunch, bundle; beam (of light).

hazaña f exploit, achievement.

hazmerreír m invar ridiculous person, laughing stock.

hebilla f buckle.

hebra f thread; vein of minerals/metals; grain of wood.

hebraico/ca adj belonging to the Hebrews.

hebreo/ea m/f Hebrew; Israeli; * m Hebrew language; * adj Hebrew; Israeli.

hechicería f witchcraft; charm.

hechicero/ra adj charming, bewitching; * m/f sorcerer/ sorceress.

hechizar vt to bewitch, to enchant; to charm.

hechizo m bewitchment, enchantment.

hecho/cha adj made; done; mature; ready-to-wear; cooked; * m action; act; fact; matter; event.

hechura f form, shape; fashion; making; workmanship; creature.

hectárea f hectare.

heder vi to stink, to smell bad.

hediondez f strong stench.

hediondo/da adj fetid, stinking.

hedor m stench, stink.

helada f frost; freeze-up.

helado/da adj frozen; glacial, icy; astonished; astounded; * m ice cream.

helar vt to freeze; to congeal; to astonish, to amaze; ~**se** vr to be frozen; to turn into ice; to congeal; * vi to freeze; to congeal.

helecho m fern.

hélice f spiral, helix; propeller.
helicóptero m helicopter.
hembra f female.
hemisferio m hemisphere.
hemorragia f hemorrhage.
hemorroides fpl hemorrhoids pl, piles pl.
henchir vt to fill up; ~**se** vr to fill/stuff oneself.
hendedura f fissure, chink, crevice.
hender vt to crack, to split; to go through; to open a passage.
hendidura f = **hendedura**.
heno m hay.
heraldo m herald.
herborizar vi to pick herbs; to collect plants.
heredad f inherited property; country estate, ranch, large farm.
heredar vt to inherit.
heredera f heiress.
heredero m heir.
hereditario/ria adj hereditary.
hereje m/f heretic.
herejía f heresy.
herencia f inheritance, heritage, heredity.
herida f wound, injury.
herido/da adj wounded, hurt.
herir vt to wound, to hurt; to beat, to strike; to affect, to touch, to move; to offend.
hermafrodita m hermaphrodite.
hermana f sister.
hermanar vt to match, to suit, to harmonize.
hermanastra f step-sister, half-sister.
hermanastro m step-brother, half-brother.
hermandad f fraternity; brotherhood.
hermano m brother; ~/**na** adj matched; resembling.
hermético/ca adj hermetic, watertight.
hermoso/sa adj beautiful, handsome, lovely; large, robust.
hermosura f beauty.
hernia f hernia, rupture.
héroe m hero.
heroicidad f heroism; heroic deed.
heroico/ca adj heroic.
heroína[1] f heroine.
heroína[2] f heroin (drug).
heroísmo m heroism.
herpes m herpes; * fpl (med) shingles.
herrador m farrier, blacksmith.
herradura f horseshoe.
herramienta f tool.
herrar vt to shoe (horses).
herrería f ironworks; forge.
herrero m smith, blacksmith.
hervidero m boiling; unrest; swarm.
hervir vt to boil; to cook; * vi to boil; to bubble; to seethe.
hervor m boiling; fervor, passion.
heterogeneidad f heterogeneousness.

heterogéneo/nea adj heterogeneous.
heterosexual adj, m/f heterosexual.
heterosexualidad f heterosexuality.
hexámetro m hexameter.
hez f sediment, dregs pl.
hidalgo m nobleman.
hidalguía f nobility.
hidra f hydra.
hidráulica f hydraulics.
hidráulico/ca adj hydraulic.
hidroavión m hydroplane, seaplane.
hidrofobia f hydrophobia.
hidrógeno m (chem) hydrogen.
hidromasaje m whirlpool bath.
hidrovía f Lat Am waterway.
hiedra f ivy.
hiel f gall, bile.
hielo m frost; ice.
hiena f hyena.
hierba f grass; herb.
hierro m iron.
hígado m liver; (fig) courage, pluck.
higiene f hygiene.
higiénico/ca adj hygienic.
higo m fig.
higuera f fig tree.
hijastro/tra m/f stepson/stepdaughter.
hijo/ja m/f son/daughter; child; offspring.
hilandero/ra m/f spinner.
hilar vt to spin.
hilera f row, line, file.
hilo m thread; wire.
hilván m tacking.
hilvanar vt to tack; to perform in a hurry.
himno m hymn.
hincada f Lat Am genuflection.
hincapié m: **hacer** ~ **en** to emphasize.
hincar vt to thrust in, to drive in.
hincha m/f (col) fan, supporter.
hinchado/da adj swollen; vain, arrogant.
hinchar vt to swell; to inflate; (fig) to exaggerate; ~**se** vr to swell; to become vain.
hinchazón f swelling, lump.
hinojo m (bot) fennel.
hipar vi to hiccup.
hipérbola f hyperbola, section of a cone.
hipérbole f hyperbole, exaggeration.
hiperbólico/ca adj hyperbolic, hyperbolical.
hipermercado, híper m hypermarket, superstore.
hípica f horseracing; showjumping.
hipnotismo m hypnotism.
hipo m hiccups pl.
hipocondria f hypochondria.
hipocondríaco/ca adj hypochondriac.
hipocresía f hypocrisy.
hipócrita adj hypocritical; * m/f hypocrite.
hipódromo m racetrack.

H

hipopótamo *m* hippopotamus.
hipoteca *f* mortgage.
hipotecar *vt* to mortgage.
hipotecario/ria *adj* belonging to a mortgage.
hipótesis *f* hypothesis.
hipotético/ca *adj* hypothetical.
hisopo *m* (*bot*) hyssop; water sprinkler; paintbrush.
hispano/na *adj* Hispanic.
Hispanoamérica *f* Spanish America.
hispanoamericano/na *adj,m/f* Spanish American.
histeria *f* hysteria.
histérico/ca *adj* hysterical.
historia *f* history; tale, story.
historiador/ra *m/f* historian.
histórico/ca *adj* historical; historic.
historieta *f* short story; short novel; comic strip.
hito *m* landmark; boundary post; target.
hocico *m* snout; **meter el ~ en todo** to meddle in everything.
hogar *m* hearth, fireplace; (*fig*) house, home; family life.
hogaza *f* large loaf of bread.
hoguera *f* bonfire; blaze.
hoja *f* leaf; petal; sheet of paper; blade.
hojalata *f* tin plate.
hojaldre *f* puff pastry.
hojarasca *f* dead leaves *pl*; rubbish.
hojear *vt* to turn the pages of.
hola *excl* hello!
holgado/da *adj* loose, wide, baggy; at leisure; idle, unoccupied, well-to-do; well-off.
holgar *vi* to rest; to be out of work; to be superfluous.
holgazán/ana *m/f* idler, loafer.
holgazanear *vt* to idle, to loaf around, to lounge around.
holgazanería *f* idleness, laziness.
holgura *f* looseness, bagginess; leisure; comfort; enjoyment.
hollín *m* soot.
holocausto *m* holocaust.
hombre *m* man; human being.
hombrera *f* shoulder pad.
hombro *m* shoulder.
hombruno/na *adj* manlike; virile, manly.
homenaje *m* homage.
homicida *m/f* murderer; * *adj* murderous, homicidal.
homicidio *m* murder.
homilía *f* homily.
homogeneidad *f* homogeneity.
homogéneo/nea *adj* homogeneous.
homólogo/ga *adj* homologous; synonymous.
homosexual *adj, m/f* homosexual.
honda *f* sling, catapult.
hondazo *m* throw with a sling.
hondo/da *adj* deep; profound; intense.

hondonada *f* dale, hollow; ravine.
hondura *f* depth, profundity.
honestidad *f* honesty; modesty; decency.
honesto/ta *adj* honest; modest.
hongo *m* mushroom; fungus; derby (hat).
honor *m* honor.
honorable *adj* honorable.
honorario/ria *adj* honorary; ~s *mpl* fees *pl*.
honorífico/ca *adj* creditable, honorable.
honra *f* honor, reverence; self-esteem; reputation; integrity; ~s **funebres** *pl* funeral honors *pl*.
honradez *f* honesty, integrity.
honrado/da *adj* honest; honorable; reputable.
honrar *vt* to honor.
honroso/sa *adj* honorable; respectable; honest.
hora *f* hour; time.
horadar *vt* to drill, to bore.
horario/ria *adj* hourly, hour *compd*; * *m* timetable.
horca *f* gallows; pitchfork; string (of garlic/ onions etc).
horcajadas *adv*: **a ~** astride.
horchata *f* a drink made from almonds/barley and orange flower water.
horero *m* *Lat Am* hour hand.
horizontal *adj* horizontal.
horizonte *m* horizon.
horma *f* mold, form.
hormiga *f* ant.
hormigón *m* concrete.
hormiguear *vi* to itch; to swarm, to team.
hormiguero *m* anthill; place swarming with people.
hormona *f* hormone.
hornada *f* batch.
horno *m* oven; furnace.
horóscopo *m* horoscope.
horqueta *f* *Lat Am* fork.
horquilla *f* pitchfork; hairpin.
horrendo/da *adj* horrible; frightful.
hórreo *m* granary.
horrible *adj* horrid, horrible.
horripilante *adj* hair-raising.
horror *m* horror, fright; atrocity.
horrorizar *vt* to horrify; ~se *vr* to be terrified.
horroroso/sa *adj* horrid, hideous, frightful.
hortaliza *f* vegetable.
hortelano/na *m/f* gardener; truck farmer.
hortera *f* shop/store assistant; (*fig*) coarse person.
hosco/ca *adj* sullen, gloomy.
hospedaje *m* board and lodging.
hospedar *vt* to put up, to lodge; to entertain.
hospedería *f* inn; guest room; hospice.
hospedero/ra *m/f* landlord/lady; host/hostess.
hospicio *m* orphanage; hospice.
hospital *m* hospital.
hospitalario/ria *adj* hospitable.

hospitalidad f hospitality.
hostal m small hotel.
hostelería f hotel business/trade.
hostería f inn, tavern, hostelry.
hostia f host; wafer; (col) whack, punch.
hostigar vt to lash, to whip; to trouble, to pester, to bore.
hostil adj hostile; adverse.
hostilidad f hostility.
hostilizar vt (mil) to harry, to harass.
hotel m hotel.
hoy adv today; now, nowadays; **de ~ en adelante** as from today.
hoya f hole, pit; Lat Am river basin.
hoyito m Lat Am dimple.
hoyo m hole, pit; excavation.
hoz f sickle; gorge.
hozar vi to grub (of pigs).
hucha f money-box.
hueco/ca adj hollow, concave; empty; vain, ostentatious; * m interval; gap, hole; vacancy.
huelga f strike.
huella f track, footstep.
huérfano/na adj, m/f orphan.
huero/ra adj empty; addled.
huerta f truck farm; irrigated region.
huerto m orchard; kitchen garden; **~ de hortalizas** truck farm.
hueso m bone; stone, core.
huésped/da m/f guest, lodger; innkeeper.
hueste f army; crowd.
huesudo/da adj bony.
huevera f eggcup.
huevo m egg.

huida f flight, escape.
huir vi to flee, to escape.
hule m oilcloth.
humanidad f humanity; corpulence; **~es** fpl humanities pl.
humano/na adj human; humane, kind.
humareda f cloud of smoke.
humeante adj smoking; steaming.
humear vi to smoke; * vt Lat Am to fumigate.
humedad f humidity, moisture; wetness.
humedecer vt to moisten; to wet; to soak.
húmedo/da adj humid; wet; moist, damp.
humildad f humility, humbleness; submission.
humilde adj humble.
humillación f humiliation, submission.
humillar vt to humble; to subdue; **~se** vr to humble oneself.
humo m smoke; fumes pl.
humor m mood, temper; humor.
hundir vt to submerge; to sink; to ruin; **~se** vr to sink, to go to the bottom; to collapse; to be ruined.
huracán m hurricane.
huraño/ña adj shy; unsociable.
hurgar vt to stir; to poke.
hurón m ferret; (fig) shy person; busybody.
huronear vt to ferret out.
hurtadillas adv: **a ~** by stealth.
hurtar vt to steal, to rob.
hurto m theft, robbery.
húsar m hussar.
husmear vt to scent; to pry into.
huso m spindle.

I

ictericia f jaundice.
ida f departure, going; (viaje de) ~ outward journey; ~ y vuelta round trip; ~s y venidas comings and goings pl.
idea f idea; scheme.
ideal adj ideal.
idealmente adv ideally.
idear vt to conceive; to think, to contrive.
ídem pn ditto.
idéntico/ca adj identical.
identidad f identity.
identificar vt to identify.
ideología f ideology.
idilio m idyll.
idioma m language.
idiosincrasla f idiosyncrasy.
idiota m/f idiot.
idiotez f idiocy.
idólatra m/f idolater.
idolatrar vt to idolize; to worship.
idolatría f idolatry.
ídolo m idol.
idoneidad f aptitude, fitness.
idóneo/nea adj suitable, fit.
iglesia f church.
ignominia f ignominy; infamy.
ignominioso/sa adj ignominious.
ignorancia f ignorance.
ignorante adj ignorant, uninformed.
ignorar vt to be ignorant of, not to know.
igual adj equal; similar; the same; al ~ equally.
igualar vt to equalize, to equal; to match; to level off; ~se vr to be equal; to agree.
igualdad f equality.
igualmente adv equally.
ijar m flank.
ilegal adj illegal, unlawful.
ilegalidad f illegality.
ilegitimidad f illegitimacy.
ilegítimo/ma adj illegal; illegitimate.
ileso/sa adj unhurt.
ilícito/ta adj illicit, unlawful; * m Lat Am crime.
ilimitado/da adj unlimited.
illustrar vt to illustrate; to instruct.
iluminación f illumination.
iluminar vt to illumine, to illuminate, to enlighten.
ilusión f illusion; hope; hacerse ~ones to build up one's hopes.
ilusionista m/f conjurer.
iluso/sa adj easily deceived.
ilusorio/ria adj illusory.

ilustración f illustration; enlightenment.
ilustre adj illustrious, famous.
imagen f image.
imaginable adj imaginable.
imaginación f imagination; fancy.
imaginar vt to imagine; to think up; * vi, ~se vr to imagine.
imán m magnet.
imbécil m/f imbecile, idiot.
imbecilidad f imbecility.
imbuir vt to imbue; to infuse.
imitable adj imitable.
imitación f imitation; a ~ de in imitation of.
imitador/ra m/f imitator.
imitar vt to imitate, to copy; to counterfeit.
impaciencia f impatience.
impacientar vt to make impatient; to irritate.
impaciente adj impatient.
impacto m impact.
impago/ga adj Lat Am unpaid.
impar adj odd.
imparcial adj impartial.
imparcialidad f impartiality.
impasibilidad f impassivity.
impasible adj impassive.
impavidez f intrepidity; cheek(iness).
impávido/da adj dauntless, intrepid; cheeky.
impecable adj impeccable.
impedimento f impediment, obstacle.
impedir vt to impede, to hinder; to prevent.
impeler vt to drive, to propel; to impel; to incite, to stimulate.
impenetrable adj impenetrable, impervious; incomprehensible.
impenitente adj impenitent.
impensado/da adj impenitent.
imperativo/va adj, m imperative.
imperceptible adj imperceptible.
imperdible m safety pin.
imperdonable adj unforgivable.
imperfección f imperfection.
imperfecto/ta adj imperfect.
imperial adj imperial.
impericia f lack of experience.
imperio m empire.
imperioso/sa adj imperious; arrogant, haughty; urgent.
impermeable adj waterproof; * m raincoat.
impermutable adj immutable.
impersonal adj impersonal.
impertérrito/ta adj intrepid, fearless.
impertinencia f impertinence; irrelevance.

impertinente adj not pertinent; touchy; impertinent.
imperturbable adj imperturbable; unruffled.
ímpetu m impetus; impetuosity.
impetuoso/sa adj impetuous.
implacable adj implacable, inexorable.
implicación f implication.
implicar vt to implicate, to involve.
implícito/ta adj implicit.
implorar vt to beg, to implore.
imponderable adj imponderable; (fig) priceless.
imponer vt to impose; to command; ~se vr to assert oneself; to prevail.
impopular adj unpopular.
importación f importing; imports pl.
importancia f importance; significance, weight; size.
importante adj important, considerable.
importar vi to be important, to matter; * vt to import; to be worth.
importe m amount, cost.
importunar vt to bother, to pester.
importunidad f pestering; annoyance.
importuno/na adj annoying; unreasonable.
imposibilidad f impossibility.
imposibilitar vt to make impossible.
imposible adj impossible; extremely difficult; slovenly.
imposición f imposition; tax; deposit.
impostor/ra m/f impostor, fraud.
impostura f imposture, deceit, cheat.
impotencia f impotence.
impotente adj impotent.
impracticable adj impracticable, unworkable.
imprecación f curse.
imprecar vt to curse.
imprecatorio/ria adj containing curses, full of evil wishes.
impreciso/sa adj imprecise, vague.
impregnarse vr to be impregnated.
imprenta f printing; press; printing office.
imprescindible adj essential.
impresión f impression; stamp; print; edition.
impresionante adj impressive; marvelous; tremendous.
impresionar vt to move; to impress; ~se vr to be impressed; to be moved.
impreso m printed paper; printed book.
impresor m printer.
impresora f printer; ~ láser laser printer.
imprevisto/ta adj unforeseen, unexpected.
imprimir vt to print; to imprint; to stamp.
improbable adj improbable, unlikely.
improperio m insult, taunt.
impropio/pia adj improper; unfit; unbecoming.
improvisar vt to extemporize; to improvize.
improviso/sa adj: de ~ unexpectedly.
imprudencia f imprudence; indiscretion; carelessness.

imprudente adj imprudent; indiscreet; unwise.
impudencia f shamelessness.
impudente adj shameless.
impúdico/ca adj shameless; lecherous.
impuesto/ta adj imposed; * m tax, duty.
impugnación f opposition, contradiction.
impugnar vt to oppose; challenge; impugn.
impulsivo/va adj impulsive.
impulso m impulse; thrust; (fig) impulse.
impune adj unpunished.
impunidad f impunity.
impureza f impurity.
impuro/ra adj impure;, foul.
imputable adj attributable, chargeable.
imputar vt to impute, to attribute.
inaccesible adj inaccessible.
inacción f inaction, inactivity.
inadmisible adj inadmissible.
inadvertencia f carelessness, inadvertence.
inadvertido/da adj unnoticed.
inagotable adj inexhaustible.
inaguantable adj unbearable, intolerable.
inalterable adj unalterable.
inapelable adj without appeal.
inapreciable adj imperceptible; invaluable.
inaudito/ta adj unheard-of.
inauguración f inauguration, opening.
inaugurar vt to inaugurate.
incalculable adj incalculable.
incandescente adj incandescent.
incansable adj untiring, tireless.
incapacidad f incapacity, inability.
incapaz adj incapable, unable.
incauto/ta adj incautious, unwary.
incendiar vt to kindle, to set on fire.
incendiario/ria adj incendiary; * m/f arsonist.
incendio m fire.
incentivo m incentive.
incertidumbre f doubt, uncertainty.
incesante adj incessant, continual.
incesto m incest.
incestuoso/sa adj incestuous.
incidencia f incidence; incident.
incidente m incident.
incidir vi: ~ en to fall upon; to influence, to affect.
incienso m incense.
incierto/ta adj uncertain, doubtful.
incineración f incineration; cremation.
incipiente adj incipient.
incisión f incision, cut.
incisivo/va adj incisive.
inciso m (gr) comma.
incitación f incitement.
incitar vt to incite; to excite.
incivil adj uncivil, rude.
inclemencia f inclemency, severity; inclemency (of the weather).

I

inclinación f inclination.
inclinar vt to incline; to nod, to bow (the head); ~**se** vr to bow; to stoop.
incluir vt to include, to comprise; to incorporate; to enclose.
inclusión f inclusion.
inclusive adv inclusive.
incluso/sa adj included; * adv inclusively; even.
incógnito/ta adj unknown; **de** ~ incognito.
incoherencia f incoherence.
incoherente adj incoherent.
incombustible adj incombustible, fireproof.
incomodar vt to inconvenience; to bother, to annoy.
incomodidad f inconvenience; annoyance; discomfort.
incómodo/da adj uncomfortable; annoying; inconvenient.
incomparable adj incomparable, matchless.
incompatibilidad f incompatibility.
incompatible adj incompatible.
incompetencia f incompetence.
incompetente adj incompetent.
incompleto/ta adj incomplete.
incomprehensible adj incomprehensible.
incomunicación f isolation; lack of communication.
incomunicado/da adj isolated, cut off; in solitary confinement.
inconcebible adj inconceivable.
incondicional adj unconditional; wholehearted; staunch.
inconexo/xa adj unconnected, disconnected.
inconfundible adj unmistakable.
incongruencia f incongruity, incongruence.
incongruo/grua adj incongruous.
inconmensurable adj immeasurable.
inconsciencia f unconsciousness; thoughtlessness.
inconsciente adj unconscious; thoughtless.
inconsecuencia f inconsequence.
inconsiderado/da adj inconsiderate, thoughtless.
inconsolable adj inconsolable.
inconstancia f inconstancy, unsteadiness.
inconstante adj inconstant, variable, fickle.
incontestable adj indisputable, incontrovertible, undeniable.
incontinencia f incontinence.
incontinente adj incontinent.
inconveniencia f inconvenience; impoliteness; unsuitability.
inconveniente adj inconvenient, unsuitable; impolite.
incorporación f incorporation, involvement.
incorporar vt to incorporate; ~**se** vr to sit up; to join (an organization), to become incorporated.
incorrecto/ta adj incorrect.
incorregible adj incorrigible.
incorruptible adj incorruptible.
incredulidad f incredulity.

incrédulo/la adj incredulous.
increíble adj incredible.
incremento m increment, increase; growth; rise.
increpar vt to reprehend, to reprimand.
incruento/ta adj bloodless.
inculcar vt to inculcate.
inculpar vt to accuse, to blame.
inculto/ta adj uncultivated; uneducated; uncouth.
incumbencia f obligation; duty.
incumbir vi: ~ **a uno** to be incumbent upon one.
incurable adj incurable; irremediable.
incurrir vt: ~ **en** to incur; to commit (a crime).
incursión f incursion, raid.
indagación f search, inquiry.
indagar vt to inquire into.
indebido/da adj undue; illegal, unlawful.
indecencia f indecency.
indecente adj indecent.
indecible adj unspeakable, unutterable.
indecisión f hesitation; indecision.
indeciso/sa adj hesitant; undecided.
indecoroso/sa adj unseemly, unbecoming.
indefectible adj infallible.
indefenso/sa adj defenseless.
indefinible adj indefinable.
indefinido/da adj indefinite.
indeleble adj indelible.
indemnización f indemnification, compensation.
indemnizar vt to indemnify, to compensate.
independencia f independence.
independiente adj independent.
indestructible adj indestructible.
indeterminado/da adj indeterminate; indefinite.
indicación f indication.
indicador m indicator; gage.
indicar vt to indicate.
indicativo/va adj, m indicative.
índice m ratio, rate; hand (of a watch/clock); index, table of contents; catalog; forefinger, index finger.
indicio m indication, mark; sign, token; clue.
indiferencia f indifference, apathy.
indiferente adj indifferent.
indígena adj indigenous, native; * m/f native.
indigencia f indigence, poverty, need.
indigente adj indigent, poor, destitute.
indigestión f indigestion.
indigesto/ta adj undigested; indigestible.
indignación f indignation, anger.
indignar vt to irritate; to provoke, to tease; ~**se** vr: ~ **por** to get indignant about.
indigno/na adj unworthy, contemptible, low.
indirecta f innuendo, hint.
indirecto/ta adj indirect.
indisciplinado/da adj undisciplined.
indiscreción f indiscretion, tactlessness; gaffe.
indiscreto/ta adj indiscreet, tactless.

indisoluble *adj* indissoluble.
indispensable *adj* indispensable.
indisponer *vt* to spoil, to upset; to make ill; ~**se** *vr* to fall ill.
indisposición *f* indisposition, slight illness.
indispuesto/ta *adj* indisposed.
indisputable *adj* indisputable, incontrovertible.
indistinto/ta *adj* indistinct.
individual *adj* individual; single (of a room); * *m* (*sport*) singles.
individualidad *f* individuality.
individualizar *vt* to specify individually.
individuo *m* individual.
indivisible *adj* indivisible.
indocilidad *f* disobedience.
índole *f* disposition, nature, character; class, kind.
indolencia *f* indolence, laziness.
indolente *adj* indolent, lazy.
indómito/ta *adj* untamed, ungoverned.
inducción *f* induction, persuasion.
inducir *vt* to induce, to persuade.
inductivo/va *adj* inductive.
indudable *adj* undoubted; unquestionable.
indulgencia *f* indulgence.
indulgente *adj* indulgent.
indultar *vt* to pardon; to exempt.
indulto *m* pardon; exemption.
industria *f* industry; skill.
industrial *adj* industrial.
industrialización *f* industrialization.
inédito/ta *adj* unpublished; (*fig*) new.
inefable *adj* ineffable, indescribable.
ineficacia *f* inefficacy.
ineficaz *adj* ineffective; inefficient.
ineptitud *f* inability; unfitness, ineptitude.
inepto/ta *adj* inept, unfit, useless.
inercia *f* inertia, inactivity.
inerme *adj* unarmed; defenseless.
inerte *adj* inert; dull; sluggish, motionless.
inescrutable *adj* inscrutable.
inesperado/da *adj* unexpected, unforeseen.
inestable *adj* unstable.
inestimable *adj* inestimable.
inevitable *adj* unavoidable.
inexactitud *f* inaccuracy.
inexacto/ta *adj* inaccurate, untrue.
inexorable *adj* inexorable.
inexperto/ta *adj* inexperienced.
infalibilidad *f* infallibility.
infalible *adj* infallible.
infame *adj* infamous.
infancia *f* infancy, childhood.
infanta *f* infanta, princess.
infante *m* infante, prince; (*mil*) infantryman.
infantería *f* infantry.
infanticida *m/f* infanticide (person).
infanticidio *m* infanticide (act).
infantil *adj* infantile; childlike; children's.

infarto *m* heart attack; ~ **de miocardio** heart attack.
infatigable *adj* tireless, untiring.
infección *f* infection.
infectar *vt* to infect.
infeliz *adj* unhappy, unfortunate.
inferior *adj* inferior.
inferioridad *f* inferiority.
inferir *vt* to infer.
infernal *adj* infernal, hellish.
infestar *vt* to harass; to infest.
infidelidad *f* infidelity, unfaithfulness.
infiel *adj* unfaithful; disloyal; inaccurate.
infierno *m* hell.
infiltración *f* infiltration.
infiltrarse *vr* to infiltrate.
ínfimo/ma *adj* lowest; of very poor quality.
infinidad *f* infinity; immensity.
infinitivo *m* (*gr*) infinitive.
infinito/ta *adj* infinite; immense.
inflación *f* inflation.
inflamable *adj* flammable.
inflamación *f* ignition; inflammation.
inflamar *vt* to inflame; to excite, to arouse; ~**se** *vr* to catch fire.
inflamatorio/ria *adj* inflammatory.
inflar *vt* to inflate, to blow up; (*fig*) to exaggerate.
inflexibilidad *f* inflexibility.
inflexible *adj* inflexible.
influencia *f* influence.
influir *vt* to influence.
influjo *m* influence.
infografía *f* computer graphics.
información *f* information; news; (*mil*) intelligence; investigation, judicial inquiry.
informal *adj* irregular, incorrect; untrustworthy; informal.
informalidad *f* irregularity; untrustworthiness; informality.
informar *vt* to inform; to reveal, to make known; ~**se** *vr* to find out; * *vi* to report; (*law*) to plead; to inform.
informática *f* computer science, information technology.
informe *m* report, statement; piece of information, account; * *adj* shapeless, formless.
infortunio *m* misfortune, ill luck.
infracción *f* infraction; breach, infringement.
infraccionar *vt* Lat Am to fine.
infractor/ra *m/f* offender.
infructuoso/sa *adj* fruitless, unproductive, unprofitable.
infundado/da *adj* groundless.
infundir *vt* to infuse, to instil.
infusión *f* infusion.
infuso/sa *adj* infused; introduced.
ingeniar *vt* to devise; ~**se** *vr:* ~ **para** to manage to.

ingeniería f engineering; ~ **genética** genetic engineering.

ingeniero/ra m/f engineer.

ingenio m talent; wit; ingenuity; engine; ~ **de azúcar** sugar mill.

ingenioso/sa adj ingenious, clever; witty.

ingenuidad f ingenuousness; candor, frankness.

ingenuo/nua adj ingenuous.

ingerir vt to ingest; to swallow; to consume.

ingle f groin.

inglés/esa adj English; * m English (language); * m/f Englishman/woman.

ingratitud f ingratitude, unthankfulness.

ingrato/ta adj ungrateful, thankless; disagreeable.

ingrediente m ingredient.

ingresar vt to deposit; * vi to come in.

ingreso m entry; admission; ~**s** mpl income; takings pl.

inhabilitar vt to disqualify, to disable.

inhabitable adj uninhabitable.

inherente adj inherent.

inhibición f inhibition.

inhibir vt to inhibit; to restrain.

inhumano/na adj inhuman.

inicial adj, f initial.

iniciar vt to initiate; to begin.

iniciativa f initiative.

inimaginable adj unimaginable, inconceivable.

inimitable adj inimitable.

ininteligible adj unintelligible.

iniquidad f iniquity, injustice.

injertar vt to graft.

injerto m graft.

injuria f offense; insult.

injuriar vt to insult, to wrong.

injurioso/sa adj insulting; offensive.

injusticia f injustice.

injusto/ta adj unjust.

inmaculado/da adj immaculate.

inmadurez f immaturity.

inmediaciones fpl neighborhood; surrounding area.

inmediatamente adv immediately, at once.

inmediato/ta adj immediate.

inmemorial adj immemorial.

inmensidad f immensity.

inmenso/sa adj immense.

inmensurable adj immeasurable.

inmigración f immigration.

inmigrante m/f immigrant.

inmigrar vi to immigrate.

inminente adj imminent.

inmobiliario/ria adj real-estate compd; * f estate agency.

inmoral adj immoral.

inmortal adj immortal.

inmortalidad f immortality.

inmortalizar vt to immortalize.

inmóvil adj immovable.

inmovilidad f immobility.

inmueble m property; * adj: **bienes** ~**s** real estate.

inmundicia f nastiness, filth.

inmundo/da adj filthy, dirty; nasty.

inmune adj (med) immune; free, exempt.

inmunidad f immunity; exemption.

inmutabilidad f immutability.

inmutable adj immutable.

inmutarse vr to turn pale.

innato/ta adj inborn, innate.

innecesario/ria adj unnecessary.

innegable adj undeniable.

innovación f innovation.

innovador/ra m/f innovator.

innovar vt to innovate.

innumerable adj innumerable, countless.

inocencia f innocence.

inocentada f practical joke.

inocente adj innocent.

inoculación f inoculation.

inocular vt to inoculate.

inoduro m lavatory.

inofensivo/va adj harmless.

inolvidable adj unforgettable.

inopinado/da adj unexpected.

inoxidable adj: **acero** ~ stainless steel.

inquietar vt to worry, to disturb; ~**se** vr to worry, to get worried.

inquieto/ta adj anxious, worried.

inquietud f uneasiness, anxiety.

inquilino/na m/f tenant; lodger.

inquirir vt to inquire into, to investigate.

insaciable adj insatiable.

insalubre adj unhealthy.

insalubridad f unhealthiness.

insano/na adj insane, mad.

inscribir vt to inscribe; to list, to register.

inscripción f inscription; enrollment, registration.

insecticida m insecticide.

insecto m insect.

inseguridad f insecurity.

inseminación f insemination; ~ **artificial** artificial insemination.

insensatez f stupidity, folly.

insensato/ta adj senseless, stupid; mad.

insensibilidad f insensitivity; callousness.

insensible adj insensitive; imperceptible; numb.

insensiblemente adv insensitively; imperceptibly.

inseparable adj inseparable.

inserción f insertion.

insertar vt to insert.

inservible adj useless.

insidioso/sa adj insidious.

insigne adj notable.

insignificante adj insignificant.

insignia f badge; ~**s** fpl insignia pl.

insinuación f insinuation.

insinuar vt to insinuate; ~**se** vr: to make advances; ~ **en** to worm one's way into.

insipidez f insipidness.
insípido/da adj insipid.
insistencia f persistence; insistence.
insistir vi to insist.
insolación f (med) sunstroke.
insolencia f insolence, rudeness, effrontery.
insolente adj insolent, rude.
insólito/ta adj unusual.
insolvencia f insolvency.
insolvente adj insolvent.
insomnio m insomnia.
insondable adj unfathomable; inscrutable.
insoportable adj unbearable.
inspección f inspection, survey; check.
inspeccionar vt to inspect; to supervise.
inspector/ra m/f inspector; superintendent.
inspiración f inspiration.
inspirar vt to inspire; (med) to inhale.
instalación f installation.
instalar vt to install; Lat Am to set up.
instancia f instance.
instantáneo/nea adj instantaneous; * f snap(shot);
    café ~ instant coffee.
instante m instant; **al** ~ immediately, instantly.
instar vt to press, to urge.
instigación f instigation.
instigar vt to instigate.
instinto m instinct.
institución f institution.
instituir vt to institute.
instituto m institute.
institutriz f governess.
instrucción f instruction.
instructivo/va adj instructive; educational.
instructor/ra m/f instructor, teacher.
instruir vt to instruct, to teach.
instrumento m instrument; tool, implement.
insuficiencia f lack, inadequacy.
insuficiente adj insufficient, inadequate.
insufrible adj insufferable, insupportable.
insulina f insulin.
insulso/sa adj insipid; dull.
insultar vt to insult.
insulto m insult.
insumos mpl Lat Am supplies pl; raw materials pl.
insuperable adj insuperable, insurmountable.
insurgente m/f insurgent.
insurrección f insurrection.
intacto/ta adj untouched; entire; intact.
integral adj integral, whole; **pan** ~ wholewheat bread.
integrar vt to make up; to integrate.
integridad f integrity; completeness.
íntegro/gra adj integral, entire.
intelectual adj, m/f intellectual.
inteligencia f intelligence; understanding.
inteligente adj intelligent.
inteligible adj intelligible.
intemperie f: **a la** ~ out in the open.

intempestivo/va adj untimely.
intención f intention, purpose; plan.
intencionado/da adj meaningful; deliberate.
intendencia f administration, management.
intendente m manager.
intensidad f intensity; strength.
intenso/sa adj intense, strong; deep.
intentar vt to try, to attempt.
intento m intent, purpose; attempt.
intercalación f insertion.
intercalar vt to insert.
intercambio m exchange, swap.
interceder vi to intercede.
interceptar vt to intercept.
intercesión f intercession, mediation.
intercesor/ra m/f intercessor, mediator.
interés m interest; share, part; concern, advantage; profit.
interesado/da adj interested; prejudiced; mercenary.
interesante adj interesting; useful, convenient.
interesar vt to be of interest to, to interest; ~**se** vr: ~**se en/por** to take an interest in; * vi to be of interest.
interfaz, interface f interface.
interferir vt to interfere with; to jam (a telephone); * vi to interfere.
interfono m intercom.
interinato m Lat Am temporary post.
interinidad f temporary holding of office.
interino/na adj provisional, temporary; * m/f temporary holder of a post; stand-in.
interior adj interior, internal; * m interior, inside.
interioridad f inwardness.
interiorismo m interior design.
interiorista m/f interior designer.
interjección f (gr) interjection.
interlocutor/ra m/f speaker.
intermediar vt to interpose.
intermedio/dia adj intermediate; * m interval.
interminable adj interminable, endless.
intermitente adj intermittent; m (auto) indicator.
internacional adj international.
internado m boarding school.
internar vt to intern; to commit; ~**se** vr to penetrate.
interno/na adj interior, internal; * m/f boarder.
interpelación f interpellation, appeal, plea.
interpelar vt to appeal to.
interpolar vt to interpolate; to interrupt.
interponer vt to interpose, to put in.
interposición f insertion; interjection.
interpretación f interpretation.
interpretar vt to interpret, to explain; (theat) to perform; to translate.
intérprete m/f interpreter; translator; (theat) performer.

interracial adj interracial.
interrogación f interrogation; question mark.
interrogante adj questioning.
interrogar vt to interrogate.
interrogatorio m questioning; (law) examination; questionnaire.
interrumpir vt to interrupt.
interrupción f interruption.
interruptor m switch.
intertanto adv Lat Am meanwhile.
intervalo m interval.
intervención f supervision, control; (com) auditing; (med) operation; intervention.
intervenir vt to control, to supervise; (com) to audit; (med) to operate on; * vi to participate; to intervene.
interventor/ra m/f inspector; (com) auditor; Lat Am administrator.
interviú f interview.
intestino/na adj internal, interior; * m intestine.
intimar vt to intimate; * vi to become friendly.
intimidad f intimacy; private life.
intimidar vt intimidate.
íntimo/ma adj internal, innermost; intimate, private.
intolerable adj intolerable, insufferable.
intolerancia f intolerance.
intolerante adj intolerant.
intranquilizarse vr to get anxious/worried.
intranquilo/la adj worried.
intransigente adj intransigent.
intransitable adj impassable.
intransitivo/va adj (gr) intransitive.
intratable adj intractable, difficult.
intrepidez f intrepidity; fearlessness.
intrépido/da adj intrepid, daring.
intriga f intrigue.
intrigante m/f intriguer.
intrigar vt, vi to intrigue.
intrínseco/ca adj intrinsic.
introducción f introduction.
introducir vt to introduce; to insert.
introductor m introducer.
introvertido/da adj, m/f introvert.
intrusión f intrusion.
intruso/sa adj intrusive; * m/f intruder.
intuición f intuition.
intuitivo/va adj intuitive.
inundación f inundation, flood(ing).
inundar vt to inundate, to overflow; to flood.
inusitado/da adj unusual.
inútil adj useless.
inutilidad f uselessness.
inutilizar vt to render useless.
invadir vt (mil) to invade; to overrun.
invalidar vt to invalidate, to render null and void.
inválido/da adj invalid, null and void; * m/f invalid.

invariable adj invariable.
invasión f invasion.
invasor/ra adj invading; * m/f invader.
invencible adj invincible.
invención f invention.
inventar vt to invent.
inventario m inventory.
invento m invention.
inventor/ra m/f inventor.
invernadero m greenhouse.
invernar vi to pass the winter.
inverosímil adj unlikely, improbable.
inverosimilitud f unlikeliness, improbability.
inversión f (com) investment; inversion.
inverso/sa adj inverse; inverted; contrary.
invertir vt (com) to invest; to invert.
investidura f investiture.
investigación f investigation, research.
investigar vt to investigate; to do research into.
investir vt to confer.
invicto/ta adj unconquerable.
invierno m winter.
inviolabilidad f inviolability.
inviolable adj inviolable.
invisible adj invisible.
invitado/da m/f guest.
invitar vt to invite; to entice; to pay for.
invocación f invocation.
invocar vt to invoke.
involucrar vt Lat Am to involve.
involuntario/ria adj involuntary.
invulnerable adj invulnerable.
inyección f injection.
ir vi to go; to walk; to travel; ~se vr to go away, to depart.
ira f anger, wrath.
iracundo/da adj irate; irascible.
iris m iris (eye); **arco** ~ rainbow.
ironía f irony.
irónico/ca adj ironic(al).
irracional adj irrational.
irradiación f irradiation.
irrazonable adj unreasonable.
irreal adj unreal.
irreconciliable adj irreconcilable.
irreflexión f rashness, thoughtlessness.
irregular adj irregular; abnormal.
irregularidad f irregularity; abnormality.
irremediable adj irremediable; incurable.
irremisible adj irretrievable; unpardonable.
irreparable adj irreparable.
irresistible adj irresistible.
irresoluto/ta adj irresolute; hesitant.
irreverencia f irreverence; disrespect.
irreverente adj irreverent; disrespectful.
irrevocable adj irrevocable.
irrisorio/ria adj derisory, ridiculous.
irritación f irritation.

irritar *vt* to irritate, to exasperate; to stir up; to inflame.

irrupción *f* irruption; invasion.

isla *f* island, isle.

Islam *m* Islam.

islámico/ca *adj* Islamic.

islote *m* small island.

istmo *m* isthmus.

italiano/na *adj* Italian; * *m* Italian (language); * *m/f* Italian man/woman.

ítem *m* item.

itemizar *vt Lat Am* to itemize.

itinerario *m* itinerary.

izar *vt* (*mar*) to hoist.

izquierda *f* left; left-hand side.

izquierdo/da *adj* left; left-handed.

J

jabalí m wild boar.
jabalina f wild sow; (*sport*) javelin.
jabón m soap.
jabonar vt to soap.
jaca f pony; *Lat Am* fighting cock.
jacinto m hyacinth.
jacuzzi m jacuzzi.
jactancia f boasting.
jactancioso/sa adj boastful.
jactarse vr to boast.
jadear vi to pant.
jaguar m jaguar.
jalea f jelly.
jaleo m racket, uproar.
jalón m pull, tug.
jamás adv never; **para siempre ~** for ever and ever.
jamón m ham; **~ de York** (cooked) ham; **~ serrano** cured ham.
jaqueca f migraine.
jarabe m syrup.
jarcia f (*mar*) ropes *pl*, rigging.
jardín m garden.
jardinería f gardening.
jardinero/ra m/f gardener; *Lat Am* outfielder.
jarra f jug, jar, pitcher; **en ~s, de ~s** with arms akimbo; with hands to the sides.
jarro m jug.
jarrón m vase.
jaspe m jasper.
jaspear vt to marble; to speckle.
jaula f cage; cell for mad people.
jauría f pack of hounds.
jazmín m jasmin.
jazz m jazz.
jean m *Lat Am* jeans.
jefatura f: **~ de policía** police headquarters.
jefe m chief, head, leader; (*rail*) **~ de tren** guard, conductor.
jején m *Lat Am* gnat.
jengibre m ginger.
jerarquía f hierarchy.
jerárquico/ca adj hierarchical.
jerga f coarse cloth; jargon.
jergón m coarse mattress.
jerigonza f jargon, gibberish.
jeringa f syringe.
jeroglífico/ca adj hieroglyphic; * m hieroglyph, hieroglyphic.
jersey m sweater, pullover.

Jesucristo m Jesus Christ.
jesuita m Jesuit.
jesuítico/ca adj Jesuitical.
jibia f cuttlefish.
jícara f small cup (for chocolate).
jilguero m goldfinch.
jinete/ta m/f horseman/woman, rider.
jipijapa m straw hat.
jirafa f giraffe.
jirón m rag, shred.
jocosidad f humor, jocularity.
jocoso/sa adj good-humored.
jol m *Lat Am* hall.
jonrón m *Lat Am* home run.
jonronear vi *Lat Am* to hit a home run.
jornada f journey; day's journey; working day.
jornal m day's wage.
jornalero m (day) laborer.
joroba f hump; * m/f hunchback.
jorobado/da adj hunchbacked.
jorobar vt to pester, to annoy.
jota f jot, iota; Spanish dance.
joven adj young; * m/f youth; young woman.
jovial adj jovial, cheerful.
jovialidad f joviality, cheerfulness.
joya f jewel; **~s** fpl jewelry.
joyería f jewelry; jeweler's place of business.
joyero/ra m/f jeweler.
juanete m (*med*) bunion.
jubilación f retirement.
jubilado/da adj retired; * m/f senior citizen.
jubilar vt to pension off; to superannuate; to discard; **~se** vr to retire.
jubileo m jubilee.
júbilo m joy, rejoicing.
judaico/ca adj Judaic, Jewish.
judaísmo m Judaism.
judía f bean; **~ verde** green bean, French bean.
judicatura f judicature; office of a judge.
judicial adj judicial.
judío/día adj Jewish; * m/f Jewish man/woman.
juego m play; amusement; sport; game; *Lat Am* match; gambling; **~s Olímpicos** Olympic Games.
juerga f binge; party.
jueves m invar Thursday.
juez m/f judge.
jugada f playing of a card; stroke, shot.
jugador/ra m/f player; gambler.
jugar vt, vi to play, to sport, to gamble.
jugarreta f bad play, unskillful play.
jugo m sap, juice.

jugoso/sa *adj* juicy, succulent.
juguete *m* toy, plaything.
juguetear *vi* to play.
juguetón/ona *adj* playful.
juicio *m* judgement, reason; sanity; opinion.
juicioso/sa *adj* judicious, prudent.
julio *m* July.
junco *m* (*bot*) rush; junk (small Chinese ship).
jungla *f* jungle.
junio *m* June.
junta *f* meeting; assembly; congress; council.
juntamente *adv* jointly; at the same time.
juntar *vt* to join; to unite; ~**se** *vr* to meet, to assemble; to draw closer.
junto/ta *adj* joined; united; near; adjacent; ~**s** together; * *adv*: **todo** ~ all at once.
juntura *f* junction; joint.
Júpiter *m* Jupiter (planet).
jurado *m* jury; juror; member of a panel.

juramento *m* oath; curse.
jurar *vt*, *vi* to swear.
jurídico/ca *adj* lawful, legal; juridical.
jurisdicción *f* jurisdiction; district.
jurisprudencia *f* jurisprudence.
jurista *m/f* jurist.
justa *f* joust, tournament.
justamente *adv* justly; just.
justicia *f* justice; equity.
justificación *f* justification.
justificante *m* voucher; receipt.
justificar *vt* to justify.
justo/ta *adj* just; fair, right; exact, correct; tight; * *adv* exactly, precisely; just in time.
juvenil *adj* youthful.
juventud *f* youthfulness, youth; young people *pl*.
juzgado *m* tribunal; court.
juzgar *vt*, *vi* to judge.

K

karaoke *m* karaoke.
ketchup *m* ketchup.
kilogramo *m* kilogram.
kilometraje *m* distance in kilometers.

kilómetro *m* kilometer.
kilovatio *m* kilowatt.
kiosco *m* kiosk.

L

la art f the; * pn her; you; it.
laberinto m labyrinth.
labia f fluency; (col) the gift of the gab.
labio m lip; edge.
labor f labor, task; needlework; farmwork; plowing.
laboratorio m laboratory.
laboriosidad f laboriousness.
laborioso/sa adj laborious; hard-working.
labrado/da adj worked; carved; wrought; * m cultivated land.
labrador/ra m/f farmer; peasant.
labranza f farming; cultivation; farmland.
labrar vt to work; to carve; to farm; (fig) to bring about.
labriego/ga m/f peasant.
laca f lacquer; hairspray.
lacayo m lackey, footman.
lacerar vt to tear to pieces, to lacerate.
lacio/cia adj faded, withered; languid; lank (hair).
lacónico/ca adj laconic.
laconismo m laconic style, terseness.
lacra f scar; blot, blemish; Lat Am scab.
lacrar vt to seal (with sealing wax).
lacre m sealing wax.
lactancia f lactation; breast-feeding.
lácteo/tea adj: **productos ~s** dairy products.
ladear vt to move to one side; to incline; **~se** vr to lean; to tilt.
ladera f slope.
ladino/na adj cunning, crafty.
lado m side; faction, party; favor, protection; (mil) flank; **al ~ de** beside; **poner a un ~** to put aside; **por todos ~s** on all sides.
ladrar vt to bark.
ladrido m bark, barking.
ladrillo m brick.
ladrón/ona m/f thief, robber, burglar.
lagar m wine press.
lagartija f (small) lizard.
lagarto m lizard.
lago m lake.
lágrima f tear.
lagrimal m corner of the eye.
lagrimoso/sa adj weeping, shedding tears.
laguna f lake; lagoon; gap.
laico/ca adj lay; * m layman.
lama f Lat Am slime; moss.
lamedura f licking.
lamentable adj lamentable, deplorable; pitiable.
lamentación f lamentation.
lamentar vt to be sorry about; to lament, to

regret; * vi, **~se** vr to lament, to complain; to mourn.
lamento m lament.
lamer vt to lick, to lap.
lámina f plate, sheet of metal; engraving.
lámpara f lamp.
lamparilla f nightlight.
lamparón m grease spot.
lampiño/na adj beardless.
lamprea f lamprey (fish).
lana f wool.
lance m cast, throw; move, play (in a game); event, incident.
lancero m (mil) lancer.
lancha f barge, lighter; launch.
langosta f locust; lobster.
langostino m king prawn.
languidez f languor.
lánguido/da adj languid, faint, weak.
lanudo/da adj wooly, fleecy.
lanza f lance, spear.
lanzada f stroke with a lance.
lanzadera f shuttle.
lanzamiento m throwing; (mar, com) launch, launching.
lanzar vt to throw; (sport) to bowl, to pitch; to launch, to fling; (law) to evict.
lapicero m pencil, ballpoint pen; Lat Am propelling pencil.
lápida f flat stone, tablet.
lapidario/ria adj, m lapidary.
lápiz m pencil; propelling pencil.
lapso m interval; error.
lapsus m error, mistake.
largamente adv for a long time.
largar vt to loosen, to slacken; to let go; to launch; to throw out; **~se** vr (col) to beat it.
largo/ga adj long; lengthy, generous; copious; **a la ~a** in the end, eventually.
largueza f liberality, generosity.
largura f length.
laringe f larynx.
laringitis f laryngitis.
las art fpl the; * pn them; you.
lascivia f lasciviousness; lewdness.
lascivo/va adj lascivious; lewd.
láser m laser.
lasitud f lassitude, weariness.
lástima f compassion, pity; shame.
lastimadura f Lat Am graze.
lastimar vt to hurt; to wound; to feel pity for; **~se** vr to hurt oneself.

lastimero/ra *adj* pitiful, pathetic.
lastimoso/sa *adj* pathetic, mournful.
lastrar *vt* to ballast (a ship).
lastre *m* ballast; good sense.
lata *f* tin; can; (*col*) nuisance.
lateral *adj* lateral.
latero/ra *m/f Lat Am* tinsmith.
latido *m* (heart)beat.
latifundio *m* large estate.
latigazo *m* lash, crack (of a whip).
látigo *m* whip.
latín *m* Latin.
latinizar *vt* to Latinize.
latino/na *adj* Latin.
Latinoamérica *f* Latin America.
latinoamericano/na *adj, m/f* Latin American.
latir *vi* to beat, to palpitate.
latitud *f* latitude.
latón *m* brass.
latoso/sa *adj* annoying; boring.
latrocinio *m* theft, robbery.
laúd *f* lute (musical instrument).
laudable *adj* laudable, praiseworthy.
láudano *m* laudanum.
laureado/da *adj* honored; * *m* laureate.
laurel *m* (*bot*) laurel; reward.
lava *f* lava.
lavabo *m* washbasin; washroom.
lavadero *m* washing place; laundry.
lavado *m* washing; laundry.
lavadora *f* washing machine.
lavanda *f* lavender.
lavandera *f* laundress.
lavandería *f* laundry; ~ **automática** Laundromat™.
lavaparabrisas *m invar* windshield washer.
lavaplatos *m invar* dishwasher.
lavar *vt* to wash; to wipe away; **~se** *vr* to wash oneself.
lavativa *f* (*med*) enema; (*fig*) nuisance.
laxante *m* (*med*) laxative.
laxitud *f* laxity, slackness, laxness.
laxo/xa *adj* lax, slack.
lazada *f* bow, knot.
lazarillo *m*: **perro ~** guide dog.
lazo *m* knot; bow; snare, trap; tie; bond.
le *pn* him; you; (*dative*) to him; to her; to it; to you.
leal *adj* loyal; faithful.
lealtad *f* loyalty.
lebrel *m* greyhound.
lebrillo *m* glazed earthenware dish.
lección *f* reading; lesson; lecture; class.
leche *f* milk.
lechera *f* milkmaid, dairymaid; milk can, milk churn.
lechería *f* dairy.
lecho *m* bed; layer.
lechón *m* sucking pig.
lechuga *f* lettuce.

lechuza *f* owl.
lector/ra *m/f* reader.
lectura *f* reading.
leer *vt, vi* to read.
legado *m* bequest, legacy; legate.
legajo *m* file.
legal *adj* legal; trustworthy.
legalidad *f* legality.
legalización *f* legalization.
legalizar *vt* to legalize.
legaña *f* sleep (in eyes).
legar *vt* to leave, to bequeath.
legible *adj* legible.
legión *f* legion.
legionario/ria *m/f* legionary.
legislación *f* legislation.
legislador/ra *m/f* legislator, lawmaker.
legislar *vt* to legislate.
legislativo/va *adj* legislative.
legislatura *f* legislature.
legitimar *vt* to legitimize.
legitimidad *f* legitimacy.
legítimo/ma *adj* legitimate, lawful; authentic.
legua *f* league.
legumbres *fpl* pulses *pl*.
leído/da *adj* well-read.
lejano/na *adj* distant, remote; far.
lejía *f* bleach.
lejos *adv* at a great distance, far off.
lelo/la *adj* stupid, ignorant; * *m/f* idiot.
lema *m* motto; slogan.
lencería *f* linen, drapery.
lengua *f* tongue; language.
lenguado *m* sole.
lenguaje *m* language.
lente *m/f* lens; ~ **de contacto** contact lense; **~s** *mpl Lat Am* glasses.
lenteja *f* lentil.
lentilla *f* contact lens.
lentitud *f* slowness.
lento/ta *adj* slow.
leña *f* wood, lumber.
leñador *m* woodsman, woodcutter.
leño *m* block, log; trunk of a tree.
leñoso/sa *adj* woody.
Leo *m* Leo (zodiac sign).
león *m* lion; *Lat Am* puma.
leona *f* lioness.
leonado/da *adj* lion-colored, tawny.
leonino/na *adj Lat Am* Leonian (zodiac sign).
leopardo *m* leopard.
leotardos *mpl* tights.
lepra *f* leprosy.
leproso/sa *adj* leprous; * *m/f* leper.
lerdo/da *adj* slow, heavy; dull; slow-witted.
les *pn* them; you; (*dativo*) to them; to you.
lesbiana *adj, f* lesbian.
lesión *f* wound; injury; damage.

letal *adj* mortal, deadly.
letanía *f* litany.
letárgico/ca *adj* lethargic.
letargo *m* lethargy.
letra *f* letter; handwriting; printing type; draft of a song; draft; ~s *fpl* letters *pl*, learning.
letrado/da *adj* learned, lettered; * *m/f* lawyer; counsel.
letrero *m* sign; label.
letrina *f* latrine.
leucemia *f* leukemia.
leva *m* (*mar*) weighing anchor; (*mil*) levy.
levadizo/za *adj* that can be lifted/raised; **puente ~** drawbridge.
levadura *f* yeast; brewer's yeast.
levantamiento *m* raising; insurrection.
levantar *vt* to raise, to lift up; to build; to elevate; to hearten, to cheer up; ~se *vr* to get up; to stand up.
levante *m* Levant; east; east wind.
leve *adj* light; trivial.
levita *f* a heavy overcoat; greatcoat, frock coat.
léxico *m* vocabulary.
ley *f* law; standard (for metal).
leyenda *f* legend.
liar *vt* to tie, to bind; to confuse.
libelo *m* petition; satire, lampoon.
libélula *f* dragonfly.
liberación *f* liberation; release.
liberal *adj* liberal, generous; * *m/f* liberal.
liberalidad *f* liberality, generosity.
libertad *f* liberty, freedom.
libertador/ra *m/f* liberator.
libertar *vt* to free, to set at liberty; to exempt, to clear from an obligation/debt.
libertinaje *m* licentiousness.
libertino/na *m/f* permissive person.
libra *f* pound; ~ **esterlina** pound sterling.
Libra *f* Libra (zodiac sign).
librano/na *adj* *Lat Am* Libran (zodiac sign).
librar *vt* to free, to deliver; (*com*) to draw; to make out (a check); (*law*) to exempt; to fight (a battle); ~se *vr* to escape.
libre *adj* free; exempt; vacant.
libremente *adv* freely.
librería *f* bookshop.
librero/ra *m/f* bookseller.
libreta *f* notebook; ~ **de ahorros** savings book.
libretista *m/f* *Lat Am* screenwriter.
libreto *m* *Lat Am* script.
libro *m* book.
licencia *f* license; licentiousness; *Lat Am* leave.
licenciado/da *adj* licensed; * *m/f* graduate.
licenciar *vt* to permit, to allow; to license; to discharge; to confer a degree upon; ~se *vr* to graduate.
licencioso/sa *adj* licentious, dissolute.
liceo *m* lyceum; secondary school.

lícitamente *adv* lawfully.
lícito/ta *adj* lawful, fair; permissible.
licor *m* liquor.
licuadora *f* blender, liquidizer.
lid *m* contest, fight; dispute.
líder *m/f* leader.
liderazgo *m* leadership.
liebre *f* hare.
lienzo *m* linen; canvas; face/front of a building.
liga *f* garter; birdlime; league; coalition; alloy.
ligadura *f* (*med*, *mus*) ligature; binding; bond, tie.
ligamento *m* ligament; tie; bond.
ligar *vt* to tie, to bind, to fasten; ~se *vr* to commit oneself; * *vi* to mix, blend; (*col*) to pick up.
ligazón *f* union, connection.
ligereza *f* lightness; swiftness; agility; superficiality.
ligero/ra *adj* light, swift; agile; superficial.
liguero *m* garter belt.
lija *f* dogfish; sandpaper.
lijar *vt* to smooth, to sandpaper.
lila *f* lilac.
lima *f* file.
limadura *f* filing.
limar *vt* to file; to polish.
limitación *f* limitation, restriction.
limitado/da *adj* limited.
limitar *vt* to limit; to restrict; to cut down.
límite *m* limit, boundary.
limítrofe *adj* neighboring, bordering.
limón *m* lemon.
limonada *f* lemonade.
limonar *m* plantation/orchard of lemon trees.
limosna *f* alms *pl*, charity.
limpiabotas *m/f* *invar* shoeshine boy/girl.
limpiaparabrisas *m* *invar* windshield wiper.
limpiar *vt* to clean; to cleanse; to purify; to polish; (*fig*) to clean up.
limpieza *f* cleanliness; cleaning; cleansing; polishing; purity.
limpio/pia *adj* clean; neat; pure.
linaje *m* lineage, family, descent.
linaza *f* linseed.
lince *m* lynx.
linchar *vt* to lynch.
lindar *vi* to be adjacent.
linde *m* boundary.
lindero *m* edge; boundary.
lindo/da *adj* pretty; lovely.
lindura *f* *Lat Am* prettiness.
línea *f* line; cable; outline.
lineal *adj* linear.
lingote *m* ingot.
lingüista *m/f* linguist.
lino *m* flax.
linterna *f* flashlight; lantern, lamp; torch.
lío *m* bundle, parcel; (*col*) muddle, mess.
liposucción *f* liposuction.
liquidación *f* liquidation.

liquidar *vt* to liquidate; to settle (accounts).
líquido/da *adj* liquid.
lira *f* (*mus*) lyre.
lirio *m* (*bot*) iris.
lirón *m* dormouse; (*fig*) sleepyhead.
lisiado/da *adj* injured; * *m/f* physically disabled person.
lisiar *vt* to injure; to hurt.
liso/sa *adj* plain, even, flat, smooth.
lisonja *f* adulation, flattery.
lisonjear *vt* to flatter.
lisonjero/ra *m/f* flatterer; * *adj* flattering; pleasing.
lista *f* list; school register; catalog; menu.
lista de correos *f* general delivery.
listo/ta *adj* ready; smart, clever.
listón *m* ribbon; strip (of wood/metal).
litera *f* berth; bunk, bunk bed.
literal *adj* literal.
literario/ria *adj* literary.
literato/ta *adj* literary; * *m/f* writer, literary person; ~s *mpl* literati *pl*.
literatura *f* literature.
litigar *vt* to fight; * *vi* (*law*) to go to law; (*fig*) to dispute.
litigio *m* lawsuit.
litografía *f* lithography.
litográfico/ca *adj* lithographic.
litoral *adj* coastal; * *m* coast.
litro *m* liter.
liturgia *f* liturgy.
litúrgico/ca *adj* liturgical.
liviandad *f* fickleness; triviality; lightness.
liviano/na *adj* light; fickle; trivial.
lívido/da *adj* livid.
llaga *f* wound; sore.
llama *f* flame; llama (animal).
llamada *f* call.
llamado *m* *Lat Am* call.
llamador *m* door-knocker.
llamamiento *m* call.
llamar *vt* to call; to name; to summon; to ring up, to telephone; * *vi* to knock at the door; to ring up, to telephone; ~se *vr* to be named.
llamarada *f* blaze; outburst.
llamativo/va *adj* showy; loud (color).
llano/na *adj* plain; even, level, smooth; clear, evident; * *m* plain.
llanta *f* (wheel) rim; tire; inner (tube); *Lat Am* tire.
llanto *m* flood of tears, crying.
llanura *f* evenness, flatness; plain, prairie.
llave *f* faucet; key; ~ **maestra** master key.
llavero *m* key ring.
llegada *f* arrival, coming.
llegar *vi* to arrive; ~ **a** to reach; ~se *vr* to come near, to approach.
llenar *vt* to fill; to cover; to fill out (a form); to satisfy, to fulfill; ~se *vr* to gorge oneself.

lleno/na *adj* full, full up; complete.
llevadero/ra *adj* tolerable.
llevar *vt* to take; to wear; to carry; to convey, to transport; to drive; to lead; to bear; ~se *vr* to carry off, to take away.
llorar *vt*, *vi* to weep, to cry.
lloriquear *vt* to whine.
lloro *m* weeping, crying.
llorón/ona *m/f* tearful person; crybaby.
lloroso/sa *adj* mournful, full of tears.
llover *vi* to rain.
lloviznar *vi* to drizzle.
lluvia *f* rain; ~ **ácida** acid rain.
lluvioso/sa *adj* rainy.
lo *pn* it; him; you; * *art* the.
loable *adj* laudable.
loar *vt* to praise.
lobato *m* young wolf.
lobo *m* wolf.
lóbrego/ga *adj* murky, dark, gloomy.
lóbulo *m* lobe.
local *adj* local; * *m* place, site.
localidad *f* locality; location.
localizar *vt* to localize.
loción *f* lotion.
loco/ca *adj* mad; * *m/f* mad person.
locomoción *f* *Lat Am* public transport.
locomotora *f* locomotive.
locuacidad *f* loquacity.
locuaz *adj* loquacious, talkative.
locución *f* expression.
locura *f* madness, folly.
locutor/ra *m/f* (*rad*) announcer; (*TV*) newsreader.
locutorio *m* telephone booth.
lodazal *m* muddy place.
lodo *m* mud, mire.
logaritmo *m* logarithm.
lógica *f* logic.
lógico/ca *adj* logical.
lograr *vt* to achieve; to gain, to obtain.
logro *m* achievement; success.
loma *f* small hill, hillock.
lombarda *f* red cabbage.
lombriz *f* worm.
lomo *m* loin; back (of an animal); spine (of a book); **llevar/traer a** ~ to carry on the back.
lona *f* canvas.
loncha *f* slice; rasher.
longaniza *f* pork sausage.
longitud *f* length; longitude.
lonja[1] *f* slice; rasher.
lonja[2] *f* market, exchange; ~ **de pescado** fish market.
loro *m* parrot.
los *art mpl* the; * *pn* them; you.
losa *f* flagstone.
lote *m* lot; portion; *Lat Am* plot of land.
lotería *f* lottery.

loza f crockery.

lozanía f luxuriance, lushness; vigor; self-assurance.

lozano/na adj luxuriant, lush; sprightly.

lubricante m lubricant.

lucero m bright star; ~ **del alba** morning star.

lucha f struggle, fight.

luchador/ra m/f fighter; * m wrestler.

luchar vi to struggle; to wrestle.

lúcido/da adj lucid.

luciérnaga f glowworm.

lucimiento m splendor, luster; brightness.

lución m slowworm.

lucir vt to light (up); to show off; * vi to shine; Lat Am to look; ~**se** vr to make a fool of oneself.

lucrativo/va adj lucrative.

lucro m gain, profit.

luego adv next; afterward(s); **desde** ~ of course.

lugar m place, spot; village; reason; **en** ~ **de** instead of, in lieu of.

lugareño/ña adj belonging to a village; * m/f inhabitant of a village.

lugarteniente m deputy.

lúgubre adj lugubrious; sad, gloomy.

lujo m luxury; abundance.

lujoso/sa adj luxurious; showy; profuse, lavish.

lujuria f lust.

lujurioso/sa adj lustful, lewd.

lumbre f fire; light.

lumbrera f luminary; skylight.

luminaria f illumination.

luminoso/sa adj luminous, shining.

luna f moon; glass plate for mirrors; lens.

lunar m mole, spot; * adj lunar.

lunático/ca adj, m/f lunatic.

lunes m invar Monday.

lupa f magnifying glass, magnifier.

lupanar m brothel.

lustre m gloss, luster; splendor.

lustro m lustrum, space of five years.

lustroso/sa adj bright, brilliant.

luteranismo m Lutheranism.

luterano/na adj, m/f Lutheran.

luto m mourning (dress); grief.

luz f light.

M

macarrones *mpl* macaroni.
macedonia *f*: ~ **de frutas** fruit salad.
macerar *vt* to macerate, to soften.
maceta *f* flowerpot.
machacar *vt* to pound, to crush; * *vi* to insist, to go on.
machacón/ona *adj* wearisome, tedious.
machete *m* machete, cutlass.
machista *adj, m* sexist.
macho *adj* male; *(fig)* virile; * *m* male; *(fig)* he-man.
machucar *vt* to pound, to bruise.
macilento/ta *adj* lean; haggard, withered.
macizo/za *adj* massive; solid; * *m* mass, chunk.
madeja *f* skein of thread; mop of hair.
madera *f* lumber, timber, wood.
madero *m* lumber beam, timber beam.
madrastra *f* stepmother.
madraza *f* loving mother.
madre *f* mother; womb.
madreperla *f* mother-of-pearl.
madreselva *f* honeysuckle.
madrigal *m* madrigal.
madriguera *f* burrow; den.
madrina *f* godmother.
madroño *m* strawberry plant.
madrugada *f* dawn; **de** ~ at day break.
madrugador/ra *m/f* early riser.
madrugar *vi* to get up early; to get ahead.
madurar *vt* to ripen; * *vi* to ripen, to grow ripe; to mature.
madurez *f* maturity; ripeness; wisdom.
maduro/ra *adj* ripe, mature.
maestra *f* mistress; schoolmistress; teacher.
maestría *f* mastery, skill; *Lat Am* master's degree.
maestro *m* master; teacher; ~/**tra** *adj* masterly, skilled; principal.
magia *f* magic.
mágico/ca *adj* magical.
magisterio *m* teaching; teaching profession; teachers *pl*.
magistrado/da *m/f* magistrate.
magistral *adj* magisterial; masterly.
magistratura *f* magistracy.
magnanimidad *f* magnanimity.
magnánimo/ma *adj* magnanimous.
magnate *m* magnate.
magnético/ca *adj* magnetic.
magnetismo *m* magnetism.
magnetizar *vt* to magnetize.
magnetofón, magnetófono *m* tape recorder.
magnetofónico/ca *adj*: **cinta magnetofónica** recording tape.

magnificencia *f* magnificence, splendor.
magnífico/ca *adj* magnificent, splendid.
magnitud *f* magnitude.
mago/ga *m/f* magician.
magro/gra *adj* thin, lean; meager.
magulladura *f* bruise.
magullar *vt* to bruise; to damage; *(col)* to bash.
magullón *m Lat Am* bruise.
mahometano/na *m/f, adj* Muslim.
mahometanismo *m* Islam.
mahonesa *f* mayonnaise.
maíz *m* corn; maize.
maizal *m* corn field.
majada *f* sheepfold.
majadería *f* absurdity; silliness.
majadero/ra *adj* dull; silly, stupid; * *m* idiot.
majestad *f* majesty.
majestuoso/sa *adj* majestic.
majo/ja *adj* nice; attractive; smart.
majuelo *m* vine (newly planted); hawthorn.
mal *m* evil; hurt; harm, damage; misfortune; illness; * *adj* (before masculine nouns) bad.
malamente *adv* badly.
malaria *f* malaria.
malcriado/da *adj* rude, ill-behaved; naughty; spoiled.
maldad *f* wickedness.
maldecir *vt* to curse.
maldición *f* curse.
maldito/ta *adj* wicked; damned, cursed.
malear *vt* to damage; to corrupt.
malecón *m* pier.
maledicencia *f* slander; scandal.
maleducado/da *adj* bad-mannered, rude.
maleficio *m* curse; spell; witchcraft.
maléfico/ca *adj* harmful, damaging, evil.
malestar *m* discomfort; *(fig)* uneasiness; unrest.
maleta *f* suitcase; *(auto)* trunk.
maletero *f (auto)* trunk.
malevolencia *f* malevolence.
malévolo/la *adj* malevolent.
maleza *f* weeds *pl*; thicket.
malgastar *vt* to waste, to ruin.
malhablado/da *adj* foul-mouthed.
malhechor/ra *m/f* malefactor; criminal.
malhumorado/da *adj* cross, bad-tempered.
malicia *f* malice, wickedness; suspicion; cunning.
malicioso/sa *adj* malicious, wicked, evil; sly, crafty; spiteful.
malignidad *f (med)* malignancy; evil nature; malice.
maligno/na *adj* malignant; malicious.

malinformar vt Lat Am to misinform.
malla f mesh, network; **~s** fpl leotard.
malo/la adj bad; ill; wicked; * m/f villain.
malograr vt to spoil; to upset (a plan); to waste; **~se** vr to fail; to die early.
malparado/da adj: **salir ~** to come off badly.
malparida f woman who has had a miscarriage.
malparir vi to miscarry, to have a miscarriage.
malsano/na adj unhealthy.
malteada f Lat Am milk shake.
maltratamiento m ill-treatment.
maltratar vt to ill-treat, to abuse, to mistreat.
malva f (bot) mallow.
malvado/da adj wicked, villainous.
malversación f embezzlement.
malversador/ra m/f embezzler.
malversar vt to embezzle.
mama f teat; breast.
mamá f (col) mom, mommy.
mamar vt, vi to suck.
mamarrachada f ridiculous sight.
mamarracho m mess, botch-up.
mamífero m mammal.
mamita f (col) Lat Am mom, mommy.
mamón/ona m/f small baby; scrounger.
mampara f partition; screen.
mampostería f masonry; stonemasonry.
maná m manna.
manada f flock, herd; pack; crowd.
manantial m source, spring; origin.
manar vt to run with, to flow; * vi to spring from; to flow; to abound.
mancha f stain, spot.
manchado/da adj spotted.
manchar vt to stain, to soil.
mancilla f spot, blemish.
manco/ca adj one-armed; one-handed; maimed; faulty.
mancomunar vt to associate, to unite; to make jointly responsible.
mancomunidad f union, fellowship; community; (law) joint responsibility.
mandado m command; errand, message.
mandamiento m order, command; commandment.
mandar vt to command, to order; to bequeath; to send.
mandarín m mandarin.
mandarina f tangerine; mandarin orange.
mandatario/ria m/f agent; leader.
mandato m mandate, order; term of office.
mandíbula f jaw.
mandil m apron.
mando m command, authority, power; term of office; **~ a distancia** remote control.
mandón/ona adj bossy, domineering.
manecilla f small hand (of a watch/meter); book-clasp.
manejable adj manageable.

manejar vt to manage; to operate; to handle; Lat Am (auto) to drive; **~se** vr to manage; to behave; Lat Am to drive.
manejo m management; handling; Lat Am driving; confidence.
manera f manner, way; fashion; kind.
manga f sleeve; hose, hosepipe.
mango[1] m handle.
mango[2] m mango.
mangonear vi to interfere; * vt to boss about.
manguera f hose; hosepipe.
manguito m muff.
maní m peanut.
manía f mania; craze; dislike; spite.
maniatar vt to tie the hands of; to handcuff.
maniático/ca adj maniac, mad, frantic; * m/f maniac.
manicomio m mental home, lunatic asylum.
manicura f manicure.
manifestación f manifestation; show; demonstration; mass meeting.
manifestar vt to manifest, to declare.
manifiesto/ta adj manifest, open, clear; * m manifesto.
manija f Lat Am handle.
maniobra f maneuvering; handling; (mil) maneuver.
maniobrar vt to maneuver; to handle.
manipulación f manipulation.
manipular vt to manipulate.
maniquí m dummy; * m/f model.
manirroto/ta adj lavish, extravagant.
manivela f crank.
manjar m (tasty) dish.
mano f hand; hand (of a clock or watch); foot, paw (of an animal); coat (of paint); lot, series; hand (at game); Lat Am bunch (of bananas); **a ~** by hand; **a ~s llenas** liberally, generously.
manojo m handful, bunch.
manopla f gauntlet; glove; washcloth.
manosear vt to handle; to finger, to mess up.
manoseo m handling; fingering.
manotazo m slap, smack.
manoteo m gesticulation.
mansalva f: **a ~** adv indiscriminately.
mansedumbre f meekness, gentleness.
mansión f mansion.
manso/sa adj tame; gentle, soft.
manta f blanket.
manteca f fat; **~ de cerdo** lard.
mantecado m cake eaten at Christmas; ice cream.
mantecoso/sa adj greasy.
mantel m tablecloth.
mantelería f table linen.
mantener vt to maintain, to support; to nourish; to keep; **~se** vr to hold one's ground; to support oneself.

M

mantenimiento *m* maintenance; subsistence.·
mantequilla *f* butter.
mantilla *f* mantilla (head covering for women);
~**s** *fpl* baby clothes *pl*.
manto *m* mantle; cloak, robe.
mantón *m* shawl.
manual *adj* manual; * *m* manual, handbook.
manubrio *m* *Lat Am* handlebars *pl*.
manufactura *f* manufacture.
manufacturar *vt* to manufacture.
manuscrito *m* manuscript; * *adj* handwritten.
manutención *f* support, maintenance.
manzana *f* apple.
manzanilla *f* chamomile; chamomile tea;
manzanilla sherry.
manzano *m* apple tree.
maña *f* handiness, dexterity, cleverness, cunning;
habit, custom; trick.
mañana *f* morning; * *adv* tomorrow.
mañoso/sa *adj* skillful, handy; cunning.
mapa *m* map.
mapamundi *f* map of the world.
maquillaje *m* make-up; making up.
maquillar *vt* to make up; ~**se** *vr* to put on make-up.
máquina *f* machine; (*rail*) engine; camera; (*fig*)
machinery; plan, project.
maquinación *f* machination.
maquinador/ra *m/f* schemer, plotter.
maquinalmente *adv* mechanically.
maquinar *vt, vi* to machinate; to conspire.
maquinaria *f* machinery; mechanism.
maquinilla *f*: ~ **de afeitar** razor.
maquinista *m* (*rail*) train driver; operator; (*mar*)
engineer.
mar *m/f* sea.
maraña *f* shrub, thicket; tangle.
maravilla *f* wonder.
maravillar *vt* to astonish, to amaze; ~**se** *vr* to be
amazed, to be astonished.
maravilloso/sa *adj* wonderful, marvelous.
marca *f* mark; stamp; (*com*) make, brand.
marcado/da *adj* strong, marked.
marcador *m* scoreboard; scorer; *Lat Am* felt-tip pen.
marcar *vt* to mark; to dial; to score; to record;
to set (hair); * *vi* to score; to dial.
marcha *f* march; running; gear; speed; (*fig*)
progress.
marchar *vi* to go; to work; ~**se** *vr* to go away.
marchitar *vt* to wither; to fade.
marchito/ta *adj* faded; withered.
marcial *adj* martial, warlike.
marciano/na *adj* Martian.
marco *m* frame; framework; (*sport*) goalposts *pl*.
marea *f* tide; ~ **negra** oil slick.
marear *vt* (*mar*) to sail, to navigate; to annoy, to
upset; ~**se** *vr* to feel sick; to feel faint; to feel
dizzy.
marejada *f* swell, heavy sea, surge.

mareo *m* sick feeling; dizziness; nuisance.
marfil *m* ivory.
margarina *f* margarine.
margarita *f* daisy.
margen *m* margin; border; * *f* bank (of river).
marginal *adj* marginal.
marginar *vt* to exclude; to leave margins on (a
page); to make notes in the margin of.
marica *m* (*col*) sissy.
maricón *m* (*col*) queer.
marido *m* husband.
mariguana, **marihuana** *f* cannabis.
marimacho *f* (*col*) mannish woman.
marina *f* navy.
marinero/ra *adj* sea *compd*; seaworthy; * *m*
sailor.
marino/na *adj* marine; * *m* sailor, seaman.
marioneta *f* puppet.
mariposa *f* butterfly.
mariquita *f* ladybug.
mariscal *m* marshal.
marisco *m* shellfish.
marital *adj* marital.
maritimo/ma *adj* maritime, marine.
marmita *f* pot.
mármol *m* marble.
marmóreo/rea *adj* marbled, marble *compd*.
marmota *f* marmot.
maroma *f* rope.
marqués *m* marquis.
marquesa *f* marchioness.
marrano *m* hog, boar; pig.
marrón *adj* brown.
marrullería *f* plausibility; plausible excuse; ~**s**
fpl cajolery.
marrullero/ra *adj* crafty, cunning.
marta *f* marten, sable.
Marte *m* Mars (planet).
martes *m invar* Tuesday.
martillar *vt* to hammer.
martillo *m* hammer.
mártir *m/f* martyr.
martirio *m* martyrdom.
martirizar *vt* to martyr.
marxismo *m* Marxism.
marxista *adj*, *m/f* Marxist.
marzo *m* March.
mas *adv* but, yet.
más *adv* more; most; besides, moreover; **a** ~
tardar at latest; **sin** ~ **ni** ~ without more ado.
masa *f* dough, paste; mortar; mass.
masacre *m* massacre.
masaje *m* massage.
mascar *vt* to chew.
máscara *m/f* masked person; * *f* mask.
mascarada *f* masquerade.
mascarilla *f* (*med*) mask.
masculino/na *adj* masculine, male.

mascullar *vt* to mumble, to mutter.
masivo/va *adj* massive, en masse.
masoquista *m/f* masochist.
masticación *f* mastication.
masticar *vt* to masticate, to chew.
mástil *m* (*mar*) mast.
mastín *m* mastiff.
masturbación *f* masturbation.
masturbarse *vr* to masturbate.
mata *f* shrub; sprig, blade; grove, group of trees; mop of hair.
matadero *m* slaughterhouse.
matador/ra *adj* killing; * *m/f* killer; * *m* bullfighter.
matanza *f* slaughtering; massacre.
matar *vt* to kill; to execute; to murder; ~**se** *vr* to kill oneself, to commit suicide.
matasanos *m invar* quack (doctor).
matasellos *m invar* postmark.
mate[1] *m* checkmate.
mate[2] *adj* matte.
matemáticas *fpl* mathematics; math.
matemático/ca *adj* mathematical; * *m/f* mathematician.
materia *m* matter, materials *pl*; subject.
material *adj* material, physical; * *m* equipment, materials *pl*.
materialidad *f* outward appearance.
materialismo *m* materialism.
materialista *m/f* materialist.
maternal *adj* maternal, motherly.
maternidad *f* motherhood.
materno/na *adj* maternal.
matinal *adj* morning *compd*.
matiz *m* shade of color; shading.
matizar *vt* to mix colors; to tinge, to tint.
matón *m* bully.
matorral *m* shrub, thicket.
matraca *f* rattle.
matricida *m/f* matricide (person).
matricidio *m* matricide (act).
matrícula *f* register, list; (*auto*) registration number; license plate.
matricular *vt* to register, to enroll.
matrimonial *adj* matrimonial.
matrimonio *m* marriage, matrimony.
matriz *f* matrix; womb; mold, form.
matrona *f* matron.
matutino/na *adj* morning.
maullar *vi* to mew.
maullido *m* mew (of a cat).
mausoleo *m* mausoleum.
máxima *f* maxim.
máxime *adv* principally.
máximo/ma *adj* maximum; top; highest.
mayo *m* May.
mayonesa *f* mayonnaise.
mayor *adj* main, chief; (*mus*) major; biggest; eldest; greater, larger; elderly; * *m* chief, boss;

adult; **al por** ~ wholesale; ~**es** *mpl* forefathers.
mayoral *m* foreman.
mayordomo *m* steward.
mayoreo *m Lat Am* wholesale.
mayoría *f* majority, greater part; ~ **de edad** coming of age.
mayorista *m/f* wholesaler.
mayormente *adv* principally, chiefly.
mayúsculo/la *adj* (*fig*) tremendous; * *f* capital letter.
maza *f* club; mace.
mazada *f* blow with a club.
mazapán *m* marzipan.
mazmorra *f* dungeon.
mazo *m* bunch, handful; club, mallet; bat.
mazorca *f* cob; corncob; ear.
me *pn* me; to me.
mear *vi* (*col*) to pee, to piss.
mecánica *f* mechanics.
mecánico/ca *adj* mechanical; * *m/f* mechanic.
mecanismo *m* mechanism.
mecanografía *f* typing.
mecanógrafo/fa *m/f* typist.
mecate *m* rope.
mecedora *f* rocking chair.
mecer *vt* to rock; to dandle (a child).
mecha *f* wick; fuse.
mechar *vt* to lard; to stuff.
mechero *m* (cigarette) lighter.
mechón *m* lock of hair; large bundle of threads/ fibers.
medalla *f* medal.
medallón *m* medallion.
media *f* stocking; sock; average.
mediación *f* mediation, intervention.
mediado/da *adj* half-full; half-complete; **a** ~**s de** in the middle of.
mediador/ra *m/f* mediator; go-between.
medialuna *f Lat Am* croissant.
mediana *f* median strip.
medianero/ra *adj* dividing; adjacent.
mediano/na *adj* medium; middling; mediocre.
medianoche *f* midnight.
mediante *prep* by means of.
mediar *vi* to intervene; to mediate.
medias *fpl* pantyhose *pl*.
medicación *f* medication.
medicamento *m* medicine.
medicina *f* medicine.
medicinal *adj* medicinal.
médico/ca *adj* medical; * *m/f* doctor.
medida *f* measure.
medidor *m Lat Am* meter.
medio/dia *adj* half; **a medias** partly; * *m* middle; average; way, means; medium.
mediocre *adj* middling; moderate; mediocre.
mediocridad *f* mediocrity.
mediodía *m* noon, midday.

M

medir vt to measure; ~**se** vr to be moderate.
meditación f meditation.
meditar vt to meditate.
mediterráneo/nea adj Mediterranean; * m: **el M~** the Mediterranean.
medrar vi to grow, to thrive, to prosper; to improve.
medroso/sa adj fearful, timid.
médula f marrow; essence, substance; pith.
medusa f jellyfish.
megafonía f public-address system.
megáfono m megaphone.
mejilla f cheek.
mejillón m mussel.
mejor adj, adv better; best.
mejora f improvement.
mejorar vt to improve, to ameliorate; to enhance; * vi to improve; (med) to recover, to get better; ~**se** vr to improve, to get better.
mejoría f improvement; recovery.
melancolía f melancholy.
melancólico/ca adj melancholy, sad, gloomy.
melena f long hair, loose hair; mane.
melenudo/da adj long-haired.
melindroso/sa adj prudish, finicky.
mella f notch in edged tools; gap.
mellado/da adj jagged; gap-toothed.
mellar vt to notch.
mellizo/za adj, m/f twin.
melocotón m peach.
melodía f melody.
melodioso/sa adj melodious.
melodrama f melodrama.
melón m melon.
melosidad f sweetness.
meloso/sa adj honeyed; mellow.
membrana f membrane.
membranoso/sa adj membranous.
membresía f Lat Am membership.
membrete m letterhead.
membrillo m quince; quince tree.
membrudo/da adj strong, robust; burly.
memorable adj memorable.
memorándum m notebook; memorandum.
memoria f memory; report; record; ~**s** fpl memoirs pl.
memorial m memorial; petition.
mención f mention.
mencionar vt to mention.
mendigar vt to beg.
mendigo/ga m/f beggar.
mendrugo m crust.
menear vt to move from place to place; (fig) to handle; ~**se** vr to move; to shake; to sway.
meneo m movement; shake; swaying.
menester m necessity; need; want; ~**es** mpl duties pl.
menesteroso/sa adj needy.

menestra f vegetable soup/stew.
menguante f decreasing.
menguar vi to diminish; to discredit.
menopausia f menopause.
menor m/f young person, juvenile; * adj less; smaller; minor; **al por ~** retail.
menoría f: **a ~** retail.
menos adv less; least; **a lo ~/por lo ~** at least; * prep except; minus.
menoscabar vt to damage; to harm; to lessen; to discredit.
menoscabo m damage; harm; loss.
menospreciar vt to undervalue; to despise, to scorn.
menosprecio m contempt, scorn; undervaluation.
mensaje m message.
mensajero/ra m/f messenger; courier.
menstruación f menstruation.
mensual adj monthly.
menta f mint.
mental adj mental; intellectual.
mentar vt to mention.
mente f mind; understanding.
mentecato/ta adj silly, stupid; * m/f idiot.
mentir vt to feign; to pretend; * vi to lie.
mentira f lie, falsehood.
mentiroso/sa adj lying; * m/f liar.
menú m menu; set meal.
menudencia f trifle, small thing; minuteness; ~**s** fpl odds and ends pl.
menudillos mpl giblets pl.
menudo/da adj small; minute; petty, insignificant; **a ~** frequently, often.
meñique m little finger.
meollo m marrow; (fig) core.
mequetrefe m good-for-nothing; busybody.
meramente adv merely, solely.
mercader m dealer, trader.
mercadería f commodity; trade; ~**s** fpl Lat Am merchandise.
mercadería f commodity; trade; ~**s** fpl merchandise.
mercado m market; marketplace.
mercancía f commodity; ~**s** fpl goods pl, merchandise.
mercantil adj commercial, mercantile.
mercenario/ria adj mercenary; * m mercenary; laborer.
mercería f dry goods store.
mercurio m mercury.
Mercurio m Mercury (planet).
merecedor/ra adj deserving.
merecer vt to deserve, to merit.
merecido/da adj deserved.
merendar vi to have tea; to have a picnic.
merengue m meringue.
meridiano m meridian.
meridional adj southern.
merienda f (light) tea; afternoon snack; picnic.

mérito m merit; worth, value.
meritorio/ria adj meritorious.
merluza f hake.
merma f waste, leakage.
mermar vi to waste, to diminish.
mermelada f jelly, jam.
mero m pollack (fish); **~/ra** adj mere, pure.
merodeador m (mil) marauder.
merodear vi to pillage, to go marauding.
mes m month.
mesa f table; desk; plateau; **~ redonda** round table.
mesada f Lat Am monthly installment.
meseta f meseta, tableland, plateau.
mesón m inn.
mestizo/za adj of mixed race; crossbred; * m/f half-caste.
mesura f gravity; politeness; moderation.
mesurado/da adj moderate; dignified; courteous.
meta f goal; finish.
metabolismo m metabolism.
metafísica f metaphysics.
metafísico/ca adj metaphysical.
metáfora f metaphor.
metafórico/ca adj metaphorical.
metal m metal; (mus) brass; timbre/timber (of the voice).
metálico/ca adj metallic.
metalurgia f metallurgy.
metamorfosis f invar metamorphosis; transformation.
meteoro m meteor.
meteorología f meteorology.
meter vt to place, to put; to insert, to put in; to involve; to make, to cause; **~se** vr to meddle, to interfere.
metódico/ca adj methodical.
método m method.
metralla f (mil) shrapnel.
metralleta f submachine-gun.
métrico/ca adj metric.
metro¹ m meter.
metro² m subway.
metrópoli f metropolis; mother country.
mezcla f mixture; medley.
mezclar vt to mix; **~se** vr to mix; to mingle.
mezquindad f meanness; pettiness; wretchedness.
mezquino/na adj mean; small-minded, petty; wretched.
mezquita f mosque.
mi adj my.
mí pn me; myself.
microbio m microbe.
microbús m minibus.
microchip m microchip.
micrófono m microphone.
microondas m inv microwave oven.
microplaqueta f microchip.
microscópico/ca adj microscopic.

microscopio m microscope.
miedo m fear, dread.
miel f honey.
miembro m member.
mientras adv meanwhile; * conj while; as long as.
miércoles m invar Wednesday.
mierda f (col) shit.
mies f harvest.
miga f crumb; **~s** fpl fried breadcrumbs pl.
migaja f scrap, crumb.
migración f migration.
mijo m (bot) millet.
mil m one thousand.
milagro m miracle, wonder.
milagroso/sa adj miraculous.
milano m kite (bird).
milésimo/ma adj, m thousandth.
mili f: **hacer la ~** (col) to do one's military service.
milicia f militia; military service.
miliciano m militiaman.
milímetro m millimeter.
militante adj militant.
militar adj military; * m soldier; * vi to serve in the army; (fig) to be a member of a party.
milla f mile.
millar m thousand.
millón m million.
millonario/ria m/f millionaire.
mimar vt to spoil, pamper.
mimbre m wicker.
mímica f sign language; mimicry.
mimo m caress; spoiling; mime.
mimoso/sa adj spoilt, pampered; delicate.
mina f mine; underground passage.
minar vt to undermine; to mine.
mineral m mineral; * adj mineral.
mineralogía f mineralogy.
minero/ra m/f miner.
miniatura f miniature.
minicadena f midi system.
minifalda f miniskirt.
mínimo/ma adj minimum.
ministerio m ministry.
ministro/ra m/f minister.
minoría f minority.
minucioso/sa adj meticulous; very detailed.
minúsculo/la adj minute; * f small letter.
minusválido/da adj (physically) handicapped; * m/f (physically) handicapped person.
minuta f minute, first draft; menu.
minutero m minute hand (of a watch/clock).
minuto m minute.
mío/mía adj mine.
miope adj short-sighted.
mira f sight of a gun; (fig) aim.
mirada f glance; gaze.
mirador m viewpoint, vantage point.

M

miramiento *m* consideration; circumspection.

mirar *vt* to look at; to observe; to consider; * *vi* to look; **~se** *vr* to look at oneself; to look at one another.

mirilla *f* peephole.

mirlo *m* blackbird.

mirón/ona *m/f* spectator, onlooker, bystander; voyeur.

misa *f* mass; **~ del gallo** midnight mass.

misal *m* missal.

misantropía *f* misanthropy.

misántropo/pa *m/f* misanthropist.

miserable *adj* miserable; mean; squalid (place); (*col*) despicable; * *m/f* rotter.

miseria *f* misery; poverty; meanness; squalor.

misericordia *f* mercy.

misil *m* missile.

misión *f* mission.

misionero/ra *m/f* missionary.

mismo/ma *adj* same; very.

misterio *m* mystery.

misterioso/sa *adj* mysterious.

mística *f* mysticism.

místico/ca *adj* mystic(al); * *m/f* mystic.

mitad *f* half; middle.

mitigación *f* mitigation.

mitigar *vt* to mitigate.

mitin *m* (political) rally.

mito *m* myth.

mitología *f* mythology.

mitológico/ca *adj* mythological.

mitones *mpl* mittens *pl*.

mixto/ta *adj* mixed.

mobiliario *m* furniture.

mochila *f* backpack.

mochuelo *m* red owl.

moción *f* motion.

moco *m* mucus; (*col*) snot.

moda *f* fashion, style.

modales *mpl* manners *pl*.

modalidad *f* kind, variety.

modelaje *m Lat Am* modeling.

modelar *vt* to model, to form.

modelo *m* model, pattern.

módem *m* modem.

moderación *f* moderation.

moderado/da *adj* moderate.

moderar *vt* to moderate.

moderno/na *adj* modern.

modestia *f* modesty, decency.

modesto,ta *adj* modest.

módico/ca *adj* moderate.

modificación *f* modification.

modificar *vt* to modify.

modisto/ta *m/f* dressmaker.

modo *m* mode, method, manner.

modorra *f* drowsiness.

modulación *f* modulation.

modular *vt* to modulate.

mofa *f* mockery.

mofarse *vr*: **~ de** to mock, to scoff at.

moflete *m* fat cheek.

moho *m* rust; mold, mildew.

mohoso/sa *adj* moldy, musty.

mojar *vt* to wet, to moisten; **~se** *vr* to get wet.

mojigato *adj* hypocritical.

mojón *m* landmark.

molde *m* mold; *Lat Am* pattern; model.

moldura *f* molding.

mole *f* bulk; pile.

molécula *f* molecule.

moler *vt* to grind, to pound; to tire out; to annoy, to bore.

molestar *vt* to annoy, to bother; to trouble; * *vi* to be a nuisance.

molestia *f* trouble; inconvenience; (*med*) discomfort.

molesto/ta *adj* annoying; inconvenient; uncomfortable; annoyed.

molinero *m* miller.

molinillo *m*: **~ de café** coffee grinder.

molino *m* mill.

molusco *m* mollusk.

momentáneo/nea *adj* momentary.

momento *m* moment.

momia *f* mummy (as in Egyptian).

monacal *adj* monastic.

monaguillo *m* acolyte.

monarca *m/f* monarch.

monarquía *f* monarchy.

monárquico/ca *adj* monarchical; * *m/f* royalist, monarchist.

monasterio *m* monastery, convent.

monástico/ca *adj* monastic.

mondadientes *m invar* toothpick.

mondar *vt* to clean; to cleanse; to peel; **~se** *vr*: **~ de risa** (*col*) to split one's sides laughing.

mondo/da *adj* clean; pure; **~ y lirondo** bare, plain; pure and simple.

moneda *f* money; currency; coin.

monedero *m* purse; *Lat Am* phone booth.

monería *f* funny face; mimicry; prank; trifle.

monetario/ra *adj* monetary, financial.

monitor *m* monitor.

monja *f* nun.

monje *f* monk.

mono[1] *m* monkey; ape.

mono[2] *m* coveralls *pl*, overalls *pl*.

mono/na[3] *adj* lovely; pretty; nice.

monólogo *m* monolog.

monopolio *m* monopoly.

monopolista *m* monopolist.

monosílabo/ba *adj* monosyllabic.

monotonía *f* monotony.

monótono/na *adj* monotonous.

monovolumen *m* people mover.

monstruo *m* monster.

monstruosidad *f* monstrosity.

monstruoso/sa *adj* monstrous.

monta *f* amount, sum total.

montaje *m* assembly; decor (of theater); montage.

montaña *f* mountain.

montañes/esa *adj* mountain *compd*; * *m/f* highlander.

montañoso/sa *adj* mountainous.

montar *vt* to mount, to get on (a bicycle, horse etc); to assemble, to put together; to overlap; to set up (a business); to beat, to whip (in cooking); * *vi* to mount; to ride; ~ **a** to amount to.

montaraz *adj* mountainous; wild, untamed.

monte *m* mountain; woodland; ~ **alto** forest; ~ **bajo** scrub.

montería *f* hunting, chase.

montés/esa *adj* wild, untamed.

montón *m* heap, pile; mass; **a ~ones**, abundantly, by the score.

montura *f* mount; saddle.

monumento *m* monument.

monzón *m* monsoon.

moño *m* bun; *Lat Am* bow.

moquillo *m* distemper (disease in dogs).

mora *f* blackberry.

morada *f* home, abode, residence.

morado/da *adj* violet, purple.

morador/ra *m/f* inhabitant.

moral¹ *m* mulberry tree.

moral² *f* morals *pl*, ethics *pl*; * *adj* moral.

moraleja *f* moral.

moralidad *f* morality.

moralista *m/f* moralist.

moralizar *vi* to moralize.

moralmente *adv* morally.

morar *vi* to inhabit, to dwell.

moratoria *f* moratorium.

mórbido/da *adj* morbid, diseased.

morboso/sa *adj* diseased, morbid.

morcilla *f* blood sausage, black pudding.

mordacidad *f* sharpness, pungency.

mordaz *adj* biting, scathing; pungent.

mordaza *f* gag; clamp.

mordedura *f* bite.

morder *vt* to bite; to nibble; to corrode, to eat away.

mordisco *m* bite.

moreno/na *adj* brown; swarthy; dark-skinned.

moribundo/da *adj* dying.

morigeración *f* temperance.

morir *vi* to die; to expire; to die down; ~**se** *vr* to die; (*fig*) to be dying.

morisco/ca *adj* Moorish.

moro/ra *adj* Moorish.

morosidad *f* slowness, sluggishness.

moroso/sa *adj* slow, sluggish; (*com*) slow to pay up.

morral *m* haversack.

morriña *f* depression; sadness.

morro *m* snout; nose (of plane etc).

morsa *f* walrus.

mortaja *f* shroud; cigarette paper.

mortal *adj* mortal; fatal, deadly.

mortalidad *f* mortality.

mortandad *f* death toll.

mortero *m* mortar (cannon).

mortífero/ra *adj* deadly, fatal.

mortificación *f* mortification.

mortificar *vt* to mortify.

mortuorio *m* mortuary.

moruno/na *adj* Moorish.

mosca *f* fly.

moscardón *m* botfly, hornet; (*col*) pest, bore.

moscatel *adj, m* muscatel.

moscón *m* (*col*) pest, bore.

mosquearse *vr* (*col*) to get cross; (*col*) to take offense.

mosquetero *m* musketeer.

mosquitero *m* mosquito net.

mosquito *m* gnat, mosquito.

mostaza *f* mustard.

mosto *m* must, new wine.

mostrador *m* counter, bar.

mostrar *vt* to show, to exhibit; to explain; ~**se** *vr* to appear, to show oneself.

mota *f* speck, tiny piece; dot; defect, fault.

mote *m* nickname.

motejar *vt* to nickname.

motín *m* revolt; mutiny.

motivar *vt* to motivate; to explain, to justify.

motivo *m* motive, cause, reason.

moto *f* (*col*) motor scooter, motorbike.

motocicleta *f* motorcycle.

motor *m* engine, motor.

movedizo/za *adj* movable; variable, changeable; fickle.

mover *vt* to move; to shake; to drive; (*fig*) to cause; ~**se** *vr* to move; (*fig*) to get a move on.

móvil *adj* mobile, movable; moving; * *m* motive; cellular phone.

movilidad *f* mobility.

movimiento *m* movement, motion.

mozo/za *adj* young; * *m/f* youth, young man/ girl; waiter/waitress.

muchacho/a *m/f* boy/girl; * *f* maid(servant).

muchedumbre *f* crowd.

mucho/cha *adj* a lot of, much; * *adv* much, a lot; long.

muda *f* change of clothes.

mudable *adj* changeable, variable; mutable.

mudanza *f* change; move.

mudar *vt* to change; to shed, to molt; ~**se** *vr* to change one's clothes; to change house; * *vi* to change;

mudo/da adj dumb; silent, mute.
mueble m piece of furniture; ~s mpl furniture.
mueca f grimace, funny face.
muela f tooth, molar.
muelle m spring; regulator; quay, wharf.
muérdago m (bot) mistletoe.
muerte f death.
muerto m corpse; ~/ta adj dead.
muesca f notch, groove.
muestra f pattern; indication; demonstration; proof; sample; token; model.
mugido m lowing (of cattle).
mugir vi to low, to bellow.
mugre m dirt, filth.
mugriento/ta adj greasy; dirty, filthy.
mujer f woman.
mulato/ta adj mulatto.
muleta f crutch.
mullido/da adj soft; springy.
mulo/la m/f mule.
multa f fine, penalty.
multar vt to fine.
multimedia adj multimedia.
múltiple adj multiple; ~s many, numerous.
multiplicación f multiplication.
multiplicado m (math) multiplicand.
multiplicar vt to multiply.
multiplicidad f multiplicity.
multitud f multitude.
mundano/na adj worldly; mundane.
mundial adj worldwide; world compd.
mundo m world.

munición f ammunition.
municipio m town council; municipality.
municipal adj municipal.
muñeca f wrist; child's doll.
muñeco m scarecrow, puppet.
muñón m stump.
muralla f rampart, wall.
murciélago m bat (animal).
murmullo m murmur, mutter.
murmuración f backbiting, gossip.
murmurador/ra m/f detractor, backbiter.
murmurar vi to murmur; to gossip, to backbite.
muro m wall.
muscular adj muscular.
músculo m muscle.
muselina f muslin.
museo m museum.
musgo m moss.
música f music.
musical adj musical.
músico/ca m/f musician; * adj musical.
muslo m thigh.
mustio/tia adj parched, withered; sad, sorrowful.
musulmán/ana adj, m/f Muslim.
mutabilidad f mutability.
mutación f mutation, change.
mutilación f mutilation.
mutilar vt to mutilate, to maim.
mutuo/tua adj mutual, reciprocal.
mutuamente adv mutually.
muy adv very; too; greatly; ~ **ilustre** most illustrious.

N

nabo *m* turnip.

nácar *m* mother-of-pearl, nacre.

nacarado/da *adj* mother-of-pearl *compd*; pearl-colored.

nacer *vi* to be born; to bud, to shoot (of plants); to rise; to grow.

nacido/da *adj* born; **recién ~** newborn.

nacimiento *m* birth; nativity.

nación *f* nation.

nacional *adj* national.

nacionalidad *f* nationality.

nacionalizar *vt* to nationalize; **~se** to become naturalized.

nada *f* nothing; * *adv* no way, not at all, by no means.

nadador/ra *m/f* swimmer.

nadar *vi* to swim.

nadie *pn* nobody, no one.

nado *adv*: **a ~** afloat.

naipe *m* (playing) card.

nalgas *fpl* buttocks *pl*.

naranja *f* orange.

naranjada *f* orangeade.

naranjal *m* orange grove.

naranjo *m* orange tree.

narciso *m* (*bot*) daffodil; narcissus (flower); fop.

narcótico/ca *adj* narcotic; * *m* drug, narcotic.

narcotraficante *m/f* drug trafficker.

nardo *m* (*bot*) spikenard, nard.

narigón/ona, narigudo/da *adj* big-nosed.

nariz *f* nose; sense of smell.

narración *f* narration.

narrar *vt* to narrate, to tell.

narrativa *f* narrative; story.

nata *f* cream.

natación *f* swimming.

natal *adj* natal, native.

natalicio *m* birthday.

natillas *fpl* custard.

natividad *f* nativity.

nativo/va *adj*, *m/f* native.

natural *m* temperament, natural disposition; native; inhabitant; * *adj* natural; native; common, usual; **al ~** unaffectedly.

naturaleza *f* nature.

naturalidad *f* naturalness.

naturalista *m* naturalist.

naturalizar *vi* to naturalize; **~se** *vr* to become naturalized; to become acclimatized.

naturalmente *adv* in a natural way; **¡~!** of course!

naturópata *m/f* naturopath.

naufragar *vi* to be shipwrecked; to suffer ruin in one's affairs.

naufragio *m* shipwreck.

náufrago/ga *adj* shipwrecked.

nauseabundo/da *adj* nauseating.

náuseas *fpl* nauseousness, nausea.

náutica *f* navigation.

navaja *f* pocketknife, penknife; razor.

naval *adj* naval.

nave *f* ship; nave.

navegable *adj* navigable.

navegación *f* navigation; sea journey.

navegador *m* (*comput*) browser.

navegante *m* navigator.

navegar *vt*, *vi* to navigate; to sail; to fly.

navidad *f* Christmas.

navideño/ña *adj* Christmas *compd*.

navío *m* ship.

nazi *adj*, *m/f* Nazi.

neblina *f* mist; fine rain, drizzle.

nebuloso/sa *adj* misty; cloudy; nebulous; foggy; hazy; drizzling; * *f* nebula.

necedad *f* gross ignorance, stupidity; imprudence.

necesario/ria *adj* necessary.

neceser *m* toilet bag; carryall.

necesidad *f* necessity, need, want.

necesitado/da *adj* necessitous, very needy.

necesitar *vt* to need; * *vi* to want, to need.

necio/cia *adj* ignorant; stupid, foolish; imprudent; *Lat Am* stubborn.

necrología *f* obituary.

nectarina *f* nectarine.

néctar *m* nectar.

nefando/da *adj* base, nefarious, abominable.

nefasto/ta *adj* unlucky.

negación *f* negation; denial.

negado/da *adj* incapable, unfit.

negar *vt* to deny; to refuse; **~se** *vr*: **~ a hacer** to refuse to do.

negativo/va *adj*, *m* negative; * *f* negative; refusal.

negligencia *f* negligence.

negligente *adj* negligent; careless, heedless.

negociación *f* negotiation; commerce.

negociante *m/f* trader, dealer.

negociar *vt*, *vi* to negotiate.

negocio *m* business, affair; transaction; firm; place of business.

negro/gra *adj* black; dark; * *m* black; * *m/f* Black person, Negro/Negress.

negrura *f* blackness.

negruzco/ca *adj* blackish.

nene *m*, **nena** *f* baby.

nenúfar *m* water lily.

neófito *m* neophyte.

Neptuno *m* Neptune (planet).
nervio *m* nerve.
nervioso/sa *adj* nervous.
neto/ta *adj* neat, pure; net.
neumático/ca *adj* pneumatic; * *m* tire.
neurona *f* neuron.
neutral *adj* neutral; neuter.
neutralidad *f* neutrality.
neutralizar *vt* to neutralize; to counteract.
neutro/tra *adj* neutral; neuter; * *m Lat Am* neutral.
neutrón *m* neutron.
nevada *f* heavy fall of snow.
nevar *vi* to snow.
nevera *f* icebox.
nevería *f* ice-cream parlor.
nexo *m* link.
ni *conj* neither, nor.
nica *m/f Lat Am* (*col*) Nicaraguan.
nicho *m* niche.
nido *m* nest; hiding place.
niebla *f* fog; mist.
nieta *f* granddaughter.
nieto *m* grandson.
nieve *f* snow.
nigromancia *f* necromancy.
nimiedad *f* small-mindedness; triviality.
nimio/mia *adj* trivial.
ninfa *f* nymph.
ningún, ninguno/na *adj* no; * *pn* nobody; none; not one; neither.
niña *f* little girl; pupil (of eye).
niñera *f* nursemaid.
niñería *f* childishness; childish act.
niñero/ra *adj* fond of children.
niñez *f* childhood.
niño/ña *adj* childish; * *m/f* child;infant; **desde ~** from infancy, from a child; * *m* boy.
níspero *m* medlar.
nitidez *f* clarity; brightness; sharpness.
nitrato *m* (*chem*) nitrate.
nitrógeno *m* nitrogen.
nivel *m* level; standard; height; **a ~** perfectly level.
niveladora *f* bulldozer.
nivelar *vt* to level; to even up; to balance.
no *adv* no; not; * *excl* no!
noble *adj* noble, illustrious; generous.
nobleza *f* nobleness, nobility.
nocaut *m Lat Am* knockout.
noción *f* notion, idea.
nocivo/va *adj* harmful.
nocturno/na *adj* nocturnal, nightly; * *m* nocturne.
noche *f* night; evening; darkness;**¡buenas ~s!** good night!
Nochebuena *f* Christmas Eve.
Nochevieja *f* New Year's Eve.

nodriza *f* nurse.
nogal *m* walnut tree.
nómada *adj* nomadic; * *m/f* nomad.
nomás *adv Lat Am* just.
nombramiento *m* nomination; appointment.
nombrar *vt* to name; to nominate; to appoint.
nombre *m* name; title; reputation.
nomenclatura *f* nomenclature.
nómina *f* list; (*com*) payroll.
nominador *m* nominator.
nominal *adj* nominal.
nominativo *m* (*gr*) nominative.
non *adj* odd, uneven; * *m* odd number.
nonagenario/ria *adj* ninety-year-old; * *m/f* nonagenarian.
no obstante *adv* nevertheless, notwithstanding.
noquear *vt Lat Am* to thrash.
nor(d)este *adj* northeast, northeastern; * *m* northeast.
nórdico/ca *adj* northern; Nordic.
noria *f* water wheel; big wheel.
normal *adj* normal; usual.
normalizar *vt* to normalize; to standardize; **~se** *vr* to return to normal.
normar *vt Lat Am* to regulate.
noroeste *adj* northwest, northwestern; * *m* northwest.
norte *adj* north, northern; * *m* north; (*fig*) rule, guide.
nos *pn* us; to us; for us; from us; to ourselves.
nosocomio *m Lat Am* hospital.
nosotros/tras *pn* we; us.
nostalgia *f* homesickness.
nota *f* note; notice, remark; mark.
notable *adj* notable, remarkable.
notar *vt* to note; to mark; to remark; **~se** *vr* to be obvious.
notaría *f* notary profession; notary's office.
notario *m* notary.
noticia *f* notice; knowledge, information; note; **~s** *fpl* news.
noticiario *m* newsreel; news bulletin.
noticiero *m* news bulletin.
notificación *f* notification.
notificar *vt* to notify, to inform.
notoriedad *f* notoriety.
notorio/ria *adj* notorious.
novato/ta *adj* inexperienced; * *m/f* beginner; freshman.
novecientos/tas *adj* nine hundred.
novedad *f* novelty; modernness; newness; piece of news; change.
novela *f* novel.
novelero/ra *adj* highly imaginative.
novelesco/ca *adj* fictional; romantic; fantastic.
noveno/na *adj* ninth.
noventa *adj, m* ninety.
novia *f* bride; girlfriend; fiancée.

noviazgo *m* engagement.
novicio *m* novice.
noviembre *m* November.
novilla *f* heifer.
novillada *f* drove of young bulls; bullfight with young bulls and novice bullfighters.
novillo *m* young bull/ox.
novio *m* bridegroom; boyfriend; fiancé.
nubarrón *m* large cloud.
nube *f* cloud.
nublado/da *adj* cloudy; * *m* storm cloud.
nublarse *vr* to grow dark.
nublazón *m* Lat Am storm cloud.
nuca *f* nape (of the neck); scruff of the neck.
nuclear *adj* nuclear; * *vt* Lat Am to bring together.
núcleo *m* core; nucleus.
nudillo *m* knuckle.
nudo *m* knot.
nuera *f* daughter-in-law.
nuestro/tra *adj* our; * *pn* ours.
nuevamente *adv* again; anew.
nueve *adj*, *m* nine.

nuevo/va *adj* new; modern; fresh; * *f* piece of news; ¿qué hay de ~? is there any news?, what's new?
nuez *f* nut; walnut; Adam's apple; ~ moscada nutmeg.
nulidad *f* incompetence; (*law*) nullity; nonentity.
nulo/la *adj* useless; drawn; null.
numeración *f* numeration.
numerador *m* numerator.
numeral *m* numeral.
numerar *vt* to number.
numérico/ca *adj* numerical.
número *m* number; cipher.
numeroso/sa *adj* numerous.
nunca *adv* never.
nuncio *m* nuncio.
nupcial *adj* nuptial.
nupcias *fpl* nuptials *pl*, wedding.
nutria *f* otter.
nutrición *f* nutrition.
nutrir *vt* to nourish; to feed.
nutritivo/va *adj* nutritious, nourishing.
nylon *m* nylon.

Ñ

ñato/ta *adj* snub-nosed.
ñoñería *f* insipidness.

ñoño/ña *adj* insipid; spineless; silly.

O

o *conj* or; either.

oasis *m invar* oasis.

obcecación *f* obduracy.

obcecar *vt* to blind; to darken.

obedecer *vt* to obey.

obediencia *f* obedience.

obediente *adj* obedient.

obelisco *m* obelisk.

obertura *f* (*mus*) overture.

obesidad *f* obesity.

obeso/sa *adj* obese, fat.

obispado *m* bishopric, episcopate.

obispo *m* bishop.

objeción *f* objection, opposition, exception.

objetar *vi* to object.

objetor *m* ~ **de conciencia** conscientious objector.

objetivo/va *adj*, *m* objective.

objeto *m* object; aim.

oblea *f* wafer.

oblicuo/cua *adj* oblique.

obligación *f* obligation; (*com*) bond.

obligar *vt* to force; ~**se** *vr* to bind oneself.

obligatorio/ria *adj* obligatory.

oblongo/ga *adj* oblong.

oboe *m* oboe.

obra *f* work; building, construction; play; **por ~ de** thanks to.

obrar *vt* to work, to operate; to put into practice; * *vi* to behave, to act; to have an effect.

obrero/ra *adj* working; labor *compd*; * *m/f* workman; laborer.

obscenidad *f* obscenity.

obsceno/na *adj* obscene.

obsequiar *vt* to lavish attention on; ~ **con** to present with.

obsequio *m* gift; courtesy.

obsequioso/sa *adj* obsequious, compliant; officious.

observación *f* observation; remark.

observador/ra *m/f* observer.

observancia *f* observance.

observar *vt* to observe; to notice.

observatorio *m* observatory.

obsesión *f* obsession.

obsesionar *vt* to obsess.

obstáculo *m* obstacle, impediment, hindrance.

obstar *vi*: ~ **a**, ~ **para** to oppose, to obstruct, to hinder.

obstetricia *f* obstetrics.

obstinación *f* obstinacy, stubbornness.

obstinado/da *adj* obstinate.

obstinarse *vr* to be obstinate; ~ **en** to persist in.

obstrucción *f* obstruction.

obstruir *vt* to obstruct; ~**se** *vr* to be blocked up, to be obstructed.

obtener *vt* to obtain; to gain.

obtuso/sa *adj* obtuse, blunt.

obús *m* (*mil*) shell.

obviar *vt* to obviate, to remove.

obvio/via *adj* obvious, evident.

ocasión *f* occasion, opportunity.

ocasional *adj* occasional.

ocasionar *vt* to cause, to occasion.

ocaso *m* (*fig*) decline.

occidental *adj* occidental, western.

occidente *m* occident, west.

océano *m* ocean.

ochenta *adj*, *m* eighty.

ocho *adj*, *m* eight.

ochocientos *m*, *adj* eight hundred.

ocio *m* leisure; pastime.

ociosidad *f* idleness, leisure.

ocioso/sa *adj* idle; useless.

ocre *m* ocher.

octavilla *f* pamphlet.

octavo/va *adj* eighth.

octogenario/ria *adj*, *m/f* octogenarian.

octubre *m* October.

ocular *adj* ocular; eye *compd*.

oculista *m/f* oculist.

ocultar *vt* to hide, to conceal.

oculto/ta *adj* hidden, concealed; secret.

ocupación *f* occupation; business; employment.

ocupado/da *adj* busy; occupied; engaged.

ocupar *vt* to occupy; to hold (an office); ~**se** *vr*: ~ **de**/~ **en** to concern oneself with; to look after.

ocurrencia *f* event; bright idea.

ocurrir *vi* to occur, to happen.

oda *f* ode.

odiar *vt* to hate; ~**se** *vr* to hate one another.

odio *m* hatred.

odioso/sa *adj* odious, hateful.

odontólogo/ga *m/f* dentist.

odorífero/ra *adj* odoriferous, odorous.

oeste *adj* west, western; * *m* west.

ofender *vt* to offend; to injure ~**se** *vr* to be vexed; to take offense.

ofensa *f* offense; injury.

ofensivo/va *adj* offensive, injurious.

ofensor *m* offender.

oferta *f* offer; offering.

oficial *adj* official; * *m* officer; official.

oficialismo *m Lat Am*: **el ~** the Government.
oficialista *adj Lat Am* pro-government.
oficiar *vi* to officiate, to minister (of clergymen etc).
oficina *f* office.
oficio *m* office; employment, occupation; ministry; function; trade, business; **~s** *mpl* divine service.
oficiosidad *f* diligence; officiousness; importunity.
oficioso/sa *adj* officious; diligent; unofficial, informal.
ofrecer *vt* to offer; to present; to exhibit; **~se** *vr* to offer oneself; to occur, to present itself.
ofrecimiento *m* offer, promise.
ofrenda *f* offering, oblation.
ofrendar *vt* to offer, to contribute.
oftalmólogo/ga *m/f* ophthalmologist.
ofuscación *f* dimness of sight; obfuscation.
ofuscar *vt* to darken, to render obscure; to bewilder.
oídas *fpl*: **de ~** by hearsay.
oído *m* hearing; ear.
oír *vt, vi* to hear; to listen (to).
ojal *m* buttonhole.
¡ojalá! *conj* if only!, would that!
ojeada *f* glance.
ojear *vt* to eye, to view; to glance.
ojera *f* bag under the eyes.
ojeriza *f* spite, grudge, ill-will.
okey *interj Lat Am* OK.
okupa *m/f* (*col*) squatter.
ojo *m* eye; sight; eye of a needle; arch of a bridge.
ola *f* wave.
oleada *f* surge; violent emotion.
oleaje *m* succession of waves, sea swell.
óleo *m* oil.
oler *vt* to smell, to scent; * *vi* to smell; **~ a** to smack of.
olfatear *vt* to smell; (*fig*) to sniff out.
olfato *m* sense of smell.
oligarquía *f* oligarchy.
oligárquico/ca *adj* oligarchical.
olimpíada *f* Olympiad; **las O~s** the Olympics.
olímpico/ca *adj* Olympic.
oliva *f* olive.
olivar *m* olive grove.
olivo *m* olive tree.
olla *f* pan; stew; **~ podrida** dish composed of different boiled meats and vegetables; **~ exprés/~ a presión** pressure cooker.
olmo *m* elm tree.
olor *m* smell, odor; scent.
oloroso/sa *adj* fragrant; odorous.
olvidadizo/za *adj* forgetful.
olvidar *vt* to forget.
olvido *m* forgetfulness.
ombligo *m* navel.
omelet *f Lat Am* omelet.

omisión *f* omission.
omitir *vt* to omit.
omnipotencia *f* omnipotence.
omnipotente *adj* omnipotent, almighty.
once *adj, m* eleven.
onda *f* wave.
ondear *vi* to undulate; to fluctuate.
ondulado/da *adj* wavy.
oneroso/sa *adj* burdensome.
onomástico *m Lat Am* birthday.
opa *f* takeover bid.
opacidad *f* opacity; gloom, darkness.
opaco/ca *adj* opaque; dark.
opción *f* option, choice.
ópera *f* opera.
operación *f* operation; **~ de cesárea** *f* cesarean section/operation.
operador/ra *m/f* operator; projectionist; cameraman/woman.
operar *vi* to operate; to act.
operativo *m Lat Am* operation.
opinar *vt* to think; * *vi* to give one's opinion.
opinión *f* opinion.
opio *m* opium.
oponente *m/f* opponent.
oponer *vt* to oppose; **~se** *vr* to be opposed, **~ a** to oppose.
oportunidad *f* opportunity.
oportunismo *m* opportunism.
oportuno/na *adj* seasonable, opportune.
oposición *f* opposition; **~ones** *fpl* public examinations *pl*.
opositor/ra *m/f* opponent; candidate (in public examination).
opresión *f* oppression.
opresivo/va *adj* oppressive.
opresor *m* oppressor.
oprimir *vt* to oppress; to crush; to press; to squeeze.
optar *vt* to choose, to elect.
optativo/va *adj* optional.
óptica *f* optics.
óptico/ca *adj* optical; * *m/f* optician.
optimista *m/f* optimist.
óptimo/ma *adj* best.
opuesto/ta *adj* opposite; contrary; adverse.
opulencia *f* wealth, riches *pl*.
opulento/ta *adj* opulent, wealthy.
oración *f* oration, speech; prayer.
orador,ra *m/f* orator.
oral *adj* oral.
orangután *m* orang-utan.
orar *vi* to pray.
oratoria *f* oratory, rhetorical skill.
órbita *f* orbit.
orden *m/f* order; **~ del día** order of the day.
ordenación *f* arrangement; ordination; edict, ordinance.

O

ordenado/da *adj* methodical; orderly.
ordenador *m* computer.
ordenanza *f* order; statute, ordinance; ordination.
ordenar *vt* to arrange; to order; to ordain; **~se** *vr* to take holy orders.
ordeña *f Lat Am* milking.
ordeñar *vt* to milk.
órdenes sagradas *fpl* holy orders *pl*.
ordinal *adj* ordinal.
ordinario/ria *adj* ordinary, common; **de ~** regularly, commonly, ordinarily.
orégano *m* oregano.
oreja *f* ear.
orejera *f* earflap.
orfanato *m* orphanage.
orfandad *f* orphanhood.
orgánico/ca *adj* organic; harmonious.
organigrama *m* flowchart.
organismo *m* organism; organization.
organista *m/f* organist.
organización *f* organization; arrangement.
organizar *vt* to organize.
órgano *m* organ.
orgasmo *m* orgasm.
orgía *f* orgy.
orgullo *m* pride, haughtiness.
orgulloso/sa *adj* proud, haughty.
orientación *f* position; direction.
oriental *adj* oriental, eastern; *Lat Am* Uruguayan.
orientar *vt* to orient; to point; to direct; to guide; **~se** *vr* to get one's bearings; to decide on a course of action.
oriente *m* orient.
orificio *m* orifice; mouth; aperture.
origen *m* origin, source; native country; family, extraction.
original *adj* original, primitive; * *m* original, first copy.
originalidad *f* originality.
originar *vt*, *vi* to originate.
originario/ria *adj* original.
orilla *f* limit, border, margin; edge (of cloth); shore.
orín *m* rust.
orina *f* urine.
orinal *m* chamber pot.
orinar *vi* to pass water, urinate.
oriundo/da *adj*: **~ de** native of.
ornamento *m* ornament, embellishment.
ornitología *f* ornithology.
oro *m* gold.
oros *mpl* diamonds *pl* (in cards).
orquesta *f* orchestra.
orquídea *f* orchid.

ortiga *f* (*bot*) nettle.
ortodoxia *f* orthodoxy.
ortodoxo/xa *adj* orthodox.
ortografía *f* orthography.
ortográfico/ca *adj* orthographic(al).
oruga *f* (*bot*) caterpillar.
orza *f* jar.
orzuelo *m* (*med*) stye,sty.
os *pn* you; to you.
osa *f* she-bear; **O~ Mayor/Menor** Great/Little Bear.
osadamente *adv* boldly, daringly.
osadía *f* boldness, intrepidity; zeal, fervor.
osamenta *f* skeleton.
osar *vi* to dare, to venture.
óscar *m* Oscar.
oscilación *f* oscillation.
oscilar *vi* to oscillate.
oscurecer *vt* to obscure; to darken; * *vi* to grow dark; **~se** *vr* to disappear.
oscuridad *f* obscurity; darkness.
oscuro/ra *adj* obscure; dark.
osificarse *vr* to ossify.
oso *m* bear; **~ blanco** polar bear.
ostensible *adj* ostensible, apparent.
ostentación *f* ostentation, ambitious display, show.
ostentar *vt* to show; * *vi* to boast, to brag.
ostentoso/sa *adj* sumptuous, ostentatious.
ostra *f* oyster.
otitis *f* earache.
otoñal *adj* fall.
otoño *m* fall.
otorgamiento *m* granting; execution.
otorgar *vt* to concede; to grant.
otorrino/na, **otorrinolaringólogo/ga** *m/f* ear, nose and throat specialist.
otro/tra *adj* another; other.
ovación *f* ovation.
ovalado/da *adj* oval.
óvalo *m* oval.
ovario *m* ovary.
oveja *f* sheep.
overol *m Lat Am* coveralls *pl*.
ovillo *m* ball of wool.
ovíparo/ra *adj* oviparous, egg-bearing.
ovulación *f* ovulation.
óvulo *m* ovum.
oxidación *f* rusting.
oxidar *vt* to rust; **~se** *vr* to go rusty.
óxido *f* (*chem*) oxide.
oxígeno *m* (*chem*) oxygen.
oyente *m/f* listener, hearer.

P

pabellón *m* pavilion; summer house; block, section.

pábilo *m* wick.

pacer *vt* to pasture, to graze.

paciencia *f* patience.

paciente *adj*, *m/f* patient.

pacificación *f* pacification.

pacificar *vt* to pacify, to appease.

pacífico/ca *adj* pacific, peaceful; * *m*: **el P~** the Pacific.

pacotilla *f*: **de ~** third-rate; cheap.

pactar *vt* to covenant; to contract; to stipulate.

pacto *m* contract, pact.

padecer *vt* to suffer; to sustain (an injury); to put up with.

padecimiento *m* suffering, sufferance.

padrastro *m* stepfather.

padrazo *m* loving, over-indulgent father.

padre *m* father; **~s** *mpl* parents *pl*.

padrino *m* godfather.

padrón *m* census; register; pattern; model.

paella *f* paella (dish of rice with shellfish, meat etc).

paga *f* payment, fee.

pagadero/ra *adj* payable.

paganismo *m* paganism, heathenism.

pagano/na *adj*, *m/f* heathen, pagan.

pagar *vt* to pay; to pay for; (*fig*) to repay; * *vi* to pay.

pagaré *m* bond, note of hand, promissory note, IOU (I owe you).

página *f* page.

pago *m* payment; reward.

país *m* country; region.

paisaje *m* landscape.

paisano/na *adj* of the same country; * *m/f* fellow countryman/woman.

paja *f* straw; (*fig*) trash.

pajar *m* straw loft.

pajarita *f* bow tie.

pájaro *m* bird; sly, acute fellow.

pajarraco *m* large bird; cunning fellow.

paje *m* page.

pajita *f* (drinking) straw.

pajizo/za *adj* straw-colored.

pala *f* spade, shovel.

palabra *f* word; **de ~** by word of mouth.

palabrota *f* swearword.

palaciego/ga *adj* pertaining/relating to the palace; * *m* courtier.

palacio *m* palace.

paladar *m* palate; taste, relish.

paladear *vt* to taste.

palanca *f* lever; **tener ~** *Lat Am* to have connections.

palanca de cambios *f* gear shift.

palangana *f* basin; *Lat Am* wooden platter.

palco *m* box (in a theater).

paleta *f* bat; palette; trowel.

paleto/ta *m/f* rustic.

paliar *vt* to mitigate.

paliativo/va *adj*, *m* palliative.

palidecer *vi* to turn pale.

palidez *f* paleness, wanness.

pálido/da *adj* pallid, pale.

palillo *m* small stick; toothpick; **~s** *mpl* chopsticks *pl*.

paliza *f* beating, thrashing.

palma *f* palm tree; palm of the hand; palm leaf.

palmada *f* slap, clap; **~s** *fpl* clapping of hands, applause.

palmatoria *f* candlestick; cane.

palmear *vi* to slap; to clap.

palmera *f* palm tree.

palmeta *f* cane.

palmo *m* palm; small amount.

palmotear *vi* to slap; to applaud.

palmoteo *m* clapping of hands.

palo *m* stick; cudgel; blow given with a stick; post; mast; bat; suit (in cards); *Lat Am* tree.

paloma *f* pigeon, dove; **~ torcaz** ring dove/wood pigeon; **~ mensajera** carrier pigeon, homing pigeon.

palomar *m* pigeon house/loft.

palomilla *f* moth; wing nut; angle iron.

palomino *m* young pigeon.

palomitas *fpl* popcorn.

palpable *adj* palpable, evident.

palpar *vt* to feel, to touch.

palpitación *f* palpitation; panting.

palpitante *adj* palpitating; (*fig*) burning.

palta *f* avocado (pear).

paludismo *m* malaria.

palpitar *vi* to palpitate.

palurdo/da *adj* rustic, clownish, rude.

pampa *f* pampa(s), prairie.

pámpano *m* vine branch.

pamplina *f* trifle.

pan *m* bread; loaf.

pana *f* corduroy.

panacea *f* panacea, universal medicine.

panadería *f* baker's (shop).

panadero/ra *m/f* baker.

panal *m* honeycomb; sweet rusk.
pancarta *f* placard.
pancito *m* Lat Am bread roll.
panda *m* panda (bear).
pandereta *f* tambourine.
pandilla *f* group; gang; clique.
panecito *m* Lat Am bread roll.
panegírico/ca *adj* panegyrical; * *m* eulogy.
panel *m* panel.
panfleto *m* pamphlet.
pánico *m* panic.
panorama *m* panorama.
panqueque *m* Lat Am pancake.
pantalla *f* screen; lampshade.
pantalón *m*, **pantalones** *mpl* pants *pl*, women's slacks *pl*.
pantano *m* swamp; marsh; reservoir; obstacle, difficulty.
pantanoso/sa *adj* swampy, marshy.
panteísta *f* pantheist.
panteón *m*: ~ **familiar** family tomb.
pantera *f* panther.
pantomima *f* pantomime.
pantorrilla *f* calf (of the leg).
pantufla *m* slipper.
panza *f* belly, paunch.
panzada *f* bellyful of food.
panzón/ona *adj* Lat Am big-bellied.
panzudo/da *adj* big-bellied.
pañal *m* diaper; ~ **desechable** disposable diaper.
paño *m* cloth; piece of cloth; duster, rag.
pañuelo *m* handkerchief.
papa *f* potato; * *m*: **el P~** the Pope.
papá *m* (col) pop, dad.
papada *f* double chin.
papagayo *m* parrot.
papal *adj* papal.
papanatas *m invar* (col) simpleton.
Papanicolau *m* Lat Am smear test.
paparrucha *f* piece of nonsense.
papaya *f* papaya, pawpaw.
papel *m* paper; writing; part, role (acted in a play); ~ **de estraza** brown paper; ~ **sellado** stamped paper.
papeleo *m* red tape.
papelera *f* writing desk; wastepaper basket.
papelería *f* stationer's (shop).
papeleta *f* slip of paper; ballot paper; report.
paperas *fpl* mumps.
papilla *f* baby food.
papista *m* papist.
paquete *m* packet; parcel; package tour.
par *adj* equal; alike; even; * *m* pair; couple; peer; **sin** ~ matchless.
para *prep* for; to, in order to; toward(s).
parabién *m* congratulations *pl*; felicitations *pl*.
parábola *f* parable; parabola.
parabólico/ca *adj* parabolic(al).

parabrisas *m invar* windshield.
paracaídas *m invar* parachute.
paracaidista *m/f* parachutist; (mil) paratrooper.
parachoques *m invar* fender; shock absorber.
parada *f* halt; suspension; pause; stop; shutdown; stopping place; ~ **a petición** flag stop; ~ **de autobús** bus stop.
paradero *m* halting place; term, end.
parado/da *adj* motionless; at a standstill; stopped; Lat Am standing (up); unemployed; * *m/f* unemployed person.
paradoja *f* paradox.
parador *m* parador, state-owned hotel.
parafrasear *vt* to paraphrase.
paráfrasis *f invar* paraphrase.
parágrafo *m* Lat Am paragraph.
paraguas *m invar* umbrella.
paraíso *m* paradise.
paraje *m* place, spot.
paralelo/la *adj*, *m* parallel.
paralítico/ca *adj* paralytic, palsied.
paralizar *vt* to paralyze; ~**se** *vr* to become paralyzed; (fig) to come to a standstill.
páramo *m* desert; wilderness.
parangón *m* paragon, model; comparison.
paranoico/ca *m/f* paranoiac.
parapente *m* paragliding.
parapeto *m* parapet.
parar *vi* to stop, to halt; * *vt* to stop, to detain; Lat Am to raise; **sin** ~ instantly, without delay; ~**se** *vr* to stop, to halt; Lat Am to stand up.
pararrayos *m invar* lightning conductor/rod.
parásito *m* parasite; (fig) sponger.
parasol *m* parasol.
parcela *f* piece of ground.
parche *m* patch.
parcial *adj* partial.
parcialidad *f* prejudice; bias.
parco/ca *adj* sober, moderate.
pardo/da *adj* gray.
parear *vt* to match, to pair, to couple.
parecer *m* opinion, advice, counsel; countenance, air, mien; * *vi* to appear; to seem; ~**se** *vr*: ~ **a** to resemble.
parecido/da *adj* resembling, like.
pared *f* wall; (law) ~ **medianera** party-wall.
pareja *f* pair, couple; a lumber/timber beam that serves as a support, brace.
parejo/ja *adj* equal; even.
parentela *f* parentage, kindred.
parentesco *m* relationship.
paréntesis *m invar* parenthesis.
parida *f* woman who has recently given birth.
paridad *f* parity, equality.
pariente/ta *m/f* relative, relation.
parir *vt* to give birth to; * *vi* to give birth.
parking *m* parking lot.
parlamentar *vi* to parley.

parlamentario/ria *m/f* member of parliament; * *adj* parliamentary.

parlamento *m* parliament.

parlanchín/ina *adj, m/f* chatterer, jabberer.

parlante *m* Lat Am speaker.

parlotear *vi* to prattle, to chatter, to gossip.

paro *m* unemployment; Lat Am strike.

parodia *f* parody.

parpadear *vi* to blink; to flicker.

párpado *m* eyelid.

parque *m* park; ~ **eólico** wind farm.

parque de bomberos *m* fire station, fire house.

parquímetro *m* parking meter.

parra *f* vine raised on stakes/nailed to a wall.

párrafo *m* paragraph.

parricida *m/f* parricide (person).

parricidio *m* parricide (act).

parrilla *f* grill; grille; Lat Am roof rack.

párroco *m* parish priest.

parroquia *f* parish; customers *pl*.

parroquial *adj* parochial.

parroquiano *m* parishioner; customer; ~/na *adj* parochial.

parsimonia *f* parsimony.

parte *m* message; report; * *f* part; side; party; **de ocho días a esta ~** within these last eight days; **de ~ a ~** from side to side, through and through.

partera *f* midwife.

partición *f* partition, division.

participación *f* participation.

participante *m/f* participant.

participar *vi* to participate, to partake.

partícipe *m/f* participant.

participio *m* participle.

partícula *f* particle.

particular *adj* particular, special; * *m* private individual; particular matter/subject.

particularidad *f* particularity.

particularizar(se) *vt* (*vr*) to particularize; to distinguish; to specify.

partida *f* departure; party; item in an account; parcel; game.

partidario/ria *adj* partisan; * *m/f* supporter.

partido *m* party; match; team.

Partido Democrático *m* Democratic Party.

Partido Republicano *m* Republican Party.

partidor *m* apportioner, divider.

partir *vt* to part; to divide, to separate; to cut; to break; * *vi* to depart; ~**se** *vr* to break (in two etc).

parto *m* birth.

parvulario *m* kindergarten.

pasa *f* raisin.

pasada *f* passage, passing; **de ~** on the way, in passing.

pasadizo *m* narrow passage; narrow, covered way.

pasado/da *adj* past; bad; overdone; out of date; ~ **mañana** the day after tomorrow; **la semana pasada** last week; * *m* past.

pasador *m* bolt; hair slide; grip.

pasaje *m* passage; fare; passengers *pl*.

pasajero/ra *adj* transient; transitory; fugitive; * *m/f* traveler; passenger.

pasamanos *m invar* (hand)rail; banister.

pasamontañas *m invar* balaclava helmet.

pasaporte *m* passport.

pasar *vt* to pass; to surpass; to suffer; to strain; to dissemble; * *vi* to pass; to happen; ~**se** *vr* to go over (to another party); to go bad/off.

pasarela *f* footbridge; gangway.

pasatiempo *m* pastime, amusement.

Pascua *f* Passover; Easter.

pase *m* pass; showing; permit.

paseante *m* walker.

pasear *vt* to walk; *vi*, ~**se** *vr* to walk; to walk about.

paseo *m* walk; Lat Am trip; shopping mall.

pasillo *m* passage.

pasión *f* passion.

pasionaria *f* passionflower, granadilla.

pasivo/va *adj* passive.

pasmar *vt* to amaze; to numb; to chill; ~**se** *vr* to be astonished.

pasmo *m* astonishment, amazement.

pasmoso/sa *adj* marvelous, wonderful.

paso *m* pace, step; passage; manner of walking; flight of steps; accident; (*rail*) ~ **a nivel** grade crossing; **al ~** on the way, in passing.

paso de peatones *m* crosswalk.

pasota *adj, m/f* (*col*) dropout; **ser un ~** not to care about anything.

pasta *f* paste; dough; pastry; (*col*) dough, money; ~**s** *fpl* pastries *pl*; pasta; ~ **de dientes** toothpaste.

pastar *vt* to pasture, to graze.

pastel *m* cake; pie; pastel drawing; crayon.

pastelería *f* shop that sells cakes and pastries.

pasteurizado/da *adj* pasteurized.

pastilla *f* bar (of soap); tablet, pill.

pasto *m* pasture; Lat Am lawn, grass; **a ~** abundantly.

pastor *m* shepherd; pastor.

pastoso/sa *adj* mellow, pleasant (voice); soft, doughy.

pata *f* leg (of animal/furniture); foot; **a la ~ coja** hopscotch (children's game); **a ~** (*col*) on foot; **meter la ~** to put one's foot in it.

patada *f* kick; Lat Am electric shock.

patalear *vi* to kick violently.

pataleo *m* act of stamping one's foot.

pataleta *f* fit, convulsion; swoon.

patán *m* clown; churl, surly person.

patata *f* potato.

patatús *m* dizzy spell, fainting fit.

paté m pâté.

patear vt to kick; to stamp on.

patente adj patent, manifest, evident; * f patent; warrant.

paternal adj paternal, fatherly.

paternidad f paternity, fatherhood.

paterno/na adj paternal, fatherly.

patético/ca adj pathetic.

patíbulo m scaffold; gallows.

patillas fpl sideburns pl.

patín m skate; runner.

patinaje m skating.

patinar vi to skate; to skid; (col) to blunder.

patinete m scooter (child's).

patio m courtyard; playground (in schools).

patizambo/ba adj knock-kneed.

pato m duck.

patochada f blunder, folly; nonsense.

patología f pathology.

patológico/ca adj pathological.

patón/ona adj Lat Am (col) clumsy.

patoso/sa adj (col) clumsy.

patraña f lie.

patria f native country.

patriarca m patriarch.

patriarcado m patriarchy.

patriarcal adj patriarchal.

patrimonial adj patrimonial.

patrimonio m patrimony.

patrio/tria adj native; paternal.

patriota m/f patriot.

patriótico/ca adj patriotic.

patriotismo m patriotism.

patrocinar vt to sponsor; to back, to support.

patrocinio m sponsorship; backing, support.

patrón/ona m/f boss, master/mistress; landlord/lady; patron saint; * m pattern.

patronal adj: **la clase ~** management.

patronato m patronage, sponsorship; trust, foundation.

patronímico m patronymic.

patrulla f patrol.

patrullar vi to patrol.

patudo/da adj Lat Am (col) clumsy.

paulatino/na adj gradual, slow.

pausa f pause; repose.

pausado/da adj slow, deliberate; calm, quiet.

pausar vi to pause.

pauta f guideline.

pavesa f embers pl, hot cinders pl.

pavimento m sidewalk; paving.

pavo m turkey; **~ real** peacock.

pavonearse vr to strut, to walk with affected dignity.

pavor m dread, terror.

pavoroso/sa adj awful, formidable.

payaso/sa m/f clown.

payo/ya m/f non-Gypsy (for a Gypsy).

paz f peace; tranquility, ease.

peaje m toll.

peal m Lat Am lasso.

peana f pedestal; footstool.

peatón m pedestrian.

peca f freckle; spot.

pecado m sin.

pecador/ra m/f sinner.

pecaminoso/sa adj sinful.

pecar vi to sin.

pecho m chest; breast(s) (pl); teat; bosom; Lat Am breaststroke; (fig) courage, valor; **dar el ~ a** to breast-feed; **tomar a ~** to take to heart.

pechuga f breast (of a fowl); (col) bosom.

pecoso/sa adj freckled.

peculiar adj peculiar; special.

pecuniario/ria adj pecuniary.

pedagogía f pedagogy.

pedagógico/ca adj pedagogic.

pedagogo/ga m/f pedagog.

pedal m pedal.

pedalear vi to pedal.

pedante adj pedantic; * m/f pedant.

pedantería f pedantry.

pedazo m piece, tidbit.

pedernal m flint.

pedestal m pedestal, foot.

pediatra m/f pediatrician.

pediatría f. pediatrics pl.

pedicurista m/f Lat Am podiatrist.

pedicuro/ra m/f podiatrist, chiropodist.

pedido m (com) order; Lat Am request.

pedir vt to ask for; to petition; to beg; to order; to need; to solicit; * vi to ask.

pedo m (col) fart; **tirarse un ~** to fart.

pedrada f throw (of a stone).

pedregal m stony place.

pedregoso/sa adj stony.

pedrería f (collection of) precious stones pl.

pedrisco m hailstone.

pedrusco m rough piece of stone.

pegadizo/za adj clammy, sticky; catchy; contagious.

pegajoso/sa adj sticky, viscous; contagious; attractive.

pegamento m glue.

pegar vt to cement; to join, to unite; to beat; **~ fuego a** to set fire to; * vi to stick; to match; **~se** vr to intrude; to steal in.

pegatina f sticker.

pegote m adhesive tape, sticking plaster; intruder; hanger-on, (col) sponger.

peinado m hairstyle.

peinador/ra m/f Lat Am hairdresser.

peinar vt to comb; to style.

peine m comb.

peineta f convex comb for women.

peladilla f sugared almond, burnt almond; small pebble.

pelado/da *adj* peeled; shorn; bare; broke; * *m* (*col*) haircut.
peladura *f* peeling; plucking.
pelaje *m* fur coat; (*fig*) appearance.
pelapapas *m inv Lat Am* potato peeler.
pelar *vt* to cut (hair); to pluck (feathers); to peel; ~**se** *vr* to peel off; to have one's hair cut.
peldaño *m* step (of a flight of stairs).
pelea *f* battle, fight; quarrel.
pelear *vt* to fight, to combat; ~**se** *vr* to scuffle.
pelele *m* dummy; man of straw.
peletería *f* fur shop.
peletero *m* furrier.
peliagudo/da *adj* tricky; arduous, difficult.
pelícano *m* pelican.
película *f* film; pellicle.
peligrar *vi* to be in danger; ~ **de** to risk.
peligro *m* danger, peril; risk.
peligroso/sa *adj* dangerous, perilous.
pelirrojo/ja *m/f* redhead; * *adj* red-haired.
pellejo *m* skin; hide, pelt; peel; wine skin, leather bag for wine; oilskin; drunkard.
pelliza *f* fur jacket.
pellizcar *vt* to pinch.
pellizco *m* pinch; nip; small bit; (*fig*) remorse.
pelmo/ma, **pelmazo/za** *m/f* (*col*) pain (in the neck).
pelo *m* hair; pile; flaw (in precious stones).
pelón/ona *adj* hairless, bald.
pelota *f* ball.
pelotazo *m* blow with a ball.
pelotera *f* quarrel.
pelotero/ra *m/f Lat Am* baseball player.
pelotón *m* large ball; crowd; posse; (*mil*) platoon.
peluca *f* wig.
peluche *m*: **muñeco de** ~ soft toy.
peludo/da *adj* hairy.
peluquería *f* hairdresser's (premises); barber shop.
peluquero/ra *m/f* hairdresser; barber.
pelusa *f* bloom (on fruit); fluff.
pena *f* punishment, pain; **a duras** ~**s** with great difficulty/trouble.
penacho *m* tuft on the heads of some birds; crest.
penal *adj* penal; * *m Lat Am* penalty (kick).
penalidad *f* suffering, trouble; hardship; penalty.
penar *vi* to suffer pain; * *vt* to chastise.
pendencia *f* quarrel, dispute.
pendenciero/ra *adj* quarrelsome.
pender *vi* to hang; to be pending; to depend.
pendiente *f* slope, declivity; * *m* earring; * *adj* pending; unsettled.
pendón *m* standard; banner.
péndulo *m* pendulum.
pene *m* penis.
penetración *f* penetration; perception.
penetrante *adj* deep; sharp; piercing; searching; biting.

penetrar *vt* to penetrate.
penicilina *f* penicillin.
península *f* peninsula.
penique *m* penny.
penitencia *f* penitence; penalty, fine.
penitenciaría *f* penitentiary.
penitente *adj* penitent, repentant; * *m* penitent.
penoso/sa *adj* painful.
pensador/ra *m/f* thinker.
pensamiento *m* thought, thinking.
pensar *vi* to think.
pensativo/va *adj* pensive, thoughtful.
pensión *f* pension; guest-house; worry; regret.
pensionista *m/f* pensioner; lodger.
Pentecostés *m* Pentecost, Whitsuntide.
penúltimo/ma *adj* penultimate, last but one.
penumbra *f* half-light.
penuria *f* penury, poverty, neediness, extreme want.
peña *f* rock, large stone.
peñasco *m* large rock.
peñón *m* rocky mountain.
peón *m* (day)laborer; foot soldier; pawn (at chess).
peonía *f* (*bot*) peony.
peonza *f* spinning top.
peor *adj*, *adv* worse; **cada vez** ~ worse and worse.
pepinillo *m* gherkin.
pepino *m* cucumber.
pepita *f* kernel; pip.
pepitoria *f* fricassee.
pequeñez *f* smallness; childhood, infancy; triviality.
pequeño/ña *adj* little, small; young.
pera *f* pear.
peral *m* pear tree.
percance *m* perquisite (perk); bad luck, setback.
percatarse *vr*: ~ **de** to notice.
percepción *f* perception; notion.
perceptible *adj* perceptible, perceivable.
percha *f* coat hook; coat hanger; perch.
percibir *vt* to receive; to perceive, to comprehend.
percusión *f* percussion.
perder *vt* to lose; to waste; to miss; ~**se** *vr* to go astray; to be lost; to be spoiled.
perdición *f* loss, losing; perdition, ruin.
pérdida *f* loss, damage; lost object.
perdido/da *adj* lost; stray.
perdigón *m* young partridge; ~**ones** *mpl* buckshot, pellets.
perdiz *f* partridge.
perdón *m* pardon; mercy; ¡~! sorry!; excuse me!
perdonable *adj* pardonable.
perdonar *vt* to pardon, to forgive; to excuse.
perdurable *adj* perpetual, everlasting.
perdurar *vi* to last; to still exist.
perecedero/ra *adj* perishable.

P

perecer vi to perish, to die; to shatter (an object).
peregrinación f pilgrimage.
peregrinar vi to go on a pilgrimage.
peregrino/na adj (fig) strange; * m/f pilgrim.
perejil m parsley.
perenne adj perennial; perpetual.
perentorio/ria adj peremptory; urgent.
pereza f laziness, idleness.
perezoso/sa adj lazy, idle.
perfección f perfection.
perfeccionar vt to perfect; to complete, to finish.
perfecto/ta adj perfect; complete.
perfidia f perfidy.
pérfido/da adj perfidious.
perfil m profile.
perfilado/da adj well-formed, delicate (of features).
perfilar vt to outline; ~se vr: ~ en to show up against.
perforar vt to perforate; to drill; to punch a hole in; * vi to drill.
performance m Lat Am performance.
perfumador m perfumer.
perfumar vt to perfume.
perfume m perfume.
perfumería f perfumery.
pergamino m parchment.
pericia f skill, knowledge; expertise.
periferia f periphery; outskirts pl.
periférico m beltway, bypass, ring road.
perífrasis f invar periphrasis, circumlocution.
perímetro m perimeter; circumference.
periódico/ca adj periodical; * m newspaper.
periodista m/f journalist.
período/periodo m period; sentence; (med) menstrual period.
peripecia f vicissitude; sudden change.
peripuesto/ta adj dressed up, very spruce.
periquito m budgie, budgerigar.
perito/ta adj skillful, experienced; * m/f expert; skilled worker; technician.
perjudicar vt to prejudice, to damage; to injure, to hurt.
perjudicial adj prejudicial, damaging.
perjuicio m damage, harm.
perjurar vi to perjure, to swear falsely; to swear.
perjurio m perjury; false oath.
perjuro/ra adj perjured; * m/f perjurer.
perla f pearl; **de ~s** fine.
permanecer vi to stay; to continue to be.
permanencia f permanence; stay.
permanente adj permanent.
permiso m permission, leave, license.
permitir vt to permit, to allow.
permuta f permutation, exchange.
permutar vt to exchange, to permute.
pernera f trouser leg.
pernicioso/sa adj pernicious, destructive; wicked.

pernio m hinge.
perno m bolt.
pernoctar vi to spend the night.
pero m kind of apple; * conj but, yet.
perogrullada f truism, platitude.
perol m large metal pan.
perorata f harangue, speech.
perpendicular adj perpendicular.
perpetrar vt to perpetrate, to commit (a crime).
perpetuar vt to perpetuate.
perpetuidad f perpetuity.
perpetuo/tua adj perpetual.
perplejidad f perplexity.
perplejo/ja adj perplexed.
perra f bitch; (col) money.
perrera f kennel.
perro m dog.
persecución f persecution; toil, trouble; fatigue.
perseguidor m persecutor.
perseguir vt to pursue; to persecute; to chase after.
perseverancia f perseverance, constancy.
perseverante adj persistent.
perseverar vi to persevere, to persist.
persiana f (Venetian) blind.
persignarse vr to make the sign of the cross.
persistencia f persistence; steadiness.
persistir vi to persist.
persona f person; **de ~ a ~** from person to person.
personaje m celebrity; character.
personal adj personal; single; * m personnel.
personalidad f personality.
personarse vr to appear in person.
personero/ra m/f Lat Am spokesperson.
personificar vt to personify.
perspectiva f perspective; view; outlook.
perspicacia f perspicacity, clear-sightedness.
perspicaz adj perspicacious, clear-sighted.
persuadir vt to persuade; ~se vr to be persuaded.
persuasión f persuasion.
persuasivo/va adj persuasive.
pertenecer vi: ~ a to belong to; to appertain, to concern.
pertenencia f ownership; ~s fpl possessions pl.
perteneciente adj: ~ a belonging to.
pértiga f long pole/rod.
pertinacia f pertinacity; obstinacy, stubbornness.
pertinaz adj pertinacious; obstinate.
pertinente adj relevant; appropriate.
pertrechar vt to supply with ammunition and other warlike stores; to dispose; to arrange, to prepare; ~se vr to be provided with the necessary defensive stores and arms.
pertrechos mpl tools pl, instruments pl; ammunition, fixings pl.
perturbación f perturbation; disturbance.
perturbado/da adj mentally unbalanced.

perturbador *m* disturber (of the peace).
perturbar *vt* to perturb, to disturb.
perversidad *f* perversity.
perversión *f* perversion; depravation, corruption.
perverso/sa *adj* perverse; extremely wicked.
pervertido/da *adj* perverted; * *m/f* pervert.
pervertir *vt* to pervert; to corrupt.
pesa *f* weight.
pesadez *f* heaviness, weight; gravity; slowness; peevishness, fretfulness; trouble; fatigue.
pesadilla *f* nightmare.
pesado/da *adj* peevish; troublesome; cumbersome; tedious; heavy, weighty.
pesadumbre *f* weightiness; gravity; quarrel, dispute; grief; trouble.
pésame *m* message of condolence.
pesar *m* sorrow, grief; repentance; **a ~ de** in spite of, notwithstanding; * *vi* to weigh; to repent; * *vt* to weigh.
pesario *m* pessary.
pesaroso/sa *adj* sorrowful, full of repentance; restless, uneasy.
pesca *f* fishing.
pescadería *f* fish market; shop that sells only fish.
pescado *m* fish (in general).
pescador *m* fisher, fisherman.
pescar *vt* to fish for, to catch (fish); * *vi* to fish.
pescuezo *m* neck.
pesebre *m* crib, manger.
peseta *f* peseta.
pesimista *m* pessimist.
pésimo/ma *adj* very bad.
peso *m* weight, heaviness; balance scales *pl*.
pespunte *m* back-stitching.
pesquero/ra *adj* fishing *compd*.
pesquisa *f* inquiry, examination.
pestaña *f* eyelash.
pestañear *vi* to blink.
pestañeo *m* blink.
peste *f* pest, plague, pestilence.
pesticida *m* pesticide.
pestífero/ra *adj* pestilential.
pestilencia *f* pestilence.
pestillo *m* bolt.
petaca *f* covered hamper; tobacco pouch.
pétalo *m* petal.
petardo *m* petard; cheat, fraud; imposition.
petate *m* straw bed; sleeping mat of the Indians; (*mar*) sailors' bedding on board ship; (*mar*) passengers' baggage; poor fellow.
petición *f* petition, demand.
peticionante *m/f Lat Am* petitioner.
peticionar *vt Lat Am* to petition.
peto *m* breastplate; bodice.
petrificar(se) *vt, vr* to petrify.
petróleo *m* oil, petroleum.
petrolero/ra *adj* petroleum *compd*; * *m* (oil) tanker; (*com*) oil man.

petulancia *f* petulance; insolence.
petulante *adj* petulant; insolent.
peyorativo/va *adj* pejorative.
pez *m* fish; * *f* pitch.
pezón *m* nipple.
pezuña *f* hoof.
piadoso/sa *adj* pious; mild; merciful; moderate.
pial *m Lat Am* lasso.
pianista *m/f* pianist.
piano *m* piano.
piar *vi* to squeak; to chirp.
piara *f* herd (of cattle); flock (of sheep).
pibe/ba *m/f* boy/girl.
pica *f* pike.
picacho *m* sharp point.
picadero *m* riding school.
picadillo *m* minced meat.
picado/da *adj* pricked; minced, chopped; bad (tooth); cross.
picador *m* riding master; picador.
picadura *f* prick; puncture.
picaflor *m Lat Am* hummingbird.
picana *f Lat Am* goad.
picanear *vt Lat Am* to goad.
picante *adj* hot, spicy; racy.
picapedrero *m* stonecutter.
picaporte *m* door handle; latch.
picar *vt* to prick; to sting; to mince; to nibble; * *vi* to prick; to sting; to itch; **~se** *vr* to be piqued; to take offense; to be moth-eaten; to begin to rot.
picardía *f* roguery; deceit; malice; lewdness.
picaresco/ca *adj* roguish; picaresque.
pícaro/ra *adj* roguish; mischievous, malicious; sly; * *m/f* rogue, knave.
picazón *f* itching; stinging; displeasure.
pichón *m* young pigeon.
pico *m* beak; bill, nib; peak; pick-ax.
picotazo *m* peck (of a bird).
picotear *vt* to peck (of birds).
picudo/da *adj* with a beak; sharp-pointed.
pie *m* foot; leg; basis; trunk (tree); foundation; occasion; **a ~** on foot.
piedad *f* piety; mercy, pity.
piedra *f* stone.
piel *f* skin; hide; peel.
pienso *m* fodder.
pierna *f* leg.
pieza *f* piece; room.
pigmeo/mea *m/f, adj* pigmy.
pijama *m* pajamas *pl*.
pila *f* battery; trough; font; sink; pile, heap; **nombre de ~** first name.
pilar¹ *m* basin.
pilar² *m* pillar, column; mainstay.
píldora *f* pill.
pileta *f* basin; swimming pool.
pillaje *m* pillage, plunder.

pillar vt to pillage, to plunder, to foray, to seize; to catch onto; to catch.

pillo/lla adj, m rascal, scoundrel.

pilotaje m pilotage.

piloto m/f pilot.

piltrafa f piece of meat that is nearly all skin.

pimentón m paprika.

pimienta f allspice; pepper, pimento.

pimiento m sweet pepper, pimiento.

pinacoteca f art gallery.

pináculo m pinnacle.

pinar m grove of pine trees.

pincel m paintbrush.

pincelada f dash with a paintbrush.

pinchar vt to prick; to puncture.

pinchazo m prick; puncture; (fig) prod.

pinchito m small snack.

pincho m thorn; snack.

pingajo m rag, tatter.

ping-pong m table tennis.

pingüe adj fat, greasy; fertile.

pingüino m penguin.

pino m pine tree.

pinta f spot, blemish; scar; mark (on playing cards); pint.

pintado/da adj painted, mottled; **venir ~** to fit exactly.

pintar vt to paint; to picture; to describe; to exaggerate; * vi to paint; (col) to count, to be important; **~se** vr to put on make-up.

pintarrajear vt to daub.

pintarrajo m daub.

pintor/-ra m/f painter.

pintoresco/ca adj picturesque.

pintura f painting.

pinza f claw; clothes peg; pincers pl; **~s** fpl tweezers pl.

piña f pineapple; fir cone; group.

piñal m Lat Am pineapple plantation.

piñón m pine nut; pinion.

pío/pía adj pious, devout; merciful.

piojo m louse; troublesome hanger-on.

piojoso/sa adj lousy; miserable, stingy.

piola f Lat Am cord.

pionero/ra adj pioneering; * m/f pioneer.

pipa f pipe (for smoking); seed; sunflower seed.

pipí m (col): **hacer ~** to have to go (urinate).

pique m pique, offense taken; rivalry; **echar a ~** to sink a ship; **a ~** in danger; **a ~ de** on the point of.

piquete m slight prick/sting; picket.

pira f funeral pyre.

piragua f canoe.

piragüismo m canoeing.

piramidal adj pyramidal.

pirámide f pyramid.

pirata m pirate.

piropo m compliment; flattery.

pirotecnia f fireworks pl.

pirueta f pirouette.

pisada f footstep; footprint.

pisar vt to tread, to trample; to stamp on (the ground); to hammer down; * vi to tread, to walk.

pisciano/na adj Lat Am Piscean (zodiac sign).

piscina f swimming pool; **~ para niños** paddling pool.

Piscis m Pisces (zodiac sign).

piso m flat, apartment; tread, trampling; floor, pavement; floor, story.

pisotear vt to trample, to tread under foot.

pista f trace, footprint; clue.

pisto m thick soup/broth.

pistola f pistol.

pistolera f pistol holster.

pistolero/ra m/f gunman/woman, gangster.

pistoletazo m pistol shot.

pistón m piston, (musical) key.

pita f (bot) any plant of the family Agavaceae, with tall flowers and thick, fleshy leaves.

pitada f Lat Am (col) puff.

pitar vt to blow; to whistle at; * vi to whistle; to toot one's horn; to smoke.

pitillo m cigarette.

pito m whistle; horn.

pitón m python.

pitonisa f sorceress, enchantress.

pitorreo m joke; **estar de ~** to be joking.

piyama m/f Lat Am pajamas.

pizarra f slate.

pizarral m slate quarry, slate pit.

pizarrón m Lat Am chalkboard.

pizca f mite; pinch.

placa f plate; badge; **~ de matrícula** license plate.

placentero/ra adj joyful, merry.

placer m pleasure; delight; * vt to please.

plácido/da adj placid.

plaga f plague.

plagar vt to plague, to torment.

plagio m plagiarism.

plan m plan; design; plot.

plana f trowel; page (of a book); level; **~ mayor** (mil) staff.

plancha f plate; iron; gangway; press-up.

planchar vt to iron.

planchuela n doorplate f.

planeador m glider.

planear vt to plan; * vi to glide.

planeta m planet.

planetario/ria adj planetary.

planicie f plain.

planificación f planning; **~ familiar** family planning, birth control.

planilla f Lat Am form.

plano/na adj plain, level, flat; * m plan; ground plot; **~ inclinado** (rail) dead level.

planta f plant; plantation.
plantación f plantation.
plantar vt to plant; to fix upright; to strike/hit (a blow); to found; to establish; ~**se** vr to stand upright.
plantear vt to plan; to implant.
plantel m Lat Am team.
plantilla f personnel; insole of a shoe.
plantón m long wait; (mil) sentry.
plañir vi to lament, to grieve, to bewail.
plasmar vt to mold; to represent.
plasta f paste, soft clay; mess.
plástico/ca adj plastic; * m plastic; * f sculpture (the art of).
plata f silver; plate (wrought silver); cash; Lat Am money; **en** ~ briefly.
plataforma f platform; ~ **giratoria** (rail) turntable.
plátano m banana tree; plane tree.
plateado/da adj silvered; silver-plated.
platería f silversmith's (premises); trade of silversmithing.
plática f discourse, conversation.
platicar vi to converse.
platillo m saucer; ~**s** mpl cymbals pl; ~ **volador**/ ~ **volante** flying saucer.
platino m platinum; ~**s** mpl contact points pl.
plato m dish; plate.
platónico/ca adj platonic.
plausible adj plausible.
playa f beach.
playera f T-shirt; ~**s** fpl sneakers pl, tennis shoes pl.
plaza f square; place; office, employment; room; seat.
plazo m term; installment; expiry date.
pleamar f (mar) high water.
plebe f common people pl, populace.
plebeyo/ya adj plebeian; * m commoner.
plebiscito m plebiscite.
plegable adj pliable; folding.
plegar vt to fold; to plait.
plegaria f prayer.
pleitear vi to plead, to litigate.
pleito m contract, bargain; dispute, controversy, Lat Am debate; lawsuit.
plenamente adv fully; completely.
plenario/ria adj complete; full.
plenilunio m full moon.
plenipotenciario m plenipotentiary.
plenitud f fullness; abundance.
pleno/na adj full; complete; * m plenum.
pliego m sheet of paper.
pliegue m fold; plait.
plisado/da adj pleated; * m pleating.
plomero m plumber.
plomizo/za adj leaden.
plomo m lead; **a** ~ perpendicularly.
pluma f feather, plume.

plumaje m plumage; plume.
plumero m bunch of feathers; feather duster.
plumón m felt-tip pen; marker; down (feathers).
plural adj (gr) plural.
pluralidad f plurality.
Plutón m Pluto (planet).
población f population; town.
poblado m town; village; inhabited place.
poblador/ra m/f populator, founder.
poblar vt to populate, to people; to fill, to occupy.
pobre adj poor.
pobreza f poverty, poorness.
pocilga f pigpen.
pocillo m coffee cup.
pócima, poción f potion.
poco/ca adj little, scanty; few pl; * adv little; ~ **a** ~ gently; little by little; * m small part; little.
poda f pruning (of trees).
podadera f pruning knife.
podadora f Lat Am pruning knife.
podar vt to prune.
podenco m hound.
poder m power, authority; command; force; * vi to be able to; to possess the power of doing/performing.
poderío m power, authority; wealth, riches pl.
poderoso/sa adj powerful; eminent, excellent.
podiatra m/f Lat Am podiatrist.
podredumbre f putrid matter; grief.
podrido/da adj rotten, bad; (fig) rotten.
podrir vt to rot, to putrefy; ~**se** vr to rot, to decay.
poema m poem.
poesía f poetry.
poeta m poet.
poético/ca adj poetical.
poetisa f poetess.
poetizar vt to poetize.
polar adj polar.
polea f pulley; (mar) tackle-block.
polémica f polemic.
polémico/ca adj polemical.
polen m pollen.
policía f police; * m/f police officer.
polideportivo m sports center.
poligamia f polygamy.
polígamo m polygamist.
polígono m polygon.
polilla f moth.
polio f polio.
pólipo m polypus.
politécnico/ca adj polytechnic.
politeísmo m polytheism.
política f politics; policy.
político/ca adj political; * m/f politician.
póliza f written order; policy.
polizón m stowaway.
pollera f skirt.
pollería f poulterer's (shop).

P

pollo m chicken.
polo m pole; Popsicle™; polo; polo neck.
polución f pollution.
polvareda f cloud of dust.
polvera f powder compact.
polvo m powder, dust.
pólvora f gunpowder.
polvoriento/ta adj dusty.
polvorín m powder reduced to the finest dust; powder flask.
pomada f cream, ointment.
pomelo m grapefruit.
pómez f: **piedra ~** pumice stone.
pompa f pomp; bubble.
pomposo/sa adj pompous.
pómulo m cheekbone.
ponchar vt Lat Am to strike out.
ponche m punch.
poncho/cha adj soft, mild; * m poncho.
ponderación f pondering, considering; exaggeration.
ponderar vt to ponder, to weigh; to exaggerate.
ponedero/ra adj egg-laying; capable of being laid/placed; * m nest; nest egg.
poner vt to put, to place; to put on; to impose; to lay (eggs); **~se** vr to oppose; to set (of stars); to become.
poniente m west; west wind.
pontificado m pontificate.
pontífice m Pope, pontiff.
pontificio/cia adj pontifical.
pontón m pontoon.
ponzoña f poison.
ponzoñoso/sa adj poisonous.
popa f (mar) poop, stern.
populacho m populace, mob.
popular adj popular.
popularidad f popularity.
popularizarse vr to become popular.
populoso/sa adj populous.
poquedad f paucity, smallness; cowardice.
por prep for; by; about; by means of; through; on account of.
porcelana f porcelain, china.
porcentaje m percentage.
porción f part, portion; lot.
porcuno/na adj hoggish, piggish; porcine.
pordiosero/ra m/f beggar.
porfiar vt to dispute obstinately; to persist in a pursuit.
pormenor f detail.
pornografía f pornography.
poro m pore.
porosidad f porosity.
poroso/sa adj porous.
porque conj because; since; so that.
porqué m cause, reason.
porquería f nastiness, foulness; brutishness; rudeness; trifle; dirty action.

porqueriza f pigpen.
porra f cudgel.
porrillo: a ~ adv copiously, abundantly.
porrón m spouted wine jar.
portada f portal, porch; frontispiece.
portador/ra m/f carrier, porter.
portaequipajes m invar trunk (in car); baggage rack.
portal m porch; portal.
portaligas m inv Lat Am garter belt.
portamonedas m invar purse.
portarse vr to behave.
portátil adj portable; * m laptop.
portaaviones m invar aircraft carrier.
portavoz m/f spokesman/woman.
portazo m bang of a door; the act of banging a door in someone's face.
porte m transportation charges pl; deportment, demeanor, conduct.
portento m prodigy, portent.
portentoso/sa adj prodigious, marvelous, strange.
portería f porter's office; goal (sport).
portero/ra m/f porter; janitor; gatekeeper; goalkeeper.
portezuela f little door.
pórtico m portico, porch, lobby.
portilla f, **portillo** m aperture in a wall; gate; gap, breach.
portón m main door (of a house).
porvenir m future.
pos prep: **en ~ de** after, behind; in pursuit of.
posada f shelter; inn, hotel.
posaderas fpl buttocks pl.
posadero m innkeeper.
posar vi to sit, to pose; * vt to lay down (a burden); **~se** vr to settle; to perch; to land.
posdata f postcript.
pose f pose.
poseedor/ra m/f owner, possessor; holder.
poseer vt to hold, to possess.
poseído/da adj possessed by the devil.
posesión f possession.
posesivo/va adj possessive.
posesor/ra m/f possessor.
posibilidad f possibility.
posibilitar vt to make possible; to make feasible.
posible adj possible.
posición f position; posture; situation.
positivo/va adj positive.
poso m sediment, dregs pl.
posponer vt to postpone.
posta f: **a ~** on purpose.
postal adj postal; * f postal card, postcard.
poste m pole, post, pillar.
póster m poster.
postergación f missing out, passing over; putting over.

postergar vt to leave behind; to postpone.
posteridad f posterity.
posterior adj posterior.
posterioridad f: **con ~** subsequently, later.
postigo m postern; small door; shutter (of a window).
postizo/za adj artificial (not natural); * m wig.
postor m bidder at a public sale; better.
postración f prostration.
postrar vt to humble, to humiliate; **~se** vr to prostrate oneself.
postre m dessert.
postrer(o)/ra adj last, hindmost.
postrimerías fpl dying moments; final stages.
póstumo/ma adj posthumous.
postulante m/f Lat Am candidate.
postura f posture, position; attitude; bet, wager; agreement, convention.
potable adj drinkable.
potaje m pottage; drink made up of several ingredients; medley of various useless things.
pote m pot, jar; flower pot.
potencia f power; mightiness.
potencial m potential.
potentado m potentate; prince.
potente adj potent, powerful, mighty.
potestad f power; dominion; jurisdiction.
potrero m Lat Am pasture.
potro/ra m/f colt; foal.
poyo m stone seat/bench.
pozo m well.
práctica f practice.
practicable adj practicable, feasible.
practicante adj practicing; * m/f practitioner.
practicar vt to practice.
práctico/ca adj practical; skillful, experienced.
pradera f meadow.
prado m lawn; meadow.
pragmático/ca adj pragmatic.
preámbulo m preamble; circumlocution.
prebenda f prebend.
precampaña f run-up to an election campaign.
precario/ria adj precarious.
precaución f precaution.
precaver vt to prevent; to guard against.
precedencia f precedence; preference; superiority.
precedente adj preceding, foregoing.
preceder vt to precede, to go before.
precepto m precept, order.
preceptor/ra m/f master, teacher, preceptor.
preciado/da adj esteemed, valued.
preciarse vr to boast; **~ de** to take pride in.
precinto m seal.
precio m price; value.
preciosidad f excellence; preciousness.
precioso/sa adj precious; (col) beautiful.
precipicio m precipice; violent, sudden fall; ruin, destruction.

precipitación f precipitation, rush.
precipitado/da adj precipitate, headlong, hasty.
precipitar vt to precipitate; **~se** vr to act hastily; to rush.
precisamente adv precisely; exactly.
precisar vt to compel, to oblige; to need.
precisión f necessity, compulsion; preciseness.
preciso/sa adj necessary, requisite; precise, exact; abstracted.
precocidad f precocity.
preconizar vt to proclaim; to recommend.
precoz adj precocious.
precursor/ra m/f harbinger, forerunner.
predecesor/ra m/f predecessor.
predecir vt to foretell.
predestinación f predestination.
predestinar vt to predestine.
predicación f preaching; sermon.
predicado m predicate.
predicador m preacher.
predicar vt to preach.
predicción f prediction.
predilección f predilection.
predilecto/ta adj darling, favorite.
predio m Lat Am building.
predisponer vt to predispose; to prejudice.
predisposición f inclination; prejudice.
predominar vi to predominate, to prevail.
predominio m predominant power, superiority.
preeminencia f pre-eminence; superiority.
preeminente adj pre-eminent; superior.
preescolar adj pre-school.
preestreno m prevue.
preexistencia f pre-existence.
preexistente adj pre-existent.
preexistir vt to pre-exist, to exist before.
prefabricado/da adj prefabricated.
prefacio m preface.
prefecto m prefect.
prefectura f prefecture.
preferencia f preference.
preferible adj preferable.
preferir vt to prefer.
prefijar vt (gr) to prefix; to fix beforehand.
prefijo m dial code.
pregón m proclamation; hue and cry.
pregonar vt to proclaim.
pregonero m town crier.
pregunta f question; inquiry.
preguntar vt to ask; to question; to demand; to inquire.
preguntón/ona m/f inquisitive person.
prehistórico/ca adj prehistoric.
prejuicio m prejudgement; preconception; prejudice.
prelado m prelate.
preliminar adj, m preliminary.
preludio m prelude.

P

prematuro/ra *adj* premature.
premeditación *f* premeditation, forethought.
premeditar *vt* to premeditate, to think out.
premiar *vt* to reward, to remunerate.
premio *m* reward, recompense; premium.
premisa *f* premise.
premura *f* pressure, haste, hurry.
prenatal *adj* pre-natal.
prenda *f* pledge; garment; sweetheart; person/
  thing dearly loved; ~**s** *fpl* accomplishments *pl*,
  talents *pl*.
prendar *vt* to enchant; ~**se** *vr*: ~ **de** to fall in
  love with.
prendedor *m* brooch.
prender *vt* to seize, to catch, to lay hold of; to
  imprison; *Lat Am* to switch on; ~**se** *vr* to catch
  fire; * *vi* to take root.
prendimiento *m* seizure; capture.
prensa *f* press.
prensar *vt* to press.
preñado/da *adj* pregnant.
preñez *f* pregnancy.
preocupación *f* worry, preoccupation.
preocupado/da *adj* worried, anxious.
preocupar(se) *vt* (*vr*) to worry.
preparación *f* preparation.
preparador/ra *m/f* trainer.
preparar *vt* to prepare; ~**se** *vr* to be prepared.
preparativo/va *adj* preparatory; preliminary;
  qualifying; * *m* preparation.
preparatorio/ria *adj* preparatory.
preponderancia *f* preponderance.
preponderar *vi* to preponderate, to prevail.
preposición *f* (*gr*) preposition.
prepucio *m* foreskin.
prerrogativa *f* prerogative, privilege.
presa *f* capture, seizure; dike, dam.
presagiar *vt* to presage, to forebode.
presagio *m* omen.
presbítero *m* priest, clergyman.
presciencia *f* prescience, foreknowledge.
prescindir *vi*: ~ **de** to do without; to dispense
  with.
prescribir *vt* to prescribe.
prescripción *f* prescription.
presencia *f* presence.
presenciar *vt* to attend; to be present at; to
  witness.
presentación *f* presentation.
presentador/ra *m/f* (*rad*, *TV*) presenter; compere.
presentar *vt* to present; to introduce; to offer;
  to show; ~**se** *vr* to present oneself; to appear;
  to run (as candidate); to apply.
presente *m* present, gift; * *adj* present.
presentemente *adv* presently, now.
presentimiento *m* presentiment.
presentir *vt* to have a premonition of.
preservación *f* preservation.

preservar *vt* to preserve; to defend.
preservativo *m* condom, sheath; *Lat Am*
  preservative.
presidencia *f* presidency.
presidente/ta *m/f* president.
presidiario/ria *m/f* convict.
presidio *m* penitentiary, prison.
presidir *vt* to preside at.
presilla *f* clip; loop (in clothes).
presión *f* pressure, pressing; ~ **de los neumáticos**
  tire pressure.
presionar *vt* to press; (*fig*) to put pressure on.
preso/sa *m/f* prisoner.
prestado/da *adj* on loan; **pedir** ~ to borrow.
prestamista *m* borrower, lender.
préstamo *m* loan.
prestar *vt* to lend.
presteza *f* quickness; haste, speed.
prestigio *m* prestige.
presto/ta *adj* quick; prompt; ready; * *adv* soon;
  quickly.
presumible *adj* presumable.
presumido/da *adj* presumptuous, arrogant.
presumir *vt* to presume, to conjecture; * *vi* to
  be conceited.
presunción *f* presumption, conjecture; conceit.
presunto/ta *adj* supposed; so-called.
presuntuoso/sa *adj* presumptuous.
presuponer *vt* to presuppose.
presupuesto *m* estimate; budget.
presuroso/sa *adj* hasty, quick; prompt; nimble.
pretencioso/sa *adj* pretentious.
pretender *vt* to pretend, to claim; to try, to
  attempt.
pretendiente *m* pretender; suitor.
pretensión *f* pretension.
pretérito/ta *adj* past.
pretextar *vt* to plead, use as an excuse.
pretexto *m* pretext; pretense; plea, excuse.
prevalacer *vi* to prevail; to triumph; to take root.
prevención *f* disposition, preparation; supply of
  provisions; foresight; prevention; (*mil*)
  guardroom, guardhouse.
prevenido/da *adj* prepared; careful, cautious;
  foreseeing.
prevenir *vt* to prepare; to foresee, to know in
  advance; to prevent; to warn; ~**se** *vr* to be
  prepared; to be predisposed.
preventivo/va *adj* preventive.
prever *vt* to foresee, to forecast.
previo/via *adj* previous.
previsión *f* foresight, prevision; forecast.
previsor/ra *adj* far-sighted.
previsivo/va *adj* *Lat Am* far-sighted.
prima *f* bonus; (female) cousin.
primacía *f* priority; primacy.
primado *m* primate.
primario/ria *adj* primary.

primavera f spring (the season).
primeramente adv in the first place, mainly.
primer(o)/ra adj first; prior; former; * adv first; rather, sooner.
primicias fpl first fruits pl.
primitivo/va adj primitive; original.
primo/ma m cousin.
primogénito/ta adj, m/f first-born.
primogenitura f primogeniture.
primor m beauty; dexterity, ability.
primordial adj basic, fundamental.
primoroso/sa adj neat, elegant; fine, excellent; handsome.
princesa f princess.
principal adj, m principal, chief.
príncipe m prince.
principiante m beginner, learner.
principiar vt, vi to commence, to begin.
principio m beginning, commencement; principle.
pringoso/sa adj greasy; sticky.
pringue m/f grease; lard, fat.
prioridad f priority.
prisa f speed; hurry; urgency; promptness.
prisión f prison; imprisonment.
prisionero m prisoner.
prisma m prism.
prismáticos mpl binoculars pl.
privación f deprivation, want.
privado/da adj private; particular.
privar vt to deprive; to prohibit; ~se vr to deprive oneself.
privativo/va adj private, one's own; particular, peculiar.
privilegiado/da adj privileged; very good.
privilegiar vt to privilege.
privilegio m privilege.
pro m/f profit; benefit; advantage.
proa f (mar) prow.
probabilidad f probability, likelihood.
probable adj probable, likely.
probado/da adj proved, tried.
probador m fitting room.
probar vt to try; to prove; to taste; * vi to try.
probeta f test tube.
problema m problem.
problemático/ca adj problematic.
procedencia m derivation.
procedente adj reasonable; proper; ~ de coming from.
proceder m procedure; * vi to proceed, to go on; to act.
procedimiento m proceeding; legal procedure.
procesado/da m/f accused.
procesador m: ~ de textos word processor.
procesar vt to put on trial.
procesión f procession.
proceso m process; lawsuit.

proclama f proclamation, publication.
proclamación f proclamation; acclamation.
proclamar vt to proclaim.
procreación f procreation, generation.
procrear vt to procreate, to generate.
procura f Lat Am search.
procurador/ra m/f procurer; attorney; solicitor.
procurar vt to try; to obtain; to produce.
prodigalidad f plenty, abundance.
prodigar vt to waste, to lavish.
prodigio m prodigy; monster.
prodigioso/sa adj prodigious, monstrous; exquisite; excellent.
pródigo/ga adj prodigal.
producción f production.
producir vt to produce; (law) to produce as evidence; ~se vr to come about; to arise; to be made; to break out.
productividad f productivity.
productivo/va adj productive.
producto m product.
productor/ra adj productive; * m/f producer.
proeza f prowess, valor, bravery.
profanación f desecration.
profanar vt to profane, to desecrate.
profano/na adj profane.
profecía f prophecy.
profesar vt to profess, to practice.
profesión f profession.
profesional adj, m/f professional.
profeso/sa adj professed.
profesor/ra m/f teacher; lecturer.
profesorado m teaching profession.
profeta m prophet.
profético/ca adj prophetic.
profetizar vt to prophesy.
prófugo/ga m/f fugitive.
profundidad f profundity, profoundness; depth; grandeur.
profundizar vt to go deeply into; to deepen; to penetrate.
profundo/da adj profound.
profusamente adv profusely.
profusión f profusion; prodigality.
progenie f progeny, offspring; race; generation.
progenitor m progenitor, ancestor, forefather.
programa m program.
programación f computer programing.
programador/ra m/f programer.
programar vt to program.
progresar vi to progress.
progresión f progression.
progresista adj, m/f progressive.
progreso m progress.
progresivo/va adj progressive.
prohibición f prohibition, ban.
prohibir vt to prohibit, to forbid; to hinder.
prójimo m fellow creature; neighbor.

P

prole f offspring, progeny; race.
proletariado m proletariat.
proletario/ria adj proletarian.
proliferación f proliferation.
proliferar vi to proliferate.
prolífico/ca adj prolific.
prolijidad f prolixity; minute attention to detail.
prolijo/ja adj long-winded; tedious.
prólogo m prolog.
prolongación f prolongation.
prolongar vt to prolong.
promedio m average; middle.
promesa f promise.
prometer vt to promise; to assure; ~**se** vr to become engaged.
prometido/da adj promised; engaged; * m/f fiancé/fiancée.
prominencia f protuberance.
prominente adj prominent, jutting out.
promiscuo/cua adj promiscuous; confusedly mingled; ambiguous.
promoción f promotion.
promontorio m promontory, cape.
promotor m promoter.
promover vt to promote, to advance; to stir up.
promulgación f promulgation.
promulgar vt to promulgate, to publish.
pronombre m (gr) pronoun.
pronosticar vt to predict, to foretell; to conjecture.
pronóstico m prediction; forecast.
prontitud f promptness.
pronto/ta adj prompt; ready; * adv promptly.
pronunciación f pronunciation.
pronunciamiento m (law) publication; insurrection, sedition.
pronunciar vt to pronounce; to deliver; ~**se** vr to rebel.
propagación f propagation; extension.
propagador/ra m/f propagator.
propaganda f propaganda; advertising.
propagar vt to propagate.
propasar vt to go beyond, to exceed.
propender vi to incline.
propensión f propensity, inclination.
propenso/sa adj prone, inclined.
propiamente adv properly; really.
propiciar vt to favor; to cause.
propiciatorio/ria adj propitiatory.
propicio/cia adj propitious.
propiedad f property, possessions pl; right of property; propriety.
propietario/ria adj proprietary; * m/f proprietor.
propina f tip.
propinar vt to hit; to give.
propio/pia adj proper; own; typical; very.
proponer vt to propose.
proporción f proportion; symmetry.

proporcionado/da adj proportionate; fit; **bien** ~ well-proportioned.
proporcional adj proportional.
proporcionar vt to provide; to adjust, to adapt.
proposición f proposition.
propósito m aim, purpose; **a** ~ on purpose.
propuesta f proposal, offer; representation.
propulsar vt to propel; (fig) to promote.
prórroga f prolongation; extension; extra time.
prorrogable adj extendable.
prorrogar vt to extend; to postpone.
prorrumpir vi to break forth, to burst forth.
prosa f prose.
prosaico/ca adj prosaic.
proscribir vt to proscribe, to outlaw.
proscripción f proscription.
proscrito/ta adj banned.
prosecución f continuation.
proseguir vt to continue; * vi to continue, to go on.
prospección f exploration; prospecting.
prospecto m prospectus.
prosperar vi to prosper, to thrive.
prosperidad f prosperity.
próspero/ra adj prosperous.
prostíbulo m brothel.
prostitución f prostitution.
prostituir vt to prostitute.
prostituta f prostitute.
protagonista m/f protagonist.
protagonizar vt to take the chief role in.
protección f protection.
protector m to protect.
proteger vt protector.
proteína f protein.
protesta f protest.
protestante m/f Protestant.
protestar vt to protest; to make a public declaration (of faith); * vi to protest.
protocolo m protocol.
prototipo m prototype.
provecho m profit; advantage.
provechoso/sa adj profitable; advantageous.
proveedor/ra m/f purveyor.
proveer vt to provide; to provision; to decree.
provenir vi to arise, to originate; to issue.
proverbial adj proverbial.
proverbio m proverb; ~**s** mpl Book of Proverbs.
providencia f providence; foresight; divine providence.
providencial adj providential.
provincia f province.
provincial adj, m provincial.
provinciano/na adj provincial; country compd.
provisión f provision; store.
provisional adj provisional.
provisionalmente adv provisionally.
provisorio/ria adj Lat Am provisional.
provocación f provocation.

provocador/ra adj provocative.
provocar vt to provoke; to lead to; to excite.
provocativo/va adj provocative.
próximamente adv soon.
proximidad f proximity, closeness.
próximo/ma adj next; neighboring; close, nearby.
proyección f projection; showing; influence.
proyectar vt to throw; to cast; to screen; to plan.
proyectil m projectile, missile.
proyecto m plan; project.
proyector m projector.
prudencia f prudence, wisdom.
prudente adj prudent.
prueba f proof; reason; argument; token; experiment; essay; attempt; relish, taste.
prurito m itching.
psicoanálisis m psychoanalysis.
psicoanalista m/f psychoanalyst.
psicología f psychology.
psicólogo/ga m/f psychologist.
psiquiatra m/f psychiatrist.
psiquiátrico/ca adj psychiatric.
psíquico/ca adj psychic(al).
púa f sharp point, prickle; shoot; pick.
pubertad f puberty.
publicación f publication.
publicar vt to publish; to make public.
publicidad f publicity.
público/ca adj public; * m public; audience; crowd.
puchero m pot; stew.
púdico/ca adj chaste, pure.
pudiente adj rich, opulent.
pudor m bashfulness.
pudrir vt to rot, to putrefy; ~**se** vr to decay, to rot.
pueblo m people pl; town, village; population; populace.
puente m bridge.
puenting m bungee-jumping.
puerco/ca adj nasty; filthy, dirty; rude, coarse; * m hog, pig; ~ **espín** porcupine.
pueril adj childish; puerile.
puerilidad f puerility.
puerro m leek.
puerta f door; doorway; gateway; ~ **trasera** back door.
puerto m port, harbor; haven; pass; narrow pass.
pues adv then; therefore; well; ¡~! well, then!
puesto m place; particular spot; post, employment; barracks pl; stand.
púgil m boxer.
pugilato m boxing.
pugna f combat, battle.
pugnar vi to fight, to combat; to struggle.
pujante adj powerful, strong; robust; stout, strapping.
pujanza f power, strength.
pujar vt to outbid; to strain.

pulcritud f beauty.
pulcro/cra adj beautiful; affected.
pulga f flea; **tener malas ~s** to be easily piqued; to be ill-tempered.
pulgada f inch.
pulgar m thumb.
pulir vt to polish; to put the last touches to.
pulla f smart repartee; obscene expression.
pulmón m lung.
pulmonía f pneumonia.
pulpa f pulp; soft part (of fruit).
pulpería f small grocery shop.
púlpito m pulpit.
pulpo m octopus.
pulsación f pulsation.
pulsador m push button.
pulsar vt to touch; to play; to press.
pulsera f bracelet.
pulso m pulse; wrist; firmness/steadiness of the hand.
pulular vi to swarm.
pulverización f pulverization.
pulverizador m spray gun.
pulverizar vt to pulverize.
puna f (med) mountain sickness.
pungir vt to punch, to prick.
punición f punishment, chastisement.
punitivo/va adj punitive.
punta f point; end; trace.
puntada f stitch.
puntaje m Lat Am grade.
puntal m prop, stay; buttress.
puntapié m kick.
puntear vt to tick; to pluck (the guitar); to stitch.
puntería f aiming.
puntero m pointer; ~/**ra** adj leading.
puntiagudo/da adj sharp-pointed.
puntilla f narrow lace edging; **de ~s** on tiptoe.
punto m point; end; spot; stitch.
puntuación f punctuation.
puntual adj punctual; exact; reliable.
puntualidad f punctuality.
puntualizar vt to fix; to specify.
puntuar vt to punctuate; to evaluate.
punzada f prick; sting; pain; compunction.
punzante adj sharp.
punzar vt to punch; to prick; to sting.
punzón m punch.
puñado m handful.
puñal m dagger.
puñalada f stab.
puñetazo m punch.
puño m fist; handful; wrist-band; cuff; handle.
pupila f pupil (of eye).
pupitre m desk.
puré m puree; (thick) soup; ~ **de patatas** mashed potatoes pl.
pureza f purity, chastity.

P

purga f purge.
purgante m purgative.
purgar vt to purge; to purify; to atone, to expiate.
purgativo/va adj purgative, purging.
purgatorio m purgatory.
purificación f purification.
purificador/ra m/f purifier; * adj purifying.
purificar vt to purify.
purismo m purism.
purista m purist.
puritano/na adj puritanical; * m/f Puritan.

puro/ra adj pure; mere; clear; genuine.
púrpura f purple.
purpúreo/rea adj purple.
purulento/ta adj purulent.
pus m pus.
pusilánime adj pusillanimous, fainthearted.
pusilanimidad f pusillanimity.
pústula f pustule, pimple.
puta f whore.
putrefacción f putrefaction.
pútrido/da adj putrid, rotten.

Q

que *pn* that; who; which; what; * *conj* that; than.
qué *adj* what; which; * *pn* what; which.
quebrada *f* broken, uneven ground; *Lat Am* stream.
quebradero *m* breaker; ~ **de cabeza** worry.
quebradizo/za *adj* brittle; flexible.
quebrado *m* (*math*) fraction.
quebradura *f* fracture; rupture, hernia.
quebrantamiento *m* fracture; rupture; breaking; weariness, fatigue; violation (of the law).
quebrantar *vt* to break; to crack; to burst; to pound, to grind; to violate; to fatigue; to weaken.
quebranto *m* weakness; great loss, severe damage.
quebrar *vt* to break; to transgress; to violate (a law); * *vi* to go bankrupt; ~**se** *vr* to break into pieces; to be ruptured.
queda *f* resting time; (*mil*) tattoo.
quedar *vi* to stay; ~**se** *vr* to remain.
quedo/da *adj* quiet, still; * *adv* softly, gently.
quehacer *m* task.
queja *f* complaint.
quejarse *vr* to complain of.
quejido *m* complaint.
quejoso/sa *adj* complaining, querulous.
quejumbroso/sa *adj* complaining, plaintive.
quema *f* burning, combustion; fire.
quemador *m* burner.
quemadura *f* burn.
quemar *vt* to burn; to kindle; ~**se** *vr* to be parched with heat; to burn oneself; * *vi* to be too hot.
quemarropa *f*: **a** ~ *adv* point-blank.
quemazón *f* burn; itch.
querella *f* charge; dispute; complaint.
querellarse *vr* to complain; to file a complaint.
querendón/ona *adj Lat Am* affectionate.
querer *vt* to want; to desire; to will; to love; * *m* will, desire.
querido/da *adj* dear, beloved; * *m/f* darling; lover; ~**do mío/~da mía** my dear, my love, my darling.
querosén *m Lat Am* kerosene/kerosine.
queroseno *m* kerosene/kerosine.
querubín *m* cherub.
quesería *f* shop that specializes in cheese.
queso *m* cheese.

quicio *m* hook, hinge (of a door).
quiebra *f* break, fracture; bankruptcy; slump.
quien *pn* who; whom.
quién *pn* who; whom.
quienquiera *adj* whoever.
quieto/ta *adj* still, peaceable.
quietud *f* quietness, peace, tranquility, calmness.
quijada *f* jaw; jawbone.
quijotada *f* quixotic action.
quijote *m* quixotic person.
quijotesco/ca *adj* quixotic.
quilate *m* carat.
quilla *f* keel.
quimera *f* chimera.
quimérico/ca *adj* chimerical, fantastic.
química *f* chemistry.
químico/ca *m/f* chemist; * *adj* chemical.
quimioterapia *f* chemotherapy.
quina *f* Peruvian bark, quinine.
quincalla *f* hardware.
quince *adj, m* fifteen; fifteenth.
quincena *f* fortnight.
quinientos/tas *adj* five hundred.
quinina *f* quinine.
quinquenal *adj* quinquennial.
quinquenio *m* space of five years.
quinqui *m* delinquent.
quinta *f* country house; levy, drafting of soldiers.
quintaesencia *f* quintessence.
quintilla *f* (*poet*) metrical composition of five verses.
quinto *adj* fifth; * *m* fifth; drafted soldier.
quíntuplo/pla *adj* quintuple, fivefold.
quiosco *m* bandstand; newsstand.
quirófano *m* operating theater.
quiromancia *f* palmistry.
quirúrgico/ca *adj* surgical.
quisquilloso/sa *adj* difficult, touchy; peevish, irritable.
quiste *m* cyst.
quitaesmalte *m* nail-polish remover.
quitamanchas *m invar* stain remover.
quitanieves *m invar* snowplow.
quitar *vt* to take away, to remove; to take off; to relieve; to annul; ~**se** *vr* to take off (clothes etc); to withdraw.
quitasol *m* parasol.
quizá, quizás *adv* perhaps.

R

rabadilla f coccyx; rump, croup (of a horse/other four-legged animal).

rábano m radish.

rabí m rabbi.

rabia f rage, fury.

rabiar vt to be furious, to rage.

rabieta f touchiness, petulance; fit of bad temper.

rabino m rabbi.

rabioso/sa adj rabid; furious.

rabo m tail.

racha f gust of wind; **buena/mala ~** spell of good/bad luck.

racial adj racial, race compd.

racimo m bunch of grapes.

raclocinio m reasoning; argument.

ración f ration.

racional adj rational; reasonable.

racionalidad f rationality.

racionar vt to ration (out).

racismo m racialism.

racista adj, m/f racist.

radar m radar.

radiación f radiation.

radiactivo/va, radioactivo/va adj radioactive.

radiador m radiator.

radiante adj radiant.

radiar vt to radiate.

radicación f taking root; becoming rooted (of a habit).

radical adj radical.

radicar vt to take root; **~se** vr to establish oneself.

radio f radio; radio (set); * m radius; ray.

radiografía f radiography; X-ray.

radioso/sa adj Lat Am radiant.

radioterapia f radiotherapy.

raer vt to scrape; to grate; to erase.

ráfaga f gust; flash; burst.

rafting m rafting.

raído/da adj scraped; worn-out; impudent.

raíz f root; base, basis; origin.

raja f splinter, chip (of wood); chink, fissure.

rajar vt to split; to chop, to cleave.

rajatabla f: **a ~** adv strictly.

ralea f race; breed, species.

rallador m grater.

rallar vt to grate.

ralo/la adj thin, rare.

rama f branch (of a tree, of a family).

ramadán m Ramadan.

ramaje m branches pl.

rambla f avenue.

ramera f whore, prostitute.

ramificación f ramification.

ramificarse vr to ramify.

ramillete m bunch.

ramo m branch (of a tree).

rampa f ramp.

rampante adj rampant.

rana f frog.

ranchera f station wagon.

ranchero m rancher;farmer.

rancho m grub; ranch; farm; settlement, camp.

rancio/cia adj rank; rancid.

rango m rank, standing.

ranúnculo m (bot) buttercup.

ranura f groove; slot.

rapacidad f rapacity.

rapadura f shaving; baldness.

rapar vt to shave; to plunder.

rapaz/za adj rapacious; * m/f young boy/girl.

rape m quick shave; monkfish.

rapé m snuff.

rapidez f speed, rapidity.

rápido/da adj quick, rapid, swift.

rapiña f robbery.

rappel m abseiling.

raptar vt to kidnap.

rapto m kidnaping; (fig) ecstasy, rapture.

raqueta f racket.

raquítico/ca adj stunted; (fig) inadequate.

rareza f rarity, rareness.

raro/ra adj rare, scarce; extraordinary.

ras m: **a ~ de** level with; **a ~ de tierra** at ground level.

rasar vt to level.

rascacielos m invar skyscraper.

rascar vt to scratch, to scrape.

rasgar vt to tear, to rip.

rasgo m dash, stroke; grand/magnanimous action; **~s** mpl features pl.

rasguear vi to form bold strokes with a pen; (mus) to strum.

rasguñar vt to scratch, to scrape.

rasguño m scratch.

rasguñón m Lat Am scratch.

raso/sa adj plain; flat; * m satin; **al raso** in the open air.

raspa f beard (of an ear of corn); backbone (of fish); stalk (of grapes); rasp.

raspadura f filing, scraping; filings pl.

raspar vt to scrape, to rasp.

rastra f rake; **a ~s** by dragging.

rastreador m tracker.

rastrear vt to trace; to inquire into; * vi to skim along close to the ground (of birds).

rastrero/ra *adj* creeping; low, humble, cringing.
rastrillar *vt* to rake.
rastrillo *m* rake.
rastro *m* track; rake; trace.
rastrojera *f* stubble field.
rastrojo *m* stubble.
rasurador/ra *m/f* electric shaver.
rasurarse *vr* to shave.
rata *f* rat.
ratería *f* larceny, petty theft.
ratero/ra *adj* creeping, mean, vile; * *m/f* pickpocket; burglar.
ratificación *f* ratification.
ratificar *vt* to ratify; to approve of.
rato *m* moment; **a ~s perdidos** in leisure time.
ratón *m* mouse.
ratonera *f* mousetrap.
raudal *m* torrent.
raya *f* stroke; line; part; frontier; ray (fish); roach (fish).
rayado/da *adj* ruled; crossed; striped.
rayar *vt* to draw lines on; to cross out; to underline; to cross; to rifle.
rayo *m* ray, beam (of light).
rayón *m* rayon.
raza *f* race, lineage; quality.
razón *f* reason; right; reasonableness; account; calculation.
razonable *adj* reasonable.
razonado/da *adj* rational; prudent.
razonamiento *m* reasoning; discourse.
razonar *vi* to reason; to discourse, to talk.
reacción *f* reaction.
reaccionar *vi* to react.
reaccionario/ria *adj* reactionary.
reacio/cia *adj* stubborn.
reactor *m* reactor.
reajuste *m* readjustment.
real *adj* real, actual; royal; * *m* (*mil*) camp.
realce *m* embossment; flash; luster, splendor.
realidad *f* reality; sincerity.
realista *m* realist; royalist.
realizador/ra *m/f* producer (in TV etc).
realizar *vt* to realize; to achieve; to undertake.
realmente *adv* really, actually.
realzar *vt* to raise, to elevate; to emboss; to heighten.
reanimar *vt* to cheer, to encourage; to reanimate.
reanudar *vt* to renew; to resume.
reaparición *f* reappearance.
reasumir *vt* to retake, to resume.
reata *f* collar, leash; string (of horses).
rebaja *f* abatement; deduction; **~s** *fpl* sale.
rebajar *vt* to abate, to lessen, to diminish; to lower.
rebanada *f* slice.
rebaño *m* flock (of sheep), herd (of cattle).
rebasar *vt* to exceed.

rebatir *vt* to resist; to parry, to ward off; to refute; to repress.
rebeca *f* cardigan.
rebelarse *vr* to revolt; to rebel; to resist.
rebelde *m/f* rebel; * *adj* rebellious.
rebeldía *f* rebelliousness, disobedience; (*law*) contumacy; **en ~** by default.
rebelión *f* rebellion, revolt.
rebosar *vi* to run over, to overflow; to abound.
rebotar *vt* to bounce; to clinch; to repel; * *vi* to rebound.
rebote *m* rebound; **de ~** on the rebound.
rebozado/da *adj* fried in batter/breadcrumbs.
rebozar *vt* to wrap up; to fry in batter/ breadcrumbs.
rebozo *m* *Lat Am* shawl.
rebullir *vi* to stir, to begin to move.
rebuscado/da *adj* affected; recherché; far-fetched.
rebuznar *vi* to bray.
rebuzno *m* braying (of an ass).
recabar *vt* to obtain by entreaty.
recado *m* message; gift.
recaer *vi* to fall back.
recaída *f* relapse.
recalcar *vt* to stress, to emphasize.
recalcitrante *adj* recalcitrant.
recalentamiento *m* overheating.
recalentar *vt* to heat again; to overheat.
recámara *f* bedroom.
recambio *m* spare; refill.
recapacitar *vt* to reflect.
recapitulación *f* recapitulation.
recapitular *vt* to recapitulate.
recargado/da *adj* overloaded.
recargar *vt* to overload; to recharge; to charge again.
recargo *m* extra load; new charge/accusation.
recatado/da *adj* prudent; circumspect; modest.
recato *m* prudence; circumspection; modesty; bashfulness.
recaudación *f* take, income; recovery of debts; tax collector's office.
recaudador *m* tax collector.
recaudar *vt* to gather; to obtain; to recover.
recelar *vt* to fear; to suspect, to doubt.
recelo *m* dread; suspicion, mistrust.
receloso/sa *adj* mistrustful; shy.
recepción *f* reception.
recepcionar *vt* *Lat Am* to receive.
recepcionista *m/f* receptionist.
receptáculo *m* receptacle.
receptor *m* receiver; investigating official.
recesión *f* (*com*) recession.
receta *f* recipe; prescription.
recetar *vt* to prescribe.
rechazar *vt* to refuse; to repulse; to contradict.
rechazo *m* rebound; denial; recoil.

R

rechifla f booing; (fig) derision.
rechiflar vt to boo.
rechinar vi to gnash (teeth).
rechistar vi: **sin ~** without a murmur.
rechoncho/cha adj chubby.
recibidor m entrance hall.
recibimiento m reception.
recibir vt to receive, to accept; to let in; to go to meet; **~se** vr: **~ de** Lat Am to qualify as.
recibo m receipt.
reciclado/da adj recycled.
reciclar vt to recycle.
recién adv recently, lately; Lat Am only.
reciente adj recent; new, fresh; modern.
recinto m district, precinct.
recio/cia adj stout; strong, robust; coarse, thick; rude; arduous, rigid; * adv strongly, stoutly; **hablar ~** to talk loud.
recipiente m container.
reciprocidad f reciprocity.
recíproco/ca adj reciprocal, mutual.
recitación f recitation.
recital m recital; reading.
recitar vt to recite.
recitativo/va adj recitative.
reclamación f claim; reclamation; protest.
reclamar vt to claim.
reclame m Lat Am advertisement.
reclamo m claim; advertisement; attraction; decoy bird; catchword (in printing); Lat Am complaint.
reclinar vt to recline; **~se** vr to lean back.
recluir vt to shut up.
reclusión f seclusion; prison.
recluta f recruitment; * m/f recruit.
reclutador m recruitment officer.
reclutar vt to recruit.
recobrar vt to recover; **~se** vr to recover (from sickness).
recodo m corner/angle jutting out.
recogedor m scraper (instrument).
recoger vt to collect; to retake, to take back; to get; to gather; to shelter; to compile; **~se** vr to take shelter/refuge; to retire; to withdraw from the world.
recogido/da adj retired, secluded; quiet.
recogimiento m collection; retreat; shelter; abstraction from all worldly concerns.
recolección f summary; recollection.
recomendación f recommendation.
recomendado/da adj Lat Am registered.
recomendar vt to recommend.
recompensa f compensation; recompense, reward.
recompensar vt to recompense, to reward.
recomponer vt to recompose; to mend.
reconcentrar vt to concentrate on.
reconciliación f reconciliation.

reconciliar vt to reconcile; **~se** vr to make one's peace.
recóndito/ta adj recondite, secret, concealed.
reconfortar vt to comfort.
reconocer vt to recognize; to examine closely; to acknowledge; to consider; (mil) to reconnoiter.
reconocido/da adj recognized; grateful.
reconocimiento m recognition; acknowledgement; gratitude; confession; search; submission; inquiry; (mil) reconnaissance.
reconquista f reconquest.
reconquistar vt to reconquer.
reconstituyente m tonic.
reconstruir vt to reconstruct.
reconvenir vt to return the accusations of.
reconversión f: **~ industrial** industrial rationalization.
recopilación f summary, abridgement.
recopilador m compiler.
recopilar vt to compile.
récord adj invar record; * m record.
recordar vt to remember; to remind; * vi to remember.
recorrer vt to run over, to peruse; to cover.
recorrida f Lat Am journey.
recortar vt to cut out.
recorte m cutting; trimming.
recostar vt to lean, to recline; **~se** vr to lie down.
recoveco m cubbyhole; bend.
recrear vt to amuse, to entertain; to delight.
recreativo/va adj recreational.
recreo m recreation; playtime (at school).
recriminación f recrimination.
recriminar vt to recriminate.
recrudecer vt, vi, **~se** vr to worsen.
recrudecimiento m upsurge.
recta f straight line.
rectángulo/la adj rectangular; * m rectangle.
rectificación f rectification.
rectificar vt to rectify.
rectilíneo/nea adj rectilinear.
rectitud f straightness; rectitude; justness, honesty; exactitude.
recto/ta adj straight; right; just, honest; * m rectum.
rector/ra m/f superior of a community or establishment; vice-chancellor (of a university); presiding judge; curate, rector; * adj governing.
rectorado m rectorship; vice-chancellorship.
rectoría f rectory; rectorship.
recua f train (of mules, pack animals).
recuadro m box; inset.
recuento m inventory.
recuerdo m souvenir; memory.
recular vi to fall back, to recoil.
recuperable adj recoverable.
recuperación f recovery.
recuperar vt to recover; **~se** vr to recover (from sickness).

recurrir *vi*: ~ **a** to resort to.
recurso *m* recourse.
recusación *f* refusal.
recusar *vt* to refuse; to refuse to admit.
red *f* net; network; snare.
redacción *f* editing; editor's office.
redactar *vt* to draft; to edit.
redactor/ra *m/f* editor.
redada *f*: ~ **policial** police raid.
redecilla *f* hairnet.
rededor *m* environs *pl*; **al** ~ round about.
redención *f* redemption.
redentor/ra *m/f* redeemer.
redescubrir *vt* to rediscover.
redicho/cha *adj* affected.
redil *m* enclosure for sheep.
redimible *adj* redeemable.
redimir *vt* to redeem; to ransom.
rédito *m* revenue, rent.
redoblado/da *adj* redoubled; stout and thick; reinforced.
redoblar *vt* to redouble; to rivet.
redoble *m* doubling, repetition; (*mil*) roll of a drum.
redomado/da *adj* sly; out-and-out.
redondear *vt* to round.
redondel *m* circle; traffic circle.
redondez *f* roundness, circular form.
redondo/da *adj* round; complete.
reducción *f* reduction.
reducible *adj* reducible; convertible.
reducido/da *adj* reduced; limited; small.
reducir *adj* to reduce; to limit; ~**se** *vr* to diminish.
reducto *m* (*mil*) redoubt.
redundancia *f* superfluity, redundancy, excess.
redundar *vi* to contribute.
reelegir *vt* to re-elect, to elect again.
reembolsar *vt* to refund; to reimburse.
reembolso *m* reimbursement; refund; **contra** ~ C.O.D.
reemplazar *vt* to replace; to restore.
reemplazo *m* replacement; reserve.
reenganchar *vt* (*mil*) to re-enlist; ~**se** *vr* to enlist again.
referencia *f* reference.
referéndum *m* referendum.
referí *m* *Lat Am* referee.
referir *vt* to refer, to relate, to report; ~**se** *vr* to refer/relate to.
refilón *m*: **de** ~ *adv* obliquely.
refinado/da *adj* refined; subtle, artful.
refinar *vt* to refine.
refinería *f* refinery.
reflejar *vt* to reflect.
reflejo *m* reflex; reflection.
reflexión *f* meditation, reflection.
reflexionar *vt* to reflect on; * *vi* to reflect, to meditate.

reflexivo/va *adj* reflexive; thoughtful.
reflujo *m* reflux, ebb; **flujo y** ~ the tides *pl*.
reforma *f* reform; correction; repair.
reformar *vt* to reform; to correct; to restore; ~**se** *vr* to mend.
reformatorio *m* reformatory.
reforzar *vt* to strengthen, to fortify; to encourage.
refracción *f* refraction.
refractario/ria *adj* refractory.
refrán *m* proverb.
refregar *vt* to scrub.
refrenar *vt* to refrain; to check.
refrendar *vt* to countersign; to approve.
refrescante *adj* refreshing.
refrescar *vt* to refresh; ~**se** *vr* to get cooler; to go out for a breath of fresh air; * *vi* to cool down.
refresco *m* refreshment.
refriega *f* affray, skirmish, fray.
refrigerador/ra *m/f* refrigerator, fridge.
refrigerar *vt* to cool; to refresh; to refrigerate; to comfort.
refrigerio *m* refrigeration; refreshment; consolation, comfort.
refuerzo *m* reinforcement.
refugiado/da *m/f* refugee.
refugiar *vt* to shelter; ~**se** *vr* to take refuge.
refugio *m* refuge, asylum.
refulgir *vi* to shine.
refunfuñar *vi* to snarl; to growl; to grumble.
refutación *f* refutation.
refutar *vt* to refute.
regadera *f* watering can.
regadío *m* irrigated land.
regalar *vt* to give (as present); to give away; to pamper; to caress.
regalía *f* regalia; bonus; royalty; privilege.
regaliz *m* licorice.
regalo *m* present, gift; pleasure; comfort.
regañadientes: **a** ~ *adv* reluctantly.
regañar *vt* to scold; * *vi* to growl; to grumble; to quarrel.
regañón/ona *adj* snarling, growling; grumbling; troublesome.
regar *vt* to water, to irrigate.
regata *f* irrigation ditch; regatta.
regatear *vt* (*com*) to bargain over; to be mean with; * *vi* to haggle; to dribble (in sport).
regateo *m* haggling; bartering; dribbling.
regazo *m* lap.
regencia *f* regency.
regeneración *f* regeneration.
regenerar *vt* to regenerate.
regentar *vt* to rule; to govern.
regente *m* regent; manager.
régimen *m* regime, management; diet; (*gr*) rules of verbs *pl*.
regimiento *m* regime; (*mil*) regiment.

R

regio/gia adj royal, regal.
región f region.
regir vt to rule, to govern; to direct; * vi to apply.
registrador/ra m/f registrar; controller.
registradora f Lat Am cash register.
registrar vt to survey; to inspect, to examine; to record, to enter in a register; ~**se** vr to register; to happen.
registro m examining; enrolling office; register; registration.
regla f rule, ruler; period.
reglamentar vt to regulate.
reglamentario/ria adj statutory.
reglamento m regulation; bylaw/bye-law.
regocijar vt to gladden; ~**se** vr to rejoice.
regocijo m joy, pleasure; merriment, rejoicing.
regodearse vr to be delighted; to trifle, to play the fool; to joke, to jest.
regodeo m joy, merriment.
regordete adj chubby, plump.
regresar vi to return, to go back.
regreso m return, regression.
reguero m small rivulet; trickle of spilt liquid; drain, gutter.
regulación f regulation.
regulador/ra m/f regulator; knob, control.
regular vt to regulate, to adjust; * adj regular; ordinary.
regularidad f regularity.
regularizar vt to regularize.
rehabilitación f rehabilitation.
rehabilitar vt to rehabilitate.
rehacer vt to repair, to make again; to redo; ~**se** vr to recover; (mil) to rally.
rehén m hostage.
rehuir vt to avoid.
rehusar vt to refuse, to decline.
reimpresión f reprint.
reimprimir vt to reprint.
reina f queen.
reinado m reign.
reinante adj (fig) prevailing.
reinar vi to reign; to govern.
reincidencia f relapse.
reincidir vi: ~ **en** to relapse into, to fall back into.
reino m kingdom, reign.
reintegración f reintegration, restoration.
reintegrar vt to reintegrate, to restore; ~**se** vr to be reinstated/restored.
reintegro m reintegration.
reír(se) vi (vr) to laugh.
reiteración f repetition, reiteration.
reiterar vt to reiterate, to repeat.
reivindicación f claim; vindication.
reivindicar vt to claim.
reja f plowshare; lattice, grating.
rejilla f grating, grille; vent; rack (for baggage).
rejoneador m mounted bullfighter.

rejonear vt to spear (bulls).
rejuvenecer vt, vi to rejuvenate.
relación f relation; relationship; report; account.
relacionar vt to relate.
relajación f relaxation; remission; laxity.
relajar vt to relax, to slacken; ~**se** vr to relax.
relajo m Lat Am (col) mess; racket.
relamerse vr to lick one's lips; to relish.
relamido/da adj affected; overdressed.
relámpago m flash of lightning.
relampaguear vi to flash.
relatar vt to relate, to tell.
relativo/va adj relative.
relato m story; recital.
relax m relaxation.
releer vt to reread.
relegación f relegation; exile.
relegar vt to relegate; to banish, to exile.
relente m evening dew.
relevante adj excellent, great; eminent.
relevar vt to emboss, to work in relief; to exonerate; to relieve; to assist.
relevo m (mil) relief.
relicario m reliquary.
relieve m relief; (fig) prominence.
religión f religion.
religiosidad f religiousness.
religioso/sa adj religious.
relinchar vi to neigh.
relincho m neigh, neighing.
reliquia f residue, remains pl; (saintly) relic.
rellano m landing (of stairs).
rellenar vt to fill up; to stuff.
relleno/na adj satiated, full up; stuffed; * m stuffing.
reloj m clock; watch.
relojero m watchmaker.
relucir vi to shine, to glitter; to excel, to be brilliant.
relumbrar vi to sparkle, to shine.
remachar vt to rivet; (fig) to drive home.
remanente m remainder; (com) balance; surplus.
remangar vt to roll up.
remansarse vr to form a pool.
remanso m stagnant water; quiet place.
remar vi to row.
rematadamente adv entirely, totally.
rematado/da adj utter, complete.
rematar vt to terminate, to finish; to sell off cheaply; * vi to end.
remate m end, conclusion; shot; tip; last/best bid.
remedar vt to copy, to imitate; to mimic.
remediable adj remediable.
remediar vt to remedy; to assist, to help; to free from danger; to avoid.
remedio m amendment, correction; recourse; refuge.
remedo m imitation, copy.

remendar *vt* to patch, to mend; to correct.
remero *m* rower, oarsman.
remesa *f* shipment; remittance.
remiendo *m* patch; mend.
remilgado/da *adj* prim; affected.
remilgo *m* primness, affectation.
reminiscencia *f* reminiscence, recollection.
remiso/sa *adj* remiss, careless; indolent.
remitente *m* sender.
remitir *vt* to remit, to send; to pardon (a fault); to suspend, to put off; * *vi*, **~se** *vr* to slacken.
remo *m* oar; rowing.
remojar *vt* to steep; to dunk.
remojo *m* steeping, soaking.
remolacha *f* beet (crop).
remolcar *vt* to tow.
remolino *m* whirlwind; whirlpool; crowd.
remolón/ona *adj* stubborn; lazy.
remolque *m* tow, towing; tow rope.
remontar *vt* to mend; **~se** *vr* to tower, to soar.
remorder *vt* to disturb.
remordimiento *m* remorse.
remoto/ta *adj* remote, distant; far.
remover *vt* to stir; to move around; *Lat Am* to dismiss.
remozar *vt* to rejuvenate; to renovate.
remuneración *f* remuneration, recompense.
remunerador/ra *m/f* remunerator.
remunerar *vt* to reward, to remunerate.
renacer *vi* to be born again; to revive.
renacimiento *m* regeneration; rebirth.
renacuajo *m* tadpole.
renal *adj* renal, kidney *compd*.
rencilla *f* quarrel.
rencor *m* rancor, grudge.
rencoroso/sa *adj* rancorous.
rendición *f* surrender; profit.
rendido/da *adj* submissive; exhausted.
rendija *f* crevice, crack, cleft.
rendimiento *m* output; efficiency.
rendir *vt* to subject, to subdue; **~se** *vr* to yield; to surrender; to be tired out.
renegado *m* apostate; wicked person.
renegar *vt* to deny; to disown; to detest, to abhor; * *vi* to apostatize; to blaspheme, to curse.
renglón *m* line; item.
reno *m* caribou, reindeer.
renombrado/da *adj* renowned.
renombre *m* renown.
renovación *f* renovation; renewal.
renovar *vt* to renew; to renovate; to reform.
renquear *vi* to limp.
renta *f* income; rent; profit.
renuncia *f* renunciation; resignation.
renunciar *vt* to renounce; * *vi* to resign.
reñido/da *adj* at variance, at odds; hard-fought.
reñir *vt*, *vi* to wrangle, to quarrel; to scold, to chide.
reo *m* offender, criminal.

reojo *m*: **mirar de ~** to look at furtively.
reparación *f* repair; reparation.
reparar *vt* to repair; to consider, to observe; to parry; * *vi*: **~ en** to notice; to pass (in cards).
reparo *m* repair, reparation; consideration; difficulty.
repartición *f* distribution.
repartidor *m/f* distributor; assessor of taxes.
repartir *vt* to distribute; to deliver.
reparto *m* distribution; delivery; cost; property development.
repasar *vt* to pass again; to revise; to check; to mend.
repaso *m* revision; check-up.
repatriar *vt* to repatriate.
repecho *m* slope.
repelente *adj* repellent, repulsive.
repeler *vt* to repel; to refute, to reject.
repente: **de ~** *adv* suddenly.
repentino/na *adj* sudden, unforeseen.
repercusión *f* reverberation.
repercutir *vi* to reverberate; to rebound.
repertorio *m* repertory; index; list.
repetición *f* repetition; (*mus*) encore.
repetidor/ra *m/f* repeater.
repetir *vt*, *vi* to repeat.
repicar *vt* to ring.
repique *m* chime.
repiquetear *vt* to ring merrily.
repisa *f* pedestal, stand; shelf; windowsill.
replegar *vt* to redouble; to fold over; **~se** *vr* (*mil*) to fall back.
repleto/ta *adj* replete, very full.
réplica *f* reply, answer; repartee.
replicar *vi* to reply.
repoblación *f* repopulation; restocking; **~ forestal** reforestation.
repoblar *vt* to repopulate; to reforest.
repollo *m* cabbage.
reponer *vt* to replace; to restore; **~se** *vr* to recover lost health/property.
reportaje *m* report, article; *Lat Am* interview.
reportero/ra *m/f* reporter.
reposado/da *adj* quiet, peaceful; settled (wine).
reposar *vi* to rest, to repose.
reposición *f* replacement; remake.
reposo *m* rest, repose.
repostería *f* confectioner's (shop).
repostero *m* confectioner.
reprender *vt* to reprimand.
represa *f* dam; lake.
represalia *f* reprisal.
representación *f* representation; authority.
representante *m/f* representative; understudy (theater).
representar *vt* to represent; to play on the stage; to look (age).
representativo/va *adj* representative.

R

represión f repression.
reprimenda f reprimand.
reprimir vt to repress; to check; to contain.
reprobable adj reprehensible.
reprobación f reprobation, reproof.
reprobar vt to reject; to condemn, to upbraid; Lat Am to fail.
réprobo m reprobate.
reprochar vt to reproach.
reproche m reproach.
reproducción f reproduction.
reproducir vt to reproduce.
reptil m reptile.
república f republic.
republicano/na adj, m/f republican.
repudiar vt to repudiate.
repudio m repudiation.
repuesto m supply; spare part.
repugnancia f reluctance; repugnance.
repugnante adj repugnant.
repugnar vt to disgust.
repulsa f refusal.
repulsar vt to reject; to decline, to refuse.
repulsión f repulsion.
repulsivo/va adj repulsive.
repuntar vi Lat Am to improve.
reputación f reputation, renown.
reputar to consider.
requebrar vt to woo, to court.
requerimiento m request; requisition; intimation; summons.
requerir vt to intimate, to notify; to request; to require, to need; to summon.
requesón m cottage cheese.
requiebro m endearing expression.
réquiem m requiem.
requisa f inspection; (mil) requisition.
requisito m requisite.
res f animal; head of cattle; **~es** Lat Am cattle.
resabio m (unpleasant) aftertaste; vicious habit, bad custom.
resaca f surge, surf; (fig) backlash; (col) hangover.
resaltar vi to rebound; to jut out; to be evident; to stand out.
resarcimiento m compensation, reparation.
resarcir vt to compensate, to make amends for.
resbalada f Lat Am slip, slide.
resbaladizo/za adj slippery.
resbalar(se) vi (vr) to slip, to slide.
resbalón m slip, slide.
rescatar vt to ransom, to redeem.
rescate m ransom.
rescindir vt to rescind, to annul.
rescisión f rescindment, revocation.
rescoldo m embers pl, cinders pl.
resecarse vr to dry up.
reseco/ca adj very dry.

resentido/da adj resentful.
resentimiento m resentment.
resentirse vr: **~ de** to suffer; **~ con** to resent.
reseña f review; account.
reseñar vt to describe; to review.
reserva f reserve; reservation.
reservado/da adj reserved, cautious, circumspect.
reservar vt to keep; to reserve; **~se** vr to preserve oneself; to keep to oneself.
resfriado m cold.
resfriarse vr to catch cold.
resguardar vt to preserve, to defend; **~se** vr to be on one's guard.
resguardo m guard; security, safety; voucher; receipt.
residencia f residence.
residente adj residing, resident; * m/f resident.
residir vi to reside, to dwell.
residuo m residue, remainder.
resignación f resignation.
resignadamente adv resignedly.
resignarse vr to resign oneself.
resina f resin.
resinoso/sa adj resinous.
resistencia f resistance, opposition.
resistente adj strong; resistant.
resistir vt to resist, to oppose; to put up with; * vi to resist; to hold out.
resma f ream (of paper).
resol m glare (of the sun).
resollar vi to wheeze; to breath with difficulty.
resolución f resolution, boldness; decision.
resolver vt to resolve, to decide; to analyze; **~se** vr to resolve, to determine.
resonar vi to resound.
resoplar vi to snore; to snort.
resoplido m heavy breathing.
resorte m spring.
respaldar vt to endorse; **~se** vr to lean back.
respaldo m backing; endorsement; back of a seat.
respectivo/va adj respective.
respecto m respect; relation; **al ~** on this matter.
respetable adj respectable.
respetar vt to respect; to revere.
respeto m respect, regard, consideration; homage.
respetuoso/sa adj respectful.
respingar vi to shy.
respingo m start; jump.
respiración f respiration, breathing.
respiradero m vent, breathing hole; rest, repose.
respirar vi to breathe.
respiratorio/ria adj respiratory.
respiro m breathing; (fig) respite.
resplandecer vi to shine; to glisten.
resplandeciente adj resplendent.
resplandor m splendor, brilliance.
responder vt to answer; * vi to answer; to correspond; **~ de** to be responsible for.

respondón/ona *adj* ever ready to reply; cheeky.

responsable *adj* responsible; accountable, answerable.

responsabilidad *f* responsibility.

responsabilizarse *vr* to take charge.

responso *m* prayer for the dead.

respuesta *f* answer, reply.

resquemor *m* resentment.

resquicio *m* crack, cleft; (*fig*) chance.

restablecer *vt* to re-establish; **~se** *vr* to recover.

restablecimiento *m* re-establishment.

restallar *vi* to crack; to click.

restante *adj* remaining.

restar *vt* to subtract, to take away; * *vi* to be left.

restauración *f* restoration.

restaurant *m Lat Am* diner.

restaurante *m* diner.

restaurar *vt* to restore.

restitución *f* restitution.

restituir *vt* to restore; to return.

resto *m* remainder, rest.

restregar *vt* to scrub, to rub.

restricción *f* restriction, limitation.

restringir *vt* to restrict, to limit; to restrain.

resucitar *vt* to resuscitate, to revive; to renew.

resuello *m* breath, breathing.

resuelto/ta *adj* resolute, determined; prompt.

resultado *m* result, consequence.

resultar *vi* to be; to turn out; to amount to.

resumen *m* summary.

resumidamente *adv* summarily.

resumir *vt* to abridge; to sum up; to summarize.

resurrección *f* resurrection, revival.

retablo *m* picture drawn on a board; splendid altarpiece.

retaguardia *f* rearguard.

retahíla *f* range, series.

retal *m* remnant.

retar *vt* to challenge.

retardar *vt* to retard; to delay.

retardo *m* delay.

retazo *m* remnant; cutting.

retén *m Lat Am* reformatory.

retención *f* retention.

retener *vt* to retain, to keep back.

retentiva *f* memory.

reticencia *f* reticence.

retina *f* retina.

retintín *m* tinkling sound; affected tone of voice.

retirada *f* (*mil*) retreat, withdrawal; recall.

retirar *vt* to withdraw, to retire; to remove; **~se** *vr* to retire, to retreat; to go to bed.

retiro *m* retreat, retirement; pension.

reto *m* challenge; threat, menace.

retocar *vt* to retouch; to mend; to finish off (work).

retoñar *vi* to sprout.

retoño *m* shoot; offspring.

retoque *m* finishing stroke; retouching.

retorcer *vt* to twist; to wring.

retorcimiento *m* twisting, contortion.

retórica *f* rhetoric.

retórico/ca *adj* rhetorical; * *f* rhetoric; affectedness.

retornar *vt*, *vi* to return.

retorno *m* return; barter, exchange.

retortero: andar al ~ to bustle about.

retortijón *m* twisting; **~ de tripas** stomach cramp.

retozar *vi* to frisk, to skip.

retozo *m* romp.

retozón/ona *adj* wanton; romping.

retracción *f* retraction.

retractar *vt* to retract.

retraer *vt* to draw back; to dissuade; **~se** *vr* to take refuge; to flee.

retraído/da *adj* shy.

retransmisión *f* broadcast.

retransmitir *vt* to broadcast; to relay; to retransmit.

retrasado/da *adj* late; (*med*) mentally handicapped; backward.

retraso *m* delay; slowness; backwardness; lateness; (*rail*): **el tren ha tenido ~** the train is overdue/late.

retratar *vt* to portray; to photograph; to describe.

retrato *m* portrait, effigy.

retreta *f* (*mil*) retreat.

retrete *m* bathroom, lavatory.

retribución *f* retribution.

retribuir *vt* to repay.

retroacción *f* retroaction.

retroactivo/va *adj* retroactive.

retroceder *vi* to go backward(s), to fly back; to back down.

retrógrado/da *adj* retrograde; reactionary.

retrospectivo/va *adj* retrospective.

retrovisor *m* rear-view mirror.

retumbar *vi* to resound, to jingle.

reuma *f* rheumatism.

reumático/ca *adj* rheumatic.

reumatismo *m* rheumatism.

reunión *f* reunion, meeting.

reunir *vt* to reunite; to unite; **~se** *vr* to gather, to meet.

revalidación *f* confirmation, ratification.

revalidar *vt* to ratify, to confirm.

revancha *f* revenge.

revelación *f* revelation.

revelado *m* developing.

revelar *vt* to reveal; to develop (photographs).

reventar *vi* to burst, to explode; to toil, to overwork.

reventón *m* (*auto*) blow-out.

reverberación *f* reverberation.

reverberar *vi* to reverberate.

reverdecer *vi* to grow green again; to revive.

reverencia *f* reverence, veneration; respect.

R

reverenciar vt to venerate, to revere.
reverendo/da adj reverend.
reverente adj respectful, reverent.
reverso m reverse.
revés m back; wrong side; disappointment, setback.
revestir vt to put on; to coat, to cover.
revisar vt to revise, to review; Lat Am to search.
revisión f revision.
revisor/ra m/f inspector; ticket collector.
revista f magazine; review, revision.
revivir vi to revive.
revocación f revocation.
revocar vt to revoke.
revolcarse vr to wallow.
revolotear vi to flutter.
revoloteo m fluttering.
revoltijo m confusion, disorder.
revoltoso/sa adj rebellious, unruly.
revolución f revolution.
revolucionario/ria adj, m/f revolutionary.
revolver vt to move about; to turn around; to mess up; to revolve; ~se vr to turn round; to change (of the weather).
revólver m revolver.
revuelo m fluttering; (fig) commotion.
revuelta f turn; disturbance, revolt.
rey m king; king (in cards/chess).
reyerta f quarrel, brawl.
rezagar vt to leave behind; to defer; ~se vr to remain behind.
rezar vi to pray, to say one's prayers.
rezo m prayer.
rezongar vi to grumble.
rezumar vt to ooze, to leak.
ría f estuary.
riada f flood.
ribera f shore, bank.
ribereño/ña adj coastal; riverside.
ribete m trimming; seam, border.
ribetear vt to hem, to border.
ricino m: **aceite de ~** castor oil.
rico/ca adj rich; delicious; lovely; cute.
ridiculez f absurdity.
ridiculizar vt to ridicule.
ridículo/la adj ridiculous.
riego m irrigation.
riel m (rail) rail.
rienda f rein of a bridle; **dar ~ suelta** to give free rein to.
riesgo m risk, danger.
riesgoso/sa adj Lat Am risky.
rifa f raffle, lottery.
rifar vt to raffle.
rifle m rifle.
rigidez f rigidity.
rígido/da adj rigid, inflexible; severe.
rigor m rigor.

riguroso/sa adj rigorous.
rima f rhyme.
rimar vi to rhyme.
rimbombante adj pompous.
rímel, rimmel m mascara.
rincón m (inside) corner.
rinoceronte m rhinoceros.
riña f quarrel, dispute.
riñón m kidney.
río m river, stream.
rioja m rioja (wine).
riqueza f riches pl, wealth.
risa f laugh, laughter.
risco m steep rock.
risible adj risible, laughable.
risotada f loud laugh.
ristra f string.
risueño/ña adj smiling.
rítmico/ca adj rhythmic.
ritmo m rhythm.
rito m rite, ceremony.
ritual adj, m ritual.
rival adj, m/f rival.
rivalidad f rivalry.
rivalizar vi: ~ **con** to rival, to vie with.
rizado/da adj curly.
rizar vt to curl (hair).
rizo m curl; ripple (on water).
robar vt to rob; to steal; to break into.
roble m oak tree.
robledal m oakwood.
robo m robbery; theft.
robot m robot.
robustez f robustness.
robusto/ta adj robust, strong.
roca f rock.
rocalla f pebbles pl.
roce m rub; brush; friction.
rociada f sprinkling; spray, shower.
rociar vt to sprinkle; to spray.
rocín m nag; hack; stupid person.
rocío m dew.
rocoso/sa adj rocky.
rodada f rut, track of a wheel.
rodador m Lat Am gnat.
rodadura f act of rolling.
rodaja f slice.
rodaje m filming; **en ~** (auto) running in.
rodar vi to roll.
rodear vi to make a detour; * vt to surround, to enclose; Lat Am to round up.
rodeo m detour; subterfuge; evasion; rodeo.
rodilla f knee; **de ~s** on one's knees.
rodillo m roller.
roedor/ra adj gnawing; * m rodent.
roedura f gnawing.
roer vt to gnaw; to corrode.
rogar vt, vi to ask for; to beg, to entreat; to pray.

rogativa f supplication, prayer.

rojez f redness.

rojizo/za adj reddish.

rojo/ja adj red; ruddy.

rol m list, roll, catalog; role.

rollizo/za adj round; plump, chubby.

rollo m roll; coil.

romance m Romance language; romance.

romancero m collection of romances/ballads.

romanticismo m romanticism.

romántico/ca adj romantic.

rombo m rhombus.

romboide m rhomboid.

romería f pilgrimage.

romero m (bot) rosemary.

romo/ma adj blunt; snub-nosed.

rompecabezas m invar riddle; jigsaw.

romper vt to break; to tear up; to wear out; to break up (land); * vi to break (of waves); to break through.

rompimiento m Lat Am tearing, breaking; crack.

ron m rum.

roncar vi to snore; to roar.

roncha f weal, bruise.

ronco/ca adj hoarse; husky; raucous.

ronda f night patrol; round (of drinks, cards etc).

rondar vt, vi to patrol; to prowl around.

ronquera f hoarseness.

ronquido m snore; roar.

ronzal m halter.

ronronear vi to purr.

roña f scab, mange; grime; rust.

roñoso/sa adj filthy; mean.

ropa f clothes pl; clothing; dress.

ropaje m gown, robes pl; drapery.

ropero m linen cupboard; closet.

rosa f rose; birthmark.

rosado/da adj pink; rosy.

rosal m rosebush.

rosario m rosary.

rosca f thread (of a screw); coil, spiral.

rosedal m Lat Am rose garden.

rosetón m rosette; rose window, wheel window.

rosquilla f doughnut, donut.

rostro m face.

rotación f rotation.

roto/ta adj broken, destroyed; debauched.

rótula f kneecap; ball-and-socket joint.

rotulador m felt-tip pen, fiber-tip pen.

rotular vt to inscribe, to label.

rótulo m inscription; label, ticket; placard, poster.

rotundo/da adj round; emphatic.

rotura f breaking; crack; tear.

roturar vt to plow.

rozadura f graze, scratch.

rozar vt to rub; to chafe; to nibble (the grass); to scrape; to touch lightly.

rubí m ruby.

rubicundo/da adj reddish.

rubio/bia adj fair-haired, blond/blonde; * m/f blond/blonde.

rubor m blush; bashfulness.

rúbrica f red mark; flourish at the end of a signature; title, heading, rubric.

rubricar vt to sign with a flourish; to sign and seal.

rubro m Lat Am heading; item.

rudeza f roughness, rudeness; stupidity.

rudimento m principle; beginning; ~s mpl rudiments pl.

rudo/da adj rough, coarse; plain, simple; stupid.

rueca f distaff.

rueda f wheel; circle; slice, round.

ruedo m rotation; border, selvage; arena, bullring.

ruego m request, entreaty.

rufián m pimp, pander; lout.

rugby m rugby.

rugido m roar.

rugir vi to roar, to bellow.

rugoso/sa adj wrinkled.

ruibarbo m rhubarb.

ruido m noise, sound; din, row; fuss.

ruidoso/sa adj noisy, loud.

ruin adj mean, despicable; mean, stingy.

ruina f ruin, collapse; downfall, destruction; ~s fpl ruins pl.

ruindad f meanness, lowness; mean act.

ruinoso/sa adj ruinous, disastrous.

ruiseñor m nightingale.

ruleta f roulette.

rulo m rolling pin; hair curler.

rumba f rumba.

rumbo m (mar) course, bearing; road, route, way; course of events, pomp, ostentation.

rumboso/sa adj generous, lavish.

rumiante m ruminant.

rumiar vt to chew; * vi to ruminate.

rumor m rumor; murmur.

runrún m rumor; sound of voices, whirr.

ruptura f rupture.

rural adj rural.

rusticidad f rusticity; coarseness.

rústico/ca adj rustic; * m/f peasant.

ruta f route, itinerary.

rutina f routine; habit.

R

S

sábado *m* Saturday; (Jewish) Sabbath.
sábana *f* sheet; altar cloth.
sabandija *f* bug, insect.
sabañón *m* chilblain.
sabelotodo *m/f invar* know-all.
saber *vt* to know; to be able to; to find out, to learn; to experience; * *vi:* ~ **a** to taste of; * *m* learning, knowledge.
sabiduría *f* learning, knowledge; wisdom.
sabiendas *adv:* **a** ~ knowingly.
sabihondo/da *adj* know-all; pedantic.
sabio/bia *adj* sage, wise; * *m/f* sage, wise person.
sablazo *m* sword wound; (*col*) sponging, scrounging.
sable *m* saber, cutlass.
sabor *m* taste, savor, flavor.
saborear *vt* to savor, to taste; to enjoy.
sabotaje *m* sabotage.
saboteador/ora *m/f* saboteur.
sabotear *vt* to sabotage.
sabroso/sa *adj* tasty, delicious; pleasant; salted.
sabueso *m* bloodhound.
sacacorchos *m invar* corkscrew.
sacapuntas *m invar* pencil sharpener.
sacar *vt* to take out, to extract; to get out; to bring out (a book etc); to take off (clothes); to receive, to get; (*sport*) to serve.
sacarina *f* saccharin.
sacerdotal *adj* priestly.
sacerdote *m* priest.
sacerdotisa *f* priestess.
saciar *vt* to satiate.
saciedad *f* satiety.
saco *m* bag, sack; *Lat Am* jacket; *Lat Am* coat; ~ **de dormir** sleeping bag.
sacramental *adj* sacramental.
sacramento *m* sacrament.
sacrificar *vt* to sacrifice.
sacrificio *m* sacrifice.
sacrilegio *m* sacrilege.
sacrílego/ga *adj* sacrilegious.
sacristán *m* sacristan, sexton.
sacristía *f* sacristy, vestry.
sacro/cra *adj* holy, sacred.
sacrosanto/ta *adj* sacrosanct.
sacudida *f* shake, jerk.
sacudir *vt* to shake, to jerk; to beat, to hit.
sacudón *m Lat Am* shake, jerk.
sádico/ca *adj* sadistic; * *m/f* sadist.
sadismo *m* sadism.
saeta *f* arrow, dart.
sagacidad *f* shrewdness, cleverness, sagacity.

sagaz *adj* shrewd, clever, sagacious.
sagitariano/na *adj Lat Am* Sagittarian (zodiac sign).
Sagitario *m* Sagittarius (zodiac sign).
sagrado/da *adj* sacred, holy.
sagrario *m* shrine; tabernacle.
sainete *m* (*theat*) farce; flavor, relish; seasoning.
saíno *m Lat Am* peccary.
sal *f* salt.
sala *f* large room; (*theat*) house, auditorium; public hall; (*law*) court; (*med*) ward.
salado/da *adj* salted; witty, amusing.
salamandra *f* salamander.
salar *vt* to salt.
salarial *adj* wage *compd*, salary *compd*.
salario *m* salary.
salazón *f* salting.
salchicha *f* sausage.
salchichón *m* salami-type sausage.
saldar *vt* to pay; to sell off; (*fig*) to settle.
saldo *m* settlement; balance; remainder; ~**s** *mpl* sale.
saledizo/za *adj* projecting, salient.
salero *m* salt cellar.
saleroso *adj* witty, amusing.
salida *f* exit, way out; leaving, departure; production, output; (*com*) sale; sales outlet.
saliente *adj* projecting; rising; (*fig*) outstanding.
salina *f* saltworks, salt mine.
salino/na *adj* saline.
salir *vi* to go out, to leave; to depart, to set out; to appear; to turn out, to prove; ~**se** *vr* to escape, to leak.
salitre *m* saltpeter.
saliva *f* saliva.
salmo *m* psalm.
salmón *m* salmon.
salmonete *m* red mullet.
salmuera *f* brine.
salobre *adj* brackish, salty.
salón *m* living room, lounge; public hall.
salpicadero *m* dashboard.
salpicar *vt* to sprinkle, to splash, to spatter.
salpimentar *vt* to season with pepper and salt.
salsa *f* sauce.
salsera *f* sauce boat; gravy boat.
saltamontes *m invar* grasshopper.
saltar *vt* to jump, to leap; to skip, to miss out; * *vi* to leap, to jump; to bounce; (*fig*) to explode, to blow up.
salteador *m* highwayman.
saltear *vt* to rob in a stick-up; to assault; to sauté (in cooking).
saltimbanqui *m/f* acrobat.

salto m leap, jump.
saltón/ona adj bulging; protruding.
salubre adj healthy.
salubridad f healthiness.
salud f health.
saludable adj healthy.
saludar vt to greet; (mil) to salute.
saludo m greeting.
salutación f salutation, greeting.
salva f (mil) salute, salvo.
salvación f salvation; rescue.
salvado m bran.
salvaguardar vt to safeguard.
salvaguardia m safeguard.
salvaje adj savage.
salvajismo m savagery.
salvar vt to save; to rescue; to overcome; to cross, to jump across; to cover, to travel; to exclude; ~**se** vr to escape from danger.
salvavidas adj invar: **bote** ~ lifeboat; **chaleco** ~ life preserver.
salvia f (bot) sage.
salvo/va adj safe; * adv save, except (for).
salvoconducto m safe-conduct.
san adj saint (as title).
sanamente adv healthily.
sanar vt, vi to heal.
sanatorio m sanitarium; nursing home.
sanción f sanction.
sancionar vt to sanction.
sandalia f sandal.
sándalo m sandal, sandalwood.
sandez f folly, stupidity.
sandía f watermelon.
sánduche m Lat Am sandwich.
sandwich m sandwich.
saneamiento m sanitation.
sanear vt to drain.
sangrar vt, vi to bleed.
sangre f blood; **a** ~ **fría** in cold blood; **a** ~ **y fuego** without mercy.
sangría f sangria (drink); bleeding.
sangriento/ta adj bloody, blood-stained, gory; cruel.
sanguijuela f leech.
sanguinario/ria adj bloodthirsty, cruel.
sanguíneo/nea adj blood compd.
sanidad f sanitation; health.
sanitario/ria adj sanitary; health; ~**s** mpl bathroom facilities pl.
sano/na adj healthy, fit; intact, sound.
santiamén m: **en un** ~ in no time at all.
santidad f sanctity.
santificar vt to sanctify; to make holy.
santiguarse vr to make the sign of the cross.
santo/ta adj holy; sacred; * m/f saint; ~ **y seña** password, watchword.
santuario m sanctuary.
saña f anger, passion.

sañudo/da adj furious, enraged.
sapo m toad.
saque m (sport) serve, service, throw-in.
saqueador/ra m/f ransacker, looter.
saquear vt to ransack, to plunder.
saqueo m looting, sacking.
sarampión m measles.
sarao m evening party, soiree.
sarcasmo m sarcasm.
sarcástico/ca adj sarcastic.
sarcófago m sarcophagus.
sardina f sardine.
sardónico/ca adj sardonic; ironic(al).
sargento m sergeant.
sarmiento m vine shoot.
sarna f itch; mange; (med) scabies.
sarnoso/sa adj itchy, scabby, mangy.
sarpullido m (med) rash.
sarro m (med) tartar.
sarta f string of beads etc; string, row.
sartén f frying pan.
sastre m tailor.
sastrería f tailor's premises.
Satanás m Satan.
satélite m satellite.
sátira f satire.
satírico/ca adj satirical.
satirizar vt to satirize.
sátiro m satyr.
satisfacción f satisfaction; apology.
satisfacer vt to satisfy; to pay (a debt); ~**se** vr to satisfy oneself; to take revenge.
satisfactorio/ria adj satisfactory.
satisfecho/cha adj satisfied.
saturación f (chem) saturation.
Saturno m Saturn (planet).
sauce m willow tree.
saúco m elder tree.
sauna f sauna.
savia f sap.
saxofón m saxophone.
sazonado/da adj flavored, seasoned.
sazonar vt to ripen; to season.
se pn reflexivo: himself; herself; itself; yourself; themselves; yourselves; each other; one another; oneself.
sebo m fat, grease.
seboso/sa adj fat, greasy.
secador m: ~ **de pelo** hairdryer.
secadora f tumble dryer.
secamente adv drily/dryly, curtly.
secano m dry, arable land which is not irrigated.
secar vt to dry; ~**se** vr to dry up; to dry oneself.
sección f section.
seco/ca adj dry; dried up; skinny; cold (of character); brusque, sharp; bare.
secretaría f secretariat.
secretario/ria m/f secretary.

S

secreto/ta adj secret; hidden; * m secret; secrecy.
secta f sect.
sectario/ria adj, m/f sectarian.
sector m sector.
secuela f sequel; consequence.
secuencia f sequence.
secuestrador/ra m/f kidnaper.
secuestrar vt to kidnap; to confiscate.
secuestro m kidnaping; confiscation.
secular adj secular.
secularización f secularization.
secularizar vt to secularize.
secundar vt to second.
secundario/ria adj secondary.
sed f thirst; **tener** ~ to be thirsty.
seda f silk.
sedal m fishing line.
sedante m sedative.
sede f see; seat; headquarters.
sedentario/ria adj sedentary.
sedición f sedition.
sedicioso/sa adj seditious, mutinous.
sediento/ta adj thirsty; eager.
sedoso/sa adj silky.
seducción f seduction.
seducir vt to seduce; to bribe; to charm, to attract.
seductor/ra adj seductive; charming; attractive; * m/f seducer.
segador/ra m/f reaper, harvester.
segadora-trilladora f combine (harvester).
segar vt to reap, to harvest; to mow.
seglar adj secular, lay.
segmento m segment.
segregación f segregation, separation.
segregar vt to segregate, to separate.
seguido/da adj continuous; successive; long-lasting; * adv straight (on); after; Lat Am often.
seguidor/ra m/f follower; supporter.
seguimiento m pursuit; continuation.
seguir vt to follow, to pursue; to continue; * vi to follow; to carry on; ~se vr to follow, to ensue.
según prep according to.
segundo/da adj second; * m second (of time).
seguramente adv surely; for sure.
seguridad f security; certainty; safety; confidence; stability.
seguro/ra adj safe, secure; sure, certain; firm, constant; * adv for sure; * m safety device; insurance; safety, certainty.
seis adj, m six; sixth.
seiscientos/tas adj six hundred.
seísmo m earthquake.
selección f selection, choice.
seleccionar vt to select, to choose.
selecto/ta adj select, choice.
sellar vt to seal; to stamp (a document).
sello m seal; stamp.
selva f forest.

semáforo m traffic lights pl; signal.
semana f week.
semanada f Lat Am weekly pocket money.
semanal adj weekly.
semanario/ria m weekly (magazine).
semblante m face; (fig) look; appearance.
sembrado m sown field.
sembrar vt to sow; to sprinkle, to scatter.
semejante adj similar, like; * m fellow man.
semejanza f resemblance, likeness.
semejar vi to resemble; ~se vr to look alike.
semen m semen.
semental m stud.
sementera f sowing time; land sown with seed.
semestral adj half-yearly.
semicircular adj semicircular.
semicírculo m semicircle.
semifinal f semifinal.
semilla f seed, bean.
semilla de soja f soybean.
semillero m seed plot.
seminario m seedbed; seminary.
seminarista m seminarist.
semitono m (mus) half step, semitone.
sémola f semolina.
sempiterno/na adj everlasting.
senado m senate.
senador/ra m/f senator.
sencillez f plainness; simplicity; naturalness.
sencillo/lla adj simple; natural; unaffected; single.
senda f m path, footpath.
senderismo m hillwalking.
senderista m/f hillwalker.
sendero m path, footpath.
senil adj senile.
seno m bosom; lap; womb; hole, cavity; sinus; ~s mpl breasts pl.
sensación f sensation, feeling; sense.
sensacional adj sensational.
sensato/ta adj sensible.
sensibilidad f sensibility, sensitivity.
sensible adj sensitive; perceptible, appreciable; regrettable.
sensitivo/va adj sense compd, sensitive.
sensorial adj sensorial, sensory.
sensual adj sensuous, sensual.
sensualidad f sensuousness; sensuality; sexiness.
sentado/da adj sitting, seated; sedate; settled.
sentar vt to seat; (fig) to establish; * vi to suit; ~se vr to sit down.
sentencia f (law) sentence; opinion; saying.
sentenciar vt (law) to sentence, to pass judgement on; * vi to give one's opinion.
sentencioso/sa adj sententious.
sentido m sense; feeling; meaning; ~/da adj regrettable; sensitive.
sentimental adj sentimental.

sentimiento *m* feeling, emotion, sentiment; sympathy; regret, grief.

sentir *vt* to feel; to hear; to perceive; to sense; to suffer from; to regret, to be sorry for; ~**se** *vr* to feel; to feel pain; to crack (of walls etc); * *m* opinion, judgement.

seña *f* sign, mark, token; signal; (*mil*) password; ~**s** *fpl* address.

señal *f* sign, token; symptom; signal; landmark; (*com*) deposit.

señalado/da *adj* distinct; special; distinguished, notable.

señalar *vt* to stamp, to mark; to signpost; to point out; to fix, to settle; ~**se** *vr* to distinguish oneself, to excel.

señor *m* man; gentleman; master; Mr; sir.

señora *f* lady; Mrs; madam; wife.

señorita *f* Miss; young lady.

señorito *m* Master; young gentleman; rich kid.

señuelo *m* decoy; bait, lure.

separable *adj* separable.

separación *f* separation.

separar *vt* to separate; ~**se** *vr* to separate; to come away, to come apart; to withdraw.

septentrional *adj* north, northern.

séptico *adj* septic.

septiembre *m* September.

séptimo/ma *adj* seventh.

sepulcral *adj* sepulchral.

sepulcro *m* sepulcher, grave, tomb.

sepultar *vt* to bury, to inter.

sepultura *f* burial, interment; grave, tomb.

sepulturero *m* gravedigger, sexton.

sequedad *f* dryness; brusqueness.

sequía *f* dryness; thirst; drought.

séquito *m* retinue, suite; group of supporters; aftermath.

ser *vi* to be; to exist; ~ **de** to come from; to be made of; to belong to; * *m* being.

serenarse *vr* to calm down.

serenata *f* (*mus*) serenade.

serenidad *f* serenity.

sereno *m* night watchman; ~/**na** *adj* serene, calm, quiet.

serial *m* serial.

serie *f* series; sequence.

seriedad *f* seriousness, gravity; reliability; sincerity.

serio/ria *adj* serious; grave; reliable.

sermón *m* sermon.

sermonear *vt* to lecture; * *vi* to sermonize.

seronegativo/va *adj* HIV-negative.

seropositivo/va *adj* HIV-positive.

serpentear *vi* to wriggle; to wind, to snake.

serpentina *f* streamer.

serpiente *f* snake.

serranía *f* range of mountains; mountainous country.

serrano/na *m/f* highlander.

serrar *vt* to saw.

serrín *m* sawdust.

serruchar *vt Lat Am* to saw up.

serrucho *m* handsaw.

servible *adj* serviceable.

servicial *adj* helpful, obliging.

servicio *m* service; service charge; service, set of dishes; ~**s** *mpl* bathroom facilities *pl*.

servidor/ra *m/f* servant.

servidumbre *f* servitude; servants *pl*, staff.

servil *adj* servile.

servilleta *f* napkin, serviette.

servir *vt* to serve; to wait on; * *vi* to serve; to be of use; to be in service; ~**se** *vr* to serve oneself, to help oneself; to deign, to please; to make use of.

sesenta *adj, m* sixty; sixtieth.

sesentón/ona *m/f* person of about sixty years of age.

sesgar *vt* to slope, to slant.

sesgo *m* slope.

sesión *f* session; sitting; performance; showing.

seso *m* brain.

sestear *vi* to take a nap.

sesudo/da *adj* sensible, prudent.

seta *f* mushroom.

setecientos/tas *adj* seven hundred.

setenta *adj, m* seventy.

setiembre *m* September.

seto *m* fence; enclosure; hedge.

seudo- *pref* pseudo-.

seudónimo *m* pseudonym.

severidad *f* severity.

severo/ra *adj* severe, strict; grave, serious.

sexagenario/ria *adj* sixty years old.

sexagésimo/ma *adj* sixtieth.

sexenio *m* space of six years.

sexo *m* sex.

sexto/ta *adj, m* sixth.

sexual *adj* sexual.

short *m Lat Am* shorts.

si *conj* whether; if.

sí *adv* yes; certainly; indeed; * *pn* oneself; himself; herself; itself; yourself; themselves; yourselves; each other; one another.

siderúrgico/ca *adj* iron and steel *compd*.

sidra *f* cider.

siega *f* harvest, mowing.

siembra *f* sowing time.

siempre *adv* always; all the time; ever; *Lat Am* still; ~ **jamás** for ever and ever.

sien *f* temple (of the head).

sierra *f* saw; range of mountains.

siervo/va *m/f* slave.

siesta *f* siesta, afternoon nap.

siete *adj, m* seven.

sietemesino/na *adj* born seven months after conception; premature; (*fig*) half-witted.

S

sífilis f syphilis.
sifón m siphon; soda.
sigilo m secrecy.
sigiloso/sa adj reserved; silent.
sigla f acronym; abbreviation.
siglo m century.
significación f significance, meaning.
significado m significance, meaning.
significar vt to signify, to mean; to make known, to express.
significativo/va adj significant.
signo m sign, mark.
siguiente adj following, successive, next.
sílaba f syllable.
silbar vt, vi to hiss; to whistle.
silbato m whistle.
silbido/silbo m hiss; whistling.
silencio m silence; ¡~! silence!, quiet!
silencioso/sa adj silent.
silla f chair; saddle; seat; ~ **de ruedas** wheelchair.
sillón m armchair, easy chair; rocking chair.
silo m silo.
silogismo m syllogism.
silueta f silhouette; outline; figure.
silvestre adj wild, uncultivated; rustic.
sima f abyss; pothole, cavern.
simbólico/ca adj symbolic.
simbolizar vt to symbolize.
símbolo m symbol.
simetría f symmetry.
simétrico/ca adj symmetrical.
simiente f seed.
similar adj similar.
similitud f similarity, similitude.
simio m ape.
simpatía f liking; kindness; solidarity; affection.
simpático/ca adj pleasant; kind.
simpatizante m/f sympathizer.
simpatizar vi: ~ **con** to get on well with.
simple adj single; simple, easy; mere; sheer; silly; * m/f simpleton.
simpleza f simpleness, gullibility; silliness.
simplicidad f simplicity.
simplificar vt to simplify.
simulación f simulation.
simulacro m simulacrum, idol.
simuladamente adv deceptively, hypocritically.
simular vt to simulate.
simultaneidad f simultaneousness.
simultáneo/nea adj simultaneous.
sin prep without.
sinagoga f synagogue.
sinceridad f sincerity.
sincero/ra adj sincere.
síncope f (med) syncope, fainting fit.
sincronizar vt to synchronize.
sindical adj union compd.
sindicato m labor union; syndicate.

sinfín m: **un ~ de** a great many.
sinfonía f symphony.
singular adj singular; exceptional; peculiar, odd.
singularidad f singularity.
singularizar vt to distinguish; to singularize; ~**se** vr to distinguish oneself; to stand out.
siniestro/tra adj left; (fig) sinister; * m accident.
sinnúmero m = **sinfín**.
sino conj but; except; save; only; * m fate.
sinónimo/ma adj synonymous; * m synonym.
sinsabor m unpleasantness; disgust.
sintaxis f syntax.
síntesis f synthesis.
sintético/ca adj synthetic.
sintetizar vt synthesize.
síntoma m symptom.
sinuosidad f sinuosity; curve, wave.
sinuoso/sa adj sinuous; wavy.
sinvergüenza m/f rogue.
siquiera conj even if, even though; * adv at least.
sirena f siren; mermaid; car horn.
sirviente/ta m/f servant.
sisa f petty theft; cut, percentage.
sisear vt, vi to hiss.
sistema m system.
sistemático/ca adj systematic.
sitiar vt to besiege.
sitio m place; spot; site, location; room, space; job, post; (mil) siege, blockade.
situación f situation, position; standing.
situar vt to place, to situate; to invest; ~**se** vr to be established in place/business.
slip m underpants pl, briefs pl.
smoking m tuxedo.
sobaco m armpit, armhole.
sobar vt to handle, to soften; to knead; to massage, to rub hard; to rumple (clothes); to fondle.
soberanía f sovereignty.
soberano/na m/f sovereign.
soberbia f pride, haughtiness; magnificence.
soberbio/bia adj proud, haughty; magnificent.
sobornar vt to suborn, to bribe.
soborno m subornation, bribery; bribe.
sobra f surplus, excess; **de ~** spare, surplus, extra.
sobradamente adv too; amply.
sobrante adj remaining; * m surplus, remainder.
sobrar vt to exceed, to surpass; * vi to be more than enough; to remain, to be left.
sobrasada f pork sausage spread.
sobre prep on; on top of; above, over; more than; besides; * m envelope; Lat Am purse, handbag.
sobreabundancia f superabundance.
sobreabundar vi to superabound.
sobrecarga f extra load; (com) surcharge.
sobrecargar vt to overload; (com) to surcharge.
sobrecoger vt to surprise.
sobredosis f invar overdose.

sobreentender vt to deduce; **~se** vr: se sobreentiende que . . . it is implied that . . . .

sobrehumano/na adj superhuman.

sobrellevar vt to carry; to tolerate.

sobremanera adv excessively.

sobremesa f: **de ~** immediately after dinner.

sobrenatural adj supernatural.

sobrenaturalmente adv supernaturally.

sobrenombre m nickname.

sobrepasar vt to surpass.

sobreponer vt to put (something) over/on top of; **~se** vr to pull through.

sobresaliente adj projecting; (fig) outstanding.

sobresalir vi to project; (fig) to stand out.

sobresaltar vt to frighten.

sobresalto m start, scare; sudden shock.

sobreseer vt: **~ una causa** (law) to stay a case; * vi: **~ de** to desist from.

sobreseimiento m dismissal, suspension.

sobrevenir vi to happen, to come unexpectedly; to supervene.

sobrevida f Lat Am survival.

sobreviviente adj surviving; * m/f survivor.

sobrevivir vi to survive.

sobrevolar vt to fly over.

sobriedad f sobriety.

sobrino/na m/f nephew/niece.

sobrio/ria adj sober, frugal.

socarrón/ona adj sarcastic; ironic(al).

socarronería f sarcasm; irony.

socavar vt to undermine.

socavón m hole.

sociabilidad f sociability.

sociable adj sociable.

social adj social.

socialdemócrata adj, m/f social democrat.

socialista adj, m/f socialist.

sociedad f society.

socio/cia m/f associate, member.

sociología f sociology.

sociólogo/ga m/f sociologist.

socorrer vt to help.

socorrido/da adj well-stocked/supplied.

socorrista m/f first aider; lifeguard.

socorro m help, aid, assistance, relief.

soda f soda; soda water.

sodomía f sodomy.

sodomita m sodomite.

soez adj dirty, obscene.

sofá m sofa.

sofisma m sophism.

sofista m/f sophist.

sofisticación f sophistication.

sofocar vt to suffocate.

software m (comput) software.

soga f rope.

sojuzgar vt to conquer, to subdue.

sol m sun; sunshine, sunlight.

solamente adv only, solely.

solapa f lapel.

solapado/da adj cunning, crafty, artful.

solar m building site; piece of land; ancestral home of a family; * adj solar.

solariego/ga adj belonging to the ancestral home of a family.

solaz m recreation, relaxation; solace, consolation.

solazar vt to provide relaxation for; to comfort.

soldada f wages pl.

soldadesca f military profession.

soldado m/f soldier; **~ raso** private.

soldador m welder; soldering iron.

soldadura f soldering; solder.

soldar vt to solder; to weld; to unite.

soleado/da adj sunny.

soledad f solitude; loneliness.

solemne adj solemn; impressive, grand.

solemnidad f solemnity.

solemnizar vt to solemnize; to praise.

soler vi to be accustomed to, to be in the habit of.

solfeo m (mus) solfa.

solicitar vt to ask for, to seek; to apply for (a job); to canvass for; to chase after, to pursue.

solícito/ta adj diligent; solicitous.

solicitud f care, solicitude; request, petition.

solidaridad f solidarity.

solidario/ria adj joint; mutually binding.

solidez f solidity.

sólido/da adj solid.

soliloquio m soliloquy, monolog.

solista m/f soloist.

solitario/ria adj lonesome, solitary; * m solitaire; * m/f hermit.

sollozar vi to sob.

sollozo m sob.

solo m (mus) solo; **~/la** adj alone, single; **a solas** alone, unaided.

sólo adv only.

solomillo m sirloin.

solsticio m solstice.

soltar vt to untie, to loosen; to set free, to let out; **~se** vr to get loose; to come undone.

soltero/ra m/f bachelor/single woman; * adj single, unmarried.

soltura f looseness, slackness; agility, activity; fluency.

soluble adj soluble; solvable.

solución f solution; denouement.

solucionar vt to solve; to resolve.

solvente adj, m solvent.

sombra f shade; shadow.

sombrear vt to shade.

sombrero m hat.

sombrilla f parasol.

sombrío/bría adj shady, gloomy; sad.

somero/ra adj superficial.

S

someter vt to conquer (a country); to subject to one's will; to submit; to subdue; ~**se** vr to give in, to submit.

sometimiento m submission.

somnífero m sleeping pill.

somnolencia f sleepiness, drowsiness.

son m sound; rumor.

sonado/da adj celebrated; famous; generally reported.

sonaja f (mus) timbrel.

sonajero m (mus) small timbrel.

sonámbulo/la m/f sleepwalker; somnambulist.

sonar vt to ring; * vi to sound; to make a noise; to be pronounced; to be talked of; to sound familiar; ~**se** vr to blow one's nose.

sonata f (mus) sonata.

sonda f sounding; (med) probe.

sondear vt (mar) to sound; to probe; to bore.

sondeo m sounding; boring; (fig) poll.

soneto m sonnet.

sónico/ca adj sonic.

sonido m sound.

sonoro/ra adj sonorous.

sonreír(se) vi (vr) to smile.

sonrisa f smile.

sonrojarse vr to blush.

sonrojo m blush.

sonsacar vt to wheedle, cajole; to obtain by cunning.

sonsear vi Lat Am to fool around.

sonsera f Lat Am nonsense.

sonso/sa m/f Lat Am fool.

sonsonete m tapping noise; monotonous voice.

soñador/ra m/f dreamer.

soñar vt, vi to dream.

soñoliento/ta adj sleepy, drowsy.

sopa f soup; sop.

sopapo m punch, thump.

sopera f soup dish.

sopero m soup plate.

sopetón m: **de** ~ suddenly.

soplar vt to blow away, to blow off; to blow up, to inflate; * vi to blow, to puff.

soplete m blowlamp.

soplo m blowing; puff of wind; (col) tip-off.

soplón/ona m/f telltale.

sopor m drowsiness, sleepiness.

soporífero/ra adj soporific; * m sleeping pill.

soportable adj tolerable, bearable.

soportal m portico.

soportar vt to suffer, to tolerate; to support.

sorber vt to sip; to inhale; to swallow; to absorb.

sorbete m sherbet; sorbet.

sorbo m sip; gulp, swallow.

sordera f deafness.

sordidez f sordidness; dirtiness; meanness.

sórdido/da adj sordid; dirty; mean.

sorda/da adj deaf; silent, quiet; * m/f deaf person.

sordomudo/da adj deaf and dumb.

sorna f slyness; sarcasm; slowness.

soroche m mountain sickness.

sorprender vt to surprise.

sorpresa f surprise.

sortear vt to draw/cast (lots); to raffle; to avoid.

sorteo m draw; raffle.

sortija f ring; ringlet, curl.

sortilegio m sorcery.

sosegado/da adj quiet, peaceful.

sosegar vt to appease, to calm; * vi to rest.

sosería f insipidness; dullness.

sosiego m tranquility, calmness.

soslayar vt to do/place (something) obliquely.

soslayo adv: **al/de** ~ obliquely, sideways.

soso/sa adj insipid, tasteless; dull.

sospecha f suspicion.

sospechar vt to suspect.

sospechoso/sa adj suspicious; suspect; * m/f suspect.

sostén m support; bra; sustenance.

sostener vt to sustain, to maintain; ~**se** vr to support/maintain oneself; to contrive, to remain.

sostenimiento m support; maintenance; sustenance.

sota f jack, knave (in cards).

sotana f cassock.

sótano m basement, cellar.

sotavento m (mar) leeward, lee.

soto m grove, thicket.

squash m squash.

status m invar status.

su pn his, her, its, one's; their; your.

suave adj smooth, soft; delicate; gentle; mild, meek.

suavidad f softness, sweetness; suavity.

suavizar vt to soften.

subalterno/na adj secondary; auxiliary.

subasta f auction.

subastar vt to sell by auction.

subcampeón/ona m/f runner-up.

subconsciente adj, m subconscious.

subdesarrollado/da adj underdeveloped.

subdesarrollo m underdevelopment.

subdirector/ora m/f assistant director.

súbdito/ta adj, m/f subject.

subdividir vt to subdivide.

subdivisión f subdivision.

subestimar vt to underestimate.

subida f climb, ascent, rise in value/price.

subido/da adj deep-colored; high (price).

subir vt, vi to raise, to lift up; to go up; to climb, to ascend; to increase, to swell; to get in, to get on, to board; to rise (in price).

súbito/ta adj sudden, hasty; unforeseen.

subjetivo/va adj subjective.

subjuntivo m (gr) subjunctive.

sublevación f sedition, revolt.

sublevar vt to excite (a rebellion); to incite (a revolt); ~**se** vr to revolt.

sublime *adj* sublime.
sublimidad *f* sublimity.
submarino/na *adj* underwater; * *m* submarine.
subnormal *adj* subnormal; * *m/f* person of low intelligence.
subordinación *f* subordination.
subrayar *vt* to underline.
subrepticio/cia *adj* surreptitious.
subsanar *vt* to excuse; to mend, to repair; to overcome.
subsidio *m* subsidy, aid; benefit, allowance.
subsistencia *f* subsistence.
subsistir *vi* to subsist.
su(b)stancia *f* substance.
su(b)stancial *adj* substantial.
su(b)stancioso/sa *adj* substantial; nutritious.
su(b)stracción *f* removal; (*math*) subtraction.
su(b)straer *vt* to remove; (*math*) to subtract; ~**se** *vr* to avoid; to withdraw.
subterfugio *f* subterfuge.
subterráneo/nea *adj* subterranean, underground; * *m* underground passage; (*rail*) subway.
suburbio *m* slum quarter; suburbs *pl*.
subvencionar *vt* to subsidize.
subversión *f* subversion, overthrow.
subversivo/va *adj* subversive.
subvertir *vt* to subvert, to overthrow.
subyugar *vt* to subdue, to subjugate.
sucedáneo/nea *adj* substitute; * *m* substitute (food).
suceder *vt* to succeed, to inherit; * *vi* to happen.
sucesión *f* succession; issue, offspring; inheritance.
sucesivamente *adv*: **y así** ~ and so on.
sucesivo/va *adj* successive.
suceso *m* event; incident.
sucesor/ra *m/f* successor; heir.
suciedad *f* dirtiness, filthiness; dirt.
sucinto/ta *adj* succinct, concise.
sucio/cia *adj* dirty, filthy; obscene; dishonest.
suculento/ta *adj* succulent, juicy.
sucumbir *vt* to succumb.
sucursal *f* branch (office).
sudar *vt, vi* to sweat.
sudeste *adj* southeast, southeastern; * *m* southeast.
sudoeste *adj* southwest, southwestern; * *m* southwest.
sudor *m* sweat.
sudorífico/ca *adj* sweaty.
suegra *f* mother-in-law.
suegro *m* father-in-law.
suela *f* sole (shoe).
sueldo *m* wages *pl*, salary.
suelo *m* ground; floor; soil, surface.
suelto/ta *adj* loose; free; detached; swift; * *m* loose change.
sueño *m* sleep; dream.
suero *m* (*med*) serum; whey.

suerte *f* fate, destiny, chance, lot, fortune, good luck; kind, sort.
suéter *m* sweater.
suficiencia *f* sufficiency, competence, fitness.
suficiente *adj* enough, sufficient; fit, capable.
sufragar *vt* to aid, to assist; * *vi Lat Am* to vote.
sufragio *m* vote, suffrage; aid, assistance.
sufrible *adj* bearable.
sufrido/da *adj* long-suffering, patient; hard-wearing.
sufrimiento *m* suffering; patience.
sufrir *vt* to suffer; to bear, to put up with; to support.
sugerencia *f* suggestion.
sugerir *vt* to suggest.
sugestión *f* suggestion.
suicida *adj* suicidal; * *m/f* suicide; suicidal person.
suicidio *m* suicide.
sujeción *f* subjection.
sujetacorbata *m Lat Am* tie-pin.
sujetador *m* fastener; bra.
sujetar *vt* to fasten, to hold down; to subdue; to subject; ~**se** *vr* to subject oneself.
sujeto/ta *adj* fastened, secure; subject, liable; * *m* subject; individual.
sulfúrico *adj* sulfuric.
sultán *m* sultan.
sultana *f* sultana.
suma *f* total, sum; adding up; summary.
sumamente *adv* extremely.
sumar *vt* to add, to add up; to collect, to gather; * *vi* to add up.
sumario/ria *adj* brief, concise; * *m* summary.
sumergir *vt* to submerge, to sink; to immerse.
sumidero *m* sewer, drain.
suministrador/ra *m/f* provider, supplier.
suministrar *vt* to supply, to furnish.
sumir *vt* to sink, to submerge; (*fig*) to plunge.
sumisión *f* submission.
sumiso/sa *adj* submissive, docile.
sumo/ma *adj* great, extreme; highest, greatest; **a lo** ~ at most.
suntuosidad *f* sumptuousness.
suntuoso/sa *adj* sumptuous.
súper *f* four-star (gas).
superable *adj* surmountable.
superabundancia *f* superabundance.
superabundar *vi* to superabound.
superar *vt* to surpass; to overcome; to exceed, to go beyond.
superficial *adj* superficial; shallow.
superficie *f* surface; area.
superfluo/lua *adj* superfluous.
superintendencia *f* supervision.
superintendente *m/f* superintendent, supervisor; floorwalker.
superior *adj* superior; upper; higher; better; * *m/f* superior.

S

superioridad f superiority.
superlativo/va adj, m (gr) superlative.
supermercado m supermarket.
superstición f superstition.
supersticioso/sa adj superstitious.
supervisor/ra m/f supervisor.
supervivencia f survival.
superviviente m/f survivor; * adj surviving.
suplantación f supplanting.
suplantar vt to supplant.
suplemento m supplement.
suplente m/f substitute.
supletorio/ria adj supplementary.
súplica f petition, request; supplication.
suplicante adj, m/f applicant; supplicant.
suplicar vt to beg (for), to plead (for); to beg; to plead with.
suplicio m torture.
suplir vt to supply; to make good, to make up for; to replace.
suponer vt to suppose; * vi to have authority.
suposición f supposition; authority.
supremo/ma adj supreme.
supresión f suppression; abolition; removal.
suprimir vt to suppress; to abolish; to remove; to delete.
supuesto m assumption; ~/ta adj supposed; ~ que conj since, granted that.
supuración f suppuration.
supurar vt to suppurate.
sur adj south, southern; * m south; south wind.
surcar vt to furrow; to cut, to score.
surco m furrow; groove.
surgir vi to emerge; to crop up.
surtido m assortment, supply.
surtir vt to supply, to furnish, to provide; * vi to spout, to spurt.

susceptible adj susceptible; impressionable.
suscitar vt to excite, to stir up.
suscribir vt to sign; to subscribe to.
suscripción f subscription.
suscriptor/ra m/f subscriber.
susodicho/cha adj above-mentioned.
suspender vt to suspend, to hang up; to stop; to fail (an exam etc).
suspensión f suspension; stoppage.
suspenso/sa adj hanging; suspended, failed; * m Lat Am suspense.
suspicacia f suspicion, mistrust.
suspicaz adj suspicious, mistrustful.
suspirar vi to sigh.
suspiro m sigh.
sustancia f = **substancia**.
sustancial adj = **substancial**.
sustancioso adj = **substancioso**.
sustantivo/va adj, m (gr) substantive, noun.
sustentar vt to sustain; to support, to nourish.
sustento m food, sustenance; support.
sustitución f substitution.
sustituir vt to substitute.
sustituto/ta adj, m/f substitute.
susto m fright, scare.
sustracción f subtraction.
sustraer vt to take away; to subtract.
susurrar vi to whisper; to murmur; to rustle; ~**se** vr to be whispered about.
susurro m whisper; murmur.
sutil adj subtle; thin; delicate; very soft; keen, observant.
sutileza f subtlety; thinness; keenness.
suyo/ya adj his; hers; theirs; one's; his; her; its own; one's own; their own; **de** ~ per se; **los** ~**s** mpl his own, near friends, relations, family, supporters.

T

tabaco m tobacco; (col) cigarettes pl.
tábano m horsefly.
tabaquería f Lat Am cigar store.
taberna f bar, tavern.
tabernero/ra m/f barman/barmaid, bartender.
tabicar vt to wall up.
tabique m thin wall; partition wall.
tabla f board; shelf; plank; slab; index of a book; bed of earth in a garden.
tablado m scaffold; platform; stage.
tablero m plank, board; chessboard; checkerboard; (auto) dashboard; bulletin board; gambling den.
tableta f tablet; (chocolate) bar.
tablilla f small board; (med) splint.
tablón m plank; beam; ~ **de anuncios** bulletin board.
tabú m taboo.
taburete m stool.
tacañería f meanness; craftiness.
tacaño/ña adj mean, stingy; crafty.
tacha f fault, defect; small nail.
tachar vt to find fault with; to cross out, to erase.
tachuela f tack, nail.
tácito/ta adj tacit, silent; implied.
taciturno/na adj tacit, silent; sulky.
taco m stopper, plug; heel (of a shoe); wad; book of coupons; billiard cue.
tacón m heel.
taconear vi to stamp with one's heels; to walk on one's heels.
taconeo m stamping of the heels in dancing.
táctica f tactics pl.
tacto m touch, feeling; tact.
tafetán m taffeta.
tafilete m morocco leather.
tahona f bakery.
tahúr m gambler; cheat.
taimado/da adj sly, cunning, crafty.
tajada f slice; (med) hoarseness.
tajante adj sharp.
tajar vt to cut; to chop; to slice.
tajo m cut, incision; cleft, sheer drop; working area; chopping block.
tal adj such; **con ~ que** provided that; **no hay ~** no such thing.
tala f felling of trees.
taladrar vt to bore; to pierce.
taladro m drill; borer.
talante m mood; appearance; aspect; will.
talar vt to fell (trees); to desolate.
talco m talc.
talego/ga m/f bag; bagful.

talento m talent.
talismán m talisman.
talla f raised work; sculpture; stature, size; measure (of anything); hand, draw, turn (in cards).
tallado/da adj cut; carved; engraved.
tallador m engraver.
tallar vt to cut, to chop; to carve in wood; to engrave; to measure.
tallarines mpl noodles.
talle m shape; size; proportion; waist.
taller m workshop, laboratory.
tallo m shoot, sprout.
talón m heel; receipt; check.
talonario m check book; receipt book.
talonear vt Lat Am to spur.
talvez adv Lat Am perhaps.
tamaño m size, shape, bulk.
tamarindo m tamarind tree.
tambalearse vr to stagger, to waver.
tambaleo m staggering, reeling.
también adv also, as well; likewise; besides.
tambor m drum; drummer; eardrum.
tamborilear vi to drum.
tamborilero m drummer.
tamiz m fine sieve.
tampoco adv neither, nor.
tampón m tampon.
tan adv so.
tanda f turn; rotation; task; gang; number of persons employed in a workforce.
tangente f tangent.
tangible adj tangible.
tanque m tank; tanker.
tantear vt to reckon (up); to measure, to proportion; to consider; to examine.
tanteo m computation, calculation; valuation; test; scoring.
tanto m certain sum/quantity; point; goal; ~/**ta** adj so much, as much; very great; * adv so much, as much; so long, as long.
tañido m tune; sound; clink.
tapa f lid, cover; snack; (col) ~ **de los sesos** skull.
tapadera f lid (of a pot), cover.
tapar vt to stop up, to cover; to conceal, to hide.
taparrabo m loincloth.
tapete m tablecloth; Lat Am carpet.
tapia f wall.
tapiar vt to brick up; to stop up (a passage).
tapicería f tapestry; upholstery; upholsterer's place of business.

tapicero *m* tapestry-maker; upholsterer.
tapiz *m* tapestry; carpet.
tapizar *vt* to upholster.
tapón *m* cork, plug, bung; *Lat Am* fuse.
taquigrafía *f* stenography, shorthand.
taquígrafo/fa *m/f* stenographer.
taquilla *f* booking office; takings *pl*.
taquillero/ra *m/f* ticket clerk.
tara *f* (*com*) tare.
tarántula *f* tarantula.
tardanza *f* slowness, delay.
tardar *vi* to delay; to take a long time; to be late.
tarde *f* afternoon; evening; * *adv* late.
tardío/dia *adj* late; slow; tardy.
tardo/da *adj* sluggish, tardy.
tarea *f* task.
tarifa *f* tariff; price list.
tarima *f* platform; step.
tarjeta *f* card; visiting card; ~ **postal** postcard; ~ **de crédito** credit card.
tarro *m* pot.
tarta *f* tart; cake.
tartamudear *vi* to stutter, to stammer.
tartamudo/da *adj* stammering.
tarugo *m* wooden peg/pin.
tasa *f* rate; measure, rule; valuation; ~**s de aeropuerto** airport tax.
tasación *f* valuation, appraisal.
tasador *m* appraiser.
tasar *vt* to appraise, to value.
tasca *f* (*col*) joint, barroom, saloon.
tata *m* *Lat Am* (*col*) pop, dad.
tatarabuelo/la *m/f* great-great-grandfather/ mother.
tataranieto/ta *m/f* great-great-grandson/daughter.
tatuaje *m* tattoo; tattooing.
tatuar *vt* to tattoo.
taurino/na *adj* bullfighting *compd*; *Lat Am* Taurean (zodiac sign).
Tauro *m* Taurus (zodiac sign).
taxi *m* taxi.
taxista *m/f* taxi driver.
taza *f* cup; basin of a fountain.
té *m* (*bot*) tea.
te *pn* you.
tea *f* torch.
teatral *adj* theatrical.
teatro *m* theater, playhouse.
tebeo *m* comic.
techo *m* roof; ceiling.
techumbre *f* upper roof, ceiling.
tecla *f* key (of an organ, piano etc).
teclado *m* keyboard.
técnico/ca *adj* technical.
tecnología *f* technology.
tedio *m* boredom; dislike, abhorrence.
teja *f* tile.
tejado *m* roof covered with tiles.

tejanos *mpl* jeans *pl*.
tejar *vt* to tile.
tejedor *m* weaver.
tejemaneje *m* artfulness, cleverness; restlessness.
tejer *vt* to weave.
tejido *m* texture; web.
tejo *m* quoit (a ring of iron, plastic etc used in the game of quoits); hopscotch; yew tree.
tejón *m* badger.
tela *f* cloth; material.
telar *m* loom.
telaraña *f* cobweb.
telebanca *f* telephone banking.
telecomedia *f* sitcom.
telediario *m* television news.
telefax *m* *invar* fax; fax (machine).
telefonear *vt* to telephone.
telefonema *m* *Lat Am* telephone call.
telefónico/ca *adj* telephone *compd*.
teléfono *m* (tele)phone.
teléfono público *m* payphone.
telegráfico/ca *adj* telegraphic.
telégrafo *m* telegraph.
telegrama *m* telegram.
telescopio *m* telescope.
teletienda *f* home shopping program.
teletrabajador/ra *m/f* teleworker.
teletrabajo *m* teleworking.
televidente *m/f* viewer.
televisar *vt* to televise.
televisión *f* television; ~ **por cable** cable television.
televisor *m* television set.
télex *m* telex.
telón *m* drape.
tema *m* theme.
temblar *vi* to tremble.
temblón/ona *adj* trembling.
temblor *m* trembling; earthquake.
temer *vt* to fear, to doubt; * *vi* to be afraid.
temerario/ria *adj* rash.
temeridad *f* temerity, imprudence.
temeroso/sa *adj* timid; frightful.
temible *adj* dreadful, terrible.
temor *m* dread, fear.
témpano *m* ice-floe.
temperamento *m* temperament.
temperatura *f* temperature.
tempestad *f* tempest, storm; violent commotion.
tempestuoso/sa *adj* tempestuous, stormy.
templado/da *adj* temperate, tempered.
templanza *f* temperance, moderation.
templar *vt* to temper, to moderate, to cool; to tune; ~**se** *vr* to be moderate.
temple *m* temperature; tempera; temperament; tuning; **al** ~ painted in distemper.
templo *m* temple.
temporada *f* time, season; epoch, period.

temporal *adj* temporary, temporal; * *m* tempest, storm.
temporariamente *adv Lat Am* temporarily.
temporario/ria *adj Lat Am* temporary.
temprano/na *adj* early, anticipated; * *adv* early; very early, prematurely.
tenacidad *f* tenacity; obstinacy.
tenacillas *fpl* small tongs *pl*.
tenaz *adj* tenacious; stubborn.
tenaza(s) *f(pl)* tongs *pl*, pincers *pl*.
tenazmente *adv* tenaciously; obstinately.
tendedero *m* clothes line.
tendencia *f* tendency.
tender *vt* to stretch out; to expand; to extend; to hang out; to lay; *Lat Am* to lay, to set; ~**se** *vr* to stretch oneself out.
tenderete *m* stall; display of goods.
tendero/ra *m/f* shopkeeper.
tendido/da *adj* lying down; hanging; * *m* row of seats for the spectators at a bullfight.
tendón *m* tendon, sinew.
tenebroso/sa *adj* dark, obscure.
tenedor *m* holder, keeper, tenant; fork.
tenencia *f* possession; tenancy; tenure.
tener *vt* to have; to take; to hold; to possess; ~**se** *vr* to stand upright; to stop, to halt; to resist; to adhere.
tenia *f* tapeworm.
teniente *m* lieutenant.
tenis *m* tennis.
tenista *m/f* tennis player.
tenor *m* meaning; (*mus*) tenor.
tensar *vt* to tauten; to draw.
tensión *f* tension.
tenso/sa *adj* tense.
tentación *f* temptation.
tentador/ra *m/f* tempter.
tentar *vt* to touch; to try; to tempt; to attempt.
tentativa *f* attempt.
tentempié *m* (*col*) snack.
tenue *adj* thin; tenuous, slender.
tenuidad *f* slenderness; weakness; trifle.
teñir *vt* to tinge, to dye.
teología *f* theology, divinity.
teológico/ca *adj* theological.
teólogo *m* theologian, divine.
teorema *f* theorem.
teoría, teórica *f* theory.
teórico/ca *adj* theoretical.
terapéutico/ca *adj* therapeutic.
terapia *f* therapy.
tercermundista *adj* Third World *compd*.
tercer(o)/ra *adj* third; * *m* (*law*) third party.
tercerización *f Lat Am* outsourcing.
tercerizar *vt Lat Am* to outsource.
terceto *m* (*mus*) trio.
terciar *vt* to put on sideways; to divide into three parts; * *vi* to mediate; to take part.

terciarización *f Lat Am* outsourcing.
terciarizar *vt Lat Am* to outsource.
tercio/cia *adj* third; * *m* third part.
terciopelo *m* velvet.
terco/ca *adj* obstinate.
tergiversación *f* distortion; evasion.
tergiversar *vt* to distort.
termal *adj* thermal.
termas *fpl* thermal waters *pl*.
terminación *f* termination; conclusion; last syllable of a word.
terminal *adj, m/f* terminal.
terminante *adj* decisive; categorical.
terminar *vt* to finish; to end; to terminate; * *vi* to end; to stop.
término *m* term; end; boundary; limit; terminus.
terminología *f* terminology.
termodinámico/ca *adj* thermodynamic.
termómetro *m* thermometer.
termo *m* flask.
termostato *m* thermostat.
ternero/ra *m/f* calf; veal; heifer.
ternilla *f* gristle.
ternilloso/sa *adj* gristly.
terno *m* three-piece suit.
ternura *f* tenderness.
terquedad *f* stubbornness, obstinacy.
terrado *m* terrace.
terraplén *m* terrace; platform.
terrateniente *m/f* landowner.
terraza *f* balcony; (flat) roof; terrace (in fields).
terremoto *m* earthquake.
terrenal *adj* terrestrial, earthly.
terreno/na *adj* earthly, terrestrial; * *m* land, ground, field.
terrestre *adj* terrestrial.
terrible *adj* terrible, dreadful; ferocious.
territorial *adj* territorial.
territorio *m* territory.
terrón *m* clod of earth; lump; ~**ones** *mpl* real estate.
terror *m* terror, dread.
terrorismo *m* terrorism.
terrorista *m/f* terrorist.
terso/sa *adj* smooth, glossy.
tersura *f* smoothness; shine.
tertulia *f* club, assembly, circle.
tesis *f invar* thesis.
tesón *m* tenacity, firmness.
tesorero *m* treasurer.
tesoro *m* treasure; exchequer.
testamentaría *f* testamentary execution.
testamentario *m* executor of a will; ~**/ria** *adj* testamentary.
testamento *m* will, testament.
testar *vt, vi* to make one's will.
testarudo/da *adj* obstinate.
testículo *m* testicle.

testificación f attestation.
testificar vt to attest, to witness.
testigo m witness, deponent.
testimoniar vt to attest, to bear witness to.
testimonio m testimony.
teta f teat.
tétanos m tetanus.
tetera f teapot.
tetilla f nipple; teat (of a bottle).
tétrico/ca adj gloomy, sullen, surly.
textil adj textile compd.
texto m text.
textual adj textual.
textura f texture.
tez f complexion, hue.
ti pn you; yourself.
tía f aunt; (col) dame.
tiara f tiara.
tibieza f lukewarmness.
tibio/bia adj lukewarm.
tiburón m shark.
tico/ca m/f Lat Am (col) Costa Rican.
tiempo m time; term; weather; (gr) tense; occasion, opportunity; season.
tienda f tent; awning; tilt; store.
tiento m touch; circumspection; **a ~/a tientas** gropingly.
tierno/na adj tender; * m Lat Am baby.
tierra f earth; land, ground; native country.
tieso/sa adj stiff, hard, firm; robust; valiant; stubborn.
tiesto m large earthenware pot.
tifón m typhoon.
tifus m typhus.
tigre m tiger; Lat Am jaguar.
tijeras fpl scissors pl.
tijeretada f cut (with scissors), clip.
tijereta f earwig.
tijeretear vt to cut (with scissors).
tildar vt to brand, to stigmatize.
tilde f tilde (ñ).
tilo m lime tree.
timar vt to steal; to swindle.
timbrar vt to stamp.
timbre m stamp; bell; timbre; stamp duty.
timidez f timidity.
tímido/da adj timid; cowardly.
timo m swindle.
timón m helm, rudder.
tímpano m eardrum; small drum.
tina f tub; bath(tub).
tinaja f large earthenware jar.
tinglado m shed; trick; intrigue.
tinieblas fpl darkness; shadows pl.
tino m skill; judgement, prudence.
tinta f ink; tint, dye; color.
tinte m tint, dye; dry cleaner's (premises).
tintero m inkwell.

tinto/ta adj dyed; * m red wine.
tintorería f dry cleaner's (place of business).
tintura f tincture; dyeing.
tiña f scab.
tiñoso/sa adj scabby, scurvy; niggardly.
tío m uncle; (col) guy.
tiovivo m merry-go-round.
tipear vt Lat Am to type.
típico/ca adj typical.
tiple m (mus) treble; * f soprano.
tipo m type; norm; pattern; guy.
tipografía f typography.
tipográfico/ca adj typographical.
tipógrafo m printer, typographer.
tiquet m ticket; cash slip.
tiquismiquis m invar fussy person.
tira f abundance; strip.
tirabuzón m curl.
tirachinas m invar catapult.
tirado/da adj dirt-cheap; (col) very easy; * f cast; distance; series; edition.
tirador m handle.
tiraje m Lat Am print run.
tiranía f tyranny.
tiránico/ca adj tyrannical.
tiranizar vt to tyrannize.
tirano/na m/f tyrant.
tirante m joist; stay; strap; brace; * adj taut, extended, drawn.
tirantez f tension; tautness.
tirar vt to throw; to pull; to draw; to drop; to tend, to aim at; * vi to shoot; to pull; to go; to tend to.
Tirita™ f Band-Aid™, adhesive tape, sticking plaster.
tiritar vi to shiver.
tiritona f shiver; shaking with cold.
tiro m throw, shot; prank; set of coach horses; **errar el ~** to miss (at shooting).
tirón m pull, haul, tug.
tirotear vt to shoot at.
tiroteo m shooting; sharpshooting.
tirria f antipathy.
tísico/ca adj consumptive.
tisis f tuberculosis.
títere m puppet; ridiculous little fellow.
titiritero/ra m/f puppeteer.
titubear vi to stammer; to stagger; to hesitate.
titubeo m staggering; hesitation.
titular adj titular; * m/f occupant; * m headline; * vt to title; **~se** vr to obtain a title.
título m title; name; **a ~** on pretense, under pretext.
tiza f chalk.
tiznar vt to stain; to tarnish.
tizne m soot; smut.
tiznón m spot, stain.
tizón m half-burnt wood.
toalla f towel; **~ higiénica** Lat Am sanitary napkin.

tobillo *m* ankle.
tobogán *m* toboggan, sled; roller-coaster; slide.
toca *f* headdress.
tocadiscos *m invar* record player.
tocado *m* headdress, headgear.
tocador *m* dressing table; dressing room.
tocante *prep:* ~ **a** concerning, relating to.
tocar *vt* to touch; to strike; (*mus*) to play; to ring (a bell); * *vi* to belong; to concern; to knock; to call; to be a duty/obligation.
tocayo/ya *m/f* namesake.
tocino *m* bacon.
todavía *adv* even; yet, still.
todo/da *adj* all, entire; every; * *pn* everything, all; * *m* whole.
todopoderoso/sa *adj* almighty.
todoterreno *m* all-terrain vehicle.
toga *f* toga; gown.
toldo *m* awning; parasol.
tolerable *adj* tolerable.
tolerancia *f* tolerance, indulgence.
tolerante *adj* tolerant.
tolerar *vt* to tolerate; to suffer.
toma *f* taking (as in the taking of vows); (*med*) dose; plug, socket.
tomacorriente *f Lat Am* socket.
tomar *vt* to take; to seize, to grasp; to understand; to interpret, to perceive; to drink; to acquire; * *vi Lat Am* to drink; to take.
tomate *m* tomato.
tomillo *m* thyme.
tomo *m* bulk; tome; volume.
ton *m:* **sin** ~ **ni son** without rhyme or reason.
tonada *f* tune, melody.
tonadilla *f* interlude of music; short tune.
tonalidad *f* tone.
tonel *m* cask, barrel.
tonelada *f* ton; (*mar*) tonnage duty.
tónico/ca *adj* tonic, strengthening; * *m* tonic; * *f* tonic (water); (*mus*) tonic; (*fig*) keynote.
tonificar *vt* to tone up.
tono *m* tone.
tono de marcar *m* dial tone.
tontada *f* nonsense.
tontear *vi* to talk nonsense; to act foolishly.
tontera *f Lat Am* foolery, nonsense.
tontería *f* foolery, nonsense.
tonto/ta *adj* stupid, foolish.
topacio *m* topaz.
topar *vt* to run into; to find.
tope *m* butt; scuffle; ~**s** *mpl* (*rail*) buffers *pl*.
topera *f* molehill.
tópico/ca *adj* topical.
topo *m* mole; stumbler.
topografía *f* topography.
topográfico/ca *adj* topographical.
toque *m* touch; bell-ringing; crisis.
toquilla *f* headscarf; shawl.

tórax *m* thorax.
torbellino *m* whirlwind.
torcedura *f* twisting.
torcer *vt* to twist, to curve; to turn; to sprain; ~**se** *vr* to bend; to go wrong; * *vi* to turn off.
torcido/da *adj* oblique; crooked.
torcimiento *m* bending; deflection; circumlocution.
tordo *m* thrush; ~/**da** *adj* speckled black and white.
torear *vt* to avoid; to tease; * *vi* to fight bulls.
toreo *m* bullfighting.
torero *m* bullfighter.
toril *m* bull pen (at bullfight).
tormenta *f* storm, tempest.
tormento *m* torment, pain, anguish; torture.
tornar *vt* to return; to restore; ~**se** *vr* to become; * *vi* to return; ~ **a hacer** to do again.
tornasolado *adj* iridescent; shimmering.
torneo *m* tournament.
tornillo *m* screw.
torniquete *m* turnstile; (*med*) tourniquet.
torno *m* winch; revolution.
toro *m* bull.
toronja *f* grapefruit.
torpe *adj* dull, heavy; stupid.
torpedo *m* torpedo.
torpeza *f* heaviness, dullness; torpor; stupidity.
torre *f* tower; turret; steeple of a church.
torrefacto/ta *adj* roasted.
torreja *f Lat Am* French toast.
torrente *m* torrent.
tórrido/da *adj* torrid, parched, hot.
torrija *f* French toast.
torso *m* torso.
torta *f* cake; (*col*) slap.
tortícolis *f invar* stiff neck.
tortilla *f* omelet; pancake; *Lat Am* tortilla.
tórtola *f* turtledove.
tortuga *f* tortoise.
tortuoso/sa *adj* tortuous, circuitous.
tortura *f* torture.
torvo/va *adj* stern, grim.
tos *f* cough.
toscamente *adv* coarsely, grossly.
tosco/ca *adj* coarse, ill-bred, clumsy.
toser *vi* to cough.
tostada *f* slice of toast.
tostado/da *adj* parched; sunburnt; light-yellow; light-brown.
tostador *m* toaster.
tostar *vt* to toast, to roast.
total *m* whole, totality; * *adj* total, entire; * *adv* in short.
totalidad *f* totality.
totalitario/ria *adj* totalitarian.
totuma *f Lat Am* calabash.
tóxico/ca *adj* toxic; * *m* poison.
toxicómano/na *m/f* drug addict.
tozudo/da *adj* obstinate.

traba f obstacle, impediment; trammel, fetter.
trabajador/ra adj working; * m/f worker.
trabajar vt to work, to labor; to persuade; to push; * vi to strive.
trabajo m work, labor, toil; difficulty; ~s mpl troubles pl.
trabajoso/sa adj laborious; painful.
trabalenguas m invar tongue twister.
trabar vt to join, to unite; to take hold of; to fetter, to shackle.
trabucarse vr to mistake.
tracción f traction; ~ **delantera/trasera** front-wheel/rear-wheel drive.
tractor m tractor.
tradición f tradition.
traducción f translation.
traducir vt to translate.
traductor,ra m/f translator.
traer vt to bring, to carry; to attract; to persuade; to wear; to cause.
traficante m merchant, dealer.
traficar vi to trade, to do business, to deal.
tráfico m traffic, trade.
tragaldabas m/f invar glutton.
tragaluz m skylight.
tragamonedas f invar Lat Am slot machine.
tragaperras f invar slot machine.
tragar vt to swallow; to swallow up.
tragedia f tragedy.
trágico/ca adj tragic.
trago m drink; gulp; adversity, misfortune.
tragón/ona adj gluttonous.
traición f treason.
traicionar vt to betray.
traicionero/ra adj treacherous.
traidor/ra m/f traitor; * adj treacherous.
traje m dress, costume; suit.
trajín m haulage; (col) bustle.
trajinar vt to carry; * vi to bustle about; to travel around.
trama f weft, woof; (fig) plot; intrigue.
tramar vt to weave; to plot.
tramitar vt to transact; to negotiate; to handle.
trámite m path; (law) procedure.
tramo m section; piece of ground; flight of stairs.
tramoya f scene, theatrical decoration; trick.
tramoyista m scene-painter; swindler.
trampa f trap, snare; trapdoor; fraud.
trampear vt to swindle, to deceive; * vi to cheat.
trampolín m trampoline; diving board.
tramposo/sa adj deceitful, swindling.
tranca f bar, crossbeam.
trance m danger; last stage of life; trance.
tranco m long step/stride.
tranquilidad f tranquility; repose, heart's ease.
tranquilizar vt to calm; to reassure.
tranquilo/la adj tranquil, calm, quiet.
transacción f transaction.

transbordador m ferry.
transbordar vt to transfer.
transbordo m transfer; **hacer** ~ to change (trains).
transcribir vt to transcribe; to copy.
transcurrir vi to pass; to turn out.
transcurso m: ~ **del tiempo** course of time.
transeúnte adj transitory; * m passerby.
transferencia f transference; (com) transfer.
transferir vt to transfer; to defer.
transfiguración f transformation, transfiguration.
transformación f transformation.
transformador m transformer.
transformar vt to transform; ~se vr to change one's sentiments/manners.
tránsfuga, tránsfugo m deserter; fugitive; defector.
transfusión f transfusion.
transgresión f transgression.
transgresor m transgressor.
transición f transition.
transido/da adj worn out with anguish; overcome.
transigir vi to compromise.
transistor m transistor.
transitar vi to travel, to pass through a place.
transitivo/va adj transitive.
tránsito m passage; transition; road, way; change; removal; death of holy/virtuous persons.
transitorio/ria adj transitory.
transmisión f transmission; transfer; broadcast.
transmitir vt to transmit; to broadcast.
transmutación f transmutation.
transmutar vt to transmute.
transparencia f transparency; clearness; slide.
transparentarse vr to be transparent; to shine through.
transparente adj transparent.
transpiración f perspiration; transpiration.
transpirar vt to perspire; to transpire.
transportar vt to transport, to convey.
transporte m transportation.
transposición f transposition, transposal.
transversal adj transverse; collateral.
tranvía m streetcar, trolley car.
trapacería f fraud, deceit.
trapacero/ra adj deceitful.
trapecio m trapeze.
trapecista m/f trapeze artist.
trapero/ra m/f ragpicker; dealer in rags.
trapicheo m (col) fiddle.
trapo m rag, tatter.
tráquea f windpipe.
traqueteo m rattling.
tras prep after, behind.
trascendencia f transcendency; penetration.
trascendental adj transcendental.

trascender vi to smell; to come out; ~ **de** to go beyond.

trasegar vt to move about; to decant.

trasero/ra adj back; * m bottom.

trasfondo m background.

trasgredir vt to contravene.

trashumante adj migrating.

trasiego m removal; decanting (of drinks).

trasladar vt to transport; to transfer; to postpone; to transcribe, to copy; ~**se** vr to move.

traslado m move; removal.

traslucirse vr to be transparent; to conjecture.

trasluz m reflected light.

trasnochar vi to watch, to sit up the whole night.

traspaperlarse vr to get mislaid among other papers.

traspasar vt to remove, to transport; to transfix, to pierce; to return; to exceed (the proper bounds); to transfer.

traspaso m transfer, sale.

traspié m trip; slip, stumble.

trasplantar vt to transplant.

trasplante m transplant.

trasquilar vt to shear (sheep); to clip.

trasquilón m cut (of the shears); badly cut hair.

traste m fret (of a guitar); **dar al ~ con algo** to ruin something.

trastear vt to move (furniture).

trastera f lumber.

trastero m lumber room.

trastienda f back room behind a shop/store.

trasto m piece of junk; useless person.

trastornado/da adj crazy.

trastornar vt to overthrow, to overturn; to confuse; ~**se** vr to go crazy.

trastorno m overturning; confusion.

trastrocar vt to invert (the order of things).

tratable adj friendly.

tratado m treaty, convention; treatise.

tratamiento m treatment; style of address.

tratante m dealer.

tratar vt to traffic, to trade; to use; to treat; to handle; to address; ~**se** vr to treat each other.

trato m treatment; manner, address; trade, traffic; conversation; (com) agreement.

trauma m trauma.

través m (fig) reverse; **de/al ~** across, crossways; **a ~ de** prep across; over; through.

travesaño m crossbeam; transom.

travesía f crossing; crossroad; side street; trajectory; (mar) crosswind.

travesura f wit; wickedness.

travieso/sa adj restless, uneasy, fidgety; turbulent; lively; naughty.

trayecto m road; journey, stretch; course.

trayectoria f trajectory; path.

traza f first sketch; trace, outline; project; manner; means; appearance.

trazar vt to plan out; to project; to trace.

trazo m sketch, plan, design.

trébedes fpl trivet, tripod.

trébol m trefoil, clover.

trece adj, m thirteen; thirteenth.

trecho m space, distance of time/place; **a ~s** at intervals.

tregua f truce, cessation of hostilities.

treinta adj, m thirty.

tremendo/da adj terrible, formidable; awful, grand.

tremolar vt to hoist (the colors); to wave.

trémulo/la adj tremulous, trembling.

tren m train, retinue; baggage; (rail) train; ~ **de alta velocidad** high-speed train; ~ **de mercancías** freight train.

trenza f plait (in hair); braid.

trenzar vt to braid, to plait.

trepar vi to climb; to crawl.

tres adj, m three.

tresillo m three-piece suite; (mus) triplet.

treta f thrust (fencing); trick.

triangular adj triangular.

triángulo m triangle.

tribu f tribe.

tribulación f tribulation, affliction.

tribuna f tribune.

tribunal m tribunal, court of justice.

tributar vt to pay; to contribute to; to pay (homage, respect).

tributario/ria adj tributary.

tributo m tribute.

tricolor adj tricolored.

tricotar vi to knit.

tridente m trident.

trienal adj triennial.

trienio m period of three years.

trigal m wheat field.

trigésimo/ma adj thirtieth.

trigo m wheat.

trigueño/ña adj corn-colored; olive-skinned.

trillado/da adj beaten; trite, stale, hackneyed; **camino ~** common routine.

trilladora f threshing machine.

trillar vt to thresh.

trimestral adj quarterly, three-monthly.

trimestre m period of three months.

trinar vi to trill, to quaver; to be angry.

trincar vt to tie up; to pinion.

trinchante m carver; carving knife.

trinchar vt to carve, to cut up (meat).

trinchera f trench, entrenchment.

trineo m sled, sleigh.

Trinidad f Trinity.

trino m trill.

trío m (mus) trio.

tripa f gut, intestine; ~**s** fpl guts; tripe.

triple adj triple, treble.

T

triplicar *vt* to treble.
trípode *m* tripod, trivet.
tripulación *f* crew.
tripulante *m/f* crewman/woman.
tripular *vt* to man; to drive.
triquiñuela *f* trick.
triquitraque *m* clack, clatter; clashing.
tris *m invar*: **estar en un ~ de** to be on the point of.
triste *adj* sad, mournful, melancholy.
tristeza *f* sadness, mourning.
trituración *f* pulverization.
triturar *vt* to reduce to powder; to grind, to pound.
triunfal *adj* triumphal.
triunfar *vi* to triumph; to trump (in cards).
triunfo *m* triumph; trump (in cards).
trivial *adj* trivial.
trivialidad *f* triviality.
triza *f*: **hacer ~s** to smash to bits; to tear to shreds.
trocar *vt* to exchange.
trocha *f* short cut.
troche: **a ~ y moche** *adv* helter-skelter.
trofeo *m* trophy.
tromba *f* whirlwind.
trombón *m* trombone.
trombosis *f invar* thrombosis.
trompa *f* trumpet; proboscis; spinning top.
trompazo *m* heavy blow; accident; *Lat Am* punch.
trompear *vt Lat Am* to punch.
trompeta *f* trumpet; * *m* trumpeter.
trompetilla *f* small trumpet; speaking-trumpet.
trompicón *m* stumble.
trompo *m* spinning top.
tronar *vi* to thunder; to rage.
troncar *vt* to truncate, to mutilate.
troncha *f Lat Am* chunk.
tronchar *vt* to cut off; to shatter; to tire out.
troncho *m* sprig, stem/stalk.
tronco *m* trunk (of the body, tree); log; stock.
tronera *m* loophole; small window; pocket (of a billiard table).
trono *m* throne.
tropa *f* troop.
tropel *m* confused noise; hurry; bustle, confusion; heap of things; crowd; **en ~** in a tumultuous and confused manner.
tropelía *f* outrage.
tropezar *vi* to stumble; * *vt* to meet accidentally.
tropezón/ona *adj* stumbling; * *m* trip; **a ~ones** by fits and starts.
tropical *adj* tropical.
trópico *m* tropic.
tropiezo *m* stumble, trip; obstacle; slip, fault; quarrel; dispute.
trotamundos *m invar* globetrotter.
trotar *vi* to trot.
trote *m* trot; traveling.

trovador/ra *m/f* troubadour.
trozar *vt Lat Am* to cut up.
trozo *m* piece.
trucha *f* trout.
truco *m* knack; trick.
trueno *m* thunderclap.
trueque *m* exchange.
trufa *f* truffle.
truhán *adj* rogue.
truncado/da *adj* truncated.
truncamiento *m* truncation.
truncar *vt* to truncate, to maim.
trunco/ca *adj Lat Am* incomplete.
tu *adj* your.
tú *pn* you.
tubérculo *m* tuber.
tuberculosis *f* tuberculosis.
tubería *f* pipe; pipeline.
tubo *m* tube.
tuerca *f* screw.
tuerto/ta *adj* one-eyed; squint-eyed; * *m/f* one-eyed person.
tuétano *m* marrow.
tufarada *f* strong scent/smell.
tufo *m* warm vapor arising from the earth; offensive smell.
tugurio *m* slum.
tul *m* tulle.
tulipán *m* tulip.
tullido/da *adj* disabled, maimed.
tumba *f* tomb.
tumbar *vt* to knock down; * *vi* to tumble (to fall down); **~se** *vr* to lie down to sleep.
tumbo *m* fall; jolt.
tumbona *f* easy chair; beach chair.
tumor *m* tumor, growth.
túmulo *m* tomb; sepulchral monument.
tumulto *m* tumult, uproar.
tumultuoso/sa *adj* tumultuous.
tuna *f* student music group; *Lat Am* prickly pear.
tunda *f* beating.
túnel *m* tunnel.
túnica *f* tunic.
tuno *m* rogue.
tupé *m* toupee, wig/hairpiece.
tupido/da *adj* dense.
tupir *vt* to press close; **~se** *vr* to stuff oneself.
turbación *f* perturbation, confusion; trouble, disorder.
turbado/da *adj* disturbed.
turbante *m* turban.
turbar *vt* to disturb, to trouble; **~se** *vr* to be disturbed.
turbina *f* turbine.
turbio/bia *adj* muddy; troubled.
turbulencia *f* turbulence; disturbance.
turbulento/ta *adj* muddy; turbulent.
turismo *m* tourism; **~ rural** rural tourism.

turista *m/f* tourist, vacationer.
turístico/ca *adj* tourist *compd*.
turnar *vi* to alternate.
turno *m* turn; shift; opportunity.
turquesa *f* turquoise.
turrón *m* nougat (almond cake).
tutear *vt* to address as **tu**.

tutela *f* guardianship, tutelage.
tutelar *adj* tutelar, tutelary.
tutor *m* guardian, tutor.
tutora *f* tutoress.
tutoría *f* tutelage.
tuyo/ya *adj* yours; ~**s** *pl* friends and relations of the party addressed.

U

u *conj* o (instead of **o** before **o** and **ho**).
ubicar *vt* to place; *Lat Am* to locate; *Lat Am* to find; **~se** *vr* to be located.
ubre *f* udder.
ufanarse *vr* to boast.
ufano/na *adj* haughty, arrogant.
ujier *m* usher.
úlcera *f* ulcer.
ulcerar *vi* to ulcerate.
ulterior *adj* ulterior; farther, further.
últimamente *adv* lately.
ultimar *vt* to finalize; to finish; *Lat Am* to kill.
ultimátum *m* ultimatum.
último/ma *adj* last; latest; bottom; top.
ultrajar *vt* to outrage; to despise; to abuse.
ultraje *m* outrage.
ultramar *adj, m* overseas.
ultramarinos *mpl* foodstuffs, groceries.
ultrasónico/ca *adj* ultrasonic.
umbilical *adj* umbilical.
umbral *m* threshold.
un/una *art* a, an; * *adj, m* one (for **uno**).
unánime *adj* unanimous.
unanimidad *f* unanimity.
unción *f* unction; extreme/last unction.
ungir *vt* to anoint.
ungüento *m* ointment.
únicamente *adv* only, simply.
único/ca *adj* only; singular, unique.
unicornio *m* unicorn.
unidad *f* unity; unit; conformity; union.
unificar *vt* to unite.
uniformar *vt* to make uniform.
uniforme *adj* uniform; * *m* (*mil*) uniform, regimentals *pl*.
uniformidad *f* uniformity.
unilateral *adj* unilateral.
unión *f* union; **U~ Europea** European Union.
unir *vt* to join, to unite; to mingle; to bind, to tie; **~se** *vr* to associate.
unísono/na *adj* unison.
universal *adj* universal.
universalidad *f* universality.
universidad *f* university.
universitario/ria *adj* university *compd*; * *m/f* student.

universo *m* universe.
uno *m* one; **~/una** *adj* one; sole, only; **~ a otro** one another; **~ a ~** one by one; **a una** jointly together.
untar *vt* to anoint; to grease; (*col*) to bribe.
uña *f* nail; hoof; claw, talon.
¡upa! up! up!
urbanidad *f* urbanity, politeness.
uranio *m* uranium.
Urano *m* Uranus (planet).
urbanismo *m* town planning.
urbanización *f* urban development.
urbano/na *adj* urban; urbane, polite.
urdimbre *f* warp; intrigue.
urdir *vt* to warp; to contrive.
urgencia *f* urgency; emergency; need, necessity.
urgente *adj* urgent.
urgentemente *adv* urgently.
urgir *vi* to be urgent.
urinario/ria *adj* urinary; * *m* urinal.
urna *f* urn; ballot box.
urraca *f* magpie.
usado/da *adj* used; experienced; worn.
usanza *f* usage, use, custom.
usar *vt* to use, to make use of; to wear; **~se** *vr* to be used.
uso *m* use, service; custom; mode.
usted *pn* you.
usuario *m* user.
usufructo *m* (*law*) usufruct, use.
usura *f* usury.
usurario/ria *adj* usurious.
usurero *m* usurer.
usurpación *f* usurpation.
usurpar *vt* to usurp.
utensilio *m* utensil.
uterino/na *adj* uterine.
útero *m* uterus, womb.
útil *adj* useful, profitable; * *m* utility.
utilidad *f* utility; **~es** *Lat Am* profits *pl*.
utilizar *vt* to use; to make useful.
utopía *f* Utopia.
utópico/ca *adj* Utopian.
uva *f* grape.

V

vaca *f* cow; beef.
vacaciones *fpl* vacation; holidays *pl*.
vacante *adj* vacant; * *f* vacancy.
vaciar *vt* to empty, to clear; to mold; * *vi* to fall, to decrease (of waters); ~se *vr* to empty.
vacilación *f* hesitation; irresolution.
vacilar *vi* to hesitate; to falter; to fail.
vacío/cía *adj* void, empty; unoccupied; concave; vain; presumptuous; * *m* vacuum; emptiness.
vacuna *f* vaccine.
vacunar *vt* to vaccinate.
vacuno/na *adj* bovine, cow *compd*.
vadear *vt* to wade, to ford.
vagabundo/da *adj* wandering; * *m* vagrant, bum, hobo.
vagancia *f* vagrancy.
vagar *vi* to rove/loiter about; to wander.
vagido *m* cry of a child; convulsive sob.
vagina *f* vagina.
vago/ga *adj* vagrant; restless; vague.
vagón *m* (*rail*) wagon; car, carriage; ~ de mercancías goods wagon.
vaguear *vi* to rove, to loiter; to wander.
vahído *m* vertigo, giddiness.
vaho *m* steam, vapor.
vaina *f* scabbard (of a sword); pod, husk.
vainilla *f* (*bot*) vanilla; *Lat Am* hemstitch.
vaivén *m* fluctuation, instability; giddiness.
vajilla *f* crockery.
vale *m* farewell; promissory note, IOU.
valedero/ra *adj* valid; efficacious; binding.
valentía *f* valor, courage.
valentón *m* braggart.
valentonada *f* brag, boast.
valer *vi* to be valuable; to be deserving; to cost; to be valid; to be worth; to produce; to be current; * *vt* to protect, to favor; to be worth; to be equivalent to; ~se *vr* to employ, to make use of; to have recourse to.
valeroso/sa *adj* valiant, brave; strong, powerful.
valía *f* valuation; worth.
validar *vt* to validate.
validez *f* validity; stability.
válido/da *adj* valid.
valiente *adj* robust, vigorous; valiant, brave; boasting.
valija *f* suitcase.
valioso/sa *adj* valuable.
valla *f* fence; hurdle; barricade.
vallar *vt* to fence in.
valle *m* valley.
valor *m* value; price; validity; force; power; courage, valor.

valoración *f* valuation.
valorar *vt* to value; to evaluate.
valuación *f* valuation.
vals *m invar* waltz.
válvula *f* valve.
vampiro *m* vampire.
vanagloriarse *vr* to boast.
vandalismo *m* vandalism.
vándalo/la *adj*, *m* vandal.
vanguardia *f* vanguard.
vanidad *f* vanity; ostentation.
vanidoso/sa *adj* vain, showy; haughty; conceited.
vano/na *adj* vain; useless, frivolous; arrogant; futile; en ~ in vain.
vapor *m* vapor, steam; breath; steamer, steamboat, steamship.
vaporizador *m* atomizer.
vaporizar *vt* to vaporize.
vaporoso/sa *adj* vaporous.
vapular *vt* to whip, to flog.
vaquerizo/za *adj* cattle *compd*; * *m* cowboy, cowhand; cowman.
vaquero *m* cowboy, cowhand; cowman; ~/ra *adj* belonging to a cowboy/cowgirl; ~s *mpl* jeans *pl*.
vara *f* rod; pole, staff; stick.
varejón *m Lat Am* thin pole.
variable *adj* variable, changeable.
variación *f* variation.
variado/da *adj* varied; variegated.
variar *vt* to vary; to modify; to change; * *vi* to vary.
várice *f Lat Am* varicose vein.
varices *fpl* varicose veins *pl*.
variedad *f* variety; inconstancy.
varilla *f* small rod; curtain rod; spindle, pivot.
vario/ria *adj* varied, different; vague; variegated; ~s *pl* some; several.
varón *m* man, male.
varonil *adj* male, masculine; manly.
vasco/ca *adj*, *m/f* Basque.
vascuence *m* Basque.
Vaselina™ *f* Vaseline™.
vasija *f* vessel.
vaso *m* glass; vessel; vase.
vástago *m* bud, shoot; offspring.
vasto/ta *adj* vast, huge.
vaticinar *vt* to divine, to foretell.
vaticinio *m* prophecy.
vatio *m* watt.
vecindad *f* inhabitants of a place; neighborhood.
vecindario *m* number of inhabitants of a place; neighborhood.

vecino/na adj neighboring; near; * m neighbor, inhabitant.

veda f prohibition.

vedar vt to prohibit, to forbid; to impede.

vegetación f vegetation.

vegetal adj vegetable.

vegetar vi to vegetate.

vegetariano/na adj, m/f vegetarian.

vehemencia f vehemence, force.

vehemente adj vehement, violent.

vehículo m vehicle.

veinte adj, m twenty.

veintena f twentieth part; score.

vejación f vexation; embarrassment.

vejar vt to vex; to humiliate.

vejestorio m old man.

vejez f old age.

vejiga f bladder.

vela f wakefulness; vigil; night work; candle; sail; **hacerse a la ~** to set sail.

velado/da adj veiled; blurred; * f soiree.

velador m night watchman, guard; observer; candlestick; pedestal table.

velar vi to stay awake; to be attentive; * vt to guard, to watch.

veleidad f feeble will; inconstancy.

velero/ra adj swift-sailing.

veleta f weather cock, weather vane.

vello m down; gossamer; short downy hair.

vellón m fleece.

velludo/da adj shaggy, woolly.

velo m veil; pretext.

velocidad f speed; velocity.

velocímetro m speedometer.

veloz(mente) adj (adv) swift(ly), fast.

vena f vein.

venado m deer; venison.

vencedor/ra m/f conqueror, victor, winner.

vencer vt to defeat; to conquer, to vanquish; * vi to win; to expire.

vencido/da adj defeated; due.

vencimiento m victory; maturity.

vendaje m bandage, dressing for wounds.

vendal f bandage.

vendar vt to bandage; to hoodwink.

vendaval m gale.

vendedor/ra m/f seller; **~ de periódicos** newsdealer; **~ ambulante** peddler.

vender vt to sell.

vendimia f grape harvest; vintage.

vendimiador/ra m/f grape harvester, vintager.

vendimiar vt to harvest; to pick (grapes); (col) to make a killing with.

veneno m poison, venom.

venenoso/sa adj venomous, poisonous.

venerable adj venerable.

veneración f veneration, worship.

venerar vt to venerate, to worship.

venéreo/rea adj venereal.

venganza f revenge, vengeance.

vengar vt to revenge, to avenge; **~se** vr to take revenge.

vengativo/va adj revengeful.

venia f pardon; leave, permission; bow.

venial adj venial.

venida f arrival; return; overflow of a river.

venidero/ra adj future; **~s** mpl posterity.

venir vi to come, to arrive; to follow, to succeed; to happen; to spring from; **~se** vr to ferment.

venta f sale.

ventaja f advantage.

ventajoso/sa adj advantageous.

ventana f window; window shutter; nostril.

ventanilla f window.

venta por correo f mail order.

ventarrón m violent wind.

ventilación f ventilation; draft.

ventilar vt to ventilate; to fan; to discuss

ventisco/sca m/f snowstorm.

ventiscar vi to drift, to lie in drifts (snow).

ventisquero m snowdrift; **~s** mpl glaciers pl.

ventolera f gust; pride, loftiness.

ventosidad f flatulence.

ventoso/sa adj windy; flatulent.

ventrículo m ventricle.

ventrílocuo m ventriloquist.

ventura f happiness; luck, chance, fortune; **por ~** by chance.

venturoso/sa adj lucky, fortunate, happy.

Venus f Venus (planet).

ver vt to see, to look at; to observe; to visit; * vi to understand; to see; **~se** vr to be seen; to be conspicuous; to find oneself; **~se con uno** to have a bone to pick with someone; * m sense of sight; appearance.

vera f edge; bank.

veracidad f truth; veracity.

veranear vi to spend the summer holiday, to vacation.

veraneo m summer vacation.

veraniego/ga adj summer.

verano m summer.

veras fpl truth, sincerity; **de ~** in truth, really.

veraz adj truthful.

verbal adj verbal.

verbena f fair; dance.

verbo m word, term; (gr) verb.

verbosidad f verbosity.

verdad f truth, veracity; reality; reliability.

verdaderamente adv truly, in fact.

verdadero/ra adj true; real; sincere.

verde adj, m green.

verdear, verdecer vi to turn green.

verdín m bright green; verdure.

verdor m greenness; verdure; youth.

verdoso/sa adj greenish, greeny.

verdugo *m* hangman; very cruel person.
verdulero/ra *m/f* produce dealer.
verdura *f* verdure; vegetables *pl*, greens *pl*.
vereda *f* path; sidewalk.
veredicto *m* verdict.
vergel *m* orchard.
vergonzoso/sa *adj* bashful; shamefaced.
vergüenza *f* shame; bashfulness; confusion.
verídico/ca *adj* truthful.
verificación *f* verification.
verificar *vt* to check, to verify; **~se** *vr* to happen.
verisímil *adj* probable.
verja *f* grate, lattice.
vermut *m* vermouth.
verosímil *adj* likely; credible.
verosimilitud *f* likeliness; credibility.
verraco *m* boar.
verruga *f* wart, pimple.
versado/da *adj* versed.
versátil *adj* versatile.
versículo *m* versicle; short verse.
versificar *vt* to versify.
versión *f* translation, version.
verso *m* verse.
vértebra *f* vertebra.
vertedero *m* sewer, drain; tip.
verter *vt* to pour; to spill; to empty; * *vi* to flow.
vertical *adj* vertical.
vértice *m* vertex, zenith; crown of the head.
vertiente *f* slope; waterfall, cascade.
vertiginoso/sa *adj* giddy.
vértigo *m* giddiness, vertigo.
vesícula *f* blister.
vespertino/na *adj* evening *compd*.
vestíbulo *m* vestibule, lobby; foyer.
vestido *m* dress; clothes *pl*.
vestidura *f* dress; clothing.
vestigio *m* vestige; footstep; trace.
vestimenta *f* clothing.
vestir *vt* to put on; to wear; to dress; to adorn; to cloak, to disguise; * *vi* to dress; **~se** *vr* to get dressed.
vestuario *m* clothes *pl*; uniform; vestry; changing room.
veta *f* vein (in mines, wood etc); streak; grain.
vetado/da *adj* striped, veined.
vetar *vt* to veto.
veterano/na *adj* experienced, practiced; * *m* veteran, old soldier.
veterinario/ria *adj* veterinary; * *m/f* veterinarian; * *f* veterinary science.
veto *m* veto.
vez *f* time; turn; return; **cada ~** each time; **una ~** once; **a veces** sometimes, by turns.
vía *f* way; road, route; mode, manner, method; (*rail*) railway line.
viajante *m* sales representative.
viajar *vi* to travel.

viaje *m* journey; voyage; travel.
viajero/ra *m/f* traveler.
vial *adj* road *compd*.
viático *m* viaticum; travel allowance.
víbora *f* viper.
vibración *f* vibration.
vibrador *m* vibrator.
vibrante *adj* vibrant.
vibrar *vt*, *vi* to vibrate.
vicaría *f* vicarship; vicarage.
vice- *pref* vice- (deputy etc).
vicealmirante *m* vice-admiral.
viceconsulado *m* vice-consulate.
vicepresidente/ta *m/f* vice-president.
viciar *vt* to vitiate, to corrupt; to invalidate.
vicio *m* vice.
vicioso/sa *adj* vicious; depraved.
vicisitud *f* vicissitude.
víctima *f* victim; sacrifice.
victimar *vt Lat Am* to kill.
victimario/ria *m/f Lat Am* killer.
victoria *f* victory.
victorioso/sa *adj* victorious.
vicuña *m* vicuna.
vid *f* (*bot*) vine.
vida *f* life.
vidriado *m* glazed earthenware, crockery.
video *m Lat Am* video.
vídeo *m* video.
videocámara *f* video camera, camcorder.
videocasete *m* video cassette.
videoclip *m* pop video.
videojuego *m* video game.
vidriar *vt* to glaze.
vidriera *f* stained-glass window; *Lat Am* shop/store window.
vidriero *m* glazier.
vidrio *m* glass; *Lat Am* window; *Lat Am* lense.
vidrioso/sa *adj* glassy; brittle; slippery; very delicate.
vieira *f* scallop.
viejo/ja *adj* old; ancient, antiquated.
viento *m* wind; air.
vientre *m* belly.
viernes *m invar* Friday; **V~ Santo** Good Friday.
viga *f* beam; girder.
vigencia *f* validity.
vigente *adj* in force.
vigésimo/ma *adj*, *m* twentieth.
vigía *f* (*mar*) lookout; * *m* watchman, guard.
vigilancia *f* vigilance, watchfulness.
vigilante *adj* watchful, vigilant.
vigilar *vt* to watch over; * *vi* to keep watch.
vigilia *f* vigil; watch.
vigor *m* vigor, strength.
vigoroso/sa *adj* vigorous.
vil *adj* mean, sordid, low; worthless; infamous; ungrateful.

vileza *f* meanness, lowness; abjectness.
vilipendiar *vt* to despise, to revile.
villa *f* villa; small town.
villancico *m* Christmas carol.
villano/na *adj* rustic, clownish; villainous; * *m* villain; rustic.
villorio *m* one-horse town; (*col*) dump; shanty town.
vilo: **en** ~ *adv* in the air; in suspense.
vinagre *m* vinegar.
vinagrera *f* vinegar bottle; ~s cruet set/stand; *Lat Am* heartburn.
vinagreta *f* vinaigrette sauce/dressing.
vinculación *f* link; linking.
vincular *vt* to link.
vínculo *m* tie, link, chain; entail.
vindicación *f* revenge.
vindicar *vt* to avenge.
vindicativo/va *adj* vindictive.
vinicultura *f* wine growing.
vino *m* wine; ~ **tinto** red wine.
viña *f* vineyard.
viñedo *m* vineyard.
viñeta *f* vignette.
viola[1] *f* (*bot*) viola.
viola[2] *f* (*mus*) viola.
violación *f* violation; rape.
violado/da *adj* violet-colored; violated.
violador/ra *m/f* rapist; violator; profaner.
violar *vt* to rape; to violate; to profane.
violencia *f* violence.
violentar *vt* to force.
violento/ta *adj* violent; forced; absurd; embarrassing.
violeta *f* violet.
violín *m* violin, fiddle.
violinista *m* violinist.
violón *m* double bass.
violoncelo, **violonchelo** *m* violoncello, cello.
vip *m/f* VIP.
viperino/na *adj* viperish.
viraje *m* turn; bend.
virar *vi* to swerve.
virgen *m/f* virgin.
virgiano/na *adj Lat Am* Virgoan (zodiac sign).
virginidad *f* virginity.
Virgo *f* Virgo (zodiac sign).
viril *adj* virile, manly.
virilidad *f* virility, manhood.
virrey *m* viceroy.
virtual *adj* virtual.
virtud *f* virtue.
virtuoso/sa *adj* virtuous.
viruela *f* smallpox.
virulencia *f* virulence.
virulento/ta *adj* virulent.
virus *m invar* virus.
visa *f*, **visado** *m* visa.

viscosidad *f* viscosity.
viscoso/sa *adj* viscous, glutinous.
visera *f* visor.
visibilidad *f* visibility.
visible *adj* visible; apparent.
visillos *mpl* lace curtains *pl*.
visión *f* sight, vision; fantasy.
visionario/ria *adj* visionary.
visita *f* visit; visitor.
visitar *vt* to visit.
vislumbrar *vt* to catch a glimpse of; to perceive indistinctly.
visón *m* mink.
víspera *f* eve; evening before; ~s *pl* vespers.
vista *f* sight, view; vision; eyesight; appearance; looks *pl*; prospect; intention; (*law*) trial; * *m* customs officer.
vistazo *m* glance.
visto: ~ **que** *conj* considering that.
vistoso/sa *adj* colorful, attractive, lively.
visual *adj* visual.
vital *adj* life *compd*; vital.
vitalicio/cia *adj* for life.
vitalidad *f* vitality.
vitamina *f* vitamin.
viticultor/ra *m/f* wine grower.
viticultura *f* wine growing.
vitorear *vt* to shout, to applaud.
vítreo/trea *adj* vitreous.
vitriolo *m* vitriol.
vitrina *f* showcase; *Lat Am* shop/store window.
vituperación *f* condemnation, censure.
vituperar *vt* to condemn, to censure.
vituperio *m* condemnation, censure; insult.
viuda *f* widow.
viudedad *f* widowhood; widow's pension.
viudez *f* widowhood.
viudo *m* widower.
vivacidad *f* vivacity, liveliness.
vivamente *adv* in lively fashion.
vivaracho/cha *adj* lively, sprightly; bright.
vivaz *adj* lively.
víveres *mpl* provisions.
vivero *m* plant nursery; fish farm.
viveza *f* liveliness; sharpness.
vividor/ra *adj* (*perj*) sharp, clever; unscrupulous.
vivienda *f* housing; apartment.
viviente *adj* living.
vivificar *vt* to vivify, to enliven.
vivíparo/ra *adj* viviparous.
vivir *vt* to live through; to go through; * *vi* to live; to last.
vivo/va *adj* living; lively; **al** ~ to the life; very realistically.
vizconde *m* viscount.
vocablo *m* word, term.
vocabulario *m* vocabulary.
vocación *f* vocation.

vocacional adj vocational.

vocal f vowel; * m/f member (of a committee); * adj vocal, oral.

vocativo m (gr) vocative.

vocear vt to cry; to shout; to cheer; to shriek; * vi to yell.

vocerío/ría m/f shouting.

vocero/ra m/f Lat Am spokesperson.

vociferar vt to shout; to proclaim in a loud voice; * vi to yell.

vodka m/f vodka.

volador/ra adj flying; fast.

volandas: **en ~** adv in the air; (fig) swiftly.

volante adj flying; * m (auto) steering wheel; note; pamphlet; shuttlecock.

volar vi to fly; to pass swiftly (of time); to rush, to hurry; * vt to blow up, to explode.

volatería f falconry; fowling; birds pl.

volátil adj volatile; changeable.

volatilizar vt to volatilize, to vaporize.

volcán m volcano.

volcánico adj volcanic.

volcar vt to upset, to overturn; to make giddy; to empty out; to exasperate; **~se** vr to tip over.

voleibol m volleyball.

vóleibol m Lat Am volleyball.

voleo m volley.

volquete m tipper truck; dump truck.

voltaje m voltage.

voltear vt to turn over; to overturn; Lat Am to knock over; * vi to roll over, to tumble.

voltereta f tumble; somersault.

voltio m volt.

voluble adj unpredictable; fickle.

volumen m volume; size.

voluminoso/sa adj voluminous.

voluntad f will, willpower; wish, desire.

voluntario/ria adj voluntary; * m/f volunteer.

voluptuoso/sa adj voluptuous.

volver vt to turn (over); to turn upside down; to turn inside out; * vi to return, to go back; **~se** vr to turn around.

vomitar vt, vi to vomit.

vómito m vomiting; vomit.

vomitona f violent vomiting.

voracidad f voracity.

voraz(mente) adj, (adv) voracious(ly).

vórtice m whirlpool.

vos pn Lat Am you.

vosotros/tras pn pl you.

votación f voting; vote.

votar vi to vow; to vote.

voto m vow; vote; opinion, advice; swearword; curse; **~s** mpl good wishes pl.

voz f voice; shout; rumor; word, term.

vuelco m overturning.

vuelo m flight; wing; projection of a building; ruffle, frill; **cazar al ~** to catch in flight; **~ chárter** charter flight.

vuelta f turn; circuit; return; row of stitches; cuff; change; bend, curve; reverse, other side; return journey.

vuelto m Lat Am change.

vuestro/tra adj your; * pn yours.

vulgar adj vulgar, common.

vulgaridad f vulgar, common.

vulgaridad f vulgarity, commonness.

vulgo m common people pl.

vulnerable adj vulnerable.

W

wáter *m* toilet.
whisky *m* whisky.

windsurf *m* windsurfing.
windsurfista *m/f* windsurfer.

X

xenofobia *f* xenophobia.
xilófono *m* xylophone.

xilógrafo *m* xylographer; wood engraver.

Y

y *conj* and.

ya *adv* already; now; immediately; at once; soon; * *conj*: ~ **que** since, seeing that; **¡~!** of course!, sure!

yacer *vi* to lie, to lie down.

yacimiento *m* deposit.

yaguré *m Lat Am* skunk.

yanqui *m/f* Yankee.

yate *m* yacht, sailing boat.

yedra *f* ivy.

yegua *f* mare.

yema *f* bud; leaf; egg yolk; ~ **del dedo** tip of the finger.

yermo *m* wasteland, wilderness; ~/**ma** *adj* waste; (*fig*) barren.

yerno *m* son-in-law.

yerro *m* error, mistake, fault.

yerto/ta *adj* stiff, inflexible; rigid.

yesca *f* tinder.

yeso *m* gypsum; plaster; ~ **mate** plaster of Paris.

yo *pn* I; ~ **mismo** I myself.

yodo *m* iodine.

yogur *m* yogurt.

yugo *m* yoke.

yugular *adj* jugular.

yunque *m* anvil.

yunta *f* yoke; ~**s** *fpl* couple, pair.

yute *m* jute.

yuxtaponer *vt* to juxtapose.

yuxtaposición *f* juxtaposition.

Z

zafado/da *adj Lat Am* crazy, mad.
zafar *vt* to loosen, to untie; to lighten (a ship); **~se** *vr* to escape; **~se de** to avoid; to free oneself from (trouble).
zafio/fia *adj* uncouth, coarse.
zafiro *m* sapphire.
zafra *f Lat Am* sugar cane harvest.
zaga *f* rear; **a la ~** behind.
zagal/la *m/f* boy/girl.
zaguán *m* porch, entrance hall.
zaherir *vt* to criticize; to upbraid.
zahorí *m* clairvoyant.
zalamería *f* flattery.
zalamero/ra *adj* flattering; * *m/f* wheedler, flatterer.
zamarra *f* sheepskin; sheepskin jacket.
zambo/ba *adj* knock-kneed.
zambomba *f* rural drum.
zambullida *f* plunge, dive; dipping, submersion.
zambullirse *vr* to plunge/dive into water.
zampar *vt* to gobble down; to put away hurriedly; **~se** *vr* to thrust oneself suddenly into any place; to crash, to hurtle.
zanahoria *f* carrot.
zancada *f* stride.
zancadilla *f* trip; trick.
zanco *m* stilt.
zancudo/da *adj* long-legged; * *m Lat Am* mosquito.
zángano *m* drone; idler, slacker.
zanja *f* ditch, trench.
zanjar *vt* to dig (ditches); (*fig*) to surmount; to resolve.
zapador *m* (*mil*) sapper.
zapata *f* boot; **~ de freno** (*auto*) brake shoe.
zapatazo *m* stamp (dancing).
zapatear *vt* to tap with the shoe; to beat time with the sole of the shoe.
zapatería *f* shoemaking; shoe shop; shoe factory.
zapatero/ra *m/f* shoemaker; **~ de viejo** cobbler.
zapatilla *f* slipper; pump (shoe); (*sport*) **~s de lona** *fpl* sneakers *pl*.
zapato *m* shoe.
zapping *m* channel-hopping.
zar *m* czar.
zarandear *vt* to shake vigorously.

zarcillo *m* earring; tendril.
zarpa *f* mud splash, dirt on clothes; claw, paw.
zarpar *vi* to weigh anchor.
zarpazo *m* thud.
zarrapastroso/sa *adj* shabby, rough-looking.
zarza *f* bramble.
zarzal *m* bramble patch.
zarzamora *f* blackberry.
zarzuela *f* Spanish light opera.
zigzag *adj* zigzag.
zigzaguear *vi* to zigzag.
zinc *m* zinc.
zócalo *m* plinth, base; base-board.
zocato/ta *adj Lat Am* stale.
zodiaco *m* zodiac.
zona *f* zone; area, belt.
zoncear *vi Lat Am* to fool around.
zoncera *f Lat Am* nonsense.
zonzo/sa *m/f Lat Am* fool.
zoo *m* zoo.
zoología *f* zoology.
zoológico/ca *adj* zoological; * *m* zoo.
zoólogo/ga *m/f* zoologist.
zopenco/ca *adj* dull, very stupid.
zoquete *m* block; crust of bread; (*col*) blockhead.
zorra *f* fox; vixen; (*col*) whore, tart.
zorro *m* male fox; cunning person.
zozobra *f* (*mar*) capsizing; uneasiness, anxiety.
zozobrar *vi* (*mar*) to founder, to capsize; (*fig*) to fail; to be anxious.
zueco *m* wooden shoe; clog.
zumba *f* banter, teasing; beating.
zumbar *vt* to hit; **~se** *vr* to hit each other; * *vi* to buzz.
zumbido *m* humming, buzzing sound.
zumbón/ona *adj* waggish, funny, teasing.
zumo *m* juice.
zurcir *vt* to darn; (*fig*) to join, to unite; to hatch (lies).
zurdo/da *adj* left; left-handed.
zurra *f* flogging; drudgery.
zurrar *vt* (*col*) to flog, to lay into; (*fig*) to criticize harshly.
zurrón *m* pouch.
zutano/na *m/f* so-and-so; **~ y fulano** such and such a one, so-and-so.

WEBSTER'S
ENGLISH–SPANISH
DICTIONARY

a *art* un, uno, una; * *prep* a, al, en.

aback *adv* detrás, atrás; **to be taken ~** *vi* quedar consternado/da.

abacus *n* ábaco *m*.

abandon *vt* abandonar, dejar.

abandonment *n* abandono *m*; desamparo *m*.

abase *vt* abatir, humillar.

abasement *n* abatimiento *m*; humillación *f*.

abash *vt* avergonzar, causar confusión.

abate *vt* disminuir, rebajar; * *vi* disminuirse.

abatement *n* rebaja, disminución *f*.

abbess *n* abadesa *f*.

abbey *n* abadía *f*.

abbot *n* abad *m*.

abbreviate *vt* abreviar, acortar.

abbreviation *n* abreviatura *f*.

abdicate *vt* abdicar; renunciar.

abdication *n* abdicación *f*; renuncia *f*.

abdomen *n* abdomen *m*.

abdominal *adj* abdominal.

abduct *vt* secuestrar.

abductor *n* músculo abductor *m*.

abed *adv* en (la) cama.

aberrant *adj* anormal.

aberration *n* error *m*; aberración *f*.

abet *vt*: **to aid and ~** ser cómplice de.

abeyance *n* desuso *m*.

abhor *vt* aborrecer, detestar.

abhorrence *n* aborrecimiento, odio *m*.

abhorrent *adj* repugnante.

abide *vt* soportar, sufrir.

ability *n* habilidad, capacidad, aptitud *f*; **~ ies** *pl* talento *m*.

abject *adj* vil, despreciable, bajo/ja; **~ly** *adv* vilmente, bajamente.

abjure *vt* abjurar; renunciar.

ablative *n* (*gr*) ablativo *m*.

ablaze *adj* en llamas.

able *adj* capaz, hábil; **to be ~** poder.

able-bodied *adj* robusto/ta, vigoroso/sa.

ablution *n* ablución *f*.

ably *adv* con habilidad.

abnegation *n* abnegación, resignación *f*.

abnormal *adj* anormal.

abnormality *n* anormalidad *f*.

aboard *adv* a bordo.

abode *n* domicilio *m*.

abolish *vt* abolir, anular, revocar.

abolition *n* abolición, anulación *f*.

abominable *adj* abominable, detestable; **~bly** *adv* abominablemente.

abomination *n* abominación *f*.

aboriginal *adj* aborigen.

aborigines *npl* aborígenes *mpl*.

abort *vi* abortar.

abortion *n* aborto *m*.

abortive *adj* fracasado/da.

abound *vi* abundar; **to ~ with** abundar en.

about *prep* acerca de, acerca; **I carry no money ~ me** no traigo dinero; * *adv* aquí y allá; **to be ~ to** estar a punto de; **to go ~** andar acá y acullá; **to go ~ a thing** emprender alguna cosa; **all ~** en todo lugar.

above *prep* encima; * *adv* arriba, *Lat Am* arriba de; **~ all** sobre todo, principalmente; **~ mentioned** ya mencionado.

aboveboard *adj* legítimo/ma.

abrasion *n* abrasión *f*.

abrasive *adj* abrasivo/va.

abreast *adv* de costado.

abridge *vt* abreviar, compendiar; acortar.

abridgement *n* compendio *m*, recopilación *f*.

abroad *adv* en el extranjero; **to go ~** salir del país.

abrogate *vt* abrogar, anular.

abrogation *n* abrogación, anulación *f*.

abrupt *adj* brusco/ca; **~ly** *adv* precipitadamente; bruscamente.

abscess *n* absceso *m*.

abscond *vi* esconderse; huir.

abseiling *n* rappel *m*.

absence *n* ausencia *f*.

absent *adj* ausente; * *vi* ausentarse.

absentee *n* ausente *m*.

absenteeism *n* absentismo *m*.

absent-minded *adj* distraído/da.

absolute *adj* absoluto/ta; categórico/ca; **~ly** *adv* totalmente.

absolution *n* absolución *f*.

absolutism *n* absolutismo *m*.

absolve *vt* absolver.

absorb *vt* absorber.

absorbent *adj* absorbente.

absorbent cotton *n* algodón hidrófilo *m*.

absorption *n* absorción *f*.

abstain *vi* abstenerse, privarse.

abstemious *adj* abstemio/mia, sobrio/ria; **~ly** *adv* moderadamente.

abstemiousness *n* sobriedad, abstinencia *f*.

abstinence *n* abstinencia *f*; templanza *f*.

abstinent *adj* abstinente, sobrio/ria.

abstract *adj* abstracto/ta; * *n* extracto *m*; sumario *m*; **in the ~** de modo abstracto.

abstraction *n* abstracción *f*.

abstractly *adv* en abstracto.

abstruse adj oscuro/ra; ~**ly** adv oscuramente.
absurd adj absurdo/da; ~**ly** adv absurdamente.
absurdity n absurdidad f.
abundance n abundancia f.
abundant adj abundante; ~**ly** adv abundantemente.
abuse vt abusar; maltratar; * n abuso m; injurias fpl.
abusive adj abusivo/va, ofensivo/va; ~**ly** adv abusivamente.
abut vi confinar.
abysmal adj abismal; insondable.
abyss n abismo m.
acacia n acacia f.
academic adj académico/ca.
academician n académico m.
academy n academia f.
accede vi acceder.
accelerate vt acelerar.
accelerator n acelerador m.
acceleration n aceleración f.
accent n acento m; tono m; * vt acentuar.
accentuate vt acentuar.
accentuation n acentuación f.
accept vt aceptar; admitir.
acceptable adj aceptable.
acceptability n aceptabilidad f.
acceptance n aceptación f.
access n acceso m; entrada f.
accessible adj accesible.
accession n acceso m.
accessory n accesorio m; (law) cómplice m.
accident n accidente m; casualidad f.
accidental adj casual; ~**ly** adv por casualidad.
acclaim vt aclamar, aplaudir.
acclamation n aclamación f; aplauso m.
acclimatize vt aclimatar.
accommodate vt alojar; complacer.
accommodating adj servicial.
accommodations npl alojamiento m.
accompaniment n (mus) acompañamiento m.
accompanist n (mus) acompañante m.
accompany vt acompañar.
accomplice n cómplice m.
accomplish vt efectuar, completar.
accomplished adj elegante, consumado/da.
accomplishment n cumplimiento m; ~**s** pl talentos, conocimientos mpl.
accord n acuerdo, convenio m; **with one ~** unánimemente; **of one's own ~** espontáneamente.
accordance n: **in ~ with** de acuerdo con.
according prep según, conforme; ~ **to** según; ~**ly** adv por consiguiente.
accordion n (mus) acordeón m.
accost vt trabar conversación con.
account n cuenta f; **on no ~** de ninguna manera; bajo ningún concepto; **on ~ of** por motivo de; **to call to ~** pedir cuenta; **to turn to ~** hacer provechoso; * vt **to ~ for** explicar.
accountability n responsabilidad f.

accountable adj responsable.
accountancy n contabilidad f, Lat Am contaduría f.
accountant n contable m, Lat Am contador m.
account book n libro m de cuentas.
account number n número m de cuenta.
accrue vi resultar, provenir.
accumulate vt acumular; amontonar; * vi crecer.
accumulation n acumulación f; amontonamiento m.
accuracy n exactitud f.
accurate adj exacto/ta; ~**ly** adv exactamente.
accursed adj maldito/ta.
accusation n acusación f.
accusative n (gr) acusativo m.
accusatory adj acusatorio/ria.
accuse vt acusar; culpar.
accused n acusado m.
accuser n acusador/a m/f.
accustom vt acostumbrar.
accustomed adj acostumbrado/da, habitual.
ace n as m; **within an ~ of**... casi, por poco no....
acerbic adj mordaz.
acetate n (chem) acetato m.
ache n dolor m; * vi doler.
achieve vt realizar; obtener.
achievement n realización f; hazaña f.
acid adj ácido/da; agrio/ria; * n ácido m.
acid rain n lluvia ácida f.
acidity n acidez f.
acknowledge vt reconocer, confesar.
acknowledgement n reconocimiento m; gratitud f.
acme n apogeo m.
acne n acne m.
acorn n bellota f.
acoustics n acústica f.
acquaint vt informar, avisar.
acquaintance n conocimiento m; conocido m.
acquiesce vi someterse, consentir, asentir.
acquiescence n consentimiento m.
acquiescent adj deferente.
acquire vt adquirir.
acquisition n adquisición, obtención f.
acquit vt absolver.
acquittal n absolución f.
acre n acre m.
acrid adj acre.
acrimonious adj mordaz.
acrimony n acrimonia, acritud f.
across adv de una parte a otra; * prep a través de; **to come ~** toparse con.
act vt representar; * vi hacer; * n acto, hecho m; acción f; ~**s of the apostles** Hechos mpl de los Apóstoles.
acting adj interino/na.
action n acción f; batalla f.
action replay n repetición f.
activate vt activar.
active adj activo/va; ~**ly** adv activamente.
activity n actividad f.

actor n actor m.
actress n actriz f.
actual adj real; efectivo/va; ~**ly** adv en efecto, realmente.
actuary n actuario m de seguros.
acumen n agudeza, perspicacia f.
acupuncture n acupuntura f.
acute adj agudo/da; ingenioso/sa; ~ **accent** n acento agudo m; ~ **angle** n ángulo agudo m; ~**ly** adv con agudeza.
acuteness n perspicacia, sagacidad f.
adage n proverbio m.
adamant adj inflexible.
adapt vt adaptar, acomodar; ajustar.
adaptability n facilidad de adaptarse f.
adaptable adj adaptable.
adaptation n adaptación f.
adapter n adaptador m.
add vt añadir, agregar; **to ~ up** sumar.
addendum n suplemento m.
adder n culebra f; víbora f.
addict n drogadicto m.
addiction n dependencia f.
addictive adj que crea dependencia.
addition n adición f.
additional adj adicional; ~**ly** adv en/por adición.
additive n aditivo m.
address vt dirigir; * n dirección f; discurso m.
adduce vt alegar, aducir.
adenoids npl vegetaciones adenoideas fpl.
adept adj hábil.
adequacy n suficiencia f.
adequate adj adecuado/da; suficiente; ~**ly** adv adecuadamente.
adhere vi adherir.
adherence n adherencia f.
adherent n adherente, partidario m.
adhesion n adhesión f.
adhesive adj pegajoso/sa.
adhesiveness n adhesividad f.
adhesive tape n esparadrapo m.
adieu adv adiós; * n despedida f.
adipose adj adiposo/sa.
adjacent adj adyacente, contiguo/gua.
adjectival adj adjetivado/da; ~**ly** adv como adjetivo.
adjective n adjetivo m.
adjoin vi estar contiguo/gua.
adjoining adj contiguo/gua.
adjourn vt aplazar.
adjournment n prórroga f.
adjudicate vt adjudicar.
adjunct n adjunto m.
adjust vt ajustar, acomodar.
adjustable adj ajustable.
adjustment n ajustamiento, arreglo m.
adjutant n (mil) ayudante m.
ad lib vt improvisar.

administer vt administrar; gobernar; **to ~ an oath** prestar juramento.
administration n administración f; gobierno m.
administrative adj administrativo/va.
administrator n administrador/a m/f.
admirable adj admirable; ~**bly** adv admirablemente.
admiral n almirante m.
admiralship n almirante f.
admiralty n almirantazgo m.
admiration n admiración f.
admire vt admirar.
admirer n admira/a m/f.
admiringly adv con admiración.
admissible adj admisible.
admission adj entrada f.
admit vt admitir; **to ~ to** confesarse culpable de.
admittance n entrada f.
admittedly adj de acuerdo que.
admixture n mixtura, mezcla f.
admonish vt amonestar, reprender.
admonition n amonestación f; consejo, aviso m.
admonitory adj exhortatorio/ria.
ad nauseam adv hasta el cansancio.
adolescence n adolescencia f.
adolescent n adolescente m/f.
adopt vt adoptar.
adopted adj adoptivo/va.
adoption n adopción f.
adoptive adj adoptivo/va.
adorable adj adorable.
adorably adv de modo adorable.
adoration n adoración f.
adore vt adorar.
adorn vt adornar.
adornment n adorno m.
adrift adv a la deriva.
adroit adj diestro/tra, hábil.
adroitness n destreza f.
adulation n adulación, zalamería f.
adulatory adj lisonjero/ra.
adult adj adulto/ta; * n adulto m; adulta f.
adulterate vt adulterar, corromper; * adj adulterado/da, falsificado/da.
adulteration n adulteración, corrupción f.
adulterer n adúltero m.
adulteress n adúltera f.
adulterous adj adúltero/ra.
adultery n adulterio m.
advance vt avanzar; promover; pagar por adelantado; * vi hacer progresos; **to make ~s** insinuarse; * n avance m; paga adelantada f.
advanced adj avanzado/da.
advancement n adelantamiento m; progreso m; promoción f.
advantage n ventaja f; **to take ~ of** sacar provecho de.
advantageous adj ventajoso/sa; ~**ly** adv ventajosamente.

advantageousness n ventaja, utilidad f.
advent n venida f.
Advent n Adviento m.
adventitious adj adventicio/cia.
adventure n aventura f.
adventurer n aventurero m.
adventurous adj intrépido/da; valeroso/sa; ~ly adv arriesgadamente.
adverb n adverbio m.
adverbial adj adverbial; ~ly adv como adverbio.
adversary n adversario, enemigo m.
adverse adj adverso/sa, contrario/ria.
adversity n calamidad f; infortunio m.
advertise/advertize vt anunciar.
advertisement/advertizement n anuncio m; Lat Am aviso m, Lat Am reclame m.
advertising n publicidad f.
advice n consejo m; aviso m.
advisability n prudencia, conveniencia f.
advisable adj prudente, conveniente.
advise vt aconsejar; avisar.
advisedly adv prudentemente, avisadamente.
advisory adj consultivo/va.
advocacy n defensa f.
advocate n abogado m; protector m; * vt abogar por.
advocateship n abogacía f.
aerial n antena f.
aerobics npl aerobic m, Lat Am aerobismo m.
aerometer n areómetro m.
aerosol n aerosol m.
aerostat n globo aerostático m.
afar adv lejos, distante; **from** ~ desde lejos.
affability n afabilidad, urbanidad f.
affable adj afable, complaciente; ~bly adv afablemente.
affair n asunto m; negocio m.
affect vt conmover; afectar.
affectation n afectación f.
affected adj afectado/da, lleno/na de afectación; ~ly adv con afectación.
affectingly adv con afecto.
affection n cariño m.
affectionate adj afectuoso/sa, Lat Am querendón/ona; ~ly adv cariñosamente.
affidavit n declaración jurada f.
affiliate vt afiliar.
affiliation n afiliación f.
affinity n afinidad f.
affirm vt afirmar, declarar.
affirmation n afirmación f.
affirmative adj afirmativo/va; ~ly adv afirmativamente.
affix vt pegar; * n (gr) afijo m.
afflict vt afligir.
affliction n aflicción f; dolor m.
affluence n abundancia f.
affluent adj opulento/ta.
afflux n confluencia, afluencia f.
afford vt dar; proveer.

affray n asalto m; tumulto m.
affront n afrenta, injuria f; * vt afrentar, insultar, ultrajar.
aflame adv en llamas.
afloat adv flotante, a flote.
afraid adj espantado/da, tímido/da; **I am** ~ temo.
afresh adv de nuevo, otra vez.
African-American adj, n afroamericano/na m/f.
aft adv (mar) a popa.
after prep después; detrás; según; * adv después; ~ **all** después de todo.
afterbirth n secundinas fpl.
after-effects npl consecuencias fpl.
afterlife n vida venidera f.
aftermath n consecuencias fpl.
afternoon n tarde f.
aftershave n aftershave m.
aftertaste n resabio m.
afterwards adv después
again adv otra vez; ~ **and** ~ muchas veces; **as much** ~ otra vez tanto.
against prep contra; ~ **the grain** a contrapelo; de mala gana.
agate n ágata f.
age n edad f; **under** ~ menor; * vt envejecer.
aged adj viejo/ja, anciano/na.
agency n agencia f.
agenda n orden del día m.
agent n agente m.
agglomerate vt aglomerar.
agglomeration n aglomeración f.
aggrandizement n engrandecimiento m.
aggravate vt agravar, exagerar.
aggravation n agravación f.
aggregate n agregado m.
aggregation n agregación f.
aggression n agresión f.
aggressive adj ofensivo/va.
aggressor n agresor m.
aggrieved adj ofendido/da.
aghast adj horrorizado/da.
agile adj ágil; diestro/tra.
agility n agilidad f; destreza f.
agitate vt agitar.
agitation n agitación f; perturbación f.
agitator n agitador, incitador m.
ago adv pasado, largo tiempo; después; **how long** ~? ¿cuánto hace?
agog adj emocionado/da.
agonizing adj atroz.
agony n agonía f.
agree vt convenir; * vi estar de acuerdo/da.
agreeable adj agradable; amable; ~bly adv agradablemente; ~ **with** según, conforme a.
agreeableness n amabilidad, gracia f.
agreed adj establecido/da, convenido/da; ~! adv ¡de acuerdo!
agreement n acuerdo m.

agricultural *adj* agrario/ria.
agriculture *n* agricultura *f.*
agriculturist *n* agricultor *m.*
agronomy *n* agronomía *f.*
aground *adv* (*mar*) encallado.
ah! *excl* iah!, iay!
ahead *adv* más allá, delante de otro; (*mar*) por la proa.
ahoy! *excl* (*mar*) iohe!
aid *vt* ayudar, socorrer; **to ~ and abet** ser cómplice de; * *n* ayuda *f;* auxilio, socorro *m.*
aide-de-camp *n* (*mil*) ayudante de campo *m.*
AIDS *n* SIDA *m.*
ail *vt* afligir, molestar.
ailing *adj* doliente.
ailment *n* dolencia, indisposición *f.*
aim *vt* apuntar aspirar a; intentar; * *n* designio *m;* puntería *f.*
aimless *adj* sin designio, sin objeto; **~ly** a la deriva.
air *n* aire *m;* * *vt* airear; ventilar.
airbag *n* airbag *m.*
air balloon *n* globo aerostático *m.*
airborne *adj* aerotransportado/da.
air-conditioned *adj* climatizado/da.
air conditioning *n* aire acondicionado *m.*
aircraft *n* avión *m.*
air cushion *n* cojinete rellenado de aire *m.*
air force *n* fuerzas aéreas *fpl.*
air freshener *n* ambientador *m.*
air gun *n* escopeta de aire comprimido *f.*
air hole *n* respiradero *m.*
airless *adj* falto de ventilación, sofocado/da.
airlift *n* puente aéreo *m.*
airline *n* línea aérea *f.*
airmail *n*: **by ~** por avión.
airplane *n* avión *m.*
airport *n* aeropuerto *m.*
airport tax *n* tasas de aeropuerto *f.*
air pump *n* bomba de aire *f.*
airsick *adj* mareado/da.
airstrip *n* pista de aterrizaje *f.*
air terminal *n* terminal *f.*
airtight *adj* herméticamente cerrado/da.
airy *adj* bien ventilado/da.
aisle *n* nave de una iglesia *f.*
ajar *adj* entreabierto/ta.
akimbo *adj* corvo/va.
akin *adj* parecido/da.
alabaster *n* alabastro *m;* * *adj* alabastrino/na.
alacrity *n* presteza *f.*
alarm *n* alarma *f;* * *vt* alarmar; inquietar.
alarm bell *n* timbre de alarma *m.*
alarmist *n* alarmista *m.*
alas *adv* desgraciadamente.
albeit *conj* aunque.
album *n* álbum *m.*
alchemist *n* alquimista *m.*

alchemy *n* alquimia *f.*
alcohol *n* alcohol *m.*
alcoholic *adj* alcohólico/ca; * *n* alcoholizado *m.*
alcove *n* nicho *m.*
alder *n* aliso *m.*
ale *n* cerveza *f.*
alert *adj* vigilante; alerto/ta; * *n* alerta *f.*
alertness *n* cuidado *m;* vigilancia *f.*
algae *npl* alga *f.*
algebra *n* álgebra *f.*
algebraic *adj* algebraico/ca.
alias *adj* alias.
alibi *n* (*law*) coartada *f.*
alien *adj* ajeno/na; * *n* forastero *m.*
alienate *vt* enajenar.
alienation *n* enajenación *f.*
alight *vi* apearse; * *adj* encendido/da.
align *vt* alinear.
alike *adj* semejante, igual; * *adv* igualmente.
alimentation *n* alimentación *f.*
alimony *n* alimentos *mpl.*
alive *adj* vivo/va, viviente; activo/va.
alkali *n* álcali *m.*
alkaline *adj* alcalino/na.
all *adj* todo/da; * *adv* totalmente; **~ at once, ~ of a sudden** de repente; **~ the same** sin embargo; **~ the better** tanto mejor; **not at ~!** ino hay de qué!; **once for ~** una vez por todas; * *n* todo *m.*
allay *vt* aliviar.
all clear *n* luz verde *f.*
allegation *n* alegación *f.*
allege *vt* alegar; declarar.
allegiance *n* lealtad, fidelidad *f.*
allegorical *adj* alegórico/ca; **~ly** *adv* alegóricamente.
allegory *n* alegoría *f.*
allegro *n* (*mus*) alegro *m.*
allergy *n* alergia *f.*
alleviate *vt* aliviar, aligerar.
alleviation *n* alivio *m;* mitigación *f.*
alley *n* callejuela *f.*
alliance *n* alianza *f.*
allied *adj* aliado/da.
alligator *n* caimán *m.*
alliteration *n* aliteración *f.*
all-night *adj* abierto/ta toda la noche.
allocate *vt* repartir.
allocation *n* cuota *f.*
allot *vt* asignar.
allow *vt* conceder; permitir; dar, pagar; **to ~ for** tener en cuenta.
allowable *adj* admisible, permitido/da.
allowance *n* concesión *f.*
alloy *n* liga, mezcla, aleación *f.*
all right *adv* bien.
all-round *adj* completo/ta.
allspice *n* pimienta de Jamaica *f.*
allude *vt* aludir.

A

allure *n* fascinación *f*.
alluring *adj* seductor/a; **~ly** *adv* seductoramente.
allurement *n* aliciente, atractivo *m*.
allusion *n* alusión *f*.
allusive *adj* alusivo/va; **~ly** *adv* de modo alusivo.
alluvial *adj* aluvial.
ally *n* aliado *m*; * *vt* aliar.
almanac *n* almanaque *m*.
almighty *adj* omnipotente, todopoderoso/sa.
almond *n* almendra *f*.
almond tree *n* almendro *m*.
almost *adv* casi; cerca de.
alms *n* limosna *f*.
aloft *prep* arriba.
alone *adj* solo; * *adv* solamente, sólo; **to leave ~** dejar en paz.
along *adv* a lo largo; **~ side** al lado.
aloof *adv* lejos.
aloud *adj* en voz alta.
alphabet *n* alfabeto *m*.
alphabetical *adj* alfabético/ca; **~ly** *adv* por orden alfabético.
alpine *adj* alpino/na.
already *adv* ya.
also *adv* también, además.
altar *n* altar *m*.
altarpiece *n* retablo *m*.
alter *vt* modificar.
alteration *n* alteración *f*.
altercation *n* altercado *m*.
alternate *adj* alterno/na; * *vt* alternar, variar; **~ly** *adv* alternativamente.
alternating *adj* alterno/na.
alternation *n* alternación *f*.
alternator *n* alternador *m*.
alternative *n* alternativa *f*; * *adj* alternative; **~ly** *adv* si no.
although *conj* aunque, no obstante.
altitude *n* altitud, altura *f*.
altogether *adv* del todo.
alum *n* alumbre *m*.
aluminous *adj* aluminoso/sa.
aluminum *n* aluminio *m*.
always *adv* siempre, constantemente.
a.m. *adv* de la mañana.
amalgam *n* amalgama *f*.
amalgamate *vt,vi* amalgamar(se).
amalgamation *n* amalgamación *f*.
amanuensis *n* amanuense, secretario *m*.
amaryllis *n* (bot) amarillas *f*.
amass *vt* acumular, amontonar.
amateur *n* aficionado *m*, amateur *m/f*.
amateurish *adj* torpe.
amatory *adj* amatorio/ria; erótico/ca.
amaze *vt* asombrar.
amazement *n* asombro *m*.
amazing *adj* pasmoso/sa; **~ly** *adv* extraordinariamente.
amazon *n* amazona *f*.

ambassador *n* embajador *m*.
ambassadress *n* embajadora *f*.
amber *n* ámbar *m*; * *adj* ambarino/na.
ambidextrous *adj* ambidextro/tra, ambidiestro/tra.
ambient *adj* ambiente.
ambiguity *n* ambigüedad, duda *f*.
ambiguous *adj* ambiguo; **~ly** *adv* ambiguamente.
ambition *n* ambición *f*.
ambitious *adj* ambicioso/sa; **~ly** *adv* ambiciosamente.
amble *vi* andar sin prisa.
ambulance *n* ambulancia *f*.
ambush *n* emboscada *f*; **to lie in ~** estar emboscado/da; * *vt* tender una emboscada a.
ameliorate *vt* mejorar.
amelioration *n* mejoramiento *m*.
amenable *adj* sensible.
amend *vt* enmendar.
amendable *adj* reparable, corregible.
amendment *n* enmienda *f*.
amends *npl* compensación *f*.
amenities *npl* comodidades *fpl*.
America *n* América *f*.
American *adj* americano/na.
amethyst *n* amatista *f*.
amiability *n* amabilidad *f*.
amiable *adj* amable.
amiableness *n* amabilidad *f*.
amiably *adv* amablemente.
amicable *adj* amigable, amistoso/sa; **~bly** *adv* amistosamente.
amid(st) *prep* entre, en medio de.
amiss *adv*: **something's ~** algo pasa.
ammonia *n* amoniaco *m*.
ammunition *n* municiones *fpl*.
amnesia *n* amnesia *f*.
amnesty *n* amnistía *f*.
among(st) *prep* entre, en medio de.
amoral *adv* amoral.
amorous *adj* amoroso/sa; **~ly** *adv* amorosamente.
amorphous *adj* informe.
amount *n* importe *m*; cantidad *f*; * *vi* sumar.
amp(ere) *n* amperio *m*.
amphibian *n* anfibio *m*.
amphibious *adj* anfibio/bia.
amphitheater *n* anfiteatro *m*.
ample *adj* amplio/lia.
ampleness *n* amplitud, abundancia *f*.
amplification *n* amplificación *f*; extensión *f*.
amplifier *n* amplificador *m*
amplify *vt* ampliar, extender.
amplitude *n* amplitud, extensión *f*.
amply *adv* ampliamente.
amputate *vt* amputar.
amputation *n* amputación *f*.
amulet *n* amuleto *m*.
amuse *vt* entretener, divertir.
amusement *n* diversión *f*, pasatiempo, entretenimiento *m*.

amusing *adj* divertido/da; **~ly** *adv* entretenidamente.
an *art* un, uno, una.
anachronism *n* anacronismo *m*.
analog *adj* (*comput*) analógico/ca.
analogous *adj* análogo.
analogy *n* analogía *f*.
analyze *vt* analizar.
analysis *n* análisis *m invar*.
analyst *n* analizador/a *m/f*.
analytical *adj* analítico/ca; **~ly** *adv* analíticamente.
anarchic *adj* anárquico/ca.
anarchist *adj* anarquista.
anarchy *n* anarquía *f*.
anatomical *adj* anatómico/ca; **~ly** *adv* anatómicamente.
anatomize *vt* anatomizar.
anatomy *n* anatomía *f*
ancestor *n*: **~s** *pl* antepasados *mpl*.
ancestral *adj* hereditario/ria.
ancestry *n* raza, alcurnia *f*.
anchor *n* ancla *f*; * *vi* anclar; **to weigh ~** zarpar.
anchorage *n* fondeadero *m*.
anchovy *n* anchoa *f*.
ancient *adj* antiguo.
ancillary *adj* auxiliar.
and *conj* y, e.
anecdotal *adj* anecdótico/ca.
anecdote *n* anécdota *f*
anemia *n* anemia *f*.
anemic *adj* (*med*) anémico/ca.
anemone *n* (*bot*) anémona *f*
anesthetic *n* anestesia *f*.
anew *adv* de nuevo, nuevamente.
angel *n* ángel *m*
angelic *adj* angélico/ca.
anger *n* cólera *f*; * *vt* enojar, irritar.
angle *n* ángulo *m*; * *vt* pescar con caña.
angled *adj* anguloso/sa.
angler *n* pescador/a de caña *m/f*.
Anglicanism *n* anglicismo *m*.
angling *n* pesca con caña *f*
angrily *adv* enojado.
angry *adj* enojado/da.
anguish *n* ansia, angustia *f*
angular *adj* angular.
angularity *n* forma angular *f*.
animal *n* adj animal *m*.
animate *vt* animar; * *adj* viviente.
animated *adj* vivo/va.
animation *n* animación *f*
animosity *n* rencor *m*.
animus *n* odio *m*
anise *n* anís *m*
aniseed *n* anís *m*
ankle *n* tobillo *m*; **~ bone** hueso del tobillo *m*
annals *n* anales *mpl*.
annex *vt* anejar; * *n* anejo *m*.
annexation *n* anexión *f*.
annihilate *vt* aniquilar.

annihilation *n* aniquilación *f*.
anniversary *n* aniversario *m*.
annotate *vi* anotar.
annotation *n* anotación *f*.
announce *vt* anunciar, publicar.
announcement *n* anuncio *m*.
announcer *n* locutor/a *m/f*.
annoy *vt* molestar.
annoyance *n* molestia *f*.
annoying *adj* molesto/ta; fastidioso/sa.
annual *adj* anual; **~ly** *adv* anualmente, cada año.
annuity *n* renta vitalicia *f*.
annul *vt* anular.
annulment *n* anulación *f*.
annunciation *n* anunciación *f*
anodyne *adj* anodino/na.
anoint *vt* untar, ungir.
anomalous *adj* anómalo.
anomaly *n* anomalía, irregularidad *f*.
anon *adv* más tarde.
anonymity *n* anonimato *f*.
anonymous *adj* anónimo/ma; **~ly** *adj* anónimamente.
anorexia *n* anorexia *f*.
another *adj* otro/tra, diferente; **one ~** uno a otro.
answer *vt* responder, replicar; corresponder; **to ~ for** responder de/por; **to ~ to** corresponder a; * *n* respuesta, réplica *f*.
answerable *adj* responsable.
answering machine *n* contestador automático *m*.
ant *n* hormiga *f*.
antagonism *n* antagonismo *m*; rivalidad *f*.
antagonist *n* antagonista *m*.
antagonize *vt* provocar.
Antarctic *adj* antártico/ca.
anteater *n* oso hormiguero *m*
antecedent *n*: **~s** *pl* antecedentes *mpl*.
antechamber *n* antecámara *f*
antedate *vt* antedatar.
antelope *n* antílope *m*.
antenna *npl* antena *f*.
anterior *adj* anterior, precedente.
anthem *n* himno *m*.
ant hill *n* hormiguero *m*.
anthology *n* antología *f*.
anthracite *n* antracita *f*.
anthropologist *n* antropólogo/ga *m/f*.
anthropology *n* antropología *f*
anti-aircraft *adj* antiaéreo/rea.
antibiotic *n* antibiótico *m*.
antibody *n* anticuerpo *m*.
Antichrist *n* Anticristo *m*.
anticipate *vt* anticipar, prevenir.
anticipation *n* anticipación *f*.
anticlockwise *adv* en sentido contrario al de las agujas del reloj.
antidote *n* antídoto *m*.
antifreeze *n* anticongelante *m*.
antimony *n* antimonio *m*.

antipathy *n* antipatía *f.*
antipodes *npl* antípodas *fpl*
antiquarian *n* anticuario *m.*
antiquated *adj* antiguo/gua; * *n* antigüedad *f.*
antiquity *n* antigüedad *f.*
antiseptic *adj* antiséptico/ca.
antisocial *adj* antisocial.
antithesis *n* antítesis *f.*
antler *n* cuerna *f.*
anvil *n* yunque *m.*
anxiety *n* ansiedad *f*, ansia *f*; afán *m*, zozobra *f.*
anxious *adj* ansioso/sa; **~ly** *adv* ansiosamente;
　to be ~ *vi* zozobrar.
any *adj pn* cualquier, cualquiera; alguno, alguna;
　todo; **~body** alguien, nadie, cualquiera; **~how**
　de cualquier manera; **~more** más; **~place** en
　ninguna parte; **~thing** algo, nada, cualquier
　cosa.
apace *adv* rápidamente.
apart *adv* aparte, separadamente.
apartment *n* apartamento, departamento *m.*
apartment house *n* casa de apartamentos *f.*
apathetic *adj* apático/ca.
apathy *n* apatía *f.*
ape *n* mono *m*; * *vt* remedar.
aperture *n* abertura *f.*
apex *n* ápice *m.*
aphorism *n* aforismo *m*; máxima *f.*
apiary *n* colmenar *m*, *Lat Am* apiario *m.*
apiece *adv* por cabeza, por persona.
aplomb *n* aplomo *m.*
Apocalypse *n* Apocalipsis *m.*
apocrypha *npl* libros apócrifos *mpl.*
apocryphal *adj* apócrifo/fa, no canónico/ca.
apologetic *adj* de disculpa.
apologist *n* apologista *m.*
apologize *vt* disculpar.
apology *n* apología, defensa *f.*
apoplexy *n* apoplejía *f*
apostle *n* apóstol *m.*
apostolic *adj* apostólico/ca.
apostrophe *n* apóstrofe *m.*
apotheosis *n* apoteosis *f.*
appall *vt* espantar, aterrar.
appalling *adj* espantoso/sa.
apparatus *n* aparato *m.*
apparel *n* traje, vestido *m.*
apparent *adj* evidente, aparente; **~ly** *adv* por lo
　visto.
apparition *n* aparición, visión *f.*
appeal *vi* apelar, recurrir a un tribunal superior;
　* *n* (*law*) apelación *f.*
appealing *adj* atractivo/va.
appear *vi* aparecer.
appearance *n* apariencia *f.*
appease *vt* aplacar.
appellant *n* (*law*) apelante *m.*
append *vt* anejar.

appendage *n* cosa accesoria *f.*
appendicitis *n* apendicitis *f.*
appendix *n* apéndice *m.*
appertain *vi* tocar a.
appetite *n* apetito *m.*
appetizing *adj* apetitivo/va.
applaud *vi* aplaudir.
applause *n* aplausos *mpl*
apple *n* manzana *f.*
apple pie *n* pastelillo de manzanas *m*; **in ~ order**
　en sumo orden.
apple tree *n* manzano *m.*
appliance *n* aparato *m.*
applicability *n* aplicabilidad *f.*
applicable *adj* aplicable.
applicant *n* aspirante, candidato *m.*
application *n* aplicación *f*; solicitud *f.*
applied *adj* aplicado/da.
apply *vt* aplicar; * *vi* dirigirse a, recurrir a.
appoint *vt* nombrar.
appointee *n* persona nombrada *f.*
appointment *n* cita *f*; nombramiento *m.*
apportion *vt* repartir.
apportionment *n* repartición *f.*
apposite *adj* adaptado/da.
apposition *n* aposición *f.*
appraisal *n* estimación *f.*
appraise *vt* tasar; estimar.
appreciable *adj* sensible.
appreciably *adv* sensiblemente.
appreciate *vt* apreciar; agradecer.
appreciation *n* aprecio *m.*
appreciative *adj* agradecido/da.
apprehend *vt* arrestar.
apprehension *n* aprensión *f.*
apprehensive *adj* aprensivo/va, tímido/da.
apprentice *n* aprendiz *m*; * *vt* poner de aprendiz.
apprenticeship *n* aprendizaje *m.*
apprise *vt* informar.
approach *vt* (*vi*) aproximar(se); * *n* acceso *m.*
approachable *adj* accesible.
approbation *n* aprobación *f.*
appropriate *vt* apropiarse de; * *adj* apropiado/da.
approval *n* aprobación *f.*
approve (of) *vt* aprobar.
approximate *vi* acercarse; * *adj* aproximativo/va;
　~ly *adv* aproximadamente.
approximation *n* aproximación *f.*
apricot *n* damasco, albaricoque *m.*
April *n* abril *m.*
apron *n* delantal *m.*
apse *n* ábside *m.*
apt *adj* apto/ta, idóneo/nea; **~ly** *adv* oportunamente.
aptitude *n* aptitud *f.*
aqualung *n* escafandra autónoma *f.*
aquarium *n* acuario *m.*
Aquarius *n* Acuario *m.*
aquatic *adj* acuático/ca.

aqueduct n acueducto m.
aquiline adj aguileño/ña.
arabesque n arabesco m.
arable adj labrantío/tía.
arbiter n árbitro m.
arbitrariness n arbitrariedad f.
arbitrary adj arbitrario/ria.
arbitrate vt arbitrar, juzgar como árbitro.
arbitration n arbitrio m.
arbitrator n árbitro m.
arbor n emparrado m; enramada f.
arcade n galería f.
arch n arco m; * adj malicioso/sa.
archaic adj arcaico/ca.
archangel n arcángel m.
archbishop n arzobispo m.
archbishopric n arzobispado m.
archeological adj arqueológico/ca.
archeologist n arqueólogo/ga m/f.
archeology n arqueología f.
archer n arquero m.
archery n tiro con arco m.
architect n arquitecto/ta m/f.
architectural adj arquitectónico/ca.
architecture n arquitectura f.
archives npl archivos mpl.
archivist n archivero/ra m/f.
archly adv maliciosamente.
archway n arcada, bóveda f.
arctic adj ártico/ca.
ardent adj apasionado/da; ~ly adv con pasión.
ardor n ardor m; vehemencia f; pasión f.
arduous adj arduo, difícil.
area n área f; espacio m, zona f.
arena n arena f.
arguably adv posiblemente.
argue vi discutir; * vt sostener.
argument n argumento m, controversia f.
argumentation n argumentación f.
argumentative adj discutidor/a.
aria n (mus) aria f.
arid adj árido/da, estéril.
aridity n sequedad f.
Aries n Aries m.
aright adv bien; **to set** ~ rectificar.
arise vi levantarse; nacer.
aristocracy n aristocracia f.
aristocrat n aristócrata m/f.
aristocratic adj aristocrático/ca; ~ally adv aristocráticamente.
arithmetic n aritmética f.
arithmetical adj aritmético/ca; ~ly adv aritméticamente.
ark n arca f.
arm n brazo m; arma f; * vt (vi) armar(se).
armament n armamento m.
armchair n sillón m.
armed adj armado/da.
armful n brazada f.

armhole n sobaco m.
armistice n armisticio m.
armor n armadura f.
armored car n carro blindado m.
armory n arsenal m.
armpit n sobaco m.
armrest n apoyabrazos m invar.
army n ejército m; tropas fpl.
aroma n aroma m.
aromatherapy n aromaterapia f.
aromatic adj aromático/ca.
around prep alrededor de; * adv alrededor.
arouse vt despertar; excitar.
arraign vt acusar.
arraignment n acusación f; proceso criminal m.
arrange vt organizar.
arrangement n colocación f; arreglo.
arrant adj consumado/da.
array n serie f.
arrears npl resto de una deuda m; atraso m.
arrest n arresto m; * vt detener, arrestar.
arrival n llegada f.
arrive vi llegar.
arrogance n arrogancia, presunción f.
arrogant adj arrogante, presuntuoso/sa; ~ly adv arrogantemente.
arrogate vt arrogarse.
arrogation n arrogación f.
arrow n flecha f.
arsenal n (mil) arsenal m; (mar) atarazana, armería f.
arsenic n arsénico m.
arson n fuego incendiario m.
art n arte m.
arterial adj arterial.
artesian well n pozo artesiano m.
artery n arteria f.
artful adj ingenioso/sa.
artfulness n astucia, habilidad f.
art gallery n pinacoteca f.
arthritis n artritis f.
artichoke n alcachofa f.
article n artículo m.
articulate vt articular, pronunciar distintamente.
articulated adj articulado/da.
articulation n articulación f.
artifice n artificio, fraude m.
artificial adj artificial; artificioso/sa; ~ly adv artificialmente; artificiosamente.
artificial insemination n inseminación artificial f.
artificiality n artificialidad f.
artillery n artillería f.
artisan n artesano/na m/f.
artist n artista m.
artistic adj artístico/ca.
artistry n habilidad f.
artless adj sencillo, simple; ~ly adv sencillamente, naturalmente.

artlessness n sencillez f.
as conj como; mientras; también; visto que, puesto que; ~ **for**, ~ **to** en cuanto a.
asbestos n asbesto, amianto m.
ascend vi ascender, subir.
ascendancy n dominio m.
ascension n ascensión f.
ascent n subida f.
ascertain vt establecer.
ascetic adj ascético/ca; * n asceta m.
ascribe vt atribuir.
ash n (bot) fresno m; ceniza f
ashcan n cubo de la basura m.
ashamed adj avergonzado/da.
ashore adv en tierra, a tierra; **to go** ~ desembarcar.
ashtray n cenicero m.
Ash Wednesday n miércoles de ceniza m.
aside adv a un lado.
ask vt pedir, rogar; **to** ~ **after** preguntar por; **to** ~ **for** pedir; **to** ~ **out** invitar.
askance adv desconfiado/da.
askew adv de lado.
asleep adj dormido/da; **to fall** ~ dormirse.
asparagus n espárrago m.
aspect n aspecto m.
aspen n álamo temblón m.
aspersion n calumnia f.
asphalt n asfalto m.
asphyxia n (med) asfixia f.
asphyxiate vt asfixiar.
asphyxiation n asfixia f.
aspirant n aspirante m.
aspirate vt aspirar, pronunciar con aspiración; * n sonido aspirado m.
aspiration n aspiración f.
aspire vi aspirar, desear.
aspirin n aspirina f.
ass n asno m; **she** ~ burra f.
assail vt asaltar, atacar.
assailant n asaltante m/f, agresor/a m/f.
assassin n asesino/na m/f.
assassinate vt asesinar.
assassination n asesinato m.
assault n asalto m; * vt acometer, asaltar.
assemblage n multitud f.
assemble vt reunir, convocar; * vi juntarse.
assembly n asamblea, junta f; congreso m.
assembly line n cadena de montaje f.
assent n asentimiento m; * vi asentir.
assert vt sostener, mantener; afirmar.
assertion n aserción f.
assertive adj perentorio/ria.
assess vt valorar.
assessment n valoración f.
assessor n asesor/a m/f.
assets npl bienes mpl.
assiduous adj diligente, aplicado/da; ~**ly** adv diligentemente.

assign vt asignar.
assignation n cita f.
assignment n asignación f; tarea f.
assimilate vt asimilar.
assimilation n asimilación f.
assist vt asistir, ayudar, socorrer.
assistance n asistencia f; socorro m.
assistant n asistente, ayudante m.
associate vt asociar; * adj asociado/da; * n socio m.
association n asociación, sociedad f.
assonance n asonancia f.
assorted adj surtido/da.
assortment n surtido m.
assuage vt mitigar, suavizar.
assume vt asumir; suponer.
assumption n supuesto m.
Assumption n Asunción f.
assurance n seguro m.
assure vt asegurar.
assuredly adv sin duda
asterisk n asterisco m.
astern adv (mar) a popa.
asthma n asma f.
asthmatic adj asmático/ca.
astonish vt pasmar, sorprender.
astonishing adj asombroso/sa; ~**ly** adv asombrosamente.
astonishment n asombro m.
astound vt pasmar.
astray adv: **to go** ~ extraviarse; **to lead** ~ llevar por mal camino.
astride adv a horcajadas.
astringent adj astringente.
astrologer n astrólogo/ga m/f.
astrological adj astrológico/ca.
astrology n astrología f.
astronaut n astronauta m/f.
astronomer n astrónomo m.
astronomical adj astronómico/ca.
astronomy n astronomía f.
astute adj astuto/ta.
asylum n asilo, refugio m.
at prep a; en; ~ **once** en seguida; ya; ~ **all** en absoluto; ~ **all events** en todo caso; ~ **first** al principio; ~ **last** por fin.
atheism n ateísmo m.
atheist n ateo m, atea f.
athlete n atleta m/f.
athletic adj atlético/ca.
atlas n atlas m invar.
atmosphere n atmósfera f.
atmospheric adj atmosférico/ca.
atom n átomo m.
atom bomb n bomba atómica f.
atomic adj atómico/ca.
atone vt expiar.
atonement n expiación f.
atop adv encima.
atrocious adj atroz; ~**ly** adv atrozmente.

atrocity n atrocidad, enormidad f.
atrophy n (med) atrofia f.
attach vt adjuntar.
attaché n agregado m.
attachment n afecto m.
attack vt atacar; acometer; * n ataque m.
attacker n asaltante m.
attain vt conseguir, obtener.
attainable adj asequible.
attempt vt intentar; probar, experimentar; * n intento m, tentativa f.
attend vt servir; asistir; **to ~ to** ocuparse de; * vi prestar atención.
attendance n presencia f.
attendant n sirviente m.
attention n atención f; cuidado m.
attentive adj atento/ta; cuidadoso/sa; ~ly adv con atención.
attenuate vt atenuar, disminuir.
attest vt atestiguar.
attic n desván m; guardilla f.
attire n atavío m.
attitude n actitud, postura f.
attorney-at-law n abogado/da m/f.
attract vt atraer.
attraction n atracción f; atractivo m.
attractive adj atractivo/va.
attribute vt atribuir; * n atributo m.
attrition n agotamiento m.
auburn adj moreno/na, castaño/ña.
auction n subasta f.
auctioneer n subastador/a, rematador/a m/f.
audacious adj audaz, temerario/ria; ~ly adv atrevidamente.
audacity n audacia, osadía f.
audible adj perceptible al oído; ~ly adv de manera audible.
audience n audiencia f; auditorio m.
audit n auditoría f; * vt auditar.
auditor n censor/a de cuentas m/f.
auditory adj auditivo/va.
augment vt aumentar, acrecentar; * vi crecer.
augmentation n aumentación f; aumento m.
August n agosto m.
august adj majestuoso/sa.
aunt n tía f.
au pair n au pair f.
aura n aura f.
auspices npl auspicios mpl.
auspicious adj propicio/cia; ~ly adv favorablemente.
austere adj austero/ra, severo/ra; ~ly adv austeramente.
austerity n austeridad f.
authentic adj auténtico/ca; ~ly adv auténticamente.
authenticate vt autenticar.
authenticity n autenticidad f.
author n autor/a m/f; escritor/a m/f.
authoress n autora; escritora f.

authoritarian adj autoritario/ria.
authoritative adj autoritativo/va; ~ly adv autoritativamente, con autoridad.
authority n autoridad f.
authorization n autorización f.
authorize vt autorizar.
authorship n autoría f.
auto, **automobile** n carro, coche, auto m.
autocrat n autócrata m.
autocratic adj autocrático/ca.
autograph n autógrafo m.
automated adj automatizado/da.
automatic adj automático/ca.
automaton n autómata m.
autonomy n autonomía f.
autopsy n autopsia f.
autumn n otoño m.
autumnal adj otoñal.
auxiliary adj auxiliar, asistente.
avail vt: to ~ **oneself of** aprovecharse de; * n: to no ~ en vano.
available adj disponible.
avalanche n alud m.
avarice n avaricia f.
avaricious adj avaro/ra.
avenge vt vengarse, castigar.
avenue n avenida f.
aver vt afirmar, declarar.
average vt tomar un término medio; * n término medio m.
aversion n aversión f, disgusto m.
avert vt desviar, apartar.
aviary n pajarera f.
avoid vt evitar, escapar, huir; * vr zafarse de.
avoidable adj evitable.
await vt aguardar.
awake vt despertar; * vi despertarse; * adj despierto/ta.
awakening n despertar.
award vt otorgar; Lat Am acordar; * n premio m; sentencia, decisión f.
aware adj consciente; vigilante.
awareness n conciencia f.
away adv ausente, fuera; ~! ¡fuera! , ¡quita de ahí!, ¡marcha! **far and ~** de mucho, con mucho.
away game n partido fuera de casa m.
awe n miedo, temor m.
awe-inspiring, **awesome** adj imponente.
awful adj tremendo/da; horroroso/sa; ~ly adv terriblemente.
awhile adv un rato, algún tiempo.
awkward adj torpe, rudo/da, poco diestro/tra; ~ly adv groseramente, toscamente.
awkwardness n tosquedad, grosería, poca habilidad f.
awl n lezna f.
awning n (mar) toldo m.
awry adv oblicuamente, torcidamente, al través.

ax *n* hacha *f*; * *vt* despedir; cortar.
axiom *n* axioma *m*.
axis *n* eje *m*.

axle *n* eje *m*.
ay(e) *excl* sí.

B

baa n balido m; * vi balar.

babble vi charlar, parlotear; ~ , **babbling** n charla, cháchara f.

babbler n charlador/a, charlatán/ana m/f.

babe, baby n niño/a, pequeño/a, nene/a, Lat Am tierno/na m/f; **small** ~ mamón/ona m/f.

baboon n babuino m.

babyhood n niñez f.

babyish adj niñero/ra; pueril.

baby carriage n cochecito m.

baby linen n ropita de niño f.

bachelor n soltero m; bachiller m.

bachelorship n soltería f; bachillerato m.

back n dorso m; revés de la mano m; * adv atrás, detrás; **a few years** ~ hace algunos años; * vt sostener, apoyar, favorecer.

backbite vt hablar mal del que está ausente; difamar.

backbiter n detractor/a m/f.

backbone n hueso dorsal, espinazo m.

backdate vt antedatar.

backdoor n puerta trasera f.

backer n partidario/ria m/f.

backgammon n backgammon m.

background n fondo m.

backlash n reacción f.

backlog n trabajo acumulado m.

back number n número atrasado m.

backpack n mochila f.

back payment n paga atrasada f.

backside n trasero m.

back-up lights npl (auto) luces de marcha atrás fpl.

backward adj tardo/da, lento/ta; * adv hacia atrás.

bacon n tocino m.

bad adj mal/malo; perverso/sa; infeliz; dañoso/sa; indispuesto/ta; ~**ly** adv malamente.

badge n señal f; símbolo m; divisa f.

badger n tejón m; * vt fatigar; cansar; atormentar.

badminton n bádminton m.

badness n maldad, mala calidad f.

baffle vt confundir, hundir; acosar.

bag n saco m; bolsa f.

baggage n bagaje, equipaje m.

bagpipe n gaita f.

bail n fianza, caución (juratoria) f; fiador m; * vt caucionar, fiar.

bailiff n alguacil m; mayordomo m.

bait vt cebar; atraer; * n cebo m; anzuelo m.

baize n bayeta f.

bake vt cocer en horno.

bakery n panadería f.

baker n hornero/ra, panadero/ra m/f; ~**'s dozen** trece piezas.

baking n cocción f.

baking powder n levadura f.

balance n balanza f; equilibrio m; saldo de una cuenta m; **to lose one's** ~ caerse, dar en tierra; * vt pesar en balanza; contrapesar; saldar; considerar, examinar.

balance sheet n balance m.

balcony n balcón m.

bald adj calvo/va.

baldness n calvicie f.

bale n bala f; * vt embalar; tirar el agua del bote.

baleful adj triste, funesto/ta; ~**ly** adv tristemente; míseramente.

ball n bola f; pelota f; baile m, balón m.

ballad n balada f.

ballast n lastre, m * vt lastrar.

ballerina n bailarina f.

ballet n ballet m.

ballistic adj balístico/ca.

balloon n globo m.

ballot n voto m; escrutinio m; * vi votar.

ballpoint (pen) n bolígrafo m.

ballroom n salón de baile m.

balm, balsam n bálsamo m; * vt untar con bálsamo.

balmy adj balsámico/ca; fragante.

balustrade n balaustrada f.

bamboo n bambú m.

bamboozle vt (col) engañar.

ban n prohibición f; * vt prohibir.

banal adj vulgar.

banana n plátano m.

band n faja f; cuadrilla f; banda (de soldados) f; orquesta f.

bandage n venda f, vendaje m; * vt vendar.

Band-Aid™ n Tirita™ f, Lat Am Curita™ f.

bandit n bandido/da m/f.

bandstand n quiosco m.

bandy vt pelotear; discutir.

bandy-legged adj patizambo/ba.

bang n golpe m; * vt golpear; cerrar con violencia.

bangle n brazalete m.

bangs npl flequillo m.

banish vt desterrar, echar fuera, proscribir, expatriar.

banishment n destierro m.

banister(s) n(pl) pasamanos m.

banjo n banjo m.

bank n orilla (de río) f; montón de tierra m; banco m; dique m; escollo m; * vt poner dinero en un banco; **to** ~ **on** contar con.

bank account n cuenta de banco f.
bank card n tarjeta bancaria f.
banker n banquero/ra m/f.
banking n banca f; **electronic ~** banca electrónica.
banknote n billete de banco m.
bankrupt adj insolvente; * n fallido/da, quebrado/da m.
bankruptcy n bancarrota, quiebra f, Lat Am valencia f.
bank statement n detalle de cuenta m.
banner n bandera f; estandarte m.
banquet n banquete m.
banter n zumba f.
baptism n bautismo m.
baptismal adj bautismal.
baptistery n bautisterio m.
baptize vt bautizar.
bar n bar m; barra f; tranca f; obstáculo m; (law) abogacía f; * vt impedir; prohibir; excluir.
barbarian n bárbaro/ra m/f; * adj bárbaro/ra, cruel.
barbaric adj bárbaro/ra.
barbarism n (gr) barbarismo m; crueldad f.
barbarity n barbaridad, inhumanidad f.
barbarous adj bárbaro/ra, cruel.
barbecue n barbacoa f.
barber n peluquero m.
barber shop n peluquería f.
bar code n código de barras m.
bard n bardo m; poeta m.
bare adj desnudo/da, descubierto/ta; simple; puro/ra; * vt desnudar, descubrir.
barefaced adj desvergonzado/da, impudente.
barefoot(ed) adj descalzo, sin zapatos.
bareheaded adj descubierto/ta.
barelegged adj con las piernas desnudas.
barely adv apenas, solamente.
bareness n desnudez f.
bargain n ganga f; contrato, pacto m; * vi pactar; negociar; **to ~ for** esperar.
barge n barcaza f.
baritone n (mus) barítono m.
bark n corteza f; ladrido m (del perro); * vi ladrar.
barley n cebada f.
barmaid n camarera f.
barman n barman m.
barn n granero, pajar m.
barnacles npl percebe m.
barometer n barómetro m.
baron n barón m.
baroness n baronesa f.
baronial adj de barón.
barracks npl cuartel m.
barrage n descarga f; (fig) lluvia f.
barrel n barril m; cañón de escopeta m.
barrel organ n organillo de cilindro m.
barren adj estéril, infructuoso/sa; (fig) yermo/ma.
barricade n barricada f; estacada f; barrera f; * vt cerrar con barreras, empalizar.

barrier n barrera f; obstáculo m.
barring adv excepto, fuera de.
barrow n carretilla f.
bartender n barman m.
barter vi baratar; * vt cambiar, trocar.
base n fondo m; base f; basa f; pedestal m; zócalo m; * vt apoyar; * adj bajo/ja, vil.
baseball n béisbol m.
base-board n zócalo m.
baseless adj sin fondo/base.
basement n sótano m.
baseness n bajeza, vileza f.
bash vt golpear.
bashful adj vergonzoso/sa, modesto/ta, tímido/da; **~ly** adv vergonzosamente.
basic adj básico/ca; **~ally** adv básicamente.
basilisk n basilisco m.
basin n jofaina, bacía f.
basis n base f; fundamento m.
bask vi ponerse a tomar el sol.
basket n cesta, canasta f.
basketball n baloncesto m, Lat Am básquetbol m.
bass n (mus) contrabajo m.
bassoon n bajón m.
bass viol n viola f.
bass voice n bajo cantante m.
bastard n, adj bastardo/da m/f.
bastardy n bastardía f.
baste vt pringar; hilvanar.
basting n hilván m; apaleamiento m; paliza f.
bastion n (mil) bastión m.
bat n murciélago m.
batch n serie f.
bath n baño m.
bathe vt (vt) bañar(se).
bathing suit n traje de baño m.
bathos n estilo bajo en la poesía m.
bathroom n (cuarto de) baño m.
baths npl piscina f.
bathtub n baño m, bañera f.
baton n batuta f.
battalion n (mil) batallón m.
batter vt apalear; batir, cañonear; * n batido m.
battering ram n (mil) ariete m.
battery n batería f.
battle n combate m; batalla f; * vi batallar, combatir.
battle array n orden de batalla f.
battlefield n campo de batalla m.
battlement n muralla almenada f.
battleship n acorazado m.
bawdy adj indecente.
bawl vi gritar, vocear.
bay n bahía f; laurel, lauro m; * vi balar; * adj bayo.
bayonet n bayoneta f.
bay window n ventana salediza f.
bazaar n bazar m.
be vi ser; estar.

beach n playa, orilla f.
beacon n almenara f.
bead n cuenta f; **~s** npl rosario m.
beagle n sabueso m.
beak n pico m.
beaker n taza con pico f.
beam n rayo de luz m; travesaño m; pareja f; * vi brillar.
bean n alubia f, frijol m, judía f; **green ~, French ~** judía verde f.
beansprouts npl brotes de soja mpl.
bear vt llevar; sostener; soportar; producir; parir; * vi sufrir (algún dolor).
bear n oso m; **she ~** osa f.
bearable adj soportable.
beard n barba f.
bearded adj barbado/da.
bearer n portador/a m/f; árbol fructífero m.
bearing n relación f.
beast n bestia f; hombre brutal m; **~ of burden** acémila f.
beastliness n bestialidad, brutalidad f.
beastly adj bestial, brutal; * adv brutalmente.
beat vt golpear; tocar (un tambor); **to ~ time** (with the sole of the shoe) zapatear; * vi pulsar, palpitar; * n golpe m; pulsación f.
beatific adj beatífico/ca.
beatify vt beatificar, santificar.
beating n paliza, zurra f, Lat Am golpiza f; pulsación f, zumba f.
beatitude n beatitud, felicidad f.
beautiful adj hermoso/sa, bello; **~ly** adv con belleza/perfección.
beautify vt hermosear; embellecer; adornar.
beauty n hermosura, belleza f; **~ salon** n salón de belleza m; **~ spot** n lunar m.
beaver n castor m.
because conj porque, a causa de.
beckon vi hacer seña con la cabeza/la mano.
become vt convenir; estar bien; * vi hacerse, convertirse, venir a parar.
becoming adj decente, conveniente.
bed n cama f.
bedclothes npl cobertores npl, mantas/colchas fpl.
bedding n ropa de cama f.
bedecked adj adornado/da.
bedlam n manicomio m.
bedpost n pilar de cama m.
bedridden adj postrado/da en cama, encamado/da.
bedroom n dormitorio m.
bedspread n colcha f.
bedtime n hora de irse a la cama f.
bee n abeja f.
beech n haya f.
beef n carne de vaca f.
beefburger n hamburguesa f.
beefsteak n bistec m.
beehive n colmena f.

beeline n línea recta f.
beer n cerveza f.
beeswax n cera f.
beet n remolacha f.
beetle n escarabajo m.
befall vi suceder, acontecer, sobrevenir.
befit vt convenir, acomodarse a.
before adv, prep antes de; delante, enfrente; ante.
beforehand adv de antemano, anticipadamente.
befriend vt proteger, amparar.
beg vt mendigar, rogar; suplicar; suponer; * vi vivir de limosna.
beget vt engendrar.
beggar n mendigo/ga m/f.
begin vt, vi comenzar, empezar.
beginner n principiante m; novicio/cia m/f.
beginning n principio, origen m.
begrudge vt envidiar.
behalf n on **~ of** de parte de.
behave vi comportarse, portarse, conducirse.
behavior n conducta f; modo de portarse m.
behead vt decapitar, cortar la cabeza.
behind prep detrás; atrás; a la, en zaga; * adv atrasadamente.
behold vt ver, contemplar, observar.
behoove vi importar, ser útil; incumbir.
beige adj color beige.
being n existencia f; estado m; ser m.
belated adj atrasado/da.
belch vi eructar, vomitar; * n eructo m.
belfry n campanario m.
belie vt desmentir, calumniar.
belief n fe, creencia f; opinión f; credo m.
believable adj creíble.
believe vt creer; * vi pensar, imaginar.
believer n creyente, fiel, cristiano/na m/f.
belittle vt minimizar.
bell n campana f.
bellicose adj belicoso/sa.
belligerent adj beligerante.
bellow vi bramar; rugir; vociferar; * n bramido m.
bellows npl fuelle m.
belly n vientre m; panza f.
bellyful n panzada f; hartura f.
belong vi pertenecer.
belongings npl pertenencias fpl.
beloved adj querido/da, amado/da.
below adv, prep debajo, inferior; abajo.
belt n cinturón, cinto m; zona f.
beltway n periférico m; carretera de circunvalación f.
bemoan vt deplorar, lamentar.
bemused adj confundido/da.
bench n banco m, banquillo m.
bend vt encorvar, inclinar, plegar; hacer una reverencia; * vi encorvarse, inclinarse; * n curva f.
beneath adv, prep debajo, abajo.
benediction n bendición f.

B

benefactor n bienhechor m.
benefice n beneficio m; beneficio eclesiástico m.
beneficent adj benéfico/ca.
beneficial adj beneficioso/sa, provechoso/sa, útil.
beneficiary n beneficiario/ria m.
benefit n beneficio m; utilidad f; provecho m; * vt beneficiar; * vi utilizarse; prevalerse.
benefit night n representación dramática a beneficio de un actor/de una actriz f.
benevolence n benevolencia f; donativo gratuito m.
benevolent adj benévolo/la.
benign adj benigno/na; afable; liberal.
bent n inclinación f.
benzene n (chem) bencina f.
bequeath vt legar en testamento.
bequest n legado m.
bereave vt privar.
bereavement n pérdida f.
beret n boina f.
berm n arcén m.
berry n baya f.
berserk adj loco/ca.
berth n (mar) amarradero m, camarote m.
beseech vt suplicar, implorar, conjurar, rogar.
beset vt acosar.
beside(s) prep al lado de; excepto; sobre; fuera de; * adv por otra parte.
besiege vt sitiar, bloquear.
best adj mejor; * adv (lo) mejor; * n lo mejor m.
bestial adj bestial, brutal; ~**ly** adv bestialmente.
bestiality n bestialidad, brutalidad f.
bestow vt dar, conferir; otorgar.
bestseller n bestseller m.
bet n apuesta f; * vt apostar.
betray vt traicionar; divulgar algún secreto.
betrayal n traición f.
betroth vt contraer esponsales.
betrothal n esponsales mpl.
better adj, adv mejor; **so much the ~** tanto mejor; * vt mejorar, reformar.
betting n juego m.
between prep entre, en medio de.
bevel n cartabón m.
beverage n bebida f; trago m.
bevy n bandada (de aves) f.
beware vi guardarse.
bewilder vt pasmar.
bewilderment n perplejidad f.
bewitch vt encantar, hechizar.
beyond prep más allá, más adelante, fuera de.
bias n propensión, inclinación f; sesgo m; prejuicio m.
bib n babador m.
Bible n Biblia f.
biblical adj bíblico/ca.
bibliography n bibliografía f.
bicarbonate of soda n bicarbonato de soda m.
bicker vi escaramucear, reñir, disputar.

bicycle n bicicleta f.
bid vt mandar, ordenar; ofrecer; * n oferta f; tentativa f.
bidding n orden f; mandato m; ofrecimiento m.
bide vt sufrir, aguantar.
biennial adj bienal.
bifocals npl gafas bifocales fpl.
bifurcated adj bifurcado/da.
big adj grande, lleno/na; inflado/da.
bigamist n bígamo/ma m/f.
bigamy n bigamia f.
big dipper n montaña rusa f.
bigheaded adj engreído/da.
bigness n grandeza f.
bigot n fanático/ca m/f.
bigoted adj fanático/ca.
bike n bici f; bicicleta f; **mountain ~** bicicleta de montaña.
bikini n bikini m.
bilberry n arándano m.
bile n bilis f.
bilingual adj bilingüe.
bilious adj bilioso/sa.
bill n pico de ave m; billete m; cuenta f.
billboard n cartelera f.
billet n alojamiento m.
billfold n cartera f.
billiards npl billar m.
billiard-table n mesa de billar f.
billion n mil millones mpl, millardo m.
billy n porra f.
bin n cubo de la basura m.
bind vt atar; unir; encuadernar.
binder n encuadernador/a m/f.
binding n venda, faja f.
binge n juerga f.
bingo n bingo m.
biochemistry n bioquímica f.
biodegradable adj biodegradable.
biodiversity n biodiversity f.
binoculars npl prismáticos mpl, Lat Am binóculos mpl.
biographer n biógrafo/fa m/f.
biographical adj biográfico/ca.
biography n biografía f.
biological adj biológico/ca.
biology n biología f.
biped n bípedo m.
birch n abedul m.
bird n ave f; pájaro m.
bird's-eye view n vista de pájaro f.
bird-watcher n ornitólogo/ga m/f.
birth n nacimiento m; origen m; parto m.
birth certificate n partida de nacimiento f.
birth control n control de natalidad m.
birthday n cumpleaños m invar, Lat Am onomástica f.
birthplace n lugar de nacimiento m.

birthright n derechos de nacimiento mpl; primogenitura f.

biscuit n bizcocho m.

bisect vt bisecar.

bishop n obispo m.

bison n bisonte m.

bit n bocado m; pedacito m.

bitch n perra f; (fig) zorra f.

bite vt morder; picar; ~ **the dust** (col) morder la tierra, morir; * n mordedura f.

bitter adj amargo/ga, áspero/ra; mordaz, satírico/ca; penoso/sa; ~**ly** adv amargamente; con pena; severamente.

bitterness n amargor m; rencor m; pena f; dolor m.

bitumen n betún m.

bizarre adj raro/ra, extravagante.

blab vi chismear.

black adj negro/gra, oscuro/ra; funesto/ta; * n color negro m.

blackberry n zarzamora f.

blackbird n mirlo m.

black box n caja negra f.

blacken vt teñir de negro; ennegrecer.

black ice n hielo invisible m.

blackjack n veintiuna f.

blackleg n esquirol m.

blacklist n lista negra f.

blackmail n chantaje m; * vt chantajear.

black market n mercado negro m.

blackness n negrura f.

black pudding n morcilla f.

black sheep n oveja negra f.

blacksmith n herrero m.

blackthorn n endrino m.

bladder n vejiga f.

blade n hoja f; filo m; escobilla f.

blame vt culpar; * n culpa f.

blameless adj inocente, irreprensible, puro/ra; ~**ly** adv inocentemente.

blanch vt blanquear.

bland adj blando/da, suave, dulce, apacible.

blank adj blanco/ca; pálido/da; * n blanco m.

blank check n cheque en blanco m.

blanket n manta f, Lat Am cobija f, Lat Am frazada f.

blare vi resonar.

blasé adj indiferente.

blaspheme vt blasfemar, jurar, decir blasfemias.

blasphemous adj blasfemo/ma.

blasphemy n blasfemia f.

blast n soplo de aire m; carga explosiva f; * vt volar.

blast-off n lanzamiento m.

blatant adj obvio.

blaze n llama f; * vi encenderse en llamas; brillar, resplandecer.

bleach vt blanquear al sol; * vi blanquear; * n lejía f.

bleached adj teñido/da de rubio; descolorado/da.

bleachers npl gradas al sol fpl.

bleak adj pálido/da, descolorido/da; frío, helado/da.

bleakness n frialdad f; palidez f.

bleary(-eyed) adj legañoso/sa.

bleat n balido m; * vi balar.

bleed vi, vt sangrar.

bleeding n sangría f.

bleeper n busca m.

blemish vt manchar, ensuciar; infamar; * n tacha f; deshonra, infamia f.

blend vt mezclar.

bless vt bendecir.

blessing n bendición f; beneficio m; ventaja f.

blight vt arruinar.

blind adj ciego/ga; ~ **alley** n callejón sin salida m; * vt cegar; deslumbrar; * n velo m; (**Venetian**) ~ persiana f.

blinders npl anteojeras fpl.

blindfold vt vendar los ojos; ~**ed** adj con los ojos vendados.

blindly adv ciegamente, a ciegas.

blindness n ceguera f.

blind side n punto ciego m.

blind spot n punto ciego m.

blink vi parpadear.

blinkers npl anteojeras fpl.

bliss n felicidad (eterna) f.

blissful adj feliz en sumo grado; beato/ta, bienaventurado/da; ~**ly** adv felizmente.

blissfulness n suprema felicidad f.

blister n ampolla f; * vi ampollarse.

blitz n bombardeo aéreo m.

blizzard n ventisca f.

bloated adj hinchado/da.

blob n gota f.

bloc n bloque m.

block n bloque m; obstáculo m; zoquete m; manzana f, Lat Am cuadra f; ~ (**up**) vt bloquear.

blockade n bloqueo m; * vt bloquear.

blockage n obstrucción f.

blockbuster n éxito de público m.

blockhead n bruto, necio, zopenco m; (col) zoquete m.

blond adj rubio/bia; * n rubio/bia m/f.

blood n sangre f.

blood donor n donante de sangre m/f.

blood group n grupo sanguíneo m.

bloodhound n sabueso m.

bloodily adv sangrientamente, inhumanamente.

bloodiness n (fig) crueldad f.

bloodless adj exangüe; sin efusión de sangre.

blood poisoning n septicemia f.

blood pressure n presión sanguínea f.

blood sausage n morcilla f.

bloodshed n efusión de sangre f; matanza f, derramamiento de sangre m.

bloodshot adj ensangrentado/da.

bloodstream n corriente sanguínea f.

bloodsucker n sanguijuela f; (fig) desollador/a m/f.

blood test n análisis de sangre m invar.

bloodthirsty adj sanguinario/ria.
blood transfusion n transfusión sanguínea f.
blood vessel n vena f; vaso sanguíneo m.
bloody adj sangriento/ta, ensangrentado/da; cruel; ~ **minded** adj sanguinario/ria.
bloom n flor f; (also fig); * vi florecer.
blossom n flor f.
blot vt manchar (lo escrito); cancelar; denigrar; * n mancha f.
blotchy adj muy manchado/da.
blotting paper n papel secante m.
blouse n blusa f.
blow vi soplar; sonar; * vt soplar; inflar; **to** ~ **up** volar; * n golpe m.
blowout n pinchazo m.
blowpipe n soplete m.
blubber n grasa de ballena f; * vi lloriquear.
bludgeon n cachiporra f; palocorto m.
blue adj azul.
bluebell, harebell n (bot) campanilla f.
blue berets npl cascos azules mpl.
bluebottle n moscarda f.
blueness n color azul m.
blueprint n (fig) anteproyecto m.
bluff n farol m; * vt farolear.
bluish adj azulado/da.
blunder n metedura de pata f; error craso m; * vi meter la pata.
blunt adj obtuso/sa; grosero/ra; * vt embotar.
bluntly adv sin artificio; claramente; obtusamente.
bluntness n embotadura, franqueza f.
blur n contorno borroso m; * vt hacer borroso.
blurt out vt descolgarse con.
blush n rubor m; sonrojo m; * vi ponerse colorado/da, sonrojarse.
blustery adj tempestuoso/sa.
boa n boa f (serpiente).
boar n verraco m; **wild** ~ jabalí m.
board n tabla f; mesa f; consejo m; * vt embarcarse en; subir a.
boarder n pensionista m/f.
boarding card n tarjeta de embarque f.
boarding house n pensión f, casa de huéspedes f.
boarding school n internado m.
boast vi jactarse; * n jactancia f; ostentación f.
boastful adj jactancioso/sa.
boat n barco m; bote m; barca f.
boating n canotaje m; paseo en barquilla m; regata f.
bobsleigh n bob m.
bode vt presagiar, pronosticar.
bodice n corsé m.
bodily adj, adv corpóreo/rea; corporalmente.
body n cuerpo m; individuo m; gremio m; **any** ~ cualquier; **every** ~ cada uno.
body-building n culturismo m.
bodyguard n guardaespaldas m/f invar.
bodywork n (auto) carrocería f.

bog n pantano m.
boggy adj pantanoso/sa, palustre.
bogus adj postizo.
boil vi hervir; bullir; hervirle a uno la sangre; * vt cocer; * n furúnculo m.
boiled egg n huevo duro m, huevo pasado por agua m.
boiled potatoes npl patatas hervidas fpl.
boiler n marmita f; caldero m.
boiling point n punto de ebullición m.
boisterous adj borrascoso/sa, tempestuoso/sa; violento/ta; ~ly adv tumultuosamente, furiosamente.
bold adj ardiente, valiente; audaz; temerario/ria; impudente; ~ly adv descaradamente.
boldness n intrepidez f; valentía f; osadía f.
bolster n travesero m; cabezal m; * vt reforzar.
bolt n cerrojo m; * vt cerrar con cerrojo.
bomb n bomba f; ~ **disposal** desactivación de explosivos f.
bombard vt bombardear.
bombardier n bombardero m.
bombardment n bombardeo m.
bombshell n (fig) bomba f.
bond n ligadura f; vínculo m; vale m; obligación f.
bondage n esclavitud, servidumbre f.
bond holder n titular de bonos m/f.
bone n hueso m; * vt desosar.
boneless adj sin huesos; desosado/da.
bonfire n hoguera f.
bonnet n gorra f; bonete m.
bonny adj bonito/ta.
bonsai n bonsái m.
bonus n cuota, prima f.
bony adj osudo/da.
boo vt abuchear.
booby trap n trampa explosiva f.
book n libro m; **to bring to** ~ vt pedir cuentas a alguien.
bookbinder n encuadernador/a m/f.
bookcase n estantería f.
bookkeeper n tenedor/a de libros m/f.
bookkeeping n teneduría de libros f.
bookmaker n corredor de apuestas m.
bookmarker n registro de un libro m.
bookseller n librero/ra m/f.
bookstore n librería f.
bookworm n polilla f; ratón de biblioteca m.
boom n trueno m; boom m; * vi retumbar.
boon n presente, regalo m; favor m.
boor n patán, villano/na m/f.
boorish adj rústico/ca, agreste.
boost n estímulo m; vt estimular.
booster n reinyección f.
boot n bota f; zapata f; **to** ~ adv además.
booth n barraca, cabaña f.
booty n botín m; presa f; saqueo m.
booze vi emborracharse; * n bebida f.

border n orilla f; borde m; margen f; frontera f;
   * vt lindar con.
borderline n frontera f.
bore vt taladrar; barrenar; fastidiar; * n taladro
   m; calibre m; pelmazo/za *m/f.*
boredom n aburrimiento m.
borehole n barreno m.
boring adj aburrido/da, Lat Am aburridor/ra.
born adj nacido/da; destinado/da.
borrow vt pedir prestado/da.
borrower n prestamista m.
bosom n seno, pecho m.
bosom friend n amigo/ga íntimo/ma m/f.
boss n jefe m; patrón/ona m/f.
botanic(al) adj botánico/ca.
botanist n botánico m.
botany n botánica f.
botch vt chapuzar.
botch-up n mamarracho m.
both adj ambos, entrambos; ambas, entrambas;
   * conj tanto como.
bother vt preocupar; fastidiar; * n molestia f.
bottle n botella f; * vt embotellar.
bottleneck n embotellamiento m.
bottle-opener n abrebotellas m invar.
bottom n fondo m; fundamento m; * adj más
   bajo/ja; último/ma.
bottomless adj insondable; excesivo/va;
   impenetrable.
bough n brazo del árbol m; ramo m.
boulder n canto rodado m.
bounce vi rebotar; ser rechazado/da; * n rebote m.
bound n límite m; salto m; repercusión f; * vi
   resaltar; * adj destinado/da.
boundary n límite m; frontera f.
boundless adj ilimitado/da, infinito/ta.
bounteous, bountiful adj liberal, generoso/sa,
   bienhechor.
bounty n liberalidad, bondad f.
bouquet n ramillete de flores m.
bourgeois adj burgués/esa.
bout n ataque m; encuentro m.
bovine adj bovino/na.
bow[1] vt encorvar, doblar; * vi encorvarse; hacer
   una reverencia; * n reverencia, inclinación f.
bow[2] n arco m; arco de violín; corbata f; Lat Am
   bow m; nudo m.
bowels npl intestinos mpl; entrañas fpl.
bowl n taza; bola f; * vi jugar a las bochas.
bowling n bolos mpl.
bowling alley n bolera f.
bowling-green n campo m para jugar a las bochas.
bowstring n cuerda del arco f.
bow tie n pajarita f.
box n caja, cajita f; palco de teatro m; ~ **on the
   ear** bofetada f; * vt encajonar; * vi boxear.
boxer n boxeador m.
boxing n boxeo m, Lat Am box m.

boxing gloves npl guantes de boxeo mpl.
boxing ring n cuadrilátero m.
box office n taquilla f.
box-seat n asiento de palco m.
boy n muchacho m; niño m; zagal m.
boycott vt boicotear; * n boicot m.
boyfriend n novio m.
boyish adj pueril; frívolo.
bra n sujetador m.
brace n abrazadera f; corrector m.
bracelet n brazalete m.
bracing adj vigorizante.
bracken n (bot) helecho m.
bracket n puntal m; paréntesis m; corchete m;
   * **to ~ with** vt unir, ligar.
bracing adj vigorizante.
brag n jactancia f; * vi jactarse, fanfarronear.
braid n trenza f; * vt trenzar.
brain n cerebro m; seso, juicio m; * vt descerebrar,
   matar a uno.
brainchild n parto del ingenio m.
brainwash vt lavar el cerebro.
brainwave n idea luminosa f.
brainy adj inteligente.
brainless adj tonto/ta, insensato/ta.
brake n freno m; * vt, vi frenar.
brake fluid n líquido de frenos m.
brake light n luz de frenado f.
brake shoe n (auto) zapata de freno f.
bramble n zarza, espina f.
bramble patch n zarzal m.
bran n salvado m.
branch n ramo m; rama f; * vt (vi) ramificar(se).
branch line n (rail) empalme, ramal m.
brand n marca f; hierro m; * vt marcar (con un
   hierro incandescente).
brandish vt blandir, ondear.
brand-new adj flamante.
brandy n coñac m.
brash adj tosco/ca; descarado/da.
brass n bronce m.
brassiere n sujetador m.
brat n crío m.
bravado n baladronada f.
brave adj bravo/va, valiente, atrevido/da; * vt
   desafiar; * n bravo m; ~**ly** adv bravamente.
bravery n valor m; magnificencia f.
brawl n pelea, camorra f; * vi pelearse.
brawn n fuerza muscular f; carne de verraco m.
bray vi rebuznar; * n rebuzno (del asno) m.
braze vt soldar con latón; broncear.
brazen adj de latón; desvergonzado/da; impudente;
   * vi hacerse descarado/da.
brazier n brasero m.
breach n rotura f; brecha f; violación f.
bread n pan m; (fig) sustento m; **brown ~** pan
   moreno m.
breadbox n panera f.

B

breadcrumbs npl migajas fpl.
breadth n anchura f.
breadwinner n sostén de la familia m.
break vt romper; quebrantar; violar; arruinar; interrumpir; * vi romperse; **to ~ into** forzar; **to ~ out** abrirse salida; * n rotura, abertura f; interrupción f; **~ of day** despuntar del día m, aurora f.
breakage n rotura f.
breakdown n avería f; descalabro m.
breakfast n desayuno m; * vi desayunar.
breaking n rompimiento m; principio de las vacaciones en las escuelas m; fractura f.
breakthrough n avance m.
breakwater n rompeolas m invar.
breast n pecho, seno m; pechuga fcorazón m.
breastbone n esternón m.
breastplate n peto m; pectoral m; coraza f.
breaststroke n braza f, Lat Am pecho m.
breath n aliento m, respiración f; soplo de aire m.
breathe vt, vi respirar; exhalar.
breathing n respiración f; aliento m.
breathing space n descanso, reposo m.
breathless adj falto/ta de aliento; desalentado/da.
breathtaking adj pasmoso/sa.
breed n casta, raza f; * vt procrear, engendrar; producir; educar; * vi multiplicarse.
breeder n criador/a m/f.
breeding n crianza f; buena educación f.
breeze n brisa f.
breezy adj refrescado/da con brisas.
brethren n pl de **brother** hermanos mpl (en estilo grave).
breviary n breviario m.
brevity n brevedad, concisión f.
brew vt hacer; tramar, mezclar; * vi hacerse; tramarse; * n brebaje m.
brewer n cervecero m.
brewery n cervecería f.
briar, brier n zarza f, espino m.
bribe n cohecho, soborno m; * vt cohechar, corromper, sobornar.
bribery n cohecho, soborno m.
bric-a-brac n baratijas fpl.
brick n ladrillo m; * vt enladrillar.
bricklayer n albañil m.
bricklaying n albañilería f.
bridal adj nupcial.
bride n novia f.
bridegroom n novio m.
bridesmaid n madrina de boda f.
bridge n puente m/f; caballete de la nariz m; puente de violín m; **to build a ~ (over)** vt construir un puente (sobre).
bridle n brida f freno m; * vt embridar; reprimir, refrenar.
brief adj breve, conciso/sa, sucinto/ta; * n compendio m; breve m.

briefcase n cartera f.
briefly adv brevemente, en pocas palabras.
brier n = **briar**.
brigade n (mil) brigada f.
brigadier n (mil) general de brigada m.
brigand n bandido m.
bright adj claro/ra, luciente, brillante; **~ly** adv espléndidamente.
brighten vt pulir, dar lustre; ilustrar; * vi aclararse.
brightness n esplendor m, brillantez f; agudeza f; claridad f.
brilliance n brillo m.
brilliant adj brillante; **~ly** adv espléndidamente.
brim n borde extremo m; orilla f.
brimful(l) adj lleno/na hasta el borde.
bring vt llevar, traer; conducir; inducir, persuadir; **to ~ about** efectuar; **to ~ forth** producir; parir; **to ~ up** educar.
brink n orilla f; margen m/f, borde m.
brisk adj vivo/va, alegre, jovial; fresco/ca.
brisket n pecho (de un animal) m.
briskly adj vigorosamente; alegremente; vivamente.
bristle n cerda, seta f; * vi erizarse.
bristly adj cerdoso/sa, lleno/na de cerdas.
brittle adj quebradizo, frágil.
broach vt comenzar a hablar de.
broad adj ancho.
broad bean n (bot) haba f; **~s** haba gruesa fpl.
broadcast n emisión f; * vt, vi emitir; transmitir.
broadcasting n radiodifusión f.
broaden vt, vi ensanchar(se).
broadly adv anchamente.
broad-minded adj tolerante.
broadness n ancho m; anchura f.
broadside n costado de navío m; andanada f.
broadways adv a lo ancho, por lo ancho.
brocade n brocado m.
broccoli n brécol m.
brochure n folleto m.
brogue n abarca f; acento irlandés m.
broil vt asar a la parrilla.
broken adj roto/ta, interrumpido/da; **~ English** inglés mal articulado m.
broker n corredor/a m/f.
brokerage n corretaje m.
bronchial adj bronquial.
bronchitis n bronquitis f.
bronze n bronce m; * vt broncear.
brooch n broche m.
brood vi empollar; meditar; * n raza f; nidada f.
brood-hen n empolladora f.
brook n arroyo m.
broom n retama f; escoba f.
broomstick n palo de escoba m.
broth n caldo m.
brothel n burdel m.
brother n hermano m.
brotherhood n hermandad f; fraternidad f.

brother-in-law n cuñado m.
brotherly adj, adv fraternal; fraternalmente.
brow n caja f; frente f; cima f.
browbeat vt intimidar.
brown adj moreno/na; castaño/ña; ~ **paper** n papel de estraza m; ~ **bread** n pan moreno m; ~ **sugar** n azúcar terciado m; * n color moreno m; * vt volver moreno/na.
browse vt ramonear; * vi pacer la hierba.
browser n navegador m.
bruise vt magullar; * n magulladura, Lat Am magullón m, contusión f; roncha f.
brunch n desayuno-almuerzo m.
brunette n morena f.
brunt n choque m.
brush n cepillo m; escobilla f; combate m; * vt cepillar, Lat Am escobillar.
brushwood n breñal, zarzal m.
brusque adj brusco/ca.
Brussels sprout n col de Bruselas f.
brutal adj brutal; ~**ly** adv brutalmente.
brutality n brutalidad f.
brutalize vt (vi) embrutecer(se).
brute n bruto m; * adj feroz, bestial; irracional.
brutish adj brutal, bestial; feroz; ~**ly** adv brutalmente.
bubble n burbuja f; * vi burbujear, bullir.
bubblegum n chicle m.
bucket n cubo, pozal m.
buckle n hebilla f; * vt hebillar; abrochar; * vi encorvarse.
buckshot n perdigones mpl.
bucolic adj bucólico/ca.
bud n pimpollo, botón, capullo m; yema f; * vi brotar.
Buddhism n Budismo m.
budding adj en ciernes.
buddy n compañero m.
budge vi moverse, menearse.
budgerigar n periquito m.
budget n presupuesto m.
buff n entusiasta m.
buffalo n búfalo m.
buffers npl (rail) parachoques m invar, topes mpl.
buffet n buffet m; * vt abofetear.
buffoon n bufón, chocarrero m.
bug n chinche m.
bugbear n espantajo, coco m.
bugle(horn) n trompa de caza f.
build vt edificar; construir.
builder n constructor/a m/f; maestro/tra de obras m/f.
building n edificio m, Lat Am predio m; construcción f.
bulb n bulbo m; cebolla f.
bulbous adj bulboso/sa.
bulge vi combarse; * n bombeo m.
bulk n masa f; volumen m; grosura f; mayor parte f; capacidad de un buque f; **in** ~ a granel.
bulky adj grueso/sa, grande.

bull n toro m.
bulldog n dogo m.
bulldozer n aplanadora f.
bullet n bala f.
bulletin board n tablón de anuncios m.
bulletproof adj a prueba de balas.
bullfight n corrida de toros f.
bullfighter n torero m.
bullfighting n toreo m.
bullion n oro/plata en barras m/f.
bullock n novillo capado m.
bullring n plaza de toros f.
bull's-eye n centro del blanco m.
bully n valentón m; * vt tiranizar.
bulwark n baluarte m.
bum n vagabundo/da m/f.
bumblebee n abejorro, zángano m.
bump n hinchazón f; jiba f; bollo m; barriga f; * vt chocar contra.
bumpkin n patán m; villano/na m/f.
bumpy adj bacheado/da.
bun n bollo m; mono m.
bunch n ramo m; grupo m.
bundle n fardo m, haz m (de leña etc); paquete m; rollo m; * vt atar, hacer un lío.
bung n tapón m; * vt atarugar.
bungalow n bungalow m.
bungee-jumping n puenting m.
bungle vt chapucear; * vi hacer algo chabacanamente.
bunion n juanete m.
bunk n litera f.
bunker n refugio m; búnker m.
buoy n (mar) boya f.
buoyancy n capacidad para flotar f.
buoyant adj boyante.
burden n carga f; * vt cargar.
bureau n armario m; escritorio m.
bureaucracy n burocracia f.
bureaucrat n burócrata m/f.
burglar n ladrón/ona m/f.
burglar alarm n alarma antirrobo f.
burglary n robo en una casa m.
burial n enterramiento m; exequias fpl; sepultura f.
burial place n cementerio m.
burlesque n, adj lengua burlesca f; burlesco/ca m/f.
burly adj fornido/da.
burn vt quemar, abrasar, incendiar; * vi arder; * n quema dura f.
burner n quemador m; mechero m.
burning adj ardiente.
burrow n madriguera f; * vi esconderse en la madriguera.
bursar n tesorero/ra m/f.
burse n bolsa, lonja f.
burst vi reventar; abrirse; **to** ~ **into tears** prorrumpir en lágrimas; **to** ~ **out laughing** estallarse de risa; * vt **to** ~ **into** irrumpir en; * n reventón m; rebosadura f.

bury vt enterrar, sepultar; esconder.
bus n autobús m.
bush n arbusto, espinal m; cola de zorro f.
bushy adj espeso/sa, lleno/na de arbustos.
busily adv diligentemente, apresuradamente.
business n asunto m; negocios mpl; empleo m; ocupación f.
businesslike adj serio/ria.
businessman n hombre de negocios m.
business trip n viaje de negocios m.
businesswoman n mujer de negocios f.
bus lane n carril bus m.
bust n busto m.
bus stop n parada de autobuses f.
bustle vi hacer ruido; menearse; andar al retortero; * n baraúnda f; ruido m.
bustling adj animado/da.
busy adj ocupado/da; entrometido/da.
busybody n entrometido m.
but conj pero; mas; excepto, menos; solamente.
butcher n carnicero/ra m/f; * vt matar atrozmente.
butcher's (**shop/store**) n carnicería f.
butchery n matadero m.
butler n mayordomo m.
butt n colilla f; cabo, extremo m; * vt topar.
butter n mantequilla f; * vt untar con mantequilla.

buttercup n (bot) ranúnculo m.
butterfly n mariposa f.
buttermilk n suero de manteca m.
buttocks npl posaderas fpl.
button n botón m; * vt abotonar.
buttonhole n ojal m.
buttress n estribo m; apoyo m; * vt estribar.
buxom adj frescachona, rolliza.
buy vt comprar.
buyer n comprador/a m/f.
buzz, buzzing n susurro, zumbido m; * vi zumbar.
buzzard n ratonero m común.
buzzer n timbre m.
by prep por; a, en; de; cerca, al lado de; ~ **and** ~ de aquí a poco, ahora; ~ **the** ~ de paso; ~ **much** con mucho; ~ **all means** por supuesto.
bygone adj pasado/da.
by-law n ordenanza municipal f.
bypass n carretera de circunvalación f.
by-product n derivado m.
by-road n camino secundario m.
bystander n mirador m.
byte n (comput) byte m.
byword n proverbio, refrán m.

C

cab n taxi m.
cabbage n berza, col f.
cabin n cabaña, cámara de navío f.
cabinet n consejo de ministros m; gabinete m; escritorio m.
cabinet-maker n ebanista m.
cable n cable m.
cable car n teleférico m.
cable television n televisión por cable f.
caboose n (mar) cocina f.
cache n alijo m.
cackle vi cacarear, graznar; * n cacareo m; charla f.
cactus n cacto m, cactus m invar.
cadence n (mus) cadencia f.
cadet n cadete m.
cadge vt mangar.
café n café m.
cafeteria n café m.
caffeine n cafeína f.
cage n jaula f; prisión f; * vt enjaular.
cagey adj cauteloso/sa.
cajole vt lisonjear, adular; sonsacar.
cake n bollo m; tortita f.
calamitous adj calamitoso/sa.
calamity n calamidad, miseria f.
calculable adj calculable.
calculate vt calcular, contar.
calculation n cálculo m.
calculator n calculadora f.
calculus n cálculo m.
calendar n calendario m.
calf n ternero m; ternera f; carne de ternero f.
caliber n calibre m.
calisthenics n calistenia f.
call vt llamar, nombrar; llamar por teléfono; convocar, citar; apelar; to ~ for preguntar por, ir a buscar; to ~ on visitar; to ~ attention llamar la atención; to ~ names insultar; * n llamada f, Lat Am llamado m; instancia f; invitación f; urgencia f; vocación f; profesión f.
caller n visitador/a m/f.
calligraphy n caligrafía f.
calling n profesión, vocación f.
callous adj calloso/sa, endurecido/da; insensible.
calm n calma, tranquilidad f; * adj quieto/ta, tranquilo/la; * vt calmar; aplacar, aquietar; ~ly adv tranquilamente.
calmness n tranquilidad, calma f.
calorie n caloría f.
calumny n calumnia f.
Calvary n calvario m.
calve vi parir.

Calvinist n calvinista m/f.
camcorder n videocámara f.
camel n camello m.
cameo n camafeo m.
camera n máquina fotográfica f; cámara f.
cameraman n cámara m.
chamomile n manzanilla f.
camouflage n camuflaje m.
camp n campo m; * vi acampar; refugee ~ campo de refugiados.
campaign n campana f; run-up-to-the-election ~ precampaña f; * vi hacer campana.
campaigner n defensor/a m/f.
camper n campista m/f.
camping n camping m.
camphor n alcanfor m.
campsite n camping m.
campus n ciudad universitaria f, campus m invar.
can vi poder; * n lata f.
canal n estanque m; canal m.
cancel vt cancelar; anular, invalidar.
cancellation n cancelación f.
cancer n cáncer m.
Cancer n Cáncer m (signo del zodiaco).
cancerous adj canceroso/sa.
candid adj cándido/da, sencillo/lla, sincero/ra; ~ly adv cándidamente, francamente.
candidate n candidato/ta m/f, Lat Am postulante m/f.
candied adj azucarado/da.
candle n candela f; vela f.
candlelight n luz de candela f.
candlestick n candelero m.
candor n candor m; sinceridad f.
candy n confitería f.
cane n cana f; bastón m.
canine adj canino/na, perruno/na.
canister n bote m.
cannabis n cannabis m.
cannibal n caníbal m/f; antropófago/ga m/f.
cannibalism n canibalismo m.
cannon n cañón m.
cannonball n bala de artillería f.
canny adj cuerdo/da, discreto/ta.
canoe n canoa f.
canon n canon m; regla f; ~law derecho canónico m.
canonization n canonización f.
canonize vt canonizar.
can opener n abrelatas m invar.
canopy n dosel, pabellón m.
cantankerous adj áspero/ra, fastidioso/sa.
canteen n cantina f.
canter n medio galope m.

canvas n cañamazo m.

canvass vt escudriñar, examinar; controvertir; * vi solicitar votos; pretender.

canvasser n solicitador/a m/f.

canyon n cañón m.

canyoning n barranquismo m.

cap n gorra f.

capability n capacidad, aptitud, inteligencia f.

capable adj capaz.

capacitate vt hacer capaz.

capacity n capacidad f; inteligencia, habilidad f.

cape n cabo, promontorio m.

caper n cabriola f; alcaparra f; * vi hacer cabriolas.

capillary adj capilar.

capital adj capital; principal; * n capital f (la ciudad principal); capital, fondo m; mayúscula f.

capitalism n capitalismo m.

capitalist n capitalista m.

capitalize vt capitalizar; **to ~ on** aprovechar.

capital punishment n pena de muerte f.

Capitol n Capitolio m.

capitulate vi capitular.

capitulation n capitulación f.

caprice n capricho m; extravagancia f.

capricious adj caprichoso/sa; **~ly** adv caprichosamente.

Capricorn n Capricornio m (signo del zodiaco).

capsize vt (mar) volcar, zozobrar.

capsizing n (mar) zozobra f.

capsule n cápsula f.

captain n capitán/ana m/f.

captaincy, captainship n capitanía f.

captivate vt cautivar.

captivation n atractivo m.

captive n cautivo/va, esclavo/va m/f.

captivity n cautividad, esclavitud f, cautiverio m.

capture n captura f; presa f; * vt apresar, capturar.

car n coche, carro m; vagón m.

carafe n garrafa f.

caramel n caramelo m.

carat n quilate m.

caravan n caravana f.

caraway n (bot) alcaravea f.

carbohydrates npl hidratos de carbono mpl.

car bomb n coche bomba m.

carbon n carbono m, carbón m.

carbon copy n copia al carbón f.

carbonize vt carbonizar.

carbon paper n papel carbón m.

carbuncle n carbúnculo, rubí m; carbunco, tumor maligno m.

carburetor n carburador m.

carcass n cadáver m.

carcinogenic adj cancerígeno/na.

card n naipe m; carta f; **pack of ~s** baraja f.

cardboard n cartón m.

card game n juego de naipes m.

cardiac adj cardíaco/ca, cardiaco/ca.

cardinal adj cardinal, principal; * n cardenal m.

card table n mesa para jugar f.

care n cuidado m; solicitud f; * vi cuidar, tener cuidado/pena, inquietarse; **what do I ~?** ¿a mí que me importa?; **to ~ for** vt cuidar a; querer.

career n carrera f; curso m; * vi correr a carrera tendida.

carefree n despreocupado/da.

careful adj cuidadoso/sa, diligente, prudente; **~ly** adv cuidadosamente.

careless adj descuidado/da, negligente; indolente; **~ly** adv descuidadamente.

carelessness n negligencia, indiferencia f.

caress n caricia f; * vt acariciar, halagar.

caretaker n portero m, conserje m/f.

car-ferry n transbordador para coches m.

cargo n cargamento m.

car hire n alquiler de coches m.

caribou n reno m.

caricature n caricatura f, Lat Am caricato m; * vt hacer caricaturas, ridiculizar.

caries n caries f.

caring adj humanitario/ria.

Carmelite n carmelita m.

carnage n carnicería, matanza f.

carnal adj carnal; sensual; **~ly** adv carnalmente.

carnation n clavel m.

carnival n carnaval m.

carnivorous adj carnívoro/ra.

carol n villancico m, canción de alegría/piedad f.

carpenter n carpintero m; **~'s bench** banco de carpintero m.

carpentry n carpintería f.

carpet n alfombra f, Lat Am tapete m; * vt cubrir con alfombras.

carpeting n alfombrado m.

car radio n autorradio m.

carriage n porte m; coche m; vehículo m.

carriage-free adj franco de porte.

carrier n portador, carretero m.

carrier pigeon n paloma correo/mensajera f.

carrion n carroña f.

carrot n zanahoria f.

carry vt llevar, conducir; **to ~ out** ejecutar; * vi oírse; **to ~ the day** quedar victorioso/sa; **to ~ on** seguir.

cart n carro m; carreta f; * vt llevar (en carro).

cartel n cartel m.

carthorse n caballo de tiro m.

Carthusian n cartujo (monje) m.

cartilage n cartílago m.

cartload n carretada f.

carton n caja f.

cartoon n dibujo animado m; tira cómica f.

cartridge n cartucho m.

carve vt cincelar; trinchar; grabar.

carving n escultura f.

carving knife n cuchillo de trinchar m.

car wash *n* lavado de coches *m*.

case *n* caja *f*; maleta *f*; caso *m*; estuche *m*; vaina *f*; **in ~** por si acaso.

cash *n* dinero contante *m*; * *vt* cobrar.

cash card *n* tarjeta de cajero automático *f*.

cash dispenser, cash machine *n* cajero automático *m*.

cashier *n* cajero *m*.

cashmere *n* cachemira *f*.

casing *n* forro *m*; cubierta *f*.

casino *n* casino *m*.

cask *n* barril, tonel *m*.

casket *n* ataúd *m*.

casserole *n* cazuela *f*.

cassette *n* cassette *m*.

cassette player, recorder *n* cassette *m*.

cassock *n* sotana *f*.

cast *vt* tirar, lanzar; modelar; * *n* reparto *m*; forma *f*.

castanets *npl* castañuelas *fpl*.

castaway *n* réprobo *m*.

caste *n* casta *f*.

castigate *vt* castigar.

casting vote *n* voto de calidad *m*.

cast iron *n* hierro colado *m*.

castle *n* castillo *m*; fortaleza *f*.

castor oil *n* aceite de ricino *m*.

castrate *vt* castrar.

castration *n* capadura *f*.

cast steel *n* acero fundido *m*.

casual *adj* casual, fortuito/ta; **~ly** *adv* casualmente, fortuitamente.

casualty *n* víctima *f*; baja *f*.

cat *n* gato *m*; gata *f*.

catalog *n* catálogo *m*.

catalyst *n* catalizador *m*.

catalytic converter *n* catalizador *m*.

catamaran *n* catamarán *m*.

catapult *n* catapulta, honda *f*.

cataract *n* cascada *f*; catarata *f*.

catarrh *n* catarro *m*; reuma *f*.

catastrophe *n* catástrofe *f*.

catcall *n* silbido *m*; reclamo *m*.

catch *vt* coger, agarrar, asir; atrapar; pillar; sorprender; **to ~ cold** resfriarse; **to ~ fire** encenderse; * *n* presa *f*; captura *f*; (*mus*) canon *m*; trampa *f*.

catching *adj* contagioso/sa.

catch phrase *n* lema *m*.

catchword *n* reclamo *m*.

catchy *adj* pegadizo/za.

catechism *n* catecismo *m*.

catechize *vt* catequizar, examinar.

categorical *adj* categórico/ca; **~ly** *adv* categóricamente.

categorize *vt* clasificar.

category *n* categoría *f*.

cater *vi* abastecer, proveer.

caterer *n* proveedor/a, abastecedor/a *m/f*.

catering *n* alimentación *f*.

caterpillar *n* oruga *f*.

catgut *n* cuerda de violón *f*.

cathedral *n* catedral *f*.

catholic *adj*, *n* católico/ca *m/f*.

Catholicism *n* catolicismo *m*.

cattle *n* ganado *m*.

cattle show *n* feria de ganado *f*.

caucus *n* junta electoral *f*.

cauliflower *n* coliflor *f*.

cause *n* causa *f*; razón *f*; motivo *m*; proceso *m*; * *vt* causar.

causeway *n* arrecife *m*.

caustic *adj*, *n* cáustico *m*.

cauterize *vt* cauterizar.

caution *n* prudencia, precaución *f*; aviso *m*; * *vt* avisar; amonestar; advertir.

cautionary *adj* de escarmiento.

cautious *adj* prudente, circunspecto/ta, cauto/ta.

cavalier *adj* arrogante.

cavalry *n* caballería *f*.

cave *n* caverna *f*; bodega *f*.

caveat *n* aviso *m*; advertencia *f*; (*law*) notificación *f*.

cavern *n* caverna *f*; bodega *f*.

cavernous *adj* cavernoso/sa.

caviar *n* caviar *m*.

cavity *n* hueco *m*; caries *f invar*.

CD-ROM *n* cederrón *m*.

cease *vt* parar, suspender; * *vi* desistir.

cease-fire *n* alto el fuego *m*, *Lat Am* cese del fuego *m*.

ceaseless *adj* incesante, continuo/nua; **~ly** *adv* perpetuamente.

cedar *n* cedro *m*.

cede *vt* ceder, transferir.

ceiling *n* techo *m*.

celebrate *vt* celebrar.

celebration *n* celebración *f*.

celebrity *n* celebridad, fama *f*.

celery *n* apio *m*.

celestial *adj* celeste, divino/na.

celibacy *n* celibato *m*, soltería *f*.

celibate *adj* soltero; soltera.

cell *n* celdilla *f*; célula *f*; cueva *f*.

cellar *n* sótano *m*; bodega *f*.

cello *n* violoncelo *m*.

Cellophane™ *n* celofán *m*.

cellular *adj* celular; **~ phone** móvil *m*, *Lat Am* celular *m*.

cellulitis *n* celulitis *f*.

cellulose *n* (*chem*) celulosa *f*.

cement *n* cemento; (*fig*) vínculo *m*; * *vt* pegar con cemento.

cemetery *n* cementerio *m*.

cenotaph *n* cenotafio *m*.

censor *n* censor/a *m/f*; crítico/ca *m/f*.

censorious *adj* severo/ra, crítico/ca.

censorship *n* censura *f*.

C

censure n censura, reprensión f; * vt censurar, reprender; criticar.

census n censo m.

cent n centavo m.

centenarian n centenario m; centenaria f.

centenary n centena f; * adj centenario/ria.

centennial adj centenario/ria.

center n centro m; * vt centrar; concentrar; * vi concentrarse.

centigrade n centígrado m.

centiliter n centilitro m.

centimeter n centímetro m.

centipede n escolopendra f.

central adj central; ~ly adv centralmente, en el centro.

centralize vt centralizar.

centrifugal adj centrífugo/ga.

century n siglo m.

ceramic adj cerámico/ca.

cereals npl cereales fpl.

cerebral adj cerebral.

ceremonial adj, n ceremonial m; rito externo m.

ceremonious adj ceremonioso/sa; ~ly adv ceremoniosamente.

ceremony n ceremonia f.

certain adj cierto/ta, evidente; seguro/ra; ~ly adv ciertamente, sin duda.

certainty, certitude n certeza f; seguridad f.

certificate n certificado, testimonio m.

certification n certificado m.

certified mail n correo certificado m.

certify vt certificar, afirmar.

cervical adj cervical.

cesarean section/operation n (med) (operación de) cesárea f.

cessation n cesación f.

cesspool n cloaca f; sumidero m.

chafe vt frotar; enojar, irritar.

chaff n paja menuda f.

chaffinch n pinzón m.

chagrin n disgusto m.

chain n cadena f; serie, sucesión f; * vt encadenar, atar con cadena.

chain reaction n reacción en cadena f.

chain store n gran almacén m.

chair n silla f; * vt presidir.

chairman n presidente m.

chalice n cáliz m.

chalk n creta f; tiza f.

chalkboard n pizarra f, Lat Am pizarrón m.

challenge n desafío m; * vt desafiar, impugnar.

challenger n desafiador/a m/f.

challenging adj desafiante.

chamber n cámara f; aposento m.

chambermaid n moza de cámara f.

chameleon n camaleón m.

chamois leather n gamuza f.

champagne n champaña m.

champion n campeón m; * vt defender.

championship n campeonato m.

chance n ventura, suerte f; oportunidad f, Lat Am chance m; **by** ~ por acaso; * vt arriesgar.

chancellor n canciller m.

chancery n chancillería f.

chandelier n araña de luces f; candelero m.

change vt cambiar; * vi variar, alterarse; * n mudanza, variedad f; vicisitud f; cambio m, Lat Am vuelto m.

changeable adj variable, inconstante; mudable.

changeless adj constante, inmutable.

changing adj cambiante.

channel n canal f; estrecho m; * vt encauzar.

channel-hopping n zapping m.

chant n canto (llano) m; * vt cantar.

chaos n caos m; confusión f.

chaotic adj confuso/sa.

chapel n capilla f.

chaplain n capellán m.

chapter n capítulo m.

char vt chamuscar.

character n carácter m; personaje m.

characteristic adj característico/ca; ~ally adv característicamente.

characterize vt caracterizar.

characterless adj sin carácter.

charade n charada f.

charcoal n carbón de leña m.

chard n (bot) acelga f.

charge vt cargar; acusar, imputar; * n cargo m; acusación f; (mil) ataque m; depósito m; carga f.

chargeable adj imputable.

charge card n tarjeta de compra f.

charitable adj caritativo/va; benigno/na, clemente; ~bly adv caritativamente.

charity n caridad, benevolencia f; limosna f.

charlatan n charlatán/tana m/f.

charm n encanto m; atractivo m; * vt encantar, embelesar, atraer.

charming adj encantado/da.

chart n carta de navegar f.

charter n carta f; privilegio m; * vt fletar un buque; alquilar.

charter flight n vuelo chárter m, charter m.

chase vt cazar; perseguir; * n caza f.

chasm n vacío m.

chaste adj casto/ta; puro/ra; honesto/ta.

chasten vt corregir, castigar.

chastise vt castigar, reformar, corregir.

chastisement n castigo m.

chastity n castidad, pureza f.

chat vi charlar; * n charla, cháchara f.

chatter vi cotorrear; rechinar; charlar; * n chirrido m; charla f.

chatterbox n parlero/ra, hablador/a, gárrulo/la m/f.

chatty adj locuaz, parlanchín/china.

chauffeur n chófer m.

chauvinist n machista m.
cheap adj barato/ta; ~**ly** adv a bajo precio.
cheapen vt regatear; abaratar.
cheaper adj más barato/ta.
cheat vt engañar, defraudar; * n trampa f; fraude, engaño m; tramposo/sa m/f.
check[1] vt comprobar; contar; reprimir, refrenar; regañar; registrar; * n restricción f; freno m.
check[2] n cheque m.
check account n cuenta corriente f.
checkerboard n tablero de damas m.
checkered adj accidentado/da.
checkers npl juego de damas m.
checkmate n mate m.
checkout n caja f.
checkpoint n control m.
checkroom n consigna f.
check-up n reconocimiento médico m.
cheek n mejilla f; (col) desvergüenza f; atrevimiento m.
cheekbone n hueso del carrillo m.
cheeky adj descarado/da.
cheer n alegría f; aplauso m; buen humor m; * vt animar, alentar.
cheerful adj alegre, vivo/va, jovial; ~**ly** adv alegremente.
cheerfulness, cheeriness n alegría f; buen humor m.
cheese n queso m.
cheese shop n quesería f.
chef n jefe de cocina m.
chemical adj químico/ca.
chemist n químico m.
chemistry n química f.
chemotherapy n quimioterapia f.
cherish vt fomentar, proteger.
cheroot n puro m.
cherry n cereza f; * adj bermejo/ja.
cherry tree n cerezo m.
cherub n querubín m.
chess n ajedrez m.
chessboard n tablero de ajedrez m.
chessman n pieza de ajedrez f.
chest n pecho m; arca f; ~ **of drawers** cómoda f.
chestnut n castaña f; color de castaña m.
chestnut tree n castaño m.
chew vt mascar, masticar.
chewing gum n chicle m.
chic adj elegante.
chicanery n quisquilla f.
chick n polluelo m; (col) chica f.
chicken n pollo m.
chickenpox n varicela f.
chickpea n garbanzo m.
chicory n achicoria f.
chide vt reprobar, regañar.
chief adj principal, capital; ~**ly** adv principalmente; * n jefe, principal m.
chief executive n director/a general m/f.

chieftain n jefe, comandante m.
chiffon n gasa f.
chilblain n sabañón m.
child n niño m; niña f; hijo m; hija f; **from a** ~ desde niño/ña; **with** ~ preñada, embarazada.
childbirth n parto m.
childhood n infancia, niñez f; pequeñez f.
childish adj frívolo/la, pueril; ~**ly** adv puerilmente.
childishness n puerilidad f.
childless adj sin hijos.
childlike adj pueril.
children npl de **child** niños mpl.
chill adj frío/ría, friolero/ra; * n frío m; * vt enfriar; helar.
chilly adj friolero/ra, Lat Am friolento/ta.
chime n armonía f; clave m; * vi sonar con armonía; concordar.
chimney n chimenea f.
chimpanzee n chimpancé m.
chin n barbilla f.
china(**ware**) n porcelana f.
chink n grieta, hendedura f; * vi resonar.
chip vt astillar; * vi picarse; * n astilla f; chip m; patata/papa frita f.
chirp vi chirriar, gorjear; * n gorjeo, chirrido m.
chirping n canto de las aves m.
chisel n cincel m; * vt cincelar, grabar.
chitchat n charla f.
chivalrous adj caballeresco/ca.
chivalry n caballería f.
chives npl cebollinos f.
chlorine n cloro m.
chloroform n cloroformo m.
chock-full adj de bote en bote, completamente lleno/na.
chocolate n chocolate m.
choice n elección, preferencia f; selecto m; * adj selecto/ta, exquisito/ta, excelente.
choir n coro m.
choke vt sofocar; oprimir; tapar.
cholera n cólera m.
choose vt escoger, elegir.
chop vt tajar, cortar; * n chuleta f; ~**s** pl (col) quijadas fpl.
chopper n helicóptero m.
chopping block n tajo de cocina m.
chopsticks npl palillos mpl.
chore n faena f.
choral adj coral.
chord n cuerda f.
chorist, chorister n corista m.
chorus n coro m.
Christ n Cristo m.
christen vt bautizar.
Christendom n cristianismo m; cristiandad f.
christening n bautismo m.
Christian adj, n cristiano/na m/f; ~ **name** nombre de pila m.
Christianity n cristianismo m; cristiandad f.

Christmas n Navidad f.
Christmas card n tarjeta de Navidad f.
Christmas Eve n Nochebuena f.
chrome n cromo m.
chronic adj crónico/ca.
chronicle n crónica f.
chronicler n cronista m.
chronological adj cronológico/ca; ~**ly** adv cronológicamente.
chronology n cronología f.
chronometer n cronómetro m.
chubby adj gordo/da.
chuck vt lanzar.
chuckle vi reírse a carcajadas.
chug vi resoplar.
chum n compañero/ra, compinche m/f.
chunk n trozo m.
church n iglesia f.
churchyard n cementerio m.
churlish adj hosco/ca, grosero/ra; tacaño/ña
churn n mantequera f; * vt batir la leche para hacer manteca.
cider n sidra f.
cigar n cigarro m.
cigarette n cigarrillo m.
cigarette case n pitillera f.
cigarette end n colilla f.
cigarette holder n boquilla f.
cinder n carbonilla f.
cinnamon n canela f.
cipher n cifra f.
circle n círculo m; corrillo m; asamblea f; * vt circundar; cercar; * vi circular.
circuit n circuito m; recinto m.
circuitous adj circular, tortuoso/sa.
circular adj circular, redondo/da; * n carta circular f.
circulate vi circular; moverse alrededor.
circulation n circulación f.
circumcise vt circuncidar.
circumcision n circuncisión f.
circumference n circunferencia f; circuito m.
circumflex n acento circunflejo m.
circumlocution n circunlocución f.
circumnavigate vt circunnavegar.
circumnavigation n circunnavegación f.
circumscribe vt circunscribir.
circumspect adj circunspecto/ta, prudente, reservado/da.
circumspection n circunspección, prudencia f.
circumstance n circunstancia, condición f; incidente m.
circumstantial adj accidental; accesorio/ria.
circumstantiate vt circunstanciar, detallar.
circumvent vt burlar.
circumvention n evasión f.
circus n circo m.
cistern n cisterna f.

citadel n ciudadela, fortaleza f.
citation n citación, cita f.
cite vt citar (a juicio); alegar; referirse a.
citizen n ciudadano/na m/f.
citizenship n ciudadanía f.
city n ciudad f.
civic adj cívico/ca.
civil adj civil, cortés; ~**ly** adv civilmente.
civil defense n protección civil f.
civil engineer n ingeniero/ra civil m/f.
civilian n paisano m.
civility n civilidad, urbanidad, cortesía f.
civilization n civilización f.
civilize vt civilizar.
civil law n derecho civil m.
civil war n guerra civil f.
clad adj vestido/da, cubierto/ta.
claim vt pedir en juicio, reclamar; * n demanda f; derecho m.
claimant n reclamante m; demandador/a m/f.
clairvoyant n clarividente m/f; zahorí m.
clam n almeja f.
clamber vi gatear, trepar.
clammy adj viscoso/sa.
clamor n clamor, grito m; * vi vociferar, gritar.
clamp n abrazadera f; * vt afianzar; **to ~ down on** reforzar la lucha contra.
clan n familia, tribu, raza f.
clandestine adj clandestino/na, oculto/ta.
clang n rechino, sonido desapacible m; * vi rechinar.
clap vt aplaudir.
clapping n palmada f; aplauso, palmoteo m.
claret n clarete m.
clarification n clarificación f.
clarify vt clarificar, aclarar.
clarinet n clarinete m.
clarity n claridad f.
clash vi chocar; * n estruendo m; choque m.
clasp n broche m; hebilla f; abrazo m; * vt abrochar; abrazar.
class n clase f; orden f; * vt clasificar, coordinar.
classic(al) adj clásico/ca; * n autor clásico m.
classification n clasificación f.
classified advertisement n anuncio por palabras m, Lat Am clasificado m.
classify vt clasificar.
classmate n compañero/ra de clase m/f.
classroom n aula f.
clatter vi resonar; hacer ruido; * n ruido m.
clause n cláusula f; artículo m; estipulación f.
claw n garra f; zarpa f; * vt desgarrar, arañar.
clay n arcilla f.
clean adj limpio/pia; casto/ta; * vt limpiar.
cleaning n limpieza f.
cleanliness n limpieza f.
cleanly adj limpio/pia; * adv limpiamente, aseadamente.
cleanness n limpieza f; pureza f.

cleanse *vt* limpiar, purificar; purgar.

clear *adj* claro/ra; neto/ta; diáfano/na; evidente; * *adv* claramente; * *vt* clarificar, aclarar; justificar, absolver; * *vi* aclararse.

clearance *n* despeje *m*; acreditación *f*.

clear-cut *adj* bien definido/da.

clearly *adv* claramente, evidentemente.

cleaver *n* cuchillo de carnicero *m*.

clef *n* clave *f*.

cleft *n* hendedura, abertura *f*.

clemency *n* clemencia *f*.

clement *adj* clemente, benigno/na.

clenched *adj* cerrado/da.

clergy *n* clero *m*.

clergyman *n* eclesiástico *m*.

clerical *adj* clerical, eclesiástico/ca.

clerk *n* dependiente *m*; oficinista *m*.

clever *adj* listo/ta; hábil, mañoso/sa; ~**ly** *adv* diestramente, hábilmente.

click *vt* chasquear; * *vi* taconear.

client *n* cliente *m/f*.

cliff *n* acantilado *m*.

climate *n* clima *m*; temperatura *f*.

climatic *adj* climático/ca.

climax *n* clímax *m*.

climb *vt* escalar, trepar; * *vi* subir.

climber *n* alpinista *m/f*.

climbing *n* alpinismo *m*.

clinch *vt* cerrar; remachar.

cling *vi* colgar, adherirse, pegarse.

clinic *n* clínica *f*.

clink *vt* hacer resonar; * *vi* resonar; * *n* retintín *m*.

clip *vt* cortar; * *n* clip *m*; horquilla *f*.

clipping *n* recorte *m*.

clique *n* camarilla *f*.

cloak *n* capa *f*; pretexto *m*; * *vi* encapotar.

cloakroom *n* guardarropa *m*.

clock *n* reloj *m*.

clockwork *n* mecanismo de un reloj *m*; * *adj* sumamente exacto y puntual.

clod *n* terrón *m*.

clog *n* zueco *m*; * *vi* atascarse.

cloister *n* claustro, monasterio *m*.

clone *n* clon *m*.

clone *vt* clonar.

cloned *adj* clónico/ca.

cloning *n* clonación *f*.

close *vt* cerrar; concluir, terminar; * *vi* cerrarse; * *n* fin *m*; conclusión *f*; * *adj* cercano/na; estrecho/cha; ajustado/da; denso/sa; reservado/da; * *adv* de cerca; ~ **by** muy cerca; junto.

closed *adj* cerrado/da.

closely *adv* estrechamente; de cerca.

closeness *n* proximidad *f*; estrechez; reclusión *f*.

closet *n* armario *m*.

close-up *n* primer plano *m*.

closure *n* cierre *m*; conclusión *f*.

clot *n* grumo *m*; embolia *f*.

cloth *n* paño *m*; mantel *m*; vestido *m*; lienzo *m*.

clothe *vt* vestir, cubrir.

clothes *npl* ropa *f*; ropaje *m*; ropa de cama *f*; **bed** ~ cobertores *mpl*.

clothes basket *n* cesta grande *f*.

clotheshorse *n* tendedero *m*.

clothesline *n* cuerda (de tendedero) *f*.

clothespin *n* pinza *f*.

clothing *n* vestidos *mpl*.

cloud *n* nube *f*; nublado *m*; (*fig*) adversidad *f*; * *vt* anublar; oscurecer; * *vi* anublarse; oscurecerse.

cloudiness *n* nubosidad *f*; oscuridad *f*.

cloudy *adj* nublado/da; oscuro/ra; sombrío/ría, melancólico/ca.

clout *n* tortazo *m*.

clove *n* clavo *m*.

clover *n* trébol *m*.

clown *n* payaso *m*.

club *n* cachiporra *f*.

club car *n* coche restaurante *m*.

clue *n* pista *f*, indicios *m*; idea *f*.

clump *n* grupo *m*.

clumsily *adv* torpemente.

clumsiness *n* torpeza *f*.

clumsy *adj* torpe, pesado/da, *Lat Am* patón/ona; sin arte.

cluster *n* racimo *m*; manada *f*; pelotón *m*; * *vt* agrupar; * *vi* arracimarse.

clutch *n* embrague *m*; apretón *m*; * *vt* empuñar.

clutter *vt* atestar.

coach *n* autocar, autobús *m*; vagón *m*; entrenador/a *m/f*; * *vt* entrenar; enseñar.

coach trip *n* excursión en autocar *f*.

coagulate *vt* coagular, cuajar; * *vi* coagularse, cuajarse, espesarse.

coal *n* carbón *m*.

coalesce *vi* juntarse, incorporarse.

coalfield *n* yacimiento de carbón *m*.

coalition *n* coalición, confederación *f*.

coalman *n* carbonero *m*.

coalmine *n* mina de carbón, carbonería *f*.

coarse *adj* basto/ta; grosero/ra; zafio/fia; ~**ly** *adv* groseramente.

coast *n* costa *f*.

coastal *adj* costero/ra; ribereño/ña.

coastguard *n* guardacostas *m invar*.

coastline *n* litoral *m*.

coat *n* chaqueta *f*; abrigo *m*, *Lat Am* saco *m*; capa *f*; * *vt* cubrir.

coat hanger *n* percha *f*.

coat hook *n* percha *f*.

coating *n* revestimiento *m*.

coax *vt* lisonjear.

cob *n* mazorca de maíz *f*.

cobbler *n* zapatero/ra *m/f*.

cobbles, cobblestones *npl* adoquines *mpl*.

cobweb *n* telaraña *f*.

cocaine *n* cocaína *f*.

coccyx n rabadilla f.
cock n gallo m; macho m; * vt armar el sombrero; amartillar, montar una escopeta.
cock-a-doodle-doo n quiquiriquí m.
cockcrow n canto del gallo m.
cockerel n gallito m.
cockfight(ing) n pelea de gallos f.
cockle n berberecho m.
cockpit n cabina f.
cockroach n cucaracha f.
cocktail n cóctel m.
cocoa n coco m; cacao m.
coconut n coco m.
cocoon n capullo (del gusano de seda) m.
cod n bacalao m.
code n código m; prefijo m.
cod-liver oil n aceite de hígado de bacalao m.
coefficient n coeficiente m.
coercion n coerción f.
coexistence n coexistencia f.
coffee n café m.
coffee break n descanso m.
coffee house n café m.
coffee-pot n cafetera f.
coffee table n mesita f.
coffer n cofre m; caja f.
coffin n ataúd m.
cog n diente (de rueda) m.
cogency n fuerza, urgencia f.
cogent adj convincente, urgente; ~ly adv de modo convincente.
cognac n coñac m.
cognate adj cognado/da.
cognition n conocimiento m; convicción f.
cognizance n conocimiento m; competencia f.
cognizant adj informado/da; (law) competente.
cogwheel n rueda dentada f.
cohabit vi cohabitar.
cohabitation n cohabitación f.
cohere vi pegarse; unirse.
coherence n coherencia, conexión f.
coherent adj coherente; consiguiente.
cohesion n coherencia f.
cohesive adj cohesivo/va.
coil n rollo m; bobina f; * vt enrollar.
coin n moneda f; * vt acuñar.
coincide vi coincidir, concurrir, convenir.
coincidence n coincidencia f.
coke¹ n coque m.
Coke² n Coca-Cola™ f.
colander n colador m, Lat Am coladera f, pasador m.
cold adj frío/ría; indiferente, insensible; reservado/da; ~ly adv fríamente; indiferentemente; * n frío m; frialdad f; resfriado m.
cold-blooded adj impasible.
coldness n frialdad f; indiferencia, insensibilidad, apatía f.
cold sore n herpes labial m.

coleslaw n ensalada de col f.
colic n cólico m.
collaborate vt cooperar.
collaboration n cooperación f.
collapse vi hundirse; * n hundimiento; (med) colapso m.
collapsible adj plegable.
collar n cuello m.
collarbone n clavícula f.
collate vt comparar, confrontar.
collateral adj colateral; * n garantía subsidiaria f.
collation n colación f.
colleague n colega, compañero/ra m/f.
collect vt recoger; coleccionar.
collection n colección f; compilación f.
collective adj colectivo/va, congregado/da; ~ly colectivamente.
collector n coleccionista m/f.
college n colegio m, Lat Am facultad f.
collide vi chocar.
collision n choque m, colisión f.
colloquial adj familiar; coloquial; ~ly adv familiarmente.
colloquialism n lengua usual f.
collusion n colusión f.
colon n dos puntos mpl; (med) colon m.
colonel n (mil) coronel m.
colonial adj colonial.
colonist n colono m.
colonize vt colonizar.
colony n colonia f.
color n color m; ~s pl bandera f; * vt colorar; pintar; * vi ponerse colorado/da.
color-blind adj daltónico/ca.
colorful adj lleno de color.
coloring n colorido m.
colorless adj descolorido/da, sin color.
color television n televisión en color f.
colossal adj colosal.
colossus n coloso m.
colt n potro m.
column n columna f.
columnist n columnista m.
coma n coma f.
comatose adj comatoso/sa.
comb n peine m; * vt peinar.
combat n combate m; batalla f; **single** ~ duelo m; * vt combatir.
combatant n combatiente m.
combative adj combativo/va.
combination n combinación, coordinación f.
combine vt combinar; * vi unirse.
combustion n combustión f.
come vi venir; **to ~ across/upon** vt topar con; dar con; **to ~ by** vt conseguir; **to ~ down** vi bajar; ser derribado/da; **to ~ from** vt ser de; **to ~ in for** vt merecer; **to ~ into** vt heredar; **to ~ round/to** vi volver en sí; **to ~ up with** vt sugerir.

comedian n comediante, cómico m.
comedienne n cómica f.
comedy n comedia f.
comet n cometa m.
comfort n confort m; ayuda f; consuelo m; comodidad f; * vt confortar; alentar, consolar.
comfortable adj cómodo/da.
comfortably adv agradablemente; cómodamente.
comforter n chupete m.
comic(al) adj cómico/ca, burlesco/ca; ~ly adv cómicamente.
coming n venida, llegada f; * adj venidero/ra.
comma n (gr) coma f.
command vt comandar, ordenar; * n orden f.
commander n comandante m.
commandment n mandamiento, precepto m.
commando n comando m.
commemorate vt conmemorar; celebrar.
commemoration n conmemoración f.
commence vt, vi comenzar.
commencement n principio m.
commend vt encomendar; alabar; enviar.
commendable adj recomendable.
commendably adv loablemente.
commendation n recomendación f.
commensurate adj proporcionado/da.
comment n comentario m; * vt comentar; glosar.
commentary n comentario m; interpretación f.
commentator n comentarista m/f.
commerce n comercio, tráfico, trato, negocio m.
commercial adj comercial.
commiserate vt compadecer, tener compasión.
commiseration n conmiseración, piedad f.
commissariat n comisaría f.
commission n comisión f; * vt comisionar; encargar.
commissioner n comisionado/da, delegado/da m/f.
commit vt cometer; depositar; encargar.
commitment n compromiso m.
committee n comité m.
commodity n comodidad f.
common adj común; bajo/ja; in ~ comúnmente; * n pastos comunales mpl.
commoner n plebeyo m.
common law n derecho consuetudinario m.
commonly adv comúnmente, frecuentemente.
commonplace n lugar común m; * adj trivial.
common sense n sentido común m.
commonwealth n república f.
commotion n tumulto m; perturbación del ánimo f.
commune vt conversar, conferir.
communicable adj comunicable, impartible.
communicate vt comunicar, participar; * vi comunicarse.
communication n comunicación f.
communicative adj comunicativo/va.
communion n comunión f.

communiqué n comunicado m.
communism n comunismo m.
communist n comunista m/f.
community n comunidad f; colectividad f.
community center n centro social m.
community chest n arca comunitaria f.
commutable adj conmutable, cambiable.
commutation ticket n billete de abono m.
commute vt conmutar.
compact adj compacto/ta, sólido/da, denso/sa; * n pacto, convenio m; ~ly adv estrechamente; en pocas palabras.
compact disc, CD n compact disc m, disco compacto m.
companion n compañero/ra, socio/cia, compinche m/f.
companionship n sociedad, compañía f.
company n compañía, sociedad f; compañía de comercio f.
comparable adj comparable.
comparative adj comparativo/va; ~ly adv comparativamente.
compare vt comparar.
comparison n comparación f.
compartment n compartimento m.
compass n brújula f.
compassion n compasión, piedad f.
compassionate adj compasivo/va.
compatibility n compatibilidad f.
compatible adj compatible.
compatriot n compatriota m/f.
compel vt compeler, obligar, constreñir.
compelling adj convicente.
compensate vt compensar.
compensation n compensación f; resarcimiento m.
compere n (rad, TV) presentador/a m/f.
compete vi concurrir, competir.
competence n competencia f; suficiencia f.
competent adj competente, adecuado/da; ~ly adv competentemente.
competition n competencia f; concurrencia f.
competitive adj competitivo/va.
competitive scheduling n contraprogramación f.
competitor n competidor/a m/f, rival m.
compilation n compilación f.
compile vt compilar.
complacency n autocomplacencia f.
complacent adj complaciente.
complain vi quejarse, lamentarse, lastimarse, dolerse.
complaint n queja f; reclamación f, Lat Am reclamo m.
complement n complemento m.
complementary adj complementario/ria.
complete adj completo/ta, perfecto/ta; ~ly adv completamente; * vt completar, acabar.
completion n terminación f.
complex adj complejo/ja.
complexion n tez f; aspecto m.

C

complexity n complejidad f.
compliance n complacencia, sumisión f.
compliant adj complaciente, oficioso/sa.
complicate vt complicar.
complication n complicación f.
complicity n complicidad f.
compliment n cumplido m; * vt cumplimentar; hacer cumplidos.
complimentary adj elogioso/sa, ceremonioso/sa.
comply vi cumplir; condescender, conformarse.
component adj componente.
compose vt componer; sosegar.
composed adj compuesto/ta, moderado/da.
composer n compositor/a m/f.
composite adj compuesto/ta.
composition n composición f.
compositor n cajista m.
compost n abono, estiércol m.
composure n composición f; tranquilidad, sangre fría f.
compound vt componer, combinar; * adj, n compuesto m.
comprehend vt comprender, contener; entender.
comprehensible adj comprensible; ~ly adv comprensiblemente.
comprehension n comprensión f; inteligencia f.
comprehensive adj comprensivo/va; ~ly adv comprensivamente.
compress vt comprimir, estrechar; * n cabezal m.
comprise vt comprender, incluir.
compromise n compromiso m; * vt comprometer.
compulsion n compulsión f; apremio m.
compulsive adj compulsivo/va; ~ly adv compulsivamente.
compulsory adj obligatorio/ria.
compunction n compunción, contrición f.
computable adj computable, calculable.
computation n computación f, cómputo m.
compute vt computar, calcular.
computer n ordenador m.
computer graphics n infografía f.
computerize vt computerizar, informatizar.
computer programing n programación f.
computer science n informática f.
computing n informática f, Lat Am computación f.
comrade n camarada, compañero/ra m/f.
comradeship n compañerismo m.
con vt estafar; * n estafa f.
concave adj cóncavo/va.
concavity n concavidad f.
conceal vt ocultar, esconder.
concealment n ocultación f; encubrimiento m.
concede vt conceder, asentir.
conceit n concepto m; capricho m; pensamiento m; presunción f.
conceited adj afectado/da, vano/na, presumido/da.
conceivable adj concebible, inteligible.
conceive vt concebir, comprender; * vi concebir.

concentrate vt concentrar.
concentration n concentración f.
concentration camp n campo de concentración m.
concentric adj concéntrico/ca.
concept n concepto m.
conception n concepción f; sentimiento m.
concern vt concernir, importar; * n negocio m; asunto m; preocupación f.
concerning prep tocante a.
concert n concierto m.
concerto n concierto m.
concession n concesión f; privilegio m.
conciliate vt conciliar.
conciliation n conciliación f.
conciliatory adj conciliador/a.
concise adj conciso/sa, sucinto/ta; ~ly adv concisamente.
conclude vt concluir; decidir; determinar.
conclusion n conclusión, determinación f; fin m.
conclusive adj decisivo/va, conclusivo/va; ~ly adv concluyentemente.
concoct vt cocer, digerir; (fig) zurcir.
concoction n confección f; cocción f.
concomitant adj concomitante.
concord n concordia, armonía f.
concordance n concordancia f.
concordant adj concordante, conforme.
concourse n concurso m; multitud f; gentío m.
concrete n hormigón m, Lat Am concreto m; * vt concretar.
concubine n concubina f.
concur vi concurrir; juntarse.
concurrence n concurrencia f; unión f; asistencia f.
concurrently adv al mismo tiempo.
concussion n conmoción cerebral f.
condemn vt condenar; desaprobar; vituperar.
condemnation n condena f.
condensation n condensación f.
condense vt condensar.
condescend vi condescender; consentir.
condescending adj condescendiente.
condescension n condescendencia f.
condiment n condimento m; salsa f.
condition vt condicionar; *n situación, condición, calidad f; estado m.
conditional adj condicional, hipotético/ca; ~ly adv condicionalmente.
conditioned adj condicionado/da.
conditioner n acondicionador m.
condolences npl pésame m.
condom n condón m.
condominium n condominio m.
condone vt perdonar.
conducive adj conducente, oportuno/na.
conduct n conducta f; manejo, proceder m; * vt conducir, guiar.
conductor n conductor m; guía, director m; conductor de electricidad m.

conduit n conducto m; caño m.
cone n cono m.
confection n confitura f; confección f.
confectioner n confitero/ra m/f.
confectioner's (**shop/store**) n pastelería f; confitería f.
confederacy n confederación f.
confederate vi confederarse; * adj, n confederado/da m/f.
confer vi conferenciar; * vt conferir, comparar.
conference n conferencia f.
confess vt, vi confesar(se).
confession n confesión f.
confessional n confesionario m.
confessor n confesor m.
confetti n confeti m.
confidant n confidente, amigo/ga íntimo/ma m/f.
confide vt, vi confiar; fiarse.
confidence n confianza, seguridad f.
confidence trick n timo m.
confident adj cierto/ta, seguro/ra; confiado/da.
confidential adj confidencial.
configuration n configuración f.
confine vt limitar; aprisionar.
confinement n prisión f; confinación f.
confirm vt confirmar; ratificar.
confirmation n confirmación f; ratificación f; prueba f.
confirmed adj empedernido/da.
confiscate vt confiscar.
confiscation n confiscación f.
conflagration n conflagración f; incendio m.
conflict n conflicto m; combate m; pelea f.
conflicting adj contradictorio/ria.
confluence n confluencia f; concurso m.
conform vt, vi conformar(se).
conformity n conformidad, conveniencia f.
confound vt turbar, confundir.
confront vt afrontar; confrontar; comparar.
confrontation n enfrentamiento m.
confuse vt confundir; desordenar.
confusing adj confuso/sa.
confusion n confusión f; perturbación f; desorden m.
congeal vt, vi helar, congelar(se).
congenial adj congenial.
congenital adj congénito/ta.
congested adj atestado/da.
congestion n congestión f; acumulación f.
conglomerate vt conglomerar, aglomerar; * adj aglomerado/da; * n (com) conglomerado m.
conglomeration n aglomeración f.
congratulate vt congratular, felicitar.
congratulations npl felicidades fpl; * interj enhorabuena, Lat Am felicitaciones.
congratulatory adj congratulatorio/ria.
congregate vt congregar, reunir.
congregation n congregación f; reunión f.
congress n congreso m; conferencia f.

congressman n miembro del Congreso m.
congruity n congruencia f.
congruous adj idóneo/nea, congruo/rua, apto/ta.
conic(al) adj cónico/ca.
conifer n conífera f.
coniferous adj (bot) conífero/ra.
conjecture n conjetura, apariencia f; * vt conjeturar; pronosticar.
conjugal adj conyugal, matrimonial.
conjugate vt (gr) conjugar.
conjugation n conjugación f.
conjunction n conjunción f; unión f.
conjuncture n coyuntura f; ocasión f; tiempo crítico m.
conjure vi conjurar, suplicar.
conjurer n conjurador/a, encantador/a m/f.
con man n timador m.
connect vt juntar, unir, enlazar.
connection n conexión f.
connivance n connivencia f.
connive vi tolerar.
connoisseur n conocedor/a m/f.
conquer vt conquistar; vencer.
conqueror n vencedor/a, conquistador/a m/f.
conquest n conquista f.
conscience n conciencia f; escrúpulo m.
conscientious adj concienzudo/da, escrupuloso/sa; ~ly adv concienzudamente.
conscientious objector n objetor de conciencia m.
conscious adj sabedor, consciente; ~ly adv a sabiendas.
consciousness n conciencia f.
conscript n conscripto m.
conscription n reclutamiento m.
consecrate vt consagrar; dedicar.
consecration n consagración f.
consecutive adj consecutivo/va; ~ly adv consecutivamente.
consensus n consenso m.
consent n consentimiento m; aprobación f; * vi consentir; aprobar.
consequence n consecuencia f; importancia f.
consequent adj consecutivo/va, concluyente; ~ly adv consiguientemente.
conservation n conservación f.
conservative adj conservador/a m/f.
conservatory n conservatorio m.
conserve vt conservar; * n conserva f.
consider vt considerar, examinar; * vi pensar, deliberar.
considerable adj considerable; importante; ~bly adv considerablemente.
considerate adj considerado/da, prudente, discreto/ta; ~ly adv juiciosamente; prudentemente.
consideration n consideración f; deliberación f; importancia f; valor, mérito m.
considering conj en vista de; ~ that a causa de; visto que, en razón a.

C

consign *vt* consignar.
consignment *n* consignación *f*.
consist *vi* consistir.
consistency *n* consistencia *f*.
consistent *adj* consistente; conveniente, conforme; solido/da, estable; **~ly** *adv* conformemente.
console *n* consola *f*.
consolable *adj* consolable.
consolation *n* consolación *f*; consuelo *m*.
consolatory *adj* consolatorio/ria.
console *vt* consolar.
consolidate *vt, vi* consolidar(se).
consolidation *n* consolidación *f*.
consonant *adj* consonante, conforme; * *n* (*gr*) consonante *f*.
consort *n* consorte, socio *m*.
conspicuous *adj* conspicuo/cua, aparente; notable; **~ly** *adv* claramente.
conspiracy *n* conspiración *f*.
conspirator *n* conspirador/a *m/f*.
conspire *vi* conspirar, maquinar.
constancy *n* constancia, perseverancia, persistencia *f*.
constant *adj* constante; perseverante; **~ly** *adv* constantemente.
constellation *n* constelación *f*.
consternation *n* consternación *f*; terror *m*.
constipated *adj* estreñido/da.
constituency *n* circunscripción electoral *f*.
constituent *n* constitutivo *m*; * *adj* constituyente.
constitute *vt* constituir; establecer.
constitution *n* constitución *f*; estado *m*; temperamento *m*.
constitutional *adj* constitucional.
constrain *vt* constreñir, forzar; restringir.
constraint *n* constreñimiento *m*; fuerza, violencia *f*.
constrict *vt* constreñir, estrechar.
construct *vt* construir, edificar.
construction *n* construcción *f*.
construe *vt* construir; interpretar.
consul *n* cónsul *m*.
consular *adj* consular.
consulate, consulship *n* consulado *m*.
consult *vt* (*vi*) consultar(se); aconsejar(se).
consultant *n* asesor *m*.
consultation *n* consulta, deliberación *f*.
consume *vt* consumir; disipar; * *vi* consumirse.
consumer *n* consumidor/a *m/f*.
consumer goods *npl* bienes de consumo *mpl*.
consumerism *n* consumismo *m*.
consumer society *n* sociedad de consumo *f*.
consummate *vt* consumar, acabar, perfeccionar; * *adj* cumplido/da, consumado/da.
consummation *n* consumación, perfección *f*.
consumption *n* consumo *m*.
contact *n* contacto *m*.
contact lenses *npl* lentes de contacto *fpl*.

contagious *adj* contagioso/sa.
contain *vt* contener, comprender; caber, reprimir, refrenar.
container *n* recipiente *m*.
contaminate *vt* contaminar; corromper; **~d** *adj* contaminado/da, corrompido/da.
contamination *n* contaminación *f*.
contemplate *vt* contemplar.
contemplation *n* contemplación *f*.
contemplative *adj* contemplativo/va.
contemporaneous, contemporary *adj* contemporáneo/nea.
contempt *n* desprecio, desdén *m*.
contemptible *adj* despreciable, vil; **~bly** *adv* vilmente.
contemptuous *adj* desdeñoso/sa, insolente; **~ly** *adv* con desdén.
contend *vi* contender, disputar, afirmar.
content *adj* contento/ta, satisfecho/cha; * *vt* contentar, satisfacer; * *n* contenido *m*; **~s** *pl* contenido *m*; tabla de materias *f*.
contentedly *adv* de un modo satisfecho/cha; con paciencia.
contention *n* contención, altercación *f*.
contentious *adj* contencioso/sa, litigioso/sa; **~ly** *adv* contenciosamente.
contentment *n* contentamiento, placer *m*.
contest *vt* contestar, disputar, litigar; * *n* concurso *m*; contestación, altercación *f*.
contestant *n* concursante/ta *m/f*.
context *n* contexto *m*; contextura *f*.
contiguous *adj* contiguo/gua, vecino/na.
continent *adj* continente; * *n* continente *m*.
continental *adj* continental.
contingency *n* contingencia *f*; acontecimiento *m*; eventualidad *f*.
contingent *n* contingente *m*; cuota *f*; * *adj* contingente, casual; **~ly** *adv* casualmente.
continual *adj* continuo/nua; **~ly** *adv* continuamente.
continuation *n* continuación, serie *f*.
continue *vt* continuar; * *vi* durar, perseverar, persistir.
continuity *n* continuidad *f*.
continuous *adj* continuo/nua, unido/da; **~ly** *adv* continuadamente.
contort *vt* torcer.
contortion *n* contorsión *f*.
contour *n* contorno *m*.
contraband *n* contrabando *m*; * *adj* prohibido/da, ilegal.
contraception *n* contracepción *f*.
contraceptive *n* anticonceptivo *m*; * *adj* anticonceptivo/va.
contract *vt* contraer; abreviar; contratar; *vi* contraerse; * *n* contrato, pacto *m*.
contraction *n* contracción *f*; abreviatura *f*.
contractor *n* contratante *m/f*.
contradict *vt* contradecir.

contradiction n contradicción, oposición f.
contradictory adj contradictorio/ria.
contraption n artilugio m.
contrariness n contrariedad, oposición f.
contrary adj contrario/ria, opuesto/ta; * n contrario m; **on the ~** al contrario.
contrast n contraste m; oposición f; * vt contrastar, oponer.
contrasting adj opuesto/ta.
contravention n contravención f.
contributory adj contributario/ria.
contribute vt contribuir, ayudar.
contribution n contribución f; tributo m.
contributor n contribuidor/a m/f.
contributory adj contribuyente.
contrite adj contrito/ta, arrepentido/da.
contrition n penitencia, contrición f.
contrivance n designio m; invención f; concepto m.
contrive vt inventar, trazar, maquinar; manejar; combinar.
control n control m; inspección f; * vt controlar; manejar; restringir; gobernar.
control room n sala de mando f.
control tower n torre de control f.
controversial adj polémico/ca.
controversy n controversia f.
contusion n contusión f, magullamiento m.
conundrum n problema m.
conurbation n conurbación f.
convalesce vi convalecer.
convalescence n convalecencia f.
convalescent adj convaleciente.
convene vt convocar; juntar, unir; * vi convenir, juntarse.
convenience n conveniencia, comodidad, conformidad f.
convenient adj conveniente, apto/ta, cómodo/da, propio/pia; **~ly** adv cómodamente, oportunamente.
convent n convento, claustro, monasterio m.
convention n convención f; contrato, tratado m.
conventional adj convencional, estipulado/da.
converge vi converger.
convergence n convergencia f.
convergent adj convergente.
conversant adj versado en; íntimo/ma.
conversation n conversación f, Lat Am conversa f.
converse vi conversar; platicar.
conversely adv mutuamente, recíprocamente.
conversion n conversión, transmutación f.
convert vt (vr) convertir(se); * n converso, convertido m.
convertible adj convertible, transmutable; * n descapotable m.
convex adj convexo/xa.
convexity n convexidad f.
convey vt transportar; transmitir, transferir.
conveyance n transporte m; conducción f; escritura de traspaso f.

conveyancer n notario m.
convict vt probar un delito; * n convicto/ta m/f.
conviction n convicción f.
convince vt convencer, poner en evidencia.
convincing adj convincente.
convincingly adv de modo convincente.
convivial adj sociable; hospitalario/ria.
conviviality n sociabilidad f.
convoke vt convocar, reunir.
convoy n convoy m.
convulse vt conmover, convulsionar.
convulsion n convulsión f; conmoción f; tumulto m.
convulsive adj convulsivo/va; **~ly** adv convulsivamente.
coo vi arrullar.
cook n cocinero/ra m/f; * vt cocinar; * vi cocinar; guisar.
cookbook n libro de cocina m.
cooker n cocina f.
cookery n arte culinario m, cocina f.
cookie n galleta f.
cool adj fresco/ca; indiferente; * n frescura f; * vt enfriar, refrescar.
coolly adv frescamente; indiferentemente.
coolness n fresco m; frialdad, frescura f.
cooperate vi cooperar.
cooperation n cooperación f.
cooperative adj cooperativo/va; cooperante.
coordinate vt coordinar.
coordination n coordinación, elección f.
cop n (col) poli m.
copartner n compañero/ra, socio/cia m/f.
cope vi arreglárselas.
copier n copiadora f.
copious adj copioso/sa, abundante; **~ly** adv en abundancia.
copper n cobre m.
coppice, **copse** n bosquecillo m.
copulate vi copular.
copy n copia f; original m; ejemplar m; * vt copiar; imitar.
copybook n copiador de cartas (libro) m.
copying machine n copiadora f.
copyist n copista m/f.
copyright n propiedad de una obra literaria f; derechos de autor mpl.
coral n coral m.
coral reef n arrecife de coral m.
cord n cuerda f; cable m.
cordial adj cordial, de corazón, amistoso/sa; **~ly** adv cordialmente.
corduroy n pana f.
core n cuesco m; interior, centro, corazón m; materia f.
cork n alcornoque m; corcho m; * vt encorchar.
corkscrew n sacacorchos m invar.
corn¹ n maíz m; borona f; granos mpl.

corn² n callo m.
corncob n mazorca f.
cornea n córnea f.
corned beef n carne acecinada f.
corner n rincón m; esquina f.
cornerstone n piedra angular f.
cornet n corneta f.
cornfield n maizal m.
cornflakes npl copos de maíz mpl.
cornice n cornisa f.
cornstarch n harina de maíz f.
corollary n corolario m.
coronary n infarto m.
coronation n coronación f.
coroner n oficial que hace la inspección jurídica de los cadáveres m.
coronet n corona pequeña f.
corporal n cabo m.
corporate adj corporativo/va.
corporation n corporación f; gremio m.
corporeal adj corpóreo/rea.
corps n cuerpo (de ejército) m; regimiento m.
corpse n cadáver m.
corpulent adj corpulento/ta, gordo/da.
corpuscle n corpúsculo, átomo m.
corral n corral m.
correct vt corregir; enmendar; * adj correcto/ta, justo/ta; ~ly adv correctamente.
correction n corrección f; enmienda f; censura f.
corrective adj correctivo/va; * n correctivo m; restricción f.
correctness n exactitud f.
correlation n correlación f.
correlative adj correlativo/va.
correspond vi corresponder; corresponderse.
correspondence n correspondencia f.
correspondent adj correspondiente, conforme; * n corresponsal m.
corridor n pasillo m.
corroborate vt corroborar.
corroboration n corroboración f.
corroborative adj corroborativo/va.
corrode vt corroer.
corrosion n corrosión f.
corrosive adj, n corrosivo m.
corrugated iron n chapa ondulada f.
corrupt vt corromper; sobornar; * vi corromperse, pudrirse; * adj corrompido/da; depravado/da.
corruptible adj corruptible.
corruption n corrupción f; depravación f.
corruptive adj corruptivo/va.
corset n corsé, corpiño m.
cortege n cortejo m.
cosmetic adj cosmético/ca; * n cosmético m.
cosmic adj cósmico/ca.
cosmonaut n cosmonauta m/f.
cosmopolitan adj cosmopolita.

cosset vt mimar.
cost n coste, precio m; * vi costar.
costly adj costoso/sa, caro/ra.
costume n traje m.
cottage n casita, casucha f.
cotton n algodón m.
cotton candy n algodón azucarado m.
cotton mill n hilandería de algodón.
cotton wool n algodón hidrófilo m.
couch n sofá m.
couchette n litera f.
cough n tos f; * vi toser.
council n concilio, consejo m.
councilor n concejal/a m/f.
counsel n consejo, aviso m; abogado/da m/f.
counselor n consejero/ra m/f; abogado/da m/f.
count vt contar, numerar; calcular; **to ~ on** contar con; * n cuenta f; cálculo m; conde m.
countdown n cuenta atrás f.
countenance n rostro m; aspecto m; (buena/mala) cara f.
counter n mostrador m; ficha f.
counteract vt contrariar, impedir, estorbar; frustrar.
counterbalance vt contrapesar; igualar, compensar; * n contrapeso m.
counterfeit vt contrahacer, imitar, falsear; * adj falsificado/da; fingido/da.
countermand vt contramandar; revocar.
counterpart n parte correspondiente f.
counterproductive adj contraproducente.
countersign vt refrendar; firmar un decreto.
countess n condesa f.
countless adj innumerable.
countrified adj rústico/ca; tosco/ca, rudo/da.
country n país m; campo m; región f; patria f; * adj rústico/ca; campestre, rural.
country house n casa de campo, granja f.
countryman n paisano m; compatriota m.
county n condado m.
coup n golpe m.
coupé n (auto) cupé m.
couple n par m; lazo m; yuntas fpl; * vt unir, parear; casar.
couplet n copla f; par m.
coupon n cupón m.
courage n coraje, valor f.
courageous adj corajudo/da, valeroso/sa; ~ly adv valerosamente.
courier n correo, mensajero/ra m/f, expreso m.
course n curso m; carrera f; camino m; ruta f; método m; **of ~** por supuesto, sin duda.
court n corte f; palacio m; tribunal de justicia m, Lat Am corte f; * vt cortejar; solicitar, adular.
courteous adj cortés; benévolo/la; ~ly adv cortésmente.
courtesan n cortesana f.
courtesy n cortesía f; benignidad f.

courthouse n palacio de justicia m.
courtly adj cortesano/na, elegante.
court martial n consejo de guerra m.
courtroom n sala de justicia f.
courtyard n patio m.
cousin n primo m; prima f; **first ~** primo hermano m.
cove n (mar) ensenada, caleta f.
covenant n contrato m; convención f; * vi pactar, estipular.
cover n cubierta f; abrigo m; pretexto m; * vt cubrir; tapar; ocultar; proteger.
coverage n alcance m.
coveralls npl mono m; Lat Am overol m.
covering n ropa f; vestido m.
cover letter n carta de explicación f.
covert adj cubierto/ta; oculto/ta, secreto/ta; ~**ly** adv secretamente.
cover-up n encubrimiento m.
covet vt codiciar, desear con ansia.
covetous adj avariento/ta, sórdido/da.
cow n vaca f.
coward n cobarde m/f.
cowardice n cobardía, timidez f.
cowardly adj, adv cobarde; pusilánime.
cowboy, cowhand n vaquero m.
cower vi agacharse.
cowherd n vaquero m; vaquerizo m.
coy adj recatado/da, modesto/ta; esquivo/va; ~**ly** adv con esquivez.
coyness n esquivez, modestia f.
cozily adv cómodamente, con facilidad.
cozy adj cómodo/da.
crab n cangrejo m; manzana silvestre f.
crab apple n manzana silvestre f; ~ **tree** n manzano silvestre m.
crack n crujido m; hendedura, quebraja f; * vt hender, rajar; romper; **to ~ down on** reprimandar fuertemente;* vi reventar.
cracker n buscapiés m invar; galleta f.
crackle vi crujir, chillar.
crackling n estallido, crujido m.
cradle n cuna f; * vt acunar.
craft n arte m; artificio m; barco m.
craftily adv astutamente.
craftiness n astucia, estratagema f.
craftsman n artífice, artesano m.
craftsmanship n artesanía f.
crafty adj astuto/ta, artificioso/sa.
crag n despeñadero m.
cram vt embutir; engordar; empujar; * vi empollar.
crammed adj atestado/da.
cramp n calambre m; * vt constreñir.
cramped adj apretado/da.
crampon n crampón m.
cranberry n arándano agrio m.
crane n grulla f; grúa f.

crash vi estallar; * vr zamparse; * n estallido m; choque m.
crash helmet n casco m.
crash landing n aterrizaje forzoso m.
crass adj craso/sa, grueso/sa, basto/ta, tosco/ca, grosero/ra.
crate n cesta grande f.
crater n cráter m; boca de volcán f.
cravat n pañuelo m.
crave vt rogar, suplicar.
craving adj insaciable, pedigüeño/ña; * n deseo ardiente m.
crawfish n cangrejo de río m.
crawl vi arrastrar; **to ~ with** hormiguear.
crayon n lápiz m.
craze n manía f.
craziness n locura f.
crazy adj loco/ca.
creak vi crujir, chirriar.
cream n crema f; * adj color crema.
creamy adj cremoso/sa.
crease n pliegue m; * vt plegar.
create vt crear; causar.
creation n creación f; elección f.
creative adj creativo/va.
creator n creador/a m/f.
creature n criatura f.
credence n creencia, fe f; renombre m.
credentials npl (cartas) credenciales fpl.
credibility n credibilidad f.
credible adj creíble.
credit n crédito m; reputación f; autoridad f; * vt creer, fiar, acreditar.
creditable adj estimable, honorífico/ca; ~**bly** adv honorablemente.
credit card n tarjeta de crédito f.
creditor n acreedor m.
credulity n credulidad f.
credulous adj crédulo/la; ~**ly** adv con credulidad.
creed n credo m.
creek n arroyo m.
creep vi arrastrar, serpear; complacer bajamente.
creeper n (bot) enredadera f.
creepy adj horripilante.
cremate vt incinerar cadáveres.
cremation n cremación f.
crematorium n crematorio m.
crescent adj creciente; * n cuarto creciente m.
cress n berro m.
crest n cresta f.
crested adj crestado/da.
crestfallen adj acobardado/da, abatido/da de espíritu.
crevasse n grieta (de glaciar) f.
crevice n raja, hendedura f.
crew n banda, tropa f; tripulación f.
crib n cuna f; pesebre m.
cricket n grillo m; críquet m.

C

crime n crimen m; culpa f.
criminal adj criminal, reo/rea; ~**ly** adv criminalmente; * n criminal m/f.
criminality n criminalidad f.
crimson adj, n carmesí m.
cripple vt lisiar; (fig) estropear.
crisis n crisis f invar.
crisp adj crujiente.
crispness n sequedad f.
criss-cross adj entrelazado/da.
criterion n criterio m.
critic n crítico m; crítica f.
critic(al) adj crítico/ca; exacto/ta; delicado/da; ~**ally** adv exactamente, rigurosamente.
criticism n crítica f.
criticize vt criticar, censurar; zaherir; (fig) zurrar.
croak vi graznar.
crochet n ganchillo m; * vt, vi hacer ganchillo.
crockery n loza f; vasijas de barro fpl.
crocodile n cocodrilo m.
crony n amigote m; compinche m.
crook n (col) ladrón m; cayado m.
crooked adj torcido/da; perverso/sa.
crop n cultivo m; cosecha f; * vt recortar.
cross n cruz f; carga f; * adj mal humorado/da; * vt atravesar, cruzar; **to ~ over** traspasar.
crossbar n travesaño m.
crossbreed n raza cruzada f.
cross-country n carrera a campo traviesa f.
cross-examine vt preguntar a un testigo.
crossfire n fuego cruzado m.
crossing n cruce m; paso a nivel m.
cross-purpose n disposición contraria f; contradicción f; **to be at ~s** entenderse mal.
cross-reference n remisión f.
crossroad n encrucijada f.
crosswalk n paso de peatones m.
crotch n entrepierna f.
crouch vi agacharse, bajarse.
crow n cuervo m; canto del gallo m; * vi cantar el gallo.
crowd n público m; muchedumbre f; * vt amontonar; * vi reunirse.
crown n corona f; cumbre f; * vt coronar.
crown prince n príncipe real m.
crucial adj crucial.
crucible n crisol m.
crucifix n crucifijo m.
crucifixion n crucifixión f.
crucify vt crucificar; atormentar.
crude adj crudo/da, imperfecto/ta; ~**ly** adv crudamente.
cruel adj cruel, inhumano/na; ~**ly** adv cruelmente.
cruelty n crueldad f.
cruet set/stand n vinagreras fpl.
cruise n crucero m; * vi hacer un crucero.
cruiser n crucero m.
crumb n miga f.

crumble vt desmigajar, desmenuzar; * vi desmigajarse.
crumple vt arrugar.
crunch vt ronzar; * n (fig) crisis f invar.
crunchy adj crujiente.
crusade n cruzada f.
crush vt apretar, oprimir; * n choque m.
crust n costra f; corteza f; zoquete m.
crusty adj costroso/sa; bronco/ca, áspero/ra.
crutch n muleta f.
crux n lo esencial.
cry vt (vi) gritar; exclamar; llorar; * n grito m; lloro m; clamor m.
crypt n cripta f.
cryptic adj enigmático/ca.
crystal n cristal m.
crystal-clear adj claro/ra como el agua.
crystalline adj cristalino/na; transparente.
crystallize vt (vi) cristalizar(se).
cub n cachorro m.
cube n cubo m.
cubic adj cúbico/ca.
cuckoo n cuco m.
cucumber n pepino m.
cud n: **to chew the ~** rumiar; (fig) reflexionar.
cuddle vt abrazar; * vi abrazarse; * n abrazo m.
cudgel n garrote, palo m.
cue n taco (de billar) m.
cuff[1] n puño m, bocamanga f, vuelta f.
cuff[2] n puñada f.
culinary adj culinario/ria, de la cocina.
cull vt escoger, elegir.
culminate vi culminar.
culmination n colmo m.
culpability n culpabilidad f.
culpable adj culpable, criminal; ~**bly** adv culpablemente, criminalmente.
culprit n culpable m/f.
cult n culto f.
cultivate vi cultivar, mejorar; perfeccionar.
cultivation n cultivo m.
cultural adj cultural.
culture n cultura f.
cumbersome adj engorroso/sa, pesado/da, confuso/sa.
cumulative adj cumulativo/va.
cunning adj astuto/ta; intrigante; ~**ly** adv astutamente; expertamente; * n astucia, sutileza f; ~ **person** zorro m.
cup n taza, jícara f; (bot) cáliz m.
cupboard n armario m.
curable adj curable.
curate n teniente de cura m; párroco m.
curator n curador/a m/f; guardián/ana m/f.
curb n freno m; bordillo m; * vt refrenar, contener, moderar.
curd n cuajada f.
curdle vt (vi) cuajar(se), coagular(se).

cure n cura f; remedio m; * vt curar, sanar.
curfew n toque de queda m.
curing n curación f.
curiosity n curiosidad f; rareza f.
curious adj curioso/sa; ~ly adv curiosamente.
curl n rizo de pelo m; * vt rizar; ondear; * vi rizarse.
curling iron n, **curling tongs** npl tenacillas de rizar fpl.
curly adj rizado/da.
currant n pasa f.
currency n moneda f; circulación f; duración f.
current adj corriente, común; * n curso, progreso m; marcha f; corriente f.
current affairs npl actualidades fpl.
currently adv actualmente.
curriculum vitae n currículum m.
curry n curry m.
curse vt maldecir; * vi imprecar; blasfemar; * n maldición f.
cursor n cursor m.
cursory adj precipitado/da, inconsiderado/da.
curt adj sucinto/ta.
curtail vt acortar.
curtsy n reverencia f; * vi hacer una reverencia.
curvature n curvatura f.
curve vt encorvar; * n curva f.
cushion n cojín m; almohada f.
custard n natillas fpl.
custodian n custodio m.
custody n custodia f; prisión f.
custom n costumbre f, uso m.
customary adj usual, acostumbrado/da, ordinario/ria.

customer n cliente m/f.
customs npl aduana f.
customs duty n derechos de aduana mpl.
customs officer n aduanero/ra m/f.
cut vt cortar; separar; herir; dividir; cortar los naipes; **to ~ short** interrumpir, cortar la palabra; **to ~ teeth** nacerle los dientes (a un niño); * vi traspasar; cruzarse; * n corte m; cortadura f; herida f; **~ and dried** adj rutinario/ria.
cutback n reducción f.
cute adj lindo/da.
cutlery n cuchillería f.
cutlet n chuleta f.
cut-rate adj a precio reducido.
cut-throat n asesino m; * adj encarnizado/da.
cutting n cortadura f; * adj cortante; mordaz.
cyanide n cianuro m.
cyberspace n ciberespacio m.
cycle n ciclo m; bicicleta f; * vi ir en bicicleta.
cycling n ciclismo m.
cyclist n ciclista m/f.
cyclone n ciclón m.
cygnet n pollo del cisne m.
cylinder n cilindro m; rollo m.
cylindric(al) adj cilíndrico/ca.
cymbals n címbalo m.
cynic(al) adj cínico/ca; obsceno/na; * n cínico m (filósofo).
cynicism n cinismo m.
cypress n ciprés m.
cyst n quiste m.
czar n zar m.

C

D

dab n pedazo pequeño m; toque m.
dabble vi chapotear.
dad(dy) n papa m.
daddy-long-legs n típula f.
daffodil n narciso m.
dagger n puñal m.
daily adj diario/ria, cotidiano/na; * adv diariamente, cada día; * n diario m.
daintily adv delicadamente.
daintiness n elegancia f; delicadeza f.
dainty adj delicado/da. elegante.
dairy n lechería f.
dairy farm n vaquería f.
dairy produce n productos lácteos mpl.
daisy n margarita, maya f.
dale n valle m.
dally vi tardar.
dam n presa f; * vt represar.
damage n daño m; perjuicio m; * dañar; perjudicar.
damask n damasco m; * adj de damasco.
damn vt condenar; * adj maldito/ta.
damnable adj maldito/ta; ~bly adv terriblemente.
damnation n perdición f.
damning adj irrecusable.
damp adj húmedo/da; * n humedad f; * vt mojar.
dampen vt mojar.
dampness n humedad f.
damson n damascena f (ciruela).
dance n danza f; baile m; * vi bailar.
dance hall n salón de baile m.
dancer n bailarín m, bailarina f.
dandelion n diente de león m.
dandruff n caspa f.
dandy adj mono/na.
danger n peligro, riesgo m.
dangerous adj peligroso/sa; ~ly adv peligrosamente.
dangle vi estar colgado/da.
dank adj húmedo/da.
dapper adj apuesto/ta.
dappled adj rodado/da.
dare vi atreverse; * vt desafiar.
daredevil n atrevido m.
daring n osadía f; * adj atrevido/da; ~ly adv atrevidamente, osadamente.
dark adj oscuro/ra; negro/gra; * n oscuridad f; ignorancia f.
darken vt (vi) oscurecer(se).
dark glasses npl gafas de sol fpl.
darkness n oscuridad f.
darkroom n cuarto oscuro m.
darling n, adj querido m.

darn vt zurcir.
dart n dardo m.
dartboard n diana f.
dash vi irse de prisa; * n pizca f; **at one ~** de un golpe.
dashboard n tablero de instrumentos m.
dashing adj gallardo/da.
dastardly adj cobarde.
data n datos mpl.
database n base de datos f.
data processing n proceso de datos m.
date n fecha f; cita f; (bot) dátil m; * vt fechar; salir con.
dated adj anticuado/da.
dative n dativo m.
daub vt manchar.
daughter n hija f; ~ **in-law** nuera f.
daunting adj desalentador/a.
dawdle vi gastar tiempo.
dawn n alba f; * vi amanecer.
day n día m; luz f; **by ~** de día; ~ **by ~** de día en día.
daybreak n alba f.
day laborer n jornalero m.
daylight n luz del día, luz natural f; ~ **saving time** n hora de verano f.
daytime n día m.
daze vt aturdir.
dazed adj aturdido/da.
dazzle vt deslumbrar.
dazzling adj deslumbrante.
deacon n diácono m.
dead adj muerto/ta. marchito/ta; ~**wood** n lastre m; ~ **silence** n silencio profundo m; **the ~** npl los muertos.
dead-drunk adj borracho como una cuba.
deaden vt amortiguar.
dead heat n empate m.
deadline n fecha tope f.
deadlock n punto muerto m.
deadly adj mortal; * adv terriblemente.
dead march n marcha fúnebre f.
deadness n inercia f.
deaf adj sordo/da.
deafen vt ensordecer.
deaf-mute n sordomudo/da m./f.
deafness n sordera f.
deal n convenio m; transacción f; **a great ~** mucho; **a good ~** bastante; * vt distribuir; dar; * vi comerciar; **to ~ in/with** tratar en/con.
dealer n comerciante m/f; traficante m/f; mano f.
dealings npl trato m.
dean n deán m.

dear *adj* querido/da. caro/ra, costoso/sa; **~ly** *adv* caro.

dearness *n* carestía *f*.

dearth *n* escasez *f*.

death *n* muerte *f*.

deathbed *n* lecho de muerte *m*.

deathblow *n* golpe mortal *m*.

death certificate *n* partida de defunción *f*.

death penalty *n* pena de muerte *f*.

death throes *npl* agonía *f*.

death warrant *n* sentencia de muerte *f*.

debacle *n* desastre *m*.

debar *vt* excluir, no admitir.

debase *vt* degradar.

debasement *n* degradación *f*.

debatable *adj* discutible.

debate *n* debate *m*; polémica *f*; * *vt* discutir; examinar.

debauched *adj* vicioso/sa.

debauchery *n* libertinaje *m*.

debilitate *vt* debilitar.

debit *n* debe *m*; * *vt* (*com*) cargar en una cuenta.

debt *n* deuda *f*; obligación *f*; **to get into ~** contraer deudas.

debtor *n* deudor/a *m/f*.

debunk *vt* desacreditar.

decade *n* década *f*.

decadence *n* decadencia *f*.

decaffeinated *adj* descafeinado/da.

decanter *n* garrafa *f*.

decapitate *vt* decapitar, degollar.

decapitation *n* decapitación *f*.

decay *vi* decaer; pudrirse; * *n* decadencia *f*; caries *f*.

deceased *adj* muerto/ta.

deceit *n* engaño *m*.

deceitful *adj* engañoso/sa; **~ly** *adv* falsamente.

deceive *vt* engañar.

December *n* diciembre *m*.

decency *n* decencia *f*; modestia *f*.

decent *adj* decente, razonable; **~ly** *adv* decentemente.

deception *n* engaño *m*.

deceptive *adj* engañoso/sa.

decibel *n* decibelio *m*.

decide *vt, vi* decidir; resolver.

decided *adj* decidido/da.

decidedly *adv* decididamente.

deciduous *adj* (*bot*) de hoja caduca.

decimal *adj* decimal.

decimate *vt* diezmar.

decipher *vt* descifrar.

decision *n* decisión, determinación *f*.

decisive *adj* decisivo/va; **~ly** *adv* de modo decisivo.

deck *n* cubierta *f*; * *vt* adornar.

deckchair *n* tumbona *f*.

declaim *vi* declamar.

declamation *n* declamación *f*.

declaration *n* declaración *f*.

declare *vt* declarar, manifestar.

declension *n* declinación *f*.

decline *vt* (*gr*) declinar; evitar; * *vi* decaer; * *n* decadencia *f*.

declutch *vi* desembragar.

decode *vt* descifrar.

decoder *n* (*TV*) descodificador *m*.

decompose *vt* descomponer.

decomposition *n* descomposición *f*.

decor *n* decoración *f*.

decorate *vt* decorar, adornar.

decoration *n* decoración *f*.

decorative *adj* decorativo/va.

decorator *n* pintor (decorador) *m*.

decorous *adj* decoroso/sa; **~ly** *adv* decorosamente.

decorum *n* decoro, garbo *m*.

decoy *n* señuelo *m*.

decrease *vt* disminuir; * *n* disminución *f*.

decree *n* decreto *m*; * *vt* decretar; ordenar.

decrepit *adj* decrépito/ta.

decry *vt* desacreditar, censurar.

dedicate *vt* dedicar; consagrar.

dedication *n* dedicación *f*; dedicatoria *f*.

deduce *vt* deducir; concluir.

deduct *vt* restar.

deduction *n* deducción *f*; descuento *m*.

deed *n* acción *f*; hecho *m*; hazaña *f*.

deem *vi* juzgar.

deep *adj* profundo/da.

deepen *vt* profundizar.

deep-freeze *n* congeladora *f*.

deeply *adv* profundamente.

deepness *n* profundidad *f*.

deer *n* ciervo *m*.

deface *vt* desfigurar, afear.

defacement *n* desfiguración *f*.

defamation *n* difamación *f*.

default *n* defecto *m*; falta *f*; * *vi* faltar.

defaulter *n* (*law*) moroso/sa *m/f*.

defeat *n* derrota *f*; * *vt* derrotar; frustrar.

defect *n* defecto *m*; falta *f*.

defection *n* deserción *f*.

defective *adj* defectuoso/sa.

defend *vt* defender; proteger.

defendant *n* acusado/da *m/f*.

defense *n* defensa *f*; protección *f*.

defenseless *adj* indefenso/sa.

defensive *adj* defensivo/va; **~ly** *adv* de modo defensivo.

defer *vt* aplazar.

deference *n* deferencia *f*; respeto *m*.

deferential *adj* respetuoso/sa.

defiance *n* desafío *m*.

defiant *adj* insolente.

deficiency *n* defecto *m*; falta *f*.

deficient *adj* insuficiente.

deficit *n* déficit *m*, *Lat Am* faltante *m*.

defile *vt* ensuciar.

D

definable *adj* definible.
define *vt* definir.
definite *adj* definido/da. preciso/sa; **~ly** *adv* no cabe duda.
definition *n* definición *f*.
definitive *adj* definitivo/va; **~ly** *adv* definitivamente.
deflate *vt* desinflar.
deflect *vt* desviar.
deflower *vt* desvirgar.
deform *vt* desfigurar.
deformity *n* deformidad *f*.
defraud *vt* estafar.
defray *vt* costear.
defrost *vt* deshelar; descongelar.
defroster *n* luneta térmica *f*.
deft *adj* diestro/tra; **~ly** *adv* hábilmente.
defunct *adj* difunto/ta.
defuse *vt* desactivar.
degenerate *vi* degenerar; * *adj* degenerado/da.
degeneration *n* degeneración *f*.
degradation *n* degradación *f*.
degrade *vt* degradar.
degree *n* grado *m*; título *m*.
dehydrated *adj* deshidratado/da.
de-ice *vt* deshelar.
deign *vi* dignarse.
deity *n* deidad, divinidad *f*.
dejected *adj* desanimado/da.
dejection *n* desaliento *m*.
delay *vt* demorar; * *n* retraso *m*.
delectable *adj* deleitoso/sa.
delegate *vt* delegar; * *n* delegado *m*.
delegation *n* delegación *f*.
delete *vt* tachar; borrar.
deliberate *vt* deliberar; * *adj* intencionado/da; **~ly** *adv* a propósito.
deliberation *n* deliberación *f*.
deliberative *adj* deliberativo/va.
delicacy *n* delicadeza *f*.
delicate *adj* delicado/da. exquisito/ta; **~ly** *adv* delicadamente.
delicious *adj* delicioso/sa. exquisito/ta; **~ly** *adv* deliciosamente.
delight *n* delicia *f*; gozo, encanto *m*; * *vt, vi* deleitar(se).
delighted *adj* encantado/da.
delightful *adj* encantador/a, **~ly** *adv* en forma encantadora.
delineate *vt* delinear.
delineation *n* delineación *f*.
delinquency *n* delincuencia *f*.
delinquent *n* delincuente *m/f*.
delirious *adj* delirante.
delirium *n* delirio *m*.
deliver *vt* entregar; pronunciar.
deliverance *n* liberación *f*.
delivery *n* entrega *f*; parto *m*.
delude *vt* engañar.

deluge *n* diluvio *m*.
delusion *n* engaño *m*; ilusión *f*.
delve *vi* hurgar.
demagog *n* demagogo/a *m/f*.
demand *n* demanda *f*; reclamación *f*; * *vt* exigir; reclamar.
demanding *adj* exigente.
demarcation *n* demarcación *f*.
demean *vi* rebajarse.
demeanor *n* conducta *f*.
demented *adj* demente.
demise *n* desaparición *f*.
democracy *n* democracia *f*.
democrat *n* demócrata *m/f*.
democratic *adj* democrático/ca.
Democratic Party *n* Partido Democrático *m*.
demolish *vt* demoler.
demolition *n* demolición *f*.
demon *n* demonio, diablo *m*.
demonstrable *adj* demostrable; **~bly** *adv* manifiestamente.
demonstrate *vt* demostrar, probar; * *vi* manifestarse.
demonstration *n* demostración *f*; manifestación *f*.
demonstrative *adj* demostrativo/va.
demonstrator *n* manifestante *m/f*.
demoralization *n* desmoralización *f*.
demoralize *vt* desmoralizar.
demote *vt* degradar.
demur *vi* objetar.
demure *adj* modesto/ta; **~ly** *adv* modestamente.
den *n* guarida *f*.
denatured alcohol *n* alcohol desnaturalizado *m*.
denial *n* negación *f*.
denims *npl* vaqueros *mpl*.
denomination *n* valor *m*.
denominator *n* (*math*) denominador *m*.
denote *vt* denotar, indicar.
denounce *vt* denunciar.
dense *adj* denso/sa, espeso/sa.
density *n* densidad *f*.
dent *n* abolladura *f*; * *vt* abollar.
dental *adj* dental.
dentifrice *n* dentífrico *m*.
dentist *n* dentista *m/f*.
dentistry *n* odontología *f*.
denture *npl* dentadura postiza *f*.
denude *vt* desnudar, despojar.
denunciation *n* denuncia *f*.
deny *vt* negar.
deodorant *n* desodorante *m*.
deodorize *vt* desodorizar.
depart *vi* partir.
department *n* departamento *m*.
department store *n* gran almacén *m*.
departure *n* partida *f*.
departure lounge *n* sala de embarque *f*.
depend *vi* depender; **~ on/upon** contar con.

dependable adj seguro/ra, serio/ria.
dependant n dependiente m.
dependency n dependencia f.
dependent adj dependiente.
depict vt pintar, retratar; describir.
depleted adj reducido/da.
deplorable adj deplorable, lamentable; ~**bly** adv deplorablemente.
deplore vt deplorar, lamentar.
deploy vt (mil) desplegar.
depopulated adj despoblado/da.
depopulation n despoblación f.
deport vt deportar.
deportation n deportación f; destierro m.
deportment n conducta f.
deposit vt depositar; * n depósito m; yacimiento m.
deposition n deposición f.
depositor n depositante m.
depot n depósito m.
deprave vt depravar, corromper.
depraved adj depravado/da.
depravity n depravación f.
deprecate vt lamentar.
depreciate vi depreciarse.
depreciation n depreciación f.
depredation n pillaje m.
depress vt deprimir.
depressed adj deprimido/da.
depression n depresión f.
deprivation n privación f.
deprive vt privar.
deprived adj necesitado/da.
depth n profundidad f.
deputation n diputación f.
depute vt diputar, delegar.
deputize vi suplir a.
deputy n diputado/da m/f.
derail vt descarrilar.
deranged adj trastornado/da.
derby n hongo m.
derelict adj abandonado/da.
deride vt burlar.
derision n mofa f.
derisive adj irrisorio/ria.
derivable adj deducible.
derivation n derivación f.
derivative n derivado m.
derive vt, vi derivar(se).
dermatologist n dermatólogo/ga m/f.
dermatology n dermatología f.
derogatory adj despectivo/va.
derrick n torre de perforación f.
desalinate vt desalinizar.
desalination plant n desalinizadora f.
descant n (mus) discante m.
descend vi descender.
descendant n descendiente m.
descent n descenso m.

describe vt describir.
description n descripción f.
descriptive adj descriptivo/va.
descry vt divisar.
desecrate vt profanar.
desecration n profanación f.
desert[1] n desierto m; * adj desierto/ta.
desert[2] vt abandonar; desertar; * n mérito m.
deserter n desertor/a m/f.
desertion n deserción f.
deserve vt merecer, Lat Am ameritar; ser digno/na.
deservedly adv merecidamente.
deserving adj meritorio/ria.
desideratum n desiderátum m.
design vt diseñar; * n diseño m; dibujo m.
designate vt nombrar; designar.
designation n designación f.
designedly adv a propósito.
designer n diseñador m; modisto m.
desirability n conveniencia f.
desirable adj deseable.
desire n deseo m; * vt desear.
desirous adj deseoso/sa, ansioso/sa.
desist vi desistir.
desk n escritorio m.
desktop publishing n autoedición f.
desolate adj desierto/ta.
desolation n desolación f.
despair n desesperación f; * vi desesperarse.
despairingly adj desesperadamente.
desperado n bandido/da m/f.
desperate adj desesperado/da; ~**ly** adv desesperadamente; sumamente.
desperation n desesperación f.
despicable adj despreciable.
despise vt despreciar.
despite prep a pesar de.
despoil vt despojar.
despondency n abatimiento m.
despondent adj abatido/da.
despot n déspota m/f.
despotic adj despótico/ca, absoluto/ta; ~**ally** adv despóticamente.
despotism n despotismo m.
dessert n postre m.
destination n destino m.
destine vt destinar.
destiny n destino m; suerte f.
destitute adj indigente.
destitution n miseria f.
destroy vt destruir, arruinar.
destruction n destrucción, ruina f.
destructive adj destructivo/va.
desultory adj irregular; sin método.
detach vt separar.
detachable adj desmontable; de quitapón.
detachment n (mil) destacamento m.

D

detail *n* detalle *m*; **in** ~ detalladamente; * *vt* detallar.

detain *vt* retener; detener.

detect *vt* detectar.

detection *n* descubrimiento *m*.

detective *n* detective *m/f*.

detector *n* detector *m*.

detention *n* detención *f*.

deter *vt* disuadir.

detergent *n* detergente *m*.

deteriorate *vt* deteriorar.

deterioration *n* deterioro *m*.

determination *n* resolución *f*.

determine *vt* determinar, decidir.

determined *adj* resuelto/ta.

deterrent *n* fuerza de disuasión *f*.

detest *vt* detestar, aborrecer.

detestable *adj* detestable, abominable.

dethrone *vt* destronar.

dethronement *n* destronamiento *m*.

detonate *vi* detonar.

detonation *n* detonación *f*.

detour *n* desviación *f*.

detract *vt* desvirtuar.

detriment *n* perjuicio *m*.

detrimental *adj* perjudicial.

deuce *n* deuce *m*.

devaluation *n* devaluación *f*.

devastate *vt* devastar.

devastating *adj* devastador.

devastation *n* devastación, ruina *f*.

develop *vt* desarrollar.

development *n* desarrollo *m*.

deviate *vi* desviarse.

deviation *n* desviación *f*.

device *n* mecanismo *m*.

devil *n* diablo, demonio *m*.

devilish *adj* diabólico/ca; ~**ly** *adv* diabólicamente.

devious *adj* taimado/da.

devise *vt* inventar; idear.

devoid *adj* desprovisto/ta.

devolve *vt* delegar.

devote *vt* dedicar; consagrar.

devoted *adj* fiel.

devotee *n* partidario/a *m/f*.

devotion *n* devoción *f*.

devotional *adj* devoto/ta.

devour *vt* devorar.

devout *adj* devoto/ta, piadoso/sa; ~**ly** *adv* piadosamente.

dew *n* rocío *m*.

dewy *adj* rociado/da.

dexterity *n* destreza *f*.

dexterous *adj* diestro/tra, hábil.

diabetes *n* diabetes *f*.

diabetic *n* diabético/ca *m/f*.

diabolic *adj* diabólico/ca; ~**ally** *adv* diabólicamente.

diadem *n* diadema *f*.

diagnosis *n* (*med*) diagnóstico *m*.

diagnostic *adj*, *n* diagnóstico *m*; ~**s** *pl* diagnóstica *f*.

diagonal *adj*, *n* diagonal *f*; ~**ly** *adv* diagonalmente.

diagram *n* diagrama *m*.

dial *n* cuadrante *m*; disco *m*.

dial code *n* prefijo *m*.

dialect *n* dialecto *m*.

dialog *n* diálogo *m*.

dial tone *n* tono de marcar *m*.

diameter *n* diámetro *m*.

diametrical *adj* diametral; ~**ly** *adv* diametralmente.

diamond *n* diamante *m*.

diamond-cutter *n* diamantista *m/f*.

diamonds *npl* (cards) diamantes *mpl*.

diaper *n* pañal *m*; **disposable** ~ pañal desechable.

diaphragm *n* diafragma *m*.

diarrhea *n* diarrea *f*.

diary *n* diario *m*.

dice *npl* dados *mpl*.

dictate *vt* dictar; * *n* dictado *m*.

dictation *n* dictado *m*.

dictatorial *adj* autoritativo/va, magistral.

dictatorship *n* dictadura *f*.

diction *n* dicción *f*

dictionary *n* diccionario *m*.

didactic *adj* didáctico/ca.

die[1] *vi* morir; **to** ~ **away** perderse; **to** ~ **down** apagarse.

die[2] *n* dado *m*.

diehard *n* reaccionario/ria *m/f*.

diesel *n* diesel *m*.

diet *n* dieta *f*; régimen *m*; * *vi* estar a dieta.

dietary *adj* dietético/ca.

differ *vi* diferenciarse.

difference *n* diferencia, disparidad *f*.

different *adj* diferente; ~**ly** *adv* diferentemente.

differentiate *vt* diferenciar.

difficult *adj* difícil.

difficulty *n* dificultad *f*.

diffidence *n* timidez *f*.

diffident *adj* desconfiado/da; ~**ly** *adv* desconfiadamente.

diffraction *n* difracción *f*.

diffuse *vt* difundir, esparcir; * *adj* difuso/sa.

diffusion *n* difusión *f*.

dig *vt* cavar; **to** ~ **ditches** zanjar; * *n* empujón *m*.

digest *vt* digerir.

digestible *adj* digerible.

digestion *n* digestión *f*.

digestive *adj* digestivo/va.

digit *n* dígito *m*.

digital *adj* digital.

digitize *vt* digitalizar.

dignified *adj* grave.

dignitary *n* dignatario *m*.

dignity *n* dignidad *f*.

digress *vi* divagar.

digression n digresión f.
dike n dique m.
dilapidated adj desmoronado/da.
dilapidation n ruina f.
dilate vt, vi dilatar(se).
dilemma n dilema m.
diligence n diligencia f.
diligent adj diligente, asiduo/dua; ~**ly** adv diligentemente.
dilute vt diluir.
dim adj turbio/bia; lerdo/da; oscuro/ra; * vt bajar.
dime n moneda de diez centavos f.
dimension n dimensión, extensión f.
diminish vt, vi disminuir(se).
diminution n disminución f.
diminutive n diminutivo m.
dimly adv indistintamente.
dimmer n interruptor m.
dimple n hoyuelo m, Lat Am hoyito m.
din n alboroto m.
dine vi cenar.
diner n restaurante (económico) m.
dinghy n lancha neumática f.
dingy adj sombrío/ría.
dinner n cena f.
dinner-jacket n smoking m.
dinner time n hora de comer f.
dinosaur n dinosaurio m.
dint n: **by ~ of** a fuerza de.
diocese n diócesis f invar.
dip vt mojar; * n zambullida f.
diphtheria n difteria f.
diphthong n diptongo m.
diploma n diploma m.
diplomacy n diplomacia f.
diplomat n diplomático/ca m/f.
diplomatic adj diplomático/ca.
dipsomania n dipsomanía f.
dipstick n (auto) varilla de nivel f.
dire adj calamitoso/sa.
direct adj directo/ta; * vt dirigir.
direction n dirección f; instrucción f.
directly adj directamente; inmediatamente.
director n director/a m/f.
directory n guía f.
dirt n suciedad f; ~ **on clothes** zarpa f.
dirtiness n suciedad f.
dirty adj sucio/cia; vil, bajo/ja.
disability n discapacidad f.
disabled adj discapacitado/da.
disabuse vt desengañar.
disadvantage n desventaja f; * vt perjudicar.
disadvantageous adj desventajoso/sa.
disaffected adj descontento/ta.
disagree vi no estar de acuerdo.
disagreeable adj desagradable; ~**bly** adv desagradablemente.

disagreement n desacuerdo m.
disallow vt rechazar.
disappear vi desaparecer; ausentarse.
disappearance n desaparición f.
disappoint vt decepcionar.
disappointed adj decepcionado/da.
disappointing adj decepcionante.
disappointment n decepción f.
disapproval n desaprobación, censura f.
disapprove vt desaprobar.
disarm vt desarmar.
disarmament n desarme m.
disarray n desarreglo m.
disaster n desastre m.
disastrous adj desastroso/sa, calamitoso/sa.
disband vt disolver.
disbelief n incredulidad f.
disbelieve vt desconfiar.
disburse vt desembolsar, pagar.
discard vt descartar.
discern vt discernir, percibir.
discernible adj perceptible.
discerning adj perspicaz.
discernment n perspicacia f.
discharge vt descargar; pagar (una deuda); cumplir; * n descarga f; descargo m.
disciple n discípulo/la m/f.
discipline n disciplina f; * vt disciplinar.
disclaim vt negar.
disclaimer n negación f.
disclose vi revelar.
disclosure n revelación f.
discolor vt descolorar.
discoloration n descolorimiento m.
discomfort n incomodidad f.
disconcert vt desconcertar.
disconnect vt desconectar.
disconsolate adj inconsolable; ~**ly** adv desconsoladamente.
discontent n descontento/ta m/f; * adj descontento/ta.
discontented adj descontento/ta.
discontinue vi interrumpir.
discord n discordia f.
discordant adj discordante.
discotheque, disco n discoteca f.
discount n descuento m; rebaja f; * vt descontar.
discourage vt desalentar, desanimar.
discouraged adj desalentado/da.
discouragement n desaliento m.
discouraging adj desalentador/a.
discourse n discurso m.
discourteous adj descortés, grosero/ra; ~**ly** adv descortésmente.
discourtesy n descortesía f.
discover vt descubrir.
discovery n descubrimiento m; revelación f.
discredit vt desacreditar.
discreditable adj ignominioso/sa.

D

discreet *adj* discreto/ta; **~ly** *adv* discretamente.
discrepancy *n* discrepancia, diferencia *f*.
discretion *n* discreción *f*.
discretionary *adj* discrecional.
discriminate *vt* distinguir.
discrimination *n* discriminación *f*.
discursive *adj* discursivo/va.
discuss *vt* discutir.
discussion *n* discusión *f*.
disdain *vt* desdeñar; * *n* desdén, desprecio *m*.
disdainful *adj* desdeñoso/sa; **~ly** *adv* desdeñosamente.
disease *n* enfermedad *f*.
diseased *adj* enfermo/ma.
disembark *vt, vi* desembarcar.
disembarkation *n* desembarco *m*.
disenchant *vt* desencantar.
disenchanted *adj* desilusionado/da.
disenchantment *n* desilusión *f*.
disengage *vt* soltar.
disentangle *vt* desenredar.
disfigure *vt* desfigurar, afear.
disgrace *n* ignominia *f*; escándalo *m*; * *vt* deshonrar.
disgraceful *adj* ignominioso/sa; **~ly** *adv* vergonzosamente.
disgruntled *adj* descontento/ta.
disguise *vt* disfrazar; * *n* disfraz *m*.
disgust *n* aversión *f*; * *vt* repugnar.
disgusting *adj* repugnante.
dish *n* fuente *f*; plato *m*; taza *f*; * *vt* servir en fuente; **to ~ up** servir.
dishabille *n* deshabillé *m*.
dishcloth *n* paño de cocina *m*.
dishearten *vt* desalentar.
disheveled *adj* desarreglado/da.
dishonest *adj* deshonesto/ta; **~ly** *adv* deshonestamente.
dishonesty *n* falta de honradez *f*.
dishonor *n* deshonra, ignominia *f*; * *vt* deshonrar.
dishonorable *adj* deshonroso/sa; **~bly** *adv* deshonrosamente.
dishtowel *n* trapo de fregar *m*.
dishwarmer *n* escalfador *m*.
dishwasher *n* lavaplatos *m/f*; lavavajillas *m invar*.
disillusion *vt* desilusionar.
disillusioned *adj* desilusionado/da.
disincentive *n* freno *m*.
disinclination *n* aversión *f*.
disinclined *adj* reacio/cia.
disinfect *vt* desinfectar.
disinfectant *n* desinfectante *m*.
disinherit *vt* desheredar.
disintegrate *vi* disgregarse.
disinterested *adj* desinteresado/da; **~ly** *adv* desinteresadamente.
disjointed *adj* inconexo/xa.
disk *n* disco.
diskette *n* disco, disquete *m*.

dislike *n* aversión *f*; * *vt* tener antipatía.
dislocate *vt* dislocar.
dislocation *n* dislocación *f*.
dislodge *vt, vi* desalojar.
disloyal *adj* desleal; **~ly** *adv* deslealmente.
disloyalty *n* deslealtad *f*.
dismal *adj* triste.
dismantle *vt* desmontar.
dismay *n* consternación *f*.
dismember *vt* despedazar.
dismiss *vt* despedir, *Lat Am* remover.
dismount *vt* desmontar; * *vi* apearse.
disobedience *n* desobediencia *f*.
disobedient *adj* desobediente.
disobey *vt* desobedecer.
disorder *n* desorden *m*; confusión *f*.
disorderly *adj* desarreglado/da, confuso/sa.
disorganization *n* desorganización *f*.
disorganized *adj* desorganizado/da.
disorientated *adj* desorientado/da.
disown *vt* desconocer.
disparage *vt* despreciar.
disparaging *adj* despreciativo/va.
disparity *n* disparidad *f*.
dispassionate *adj* desapasionado/da.
dispatch *vt* enviar; * *n* envío *m*; informe *m*.
dispel *vt* disipar.
dispensary *n* dispensario *m*.
dispense *vt* dispensar; distribuir.
disperse *vt* dispersar.
dispirited *adj* desalentado/da.
displace *vt* desplazar.
display *vt* exponer; * *n* ostentación *f*; despliegue *m*.
displeased *adj* disgustado/da.
displeasure *n* disgusto *m*.
disposable *adj* desechable.
disposal *n* disposición *f*.
dispose *vt* disponer; arreglar.
disposed *adj* dispuesto/ta.
disposition *n* disposición *f*.
dispossess *vt* desposeer.
disproportionate *adj* desproporcionado/da.
disprove *vt* refutar.
dispute *n* disputa, controversia *f*; * *vt* disputar.
disqualify *vt* incapacitar.
disquiet *n* inquietud *f*.
disquieting *adj* inquietante.
disquisition *n* disquisición *f*.
disregard *vt* desatender; * *n* desdén *m*.
disreputable *adj* de mala fama.
disrespect *n* irreverencia *f*.
disrespectful *adj* irreverente; **~ly** *adv* irreverentemente.
disrobe *vt* desnudar.
disrupt *vt* interrumpir.
disruption *n* interrupción *f*.
dissatisfaction *n* descontento/ta, disgusto *m*.
dissatisfied *adj* insatisfecho/cha.

dissect vt disecar.
dissection n disección f.
disseminate vt diseminar.
dissension n disensión f.
dissent vi disentir; * n disensión f.
dissenter n disidente m.
dissertation n disertación f.
dissident n disidente m.
dissimilar adj distinto/ta.
dissimilarity n disimilitud f.
dissimulation n disimulo m.
dissipate vt disipar.
dissipation n disipación f.
dissociate vt disociar.
dissolute adj libertino/na.
dissolution n disolución f.
dissolve vt disolver; * vi disolverse, derretirse.
dissonance n disonancia f.
dissuade vt disuadir.
distance n distancia f; **at a ~** de lejos; * vt apartar.
distant adj distante.
distaste n disgusto m.
distasteful adj desagradable.
distend vt hinchar.
distill vt destilar.
distillation n destilación f.
distillery n destilería f.
distinct adj distinto/ta, diferente; claro/ra; **~ly** adv distintamente.
distinction n distinción f.
distinctive adj distintivo/va.
distinctness n claridad f.
distinguish vt distinguir; discernir.
distort vt retorcer.
distorted adj distorsionado/da.
distortion n distorción f.
distract vt distraer.
distracted adj distraído/da; **~ly** adj distraídamente.
distraction n distracción f; confusión f.
distraught adj enloquecido/da.
distress n angustia f; * vt angustiar.
distressing adj penoso/sa.
distribute vt distribuir, repartir.
distribution n distribución f.
distributor n distribuidor m.
district n distrito m.
district attorney n fiscal del distrito m/f.
distrustful adj desconfiado/da. sospechoso/sa.
disturb vt molestar.
disturbance n disturbio m.
disturbed adj preocupado/da.
disturbing adj inquietante.
disuse n desuso m.
disused adj abandonado/da.
ditch n zanja f.
dither vi vacilar.
ditto adv ídem.
ditty n cancioneta f.

diuretic adj (med) diurético/ca.
dive vi sumergirse; bucear; * vr zambullirse; * n zambullida f.
diver n buzo m.
diverge vi divergir.
divergence n divergencia f.
divergent adj divergente.
diverse adj diverso/sa, diferente; **~ly** adv diversamente.
diversion n diversión f.
diversity n diversidad f.
divert vt desviar; divertir.
divest vt desnudar; despojar.
divide vt dividir; * vi dividirse.
dividend n dividendo m.
dividers npl (math) compás de puntas m.
divine adj divino/na.
divinity n divinidad f.
diving n salto m; buceo m.
diving board n trampolín m.
divisible adj divisible.
division n (math) división f; desunión f.
divisor n (math) divisor m.
divorce n divorcio m; * vi divorciarse.
divorced adj divorciado/da.
divulge vt divulgar, publicar.
dizziness n vértigo m.
dizzy adj mareado/da.
DJ n pinchadiscos m.
do vt hacer, obrar.
docile adj dócil, apacible.
dock n muelle m; * vi atracar.
docker n estibador m.
dockyard n (mar) astillero m.
doctor n médico/ca m/f.
doctrinal adj doctrinal.
doctrine n doctrina f.
document n documento m.
documentary adj documental.
dodge vt esquivar.
doe n gama f; **~ rabbit** coneja f.
dog n perro m.
dogged adj tenaz; **~ly** adv tenazmente.
dog kennel n perrera f.
dogmatic adj dogmático/ca; **~ly** adv dogmáticamente.
doings npl hechos mpl; eventos mpl.
do-it-yourself n bricolaje m.
doleful adj lúgubre, triste.
doll n muñeca f.
dollar n dólar m.
dolphin n delfín m.
domain n campo m.
dome n cúpula f.
domestic adj doméstico/ca.
domesticate vt domesticar.
domestication n domesticación f.
domesticity n domesticidad f.
domicile n domicilio m.

D

dominant *adj* dominante.
dominate *vi* dominar.
domination *n* dominación *f.*
domineer *vi* dominar.
domineering *adj* dominante.
dominion *n* dominio *m.*
dominoes *npl* dominó *m.*
donate *vt* donar.
donation *n* donación *f.*
done *adj* hecho/cha; cocido/da.
donkey *n* asno, borrico *m.*
donor *n* donante *m/f.*
doodle *vi* garabatear.
doom *n* suerte *f.*
door *n* puerta *f.*
doorbell *n* timbre *m.*
door handle *n* tirador *m.*
doorman *n* portero *m.*
doormat *n* felpudo *m.*
doorplate *n* planchuela *f.*
doorstep *n* peldaño *m.*
doorway *n* entrada *f.*
dormant *adj* latente.
dormer window *n* buhardilla *f.*
dormitory *n* dormitorio *m.*
dormouse *n* lirón *m.*
dosage *n* dosis *f invar.*
dose *n* dosis *f invar, Lat Am* dosaje *m;* * *vt* disponer la dosis de.
dossier *n* expediente *m.*
dot *n* punto *m.*
dote *vi* adorar.
dotingly *adv* con cariño excesivo.
double *adj* doble; * *vt* doblar; duplicar; * *n* doble *m.*
double bed *n* cama matrimonial *f.*
double-breasted *adj* cruzado/da.
double chin *n* papada *f.*
double-dealing *n* duplicidad *f.*
double-edged *adj* de doble filo.
double entry *n* (*com*) partida doble *f.*
double-lock *vt* echar la segunda vuelta a la llave a.
double room *n* habitación doble *f.*
doubly *adj* doblemente.
doubt *n* duda, sospecha *f;* * *vt* dudar; sospechar.
doubtful *adj* dudoso/sa.
doubtless *adv* sin duda.
dough *n* masa *f.*
douse *vt* apagar.
dove *n* paloma *f.*
dovecot(e) *n* palomar *m.*
dowdy *adj* mal vestido/da.
down *n* plumón *m;* flojel *m;* * *prep* abajo; **to sit ~** sentarse; **upside ~** al revés.
downcast *adj* cabizbajo/ja.
downfall *n* ruina *f.*
downhearted *adj* desanimado/da.
downhill *adv* cuesta abajo/ja.
down payment *n* entrada *f.*

downpour *n* aguacero *m.*
downright *adj* manifiesto/ta.
downstairs *adv* abajo/ja.
down-to-earth *adj* práctico/ca.
downtown *adv* al centro (de la ciudad).
downward(s) *adv* hacia abajo.
dowry *n* dote *f.*
doze *vi* dormitar.
dozen *n* docena *f.*
dozy *adj* somnoliento/ta.
drab *adj* gris.
draft *n* borrador *m;* quinta *f;* corriente de aire *f.*
drafty *adj* expuesto/ta al aire.
drag *vt* arrastrar; tirar con fuerza; * *n* lata *f.*
dragnet *n* red barredera *f.*
dragon *n* dragón *m.*
dragonfly *n* libélula *f.*
drain *vt* desaguar; secar; * *n* desaguadero *m.*
drainage *n* desagüe *m.*
draining board *n* escurridor *m.*
drainpipe *n* desagüe *m.*
drake *n* ánade macho *m.*
dram *n* traguito *m.*
drama *n* drama *m.*
dramatic *adj* dramático/ca; **~ally** *adv* dramáticamente.
dramatist *n* dramaturgo/ga *m/f.*
dramatize *vt* dramatizar.
drape *vt* cubrir; * *n* cortina *f;* telón (en teatro) *m;* **~s** *npl* cortinas *fpl.*
drastic *adj* drástico/ca.
draw *vt* tirar; dibujar; **to ~ nigh** acercarse.
drawback *n* desventaja *f.*
drawer *n* cajón *m.*
drawing *n* dibujo *m.*
drawing board *n* tablero de dibujo *m.*
drawing room *n* salón *m.*
drawl *vi* hablar con pesadez.
dread *n* terror, espanto *m;* * *vt* temer.
dreadful *adj* espantoso/sa; **~ly** *adv* terriblemente.
dream *n* sueño *m;* * *vi* sonar.
dreary *adj* triste.
dredge *vt* dragar.
dregs *npl* heces *fpl.*
drench *vt* empapar.
dress *vt* vestir; vendar; * *vi* vestirse; * *n* vestido *m.*
dresser *n* aparador *m.*
dressing *n* vendaje *m;* aliño *m.*
dressing gown *n* bata *f.*
dressing room *n* tocador *m.*
dressing table *n* tocador *m.*
dressmaker *n* modista *f.*
dressy *adj* elegante.
dribble *vi* caer gota a gota, babear.
dribbling *n* regateo *m.*
dried *adj* seco/ca.
drift *n* montón *m;* ventisquero *m;* significado *m;* * *vi* ir a la deriva.

driftwood n madera de deriva f.
drill n taladro m; (mil) instrucción f; * vt taladrar.
drink vt, vi beber; * n bebida f.
drinkable adj potable.
drinker n bebedor/a m/f.
drinking bout n borrachera f.
drinking water n agua potable f.
drip vi gotear; * n gota f; goteo m.
drive vt conducir, Lat Am manejar; empujar; * vi conducir, Lat Am manejar; * n paseo en coche m; entrada f.
drivel n baba f; * vi babear.
driver n conductor/a m/f; Lat Am chofer m.
driver's license n carnet m de conducir, carnet m de manejar.
driveway n entrada f.
driving n conducción f, Lat Am manejo m.
driving instructor n profesor/a de autoescuela m/f.
driving school n autoescuela f.
driving test n examen de conducir, examen de manejo m.
drizzle vi lloviznar.
droll adj gracioso/sa.
drone n zumbido m; zángano m.
drool vi babear.
droop vi decaer.
drop n gota f; * vt dejar caer; * vi bajar; **to ~ out** retirarse.
drop-out n marginado m.
dropper n cuentagotas m invar.
dross n escoria f.
drought n sequía f.
drove n: in ~s en tropel.
drown vt anegar; * vi anegarse.
drowsiness n somnolencia f.
drowsy adj somnoliento/ta.
drudgery n trabajo monótono m; zurra f.
drug n droga f; * vt drogar.
drug addict n drogadicto/ta m/f.
drug addiction n drogadicción f.
druggist n farmacéutico/ca m/f.
drugstore n farmacia f.
drug trafficker n narcotraficante m/f.
drum n tambor m; **rural ~** zambomba f; * vi tocar el tambor.
drum majorette n batonista f.
drummer n batería m/f, Lat Am baterista m/f.
drumstick n palillo de tambor m.
drunk adj borracho/cha.
drunkard n borracho m.
drunken adj borracho/cha.
drunkenness n borrachera f.
dry adj seco/ca; * vt secar; * vi secarse.
dry-cleaning n lavado en seco m.
dry-goods store n mercería f.
dryness n sequedad f.
dry rot n podredumbre f.

dual adj doble.
dual-purpose adj de doble uso.
dubbed adj doblado/da.
dubious adj dudoso/sa.
duck n pato m; * vt (vi) zambullir(se).
duckling n patito m.
dud adj estropeado/da.
due adj debido/da, apto/ta; * adv exactamente; * n derecho m.
duel n duelo m.
duet n (mus) dúo m.
dull adj lerdo/da; insípido/da; zopenco/ca; gris; * vt aliviar.
duly adv debidamente; puntualmente.
dumb adj mudo/da; ~**ly** adv sin chistar.
dumbbell n pesa f.
dumbfounded adj pasmado/da.
dump n montón m; * vt dejar.
dumping n (com) dumping m.
dumpling n bola de masa f.
dumpy adj gordito/ta.
dunce n zopenco m.
dune n duna f.
dung n estiércol m.
dungeon n calabozo m.
dupe n bobo m; * vt engañar, embaucar.
duplex n dúplex m.
duplicate n duplicado m; copia f; * vt multicopiar.
duplicity n duplicidad f.
durability n durabilidad f.
durable adj duradero/ra.
duration n duración f.
during prep mientras, durante el tiempo que.
dusk n crepúsculo m.
dust n polvo m; * vt desempolvar.
duster n plumero m.
dusty adj polvoriento/ta.
Dutch courage n valor fingido m.
duteous adj fiel, leal.
dutiful adj obediente, sumiso/sa; ~**ly** adv obedientemente.
duty n deber m; obligación f.
duty-free adj libre de derechos de aduana.
dwarf n enano m; enana f; * vt empequeñecer.
dwell vi habitar, morar.
dwelling n habitación f; domicilio m.
dwindle vi mermar, disminuirse.
dye vt teñir; * n tinte m.
dyer n tintorero/ra m/f.
dyeing n tintorería f; tintura f.
dye-works npl taller del tintorero m.
dying adj agonizante, moribundo/da; * n muerte f; ~ **moments** postrimerías fpl.
dynamic adj dinámico/ca.
dynamics n dinámica f.
dynamite n dinamita f.
dynamiter n dinamitero/ra m/f.

D

dynamo *n* dinamo *f*, *Lat Am* dinamo *m*.
dynasty *n* dinastía *f*.
dysentery *n* disentería *f*.

dyspepsia *n* (*med*) dispepsia *f*.
dyspeptic *adj* dispéptico/ca.

E

each *pn* cada uno, cada una; ~ **other** unos a otros, unas a otras, mutuamente.

eager *adj* entusiasmado/da; ~**ly** *adv* con entusiasmo.

eagerness *n* ansia *f*; anhelo *m*.

eagle *n* águila *f*.

eagle-eyed *adj* con vista de lince.

eaglet *n* aguilucho *m*.

ear *n* oreja *f*; oído *m*; espiga *f*; **by** ~ de oreja.

earache *n* dolor de oídos *m*.

eardrum *n* tímpano (del oído) *m*.

early *adj* temprano/na; *adv* temprano.

earmark *vt* destinar a.

earn *vt* ganar; conseguir.

earnest *adj* serio/ria; en serio; ~**ly** *adv* seriamente.

earnestness *n* seriedad *f*.

earnings *npl* ingresos *mpl*.

earphones *npl* auriculares *mpl*.

earring *n* zarcillo, pendiente *m*.

earth *n* tierra *f*; * *vt* conectar a tierra.

earthen *adj* de tierra.

earthenware *n* loza de barro *f*.

earthquake *n* terremoto *m*.

earthworm *n* lombriz *f*.

earthy *adj* sensual.

earwig *n* tijereta *f*.

ease *n* comodidad *f*; facilidad *f*; **at** ~ con desahogo; * *vt* aliviar; mitigar.

easel *n* caballete *m*.

easily *adv* fácilmente.

easiness *n* facilidad *f*.

east *n* este *m*; oriente *m*.

Easter *n* Pascua de Resurrección; Semana Santa *f*.

Easter egg *n* huevo de Pascua *m*.

easterly *adj* del este.

eastern *adj* del este, oriental.

eastward(s) *adv* hacia el este.

easy *adj* fácil; cómodo/da, ~ **going** acomodadizo/za.

easy chair *n* sillón *m*.

eat *vt* comer; * *vi* alimentarse.

eatable *adj* comestible; * ~**s** *npl* víveres *mpl*.

eaves *npl* alero *m*.

eau de Cologne *n* agua de Colonia *f*.

eavesdrop *vt* escuchar a escondidas.

ebb *n* reflujo *m*; * *vi* menguar; decaer, disminuir.

ebony *n* ébano *m*.

eccentric *adj* excéntrico/ca.

eccentricity *n* excentricidad *f*.

ecclesiastic *adj* eclesiástico/ca.

echo *n* eco *m*; * *vi* resonar, repercutir.

eclectic *adj* ecléctico/ca.

eclipse *n* eclipse *m*; * *vt* eclipsar.

ecologist, environmentalist *n* ecologista *m/f*.

ecology *n* ecología *f*.

e-commerce *n* comercio electrónico *m*.

economic(al) *adj* económico/ca, frugal, moderado/da.

economics *npl* economía *f*.

economist *n* economista *m/f*.

economize *vt* economizar.

economy *n* economía *f*; frugalidad *f*.

ecosystem *n* ecosistema *m*.

ecotax *n* ecotasa *f*.

ecotourism *n* ecoturismo *m*.

ecstasy *n* éxtasis *m*; rapto *m*.

ecstatic *adj* extático/ca; ~**ally** *adv* en éxtasis.

eczema *n* eczema *m*.

eddy *n* reflujo de agua *m*; remolino *m*; * *vi* arremolinarse.

edge *n* filo *m*; punta *f*; margen *m/f*; acrimonia *f*; * *vt* ribetear; introducir.

edgeways, edgewise *adv* de lado.

edging *n* orla, orilla *f*.

edgy *adj* nervioso/sa.

edible *adj* comestible.

edict *n* edicto, mandato *m*.

edification *n* edificación *f*.

edifice *n* edificio *m*; fábrica *f*.

edify *vt* edificar.

edit *vt* dirigir; redactar; cortar.

edition *n* edición *f*; publicación *f*; impresión *f*.

editor *n* director/a *m/f*; redactor/a *m/f*.

editorial *adj*, *n* editorial *m*.

educate *vt* educar; enseñar.

education *n* educación *f*.

eel *n* anguila *f*.

eerie *adj* espeluznante.

efface *vt* borrar, destruir.

effect *n* efecto *m*; realidad *f*; ~**s** *npl* efectos, bienes *mpl*; * *vt* efectuar, ejecutar.

effective *adj* eficaz; efectivo/va; ~**ly** *adv* efectivamente, en efecto.

effectiveness *n* eficacia *f*.

effectual *adj* eficiente, eficaz; ~**ly** *adv* eficazmente.

effeminacy *n* afeminación *f*.

effeminate *adj* afeminado/da.

effervescence *n* efervescencia *f*; hervor *m*.

effete *adj* estéril.

efficacy *n* eficacia *f*.

efficiency *n* eficiencia, virtud *f*.

efficient *adj* eficaz.

effigy *n* efigie, imagen *f*; retrato *m*.

effort *n* esfuerzo, empeño *m*.

effortless adj sin esfuerzo.
effrontery n descaro m; impudencia, desvergüenza f.
effusive adj efusivo/va.
egg n huevo m; * **to ~ on** vt animar.
eggcup n huevera f.
eggplant n berenjena f.
eggshell n cáscara de huevo f.
ego(t)ism n egoísmo m.
ego(t)ist n egoísta m/f.
ego(t)istical adj egotista.
eiderdown n edredón m.
eight adj, n ocho.
eighteen adj, n dieciocho.
eighteenth adj, n decimoctavo.
eighth adj, n octavo.
eightieth adj, n octogésimo/ma.
eighty adj, n ochenta.
either pn cualquiera; * conj o, sea, ya.
ejaculate vt exclamar; eyacular.
ejaculation n exclamación f; eyaculación f.
eject vt expeler, desechar.
ejection n expulsión f.
ejector seat n asiento eyectable m.
eke vt alargar; prolongar; hacer crecer.
elaborate vt elaborar; * adj elaborado/da; ~ly adv cuidadosamente.
elapse vi pasar, correr (el tiempo).
elastic adj elástico/ca.
elasticity n elasticidad f.
elated adj regocijado/da.
elation n regocijo m.
elbow n codo m; * vt codear.
elbow-room n anchura f; espacio suficiente m; (fig) libertad, latitud f.
elder n saúco m (árbol); * adj mayor.
elderly adj anciano/na.
elders npl ancianos, antepasados mpl.
eldest adj el mayor, la mayor.
elect vt elegir; * adj elegido/da, escogido/da.
election n elección f.
electioneering n electoralismo m.
elective adj facultativo/va.
elector n elector/a m/f.
electoral adj electoral, Lat Am eleccionario/a.
electorate n electorado m.
electric(al) adj eléctrico/ca; ~ **domestic appliance** electrodoméstico m.
electric blanket n manta eléctrica f.
electric cooker n cocina eléctrica f.
electric fire n estufa eléctrica f.
electrician n electricista m/f.
electricity n electricidad f.
electrify vt electrizar.
electrocardiogram n electrocardiograma m.
electron n electrón m.
electronic adj electrónico/ca; ~s npl electrónica f.
elegance n elegancia f.

elegant adj elegante, delicado/da; ~ly adv elegantemente.
elegy n elegía f.
element n elemento m; fundamento m.
elemental, **elementary** adj elemental.
elephant n elefante m.
elephantine adj inmenso/sa.
elevate vt elevar, alzar, exaltar.
elevation n elevación f; altura f; alteza (de pensamientos) f.
elevator n ascensor m.
eleven adj, n once.
eleventh adj, n undécimo.
elf n duende m.
elicit vt sacar de.
eligibility n elegibilidad f.
eligible adj elegible.
eliminate vt eliminar, descartar.
elk n alce m.
elliptic(al) adj elíptico/ca.
elm n olmo m.
elocution n elocución f.
elocutionist n profesor de elocución m.
elongate vt alargar.
elope vi escapar, huir, evadirse.
elopement n fuga, huida, evasión f.
eloquence n elocuencia f.
eloquent adj elocuente; ~ly adv elocuentemente.
else pn otro/ra.
elsewhere adv en otra parte.
elucidate vt explicar.
elucidation n elucidación, explicación f.
elude vt eludir, evitar.
elusive adj esquivo/va.
emaciated adj demacrado/da.
e-mail n correo electrónico m.
emanate (from) vi emanar.
emancipate vt emancipar; dar libertad.
emancipation n emancipación f.
embalm vt embalsamar.
embankment n terraplén m.
embargo n embargo m.
embark vt embarcar.
embarkation n embarque m.
embarrass vt avergonzar.
embarrassed adj avergonzado/da.
embarrassing adj violento/ta; embarazoso/sa.
embarrassment n desconcierto m.
embassy n embajada f.
embed vt empotrar; clavar.
embellish vt hermosear, adornar.
embellishment n adorno m.
embers npl rescoldo m.
embezzle vt desfalcar.
embezzlement n desfalco m.
embitter vt amargar.
emblem n emblema m.
emblematic(al) adj emblemático/ca, simbólico/ca.

embodiment n incorporación f.
embody vt incorporar.
embrace vt abrazar; contener; * n abrazo m.
embroider vt bordar.
embroidery n bordado m; bordadura f.
embroil vt embrollar; confundir.
embryo n embrión m.
emendation n enmienda, corrección f.
emerald n esmeralda f.
emerge vi salir, proceder.
emergency n emergencia f; necesidad urgente f.
emergency cord n timbre de alarma m.
emergency exit n salida de emergencia f.
emergency landing n aterrizaje forzoso m.
emergency meeting n reunión extraordinaria f.
emery n esmeril m.
emigrant n emigrante m/f.
emigrate vi emigrar.
emigration n emigración f.
eminence n altura f; eminencia, excelencia f.
eminent adj eminente, elevado/da; distinguido/da; ~ly adv eminentemente.
emission n emisión f.
emit vt emitir; arrojar, despedir.
emolument n emolumento, provecho m.
emotion n emoción f.
emotional adj emocional.
emotive adj emotivo/va.
emperor n emperador m.
emphasis n énfasis m.
emphasize vt hablar con énfasis.
emphatic adj enfático/ca; ~ally adv enfáticamente.
empire n imperio m.
employ vt emplear, ocupar.
employee n empleado/da m/f.
employer n patrón m; empresario/ria m/f.
employment n empleo m; trabajo m.
emporium n emporio m.
empress n emperatriz f.
emptiness n vaciedad f; futilidad f.
empty adj vacío/cía; vano/na; ignorante; * vt vaciar, evacuar.
empty-handed adj con las manos vacías.
emulate vt emular, competir; imitar.
emulsion n emulsión f.
enable vt capacitar.
enact vt promulgar; representar; hacer.
enamel n esmalte m; * vt esmaltar.
enamor vt enamorar.
encamp vi acamparse.
encampment n campamento m.
encase vt encajar, encajonar.
enchant vt encantar.
enchanting adj encantador/a.
enchantment n encanto m.
encircle vt cercar, circundar.
enclose vt cercar, circunvalar, circundar; incluir.
enclosure n cercamiento m; cercado m.

encompass vt abarcar.
encore adv otra vez, de nuevo.
encounter n encuentro m; duelo m; pelea f; * vt encontrar.
encourage vt animar, alentar.
encouragement n estímulo, patrocinio m.
encroach vt usurpar, avanzar gradualmente.
encroachment n usurpación, intrusión f.
encrusted adj incrustado/da.
encumber vt embarazar, cargar.
encumbrance n embarazo, impedimento m.
encyclical adj encíclico/ca, circular.
encyclopedia n enciclopedia f.
end n fin m; extremidad f; término m; resolución f; **to the ~ that** para que; **to no ~** en vano; **on ~** en pie, de pie; * vt terminar, concluir, fenecer; * vi acabar, terminar.
endanger vt peligrar, arriesgar.
endear vt encarecer.
endearing adj simpático/ca.
endearment n ternura f.
endeavor vi esforzarse; intentar; * n esfuerzo m.
endemic adj endémico/ca.
ending n conclusión; f; desenlace m; terminación f.
endive n (bot) endibia f.
endless adj infinito/ta, perpetuo/tua; ~ly adv sin fin, perpetuamente.
endorse vt endosar; aprobar.
endorsement n endoso m; aprobación f.
endow vt dotar.
endowment n dote, dotación f.
endurable adj sufrible, tolerable.
endurance n duración f; paciencia f; sufrimiento m.
endure vt sufrir, soportar; * vi durar.
endways, endwise adv de punta, derecho.
enemy n enemigo/ga, antagonista m/f.
energetic adj enérgico/ca, vigoroso/sa.
energy n energía, fuerza f; **renewable forms of ~** energía renovables.
enervate vt enervar, debilitar.
enfeeble vt debilitar.
enfold vt envolver.
enforce vt hacer cumplir.
enforced adj forzoso/sa.
enfranchise vt emancipar.
engage vt llamar; abordar; contratar.
engaged adj prometido/da.
engagement n empeño m; combate m; pelea f; obligación f.
engagement ring n anillo de prometida m.
engaging adj atractivo/va.
engender vt engendrar; producir.
engine n motor m; locomotora f.
engine driver n maquinista m/f.
engineer n ingeniero/ra m/f; maquinista m/f.
engineering n ingeniería f.
engrave vt grabar; esculpir; tallar.

E

engraving n grabado m; estampa f.
engrossed adj absorto/ta.
engulf vt sumergir.
enhance vt aumentar, realzar.
enigma n enigma m.
enjoy vt gozar; poseer.
enjoyable adj agradable; divertido/da.
enjoyment n disfrute m; placer m; fruición f.
enlarge vt engrandecer, dilatar, extender.
enlargement n aumento m; ampliación f, soltura f.
enlighten vt iluminar; instruir.
enlightened adj iluminado/da.
Enlightenment n: the ~ el Siglo de las Luces m, la Ilustración f.
enlist vt alistar.
enlistment n alistamiento m.
enliven vt animar; avivar; alegrar.
enmity n enemistad f; odio m.
enormity n enormidad f; atrocidad f.
enormous adj enorme; ~ly adv enormemente.
enough adv bastante; basta; * n bastante m.
enounce vt declarar.
enquiry n pesquisa f.
enrage vt enfurecer, irritar.
enrapture vt arrebatar, entusiasmar; encantar.
enrich vt enriquecer; adornar.
enrichment n enriquecimiento m.
enroll vt registrar; arrollar.
enrollment n inscripción f.
en route adv durante el viaje.
ensign n (mil) bandera f; abanderado m; (mar) alférez m.
enslave vt esclavizar, cautivar.
ensue vi seguirse; suceder.
ensure vt asegurar.
entail vt suponer.
entangle vt enmarañar, embrollar.
entanglement n enredo m.
enter vt entrar; admitir; registrar; **to ~ for** presentarse para; **to ~ into** establecer; formar parte de/en; firmar.
enterprise n empresa f.
enterprising adj emprendedor/a.
entertain vt divertir; hospedar; mantener.
entertainer n artista m/f.
entertaining adj divertido/da.
entertainment n entretenimiento, pasatiempo m.
enthralled adj encantado/da.
enthralling adj cautivador/a.
enthrone vt entronizar.
enthusiasm n entusiasmo m.
enthusiast n entusiasta m/f.
enthusiastic adj entusiasta.
entice vt tentar; seducir.
entire adj entero/ra, completo/ta, perfecto/ta; ~ly adv enteramente.
entitle vt intitular; conferir algún derecho.
entitled adj titulado/da.

entity n entidad, existencia f.
entourage n séquito m.
entrails npl entrañas fpl; asadura f.
entrance n entrada f; admisión f; principio m.
entrance examination n examen de ingreso m.
entrance fee n cuota f.
entrance hall n pórtico, vestíbulo m.
entrance ramp, on ramp n rampa de acceso f.
entrant n participante m; candidato m.
entrap vt enredar; engañar.
entreat vt rogar, suplicar.
entreaty n petición, suplica, instancia f.
entrepreneur n empresario/ria m/f.
entrust vt confiar.
entry n entrada f.
entry phone n portero automático m.
entwine vt entrelazar, enroscar, torcer.
enumerate vt enumerar, numerar.
enunciate vt enunciar, declarar.
enunciation n enunciación f.
envelop vt envolver.
envelope n sobre m.
enviable adj envidiable.
envious adj envidioso/sa; ~ly adv envidiosamente.
environment n medio ambiente m.
environmental adj ambiental, medioambiental.
environs npl vecindad f; contornos mpl.
envisage vt prever; concebir.
envoy n enviado/da m/f; mensajero/ra m/f.
envy n envidia, malicia f; * vt envidiar.
ephemeral adj efímero/ra.
epic adj épico/ca; * n épica f.
epidemic adj epidémico/ca; * n epidemia f.
epilepsy n epilepsia f.
epileptic adj epiléptico/ca.
epilog n epílogo m.
Epiphany n Epifanía f.
episcopacy n episcopado m.
Episcopal adj episcopal.
Episcopalian n anglicano/na m/f.
episode n episodio m.
epistle n epístola f.
epistolary adj epistolar.
epithet n epíteto m.
epitome n epítome, compendio m.
epitomize vt epitomar, abreviar.
epoch n época f.
equable adj uniforme; ~bly adv uniformemente.
equal adj igual; justo/ta; semejante; * n igual m; compañero m; * vt igualar; compensar.
equalize vt igualar.
equalizer n igualada f.
equality n igualdad, uniformidad f.
equally adv igualmente.
equanimity n ecuanimidad f.
equate vt equiparar (con).
equation n ecuación f.
equator n ecuador m.

equatorial adj ecuatorial, ecuatorio/ria.
equestrian adj ecuestre.
equilateral adj equilátero/ra.
equilibrium n equilibrio m.
equinox n equinoccio m.
equip vt equipar, pertrechar.
equipment n equipaje m.
equitable adj equitativo/va, imparcial; **~bly** adv equitativamente.
equity n equidad, justicia, imparcialidad f.
equivalent adj, n equivalente m.
equivocal adj equívoco/ca, ambiguo/gua; **~ly** adv equivocadamente, ambiguamente.
equivocate vt equivocar, usar equívocos.
equivocation n equívoco m.
era n era f.
eradicate vt desarraigar, extirpar.
eradication n extirpación f.
erase vt borrar.
eraser n goma de borrar f.
erect vt erigir; establecer; * adj derecho/ha, erguido/da, vertical.
erection n establecimiento m; estructura f; erección f.
ermine n armiño m.
erode vt erosionar; corroer.
erotic adj erótico/ca.
err vi vagar, errar; desviarse.
errand n recado, mensaje m.
errand boy n recadero m.
errata npl fe de erratas f.
erratic adj errático/ca, errante; irregular.
erroneous adj erróneo/nea; falso/sa; **~ly** adv erróneamente.
error n error m; yerro m.
erudite adj erudito/ta.
erudition n erudición f; doctrina f.
erupt vi entrar en erupción; hacer erupción.
eruption n erupción f.
escalate vi extenderse.
escalation n intensificación f.
escalator n escalera mecánica f.
escapade n travesura f.
escape vt evitar; escapar; * vi evadirse, salvarse; * vr zafarse; * n escapada, huida, fuga f; inadvertencia f; **to make one's ~** poner los pies en polvorosa.
escapism n escapismo m.
eschew vt huir, evitar, evadir.
escort n escolta f; * vt escoltar.
esoteric adj esotérico/ca.
especial adj especial; **~ly** adv especialmente.
espionage n espionaje m.
esplanade n (mil) esplanada f.
espouse vt desposar.
essay n ensayo m.
essence n esencia f.
essential n esencia f; * adj esencial, substancial, principal; **~ly** adv esencialmente.

establish vt establecer, fundar, fijar; confirmar.
establishment n establecimiento m; fundación f; institución f.
estate n estado m; hacienda f; bienes mpl.
esteem vt estimar, apreciar; pensar; * n estima f; consideración f.
esthetic adj estético/ca; **~s** npl estética f.
estimate vt estimar, apreciar, tasar; * n presupuesto m.
estimation n estimación, valuación f; opinión f.
estrange vt extrañar, apartar, enajenar.
estranged adj separado/da.
estrangement n enajenación f; extrañeza, distancia f.
estuary n estuario m, ría f.
etch vt grabar al aguafuerte.
etching n grabado al aguafuerte m.
eternal adj eterno/na, perpetuo/tua, inmortal; **~ly** adv eternamente.
eternity n eternidad f.
ether n éter m.
ethical adj ético/ca; **~ly** adv moralmente.
ethics npl ética f.
ethnic adj étnico/ca.
ethos n genio m.
etiquette n etiqueta f.
etymological adj etimológico/ca.
etymologist n etimólogo/ga m/f, etimologista m/f.
etymology n etimología f.
Eucharist n Eucaristía f.
eulogy n elogio, encomio m; alabanza f.
eunuch n eunuco m.
euphemism n eufemismo m.
euro n euro m.
Euro MP n eurodiputado/da m/f.
Europe n Europa f.
European Community n Comunidad Europea f.
European Parliament n eurocámara f.
European Union n unión Europea f.
Euroskeptic n euroescéptico/ca m/f.
Eurotunnel, Channel Tunnel n eurotúnel m.
evacuate vt evacuar.
evacuation n evacuación f.
evade vt evadir, escapar, evitar.
evaluate vt evaluar; interpretar.
evangelic(al) adj evangélico/ca.
evangelist n evangelista m.
evaporate vt evaporar; * vi evaporarse; disiparse.
evaporated milk n leche evaporada f.
evaporation n evaporación f.
evasion n evasión f; escape m.
evasive adj evasivo/va; **~ly** adv con evasivas.
eve n víspera f.
even adj llano/na, igual; par, semejante; * adv aun; aun cuando, supuesto que; no obstante; * vt igualar, allanar; * vi: **to ~ out** nivelarse.
even-handed adj imparcial, equitativo/va.
evening n tarde f.

E

evening class n clase nocturna f.
evening dress n traje de etiqueta m; traje de noche m.
evenly adv igualmente, llanamente.
evenness n igualdad f; uniformidad f; llanura f; imparcialidad f.
event n acontecimiento, evento m; suceso m.
eventful adj lleno de acontecimientos.
eventual adj final; ~ly adv por fin.
eventuality n eventualidad f.
ever adv siempre; **for** ~ **and** ~ siempre jamás, eternamente; ~ **since** después.
evergreen adj de hoja perenne; * n árbol de hoja perenne m.
everlasting adj eterno/na.
evermore adv eternamente, para siempre jamás.
every adj cada uno, cada una; ~ **where** en/por todas partes; ~ **thing** todo; ~ **one**, ~ **body** todos, todo el mundo.
evict vt desahuciar.
eviction n desahucio m.
evidence n evidencia f; testimonio m; prueba f; * vt evidenciar.
evident adj evidente; patente, manifiesto/ta; ~**ly** adv evidentemente.
evil adj malo/la, depravado/da, pernicioso/sa; dañoso/sa; * n mal m; maldad f.
evil-minded adj malicioso/sa, mal intencionado/da.
evocative adj sugestivo/va.
evoke vt evocar.
evolution n evolución f.
evolve vt, vi evolucionar; desenvolver; desplegarse.
ewe n oveja f.
exacerbate vt exacerbar.
exact adj exacto/ta; * vt exigir.
exacting adj exigente.
exaction n exacción, extorsión f.
exactly adj exactamente.
exactness, exactitude n exactitud f.
exaggerate vt exagerar.
exaggeration n exageración f.
exalt vt exaltar, elevar; alabar; realzar.
exaltation n exaltación, elevación f.
exalted adj exaltado/da; muy animado/da.
examination n examen m.
examine vt examinar; escudriñar.
examiner n inspector/a m/f.
example n ejemplar m; ejemplo m.
exasperate vt exasperar, irritar, enojar, provocar; agravar; amargar.
exasperation n exasperación, irritación f.
excavate vt excavar, ahondar.
excavation n excavación f.
excavator n excavadora f.
exceed vt exceder; sobrepujar.
exceedingly adv extremamente, en sumo grado.
excel vt sobresalir, exceder; * vi descollar.
excellence n excelencia f; preeminencia f.

Excellency n Excelencia (título) f.
excellent adj excelente; ~**ly** adv excelentemente.
except vt exceptuar, excluir; ~(**ing**) prep excepto, a excepción de.
exception n excepción, exclusión f.
exceptional adj excepcional.
excerpt n extracto m.
excess n exceso m.
excessive adj excesivo/va; ~**ly** adv excesivamente.
exchange vt cambiar; trocar, permutar; * n cambio m; bolsa f.
exchange rate n tipo de cambio m.
excise n impuestos sobre el consumo mpl.
excitability n excitabilidad f.
excitable adj excitable.
excite vt excitar; estimular.
excited adj emocionado/da.
excitement n estímulo, excitación f.
exciting adj emocionante.
exclaim vi exclamar.
exclamation n exclamación f; clamor m.
exclamation mark n punto de admiración m.
exclamatory adj exclamatorio/ria.
exclude vt excluir; exceptuar.
exclusion n exclusión, exclusiva, excepción f.
exclusive adj exclusivo/va; ~**ly** adv exclusivamente.
excommunicate vt excomulgar.
excommunication n excomunión f.
excrement n excremento m.
excruciating adj atroz, enorme, grave.
exculpate vt disculpar; justificar.
excursion n excursión f; digresión f.
excusable adj excusable.
excuse vt disculpar; perdonar; * n disculpa, excusa f; pretexto m; ~ **me!** interj ¡perdón!.
execute vt ejecutar.
execution n ejecución f.
executioner n ejecutor/a m/f; verdugo m.
executive adj ejecutivo/va.
executor n testamentario/ria, albacea m/f.
exemplary adj ejemplar.
exemplify vt ejemplificar.
exempt adj exento/ta.
exemption n exención f.
exercise n ejercicio m; ensayo m; tarea f; practica f; * vi hacer ejercicio; * vt ejercer; valerse de.
exercise book n cuaderno m.
exert vt emplear; **to** ~ **oneself** esforzarse.
exertion n esfuerzo m.
exhale vt exhalar.
exhaust n escape m; * vt agotar.
exhausted adj agotado/da.
exhaustion n agotamiento m; extenuación f.
exhaustive adj comprensivo/va.
exhibit vt exhibir; mostrar; * n (law) objeto expuesto m.
exhibition n exposición, presentación f.
exhilarating adj estimulante.

exhilaration n alegría f; buen humor, regocijo m.
exhort vt exhortar, excitar.
exhortation n exhortación f.
exhume vt exhumar, desenterrar.
exile n destierro m; * vt desterrar, deportar.
exist vi existir.
existence n existencia f.
existent adj existente.
existing adj actual, presente.
exit n salida f; * vi hacer mutis.
exit ramp, off ramp n vía de acceso f.
exodus n éxodo m.
exonerate vt exonerar, descargar.
exoneration n exoneración f.
exorbitant adj exorbitante, excesivo/va.
exorcise vt exorcizar, conjurar.
exorcism n exorcismo m.
exotic adj exótico/ca, extranjero/ra.
expand vt extender, dilatar.
expanse n extensión f.
expansion n expansión f.
expansive adj expansivo/va.
expatriate vt expatriar.
expect vt esperar, aguardar.
expectance, expectancy n expectación, esperanza f.
expectant adj expectante.
expectant mother n mujer encinta f.
expectation n expectación, expectativa f.
expediency n conveniencia, oportunidad f.
expedient adj oportuno/na, conveniente; * n
    expediente m; ~**ly** adv convenientemente.
expedite vt acelerar; expedir.
expedition n expedición f.
expeditious adj pronto/ta, expedito/ta; ~**ly** adv
    prontamente.
expel vt expeler, desterrar.
expend vt expender; desembolsar.
expendable adj prescindible.
expenditure n gasto, desembolso m.
expense n gasto m; coste m.
expense account n cuenta de gastos f.
expensive adj caro/ra; costoso/sa; ~**ly** adv
    costosamente.
experience n experiencia f; práctica f; * vt
    experimentar.
experienced adj experimentado/da.
experiment n experimento m; * vt experimentar.
experimental adj experimental; ~**ly** adv
    experimentalmente.
expert adj experto/ta, diestro/tra.
expertise n pericia f.
expiration n expiración f; muerte f.
expire vi expirar.
explain vt explanar, explicar.
explanation n explicación f.
explanatory adj explicativo/va.
expletive adj expletivo/va.
explicable adj explicable.

explicit adj explícito/ta; ~**ly** adv explícitamente.
explode vt, vi estallar, explotar.
exploit vt explotar; * n hazaña f; hecho heroico m.
exploitation n explotación f.
exploration n exploración f; examen m.
exploratory adj exploratorio/ria.
explore vt explorar, examinar; sondear.
explorer n explorador/a m/f.
explosion n explosión f.
explosive adj, n explosivo m.
exponent n (math) exponente m.
export vt exportar.
export, exportation n exportación f.
exporter n exportador/a m/f.
expose vt exponer; mostrar; descubrir; poner en
    peligro.
exposed adj expuesto/ta.
exposition n exposición f; interpretación f.
expostulate vi debatir, contender.
exposure n exposición f; velocidad de obturación f;
    fotografía f.
exposure meter n fotómetro m.
expound vt exponer; interpretar.
express vt exprimir; representar; * adj
    expreso/sa, claro/ra; a propósito; * n
    expreso, correo m; (rail) tren expreso m.
expression n expresión f; locución f.
expressionless adj sin expresión (cara).
expressive adj expresivo/va; ~**ly** adv expresivamente.
expressly adv expresamente.
expressway n autopista f.
expropriate vt expropiar (por causa de utilidad
    pública).
expropriation n (law) expropiación f.
expulsion n explosión f.
expurgate vt expurgar.
exquisite adj exquisito/ta, perfecto/ta, excelente;
    ~**ly** adv exquisitamente.
extant adj existente.
extempore adv de improviso.
extemporize vi improvisar.
extend vt extender; amplificar; * vi extenderse.
extension n extensión f.
extensive adj extenso/sa, dilatado/da; ~**ly** adv
    extensivamente.
extent n extensión f.
extenuate vt extenuar, disminuir, atenuar.
extenuating adj atenuante.
exterior adj, n exterior m.
exterminate vt exterminar; extirpar.
extermination n exterminación, extirpación f.
external adj externo/na; ~**ly** adv exteriormente;
    ~**s** npl exterior m.
extinct adj extinto/ta; abolido/da.
extinction n extinción f; abolición f.
extinguish vt extinguir; suprimir.
extinguisher n extintor m, Lat Am extinguidor m.
extirpate vt extirpar.

E

extoll *vt* alabar, magnificar, alzar, exaltar.

extort *vt* sacar por la fuerza.

extortion *n* extorsión *f*.

extortionate *adj* excesivo/va.

extra *adv* extra; * *n* extra *m*.

extract *vt* extraer; extractar; * *n* extracto *m*; compendio *m*.

extraction *n* extracción *f*; descendencia *f*.

extracurricular *adj* extraescolar.

extradite *vt* extraditar.

extradition *n* (*law*) extradición *f*.

extramarital *adj* extramatrimonial.

extramural *adj* extraescolar.

extraneous *adj* extraño/ña, ajeno/na.

extraordinarily *adv* extraordinariamente.

extraordinary *adj* extraordinario/ria.

extravagance *n* extravagancia *f*; gastos, excesivos *mpl*.

extravagant *adj* extravagante, exorbitante; pródigo/ga; **~ly** *adv* extravagantemente.

extreme *adj* extremo/ma, supremo/ma; último/ma; * *n* extremo *m*, **~ly** *adv* extremamente.

extremist *adj*, *n* extremista *m/f*.

extremity *n* extremidad *f*.

extricate *vt* desembarazar, desenredar.

extrinsic(al) *adj* extrínseco/ca, exterior.

extrovert *adj*, *n* extrovertido *m*.

exuberance *n* exuberancia, suma abundancia *f*.

exuberant *adj* exuberante, abundantísimo/ma; **~ly** *adv* exuberantemente.

exude *vi* transpirar.

exult *vt* exultar, regocijarse, triunfar.

exultation *n* exultación *f*; regocijo *m*.

eye *n* ojo *m*; * *vt* ojear, contemplar, observar.

eyeball *n* globo del ojo *m*.

eyebrow *n* ceja *f*.

eyelash *n* pestaña *f*.

eyelid *n* párpado *m*.

eyesight *n* vista *f*.

eyesore *n* monstruosidad *f*.

eyetooth *n* colmillo *m*.

eyewitness *n* testigo ocular *m*.

eyrie *n* nido de águila *m*.

F

fable n fábula f; ficción f.
fabric n tejido m.
fabricate vt fabricar, edificar.
fabrication n fabricación f.
fabulous adj fabuloso/sa; **~ly** adv fabulosamente.
facade n fachada f.
face n cara, faz f; superficie f; fachada f; aspecto m; apariencia f; * vt encararse; hacer frente; **to ~ up to** hacer frente a.
face cream n crema facial f.
face-lift n lifting m.
face powder n polvos mpl.
facet n faceta f.
facetious adj chistoso/sa, alegre, gracioso/sa; **~ly** adv chistosamente.
face value n valor nominal m.
facial adj facial.
facile adj fácil, afable.
facilitate vt facilitar.
facility n facilidad, ligereza f; afabilidad f.
facing n paramento m; * prep enfrente.
facsimile n facsímil m; fax m.
fact n hecho m; realidad f; **in ~** en efecto.
faction n facción f; disensión f.
factor n factor m.
factory n fábrica f.
factual adj basado/da en hechos reales.
faculty n facultad f; personal docente m.
fad n moda f.
fade vi decaer, marchitarse, fallecer.
fail vt suspender, Lat Am reprobar; fallar a; * vi suspender; fracasar; fallar; (fig) zozobrar.
failing n falta f; defecto m.
failure n falta f; culpa f; descuido m; quiebra, bancarrota f.
faint vi desmayarse, debilitarse; * n desmayo m; * adj débil; **~ly** adv débilmente.
fainthearted adj cobarde, medroso/sa, pusilánime.
faintness n flaqueza f; desmayo m.
fair adj hermoso/sa, bello/la; blanco/ca; rubio/bia; claro/ra, sereno/na; favorable; recto/ta, justo/ta; franco/ca; * adv limpio; * n feria f.
fairly adv justamente; completamente.
fairness n hermosura f; justicia f.
fair play n juego limpio m.
fair trade n comercio justo m.
fairy n hada f.
fairy tale n cuento de hadas m.
faith n fe f; dogma de fe m; fidelidad f.
faithful adj fiel, leal; **~ly** adv fielmente.
faithfulness n fidelidad, lealtad f.

fake n falsificación f; impostor/a m/f; * adj falso/sa; * vt fingir; falsificar.
falcon n halcón m.
falconry n cetrería f.
fall vi caer(se); perder el poder; disminuir, decrecer en precio; **to ~ asleep** dormirse; **to ~ back** retroceder; **to ~ back on** recurrir a; **to ~ behind** quedarse atrás; **to ~ down** caerse; **to ~ for** dejarse engañar; enamorarse de; **to ~ in** hundirse; **to ~ short** faltar; **to ~ sick** enfermar; **to ~ in love** enamorarse; **to ~ off** caerse; disminuir; **to ~ out** reñir, disputar; * n caída f; otoño m.
fallacious adj falaz, fraudulento/ta; **~ly** adv falazmente.
fallacy n falacia, sofistería f; engaño m.
fallibility n falibilidad f.
fallible adj falible.
fallow adj en barbecho; **~ deer** n gamo m.
false adj falso/sa; **~ly** adv falsamente.
false alarm n falsa alarma f.
falsehood, falseness n falsedad f.
falsify vt falsificar.
falsity n falsedad, mentira f.
falter vi tartamudear; faltar.
faltering adj vacilante.
fame n fama f; renombre m.
famed adj celebrado/da, famoso/sa.
familiar adj familiar; casero/ra; **~ly** adv familiarmente.
familiarity n familiaridad f.
familiarize vt familiarizar.
family n familia f; linaje m; clase, especie f.
family business n negocio familiar m.
family doctor n médico de familia m.
famine n hambre f; carestía f.
famished adj hambriento/ta.
famous adj famoso/sa, afamado/da; **~ly** adv famosamente.
fan n abanico m; aficionado m; fan m/f; * vt abanicar; atizar.
fanatic adj, n fanático/ca m/ca.
fanaticism n fanatismo m.
fan belt n correa del ventilador f.
fanciful adj imaginativo/va, caprichoso/sa; **~ly** adv caprichosamente.
fancy n fantasía, imaginación f; capricho m; * vt tener ganas de; imaginarse.
fancy-goods npl novedades, modas fpl.
fancy-dress ball n baile de disfraces m.
fanfare n (mus) fanfarria f.
fang n colmillo m.

fantastic adj fantástico/ca; caprichoso/sa; **~ally** adv fantásticamente.

fantasy n fantasía f.

far adv lejos, a una gran distancia; * adj lejano/na, distante, remoto/ta; **~ and away** con mucho, de mucho; **~ off** lejano/na.

faraway adj remoto/ta.

farce n farsa f.

farcical adj burlesco/ca.

fare n precio m; tarifa f; comida f; viajero m; pasaje m.

farewell n despedida f; **~!** excl ¡adiós!

farm n finca f, granja f; * vt cultivar.

farmer n agricultor/a m/f; granjero/ra m/f.

farmhand n peón m.

farmhouse n casa de hacienda f, granja f.

farming n agricultura f.

farmland n tierra de cultivo f.

farmyard n corral m.

far-reaching adj de gran alcance.

fart n (col) pedo; * vi tirarse un pedo.

farther adv más lejos; más adelante; * adj más lejos, ulterior.

farthest adv lo más lejos; lo más tarde; a lo más.

fascinate vt fascinar, encantar.

fascinating adj fascinante.

fascination n fascinación f; encanto m.

fascism n fascismo.

fascist n fascista m/f.

fashion n moda f; forma, figura f; uso m; manera f; estilo m; **people of ~** gente de tono f; * vt formar, amoldar.

fashionable adj a la moda; elegante; **the ~ world** el gran mundo; **~bly** adv a/segun la moda.

fashion show n desfile de modelos m.

fast vi ayunar; * n ayuno m; * adj rápido/da; firme, estable; * adv rápidamente; firmemente; estrechamente.

fasten vt abrochar; afirmar, asegurar, atar; fijar; * vi fijarse, establecerse.

fastener, fastening n cierre m; cerrojo m.

fast food n comida rápida f.

fastidious adj fastidioso/sa, desdeñoso/sa; **~ly** adv fastidiosamente.

fat adj gordo/da; * n grasa f.

fatal adj fatal; funesto/ta; **~ly** adv fatalmente.

fatalism n fatalismo m.

fatalist n fatalista m/f.

fatality n fatalidad, predestinación f.

fate n hado, destino m.

fateful adj fatídico/ca.

father n padre m; **loving (over-indulgent) ~** padrazo m.

fatherhood n paternidad f.

father-in-law n suegro m.

fatherland n patria f.

fatherly adj paternal.

fathom n braza (medida) f; * vt sondar; penetrar.

fatigue n fatiga f; * vt fatigar, cansar.

fatten vt, vi engordar.

fatty adj graso/sa.

fatuous adj fatuo/tua, tonto/ta, imbécil.

faucet n grifo m, llave f.

fault n falta, culpa f; delito m; defecto m; yerro m.

faultfinder n censurador/a m/f.

faultless adj perfecto/ta, cumplido/da.

faulty adj defectuoso/sa.

fauna n fauna f.

faux pas n metedura de pata f.

favor n favor, beneficio m; patrocinio m; blandura f; * vt favorecer, proteger.

favorable adj favorable, propicio/cia; **~bly** adv favorablemente.

favored adj favorecido/da.

favorite n favorito/ta m/f; * adj favorecido/da.

favoritism n favoritismo m.

fawn n cervatillo m; * vi adular servilmente.

fawningly adv lisonjeramente, con adulación servil.

fax n facsímil(e) m; fax m; * vt mandar por fax.

fear vi temer; * n miedo m.

fearful adj medroso/sa, temeroso/sa; tímido/da; **~ly** adv medrosamente, temerosamente.

fearless adj intrépido/da, atrevido/da; **~ly** adv sin miedo.

fearlessness n intrepidez f.

feasibility n posibilidad f.

feasible adj factible, viable.

feast n banquete, festín m; fiesta f; * vi banquetear.

feat n hecho m; acción, hazaña f.

feather n pluma f;.

feather bed n plumón m.

feature n característica f; rasgo m; forma f; * vi figurar.

feature film n largometraje m.

February n febrero m.

federal adj federal.

federalist n federalista m/f.

federate vt, vi federar(se).

federation n federación f.

fed-up adj harto/ta.

fee n honorarios mpl; cuota f.

feeble adj flaco/ca, débil.

feebleness n debilidad f.

feebly adv débilmente.

feed vt nutrir; alimentar; **to ~ on** alimentarse de; * vi nutrirse; engordar; * n comida f; pasto m.

feedback n reacción f.

feel vt sentir; tocar; creer; **to ~ around** tantear; * n sensación f; tacto, sentido m.

feeler n antena f; (fig) tentativa f.

feeling n tacto m; sensibilidad f; corazonada f.

feelingly adv sensiblemente.

feign vt inventar, fingir; disimular.

feline adj felino/na.

fellow n tipo, tío m; socio/cia m/f.
fellow citizen n conciudadano/na m/f..
fellow countryman n compatriota m/f.
fellow feeling n simpatía f.
fellow men npl semejantes mpl.
fellowship n compañerismo m; beca (en un colegio) f.
fellow student n compañero/ra de curso m/f.
fellow traveler n compañero/ra de viaje m/f.
felon n criminal m/f.
felony n crimen m.
felt n fieltro m.
felt-tip pen, fiber-tip pen n rotulador m, Lat Am marcador m.
female n hembra f; * adj femenino/na.
feminine adj femenino/na.
feminism n feminismo m.
feminist n feminista m/f.
fence n cerca f, Lat Am cerco m; defensa f; * vt cercar; * vi esgrimir.
fencing n esgrima f.
fender n parachoques m invar.
fennel n (bot) hinojo m.
ferment n agitación f; * vi fermentar.
fern n (bot) helecho m.
ferocious adj feroz; fiero/ra; ~ly adv ferozmente.
ferocity n ferocidad, fiereza f.
ferret n hurón m; * vt huronear; **to ~ out** descubrir, echar fuera.
ferryboat, ferry n transbordador, ferry m; * vt transportar.
fertile adj fértil, fecundo/da.
fertility n fertilidad, fecundidad f.
fertilization n fertilización f.
fertilize vt fertilizar.
fertilizer n abono m.
fervent adj ferviente; fervoroso/sa; ~ly adv con fervor.
fervid adj ardiente, vehemente.
fervor n fervor, ardor m.
fester vi enconarse, inflamarse.
festival n fiesta f; festival m.
festive adj festivo/va.
festivity n festividad f.
fetch vt ir a buscar.
fetching adj atractivo/va.
fete n fiesta f.
fetid adj fétido/da, hediondo/da.
fetus n feto m.
feud n riña, contienda f.
feudal adj feudal.
feudalism n feudalismo m.
fever n fiebre f.
feverish adj febril, Lat Am afiebrado/da.
few adj poco/ca; **a ~** algunos; **~ and far between** pocos.
fewer adj menor; * adv menos.
fewest adj los menos.

fiancé n novio m.
fiancée n novia f.
fib n mentira f; * vi mentir.
fiber n fibra, hebra f.
fiberglass n fibra de vidrio f.
fickle adj voluble, inconstante, mudable, ligero/ra.
fiction n ficción f; invención f.
fictional adj novelesco/ca.
fictitious adj ficticio/cia; fingido/da; ~ly adv fingidamente.
fiddle n violín m; trampa f; * vi tocar el violín.
fiddler n violinista m/f.
fidelity n fidelidad, lealtad f.
fidget vi inquietarse.
fidgety adj inquieto/ta, impaciente.
field n campo m; campaña f; espacio m.
field day n (mil) día de maniobras m.
fieldmouse n ratón de campo m.
fieldwork n trabajo de campo m.
fiend n enemigo m; demonio m.
fiendish adj demoniaco/ca.
fierce adj fiero/ra, feroz; cruel, furioso/sa; ~ly adv furiosamente.
fierceness n fiereza, ferocidad f.
fiery adj ardiente; apasionado/da.
fifteen adj, n quince.
fifteenth adj, n decimoquinto/ta.
fifth adj, n quinto/ta; ~ly adv en quinto lugar.
fiftieth adj, n quincuagésimo/ma.
fifty adj, n cincuenta.
fig n higo m.
fight vt, vi reñir; batallar; combatir; * n batalla f; combate m; pelea f.
fighter n combatiente m; luchador/a m/f; caza m.
fighting n combate m.
fig-leaf n hoja de higuera f.
fig tree n higuera f.
figurative adj figurativo/va; ~ly adv figuradamente.
figure n figura, forma f; imagen f; cifra f; * vi figurar; ser lógico/ca; **to ~ out** comprender.
figurehead n testaferro m.
filament n filamento m; fibra f.
filch vi ratear.
filcher n ratero/ra, ladroncillo/lla m/f.
file n hilo m; lista f; (mil) fila, hilera f; lima f; carpeta f; fichero m; * vt enhilar; limar; clasificar; presentar; * vi **to ~ in/out** entrar/salir en fila; **to ~ past** desfilar ante.
filing cabinet n archivador m.
fill vt llenar; hartar; **to ~ in** rellenar; **to ~ up** llenar (hasta el borde).
fillet n filete m.
fillet steak n filete de ternera m.
fillip n (fig) estímulo m.
filly n potra f.
film n película f; film m; capa f; * vt filmar; * vi rodar.

F

film star n estrella de cine f.
film strip n tira de película f.
filter n filtro m; * vt filtrar.
filter-tipped adj con filtro.
filth(iness) n inmundicia, porquería f; fango, lodo m.
filthy adj sucio/cia, puerco/ca.
fin n aleta f.
final adj final, último/ma; ~ly adv finalmente; ~ **stages** postrimerías fpl.
finale n final m.
finalist n finalista m/f.
finalize vt concluir.
finance n fondos mpl.
financial adj financiero/ra.
financier n financiero/ra m/f, Lat Am financista m/f.
find vt hallar, descubrir, Lat Am ubicar; **to ~ out** averiguar; descubrir; **to ~ one's self** hallarse; * n hallazgo m.
findings npl fallo m; recomendaciones fpl.
fine adj fino/na; agudo/da, cortante; claro/ra, trasparente; delicado/da; astuto/ta; elegante; bello/la; * n multa f; * vt multar, Lat Am infraccionar.
fine arts npl bellas artes fpl.
finely adv con elegancia.
finery n adorno, atavío m.
finesse n sutileza f.
finger n dedo m; * vt tocar, manosear; manejar.
fingernail n uña f.
fingerprint n huella dactilar f.
fingertip n yema del dedo f.
finicky adj delicado/da.
finish vt acabar, terminar, concluir; **to ~ off** acabar (con); **to ~ up** terminar; * vi: **to ~ up** ir a parar.
finishing line n línea de llegada, línea de meta f.
finishing school n academia para señoritas f.
finite adj finito/ta; conjugado/da.
fir tree n abeto m
fire n fuego m; incendio m; * vt disparar; incendiar; despertar; * vi encenderse.
fire alarm n alarma de incendios f.
firearm n arma de fuego f.
fireball n bola f de fuego.
firebreak, **fire line** n cortafuegos m.
fire department n cuerpo de bomberos m.
fire engine n coche de bomberos m.
fire escape n escalera de incendios f.
fire extinguisher n extintor m.
firefly n luciérnaga f.
fireman n bombero m.
fireplace n hogar, fogón m.
fireproof adj a prueba de fuego.
fireside n chimenea f.
fire station, **fire house** n parque de bomberos m.
firewater n aguardiente m.
firewood n leña f.

fireworks npl fuegos artificiales mpl.
firing n disparos mpl.
firing squad n pelotón de ejecución m.
firm adj firme, estable, constante; * n (com) firma f; ~**ly** adv firmemente.
firmament n firmamento m.
firmness n firmeza f; constancia f.
first adj primero/ra; * adv primeramente; **at ~** al principio; ~**ly** adv en primer lugar.
first aid n primeros auxilios mpl.
first-aid kit n botiquín m.
first-class adj de primera (clase).
first-hand adj de primera mano.
First Lady n primera dama f.
first name n nombre de pila m.
first-rate adj de primera (clase).
fiscal adj fiscal.
fish n pez m; * vi pescar.
fishbone n espina f.
fisherman n pescador m.
fish farm n piscifactoría f.
fishing n pesca f.
fishing line n sedal m.
fishing rod n caña de pescar f.
fishing tackle n aparejo m.
fish market n lonja de pescado f.
fishseller n pescadero/ra m/f.
fish shop n pescadería f.
fishy adj (fig) sospechoso/sa.
fissure n grieta, hendedura f.
fist n puño m.
fit n paroxismo m; convulsión f; * adj en forma; apto/ta, idóneo/nea, justo/ta; * vt ajustar, acomodar, adaptar; **to ~ out** proveer; * vi convenir; **to ~ in** encajarse; llevarse bien (con todos).
fitness n salud f; aptitud, conveniencia f.
fitted carpet n moqueta f.
fitted kitchen n cocina amueblada f.
fitter n ajustador m.
fitting adj conveniente, idóneo/nea, justo/ta; * n conveniencia f; ~**s** pl guarnición f.
five adj, n cinco.
fix vt fijar, establecer; **to ~ up** arreglar.
fixation n obsesión f.
fixed adj fijo/ja.
fixings npl equipajes mpl; pertrechos mpl; ajuar m.
fixture n encuentro m.
fizz(le) vi silbar.
fizzy adj gaseoso/sa.
flabbergasted adj pasmado/da.
flabby adj blando/da, flojo/ja, lacio/cia.
flaccid adj flojo/ja, flaco/ca; fláccido/da.
flag n bandera f; losa f; * vi debilitarse.
flagpole n asta de bandera f.
flagrant adj flagrante; notorio/ria.
flagship n buque insignia m.
flag stop n parada a petición f.

flair n aptitud especial f.

flak n fuego antiaéreo m; lluvia de críticas.

flake n copo m; lámina f; * vi romperse en láminas.

flaky adj escamoso/sa, desmenuzable.

flamboyant adj vistoso/sa.

flame n llama f; fuego (del amor) m.

flamingo n flamenco m.

flammable adj inflamable.

flank n ijada f; (mil) flanco m; * vt flanquear.

flannel n franela, flanela f.

flap n solapa f; hoja f; aletazo m; * vt aletear; * vi ondear.

flare vi lucir, brillar; **to ~ up** encenderse; encolerizarse; estallar; * n llama f.

flash n flash m; relámpago m; * vt **to ~ on and off** encender y apagar.

flashbulb n bombilla de flash f.

flash cube n cubo de flash m.

flashlight n linterna f;antorcha f.

flashy adj superficial.

flask n frasco m; botella f.

flat adj llano/na, plano/na; insípido/da; * n llanura f; plano m; (mus) bemol m; **~ly** adv horizontalmente; llanamente; enteramente; de plano, de nivel; francamente.

flatness n llanura f; insipidez f.

flatten vt allanar; abatir.

flatter vt adular, lisonjear.

flattering adj halagüeño/ña, zalamero/ra.

flattery n adulación, lisonja f; zalamería f.

flatulence n (med) flatulencia f.

flaunt vt ostentar.

flavor n sabor m; * vt sazonar.

flavored adj con sabor (a).

flavorless adj soso/sa.

flaw n falta, tacha f; defecto m.

flawless adj sin defecto.

flax n lino m.

flea n pulga f.

flea bite n picadura de pulga f.

fleck n mota f; punto m.

flee vt huir de; * vi escapar; huir.

fleece n vellón m; * vt (col) pelar.

fleet n flota f; escuadra f.

fleeting adj pasajero/ra, fugitivo/va.

flesh n carne f.

flesh wound n herida superficial f.

fleshy adj carnoso/sa, pulposo/sa.

flex n cordón m; * vt tensar.

flexibility n flexibilidad f.

flexible adj flexible.

flick n golpecito m; * vt dar un golpecito a.

flicker vt aletear; fluctuar.

flier n aviador/a m/f.

flight n vuelo m; huida, fuga f; bandada (de pájaros) f; (fig) elevación f.

flight attendant n auxiliar de vuelo m/f.

flight deck n cabina de mandos f.

flimsy adj débil; fútil.

flinch vi encogerse.

fling vt lanzar, echar.

flint n pedernal m.

flip vt arrojar, lanzar.

flippant adj petulante, locuaz.

flipper n aleta f.

flirt vi coquetear; * n coqueta f.

flirtation n coquetería f.

flit vi volar, huir; aletear.

float vt hacer flotar; lanzar; * vi flotar; * n flotador m; carroza f; reserva f.

flock n manada f; rebaño m; gentío m; * vi congregarse.

flog vt azotar; (col) zurrar.

flogging n tunda, zurra f.

flood n diluvio m; inundación f; flujo m; * vt inundar.

flooding n inundación f.

floodlight n foco m.

floor n suelo, piso m; piso (de una casa); * vt dejar sin respuesta.

floorboard n tabla f.

floor lamp n lámpara de pie f.

floor show n cabaret m.

flop n fracaso m.

floppy adj flojo/ja

floppy disk n floppy m, disquete m.

flora n flora f.

floral adj floral.

florescence n florescencia f.

florid adj florido/da.

florist n florista m/f.

florist's (shop) n floristería f.

flotilla n (mar) flotilla f.

flounder n platija (pez de mar) f; * vi tropezar.

flour n harina f.

flourish vi florecer; gozar de prosperidad; * n belleza f; lazo m; (mus) floreo, preludio m.

flourishing adj floreciente.

flout vt burlarse de.

flow vi fluir, manar; crecer la marea; ondear; * n flujo de la marea m ; abundancia f; flujo m.

flow chart n organigrama m.

flower n flor f; * vi florear; florecer.

flowerbed n parterre m.

flowerpot n tiesto m, maceta f.

flowery adj florido/da.

flower show n exposición de flores f.

fluctuate vi fluctuar.

fluctuation n fluctuación f.

fluency n fluidez f.

fluent adj fluido/da; fácil; **~ly** adv con fluidez.

fluff n pelusa f; **~y** adj velloso/sa.

fluid adj, n fluido/da m.

fluidity n fluidez f.

fluke n (col) chiripa f.

F

fluoride n fluoruro m.
flurry n ráfaga f; agitación f.
flush vt: **to ~ out** levantar; desalojar; * vi ponerse colorado/da; * n rubor m; resplandor m.
flushed adj ruborizado/da.
fluster vt confundir.
flustered adj aturdido/da.
flute n flauta f.
flutter vi revolotear; estar en agitación; * n confusión f; agitación f.
flux n flujo m.
fly vt pilotar; transportar; * vi volar; huir, escapar; **to ~ away/off** emprender el vuelo; * n mosca f; bragueta f.
flying n aviación f.
flying saucer n platillo volante m.
flypast n desfile aéreo m.
flysheet n doble techo m.
foal n potro m.
foam n espuma f; * vi espumar.
foam rubber n espuma de caucho f.
foamy adj espumoso/sa.
focus n foco m.
fodder n forraje m.
foe n adversario/ria m/f, enemigo/ga m/f.
fog n niebla f.
foggy adj nebuloso/sa, brumoso/sa.
fog light n faro antiniebla m.
foible n debilidad, parte flaca f.
foil vt frustrar; * n hoja f; florete m.
fold n redil m; pliegue m; * vt plegar; * vi: **to ~ up** plegarse, doblarse; quebrar.
folder n carpeta f; folleto m.
folding adj plegable.
folding chair n silla de tijera f.
foliage n follaje m.
folio n folio m.
folk n gente f.
folklore n folklore m.
folk music n folk m.
folk song n canción folklórica f.
follow vt seguir; acompañar; imitar; **to ~ up** responder a; investigar; * vi seguir, resultar, provenir.
follower n seguidor/a m/f; imitador/a m/f; secuaz, partidario/ria m/f; adherente m; compañero/ra m/f.
following adj siguiente; * n afición f.
folly n extravagancia, bobería f.
foment vt fomentar; proteger.
fond adj cariñoso/sa; **~ly** adv cariñosamente.
fondle vt acariciar.
fondness n gusto m; cariño m.
font n pila bautismal f.
food n comida f.
food mixer n batidora f.
food poisoning n intoxicación alimentaria f.
food processor n robot de cocina m.

foodstuffs npl comestibles mpl.
fool n loco/ca, tonto/ta, Lat Am sonso/sa, Lat Am zonzo/za m/f; * vt engañar.
foolhardy adj temerario/ria.
foolish adj bobo/ba, tonto/ta; **~ly** adv tontamente.
foolproof adj infalible.
foolscap n papel tamaño folio m.
foot n pie m; pata f; paso m; **on,by ~** a pie.
footage n imágenes fpl.
football n balón m; fútbol m.
footballer n futbolista m/f; jugador/a de fútbol m/f.
footbrake n freno de pie m.
footbridge n puente peatonal m.
foothills npl estribaciones fpl.
foothold n pie firme m.
footing n base f; estado m; condición f; fundamento m.
footlights npl candilejas fpl.
footman n lacayo m; soldado de infantería m.
footnote n nota de pie f.
footpath n senda f.
footprint n huella, pisada f.
footsore adj con los pies doloridos.
footstep n paso m; huella f.
footwear n calzado m.
for prep por, a causa de; para; * conj porque, para que; por cuanto; **as ~ me** tocante a mí; **what ~?** ¿para qué?
forage n forraje m; * vt forrajear; saquear.
foray n incursión f.
forbid vt prohibir, vedar; impedir; **God ~!** ¡Dios no quiera!
forbidding adj inhóspito/ta; severo/ra.
force n fuerza f; poder, vigor m; violencia f; necesidad f; **~s** pl tropas fpl; * vt forzar; violentar; esforzar; constreñir.
forced adj forzado/da.
forced march n (mil) marcha forzada f.
forceful adj enérgico/ca.
forceps n fórceps m.
forcible adj fuerte, eficaz, poderoso/sa; **~bly** adv fuertemente, forzadamente.
ford n vado m; * vt vadear.
fore n: **to the ~** en evidencia.
forearm n antebrazo m.
foreboding n presentimiento m.
forecast vt pronosticar; * n pronóstico m.
forecourt n patio m.
forefather n abuelo, antecesor m.
forefinger n índice m.
forefront n: **in the ~ of** en la vanguardia de.
forego vt ceder, abandonar; preceder.
foregone adj pasado/da; anticipado/da.
foreground n delantera f.
forehead n frente f; insolencia f.
foreign adj extranjero/ra; extraño/ña.
foreigner n extranjero/ra, forastero/ra m/f.

foreign exchange n divisas fpl.
foreleg n pata delantera f.
foreman n capataz m; (law) presidente del jurado m.
foremost adj principal.
forenoon n mañana f.
forensic adj forense; ~ **scientist** n forense m/f.
forerunner n precursor/a m/f; predecesor/a m/f.
foresee vt prever.
foreshadow vt pronosticar; simbolizar.
foresight n previsión f; presciencia f.
forest n bosque m; selva f.
forestall vt anticipar; prevenir.
forester n guardabosque m/f.
forestry n silvicultura f.
foretaste n muestra f.
foretell vt predecir, profetizar.
forethought n providencia f; premeditación f.
forever adv para siempre.
forewarn vt prevenir de antemano.
foreword n prefacio m.
forfeit n confiscación f; * vt perder derecho a.
forge n fragua f; fábrica de metales f; * vt forjar; falsificar; inventar; * vi: **to ~ ahead** avanzar constantemente.
forger n falsificador/a m/f.
forgery n falsificación f.
forget vt olvidar; * vi olvidarse.
forgetful adj olvidadizo/za; descuidado/da.
forgetfulness n olvido m; negligencia f.
forget-me-not n (bot) nomeolvides m.
forgive vt perdonar.
forgiveness n perdón m; remisión f.
fork n tenedor m; horca f, Lat Am horqueta f; * vi bifurcarse; **to ~ out** (col) desembolsar.
forked adj horcado/da.
fork-lift truck n carretilla elevadora f.
forlorn adj abandonado/da, perdido/da.
form n forma f; modelo m; modo m; formalidad f; método m; molde m; * vt formar.
formal adj formal, metódico/ca; ceremonioso/sa; ~**ly** adv formalmente.
formality n formalidad f; ceremonia f.
format n formato m; * vt formatear.
formation n formación f.
formative adj formativo/va.
former adj precedente; anterior, pasado/da; ~**ly** adv antiguamente, en tiempos pasados.
formidable adj formidable, terrible.
formula n fórmula f.
formulate vt formular, articular.
forsake vt dejar, abandonar.
fort n castillo m; fortaleza f.
forte adj (mus) fuerte m.
forthcoming adj venidero/ra.
forthright adj franco/ca.
forthwith adj inmediatamente, sin tardanza.
fortieth adj, n cuadragésimo m.

fortification n fortificación f.
fortify vt fortificar; corroborar.
fortitude n fortaleza f; valor m.
fortnight n quince días mpl; dos semanas fpl; ~**ly** adj, adv cada quince días.
fortress n (mil) fortaleza f.
fortuitous adj impensado/da; casual; ~**ly** adv fortuitamente.
fortunate adj afortunado/da; ~**ly** adv felizmente.
fortune n fortuna, suerte f.
fortune-teller n sortílego/ga, adivino/na m/f.
forty adj, n cuarenta.
forum n foro m.
forward adj avanzado/da; delantero/ra; presumido/da; ~(**s**) adv adelante, más allá; * vt remitir; promover, patrocinar.
forwardness n precocidad f; audacia f.
fossil adj, n fósil m.
foster vt criar, nutrir.
foster child n hijo/ja adoptivo/va m/f.
foster father n padre adoptivo m.
foster mother n madre adoptiva f.
foul adj sucio/cia, puerco/ca; impuro/ra, detestable; ~ **copy** n borrador m; ~**ly** adv suciamente; ilegítimamente; * vt ensuciar.
foul play n mala jugada f; muerte violenta f.
found vt fundar, establecer; edificar; fundir.
foundation n fundación f; fundamento m.
founder n fundador/a m/f; fundidor m; * vi (mar) irse a pique; zozobrar.
foundling n niño/ña expósito/ta m/f.
foundry n fundición f.
fount, fountain n fuente f.
fountainhead n origen de fuente m.
four adj, n cuatro.
fourfold adj cuádruple.
four-poster (**bed**) n cama de dosel f.
foursome n grupo de cuatro personas m.
fourteen adj, n catorce.
fourteenth adj, n decimocuarto/ta.
fourth adj, n cuarto/ta; * n cuarto m; ~**ly** adv en cuarto lugar.
fowl n ave f de corral.
fox n zorra f; (fig) zorro m.
foyer n vestíbulo m.
fracas n riña f.
fraction n fracción f.
fracture n fractura f; * vt fracturar, romper.
fragile adj frágil; débil.
fragility n fragilidad f; debilidad, flaqueza f.
fragment n fragmento m.
fragmentary adj fragmentario/ria.
fragrance n fragancia f.
fragrant adj fragante, oloroso/sa; ~**ly** adv con fragancia.
frail adj frágil, débil.
frailty n fragilidad f; debilidad f.

F

frame n armazón m; marco, cerco m; cuadro de vidriera m; estructura f; montura f; * vt encuadrar; componer, construir, formar.
frame of mind n estado de ánimo m.
framework n estructura f; esqueleto m, armazón f.
franchise n sufragio m; concesión f.
frank adj franco/ca, liberal.
frankly adv francamente.
frankness n franqueza f.
frantic adj frenético/ca, furioso/sa.
fraternal adj, ~ly adv fraternal(mente).
fraternity n fraternidad f.
fraternize vi hermanarse.
fratricide n fratricidio m; fratricida m/f.
fraud n fraude, engaño m.
fraudulence n fraudulencia f.
fraudulent adj fraudulento/ta; ~ly adv fraudulentamente.
fraught adj cargado/da, lleno/na.
fray n riña, disputa, querella f.
freak n fantasía f; fenómeno m.
freckle n peca f.
freckled adj pecoso/sa.
free adj libre; liberal; suelto/ta; exento/ta; desocupado/da; gratis; * vt soltar; librar; eximir; * vr: **to ~ oneself from trouble** zafarse de.
freedom n libertad f.
freehold n propiedad absoluta f.
free-for-all n trifulca f.
free gift n prima f.
free kick n tiro libre m.
freelance adj, adv por cuenta propia.
freely adv libremente; espontáneamente; liberalmente, gratis.
freemason n francmasón m, masón m.
freemasonry n francmasonería f, masonería f.
Freepost™ n franqueo pagado m.
free-range adj de granja.
freethinker n librepensador/a m/f.
freethinking n librepensamiento m.
free trade n libre comercio m.
freeway n autopista f.
freewheel vi ir en punto muerto.
free will n libre albedrío m.
freeze vi helar(se); * vt congelar; helar.
freeze-dried adj liofilizado/da.
freezer n congelador m, Lat Am freezer m.
freezing adj helado/da.
freezing point n punto de congelación m.
freight n carga f; flete m.
freighter n fletador m.
freight train n tren de mercancías m.
French bean n judía verde f.
French fries npl patatas/papas fritas fpl.
French window n puertaventana f.
frenzied adj loco/ca, delirante.
frenzy n frenesí m; locura f.

frequency n frecuencia f.
frequent adj, ~ly adv frecuente(mente); * vt frecuentar.
fresco n fresco m.
fresh adj fresco/ca; nuevo/va, reciente; ~ **water** n agua dulce f.
freshen vt (vi) refrescar(se).
freshly adv nuevamente; recientemente.
freshman n novato m.
freshness n frescura f; fresco m.
freshwater adj de agua dulce.
fret vi agitarse, enojarse.
friar n fraile m.
friction n fricción f.
Friday n viernes m; **Good ~** Viernes Santo m.
friend n amigo/ga m/f.
friendless adj sin amigos.
friendliness n amistad, benevolencia, bondad f.
friendly adj amistoso/sa.
friendship n amistad f.
frieze n friso m.
frigate n (mar) fragata f.
fright n espanto, terror m.
frighten vt espantar.
frightened adj asustado/da.
frightening adj espantoso/sa.
frightful adj espantoso/sa, horrible; ~ly adv espantosamente, terriblemente.
frigid adj frío/ría, frígido/da; ~ly adv fríamente.
fringe n franja f.
fringe benefits npl ventajas adicionales fpl.
frisk vt cachear.
frisky adj juguetón/ona.
fritter vt: **to ~ away** desperdiciar.
frivolity n frivolidad f.
frivolous adj frívolo/la, vano/na.
frizz(le) vt frisar; rizar.
frizzy adj rizado/da.
fro adv: **to go to and ~** ir y venir.
frog n rana f.
frolic vi juguetear.
frolicsome adj juguetón/ona, travieso/sa.
from prep de; después; desde.
front n parte delantera f; fachada f; paseo marítimo m; frente m; apariencias fpl; * adj delantero/ra; primero/ra.
frontal adj de frente.
front door n puerta principal f.
frontier n frontera f.
front page n primera plana f.
front-wheel drive n (auto) tracción delantera f.
frost n helada f; hielo m; * vt escarchar.
frostbite n congelación f.
frostbitten adj helado/da, con síntomas de congelación.
frosted adj deslustrado/da.
frosty adj helado/da, frío/ría como el hielo.

froth n espuma (de algún líquido) f; * vi espumar.
frothy adj espumoso/sa.
frown vt mirar con ceño; * n ceño m.
frozen adj helado/da.
frugal adj frugal; económico/ca; sobrio/ria; ~ly adv frugalmente.
fruit n fruta f; fruto m; producto m.
fruiterer n frutero/ra m/f.
fruitful adj fructífero/ra, fértil; provechoso/sa, útil; ~ly adv con fertilidad.
fruitfulness n fertilidad f.
fruition n realización f.
fruit juice n zumo de fruta m.
fruitless adj estéril; inútil; ~ly adv vanamente, inútilmente.
fruit salad n ensalada de frutas f, macedonia f.
fruit seller n frutero/ra m.
fruit shop/store n frutería f.
fruit tree n frutal m.
frustrate vt frustrar; anular.
frustrated adj frustrado/da.
frustration n frustración f.
fry vt freír, Lat Am fritar.
frying pan n sartén f.
fuchsia n (bot) fucsia f.
fudge n caramelo blando m.
fuel n combustible m.
fuel tank n depósito de combustible m.
fugitive adj, n fugitivo/va m/f.
fugue n (mus) fuga f.
fulcrum n fulcro m.
fulfill vt cumplir; realizar.
fulfillment n cumplimiento m.
full adj lleno/na, repleto/ta, completo/ta; perfecto/ta; * adv enteramente, del todo.
full-blown adj hecho/cha y derecho/cha.
full-fledged adj hecho/cha y derecho/cha.
full-length adj de cuerpo entero/ra; completo/ta.
full moon n plenilunio m; luna llena f.
fullness n plenitud, abundancia f.
full-scale adj en gran escala; de tamaño natural.
full-time adj de tiempo completo.
fully adv llenamente, enteramente, ampliamente.
fulsome adj exagerado/da.
fumble vi manejar torpemente.
fume vi humear; encolerizarse.
fumes npl humo m.

fumigate vt fumigar, Lat Am humear.
fun n diversión f; alegría f.
function n función f.
functional adj funcional.
fund n fondo m; fondos públicos mpl; * vt costear.
fundamental adj fundamental; ~ly adv fundamentalmente.
fundamentalism n fundamentalismo m.
fundamentalist n fundamentalista m/f.
funeral service n misa de difuntos f, funeral m.
funeral n funeral m.
funereal adj funeral, fúnebre.
fungus n hongo m; seta f.
funnel n embudo m; cañón (de chimenea) m.
funny adj divertido/da; curioso/sa; zumbón/ona.
fur n piel f.
fur coat n abrigo de pieles m.
furious adj furioso/sa, frenético/ca; ~ly adv con furia.
furlong n estadio m; (octava parte de una milla).
furlough n (mil) licencia f; permiso m.
furnace n horno m; hornaza f.
furnish vt amueblar, Lat Am amoblar; facilitar; suministrar.
furniture n muebles mpl.
furrow n surco m; * vt surcar; estriar.
furry adj peludo/da.
further adj nuevo/va; más lejano/na; * adv más lejos, más allá; aún; además; * vt adelantar, promover, ayudar.
further education n educación para adultos f.
furthermore adv además.
furthest adv lo más lejos, lo más remoto.
furtive adj furtivo/va; secreto/ta; ~ly adv furtivamente.
fury n furor m; furia f; ira f.
fuse vt, vi fundir; derretirse; * n fusible m, Lat Am tapón m; mecha f.
fuse box n caja de fusibles f.
fusion n fusión f.
fuss n lío m; alboroto m.
fussy adj jactancioso/sa.
futile adj fútil, frívolo/la.
futility n futilidad, vanidad f.
future adj futuro/ra; * n futuro m; porvenir m.
fuzzy adj borroso/sa; muy rizado/da.

F

G

gab n (col) charla f.
gabble vi charlar, parlotear; * n algarabía f.
gable n gablete m.
gadget n dispositivo m.
gaffe n plancha f.
gag n mordaza f; chiste m; * vt amordazar.
gage n calibre m; entrevía f; indicador m; * vt medir.
gaiety n alegría f.
gaily adv alegremente.
gain n ganancia f; interés, provecho m; * vt ganar; conseguir.
gait n marcha f; porte m.
gala n fiesta f.
galaxy n galaxia f.
gale n vendaval m.
gall n hiel f.
gallant adj galante.
gall bladder n vesícula biliar f.
gallery n galería f.
galley n cocina f; galera f.
gallon n galón m (medida).
gallop n galope m; * vi galopar.
gallows n horca f.
gallstone n cálculo biliar m.
galore adv en abundancia.
galvanize vt galvanizar.
gambit n estrategia f.
gamble vi jugar; especular; * n riesgo m; apuesta f.
gambler n jugador/a m/f.
gambling n juego m.
game n juego m; pasatiempo m; partido m; partida f; caza f; * vi jugar.
gamekeeper n guardabosques m invar.
gaming n juego m.
gammon n jamón m.
gamut n (mus) gama f.
gander n ganso m.
gang n pandilla, banda f.
gangrene n gangrena f.
gangster n gángster m.
gangway n pasarela f.
gap n hueco m; claro m; intervalo m.
gape vi boquear; estar con la boca abierta.
gaping adj muy abierto/ta.
garage n garaje m, Lat Am garage m.
garbage can n cubo de la basura m.
garbageman n basurero m.
garbled adj falsificado/da.
garden n jardín m.
garden-hose n regadera f.
gardener n jardinero/ra m/f.

gardening n jardinería f.
gargle vi hacer gárgaras.
gargoyle n gárgola f.
garish adj ostentoso/sa.
garland n guirnalda f.
garlic n ajo m.
garment n prenda f.
garnish vt guarnecer, adornar; * n guarnición f; adorno m.
garret n guardilla f; desván m.
garrison n (mil) guarnición f; * vt (mil) guarnecer.
garrote vt estrangular.
garrulous adj gárrulo/la, locuaz, charlador/a.
garter n liga f.
garter belt n liguero m.
gas n gas m; gasolina f.
gas burner n mechero de gas m.
gas cylinder n bombona de gas f.
gaseous adj gaseoso/sa.
gas fire n estufa de gas f.
gash n cuchillada f; raja f; * vt acuchillar.
gasket n junta de culata f.
gas mask n careta antigás f.
gas meter n contador de gas m.
gasoline n gasolina f; four-star ~ súper f.
gasp vi jadear; * n boqueada f.
gas pedal n acelerador f.
gas ring n hornillo de gas m.
gassy adj gaseoso/sa.
gas tap n llave del gas f.
gastric adj gástrico/ca.
gastronomic adj gastronómico/ca.
gasworks npl fábrica de gas f.
gate n puerta f.
gateway n puerta f.
gather vt recoger, amontonar; entender; plegar; * vi juntarse.
gathering n reunión f; colecta f.
gauche adj torpe.
gaudy adj chillón/ona.
gaunt adj flaco/ca, delgado/da.
gauze n gasa f.
gay adj alegre; vivo/va; gay.
gaze vi contemplar, considerar; * n mirada f.
gazelle n gacela f.
gazette n gaceta f.
gazetteer n gacetero m; diccionario geográfico m.
gear n atavío m; vestido m; aparejo m; tirantes mpl; velocidad f.
gearbox n caja de cambios f.
gear wheel n rueda dentada f.

gel n gel m.

gelatin(e) n gelatina, jalea f.

gelignite n gelignita f.

gem n gema f.

Gemini n Géminis m (signo del zodiaco).

gender n género m.

gene n gen m.

genealogical adj genealógico/ca.

genealogy n genealogía f.

general adj general, común, usual; **in ~** por lo general; **~ly** adv generalmente; * n general m; generala f.

general delivery n lista de correos f.

generality n generalidad, mayor parte f.

generalization n generalización f.

generalize vt generalizar.

generate vt engendrar; producir; causar.

generation n generación f.

generator n generador m.

generic adj genérico/ca.

generosity n generosidad, liberalidad f.

generous adj generoso/sa.

genetic engineering n ingeniería genética f.

genetics npl genética f.

genial adj genial, natural; alegre.

genitals npl genitales mpl.

genitive n genitivo m.

genius n genio m.

genteel adj refinado/da, elegante.

gentile n gentil, pagano/na m/f.

gentle adj suave, dócil, manso/sa, moderado/da; benigno/na.

gentleman n caballero m.

gentleness n dulzura, suavidad f.

gently adv suavemente.

gentry n alta burguesía f.

gents n aseos mpl.

genuflection n genuflexión f, Lat Am hincada f.

genuine adj genuino/na, puro/ra; **~ly** adv puramente, naturalmente.

genus n género m.

geographer n geógrafo/fa m/f.

geographical adj geográfico/ca.

geography n geografía f.

geological adj geológico/ca.

geologist n geólogo/ga m/f.

geology n geología f.

geometric(al) adj geométrico/ca.

geometry n geometría f.

geranium n (bot) geranio m.

geriatric n, adj geriátrico/ca m/f.

germ n germen m.

germinate vi brotar.

gesticulate vi gesticular.

gesture n gesto, movimiento expresivo m.

get vt ganar; conseguir, obtener, alcanzar; coger; agarrar; * vi hacerse, ponerse; prevalecer; introducirse; **to ~ the better** salir vencedor/a, sobrepujar.

geyser n géiser m; calentador de agua m.

ghastly adj espantoso/sa.

gherkin n pepinillo, cohombrillo m.

ghetto n gueto m.

ghost n fantasma m, Lat Am espanto m; espectro m.

ghostly adj fantasmal.

giant n gigante m.

gibberish n jerigonza f.

gibe vi escarnecer, burlarse, mofar; * n mofa, burla f.

giblets npl menudillos mpl.

giddiness n vértigo m.

giddy adj vertiginoso/sa.

gift n regalo m; don m; dádiva f; talento m.

gifted adj dotado/da.

gift voucher n vale de regalo m.

gigantic adj gigantesco/ca.

giggle vi reírse tontamente.

gild vt dorar.

gilding, gilt n doradura f.

gill n cuarta parte de pinta f; **~s** pl agallas fpl.

gilt-edged adj de máxima garantía.

gimmick n truco m.

gin n ginebra f.

ginger n jengibre m.

gingerbread n pan de jengibre m.

ginger-haired adj pelirrojo/ja.

giraffe n jirafa f.

girder n viga f.

girdle n faja f; cinturón m.

girl n muchacha, chica f, zagala f.

girlfriend n amiga; novia f.

girlish adj de niña.

giro n giro postal m.

girth n cincha f; circunferencia f.

gist n punto principal m.

give vt, vi dar, donar; conceder; abandonar; pronunciar; aplicarse, dedicarse; **to ~ away** regalar; traicionar; revelar; **to ~ back** devolver; **to ~ in** vi ceder; vt entregar; **to ~ off** despedir; **to ~ out** distribuir; **to ~ up** vi rendir; vt renunciar a.

gizzard n molleja f.

glacial adj glacial.

glacier n glaciar m.

glad adj alegre, contento/ta, agradable; **I am ~ to see** me alegro de ver; **~ly** adv alegremente.

gladden vt alegrar.

gladiator n gladiador m.

glamor n encanto, atractivo m.

glamorous adj atractivo/va.

glance n ojeada f; * vi mirar; echar una ojeada.

glancing adj oblicuo/cua.

gland n glándula f.

glare n deslumbramiento m; mirada feroz y penetrante f; * vi deslumbrar, brillar; echar miradas de indignación.

glaring adj deslumbrante; manifiesto/ta; notorio/ria.

G

glass n vidrio m, cristal m; telescopio m; vaso m; espejo m; **~es** pl gafas fpl; * adj vítreo/rea.

glassware n cristalería f.

glassy adj vítreo/rea, cristalino/na, vidrioso/sa.

glaze vt vidriar; embarnizar.

glazier n vidriero m, cristalero m.

gleam n relámpago, rayo m; * vi relampaguear, brillar.

gleaming adj reluciente.

glean vt espigar; recoger.

glee n alegría f; gozo m; jovialidad f.

glen n valle m; llanura f.

glib adj con lab; **~ly** adv con labia.

glide vi resbalar; planear.

gliding n vuelo sin motor m.

glimmer n vislumbre f; * vi vislumbrarse.

glimpse n vislumbre f; relámpago m; ojeada f; * vt entrever, percibir.

glint vi centellear.

glisten, **glitter** vi relucir, brillar.

gloat vi relamerse; saborear.

global adj mundial.

globalization n globalización f.

global warming n calentamiento global m.

globe n globo m; esfera f.

gloom, **gloominess** n oscuridad f; melancolía, tristeza f; **~ily** adv oscuramente; tristemente.

gloomy adj sombrío/ría, oscuro/ra; cubierto de nubes; triste, melancólico/ca.

glorification n glorificación, alabanza f.

glorify vt glorificar, celebrar.

glorious adj glorioso/sa, ilustre; **~ly** adv gloriosamente.

glory n gloria, fama, celebridad f.

gloss n glosa f; lustre m; * vt glosar, interpretar; **to ~ over** encubrir.

glossary n glosario m.

glossy adj lustroso/sa, brillante.

glove n guante m.

glove compartment n guantera f.

glow vi arder; inflamarse; relucir; * n color vivo m; viveza de color f; vehemencia de una pasión f.

glower vi mirar con ceño.

glue n cola f; Lat Am cemento m; * vt pegar.

gluey adj viscoso/sa, pegajoso/sa.

glum adj abatido/da, triste.

glut n hartura, abundancia f.

glutinous adj glutinoso/sa, viscoso/sa.

glutton n glotón/ona, tragón/ona m/f.

gluttony n glotonería f.

glycerin n glicerina f.

gnarled adj nudoso/sa.

gnash vt, vi rechinar.

gnat n mosquito m, Lat Am jején m.

gnaw vt roer.

gnome n gnomo m.

go vi ir, irse, andar, caminar; partir(se), marchar; huir; pasar; **to ~ ahead** seguir adelante; **to ~**

away marcharse; **to ~ back** volver; **to ~ by** pasar; **to ~ for** ir por; gustar; **to ~ in** entrar; **to ~ off** irse; pasarse; **to ~ on** seguir; pasar; **to ~ out** salir; apagarse; **to ~ up** subir.

goad n aguijada, aijada f, Lat Am picana f; * vt aguijar, Lat Am picanear; estimular, incitar.

go-ahead adj emprendedor/a; * n luz verde f.

goal n meta f; fin m.

goalkeeper n portero/ra m/f, Lat Am arquero/ra m/f, Lat Am guardavallas m/f invar.

goalpost n poste (de la portería) m.

goatherd n cabrero/ra m/f.

gobble vt engullir, tragar; **to ~ down** zampar.

go-between n mediador/a m/f.

goblet n copa f.

goblin n espíritu ambulante, duende m.

God n Dios m.

godchild n ahijado, hijo de pila m.

goddaughter n ahijada, hija de pila f.

goddess n diosa f.

godfather n padrino m.

godforsaken adj dejado/da de la mano de Dios.

godhead n deidad, divinidad f.

godless adj infiel, impío/pía, sin Dios, ateo/tea.

godlike adj divino/na.

godliness n piedad, devoción, santidad f.

godly adj piadoso/sa, devoto/ta, religioso/sa; recto/ta, justificado/da.

godmother n madrina f.

godsend n don del cielo m.

godson n ahijado m.

goggle-eyed adj con ojos desorbitados.

goggles npl gafas fpl; gafas de bucear fpl.

going n ida f; salida f; partida f; progreso m.

gold n oro m.

golden adj áureo/rea, de oro; excelente; **~ rule** n regla de oro f.

goldfish n pez de colores m.

gold-plated adj chapado/da en oro.

goldsmith n orfebre m.

golf n golf m.

golf ball n pelota de golf f.

golf club n club de golf m.

golf course n campo de golf m.

golfer n golfista m/f.

gondolier n gondolero/ra m/f.

gone adj ido/da; perdido/da; pasado/da; gastado/da; muerto/ta.

gong n atabal chino, gong m.

good adj bueno/na, benévolo/la, cariñoso/sa; conveniente, apto/ta; * adv bien; * n bien m; prosperidad, ventaja f; **~s** pl bienes muebles mpl; mercaderías fpl.

goodbye ! excl ¡adiós!

Good Friday n Viernes Santo m.

goodies npl golosinas fpl.

good-looking adj guapo/pa.

good nature n bondad f.

good-natured adj bondadoso/sa.
goodness n bondad f.
goodwill n benevolencia, bondad f.
goose n ganso m; oca f.
gooseberry n grosella espinosa f.
goose bumps, goose flesh npl carne de gallina f.
goose-step n paso de la oca m.
gore n sangre cuajada f; * vt cornear.
gorge n barranco m; * vt engullir, tragar.
gorgeous adj maravilloso/sa.
gorilla n gorila m.
gorse n aulaga f.
gory adj sangriento/ta.
goshawk n azor m.
gospel n evangelio m.
gossamer n vello m; pelusa (de frutas) f.
gossip n cotilleo m; * vi cotillear.
gothic adj gótico/ca.
gout n gota f (enfermedad).
govern vt gobernar, dirigir, regir.
governess n gobernadora f.
government n gobierno m; administración publica f.
governor n gobernador/a m/f.
gown n toga f; vestido de mujer m; bata f.
grab vt agarrar.
grace n gracia f; favor m; merced f; perdón m; gracias fpl; **to say ~** bendecir la mesa; * vt adornar; agraciar.
graceful adj gracioso/sa, primoroso/sa; **~ly** adv elegantemente, con gracia.
gracious adj gracioso/sa; favorable; **~ly** adv graciosamente.
gradation n gradación f.
grade n grado m; curso m.
grade crossing n paso a nivel m.
grade school n escuela primaria f.
gradient n (rail) pendiente.
gradual adj gradual; **~ly** adv gradualmente.
graduate vi graduarse, Lat Am egresar.
graduation n graduación f, Lat Am egreso m.
graffiti n pintadas fpl.
graft n injerto m; * vt injertar, ingerir.
grain n grano m; semilla f; cereales mpl.
gram n gramo m (peso).
grammar n gramática f.
grammatical adj gramatical; **~ly** adv gramaticalmente.
granary n granero m.
grand adj grande, ilustre.
grandchild n nieto/ta m/f.
granddad n abuelo m.
granddaughter n nieta f; **great ~** bisnieta f.
grandeur n grandeza f; pompa f.
grandfather n abuelo m; **great ~** bisabuelo m.
grandiose adj grandioso/sa.
grandma n abuelita f.
grandmother n abuela f; **great ~** bisabuela f.
grandparents npl abuelos mpl.

grand piano n piano de cola m.
grandson n nieto m; **great ~** bisnieto m.
grandstand n tribuna f.
granite n granito m.
grant vt conceder; **to take for ~ed** presuponer; * n beca f; concesión f.
granulate vt granular.
granule n gránulo m.
grape n uva f; **bunch of ~s** racimo de uvas m.
grapefruit n toronja f, pomelo m.
graph n gráfica f.
graphic(al) adj gráfico/ca; pintoresco/ca; **~ally** adv gráficamente.
graphics n artes gráficas fpl; gráficos mpl.
grapnel n (mar) arpeo m.
grasp vt empuñar, asir, agarrar; * n puño m; comprensión f; poder m.
grasping adj avaro/ra.
grass n hierba f, Lat Am pasto m.
grasshopper n saltamontes m invar.
grassland n pampa, pradera f.
grass-roots adj popular.
grass snake n culebra de agua f.
grassy adj herboso/sa.
grate n reja, verja, rejilla f; * vt rallar; rechinar (los dientes); enrejar.
grateful adj grato/ta, agradecido/da; **~ly** adv agradecidamente.
gratefulness n gratitud f.
grater n rallador m.
gratification n gratificación f.
gratify vt contentar; gratificar.
gratifying adj grato/ta.
grating n rejado m; * adj áspero/ra; ofensivo/va.
gratis adv gratis.
gratitude n gratitud f.
gratuitous adj gratuito/ta, voluntario/ria; **~ly** adv gratuitamente.
gratuity n gratificación, recompensa f.
grave n sepultura f; * adj grave, serio/ria; **~ly** adv con gravedad, seriamente.
grave digger n sepulturero m.
gravel n cascajo m.
gravestone n lápida f.
graveyard n cementerio m.
gravitate vi gravitar.
gravitation n gravitación f.
gravity n gravedad f.
gravy n jugo de la carne f; salsa f.
gray adj gris; cano/na; * n gris m.
gray-haired adj canoso/sa.
grayish adj grisáceo/a; entrecano/na.
grayness n color gris m.
graze vt pastorear; tocar ligeramente; * vi pacer.
grease n grasa f; * vt untar.
greaseproof adj a prueba de grasa.
greasy adj grasiento/ta, Lat Am grasoso/sa.

G

great adj gran, grande; principal; ilustre; noble, magnánimo/ma; **~ly** adv muy, mucho.

greatcoat n sobretodo m.

greatness n grandeza f; dignidad f; poder m; magnanimidad f.

greedily adv vorazmente, ansiosamente.

greediness, greed n gula f; codicia f.

greedy adj avaro/ra, codicioso/sa, Lat Am abusador/ra; goloso/sa, glotón/ona.

Greek n griego (idioma) m.

green adj verde, fresco/ca, reciente; no maduro/ra; * n verde m; llanura verde f; **~s** pl verduras fpl.

greenback n billete m.

green belt n zona verde f.

green card n carta verde f.

greenery n verdura f.

greenhouse n invernadero m

greenhouse effect n efecto invernadero m.

greenish adj verdoso/sa.

green movement n ecologismo m.

greenness n verdor, vigor m; frescura, falta de experiencia f; novedad f.

greet vt saludar, congratular.

greeting n saludo m.

greeting(s) card n tarjeta de felicitación f.

grenade n (mil) granada f.

grenadier n granadero m.

greyhound n galgo m.

grid n reja f; red f.

gridiron n parrilla f; campo de fútbol americano m.

grief n dolor m; aflicción, pena f.

grievance n pesar m; molestia f; agravio m; injusticia f; perjuicio m.

grieve vt agraviar, afligir; * vi afligirse; llorar.

grievous adj doloroso/sa; enorme, atroz; **~ly** adv penosamente; cruelmente.

griffin n grifo m.

grill n parrilla f; * vt interrogar.

grille n reja f.

grim adj feo, fea; horrendo/da; ceñudo/da.

grimace n mueca f.

grime n porquería f.

grimy adj ensuciado/da.

grin n mueca f; * vi sonreír.

grind vt moler; pulverizar; afilar; picar; rechinar los dientes.

grinder n molinero m; molinillo m; amolador m.

grip n asimiento m; asidero m; maletín m; * vt agarrar.

gripping adj absorbente.

grisly adj horroroso/sa.

gristle n tendón, cartílago m.

gristly adj tendinoso/sa, cartilaginoso/sa.

grit n gravilla f; valor m.

groan vi gemir, suspirar; * n gemido, suspiro m.

grocer n tendero/ra, abarrotero/ra m/f.

groceries npl comestibles mpl.

grocery store n tienda de comestibles f.

groggy adj atontado/da.

groin n ingle f.

groom n establero m; criado m; novio m; * vt cuidar, almohazar.

groove n ranura f.

grope vt, vi tentar, buscar a oscuras; andar a tientas.

gross adj grueso/sa, corpulento/ta, espeso/sa; grosero/ra; estúpido/da; **~ly** adv enormemente.

grotesque adj grotesco/ca.

grotto n gruta f.

ground n tierra f; terreno, suelo, pavimento m; fundamento m; razón fundamental f; campo (de batalla) m; fondo m; * vt mantener en tierra; conectar con tierra.

ground floor n planta baja f.

grounding n conocimientos básicos mpl.

groundless adj infundado/da; **~ly** adv sin motivo.

ground staff n personal de tierra m.

groundwork n preparación f.

group n grupo m; * vt agrupar.

grouse n lagópodo escocés m; * vi quejarse.

grove n arboleda f.

grovel vi arrastrarse.

grow vt cultivar; * vi crecer, aumentarse; **~ up** crecer.

grower n cultivador/a m/f; productor/a m/f.

growing adj creciente.

growl vi regañar, gruñir; * n gruñido m.

grown-up n adulto/ta m/f.

growth n crecimiento m.

grub n gusano m.

grubby adj sucio/cia.

grudge n rencor, odio m; envidia f; * vt, vi envidiar.

grudgingly adv de mala gana.

grueling adj penoso/sa, duro/ra.

gruesome adj horrible.

gruff adj brusco/ca; **~ly** adv bruscamente.

gruffness n aspereza, severidad f.

grumble vi gruñir; murmurar.

grumpy adj regañón/ona.

grunt vi gruñir; * n gruñido m.

G-string n taparrabo m.

guarantee n garantía f; * vt garantizar.

guard n guardia f; * vt guardar; defender.

guarded adj cauteloso/sa, mesurado/da.

guardroom n (mil) cuarto de guardia m.

guardian n tutor/ra m/f; curador/a m/f; guardián/dana m/f.

guardianship n tutela f.

guerrilla n guerrillero/ra m/f.

guerrilla group n guerrilla f.

guerrilla warfare n guerra de guerrillas f.

guess v, vi conjeturar; adivinar; suponer; * n conjetura f.

guesswork n conjeturas fpl.

guest *n* huésped/a, convidado/da *m/f*.
guest room *n* cuarto de huéspedes *m*.
guffaw *n* carcajada *f*.
guidance *n* gobierno *m*; dirección *f*.
guide *vt* guiar, dirigir; * *n* guía *m*.
guide dog *n* perro lazarillo *m*.
guidelines *npl* directiva *f*.
guidebook *n* guía *f*.
guild *n* gremio *m*; corporación *f*.
guile *n* astucia *f*.
guillotine *n* guillotina *f*; * *vt* guillotinar.
guilt *n* culpabilidad *f*.
guiltless *adj* inocente, libre de culpa.
guilty *adj* reo, rea, culpable.
guinea pig *n* cobaya *f*, conejillo de Indias *m*.
guise *n* manera *f*.
guitar *n* guitarra *f*.
gulf *n* golfo *m*; abismo *m*.
gull *n* gaviota *f*.
gullet *n* esófago *m*.
gullibility *n* credulidad *f*; simpleza *f*.
gullible *adj* crédulo/la.
gully *n* barranco *m*.
gulp *n* trago *m*; * *vi* tragar saliva; * *vr* tragarse.
gum *n* goma *f*; cemento *m*; encía *f*; chicle *m*; * *vt* pegar con goma.
gum tree *n* árbol gomero *m*.
gun *n* pistola *f*; escopeta *f*.
gunboat *n* cañonera *f*.
gun carriage *n* cureña *f*.

gunfire *n* disparos *mpl*.
gunman *n* pistolero *m*.
gunmetal *n* bronce de cañones *m*.
gunner *n* artillero *m*.
gunnery *n* artillería *f*.
gunpoint *n*: **at ~** a punta de pistola; a mano armada.
gunpowder *n* pólvora *f*.
gunshot *n* escopetazo *m*.
gunsmith *n* armero/ra *m/f*.
gurgle *vi* gorgotear.
guru *n* gurú *m*.
gush *vi* brotar; chorrear; * *n* chorro *m*
gushing *adj* superabundante.
gusset *n* escudete *m*.
gust *n* ráfaga *f*; soplo de aire *m*, racha *f*.
gusto *n* entusiasmo *m*.
gusty *adj* tempestuoso/sa.
gut *n* intestino *m*; **~s** *npl* valor *m*; * *vt* destripar.
gutter *n* canalón *m*; arroyo *m*.
guttural *adj* gutural.
guy *n* tío *m*; tipo *m*.
guzzle *vt* engullir.
gym(**nasium**) *n* gimnasio *m*.
gymnast *n* gimnasta *m/f*.
gymnastic *adj* gimnástico/ca; **~s** *npl* gimnástica *f*.
gynecologist *n* ginecólogo/ga *m/f*.
Gypsy *n* gitano/na *m/f*.
gypsum *n* yeso *m*.
gyrate *vi* girar.

G

H

haberdasher *n* camisero/ra *m/f*.
haberdashery *n* camisería *f*; mercería *f*; prendas de caballero *fpl*.
habit *n* costumbre *f*.
habitable *adj* habitable.
habitat *n* hábitat *m*.
habitual *adj* habitual; **~ly** *adv* por costumbre.
hack *n* corte *m*; gacetillero/ra *m/f*; * *vt* tajar, cortar.
hackneyed *adj* trillado/da.
haddock *n* especie de bacalao *f*.
hag *n* bruja *f*.
haggard *adj* ojeroso/sa.
haggle *vi* regatear.
hail *n* granizo *m*; * *vt* saludar, * *vi* granizar.
hailstone *n* piedra de granizo *f*.
hair *n* pelo; cabello *m*.
hairbrush *n* cepillo *m*.
haircut *n* corte de pelo *m*.
hairdresser *n* peluquero/ra *m/f*, *Lat Am* peinador/ra *m/f*.
hairdryer *n* secador de pelo *m*.
hairless *adj* calvo/va.
hairnet *n* redecilla *f*.
hairpiece *n* tupé *m*.
hairpin *n* horquilla *f*.
hairpin curve *n* curva muy cerrada *f*.
hair remover *n* depilatorio *m*.
hairspray *n* laca *f*.
hairstyle *n* peinado *m*.
hairy *adj* peludo/da, cabelludo/da.
hale *adj* sano/na, vigoroso/sa.
half *n* mitad *f*; * *adj* medio/dia.
half-caste *adj* mestizo/za.
half-hearted *adj* indiferente.
half-hour *n* media hora *f*.
half-moon *n* media luna *f*.
half-price *adj* a mitad de precio.
half step *n* (*mus*) semitono *m*.
half-time *n* descanso *m*.
halfway *adv* a medio camino.
hall *n* vestíbulo *m*; hall *m*, *Lat Am* jol *m*.
hallmark *n* contraste *m*.
hallow *vt* consagrar, santificar.
hallucination *n* alucinación *f*.
halo *n* halo *m*.
halt *vi* parar; * *n* parada *f*; alto *m*.
halve *vt* partir por la mitad.
ham *n* jamón *m*.
hamburger *n* hamburguesa *f*.
hammer *n* martillo *m*; * *vt* martillar.
hammock *n* hamaca *f*.

hamper *n* cesto *f*; * *vt* estorbar.
hamstring *vt* desjarretar.
hand *n* mano *f*; brazo *m*; aguja *f*; **at ~** a mano; * *vt* alargar.
handbag *n* cartera *f*, *Lat Am* sobre *m*.
handbell *n* campanilla *f*.
handbook *n* manual *m*.
handbrake *n* freno de mano *m*.
handcuff *n* esposa *f*.
handful *n* puñado *m*.
handicap *n* desventaja *f*.
handicapped *adj* minusválido/da.
handicraft *n* artesanía *f*.
handiwork *n* obra *f*.
handkerchief *n* pañuelo *m*.
handle *n* mango, puño *m*; asa; *Lat Am* manija *f*; * *vt* manejar; tratar.
handlebars *npl* manillar *m*, *Lat Am* manubrio *m*.
handling *n* manejo *m*.
handrail *n* pasamanos *m*.
handshake *n* apretón de manos *m*.
handsome *adj* guapo/pa; **~ly** *adv* primorosamente.
handwriting *n* letra *f*.
handy *adj* práctico/ca; diestro/tra.
hang *vt* colgar; ahorcar; * *vi* colgar; ser ahorcado/da.
hanger *n* percha *f*.
hanger-on *n* parásito *m*.
hangings *npl* tapicería *f*.
hangman *n* verdugo *m*.
hangover *n* resaca *f*.
hang-up *n* complejo *m*.
hanker *vi* ansiar, apetecer.
haphazard *adj* fortuito/ta.
hapless *adj* desgraciado/da.
happen *vi* pasar; acontecer, acaecer.
happening *n* suceso *m*.
happily *adv* felizmente.
happiness *n* felicidad *f*.
happy *adj* feliz.
harangue *n* arenga *f*; * *vi* arengar.
harass *vt* cansar, fatigar.
harbinger *n* precursor *m*.
harbor *n* puerto *m*; * *vt* albergar.
hard *adj* duro/ra, firme; difícil; penoso/sa; severo/ra, rígido/da; **~ of hearing** medio sordo/da; **~ by** muy cerca.
harden *vt* (*vi*) endurecer(se).
hard-headed *adj* realista.
hard-hearted *adj* duro de corazón, insensible.
hardiness *n* robustez *f*.
hardly *adv* apenas.

hardness n dureza f; dificultad f; severidad f.
hardship n penas fpl.
hard-up adj sin plata.
hardware n hardware m; quincallería f.
hardwearing adj resistente.
hardy adj fuerte, robusto/ta.
hare n liebre f.
hare-brained adj atolondrado/da.
hare-lipped adj labihendido/da.
haricot n alubia f.
harlequin n arlequín m.
harm n mal, daño m; perjuicio m; * vt dañar.
harmful adj perjudicial.
harmless adj inocuo/cua.
harmonic adj armónico/ca.
harmonious adj armonioso/sa; ~ly adv armoniosamente.
harmonize vt armonizar.
harmony n armonía f.
harness n arreos de un caballo mpl; * vt enjaezar.
harp n arpa f.
harpist n arpista m/f.
harpoon n arpón m.
harpsichord n clavicordio m.
harrow n grada f; rastro m.
harry vt hostigar.
harsh adj duro/ra; austero/ra; ~ly adv severamente.
harshness n aspereza, dureza f; austeridad f.
harvest n cosecha f; * vt cosechar.
harvester n cosechadora f.
hash n hachís m; picadillo m.
hassock n cojín de paja m.
haste n apuro m; **to be in** ~ estar apurado/da.
hasten vt acelerar, apresurar; * vi tener prisa.
hastily adv precipitadamente.
hastiness n precipitación f.
hasty adj apresurado/da.
hat n sombrero m.
hatbox n sombrerera f.
hatch vt incubar; tramar; **to ~ a plot/scheme** zurcir; * n escotilla f.
hatchback n tres puertas, cinco puertas m invar.
hatchet n hacha f.
hatchway n (mar) escotilla f.
hate n odio, aborrecimiento m; * vt odiar, detestar.
hateful adj odioso/sa.
hatred n odio, aborrecimiento m.
hatter n sombrerero m.
haughtily adv orgullosamente.
haughtiness n orgullo m; altivez f.
haughty adj altanero/ra, orgulloso/sa.
haul vt tirar; * n botín m.
hauler n transportista m/f.
haunch n anca f.
haunt vt frecuentar, rondar; * n guarida f; costumbre f.

have vt haber; tener, poseer.
haven n asilo m; puerto m.
haversack n mochila f.
havoc n estrago m.
hawk n halcón m; * vi cazar con halcón.
hawthorn n espino blanco m.
hay n heno m.
hay fever n fiebre del heno f.
hayloft n henil m.
haystack n almiar m.
hazard n riesgo m; * vt arriesgar.
hazardous adj arriesgado/da, peligroso/sa.
haze n niebla f.
hazel n avellano m; * adj castaño/ña.
hazelnut n avellana f.
hazy adj oscuro/ra.
he pn él.
head n cabeza f; jefe m; juicio m; * vt encabezar; **to ~ for** dirigirse a.
headache n dolor de cabeza m.
headdress n cofia f; tocado m.
headland n promontorio m.
headlight n faro m, Lat Am foco m.
headline n titular m.
headlong adv precipitadamente.
headmaster n director m.
head office n oficina central f.
headphones npl auriculares mpl, Lat Am audífonos mpl.
headquarters npl (mil) cuartel general m; sede central f.
headroom n altura f.
headstrong adj testarudo/da, cabezudo/da.
headwaiter n maître m.
headway n progresos mpl.
heady adj cabezón/ona.
heal vt, vi curar.
health n salud f; brindis m invar.
healthiness n sanidad f.
healthy adj sano/na.
heap n montón m; * vt amontonar.
hear vt oír; escuchar; * vi oír; escuchar.
hearing n oído m.
hearing aid n audífono m.
hearsay n rumor m; fama f.
hearse n coche fúnebre m.
heart n corazón m; **by** ~ de memoria; **with all my** ~ con toda mi alma.
heart attack n infarto, infarto de miocardio m.
heartbreaking adj desgarrador.
heartburn n ardor de estómago m
heart failure n fallo cardíaco m.
heartfelt adj sincero/ra.
hearth n hogar m.
heartily adv sinceramente, cordialmente.
heartiness n cordialidad, sinceridad f.
heartless adj cruel; ~ly adv cruelmente.
hearty adj cordial.

heat n calor m; * vt calentar.
heater n calentador m.
heather n (bot) brezo m.
heathen n pagano/na m/f; ~**ish** adj salvaje.
heating n calefacción f.
heat wave n ola de calor f.
heave vt alzar; tirar; * n tirón m.
heaven n cielo m.
heavenly adj divino/na.
heavily adv pesadamente.
heaviness n pesadez f.
heavy adj pesado/da; opresivo/va.
Hebrew n hebreo m.
heckle vt interrumpir.
hectic adj agitado/da.
hedge n seto m; * vt cercar con seto.
hedgehog n erizo m.
heed vt hacer caso de; * n cuidado m; atención f.
heedless adj descuidado/da, negligente; ~**ly** adv negligentemente.
heel n talón m; **to take to one's** ~**s** apretar los talones, huir.
hefty adj grande.
heifer n ternera f.
height n altura f; altitud f.
heighten vt realzar; adelantar, mejorar; exaltar.
heinous adj atroz.
heir n heredero/ra m/f; ~ **apparent** heredero/ra forzoso/sa m/f.
heiress n heredera f.
heirloom n reliquia de familia f.
helicopter n helicóptero m.
hell n infierno m.
hellish adj infernal.
helm n (mar) timón m.
helmet n casco m.
help vt, vi ayudar, socorrer; **I cannot** ~ **it** no puedo remediarlo; no lo puedo evitar; * n ayuda f; socorro, remedio m.
helper n ayudante m/f.
helpful adj útil.
helping n ración f.
helpless adj indefenso/sa; ~**ly** adv irremediablemente.
helter-skelter adv a trochemoche, en desorden.
hem n ribete m; * vt ribetear.
he-man n macho m.
hemisphere n hemisferio m.
hemorrhage n hemorragia f.
hemorrhoids npl hemorroides mpl.
hemp n cáñamo m.
hen n gallina f.
henchman n secuaz m.
henceforth, **henceforward** adv de aquí en adelante.
henhouse n gallinero m.
hepatitis n hepatitis f.
her pn su; ella; de ella; a ella.
herald n heraldo m.

heraldry n heráldica f.
herb n hierba f; ~**s** pl hierbas fpl.
herbaceous adj herbáceo/cea.
herbalist n herbolario m.
herbivorous adj herbívoro/ra.
herd n rebaño m.
here adv aquí, acá.
hereabout(s) adv aquí alrededor.
hereafter adv en el futuro.
hereby adv por esto.
hereditary adj hereditario/ria.
heredity n herencia f.
heresy n herejía f.
heretic n hereje m/f; * adj herético/ca.
herewith adv con esto.
heritage n patrimonio m.
hermetic adj hermético/ca; ~**ly** adv herméticamente.
hermit n ermitaño/ña m/f.
hermitage n ermita f.
hernia n hernia f.
hero n héroe m.
heroic adj heroico/ca; ~**ally** adv heroicamente.
heroine n heroína f.
heroism n heroísmo m.
heron n garza f.
herring n arenque m.
hers pn suyo, de ella.
herself pn ella misma.
hesitant adj vacilante.
hesitate vt dudar; tardar.
hesitation n duda, irresolución f.
heterogeneous adj heterogéneo/nea.
heterosexual adj, n heterosexual m.
hew vt tajar; cortar; picar.
heyday n apogeo m.
hi! excl ¡hola!
hiatus n (gr) hiato m.
hibernate vi invernar.
hiccup n hipo m; * vi tener hipo.
hickory n nogal americana m.
hide vt esconder; * n cuero m; piel f.
hideaway n escondite m.
hideous adj horrible; ~**ly** adv horriblemente.
hiding place n escondite, escondrijo m.
hierarchy n jerarquía f.
hieroglyphic adj jeroglífico/ca; * n jeroglífico m.
hi-fi n estéreo, hi-fi m.
higgledy-piggledy adv confusamente.
high adj alto/ta; elevado/da.
high altar n altar mayor m.
highchair n silla alta f.
high-handed adj despótico/ca.
highlands npl tierras montañosas, tierras altas fpl.
highlight n punto culminante m.
highly adv en sumo grado.
highness n altura f; alteza f.
high school n centro de enseñanza secundaria m; escuela secundaria f.

highly strung adj hipertenso/sa.
high water n marea alta f.
highway n carretera f.
hike vi ir de excursión.
hijack vt secuestrar.
hijacker n secuestrador/a m/f.
hilarious adj alegre.
hill n colina f.
hillock n colina f.
hillside n ladera f.
hilly adj montañoso/sa.
hilt n puño de espada m.
him pn le, lo, el.
himself pn él mismo, se, si mismo.
hind adj trasero/ra, posterior; * n cierva f.
hinder vt impedir.
hindrance n impedimento, obstáculo m.
hindmost adj postrero/ra.
hindquarter n cuarto trasero m.
hindsight n: **with ~** en retrospectiva.
hinge n bisagra f.
hint n indirecta f; * vt insinuar; sugerir.
hip n cadera f.
hippopotamus n hipopótamo m.
hire vt alquilar; * n alquiler m.
his pn su, suyo, de él.
Hispanic adj hispano/na; hispánico/ca; * n hispanoamericano/na m/f.
hiss vt, vi silbar.
historian n historiador/a m/f.
historic(al) adj histórico/ca; **~ally** adv históricamente.
history n historia f.
histrionic adj teatral.
hit vt golpear; alcanzar; zumbar; **to ~ each other** vr zumbarse; * n golpe m; éxito m.
hitch vt atar; * n problema m.
hitch-hike vi hacer autoestop.
hitch-hiker n autoestopista m/f.
hitch-hiking n autoestop f.
hitherto adv hasta ahora, hasta aquí.
hive n colmena f.
HIV-negative adj seronegativo/va.
HIV-positive adj seropositivo/va.
hoard n montón m; tesoro escondido m; * vt acumular.
hoarfrost n escarcha f.
hoarse adj ronco/ca; **~ly** adv roncamente.
hoarseness n ronquera, carraspera f.
hoax n trampa f; * vt engañar, burlar.
hobble vi cojear.
hobby n pasatiempo m, afición f.
hobbyhorse n caballo de batalla m.
hobo n vagabundo/da m/f.
hockey n hockey m.
hodgepodge n mezcolanza f.
hoe n azadón m; * vt azadonar.
hog n cerdo, puerco m, Lat Am chancho m; (col) cochino m.

hoist vt alzar; * n grúa f.
hold vt tener; detener; contener; celebrar; **to ~ on to** agarrarse a; * vi valer; * n presa f; poder m.
holder n poseedor/a m/f; titular m/f.
holding n tenencia, posesión f.
stick-up n atraco m; retraso m.
hole n agujero m.
holiness n santidad f.
hollow adj hueco/ca; * n hoyo m; * vt excavar, ahuecar.
holly n (bot) acebo m.
hollyhock n malva hortense f.
holocaust n holocausto m.
holster n pistolera f.
holy adj santo/ta, pío, pía; consagrado/da.
holy water n agua bendita f.
holy week n semana santa f.
homage n homenaje m.
home n casa f; patria f; domicilio m; **~ly** adj casero/ra.
home address n domicilio m.
home improvement n bricolaje m.
homeless adj sin casa.
homeliness n simpleza f.
homely adj casero/ra.
home-made adj casero/ra.
homeopathist n homeópata m/f.
homeopathy n homeopatía f.
home shopping program (TV) n teletienda f.
homesick adj nostálgico/ca.
homesickness n nostalgia f.
hometown n ciudad natal f.
homeward adj hacia casa; hacia su país.
homework n deberes mpl.
homicidal adj homicida.
homicide n homicidio m; homicida m/f.
homogeneous adj homogéneo/nea.
homosexual adj, n homosexual m.
honest adj honrado/da; **~ly** adv honradamente.
honesty n honradez f.
honey n miel f.
honeycomb n panal m.
honeymoon n luna de miel f.
honeysuckle n (bot) madreselva f.
honor n honra f; honor m; * vt honrar.
honorable adj honorable; ilustre.
honorably adv honorablemente.
honorary adj honorario/ria.
hood n capo m; capucha f.
hoodlum n matón m.
hoof n pezuña f.
hook n gancho m; anzuelo m; **by ~ or by crook** de un modo u otro; * vt enganchar.
hooked adj encorvado/da.
hooligan n gamberro/rra m/f.
hoop n aro m.
hop n (bot) lúpulo m; salto m; * vi saltar, brincar.

H

hope n esperanza f; * vi esperar.
hopeful adj esperanzador/a; ~ly adv con esperanza.
hopefulness n buena esperanza f.
hopeless adj desesperado/da; ~ly adv sin esperanza.
hopscotch n tejo m.
horde n horda f.
horizon n horizonte m.
horizontal adj horizontal; ~ly adv horizontalmente.
hormone n hormona f.
horn n cuerno m; (auto) sirena f.
horned adj cornudo/da.
hornet n avispón m.
horny adj calloso/sa.
horoscope n horóscopo m.
horrendous adj horrendo/da.
horrible adj horrible, terrible.
horribly adv horriblemente; enormemente.
horrid adj horrible.
horrific adj horroroso/sa.
horrify vt horrorizar.
horror n horror, terror m.
horror film n película de horror f.
hors d'oeuvre n entremeses mpl.
horse n caballo m; caballete m.
horseback adv: on ~ a caballo.
horse-breaker n domador/a de caballos m/f.
horse chestnut n castaño de Indias m.
horsefly n moscarda f; moscardón m.
horseman n jinete m.
horsemanship n equitación f.
horsepower n caballo de fuerza m.
horse race n carrera de caballos f.
horseracing n hípica f.
horseradish n rábano silvestre m.
horseshoe n herradura de caballo f.
horsewoman n jineta f.
horticulture n horticultura, jardinería f.
horticulturist n jardinero/ra m/f.
hosepipe n manguera f.
hosiery n calcetería f.
hospitable adj hospitalario/ria.
hospitably adv con hospitalidad.
hospital n hospital m.
hospitality n hospitalidad f.
host n anfitrión m; hostia f.
hostage n rehén m.
hostess n anfitriona f.
hostile adj hostil.
hostility n hostilidad f.
hot adj caliente; cálido/da.
hotbed n semillero m.
hotdog n perro caliente m.
hotel n hotel m.
hotelier n hotelero/ra m/f.
hot-headed adj exaltado/da.
hothouse n invernadero m.

hotline n línea directa f.
hotplate n hornillo m.
hotly adv con calor; violentamente.
hound n perro de caza m.
hour n hora f.
hour-glass n reloj de arena m.
hourly adv cada hora.
house n casa f; familia f; * vt alojar.
houseboat n casa flotante f.
housebreaker n ladrón/ona de casa m/f.
housebreaking n allanamiento de morada m.
household n familia f.
householder n amo de casa, padre de familia m; dueño/ña de la casa m/f.
housekeeper n ama de llaves f.
housekeeping n trabajos domésticos mpl.
house-warming party n fiesta de estreno de una casa f.
housewife n ama de casa f.
housework n facnas de la casa fpl.
housing n vivienda f.
housing development n urbanización f.
hovel n choza, cabaña f.
hover vi flotar.
how adv cómo, como; ~ do you do! ¡encantado!
however adv comoquiera, comoquiera que sea; aunque; no obstante.
howl vi aullar; * n aullido m.
hub n centro m.
hubbub n barullo m.
hubcap n tapacubos m invar.
hue n color m; matiz m.
huff n: in a ~ picado/da.
hug vt abrazar; * n abrazo m.
huge adj vasto/ta, enorme; ~ly adv inmensamente.
hulk n (mar) casco m; armatoste m.
hull n (mar) casco m.
hum vi canturrear.
human adv humano/na.
humane adv humano/na; benigno/na; ~ly adv humanamente.
humanist n humanista m/f.
humanitarian adj humanitario/ria.
humanity n humanidad f.
humanize vt humanizar.
humanly adv humanamente.
humble adj humilde, modesto/ta; * vt humillar, postrar.
humbleness n humildad f.
humbly adv con humildad.
humbug n tonterías fpl.
humdrum adj monótono/na.
humid adj húmedo/da.
humidity n humedad f.
humiliate vt humillar.
humiliation n humillación f.

humility *n* humildad *f*.
humming *n* zumbido *m*.
humming-bird *n* colibrí *m*, *Lat Am* chupaflor *m*, *Lat Am* picaflor *m*.
humor *n* sentido del humor *m*, humor *m*; jocosidad *f*; * *vt* complacer.
humorist *n* humorista *m/f*
humorous *adj* gracioso/sa; ~**ly** *adv* con gracia.
hump *n* giba, joroba *f*.
hunch *n* corazonada *f*; ~**backed** *adj* jorobado/da, jiboso/sa.
hundred *adj* ciento; * *n* centenar *m*; un ciento.
hundredth *adj* centésimo.
hundredweight *n* quintal *m*.
hunger *n* hambre *f*; * *vi* hambrear.
hunger strike *n* huelga de hambre *f*.
hungrily *adv* con apetito.
hungry *adj* hambriento/ta, *Lat Am* hambreado/da.
hunt *vt* cazar; perseguir; buscar; * *vi* andar a caza; * *n* caza *f*.
hunter *n* cazador/a *m/f*.
hunting *n* caza *f*.
huntsman *n* cazador *m*.
hurdle *n* valla *f*.
hurl *vt* tirar con violencia; arrojar.
hurricane *n* huracán *m*.
hurried *adj* hecho/cha de prisa; ~**ly** *adv* con prisa.
hurry *vt* acelerar, apresurar; * *vi* apresurarse; * *n* prisa *f*.
hurt *vt* hacer daño; ofender; * *n* mal, daño *m*.
hurtful *adj* dañoso/sa; ~**ly** *adv* dañosamente.
hurtle *vr* zamparse.
husband *n* marido *m*.
husbandry *n* agricultura *f*.

hush! ¡chitón!, ¡silencio!; * *vt* hacer callar; * *vi* estar quieto/ta.
husk *n* cáscara *f*.
huskiness *n* ronquedad *f*.
husky *adj* ronco/ca.
hustings *n* tribuna para las elecciones *f*.
hustle *vt* empujar con fuerza.
hut *n* cabaña, barraca *f*.
hutch *n* conejera *f*.
hyacinth *n* jacinto *m*.
hydrant *n* boca de incendios *f*.
hydraulic *adj* hidráulico/ca; ~**s** *npl* hidráulica *f*.
hydroelectric *adj* hidroeléctrico/ca.
hydrofoil *n* hidroala *f*.
hydrogen *n* hidrógeno *m*.
hydrophobia *n* hidrofobia *f*.
hydroplane *n* hidroavión *m*.
hyena *n* hiena *f*.
hygiene *n* higiene *f*.
hygienic *adj* higiénico/ca.
hymn *n* himno *m*.
hyperbole *n* hipérbole *f*; exageración *f*.
hypermarket *n* hipermercado *m*.
hyphen *n* (*gr*) guión *m*.
hypochondria *n* hipocondria *f*.
hypochondriac *adj*, *n* hipocondríaco/ca *m/f*.
hypocrisy *n* hipocresía *f*.
hypocrite *n* hipócrita *m/f*.
hypocritical *adj* hipócrita.
hypothesis *n* hipótesis *f*.
hypothetical *adj* hipotético/ca; ~**ly** *adv* hipotéticamente.
hysterical *adj* histérico/ca.
hysterics *npl* histeria *f*.

H

I

I *pn* yo; ~ **myself** yo mismo.
ice *n* hielo *m*; * *vt* helar.
ice-axe *n* piqueta *f*.
iceberg *n* iceberg *m*.
ice-bound *adj* rodeado/da de hielos.
icebox *n* nevera *f*.
ice cream *n* helado *m*.
ice rink *n* pista de hielo *f*.
ice skating *n* patinaje sobre hielo *m*.
icicle *n* carámbano *m*.
iconoclast *n* iconoclasta *m/f*.
icy *adj* helado/da; frío/ría.
idea *n* idea *f*.
ideal *adj* ideal; ~**ly** *adv* idealmente.
idealist *n* idealista *m/f*.
identical *adj* idéntico/ca.
identification *n* identificación *f*.
identify *vt* identificar.
identity *n* identidad *f*.
identity card *n* carnet *m* de identidad, *Lat Am* cédula *f* de identidad.
ideology *n* ideología *f*.
idiom *n* idioma *m*.
idiomatic *adj* idiomático/ca.
idiosyncrasy *n* idiosincrasia *f*.
idiot *n* idiota, necio/cia *m/f*.
idiotic *adj* tonto/ta, bobo/ba.
idle *adj* desocupado/da; holgazán/zana; inútil.
idleness *n* pereza *f*.
idler *n* holgazán/zana *m/f*; zángano *m*.
idly *adv* ociosamente; vanamente.
idol *n* ídolo *m*.
idolatry *n* idolatría *f*.
idolize *vt* idolatrar.
idyllic *adj* idílico/ca.
i.e. *adv* esto es.
if *conj* si, aunque; ~ **not** si no.
igloo *n* iglú *m*.
ignite *vt* encender.
ignition *n* (*chem*) ignición *f*; encendido *m*.
ignition key *n* llave de contacto *f*.
ignoble *adj* innoble; bajo/ja.
ignominious *adj* ignominioso/sa; ~**ly** *adv* ignominiosamente.
ignominy *n* ignominia, infamia *f*.
ignoramus *n* ignorante, tonto/ta *m/f*.
ignorance *n* ignorancia *f*.
ignorant *adj* ignorante; ~**ly** *adv* ignorantemente.
ignore *vt* no hacer caso de.
ill *adj* malo/la, enfermo/ma; * *n* mal, infortunio *m*; * *adv* mal.
ill-advised *adj* imprudente.

illegal *adj*, ~**ly** *adv* ilegal(mente).
illegality *n* ilegalidad *f*.
illegible *adj* ilegible.
illegibly *adv* de modo ilegible.
illegitimacy *n* ilegitimidad *f*.
illegitimate *adj* ilegítimo/ma; ~**ly** *adv* ilegítimamente.
ill feeling *n* rencor *m*.
illicit *adj* ilícito/ta.
illiterate *adj* analfabeto/ta.
illness *n* enfermedad *f*.
illogical *adj* ilógico/ca.
ill-timed *adj* inoportuno/na.
ill-treat *vt* maltratar.
illuminate *vt* iluminar.
illumination *n* iluminación *f*.
illusion *n* ilusión *f*.
illusory *adj* ilusorio/ria.
illustrate *vt* ilustrar; explicar.
illustration *n* ilustración *f*; elucidación *f*.
illustrative *adj* explicativo/va.
illustrious *adj* ilustre, insigne.
ill-will *n* rencor *m*.
image *n* imagen *f*.
imagery *n* imágenes *fpl*.
imaginable *adj* concebible.
imaginary *adj* imaginario/ria.
imagination *n* imaginación *f*.
imaginative *adj* imaginativo/va.
imagine *vt* imaginarse; idear, inventar.
imbalance *n* desequilibrio *m*.
imbecile *adj* imbécil, necio/cia.
imbibe *vt* beber.
imbue *vt* infundir.
imitate *vt* imitar, copiar.
imitation *n* imitación, copia *f*.
imitative *adj* imitativo/va.
immaculate *adj* inmaculado/da, puro/ra.
immaterial *adj* poco importante.
immature *adj* inmaduro/ra.
immeasurable *adj* inconmensurable.
immeasurably *adv* inmensamente.
immediate *adj* inmediato/ta; ~**ly** *adv* inmediatamente; ya.
immense *adj* inmenso/sa; vasto/ta; ~**ly** *adv* inmensamente.
immensity *n* inmensidad *f*.
immerse *vt* sumergir.
immersion *n* inmersión *f*.
immigrant *n* inmigrante *m/f*.
immigrate *vi* inmigrar.
immigration *n* inmigración *f*.
imminent *adj* inminente.

immobile *adj* inmóvil.
immobility *n* inmovilidad *f*.
immoderate *adj* inmoderado/da, excesivo/va;
~**ly** *adv* inmoderadamente.
immodest *adj* inmodesto/ta.
immoral *adj* inmoral.
immorality *n* inmoralidad *f*.
immortal *adj* inmortal.
immortality *n* inmortalidad *f*.
immortalize *vt* inmortalizar, eternizar.
immune *adj* inmune.
immunity *n* inmunidad *f*.
immunize *vt* inmunizar.
immutable *adj* inmutable.
imp *n* diablillo, duende *m*.
impact *n* impacto *m*.
impair *vt* disminuir.
impale *vt* empalar.
impalpable *adj* impalpable.
impart *vt* comunicar.
impartial *adj*, ~**ly** *adv* imparcial(mente).
impartiality *n* imparcialidad *f*.
impassable *adj* intransitable.
impasse *n* punto muerto *m*.
impassive *adj* impasible.
impatience *n* impaciencia *f*.
impatient *adj*, ~**ly** *adv* impaciente(mente).
impeach *vt* acusar, denunciar.
impeccable *adj* impecable.
impecunious *adj* indigente.
impede *vt* estorbar.
impediment *n* obstáculo *m*.
impel *vt* impeler, impulsar.
impending *adj* inminente.
impenetrable *adj* impenetrable.
imperative *adj* imperativo/va.
imperceptible *adj* imperceptible.
imperceptibly *adv* imperceptiblemente.
imperfect *adj* imperfecto/ta, defectuoso/sa; ~**ly**
imperfectamente *adv*; * *n* (*gr*) pretérito
imperfecto *m*.
imperfection *n* imperfección *f*, defecto *m*.
imperial *adj* imperial.
imperialism *n* imperialismo *m*.
imperious *adj* imperioso/sa; arrogante; ~**ly** *adv*
imperiosamente, arrogantemente.
impermeable *adj* impermeable.
impersonal *adj*, ~**ly** *adv* impersonal(mente).
impersonate *vt* hacerse pasar por; imitar.
impertinence *n* impertinencia *f*; descaro *m*.
impertinent *adj* impertinente; ~**ly** *adv*
impertinentemente.
imperturbable *adj* imperturbable.
impervious *adj* impermeable.
impetuosity *n* impetuosidad *f*.
impetuous *adj* impetuoso/sa; ~**ly** *adv*
impetuosamente.
impetus *n* ímpetu *m*.

impiety *n* impiedad *f*.
impinge (**on**) *vt* tener influjo en.
impious *adj* impío/pía, irreligioso/sa.
implacable *adj* implacable.
implacably *adv* implacablemente.
implant *vt* implantar; plantear.
implement *n* herramienta *f*; utensilio *m*.
implicate *vt* implicar.
implication *n* implicación *f*.
implicit *adj* implícito/ta; ~**ly** *adv*
implícitamente.
implore *vt* suplicar.
imply *vt* suponer.
impolite *adj* maleducado/da.
impoliteness *n* falta de educación *f*.
impolitic *adj* imprudente; impolítico/ca.
import *vt* importar; * *n* importación *f*.
importance *n* importancia *f*.
important *adj* importante.
importation *n* importación *f*.
importer *n* importador/a *m/f*.
importunate *adj* importuno/na.
importune *vt* importunar.
importunity *n* importunidad *f*.
impose *vt* imponer.
imposing *adj* imponente.
imposition *n* imposición, carga *f*.
impossibility *n* imposibilidad *f*.
impossible *adj* imposible.
impostor *n* impostor *m*.
impotence *n* impotencia *f*.
impotent *adj* impotente; ~**ly** *adv* sin poder.
impound *vt* embargar.
impoverish *vt* empobrecer.
impoverished *adj* necesitado/da.
impoverishment *n* empobrecimiento *m*.
impracticability *n* inviabilidad *f*.
impracticable *adj* impracticable, inviable.
impractical *adj* poco práctico/ca.
imprecation *n* imprecación, maldición *f*.
imprecise *adj* impreciso/sa.
impregnable *adj* inexpugnable.
impregnate *vt* impregnar.
impregnation *n* fecundación *f*; impregnación *f*.
impress *vt* impresionar.
impression *n* impresión *f*; edición *f*.
impressionable *adj* impresionable.
impressive *adj* impresionante.
imprint *n* sello *m*; * *vt* imprimir; estampar.
imprison *vt* encarcelar.
imprisonment *n* encarcelamiento *m*.
improbability *n* improbabilidad *f*.
improbable *adj* improbable.
impromptu *adj* de improviso.
improper *adj* impropio/pia, indecente; ~**ly** *adv*
impropiamente.
impropriety *n* impropiedad *f*.
improve *vt*, *vi* mejorar, *Lat Am* repuntar.

I

improvement n progreso m, mejora f.
improvident adj impróvido/da, imprudente.
improvise vt improvisar.
imprudence n imprudencia f.
imprudent adj imprudente.
impudence n impudencia f.
impudent adj impudente; ~**ly** adv desvergonzadamente.
impugn vt impugnar.
impulse n impulso m.
impulsive adj impulsivo/va.
impunity n impunidad f.
impure adj impuro/ra; ~**ly** adv impuramente.
impurity n impureza f.
in prep en.
inability n incapacidad f.
inaccessible adj inaccesible.
inaccuracy n inexactitud f.
inaccurate adj inexacto/ta.
inaction n inacción f.
inactive adj inactivo/va, perezoso/sa.
inactivity n inactividad f.
inadequate adj inadecuado/da, defectuoso/sa.
inadmissible adj inadmisible.
inadvertently adv sin querer.
inalienable adj inalienable.
inane adj necio/cia.
inanimate adj inanimado/da.
inapplicable adj inaplicable.
inappropriate adj impropio/pia.
inasmuch adv visto que; en tanto en cuanto.
inattentive adj desatento/ta.
inaudible adj inaudible.
inaugural adj inaugural.
inaugurate vt inaugurar.
inauguration n inauguración f.
inauspicious adj poco propicio/cia.
in-between adj intermedio/dia.
inborn, inbred adj innato/ta.
incalculable adj incalculable.
incandescent adj incandescente.
incantation n conjuro m.
incapable adj incapaz.
incapacitate vt inhabilitar.
incapacity n incapacidad f.
incarcerate vt encarcelar.
incarnate adj encarnado/da.
incarnation n encarnación f.
incautious adj incauto/ta; ~**ly** adv incautamente.
incendiary n bomba incendiaria f.
incense n incienso m; * vt exasperar.
incentive n incentivo m.
inception n principio m.
incessant adj incesante, constante; ~**ly** adv continuamente.
incest n incesto m.
incestuous adj incestuoso/sa.
inch n pulgada f; ~ **by** ~ palmo a palmo.

incidence n frecuencia f.
incident n incidente m.
incidental adj casual; ~**ly** adv a propósito.
incinerator n incinerador m.
incipient adj incipiente.
incise vt tajar, cortar.
incision n incisión f.
incisive adj incisivo/va.
incisor n incisivo m.
incite vt incitar, estimular.
inclement adj feo, fea.
inclination n inclinación, propensión f.
incline vt (vi) inclinar(se); * n cuesta f.
include vt incluir, comprender.
including prep incluso.
inclusion n inclusión f.
inclusive adj inclusivo/va.
incognito adv de incógnito.
incoherence n incoherencia f.
incoherent adj incoherente, inconsecuente; ~**ly** adv de modo incoherente.
income n renta f; ingresos mpl.
income tax n impuesto sobre la renta m.
incoming adj entrante.
incomparable adj incomparable.
incomparably adv incomparablemente.
incompatibility n incompatibilidad f.
incompatible adj incompatible.
incompetence n incompetencia f.
incompetent adj, ~**ly** adv incompetente(mente).
incomplete adj incompleto/ta.
incomprehensibility n incomprensibilidad f.
incomprehensible adj incomprensible.
inconceivable adj inconcebible.
inconclusive adj no concluyente; ~**ly** adv sin conclusión.
incongruity n incongruencia f.
incongruous adj incongruo/rua; ~**ly** adv incongruamente.
inconsequential adj inconsecuente.
inconsiderate adj desconsiderado/da; ~**ly** adv desconsideradamente.
inconsistency n inconsecuencia f.
inconsistent adj inconsecuente.
inconsolable adj inconsolable.
inconspicuous adj discreto/ta.
incontinence n incontinencia f.
incontinent adj incontinente.
incontrovertible adj incontrovertible.
inconvenience n incomodidad f; * vt incomodar.
inconvenient adj incómodo/da; ~**ly** adv incómodamente.
incorporate vt (vi) incorporar(se).
incorporated company (**inc**) n sociedad anónima f.
incorporation n incorporación f.
incorrect adj incorrecto/ta; ~**ly** adv incorrectamente.
incorrigible adj incorregible.

incorruptibility *n* incorruptibilidad *f*.
incorruptible *adj* incorruptible.
increase *vt* acrecentar, aumentar; * *vi* crecer; * *n* aumento *m*.
increasing *adj* creciente; ~**ly** *adv* cada vez más.
incredible *adj* increíble.
incredulity *n* incredulidad *f*.
incredulous *adj* incrédulo/la.
increment *n* incremento *m*.
incriminate *vt* incriminar.
incrust *vt* incrustar.
incubate *vi* incubar.
incubator *n* incubadora *f*.
inculcate *vt* inculcar.
incumbent *adj* obligatorio/ria; * *n* beneficiado/da *m/f*.
incur *vt* incurrir.
incurability *n* lo incurable.
incurable *adj* incurable.
incursion *n* incursión, invasión *f*.
indebted *adj* agradecido/da.
indecency *n* indecencia *f*.
indecent *adj* indecente; ~**ly** *adv* indecentemente.
indecision *n* irresolución *f*.
indecisive *adj* indeciso/sa.
indecorous *adj* indecente.
indeed *adv* verdaderamente, de veras.
indefatigable *adj* incansable.
indefinite *adj* indefinido/da; ~**ly** *adv* indefinidamente.
indelible *adj* indeleble.
indelicacy *n* falta de delicadeza, grosería *f*.
indelicate *adj* poco delicado/da.
indemnify *vt* indemnizar.
indemnity *n* indemnidad *f*.
indent *vt* mellar.
independence *n* independencia *f*.
independent *adj* independiente; ~**ly** *adv* independientemente.
indescribable *adj* indescriptible.
indestructible *adj* indestructible.
indeterminate *adj* indeterminado/da.
index *n* índice *m*.
index card *n* ficha *f*.
indexed *adj* indexado/da.
index finger *n* dedo índice *m*.
indicate *vt* indicar.
indication *n* indicación *f*; indicio *m*.
indicative *adj*, *n* (*gr*) indicativo *m*.
indicator *n* indicador *m*.
indict *vt* acusar.
indictment *n* acusación *f*.
indifference *n* indiferencia *f*.
indifferent *adj* indiferente; ~**ly** *adv* indiferentemente.
indigenous *adj* indígena.
indigent *adj* indigente.
indigestible *adj* indigerible.
indigestion *n* indigestión *f*.
indignant *adj* indignado/da.

indignation *n* indignación *f*.
indignity *n* indignidad *f*.
indigo *n* añil *m*.
indirect *adj* indirecto/ta; ~**ly** *adv* indirectamente.
indiscreet *adj* indiscreto/ta; ~**ly** *adv* indiscretamente.
indiscretion *n* indiscreción *f*.
indiscriminate *adj* indistinto/ta; ~**ly** *adv* sin distinción.
indispensable *adj* indispensable.
indisposed *adj* indispuesto/ta.
indisposition *n* indisposición *f*.
indisputable *adj* indiscutible.
indisputably *adv* indisputablemente.
indistinct *adj* indistinto/ta, confuso/sa; ~**ly** *adv* indistintamente.
indistinguishable *adj* indistinguible.
individual *adj* individual; ~**ly** *adv* individualmente; * *n* individuo *m*.
individuality *n* individualidad *f*.
indivisible *adv* indivisible; ~**bly** *adv* indivisiblemente.
indoctrinate *vt* adoctrinar.
indoctrination *n* adoctrinamiento *m*.
indolence *n* indolencia, pereza *f*.
indolent *adj* indolente; ~**ly** *adv* con negligencia.
indomitable *adj* indomable.
indoors *adv* dentro.
indubitably *adv* indudablemente.
induce *vt* inducir, persuadir; causar.
inducement *n* aliciente *m*.
induction *n* inducción *f*.
indulge *vt*, *vi* conceder; ser indulgente.
indulgence *n* indulgencia *f*.
indulgent *adj* indulgente; ~**ly** *adv* de modo indulgente.
industrial *adj* industrial.
industrialist *n* industrial *m/f*.
industrialization *n* industrialización *f*.
industrialize *vt* industrializar.
industrial park *n* polígono industrial *m*.
industrious *adj* trabajador/a.
industry *n* industria *f*.
inebriated *adj* embriagado/da.
inebriation *n* embriaguez *f*.
inedible *adj* incomestible.
ineffable *adj* inefable.
ineffective, ineffectual *adj* ineficaz; ~**ly** *adv* sin efecto.
inefficiency *n* ineficacia *f*.
inefficient *adj* ineficaz.
ineligible *adj* ineligible.
inept *adj* incompetente.
ineptitude *n* incompetencia *f*.
inequality *n* desigualdad *f*.
inert *adj* inerte, perezoso/sa.
inertia *n* inercia *f*.
inescapable *adj* ineludible.
inestimable *adj* inestimable, inapreciable.
inevitable *adj* inevitable.

inevitably adv inevitablemente.
inexcusable adj inexcusable.
inexhaustible adj inagotable.
inexorable adj inexorable.
inexpedient adj imprudente.
inexpensive adj económico/ca.
inexperience n inexperiencia f.
inexperienced adj inexperto/ta.
inexpert adj inexperto/ta.
inexplicable adj inexplicable.
inexpressible adj indecible.
inextricably adv indisolublemente.
infallibility n infalibilidad f.
infallible adj infalible; indefectible.
infamous adj vil, infame; ~**ly** adv infamemente.
infamy n infamia f.
infancy n infancia f; pequeñez f.
infant n niño/ña m/f.
infanticide n infanticidio m; infanticida m/f.
infantile adj infantil.
infantry n infantería f.
infatuated adj chiflado/da.
infatuation n infatuación f.
infect vt infectar.
infection n infección f.
infectious adj contagioso/sa; infeccioso/sa.
infer vt inferir.
inference n inferencia f.
inferior adj inferior; * n subordinado/da m/f.
inferiority n inferioridad f.
infernal adj infernal.
inferno n infierno m.
infest vt infestar.
infidel n infiel, pagano m.
infidelity n infidelidad f.
infiltrate vi infiltrarse.
infinite adj infinito/ta; ~**ly** adv infinitamente.
infinitive n infinitivo m.
infinity n infinito m; infinidad f.
infirm adj enfermo/ma, débil.
infirmary n enfermería f.
infirmity n fragilidad, enfermedad f.
inflame vt (vi) inflamar(se).
inflammation n inflamación f.
inflammatory adj inflamatorio/ria.
inflatable adj inflable.
inflate vt inflar, hinchar.
inflation n inflación f.
inflection n inflexión f; modulación de la voz f.
inflexibility n inflexibilidad f.
inflexible adj inflexible; yerto/ta.
inflexibly adv inflexiblemente.
inflict vt imponer.
influence n influencia f; * vt influir.
influential adj influyente.
influenza n gripe f.
influx n afluencia f.
inform vt informar.

informal adj informal.
informality n informalidad f.
informant n informante m/f.
information n información f; ~ **superhighway**
autopista de la información f.
infraction n infracción f.
infra-red adj infrarrojo/ja.
infrastructure n infraestructura f.
infrequent adj raro/ra; ~**ly** adv raramente.
infringe vt infringir; violar.
infringement n infracción f.
infuriate vt enfurecer.
infuse vt infundir.
infusion n infusión f.
ingenious adj ingenioso/sa; ~**ly** adv ingeniosamente.
ingenuity n ingeniosidad f.
ingenuous adj ingenuo/nua, sincero/ra; ~**ly** adv
ingenuamente.
inglorious adj ignominioso/sa, vergonzoso/sa;
~**ly** adv ignominiosamente.
ingot n lingote m.
ingrained adj inveterado/da.
ingratiate vi congraciarse.
ingratitude n ingratitud f.
ingredient n ingrediente m.
inhabit vt, vi habitar.
inhabitable adj habitable.
inhabitant n habitante m/f.
inhale vt inhalar.
inherent adj inherente.
inherit vt heredar.
inheritance n herencia f.
inheritor n heredero/a m/f.
inhibit vt inhibir.
inhibited adj cohibido/da.
inhibition n inhibición f.
inhospitable adj inhospitalario/ria.
inhospitality n inhospitalidad f.
inhuman adj inhumano/na, cruel; ~**ly** adv
inhumanamente.
inhumanity n inhumanidad, crueldad f.
inimical adj enemigo/ga.
inimitable adj inimitable.
iniquitous adj inicuo/cua, injusto/ta.
iniquity n iniquidad, injusticia f.
initial adj inicial; * n inicial f.
initially adv al principio.
initiate vt iniciar.
initiation n principio m; iniciación f.
initiative n iniciativa f.
inject vt inyectar.
injection n inyección f.
injudicious adj poco juicioso/sa.
injunction n entredicho m.
injure vt herir.
injury n daño m.
injury time n descuento m.
injustice n injusticia f.

ink n tinta f.
inkling n sospecha f.
inkstand n tintero m.
inlaid adj taraceado/da.
inland adj interior; * adv tierra adentro.
in-laws npl suegros mpl.
inlay vt taracear.
inlet n ensenada f.
inmate n preso m.
inmost adj más íntimo/ma.
inn n posada f; mesón m.
innate adj innato/ta.
inner adj interior.
innermost adj más íntimo/ma.
inner tube n cámara f.
innkeeper n posadero/ra, mesonero/ra m/f.
innocence n inocencia f.
innocent adj inocente; ~ly adv inocentemente.
innocuous adj inocuo/cua; ~ly adv inocentemente.
innovate vt innovar.
innovation n innovación f.
innuendo n indirecta, insinuación f.
innumerable adj innumerable.
inoculate vt inocular.
inoculation n inoculación f.
inoffensive adj inofensivo/va.
inopportune adj inconveniente, inoportuno/na.
inordinately adv desmesuradamente.
inorganic adj inorgánico/ca.
inpatient n paciente interno/na m/f.
input n entrada f.
inquest n encuesta judicial f.
inquire, enquire vt, vi preguntar; **to ~ about** informarse de; **to ~ after** vt preguntar por; **to ~ into** vt investigar, indagar, inquirir.
inquiry n pesquisa f.
inquisition n inquisición f.
inquisitive adj curioso/sa.
inroad n incursión, invasión f.
insane adj loco/ca, demente.
insanity n locura f.
insatiable adj insaciable.
inscribe vt inscribir; dedicar.
inscription n inscripción f; dedicatoria f.
inscrutable adj inescrutable.
insect n insecto m.
insecticide n insecticida m.
insecure adj inseguro/ra.
insecurity n inseguridad f.
insemination n inseminación f.
insensible adj inconsciente.
insensitive adj insensible.
inseparable adj inseparable.
insert vt introducir.
insertion n inserción f.
inshore adj costero/ra.
inside n interior m; * adv dentro; Lat Am adentro de.
inside out adv al revés; a fondo.

insidious adj insidioso/sa; ~ly adv insidiosamente.
insight n perspicacia f.
insignia npl insignias fpl.
insignificant adj insignificante, frívolo/la.
insincere adj poco sincero/ra.
insincerity n falta de sinceridad f.
insinuate vt insinuar.
insinuation n insinuación f.
insipid adj insípido/da; insulso/sa; ñoño/ña.
insipidness n ñoñería f.
insist vi insistir.
insistence n insistencia f.
insistent adj insistente.
insole n plantilla f.
insolence n insolencia f.
insolent adj insolente; ~ly adv insolentemente.
insoluble adj insoluble.
insolvency n insolvencia f.
insolvent adj insolvente.
insomnia n insomnio m.
insomuch conj puesto que.
inspect vt examinar, inspeccionar.
inspection n inspección f.
inspector n inspector, superintendente m.
inspiration n inspiración f.
inspire vt inspirar.
instability n inestabilidad f.
install vt instalar.
installation n instalación f.
installment n instalación f; plazo m, Lat Am cuota f.
installment plan n compra a plazos f.
instance n ejemplo m; **for ~** por ejemplo.
instant adj inmediato/ta; ~ly adv en seguida; * n instante, momento m.
instantaneous adj instantáneo/nea; ~ly adv instantáneamente.
instead (of) prep por, en lugar de, en vez de.
instep n empeine m.
instigate vt instigar.
instigation n instigación f.
instill vt inculcar.
instinct n instinto m.
instinctive adj instintivo/va; ~ly adv por instinto.
institute vt establecer; * n instituto m.
institution n institución f.
instruct vt instruir, enseñar; illustrar.
instruction n instrucción f.
instructive adj instructivo/va.
instructor n instructor/a m/f.
instrument n instrumento m.
instrumental adj instrumental.
insubordinate adj insubordinado/da.
insubordination n insubordinación f.
insufferable adj insoportable.
insufferably adv de modo insoportable.
insufficiency n insuficiencia f.
insufficient adj insuficiente; ~ly adv insuficientemente.

insular *adj* insular.
insulate *vt* aislar.
insulating tape *n* cinta aislante *f*.
insulation *n* aislamiento *m*.
insulin *n* insulina *f*.
insult *vt* insultar; * *n* insulto *m*.
insulting *adj* insultante.
insuperable *adj* insuperable.
insurance *n* (*com*) seguro *m*.
insurance policy *n* póliza de seguros *f*.
insure *vt* asegurar.
insurgent *n* insurgente, rebelde *m*.
insurmountable *adj* insuperable.
insurrection *n* insurrección *f*.
intact *adj* intacto/ta.
intake *n* admisión *f*; entrada *f*.
integral *adj* íntegro/gra; (*chem*) integrante; * *n* todo *m*.
integrate *vt* integrar.
integration *n* integración *f*.
integrity *n* integridad *f*.
intellect *n* intelecto *m*.
intellectual *adj* intelectual.
intelligence *n* inteligencia *f*.
intelligent *adj* inteligente.
intelligentsia *n* intelectualidad *f*.
intelligible *adj* inteligible.
intelligibly *adv* inteligiblemente.
intemperate *adj* inmoderado/da; ~**ly** *adv* inmoderadamente.
intend *vi* tener intención de.
intendant *n* intendente *m*.
intended *adj* deseado/da.
intense *adj* intenso/sa, hondo/da; ~**ly** *adv* intensamente.
intensify *vt* intensificar.
intensity *n* intensidad *f*.
intensive *adj* intensivo/va.
intensive care unit *n* unidad de vigilancia intensiva, unidad de cuidados intensivos *f*.
intent *adj* atento/ta, cuidadoso/sa; ~**ly** *adv* con aplicación; * *n* designio *m*.
intention *n* intención *f*; designio *m*.
intentional *adj* intencional; ~**ly** *adv* a propósito.
inter *vt* enterrar.
interaction *n* interacción *f*.
intercede *vi* interceder.
intercept *vt* interceptar.
intercession *n* intercesión, mediación *f*.
interchange *n* intercambio *m*.
intercom *n* interfono *m*.
intercourse *n* coito *m*.
interest *vt* interesar; * *n* interés *m*.
interesting *adj* interesante.
interest rate *n* tipo de interés *m*.
interface *n* interfaz, interface *f*.
interfere *vi* entrometerse.
interference *n* interferencia *f*.

interim *adj* provisional.
interior *adj* interior.
interior design *n* interiorismo *m*.
interior designer *n* interiorista *m/f*.
interjection *n* (*gr*) interjección *f*.
interlock *vi* endentarse.
interlocutor *n* interlocutor/a *m/f*.
interloper *n* intruso/sa *m/f*.
interlude *n* intermedio *m*.
intermarriage *n* matrimonio mixto *m*.
intermediary *n* intermediario/ria *m/f*.
intermediate *adj* intermedio/dia.
interment *n* entierro *m*; sepultura *f*.
interminable *adj* inacabable.
intermingle *vt, vi* entremezclar; mezclarse.
intermission *n* descanso *m*.
intermittent *adj* intermitente.
intern *n* interno *m*.
internal *adj* interno/na, ~**ly** *adv* internamente.
international *adj* internacional.
Internet café *n* cibercafé *m*.
interplay *n* interacción *f*.
interpose *vt* interponer.
interpret *vt* interpretar.
interpretation *n* interpretación *f*.
interpreter *n* intérprete *m/f*.
interracial *adj* interracial.
interregnum *n* interregno *m*.
interrelated *adj* interrelacionado/da.
interrogate *vt* interrogar.
interrogation *n* interrogatorio *m*.
interrogative *adj* interrogativo/va.
interrupt *vt* interrumpir.
interruption *n* interrupción *f*.
intersect *vi* cruzarse.
intersection *n* cruce *m*.
intersperse *vt* esparcir.
intertwine *vt* entretejer.
interval *n* intervalo *m*.
intervene *vi* intervenir; ocurrir.
intervention *n* intervención *f*.
interview *n* entrevista *f*, *Lat Am* reportaje *m*; * *vt* entrevistar.
interviewer *n* entrevistador/a *m/f*.
interweave *vt* entretejer.
intestate *adj* intestado/da.
intestinal *adj* intestinal.
intestine *n* intestino *m*.
intimacy *n* intimidad *f*.
intimate *n* amigo/ga íntimo/ma *m/f*; * *adj* íntimo/ma; ~**ly** *adv* íntimamente; * *vt* insinuar, dar a entender.
intimidate *vt* intimidar.
into *prep* en, dentro, adentro.
intolerable *adj* intolerable.
intolerably *adv* intolerablemente.
intolerance *n* intolerancia *f*.
intolerant *adj* intolerante.

intonation n entonación f.
intoxicate vt embriagar.
intoxication n embriaguez f.
intractable adj intratable.
intransitive adj (gr) intransitivo/va.
intravenous adj intravenoso/sa.
in-tray n bandeja de entrada f.
intrepid adj intrépido/da; ~**ly** adv intrépidamente.
intrepidity n intrepidez f.
intricacy n complejidad f.
intricate adj intrincado/da, complicado/da; ~**ly** adv intrincadamente.
intrigue n intriga f; * vi intrigar.
intriguing adj fascinante.
intrinsic adj intrínseco/ca; ~**ally** adv intrínsecamente.
introduce vt introducir.
introduction n introducción f.
introductory adj introductorio/ria.
introspection n introspección f.
introvert n introvertido/da m/f.
intrude vi entrometerse.
intruder n intruso/sa m/f.
intrusion n invasión f.
intuition n intuición f.
intuitive adj intuitivo/va.
inundate vt inundar.
inundation n inundación f.
inure vt acostumbrar, habituar.
invade vt invadir.
invader n invasor/a m/f.
invalid adj inválido/da, nulo/la; * n minusválido m.
invalidate vt invalidar, anular.
invaluable adj inapreciable.
invariable adj invariable.
invariably adv invariablemente.
invasion n invasión f.
invective n invectiva f.
inveigle vt seducir, persuadir.
invent vt inventar.
invention n invento m.
inventive adj inventivo/va.
inventor n inventor m.
inventory n inventario m.
inverse adj inverso/sa.
inversion n inversión f.
invert vt invertir.
invest vt invertir.
investigate vt investigar.
investigation n investigación, pesquisa f.
investigator n investigador/a m/f.
investment n inversión f.
inveterate adj inveterado/da.
invidious adj odioso/sa.
invigilate vt vigilar.
invigorating adj vigorizante.
invincible adj invencible.
invincibly adv invenciblemente.
inviolable adj inviolable.

invisible adj invisible.
invisibly adv invisiblemente.
invitation n invitación f.
invite vt invitar.
inviting adj atractivo/va.
invoice n (com) factura f.
invoke vt invocar.
involuntarily adv involuntariamente.
involuntary adj involuntario/ria.
involve vt implicar, Lat Am involucrar.
involved adj complicado/da.
involvement n compromiso m.
invulnerable adj invulnerable.
inward adj interior; interno/na; ~, ~**s** adv hacia dentro.
iodine n (chem) yodo m.
IOU (**I owe you**) n pagaré m.
irascible adj irascible.
irate, ireful adj enojado/da.
iris n iris m.
irksome adj fastidioso/sa.
iron n hierro m, Lat Am fierro m, plancha f; * adj férreo/rea; * vt planchar.
ironic adj irónico/ca; ~**ly** adv con ironía.
ironing n planchado m.
ironing board n tabla de planchar f.
iron ore n mineral de hierro m.
ironwork n herraje m; ~**s** pl herrería f.
irony n ironía f.
irradiate vt irradiar.
irrational adj irracional.
irreconcilable adj irreconciliable.
irregular adj, ~**ly** adv irregular(mente).
irregularity n irregularidad f.
irrelevant adj impertinente.
irreligious adj irreligioso/sa.
irreparable adj irreparable.
irreplaceable adj irreemplazable.
irrepressible adj incontenible.
irreproachable adj irreprensible.
irresistible adj irresistible.
irresolute adj irresoluto/ta; ~**ly** adv irresolutamente.
irresponsible adj irresponsable.
irretrievably adv irreparablemente.
irreverence n irreverencia f.
irreverent adj irreverente; ~**ly** adv irreverentemente.
irrigate vt regar.
irrigation n riego m.
irritability n irritabilidad f.
irritable adj irritable.
irritant n (med) irritante m.
irritate vt irritar.
irritating adj fastidioso/sa.
irritation n fastidio m; picazón f.
Islam n islam m.
Islamic adj islámico/ca.
island n isla f.

islander n isleño/ña m/f.
isle n isla f.
isolate vt aislar.
isolation n aislamiento m.
issue n asunto m; * vt expedir; publicar; repartir.
isthmus n istmo m.
it pn él, ella, ello, lo, la, le.
italic n cursiva f.
itch n picazón f; * vi picar.

item n artículo m.
itemize vt detallar, *Lat Am* itemizar.
itinerant n ambulante, errante m.
itinerary n itinerario m.
its pn su, suyo.
itself pn se, por sí mismo.
ivory n marfil m.
ivy n hiedra f; yedra f.

J

jab vt clavar.
jabber vi farfullar.
jack n gato m; sota f.
jackal n chacal m.
jackboots npl botas militares fpl.
jackdaw n grajo m.
jacket n chaqueta f, Lat Am saco m; funda f.
jack-knife vi colear.
jackpot n premio gordo m.
jacuzzi n jacuzzi m.
jade n jade m.
jagged adj dentado/da.
jaguar n jaguar m, Lat Am tigre m.
jail n cárcel f.
jailbird n preso/sa m/f.
jailer n carcelero/ra m/f.
jam n conserva f; mermelada de frutas f; (auto)
   embotellamiento m
jangle vi sonar.
janitor n portero/ra m/f, bedel m.
January n enero m.
jar vi chocar; (mus) discordar; reñir; * n jarra f.
jargon n jerigonza f.
jasmine n jazmín m.
jaundice n ictericia f.
jaunt n excursión f.
jaunty adj alegre.
javelin n jabalina f.
jaw n mandíbula f.
jay n arrendajo m.
jazz n jazz m.
jealous adj celoso/sa; envidioso/sa.
jealousy n celos mpl; envidia f.
jeans npl vaqueros mpl, jeans mpl, Lat Am jean m.
Jeep™ n jeep m.
jeer vi befar, mofar; * n burla f.
jelly n jalea, gelatina f.
jellyfish n medusa f, aguamar m.
jeopardize vt arriesgar, poner en riesgo.
jerk n sacudida f; * vt tirar.
jerky adj espasmódico/ca.
jersey n jersey m.
jest n broma f.
jester n bufón/ona m/f.
jestingly adv de burlas.
Jesuit n jesuita m.
Jesus n Jesús m.
jet n avión a reacción m; azabache m.
jet engine n motor a reacción m, reactor m.
jettison vt desechar.
jetty n muelle m.
Jew n judío/día m/f.

jewel n joya f.
jeweler n joyero/ra m/f.
jewelry n joyería f.
jeweler's (**shop**/**store**) n joyería f.
Jewish adj judío/día.
jib n (mar) foque m.
jibe n mofa f.
jig n giga f.
jigsaw n rompecabezas m invar.
jilt vt dejar.
jinx n gafe m.
job n trabajo m.
jockey n jinete m/f.
jocular adj jocoso/sa, alegre.
jocularity n jocosidad f.
jog vi hacer footing.
jogging n footing m.
join vt juntar, unir; (fig) zurcir; **to ~ in** participar
   en; * vi unirse, juntarse.
joiner n carpintero/ra m/f.
joinery n carpintería f.
joint n articulación f; * adj común.
jointly adv conjuntamente.
joint-stock company n (com) sociedad por
   acciones f.
joke n broma f; * vi bromear.
joker n comodín m.
jollity n alegría f.
jolly adj alegre.
jolt vt sacudir; * n sacudida f.
jostle vt codear.
journal n revista f.
journalism n periodismo m.
journalist n periodista m/f.
journey n viaje m; * vt viajar.
jovial adj jovial, alegre; ~ly adv con jovialidad.
joy n alegría f; júbilo m.
joyful, joyous adj alegre, gozoso/sa; ~ly adv
   alegremente.
joystick n palanca de control f, joystick m.
jubilant adj jubiloso/sa.
jubilation n júbilo/la, regocijo m.
jubilee n jubileo m.
Judaism n judaísmo m.
judge n juez/a m/f; * vt juzgar.
judgement n juicio m.
judicial adj, ~ly adv judicial(mente).
judiciary n poder judicial m, judicatura f.
judicious adj, prudente.
judo n judo m.
jug n jarro m.
juggle vi hacer juegos malabares.

juggler n malabarista m/f.
jugular adj yugular.
juice n zumo, jugo m.
juicy adj jugoso/sa.
jukebox n gramola f.
July n julio m.
jumble vt mezclar; * n revoltijo m.
jump vi saltar, brincar; * n salto m.
jumper n suéter, jersey m.
jumpy adj nervioso/sa.
juncture n coyuntura f.
June n junio m.
jungle n selva f.
junior adj más joven.
juniper n (bot) enebro m.
junk n basura f; baratijas fpl.
junk food n comida basura f.
junkman n trapero m.
junta n junta f.

jurisdiction n jurisdicción f.
jurisprudence n jurisprudencia f.
jurist n jurista m/f.
juror, juryman n jurado/da m/f.
jury n jurado m.
just adj justo/ta; * adv justamente, exactamente; ~ **as** como; ~ **now** ahora mismo.
justice n justicia f.
justifiably adv con justificación.
justification n justificación f.
justify vt justificar.
justly adv justamente.
justness n justicia f.
jut vi; **to ~ out** sobresalir.
jute n yute m.
juvenile adj juvenil.
juxtapose vt yuxtaponer.
juxtaposition n yuxtaposición f.

K

kaleidoscope n caleidoscopio m.
kangaroo n canguro m.
karaoke n karaoke m.
karate n kárate m.
kebab n pincho m moruno.
keel n (mar) quilla f.
keen adj agudo/da; vivo/va.
keenness n entusiasmo m.
keep vt mantener; guardar; conservar.
keeper n guardián/ana m/f.
keepsake n recuerdo m.
keg n barril m.
kennel n perrera f.
kernel n fruta f; meollo m.
kerosene n queroseno m, Lat Am querosén m.
ketchup n catsup, ketchup m.
kettle n hervidor m.
kettle-drum n timbal m.
key n llave f; (mus) clave f; tecla f.
keyboard n teclado m.
keyhole n ojo de la cerradura m.
keynote n (mus) tónica f.
key ring n llavero m.
keystone n piedra clave f.
khaki n caqui m.
kick vt, vi patear; * n puntapié m; patada f.
kid n chico/ca m/f.
kidnap vt secuestrar.
kidnaper n secuestrador/a m/f.
kidnaping n secuestro m; rapto m.
kidney n riñón m.
killer n asesino/a m/f.
killing n asesinato m.
kiln n horno m.
kilo n kilo m.
kilobyte n kilobyte m.
kilogram n kilo m.
kilometer n kilómetro m.
kilt n falda escocesa f.
kin n parientes mpl; next of ~ pariente próximo
  m, pariente próxima f.
kind adj cariñoso/sa; * n género m.
kindergarten n parvulario m.
kind-hearted adj bondadoso/sa.
kindle vt, vi encender.
kindliness n benevolencia f.
kindly adj bondadoso/sa.
kindness n bondad f.

kindred adj emparentado/da.
kinetic adj cinético/ca.
king n rey m.
kingdom n reino m.
kingfisher n martín pescador m.
king prawn n langostino m.
kiosk n quiosco m.
kiss n beso m; * vt besar.
kissing n besos mpl.
kit n equipo m.
kitchen n cocina f.
kitchen garden n huerta f.
kitchen maid n fregona f.
kite n cometa f.
kitten n gatito m.
knack n don m.
knapsack n mochila f.
knave n bribón, pícaro m; (cards) sota f.
knead vt amasar.
knee n rodilla f.
knee-deep adj metido hasta las rodillas.
kneel vi arrodillarse.
knell n toque de difuntos m.
knife n cuchillo m.
knight n caballero m.
knit vt, vi tejer, tricotear; to ~ the brows fruncir
  el ceño.
knitter n calcetero/ra, mediero/ra m/f.
knitting needle n aguja de tejer f.
knitwear n prendas de punto fpl.
knob n bulto m; nudo en la madera m; botón de
  las flores m.
knock vt, vi golpear, tocar; to ~ down derribar;
  * n golpe m.
knocker n aldaba f.
knock-kneed adj patizambo/ba; zambo/ba.
knock-out n KO m, Lat Am nocaut m.
knoll n cima de una colina f.
knot n nudo m; lazo m; * vt anudar.
knotty adj escabroso/sa.
know vt, vi conocer; saber.
know-all n sabelotodo m/f.
know-how n conocimientos mpl.
knowing adj entendido/da; ~ly adv a sabiendas.
knowledge n conocimiento m.
knowledgeable adj bien informado/da.
knuckle n nudillo m.

L

label n etiqueta f.
labor n trabajo m; **to be in** ~ estar de parto; * vt trabajar.
laboratory n laboratorio m.
laborer n peón m.
laborious adj laborioso/sa; difícil; ~**ly** adv laboriosamente.
labor union n sindicato m, Lat Am gremial f.
labor unionist n sindicalista m/f, Lat Am gremialista m/f.
labyrinth n laberinto m.
lace n cordón; encaje m; * vt abrochar.
lacerate vt lacerar.
lack vt, vi faltar; * n falta f.
lackadaisical adj descuidado/da.
lackey n lacayo m.
laconic adj lacónico/ca.
lacquer n laca f.
lad n muchacho m.
ladder n escalera f.
ladle n cucharón m.
ladleful n cucharada f.
lady n señora f.
ladybug n mariquita f.
lady-killer n casanova m.
ladylike adj fino/na.
ladyship n señoría f.
lag vi quedarse atrás.
lager n cerveza (rubia) f.
lagoon n laguna f.
laid-back adj relajado/da.
lair n guarida f.
laity n laicado m.
lake n lago m; laguna f.
lamb n cordero m; * vi parir.
lame adj cojo/ja.
lament vt (vi) lamentar(se); * n lamento m.
lamentable adj lamentable, deplorable.
lamentation n lamentación f.
laminated adj laminado/da; plastificado/da.
lamp n lámpara f.
lampoon n sátira f.
lampshade n pantalla f.
lance n lanza f; * vt abrir con lanceta.
lancet n lanceta f.
land n país m; tierra f; * vt, vi desembarcar.
land forces npl tropas de tierra fpl.
land-holder n hacendado m.
landing n desembarco m.
landing strip n pista de aterrizaje f.
landlady n propietaria f.
landlord n propietario m.

landlubber n marinero de agua dulce m.
landmark n lugar conocido; hito m.
landowner n terrateniente m/f.
landscape n paisaje m.
landslide n corrimiento de tierras m, Lat Am deslave m.
lane n callejuela f.
langoustine n langostino m.
language n lengua f; lenguaje m.
languid adj lánguido/da, débil; ~**ly** adv lánguidamente, débilmente.
languish vi languidecer.
lank adj lacio/cia.
lanky adj larguirucho/cha.
lantern n linterna f; farol m.
lap n regazo m; * vt lamer.
lapdog n perro faldero m.
lapel n solapa f.
lapse n lapso m; * vi transcurrir.
laptop n portátil m.
larceny n latrocinio m.
larch n alerce m.
lard n manteca de cerdo f.
larder n despensa f.
large adj grande; **at** ~ en libertad; ~**ly** adv en gran parte.
large-scale adj en gran escala.
largesse n liberalidad f.
lark n alondra f.
larva n larva, oruga f.
laryngitis n laringitis f.
larynx n laringe f.
lascivious adj lascivo/va; ~**ly** adv lascivamente.
laser n láser m.
laser printer n impresora láser f.
lash n latigazo m, Lat Am cuerazo m; * vt dar latigazos, Lat Am cuerear; atar.
lasso n lazo m, Lat Am peal m.
last adj último/ma; pasado/da; **at** ~ por fin; ~**ly** adv finalmente; * n horma de zapatero f; * vi durar.
last-ditch adj último/ma.
lasting adj duradero/ra, permanente; ~**ly** adv perpetuamente.
last-minute adj de última hora.
latch n picaporte m.
latch-key n llave maestra f.
late adj tarde; difunto/ta; (rail) **the train is ten minutes** ~ el tren tiene un retraso de diez minutos; * adv tarde; ~**ly** adv recientemente.
latecomer n recién llegado/da m/f.
latent adj latente.

lateral adj, **~ly** adv lateral(mente).
lathe n torno m.
lather n espuma f.
latitude n latitud f.
latrine n letrina f.
latter adj último/ma; **~ly** adv últimamente, recientemente.
lattice n celosía f.
laudable adj loable.
laudably adv loablemente.
laugh vi reir; **to ~ at** vt reírse de; * n risa f.
laughable adj absurdo/da.
laughing stock n hazmerreír m.
laughter n risa f.
launch vt (vi) lanzar(se); * n (mar) lancha f.
launching n lanzamiento m.
launching pad n plataforma de lanzamiento f.
launder vt lavar.
Launderette™ n lavandería automática f.
laundry n lavandería f.
laurel n laurel m.
lava n lava f.
lavatory n cuarto de baño m.
lavender n (bot) espliego m, lavanda f.
lavish adj pródigo/ga; **~ly** adv pródigamente; * vt disipar.
law n ley f; derecho m.
law-abiding adj respetuoso/sa con la ley.
law and order n orden público m.
law court n tribunal m.
lawful adj legal; legítimo/ma; **~ly** adv legalmente.
lawless adj anárquico/ca.
lawlessness n anarquía f.
lawmaker n legislador/a m/f.
lawn n pasto m, Lat Am grama f.
lawnmower n cortacésped m.
law school n facultad de derecho f.
lawsuit n proceso m.
lawyer n abogado/da m/f.
lax adj laxo/xa; flojo/ja.
laxative n laxante m.
laxity n laxitud f; flojedad f.
lay vt poner; **to ~ claim** reclamar; pretender; **to ~ into** (col) zurrar; * vi poner.
layabout n vago/ga m/f.
layer n capa f.
layette n ajuar de niño m.
layman n lego, seglar m.
layout n composición f.
laze vi holgazanear.
lazily adv perezosamente; lentamente.
laziness n pereza f.
lazy adj perezoso/sa.
lead[1] n plomo m.
lead[2] vt conducir, guiar; * vi mandar.
leader n jefe/fa m/f.
leadership n dirección f; liderazgo m.

leading adj principal; capital; **~ article** n artículo principal m.
leaf n hoja f, yema f.
leaflet n folleto m.
leafy adj frondoso/sa.
league n liga, alianza f; legua f.
leak n escape m; * vi (mar) hacer agua.
leaky adj agujereado/da.
lean vt (vi) apoyar(se); * adj magro/ra.
leap vi saltar; * n salto m.
leapfrog n pídola f.
leap year n año bisiesto m.
learn vt, vi aprender.
learned adj docto/ta.
learner n aprendiz m.
learning n erudición f.
lease n arriendo m; * vt arrendar.
leasehold n arriendo m.
leash n correa f.
least adj mínimo/ma; **at ~** por lo menos; **not in the ~** en absoluto.
leather n cuero m.
leathery adj correoso/sa.
leave n licencia f; permiso m; **to take ~** despedirse; * vt dejar, abandonar.
leaven n levadura f; * vt fermentar.
leavings npl sobras fpl.
lecherous adj lascivo/va.
lecture n conferencia f; * vt dar una conferencia.
lecturer n conferenciante m/f; profesor/ra m/f.
ledge n reborde m.
ledger n (com) libro mayor m.
lee n (mar) sotavento m.
leech n sanguijuela f.
leek n (bot) puerro m.
leer vt mirar de manera lasciva.
lees npl sedimento, poso m.
leeward adj (mar) sotavento.
leeway n libertad de acción f.
left adj izquierdo/da; zurdo/da; **on the ~** a la izquierda.
left-handed adj zurdo/da.
leftovers npl sobras fpl.
leg n pierna f; pie m.
legacy n herencia f.
legal adj legal, legítimo/ma; **~ly** adv legalmente.
legal holiday n fiesta oficial f.
legality n legalidad, legitimidad f.
legalize vt legalizar.
legal tender n moneda de curso legal f.
legate n legado m.
legatee n legado m.
legation n legación f.
legend n leyenda f.
legendary adj legendario/ria.
legible adj legible.
legibly adv legiblemente.
legion n legión f.

legislate *vt* legislar.
legislation *n* legislación *f*.
legislative *adj* legislativo/va.
legislator *n* legislador/a *m/f*.
legislature *n* cuerpo legislativo *m*.
legitimacy *n* legitimidad *f*.
legitimate *adj* legítimo/ma; ~**ly** *adv* legítimamente; * *vt* legitimar.
leisure *n* ocio *m*; ~**ly** *adj* sin prisa; **at** ~ desocupado/da.
lemon *n* limón *m*.
lemonade *n* limonada *f*.
lemon tea *n* te con limón *m*.
lemon tree *n* limonero *m*.
lend *vt* prestar.
length *n* largo *m*; duración *f*; **at** ~ finalmente.
lengthen *vt* alargar; * *vi* alargarse.
lengthways, lengthwise *adv* a lo largo.
lengthy *adj* largo/ga.
lenient *adj* indulgente.
lens *n* lente *f*.
Lent *n* Cuaresma *f*.
lentil *n* lenteja *f*.
leopard *n* leopardo *m*; mallas *fpl*.
leotard *n* leotardo *m*.
leper *n* leproso/sa *m/f*.
leprosy *n* lepra *f*.
lesbian *n* lesbiana *f*.
less *adj* menor; * *adv* menos.
lessen *vt* disminuir; * *vi* disminuirse.
lesser *adj* más pequeño/ña.
lesson *n* lección *f*.
lest *conj* para que no.
let *vt* dejar, permitir; alquilar.
lethal *adj* mortal.
lethargic *adj* letárgico/ca.
lethargy *n* letargo *m*.
letter *n* letra *f*; carta *f*.
letter bomb *n* carta bomba *f*.
lettering *n* letras *fpl*.
letter of credit *n* carta de crédito *f*.
lettuce *n* lechuga *f*.
leukemia *n* leucemia *f*.
level *adj* llano/na, igual; nivelado/da; * *n* nivel *m*; * *vt* allanar; nivelar.
level-headed *adj* sensato/ta.
lever *n* palanca *f*.
leverage *n* influencia *f*.
levity *n* ligereza *f*.
levy *n* leva (de tropas) *f*; * *vt* recaudar.
lewd *adj* obsceno/na.
lexicon *n* lexicón *m*.
liability *n* responsabilidad *f*.
liable *adj* sujeto/ta; responsable.
liaise *vi* enlazar.
liaison *n* enlace *m*.
liar *n* embustero *m*.
libel *n* difamación *f*; * *vt* difamar.

libelous *adj* difamatorio/ria.
liberal *adj* liberal, generoso/sa; ~**ly** *adv* liberalmente.
liberality *n* liberalidad, generosidad *f*.
liberate *vt* libertar.
liberation *n* liberación *f*.
libertine *n* libertino *m*.
liberty *n* libertad *f*.
Libra *n* Libra *f*.
librarian *n* bibliotecario/ria *m/f*.
library *n* biblioteca *f*.
libretto *n* libreto *m*.
license *n* licencia *f*; permiso *m*; * *vt* autorizar, licenciar.
license plate *n* placa de matrícula *f*.
licentious *adj* licencioso/sa.
lichen *n* (*bot*) liquen *m*.
lick *vt* lamer.
lid *n* tapa *f*.
lie *n* mentira *f*; * *vi* mentir; echarse.
lie down *vi* yacer.
lieu *n*: **in** ~ **of** en vez de.
lieutenant *n* lugarteniente *m/f*; teniente *m/f*.
life *n* vida *f*; **for** ~ para toda la vida.
lifeboat *n* lancha de socorro *f*; bote salvavidas *m*.
lifeguard *n* socorrista *m/f*.
lifeless *adj* muerto/ta; sin vida.
lifelike *adj* natural.
lifeline *n* cordón umbilical *m*.
life preserver *n* chaleco salvavidas *m*.
life sentence *n* cadena perpetua *f*.
life-sized *adj* de tamaño natural.
life span *n* vida *f*.
lifestyle *n* estilo de vida *f*.
life-support system *n* sistema de respiración asistida *m*.
lifetime *n* vida *f*.
lift *vt* levantar.
ligament *n* ligamento *m*.
light *n* luz *f*; * *adj* ligero/ra; claro/ra; * *vt* encender; alumbrar.
light bulb *n* foco *m*; bombilla *f*.
lighten *vi* relampaguear; * *vt* iluminar; aligerar; (*mar*) zafar.
lighter *n* encendedor *m*.
light-headed *adj* mareado/da.
light-hearted *adj* alegre.
lighthouse *n* (*mar*) faro *m*.
lighting *n* iluminación *f*.
lightly *adv* ligeramente.
lightning *n* relámpago *m*.
lightning-rod *n* pararrayos *m invar*.
light pen *n* lápiz óptico *m*.
lightweight *adj* ligero/ra.
light year *n* año luz *m*.
ligneous *adj* leñoso/sa.
like *adj* semejante; igual; * *adv* como, del mismo modo que; * *vt, vi* gustar.

likeable *adj* simpático/ca.
likelihood *n* probabilidad *f*.
likely *adj* probable, verosímil.
liken *vt* comparar.
likeness *n* semejanza *f*.
likewise *adv* igualmente.
liking *n* agrado *m*.
lilac *n* lila *f*.
lily *n* lirio *m*; ~ **of the valley** lirio de los valles.
limb *n* miembro *m*.
limber *adj* flexible.
lime *n* cal *f*; lima *f*; ~ **tree** tilo *m*.
limestone *n* piedra caliza *f*; caliza *f*.
limit *n* límite, término *m*; * *vt* restringir.
limitation *n* limitación *f*; restricción *f*.
limitless *adj* inmenso/sa.
limousine *n* limusina *f*.
limp *vi* cojear; * *n* cojera *f*; * *adj* flojo/ja.
limpet *n* lapa *f*.
limpid *adj* claro/ra, transparente.
line *n* línea *f*; raya *f*; * *vt* forrar; revestir.
lineage *n* linaje *m*; filiación *f*.
linear *adj* lineal.
lined *adj* rayado/da; arrugado/da.
linen *n* lino *m*.
liner *n* transatlántico *m*.
linesman *n* juez de línea *m*.
linger *vi* persistir.
lingerie *n* ropa interior *f*.
lingering *adj* lento/ta.
linguist *n* lingüista *m/f*.
linguistic *adj* lingüístico/ca.
linguistics *n* lingüística *f*.
liniment *n* linimento *m*.
lining *n* forro *m*.
link *n* eslabón *m*; * *vt* enlazar.
linnet *n* pardillo *m*.
linoleum *n* linóleo *m*.
linseed *n* linaza *f*.
lint *n* hilas *fpl*.
lintel *n* dintel, tranquero *m*.
lion *n* león *m*.
lioness *n* leona *f*.
lip *n* labio *m*; borde *m*.
liposuction *n* liposucción *f*.
lip read *vi* leer los labios.
lip salve *n* crema protectora para labios *f*.
lipstick *n* lápiz de labios *m*.
liqueur *n* licor *m*.
liquid *adj* líquido/da; * *n* líquido *m*.
liquidate *vt* liquidar.
liquidation *n* liquidación *f*.
liquidize *vt* licuar.
liquor *n* licor *m*.
liquorice *n* regaliz *m*.
lisp *vi* cecear; * *n* ceceo *m*.
list *n* lista *f*; * *vt* hacer una lista de.
listen *vi* escuchar.

listless *adj* indiferente.
litany *n* letanía *f*.
liter *n* litro *m*.
literal *adj*, ~**ly** *adv* literal(mente).
literary *adj* literario/ria.
literate *adj* culto/ta.
literature *n* literatura *f*.
lithe *adj* ágil.
lithograph *n* litografía *f*.
lithography *n* litografía *f*.
litigation *n* litigio *m*.
litigious *adj* litigioso/sa.
litter *n* litera *f*; camada *f*; * *vt* parir.
little *adj* pequeño/ña, poco/ca; ~ **by** ~ poco a poco; * *n* poco *m*.
liturgy *n* liturgia *f*.
live *vi* vivir; habitar; **to** ~ **on** alimentarse de; **to** ~ **up to** *vt* cumplir con; * *adj* vivo/va.
livelihood *n* vida *f*.
liveliness *n* vivacidad *f*; belleza *f*.
lively *adj* vivo/va.
liven up *vt* animar.
liver *n* hígado *m*.
livery *n* librea *f*.
livestock *n* ganado *m*.
livid *adj* lívido/da, cárdeno/na.
living *n* vida *f*; * *adj* vivo/va.
living room *n* sala de estar *f*.
lizard *n* lagarto *m*.
load *vt* cargar; * *n* carga *f*.
loaded *adj* cargado/da.
loaf *n* pan *m*.
loafer *n* holgazán, gandul *m*.
loam *n* marga *f*.
loan *n* préstamo *m*.
loathe *vt* aborrecer; tener hastío; * *vi* fastidiar.
loathing *n* aversión *f*.
loathsome *adj* asqueroso/sa.
lobby *n* vestíbulo *m*.
lobe *n* lóbulo *m*.
lobster *n* langosta *f*.
local *adj* local.
local anesthetic *n* anestesia local *f*.
local government *n* gobierno municipal *m*.
locality *n* localidad *f*.
localize *vt* localizar.
locally *adv* en la vecindad.
locate *vt* localizar, *Lat Am* ubicar.
location *n* situación *f*.
loch *n* lago *m*.
lock *n* cerradura *f*; * *vt* cerrar con llave.
locker *n* vestuario *m*.
locket *n* medallón *m*.
lockout *n* cierre patronal *m*.
locksmith *n* cerrajero *m*.
locomotive *n* locomotora *f*.
locust *n* langosta *f*.
lodge *n* casa del guarda *f*; * *vi* alojarse.

lodger n inquilino/na m/f.
loft n desván m.
lofty adj alto/ta.
log n leño m.
logbook n (mar) diario de a bordo m.
logic n lógica f.
logical adj lógico/ca.
logo n logotipo m.
loin n lomo m.
loiter vi merodear.
loll vi repantigarse.
lollipop n pirulí m, piruleta f.
loneliness n soledad f.
lonesome adj solitario/ria; solo/la.
long adj largo/ga; * vi anhelar.
long-distance n: ~ **call** llamada interurbana f.
longevity n longevidad f.
long-haired adj de pelo largo.
longing n anhelo m.
longitude n longitud f.
longitudinal adj longitudinal.
long jump n salto de longitud m.
long-legged adj zancudo/da.
long-playing record n elepé m.
long-range adj de gran alcance.
long-term adj a largo plazo.
long wave n onda larga f.
long-winded adj prolijo/ja.
look vi mirar; parecer; **to ~ after** vt cuidar; **to ~ for** vt buscar; **to ~ forward to** vt esperar con impaciencia; **to ~ out for** vt aguardar; * n aspecto m; mirada f.
looking glass n espejo m.
lookout n (mil) centinela f; vigía f.
loom n telar m; * vi amenazar.
loop n lazo m.
loophole n escapatoria f.
loose adj suelto/ta; flojo/ja; ~**ly** adv aproximadamente.
loosen vt aflojar, zafar.
loot vt saquear; * n botín m.
lop vt desmochar.
lop-sided adj desequilibrado/da.
loquacious adj locuaz.
loquacity n locuacidad f.
lord n señor m.
lore n saber popular m.
lose vt perder; * vi perder; **to ~ weight** vi adelgazar.
loss n pérdida f; **to be at a ~** no saber qué hacer.
lost and found n objetos perdidos mpl.
lot n suerte f; lote m; **a ~** mucho.
lotion n loción f.
lottery n lotería, rifa f.
loud adj fuerte; ~**ly** adv fuerte.
loudspeaker n altavoz m, Lat Am altoparlante m.
lounge n salón m.
louse n (pl **lice**) piojo m.

lousy adj vil.
lout n gamberro m.
lovable adj amable.
love n amor, cariño m; **to fall in ~** enamorarse; * vt amar; gustar.
love letter n carta de amor f.
love life n vida sentimental f.
lovely adj hermoso/sa.
lover n amante m.
lovesick adj enamorado/da.
loving adj amoroso/sa.
low adj bajo/ja; * vi mugir.
low-cut adj escotado/da.
lower adj más bajo/ja; * vt bajar.
lowest adj más bajo/ja, ínfimo/ma.
lowland n tierra baja f.
lowliness n humildad f.
lowly adj humilde.
low water, low tide n bajamar f.
loyal adj leal; fiel; ~**ly** adv lealmente.
loyalty n lealtad f; fidelidad f.
lozenge n pastilla f.
lubricant n lubricante m.
lubricate vt lubricar.
lucid adj lúcido/da.
luck n suerte; fortuna f.
luckily adv afortunadamente.
luckless adj desdichado/da.
lucky adj afortunado/da.
lucrative adj lucrativo/va.
ludicrous adj absurdo/da.
lug vt arrastrar.
luggage n equipaje m.
lugubrious adj lúgubre, triste.
lukewarm adj tibio/bia.
lull vt acunar; * n tregua f.
lullaby n nana f.
lumbago n lumbago m.
lumber n trastera f.
lumberjack n maderero/ra m/f.
lumber room n trastero m.
luminous adj luminoso/sa.
lump n terrón m; bulto m; chichón m; * vt juntar.
lump sum n suma global f.
lunacy n locura f.
lunar adj lunar.
lunatic adj loco/ca.
lunch, luncheon n almuerzo m, comida f; * vt, vi almorzar.
lungs npl pulmones mpl.
lurch n sacudida f.
lure n señuelo m; cebo m; * vt inducir.
lurid adj sensacional.
lurk vi esconderse.
luscious adj delicioso/sa.
lush adj exuberante.
lust n lujuria, sensualidad f; concupiscencia f; * vi lujuriar; **to ~ after** vt codiciar.

luster n lustre m.
lustful adj lujurioso/sa, voluptuoso/sa; ~**ly** adv lujuriosamente.
lustily adv vigorosamente.
lusty adj fuerte, vigoroso/sa.
lute n laúd m.
Lutheran n luterano/na m/f.
luxuriance n exuberancia, superabundancia f.
luxuriant adj exuberante, superabundante.
luxuriate vi crecer con exuberancia.

luxurious adj lujoso/sa; exuberante; ~**ly** adv lujosamente.
luxury n lujo m, voluptuosidad f; exuberancia f.
lying n mentiras fpl.
lymph n linfa f.
lynch vt linchar.
lynx n lince m.
lyrical adj lírico/ca.
lyrics npl letra f.

M

macaroni *n* macarrones *mpl*.
macaroon *n* almendrado *m*.
mace *n* maza *f*; macis *f invar*.
macerate *vt* macerar; mortificar.
machination *n* maquinación, trama *f*.
machine *n* máquina *f*.
machine gun *n* ametralladora *f*.
machinery *n* maquinaria, mecánica *f*.
mackerel *n* caballa *f*.
mad *adj* loco/ca, furioso/sa, rabioso/sa, insensato/ta.
madam *n* madama, señora *f*.
madden *vt* enloquecer.
madder *n* (*bot*) rubia *f*.
madhouse *n* casa de locos *f*.
madly *adv* locamente.
madman *n* loco *m*.
madness *n* locura *f*.
magazine *n* revista *f*; almacén *m*.
maggot *n* gusano *m*.
magic *n* magia *f*; * *adj* mágico/ca; **~ally** *adv* mágicamente.
magician *n* mago/ga *m/f*; prestidigitador/a *m/f*.
magisterial *adj* magistral; **~ly** *adv* magistralmente.
magistracy *n* magistratura *f*.
magistrate *n* magistrado/da *m/f*.
magnanimity *n* magnanimidad *f*.
magnanimous *adj* magnánimo; **~ly** *adv* magnanimaménte.
magnet *n* iman *m*.
magnetic *adj* magnetico/ca.
magnetism *n* magnetismo *m*.
magnificence *n* magnificencia *f*.
magnificent *adj* magnifico; **~ly** *adv* magníficamente.
magnify *vt* aumentar; exagerar.
magnifying glass *n* lupa *f*.
magnitude *n* magnitud *f*.
magpie *n* urraca *f*.
mahogany *n* caoba *f*.
maid *n* criada *f*, *Lat Am* chinita *f*.
maiden *n* doncella *f*.
maiden name *n* nombre de soltera *m*.
mail *n* correo *m*.
mailbox *n* buzón *m*.
mailing list *n* lista de direcciones *f*.
mail order *n* venta por correo *f*.
mail train *n* (*rail*) tren correo *m*.
maim *vt* mutilar.
main *adj* principal; esencial; **in the ~** en general.
mainland *n* continente *m*.
main line *n* (*rail*) línea principal *f*.
mainly *adv* principalmente.

main street *n* calle mayor *f*.
maintain *vt* mantener; sostener.
maintenance *n* mantenimiento *m*.
maize *n* maíz *m*; borona *f*.
majestic *adj* majestuoso/sa; **~ally** *adv* majestuosamente.
majesty *n* majestad *f*.
major *adj* principal; * *n* (*mil*) comandante/a *m/f*.
majority *n* mayoría *f*.
make *vt* hacer, crear; **to ~ for** dirigirse hacia; **to ~ up** inventar; **to ~ up for** compensar; **to ~ off with something** alzar; * *n* marca *f*.
make-believe *n* invención *f*.
makeshift *adj* improvisado.
make-up *n* maquillaje *m*.
make-up remover *n* desmaquillador *m*.
malady *n* enfermedad *f*.
malaise *n* malestar *m*.
malaria *n* malaria *f*.
malcontent *adj*, *n* malcontento/ta *m/f*.
male *adj* masculino/na; * *n* macho *m*.
malevolence *n* malevolencia *f*.
malevolent *adj* malévolo/la; **~ly** *adv* malignamente.
malfunction *n* mal funcionamiento, fallo *m*.
malice *n* malicia *f*.
malicious *adj* malicioso/sa; **~ly** *adv* maliciosamente.
malign *adj* maligno; * *vt* calumniar.
malignant *adj* maligno/na; **~ly** *adv* malignamente.
mall (**shopping**) *n* centro comercial; paseo *m*.
malleable *adj* maleable.
mallet *n* mazo *m*.
mallow *n* (*bot*) malva *f*.
malnutrition *n* desnutrición *f*.
malpractice *n* negligencia *f*.
malt *n* malta *f*.
maltreat *vt* maltratar.
mammal *n* mamífero *m*.
mammoth *adj* gigantesco/ca.
man *n* hombre *m*; * *vt* (*mar*) tripular.
manacle *n* manilla *f*; **~s** *npl* esposas *fpl*.
manage *vt*, *vi* manejar, dirigir, *Lat Am* gerenciar.
manageable *adj* manejable.
management *n* dirección *f*.
manager *n* director/a *m/f*.
manageress *n* directora *f*.
managerial *adj* directivo/va.
managing director *n* director/a general *m/f*.
mandarin *n* (*bot*) mandarina *f*; mandarín *m*.
mandate *n* mandato *m*.
mandatory *adj* obligatorio/ria.
mane *n* crines *fpl*, melena *f*.
maneuver *n* maniobra *f*.

manfully adv valerosamente.
manger n pesebre m.
mangle n rodillo m; * vt mutilar.
mangy adj sarnoso/sa.
manhandle vt maltratar.
manhood n madurez; hombría f.
man-hour n hora hombre f.
mania n manía f.
maniac n maníaco/ca m/f.
manic adj frenético/ca.
manicure n manicura f.
manifest adj manifiesto/ta, patente; * vt manifestar.
manifestation n manifestación f.
manifesto n manifiesto m.
manipulate vt manejar; manipular.
manipulation n manejo; manipulación f.
mankind n género humano m.
manlike adj varonil.
manliness n valentía, hombría f.
manly adj varonil.
man-made adj artificial.
manner n manera f; modo m; forma f; ~s pl modales mpl.
manpower n mano de obra f.
mansion n palacio m, mansión f.
manslaughter n homicidio (sin premeditación) m.
mantelpiece n repisa (de chimenea) f.
manual adj, n manual m.
manufacture n fabricación f; * vt fabricar.
manufacturer n fabricante m/f.
manure n abono m; estiércol m; fiemo m; * vt abonar.
manuscript n manuscrito m.
many adj muchos, muchas; ~ a time muchas veces; **how ~?** ¿cuantos?; **as ~ as** tantos como.
map n mapa m; * vt planear, trazar el mapa de; **to ~ out** proyectar.
maple n arce m.
mar vt estropear.
marathon n maratón m.
marauder n merodeador/a m/f.
marble n mármol m; * adj marmóreo/rea.
March n marzo m.
march n marcha f; * vi marchar.
march past n desfile m.
mare n yegua f.
margarine n margarina f.
margin n margen m; borde m.
marginal adj marginal.
marigold n (bot) caléndula f.
marijuana n marihuana f.
marinate vt adobar.
marine adj marino/na; * n infante de marina m.
mariner n marinero/ra m/f.
marital adj marital.
maritime adj marítimo/ma.
marjoram n mejorana f.

mark n marca f; señal f; * vt marcar.
marker n registro m.
market n mercado m.
marketable adj vendible.
marketing n márketing m.
marketplace n mercado m.
market research n análisis de mercados m invar.
market value n valor de mercado m.
marksman n tirador m.
marmalade n mermelada de naranja f.
maroon adj marrón.
marquee n entoldado/da m/f.
marriage n matrimonio m; casamiento m.
marriageable adj casadero/ra.
marriage certificate n partida de casamiento f.
married adj casado/da; conyugal.
marrow n médula f.
marry vi casarse.
marsh n pantano m.
marshal n mariscal/a m/f.
marshy adj pantanoso/sa.
marten n marta f.
martial adj marcial; ~ **law** n ley marcial f.
martyr n mártir m.
martyrdom n martirio m.
marvel n maravilla f; * vi maravillar(se).
marvelous adj maravilloso/sa; ~**ly** adv maravillosamente.
marzipan n mazapán m.
mascara n rímel m.
masculine adj masculino/na, varonil.
mash n mezcla f.
mask n máscara f; * vt enmascarar.
masochist n masoquista m/f.
mason n albañil m.
masonry n mampostería f.
masquerade n mascarada f.
mass n masa f; misa f; montón m.
massacre n carnicería, matanza f; * vt hacer una carnicería.
massage n masaje m.
masseur n masajista m.
masseuse n masajista f.
massive adj enorme.
mass-media npl medios de comunicación de masas mpl.
mast n mástil m.
master n amo/ma, dueño/ña m/f; maestro/tra m/f; * vt dominar.
masterly adj magistral.
mastermind vt dirigir.
masterpiece n obra maestra f.
mastery n maestría f.
masticate vt masticar.
mastiff n mastín m.
mat n estera f; felpudo m.
match n fósforo m, cerilla f; partido m, Lat Am juego m; * vt igualar; * vi hacer juego.

M

matchbox n caja de fósforos f.
matchless adj incomparable, sin par.
matchmaker n casamentero/ra m/f.
mate n compañero/ra m/f; * vt acoplar.
material adj, ~ly adv material(mente).
materialism n materialismo m.
maternal adj maternal.
maternity clothes npl vestido premamá m.
maternity hospital n hospital de maternidad m.
math n mates, matemáticas fpl.
mathematical adj matemático/ca; ~ly adv matemáticamente.
mathematician n matemático/ca m/f.
mathematics npl matemáticas fpl.
matinee n función de la tarde f.
mating n aparejamiento m.
matins npl maitines mpl.
matriculate vt matricular.
matriculation n matriculación f.
matrimonial adj matrimonial.
matte adj mate.
matted adj enmarañado/da.
matter n materia, substancia f; asunto m; cuestión f; **what is the ~?** ¿qué pasa?; **as a ~ of fact** en realidad; * vi importar.
mattress n colchón m.
mature adj maduro/ra; * vt madurar.
maturity n madurez f.
maul vt magullar.
mausoleum n mausoleo m.
mauve adj malva.
maxim n máxima f.
maximum n máximo m.
may vi poder; ~**be** acaso, quizá.
May n mayo m.
Mayday n primero de mayo m.
mayonnaise n mayonesa f.
mayor n alcalde m.
mayoress n alcaldesa f.
maze n laberinto m.
me pn me; mí.
meadow n pradera f; prado m.
meager adj pobre.
meagerness n escasez f.
meal n comida f; harina f.
mealtime n hora de comer f.
mean adj tacaño/ña; **in the ~time**, ~**while** mientras tanto; ~**s** npl medios mpl; * vt, vi significar.
meander vi serpentear.
meaning n sentido, significado m.
meaningful adj significativo/va.
meaningless adj sin sentido.
meanness n tacañería f.
meantime, **meanwhile** adv mientras tanto, Lat Am intertanto.
measles npl sarampión m.
measure n medida f; (mus) compás m; * vt medir.

measurement n medida f.
meat n carne f.
meatball n albóndiga f.
meaty adj sustancioso/sa.
mechanic n mecánico/ca m/f.
mechanical adj mecánico; ~**ly** adv mecánicamente.
mechanics npl mecánica f.
mechanism n mecanismo m.
medal n medalla f.
medallion n medallón m.
medallist n medallero/ra m/f.
meddle vi entrometerse.
meddler n entrometido m.
media npl medios de comunicación mpl.
median strip n mediana f.
mediate vi mediar.
mediation n mediación, interposición f.
mediator n intermediario/ria m/f.
medical adj médico/ca.
medicate vt medicar.
medicated adj medicinal.
medicinal adj medicinal.
medicine n medicina f; medicamento m.
medieval adj medieval.
mediocre adj mediocre.
mediocrity n mediocridad f.
meditate vi meditar.
meditation n meditación f.
meditative adj contemplativo/va.
Mediterranean adj mediterráneo/nea; **the ~** el Mediterráneo/nea m.
medium n medio m; * adj mediano/na.
medium wave n onda media f.
medley n mezcla m.
meek adj manso/sa; ~**ly** adv mansamente.
meekness n mansedumbre f.
meet vt encontrar; **to ~ with** reunirse con; * vi encontrarse; juntarse.
meeting n reunión f; congreso m.
megaphone n megáfono m.
melancholy n melancolía f; * adj melancólico/ca.
mellow adj maduro/ra; suave; * vi madurar.
mellowness n madurez f.
melodious adj melodioso/sa; ~**ly** adv melodiosamente.
melody n melodía f.
melon n melón m.
melt vt derretir; * vi derretirse.
melting point n punto de fusión m.
member n miembro m/f.
membership n número de miembros m, Lat Am membresía f.
membrane n membrana f.
memento n recuerdo m.
memo n memorándum m.
memoir n memoria f.
memorable adj memorable.
memorandum n memorándum m.
memorial n monumento conmemorativo m.

memorize vt memorizar, aprender de memoria.
memory n memoria f; recuerdo m.
menace n amenaza f; * vt amenazar.
menacing adj amenazador/ra.
menagerie n casa de fieras f.
mend vt reparar.
mending n reparación f.
menial adj doméstico/ca.
meningitis n meningitis f.
menopause n menopausia f.
menstruation n menstruación f.
mental adj mental, intelectual.
mentality n mentalidad f.
mentally adv mentalmente, intelectualmente.
mention n mención f; * vt mencionar.
mentor n mentor m.
menu n menú m; carta f.
mercantile adj mercantil.
mercenary adj, n mercenario/ria m/f.
merchandise n mercancía f.
merchant n comerciante m/f.
merchantman n navío mercante m.
merchant marine n marina mercante f.
merciful adj compasivo/va.
merciless adj despiadado/da; ~ly adv
　despiadadamente.
mercury n mercurio m.
mercy n compasión f.
mere adj mero/ra; ~ly adv simplemente.
merge vt fundir.
merger n fusión f.
meridian n meridiano m.
meringue n merengue m.
merit n mérito m; * vt merecer.
meritorious adj meritorio/ria.
mermaid n sirena f.
merrily adv alegremente.
merriment n diversión f; regocijo m.
merry adj alegre.
merry-go-round n tiovivo m.
mesh n malla f.
mesmerize vt hipnotizar.
mess n lío m, Lat Am relajo m; mamarracho m;
　(mil) comedor m; **to ~ up** vt desordenar.
message n mensaje m.
messenger n mensajero/ra m/f.
metabolism n metabolismo n.
metal n metal m.
metallic adj metálico/ca.
metallurgy n metalurgía f.
metamorphosis n metamorfosis f invar.
metaphor n metáfora f.
metaphoric(al) adj metafórico/ca.
metaphysical adj metafísico/ca.
metaphysics npl metafísica f.
mete (out) vt imponer.
meteor n meteoro m.
meteorological adj meteorológico/ca.

meteorology n meteorología f.
meter[1] n contador m, Lat Am medidor m.
meter[2] n metro m.
method n método m.
methodical adj metódico/ca; ~ly adv
　metódicamente.
Methodist n metodista m/f.
metric adj métrico/ca.
metropolis n metrópoli f.
metropolitan adj metropolitano/na.
mettle n valor m.
mettlesome adj brioso/sa.
mew vi maullar.
mezzanine n entresuelo m.
microbe n microbio m.
microphone n micrófono m.
microchip n microchip m.
microscope n microscopio m.
microscopic adj microscópico/ca.
microwave n microondas m invar; ~ **oven**
　microondas m.
mid adj medio/dia.
midday n mediodía m.
middle adj medio/dia; * n medio, centro m.
middle name n segundo nombre m.
middleweight n peso medio m.
middling adj mediano/na.
midge n mosquito m.
midget n enano/na m/f.
midi system n minicadena f.
midnight n medianoche f.
midriff n diafragma m.
midst n medio, centro m.
midsummer n pleno verano m.
midway adv a medio camino.
midwife n partera f.
midwifery n obstetricia f.
might n poder m; fuerza f.
mighty adj fuerte.
migraine n jaqueca f.
migrate vi emigrar, migrar.
migration n emigración, migración f.
migratory adj migratorio/ria.
mike n micrófono m.
mild adj apacible; suave; ~ly adv suavemente.
mildew n moho m.
mildness n dulzura f.
mile n milla f.
mileage n kilometraje m.
milieu n ambiente m.
militant adj militante.
military adj militar.
militate vi militar.
militia n milicia f.
milk n leche f; * vt ordenar.
milkshake n batido de leche m, Lat Am malteada f.
milky adj lechoso/sa; **M~ Way** n Via Lactea f.
mill n molino m; * vt moler.

millennium n milenio m.
miller n molinero/ra m/f.
millet n (bot) mijo m.
milligram n miligramo m.
milliliter n mililitro m.
millimeter n milímetro m.
milliner n sombrerero/ra m/f.
millinery n sombrerería f.
million n millón m.
millionaire n millonario/ria m/f.
millionth adj, n millonésimo/ma m/f.
millstone n piedra de molino f.
mime n mimo m.
mimic vt imitar.
mimicry n mímica f.
mince vt picar.
mind n mente f; * vt cuidar; * vi molestar.
minded adj dispuesto/ta.
mindful adj consciente.
mindless adj sin motivo.
mine pn mío, mía, mi; * n mina; * vi minar.
minefield n campo de minas m.
miner n minero/ra m/f.
mineral adj, n mineral m.
mineralogy n mineralogia f.
mineral water n agua mineral f.
minesweeper n dragaminas m invar.
mingle vt mezclar.
miniature n miniatura f.
minimal adj mínimo/ma.
minimize vt minimizar.
minimum n mínimo m.
mining n minería f.
minion n favorito/ta m/f.
minister n ministro/tro m/f; * vt servir.
ministerial adj ministerial.
ministry n ministerio m.
mink n visón m.
minnow n vario m (pez).
minor adj menor; * n menor (de edad) m/f.
minority n minoría f.
minstrel n juglar m.
mint n (bot) menta f; casa de la moneda f; * vt
  acuñar.
minus adv menos.
minute¹ adj diminuto/ta; ~ly adv minuciosamente.
minute² n minuto m.
miracle n milagro m.
miraculous adj milagroso/sa.
mirage n espejismo m.
mire n fango m.
mirky adj turbio/bia.
mirror n espejo m.
mirth n alegría f.
mirthful adj alegre.
misadventure n desgracia f.
misanthrope, misanthropist n misántropo m.
misapply vt aplicar mal.

misapprehension n error m.
misbehave vi portarse mal.
misbehavior n mala conducta f.
miscalculate vt calcular mal.
miscarriage n aborto (espontáneo) m.
miscarry vi abortar (espontáneamente); malograrse.
miscellaneous adj varios, varias.
miscellany n miscelánea f.
mischief n mal, daño m.
mischievous adj dañoso/sa; travieso/sa.
misconception n equivocación f.
misconduct n mala conducta f.
misconstrue vt interpretar mal.
miscount vt contar mal.
miscreant n malvado/da m/f.
misdeed n delito m.
misdemeanor n delito m.
misdirect vt dirigir mal.
miser n avaro/ra m/f.
miserable adj miserable, infeliz.
miserly adj mezquino/na, tacaño/ña.
misery n miseria f.
misfit n inadaptado/da m/f.
misfortune n desgracia f.
misgiving n recelo m; presentimiento m.
misgovern vt gobernar mal.
misguided adj equivocado/da.
mishandle vt manejar mal.
mishap n desgracia f.
misinform vt informar mal, Lat Am malinformar.
misinterpret vt interpretar mal.
misjudge vi juzgar mal.
mislay vt extraviar.
mislead vt engañar.
mismanage vt manejar mal.
mismanagement n mala administración f.
misnomer n nombre inapropriado m.
misogynist n misógino/na m/f.
misplace vt extraviar.
misprint vt imprimir mal; * n errata f.
misrepresent vt representar mal.
Miss n señorita f.
miss vt perder; echar de menos.
missal n misal m.
misshapen adj deforme.
missile n misil m.
missing adj perdido/da; ausente.
mission n misión f.
missionary n misionero/ra m/f.
misspent adj disipado/da.
mist n niebla f.
mistake vt entender mal; * vi equivocarse,
  engañarse; to be mistaken equivocarse; * n
  equivocación f; error m, Lat Am falla f, yerro m.
Mister n Señor m.
mistletoe n (bot) muérdago m.
mistress n amante f.
mistrust vt desconfiar; * n desconfianza f.

mistrustful adj desconfiado/da.
misty adj nebuloso/sa.
misunderstand vt entender mal.
misunderstanding n malentendido m.
misuse vt maltratar; abusar de.
miter n mitra f.
mitigate vt mitigar.
mitigation n mitigación f.
mittens npl manoplas fpl.
mix vt mezclar.
mixed adj surtido/da; mixto/ta.
mixed-up adj confuso/sa.
mixer n licuadora f.
mixture n mezcla f.
mix-up n confusión f.
moan n gemido m; * vi gemir; quejarse.
moat n foso m.
mob n multitud f.
mobile adj móvil; ~/**cell phone** móvil m, Lat Am celular m.
mobile home n caravana f.
mobility n movilidad f.
mobilize vt (mil) movilizar.
moccasin n mocasín m.
mock vt burlarse.
mockery n mofa f.
mode n modo m.
model n modelo m; * vt modelar.
modem n módem m.
moderate adj moderado/da; ~**ly** adv medianamente; * vt moderar.
moderation n moderación f.
modern adj moderno/na.
modernize vt modernizar.
modest adj modesto/ta; ~**ly** adv modestamente.
modesty n modestia f.
modicum n mínimo m.
modification n modificación f.
modify vt modificar.
modulate vt modular.
modulation n (mus) modulación f.
module n módulo m.
mogul n magnate m/f.
mohair n mohair m.
moist adj húmedo/da.
moisten vt humedecer.
moisture n humedad f.
molars npl muelas fpl.
molasses npl melaza f.
mold n molde m; moho m; * vt moldear.
molder vi decaer.
moldy adj enmohecido/da.
mole n topo m.
molecule n molécula f.
molehill n topera f.
molest vt importunar.
mollify vt apaciguar.
mollusk n molusco m.

mollycoddle vt mimar.
molt vt mudar.
molten adj derretido/da.
moment n momento m.
momentarily adv momentáneamente.
momentary adj momentáneo/nea.
momentous adj importante.
momentum n ímpetu m.
mommy n mamá f.
monarch n monarca m.
monarchy n monarquía f.
monastery n monasterio m.
monastic adj monástico/ca.
Monday n lunes m.
monetary adj monetario/ria.
money n dinero m, Lat Am plata f.
money box n hucha f, Lat Am alcancía f.
money laundering n blanqueo m.
money order n giro m.
Mongol n mongólico/ca m/f.
mongrel adj, n mestizo/za m/f.
monitor n monitor m.
monk n monje m.
monkey n mono m.
monochrome adj monocromo/ma.
monocle n monóculo m.
monolog n monólogo m.
monopolize vt monopolizar.
monopoly n monopolio m.
monosyllable n monosílabo m.
monotonous adj monótono/na.
monotony n monotonía f.
monsoon n (mar) monzón m.
monster n monstruo m.
monstrosity n monstruosidad f.
monstrous adj monstruoso/sa; ~**ly** adv monstruosamente.
montage n montaje m.
month n mes m.
monthly adj, adv mensual(mente).
monument n monumento m.
monumental adj monumental.
moo vi mugir.
mood n humor m.
moodiness n mal humor m.
moody adj malhumorado/da.
moon n luna f.
moonbeams npl rayos lunares mpl.
moonlight n luz de la luna f.
moor vt (mar) atracar.
mooring rope n amarra f.
moorland, moor n páramo m.
moose n alce m.
mop n fregona f; * vt fregar.
mope vi estar triste.
moped n ciclomotor m.
moral adj, ~**ly** adv moral(mente); ~**s** npl moralidad f.

M

morale n moral f.
moralist n moralista m/f.
morality n ética, moralidad f.
moralize vt, vi moralizar.
morass n pantano m.
morbid adj morboso/sa.
more adj, adv más; **never** ~ nunca más; **once** ~ otra vez; ~ **and** ~ más y más, cada vez más; **so much the** ~ cuanto más.
moreover adv además.
morgue n depósito de cadáveres m.
morning n mañana f; **good** ~ buenos días mpl.
moron n imbécil m/f.
morose adj hosco/ca.
morphine n morfina f.
morsel n bocado m.
mortal adj mortal; ~**ly** adv mortalmente; * n mortal m/f.
mortality n mortalidad f.
mortar n mortero m.
mortgage n hipoteca f; * vt hipotecar.
mortgage company n banco hipotecario m.
mortgager n deudor hipotecario m, deudora hipotecaria f.
mortician n director de pompas fúnebres.
mortification n mortificación f.
mortuary n depósito de cadáveres m.
mosaic n mosaico m.
mosque n mezquita f.
mosquito n mosquito m; zancudo/da m.
moss n (bot) musgo m, Lat Am lama f.
mossy adj cubierto/ta de musgo.
most adj la mayoría de; * adv sumamente; **at** ~ a lo sumo; ~**ly** adv principalmente.
motel n motel m.
moth n polilla f.
mothball n bola de naftalina f.
mother n madre f; **loving** ~ madraza f.
motherhood n maternidad f.
mother-in-law n suegra f.
motherless adj sin madre.
motherly adj maternal.
mother-of-pearl n nácar m.
mother-to-be n futura madre f.
mother tongue n lengua materna f.
motif n tema m.
motion n movimiento m.
motionless adj inmóvil.
motion picture n película f.
motivated adj motivado/da.
motive n motivo m.
motley adj abigarrado/da.
motor n motor m.
motorbike n moto f.
motorboat n lancha motora f.
motorcycle n motocicleta f.
motor scooter n moto f.
motor vehicle n automóvil m.

mottled adj multicolor.
motto n lema m.
mound n montón m.
mount n monte m; * vt subir.
mountain n montaña f.
mountaineer n montañero/ra m/f, alpinista m/f, Lat Am andinista m/f.
mountaineering n montañismo m, alpinismo m, Lat Am andinismo m.
mountainous adj montañoso/sa.
mourn vt lamentar.
mourner n doliente m/f.
mournful adj triste; ~**ly** adv tristemente.
mourning n luto m.
mouse n (pl **mice**) ratón m.
mouse mat n alfombrilla f.
mousse n mousse f.
mouth n boca f; desembocadura f.
mouthful n bocado m.
mouth organ n harmónica f.
mouthpiece n boquilla f.
mouthwash n enjuague m.
mouthwatering adj apetitoso/sa.
movable adj movible.
move vt mover; proponer; * vi moverse; * n movimiento m.
movement n movimiento m.
movie n película f.
movie camera n cámara cinematográfica f.
movie theater, **movie house** n cine m.
moving adj conmovedor/a.
mow vt segar.
mower n cortacésped m.
Mrs n señora f.
much adj, adv mucho/cha; con mucho.
muck n suciedad f.
mucous adj mocoso/sa.
mucus n moco m.
mud n barro m.
muddle vt confundir m; confusión f.
muddy adj fangoso/sa.
mudguard n guardabarros m invar.
muffle vt embozar.
mug n jarra f.
muggy adj bochornoso/sa.
mulberry n mora f; ~ **tree** morera f.
mule n mulo m, mula f.
mull vt meditar.
multifarious adj múltiple.
multimedia adj multimedia.
multiple adj múltiplo m.
multiplication n multiplicación f; ~ **table** tabla de multiplicar f.
multiply vt multiplicar.
multitude n multitud f.
mumble vt, vi refunfuñar.
mummy n momia f.
mumps npl paperas fpl.

munch vt mascar.
mundane adj trivial.
municipal adj municipal.
municipality n municipalidad f.
munificence n munificencia f.
munitions npl municiones fpl.
mural n mural m.
murder n asesinato m; homicidio m; * vt asesinar.
murderer n asesino/na m/f.
murderess n asesina f.
murderous adj homicida.
murky adj sombrío/ría.
murmur n murmullo m;* vi murmurar.
muscle n músculo m.
muscular adj muscular.
muse vi meditar.
museum n museo m.
mushroom n (bot) seta f; champiñón m.
music n musica f.
musical adj musical; melodioso/sa.
musician n músico/ca m/f.
musk n almizcle m.
muslin n muselina f.
mussel n mejillón m.
must v aux tener que, deber; deber de.
mustache n bigote m.
mustard n mostaza f.

muster vt agregar.
musty adj mohoso/sa, añejo/ja.
mute adj mudo/da, silencioso/sa.
muted adj callado/da.
mutilate vt mutilar.
mutilation n mutilación f.
mutiny n motin, tumulto m; * vi amotinarse, rebelarse.
mutter vt, vi murmurar, musitar; * n murmuración f.
mutton n carnero m.
mutual adj mutuo/tua, mutual, recíproco/ca; ~ly adv mutuamente, recíprocamente.
muzzle n bozal m; hocico m; * vt embozar.
my pn mi, mis; mio, mia; mios, mias.
myriad n miríada f; gran número m.
myrrh n mirra f.
myrtle n mirto, arrayán m
myself pn yo mismo/ma.
mysterious adj misterioso/sa; ~ly adv misteriosamente.
mystery n misterio m.
mystic(al) adj místico/ca.
mystify vt dejar perplejo/ja.
mystique n misterio m.
myth n mito m.
mythology n mitología f.

M

N

nab vt agarrar.
nag n jaca f; * vt regañar.
nagging adj persistente; * npl quejas fpl.
nail n uña f; garra f; clavo m; * vt clavar.
nailbrush n cepillo de uñas m.
nailfile n lima de uñas f.
nail polish n esmalte de uñas m.
nail scissors npl tijeras de manicura fpl.
naïve adj ingenuo/nua.
naked adj desnudo/da evidente; puro/ra, simple.
name n nombre m; fama, reputación f; * vt nombrar; mencionar.
nameless adj anónimo/ma.
namely adv a saber.
namesake n tocayo/ya m/f.
nanny n niñera f.
nap n sueño ligero m.
napalm n napalm m.
nape n nuca f.
napkin n servilleta f.
narcissus n (bot) narciso m.
narcotic adj narcótico/ca; * n narcótico m.
narrate vt narrar, relatar.
narrative adj narrativo/va; * n narrativa f.
narrow adj angosto/ta, estrecho/cha; ~ly adv estrechamente; * vt estrechar; limitar.
narrow-minded adj estrecho/cha de miras.
narrow pass n puerto m.
nasal adj nasal.
nasty adj sucio/cia, puerco/ca; obsceno/na; sórdido/da.
natal adj nativo/va; natal.
nation n nación f.
national adj, ~ly adv nacional(mente).
nationalism n nacionalismo m.
nationalist adj, n nacionalista m/f.
nationality n nacionalidad f.
nationalize vt nacionalizar.
nationwide adj a nivel nacional.
native adj nativo/va; * n natural m/f.
native language n lengua materna f.
Nativity n Navidad f.
natural adj natural; sencillo/lla; ~ly adv naturalmente.
natural gas n gas natural m.
naturalist n naturalista m/f.
naturalize vt naturalizar.
nature n naturaleza f; índole f.
naturopath n naturópata m/f.
naught, nought n cero m.
naughty adj malo/la, malvado/da.
nausea n náuseas fpl, gana de vomitar f.

nauseate vt dar náuseas a.
nauseous adj fastidioso/sa.
nautical, naval adj náutico/ca, naval.
nave n nave (de la iglesia) f.
navel n ombligo m.
navigate vi navegar.
navigation n navegación f.
navy n marina f; armada f.
Nazi n nazi m/f.
near prep cerca de, junto a; * adv casi; cerca, cerca de; * adj cercano/na, proximo/ma.
nearby adj cercano/na.
nearly adv casi.
near-sighted adj miope.
neat adj hermoso/sa, pulido/da; puro/ra; neto/ta; ~ly adv elegantemente.
nebulous adj nebuloso/sa.
necessarily adv necesariamente.
necessary adj necesario/ria.
necessitate vt necesitar.
necessity n necesidad f.
neck n cuello m, Lat Am cogote m; * vi besuquearse.
necklace n collar m.
nectar n néctar m.
née, nee adj: ~ Brown de soltera Brown.
need n necesidad f; pobreza f; * vt necesitar.
needle n aguja f.
needless adj superfluo/lua, inútil.
needlework n costura f; bordado de aguja m; obra de punto m.
needy adj necesitado/da, pobre.
negation n negación f.
negative adj negativo/va; ~ly adv negativamente; * n negativa f.
neglect vt descuidar, desatender; * n negligencia f.
negligee n salto de cama m.
negligence n negligencia f; descuido m.
negligent adj negligente, descuidado/da; ~ly adv negligentemente.
negligible adj insignificante.
negotiate vt, vi negociar (con).
negotiation n negociación f; negocio m.
Negress n negra f.
Negro adj negro/gra; * n negro m.
neigh vi relinchar; * n relincho m.
neighbor n vecino/na m/f; * vt confinar.
neighborhood n vecindad f; vecindario m.
neighboring adj vecino/na.
neighborly adj sociable.
neither conj ni; * pn ninguno/na, ni uno ni otro, ni una ni otra.

neon n neón m.
neon light n luz de neón f.
nephew n sobrino m.
nepotism n nepotismo m.
nerve n nervio m; valor m.
nerve-racking adj espantoso/sa.
nervous adj nervioso/sa; nervudo/da.
nervous breakdown n crisis nerviosa f.
nest n nido m; nidada f.
nest egg n (fig) ahorros mpl.
nestle vt anidarse.
net n red f.
netball n nétbol m.
net curtain n visillo m.
netting n mallado m.
nettle n ortiga f.
network n red f, malla f.
neuron n neurona f.
neurosis n neurosis f invar.
neurotic adj, n neurótico/ca m/f.
neuter adj (gr) neutro/tra.
neutral adj neutral.
neutrality n neutralidad f.
neutralize vt neutralizar.
neutron n neutrón m.
neutron bomb n bomba de neutrones f.
never adv nunca, jamás; ~ **mind** no importa.
never-ending adj sin fin.
nevertheless adv no obstante.
new adj nuevo/va, fresco/sca, reciénte; ~**ly** adv nuevamente.
newborn adj recién nacido/da.
newcomer n recién llegado/da m.
new-fangled adj inventado/da por novedad.
news npl novedad, noticias fpl.
news agency n agencia de noticias f.
newscaster n presentador/a m/f.
newsdealer n vendedor/a de periódicos m/f.
news flash n noticia de última hora f.
newsletter n boletín n.
newspaper n periódico m.
newsreel n noticiario m.
New Year n Año Nuevo m; ~**'s Day** Día de Año Nuevo m; ~**'s Eve** Nochevieja f.
next adj próximo/ma; **the ~ day** el día siguiente; * adv luego, inmediatamente después.
nib n pico m; punta f.
nibble vt picar, mordiscar.
nice adj simpático/ca; agradable; lindo/da; ~**ly** adv bien.
nice-looking adj guapo/pa.
niche n nicho m.
nick n mella f; * vt (col) robar.
nickel n níquel m; moneda de cinco centavos f.
nickname n mote, apodo m; * vt poner apodos.
nicotine n nicotina f.
niece n sobrina f.
niggling adj insignificante.

night n noche f; velador m; **by** ~ de noche; **good** ~ buenas noches.
nightclub n cabaret m.
nightfall n anochecer m.
nightingale n ruiseñor m.
nightly adv por las noches, todas las noches; * adj nocturno/na.
nightmare n pesadilla f.
night school n clases nocturnas fpl.
night shift n turno de noche m.
night-time n noche f.
night work n vela f.
nihilist n nihilista m/f.
nimble adj ligero/ra, activo/va, listo/ta, ágil.
nine adj, n nueve.
ninepin n bolo m.
nineteen adj, n diecinueve.
nineteenth adj, n decimonoveno/na.
ninetieth adj, n nonagésimo/ma.
ninety adj, n noventa.
ninth adj, n nono/na, noveno/na.
nip vt pellizcar; morder.
nipple n pezón m; tetilla f.
nit n liendre f.
nitrogen n nitrógeno m.
no adv no; * adj ningún, ninguno/na.
nobility n nobleza f.
noble adj noble; insigne; * n noble m/f.
nobleman n noble m.
nobody n nadie, ninguna persona f.
nocturnal adj nocturnal, nocturno/na.
nod n cabeceo m; señal f; * vi cabecear; amodorrarse.
noise n ruido, estruendo m; rumor m.
noisily adv con ruido.
noisiness n ruido, tumulto, alboroto m.
noisy adj ruidoso/sa, turbulento/ta.
nominal adj, ~**ly** adv nominal(mente).
nominate vt nombrar.
nomination n nominación f.
nominative n (gr) nominativo m.
nominee n candidato/ta m/f.
nonalcoholic adj no alcóholico/ca.
nonaligned adj no alineado/da.
nonchalant adj indiferente.
noncommittal adj reservado/da.
nonconformist n inconformista m/f.
nondescript adj no descrito/ta.
none adj nadie, ninguno/na.
nonentity n nulidad f.
nonetheless adv sin embargo.
nonexistent adj inexistente.
nonfiction n no ficción f.
nonplussed adj confuso/sa.
nonsense n disparate, absurdo m, Lat Am sonsera f.
nonsensical adj absurdo/da.
nonsmoker n no fumador/a m/f.

N

nonstick *adj* antiadherente.
nonstop *adj* directo/ta; * *adv* sin parar.
noodles *npl* fideos (chinos) *mpl*.
noon *n* mediodía *m*.
noose *n* nudo corredizo *m*.
nor *conj* ni.
normal *adj* normal.
north *n* norte *m*; * *adj* del norte.
North America *n* América del Norte, Norteamérica *f*.
northeast *n* nor(d)este *m*.
northerly, northern *adj* norteño/ña.
North Pole *n* polo norte *m*.
northward(s) *adv* hacia el norte.
northwest *n* nor(d)oeste *m*.
nose *n* nariz *f*; olfato *m*.
nosebleed *n* hemorragia nasal *f*.
nosedive *n* picado vertical *m*.
nostalgia *n* nostalgia *f*.
nostril *n* ventana de la nariz *f*.
not *adv* no.
notable *adj* notable; memorable.
notably *adv* especialmente.
notary *n* notario/ria *m/f*.
notch *n* muesca *f*; * *vt* hacer muescas.
note *n* nota, marca *f*; señal *f*; aprecio *m*; billete *m*; consecuen cia *f*; noticia *f*; indirecta *f*; * *vt* notar, marcar; observar.
notebook *n* cuaderno *m*, libreta *f*.
noted *adj* afamado/da, celebre.
notepad *n* bloc *m*.
notepaper *n* papel de cartas *m*.
nothing *n* nada *f*; **good for** ~ lo que sirve para nada.
notice *n* noticia *f*; aviso *m*; * *vt* observar.
noticeable *adj* notable, reparable.
notification *n* notificación *f*.
notify *vt* notificar.
notion *n* noción *f*; opinión *f*; idea *f*.
notoriety *n* mala fama *f*.
notorious *adj* tristemente célebre; ~**ly** *adv* notoriamente.
notwithstanding *conj* no obstante, aunque.
nougat *n* turrón *m*.
noun *n* (*gr*) sustantivo *m*.
nourish *vt* nutrir, alimentar.
nourishing *adj* nutritivo/va.

nourishment *n* nutrimiento, alimento *m*.
novel *n* novela *f*.
novelist *n* novelista *m/f*.
novelty *n* novedad *f*.
November *n* noviembre *m*.
novice *n* novicio/cia *m/f*.
now *adv* ya, ahora, hoy (en) día; ~ **and then** de vez en cuando.
nowadays *adv* hoy (en) día.
nowhere *adv* en ninguna parte.
noxious *adj* nocivo/va, dañoso/sa.
nozzle *n* boquilla *f*.
nuance *n* matiz *m*.
nuclear *adj* nuclear; ~ **power** energía nuclear *f*; ~ **power station** *n* central nuclear *f*.
nucleus *n* núcleo *m*.
nude *adj* desnudo/da, en carnes, en cueros, sin vestido.
nudge *vt* dar un codazo a.
nudist *n* nudista *m/f*.
nudity *n* desnudez *f*.
nuisance *n* daño, perjuicio *m*; incomodidad *f*.
nuke *n* (*col*) bomba atómica *f*; * *vt* atacar con arma nuclear.
null *adj* nulo/la, inválido/da.
nullify *vt* anular, invalidar.
numb *adj* entorpecido/da; * *vt* entorpecer.
number *n* número *m*; cantidad *f*; * *vt* numerar.
numbness *n* entumecimiento *m*.
numeral *n* número *m*.
numerical *adj* numérico/ca.
numerous *adj* numeroso/sa.
nun *n* monja, religiosa *f*.
nunnery *n* convento de monjas *m*.
nuptial *adj* nupcial; ~**s** *npl* nupcias *fpl*.
nurse *n* enfermera *f*; * *vt* cuidar; amamantar.
nursery *n* guardería infantil *f*; criadero *m*.
nursery rhyme *n* canción infantil *f*.
nursing home *n* clinica de reposo *f*.
nurture *vt* criar, educar.
nut *n* nuez *f*.
nutcrackers *npl* cascanueces *m invar*.
nutmeg *n* nuez moscada *f*.
nutritious *adj* nutritivo/va.
nutshell *n* cascara de nuez *f*.
nylon *n* nylon, nailon *m*; * *adj* de nylon, de nailon.

O

oak n roble m.

oar n remo m.

oasis n oasis f invar.

oath n juramento m.

oatmeal n harina de avena f.

oats npl avena f.

obedience n obediencia f.

obedient adj, ~ly adv obediente(mente).

obese adj obeso/sa, gordo/da.

obesity n obesidad f.

obey vt obedecer.

obituary n necrología f.

object n objeto m; * vt objetar.

objection n oposición, objeción, réplica f.

objectionable adj desagradable.

objective adj objetivo/va; * n objetivo m.

obligation n obligación f.

obligatory adj obligatorio/ria.

oblige vt obligar; complacer, favorecer.

obliging adj servicial.

oblique adj oblicuo/cua; indirecto/ta; ~ly adv oblicuamente.

obliterate vt borrar.

oblivion n olvido m.

oblivious adj olvidadizo/za.

oblong adj oblongo/ga.

obnoxious adj odioso/sa.

oboe n oboe m.

obscene adj obsceno/na, impudico/ca.

obscenity n obscenidad f.

obscure adj oscuro/ra; ~ly adv oscuramente; * vt oscurecer.

obscurity n oscuridad f.

observance n observancia f; reverencia f.

observant adj observante, respetuoso/sa.

observantly adv cuidadosamente, atentamente.

observation n observación f.

observatory n observatorio m.

observe vt observar, mirar.

observer n observador/a m/f.

obsess vt obsesionar.

obsessive adj obsesivo/va.

obsolete adj obsoleto/ta.

obstacle n obstáculo m.

obstinacy n tenacidad f.

obstinate adj obstinado/da; ~ly adv obstinadamente.

obstruct vt obstruir; impedir.

obstruction n obstrucción f; impedimento m.

obtain vt obtener, adquirir; ~ by cunning sonsacar.

obtainable adj asequible.

obtrusive adj intruso/sa, importuno/na.

obtuse adj obtuso/sa, sin punta; lerdo/da, torpe.

obvious adj obvio/via, evidente; ~ly adv naturalmente.

occasion n ocasión f; momento oportuno m; * vt ocasionar, causar.

occasional adj ocasional, casual; ~ly adv ocasionalmente.

occupant, occupier n ocupante m/f; poseedor/a m/f; inquilino/na m/f.

occupation n ocupación f; empleo m.

occupy vt ocupar, emplear.

occur vi pasar, ocurrir.

occurrence n incidente m.

ocean n océano m; alta mar f.

ocean-going adj de alta mar.

oceanic adj oceánico/ca.

ocher n ocre m.

octave n octava f.

October n octubre m.

octopus n pulpo m.

odd adj impar; particular; extravagante; extraño/ña; ~ly adv extrañamente.

oddity n singularidad, particularidad, rareza f.

oddness n desigualdad f; singularidad f.

odds npl probabilidades fpl; apuestas fpl.

odious adj odioso/sa.

odometer n cuentakilómetros m invar.

odor n olor m; fragancia f.

odorous, odoriferous adj odorífero/ra.

of prep de; tocante; segun.

of course! interj inaturalmente!

off adv desconectado/da; apagado/da; cerrado/da; cancelado/da; ~! excl ifuera!

offend vt ofender, irritar; injuriar; * vi pecar.

offender n delincuente m.

offense n ofensa f; injuria f.

offensive adj ofensivo/va; injurioso/sa; ~ly adv ofensivamente.

offer vt ofrecer; * n oferta f.

offering n sacrificio m; oferta f.

offhand adj descortés; * adv de repente.

office n oficina f; oficio, empleo m; servicio m.

office building n bloque de oficinas m.

office hours npl horas de oficina fpl.

officer n oficial/a, empleado/da m/f.

office worker n oficinista m/f.

official adj oficial; ~ly adv de oficio; * n empleado m.

officiate vi oficiar.

officious adj oficioso/sa; ~ly adv oficiosamente.

off-line adj, adv fuera de línea.

off-peak adj de temporada baja.
off-season adj, adv fuera de temporada, en tarifa reducida.
offset vt contrarrestar.
offshoot n ramificación f.
offshore adj costero/ra.
offside adj fuera de juego.
offspring n prole f; linaje m; descendencia f.
offstage adv entre bastidores.
off-the-peg adj confeccionado/da.
ogle vt comerse con los ojos.
oil n aceite m; óleo m; * vt engrasar.
oilcan n lata de aceite f.
oilfield n campo petrolífero m.
oil filter n filtro de aceite m.
oil painting n pintura al óleo f.
oil rig n torre de perforación f.
oil slick n marea negra f.
oil tanker n petrolero m.
oil well n pozo petrolífero m.
oily adj aceitoso/sa; grasiento/ta.
ointment n ungüento m.
OK, okay excl vale, Lat Am okey; * adj bien; * vt dar el visto bueno a.
old adj viejo/ja; antiguo/gua.
old age n vejez f.
old-fashioned adj pasado/da de moda.
olive n olivo m; oliva f.
olive oil n aceite de oliva m.
Olympic Games npl las Olímpicos fpl.
omelet n tortilla (francesa) f, Lat Am omelet f.
omen n agüero, presagio m.
ominous adj ominoso/sa.
omission n omisión f; descuido m.
omit vt omitir.
omnipotence n omnipotencia f.
omnipotent adj omnipotente, todopoderoso/sa.
on prep sobre, encima, en; de; a; * adj encendido/da; prendido/da; abierto/ta; puesto/ta.
once adv una vez; **at ~** en seguida; **all at ~** de una vez, en seguida; **~ more** otra vez.
oncoming adj que viene de frente.
one adj un, uno, una; **~ by ~** uno a uno, una a una, uno por uno, una por una.
one-day excursion n billete de ida y vuelta en un día m.
one-man adj individual.
onerous adj oneroso/sa, molesto/ta.
oneself pn sí mismo; sí misma.
one-sided adj parcial.
one-to-one adj de uno a uno; cara a cara.
ongoing adj continuo/nua.
onion n cebolla f.
on line adj, adv en línea.
onlooker n espectador/a m/f.
only adj único/ca, solo/la; * adv solamente.
onset, onslaught n acometida f; ataque m.
onus n responsabilidad f.

onward(s) adv adelante.
ooze vi manar suavemente, rezumar.
opaque adj opaco/ca.
open adj abierto/ta; patente, evidente; sincero/ra, franco/ca; **~ly** adv con franqueza; * vt (vi) abrir(se); descubrir(se); **to ~ on to** dar a; **to ~ up** vt abrir; vi abrirse.
opening n abertura f; (com) salida f; principio m.
open-minded adj de mentalidad abierta.
openness n claridad f; franqueza, sinceridad f.
opera n ópera f.
opera house n teatro de la ópera m.
operate vi obrar, operar.
operating theater n quirófano m.
operation n operación f; efecto m.
operational adj operacional.
operative adj operativo/va.
operator n operario/ria m/f; operador/a m/f.
ophthalmic adj oftálmico/ca.
opine vi opinar, juzgar.
opinion n opinión f; juicio m.
opinionated adj testarudo/da.
opinion poll n sondeo m.
opponent n antagonista m/f; adversario/ria m/f.
opportune adj oportuno/na.
opportunist n oportunista m/f.
opportunity n oportunidad f.
oppose vt oponerse.
opposing adj opuesto/ta.
opposite adj opuesto/ta; contrario/ria; * adv enfrente; prep frente a; * n lo contrario.
opposition n oposición f; resistencia f; impedimento m.
oppress vt oprimir.
oppression n opresión f.
oppressive adj opresivo/va, cruel.
oppressor n opresor/a m/f.
optic(al) adj óptico/ca; **~s** npl óptica f.
optician n óptico/ca m/f.
optimist n optimista m/f.
optimistic adj optimista.
optimum adj óptimo/ma.
option n opción f; deseo m.
optional adj facultativo/va.
opulent adj opulento/ta.
or conj o; u.
oracle n oráculo m.
oral adj oral, vocal; **~ly** adv verbalmente, de palabra.
orange n naranja f.
orator n orador/a m/f.
orbit n órbita f.
orchard n huerto m.
orchestra n orquesta f.
orchestral adj orquestal.
orchid n orquídea f.
ordain vt ordenar; establecer.
ordeal n prueba rigurosa f.

order n orden m/f; regla f; mandato m; serie, clase f; * vt ordenar, arreglar; mandar.
order form n hoja de pedido f.
orderly adj ordenado/da, regular.
ordinarily adv ordinariamente.
ordinary adj ordinario/ria.
ordination n ordenación f.
ordnance n armamento m; pertrechos mpl.
ore n mineral m.
organ n órgano m.
organic adj orgánico/ca.
organic farming n agricultura biológica f.
organism n organismo m.
organist n organista m/f.
organization n organización f.
organize vt organizar.
orgasm n orgasmo m.
orgy n orgía f.
oriental adj oriental.
orifice n orificio m.
origin n origen, principio m.
original adj original, primitivo/va; ~ly adv originalmente.
originality n originalidad f.
originate vi originar.
ornament n ornamento m; * vt ornamentar, adornar.
ornamental adj ornamental, decorativo/va.
ornate adj adornado/da, ataviado/da.
ornithology n ornitología f.
orphan adj, n huérfano/na m/f.
orphanage n orfanato m.
orthodox adj ortodoxo/xa.
orthodoxy n ortodoxia f.
orthography n ortografía f.
orthopedic adj ortopédico/ca.
Oscar n óscar m.
oscillate vi oscilar, vibrar.
osprey n águila pescadora f.
ostensibly adv aparentemente.
ostentatious adj ostentoso/sa.
osteopath n osteópata m/f.
ostracize vt condenar al ostracismo.
ostrich n avestruz m.
other pn otro, otra.
otherwise adv de otra manera, por otra parte.
otter n nutria f.
ouch excl ¡ay!
ought v aux deber, ser menester.
ounce n onza f.
our, ours pn nuestro, nuestra, nuestros, nuestras.
ourselves pn pl nosotros mismos, nosotras mismas.
oust vt quitar; desposeer.
out adv fuera, afuera; apagado/da.
outboard adj: ~ **motor** fueraborda m.
outbreak n erupción f.
outburst n explosión f.

outcast n paria m/f.
outcome n resultado m.
outcry n clamor m; griterío m.
outdated adj fuera de moda.
outdo vt exceder a otro, sobrepujar.
outdoor adj, ~s adv al aire libre.
outer adj exterior.
outermost adj extremo/ma; lo más exterior.
outer space n espacio exterior m.
outfit n vestidos mpl; ropa f.
outfitter n sastre m.
outgoing adj extrovertido/da.
outgrow vt sobrecrecer.
outhouse n dependencia (de una casa) f.
outing n excursión f.
outlandish adj estrafalario/ria.
outlaw n bandido m; * vt proscribir.
outlay n despensa f, gastos mpl.
outlet n salida f.
outline n contorno m; bosquejo m.
outlive vt sobrevivir.
outlook n perspectiva f.
outlying adj distante, lejos.
outmoded adj anticuado/da.
outnumber vt superar en número.
out-of-date adj caducado/da; pasado/da de moda.
outpatient n paciente externo/na m/f.
outpost n puesto avanzado m.
output n rendimiento m; salida f.
outrage n ultraje m; * vt ultrajar.
outrageous adj escandaloso/sa; atroz; ~ly adv escandalosamente; injuriosamente; enormemente.
outright adv absolutamente; * adj completo/ta.
outrun vt correr más que.
outset n principio m.
outshine vt exceder en brillantez, eclipsar.
outside n superficie f; exterior m; apariencia f; * adv fuera, Lat Am afuera de; * prep fuera de.
outsider n forástero m/f.
outsize adj de talla grande.
outskirts npl alrededores mpl.
outspoken adj muy franco/ca.
outstanding adj excepcional; pendiente.
outstretch vt extenderse, alargar.
outstrip vt dejar atrás; superar.
out-tray n bandeja de salida f.
outward adj exterior, externo/na; de ida; ~ly adv por fuera; exteriormente.
outweigh vt pesar más que.
outwit vt burlar.
oval n óvalo m; * adj oval.
ovary n ovario m.
oven n horno m.
ovenproof adj resistente al horno.
over prep sobre, encima; más de; durante; **all ~** por todos lados; * adj terminado/da; de sobra; **~ again** otra vez; **~ and ~** repetidas veces.
overall adj total; * adv en conjunto.

O

overalls *npl* mono *m*; *Lat Am* overol *m*.
overawe *vt* imponer respeto.
overbalance *vi* perder el equilibrio.
overbearing *adj* despótico/ca.
overboard *adv* (*mar*) por la borda, al mar.
overbook *vt* sobrereservar.
overcast *adj* encapotado/da.
overcharge *vt* sobrecargar; cobrar de más.
overcoat *n* abrigo *m*.
overcome *vt* vencer; superar.
overconfident *adj* demasiado confiado/da.
overcrowded *adj* atestado/da; superpoblado/da.
overdo *vi* hacer más de lo necesario; exagerar.
overdose *n* sobredosis *f invar*.
overdraft *n* saldo deudor, descubierto *m*.
overdrawn *adj* en descubierto.
overdress *vt* engalanar con exceso.
overdue *adj* retrasado/da.
overeat *vi* comer demasiado.
overestimate *vt* sobreestimar.
overflow *vt*, *vi* inundar; rebosar; * *n* inundación *f*; superabundancia *f*.
overgrown *adj* invadido/da.
overgrowth *n* vegetación exuberante *f*.
overhang *vt* colgar sobre.
overhaul *vt* revisar; * *n* revisión *f*.
overhead *adv* sobre la cabeza, en lo alto.
overhear *vt* oír por casualidad.
overjoyed *adj* muy gozoso/sa.
overkill *n* exceso de medios *m*.
overland *adj*, *adv* por tierra.
overlap *vi* traslaparse.
overleaf *adv* al dorso.
overload *vt* sobrecargar.
overlook *vt* mirar desde lo alto; examinar; repasar; pasar por alto, tolerar; descuidar.
overnight *adv* durante la noche; * *adj* de noche.
overpass *n* paso superior *m*.
overpower *vt* predominar, oprimir.
overpowering *adj* agobiante.
overrate *vt* sobrevalorar.

override *vt* no hacer caso de; anular.
overriding *adj* predominante.
overrule *vt* denegar.
overrun *vt* inundar; infestar; rebasar.
overseas *adv* fuera del país; * *adj* extranjero/ra.
oversee *vt* inspeccionar.
overseer *n* superintendente *m*.
overshadow *vt* eclipsar.
overshoot *vt* excederse.
oversight *n* yerro *m*; equivocación *f*.
oversleep *vi* dormir demasiado.
overspill *n* exceso de población *m*.
overstate *vi* exagerar.
overstep *vt* traspasar, exceder.
overt *adj* abierto/ta; publico/ca; ~**ly** *adv* abiertamente.
overtake *vt* adelantar, sobrepasar.
overthrow *vt* trastornar; demoler; destruir; * *n* trastorno *m*; ruina, derrota *f*.
overtime *n* horas extra *fpl*.
overtone *n* trasfondo *m*.
overture *n* abertura *f*; (*mus*) obertura *f*.
overturn *vt* subvertir, trastornar.
overweight *adj* demasiado pesado/da.
overwhelm *vt* abrumar; oprimir; sumergir.
overwhelming *adj* arrollador/a; irresistible.
overwork *vi* trabajar demasiado.
owe *vt* deber, tener deudas; estar obligado/da.
owing *adj* que es debido/da; ~ **to** por causa de.
owl *n* búho *m*.
own *adj* propio/pia; **my** ~ mío, mía; * *vt* tener; poseer; **to** ~ **up** *vi* confesar.
owner *n* dueño/ña, propietario/ria *m/f*.
ownership *n* posesión *f*.
ox *n* buey *m*; ~**en** *pl* ganado vacuno *m*.
oxidize *vt* oxidar.
oxygen *n* oxígeno *m*.
oxygen mask *n* máscara de oxígeno *f*.
oxygen tent *n* tienda de oxígeno *f*.
oyster *n* ostra *f*.
ozone *n* ozono *m*.

P

pa n papá m.

pace n paso m; * vt regular el ritmo de; * vi pasear.

pacemaker n marcapasos m invar.

pacific adj pacífico/ca; **P~ Ocean** el Pacífico m.

pacification n pacificación f.

pacifier n chupete m.

pacify vt pacificar.

pack n lío, fardo m; baraja (de naipes) f; cuadrilla f; * vt empaquetar; hacer la maleta; llenar.

package n paquete m; acuerdo m.

package tour n viaje organizado m.

packet n paquete m.

packing n embalaje m.

pact n pacto m.

pad n bloc m; plataforma f; (col) casa f; * vt rellenar.

padding n relleno m; paja f.

paddle vivadear; remar; chapotear; * n canalete m.

paddle steamer n vapor de ruedas m.

paddling pool n piscina para niños f.

paddock n corral m.

paddy field n arrozal m.

pagan adj, n pagano/na m/f.

page n página f; paje m.

pageant n espectáculo público m.

pageantry n pompa f.

pail n cubo, pozal m.

pain n pena f; castigo m; dolor m; * vt afligir.

pained adj afligido/da.

painful adj dolorido/da; penoso/sa; ~ly adv dolorosamente, con pena.

painkiller n analgésico m.

painless adj sin pena; indoloro/ra.

painstaking adj laborioso/sa, meticuloso/sa.

paint vt pintar.

paintbrush n pincel m; brocha f.

painter n pintor m/f.

painting n pintura f.

paintwork n pintura f.

pair n par m; yuntas fpl.

pajamas npl pijama m.

pal n compañero/ra m/f.

palatable adj sabroso/sa.

palate n paladar m; gusto m.

palatial adj palatino/na.

palaver n lío m.

pale adj palido/da; claro/ra.

palette n paleta f.

paling n estacada, palizada f.

pall n cortina de humo f; * vi perder el sabor.

palliative adj paliativo/va; * n paliativo m.

pallid adj pálido/da.

pallor n palidez f.

palm n (bot) palma f.

palmistry n quiromancia f.

Palm Sunday n Domingo de Ramos m.

palpable adj palpable; evidente.

palpitation n palpitación f.

paltry adj irrisorio/ria; mezquino/na.

pamper vt mimar.

pamphlet n folleto m.

pan n cazuela f; sartén f; olla f.

panacea n panacea f.

panache n estilo m.

pancake n crepe f, Lat Am panqueque m.

pandemonium n jaleo m.

pane n cristal m.

panel n panel m; paño m.

paneling n paneles mpl.

pang n angustia, congoja f.

panic adj, n pánico/ca m.

panicky adj asustadizo/za.

panic-stricken adj preso/sa del pánico.

pansy n (bot) pensamiento m.

pant vi jadear.

panther n pantera f.

pantihose npl medias fpl.

pants npl bragas fpl.

pantry n despensa f.

papacy n papado m.

papal adj papal.

papaw, pawpaw, papaya n papaya f.

paper n papel m; periódico m; examen m; estudio m; ~s pl escrituras fpl; (com) fondos mpl; * adj de papel; * vt empape lar; tapizar.

paperback n libro en rústica m.

paper bag n bolsa de papel f.

paperclip n clip m.

paperweight n sujetapapeles m invar.

paperwork n papeleo m.

paprika n pimentón m, paprika f.

par n equivalencia f; igualdad f; par m; **at ~** (com) a la par.

parable n parábola f.

parachute n paracaídas m invar; * vi lanzarse en paracaídas.

parade n ostentación, pompa f; (mil) parada f; * vt, vi desfilar; pasear; hacer gala.

paradise n paraíso m.

paradox n paradoja f.

paradoxical adj paradójico/ca.

paragliding n parapente m.

paragon n dechado m.

paragraph n párrafo m, Lat Am acápite m.
parallel adj paralelo/la; * n línea paralela f; * vt paralelizar; parangonar.
paralyze vt paralizar.
paralysis n parálisis f.
paralytic adj paralítico/ca.
paramedic n auxiliar sanitario/ria m/f.
paramount adj supremo/ma, superior.
paranoid adj paranoico/ca.
paraphernalia n parafernalia f.
parasite n parásito m.
parasol n parasol, quitasol m.
paratrooper n paracaidista m.
parcel n paquete m; porción, cantidad f; equipajes, bultos mpl; * vt empaquetar, embalar.
parch vt resecar.
parched adj reseco/ca; muerto/ta de sed.
parchment n pergamino m.
pardon n perdón m; * vt perdonar.
parent n padre m; madre f.
parentage n parentela f; extracción f.
parental adj de los padres.
parenthesis n paréntesis m invar.
parish n parroquia f; * adj parroquial.
parishioner n parroquiano/na m/f.
parity n paridad f.
park n parque m; * vt, vi aparcar, estacionar.
parking n aparcamiento, estacionamiento m.
parking lot n aparcamiento, estacionamiento m.
parking meter n parquímetro m.
parking ticket n multa de estacionamiento f.
parlance n lenguaje m.
parliament n parlamento m.
parliamentary adj parlamentario/ria.
parlor n salón m.
parody n parodia f; * vt parodiar.
parole n: on ~ en libertad bajo palabra.
parricide n parricidio m; parricida m/f.
parrot n papagayo m.
parry vt parar.
parsley n (bot) perejil m.
parsnip n (bot) chirivía f.
part n parte f; partido m; oficio m; papel (de un actor) m; obligación f; raya f; ~s pl partes fpl; paraje, distrito m; * vt partir, separar, desunir; * vi partirse, separarse; to ~ with entregar; pagar; deshacerse de; ~ly adv en parte.
partial adj, ~ly adv parcial(mente).
participant n concursante m.
participate vi participar (en).
participation n participación f.
participle n (gr) participio m.
particle n partícula f.
particular adj particular, singular; ~ly adv particularmente; * n particular m; particularidad f.
parting n separación, partida f; raya (en los cabellos) f.

partisan n partidario/ria m/f.
partition n partición, separación f; * vt partir, dividir en varias partes.
partner n socio/cia, compañero/ra m/f.
partnership n compañía, sociedad de comercio f.
partridge n perdiz f.
party n partido m; fiesta f.
pass vt pasar; traspasar; transferir; adelantarse a; * vi pasar, aprobar; * n permiso m; puerto m; to ~ away vi fallecer; to ~ by vi pasar; vt pasar por alto; to ~ on vt transmitir.
passable adj pasadero/ra, transitable.
passage n pasaje m; travesía f; pasadizo m.
passbook n libreta de depósitos f.
passenger n pasajero/ra m/f.
passer-by n transeúnte m/f.
passing adj pasajero/ra.
passion n pasión f; amor m; celo, ardor m.
passionate adj apasionado/da; ~ly adv apasionadamente; ardientemente.
passive adj pasivo/va; ~ly adv pasivamente.
passkey n llava maestra f.
Passover n Pascua f.
passport n pasaporte m.
passport control n control de pasaportes m.
password n contraseña f.
past adj pasado/da; gastado/da; * n (gr) pretérito m; el pasado; * prep más allá de; después de.
pasta n pasta f.
paste n pasta f; engrudo m; * vt engrudar.
pasteurized adj pasteurizado/da.
pastime n pasatiempo m; diversión f.
pastor n pastor m.
pastoral adj pastoril; pastoral.
pastry n pastelería f.
pasture n pasto m, Lat Am potrero m.
pasty adj pastoso/sa; pálido/da.
pat vt dar golpecillos.
patch n remiendo m; parche m; terreno m; * vt remendar; to ~ up reparar; hacer las paces en.
patchwork n obra de retacitos f; chapucería f.
pâté n paté m.
patent adj patente; privilegiado/da; * n patente f; * vt privilegiar.
patentee n poseedor/a de una patente m/f.
patent leather n charol m.
paternal adj paternal.
paternity n paternidad f.
path n senda f.
pathetic adj patético/ca; ~ally adv patéticamente.
pathological adj patológico/ca.
pathology n patología f.
pathos n patetismo m.
pathway n sendero m.
patience n paciencia f.
patient adj paciente, sufrido/da, Lat Am aguantador/ra; ~ly adv con paciencia; * n enfermo/ma m/f.

patio *n* patio *m*.
patriarch *n* patriarca *m*.
patriot *n* patriota *m*.
patriotic *adj* patriotico/ca.
patriotism *n* patriotismo *m*.
patrol *n* patrulla *f*; * *vi* patrullar.
patrol car *n* coche patrulla *m*.
patrolman *n* policía *m*.
patron *n* patrón/ona, protector *m/f*.
patronage *n* patrocinio *m*; patronato, patronazgo *m*.
patronize *vt* patrocinar, proteger.
patter *n* golpeteo *m*; labia *f*; * *vi* tamborilear.
pattern *n* patrón *m*; dibujo *m*; *Lat Am* molde *m*.
paunch *n* panza *f*; vientre *m*.
pauper *n* pobre *m/f*.
pause *n* pausa *f*; * *vt* pausar; deliberar.
pave *vt* empedrar; enlosar, embaldosar.
pavilion *n* pabellón *m*.
paving stone *n* ladrillo *m*; losa *f*.
paw *n* pata *f*; garra *f*; * *vt* manosear.
pawn *n* peón *m*; * *vt* empeñar.
pawnbroker *n* prestamista *m/f*.
pawnshop *n* casa de empeños *f*.
pay *vt* pagar; sufrir por; **to ~ back** *vt* reembolsar; **to ~ for** pagar; **to ~ off** *vt* liquidar; *vi* dar resultados; * *n* paga *f*; salario *m*.
payable *adj* pagadero/ra.
payday *n* día de paga *m*.
payee *n* portador/a *m/f*.
pay envelope *n* sobre (de paga) *m*.
paymaster *n* pagador/a *m/f*.
payment *n* paga *f*; pagamento, pago *m*.
payphone *n* teléfono público *m*.
payroll *n* nómina *f*.
pea *n* guisante *m*, *Lat Am* chícharro *m*.
peace *n* paz *f*.
peaceful *adj* tranquilo/la, pacífico/ca.
peach *n* melocotón *m*, *Lat Am* durazno *m*.
peacock *n* pavón, pavo real *m*.
peak *n* cima *f*.
peak hours, peak period *n* horas punta *fpl*.
peal *n* campaneo *m*; estruendo *m*.
peanut *n* cacahuete *m*; maní *m*.
pear *n* pera *f*.
pearl *n* perla *f*.
peasant *n* campesino/na *m/f*.
peat *n* turba *f*.
pebble *n* guija *f*; guijarro *m*.
peck *n* picotazo *m*; * *vt* picotear; picar.
pecking order *n* orden de jerarquía *m*.
peculiar *adj* peculiar, particular, singular; **~ly** *adv* peculiarmente.
peculiarity *n* particularidad, singularidad *f*.
pedal *n* pedal *m*; * *vi* pedalear.
pedant *n* pedante *m/f*.
pedantic *adj* pedante.
pedestal *n* pedestal *m*.
pedestrian *n* peatón/ona *m/f*; * *adj* pedestre.

pedigree *n* genealogía *f*; * *adj* de raza.
peddler *n* vendedor/a ambulante *m/f*.
peek *vi* mirar de soslayo.
peel *vt* pelar; * *vi* desconcharse; * *n* piel *f*; cáscara *f*.
peer *n* compañero/ra *m/f*; par *m*.
peerless *adj* incomparable.
peeved *adj* enojado/da.
peevish *adj* regañón/ona, bronco/ca; enojadizo/za.
peg *n* clavija *f*; gancho *m*; * *vt* clavar.
pelican *n* pelícano *m*.
pellet *n* bolita *f*; **~s** perdigones *mpl*.
pelt *n* pellejo, cuero *m*; * *vt* arrojar; * *vi* llover a cántaros.
pen *n* bolígrafo *m*; pluma *f*; redil *m*.
penal *adj* penal.
penalty *n* pena *f*; castigo *m*; multa *f*.
penance *n* penitencia *f*.
pence *n pl* de **penny**.
pencil *n* lápiz *m*; lapicero *m*.
pencil case *n* estuche *m*.
pendant *n* pendiente *m*.
pending *adj* pendiente.
pendulum *n* péndulo *m*.
penetrate *vt* penetrar.
penguin *n* pingüino *m*.
penicillin *n* penicilina *f*.
peninsula *n* península *f*.
penis *n* pene *m*.
penitence *n* penitencia *f*.
penitent *adj*, *n* penitente *m*.
penitentiary *n* penitenciaría *f*.
penknife *n* navaja *f*.
pennant *n* banderola *f*.
penniless *adj* sin dinero.
penny *n* penique *m*.
penpal *n* amigo/ga por carta *m/f*.
pension *n* pensión *f*; * *vt* dar pensión a.
pensive *adj* pensativo/va; **~ly** *adv* pensativamente.
pentagon *n*: **the P~** el Pentágono.
Pentecost *n* Pentecostés *m*.
penthouse *n* ático *m*.
pent-up *adj* reprimido/da.
penultimate *adj* penúltimo/ma.
penury *n* penuria, carestia *f*.
people *n* pueblo *m*; nación *f*; gente *f*; * *vt* poblar.
people mover *n* monovolumen *m*.
pep *n* energía *f*; **to ~ up** *vt* animar.
pepper *n* pimienta *f*; * *vt* sazonar con pimienta.
peppermint *n* menta *f*.
per *prep* por.
per annum *adv* al año.
per capita *adj*, *adv* per cápita.
perceive *vt* percibir, comprender.
percentage *n* porcentaje *m*.
perception *n* percepción, idea, noción *f*.
perch *n* percha *f*.
perchance *adv* acaso, quizá.
percolate *vt* colar; filtrar.

P

percolator *n* cafetera de filtro *f*.
percussion *n* percusión *f*; golpe *m*.
perdition *n* pérdida, ruina *f*.
peremptory *adj* perentorio/ria; decisivo/va.
perennial *adj* perenne; perpetuo/tua.
perfect *adj* perfecto/ta, acabado/da; puro/ra; ~ly *adv* perfectamente; * *vt* perfeccionar, acabar.
perfection *n* perfección *f*.
perforate *vt* horadar.
perforated *adj* (of stamps) dentado/da.
perforation *n* perforación *f*.
perform *vt* ejecutar; efectuar; * *vi* representar, hacer papel.
performance *n* ejecución *f*; cumplimiento *m*, *Lat Am* performance *m*; obra *f*; representación teatral, función *f*.
performer *n* ejecutor/a *m/f*; actor *m*, actriz *f*.
perfume *n* perfume *m*; fragancia *f*; * *vt* perfumar.
perhaps *adv* quizá, quizás.
peril *n* peligro, riesgo *m*.
perilous *adj* peligroso/sa; ~ly *adv* peligrosamente.
perimeter *n* perímetro *m*.
period *n* período *m*; época *f*; regla *f*.
periodic *adj* periódico/ca; ~ally *adv* periódicamente.
periodical *n* periódico *m*.
peripheral *adj* periférico/ca; * *n* periférico *m*.
perish *vi* perecer.
perishable *adj* perecedero/ra.
perjure *vt* perjurar.
perjury *n* perjurio *m*.
perk *n* extra *m*.
perky *adj* animado/da.
perm *n* permanente *f*.
permanent *adj*, ~ly *adv* permanente(mente).
permeate *vt* penetrar, atravesar.
permissible *adj* lícito/ta, permiso.
permission *n* permiso *m*.
permissive *adj* permisivo/va.
permit *vt* permitir; * *n* permiso *m*.
permutation *n* permutación *f*.
perpendicular *adj*, ~ly *adv* perpendicular(mente); * *n* línea perpendicular *f*.
perpetrate *vt* perpetrar, cometer.
perpetual *adj* perpetuo/tua; ~ly *adv* perpetuamente.
perpetuate *vt* perpetuar, eternizar.
perplex *vt* confundir.
persecute *vt* perseguir, importunar.
persecution *n* persecución *f*.
perseverance *n* perseverancia *f*.
persevere *vi* perseverar.
persist *vi* persistir.
persistence *adj* persistencia *f*.
persistent *adj* persistente.
person *n* persona *f*.
personable *adj* atractivo/va.
personage *n* personaje *m*.
personal *adj*, ~ly *adv* personal(mente).
personal assistant *n* secretario/ria personal *m/f*.

personal column *n* anuncios personales *mpl*.
personal computer *n* ordenador personal *m*, computadora personal *f*.
personality *n* personalidad *f*.
personification *n* personificación *f*.
personify *vt* personificar.
personnel *n* personal *m*.
perspective *n* perspectiva *f*.
perspiration *n* transpiración *f*.
perspire *vi* transpirar.
persuade *vt* persuadir.
persuasion *n* persuasión *f*.
persuasive *adj* persuasivo/va; ~ly *adv* de modo persuasivo.
pert *adj* listo/va, vivo/va; petulante.
pertaining: ~ to *prep* relacionado/da con.
pertinent *adj* pertinente; ~ly *adv* oportunamente.
pertness *n* impertinencia *f*; vivacidad *f*.
perturb *vt* perturbar.
perusal *n* lectura, lección *f*.
peruse *vt* leer; examinar atentamente.
pervade *vt* atravesar, penetrar.
perverse *adj* perverso/sa, depravado/da; ~ly *adv* perversamente.
pervert *vt* pervertir, corromper.
pessimist *n* pesimista *m*.
pest *n* plaga *f*; molestia *f*.
pester *vt* molestar, cansar.
pestilence *n* pestilencia *f*.
pet *n* animal doméstico *m*; favorito/ta *m/f*; * *vt* mimar; * *vi* besuquearse.
petal *n* (bot) pétalo *m*.
petite *adj* chiquito/ta.
petition *n* presentación, petición *f*; * *vt* suplicar, *Lat Am* peticionar; requerir en justicia.
petrified *adj* horrorizado/da.
petroleum *n* petróleo *m*.
petticoat *n* enaguas *fpl*.
pettiness *n* mezquindad *f*; pequeñez *f*.
petty *adj* mezquino/na; insignificante.
petty cash *n* dinero para gastos menores *m*.
petty officer *n* contramaestre *m*.
petulant *adj* petulante.
pew *n* banco *m*.
pewter *n* peltre *m*.
phantom *n* fantasma *m*.
Pharisee *n* fariseo/sea *m/f*.
pharmaceutical *adj* farmacéutico/ca.
phase *n* fase *f*.
pheasant *n* faisán *m*.
phenomenal *adj* fenomenal.
phenomenon *n* fenómeno *m*.
phial *n* vial *m*.
philanthropic *adj* filantrópico/ca.
philanthropist *n* filántropo/pa *m/f*.
philanthropy *n* filantropía *f*.
philologist *n* filólogo/ga *m/f*.
philology *n* filología *f*.

philosopher n filósofo/fa m/f.
philosophic(al) adj filosófico/ca; **~ally** adv filosóficamente.
philosophize vi filosofar.
philosophy n filosofía f; **natural ~** filosofía natural f.
phlegm n flema f.
phlegmatic(al) adj flemático/ca.
phobia n fobia f.
phone n teléfono m; * vt telefonear; **to ~ back** vt, vi volver a llamar; **to ~ up** llamar por teléfono.
phone book n guía telefónica f.
phone box n cabina telefónica f, Lat Am monedero m.
phone call n llamada (telefonica) f.
phosphorus n fosforo m.
photocopier n fotocopiadora f.
photocopy n fotocopia f.
photograph n fotografía f; * vt fotografiar.
photographer n fotógrafo/fa m/f.
photographic adj fotográfico/ca.
photography n fotografía f.
phrase n frase f; estilo m; * vt expresar.
phrase book n libro de frases m.
physical adj físico/ca; **~ly** adv físicamente.
physical education n educación física f.
physician n médico/ca m/f.
physicist n físico/ca m/f.
physiological adj fisiológico/ca.
physiologist n fisiólogo/ga m/f.
physiology n fisiología f.
physiotherapy n fisioterapia f.
physique n físico m.
pianist n pianista m/f.
piano n piano m.
piccolo n flautín m.
pick vt escoger, elegir; recoger; mondar, limpiar; **to ~ on** vt meterse con; **to ~ out** vt escoger; **to ~ up** vi ir mejor; recobrarse; * vt recoger; comprar; aprender; * n pico m; **the ~ of** lo más escogido de.
pickax n pico m.
picket n piquete m.
pickle n escabeche m; *vt escabechar.
pickpocket n carterista m/f.
pick-up n (auto) furgoneta f.
picnic n picnic m.
pictorial adj pictórico/ca.
picture n pintura f; retrato m; * vt pintar; figurar.
picture book n libro de dibujos m.
picturesque adj pintoresco/ca.
pie n pastel m; tarta f; empanada f.
piece n pedazo m; pieza, obra f; * vt remendar.
piecemeal adv en pedazos; * adj dividido/da.
piecework n destajo m; * vi **to do ~** trabajar a destajo.
pier n pilar m; muelle m.

pierce vt penetrar, agujerear, taladrar.
piercing adj penetrante.
piety n piedad, devoción f.
pig n cerdo m, Lat Am chancho m; (col) cochino m.
pigeon n paloma f; **carrier/homing ~** paloma mensajera f.
pigeonhole n casillero m.
piggy bank n hucha f.
pig-headed adj terco/ca.
pigpen n pocilga f.
pigtail n trenza f.
pike n lucio m; pica f.
pile n estaca f; pila f; montón m; pelo m; pelillo m; **~s** pl almorranas fpl; * vt amontonar, apilar.
pile-up n colisión múltiple f.
pilfer vt hurtar.
pilgrim n peregrino/na m/f.
pilgrimage n peregrinación f.
pill n píldora f.
pillage vt saquear.
pillar n pilar m.
pillion n asiento trasero m.
pillow n almohada f.
pillowcase n funda de almohada f.
pilot n piloto m/f; * vt pilotar; (fig) guiar.
pilot light n piloto m.
pimp n chulo, cafiche m.
pimple n grano m.
pin n alfiler m; **~s and needles** npl hormigueo m; * vt prender con alfileres; fijar con clavija.
pinafore n delantal m.
pinball n flíper m.
pincers n pinzas, tenazuelas fpl.
pinch vt pellizcar; (col) birlar; * vi apretar; * n pellizco m.
pincushion n acerico m.
pine[1] n (bot) pino m.
pine[2] vi ansiar por.
pineapple n piña f, ananás m invar.
ping n sonido agudo m.
pink n rosa f; * adj color de rosa.
pinnacle n cumbre f.
pinpoint vt precisar.
pint n pinta f.
pioneer n pionero/ra m/f.
pious adj pío, pía, devoto/ta; **~ly** adv piadosamente.
pip n pepita f.
pipe n tubo, caño m; pipa f, Lat Am cachimbo m; **~s** cañería f.
pipe cleaner n limpiapipas m invar.
pipe dream n sueño imposible m.
pipeline n tubería f; oleoducto m; gasoducto m.
piper n gaitero/ra m/f.
piping adj hirviente.
pique n pique m; desazón f; ojeriza f.
piracy n piratería f.
pirate n pirata m/f.
pirouette n pirueta; vi piruetear.

P

Pisces n Piscis m (signo del zodiaco).
piss n (col) meada f; * vi mear.
pistol n pistola f.
piston n émbolo m.
pit n hoyo m; mina f.
pitch n lanzamiento m; tono m; campo m, Lat Am cancha f; * vt tirar, arrojar; * vi caerse; caer de cabeza.
pitch-black adj negro/gra como boca de lobo.
pitcher n cántaro m.
pitchfork n horca f.
pitfall n trampa f.
pithy adj meduloso/sa.
pitiable adj lastimoso/sa.
pitiful adj lastimoso/sa, compasivo/va; ~ly adv lastimosamente.
pittance n pitanza, ración f; porcioncilla f.
pity n piedad, compasión f; * vt compadecer.
pivot n eje m.
pizza n pizza f.
placard n pancarta f.
placate vt apaciguar.
place n lugar, sitio m; rango, empleo m; * vt colocar; poner.
placid adj plácido/da, quieto/ta; ~ly adv plácidamente.
plagiarism n plagio m.
plague n peste, plaga f; * vt atormentar; infestar, apestar.
plaice n platija f (pez).
plaid n tartán m.
plain adj liso/so, llano/na, abierto/ta; sincero/ra; puro/ra, simple, común; claro/ra, evidente, distinto/ta; ~ly adv llanamente; claramente; * n llano m.
plaintiff n (law) demandante m/f.
plait n pliegue m; trenza f; * vt plegar; trenzar.
plan n plano m; plan m; * vt proyectar.
plane n avión m; plano m; cepillo m; * vt allanar; acepillar.
planet n planeta m.
planetary adj planetario/ria.
plank n tabla f.
planner n planificador/a m/f.
planning n planificación f.
plant n planta f; fábrica f; maquinaria f; * vt plantar.
plantation n plantación f; colonia f.
plaque n placa f.
plaster n yeso m; emplasto m; * vt enyesar; emplastar.
plastered adj (col) borracho/cha.
plasterer n yesero/ra m/f.
plaster of Paris n yeso mate m.
plastic adj plástico/ca.
plastic surgery n cirugía plástica f.
plate n plato m; lámina f; placa f.
plateau n meseta f.

plate glass n vidrio cilindrado m.
platform n plataforma f.
platinum n platino m.
platitude n tópico m.
platoon n (mil) pelotón m.
platter n fuente f; plato grande m.
plaudit n aplauso m.
plausible adj plausible.
play n juego m; comedia f; * vt, vi jugar; juguetear; representar; (mus) tocar; **to ~ down** vt quitar importancia a.
playboy n playboy m.
player n jugador/a m/f; comediante/ta m/f, actor m, actriz f.
playful adj juguetón/ona, travieso/sa; ~ly adv juguetonamente, reto zando.
playmate n camarada m/f.
playground n patio m.
playgroup n parvulario m.
play-off n desempate m.
playpen n corral (de niños) m.
plaything n juguete m.
playwright n dramaturgo/ga m/f.
plea n defensa f; excusa f; pretexto m; * vt pretextar.
plead vt defender en juicio; alegar.
pleasant adj agradable; placentero/ra, alegre; ~ly adv alegremente, placenteramente.
please vt agradar, complacer.
pleased adj contento/ta.
pleasing adj agradable, placentero/ra.
pleasure n gusto, placer m; recreo m.
pleat n pliegue m.
pledge n prenda f; fianza f; * vt empeñar, prometer.
plentiful adj copioso/sa, abundante.
plenty n copia, abundancia f.
plethora n plétora f.
pleurisy n pleuresía f.
pliable, **pliant** adj flexible, dócil.
pliers npl alicates mpl.
plight n situación difícil f.
plinth n plinto m; zócalo m.
plod vi afanarse mucho, ajetrearse.
plot n terreno m; plano m; conspiración, trama f; estratagema f; * vi trazar; conspirar; tramar.
plow n arado m; * vt arar, labrar la tierra; **to ~ back** vt reinvertir; **to ~ through** abrirse paso; roer.
ploy n truco m.
pluck vt tirar con fuerza; arrancar; desplumar; * n ánimo m.
plucky adj gallardo/da.
plug n tapón m; enchufe m; bujía f; * vt tapar.
plum n ciruela f.
plumage n plumaje m.
plumb n plomada f; * adv a plomo; * vt aplomar.
plumber n fontanero/ra, plomero/ra m/f.

plume n pluma f.
plump adj gordo/da, rollizo/za.
plum tree n ciruelo m.
plunder vt saquear, pillar, robar; * n pillaje, botín m.
plunge vi sumergir(se), precipitarse; * n zambullida f.
plunger n desatascador m.
pluperfect n (gr) pluscuamperfecto m.
plural adj, n plural m.
plurality n pluralidad f.
plus n signo de más m; * prep más, y, además de.
plush adj de felpa.
plutonium n plutonio m.
ply vt trabajar con ahínco; * vi aplicarse; (mar) ir y venir.
plywood n madera contrachapada f.
pneumatic adj neumático/ca.
pneumatic drill n martillo neumático m.
pneumonia n pulmonía f.
poach vt escalfar; cazar en vedado; * vi cazar en vedado.
poached adj escalfado/da.
poacher n cazador furtivo m.
poaching n caza furtiva f.
pocket n bolsillo m; bolsa f; * vt embolsar.
pocketbook n cartera f.
pocket money n dinero para gastos m.
pod n vaina f.
podgy adj gordinflón/ona.
podiatrist n pedicuro/ra m/f, Lat Am pedicurista m/f.
poem n poema m.
poet n poeta m, poetisa f.
poetic adj poético/ca.
poetry n poesía f.
poignant adj punzante.
point n punta f; punto m; promontorio m; puntillo m; estado m; ~ **of view** n punto de vista m; * vt apuntar; aguzar; puntuar; **to ~ a gun** encañonar.
point-blank adv directamente.
pointed adj puntiagudo/da; epigramático/ca; ~**ly** adv sutilmente.
pointer n apuntador/a m/f; perro de muestra m.
pointless adj sin sentido.
poise n peso m; equilibrio m.
poison n veneno m; * vt envenenar.
poisoning n envenenamiento m.
poisonous adj venenoso/sa.
poke vt hurgar; empujar.
poker n atizador m; póker m.
poker-faced adj con cara de póker.
poky adj estrecho/cha.
polar adj polar.
pole n polo m; palo m; pértiga f.
pole bean n judía trepadora f.
pole vault n salto con pértiga m.
police n policía f.

police car n coche patrulla m.
police officer, **policeman** n policía m.
police station n comisaría f, Lat Am destacamento m de policía.
policewoman n mujer policía f.
policy n política f.
polio n polio f.
polish vt pulir, alisar; limar; **to ~ off** vt terminar; despachar; * n pulimento m.
polished adj elegante, pulido/da.
polite adj pulido/da, cortés; ~**ly** adv cortésmente.
politeness n cortesía f.
politic adj político/ca; astuto/ta.
political adj político/ca.
political asylum n asilo político m.
politician n político/ca m/f.
politics npl política f.
polka n polca f; ~ **dot** n lunar m.
poll n voto m; encuesta f, sondeo m.
pollen n (bot) polen m.
pollute vt contaminar.
pollution n polución, contaminación f.
polo n polo m.
polyester n poliéster m.
polyethylene, **polythene** n polietileno m.
polygamy n poligamia f.
polystyrene n poliestireno m.
polytechnic n politécnico m.
pomegranate n granada f.
pomp n pompa f; esplendor m.
pompom n borla f.
pompous adj pomposo/sa.
pond n estanque m.
ponder vt ponderar, considerar.
ponderous adj ponderoso/sa, pesado/da.
pontiff n pontífice, papa m.
pontoon n pontón m.
pony n jaca f; potro m.
ponytail n cola de caballo f.
pool n charca f; piscina, alberca f; * vt juntar; **to form a ~** remansarse.
poor adj pobre; humilde; de poco valor; ~**ly** adv pobremente; **the ~** n los pobres mpl.
pop n pop m; papá m; gaseosa f; chasquido m; * **to ~ in/out** vi entrar/salir un momento.
pop concert n concierto pop m.
popcorn n palomitas fpl.
Pope n Papa m.
poplar n álamo m.
poppy n (bot) amapola f.
populace n populacho m.
popular adj, ~**ly** adv popular(mente).
popularity n popularidad f.
popularize vt popularizar.
populate vi poblar.
population n población f.
populous adj populoso/sa.
pop video n videoclip m.

P

porcelain *n* porcelana, china, loza fina *f*.
porch *n* pórtico, vestíbulo *m*, zaguán *m*.
porcupine *n* puerco espín *m*.
pore *n* poro *m*.
pork *n* carne de cerdo, carne de puerco *f*.
pornography *n* pornografía *f*.
porous *adj* poroso/sa.
porpoise *n* marsopa *f*.
porridge *n* gachas de avena *fpl*.
port *n* puerto *m*; (*mar*) babor *m*; vino de Oporto *m*.
portable *adj* portátil.
portal *n* portal *m*; portada *f*.
porter *n* portero *m*; mozo *m*; conserje *m/f*.
portfolio *n* cartera *f*.
porthole *n* portilla *f*.
portico *n* pórtico, portal *m*.
portion *n* porción, parte *f*.
portly *adj* rollizo/za.
portrait *n* retrato *m*.
portray *vt* retratar.
pose *n* postura *f*; posc *f*, * *vi* posar; * *vt* plantear.
posh *adj* elegante.
position *n* posición, situación *f*; * *vt* colocar.
positive *adj* positivo/va, real, verdadero/ra; **~ly** *adv* positivamente; ciertamente.
posse *n* pelotón *m*.
possess *vt* poseer; gozar.
possession *n* posesión *f*.
possessive *adj* posesivo/va.
possibility *n* posibilidad *f*.
possible *adj* posible; **~ly** *adv* quizá, quizás.
post *n* correo *m*; puesto *m*; empleo *m*; poste *m*; * *vt* apostar; fijar.
postage *n* franqueo *m*.
postage stamp *n* sello de correos *m*; *Lat Am* estampilla *f*.
postal box, PO Box *n* apartado de correos *m*.
postcard, postal card *n* tarjeta *f* postal, *Lat Am* carta *f* postal.
post code *n* código postal *m*.
postdate *vt* posfechar.
poster *n* cartel *m*, *Lat Am* afiche *m*.
posterior *n* trasero *m*.
posterity *n* posteridad *f*.
postgraduate *n* posgraduado/da *m/f*.
posthumous *adj* póstumo/ma.
postman *n* cartero *m*.
postmark *n* matasellos *m*.
postmaster *n* administrador/a de correos *m/f*.
post office *n* correos *m*.
postpone *vt* diferir, suspender; posponer.
postscript *n* posdata *f*.
posture *n* postura *f*.
post-war *adj* de posguerra.
postwoman *n* cartera *f*.
posy *n* ramillete de flores *m*.
pot *n* marmita *f*; olla *f*; (*col*) marihuana *f*; * *vt* preservar en marmitas.

potato *n* patata *f*, *Lat Am* papa *f*.
potato peeler *n* pelapatatas *m invar*, *Lat Am* pelapapas *m invar*.
potbellied *adj* panzudo/da.
potent *adj* potente, poderoso/sa, eficaz.
potential *adj* potencial, poderoso/sa.
pothole *n* bache *m*.
potion *n* poción, bebida medicinal *f*.
potted *adj* en conserva; en tiesto.
potter *n* alfarero/ra *m/f*.
pottery *n* cerámica *f*.
potty *adj* chiflado/da.
pouch *n* bolsa *f*; petaca *f*; zurrón *m*.
poultice *n* cataplasma *f*.
poultry *n* aves de corral *fpl*.
pound *n* libra *f*; libra esterlina *f*; corral *m*; * *vt* machacar; * *vi* dar golpes.
pour *vt* echar; servir; * *vi* fluir con rapidez; llover a cántaros.
pout *vi* fruncir el ceño.
poverty *n* pobreza *f*.
powder *n* polvo *m*; pólvora *f*; * *vt* polvorear.
powder compact *n* polvera *f*.
powdered milk *n* leche en polvo *f*.
powder puff *n* borla *f*.
powder room *n* aseos *mpl*.
powdery *adj* polvoriento/ta.
power *n* poder *m*; potestad *f*; imperio *m*; potencia *f*; autoridad *f*; fuerza *f*; * *vt* impulsar.
powerful *adj* poderoso/sa; **~ly** *adv* poderosamente, con mucha fuerza.
powerless *adj* impotente.
power station *n* central eléctrica *f*.
practicable *adj* factible; viable.
practical *adj* práctico/ca; **~ly** *adv* prácticamente.
practicality *n* viabilidad *f*.
practical joke *n* broma pesada *f*.
practice *n* práctica *f*; uso *m*; costumbre *f*; **~s** *pl* intrigas *fpl*; * *vi* practicar, ejercer.
practice *vi* practicar, ejercer.
practitioner (medical) *n* médico/ca *m/f*.
pragmatic *adj* pragmático/ca.
prairie *n* pampa *f*.
praise *n* renombre *m*; alabanza *f*; * *vt* celebrar, alabar.
praiseworthy *adj* digno/na de alabanza; laudable.
prance *vi* cabriolar.
prank *n* travesura, extravagancia *f*.
prattle *vi* charlar; * *n* charla *f*.
prawn *n* gamba *f*.
pray *vi* rezar; rogar; orar.
prayer *n* oración, súplica *f*.
prayer book *n* devocionario *m*.
preach *vi* predicar.
preacher *n* pastor/a; predicador/a *m/f*.
preamble *n* preámbulo *m*.
precarious *adj* precario, incierto/ta; **~ly** *adv* precariamente.

precaution n precaución f.
precautionary adj preventivo/va.
precede vt anteceder, preceder.
precedence n precedencia f.
precedent adj, n precedente m.
precinct n límite, lindero m; barrio m; distrito electoral m.
precious adj precioso/sa.
precipice n precipicio m.
precipitate vt precipitar; * adj precipitado/da.
precise adj preciso/sa, exacto/ta; ~**ly** adv precisamente, exactamente.
precision n precisión, limitación exacta f.
preclude vt prevenir, impedir.
precocious adj precoz, temprano/na, prematuro/ra.
preconceive vt preconcebir.
preconception n preconcepción f.
precondition n condición previa f.
precursor n precursor/a m/f.
predator n depredador/a m/f.
predecessor n predecesor/a, antecesor/a m/f.
predestination n predestinación f.
predicament n aprieto m; dilema m.
predict vt predecir.
predictable adj previsible.
prediction n predicción f.
predilection n predilección f.
predominant adj predominante.
predominate vt predominar.
preen vt limpiarse (las plumas).
prefab n casa prefabricada f.
preface n prefacio m.
prefer vt preferir.
preferable adj preferible.
preferably adv de preferencia.
preference n preferencia f.
preferential adj preferente.
preferment n promoción f; preferencia f.
prefix vt prefijar; * n (gr) prefijo m.
pregnancy n embarazo m.
pregnant adj embarazada.
prehistoric adj prehistórico/ca.
prejudice n perjuicio, daño m; * vt perjudicar, hacer daño.
prejudiced adj predispuesto/ta; parcial.
prejudicial adj perjudicial, dañoso/sa.
preliminary adj preliminar.
prelude n preludio m.
premarital adj premarital.
premature adj prematuro/ra; ~**ly** adv anticipadamente.
premeditation n premeditación f.
premier n primer ministro m, primera ministra f.
première n estreno m.
premise n premisa f.
premises npl establecimiento m.
premium n premio m; remuneración f; prima f.
premonition n presentimiento m.
preoccupied adj preocupado/da; ensimismado/da.

prepaid adj con el porte pagado.
preparation n preparación f; cosa preparada f.
preparatory adj preparatorio/ria.
prepare vt (vi) preparar(se).
prepared adj abonado/da.
preponderance n preponderancia f.
preposition n preposición f.
preposterous adj absurdo/da.
prerequisite n requisito m.
prerogative n prerrogativa f.
prescribe vi prescribir; recetar.
prescription n prescripción f; receta medicinal f.
presence n presencia f; asistencia f.
present n regalo m; * adj presente; ~**ly** adv al presente; * vt ofrecer, presentar; regalar; acusar.
presentable adj decente, decoroso/sa.
presentation n presentación f.
present-day adj actual.
presenter n presentador/a m/f.
presentiment n presentimiento m.
preservation n preservación f.
preservative n preservativo m.
preserve vt preservar, conservar; poner en conserva; * n conserva, confitura f.
preside vi presidir; dirigir.
presidency n presidencia f.
president n presidente m/f.
presidential adj presidencial.
press vt empujar; apretar; compeler; * vi apretar; * n prensa f; armario m; apretón m; imprenta f.
press agency n agencia de prensa f.
press conference n rueda de prensa f.
pressing adj, ~**ly** adv urgente(mente).
press-up n plancha f.
pressure n presión f; opresión f.
pressure cooker n olla exprés, olla a presión f.
pressure group n grupo de presión m.
pressurized adj a presión.
prestige n prestigio m.
presumable adj presumible.
presumably adv es de suponer que.
presume vt presumir, suponer.
presumption n presunción f.
presumptuous adj presuntuoso/sa.
presuppose vt presuponer.
pretend vi pretender; presumir.
pretender n pretendiente m/f.
pretense n pretexto m; pretensión f.
pretension n pretensión f.
pretentious adj presumido/da; ostentoso/sa.
preterit n pretérito m.
pretext n pretexto m; **to find a ~ for** pretextar.
pretty adj lindo/da, bien parecido/da; hermoso/sa; * adv algo, un poco.
prevail vi prevalecer, predominar.
prevailing adj dominante (uso, costumbre).
prevalent adj predominante, eficaz.
prevent vt prevenir; impedir.

P

prevention n prevención f.
preventive adj preventivo/va.
previous adj previo/via; antecedente; **~ly** adv antes.
prevue n preestreno m.
prewar adj de antes de la guerra.
prey n presa f.
price n precio m.
priceless adj inapreciable.
price list n tarifa, lista de precios f.
pricey adj carero/ra.
prick vt punzar, picar; apuntar; excitar; * n puntura f; pica dura f; punzada f.
prickle n pincho m; espina f.
prickly adj espinoso/sa.
pride n orgullo m; vanidad f; jactancia f.
priest n sacerdote m.
priestess n sacerdotisa f.
priesthood n sacerdocio m.
priestly adj sacerdotal.
priggish adj afectado/da.
prim adj peripuesto/ta, afectado/da.
primacy n primacía f.
primarily adv primariamente, sobre todo.
primary adj primario/ria, principal, primero/ra.
primate n primadoprimate m.
prime n (fig) flor, nata f; primavera f; principio m; * adj primero/ra; primoroso/sa, excelente; * vt cebar.
prime minister n primer ministro m, primera ministra f.
primeval adj primitivo/va.
priming n cebo m; imprimación f.
primitive adj primitivo/va; **~ly** adv primitivamente.
primrose n (bot) primavera f.
prince n príncipe m.
princess n princesa f.
principal adj, **~ly** adv principal(mente); * n principal, jefe m.
principality n principado/da m.
principle n principio m; causa primitiva f; fundamento, motivo m.
print vt imprimir; * n impresión, estampa, edición f; impreso m; **out of ~** vendido/da, agotado/da.
printed matter n impresos mpl.
printer n impresor/a m/f.
printing n imprenta f.
prior adj anterior, precedente; * n prior (prelado) m.
priority n prioridad f.
priory n priorato m.
prism n prisma m.
prison n prisión, carcel f.
prisoner n prisionero/ra m/f.
pristine adj prístino/na, antiguo/gua.
privacy n soledad f.
private adj secreto/ta, privado/da; particular; **~ soldier** n soldado raso m; **~ly** adv en secreto.

private eye n detective privado/da m/f.
private school n instituto; colegio privado m.
privet n (bot) alheña f.
privilege n privilegio m.
prize n premio m; presa f; * vt apreciar, valuar; **to ~ open** abrir por fuerza.
prize-giving n entrega de premios f.
prizewinner n premiado/da m/f, Lat Am favorecido/da m/f.
pro prep para.
probability n probabilidad, verosimilitud f.
probable adj probable, verosímil; **~bly** adv probablemente.
probation n prueba f.
probationary adj de prueba.
probe n sonda f; encuesta f; * vt sondar; investigar.
problem n problema m.
problematical adj problemático/ca; **~ly** adv problemáticamente.
procedure n procedimiento m; progreso, proceso m.
proceed vi proceder; provenir; originarse; **~s** npl producto m; rédito m; **gross ~s** producto íntegro; **net ~s** producto neto.
proceedings n procedimiento m; proceso m; conducta f.
process n proceso m.
procession n procesión f.
proclaim vt proclamar, promulgar; publicar.
proclamation n proclamación f; decreto m.
procrastinate vt diferir, retardar.
proctor n censor/a m/f.
procure vt procurar.
procurement n procuración f.
prod vt empujar.
prodigal adj pródigo/ga.
prodigious adj prodigioso/sa; **~ly** adv prodigiosamente.
prodigy n prodigio m.
produce vt producir, criar; causar; * n producto m; verdura f.
produce dealer n verdulero/ra m/f.
producer n productor/a m/f.
product n producto m; obra f; efecto m.
production n producción f; producto m.
production line n línea de producción f.
productive adj productivo/va.
productivity n productividad f.
profane adj profano/na.
profess vt profesar; ejercer; declarar.
profession n profesión f.
professional adj profesional.
professor n profesor/a, catedratico/ca m/f.
proficiency n capacidad f.
proficient adj proficiente, adelantado/da.
profile n perfil m.
profit n ganancia f, Lat Am utilidad f; provecho m; ventaja f; * vi aprovechar.

profitability n rentabilidad f.
profitable adj provechoso/sa, ventajoso/sa.
profiteering n explotación f.
profound adj profundo/da; **~ly** adv profundamente.
profuse adj profuso/sa, prodigo/ga; **~ly** adv profusamente.
program n programa m.
programer n programador/a m/f.
programing n programación f.
progress n progreso m; curso m; * vi hacer progresos.
progression n progresión f; adelantamiento m.
progressive adj progresivo/va; **~ly** adv progresivamente.
prohibit vt prohibir, vedar; impedir.
prohibition n prohibición f.
project vt proyectar, trazar; * n proyecto m.
projectile n proyectil m.
projection n proyección f; estimación f.
projector n proyector m.
proletarian adj proletario/ria.
proletariat n proletariado m.
prolific adj prolifico/ca, fecundo/da.
prolog n prólogo m.
prolong vt prolongar; diferir.
prom n baile de gala.
promenade n paseo m.
prominence n prominencia f.
prominent adj prominente, saledizo/za.
promiscuous adj promiscuo/cua.
promise n promesa f; * vt prometer.
promising adj prometedor/a.
promontory n promontorio m.
promote vt promover.
promoter n promotor/a, promovedor/a m/f.
promotion n promoción f.
prompt adj pronto/ta; **~ly** adv prontamente; * vt sugerir, insinuar; (theat) apuntar.
prompter n apuntador/a m/f.
prone adj inclinado/da.
prong n diente m.
pronoun n pronombre m.
pronounce vt pronunciar; recitar.
pronounced adj marcado/da.
pronouncement n declaración f.
pronunciation n pronunciación f.
proof n prueba f; * adj impenetrable; de prueba.
prop vt sostener; * n apoyo, puntal m; sostén m.
propaganda n propaganda f.
propel vt impeler.
propeller n hélice f.
propensity n propensión, tendencia f.
proper adj propio/pia; conveniente; exacto/ta; bien parecido/da; **~ly** adv propiamente, justamente.
property n propiedad f.
prophecy n profecía f.
prophesy vt profetizar.

prophet n profeta m.
prophetic adj profético/ca.
proportion n proporción f; simetría f.
proportional adj proporcional.
proportionate adj proporcionado/da.
proposal n propuesta, proposición f; oferta f.
propose vt proponer.
proposition n proposición, propuesta f.
proprietor n propietario/ria m/f.
propriety n propiedad f.
pro rata adv de forma prorrateada.
prosaic adj prosaico/ca, en prosa.
prose n prosa f.
prosecute vt proseguir.
prosecution n prosecución f; acusación f.
prosecutor n fiscal m/f.
prospect n perspectiva f; esperanza f; * vt explorar; * vi buscar.
prospecting n prospección f.
prospective adj probable; futuro/ra.
prospector n explorador/a m/f.
prospectus n prospecto m.
prosper vi prosperar.
prosperity n prosperidad f.
prosperous adj próspero/ra, feliz.
prostitute n prostituta f.
prostitution n prostitución f.
prostrate adj postrado/da.
protagonist n protagonista m.
protect vt proteger; amparar.
protection n protección f.
protective adj protectorio/ria.
protector n protector/a, patrono/na m/f.
protégé(e) n protegido/da m/f.
protein n proteína f.
protest vi protestar; * n protesta f.
Protestant n protestante m/f.
protester n manifestante m/f.
protocol n protocolo m.
prototype n prototipo m.
protracted adj prolongado/da.
protrude vi sobresalir.
proud adj soberbio/bia, orgulloso/sa; **~ly** adv soberbiamente.
prove vt probar, justificar; * vi resultar; salir (bien/mal).
proverb n proverbio m.
proverbial adj, **~ly** adv proverbial(mente).
provide vt proveer; **to ~ for** mantener a; tener en cuenta.
provided conj: **~ that** con tal que.
providence n providencia f.
province n provincia f; campo de acción m.
provincial adj provincial; * n provincial/a m/f.
provision n provisión f; precaución f.
provisional adj provisional, Lat Am provisorio/a; **~ly** adv provisionalmente, Lat Am provisoriamente.

P

proviso n estipulación f.
provocation n provocación f; apelación f.
provocative adj provocativo/va.
provoke vt provocar; apelar.
prow n (mar) proa f.
prowess n proeza, valentia f.
prowl vi rondar, vagar.
prowler n merodeador/a m/f.
proximity n proximidad f.
proxy n poder m; apoderado/da m/f.
prudence n prudencia f.
prudent adj prudente, circunspecto/ta; ~ly adv con juicio.
prudish adj gazmoño/ña, mojigato/ta.
prune vt podar; * n ciruela pasa f.
prussic acid n ácido prúsico m.
pry vi espiar, acechar; **to ~ open** vt abrir por fuerza.
psalm n salmo m.
pseudonym n seudónimo m.
psyche n psique f.
psychiatric adj psiquiátrico/ca.
psychiatrist n psiquiatra m/f.
psychiatry n psiquiatría f.
psychic adj psíquico/ca.
psychoanalysis n psicoanálisis m.
psychoanalyst n psicoanalista m/f.
psychological adj psicológico/ca.
psychologist n psicólogo/ga m/f.
psychology n psicología f.
puberty n pubertad f.
public adj público/ca; común; notorio/ria; ~ly adv publicamente; * n público m.
public-address system n megafonía f.
publican n publicano m; tabernero/ra m/f.
publication n publicación f; edición f.
publicity n publicidad f.
publicize vt publicitar; hacer propaganda para.
public opinion n opinión pública f.
publish vt publicar.
publisher n editorial f; editor/a m/f.
publishing n industria del libro f.
pucker vt arrugar, hacer pliegues.
pudding n pudín m; morcilla f.
puddle n charco m.
puerile adj pueril.
puff n soplo m; bocanada f, Lat Am pitada f; resoplido m; * vt chupar; * vi bufar; resoplar.
puff pastry n hojaldre m.
puffy adj hinchado/da, entumecido/da.
pull vt tirar; coger; rasgar, desgarrar; **to ~ down** derribar; **to ~ in** parar; llegar a la estación; **to ~ off** cerrar; **to ~ out** vi irse; salir; * vt arrancar; **to ~ through** salir adelante; **to ~ up** vi parar; * vt arrancar; parar; * n tirón m; sacudida f.
pulley n polea, garrucha f.
pullover n jersey m.

pulp n pulpa f; pasta f.
pulpit n púlpito m.
pulsate vi pulsar, latir.
pulse n pulso m; legumbres fpl.
pulverize vt pulverizar.
pumice n piedra pómez f.
pummel vt aporrear.
pump n bomba f; zapatilla f; * vt bombear; sondear; sonsacar.
pumpkin n calabaza f.
pun n juego de palabras m; * vi hacer juegos de palabras.
punch n puñetazo m; punzón m; taladro m; ponche m; * vt golpear; perforar.
punctual adj puntual, exacto/ta; ~ly adv puntualmente.
punctuate vi puntuar.
punctuation n puntuación f.
pundit n experto/ta m/f.
pungent adj picante, acre, mordaz.
punish vt castigar.
punishment n castigo m; pena f.
punk n punk m/f; música punk f; rufián/fiana m/f.
punt n barco llano m.
puny adj joven, pequeño/ña; inferior.
pup n cachorro m; * vi parir (la perra).
pupil n alumno/na m/f; pupila f.
puppet n títere, muñeco m.
puppy n perrito m.
purchase vt comprar; * n compra f; adquisición f.
purchaser n comprador/a m/f.
pure adj puro/ra; ~ly adv puramente.
purée n puré m.
purge vt purgar.
purification n purificación f.
purifier n depuradora f.
purify vt purificar.
purist n purista m/f.
puritan n puritano/na m/f.
purity n pureza f.
purl n punto del revés m.
purple adj purpureo/rea; * n púrpura f.
purport vi: **to ~ to** dar a entender que.
purpose n intención f; designio, proyecto m; **to the ~** al propósito; **to no ~** inútilmente; **on ~** a propósito.
purposeful adj resuelto/ta.
purr vi ronronear.
purse n bolsa f; cartera f, Lat Am sobre m.
purser n comisario m/f.
pursue vi perseguir; seguir, acosar.
pursuit n perseguimiento m; ocupación f.
purveyor n abastecedor m.
push vt empujar; estrechar, apretar; **to ~ aside** apartar; **to ~ off** (col) largarse; **to ~ on** seguir adelante; * n impulso m; empujón m; esfuerzo m; asalto m.
pusher (**drug**) n traficante de drogas m/f.

put vt poner, colocar; proponer; imponer, obligar; **to ~ away** guardar; **to ~ away hurriedly** zampar; **to ~ down** poner en el suelo; sacrificar; apuntar; sofocar; **to ~ forward** adelantar; **to ~ off** aplazar; desanimar; **to ~ on** ponerse; encender; presentar; ganar; echar; **to ~ out** apagar; extender; molestar; **to ~ up** alzar; aumentar; alojar.

putrid adj podrido/da.

putt n putt m; vt hacer un putt.

putty n masilla f.

puzzle n acertijo m; rompecabezas m inv ar.

puzzling adj extraño/ña.

pylon n torre de alta tensión f.

pyramid n pirámide f.

python n pitón m.

P

Q

quack vi graznar; * n graznido m; (col) curandero/ra m/f.
quadrangle n cuadrángulo m.
quadrant n cuadrante m.
quadrilateral adj cuadrilátero/ra.
quadruped n cuadrúpedo m.
quadruple adj cuádruplo.
quadruplet n cuatrillizo/za m/f.
quagmire n barrizal m, cenagal m.
quail n codorniz f.
quaint adj pulido/da; exquisito/ta.
quake vi temblar; tiritar.
Quaker n cuáquero/ra m/f.
qualification n calificación f; título m.
qualified adj capacitado/da; titulado/da.
qualify vt calificar; modificar; * vi clasificarse.
quality n calidad f.
qualm n escrupúlo m.
quandary n incertidumbre, duda f.
quantitative adj cuantitativo/va.
quantity n cantidad f.
quarantine n cuarentena f.
quarrel n riña, contienda f; * vi reñir, disputar.
quarrelsome adj pendenciero/ra.
quarry n cantera f.
quarter n cuarto m; cuarta parte f; ~ of an hour cuarto de hora; * vt cuartear.
quarterly adj trimestral; * adv trimestralmente.
quartermaster n (mil) comisario/ria m/f.
quartet n (mus) cuarteto m.
quartz n cuarzo m.
quash vt fracasar; anular, abrogar.
quay n muelle m.
queasy adj nauseabundo/da.
queen n reina f; dama f.
queer adj extraño/ña; ridículo/la; * n (col) maricón m.
quell vt calmar; sosegar.
quench vt apagar; extinguir.

query n cuestión, pregunta f; * vt preguntar.
quest n pesquisa, inquisición, busca f.
question n pregunta f; cuestión f; asunto m; duda f; * vt dudar de; interrogar.
questionable adj cuestionable, dudoso/sa.
questioner n interrogador/a m/f.
question mark n signo de interrogación m.
questionnaire n cuestionario m.
quibble vi buscar evasivas.
quick adj rapido/da; vivo/va; pronto/ta; ágil; ~ly adv rápidamente.
quicken vt apresurar; * vi darse prisa.
quicksand n arenas movedizas f/pl.
quicksilver n azogue, mercurio m.
quick-witted adj agudo/da, perspicaz.
quiet adj callado/da; ~ly adv tranquilamente.
quietness n tranquilidad f.
quinine n quinina f.
quintet n (mus) quinteto m.
quintuple adj quíntuplo.
quintuplet n quintillizo/za m/f.
quip n indirecta f; * vt echar pullas.
quirk n peculiaridad f.
quit vt dejar; desocupar; * vi renunciar; irse; * adj libre, descargado/da.
quite adv bastante; totalmente, enteramente, absolutamente.
quits adv ¡en paz!
quiver vi temblar.
quixotic adj quijotesco/ca.
quiz n concurso m; programa concurso m; * vt interrogar.
quizzical adj burlón/ona.
quota n cuota f.
quotation n citación, cita f.
quotation marks npl comillas fpl.
quote vt citar.
quotient n cociente m.

R

rabbi n rabino/na m/f.

rabbit n conejo m.

rabbit hutch n conejera f.

rabble n gentuza f.

rabid adj rabioso/sa; furioso/sa.

rabies n rabia f.

race n raza, casta f; carrera f; * vt hacer correr a; competir contra; acelerar; * vi correr; competir; latir rápidamente.

racehorse n caballo de carreras m.

racial adj racial.

raciness n vivacidad f.

racing n carreras fpl.

racist adj, n racista m/f.

rack n rejilla f; estante m; * vt atormentar; trasegar.

racket n ruido m; raqueta f.

rack-rent n alquiler abusivo m.

racy adj picante, vivo/va.

radiance n brillantez f, resplandor m.

radiant adj radiante, brillante, Lat Am radioso/sa.

radiate vt, vi radiar, irradiar.

radiation n radiación f.

radiator n radiador m.

radical adj radical; ~ly adv radicalmente.

radicalism n radicalismo m.

radio n radio f.

radioactive adj radioactivo/va; ~ **fallout** lluvia radioactiva f.

radish n rábano m.

radius n radio f.

raffle n rifa f (juego); * vt rifar.

raft n balsa, almadía f.

rafter n par m; viga f.

rafting n rafting m.

rag n trapo, andrajo m.

ragamuffin n granuja, galopín/ina m/f.

rage n rabia f; furor m; * vi rabiar; encolerizarse.

ragged adj andrajoso/sa.

raging adj furioso/sa, rabioso/sa.

ragpicker n trapero m.

raid n incursión f; * vt invadir.

raider n invasor/a m/f.

rail n baranda, barandilla f; (rail) raíl, carril m; * vt cercar con barandillas.

raillery n burlas fpl.

railroad n ferrocarril m.

raiment n vestido m.

rain n lluvia f; * vi llover.

rainbow n arco iris m.

rainwater n agua de lluvia f.

rainy adj lluvioso/sa.

raise vt levantar, alzar, Lat Am parar; fabricar, edificar; elevar.

raisin n pasa f.

rake n rastro, rastrillo m; libertino/na m/f; * vt rastrillar.

rakish adj libertino/na, disoluto/ta.

rally vt (mil) reunir; * vi reunirse.

ram n carnero, morueco m; ariete m; * vt chocar con.

ramble vi divagar; salir de excursión a pie; * n excursión a pie, caminata f.

rambler n excursionista m/f.

ramification n ramificación f.

ramify vi ramificarse.

ramp n rampa f.

rampant adj exuberante.

rampart n terraplén m; (mil) muralla f.

ramrod n baqueta f; atacador m.

ramshackle adj en ruina.

ranch n hacienda, estancia f.

rancid adj rancio/cia.

rancor n rencor m.

random adj fortuito/ta, sin orden; **at ~** al azar.

range vt colocar, ordenar; *vi vagar; * n clase f; orden m; hilera f; cordillera f; campo abierto m; campo de tiro m; reja de cocina f.

ranger n guardabosques m invar.

rank adj exuberante; rancio/cia; fétido/da; * n fila, hilera, clase f.

rankle vi doler.

rankness n exuberancia f; olor/gusto rancio m.

ransack vt saquear, pillar.

ransom n rescate m.

rant vi vociferar.

rap vi dar un golpecito; * n golpecito m.

rapacious adj rapaz; ~ly adv con rapacidad.

rapacity, rapaciousness n rapacidad f.

rape n violación f; estupro m; (bot) colza f; * vt violar.

rapid adj rápido/da; ~ly adv rápidamente.

rapidity n rapidez f.

rapier n espadín m.

rapist n violador m.

rapt adj arrebatado/da; absorto/ta.

rapture n rapto m; éxtasis m invar.

rapturous adj arrebatado/da.

rare adj raro/ra, extraordinario/ria; ~ly adv raramente.

rarity n raridad, rareza f.

rascal n pícaro/ra m/f.

rash adj precipitado/da, temerario/ria; ~ly adv temerariamente; * n salpullido m; erupción (cutánea) f.

R

rashness n temeridad f.
rasp n raspador m; * vt raspar, escofinar.
raspberry n frambuesa f; ~ **bush** frambueso m.
rat n rata f.
rate n tasa f, precio, valor m; grado m; * vt tasar, apreciar.
rather adv más bien; antes.
ratification n ratificación f.
ratify vt ratificar.
rating n tasación f; clasificación f; índice m.
ratio n razón f.
ration n ración f; (mil) víveres mpl.
rational adj racional; razonable; ~**ly** adv racionalmente.
rationality n racionalidad f.
rattan n (bot) rota f.
rattle vi golpear; traquetear; * vt sacudir; * n traqueteo m; sonajero m.
rattlesnake n serpiente de cascabel f.
ravage vt saquear, pillar; estragar; * n saqueo m.
rave vi delirar.
rave music n (col) bakalao m.
raven n cuervo m.
ravenous adj, ~**ly** adv voraz(mente).
ravine n barranco m.
ravish vt encantar; raptar.
ravishing adj encantador/a.
raw adj crudo/da; puro/ra; novato/ta.
rawboned adj huesudo/da; magro/gra.
rawness n crudeza f; falta de experiencia f.
ray n rayo de luz m; raya f (pez).
raze vt arrasar.
razor n navaja; máquina de afeitar f.
reach vt alcanzar; llegar hasta; * vi extenderse, llegar; alcanzar, penetrar; * n alcance m.
react vi reaccionar.
reaction n reacción f.
read vt leer; * vi estudiar.
readable adj legible.
reader n lector/a m/f.
readily adv pronto; de buena gana.
readiness n voluntad, gana f; prontitud f.
reading n lectura f.
reading room n sala de lectura f.
readjust vt reajustar.
ready adj listo/ta, pronto/ta; inclinado/da; abonado/da; fácil.
real adj real, verdadero/ra; ~**ly** adv realmente.
reality n realidad f.
realization n realización f.
realize adv darse cuenta de; realizar.
realm n reino m.
ream n resma f.
reap vt segar.
reaper n segador/a m/f.
reappear vi reaparecer.
rear n parte trasera f; retaguardia f; zaga f; * vt levantar, alzar.

rearmament n rearme m.
reason n razon f; causa f; * vt, vi razonar.
reasonable adj razonable.
reasonableness n lo razonable.
reasonably adv razonablemente.
reasoning n razonamiento m.
reassure vt tranquilizar, alentar; (com) asegurar.
rebel n rebelde m/f; * vi rebelarse.
rebellion n rebelión f.
rebellious adj rebelde.
rebound vi rebotar.
rebuff n desaire m; * vt rechazar.
rebuild vt reedificar.
rebuke vt reprender; * n reprensión f.
rebut vi repercutir.
recalcitrant adj recalcitrante.
recall vt recordar; retirar; * n retirada f.
recant vt retractar, desdecirse.
recantation n retractación f.
recapitulate vt, vi recapitular.
recapitulation n recapitulación f.
recapture n recobra f.
recede vi retroceder.
receipt n recibo m; recepción f; ~**s** npl ingresos mpl.
receivable adj por cobrar.
receive vt recibir, Lat Am recepcionar; aceptar, admitir.
recent adj reciente, nuevo/va; ~**ly** adv recientemente.
receptacle n receptáculo m.
reception n recepción f.
recess n descanso m; recreo m; hueco m.
recession n retirada f; (com) recesión f.
recipe n receta f.
recipient n recipiente m.
reciprocal adj recíproco/ca; ~**ly** adv recíprocamente.
reciprocate vi reciprocar.
reciprocity n reciprocidad f.
recital n recital m.
recite vt recitar; referir, relatar.
reckless adj temerario/ria; ~**ly** adv temerariamente.
reckon vt contar, computar; * vi calcular.
reckoning n cuenta f; cálculo m.
reclaim vt reformar; reclamar.
reclaimable adj reclamable.
recline vt (vi) reclinar(se); recostar(se).
recluse n recluso/sa m/f.
recognition n reconocimiento; recuerdo m.
recognize vt reconocer.
recoil vi recular.
recollect vt acordarse de; recordar.
recollection n recuerdo m.
recommence vt empezar de nuevo.
recommend vt recomendar.
recommendation n recomendación f.
recompense n recompensa f; * vt recompensar.
reconcilable adj reconciliable.
reconcile vt reconciliar.
reconciliation n reconciliación f.

recondite adj recóndito/ta, reservado/da.

reconnaissance n (mil) reconocimiento m.

reconnoiter vt (mil) reconocer.

reconsider vt reconsiderar.

reconstruct vt reedificar.

record vt registrar; grabar; * n registro, archivo m; disco; récord m; ~s pl anales mpl.

recorder n registrador/a, archivero/ra m/f; (mus) flauta de pico f.

recount vt contar de nuevo; relatar.

recourse n recurso m; remedio m.

recover vt recobrar; recuperar; restablecer; * vi convalecer, restablecerse.

recoverable adj recuperable.

recovery n convalecencia; recuperación f.

recreation n recreación f; recreo m.

recriminate vi recriminar.

recrimination n recriminación f.

recruit vt reclutar; * n (mil) recluta m/f.

recruiting n recluta f.

rectangle n rectángulo m.

rectangular adj rectangular.

rectification n rectificación f.

rectify vt rectificar.

rectilinear adj rectilíneo/nea.

rectitude n rectitud f.

rector n rector/a m/f.

recumbent adj recostado/da, reclinado/da.

recur vi repetirse.

recurrence n repetición f.

recurrent adj repetido/da.

recycle vt reciclar.

recycled adj reciclado/da.

red adj rojo/ja; tinto/ta; * n rojo m.

redden vt enrojecer; * vi ponerse colorado/da.

reddish adj rojizo/za.

redeem vt redimir, rescatar.

redeemable adj redimible.

redeemer n redentor/a m/f.

redemption n redención f.

redeploy vt reorganizar.

red-handed adj: **to catch somebody** ~ pillar a alguien con las manos en la masa.

red-hot adj candente, ardiente.

red-letter day n dia señalado m.

redness n rojez, bermejura f.

redolent adj fragante, oloroso/sa.

redouble vt (vi) redoblar(se).

redress vt corregir; reformar; rectificar; * n reparación, compensación f.

red tape n (fig) trámites mpl.

reduce vt reducir; disminuir; rebajer.

reducible adj reducible.

reduction n reducción f; rebaja f.

redundancy n despido m.

redundant adj superfluo/lua.

reed n caña f.

reedy adj lleno de canas.

reef n (mar) rizo m; arrecife m.

reek n mal olor m; * vi humear; vahear.

reel n carrete m; bobina f; rollo m; * vi tambalear(se).

re-election n reelección f.

re-engage vt empeñar de nuevo.

re-enter vt volver a entrar.

re-establish vt restablecer, volver a establecer.

re-establishment n restablecimiento m; restauración f.

refectory n refectorio; comedor m.

refer vt, vi referir, remitir; referirse.

referee n arbitro/ra m/f, Lat Am referí m/f.

reference n referencia, relación f.

refine vt refinar, purificar.

refinement n refinación f; refinadura f; cultura f.

refinery n refinería f.

refit vt reparar; (mar) reparar.

reflect vt, vi reflejar; reflexionar.

reflection n reflexión, meditación f.

reflector n reflector m; captafaros m invar.

reflex adj reflejo.

reform vt (vi) reformar(se).

reform, reformation n reformación f.

reformer n reformador/a m/f.

reformist n reformista m/f.

refract vt refractar.

refraction n refracción f.

refrain vi: **to ~ from something** abstenerse de algo.

refresh vt refrescar.

refreshment n refresco, refrigerio m.

refrigerator n nevera f; refrigerador m.

refuel vi repostar (combustible).

refuge n refugio, asilo m.

refugee n refugiado/da m/f.

refund vt devolver; * n reembolso m.

refurbish vt restaurar, renovar.

refusal n negativa f.

refuse[1] vt rehusar.

refuse[2] n basura f.

refuse collector n basurero m.

refute vt refutar.

regain vt recobrar, recuperar.

regal adj real.

regale vt regalar.

regalia n insignias fpl.

regard vt estimar; considerar; * n consideración f; respeto m.

regarding pr en cuanto a.

regardless adv a pesar de todo.

regatta n regata f.

regency n regencia f.

regenerate vt regenerar; * adj regenerado/da.

regeneration n regeneración f.

regent n regente m/f.

regime n régimen m.

regiment n regimiento m.

region n región f.

R

register *n* registro *m*; * *vt* registrar.
registrar *n* registrador/a *m/f*.
registration *n* registro *m*.
registry *n* registro *m*.
regressive *adj* regresivo/va.
regret *n* sentimiento *m*; remordimiento *m*; pensión *f*; * *vt* sentir.
regretful *adj* pesaroso/sa.
regular *adj* regular; ordinario/ria; ~ly *adv* regularmente; * *n* regular *m*.
regularity *n* regularidad *f*.
regulate *vt* regular, ordenar; *Lat Am* normar.
regulation *n* regulación *f*; arreglo *m*.
regulator *n* regulador *m*.
rehabilitate *vt* rehabilitar.
rehabilitation *n* rehabilitación *f*.
rehearsal *n* repetición *f*; ensayo *m*.
rehearse *vt* repetir; ensayar.
reign *n* reinado, reino *m*; * *vi* reinar; prevalecer.
reimburse *vt* reembolsar.
reimbursement *n* reembolso *m*.
rein *n* rienda *f*; * *vt* refrenar.
reindeer *n* reno *m*.
reinforce *vt* reforzar.
reinstate *vt* reintegrar.
reinsure *vt* (*com*) reasegurar.
reissue *n* reedición *f*.
reiterate *vt* reiterar.
reiteration *n* reiteración, repetición *f*.
reject *vt* rechazar.
rejection *n* rechazo *m*.
rejoice *vt* (*vi*) regocijar(se).
rejoicing *n* regocijo *m*.
relapse *vi* recaer; * *n* reincidencia *f*; recaída *f*.
relate *vt*, *vi* relatar, referirse.
related *adj* emparentado/da.
relation *n* relación *f*; pariente *m*.
relationship *n* parentesco *m*; relación *f*.
relative *adj* relativo/va; ~ly *adv* relativamente; * *n* pariente *m/f*.
relax *vt*, *vi* relajar; descansar.
relaxation *n* relajación *f*; descanso *m*; relax *m*.
relay *n* relevo *m*; * *vt* retransmitir.
release *vt* soltar, libertar; * *n* liberación *f*; descargo *m*.
relegate *vt* relegar.
relegation *n* relegación *f*, descenso *m*.
relent *vi* ablandarse.
relentless *adj* implacable.
relevant *adj* pertinente.
reliable *adj* fiable, de confianza, *Lat Am* confiable.
reliance *n* confianza *f*.
relic *n* reliquia *f*.
relief *n* relieve *m*; alivio *m*.
relieve *vt* aliviar, consolar; socorrer.
religion *n* religión *f*.
religious *adj* religioso/sa; ~ly *adv* religiosamente.
relinquish *vt* abandonar, dejar.

relish *n* sabor *m*; gusto *m*; salsa *f*; * *vt* gustar de, agradar.
reluctance *n* repugnancia *f*.
reluctant *adj* reticente.
rely *vi* confiar en; contar con.
remain *vi* quedar, restar, permanecer, durar.
remainder *n* resto, residuo *m*.
remains *npl* restos, residuos *mpl*; sobras *fpl*.
remand *vt*: to ~ in custody mantener bajo prisión preventiva.
remark *n* observación, nota *f*; * *vt* notar, observar.
remarkable *adj* notable, interesante.
remarkably *adv* notablemente.
remarry *vi* volver a casarse.
remedial *adv* curativo/va.
remedy *n* remedio, recurso *m*; * *vt* remediar.
remember *vt* acordarse de; recordar.
remembrance *n* memoria *f*; recuerdo *m*.
remind *vt* recordar.
reminiscence *n* reminiscencia *f*.
remiss *adj* negligente.
remission *n* remisión *f*.
remit *vt*, *vi* remitir, perdonar; disminuir.
remittance *n* remesa *f*.
remnant *n* resto, residuo *m*.
remodel *vt* remodelar.
remonstrate *vi* protestar.
remorse *n* remordimiento *m*; compunción *f*.
remorseless *adj* implacable.
remote *adj* remoto/ta, lejano/na; ~ly *adv* remotamente, lejos.
remote control *n* mando a distancia *m*.
remoteness *n* alejamiento *m*; distancia *f*.
removable *adj* de quita y pon, de quitapón.
removal *n* remoción *f*; mudanza *f*.
remove *vt* quitar; * *vi* mudarse.
remunerate *vt* remunerar.
remuneration *n* remuneración *f*.
render *vt* devolver, restituir; traducir; rendir.
rendezvous *n* cita *f*; lugar de encuentro *m*.
renegade *n* renegado/da *m/f*.
renew *vt* renovar, restablecer.
renewal *n* renovación *f*.
rennet *n* cuajo *m*.
renounce *vt* renunciar.
renovate *vt* renovar.
renovation *n* renovación *f*.
renown *n* renombre *m*; celebridad *f*.
renowned *adj* célebre.
rent *n* renta *f*; arrendamiento *m*; alquiler *m*; * *vt* alquilar.
rental *n* alquiler *m*.
renunciation *n* renuncia *f*.
reopen *vt* reabrir.
reorganization *n* reorganización *f*.
reorganize *vt* reorganizar.
repair *vt* reparar; resarcir; * *n* reparación *f*.

reparable *adj* reparable.

reparation *n* reparación *f*.

repartee *n* réplica aguda/picante *f*.

repatriate *vt* repatriar.

repay *vt* devolver; pagar, restituir.

repayment *n* pago *m*.

repeal *vt* abrogar, revocar; * *n* revocación, anulación *f*.

repeat *vt* repetir.

repeatedly *adv* repetidamente.

repeater *n* reloj de repetición *m*.

repel *vt* repeler, rechazar.

repent *vi* arrepentirse.

repentance *n* arrepentimiento *m*.

repentant *adj* arrepentido/da.

repertory *n* repertorio *m*.

repetition *n* repetición, reiteración *f*.

replace *vt* reemplazar; reponer.

replenish *vt* llenar, surtir.

replete *adj* repleto/ta, lleno/na.

reply *n* respuesta *f*; * *vi* responder.

report *vt* referir, contar; dar cuenta de; * *n* informe *m*; repor taje *m*; relación *f*.

reporter *n* reportero/ra *m/f*.

repose *vt*, *vi* reposar; * *n* reposo *m*.

repository *n* depósito *m*.

repossess *vt* reobrar.

reprehend *vt* reprender.

reprehensible *adj* reprensible.

represent *vt* representar.

representation *n* representación *f*.

representative *adj* representativo/va; * *n* representante *m/f*.

repress *vt* reprimir, domar.

repression *n* represión *f*.

repressive *adj* represivo/va.

reprieve *vt* suspender una ejecución; indultar; * *n* indulto *m*.

reprimand *vt* reprender, corregir; * *n* reprensión *f*; repri menda *f*.

reprint *vt* reimprimir.

reprisal *n* represalia *f*.

reproach *n* improperio, oprobio *m*; * *vt* hacer reproches a.

reproachful *adj* ignominioso/sa; ~ly *adv* ignominiosamente.

reproduce *vt* reproducir.

reproduction *n* reproducción *f*.

reptile *n* reptil *m*.

republic *n* república *f*.

republican *adj*, *n* republicano/a *m/f*.

republicanism *n* republicanismo *m*.

Republican Party *n* Partido Republicano *m*.

repudiate *vt* repudiar.

repugnance *n* repugnancia *f*.

repugnant *adj* repugnante; ~ly *adv* con repugnancia.

repulse *vt* repulsar, desechar; * *n* repulsa *f*; rechazo *m*.

repulsion *n* repúlsión, repulsa *f*.

repulsive *adj* repulsivo/va.

reputable *adj* honroso/sa.

reputation *n* reputación *f*.

repute *vt* reputar.

request *n* petición, súplica *f*, *Lat Am* pedido *m*; * *vt* rogar, suplicar.

require *vt* requerir, demandar.

requirement *n* requisito *m*; exigencia *f*.

requisite *adj* necesario/ria, indispensable; * *n* requisito *m*.

requisition *n* petición, demanda *f*.

requite *vt* recompensar.

rescind *vt* rescindir, abrogar.

rescue *vt* librar, rescatar; * *n* libramiento, recobro *m*.

research *vt* investigar; * *n* investigación *f*.

resemblance *n* semejanza *f*.

resemble *vt* asemejarse.

resent *vt* resentirse.

resentful *adj* resentido/da; vengativo/va; ~ly *adv* con resentimi ento.

resentment *n* resentimiento *m*.

reservation *n* reserva *f*.

reserve *vt* reservar; * *n* reserva *f*.

reservedly *adv* con reserva.

reservoir *n* depósito *m*; pantano *m*.

reside *vi* residir, morar.

residence *n* residencia, morada *f*.

resident *adj* residente.

residuary *adj* sobrado/da; ~ **legatee** *n* (*law*) legatario/ria universal *m/f*.

residue *n* residuo, resto *m*.

resign *vt*, *vi* resignar, renunciar, ceder; resignarse, rendirse.

resignation *n* resignación *f*; dimisión *f*.

resin *n* resina *f*.

resinous *adj* resinoso/sa.

resist *vt* resistir, oponerse.

resistance *n* resistencia *f*.

resolute *adj* resuelto/ta; ~ly *adv* resueltamente.

resolution *n* resolución *f*.

resolve *vt* (*vr*) resolver(se); (*fig*) zanjar.

resonance *n* resonancia *f*.

resonant *adj* resonante.

resort *vi* recurrir, frecuentar; * *n* recurso *m*; resorte *m*.

resound *vi* resonar.

resource *n* recurso *m*; expediente *m*.

respect *n* respecto *m*; respeto *m*; motivo *m*; ~s *pl* recuerdos *mpl*; * *vt* apreciar; respetar; venerar.

respectability *n* respetabilidad *f*.

respectable *adj* respetable; considerable; ~bly *adv* notablemente.

respectful *adj* respetuoso/sa; ~ly *adv* respetuosamente.

respecting *prep* con respecto a.

R

respective *adj* respectivo/va, relativo/va; **~ly** *adv* respectivamente.
respirator *n* respirador *m*.
respiratory *adj* respiratorio/ria.
respite *n* suspensión *f*; respiro *m*; * *vt* suspender, diferir.
resplendence *n* resplandor, brillo *m*.
resplendent *adj* resplandeciente.
respond *vt* responder; corresponder.
respondent *n* (*law*) defensor/a *m*.
response *n* respuesta, réplica *f*.
responsibility *n* responsabilidad *f*.
responsible *adj* responsable.
responsive *adj* sensible.
rest *n* reposo *m*; sueño *m*; quietud *f*; (*mus*) pausa *f*; resto, residuo *m*; * *vt* descansar; apoyar; * *vi* dormir, reposar; descansarse.
restaurant *n* restaurante, restorán *m*.
resting place (**last**) *n* última morada *f*.
restitution *n* restitución *f*.
restive *adj* inquieto/ta; obstinado/da.
restless *adj* insomne; inquieto/ta.
restoration *n* restauración *f*.
restorative *adj* restaurativo/va.
restore *vt* restaurar, restituir.
restrain *vt* restringir, restriñir.
restraint *n* refrenamiento, constreñimiento *m*.
restrict *vt* restringir, limitar.
restriction *n* restricción *f*.
restrictive *adj* restrictivo/va.
result *vi* resultar; * *n* resultado *m*.
resume *vt* resumir; empezar de nuevo.
resurrection *n* resurrección *f*.
resuscitate *vt* resucitar.
retail *vt* vender al por menor; * *n* venta por menor *f*.
retain *vt* retener, guardar.
retainer *n* adherente, partidario/ria *m/f*; **~s** *pl* comitiva *f*; séquito *m*.
retake *vt* volver a tomar.
retaliate *vt* tomar represalias.
retaliation *n* represalias *fpl*.
retardation *n* retraso *m*.
retarded *adj* retrasado/da.
retch *vi* tener arcadas.
retention *n* retención *f*.
retentive *adj* retentivo/va.
reticence *n* reticencia *f*.
retina *n* retina *f*.
retire *vt* (*vi*) retirar(se); jubilar(se).
retired *adj* apartado/da, retirado/da; jubilado/da.
retirement *n* retiro *m*, jubilación *f*.
retort *vt* replicar; * *n* réplica *f*.
retouch *vt* retocar.
retrace *vt* volver a trazar.
retract *vt* retraer; retractar.
retrain *vt* reciclar.
retraining *n* reciclaje profesional *m*.

retreat *n* retirada *f*; * *vi* retirarse.
retribution *n* retribución, recompensa *f*.
retrievable *adj* recuperable; reparable.
retrieve *vt* recuperar, recobrar.
retriever *n* sabueso *m*.
retrograde *adj* retrógrado/da.
retrospect, retrospection *n* reflexión *f*.
retrospective *adj* retrospectivo/va.
return *vt* retribuir; restituir; devolver; * *n* retorno *m*; vuelta *f*; recompensa, rendimiento *m*; recaída *f*.
reunion *n* reunión *f*.
reunite *vt* (*vi*) reunir(se).
reveal *vt* revelar.
revel *vi* andar de juerga.
revelation *n* revelación *f*.
reveler *n* juerguista *m/f*.
revelry *n* juerga *f*.
revenge *vt* vengar; * *n* venganza *f*.
revengeful *adj* vengativo/va.
revenue *n* renta *f*; rédito *m*.
reverberate *vt, vi* reverberar; resonar, retumbar.
reverberation *n* rechazo *m*; reverberación *f*.
revere *vt* reverenciar, venerar.
reverence *n* reverencia *f*; * *vt* reverenciar.
reverend *adj* reverendo/da; venerable; * *n* padre *m*.
reverent, reverential *adj* reverencial, respetuoso/sa.
reversal *n* revocación *f*; cambio total *m*.
reverse *vt* trastrocar; abolir; poner en marcha atrás; * *n* vicisitud *f*; contrario *m*; reverso *m* (de una moneda).
reversible *adj* revocable; reversible.
reversion *n* reversión *f*.
revert *vt, vi* trastrocar; volverse atrás.
review *vt* rever; (*mil*) revistar; * *n* revista *f*; reseña *f*.
reviewer *n* revisor/a *m/f*; crítico/ca *m/f*.
revile *vt* ultrajar; difamar.
revise *vt* rever; repasar.
reviser *n* revisor/a *m/f*.
revision *n* revisión *f*.
revisit *vt* volver a visitar.
revival *n* restauración *f*; restablecimiento *m*.
revive *vt* avivar; restablecer; * *vi* revivir.
revocation *n* revocación *f*.
revoke *vt* revocar, anular.
revolt *vi* rebelarse; * *n* rebelión *f*.
revolting *adj* asqueroso/sa.
revolution *n* revolución *f*.
revolutionary *adj, n* revolucionario/a *m/f*.
revolve *vt* revolver; meditar; * *vi* girar.
revolver *n* revólver *m*.
revolving *adj* giratorio/ria.
revue *n* revista *f*.
revulsion *n* revulsión *f*.
reward *n* recompensa *f*; * *vt* recompensar.
rhapsody *n* rapsodia *f*.
rhetoric *n* retórica *f*.

rhetorical *adj* retórico/ca.
rheumatic *adj* reumático/ca.
rheumatism *n* reumatismo *m*.
rhinoceros *n* rinoceronte *m*.
rhomboid *n* romboide *m*.
rhombus *n* rombo *m*.
rhubarb *n* ruibarbo *m*.
rhyme *n* rima *f*; poema *m*; * *vi* rimar.
rhythm *n* ritmo *m*.
rhythmical *adj* rítmico/ca.
rib *n* costilla *f*.
ribald *adj* escabroso/sa.
ribbon *n* listón *m*; cinta *f*.
rice *n* arroz *m*.
rich *adj* rico/ca; opulento/ta; abundante; ~ly *adv* ricamente.
riches *npl* riqueza *f*.
richness *n* riqueza *f*; abundancia *f*.
rickets *n* raquitismo *m*.
rickety *adj* raquítico/ca.
rid *vt* librar, desembarazar.
riddance *n*: good ~! ¡enhoramala!
riddle *n* enigma *m*; criba *f*; * *vt* cribar.
ride *vi* cabalgar; andar en coche; * *n* paseo a caballo/en coche *m*.
rider *n* caballero/ra, jinete *m*, amazona *f*.
ridge *n* espinazo, lomo *m*; cumbre *f*; * *vt* formar lomos/surcos.
ridicule *n* ridiculez *f*; ridiculo *m*; * *vt* ridiculizar.
ridiculous *adj* ridículo/la; ~ly *adv* ridiculamente.
riding *n* equitación *f*.
riding habit *n* traje de amazona *m*.
riding school *n* picadero *m*.
rife *adj* común, frecuente.
riffraff *n* desecho, desperdicio *m*.
rifle *vt* robar, pillar; estriar, rayar; * *n* rifle *m*.
rifleman *n* fusilero *m*.
rig *vt* ataviar; (*mar*) aparejar; * *n* torre de perforación *f*; **oil** ~ plataforma petrolera *f*.
rigging *n* (*mar*) aparejo *m*.
right *adj* derecho/cha, recto/ta; justo/ta; honesto/ta; ~! ¡bien!, ¡bueno!; ~ly *adv* rectamente, justamente; * *n* justicia *f*; razón *f*; derecho *m*; mano derecha *f*; * *vt* hacer justicia.
righteous *adj* justo/ta, honrado/da; ~ly *adv* justamente.
righteousness *n* equidad *f*; honradez *f*.
rigid *adj* rígido/da; austero/ra, severo/ra; yerto/ta; ~ly *adv* con rigidez.
rigidity *n* rigidez, austeridad *f*.
rigmarole *n* galimatías *m*.
rigor *n* rigor *m*; severidad *f*.
rigorous *adj* riguroso/sa; ~ly *adv* rigorosamente.
rim *n* margen *m*/*f*; orilla *f*.
rind *n* corteza *f*.
ring *n* círculo, cerco *m*; anillo *m*; campaneo *m*; * *vt* sonar; * *vi* retiñir, retumbar; **to** ~ **the bell** pulsar el timbre.

ringer (**bell**) *n* campanero/ra *m*/*f*.
ringleader *n* cabecilla *m*/*f*.
ringlet *n* anillejo *m*.
ringworm *n* (*med*) tina favosa *f*.
rink *n* (*also* **ice** ~) pista de hielo *f*.
rinse *vt* lavar, limpiar.
riot *n* tumulto, bullicio *m*; * *vi* amotinarse.
rioter *n* amotinado/da *m*/*f*.
riotous *adj* bullicioso/sa, sedicioso/sa; disoluto/ta; ~ly *adv* disolutamente.
rip *vt* rasgar, lacerar; descoser.
ripe *adj* maduro/ra, sazonado/da.
ripen *vt*, *vi* madurar.
ripeness *n* madurez *f*.
rip-off *n* (*col*): **it's a** ~! ¡es una estafa!
ripple *vi* rizarse; * *vt* rizar; * *n* onda *f*, rizo *m*.
rise *vi* levantarse; nacer, salir; rebelarse; ascender; hincharse; elevarse; resucitar; * *n* levantamiento *m*; elevación *f*; subida *f*; salida (del sol) *f*; causa *f*.
rising *n* salida (del sol) *f*; fin (de una junta/sesión) *m*.
risk *n* riesgo, peligro *m*; * *vt* arriesgar.
risky *adj* peligroso/sa, *Lat Am* riesgoso/sa.
rissole *n* croqueta *f*.
rite *n* rito *m*.
ritual *adj*, *n* ritual *m*.
rival *adj*, *n* rival *m*/*f*; * *vt* competir, emular.
rivalry *n* rivalidad *f*.
river *n* río *m*.
riverside *adj* ribereño/ña.
rivet *n* remache *m*; * *vt* remachar, roblar.
rivulet *n* riachuelo *m*.
road *n* camino *m*.
road sign *n* señal de trafico *f*.
roadstead *n* (*mar*) rada *f*.
roadworks *npl* obras *fpl*.
roam *vt*, *vi* corretear; vagar.
roan *adj* ruano/na.
roar *vi* rugir, aullar; bramar; * *n* rugido *m*; bramido, truendo *m*; mugido *m*.
roast *vt* asar; tostar.
roast beef *n* rosbif *m*.
rob *vt* robar, hurtar.
robber *n* ladrón/ona *m*/*f*.
robbery *n* robo *m*.
robe *n* manto *m*; toga *f*; * *vt* vestir de gala.
robin (**redbreast**) *n* petirrojo *m*.
robust *adj* robusto/ta.
robustness *n* robustez *f*.
rock *n* roca *f*; escollo *m*; rueca *f*; * *vt* mecer; arrullar; ape drear; * *vi* bambolear.
rock and roll *n* rocanrol *m*.
rock crystal *n* cuarzo *m*.
rocking chair *n* mecedora *f*.
rocket *n* cohete *m*, *Lat Am* cuete *m*.
rock salt *n* sal gema *f*.
rocky *adj* peñascoso/sa.
rod *n* varilla, verga, cana *f*.

R

rodent n roedor/a m/f.

roe[1] n corzo m.

roe[2] n hueva f.

roebuck n corzo m.

rogation n rogaciones fpl.

rogue n bribón/ona, pícaro/ra, villano/na m/f.

roguish adj pícaro/ra.

roll vt rodar; volver; arrollar; * vi rodar; girar; * n rodadura f; rollo m; lista f; catalogo m; bollo m; panecillo m.

roller n rodillo, cilindro m.

roller skates npl patines de rueda mpl.

rolling pin n rodillo de cocina m.

Roman Catholic adj, n católico/ca m/f (romano/na).

romance n romance m; ficción f; cuento m; fábula f.

romantic adj romántico/ca.

romp vi retozar.

roof n tejado m; paladar m; * vt techar.

roofing n techado, tejado m.

rook[1] n grajo m.

rook[2] n torre f (en el juego de ajedrez).

room n habitación, sala f; lugar, espacio m; aposento m.

roominess n espaciosidad, capacidad f.

roomy adj espacioso/sa.

roost n pértiga del gallinero f; * vi dormir en una pértiga.

root n raíz f; origen m; * vt, vi: to ~ out desarraigar; arraigar.

rooted adj inveterado/da.

rope n cuerda f; cordel m; * vi hacer hebras.

rope maker n cordelero/ra m/f.

rosary n rosario m.

rose n rosa f.

rose bed n campo de rosales m.

rosebud n capullo de rosa m.

rosemary n (bot) romero m.

rose tree n rosal m.

rosette n roseta f.

rosé wine n vino rosado m.

rosewood n palo de rosa m.

rosiness n color rosado m.

rosy adj rosado/da.

rot vi pudrirse; * n putrefacción f.

rotate vt, vi girar.

rotation n rotación f.

rote n uso m; práctica f.

rotten adj podrido/da, corrompido/da.

rottenness n podredumbre, putrefacción f.

rotund adj rotundo/da, redondo/da, circular, esférico/ca.

rouge n arrebol, colorete m.

rough adj áspero/ra, tosco/ca; bronco/ca; bruto/ta, brusco/ca; tempestuoso/sa; ~-looking zarrapastroso/sa; ~ly adv rudamente.

roughcast n mezcla gruesa f.

roughen vt poner áspero/ra.

roughness n aspereza f; rudeza, tosquedad f; tempestad f.

roulette n ruleta f.

round adj redondo/da; cabal; franco/ca, sincero/ra; * n círculo m; redondez f; vuelta f; giro m; escalón m; ronda f; andanada de canones f; descarga f; * adv alrededor; por todos lados; ~ly adv redondamente; francamente; * vt cercar, rodear; redondear.

roundabout adj amplio/lia; indirecto/ta, vago/ga; * n tiovivo m.

roundness n redondez f.

rouse vt despertar; excitar.

rout n derrota f; * vt derrotar.

route n ruta f; camino m.

routine adj rutinario/ria; * n rutina f; número m.

rove vi vagar, vaguear.

rover n vagabundo/da m/f; pirata m/f.

row[1] n camorra f; rina f.

row[2] n hilera, fila f.

row[3] vt (mar) remar, bogar.

rowdy n alborotador/a, bullanguero/ra m/f.

rower n remero/ra m/f.

royal adj real; regio/gia; ~ly adv regiamente.

royalist n realista m/f.

royalty n realeza, dignidad real f; honorarios que paga el editor al autor por cada ejemplar vendido de su obra mpl.

royalties npl regalías fpl.

rub vt estregar, fregar, frotar; raspar; * n frotamiento m; (fig) embarazo m; dificultad f.

rubber n caucho m, goma f; (col) condón m.

rubber-band n goma, gomita f.

rubbish n basura f; tonterías fpl; escombro m; ruinas fpl.

rubble n escombros mpl; cascote m.

ruble n rublo m.

rubric n rúbrica f.

ruby n rubí m.

rucksack n mochila f.

rudder n timón m.

ruddiness n tez encendida; rubicundez f.

ruddy adj colorado/da, rubio/bia.

rude adj rudo/da, brutal, rústico/ca, grosero/ra; tosco/ca; ~ly adv rudamente, groseramente.

rudeness n descortesía f; rudeza, insolencia f.

rudiment n rudimentos mpl.

rue vi compadecerse; * n (bot) ruda f.

rueful adj lamentable, triste.

ruffian n malhechor/a, bandolero/ra m/f; * adj brutal.

ruffle vt desordenar, desazonar; rizar.

rug n alfombra f.

rugby n rugby m.

rugged adj áspero/ra, tosco/ca; brutal; peludo/da.

ruin n ruina f; perdición f; escombros mpl; * vt arruinar; destruir.

ruinous adj ruinoso/sa.

rule *n* mando *m*; regla *f*; regularidad *f*; dominio *m*; * *vt* gobernar; reglar, arreglar, dirigir.

ruler *n* gobernador/a *m/f*; regla *f*.

rum *n* ron *m*.

rumble *vi* crujir, rugir.

ruminate *vt* rumiar.

rummage *vt* rebuscar.

rumor *n* rumor *m*; * *vt* rumorearse.

rump *n* ancas *fpl*.

run *vt* dirigir; organizar; llevar; pasar; **to ~ the risk** aventurar, arriesgar; * *vi* correr; fluir, manar; pasar rápidamente; proceder; ir; desteñirse; ser candidato/ta; * *n* corrida, carrera *f*; paseo *m*; curso *m*; serie *f*; moda *f*; ataque *m*.

runaway *n* fugitivo/va, desertor/a *m/f*.

rung *n* escalón, peldaño *m* (de escalera de mano).

runner *n* corredor/a *m/f*; correo, mensajero/ra *m/f*.

running *n* carrera, corrida *f*; curso *m*.

runway *n* pista de aterrizaje *f*.

rupture *n* rotura *f*; hernia, quebradura *f*; * *vt* reventar, romper.

rural *adj* rural, campestre, rústico/ca.

ruse *n* astucia, maña *f*.

rush *n* junco *m*; ráfaga *f*; ímpetu *m*; * *vt* apresurar; * *vi* abalanzarse, tirarse.

rusk *n* galleta *f*.

russet *adj* bermejo/ja.

rust *n* herrumbre *f*; * *vi* oxidarse.

rustic *adj* rústico/ca; * *n* patán/ana, rústico/ca *m/f*.

rustiness *n* herrumbre *f*.

rustle *vi* crujir, rechinar; * *vt* hacer crujir.

rustling *n* estruendo *m*; crujido *m*.

rusty *adj* oriniento/ta, mohoso/sa; oxidado/da.

ruthless *adj* cruel, insensible; ~**ly** *adv* inhumanamente.

rye *n* (*bot*) centeno *m*.

S

Sabbath n sábado m.
sable n cebellina f.
sabotage n sabotaje m.
saber n sable m.
saccharin n sacarina f.
sachet n sobrecito m.
sack n saco m; * vt despedir; saquear.
sacrament n sacramento m; Eucaristía f.
sacramental adj sacramental.
sacred adj sagrado/da, sacro/cra; inviolable.
sacredness n santidad f.
sacrifice n sacrificio m; * vt, vi sacrificar.
sacrificial adj de sacrificio.
sacrilege n sacrilegio m.
sacrilegious adj sacrílego/ga.
sad adj trıste, melanólico/ca; infausto/ta; obscuro/ra; ~ly adv tristemente.
sadden vt entristecer.
saddle n silla f; sillín m; * vt ensillar.
saddlebag n alforja f.
saddler n sillero m/f.
sadness n tristeza f.
safari n safari m.
safe adj seguro/ra; ileso/sa; fuera de peligro; de fiar; ~ly adv seguramente; ~ and sound sano y salvo; * n caja fuerte f.
safe-conduct n salvoconducto m.
safeguard n salvaguardia f; * vt proteger, defender.
safety n seguridad f; salvamento m.
safety belt n cinturón (de seguridad) m.
safety match n cerilla f.
safety pin n imperdible, seguro m.
saffron n azafrán m.
sage n (bot) salvia f; sabio/bia m/f; * adj sabio/bia; ~ly adv sabiamente.
Sagittarius n Sagitario m (signo del zodíaco).
sago n (bot) sagú m.
sail n vela f; * vt gobernar; * vi dar a la vela, navegar.
sailing n navegación f.
sailing boat n yate m.
sailor n marinero/ra m/f.
saint n santo/ta m/f.
sainted, saintly adj santo/ta.
sake n causa, razón f; **for God's** ~ por amor de Dios.
salable adj vendible.
salad n ensalada f.
salad bowl n ensaladera f.
salad dressing n aliño m.
salad oil n aceite para ensaladas m.

salamander n salamandra f.
salary n sueldo m.
sale n venta f; liquidación f.
salesman n vendedor m.
saleswoman n vendedora f.
salient adj saliente, saledizo/za.
saline adj salino/na.
saliva n saliva f.
sallow adj cetrino/na, pálido/da.
sally n (mil) salida, surtida f; * vi salir.
salmon n salmón m.
salmon trout n trucha salmonada f.
saloon n bar m.
salt n sal f; * vt salar.
salt cellar n salero m.
salting n saladura f.
saltpeter n salitre m.
saltworks npl salinas fpl.
salubrious adj salubre, saludable.
salubrity n salubridad f.
salutary adj salubre, salutífero/ra.
salutation n salutación f.
salute vt saludar; * n saludo m.
salvage n (mar) salvamento, rescate m.
salvation n salvación f.
salve n emplasto, ungüento m.
salver n salvilla, bandeja f.
salvo n salva, excusa f.
same adj mismo/ma, idéntico/ca.
sameness n identidad f.
sample n muestra f; ejemplo m; * vt probar.
sampler n muestra f; dechado, modelo m.
sanctify vt santificar.
sanctimonious adj santurrón/ona.
sanction n sanción f; * vt sancionar.
sanctity n santidad f.
sanctuary n santuario m; asilo m.
sand n arena f; * vt lijar.
sandal n sandalia f.
sandbag n (mil) saco de tierra m.
sandpit n arenal m.
sandstone n arenisca f.
sandwich n bocadillo, sandwich m, Lat Am sánduche m.
sandy adj arenoso/sa.
sane adj sano/na.
sanguinary adj sanguinario/ria.
sanguine adj sanguíneo/nea.
sanitarium n sanatorio m.
sanitary napkin n compresa f, Lat Am toalla f higiénica.
sanity n juicio sano, sentido común m.

sap *n* savia *f*; * *vt* minar.
sapient *adj* sabio/bia, cuerdo/da.
sapling *n* arbolito *m*.
sapper *n* (*mil*) zapador *m*.
sapphire *n* zafiro *m*.
sarcasm *n* sarcasmo *m*.
sarcastic *adj* sarcástico/ca; ~**ally** *adv* sarcásticamente.
sarcophagus *n* sarcófago, sepulcro *m*.
sardine *n* sardina *f*.
sash *n* cingulo *m*, cinta *f*.
sash window *n* ventana/vidriera corrediza *f*.
Satan *n* Satanás *m*.
satanic(al) *adj* diabólico/ca.
satchel *n* mochila *f*.
satellite *n* satélite *m*.
satellite dish *n* antena parabólica *f*.
satiate, sate *vt* saciar, hartar.
satin *n* raso *m*; * *adj* de raso.
satire *n* satira *f*.
satiric(al) *adj* satírico/ca; ~**ly** *adv* satíricamente.
satirist *n* autor satírico *m*, autora satírica *f*.
satirize *vt* satirizar.
satisfaction *n* satisfacción *f*.
satisfactorily *adv* satisfactoriamente.
satisfactory *adj* satisfactorio/ria.
satisfy *vt* satisfacer; convencer.
saturate *vt* saturar.
Saturday *n* sábado *m*.
saturnine *adj* saturnino/na, melancólico/ca.
satyr *n* sátiro *m*.
sauce *n* salsa *f*; crema *f*; compota de frutas *f*; * *vt* condimentar.
saucepan *n* cazo *m*.
saucer *n* platillo *m*.
saucily *adv* desvergonzadamente.
sauciness *n* insolencia, impudencia *f*.
saucy *adj* insolente.
saunter *vi* callejear, corretear.
sausage *n* salchicha *f*.
savage *adj* salvaje, bárbaro/ra; ~**ly** *adv* bárbaramente; * *n* salvaje *m/f*.
savageness *n* salvajería, *f*; crueldad *f*.
savagery *n* crueldad *f*.
savanna(h) *n* sabana *f*.
save *vt* salvar; economizar; ahorrar; evitar; conservar; * *adv* salvo, excepto; * *n* parada *f*, *Lat Am* atajada *f*.
saveloy sausage *n* chorizo *m*.
saver *n* ahorrador/a *m/f*.
saving *adj* frugal, económico/ca; * *prep* fuera de, excepto; * *n* salvamiento *m*; ~**s** *pl* ahorro *m*, economía *f*.
savings account *n* cuenta de ahorros *f*.
savings bank *n* caja de ahorros *f*.
Savior *n* Salvador *m*.
savior *n* libertador/a *m/f*.
savor *n* olor *m*; sabor *m*; * *vt* gustar, saborear.

savoriness *n* paladar; sabor *m*.
savory *adj* sabroso/sa.
saw *n* sierra *f*; * *vt* serrar, *Lat Am* serruchar.
sawdust *n* serrín *m*.
sawfish *n* pez sierra *m*.
sawmill *n* aserradero *m*.
sawyer *n* aserrador/a *m/f*.
saxophone *n* saxofóno *m*.
say *vt* decir, hablar.
saying *n* dicho, proverbio *m*.
scab *n* roña *f*; roñoso *m*.
scabbard *n* vaina (de espada) *f*; cobertura *f*.
scabby *adj* sarnoso/sa.
scaffold *n* tablado *m*; cadalso *m*.
scaffolding *n* andamio *m*.
scald *vt* escaldar; * *n* escaldadura *f*.
scale *n* balanza *f*; escama *f*; escala *f*; gama *f*; * *vt*, *vi* escalar; descostrarse.
scallop *n* vieira *f*; festón *m*; * *vt* festonear.
scalp *n* cuero cabelludo *m*; * *vt* escalpar.
scamp *n* bribón/ona, ladrón/ona *m/f*.
scamper *vi* escapar, huir.
scampi *npl* gambas *fpl*.
scan *vt* escudriñar; registrar; escandir; escanear.
scandal *n* escándalo *m*; infamia *f*.
scandalize *vt* escandalizar.
scandalous *adj* escandaloso/sa; ~**ly** *adv* escandalosamente.
scanner *n* escáner *m*.
scant, scanty *adj* escaso/sa, parco/ca.
scantily *adv* escasamente, estrechamente.
scantness *n* estrechez, escasez *f*.
scapegoat *n* chivo expiatorio *m*.
scar *n* cicatriz *f*; * *vt* dejar cicatriz en.
scarce *adj* raro/ra; ~**ly** *adv* apenas.
scarcity *n* escasez *f*; raridad *f*.
scare *vt* espantar; * *n* susto *m*.
scarecrow *n* espantapájaros *m invar*.
scarf *n* bufanda *f*.
scarlet *n* escarlata *f*; * *adj* escarlata.
scarlet fever *n* escarlatina *f*.
scarp *n* escarpa *f*.
scat *interj* (*col*) izape!
scatter *vt* esparcir; disipar.
scavenger *n* basurero/ra *m/f*; carroñero/ra *m/f*.
scenario *n* argumento *m*; guión *m*; (*fig*) escenario *m*.
scene *n* escena *f*; panorama *m*; escándalo *m*; paisaje *m*.
scenery *n* vista *f*; decoración (de teatro) *f*.
scenic *adj* escénico/ca.
scent *n* olfato *m*; olor *m*; rastro *m*; * *vt* oler.
scent bottle *n* frasco de perfume *m*.
scentless *adj* sin olfato; inodoro/ra.
scepter *n* cetro *m*.
schedule *n* horario *m*; programa *m*; lista *f*.
scheme *n* proyecto, plan *m*; esquema *m*; sistema *m*; modelo *m*; * *vt* proyectar; * *vi* intrigar.
schemer *n* proyectista, intrigante *m/f*.

S

schism *n* cisma *m.*
schismatic *adj* cismático/ca.
scholar *n* estudiante *m/f;* erudito/ta *m/f,* escolástico/ca *m/f.*
scholarship *n* ciencia *f;* erudición *f.*
scholastic *adj* escolástico/ca.
school *n* escuela *f,* colegio *m;* * *vt* enseñar.
schoolboy *n* alumno *m.*
schoolgirl *n* alumna *f.*
schooling *n* instrucción *f.*
schoolmaster *n* maestro de escuela *m.*
schoolmistress *n* maestra de niños/niñas *f.*
schoolteacher *n* maestro/tra *m/f;* profesor/a *m/f.*
schooner *n* (*mar*) goleta *f.*
sciatica *n* ciática *f.*
science *n* ciencia *f.*
scientific *adj* científico/ca; ~**ally** *adv* científicamente.
scientist *n* científico/ca *m/f.*
scimitar *n* cimitarra *f.*
scintillate *vi* chispear, centellar.
scintillating *adj* brillante, ingenioso/sa.
scissors *npl* tijeras *fpl.*
scoff *vi* mofarse, burlarse.
scold *vt, vi* regañar, reñir, refunfuñar.
scoop *n* cucharón *m;* pala *f;* exclusiva *f;* * *vt* cavar, socavar.
scooter (**child's**) *n* patinete *m.*
scope *n* objeto, intento, designio, blanco, espacio *m;* alcance *m;* libertad *f.*
scorch *vt* quemar; tostar; * *vi* quemarse, secarse.
score *n* muesca, canalita *f;* consideración *f;* cuenta *f;* puntuación *f;* razón *f;* motivo *m;* veintena *f;* * *vt* ganar; señalar con una línea; * *vi* marcar.
scoreboard *n* marcador *m.*
scorn *vt, vi* despreciar; mofar; * *n* desdén, menosprecio *m.*
scornful *adj* desdeñoso/sa; ~**ly** *adv* con desdén.
Scorpio *n* Escorpión *m* (signo del zodíaco).
scorpion *n* escorpión *m.*
scotch *vt* descartar.
Scotch *n* whisky escocés *m.*
scoundrel *n* pícaro/ra *m/f.*
scour *vt* fregar, estregar; limpiar; * *vi* corretear.
scourge *n* azote *m;* castigo *m;* * *vt* azotar, castigar.
scout *n* (*mil*) explorador/a *m/f;* espía *m/f;* * *vi* ir de reconocimiento.
scowl *vi* fruncir el ceño; * *n* ceño, semblante ceñudo *m.*
scragginess *n* flaqueza, aspereza *f.*
scraggy *adj* áspero/ra; macilento/ta.
scramble *vi* arrapar; trepar; disputar; * *n* disputa *f;* subida *f.*
scrap *n* migaja *f;* sobras *fpl;* pedacito *m;* riña *f;* chatarra *f.*
scrape *vt, vi* raer, raspar; arañar; tocar mal un instrumento; * *n* embarazo *m;* dificultad *f.*
scraper *n* rascador *m.*

scratch *vt* rascar, raspar; raer, garrapatear; * *n* rasguño *m, Lat Am* rasguñón *m.*
scrawl *vt, vi* garrapatear; * *n* garabatos *mpl.*
scream, screech *vi* chillar, dar alaridos; * *n* chillido, grito, alarido *m.*
screen *n* pantalla *f;* biombo *m;* mampara *f;* abanico de chimenea *m;* * *vt* abrigar, esconder; proyectar; cribar, cerner.
screenplay *n* guión *m, Lat Am* libreto *m.*
screw *n* tornillo *m;* * *vt* atornillar; forzar, apretar, estrechar.
screwdriver *n* destornillador *m.*
scribble *vt* escarabajear; * *n* escrito de poco mérito *m.*
scribe *n* escritor/a *m/f;* escriba *m/f.*
scrimmage *n* tumulto *m,* scrimmage *m.*
script *n* guión *m;* letra *f.*
scriptural *adj* bíblico/ca.
Scripture *n* Sagrada Escritura *f.*
scroll *n* rollo (de papel/pergamino) *m.*
scrounger *n* mamón/ona *m/f.*
scrub *vt* restregar; anular; * *n* maleza *f.*
scruffy *adj* desaliñado/da.
scruple *n* escrúpulo *m.*
scrupulous *adj* escrupuloso/sa; ~**ly** *adv* escrupulosamente.
scrutinize *vt* escudriñar, examinar.
scrutiny *n* escrutinio, examen *m.*
scuffle *n* quimera, riña *f;* * *vi* reñir, pelear.
scull *n* barquillo *m.*
sculptor *n* escultor/a *m/f.*
sculpture *n* escultura *f;* * *vt* esculpir.
scum *n* espuma *f;* escoria *f;* canalla *m/f.*
scurrilous *adj* vil, bajo/ja; injurioso/sa; ~**ly** *adv* injuriosamente.
scurvy *n* escorbuto *m;* * *adj* escorbútico/ca; vil, despreciable.
scuttle[1] *n* carbonera *f.*
scuttle[2] *vt* barrenar.
scythe *n* guadaña *f.*
sea *n* mar *m/f;* * *adj* de mar; **heavy** ~ oleada *f.*
sea breeze *n* viento de mar *m.*
seacoast *n* costa marítima *f.*
sea fight *n* combate naval *m.*
seafood *n* mariscos *mpl.*
sea front *n* paseo marítimo *m.*
sea-green *adj* verdemar.
seagull *n* gaviota *f.*
sea horse *n* caballito de mar *m.*
seal *n* sello *m;* foca *f;* * *vt* sellar.
sealing wax *n* lacre *m.*
seam *n* costura *f;* * *vt* coser.
seaman *n* marinero *m.*
seamanship *n* pericia en la navegación *m.*
seamstress *n* costurera *f.*
seamy *adj* sórdido/da.
seaport *n* puerto de mar *m.*
sear *vt* cauterizar.

search vt examinar; escudriñar; inquirir, tentar; investigar, buscar; * n pesquisa f; busca f, Lat Am procura f; buscada f.
searchlight n reflector m.
seashore n ribera f, litoral m.
seasick adj mareado/da.
seasickness n mareo m.
seaside n orilla/ribera del mar f.
season n estación f; tiempo oportuno m; sazón f; * vt sazonar; imbuir.
seasonable adj oportuno/na, a propósito.
seasonably adv oportunamente.
seasoning n condimento m.
season ticket n abono m.
season ticket holder n abonado/da m/f.
seat n asiento m; silla f; escaño m; situación f; * vt situar; colocar; asentar.
seat belt n cinturón de seguridad m.
seaward adj del litoral; ~s adv hacia el mar.
seaweed n alga marina f.
seaworthy adj en condiciones de navegar.
secede vi apartarse, separarse.
secession n secesión f; separación f.
seclude vt apartar, excluir.
seclusion n separación f; exclusión f.
second adj segundo/da; ~(ly) adv en segundo lugar; * n defensor/a m/f; segundo m; (mus) segunda f; * vt ayudar; segundar.
secondary adj secundario/ria.
secondary school n escuela secundaria f.
secondhand adj de segunda mano.
secrecy n secreto m, confidencialidad f.
secret adj secreto/ta; * n secreto m; ~ly adv secretamente.
secretary n secretario/ria m/f.
secrete vt esconder; (med) secretar.
secretion n secreción f.
secretive adj misterioso/sa.
sect n secta f.
sectarian n sectario/ria m/f.
section n sección f.
sector n sector m.
secular adj secular, seglar.
secularize vt secularizar.
secure adj seguro/ra; salvo/va; ~ly adv seguramente; * vt asegurar; salvar.
security n seguridad f; defensa f; confianza f; fianza f.
sedan, saloon n sedán m.
sedate adj sosegado/da, tranquilo/la; ~ly adv tranquilamente.
sedateness n tranquilidad f.
sedative n sedativo m.
sedentary adj sedentario/ria.
sedge n (bot) juncia f.
sediment n sedimento m; hez f; poso m.
sedition n sedición f; tumulto, alboroto, motín m; revuelta f.

seditious adj sedicioso/sa.
seduce vt seducir; engañar.
seducer n seductor/a m/f.
seduction n seducción f.
seductive adj seductor/a.
sedulous adj asiduo/dua; ~ly adv asiduamente.
see vt, vi ver, observar, descubrir; advertir; conocer, juzgar; comprender; ~! ¡mira!
seed n semilla, simiente f; * vi granar.
seedling n plantón m.
seedsman n tratante en semillas m.
seedy adj desaseado/da.
seeing conj: ~ that visto que, ya que.
seek vt, vi buscar; pretender.
seem vi parecer, semejarse.
seeming n apariencia f; ~ly adv al parecer.
seemliness n decensia f.
seemly adj decente, propio/pia.
seer n proféta m, profetisa f.
seesaw n vaivén m; * vi balancear.
seethe vi hervir, bullir.
segment n segmento m.
seize vt asir, agarrar; secuestrar (bienes/efectos).
seizure n captura f; secuestro m.
seldom adv raramente, rara vez.
select vt elegir, escoger; * adj selecto/ta, escogido/da.
selection n selección f.
self n uno/na mismo/ma; **the** ~ el yo; * pref auto-.
self-command n autocontrol m.
self-conceit n presunción f.
self-confident adj que tiene confianza en sí mismo/ma.
self-defense n defensa propia f.
self-denial n abnegación de sí mismo/ma f.
self-employed adj autónomo/ma, Lat Am cuentapropista.
self-evident adj obvio/via.
self-governing adj autónomo/ma.
self-interest n interés propio m.
selfish adj egoísta; ~ly adv interesadamente.
selfishness n egoísmo m.
self-medication n automedicación f.
self-pity n lástima de sí mismo/ma f.
self-portrait n autorretrato m.
self-possession n sangre fría, tranquilidad de ánimo f.
self-reliant adj independiente.
self-respect n amor propio m.
selfsame adj mismísimo/ma.
self-satisfied adj pagado/da de sí mismo/ma.
self-seeking adj egoísta.
self-service adj de autoservicio.
self-styled adj autoproclamado/da.
self-sufficient adj autosuficiente.
self-taught adj autodidacta.
self-willed adj obstinado/da.

S

sell *vt, vi* vender; traficar.
seller *n* vendedor/a *m/f.*
selling-off *n* privatización *f.*
Sellotape™ *n* celo *m.*
semblance *n* semejanza, apariencia *f.*
semen *n* semen *m.*
semester *n* semestre *m.*
semicircle *n* semicírculo *m.*
semicircular *adj* semicircular.
semicolon *n* punto y coma *m.*
semiconductor *n* semiconductor *m.*
semifinal *n* semifinal *f.*
seminarist *n* seminarista *m.*
seminary *n* seminario *m.*
semitone *n* (*mus*) semitono *m.*
senate *n* senado *m.*
senator *n* senador/a *m/f.*
senatorial *adj* senatorio/ria.
send *vt* enviar, despachar, mandar; enviar; producir.
sender *n* remitente *m/f.*
senile *adj* senil.
senility *n* senectud *f*; vejez *f.*
senior *n* mayor *m*; * *adj* mayor; superior.
seniority *n* antigüedad, ancianidad *f.*
senna *n* (*bot*) sena *f.*
sensation *n* sensación *f.*
sense *n* sentido *m*; entendimiento *m*; razón *f*; juicio *m*; sentimiento *m.*
senseless *adj* insensible; insensato/ta; ~ly *adv* insensatamente.
senselessness *n* tontería, insensatez *f.*
sensibility *n* sensibilidad *f.*
sensible *adj* sensato/ta; juicioso/sa.
sensibly *adv* sensatamente.
sensitive *adj* sensible.
sensual, sensuous *adj*, ~ly *adv* sensual(mente).
sensuality *n* sensualidad *f.*
sentence *n* oración *f*; sentencia *f*; * *vt* sentenciar, condenar.
sententious *adj* sentencioso/sa; ~ly *adv* sentenciosamente.
sentient *adj* sensitivo/va.
sentiment *n* sentimiento *m*; opinión *f.*
sentimental *adj* sentimental.
sentinel, sentry *n* centinela *m.*
sentry box *n* garita *f.*
separable *adj* separable.
separate *vt* (*vi*) separar(se); * *adj* separado/da; distinto/ta; ~ly *adv* separadamente.
separation *n* separación *f.*
September *n* septiembre *m.*
septennial *adj* sieteñal.
septuagenarian *n* septuagenario/ria *m/f.*
sepulcher *n* sepulcro *m.*
sequel *n* continuación *f*; consecuencia *f.*
sequence *n* serie, continuación *f.*
sequester, sequestrate *vt* secuestrar.

sequestration *n* secuestro *m.*
seraglio *n* serallo *m.*
seraph *n* serafín *m.*
serenade *n* serenata *f*; * *vt* dar serenatas.
serene *adj* sereno/na; ~ly *adv* serenamente.
serenity *n* serenidad *f.*
serf *n* siervo/va, esclavo/va *m/f.*
serge *n* sarga *f.*
sergeant *n* sargento/ta *m/f*; alguacil *m/f.*
serial *adj* consecutivo/va, en serie; * *n* serial *m*; telenovela *f.*
series *n* serie *f.*
serious *adj* serio/ria, grave; ~ly *adv* seriamente.
sermon *n* sermón *f*; oración evangélica *f.*
serpent *n* serpiente, sierpe *f.*
serpentine *adj* serpentino/na; * *n* (*chem*) serpentina *f.*
serrated *adj* serrado/da.
serum *n* suero *m.*
servant *n* criado *m*; criada *f.*
servant girl *n* criada *f.*
serve *vt, vi* servir; asistir (a la mesa); hacer; cumplir; sacar; ser a propósito; **to ~ a warrant** ejecutar un auto de prisión.
service *n* servicio *m*; servidumbre, utilidad *f*; culto divino *m*; acomodo *m*; * *vt* mantener; reparar.
serviceable *adj* servible; oficioso/sa.
service station *n* estación de servicio *f*; gasolinera *f.*
servile *adj* servil.
servitude *n* servidumbre, esclavitud *f.*
session *n* junta *f*; sesión *f.*
set *vt* poner, colocar, fijar; establecer, determinar; * *vi* ponerse (el sol/los astros); cuajarse; aplicarse; * *n* juego, conjunto *m*; servicio (de plata) *m*; conjunto/agregado de muchas cosas *m*; decorado *m*; set *m*; cuadrilla, bandada *f*; * *adj* puesto/ta, fijo/ja; listo/ta; decidido/da.
settee *n* sofá *m.*
setter *n* setter *m.*
setting *n* establecimiento *m*; marco *m*; montadura *f*; ~ **of the sun** puesta del sol *f.*
settle *vt* colocar, fijar, afirmar; arreglar; calmar; * *vi* reposarse; establecerse; sosegarse.
settlement *n* establecimiento *m*; domicilio *m*; contrato *m*; empleo *m*; poso *m*; colonia *f.*
settler *n* colono/na *m/f.*
set-to *n* riña *f*; combate *m.*
seven *adj, n* siete.
seventeen *adj, n* diecisiete.
seventeenth *adj, n* decimoséptimo/ma.
seventh *adj, n* séptimo/ma.
seventieth *adj, n* septuagésimo/ma.
seventy *adj, n* setenta.
sever *vt, vi* separar.
several *adj, pn* varios/as, algunos/nas.
severance *n* separación *f.*

severe adj severo/ra, riguroso/sa, áspero/ra, duro/ra; ~**ly** adv severamente.

severity n severidad f.

sew vt, vi coser.

sewer n alcantarilla f.

sewerage n alcantarillado m.

sewing machine n máquina de coser f.

sex n sexo m.

sexist adj, n sexista m/f.

sextant n sextante m.

sexton n sepulturero/ra m/f.

sexual adj sexual.

sexy adj sexy.

shabbily adv vilmente, mezquinamente.

shabbiness n miseria f.

shabby adj desharrapado/da, zarrapastroso/sa.

shackle vt poner grilletes; ~**s** npl grilletes mpl.

shade n sombra, oscuridad f; matiz m; sombrilla f; * vt dar sombra a; abrigar; proteger.

shadiness n sombraje m; umbría f.

shadow n sombra f; protección f.

shadowy adj umbroso/sa; oscuro/ra; quimerico/ca.

shady adj opaco/ca, oscuro/ra, sombrío/ría.

shaft n flecha, saeta f; fuste de columna m; pozo m; hueco m; rayo m.

shag n tabaco picado m; cormorán moñudo m.

shaggy adj lanoso/sa.

shake vt sacudir; agitar; **to ~ vigorously** zarandear; **to ~ hands** darse las manos; * vi vacilar; temblar; * n sacudida f, Lat Am sacudón m; vibración f.

shaking n temblor m.

shaky adj titubeante.

shallow adj somero/ra, superficial; trivial.

shallowness n poca profundidad f; necedad f.

sham vt engañar; * n fingimiento m; impostura f; * adj fingido/da, disimulado/da.

shambles npl confusión f.

shame n vergüenza f; deshonra f; * vt avergonzar, deshonrar.

shamefaced adj vergonzoso/sa, pudoroso/sa.

shameful adj vergonzoso/sa; deshonroso/sa; ~**ly** adv ignominiosamente.

shameless adj desvergonzado/da; ~**ly** adv desvergonzadamente.

shamelessness n desvergüenza, impudencia f.

shammy, chamois n gamuza f.

shampoo vt lavar con champú; * n champú m.

shamrock n trébol m.

shank n caña f; asta (de ancla) f; cañón (de pipa) m.

shanty n chabola f.

shanty town n barrio de chabolas m, Lat Am barriada f.

shape vt, vi formar; proporcionar; concebir; * n forma, figura f; modelo m.

shapeless adj informe.

shapely adj bien hecho/cha.

share n parte, porción f; (com) acción f; reja del arado f; * vt, vi repartir; compartir.

sharer n partícipe m/f.

shark n tiburón m.

sharp adj agudo/da, aguzado/da; afilado/da, Lat Am filoso/sa; astuto/ta; perspicaz; penetrante; acre, mordaz, severo/ra, rígido/da; vivo/va, violento/ta; * n (mus) sostenido m; * adv en punto.

sharpen vt afilar, aguzar.

sharply adv con filo; severamente, agudamente; ingenios amente.

sharpness n agudeza f; sutileza, perspicacia f; acrimonia f.

shatter vt destrozar, estrellar; * vi hacerse pedazos.

shave vt afeitar, rasurar; * vi afeitarse, rasurarse; * n afeite m, Lat Am afeitada f.

shaver n máquina de afeitar f.

shaving n rasurado m.

shaving brush n brocha de afeitar f.

shaving cream n crema de afeitar f.

shawl n chal m, Lat Am rebozo m.

she pn ella.

sheaf n gavilla f; haz m.

shear vt atusar; tundir; ~**s** npl tijeras de podar fpl.

sheath n vaina f.

shed vt verter, derramar; esparcir; * n tejadillo m; cabaña f.

sheen n resplandor m.

sheep n oveja f.

sheepfold n redil m.

sheepish adj vergonzoso/sa; tímido/da.

sheepishness n timidez, cortedad de genio f.

sheepskin n piel de carnero m; zamarra f; ~ **jacket** zamarra f.

sheer adj puro/ra, claro/ra, sin mezcla; escarpado/da; * adv verticalmente.

sheet n sábana f; lámina f; pliego de papel f; (mar) escota f.

sheet anchor n áncora mayor de un navio f.

sheeting n tela para sábanas f.

sheet iron n chapa de hierro batido f.

sheet lightning n relampagueamiento m.

shelf n anaquel m; (mar) arrecife m; escollera f; **on the ~** desecho/cha.

shell n cáscara f; proyectil m; concha f; corteza f; * vt descas carar, descortezar; bombardear; * vi descascararse.

shellfish npl invarcrustáceo m; marisco m.

shelter n guardia f; amparo, abrigo m; asilo, refugio m; * vt guarecer, abrigar; acoger; * vi abrigarse.

shelve vt echar a un lado, arrinconar.

shelving n estantería f.

shepherd n pastor m.

shepherdess n pastora f.

sherbet n sorbete m.

sheriff n sheriff m/f.
sherry n jerez m.
shield n escudo m; patrocinio m; * vt defender.
shift vi cambiarse; moverse; * vt mudar, cambiar; transpor tar; * n cambio m; turno m.
shinbone n espinilla f.
shine vi lucir, brillar, resplandecer; * vt lustrar; * n brillo m.
shingle[1] n guijarros mpl.
shingle[2] n letrero con nombre del dueno m.
shingles npl (med) herpes m invar.
shining adj resplandeciente; * n esplendor m.
shiny adj brillante, luciente.
ship n nave f; barco m; navío, buque m; * vt embarcar; transportar.
shipbuilding n construcción naval f.
shipmate n (mar) ayudante m/f.
shipment n cargamento mf.
shipowner n naviero/ra m/f.
shipwreck n naufragio m.
shirt n camisa f.
shit excl (col) ¡mierda!
shiver vi tiritar de frío.
shoal n banco m.
shock n choque m; descarga f; susto m; * vt asustar; ofender.
shock absorber n amortiguador m.
shoddy adj de pacotilla.
shoe n zapato m; herradura f; * vt calzar; herrar.
shoe factory n zapatería f.
shoehorn n calzador m.
shoelace n cordón de zapato m.
shoemaker n zapatero/ra m/f.
shoemaking n zapatería f.
shoe shop/store n zapatería f.
shoestring n lazo de zapato m.
shoot vt tirar, arrojar, lanzar, disparar, Lat Am balacear, Lat Am balear; * vi brotar, germinar; sobresalir; lanzarse; * n vástago m.
shooter n tirador m.
shooting n caza con escopeta f; tiroteo m.
shop front, **shop window** n escaparate m, Lat Am vidriera f, Lat Am vitrina f.
shopkeeper n tendero/ra m/f.
shoplifter n ladrón/ona de tiendas m/f.
shopper n comprador/a m/f.
shopping n compras fpl.
shopping center n centro comercial m.
shopping mall n paseo m.
shore n costa, ribera, playa f.
short adj corto/ta, breve, sucinto/ta, conciso/sa; ~**ly** adv brevemente; pronto; en pocas palabras.
shortcoming n insuficiencia f; déficit m.
shorten vt acortar; abreviar.
shortness n cortedad f; brevedad f.
short-sighted adj miope, corto de vista.
short-sightedness n miopía f.
short wave n onda corta f.

shot n tiro m; alcance m; perdigones mpl; tentativa f; toma f.
shotgun n escopeta f.
shoulder n hombro m; brazuelo m; * vt cargar al hombro.
shout vi gritar, aclamar; * vt gritar; * n aclamación f, grito m.
shouting n gritos mpl.
shove vt, vi empujar; impeler; * n empujon m.
shovel n pala f; * vt traspalar.
show vt mostrar; descubrir, manifestar; probar; ensenar, explicar; * vi parecer; * n espectaculo m; muestra f; exposición, parada f.
show business n el mundo del espectaculo m.
shower n nubada f; llovizna f; ducha f, Lat Am baño m; (fig) abundancia f; * vi llover.
showery adj lluvioso/sa.
showjumping n hípica f.
showroom n sala de muestras f.
showy adj ostentoso/sa, suntuoso/sa.
shred n cacho, pedazo pequeño m; * vt hacer trizas.
shrew n mujer de mal genio f; musaraña f.
shrewd adj astuto/ta; maligno/gna; ~**ly** adv astutamente.
shrewdness n astucia f.
shriek vt, vi chillar; * n chillido m.
shrill adj agudo/da, penetrante.
shrillness n aspereza (del sonido/de la voz) f.
shrimp n camarón m; enano/na m/f, hombrecillo m.
shrine n relicario m.
shrink vi encogerse; angostarse, acortarse.
shrivel vi arrugarse, encogerse; * vt encoger.
shroud n cubierta f; mortaja f; * vt cubrir, defender; amortajar; proteger.
Shrove Tuesday n martes de carnaval m.
shrub n arbusto m.
shrubbery n plantio de arbustos m.
shrug vt encogerse de hombros; * n encogimiento de hombros m.
shudder vi estremecerse; * n temblor m.
shuffle vt desordenar; barajar.
shun vt huir, evitar.
shunt vt (rail) maniobrar.
shut vt cerrar, encerrar; vi cerrarse.
shutter n contraventana f.
shuttle n lanzadera f.
shuttlecock n volante, rehilete m.
shy adj tímido/da; reservado/da; vergonzoso/sa, contenido/da; ~**ly** adv tímidamente.
shyness n timidez f.
sibling n hermano/na m/f.
sibyl n sibila, profetisa f.
sick adj malo/la, enfermo/ma; disgustado/da.
sicken vt enfermar; * vi caer enfermo/ma.
sickle n hoz f.
sick leave n baja por enfermedad f.
sickliness n indisposición habitual f.

sickly adj enfermizo/za.
sickness n enfermedad f.
sick pay n subsidio por enfermedad m.
side n lado m; costado m; facción f; partido m; * adj lateral; oblicuo/cua; * vi unirse.
sideboard n aparador m; alacena f.
sidelight n luz lateral f.
sidelong adj lateral.
sidewalk n acera f.
sideways adv de lado, al través.
siding n toma de partido f; (rail) aguja f.
sidle vi ir de lado.
siege n (mil) sitio m.
sieve n tamiz m; criba f; colador m; * vt cribar.
sift vt cerner; cribar; examinar; investigar.
sigh vi suspirar, gemir; * n suspiro m.
sight n vista f; mira f; espectáculo m.
sightless adj ciego/ga.
sightly adj vistoso/sa, hermoso/sa.
sightseeing n excursionismo, turismo m.
sign n señal f, indicio m; letrero m; signo m; firma f; seña f; * vt firmar.
signal n señal f, aviso m; * adj insigne, señalado/da.
signalize vt señalar.
signal lamp n (rail) reflector de señales m.
signalman n (rail) guardavía m.
signature n firma f.
signet n sello m.
significance n importancia f.
significant adj significante.
signify vt significar.
signpost n indicador m.
silence n silencio m; * vt imponer silencio.
silent adj silencioso/sa; ~ly adv silenciosamente.
silex n sílex m.
silicon chip n chip de silicio m.
silk n seda f.
silken adj hecho/cha de seda; sedeño/ña.
silkiness n blandura, molicie f.
silkworm n gusano de seda m.
silky adj hecho/cha de seda; sedoso/sa.
sill n repisa f; umbral de puerta m.
silliness n simpleza, bobería, tontería, necedad f.
silly adj tonto/ta, imbécil; ñoño/ña.
silver n plata f; * adj de plata.
silversmith n platero/ra m/f.
silvery adj plateado/da.
similar adj similar; semejante; ~ly adv del mismo modo.
similarity n semejanza f.
simile n símil m.
simmer vi hervir a fuego lento.
simony n simonía f.
simper vi sonreír; * n sonrisa f.
simple adj simple, puro/ra, sencillo/lla.
simpleton n simplón/ona, simplonazo/za m/f.
simplicity n sencillez f; simpleza f.

simplification n simplificación f.
simplify vt simplificar.
simply adv sencillamente; solo.
simulate vt simular, fingir.
simulation n simulación f.
simultaneous adj simultáneo/nea.
sin n pecado m; * vi pecar, faltar.
since adv desde, entonces, después; * prep desde; * conj desde que; ya que.
sincere adj sencillo/lla; sincero/ra; ~ly adv sinceramente; **yours** ~**ly** le saluda atentamente.
sincerity n sinceridad f.
sinecure n sinecura f.
sinew n tendón m; nervio m.
sinewy adj nervioso/sa, robusto/ta.
sinful adj pecaminoso/sa, malvado/da; ~ly adv malvadamente.
sinfulness n corrupción f.
sing vi, vt cantar; gorjear; (poet) celebrar.
singe vt chamuscar.
singer n cantante m/f.
singing n canto m.
single adj sencillo/lla, simple, solo/la; soltero/ra; * n billete sencillo m; sencillo m; * vt singularizar; separar.
singly adv separadamente.
singular adj singular, peculiar; * n singular m; ~ly adv singularmente.
singularity n singularidad f.
sinister adj siniestro/tra, izquierdo/da; infeliz, funesto/ta.
sink vi hundirse; sumergirse; bajarse; arruinarse, decaer; * vt hundir, echar a lo hondo; destruir; * n fregadero m.
sinking fund n fondo de amortización m.
sinner n pecador/a m/f.
sinuosity n sinuosidad f.
sinuous adj sinuoso/sa.
sinus n seno m.
sip vt sorber; * n sorbo m.
siphon n sifón m.
sir n señor m.
sire n caballo padre m.
siren n sirena f.
sirloin n solomillo m.
sister n hermana f.
sisterhood n hermandad f.
sister-in-law n cuñada f.
sisterly adj de hermana.
sit vi sentarse; estar situado/da; * vt presentarse a.
sitcom n telecomedia f.
site n sitio m; situación f.
sit-in n ocupación f.
sitting n sesión, junta f; sentada f.
sitting room n sala de estar f.
situated adj situado/da.
situation n situación f.
six adj, n seis.

S

sixteen *adj, n* dieciséis.
sixteenth *adj, n* decimosexto/ta.
sixth *adj, n* sexto/ta.
sixtieth *adj, n* sexagésimo/ma.
sixty *adj, n* sesenta.
size *n* tamaño, talle *m*; calibre *m*; dimensión *f*; estatura *f*; condición *f*.
sizeable *adj* considerable.
skate *n* patín *m*; * *vi* patinar.
skateboard *n* monopatín *m*.
skating *n* patinaje *m*.
skating rink *n* pista de patinaje *f*.
skein *n* madeja *f*.
skeleton *n* esqueleto *m*.
skeleton key *n* llave maestra *f*.
skeptic *n* escéptico/ca *m/f*.
skeptic(al) *adj* escéptico/ca.
skepticism *n* escepticismo *m*.
sketch *n* esbozo *m*; esquicio *m*; * *vt* esquiciar, bosquejar.
skewer *n* aguja de lardear *f*; espetón *m*; * *vt* espetar.
ski *n* esquí *m*; * *vi* esquiar.
ski boot *n* bota de esquí *f*.
skid *n* patinazo *m*; * *vi* patinar.
skier *n* esquiador/a *m/f*.
skiing *n* esquí *m*.
skill *n* destreza, arte, pericia *f*.
skilled *adj* práctico/ca, instruido/da.
skillful *adj* práctico/ca, diestro/tra; ~ly *adv* diestramente.
skillfulness *n* destreza *f*.
skim *vt* espumar; tratar superficialmente.
skimmed milk *n* leche desnatada *f*.
skimmer, skimming ladle *n* espumadera *f*.
skin *n* piel *f*; cutis *m*; * *vt* desollar.
skin diving *n* buceo *m*.
skinned *adj* desollado/da.
skinny *adj* flaco/ca, macilento/ta.
skip *vi* saltar, brincar; * *vt* pasar, omitir; * *n* salto, brinco *m*; cuba *f*.
ski pants *npl* pantalones de esquí *mpl*.
skipper *n* capitán/ana *m/f*.
skirmish *n* escaramuza *f*; * *vi* escaramuzar.
skirt *n* falda, orla *f*; * *vt* orillar.
skit *n* burla, zumba *f*.
skittish *adj* espantadizo/za, retozón/ona; terco/ca; inconstante; ~ly *adv* caprichosamente.
skulk *vi* escuchar, acechar.
skull *n* cráneo *m*.
skullcap *n* casquete *m*.
sky *n* cielo, firmamento *m*.
skylight *n* claraboya *f*.
skyrocket *n* cohete *m*.
skyscraper *n* rascacielos *m invar*.
slab *n* losa *f*.
slack *adj* flojo/ja, perezoso/sa, negligente, lento/ta.

slack(en) *vt, vi* aflojar; ablandar; entibiarse; decaer; relajar; aliviar.
slacker *n* zángano *m*.
slackness *n* flojedad, remisión *f*; descuido *m*.
slag *n* escoria *f*.
slam *vt* cerrar de golpe; * *vi* cerrarse de golpe.
slander *vt* calumniar, infamar; * *n* calumnia *f*.
slanderer *n* calumniador/a, maldiciente *m/f*.
slanderous *adj* calumnioso/sa; ~ly *adv* calumniosamente.
slang *n* argot *m*; jerigonza *f*.
slant *vi* pender oblicuamente; * *n* sesgo *m*; interpretación *f*.
slanting *adj* sesgado/da, oblicuo/cua.
slap *n* manotazo *m*; bofetada *f*; * *adv* directamente; * *vt* golpear, dar una bofetada.
slash *vt* acuchillar; * *n* cuchillada *f*.
slate *n* pizarra *f*.
slater *n* pizarrero/ra *m/f*.
slating *n* techo de pizarras *m*.
slaughter *n* carnicería, matanza *f*; * *vt* matar atrozmente; hacer una matanza de.
slaughterer *n* matador/a, asesino/na *m/f*.
slaughterhouse *n* matadero *m*, *Lat Am* cuadro *m*.
slave *n* esclavo/va *m/f*; * *vi* trabajar como esclavo/va.
slaver *n* baba *f*; * *vi* babosear.
slavery *n* esclavitud *f*.
slavish *adj* servil, humilde; ~ly *adv* servilmente.
slavishness *n* bajeza, servidumbre *f*.
slay *vt* matar, quitar la vida.
slayer *n* matador/a *m/f*.
sleazy *adj* de mala fama.
sled, sleigh *n* trineo *m*.
sledgehammer *n* mazo *m*.
sleek *adj* liso/sa, brunido/da.
sleep *vi* dormir; * *n* sueño *m*.
sleeper *n* durmiente *m*.
sleepily *adv* con somnolencia/torpeza.
sleepiness *n* sueño *m*.
sleeping bag *n* saco *m* de dormir, *Lat Am* bolsa *f* de dormir.
sleeping pill *n* somnífero *m*.
sleepless *adj* desvelado/da.
sleepwalking *n* sonambulismo *m*.
sleepy *adj* soñoliento/ta.
sleet *n* aguanieve *f*.
sleeve *n* manga *f*.
sleight *n*: ~ of hand escamoteo *m*.
slender *adj* delgado/da, débil, pequeño/ña, escaso/sa; ~ly *adv* delgadamente.
slenderness *n* delgadez *f*; tenuidad *f*; pequeñez *f*.
slice *n* rebanada *f*; espátula *f*; * *vt* rebanar.
slide *vi* resbalar, deslizarse; correr por encima del hielo; * *n* resbalón *m*; corredera *f*; diapositiva *f*; tobogán *m*.
sliding *adj* corredizo/za.

slight adj ligero/ra, leve, pequeño/ña; * n descuido m; * vt despreciar.

slightly adv ligeramente.

slightness n debilidad f; negligencia f.

slim adj delgado/da; * vi adelgazar.

slime n lodo m, Lat Am lama f; substancia viscosa f.

sliminess n viscosidad f.

slimming n adelgazamiento m.

slimy adj viscoso/sa, pegajoso/sa.

sling n honda f; cabestrillo m; * vt tirar.

slink vi escaparse; esconderse.

slip vi resbalar; escapar, huirse; * vt deslizar; * n resbalón m, Lat Am resbalada f; tropiezo m; escapada f; papelito m.

slipper n zapatilla f.

slippery adj resbaladizo/za.

slipshod adj descuidado/da.

slipway n grada f, gradas fpl.

slit vt rajar, hender; * n raja, hendedura f.

slobber n baba f.

sloe n endrina f.

slogan n eslogan, lema m.

sloop n (mar) balandro m.

slop n aguachirle f; lodazal m; ~s pl gachas fpl.

slope n cuesta f; sesgo m; declivio m; escarpa f; * vt sesgar.

sloping adj oblicuo/cua; en declive.

sloppy adj descuidado/da; desaliñado/da.

sloth n pereza f.

slouch vt, vi estar cabizbajo/ja; bambolearse pesadamente.

slovenliness n desaliño m; porquería f.

slovenly adj desaliñado/da, puerco/ca, sucio/cia.

slow adj tardío/día, lento/ta, torpe, perezoso/sa; ~ly adv lentamente, despacio.

slowness n lentitud, tardanza, pesadez f.

slowworm n lución m.

slug n holgazán/ana m/f, zángano m; babosa f; ficha f; trago m.

sluggish adj perezoso/sa; lento/ta; ~ly adv perezosamente.

sluggishness n pereza f.

sluice n compuerta f; * vt soltar la compuerta de.

slum n tugurio m; barrio bajo m.

slumber vi dormitar; * n sueño ligero m.

slump n depresión f.

slur vt ensuciar; calumniar; pronunciar mal; * n calumnia f.

slush n lodo, barro, cieno m.

slut n marrana f.

sly adj astuto/ta; ~ly adv astutamente.

slyness n astucia, maña f.

smack n sabor, gusto m; beso fuerte (que se oye) m; chasquido de latigo m; * vi saber; besar con ruido; * vt golpear.

small adj pequeño/ña, menudo/da.

smallish adj algo pequeño/ña.

smallness n pequeñez f.

smallpox n viruelas fpl.

small talk n charla, prosa f.

smart adj elegante; listo/ta, ingenioso/sa; vivo/va; * vi escocer.

smartly adv agudamente, vivamente; elegantemente; inteligentemente.

smartness n agudeza, viveza, sutileza f.

smash vt romper, quebrantar; estrellar; batir; * vi hacerse pedazos; estrellarse; * n fracaso m; choque m.

smattering n conocimiento superficial m.

smear n mancha f; (med) frotis m invar; ~ test Lat Am Papanicolau m; * vt untar; difamar.

smell vt, vi oler; * n olfato m; olor m; hediondez f.

smelly adj maloliente.

smelt n espirenque de mar m; * vt fundir (el metal).

smelter n fundidor/a m/f.

smile vi sonreír; * n sonrisa f.

smirk vi sonreír.

smite vt herir; afligir.

smith n herrero/ra m/f.

smithy n herrería f.

smock n camisa de mujer f.

smoke n humo m; vapor m; * vt, vi ahumar; humear; fumar.

smoked herring, kipper n arenque ahumado m.

smokeless adj sin humo.

smoker n fumador/a m/f.

smoking: no ~ prohibido fumar.

smoky adj humeante; humoso/sa.

smooth adj liso/sa, pulido/da, llano/na; suave; afable; * vt allanar; alisar; lisonjear.

smoothly adv llanamente; con blandura.

smoothness n lisura f; llanura f; suavidad f.

smother vt sofocar; suprimir.

smolder vi arder debajo la ceniza.

smudge vt manchar; * n mancha f.

smug adj presumido/da.

smuggle vt pasar de contrabando.

smuggler n contrabandista m/f.

smuggling n contrabando m.

smut n tiznón m; suciedad f.

smuttiness n obscenidad f.

smutty adj tiznado/da; obsceno/na.

snack n bocado, bocadillo m, pinchito m.

snack bar n cafetería f.

snag n problema m.

snail n caracol m.

snake n serpiente, culebra f.

snaky adj serpentino/na.

snap vt, vi romper; agarrar; morder; insultar; **to ~ one's fingers** castañetear; * n estallido m; foto f.

snapdragon n (bot) boca de dragón f.

snare n lazo m; trampa f.

snarl vi regañar, gruñir.

snatch vt arrebatar; agarrar; * n arrebatamiento m; robo m; bocado m.

S

sneak vi arrastrar; * n soplón/ona m/f.
sneakers npl zapatillas de lona fpl.
sneer vi hablar con desprecio.
sneeringly adv con desprecio.
sneeze vi estornudar.
sniff vt oler; * vi resollar con fuerza.
snigger vi reír disimuladamente.
snip vt tijeretear; * n tijeretada f, pedazo pequeño m; porción f.
snipe n agachadiza f; zopenco m.
sniper n francotirador/a m/f.
snivel n moquita f; * vi moquear.
sniveler n lloraduelos m invar.
snob n (e)snob m/f.
snobbish adj esnob.
snooze n sueño ligero m; * vi echar una siesta.
snore vi roncar.
snorkel n (tubo)respirador m.
snort vi resoplar.
snout n hocico m; morro m.
snow n nieve f; * vi nevar.
snowball n bola de nieve f.
snowdrop n (bot) campanilla blanca f.
snowman n muñeco de nieve m.
snowplow n quitanieves m invar.
snowy adj nevoso/sa; nevado/da.
snub vt reprender, regañar.
snub-nosed adj chato/ta; ñato/ta.
snuff n rapé m.
snuffbox n tabaquera f.
snuffle vi ganguear, hablar gangoso.
snug adj abrigado/da; conveniente, cómodo/da, agradable, grato/ta.
so adv así; de este modo; tan.
soak vi, vt remojarse; calarse; empapar, remojar.
so-and-so n zutano/na m/f.
soap n jabón m; * vt jabonar.
soap bubble n burbuja de jabón f.
soap opera n telenovela f.
soap powder n jabón en polvo m.
soapsuds n jabonaduras fpl.
soapy adj jabonoso/sa.
soar vi remontarse, sublimarse.
sob n sollozo m; * vi sollozar.
sober adj sobrio/ria; serio/ria; ~ly adv sobriamente; juiciosamente.
sobriety n sobriedad f; seriedad, sangre fria f.
soccer n fútbol m.
sociability n sociabilidad f.
sociable adj sociable, comunicativo/va.
sociably adv sociablemente.
social adj social, sociable; ~ly adv sociablemente.
socialism n socialismo m.
socialist n socialista m/f.
social work n asistencia social f.
social worker n asistente/ta social m/f.
society n sociedad f; compañia f.
sociologist n sociólogo/ga m/f.

sociology n sociología f.
sock n calcetín m; media f.
socket n enchufe m, Lat Am tomacorriente f.
socket n enchufe m.
sod n césped m.
soda n sosa f; gaseosa f.
sofa n sofá m.
soft adj blando/da, suave; benigno/na, tierno/na; afeminado/da; mullido/da; ~ly adv suavemente; paso a paso.
soften vt ablandar, mitigar; enternecer.
soft-hearted adj compasivo/va.
softness n blandura, dulzura f.
soft-spoken adj de voz suave.
software n (comput) software m.
soil vt ensuciar, emporcar; * n mancha, porquería f; terreno m; tierra f.
sojourn vi residir, morar; * n morada f; residencia f.
solace vt solazar, consolar; * n consuelo m.
solar adj solar; ~ energy energía solar f.
solder vt soldar; * n soldadura f.
soldier n soldado/da m/f; militar m.
soldierly adj soldadesco/ca.
sole n planta (del pie) f; suela (del zapato) f; lenguado m; * adj único/ca, solo/la.
solecism n (gr) solecismo m.
solemn adj, ~ly adv solemne(mente).
solemnity n solemnidad f.
solemnize vt solemnizar.
solicit vt solicitar; implorar.
solicitation n solicitación f.
solicitor n representante, agente m/f.
solicitous adj solícito/ta, diligente; ~ly adv solícitamente.
solicitude n solicitud f.
solid adj sólido/da, compacto/ta; * n sólido m; ~ly adv sólidamente.
solidify vt solidificar.
solidity n solidez f.
soliloquy n soliloquio m.
solitaire n solitario m.
solitary adj solitario/ria, retirado/da; * n ermitaño/ña m/f.
solitude n soledad f; vida solitaria f.
solo n (mus) solo/la m.
solstice n solsticio m.
soluble adj soluble.
solution n solución f.
solve vt resolver.
solvency n solvencia f.
solvent adj solvente; n (chem) solvente m.
some adj algo de, un poco, algún, alguno, alguna, unos, pocos, ciertos.
somebody n alguien m.
somehow adv de algún modo.
someplace adv en alguna parte; a alguna parte.
something n alguna cosa, algo.
sometime adv algún día.

sometimes adv a veces.
somewhat adv algo; algún tanto, un poco.
somewhere adv en alguna parte; a alguna parte.
somnambulism n sonambulismo m.
somnambulist n sonámbulo/la m/f.
somnolence n somnolencia f.
somnolent adj somnoliento/ta.
son n hijo m.
sonata n (mus) sonata f.
song n canción f.
son-in-law n yerno m.
sonnet n soneto m.
sonorous adj sonoro/ra.
soon adv ya, pronto; **as ~ as** luego que.
sooner adv antes, más pronto.
soot n hollín m.
soothe vt adular; calmar.
soothsayer n adivino/na m/f.
sop n sopa f.
sophism n sofisma m.
sophist n sofista m/f.
sophistical adj sofístico/ca.
sophisticate vt sofisticar; falsificar.
sophisticated adj sofisticado/da.
sophistry n sofistería f.
soporific adj soporífero/ra.
sorcerer n hechicero m.
sorceress n hechicera f.
sorcery n hechizo, encanto m.
sordid adj sórdido/da, sucio/cia; asqueroso/sa.
sordidness n sordidez, suciedad f.
sore n llaga, úlcera f; * adj doloroso/sa, penoso/sa; resentido/da; ~**ly** adv penosamente.
sorrel n (bot) acedera f; * adj alazán rojo/ja.
sorrow n pesar m; tristeza f; * vi entristecerse.
sorrowful adj pesaroso/sa, afligido/da; ~**ly** adv con aflicción.
sorry adj triste, afligido/da; arrepentido/da; **I am ~** lo siento.
sort n suerte f; género m; especie f; calidad f; manera f; * vt separar en distintas clases; escoger, elegir.
soul n alma f; esencia f; persona f.
sound adj sano/na; entero/ra; puro/ra; firme; ~**ly** adv sanamente, vigo rosamente; * n sonido, ruido m; estrecho m; * vt sonar; tocar; celebrar; sondar; * vi sonar, resonar; parecer.
sounding board n diapasón m; sombrero de púlpito m.
sound effects npl efectos sonoros mpl.
soundings npl (mar) sondeo m; (mar) surgidero m.
soundness n sanidad f; fuerza, solidez f.
soundtrack n banda sonora f.
soup n sopa f.
sour adj agrio/ria, ácido/da; cortado/da; áspero/ra; ~**ly** adv agriamente; * vt, vi agriar, acedar; agriarse.
source n manantial m; principio m.

sourness n acedía, agrura f; acrimonia f.
souse n (col) borracho/cha m/f; * vt escabechar; chapuzar.
souvenir n recuerdo m.
south n sur m; * adj del sur; * adv al sur.
southerly, **southern** adj del sur, meridional.
southward(s) adv hacia el sur.
southwester n (mar) viento de sudoeste m; sombrero grande de los marineros m.
sovereign adj, n soberano/na m/f.
sovereignty n soberanía f.
sow[1] n puerca, marrana f.
sow[2] vt sembrar; esparcir.
sowing time n sementera, siembra f.
soybean n semilla de soja f.
space n espacio m; intersticio m; * vt espaciar.
spacecraft n nave espacial f.
spaceman n astronauta m.
spacewoman n astronauta f.
spacious adj espacioso/sa, amplio/lia; ~**ly** adv con bastante espacio.
spaciousness n espaciosidad f.
spade n laya, azada f; pica (en los naipes) f.
spaghetti n espaguetis mpl.
span n palmo m; envergadura f; * vt cruzar; abarcar.
spangle n lentejuela f; * vt adornar con lentejuelas.
spaniel n perro de aguas m.
Spanish adj, n español/a m/f; ~ **musical comedy/ light opera** zarzuela f.
Spanish America n Hispanoamérica f.
Spanish American adj hispanoamericano/na; * n hispanoamericano/na m/f.
spar n palo m; * vi entrenarse.
spare vt, vi ahorrar, economizar; perdonar; pasarse sin; vivir con economía; * adj de más; de reserva.
sparing adj escaso/sa, raro/ra, económico/ca; ~**ly** adv parcamente, frugalmente.
spark n chispa f.
sparkle n centella, chispa f; * vi chispear; espumar.
spark plug n bujía f.
sparrow n gorrión m.
sparrowhawk n gavilán m.
sparse adj delgado/da; tenue; ~**ly** adv tenuemente.
spasm n espasmo m.
spasmodic adj espasmódico/ca.
spatter vt salpicar, manchar.
spatula n espátula f.
spawn n freza f; * vt, vi desovar; engendrar.
spawning n freza f.
speak vt, vi hablar; decir; conversar; pronunciar.
speaker n altavoz m, Lat Am parlante m; bafle m; orador/a m/f.
spear n lanza f; arpón m; * vt herir con lanza.

S

special adj especial, particular; **~ly** adv especialmente.

specialty n especialidad f.

species n especie f.

specific adj específico/ca; *,* n específico m.

specifically adv específicamente.

specification n especificación f.

specify vt especificar.

specimen n muestra f; prueba f.

specious adj especioso/sa.

speck(le) n mácula, tacha f; * vt abigarrar, manchar.

spectacle n espectáculo m.

spectacles npl gafas fpl.

spectator n espectador/a m/f.

spectral adj espectral; **~ analysis** n análisis espectral m invar.

specter n espectro m.

speculate vi especular; reflexionar.

speculation n especulación f; especulativa f; meditación f.

speculative adj especulativo/va, teórico/ca.

speculum n espéculo m.

speech n habla m; discurso m; lenguaje m; conversación f.

speechify vi arengar.

speechless adj sin habla.

speed n prisa f; velocidad f; * vt apresurar; despachar; * vi darse prisa.

speedboat n lancha motora f.

speedily adv aceleradamente, deprisa.

speediness n celeridad, prontitud, precipitación f.

speed limit n límite de velocidad m, velocidad maxima f.

speedometer n velocímetro m.

speedway n pista de carreras f.

speedy adj veloz, pronto/ta, diligente.

spell n hechizo, encanto m; período m; * vt, vi escribir correc tamente; deletrear; hechizar, encantar.

spelling n ortografía f.

spend vt gastar; pasar; disipar; consumir.

spendthrift n despilfarrador/a m/f.

spent adj agotado/da.

sperm n esperma f.

spermaceti n espermaceti m.

spew vi (col) vomitar.

sphere n esfera f.

spherical adj esférico/ca; **~ly** adv en forma esférica.

spice n especia f; * vt especiar.

spick-and-span adj aseado/da, (bien) arreglado/da.

spicy adj aromático/ca.

spider n araña f.

spigot n grifo m.

spike n espiga de grano f; espigón m; * vi clavar con espi gones.

spill vt derramar, verter; * vi derramarse.

spin vt hilar; alargar, prolongar; girar; * vi dar vueltas; * n vuelta f; paseo (en coche) m.

spinach n espinaca f.

spinal adj espinal.

spindle n huso m; quicio m.

spine n espinazo m, espina f.

spineless adj ñoño/ña.

spinet n (mus) espineta f.

spinner n hilador/a m/f; hilandero/ra m/f.

spinning top n trompa f.

spinning wheel n rueca f.

spin-off n derivado, producto secundario m.

spinster n soltera f.

spiral adj espiral; **~ly** adv en figura de espiral.

spire n espira f; pirámide m; aguja f (de una torre).

spirit n aliento m; espíritu m; ánimo, valor m; brío m; humor m; fantasma m; * vt incitar, animar; **to ~ away** quitar secretamente.

spirited adj vivo/va, brioso/sa; **~ly** adv con espíritu.

spirit lamp n velón/quinque de alcohol m.

spiritless adj abatido/da, sin espíritu.

spiritual adj, **~ly** adv espiritual(mente).

spiritualist n espiritista m/f.

spirituality n espiritualidad f.

spit n asador m; saliva f; * vt, vi espetar; escupir.

spite n rencor m, malevolencia f; **in ~ of** a pesar de, a despe cho; * vt dar pesar.

spiteful adj rencoroso/sa, malicioso/sa; **~ly** adv malignamente, con tirria.

spitefulness n malicia f; rencor m.

spittle n saliva f; baba f, esputo m.

splash vt salpicar, enlodar; * vi chapotear; * n chapoteo m; mancha f.

spleen n bazo m; esplín m.

splendid adj espléndido/da, magnífico/ca; **~ly** adv espléndidamente.

splendor n esplendor m; pompa f.

splice vt (mar) empalmar, empleitar.

splint n tablilla f.

splinter n cacho m; astilla f; brisna f; * vt (vi) hender(se).

split n hendedura f; división f; * vt hender, rajar; * vi hen derse.

splutter, sputter vi escupir con frecuencia; babosear; barbotar.

spoil vt despojar; arruinar; mimar.

spoiled adj pasado/da; cortado/da.

spoke n radio (de la rueda) m.

spokesman n portavoz m, Lat Am personero m, Lat Am vocero m.

spokeswoman n portavoz f, Lat Am personera f, Lat Am vocera f.

sponge n esponja f; * vt limpiar con esponja; * vi meterse de mogollón.

sponger n mogollón m.

sponginess n esponjosidad f.

spongy adj esponjoso/sa.

sponsor *n* patrocinador/a *m/f*; padrino *m*; madrina *f*.

sponsorship *n* patrocinio *m*.

spontaneity *n* espontaneidad, voluntariedad *f*.

spontaneous *adj* espontáneo/nea; **~ly** *adv* espontaneamente.

spool *n* carrete *m*; canilla, broca *f*.

spoon *n* cuchara *f*.

spoonful *n* cucharada *f*.

sporadic(al) *adj* esporádico/ca.

sport *n* deporte *m*; juego, retozo *m*; juguete, divertimiento, recreo, pasatiempo *m*.

sports car *n* coche deportivo *m*.

sports coat, sports jacket *n* chaqueta deportiva *f*.

sportsman *n* deportista *m*.

sportswear *n* ropa de deporte/sport *f*.

sportswoman *n* deportista *f*.

spot *n* mancha *f*; borrón *m*; sitio, lugar *m*; grano *m*; * *vt* notar; manchar.

spotless *adj* limpio/pia, inmaculado/da.

spotlight *n* foco, reflector *m*.

spotted, spotty *adj* lleno/na de manchas; con granos.

spouse *n* esposo/a *m/f*.

spout *vi* borbotar; chorrear; * *vt* arrojar; vomitar; *(fig)* declamar; * *n* pitón *m*, pico *m*.

sprain *adj* descoyuntar; * *n* dislocación *f*.

sprat *n* meleta, nuesa (pez) *f*.

sprawl *vi* revolcarse.

spray *n* rociada *f*; espray *m*; ramita *f*; espuma de la mar *f*.

spread *vt* extender, desplegar; esparcir, divulgar; * *vi* extenderse, desplegarse; * *n* extensión, dilatación *f*.

spree *n* fiesta *f*; juerga *f*.

sprig *n* ramito *m*.

sprightliness *n* alegría, vivacidad *f*.

sprightly *adj* alegre, despierto/ta, vivaracho/cha.

spring *vi* brotar, arrojar; nacer, provenir; dimanar, originarse; saltar, brincar; * *n* primavera *f*; elasticidad *f*; muelle, resorte *m*; salto *m*; manantial *m*.

springiness *n* elasticidad *f*.

spring onion *n* cebolleta *f*.

springtime *n* primavera *f*.

spring water *n* agua de fuente *f*.

springy *adj* elástico/ca; mullido/da.

sprinkle *vt* rociar.

sprinkling *n* rociadura *f*.

sprout *n* vástago, renuevo *m*; **~s** *npl* coles de Bruselas *fpl*; * *vi* brotar.

spruce *adj* pulido/da, gentil; **~ly** *adv* bellamente, lindamente; * *vr* vestirse con afectación.

spruceness *n* lindeza, hermosura *f*.

spur *n* espuela *f*; espolón (del gallo) *m*; estímulo *m*; * *vt* espolear, *Lat Am* talonear; estimular.

spurious *adj* espurio/ria, falso/sa; contrahecho/cha; supuesto/ta; bastardo/da.

spurn *vt* despreciar.

spy *n* espía *m/f*; * *vt, vi* espiar.

squabble *vi* reñir, disputar; * *n* riña, disputa *f*.

squad *n* escuadra *f*; brigada *f*; equipo *m*.

squadron *n* *(mil)* escuadrón *m*.

squalid *adj* sucio/cia, puerco/ca.

squall *n* ráfaga *f*; chubasco *m*; * *vi* chillar.

squally *adj* borrascoso/sa.

squalor *n* porquería, suciedad *f*.

squander *vt* malgastar, disipar.

square *adj* cuadrado/da, cuadrángulo/la; exacto/ta; cabal; * *n* cuadro *m*; plaza *f*; escuadra *f*; * *vt* cuadrar; ajustar, arreglar; * *vi* ajustarse.

squareness *n* cuadratura *f*.

squash *vt* aplastar; * *n* squash *m*.

squat *vi* agacharse; * *adj* agachado/da; rechoncho/cha.

squatter *n* ocupante ilegal *m/f*; *(col)* okupa *m/f*.

squaw *n* mujer de un indio *f*.

squeak *vi* plañir, chillar; * *n* grito, plañido *m*.

squeal *vi* plañir, gritar.

squeamish *adj* fastidioso/sa; demasiado delicado/da.

squeeze *vt* apretar, comprimir; estrechar; * *n* presión *f*; apretón *m*; restricción *f*.

squid *n* calamar *m*.

squint *adj* bizco/ca; * *vi* bizquear; * *n* estrabismo.

squirrel *n* ardilla *f*.

squirt *vt* jeringar; * *n* jeringa *f*; chorro *m*; pisaverde *m*.

stab *vt* apuñalar; * *n* puñalada *f*.

stability *n* estabilidad, solidez *f*.

stable *n* establo *m*; * *vt* poner en el establo; * *adj* estable.

stack *n* pila *f*; * *vt* hacinar.

staff *n* personal *m*, plantilla *f*; palo *m*; apoyo *m*.

stag *n* ciervo *m*.

stage *n* etapa *f*; escena *f*; tablado *m*; teatro *m*; parada *f*; escalón *m*.

stagger *vi* vacilar, titubear; estar incierto/ta; * *vt* asustar; escalonar.

stagnant *adj* estancado/da.

stagnate *vi* estancarse.

stagnation *n* estancamiento *m*.

staid *adj* grave, serio/ria.

stain *vt* manchar; empañar la reputación de; * *n* mancha *f*; deshonra *f*.

stainless *adj* limpio/pia; inmaculado/da.

stair *n* escalón *m*; **~s** *pl* escalera *f*.

staircase *n* escalera *f*.

stake *n* estaca *f*; apuesta (en el juego) *f*; * *vt* estacar; apostar.

stale *adj* añejo/ja, viejo/ja, rancio/cia, *Lat Am* zocato/ta.

staleness *n* vejez *f*; rancidez *f*.

stalk *vi* andar con paso majestuoso; * *n* tallo, pie, tronco *m*; troncho *m* (de ciertas hortalizas).

S

stall n pesebre m; puesto m; tabanco m; emplazamiento m; * vt parar; * vi pararse; buscar evasivas.

stallion n semental m; caballo entero m.

stalwart n partidario/ria leal m/f.

stamen n estambre m; fundamento m.

stamina n resistencia f.

stammer vi tartamudear; * n tartamudeo m.

stamp vt patear; estampar, imprimir; acuñar; andar con mucha pesadez; * vi patear; * n cuño m; sello m; impresión f; huella f; Lat Am estampilla f; zapatazo m.

stampede n estampida f.

stand vi estar de pie; ponerse de pie, Lat Am pararse; sostenerse; permanecer; pararse, hacer alto, estar situado/da; hallarse; erizarse (el pelo); * vt poner; aguantar; sostener, defender; * n puesto, sitio m; posición, situación f; parada f; estado m (fijo); tribuna f; stand m.

standard n estandarte m; modelo m; precio ordinario m; norma f; * adj normal.

standing adj permanente, fijado/da, establecido/da; de pie, Lat Am parado/da; estancado/da; * n duración f; posición f; puesto m.

standstill n pausa f; alto m.

staple n grapa f; * adj básico/ca, establecido/da; * vt grapar, Lat Am engrapar.

star n estrella f; asterisco m.

starboard n estribor m.

starch n almidón m; * vt almidonar.

stare vi: **to ~ at** clavar la vista en; * n mirada fija f.

stark adj fuerte, áspero/ra; puro/ra; * adv del todo.

starling n estornino m.

starry adj estrellado/da.

start vi empezar; sobrecogerse, sobresaltarse; levantarse de repente; salir; * vt empezar; causar; fundar; poner en marcha; * n principio m; salida f; sobresalto m; ímpetu m; paso primero m.

starter n estárter m; juez de salida m.

starting point n punto de partida m.

startle vt sobresaltar.

startling adj alarmante.

starvation n hambre, inanición f.

starve vi pasar hambre.

state n estado m; condición f; estado (político); pompa, gran deza f; **the S~s** los Estados Unidos mpl; * vt afirmar; exponer.

stateliness n grandeza, pompa f.

stately adj augusto/ta, majestuoso/sa.

statement n afirmación, cuenta f.

statesman n estadista, político m.

statesmanship n política f.

static adj estático/ca; * n parásitos mpl.

station n estación f; emisora f; empleo, puesto m; situación f; condición f; (rail) estación f; * vt apostar.

stationary adj estacionario/ria, fijo/ja.

stationer n papelero/ra m/f.

stationery n papelería f.

station wagon n ranchera f.

statistical adj estadístico/ca.

statistics npl estadística f.

statuary n estatuario/ria, escultor/a m/f.

statue n estatua f.

stature n estatura, talla f.

statute n estatuto m; reglamento m.

stay n estancia f, Lat Am estadía f; **~s** npl corsé, justillo m; * vi quedarse, estarse; detenerse; esperarse; **to ~ in** quedarse en casa; **to ~ on** quedarse; **to ~ up** velar.

steadfast adj firme, estable, sólido/da; **~ly** adv firmemente, con constancia.

steadily adv firmemente; invariablemente.

steadiness n firmeza, estabilidad f.

steady adj firme, fijo/ja; * vt hacer firme.

steak n filete m; bistec m.

steal vt, vi robar.

stealth n hurto m; **by ~** a hurtadillas.

stealthily adv furtivamente.

stealthy adj furtivo/va.

steam n vapor m; humo m; * vt cocer al vapor; * vi echar humo.

steam-engine n máquina de vapor f.

steamer, **steamboat** n vapor, buque de vapor m.

steel n acero m; * adj de acero.

steelyard n romana f.

steep adj escarpado/da; excesivo/va; * vt empapar.

steeple n torre f; campanario m.

steeplechase n carrera de obstáculos f.

steepness n lo escarpado; lo abrupto.

steer[1] n novillo m.

steer[2] vt manejar, conducir; dirigir; gobernar; * vi conducir.

steering n dirección f.

steering wheel n volante m.

stellar adj estrellado/da.

stem n vástago, tallo m; estirpe f; pie m; cañón m; * vt cortar la corriente.

stench n hedor m.

stencil n cliché m.

stenographer n taquígrafo/fa m/f.

stenography n taquigrafía f.

step n paso, escalón m; huella f; * vi dar un paso; andar.

stepbrother n hermanastro m.

stepdaughter n hijastra f.

stepfather n padrastro m.

stepmother n madrastra f.

stepping stone n pasadera f.

stepsister n hermanastra f.

stepson n hijastro m.

stereo n estérreo m.

stereotype n estereotipo m; * vt estereotipar.

sterile adj estéril.

sterility n esterilidad f.

sterling *adj* esterlín/ina, genuino/na, verdadero/ra; * *n* libras esterlinas *fpl*.

stern *adj* austero/ra, rígido/da, severo/ra; * *n* (*mar*) popa *f*; **~ly** *adv* austeramente.

stethoscope *n* (*med*) estetoscopio *m*.

stevedore *n* (*mar*) estibador/a *m/f*.

stew *vt* estofar; * *n* estufa, olla *f*.

steward *n* mayordomo *m*; (*mar*) despensero *m*.

stewardess *n* azafata *f*, *Lat Am* aeromoza *f*.

stewardship *n* mayordomía *f*.

stick *n* palo, palillo, bastón *m*; vara *f*; * *vt* pegar, hincar; aguantar; picar; * *vi* pegarse; detenerse; perseverar; dudar.

stickiness *n* viscosidad, gomosidad *f*.

sticking plaster *n* esparadrapo *m*.

stick shift *n* palanca de cambios *f*.

stick-up *n* asalto, atraco *m*.

sticky *adj* viscoso/sa, tenaz.

stiff *adj* tieso/sa; duro/ra, torpe; rígido/da; yerto/ta; obstinado/da; **~ly** *adv* obstinadamente.

stiffen *vt* atiesar, endurecer; * *vi* endurecerse.

stiff neck *n* tortícolis *m*.

stiffness *n* tesura, rigidez *f*; obstinación *f*.

stifle *vt* suofocar.

stifling *adj* bochornoso/sa.

stigma *n* estigma *m*.

stigmatize *vt* estigmatizar.

stile *n* portillo con escalones *m* (para pasar de un cercado a otro).

stiletto *n* estilete *m*; tacón de aguja *m*.

still *vt* aquietar, aplacar; destilar; * *adj* silencioso/sa, tranquilo/la; * *n* alambique *m*; * *adv* todavía; hasta ahora; no obstante; aún así.

stillborn *adj* nacido/da muerto/ta.

stillness *n* calma, quietud *f*.

stilts *npl* zancos *mpl*.

stimulant *n* estimulante *m*.

stimulate *vt* estimular, aguijonear.

stimulation *n* estímulo *m*; estimulación *f*.

stimulus *n* estímulo *m*.

sting *vt* picar/morder (un insecto); * *vi* escocer; * *n* aguijón *m*; punzada, picadura, picada *f*; timo *m*.

stingily *adv* avaramente.

stinginess *n* tacañería, avaricia *f*.

stingy *adj* mezquino/na, tacaño/ña, avaro/ra.

stink *vi* heder; * *n* hedor *m*.

stint *n* tarea *f*.

stipulate *vt* estipular.

stipulation *n* estipulación *f*; condición *f*.

stir *vt* remover; agitar; incitar; * *vi* moverse; * *n* tumulto *m*; turbulencia *f*.

stirrup *n* estribo *m*.

stitch *vt* coser; * *n* punzada *f*; punto *m*.

stoat *n* armiño *m*.

stock *n* existencias *fpl*; ganado *m*; caldo *m*; estirpe *f*, linaje *m*; capital, principal *m*; fondo *m*; **~s** *pl* acciones en los fondos públicos *fpl*; * *vt* proveer, abastecer.

stockade *n* prisión militar *f*.

stockbroker *n* agente de bolsa *m/f*.

stock exchange *n* bolsa *f*.

stockholder *n* accionista *m/f*.

stocking *n* media *f*.

stock market *n* bolsa *f*.

stoic *n* estoico/ca *m/f*.

stoical *adj* estoico/ca; **~ly** *adv* estoicamente.

stoicism *n* estoicismo *m*.

stole *n* estola *f*.

stomach *n* estómago *m*; apetito *m*; * *vt* aguantar.

stone *n* piedra *f*; pepita *f*; hueso de fruta *m*; * *adj* de piedra; * *vt* apedrear; deshuesar; empedrar; trabajar de albañil.

stone deaf *adj* sordo/da como una tapia.

stoning *n* apedreamiento *m*.

stony *adj* de piedra, pétreo/rea; duro/ra.

stool *n* banquillo, taburete *m*.

stoop *vi* encorvarse, inclinarse; bajarse; * *n* inclinación hacia abajo *f*.

stop *vt* detener, parar; tapar; * *vi* pararse, hacer alto; * *n* parada *f*; punto *m*; pausa *f*; obstáculo *m*.

stopover *n* parada; rescala *f*.

stoppage *n* obstrucción *f*; impedimiento *m*.

stopwatch *n* cronómetro *m*.

storage *n* almacenamiento *m*; almacenaje *m*.

store *n* abundancia *f*; provisión *f*; almacén *m*, taller *m*, tienda *f*; * *vt* surtir, proveer, abastecer.

store front, **store window** *n* escaparate *m*.

store owner *n* tendero/ra *m/f*.

storm *n* tempestad, borrasca *f*; asalto *m*; * *vt* tomar por asalto; * *vi* rabiar.

stormily *adv* violentamente.

stormy *adj* tempestuoso/sa; violento/ta.

story[1] *n* historia *f*; chiste *m*.

story[2] *n* piso (de una casa) *m*.

stout *adj* robusto/ta, corpulento/ta, vigoroso/sa; terco/ca; **~ly** *adv* valientemente; obstinadamente.

stork *n* cigüeña *f*.

stoutness *n* valor *m*; fuerza *f*; corpulencia *f*.

stove *n* cocina *f*; estufa *f*.

stow *vt* ordenar, colocar; (*mar*) estibar.

straggle *vi* rezagarse.

straggler *n* rezagado/da *m/f*.

straight *adj* derecho/cha; estrecho/cha; franco/ca; * *adv* directamente.

straightaway *adv* inmediatamente.

straighten *vt* enderezar.

straightforward *adj* derecho/cha; franco/ca; leal.

straightforwardness *n* derechura *f*, franqueza *f*.

strain *vt* colar, filtrar; apretar (a uno contra sí); forzar, violen tar; * *vi* esforzarse; * *n* tensión *f*; retorcimiento *m*; raza *f*; linaje *m*; estilo *m*; sonido *m*; armonía *f*.

strainer *n* colador *m*, *Lat Am* coladera *f*.

S

strait n estrecho m; aprieto, peligro m; penuria f.
straitjacket n camisa de fuerza f.
strand n hebra f; costa, playa f.
strange adj raro/ra; extraño/ña; ~ly adv extrañamente, extraordinariamente.
strangeness n rareza f; extrañeza f.
stranger n desconocido/da m/f; extranjero/ra m/f.
strangle vt estrangular.
strangulation n estrangulamiento m.
strap n correa, tira de cuero f; tirante de bota m; * vt atar con correa.
strapping adj abultado/da, corpulento/ta.
stratagem n estratagema f; astucia f.
strategic adj estratégico/ca.
strategy n estrategia f.
stratum n estrato m.
straw n paja m; pajita f.
strawberry n fresa f.
stray vi extraviarse; perder el camino; * adj extraviado/da; perdido/da.
streak n raya, lista f; vena f; * vt rayar.
stream n arroyo m, río m, Lat Am quebrada f, torrente m; * vi correr.
streamer n serpentina f.
street n calle f.
strength n fuerza, robustez f; vigor m; fortaleza f.
strengthen vt fortificar; corroborar.
strenuous adj arduo/dua; ágil.
stress n presión f; estrés m; fuerza f; peso m; importancia f; acento m; * vt subrayar; acentuar.
stretch vt, vi extender, alargar; estirar; extenderse; esfor zarse; * n extensión f; trecho m; estirón m.
stretcher n camilla f.
strew vt esparcir; sembrar.
strict adj estricto/ta, estrecho/cha; exacto/ta, riguroso/sa, severo/ra; ~ly adv exactamente, con severidad.
strictness n exactitud f; severidad f, Lat Am estrictez f, estrechez f.
stride n tranco m; zancada f; * vi atrancar.
strife n contienda, disputa f.
strike vt, vi golpear; herir; castigar; tocar; chocar; sonar; cesar de trabajar; * n ataque m; descubrimiento m; huelga f, Lat Am paro m.
striker n huelguista m/f.
striking adj llamativo/va; notorio/ria; ~ly adv sorprendentemente.
string n cordón m; hilo m; cuerda f; hilera f; fibra f; * vt encordar; enhilar; estirar.
stringent adj astringente.
stringy adj fibroso/sa.
strip vt desnudar, despojar; * vi desnudarse; * n tira f; franja f; faja f; cinta f.
stripe n raya, lista f; azote m; * vt rayar.
strive vi esforzarse; empeñarse; disputar, contender; oponerse.
stroke n golpe m; toque (en la pintura) m; sonido

(del reloj) m; plumada f; acaricia f; apoplejía f; * vt acariciar.
stroll n paseo; * vi dar un paseo.
strong adj fuerte, vigoroso/sa, robusto/ta; poderoso/sa; violento/ta; ~ly adv fuertemente, con violencia.
strongbox n caja fuerte f.
stronghold n plaza fuerte f.
strophe n estrofa f.
structure n estructura f; edificio m.
struggle vi esforzarse; luchar; agitarse; * n lucha f.
strum vt (mus) rasguear.
strut vi pavonearse; * n contoneo m.
stub n talón m; colilla f; tronco m.
stubble n rastrojo m; cerda f.
stubborn adj obstinado/da, testarudo/da, Lat Am necio/a; ~ly adv obstinadamente.
stubbornness n obstinación, pertinacia f.
stucco n estuco m.
stud¹ n corchete m; taco m.
stud² caballeriza f.
student n estudiante m/f; * adj estudiantil.
studio n estudio m.
studio flat n estudio m.
studious adj estudioso/sa; diligente; ~ly adv estudiosamente, diligentemente.
study n estudio m; aplicación f; meditación profunda f; * vt estudiar; observar; * vi estudiar; aplicarse.
stuff n materia f; material m; estofa f; * vt henchir, llenar; disecar.
stuffing n relleno m.
stuffy adj cargado/da; de miras estrechas.
stumble vi tropezar; * n traspié, tropiezo m.
stumbling block n tropiezo m; escollo m.
stump n tronco m; tocón m; muñón m.
stun vt aturdir, ensordecer.
stunner n cosa estupenda f.
stunt n vuelo acrobático m; truco publicitario m; * vt no dejar crecer.
stuntman n especialista m.
stuntwoman n especialista f.
stupefy vt atontar, atolondrar.
stupendous adj estupendo/da, maravilloso/sa.
stupid adj estúpido/da; very ~ zopenco/ca; ~ly adv estúpidamente.
stupidity n estupidez f.
stupor n estupor m.
sturdily adv fuertemente.
sturdiness n fuerza, fortaleza f; obstinación f.
sturdy adj fuerte, tieso/sa, robusto/ta; bronco/ca, insolente.
sturgeon n esturión m.
stutter vi tartamudear.
sty n zahurda f; pocilga f.
stye, sty n orzuelo m.
style n estilo m; moda f; * vt titular; nombrar; estilizar.

stylish *adj* elegante, en buen estilo.
suave *adj* afable.
subdivide *vt* subdividir.
subdivision *n* subdivisión f.
subdue *vt* sojuzgar, sujetar; conquistar; mortificar.
subject *adj* sujeto/ta; sometido/da; * *n* sujeto m; súbdito/ta m/f; tema m; * *vt* sujetar; exponer.
subjection *n* sujeción f.
subjugate *vt* sojuzgar, subyugar.
subjugation *n* subyugación f.
subjunctive *n* subjuntivo m.
sublet *vt* subarrendar.
sublimate *vt* sublimar.
sublime *adj* sublime, excelso/sa; ~**ly** *adv* de modo sublime; * *n* sublime m.
sublimity *n* sublimidad f.
submachine gun *n* metralleta f.
submarine *adj* submarino/na; * *n* submarino m.
submerge *vt* sumergir.
submersion *n* inmersión f; zambullida f.
submission *n* sumisión f.
submissive *adj* sumiso/sa, obsequioso/sa; ~**ly** *adv* con sumisión.
submissiveness *n* obsequio m; sumisión f.
submit *vt* (*vi*) someter(se).
subordinate *adj* subordinado/da, inferior; * *vt* subordinar.
subordination *n* subordinación f.
subpoena *n* citación f; * *vt* citar.
subscribe *vt, vi* suscribir, certificar con su firma; consentir.
subscriber *n* suscriptor/a m/f.
subscription *n* suscripción f.
subsequent *adj*, ~**ly** *adv* subsiguiente(mente).
subservient *adj* subordinado/da; servil.
subside *vi* sumergirse, irse a fondo.
subsidence *n* derrumbamiento m.
subsidiary *adj* subsidiario/ria.
subsidize *vt* subvencionar, dar subsidios.
subsidy *n* subvención f; subsidio, socorro m.
subsist *vi* subsistir; existir.
subsistence *n* existencia f; subsistencia f.
substance *n* substancia f; entidad f; esencia f.
substantial *adj* substancial; real, material; substancioso/sa; fuerte; ~**ly** *adv* substancialmente.
substantiate *vt* probar.
substantive *n* sustantivo m.
substitute *vt* sustituir; * *n* suplente m/f.
substitution *n* sustitución f.
substratum *n* sustrato m.
subterfuge *n* subterfugio m; evasión f.
subterranean *adj* subterráneo/nea.
subtitle *n* subtítulo m.
subtle *adj* sutil, astuto/ta.
subtlety *n* sutileza, astucia f.
subtly *adv* sutilmente.
subtract *vt* (*math*) sustraer.

suburb *n* zona residencial f.
suburban *adj* suburbano/na.
subversion *n* subversión f.
subversive *adj* subversivo/va.
subvert *vt* subvertir, destruir.
succeed *vt, vi* seguir; conseguir, lograr, tener exito.
success *n* éxito m.
successful *adj* exitoso/sa; próspero/ra, dichoso/sa; ~**ly** *adv* con éxito; prósperamente.
succession *n* sucesión f; descendencia f; herencia f.
successive *adj* sucesivo/va; ~**ly** *adv* sucesivamente.
successor *n* sucesor/a m/f.
succinct *adj* sucinto/ta, compendioso/sa; ~**ly** *adv* con brevedad.
succulent *adj* suculento/ta, jugoso/sa.
succumb *vi* sucumbir.
such *adj* tal, semejante; ~ **as** tal como.
such and such a one *n* zutano/na y fulano m/f.
suck *vt, vi* chupar; mamar.
suckle *vt* amamantar.
suckling *n* mamantón/ona m/f.
suction *n* (*med*) succión f.
sudden *adj* repentino/na, no previsto/ta; ~**ly** *adv* de repente, súbitamente.
suddenness *n* precipitación f.
sue *vt* demandar.
suede *n* ante m, gamuza f.
suet *n* sebo m.
suffer *vt, vi* sufrir, padecer; tolerar, permitir.
suffering *n* pena f; dolor m.
suffice *vi* bastar, ser suficiente.
sufficiency *n* suficiencia f; capacidad f.
sufficient *adj* suficiente; ~**ly** *adv* bastante.
suffocate *vt* asfixiar; sofocar; * *vi* asfixiarse.
suffocation *n* asfixia f.
suffrage *n* sufragio, voto m.
suffuse *vt* difundir, derramar.
sugar *n* azúcar m; * *vt* azucarar.
sugar beet *n* remolacha f.
sugar cane *n* caña de azúcar f.
sugar loaf *n* pan de azúcar m.
sugary *adj* azucarado/da.
suggest *vt* sugerir.
suggestion *n* sugestión f.
suicidal *adj* suicida.
suicide *n* suicidio m; suicida m/f.
suit *n* conjunto m; petición f; traje m; pleito m; surtido m; * *vt* convenir; sentar a; adaptar.
suitable *adj* conforme, conveniente.
suitably *adv* convenientemente.
suitcase *n* maleta, valija f.
suite *n* suite f; serie f; tren m, comitiva f.
suitor *n* suplicante m; amante, cortejo m; pleiteante m/f; galanteador m.
sulkiness *n* mal humor m.
sulky *adj* regañón, terco/ca.

S

sullen *adj* hosco/ca; intratable; **~ly** *adv* de mal humor; tercamente.

sullenness *n* hosquedad *f*; obstinación, pertinacia, terquedad *f*.

sulfur *n* azufre *m*.

sulfurous *adj* sulfúreo, azufroso/sa.

sultan *n* sultán *m*.

sultana *n* sultana *f*; pasa *f*.

sultry *adj* caluroso/sa; sofocante.

sum *n* suma *f*; total *m*; * **to ~ up** *vt* sumar; recopilar; * *vi* hacer un resumen.

summarily *adv* sumariamente.

summary *adj* sumario/ria; * *n* sumario *m*.

summer *n* verano, estío *m*.

summerhouse *n* glorieta de jardín *f*.

summit *n* ápice *m*; cima *f*.

summon *vt* citar, requerir por auto de juez; convocar, convidar; (*mil*) intimar la rendición.

summons *n* citación *f*; requerimiento *m*.

sumptuous *adj* suntuoso/sa; **~ly** *adv* suntuosamente.

sun *n* sol *m*.

sunbathe *vi* tomar el sol.

sunburnt *adj* quemado/da por el sol.

Sunday *n* domingo *m*; * *adj* dominical; **done/ worn on ~** dominguero/ra.

Sunday driver *n* dominguero/ra *m/f*.

sundial *n* reloj de sol, cuadrante *m*.

sundry *adj* diversos/sas.

sunflower *n* girasol *m*.

sunglasses *npl* gafas de sol *fpl*.

sunless *adj* sin sol; sin luz.

sunlight *n* luz del sol *f*.

sunny *adj* soleado/da; brillante.

sunrise *n* salida del sol *f*; amanecer *m*.

sunroof *n* techo corredizo *m*.

sunset *n* puesta del sol *f*.

sunshade *n* quitasol *m*.

sunshine *n* solana *f*; claridad del sol *f*.

sunstroke *n* insolación *f*.

suntan *n* bronceado *m*.

suntan oil *n* aceite bronceador *m*.

super *adj* (*col*) bárbaro/ra.

superannuated *adj* añejado/da; pensionado/da.

superannuation *n* pensión, jubilación *f*; retiro *m*.

superb *adj* magnífico/ca; **~ly** *adv* magníficamente.

supercargo *n* (*mar*) sobrecargo *m*.

supercilious *adj* arrogante, altanero/ra; **~ly** *adv* con altivez.

superficial *adj*, **~ly** *adv* superficial(mente).

superfluity *n* superfluidad *f*.

superfluous *adj* superfluo/lua.

superhuman *adj* sobrehumano/na.

superintendent *n* superintendente *m/f*.

superior *adj* superior; * *n* superior/a *m/f*.

superiority *n* superioridad *f*.

superlative *adj* superlativo/va; * *n* superlativo

m; **~ly** *adv* superlativamente, en sumo grado.

supermarket *n* supermercado *m*.

supernatural *adj* sobrenatural.

supernumerary *adj* supernumerario/ria.

superpower *n* superpotencia *f*.

supersede *vt* sobreseer; sustituir; invalidar.

supersonic *adj* supersónico/ca.

superstition *n* superstición *f*.

superstitious *adj* supersticioso/sa; **~ly** *adv* supersticiosamente.

superstructure *n* superestructura *f*.

supertanker *n* superpetrolero *m*.

supervene *vi* sobrevenir.

supervise *vt* supervisar, revistar.

supervision *n* supervisión *f*.

supervisor *n* supervisor/a *m/f*.

supine *adj* supino/na; negligente.

supper *n* cena *f*.

supplant *vt* suplantar.

supple *adj* flexible, manejable; blando/da.

supplement *n* suplemento *m*.

supplementary *adj* adicional.

suppleness *n* flexibilidad *f*.

supplicant, suppliant *n* suplicante *m/f*.

supplicate *vt* suplicar.

supplication *n* súplica, suplicación *f*.

supplier *n* proveedor/a *m/f*.

supply *vt* suministrar; suplir, completar; surtir; * *n* provisión *f*; suministro *m*.

support *vt* sostener; soportar, asistir; * *n* apoyo *m*.

supportable *adj* soportable.

supporter *n* partidario/ria *m/f*; aficionado/da *m/f*.

suppose *vt*, *vi* suponer.

supposition *n* suposición *f*.

suppress *vt* suprimir.

suppression *n* supresión *f*.

supremacy *n* supremacía *f*.

supreme *adj* supremo/ma; **~ly** *adv* supremamente.

surcharge *vt* sobrecargar; * *n* sobretasa *f*.

sure[1] *adj* seguro/ra, cierto/ta; firme; estable; **to be ~** estar seguro/ra; **~ly** *adv* ciertamente, seguramente, sin duda.

sure![2] *interj* ¡ya!

sureness *n* certeza, seguridad *f*.

surety *n* seguridad *f*; fiador *m/f*.

surf *n* (*mar*) resaca *f*.

surface *n* superficie *f*; * *vt* revestir; * *vi* salir a la superficie.

surfboard *n* plancha de surf *f*.

surfeit *n* exceso *m*.

surge *n* ola, onda *f*; * *vi* avanzar en tropel.

surgeon *n* cirujano/na *m/f*.

surgery *n* cirugía *f*.

surgical *adj* quirúrgico/ca.

surliness *n* mal humor *m*.

surly *adj* hosco/ca.

surmise *vt* sospechar; * *n* sospecha *f*.

surmount *vt* sobrepujar; (*fig*) zanjar.

surmountable *adj* superable.

surname *n* apellido, sobrenombre *m*.

surpass *vt* sobresalir, sobrepujar, exceder, aventajar.

surpassing *adj* sobresaliente.

surplice *n* sobrepelliz *f*.

surplus *n* excedente *m*; sobrante *m*; * *adj* sobrante.

surprise *vt* sorprender; * *n* sorpresa *f*.

surprising *adj* sorprendente.

surrender *vt, vi* rendir; ceder; rendirse; * *n* rendición *f*.

surreptitious *adj* subrepticio/cia; ~ly *adv* subrepticiamente.

surrogate *vt* subrogar; * *n* subrogado/da *m/f*.

surrogate mother *n* madre de alquiler *f*.

surround *vt* circundar, cercar, rodear.

surrounding area *n* inmediaciones *fpl*.

survey *vt* inspeccionar, examinar; apear; * *n* inspección *f*; apeo (de tierras) *m*.

survive *vi* sobrevivir; * *vt* sobrevivir a.

survivor *n* superviviente *m/f*.

susceptibility *n* susceptibilidad *f*.

susceptible *adj* susceptible.

suspect *vt, vi* sospechar; * *n* sospechoso/sa *m/f*.

suspend *vt* suspender.

suspense *n* suspense *m*, *Lat Am* suspenso *m*; detención *f*; incertidumbre *f*.

suspension *n* suspensión *f*.

suspension bridge *n* puente colgante *m*.

suspicion *n* sospecha *f*.

suspicious *adj* suspicaz; ~ly *adv* sospechosamente.

suspiciousness *n* suspicacia *f*.

sustain *vt* sostener, sustentar, mantener; apoyar; sufrir.

sustenance *n* sostenimiento, sustento *m*.

suture *n* sutura, costura *f*.

swab *n* algodón *m*; frotis *m invar*.

swaddle *vt* fajar.

swaddling-clothes *npl* pañales *mpl*.

swagger *vi* baladronear.

swallow *n* golondrina *f*; * *vt* tragar, engullir.

swamp *n* pantano *m*.

swampy *adj* pantanoso/sa.

swan *n* cisne *m*.

swap *vt* canjear; * *n* intercambio *m*.

swarm *n* enjambre *m*; gentío *m*; hormiguero *m*; * *vi* enjambrar; hormiguear de gente; abundar.

swarthy *adj* atezado/da.

swarthiness *n* tez morena *f*.

swashbuckling *adj* fanfarrón/ona.

swathe *vt* fajar.

sway *vt* mover; * *vi* ladearse, inclinarse; * *n* balanceo *m*; poder, imperio, influjo *m*.

swear *vt, vi* jurar; hacer jurar; juramentar.

sweat *n* sudor *m*; * *vi* sudar; trabajar con fatiga.

sweater, sweatshirt *n* suéter *m*.

sweep *vt, vi* barrer; arrebatar; deshollinar; pasar/ tocar liger amente; oscilar; * *n* barredura *f*; vuelta *f*; giro *m*.

sweeping *adj* rápido/da; ~s *pl* barreduras *fpl*.

sweepstake *n* lotería *f*.

sweet *adj* dulce, grato/ta, gustoso/sa; suave; oloroso/sa; melodioso/sa; hermoso/sa; amable; * *adv* dulcemente, suavemente; * *n* dulce, caramelo *m*.

sweetbread *n* mellejas de ternera *fpl*.

sweeten *vt* endulzar; suavizar; aplacar; perfumar.

sweetener *n* edulcorante *m*.

sweetheart *n* novio/via *m/f*; querida *f*.

sweetmeats *npl* dulces secos *mpl*.

sweetness *n* dulzura, suavidad *f*.

swell *vi* hincharse; ensoberbecerse; embravecerse; * *vt* hinchar, inflar, agravar; * *n* marejada *f*; * *adj* (*col*) estupendo/da, fenomenal.

swelling *n* hinchazón *f*; tumor *m*.

swelter *vi* ahogarse de calor.

swerve *vi* vagar; desviarse.

swift *adj* veloz, ligero/ra, rápido/da; * *n* vencejo *m*.

swiftly *adv* velozmente.

swiftness *n* velocidad, rapidez *f*.

swill *vt* beber en exceso; * *n* bazofia *f*.

swim *vi* nadar; abundar en; * *vt* pasar a nado; * *n* nadada *f*.

swimming *n* natación *f*.

swimming pool *n* piscina *f*.

swimsuit *n* traje de baño *m*.

swindle *vt* estafar.

swindler *n* estafador/a *m/f*.

swine *n* puerco, cochino *m*.

swing *vi* balancear, columpiarse; vibrar; agitarse; * *vt* colum piar; balancear; girar; * *n* vibración *f*; balanceo *m*.

swinging *adj* (*col*) alegre.

swing (ing) door *n* puerta giratoria *f*.

swirl *n* remolino.

switch *n* varilla *f*; interruptor *m*; (*rail*) aguja *f*; * *vt* cambiar de; **to ~ off** apagar; parar; **to ~ on** encender, *Lat Am* prender.

switchboard *n* centralita *f*, *Lat Am* conmutador *m*.

swivel *vt* girar.

swoon *vi* desmayarse; * *n* desmayo, deliquio, pasmo *m*.

swoop *vi* calarse; * *n* calada; redada *f*; **in one ~** de un golpe.

sword *n* espada *f*.

swordfish *n* pez espada *f*.

swordsman *n* guerrero, espadachín *m*.

sycamore *n* sicomoro *m* (árbol).

sycophant *n* sicofante *m*.

syllabic *adj* silábico/ca.

syllable *n* sílaba *f*.

syllabus *n* programa de estudios *m*.

syllogism *n* silogismo *m*.

S

sylph n silfio m; sílfide f.
symbol n simbolo m.
symbolic(al) adj simbólico/ca.
symbolize vt simbolizar.
symmetrical adj simétrico/ca; ~ly adv con simetría.
symmetry n simetría f.
sympathetic adj simpático/ca; ~ally adv simpáticamente.
sympathize vi compadecerse.
sympathy n simpatía f.
symphony n sinfonía f.
symposium n simposio m.
symptom n síntoma m.
synagogue n sinagoga f.
synchronism n sincronismo m.

syndicate n sindicato m.
syndrome n síndrome m.
synod n sínodo m.
synonym n sinónimo m.
synonymous adj sinónimo/ma; ~ly adv con sinonimia.
synopsis n sinopsis f invar; sumario m.
synoptic adj sinóptico/ca.
syntax n sintaxis f.
synthesis n síntesis f invar.
syringe n jeringa, lavativa f; * vt jeringar.
system n sistema m.
systematic adj sistemático/ca; ~ally adv sistemáticamente.
systems analyst n analista de sistemas m/f.

T

tab n lengüeta f; etiqueta f.
tabernacle n tabernáculo m.
table n mesa f; tabla f; * vt someter a discusión; poner sobre la mesa; ~ **d'hôte** menu m.
tablecloth n mantel m.
tablespoon n cuchara para comer f.
tablet n tableta f; pastilla f; comprimido m.
table tennis n ping-pong, tenis de mesa m.
taboo adj tabú; * n tabú m; * vt interdecir.
tabular adj tabular.
tachometer n cuentarrevoluciones m invar.
tacit adj tácito/ta; ~ly adv tácitamente.
taciturn adj taciturno/na, callado/da.
tack n bordo m; n tachuela f; * vt atar; pegar; * vi virar.
tackle n equipo m, aparejos mpl; placaje m; (mar) cordaje m, jarcia f.
tact n tacto m.
tactician n táctico/ca m/f.
tactics npl táctica f.
tadpole n renacuajo m.
taffeta n tafetán m.
tag n herrete m; * vt herretear.
tail n cola f; rabo m; * vt vigilar a.
tailgate, tailboard n puerta trasera f.
tailor n sastre m.
tailoring n corte m.
tailor-made adj hecho/cha a la medida.
tailwind n viento de cola m.
taint vt tachar, manchar; viciar; * n mancha f.
tainted adj contaminado/da; manchado/da.
take vt tomar, coger, asir; recibir, aceptar; pillar; prender; admitir; entender; * vi prender el fuego; **to ~ apart** vt descoser; **to ~ away** quitar; llevar; **to ~ back** devolver; retractar; **to ~ down** derribar; apuntar; **to ~ in** entender, abarcar; acoger; **to ~ off** vi despegar, Lat Am decolar; vt quitar; imitar; **to ~ on** aceptar; contratar; desafiar; **to ~ out** sacar; quitar; **to ~ to** encariñarse con; **to ~ up** acortar; ocupar; dedicarse a; * n toma f.
takeoff n despegue m, Lat Am decolaje m.
takeover n absorción f; ~ **bid** opa f.
takings npl ingresos mpl.
talc n talco m.
talent n talento m; capacidad f.
talented adj con talento.
talisman n talismán m.
talk vi hablar, conversar; charlar; * n habla f; charla f, Lat Am conversa f; fama f.
talkative adj locuaz.
talk show n programa de entrevistas m.

tall adj alto/ta, elevado/da; robusto/ta.
tally vi corresponder.
talon n garra f.
tambourine n pandereta f.
tame adj amansado/da, domado/da, domesticado/da; ~ly adv mansamente; bajamente; * vt domar; domesticar.
tameness n domesticidad f; sumisión f.
tamper vi tocar.
tampon n tampón m.
tan vt broncear; * vi broncearse, ponerse moreno/na; * n bronceado m.
tang n sabor fuerte m.
tangent n tangente f.
tangerine n mandarina f.
tangible adj tangible.
tangle vt enredar, embrollar.
tank n cisterna f; aljibe m.
tanker n petrolero m; camión cisterna m.
tanned adj bronceado/da.
tantalizing adj tentador/a.
tantamount adj equivalente.
tantrum n rabieta f.
tap vt tocar ligeramente; utilizar; intervenir; zapatear; * n grifo m; palmada suave f; toque ligero m; espita f.
tape n cinta f; * vt grabar.
tape measure n metro m.
taper n cirio m.
tape recorder n grabadora f.
tapestry n tapiz m; tapicería f.
tar n brea f.
target n blanco m (para tirar).
tariff n tarifa f.
Tarmac™ n alquitranado m.
tarnish vt deslustrar.
tarpaulin n alquitranado m.
tarragon n (bot) estragón m.
tart adj acedo/da, acre; * n tarta, torta f; (col) zorra f.
tartan n tela escocesa f.
tartar n tártaro m.
task n tarea f.
tassel n borlita f.
taste n gusto m; sabor m; saboreo m; ensayo m; * vt, vi gustar; probar; experimentar; agradar; tener sabor.
tasteful adj sabroso/sa; ~ly adv sabrosamente.
tasteless adj insípido/da, sin sabor.
tasty adj sabroso/sa.
tattoo n tatuaje m; * vt tatuar.
taunt vt mofar; ridiculizar; * n mofa, burla f.

Taurus n Tauro m (signo del zodíaco).
taut adj tieso/sa.
tautological adj tautológico/ca.
tautology n tautología f.
tawdry adj jarifo/fa, vistoso/sa, chabacano/na.
tax n impuesto m; contribución f; * vt gravar; poner a prueba.
taxable adj sujeto/ta a impuestos.
taxation n imposición de impuestos f.
tax collector n recaudador/a m/f de impuestos.
tax-free adj libre de impuestos.
taxi n taxi m; * vi rodar por la pista.
taxi driver n taxista m/f.
taxi rank n parada de taxis f.
tax payer n contribuyente m/f.
tax relief n desgravación fiscal f.
tax return n declaración de la renta f.
tea n té m.
teach vt enseñar, instruir, Lat Am dictar; * vi enseñar.
teacher n profesor/a m/f; maestro/tra m/f.
teaching n enseñanza f.
teacup n taza de té f.
teak n teca f (árbol).
team n equipo m.
teamster n camionero/ra m/f.
teamwork n trabajo de equipo m.
teapot n tetera f.
tear[1] vt despedazar, rasgar; **to ~ up** hacer trizas.
tear[2] n lágrima f; gota f.
tearful adj lloroso/sa; **~ly** adv con lloro.
tear gas n gas lacrimógeno m.
tease vt tomar el pelo.
tea service, tea set n servicio para té m.
teasing adj zumbón/ona; * n zumba f.
teaspoon n cucharita f.
teat n ubre, teta f.
technical adj técnico/ca.
technicality n detalle técnico m.
technician n técnico/ca m
technique n técnica f.
technological adj tecnológico/ca.
technology n tecnología f.
teddy (**bear**) n osito de felpa m.
tedious adj tedioso/sa, fastidioso/sa; **~ly** adv fastidiosamente.
tedium n tedio, fastidio m.
tee n tee m.
teem vi rebosar de.
teenage adj juvenil; **~r** n adolescente m/f.
teens npl adolescencia f.
tee-shirt, T-shirt n camiseta f.
teeth npl de tooth.
teethe vi echar los dientes.
teetotal adj abstemio/mia, sobrio/ria.
teetotaler n abstemio/mia m/f.
telegram n telegrama m.
telegraph n telégrafo m.

telegraphic adj telegráfico/ca.
telegraphy n telegrafía f.
telepathy n telepatía f.
telephone n teléfono m.
telephone banking n telebanca f.
telephone booth n cabina telefónica f.
telephone call n llamada telefónica f, Lat Am telefonema m.
telephone directory n guía f telefónica.
telephone number n número de teléfono m.
telescope n telescopio m.
telescopic adj telescópico/ca.
televise vt televisar.
television n televisión f.
television news n telediario m.
television set n televisor m.
teleworker n teletrabajador/ra m/f.
teleworking n teletrabajo m.
telex n télex m; vt, vi enviar un télex.
tell vi decir; informar, contar.
teller n cajero/ra m/f.
telling adj contundente; revelador/a.
telltale adj indicador/a.
temper vt templar, moderar; * n mal genio m.
temperament n temperamento m.
temperance n templanza, moderación f.
temperate adj templado/da, moderado/da, sobrio/ria.
temperature n temperatura f.
tempest n tempestad f.
tempestuous adj tempestuoso/sa.
template n plantilla f.
temple n templo m; sien f.
temporarily adv temporalmente, Lat Am temporariamente.
temporary adj temporal, Lat Am temporario/ria.
tempt vt tentar; provocar.
temptation n tentación f.
tempting adj tentador/a.
ten adj, n diez.
tenable adj defendible.
tenacious adj, **~ly** adv tenaz(mente).
tenacity n tenacidad f; porfía f.
tenancy n tenencia f.
tenant n arrendatario/ria, inquilino/na m/f.
tend vt guardar, velar; * vi tener tendencia a.
tendency n tendencia f.
tender adj tierno/na, delicado/da; sensible; **~ly** adv tiernamente; * n oferta f; * vt ofrecer; estimar.
tenderness n ternura f.
tendon n tendón m.
tendril n zarcillo m.
tenement n casa de pisos f.
tenet n dogma m; aserción f.
tennis n tenis m.
tennis court n cancha de tenis f.
tennis player n tenista m/f.

tennis racket n raqueta de tenis f.
tennis shoes npl zapatillas de tenis fpl.
tenor n (mus) tenor m; contenido m; substancia f.
tense adj tieso/sa, tenso/sa; * n (gr) tiempo m.
tension n tensión, tirantez f.
tent n tienda de campaña f, Lat Am carpa f.
tentacle n tentáculo m.
tentative adj de ensayo, de prueba; ~**ly** adv como prueba.
tenth adj, n décimo/ma.
tenuous adj tenue.
tenure n tenencia f.
tepid adj tibio/bia.
term n término m; dicción f; vocablo m; condición, estipulación f; * vt nombrar, llamar.
terminal adj mortal; * n terminal m; terminal f.
terminate vt terminar.
termination n terminación, conclusión f.
terminus n terminal f.
terrace n terraza f.
terrain n terreno m.
terrestrial adj terrestre, terreno/na.
terrible adj terrible.
terribly adv terriblemente.
terrier n terrier m.
terrific adj fantástico/ca; maravilloso/sa.
terrify vt aterrar, espantar.
territorial adj territorial.
territory n territorio, distrito m.
terror n terror m.
terrorism n terrorismo m.
terrorist n terrorista m/f.
terrorist attack n atentado m.
terrorize vt aterrorizar.
terse adj tajante.
test n examen m; prueba f; * vt probar; examinar.
testament n testamento m.
tester n ensayador/a m/f.
testicles npl testículos mpl.
testify vt testificar, atestiguar.
testimonial n atestación f.
testimony n testimonio m.
test pilot n piloto de pruebas m/f.
test tube n probeta f.
testy adj tétrico/ca.
tetanus n tétanos m invar.
tether vt atar.
text n texto m.
textbook n libro de texto m.
textiles npl textiles mpl.
textual adj textual.
texture n textura f; tejido m.
than adv que, de.
thank vt agradecer, dar las gracias a.
thankful adj grato/ta, agradecido/da; ~**ly** adv con gratitud.
thankfulness n gratitud f.
thankless adj ingrato/ta.

thanks npl gracias fpl.
Thanksgiving n día de acción de gracias m.
that pn aquel, aquello, aquella; que; este; * conj porque; para que; **so** ~ de modo que.
thatch n techo de paja m; * vt techar con paja.
thaw n deshielo m; * vi deshelarse.
the art el, la, lo; los, las.
theater n teatro m.
theatergoer n aficionado/da al teatro m/f.
theatrical adj teatral.
theft n robo m.
their pn su, suyo, suya; de ellos, de ellas; ~**s** el suyo, la suya, los suyos, las suyas; de ellos, de ellas.
them pn los, las, les; ellos, ellas.
theme n tema m.
themselves pn pl ellos mismos, ellas mismas; sí mismos; se.
then adv entonces, después; en tal caso; * conj en ese caso; * adj entonces; **now and** ~ de vez en cuando.
theologian n teólogo/ga m/f.
theological adj teológico/ca.
theology n teología f.
theorem n teorema m.
theoretic(al) adj teórico/ca; ~**ly** adv teóricamente.
theorist n teórico/ca m/f.
theorize vt teorizar.
theory n teoría f.
therapeutics n terapéutica f.
therapist n terapeuta m/f.
therapy n terapia f.
there adv allí, allá.
thereabout(s) adv por ahí, acerca de.
thereafter adv después; según.
thereby adv así; de ese modo.
therefore adv por eso, por lo tanto.
thermal adj termal.
thermal printer n impresora térmica f.
thermometer n termómetro m.
thermostat n termostato m.
thesaurus n diccionario de sinónimos m.
these pn pl éstos, éstas; adj estos, estas.
thesis n tesis f invar.
they pn pl ellos, ellas.
thick adj espeso/sa, denso/sa; grueso/sa; torpe.
thicken vi espesar, condensar; condensarse.
thicket n espesura f.
thickness n espesor m.
thickset adj grueso/sa; rechoncho/cha.
thick-skinned adj duro/ra de pellejo.
thief n ladrón/ona m/f.
thigh n muslo m.
thimble n dedal m.
thin adj delgado/da, delicado/da, flaco/ca; claro/ra; * vt atenuar; adelgazar; aclarar.
thing n cosa f; objeto m; chisme m.

T

think *vi* pensar, imaginar, meditar, considerar; creer, juzgar; **to ~ over** reflexionar; **to ~ up** imaginar.

thinker *n* pensador/a *m/f*.

thinking *n* pensamiento *m*; juicio *m*; opinión *f*.

third *adj* tercero/ra; * *n* tercio *m*; **~ly** *adv* en tercer lugar.

third rate *adj* mediocre.

thirst *n* sed *f*.

thirsty *adj* sediento/ta.

thirteen *adj*, *n* trece.

thirteenth *adj*, *n* decimotercero/ra.

thirtieth *adj*, *n* trigésimo/ma.

thirty *adj*, *n* treinta.

this *adj* este, esta; * *pn* éste, ésta, esto.

thistle *n* cardo *m*.

thorn *n* espino *m*; espina *f*.

thorny *adj* espinoso/sa; arduo/dua.

thorough *adj* entero/ra, perfecto/ta; **~ly** *adv* enteramente, profundamente.

thoroughbred *adj* de sangre, de casta.

thoroughfare *n* paso, tránsito *m*.

those *pn pl* ésos, ésas; aquéllos, aquéllas; * *adj* esos, esas; aquellos, aquellas.

though *conj* aunque, no obstante; * *adv* sin embargo.

thought *n* pensamiento, juicio *m*; opinión *f*; cuidado *m*.

thoughtful *adj* pensativo/va.

thoughtless *adj* descuidado/da; insensato/ta; **~ly** *adv* descuidadamente, sin reflexión.

thousand *adj*, *n* mil.

thousandth *adj*, *n* milésimo/ma.

thrash *vt* golpear; derrotar.

thread *n* hilo *m*; rosca *f*; * *vt* enhebrar.

threadbare *adj* raído/da, muy usado/da.

threat *n* amenaza *f*.

threaten *vt* amenazar.

three *adj*, *n* tres.

three-dimensional *adj* tridimensional.

three-monthly *adj* trimestral.

three-ply *adj* triple.

threshold *n* umbral *m*.

thrifty *adj* económico/ca.

thrill *vt* emocionar; * *n* emoción *f*.

thriller *n* película/novela de suspense *f*.

thrive *vi* prosperar; crecer.

throat *n* garganta *f*.

throb *vi* palpitar; vibrar; dar punzadas.

throne *n* trono *m*.

throng *n* tropel de gente *m*; * *vt* venir en tropel.

throttle *n* acelerador *m*; * *vt* estrangular.

through *prep* por; durante; mediante; * *adj* directo/ta; * *adv* completamente.

throughout *prep* por todo; * *adv* en todas partes.

throw *vt* echar, arrojar, tirar, lanzar; * *n* tiro *m*; golpe *m*; **to ~ away** tirar; **to ~ off** desechar; **to ~ out** tirar; **to ~ up** vomitar, devolver.

throwaway *adj* desechable.

thrush *n* tordo (ave) *m*.

thrust *vt* empujar, introducir; * *vr* zamparse; * *n* empuje *m*.

thud *n* ruido sordo *m*; zarpazo *m*.

thug *n* gamberro/rra *m/f*.

thumb *n* pulgar *m*.

thumbtack *n* chincheta *f*, *Lat Am* chinche *f*.

thump *n* golpe *m*; * *vt*, *vi* golpear.

thunder *n* trueno *m*; * *vi* tronar.

thunderbolt *n* rayo *m*.

thunderclap *n* trueno *m*.

thunderstorm *n* tormenta *f*.

thundery *adj* tormentoso/sa.

Thursday *n* jueves *m invar*.

thus *adv* así, de este modo.

thwart *vt* frustrar.

thyme *n* (*bot*) tomillo *m*.

thyroid *n* tiroides *m invar*.

tiara *n* tiara *f*.

tic *n* tic *m*.

tick *n* tictac *m*; palomita *f*; marca *f*; * *vt* marcar; **to ~ over** girar en marcha; ir tirando.

ticket *n* billete, *Lat Am* boleto *m*; etiqueta *f*; tarjeta *f*.

ticket collector *n* (*rail*) revisor/a *m/f*.

ticket office *n* taquilla *f*, *Lat Am* boletería *f*; *Lat Am* despacho *m* de boletos.

tickle *vt* hacer cosquillas.

ticklish *adj* con cosquillas, *Lat Am* cosquilloso/sa.

tidal *adj* de marea.

tidal wave *n* maremoto *m*.

tidbit *n* golosina *f*; pedazo *m*.

tide *n* curso *m*; marea *f*.

tidy *adj* ordenado/da; arreglado/da; aseado/da.

tie *vt* anudar, atar; * *vi* empatar; **to ~ up** envolver; atar; amarrar; concluir; * *n* atadura *f*; lazo *m*; corbata *f*; empate *m*.

tier *n* grada *f*; piso *m*.

tiger *n* tigre *m*.

tight *adj* tirante, tieso/sa, tenso/sa; cerrado/da; apretado/da; * *adv* con fuerza.

tighten *vt* tirar, estirar.

tightfisted *adj* tacaño/ña.

tightly *adv* muy fuerte.

tightrope *n* cuerda floja *f*.

tigress *n* tigresa *f*.

tile *n* teja *f*; baldosa *f*; azulejo *m*; * *vt* tejar.

tiled *adj* embaldosado/da.

till¹ *n* caja registradora *f*.

till² *vt* cultivar, labrar.

tiller *n* cana del timón *f*.

tilt *vt* inclinar; * *vi* inclinarse.

timber *n* madera de construcción *f*; árboles *mpl*.

time *n* tiempo; época *f*; hora *f*; momento *m*; (*mus*) compás *m*; **in ~** a tiempo; **from ~ to ~** de vez en cuando; * *vt* medir el tiempo; cronometrar.

time bomb n bomba de relojería f.
time lag n desfase m.
timeless adj eterno/na.
timely adj oportuno/na.
time off n tiempo libre m.
timer n interruptor m; programador horario m.
time scale n escala de tiempo f.
time trial n contrarreloj f.
time zone n huso horario m.
timid adj tímido/da, temeroso/sa; **~ly** adv con timidez.
timidity n timidez f.
timing n cronometraje m; oportunidad f.
tin n estaño m; hojalata f.
tinder n yesca f.
tinfoil n papel de estaño m.
tinge n matiz m.
tingle vi zumbar; latir, punzar.
tingling n zumbido m; latido m.
tinker n calderero remendón m; gitano/na m/f.
tinkle vi tintinear.
tin plate n hojalata f.
tinsel n oropel m.
tint n tinte m; * vt teñir.
tinted adj teñido/da; ahumado/da.
tiny adj pequeño/ña, chico/ca.
tip[1] n punta, extremidad f.
tip[2] propina f; consejo m; * vt dar una propina a.
tip[3] vt inclinar; vaciar.
tip-off n advertencia f.
tipsy adj alegre.
tiptop adj excelente, perfecto/ta.
tirade n invectiva f.
tire[1] vt cansar, fatigar; * vi cansarse; fastidiarse.
tire[2] n neumático m; llanta f.
tireless adj incansable.
tire pressure n presión de los neumáticos f.
tiresome adj tedioso/sa, molesto/ta.
tiring adj cansado/da.
tissue n tejido m; pañuelo de papel m.
tissue paper n papel de seda m.
titillate vt estimular.
title n título m.
title deed n derecho de propiedad m.
title page n portada f.
titter vi reírse disimuladamente; * n risa disimulada f.
titular adj titular.
to prep a; para; por; de; hasta; en; con; que.
toad n sapo m.
toadstool n (bot) seta venenosa f.
toast vt tostar; brindar; * n tostada f; brindis m.
toaster n tostadora f.
tobacco n tabaco m.
tobacconist n tabaquero/ra, estanquero/ra m/f.
tobacconist's (shop) n estanco m, tabaquería f, Lat Am cigarrería f.
tobacco pouch n petaca f.

toboggan n tobogán m.
today adv hoy.
toddler n niño/ña (que empieza a andar) m/f.
toddy n ponche m.
toe n dedo del pie m; punta f.
toffee n caramelo m.
together adv juntamente, juntos; al mismo tiempo.
toil vi fatigarse, trabajar mucho; afanarse; * n trabajo m; fatiga f; afán m.
toilet n servicios mpl; sanitario m; * adj de aseo.
toilet bag n bolsa de aseo f.
toilet bowl n taza del retrete f.
toilet paper n papel higiénico m.
toiletries npl artículos de aseo mpl.
token n senal f; muestra f; recuerdo m; vale m; ficha f.
tolerable adj soportable; pasable.
tolerance n tolerancia f.
tolerant adj tolerante.
tolerate vt tolerar.
toll[1] n peaje m; número de victimas m.
toll[2] vi doblar.
tomato n tomate m.
tomb n tumba f; sepulcro m, sepultura f.
tomboy n muchachota f.
tombstone n piedra sepulcral f.
tomcat n gato m.
tomorrow adv mañana; * n mañana f.
ton n tonelada f.
tone n tono m; acento m; * vi armonizar; **to ~ down** suavizar.
tone-deaf adj sin oído musical.
tongs npl tenacillas fpl.
tongue n lengua f.
tongue-tied adj mudo/da.
tongue-twister n trabalenguas m invar.
tonic n (med) tónico m.
tonight adv, n esta tarde (f).
tonnage n tonelaje m.
tonsil n amígdala f; **~s** npl agallas fpl.
tonsillitis n agalla f.
tonsure n tonsura f.
too adv demasiado; también.
tool n herramienta f; utensilio m.
tool box n caja de herramientas f.
toot vi tocar la bocina.
tooth n diente m.
toothache n dolor de muelas m.
toothbrush n cepillo de dientes m.
toothless adj desdentado/da.
toothpaste n pasta de dientes f.
toothpick n palillo m.
top n cima, cumbre f; último grado m; lo alto; superficie f; tapa f; cabeza f; * adj de arriba; primero/ra; * vt elevarse por encima; sobrepujar, exceder; **to ~ off** llenar.
topaz n topacio m.

T

top floor n último piso m.
top-heavy adj inestable.
topic n tema m; ~**al** adj actual.
topless adj topless.
top-level adj al más alto nivel.
topmost adj lo más alto.
topographic(al) adj topográfico/ca.
topography n topografía f.
topple vt derribar; * vi volcarse.
top-secret adj de alto secreto.
topsy-turvy adv al revés.
torment vt atormentar; * n tormento m.
tornado n tornado m.
torrent n torrente m.
torrid adj apasionado/da.
tortoise n tortuga f.
tortoiseshell adj de carey.
tortuous adj tortuoso/sa, sinuoso/sa.
torture n tortura f; * vt torturar.
toss vt tirar, lanzar, arrojar; agitar, sacudir.
total adj total, entero/ra; ~**ly** adv totalmente.
totalitarian adj totalitario/ria.
totality n totalidad f.
totter vi vacilar.
touch vt tocar, palpar; **to ~ on** aludir a; **to ~ up** retocar; * n contacto m; tacto m; toque m; prueba f.
touch-and-go adj arriesgado/da.
touchdown n aterrizaje m; ensayo m.
touched adj conmovido/da; chiflado/da.
touching adj patético/ca, conmovedor/a.
touchstone n piedra de toque f.
touchwood n yesca f.
touchy adj quisquilloso/sa.
tough adj duro/ra; difícil; resistente; fuerte; * n gorila m.
toughen vt endurecer.
toupee n tupé m.
tour n viaje m; visita f; * vt visitar.
touring n viajes turísticos mpl.
tourism n turismo m; **bicycle ~** cicloturismo; **rural ~** turismo rural.
tourist n turista m/f.
tourist office n oficina de turismo f.
tournament n torneo m.
tow n remolque m; * vt remolcar.
toward(s) prep, adv hacia, con dirección a; cerca de, respecto a.
towel n toalla f.
toweling n toalla f.
towel rack n toallero m.
tower n torre f.
towering adj imponente.
town n ciudad f.
town clerk n secretario/ria del ayuntamiento m/f.
town hall n ayuntamiento m.
towrope n cable de remolque m.
toy n juguete m.

toy store n juguetería f.
trace n huella, pisada f; * vt trazar, delinear; encontrar.
track n vestigio m; huella f; camino m; vía f; pista f; canción f; * vt rastrear.
tracksuit n chándal m.
tract n región, comarca f; serie f; tratado m.
traction n tracción f.
trade n comercio, tráfico m; negocio, trato m; ocupación f; * vi comerciar, traficar.
trade fair n feria de muestras f.
trademark n marca comercial f.
trade name n nombre comercial m.
trader n comerciante, traficante m.
tradesman n tendero m.
trading n comercio m; * adj comercial.
tradition n tradición f
traditional adj tradicional.
traffic n tráfico m; tránsito m; * vi traficar, comerciar.
traffic circle n glorieta f.
traffic jam n embotellamiento m, aglomeración f de tráfico.
trafficker n traficante, comerciante m/f.
traffic lights npl semáforo m.
tragedy n tragedia f.
tragic adj trágico/ca; ~**ally** adv trágicamente.
tragicomedy n tragicomedia f.
trail vt, vi rastrear; arrastrar; * n rastro m; pista f; cola f.
trailer n tráiler m; remolque m; avance m.
train vt entrenar; amaestrar, enseñar, criar, adiestrar; disciplinar; * vr ejercitarse; * n tren m; cola f; serie f; **high-speed ~** tren de alta velocidad m.
trained adj cualificado/da; amaestrado/da.
trainee n aprendiz/a m/f.
trainer n entrenador/a m/f.
training n entrenamiento m; formación f.
trait n rasgo m.
traitor n traidor/a m/f.
tram n tranvía f.
tramp n vagabundo/da m/f; (col) puta f; * vi andar pesadamente; * vt pisotear.
trample vt pisotear.
trampoline n cama elástica f.
trance n rapto m; éxtasis m.
tranquil adj tranquilo/la.
tranquilize vt tranquilizar.
tranquilizer n tranquilizante m.
transact vt negociar.
transaction n transacción f; negociación f.
transatlantic adj transatlántico/ca.
transcend vt trascender, pasar; exceder.
transcription n transcripción f.
transfer vt transferir, trasladar; * n transferencia f; traspaso m; calcomanía f.
transform vt transformar.

transformation n transformación f.
transfusion n transfusión f.
transient adj pasajero/ra, transitorio/ria.
transit n tránsito m.
transition n tránsito m; transición f.
transitional adj de transición.
transitive adj transitivo/va.
translate vt traducir.
translation n traducción f.
translator n traductor/ra m/f.
transmission n transmisión f.
transmit vt transmitir.
transmitter n transmisor m; emisora f.
transparency n transparencia f.
transparent adj transparente, diáfano/na.
transpire vi resultar; ocurrir.
transplant vt trasplantar; * n trasplante m.
transport vt transportar; * n transporte m.
transportation n transporte m.
trap n trampa f; * vt atrapar, bloquear.
trap door n trampilla f; escotillón m.
trapeze n trapecio m.
trappings npl adornos mpl.
trash n basura f; tonterías fpl.
trash can n cubo de la basura m.
trashy adj vil, despreciable, de ningún valor.
travel vi viajar; * vt recorrer; * n viaje m.
travel agency n agencia de viajes f.
travel agent n agente de viajes m.
traveler n viajante, viajero/ra m/f.
traveler's check n cheque de viaje m.
travel-sickness n mareo m.
travesty n parodia f.
trawler n arrastrero m.
tray n bandeja f; cajón m.
treacherous adj traidor/a, perfido/da.
treachery n traición f.
tread vi pisar; pistoear; * n pisada f; ruido de pasos m; banda de rodadura f.
treason n traición f; **high** ~ alta traición f.
treasure n tesoro m; * vt atesorar.
treasurer n tesorero/ra m/f.
treat vt tratar; regalar; * n regalo m; placer m.
treatise n tratado m.
treatment n trato m.
treaty n tratado m.
treble adj triple; * vt (vi) triplicar(se); * n (mus) tiple m.
treble clef n clave de sol f.
tree n árbol m.
trek n caminata f; expedición f.
trellis n enrejado m.
tremble vi temblar.
trembling n temor m; trino m.
tremendous adj tremendo/da; enorme; estupendo/da.
tremor n temblor m.
trench n foso m; (mil) trinchera f; zanja f.

trend n tendencia f; curso m; moda f.
trendy adj de moda.
trepidation n inquietud f.
trespass vt transpasar, violar.
tress n trenza f; rizo de pelo m.
trestle n caballete de serrador m.
trial n proceso m; prueba f; ensayo m; desgracia f.
triangle n triángulo m.
triangular adj triangular.
tribal adj tribal.
tribe n tribu f; raza, casta f.
tribulation n tribulación f.
tribunal n tribunal m.
tributary adj, n tributario/ria m/f.
tribute n tributo m.
trice n momento, tris m.
trick n engaño, fraude m; burla f; baza f; zancadilla f; * vt engañar.
trickery n engaño m.
trickle vi gotear; * n reguero m.
tricky adj difícil; delicado/da.
tricycle n triciclo m.
trifle n bagatela, nineria f; * vi bobear; juguetear.
trifling adj frívolo/la, inútil.
trigger n gatillo m; * **to** ~ **off** vt desencadenar.
trigonometry n trigonometría f.
trill n trino m; * vi trinar.
trillion n billón m.
trim adj aseado/da; en buen estado; arreglado/da; * vt arreglar; recortar; adornar.
trimester n trimestre m.
trimmings npl accesorios mpl.
Trinity n Trinidad f.
trinket n joya, alhaja f; adorno m.
trio n (mus) trío m.
trip vt hacer caer; * vi tropezar; resbalar; * n resbalón m; viaje corto m, Lat Am paseo m; zancadilla f.
tripe n callos mpl; bobadas fpl.
triple adj triple; * vt triplicar.
triplets npl trillizos/zas m/fpl.
triplicate n triplicado m.
tripod n trípode m.
trite adj trivial; usado/da.
triumph n triunfo m; * vi triunfar.
triumphal adj triunfal.
triumphant adj triunfante; victorioso/sa; ~**ly** adv en triunfo.
trivia npl trivialidades fpl.
trivial adj trivial, vulgar; ~**ly** adv trivialmente.
triviality n trivialidad f.
trolley n carrito m.
trombone n trombón m.
troop n grupo m; ~**s** npl tropas fpl.
trooper n soldado a caballo m.
trophy n trofeo m.
tropical adj trópico/ca.
trot n trote m; * vi trotar.

T

trouble *vt* afligir; molestar; * *n* problema *m*; disturbio *m*; inquietud *f*; aflicción, pena *f*.

troubled *adj* preocupado/da; agitado/da.

troublemaker *n* agitador/a *m/f*.

troubleshooter *n* conciliador/a *m/f*.

troublesome *adj* molesto/ta.

trough *n* abrevadero *m*; comedero *m*.

troupe *n* grupo *m*.

trousers *npl* pantalones *mpl*.

trout *n* trucha *f*.

trowel *n* paleta *f*.

truce *n* tregua *f*.

truck *n* camión *m*; vagón *m*.

truck driver *n* camionero/ra *m/f*.

truculent *adj* truculento/ta, cruel.

trudge *vi* andar fatigosamente, andar con dificultad.

true *adj* verdadero/ra, cierto/ta; sincero/ra; exacto/ta.

truelove *n* amor verdadero *m*.

truffle *n* trufa *f*.

truly *adv* en verdad; sinceramente.

trump *n* triunfo (en el juego de naipes) *m*.

trumpet *n* trompeta *f*.

trunk *n* baúl, cofre *m*; trompa *f*.

truss *n* braguero *m*; * *vt* atar; espetar.

trust *n* confianza *f*; trust *m*; fideicomiso *m*; * *vt* tener confianza en; confiar algo a.

trusted *adj* de confianza.

trustee *n* fideicomisario/ria, curador/a *m/f*.

trustful *adj* fiel; confiado/da.

trustily *adv* fielmente.

trusting *adj* confiado/da.

trustworthy *adj* digno/na de confianza.

trusty *adj* fiel, leal; seguro/ra.

truth *n* verdad *f*; fidelidad *f*; realidad *f*; **in ~** en verdad.

truthful *adj* verídico/ca; veraz.

truthfulness *n* veracidad *f*.

try *vt* examinar, ensayar, probar; experimentar; tentar; inte ntar; juzgar; * *vi* probar; **to ~ on** probarse; **to ~ out** probar; * *n* tentativa *f*; ensayo *m*.

trying *adj* pesado/da; cansado/da.

tub *n* balde *m*, barreño *m*, cubo *m*; tina *f*.

tuba *n* tuba *f*.

tube *n* tubo, cañon, canuto *m*.

tuberculosis *n* tuberculosis *f invar*.

tubing *n* caería *f*.

tuck *n* pliegue *m*; * *vt* poner.

Tuesday *n* martes *m invar*.

tuft *n* mechón *m*; manojo *m*.

tug *vt* remolcar; * *n* remolcador *m*.

tuition *n* matrícula *f*; enseñanza *f*.

tulip *n* tulipán *m*.

tumble *vi* caer, hundirse; revolcarse; * *vt* revolver; volcar; * *n* caída *f*; vuelco *m*.

tumbledown *adj* destartalado/da.

tumbler *n* vaso *m*.

tummy *n* barriga *f*.

tumor *n* tumor *m*.

tumultuous *adj* tumultuoso/sa.

tuna *n* atún *m*.

tune *n* tono *m*; armonia *f*; aria *f*; * *vt* afinar; sintonizar.

tuneful *adj* armonioso/sa, acorde, melodioso/sa.

tuner *n* sintonizador/a *m*.

tunic *n* túnica *f*.

tuning fork *n* (*mus*) diapasón *m*.

tunnel *n* túnel *m*; * *vt* construir un tunel por.

turban *n* turbante *m*.

turbine *n* turbina *f*.

turbulence *n* turbulencia, confusión *f*.

turbulent *adj* turbulento/ta, tumultuoso/sa.

tureen *n* sopera *f*.

turf *n* césped *m*; * *vt* cubrir con césped.

turgid *adj* pesado/da.

turkey *n* pavo *m*.

turmoil *n* disturbio *m*; baraúnda *f*.

turn *vi* volver; cambiar; girar; dar vueltas; volverse a, mudarse, transformarse; **to ~ around** volverse; girar; **to ~ back** volverse; **to ~ down** rechazar; doblar; **to ~ in** acostarse; **to ~ off** *vi* desviarse; *vt* apagar; parar; **to ~ on** encender, prender; poner en marcha; **to ~ out** apagar; **to ~ over** *vi* volverse; *vt* volver; **to ~ up** *vi* llegar; aparecer; *vt* subir; * *n* vuelta *f*; giro *m*; rodeo *m*; turno *m*; vez *f*; inclinación *f*.

turncoat *n* desertor/a, renegado/da *m/f*.

turning *n* vuelta *f*.

turnip *n* nabo *m*.

turn-off *n* salida *f*.

turnout *n* concurrencia *f*.

turnover *n* facturación *f*.

turnpike *n* autopista de peaje *f*.

turnstile *n* torniquete *m*.

turntable *n* plato *m*.

turpentine *n* trementina *f*.

turquoise *n* turquesa *f*.

turret *n* torrecilla, torreta *f*.

turtle *n* tortuga marina *f*.

turtledove *n* tórtola *f*.

tusk *n* colmillo *m*.

tussle *n* pelea *f*.

tutor *n* tutor/a *m/f*; profesor/a *m/f*; * *vt* enseñar, instruir.

tuxedo *n* smoking *m*.

twang *n* gangueo *m*; sonido agudo *m*.

tweezers *npl* tenacillas *fpl*.

twelfth *adj*, *n* duodécimo/ma.

twelve *adj*, *n* doce.

twentieth *adj*, *n* vigésimo/ma.

twenty *adj*, *n* veinte.

twice *adv* dos veces.

twig *n* ramita *f*; * *vi* caer en la cuenta.

twilight *n* crepúsculo *m*.

twin *n* gemelo/la *m/f*.
twine *vi* entrelazarse; caracolear; * *n* bramante *m*.
twinge *vt* punzar, pellizcar; * *n* dolor agudo/punzante *m*; punzada *f*.
twinkle *vi* centellear; parpadear.
twirl *vt* dar vueltas a; * *vi* piruetear; * *n* rotación *f*.
twist *vt* torcer, retorcer; entretejer; * *vi* serpentear; * *n* torsión *f*; vuelta *f*; doblez *f*.
twit *n* (*col*) tonto/ta *m/f*.
twitch *vi* moverse nerviosamente; * *n* tirón; tic *m*.
twitter *vi* gorjear; * *n* gorjeo *m*.
two *adj*, *n* dos.
two-door *adj* de dos puertas.
two-faced *adj* falso/sa.
twofold *adj* doble, duplicado/da; * *adv* al doble.
two-seater *n* avión/coche de dos plazas *m*.

twosome *n* pareja *f*.
tycoon *n* magnate *m*.
type *n* tipo *m*; letra *f*; modelo *m*; * *vt* escribir a máquina, *Lat Am* tipear.
typecast *adj* encasillado/da.
typeface *n* tipo *m*.
typescript *n* texto mecanografiado *m*.
typewriter *n* máquina de escribir *f*.
typewritten *adj* mecanografiado/da.
typical *adj* típico/ca.
typographer *n* tipógrafo *m*.
typographical *adj* tipográfico/ca
typography *n* tipografía *f*.
tyrannical *adj* tiránico/ca.
tyranny *n* tiranía *f*; crueldad *f*.
tyrant *n* tirano/na *m/f*.

U

ubiquitous *adj* ubicuo/cua.
udder *n* ubre *f.*
ugh *excl* ¡puaj!
ugliness *n* fealdad *f.*
ugly *adj* feo, fea; peligroso/sa.
ulcer *n* úlcera *f.*
ulterior *adj* ulterior.
ultimate *adj* último/ma; ~**ly** *adv* al final; a fin de cuentas.
ultimatum *n* ultimátum *m.*
ultramarine *n* ultramar *m*; * *adj* ultramarino/na.
ultrasound *n* ultrasonido *m.*
ultrasound scan *n* ecografía *f.*
umbilical cord *n* cordón umbilical *m.*
umbrella *n* paraguas *m invar.*
umpire *n* árbitro/tra *m/f.*
umpteen *adj* enésimos/mas.
unable *adj* incapaz.
unaccompanied *adj* solo/la, sin acompañamiento.
unaccomplished *adj* incompleto/ta, no acabado/da.
unaccountable *adj* inexplicable, extraño/ña.
unaccountably *adv* extrañamente.
unaccustomed *adj* desacostumbrado/da, desusado/da.
unacknowledged *adj* desconocido/da; negado/da.
unacquainted *adj* desconocido/da; ignorado/da.
unadorned *adj* sin adorno.
unadulterated *adj* genuino/na, puro/ra; sin mezcla.
unaffected *adj* sincero/ra, sin afectación.
unaided *adj* sin ayuda.
unaltered *adj* invariado/da.
unambitious *adj* poco/ca ambicioso/sa.
unanimity *n* unanimidad *f.*
unanimous *adj* unánime; ~**ly** *adv* unánimemente.
unanswerable *adj* incontrovertible, incontestable.
unanswered *adj* no contestado/da.
unapproachable *adj* inaccesible.
unarmed *adj* inerme, desarmado/da.
unassuming *adj* nada presuntuoso/sa, modesto/ta.
unattached *adj* independiente; disponible.
unattainable *adj* inasequible.
unattended *adj* sin atender.
unauthorized *adj* no autorizado/da.
unavoidable *adj* inevitable.
unavoidably *adv* inevitablemente.
unaware *adj* ignorante.
unawares *adv* inadvertidamente; de improviso.
unbalanced *adj* desequilibrado/da; trastornado/da.
unbearable *adj* insoportable.
unbecoming *adj* indecente, indecoroso/sa.

unbelievable *adj* increíble.
unbend *vi* relajarse; * *vt* enderezar.
unbiased *adj* imparcial.
unblemished *adj* sin mancha, sin tacha, irreprensible.
unborn *adj* no nacido/da.
unbreakable *adj* irrompible.
unbroken *adj* intacto/ta; indómito/ta; entero/ra; no batido/da.
unbutton *vt* desabotonar.
uncalled-for *adj* fuera de lugar.
uncanny *adj* extraordinario/ria.
unceasing *adj* sin cesar, continuo/nua.
unceremonious *adj* brusco/ca.
uncertain *adj* incierto/ta, dudoso/sa.
uncertainty *n* incertidumbre *f.*
unchangeable *adj* inmutable.
unchanged *adj* no alterado/da.
unchanging *adj* inalterable, immutable.
uncharitable *adj* nada caritativo/va, duro/ra.
unchecked *adj* desenfrenado/da, incontrolado/da.
unchristian *adj* poco cristiano/na.
uncivil *adj* grosero/ra, descortés.
uncivilized *adj* tosco/ca, salvaje, incivilizado/da.
uncle *n* tío.
uncomfortable *adj* incómodo/da; molesto/ta.
uncomfortably *adv* incómodamente; inquietantemente.
uncommon *adj* raro/ra, extraordinario/ria.
uncompromising *adj* irreconciliable.
unconcerned *adj* indiferente.
unconditional *adj* sin condiciones, incondicional.
unconfined *adj* libre, ilimitado/da.
unconfirmed *adj* no confirmado/da.
unconnected *adj* inconexo/xa.
unconquerable *adj* invencible, insuperable.
unconscious *adj* inconsciente; ~**ly** *adv* inconscientemente.
unconstrained *adj* libre, voluntario/ria.
uncontrollable *adj* incontrolable; desenfrenado/da.
unconventional *adj* poco convencional.
unconvincing *adj* no convincente.
uncork *vt* destapar.
uncorrected *adj* sin corregir, no corregido/da.
uncouth *adj* grosero/ra, zafio/fia.
uncover *vt* descubrir.
uncultivated *adj* inculto/ta.
uncut *adj* no cortado/da, entero/ra.
undamaged *adj* ileso/sa, libre de daño.
undaunted *adj* intrépido/da.
undecided *adj* indeciso/sa.
undefiled *adj* impoluto/ta, puro/ra.

undeniable *adj* innegable, incontestable; ~**bly** *adv* indubitablemente.

under *prep* debajo de; menos de; segun; * *adv* debajo.

under-age *adj* menor de edad.

undercharge *vt* cobrar de menos.

underclothing *n* ropa íntima *f*.

undercoat *n* primera mano *f*.

undercover *adj* clandestino/na.

undercurrent *n* corriente subyacente *f*.

undercut *vt* vender más barato que.

underdeveloped *adj* subdesarrollado/da.

underdog *n* desvalido/da *m/f*.

underdone *adj* poco cocido/da.

underestimate *vt* subestimar.

undergo *vt* sufrir; sostener.

undergraduate *n* estudiante universitario/ria *m/f*.

underground *n* movimiento clandestino *m*.

undergrowth *n* soto *m*, maleza *f*.

underhand *adv* clandestinamente; * *adj* secreto/ta, clandestino/na.

underlie *vi* estar debajo.

underline *vt* subrayar.

undermine *vt* minar.

underneath *adv* debajo; * *prep* debajo de.

underpaid *adj* mal pagado/da.

underpants *npl* calzoncillos *mpl*.

underprivileged *adj* desvalido/da.

underrate *vt* menospreciar.

undersecretary *n* subsecretario/ria *m/f*.

undershirt *n* camiseta *f*.

underside *n* revés *m*.

understand *vt* entender, comprender.

understandable *adj* comprensible.

understanding *n* entendimiento *m*; inteligencia *f*; conocimiento *m*; correspondencia *f*; * *adj* comprensivo/va.

understatement *n* subestimación *f*; modestia *f*.

undertake *vt*, *vi* emprender.

undertaking *n* empresa *f*; empeño *m*.

undervalue *vt* menospreciar.

underwater *adj* submarino/na; * *adv* bajo el agua.

underwear *n* ropa íntima *f*.

underworld *n* hampa *f*.

underwrite *vt* suscribir; asegurar contra riesgos.

underwriter *n* asegurador/a *m/f*.

undeserved *adj* inmerecido/da; ~**ly** *adv* sin haberlo merecido.

undeserving *adj* indigno/na.

undesirable *adj* indeseable.

undetermined *adj* indeterminado/da, indeciso/sa.

undigested *adj* no digerido/da.

undiminished *adj* entero/ra, no disminuido/da.

undisciplined *adj* indisciplinado/da.

undisguised *adj* sin disfraz, cándido/da, sincero/ra.

undismayed *adj* intrépido/da.

undisputed *adj* incontestable.

undisturbed *adj* quieto/ta, tranquilo/la.

undivided *adj* indiviso/sa, entero/ra.

undo *vt* deshacer, destar, descoser.

undoing *n* ruina *f*.

undoubted *adj* indudable; ~**ly** *adv* indudablemente.

undress *vi* desnudarse.

undue *adj* indebido/da; injusto/ta.

undulating *adj* ondulante.

unduly *adv* indebidamente.

undying *adj* inmortal.

unearth *vt* desenterrar.

unearthly *adj* inverosímil.

uneasiness *n* inquietud *f*; zozobra *f*.

uneasy *adj* inquieto/ta, desasosegado/da; incomodo/da.

uneducated *adj* ignorante.

unemployed *adj* desmpleado/da, parado/da; ~ **person** parado/da *m/f*.

unemployment *n* desempleo, paro *m*.

unending *adj* interminable.

unenlightened *adj* no iluminado/da.

unenviable *adj* poco envidiable.

unequal *adj*, ~**ly** *adv* desigual(mente).

unequaled *adj* incomparable.

unerring *adj*, ~**ly** *adv* infalible(mente).

uneven *adj* desigual; impar; ~**ly** *adv* desigualmente.

unexpected *adj* inesperado/da; inopinado/da; ~**ly** *adv* de repente; inopinadamente.

unexplored *adj* inexplorado/da, no descubierto/ta.

unfailing *adj* infalible, seguro/ra.

unfair *adj* falso/sa; injusto/ta; ~**ly** *adv* injustamente.

unfaithful *adj* infiel, pérfido/da.

unfaithfulness *n* infidelidad, perfidia *f*.

unfaltering *adj* firme, asegurado/da.

unfamiliar *adj* desacostumbrado/da, poco común.

unfashionable *adj* pasado/da de moda; ~**bly** *adv* contra la moda.

unfasten *vt* desatar, soltar, aflojar.

unfathomable *adj* insondable, impenetrable.

unfavorable *adj* desfavorable.

unfeeling *adj* insensible, duro/ra de corazón.

unfinished *adj* imperfecto/ta, no acabado/da.

unfit *adj* indispuesto/ta; incapaz.

unfold *vt* desplegar; revelar; * *vi* abrirse.

unforeseen *adj* imprevisto/ta.

unforgettable *adj* inolvidable.

unforgivable *adj* imperdonable.

unforgiving *adj* implacable.

unfortunate *adj* desafortunado/da, infeliz; ~**ly** *adv* por desgracia, infelizmente.

unfounded *adj* sin fundamento.

unfriendly *adj* antipático/ca.

U

unfruitful adj estéril; infructuoso/sa.
unfurnished adj sin muebles; desprovisto/ta.
ungainly adj desmañado/da.
ungentlemanly adj indigno/na de un hombre bien criado.
ungovernable adj indomable, ingobernable.
ungrateful adj ingrato/ta; desagradable; ~ly adv ingratamente.
ungrounded adj infundado/da.
unhappily adv infelizmente.
unhappiness n infelicidad f.
unhappy adj infeliz.
unharmed adj ileso/sa, sano/na y salvo/va.
unhealthy adj malsano/na; enfermizo/za.
unheard-of adj inaudito/ta, extraño/ña, sin ejemplo.
unheeding adj negligente; distraído/da.
unhitch vt desaparejar.
unhook vt desenganchar; descolgar; desabrochar.
unhoped (for) adj inesperado/da.
unhurt adj ileso/sa.
unicorn n unicornio m.
uniform adj, ~ly adv uniforme(mente); * n uniforme m.
uniformity adj uniformidad f.
unify vt unificar.
unimaginable adj inimaginable.
unimpaired adj no disminuido/da, no alterado/da.
unimportant adj poco importante.
uninformed adj desinformado/da.
uninhabitable adj inhabitable.
uninhabited adj inhabitado/da, desierto/ta.
uninjured adj ileso/sa, no dañado/da.
unintelligible adj ininteligible.
unintelligibly adv de modo ininteligible.
unintentional adj involuntario/ria, no intencionado/da.
uninterested adj desinteresado/da.
uninteresting adj poco interesante.
uninterrupted adj sin interrupción, continuo/nua.
uninvited adj no convidado/da.
union n unión f; sindicato m.
unionist n sindicalista m/f.
unique adj único/ca, uno/na, singular.
unison n unísono m.
unit n unidad f.
Unitarian n unitario/ria m/f.
unite vt (vi) unir(se), juntarse; (fig) zurcir.
unitedly adv unidamente, de acuerdo.
United States (**of America**) npl Estados Unidos (de América) mpl.
unity n unidad, concordia, conformidad f.
universal adj, ~ly adv universal(mente).
universe n universo m.
university n universidad f.
unjust adj injusto/ta; ~ly adv injustamente.
unkempt adj despeinado/da; descuidado/da.
unkind adj poco amable; severo/ra.

unknowingly adv sin saberlo.
unknown adj incógnito/ta.
unlawful adj ilegal; ~ly adv ilegalmente.
unlawfulness n ilegalidad f.
unleash vt desencadenar.
unless conj a menos que, si no.
unlicensed adj sin licencia.
unlike, unlikely adj diferente; improbable; inverosímil.
unlikelihood n inverisimilitud f.
unlimited adj ilimitado/da.
unlisted adj que no viene en la guía.
unload vt descargar.
unlock vt abrir.
unluckily adv desafortunadamente.
unlucky adj desafortunado/da.
unmanageable adj inmanejable, intratable.
unmannered adj rudo/da, brutal, grosero/ra.
unmannerly adj malcriado/da, descortés.
unmarried adj soltero/ra.
unmask vt desenmascarar.
unmentionable adj que no se puede mencionar.
unmerited adj desmerecido/da.
unmindful adj olvidadizo/za, negligente.
unmistakable adj inconfundible; ~ly adv indudablemente.
unmitigated adj absoluto/ta.
unmoved adj inmoto, firme.
unnatural adj antinatural; perverso/sa; afectado/da.
unnecessary adj inútil, innecesario/ria.
unneighborly adj poco atento/ta con sus vecinos; descortés.
unnoticed adj inadvertido/da.
unnumbered adj innumerable.
unobserved adj no observado/da.
unobtainable adj inconseguible; inexistente.
unobtrusive adj modesto/ta.
unoccupied adj desocupado/da.
unoffending adj sencillo/lla, inocente.
unofficial adj no oficial.
unorthodox adj heterodoxo/xa.
unpack vt desempacar; desenvolver.
unpaid adj no pagado/da, Lat Am impago/ga.
unpalatable adj desabrido/da, desgradable.
unparalleled adj sin paralelo; sin par.
unpleasant adj , ~ly adv desagradable(mente).
unpleasantness n desagrado m.
unplug vt desconectar.
unpolished adj que no está pulido/da; rudo/da, grosero/ra.
unpopular adj impopular.
unpracticed adj inexperto/ta, no versado/da.
unprecedented adj sin precedentes.
unpredictable adj imprevisible.
unprejudiced adj imparcial.
unprepared adj no preparado/da.
unprofitable adj inútil, vano/na; poco lucrativo/va.

unprotected *adj* desvalido/da, sin protección.
unpublished *adj* no publicado/da; inédito/ta.
unpunished *adj* impune.
unqualified *adj* sin títulos; total.
unquestionable *adj* indubitable, indisputable; ~**ly** *adv* sin duda, sin disputa.
unquestioned *adj* incontestable, no preguntado/da.
unravel *vt* desenredar.
unread *adj* no leído/da; ignorante.
unreal *adj* irreal.
unrealistic *adj* poco realista.
unreasonable *adj* poco razonable; disparatado/da.
unreasonably *adv* poco razonablemente; disparatadamente.
unrelated *adj* sin relación; inconexo/xa.
unrelenting *adj* implacable.
unreliable *adj* poco fiable.
unremitting *adj* constante, incansable.
unrepentant *adj* impenitente.
unreserved *adj* sin restricción; franco/ca; ~**ly** *adv* abiertamente.
unrest *n* malestar *m*; disturbios *mpl*.
unrestrained *adj* desenfrenado/da; ilimitado/da.
unripe *adj* inmaduro/ra.
unrivaled *adj* sin rival, sin igual.
unroll *vt* desenrollar.
unruliness *n* turbulencia *f*; desenfreno *m*.
unruly *adj* desenfrenado/da.
unsafe *adj* inseguro/ra, peligroso/sa.
unsatisfactory *adj* insatisfactorio/ria.
unsavory *adj* desabrido/da, insípido/da.
unscathed *adj* ileso/sa.
unscrew *vt* destornillar.
unscrupulous *adj* sin escrúpulos.
unseasonable *adj* intempestivo/va, fuera de propósito.
unseemly *adj* indecente.
unseen *adj* invisible.
unselfish *adj* desinteresado/da.
unsettle *vt* perturbar.
unsettled *adj* inquieto/ta; inestable; variable.
unshaken *adj* firme, estable.
unshaven *adj* sin afeitar.
unsightly *adj* desagradable a la vista, feo/a.
unskillful *adj* inhábil, poco mañoso/sa.
unskilled *adj* no cualificado/da.
unsociable *adj* insociable, intratable.
unspeakable *adj* inefable, indecible.
unstable *adj* instable, inconstante.
unsteadily *adv* ligeramente, inconstantemente.
unsteady *adj* inestable.
unstudied *adj* no estudiado/da; no premeditado/da.
unsuccessful *adj* infeliz, desafortunado/da; ~**ly** *adv* sin éxito.
unsuitable *adj* inapropiado/da; inoportuno/na.

unsure *adj* ineguro/ra.
unsympathetic *adj* poco comprensivo/va.
untamed *adj* indomado/da.
untapped *adj* sin explotar.
untenable *adj* insostenible.
unthinkable *adj* inconcebible.
unthinking *adj* desatento/ta, irreflexivo/va.
untidiness *n* desaliño *m*.
untidy *adj* desordenado/da; sucio/cia.
untie *vt* desatar, deshacer, soltar, zafar.
until *prep* hasta; * *conj* hasta que.
untimely *adj* intempestivo/va.
untiring *adj* incansable.
untold *adj* nunca dicho/cha; indecible; incalculable.
untouched *adj* intacto/ta.
untoward *adj* impropio/pia; adverso/sa.
untried *adj* no ensayado/da/probado/da.
untroubled *adj* no perturbado/da, tranquilo/la.
untrue *adj* falso/sa.
untrustworthy *adj* indigno/na de confianza.
untruth *n* falsedad, mentira *f*.
unused *adj* sin usar, no usado/da.
unusual *adj* inusual, inusitado/da, raro/ra; ~**ly** *adv* inusitadamente, raramente.
unveil *vt* quitar el velo, descubrir.
unwavering *adj* inquebrantable.
unwelcome *adj* desagradable, inoportuno/na.
unwell *adj* enfermizo/za, malo/la.
unwieldy *adj* pesado/da.
unwilling *adj* desinclinado/da; ~**ly** *adv* de mala gana.
unwillingness *n* mala gana, repugnancia *f*.
unwind *vt* desenredar, desenmarañar; * *vi* relajarse.
unwise *adj* imprudente.
unwitting *adj* inconsciente.
unworkable *adj* poco práctico/ca.
unworthy *adj* indigno/na.
unwrap *vt* desenvolver.
unwritten *adj* no escrito/ta.
up *adv* arriba, en lo alto; levantado/da; * *prep* hacia; hasta.
upbraid *vt* zaherir.
upbringing *n* educación *f*.
update *vt* poner al dia.
upheaval *n* agitación *f*.
uphill *adj* difícil, penoso/sa; * *adv* cuesta arriba.
uphold *vt* sos tener, apoyar.
upholstery *n* tapicería *f*.
upkeep *n* mantenimiento *m*.
uplift *vt* levantar.
upon *prep* sobre, encima.
upper *adj* superior; más elevado/da.
upper-class *adj* de la clase alta.
upper-hand *n* (*fig*) superioridad *f*.
uppermost *adj* más alto/ta, supremo/ma; **to be** ~ predominar.

U

upright *adj* derecho/cha, perpendicular, recto/ta; puesto/ta en pie; honrado/da.
uprising *n* sublevación *f*.
uproar *n* tumulto, alboroto *m*.
uproot *vt* desarraigar.
upset *vt* trastornar; derramar, volcar; * *n* revés *m*; trastorno *m*; * *adj* molesto/ta; revuelto/ta.
upshot *n* remate *m*; fin *m*; conclusión *f*.
upside-down *adv* al revés.
upstairs *adv* arriba.
upstart *n* advenedizo/za *m/f*.
uptight *adj* nervioso/sa.
up-to-date *adj* al día.
upturn *n* mejora *f*.
upward *adj* ascendente; ~s *adv* hacia arriba.
urban *adj* urbano/na.
urbane *adj* cortés.
urchin *n* golfillo/lla *m/f*.
urge *vt* animar; * *n* impulso *m*; deseo *m*.
urgency *n* urgencia *f*.
urgent *adj* urgente.
urinal *n* orinal *m*.
urinate *vi* orinar.
urine *n* orina *f*.
urn *n* urna *f*.
us *pn* nos; nosotros, nosotras.

usage *n* tratamiento *m*; uso *m*.
use *n* uso *m*; utilidad, práctica *f*; * *vt* usar, emplear.
used *adj* usado/da.
useful *adj* , ~ly *adv* útil(mente).
usefulness *n* utilidad *f*.
useless *adj* inútil; ~ly *adv* inútilmente.
uselessness *n* inutilidad *f*.
user-friendly *adj* fácil de utilizar.
usher *n* ujier *m/f*; acomodador/a *m/f*.
usherette *n* acomodadora *f*.
usual *adj* usual, común, normal; ~ly *adv* normalmente.
usurer *n* usurero/ra *m/f*.
usurp *vt* usurpar.
usury *n* usura *f*.
utensil *n* utensilio *m*.
uterus *n* útero *m*.
utility *n* utilidad *f*.
utilize *vt* utilizar.
utmost *adj* extremo/ma, sumo/ma; último/ma.
utter *adj* total; todo; entero/ra; * *vt* proferir; expresar; publicar.
utterance *n* expresion *f*.
utterly *adv* enteramente, del todo.

V

vacancy n cuarto libre m, vacante f.
vacant adj vacío/cía; desocupado/da; vacante.
vacant lot n solar m.
vacate vt desocupar; dejar.
vacation n vacaciones fpl.
vaccinate vt vacunar.
vaccination n vacunación f.
vaccine n vacuna f.
vacuous adj vacío/cía, vacuo/cua.
vacuum n vacío m.
vacuum flask n termo m.
vagina n vagina f.
vagrant n vagabundo/da m/f.
vague adj vago/ga; ~ly adv vagamente.
vain adj vano/na, inútil; vanidoso/sa.
valet n criado m.
valiant adj valiente, valeroso/sa.
valid adj válido/da.
valley n valle m.
valor n valor, aliento, brío, esfuerzo m.
valuable adj valioso/sa; ~s npl objetos de valor mpl.
valuation n tasa, valuación f.
value n valor, precio m; * vt valuar, Lat Am avaluar; estimar, apreciar.
valued adj apreciado/da.
valve n válvula f.
vampire n vampiro m.
van n camioneta f.
vandal n gamberro/rra m/f.
vandalism n vandalismo m.
vandalize vt dañar.
vanguard n vanguardia f.
vanilla n vainilla f.
vanish vi desvanecerse, desaparecer.
vanity n vanidad f.
vanity case n neceser m.
vanquish vt vencer, conquistar.
vantage point n punto panorámico m.
vapor n vapor m; exhalación f.
variable adj variable; voluble.
variance n discordia, desavenencia f.
variation n variación f.
varicose vein n variz f, Lat Am várice f.
varied adj variado/da.
variety n variedad f.
variety show n espectáculo de variedades m.
various adj vario/ria, diverso/sa, diferente.
varnish n barniz m; * vt barnizar.
vary vt, vi variar; cambiar.
vase n florero, jarrón m.
vast adj vasto/ta; inmenso/sa.
vat n tina f.

vault n bóveda f; cueva f; caverna f; * vt saltar.
veal n ternera f.
veer vi (mar) virar.
vegetable adj vegetal; * n vegetal m; ~s pl verduras fpl.
vegetable garden n huerta f.
vegetarian n vegetariano/na m/f.
vegetate vi vegetar.
vegetation n vegetación f.
vehemence n vehemencia, violencia f.
vehement adj vehemente, violento/ta; ~ly adv vehementemente.
vehicle n vehículo m; **all-terrain** ~ todoterreno m.
veil n velo m; * vt encubrir, ocultar.
vein n vena f; cavidad f; inclinación del ingenio f.
velocity n velocidad f.
velvet n terciopelo m.
vending machine n máquina expendedora f.
vendor n vendedor/a m/f.
veneer n chapa f; barniz m.
venerable adj venerable.
venerate vt venerar, honrar.
veneration n veneración f.
venereal adj venéreo.
vengeance n venganza f.
venial adj venial.
venison n (carne de) venado f.
venom n veneno m.
venomous adj venenoso/sa; ~ly adv venenosamente.
vent n respiradero m; salida f; * vt desahogar.
ventilate vt ventilar.
ventilation n ventilación f.
ventilator n ventilador m.
ventriloquist n ventrílocuo/cua m/f.
venture n empresa f; * vi aventurarse; * vt aventurar, arriesgar.
venue n lugar de reunión, local m.
veranda(h) n terraza f, porche m.
verb n (gr) verbo m.
verbal adj verbal, literal; ~ly adv verbalmente.
verbatim adv literalmente.
verbose adj verboso/sa.
verdant adj verde.
verdict n (law) veredicto m; opinión f.
verification n verificación f.
verify vt verificar.
veritable adj verdadero/ra.
vermicelli npl fideos mpl.
vermin n bichos mpl.
vermouth n vermut m.
versatile adj versátil; polifacético/ca.
verse n verso m; versículo m.

versed *adj* versado/da.
version *n* versión f.
versus *prep* contra.
vertebra *n* vértebra f.
vertebral, **vertebrate** *adj* vertebral.
vertex *n* cenit, vértice *m*.
vertical *adj* , ~**ly** *adv* vertical(mente).
vertigo *n* vértigo *m*.
verve *n* brío *m*.
very *adj* idéntico/ca, mismo/ma; * *adv* muy,
   mucho, sumamente.
vessel *n* vasija f; vaso *m*; barco *m*.
vest *n* chaleco *m*.
vestibule *n* vestíbulo *m*.
vestige *n* vestigio *m*.
vestment *n* vestido *m*; vestidura f.
vestry *n* sacristía f.
veteran *adj*, *n* veterano/na *m/f*.
veterinarian, **vet** *n* veterinario/ria *m/f*.
veterinary *adj* veterinario/ria.
veterinary science *n* veterinaria f.
veto *n* veto *m*; * *vt* vetar.
vex *vt* molestar.
vexed *adj* molesto/ta; controvertido/da.
via *prep* por.
viaduct *n* viaducto *m*.
vial *n* ampolla f, vial *m*.
vibrate *vi* vibrar.
vibration *n* vibración f.
vicarious *adj* sustituto/ta.
vice *n* vicio *m*; culpa f; tornillo *m*.
vice-chairman *n* vice-presidente *m*.
vice-chancellor (**of a university**) *n* rector/ra *m/f*.
vice-chancellorship *n* rectorado *m*.
vice versa *adv* viceversa.
vicinity *n* vecindad, proximidad f; **immediate ~**
   inmediaciones *fpl*.
vicious *adj* vicioso/sa; ~**ly** *adv* de manera viciosa.
victim *n* víctima f.
victimize *vt* victimizar.
victor *n* vencedor/a *m/f*.
victorious *adj* victorioso/sa.
victory *n* victoria f.
video *n* vídeo *m*, *Lat Am* video *m*.
video camera *n* videocámara f.
video cassette *n* videocasete *m*.
video game *n* videojuego *m*.
video tape *n* cinta de vídeo f.
vie *vi* competir.
view *n* vista f; perspectiva f; aspecto *m*; opinión
   f; paisaje *m*; * *vt* mirar, ver; examinar.
viewer *n* televidente *m/f*.
viewfinder *n* visor *m*.
viewpoint *n* punto de vista *m*.
vigil *n* vela f; vigilia f.
vigilance *n* vigilancia f.
vigilant *adj* vigilante, atento/ta.
vigorous *adj* vigoroso/sa; ~**ly** *adv* vigorosamente.

vigor *n* vigor *m*; energía f.
vile *adj* vil, bajo/ja; asqueroso/sa.
vilify *vt* envilecer.
villa *n* chalet *m*; casa de campo f.
village *n* aldea f.
villager *n* aldeano/na *m/f*.
villain *n* malvado/da *m/f*.
vindicate *vt* vindicar, defender.
vindication *n* vindicación f; justificación f.
vindictive *adj* vengativo/va.
vine *n* vid f.
vinegar *n* vinagre *m*.
vineyard *n* viña f.
vintage *n* vendimia f.
vinyl *n* vinilo *m*.
viola *n* (*mus*) viola f.
violate *vt* violar.
violation *n* violación f.
violence *n* violencia f.
violent *adj* violento/ta; ~**ly** *adv* violentamente.
violet *n* (*bot*) violeta f.
violin *n* (*mus*) violín *m*.
violinist *n* violinista *m/f*.
violoncello, **cello** *n* (*mus*) violoncelo, violonchelo *m*.
VIP *n* vip *m/f*.
viper *n* víbora f.
virgin *n* virgen f; * *adj* virgen.
virginity *n* virginidad f.
Virgo *n* Virgo f (signo del zodiaco).
virile *adj* viril.
virility *n* virilidad f.
virtual *adj*, ~**ly** *adv* virtual(mente).
virtue *n* virtud f.
virtuous *adj* virtuoso/sa.
virulent *adj* virulento/ta.
virus *n* virus *m invar*.
visa *n* visado *m*, visa f.
vis-à-vis *prep* con respecto a.
viscous *adj* viscoso/sa, glutinoso/sa.
visibility *n* visibilidad f.
visible *adj* visible.
visibly *adv* visiblemente.
vision *n* vista f; visión f.
visit *vt* visitar; * *n* visita f.
visitation *n* visitación, visita f.
visiting hours *npl* horas de visita *fpl*.
visitor *n* visitante *m/f*; turista *m/f*.
visor *n* visera f.
vista *n* vista, perspectiva f.
visual *adj* visual.
visual aid *n* medio visual *m*.
visualize *vt* imaginarse.
vital *adj* vital; esencial; imprescindible; ~**ly** *adv*
   vitalmente; ~**s** *npl* partes vitales *fpl*.
vitality *n* vitalidad f.
vital statistics *npl* medidas vitales *fpl*.
vitamin *n* vitamina f.
vitiate *vt* viciar, corromper.

vivacious adj vivaz.
vivid adj vivo/va; gráfico/ca; intenso/sa; ~**ly** adv vivamente; gráficamente.
vivisection n vivisección f.
vixen n zorra f.
vocabulary n vocabulario m.
vocal adj vocal.
vocation n vocación f; oficio m; carrera, profesión f; ~**al** adj profesional.
vocative n vocativo m.
vociferous adj vocinglero/ra, clamoroso/sa.
vodka n vodka m.
vogue n moda f; boga f.
voice n voz f; * vt expresar.
void adj nulo* n vacio m.
volatile adj volátil; voluble.
volcanic adj volcánico/ca.
volcano n volcán m.
volition n voluntad f.
volley n descarga f; salva f; rociada f; volea f.
volleyball n voleibol m, Lat Am vóleibol m.
volt n voltio m.
voltage n voltaje m.

voluble adj locuaz.
volume n volumen m; libro m.
voluntarily adv voluntariamente.
voluntary adj voluntario/ria.
volunteer n voluntario/ria m/f; * vi ofrecerse voluntariamente.
voluptuous adj voluptuoso/sa.
vomit vt, vi vomitar; * n vómito m.
voracious adj, ~**ly** adv voraz(mente).
vortex n remolino, torbellino m.
vote n voto, sufragio m; votación f; * vt votar, Lat Am sufragar.
voter n votante m/f.
voting n votación f.
voucher n vale m.
vow n voto m; * vi jurar.
vowel n vocal f.
voyage n viaje m; travesía f.
vulgar adj vulgar, ordinario/ria; de mal gusto.
vulgarity n vulgaridad f, grosería f; mal gusto m.
vulnerable adj vulnerable.
vulture n buitre m.

W

wad n fajo m; bolita f.
waddle vi anadear.
wade vi vadear.
wafer n galleta f; oblea f.
waffle n gofre m.
waft vt hacer flotar; * vi flotar.
wag vt menear; * vi menearse.
wage n salario m.
wage earner n asalariado/da m/f.
wager n apuesta f; * vt apostar.
wages npl salario m.
waggish adj zumbón/ona.
waggle vt menear.
wagon n carro m; (rail) vagón m.
wail n lamento, gemido m; * vi gemir.
waist n cintura f.
waistline n talle m.
wait vi esperar; * n espera f; pausa f.
waiter n camarero m.
waiting list n lista de espera f.
waiting room n sala de espera f.
waive vt suspender.
wake[1] vi despertarse; * vt despertar; * n vela f.
wake[2] n (mar) estela f.
wakefulness n vela f.
waken vt (vi) despertar(se).
walk vt, vi pasear, ir; andar, caminar; * n paseo m; caminata f.
walker n paseante m/f.
walkie-talkie n walkie-talkie m.
walking n paseos mpl.
walking stick n bastón m.
walkout n huelga f.
walkover n (col) pan comido m.
walkway n paseo m.
wall n pared f; muralla f; muro m.
walled adj amurallado/da.
wallflower n (bot) alhelí m.
wallow vi revolcarse.
wallpaper n papel pintado m.
walnut n nogal m; nuez f.
walrus n morsa f.
waltz n vals m invar.
wan adj pálido/da.
wand n varita mágica f.
wander vt, vi errar; vagar.
wane vi menguar.
want vt querer; necesitar; faltar; * n necesidad f; falta f.
wanting adj falto/ta, defectuoso/sa.
wanton adj lascivo/va; juguetón/ona.
war n guerra f.

ward n sala f; pupilo/la m/f.
wardrobe n guardarropa f, ropero m.
warehouse n almacén m.
warfare n guerra f.
warhead n ojiva f.
warily adv prudentemente.
wariness n cautela, prudencia f.
warm adj cálido/da; caliente; efusivo/va; * vt calentar; to ~ up vi calentarse; entrar en calor; acalorarse; vt calentar.
warm-hearted adj afectuoso/sa.
warmly adv con calor, ardientemente.
warmth n calor m.
warn vt avisar; advertir.
warning n aviso m.
warning light n luz de advertencia f.
warp vi torcerse; * vt torcer; pervertir.
warrant n orden judicial f; mandamiento judicial m.
warranty n garantía f.
warren n conejero m.
warrior n guerrero/ra, soldado/da m/f.
warship n barco de guerra m.
wart n verruga f.
wary adj cauto/ta, prudente.
wash vt lavar; bañar; * vi lavarse; * n lavado m; baño m.
washable adj lavable.
washbowl, washbasin n lavabo m.
washcloth n manopla f.
washer n arandela f.
washing n ropa sucia f; colada f.
washing machine n lavadora f.
washing-up n fregado m.
wash out n (col) fracaso m.
washroom n aseos mpl.
wasp n avispa f.
wastage n desgaste m; pérdida f.
waste vt malgastar; destruir, arruinar; perder; * vi gastarse; * n desperdicio m; destrucción f; despilfarro m; basura f; yermo m.
wasteful adj destructivo/va; pródigo/ga; ~ly adv pródigamente.
wasteland n yermo m.
waste paper n papel usado m.
waste pipe n tubo de desagüe m.
watch n reloj m; centinela f; guardia f; * vt mirar; ver; vigilar; tener cuidado; * vi ver; montar guardia.
watchdog n perro guardián m.
watchful adj vigilante; ~ly adv vigilantemente.
watchmaker n relojero/ra m/f.
watchman n sereno m; vigilante m.

watchtower n atalaya, garita f.
watchword n santo y seña m.
water n agua f; * vt regar, humedecer, mojar; * vi hacerse agua.
water closet, WC n váter m.
watercolor n acuarela f.
waterfall n cascada f.
water heater n calentador de agua m.
watering-can n regadera f.
water level n nivel del agua m.
water lily n ninfea f.
water line n línea de flotación f.
waterlogged adj anegado/da.
water main n cañería del agua f.
watermark n filigrana f.
water melon n sandía f.
watershed n momento crítico m.
watertight adj impermeable.
waterworks npl depuradora de agua f.
watery adj aguado/da, Lat Am aguachento/ta; desvaído/da; lloroso/sa.
watt n vatio m.
wave n ola, onda f; oleada f; senal f; * vi agitar la mano; ondear; * vt agitar.
wavelength n longitud de onda f.
waver vi vacilar, balancear.
wavering adj inconstante.
wavy adj ondulado/da.
wax n cera f; * vt encerar; * vi crecer.
wax paper n papel de cera m.
waxworks n museo de cera m.
way n camino m; vía f; ruta f; modo m; recorrido m; **to give ~** ceder.
waylay vt salir al paso.
wayward adj caprichoso/sa.
we pn nosotros, nosotras.
weak adj , **~ly** adv débil(mente).
weaken vt debilitar.
weakling n enclenque m/f.
weakness n debilidad f; punto débil m.
weal, wheal n roncha f.
wealth n riqueza f; bienes mpl.
wealthy adj rico/ca.
wean vt destetar.
weapon n arma f.
wear vt gastar, consumir; usar, llevar; * vi consumirse; **to ~ away** vt gastar; vi desgastarse; **to ~ down** gastar; agotar; **to ~ off** pasar; **to ~ out** desgastar; agotar; * n uso m; desgaste m.
weariness n cansancio m; fatiga f; enfado m.
wearisome adj tedioso/sa.
weary adj cansado/da, fatigado/da; tedioso/sa.
weasel n comadreja f.
weather n tiempo m; * vt (out) sufrir, superar.
weather-beaten adj curtido/da.
weather cock n gallo de campanario m; veleta f.
weather forecast n boletín meteorológico m.

weave vt tejer; trenzar; (fig) zurcir.
weaving n tejido m.
web n telarana f; membrana f; red f.
wed vt (vi) casar(se).
wedding n boda f; nupcias fpl; casamiento m.
wedding day n día de la boda m.
wedding dress n traje de novia m.
wedding present n regalo de boda m.
wedding ring n alianza f.
wedge n cuña f; * vt acuñar; apretar.
wedlock n matrimonio m.
Wednesday n miércoles m invar.
wee adj pequeñito/ta.
weed n mala hierba f; * vt escardar.
weedkiller n herbicida m.
weedy adj lleno/na de malas hierbas.
week n semana f; **tomorrow ~** mañana en una semana; **yesterday ~** ayer hace ocho dias.
weekday n día laborable m.
weekend n fin de semana m.
weekly adj semanal; * adv semanalmente, por semana.
weep vt, vi llorar; lamentar.
weeping willow n sauce llorón m.
weigh vt, vi pesar.
weight n peso m.
weightily adv pesadamente.
weightlifter n levantador/a m/f de pesas, Lat Am fierrero/ra m/f.
weighty adj ponderoso/sa; importante.
welcome adj bienvenido/da; **~!** ¡bienvenido!; * n bienvenida f; * vt dar la bienvenida a.
weld vt soldar; * n soldadura f.
welfare n prosperidad f; bienestar m; subsidio de paro m.
welfare state n estado del bienestar m.
well n fuente f; manantial m; pozo m; * adj bueno/na, sano/na; * adv bien, felizmente; favorablemente; suficientemente; convenientemente; **as ~ as** así como, además de, lo mismo que.
well-behaved adj bien educado/da.
wellbeing n felicidad, prosperidad f.
well-bred adj bien criado/da, bien educado/da.
well-built adj fornido/da.
well-deserved adj merecido/da.
well-dressed adj bien vestido/da.
well-known adj conocido/da.
well-mannered adj educado/da.
well-meaning adj bien intencionado/da.
well-off adj acomodado/da.
well-to-do adj acomodado/da.
well-wisher n partidario/ria m/f.
wench n mozuela, cantonera f.
west n oeste, occidente m; * adj occidental; * adv hacia el oeste.
westerly, western adj occidental.
westward adv hacia el oeste.

W

wet adj húmedo/da, mojado/da; * n humedad f;
* vt mojar, hume decer.

wet-nurse n ama de leche f.

wet suit n traje de buzo m.

whack vt aporrear; * n golpe m.

whale n ballena f.

wharf n muelle m.

what pn que, ¿qué?, el que, la que, lo que; * adj
¿qué?; * excl ¡cómo!

whatever pn cualquier, cualquiera cosa que, lo
que sea.

wheat n trigo m.

wheedle vt halagar, engañar con lisonjas,
sonsacar.

wheedler n zalamero/ra m/f.

wheel n rueda f; volante m; timón m; * vt (hacer)
rodar; volver, girar; * vi rodar.

wheelbarrow n carretilla f.

wheelchair n silla de ruedas f.

wheel clamp n cepo m.

wheeze vi jadear.

when adv ¿cuándo?; mientras que; * conj
cuando.

whenever adv cuando; cada vez que.

where adv ¿dónde?; * conj donde; **any~** en
cualquier parte; **every~** en todas partes.

whereabout(s) adv ¿dónde?

whereas conj mientras que; pues que, ya que.

whereby pn por lo cual, con lo cual.

whereupon conj con lo cual.

wherever adv dondequiera que.

wherewithal npl recursos mpl.

whet vt excitar.

whether conj si.

which pn qué; lo que; el que, el cual; cuál; * adj
¿qué?; cuyo.

whiff n bocanada de humo f.

while n rato m; vez f; * conj durante; mientras;
aunque.

whim n antojo, capricho m.

whimper vi sollozar, gemir.

whimsical adj caprichoso/sa, fantástico/ca.

whine vi llorar, lamentar; * n quejido, lamento m.

whinny vi relinchar.

whip n azote m; látigo m, Lat Am chicote m, Lat
Am cuero m; * vt azotar; batir.

whipped cream n nata montada f.

whirl vt, vi girar; hacer girar; mover(se)
rápidamente.

whirlpool n remolino m.

whirlpool bath n hidromasaje m.

whirlwind n torbellino m.

whisky n whisky m.

whisper vi cuchichear; susurrar.

whispering n cuchicheo m; susurro m.

whistle vi silbar; * n silbido m.

white adj blanco/ca, pálido/da; cano/na; puro/ra;
* n color blanco m; clara del huevo f.

white elephant n maula f.

white-hot adj incandescente.

white lie n mentirijilla f.

whiten vt, vi blanquear; emblanquecerse.

whiteness n blancura f; palidez f.

whitewash n enlucimiento m; * vt encalar;
jalbegar.

whiting n pescadilla f.

whitish adj blanquecino/na.

who pn ¿quién?, que.

whoever pn quienquiera, cualquiera.

whole adj todo/da, total; sano/na, entero/ra; * n
total m; conjunto m.

wholehearted adj sincero/ra.

wholesale n venta al por mayor f, Lat Am
mayoreo m.

wholesome adj sano/na, saludable.

wholewheat adj integral.

wholly adv enteramente.

whom pn ¿quién?; que.

whooping cough n tos ferina f.

whore n puta f; (col) zorra f.

why n ¿por qué?; * conj por qué; * excl ¡hombre!

wick n mecha f.

wicked adj malvado/da, perverso/sa; **~ly** adv
malamente.

wickedness n perversidad, malignidad f.

wicker n mimbre m; * adj tejido/da de mimbre.

wide adj ancho/cha, vasto/ta; grande; **~ly** adv
muy; **far and ~** por todos lados.

wide-awake adj despierto/ta.

widen vt ensanchar, extender.

wide open adj de par en par.

widespread adj extendido/da.

widow n viuda f.

widower n viudo m.

width n anchura f.

wield vt manejar, empuñar.

wife n esposa f; mujer f.

wig n peluca f; tupé m.

wiggle vt menear; * vi menearse.

wild adj silvestre, feroz; desierto/ta;
descabellado/da; salvaje.

wilderness n desierto m; yermo m.

wild life n fauna f.

wildly adv violentamente; locamente;
desatinadamente.

willful adj deliberado/da; testarudo/da.

willfulness n obstinación f.

wiliness n fraude, engaño m.

will n voluntad f; testamento m; * vt querer,
desear.

willing adj inclinado/da, dispuesto/ta; **~ly** adv
de buena gana.

willingness n buena voluntad, buena gana f.

willow n sauce m (árbol).

willpower n fuerza de voluntad f.

wilt vi marchitarse.

wily adj astuto/ta.

win vt ganar, conquistar; alcanzar; lograr.

wince vi encogerse, estremecerse.

winch n torno m.

wind n viento m; aliento m; flatulencia f.

wind vt enrollar; envolver; dar cuerda a; * vi serpentear.

windfall n golpe de suerte m.

wind farm n parque eólico m.

winding adj tortuoso/sa.

windmill n molino de viento m.

window n ventana f.

window box n jardinera de ventana f.

window cleaner n limpiacristales m invar.

window ledge n repisa f.

windowpane n cristal m.

windowsill n repisa f.

windpipe n tráquea f.

windshield n parabrisas m invar.

windshield washer n lavaparabrisas m invar.

windshield wiper n limpiaparabrisas m invar.

windsurfer n windsurfista m/f.

windsurfing n windsurf m.

wind turbine n aerogenerador m.

windy adj de mucho viento.

wine n vino m.

wine cellar n bodega f.

wine glass n copa de vino f.

wine list n carta de vinos f.

wine merchant n vinatero/ra m/f.

wine-tasting n degustación de vinos f.

wing n ala f.

winged adj alado/da.

winger n extremo m.

wink vi guiñar; * n pestañeo m; guino m.

winner n ganador/a m/f; vencedor/a m/f.

winning post n meta f.

winter n invierno m; * vi invernar.

winter sports npl deportes de invierno mpl.

wintry adj invernal.

wipe vt limpiar; borrar.

wire n alambre m; telegrama m; * vt instalar el alambrado en; conectar.

wiring n alambrada m, Lat Am alambrado m.

wiry adj delgado/da y fuerte.

wisdom n sabiduría, prudencia f.

wisdom teeth npl muelas del juicio fpl.

wise adj sabio/bia, docto/ta, juicioso/sa, prudente.

wisecrack n broma f.

wish vt querer, desear, anhelar; * n anhelo, deseo m.

wishful adj deseoso/sa.

wisp n mechón m; voluta f.

wistful adj pensativo/va, atento/ta.

wit n entendimiento, ingenio m.

witch n bruja, hechicera f.

witchcraft n brujería f; sortilegio m.

with prep con; por, de, a.

withdraw vt quitar; privar; retirar; * vi retirarse, apartarse.

withdrawal n retirada f.

withdrawn adj reservado/da.

wither vi marchitarse, secarse.

withhold vt detener, impedir, retener.

within prep dentro de, adentro; * adv interiormente; en casa.

without prep sin.

withstand vt resistir.

witless adj necio/cia, tonto/ta, falto/ta de ingenio.

witness n testimonio m; testgo m/f; * vt atestiguar, testificar.

witness stand n estrado de los testigos m.

witticism n ocurrencia f.

wittily adv ingeniosamente.

wittingly adv adrede, de propósito.

witty adj ingenioso/sa, agudo/da, chistoso/sa.

wizard n brujo, hechicero m.

wobble vi tambalearse.

woe n dolor m; miseria f.

woeful adj triste, funesto/ta; ~ly adv tristemente.

wolf n lobo m; **she ~** loba f.

woman n mujer f.

womanish adj mujeril.

womanly adj mujeril, mujeriego/ga.

womb n útero m.

women's lib n la liberación de la mujer f.

wonder n milagro m; maravilla f; asombro m; * vi maravil larse de; preguntarse si.

wonderful adj maravilloso/sa; ~ly adv maravillosamente.

wondrous adj maravilloso/sa.

won't abbrev will not.

wont n uso m; costumbre f.

woo vt cortejar.

wood n bosque m; selva f; madera f; leña f.

wood alcohol n alcohol metílico m.

wood carving n tallado en madera m.

woodcut n estampa de madera f.

woodcutter n leñador/a m/f; grabador en láminas de madera, xilógrafo m/f.

wooded adj arbolado/da.

wooden adj de madera.

wood engraver n xilógrafo m.

wooden shoe n zueco m.

woodland n arbolado m.

woodlouse n cochinilla f.

woodpecker n pájaro carpintero m.

woodsman n cazador m; guardabosque m.

woodwind n intrumento de viento de madera m.

woodwork n carpintería f.

woodworm n carcoma f.

wool n lana f.

woolen adj de lana.

woolens npl géneros de lana mpl.

woolly, wooly adj lanudo/da, lanoso/sa.

word n palabra f; noticia f; * vt expresar; componer en escri tura.
wordiness n verbosidad f.
wording n redacción f.
word processing n tratamiento de textos m.
word processor n procesador de textos m.
wordy adj verboso/sa.
work vi trabajar; obrar; estar en movimiento/en acción; fermentar; * vt trabajar, labrar; fabricar, manufacturar; **to ~ out** vi salir bien; * vt resolver; * n trabajo m; fábrica f; obra f; empleo m.
workable adj práctico/ca.
workaholic n trabajador obsesivo m, trabajadora obsesiva f.
worker n trabajador/a m/f; obrero/ra m/f.
workforce n mano de obra f.
working-class adj obrero/ra, de clase trabajadora.
workman n labrador m.
workmanship n manufactura f; destreza del artífice f.
workmate n compañero/ra de trabajo m/f.
workshop n taller, obrador m.
world n mundo m; * adj del mundo; mundial.
worldliness n mundanería f.
worldly adj mundano/na, terreno/na.
worldwide adj mundial.
worm n gusano m; (tec) rosca de tornillo f.
worn-out adj gastado/da; rendido/da.
worried adj preocupado/da.
worry vt preocupar; * n preocupación f; pensión f.
worrying adj inquietante.
worse adj, adv peor; **~ and ~** cada vez peor; * n lo peor.
worship n culto m; adoración f; **your ~** su señoría; * vt adorar, venerar.
worst adj el/la peor; * adv peor; * n lo peor m.
worth n valor, precio m; mérito m.
worthily adv dignamente, convenientemente.
worthless adj sin valor; inútil.
worthwhile adj que vale la pena; valioso/sa.

worthy adj digno/na; respetable; honesto/ta.
would-be adj aspirante.
wound n herida, llaga f; * vt herir, llagar.
wrangle vi reñir; * n riña f.
wrap vt envolver.
wrath n ira, rabia, cólera f.
wreath n corona, guirnalda f.
wreck n naufragio m; ruina f; destrucción f; navío naufragado m; * vt naufragar; arruinar.
wreckage n restos mpl; escombros mpl.
wren n chochín m.
wrench vt arrancar; dislocar; torcer; * n llave inglesa f; tirón m.
wrest vt arrancar, arrebatar.
wrestle vi luchar; disputar.
wrestling n lucha f.
wretched adj infeliz, miserable.
wriggle vi menearse, agitarse.
wring vt torcer; arrancar; estrujar.
wrinkle n arruga f; * vt arrugar; * vi arrugarse.
wrist n muñeca f.
wristband n puno de camisa m.
wristwatch n reloj de pulsera m.
writ n escrito m; escritura f; orden f.
write vt escribir; componer; **to ~ down** apuntar; **to ~ off** borrar; desechar; **to ~ up** redactar.
write-off n pérdida total f.
writer n escritor/a, m/f; autor/a m/f.
writhe vi retorcerse.
writing n escritura f; letra f; obras fpl; escrito m.
writing desk n escritorio m.
writing paper n papel para escribir m.
wrong n injuria f; injusticia f; perjuicio m; error m; * adj malo/la; injusto/ta; equivocado/da, inoportuno/na; falso/sa; * adv mal, equivocadamente; * vt agraviar, injuriar.
wrongful adj injusto/ta.
wrongly adv injustamente.
wry adj irónico/ca.

X

xenophobia *n* xenofobia *f.*
Xmas *n* Navidad *f.*
X-ray *n* radiografía *f.*

xylographer *n* xilógrafo *m.*
xylophone *n* xilófano *m.*

Y

yacht *n* yate *m*.
yachting *n* vela *f*.
Yankee *n* yanqui *m/f*.
yard *n* corral *m*; yarda *f*.
yardstick *n* criterio *m*.
yarn *n* estambre *m*; hilo de lino *m*.
yawn *vi* bostezar; * *n* bostezo *m*.
yawning *adj* muy abierto/ta.
yeah *adv* sí.
year *n* año *m*.
yearbook *n* anuario *m*.
yearling *n* añal *m*.
yearly *adj* anual; * *adv* anualmente, todos los años.
yearn *vi* añorar.
yearning *n* añoranza *f*.
yeast *n* levadura *f*.
yell *vi* aullar; * *n* aullido *m*.
yellow *adj* amarillo/lla; * *n* amarillo *m*.
yellowish *adj* amarillento/ta.
yelp *vi* latir, gañir; * *n* aullido *m*.
yes *adv* sí; * *n* sí *m*.
yesterday *adv* ayer; * *n* ayer *m*.
yet *conj* sin embargo; pero; * *adv* todavía.

yew *n* tejo *m*.
yield *vt* dar, producir; rendir; * *vi* rendirse; ceder el paso; * *n* producción *f*; cosecha *f*; rendimiento *m*.
yoga *n* yoga *m*.
yogurt *n* yogur *m*.
yoke *n* yugo *m*; yunta *f*.
yolk *n* yema (de huevo) *f*.
yonder *adv* allá.
you *pn* vosotros/tras, tú, usted, *Lat Am* vos, ustedes.
young *adj* joven, mozo/za; **~er** *adj* menor.
youngster *n* jovencito/ta *m/f*; joven *m/f*.
your(s) *pn* tuyo, tuya, vuestro, vuestra, suyo, suya.
yourself *pn* tú mismo, tú misma, usted mismo, usted misma.
yourselves *pn pl* vosotros mismos, vosotras mismas, ustedes mismos, ustedes mismas.
youth *n* juventud, adolescencia *f*; joven *m/f*.
youthful *adj* juvenil.
youthfulness *n* juventud *f*.
yuppie *adj*, *n* yupi *m/f*.

Z

zany *adj* estrafalario/ria.
zap *vt* borrar.
zeal *n* celo *m*; ardor *m*.
zealous *adj* celoso/sa.
zebra *n* cebra *f*.
zenith *n* cénit *m*.
zero *n* zero, cero *m*.
zest *n* ánimo *m*.
zigzag *n* zigzag *m*; * *adj* zigzag; * *vi* zigzaguear.
zinc *n* zinc *m*.

zipper *n* cremallera *f*; cierre de cremallera *m*.
zodiac *n* zodíaco *m*.
zone *n* banda, faja *f*; zona *f*.
zoo *n* zoo, zoológico *m*.
zoological *adj* zoológico/ca.
zoologist *n* zoólogo/ga *m/f*.
zoology *n* zoología *f*.
zoom *vi* zumbar.
zoom lens *n* zoom *m*.

Z

SPANISH PHRASES

Getting Started

Everyday words and phrases

Yes	Sí *see*	**OK**	Vale *ba-lay*	**Good**	Bueno *bway-no*
Yes, please	Sí, por favor *see, por fa-bor*	**Please**	Por favor *por fa-bor*	**I am very sorry**	Lo siento mucho *lo syen-to moo-cho*
No	No *no*	**Thank you**	Gracias *gra-thee-as*		
No, thank you	No, gracias *no, gra-thee-as*	**Excuse me**	¡Perdón! *pair-don*		

Being understood

Please repeat that slowly
Por favor repítame eso
lentamente
*por fa-bor, re-pee-ta-may e-so
len-ta-men-tay*
I do not speak Spanish
No hablo castellano
no a-blo kas-te-ya-no
I do not understand
No entiendo
no en-tyen-do

**Can you find someone who
speaks English?**
¿Puede encontrar a alguien
que hable inglés?
*pwe-day en-kon-trar al- gee-en
kay a-blay een-glays*
Can you help me, please?
¿Puede ayudarme, por favor?
pwe-day a-yoo-dar-may, por fa-bor

It does not matter
No importa
no eem-por-ta
I do not mind
No me importa
no may eem-por-ta

Greetings and exchanges

Hello
Hola
o-la
Hi
Hola
o-la
Good evening
Buenas tardes
bway-nas tar-des
Good morning
Buenos días
bway-nos dee-as
Good night
Buenas noches
bway-nas no-ches
Good-bye
Adiós
a-dee-os
It is nice to meet you
Encantado/Encantada de
conocerle
*en-kan-ta-do /en-kan-ta-da day
ko-no-thair-lay*

How are you?
¿Qué tal estás? ?
kay tal es-tas
¿Cómo estás?
I am very well, thank you
Muy bien, gracias
mwee byen, gra-thee-as
It is good to see you
Me alegro de verlo
may a-le-gro day bair-lo
There are five of us
Somos cinco
so-mos theen-ko
This is — my son
Este es — mi hijo
es-tay es — mee ee-ho
— my husband
— mi marido
— mee ma-ree-do
This is — my daughter
Ésta es — mi hija
es-ta es — mee ee-ha

— my wife
— mi esposa
— mee es-po-sa
My name is...
Me llamo...
may ya-mo...
What is your name?
¿Cómo te llamas?
ko-mo tay ya-mas
I am a student
Soy estudiante
soy es-too-dee-an-tay
I am on vacation
Estoy de vacaciones
es-toy day ba-ka-thyo-nes
I live in...
Vivo en...
bee-bo en...
You are very kind
Es usted muy amable
es oo-sted mwee a-ma-blay
You're welcome!
¡De nada!
day na-da!

See you soon	— *gran bre-tan-ya*	— Nueva Zelanda
Hasta pronto	— **Canada**	— *nway-ba the-lan-da*
a-sta pron-to	— Canadá	— **Scotland**
I am from — America	— *ka-na-da*	— Escocia
Soy de — los Estados Unidos	— **England**	— *es-ko-thee-a*
soy day— los es-ta-dos oo-nee-dos	— Inglaterra	— **South Africa**
— **Australia**	— *een-gla-te-ra*	— Sudáfrica
— Australia	— **Ireland**	— *soo-da-free-ka*
— *ow-stra-lee-a*	— Irlanda	— **Wales**
— **Britain**	— *eer-lan-da*	— Gales
— Gran Bretaña	— **New Zealand**	— *ga-les*

Common questions

Where?	**How can I contact American**	**Where can I buy currency?**
¿Dónde?	**Express/Diners Club?**	¿Dónde puedo cambiar
don-day	¿Cómo puedo contactar la	efectivo?
Where is...?	oficina de American Express/	*don-day pwe-do kam-byar dee-*
¿Dónde está...?	Diners Club?	*ne-ro en e-fek-tee-bo*
don-day es-ta...	*ko-mo pwe-do kon-tak-tar la o-*	**Where can I change**
Where are...?	*fee-thee-na day American*	**traveler's checks?**
¿Dónde están...?	*Express/Diners Club*	¿Dónde puedo cambiar
don-day es-tan...	**What is the problem?**	cheques de viajero?
When?	¿Cuál es el problema?	*don-day pwe-do kam-byar che-*
¿Cuándo?	*kwal es el pro-blay-ma*	*kays day bee-a-hay*
kwan-do	**Do you know a good**	**Where can we sit down?**
What?	**restaurant?**	¿Dónde podemos sentarnos?
¿Qué?	¿Conoce algún buen	*don-day po-day-mos sen-tar-nos*
kay	restaurante?	**Where is the bathroom?**
How?	*ko-no-thay al-goon bwen res-to-*	¿Dónde están los servicios?
¿Cómo?	*ran-tay*	*don-day es-tan los sair-bee-thee-*
ko-mo	**Do you mind if I...?**	*os*
How much?	¿Le importa que yo...?	**Who did this?**
¿Cuánto?	*lay eem-por-ta kay yo...*	¿Quién ha hecho esto?
kwan-to	**What is wrong?**	*kee-en a e-cho es-to*
Who?	¿Qué ocurre?	**Who should I see about**
¿Quién?	*kay o-koo-ray*	**this?**
kee-en	**What time do you close?**	¿Con quién debo hablar sobre
Why?	¿A qué hora cierran?	esto?
¿Por qué?	*a kay o-ra thee-e-ran*	*kon kee-en de-bo a-blar so-bray*
por kay	**Where can I buy a postcard?**	*es-to*
Which?	¿Dónde puedo comprar una	**Will you come also?**
¿Cuál?	postal?	¿Va a venir usted también?
kwal	*don-day pwe-do kom-prar oo-na*	*ba a be-neer oo-sted tam-byen*
How long will it take?	*po-stal*	
¿Cuánto tardará?		
kwan-to tar-da-ra		

Asking the time

What time is it?	— las dieciocho quince	— *las on-thay me-nos kwar-to*
¿Qué hora es?	— *las dee-eth-ee-o-cho keen-thay*	— **after three o'clock**
kay o-ra es	— **a quarter past ten**	— después de las tres
It is — nine-thirty p.m. (21:30)	— las diez y cuarto	— *des-pwes day las tres*
Son — las veintiuna trenta	— *las dee-eth ee kwar-to*	— **nearly five o'clock**
son — las bain-tee-oo-na trayn-ta	— **a quarter to eleven**	— casi las cinco
— **six-fifteen p.m. (18:15)**	— las once menos cuarto	— *ka-see las theen-co*

— twenty-five past ten
— las diez y veinticinco
— *las dee-eth ee bain-tee-theen-ko*
— twenty-five to eleven
— las once menos veinticinco
— *las on-thay me-nos bain-tee-theen-ko*
— eleven o'clock
— las once/las once en punto
— *las on-thay/las on-thay en poon-to*
— five past ten
— las diez y cinco
— *las dee-eth ee theen-ko*
— half past ten
— las diez y media
— *las dee-eth ee me-dee-a*
— five to eleven
— las once menos cinco
— *las on-thay me-nos theen-ko*
— ten o' clock
— las diez/las diez en punto
— *las dee-eth/las dee-eth en poon-to*
— ten past ten
— las diez y diez
— *las dee-eth ee dee-eth*

— twenty past ten
— las diez y veinte
— *las dee-eth ee bain-tay*
— twenty to eleven
— las once menos veinte
— *las on-thay me-nos bain-tay*
It is — early
Es — temprano
es— tem-pra-no
— late
— tarde
— *tar-day*
— one o'clock
— la una
— *la oo-na*
— midday
— mediodía
— *me-dee-o-dee-a*
— midnight
— medianoche
— *me-dee-a-no-chay*
at about one o'clock
sobre la una
so-bray la oo-na
at half past six
a las seis y media
a las says ee me-dee-a

at half past eight exactly
a las ocho y media en punto
a las o-cho ee me-dee-a en poon-to
in an hour's time
dentro de una hora
den-tro day oo-na o-ra
in half an hour
dentro de media hora
den-tro day me-dee-a o-ra
soon
pronto
pron-to
this afternoon
esta tarde
es-ta tar-day
this evening
esta tarde
es-ta tar-day
this morning
por la mañana
por la man-ya-na
tonight
esta noche
es-ta no-chay
at night
por la noche
por la no-chay

At the Airport

Arrival

Here is my passport
Aquí está mi pasaporte
a-kee es-ta mee pa-sa-por-tay
How long will this take?
¿Cuánto tardará esto?
kwan-to tar-da-ra es-to
I am attending a convention
Voy a asistir a un congreso
boy a a-see-steer a oon kon-gre-so
I am here on business
Estoy aquí en viaje de
negocios
es-toy a-kee en bee-a-hay day ne-go-thee-os

I will be staying here for
eight weeks
Me quedaré aquí ocho
semanas
may kay-da-ray a-kee o-cho se-ma-nas
We are visiting friends
Estamos visitando unos
amigos
es-ta-mos bee-see-tan-do oon-os a-mee-gos
We have a joint passport
Tenemos un pasaporte familiar
te-nay-mos oon pa-sa-por-tay fa-mee-lyar

How much do I have to
pay?
¿Cuánto tengo que pagar?
kwan-to ten-go kay pa-gar
I have nothing to declare
No tengo nada que declarar
no ten-go na-da kay de-kla-rar
I have the usual allowances
Tengo los artículos permitidos
ten-go los ar-tee-koo-los pair-mee-tee-dos
This is for my own use
Esto es para mi uso personal
es-to es pa-ra mee oo-so pair-so-nal

Common problems and requests

Can I upgrade to first class?
¿Puedo cambiar mi billete a primera clase?
pway-do kam-byar mee bee-ye-tay a pree-me-ra kla-say

I have lost my ticket
He perdido el billete
ay pair-dee-do el bee-ye-tay

I have missed my connection
He perdido el vuelo de enlace
ay pair-dee-do el bway-lo day en-la-thay

Please give me back my passport
Devuélvame el pasaporte, por favor
de-bwel-ba-may el pa-sa-por-tay, por fa-bor

The people who were to meet me have not arrived
No ha llegado la gente que iba a recibirme
no a ye-ga-do la hen-tay kay ee-ba a re-thee-beer-may

I was held up at immigration
Me entretuvieron en el control de pasaportes
may en-tray-too-byair-on en el kon-trol day pa-sa-por-tes

Where can I find the airline representative?
¿Dónde puedo encontrar al representante de la compañía aérea?
don-day pwe-do en-kon-trar al re-pre-zen-tan-tay day la kom-pan-yee-a a-air-ay-a

Where do I get the connecting flight to Santiago?
¿Dónde puedo enlazar con el vuelo a Santiago?
don-day pwe-do en-la-thar kon el bway-lo a san-tee-a-go

Where is — the bar?
¿Dónde está — el bar?
don-day es-ta — el bar

— the departure lounge?
— la sala de embarque?
— la sa-la day em-bar-kay

— the information desk?
— la oficina de información?
— la o-fee-thee-na day een-for-ma-thyon

— the transfer desk?
— el mostrador de transbordos?
— el mos-tra-dor day trans-bor-dos

Where is the rest room?
¿Dónde están los servicios?
don-day es-tan los sair-bee-thee-os

Is there a bus into town?
¿Hay autobús a la ciudad?
eye ow-to-boos a la thee-oo-dad

How long will the delay be?
¿Cuánto se retrasará?
kwan-to say re-tra-sa-ra

I was delayed at the airport
Me entretuvieron en el aeropuerto
may en-tray-too-byair-on en el a-air-o-pwair-to

My flight was late
Mi vuelo se retrasó
mee bway-lo say re-tra-so

Baggage

Where is the baggage from flight number…?
¿Dónde están los equipajes del vuelo número…?
don-day es-tan los e-kee-pa-hays del bway-lo noo-me-ro…

I have lost my bag
He perdido la bolsa
ay pair-dee-do la bol-sa

These bags are not mine
Estas bolsas no son mías
es-tas bol-sas no son mee-as

Are there any baggage trolleys?
¿Hay carritos de equipaje?
eye ka-ree-tos day e-kee-pa-hay

Can I have help with my bags?
¿Puedo obtener ayuda para llevar el equipaje?
pwe-do ob-te-nair a-yoo-da pa-ra ye-bar el e-kee-pa-hay

Is there any charge?
¿Hay que pagar algo?
eye kay pa-gar al-go

I will carry that myself
Esto lo llevaré yo mismo/misma
es-to lo ye-ba-ray yo miz-mo / miz-ma

My baggage has not arrived
No ha llegado mi equipaje
no a ye-ga-do mee e-kee-pa-hay

Where is my bag?
¿Dónde está mi bolsa?
don-day es-ta mee bol-sa

It is — a large suitcase
Es — una maleta grande
es — oo-na ma-lay-ta gran-day

— a rucksack
— una mochila
— oo-na mo-chee-la

— a small bag
— una bolsa pequeña
— oo-na bol-sa pe-ken-ya

No, do not put that on top
No, no ponga eso encima de todo
no, no pon-ga e-so en-thee-ma day to-do

Please take these bags to a taxi
Por favor lleve estas bolsas a un taxi
por fa-bor, ye-bay es-tas bol-sas a oon tak-see

Careful, the handle is broken
Cuidado, el mango está roto
kwee-da-do, el man-go es-ta ro-to

This package is fragile
Este paquete es frágil
es-tay pa-ke-tay es fra-heel

At the Hotel

Reservations and inquiries

I am sorry I am late
Siento llegar tarde
syen-to ye-gar tar-day
I have a reservation
Tengo una reserva hecha
ten-go oo-na re-sair-ba ay-cha
I shall be staying until July 4th
Me quedaré hasta el cuatro de julio
may ke-da-ray a-sta el kwa-tro day hoo-lee-o
I want to stay for five nights
Quiero quedarme cinco noches
kee-e-ro ke-dar-may theen-ko no-ches
Do you have a double room with a bath?
¿Tiene una habitación doble con baño?
tee-e-nay oo-na a-bee-ta-thyon do-blay kon ban-yo
Do you have a room with twin beds and a shower?
¿Tiene una habitación con camas gemelas y ducha?
tee-e-nay oo-na a-bee-ta-thyon kon ka-mas he-may-las ee doo-cha
Do you have a single room?
¿Tiene una habitación individual?
tee-e-nay oo-na a-bee-ta-thyon een-dee-bee-dwal
I need — a double room with a bed for a child
Necesito — una habitación doble con una cama para un niño
ne-the-see-to — oo-na a-bee-ta-thyon do-blay kon oo-naka-ma pa-ra oon neen-yo
— a room with a double bed
— una habitación con cama doble
— oo-na a-bee-ta-thyon kon ka-ma do-blay

— a room with twin beds and bath
— una habitación con camas gemelas y baño
— oo-na a-bee-ta-thyon kon ka-mas he-may-las ee ban-yo
— a single room
— una habitación individual
— oo-na a-bee-ta-thyon een-dee-bee-dwal
— a single room with a shower or bath
— una habitación individual con ducha o baño
— oo-na a-bee-ta-thyon een-dee-bee-dwal kon doo-cha o ban-y
How much is — full board?
¿Cuánto es — la pensión completa?
kwan-to es — la pen-syon kom-play-ta
— half-board?
— la media pensión?
— la me-dee-a pen-syon
How much is it per night?
¿Cuánto cuesta por noche?
kwan-to kwes-ta por no-chay
Does the price include room and breakfast?
¿Están incluidos en el precio la habitación y el desayuno?
es-tan een-kloo-ee-dos en el pre-thee-o la a-bee-ta-thyon ee el des-a-yoo-no
Does the price include room and all meals?
¿Están incluidos en el precio la habitación y todas las comidas?
es-tan een-kloo-ee-dos en el pre-thee-o la a-bee- ta-thyon ee to-das las ko-mee-das
Does the price include room and dinner?
¿Están incluidos en el precio la habitación y la cena?
es-tan een-kloo-ee-dos en el pre-thee-o la a- bee-ta-thyon ee la thay-na

Can we have adjoining rooms?
¿Nos puede dar habitaciones contiguas?
nos pwe-day dar a-bee-ta-thyo-nes kon-tee- gwas
Are there other children staying at the hotel?
¿Hay más niños hospedados en el hotel?
eye mas neen-yos os-pe-da-dos en el o-tel
Are there supervised activities for the children?
¿Hay actividades vigiladas para los niños?
eye ak-tee-bee-da-des bee-hee-la-das pa-ra los neen-yos
Can my son sleep in our room?
¿Puede dormir mi hijo en nuestra habitación?
pwe-day dor-meer mee ee-ho en nwes-tra a- bee-ta-thyon
Do you take traveler's checks?
¿Acepta cheques de viaje?
a-thep-ta che-kays day bee-a-hay
Which floor is my room on?
¿En qué piso está mi habitación?
en kay pee-so es-ta mee a-bee-ta-thyon
Do you have a fax machine?
¿Tiene fax?
tee-e-nay faks
Do you have a laundry service?
¿Tienen servicio de lavandería?
tee-e-nen sair-bee-thee-o day la-ban-de-ree-a
Do you have a safe for valuables?
¿Tiene caja fuerte para objetos de valor?
tee-e-nay ka-ha fwair-tay pa-ra ob-he-tos day ba-lor

Do you have any English
newspapers?
¿Tiene periódicos en inglés?
*tee-e-nay pe-ree-o-dee-kos en een-
gles*

Do you have a parking lot?
¿Tienen aparcamiento?
tee-e-nen a-par-ka-myen-to

Do you have a cot for my
baby?
¿Tiene una cuna para el bebé?
*tee-e-nay oo-na coo-na pa-ra el
be-bay*

Do you have satellite TV?
¿Tiene antena parabólica?
tee-e-nay an-te-na pa-ra-bo-lee-ka

What is the voltage here?
¿Qué voltaje hay aquí?
kay bol-ta-hay eye a-kee

Is the voltage 220 or 110?
¿Es el voltaje de doscientos
veinte o de ciento diez?
*es el bol-ta-hay day dos-thee-en-
tos bain-tay o day thee-en-to
dee-eth*

Is there — a casino?
¿Hay — casino?
eye — ka-see-no

— a hairdryer?
— secador de pelo?
— se-ka-dor day pay-lo

— an elevator?
— ascensor?
— as-then-sor

— a minibar?

— minibar?
— mee-nee-bar

— a sauna?
— sauna?
— sow-na

— a swimming pool?
— piscina?
— pees-thee-na

— a telephone?
— teléfono?
— te-le-fo-no

— a television?
— televisión?
— te-lay-bee-syon

Is there a room service
menu?
¿Hay menú para el servicio de
habitaciones?
*eye me-noo pa-ra el sair-bee-
theo o day u-bee- ta-thyo-nes*

Is there a market in the
town?
¿Hay algún mercado en la
ciudad?
*eye al-goon mair-ka-do en la
thee-oo-dad*

Is there a Chinese restaurant?
¿Hay algún restaurante chino?
*eye al-goon re-sto-ran-tay chee-
no*

Is there an Indian restaurant?
¿Hay algún restaurante indio?
*eye al-goon re-sto-ran-tay een-
dee-o*

Is this a safe area?
¿Es ésta una zona segura?
es es-ta oo-na tho-na se-goo-ra

Where is the socket for my
razor?
¿Dónde está el enchufe para la
máquina de afeitar?
*don-day es-ta el en-choo-fay day
la ma-kee-nee-ya day a-fay-tar*

What time does the hotel
close?
¿A qué hora cierra el hotel?
a kay o-ra thee-e-ra el o-tel

What time does the restaurant
close?
¿A qué hora cierra el
restaurante?
*a kay o-ra thee-e-ra el re-sto-
ran-tay*

When does the bar open?
¿Cuándo se abre el bar?
kwan-do say a-bray el bar
¿A qué hora abre el bar?

What time is — breakfast?
¿A qué hora es — el desayuno?
a kay o-ra es — el des-a-yoo-no

— dinner?
— la cena?
— la thay-na

— lunch?
— la comida?
— la ko-mee-da

Service

Can I charge this to my
room?
¿Puede cargar esto a mi
cuenta?
*pwe-day kar-gar es-to a mee
kwen-ta*

Can I dial direct from my
room?
¿Puedo marcar directamente
desde mi habitación?
*pwe-do mar-kar dee-rek-ta-
men-tay dez-day mee a-bee-ta-
thyon*

Can I have a newspaper?
¿Me da un periódico?
may da oon pe-ree-o-dee-ko

Can I have an outside line?
¿Me da línea, por favor?
may da lee-nay-a, por fa-bor

Can I have my billfold from
the safe?
¿Puedo sacar mi cartera de la
caja fuerte?
*pwe-do sa-kar mee kar-tair-a
day la ka-ha fwair-tay*

Can I have the check, please
¿Puede darme la factura, por
favor?
*pwe-day dar-may la fak-too-ra,
por fa-bor*

Can I make a telephone call
from here?
¿Puedo hacer una llamada
telefónica desde aquí?
*pwe-do a-thair oo-na ya-ma-da
te-le-fo-nee-ka dez-day a-kee*

Can I send this by courier?
¿Puedo enviar esto por
mensajero?
*pwe-do en-byar es-to por men-sa-
hair-o*
¿Puedo enviar esto por correo
urbano? (*Lat Am*)

Can I use my credit card?
¿Puedo utilizar mi tarjeta de
pago?
*pwe-do oo-tee-lee-thar mee tar-
hay-ta day pa-go*

Can I use my personal
computer here?
¿Puedo utilizar aquí mi
ordenador personal?
*pwe-do oo-tee-lee-thar a-kee mee
or-de-na-dor pair-so-nal*

Can I use traveler's checks?
¿Puedo utilizar cheques de viaje?
pwe-do oo-tee-lee-thar che-kays day bee-a-hay

Can we have breakfast in our room, please?
¿Podemos desayunar en la habitación, por favor?
po-day-mos des-a-yoo-nar en la a-bee-ta- thyon, por fa-bor

Can you recommend a good local restaurant?
¿Puede recomendar un buen restaurante cercano?
pwe-day re-ko-men-dar oon bwen re-sto-ran- tay thair-ka-no

I want to stay an extra night
Quiero quedarme una noche más
kee-e-ro ke-dar-may oo-na no-chay mas

Do I have to change rooms?
¿Tengo que cambiarme de habitación?
ten-go kay kam-byar may day a-bee-ta-thyon

I need an early morning call
Necesito que me llame por la mañana temprano
ne-the-see-to kay may ya-may por la man-ya- na tem-pra-no

I need — a razor
Necesito — una maquinilla de afeitar
ne-the-see-to — oo-na ma-kee-nee-ya day a- fay-tar

— some soap
— jabón
— ha-bon

— some toilet paper

— papel higiénico
— pa-pel ee-hyen-ee-ko

— some towels
— toallas
— to-a-yas

I need to charge these batteries
Tengo que cargar estas pilas
ten-go kay kar-gar es-tas pee-las

I want to press these clothes
Quiero planchar esta ropa
kee-e-ro plan-char es-ta ro-pa

Please fill the minibar
Por favor llene el minibar
por fa-bor, ye-nay el mee-nee-bar

Please leave the bags in the lobby
Por favor deje las bolsas en el vestíbulo
por fa-bor, de-hay las bol-sas en el bes-tee-boo-lo

Please send this fax for me
Por favor envíe este fax de mi parte
por fa-bor, en-bee-ay es-tay faks day mee par-tay

Please turn the heating off
Apague la calefacción, por favor
a-pa-gay la ka-le-fak-thyon, por fa-bor

Please wake me at seven o'clock in the morning
Por favor, llámeme a las siete de la mañana
por fa-bor, ya-may-may a las see-e-tay day la man-ya-na

Where can I send a fax?
¿Dónde puedo enviar un fax?
don-day pwe-do en-byar oon faks

Can I have — my key, please?
¿Puede darme — mi llave, por favor?
pwe-day dar-may — mee ya-bay, por fa-bor

— an ashtray?
— un cenicero?
— oon the-nee-thair-o

— another blanket?
— otra manta?
— o-tra man-ta

— another pillow?
— otra almohada?
— o-tra al-mo-a-da

— some coat hangers?
— algunas perchas?
— al-goo-nas pair-chas

— some notepaper?
— papel de cartas?
— pa-pel day kar-tas

Has my colleague arrived yet?
¿Ha llegado mi compañero?
a ye-ga-do mee kom-pan-ye-ro

I am expecting a fax
Estoy esperando un fax
es-toy es-pe-ran-do oon faks

My room number is 22
El número de mi habitación es el veintidós
el noo-me-ro day mee a-bee-ta-thyon es el bain-tee-dos

Please can I leave a message?
¿Puedo dejar un mensaje, por favor?
pwe-do de-har oon men-sa-hay, por fa-bor

Problems

Where is the manager?
¿Dónde está el gerente?
don-day es-ta el he-ren-tay

I cannot close the window
No puedo cerrar la ventana
no pwe-do the-rar la ben-ta-na

I cannot open the window
No puedo abrir la ventana
no pwe-do a-breer la ben-ta-na

The heating is not working
No funciona la calefacción
no foon-thyo-na la ka-le-fak-thyon

The room is not serviced
La habitación no está preparada
la a-bee-ta-thyon no es-ta pre-pa-ra-da

The air conditioning is not working
No funciona el aire acondicionado
no foon-thyo-na el eye-ray a-kon-dee-thyo-na-do

The room key does not work
No funciona la llave de la habitación
no foon-thyo-na la ya-bay day la a-bee-ta-thyon

The bathroom is dirty
El cuarto de baño está sucio
el kwar-to day ban-yo es-ta soo-thyo

The light is not working
No funciona la luz
no foon-thyo-na la looth
The room is too noisy
La habitación es demasiado
ruidosa
la a-bee-ta-thyon es de-ma-sya-do roo-ee-do-so

There are no towels in the
room
No hay toallas en la habitación
no eye to-a-yas en la a-bee-ta-thyon
There is no hot water
No hay agua caliente
no eye a-gwa ka-lee-en-tay

There is no plug for the
washbasin
No hay tapón en el lavabo
no eye ta-pon en el la-ba-bo

Checking out

I have to leave tomorrow
Tengo que irme mañana
ten-go kay eer-may man-ya-na
We will be leaving early
tomorrow
Nos iremos mañana temprano
nos ee-ray-mos man-ya-na tem-pra-no

Could you have my bags
brought down?
¿Podría hacer que me bajen las
bolsas?
po-dree-a a-thair kay may ba-hen las bol-sas

Could you order me a taxi?
¿Puede pedirme un taxi?
pwe-day pe-deer-may oon tak-see
Thank you, we enjoyed our
stay
Gracias, hemos disfrutado de
nuestra estancia
gra-thee-as, ay-mos dees-froo-ta-do day nwes-tra e-stan-thee-a

Childcare

Can you warm this milk for
me?
¿Puede calentarme esta leche?
pwe-day ka-len-tar-may es-ta le-chay
Do you have a high chair?
¿Tiene alguna silla alta?
tee-e-nay al-goo-na see-ya al-ta
Is there a baby-sitter?
¿Hay una canguro?
eye oo-na kan-goo-ro
Is there a cot for our baby?
¿Hay alguna cuna para nuestro
bebé?
eye al-goo-na coo-na pa-ra nwes-tra be-bay
Is there a paddling pool?
¿Hay piscina para niños?
eye pees-thee-na pa-ra neen-yos
Is there a swimming pool?
¿Hay piscina?
eye pees-thee-na
Is there a swing park?
¿Hay parque de columpios?
eye par-kay day ko-loom-pyos

I am very sorry. That was
very naughty of him
Lo siento mucho. Ha sido una
travesura suya
lo syen-to moo-cho. A see-do oo-na tra-be-soo-ra soo-ya
It will not happen again
No volverá a ocurrir
no bol-bair-a a o-koo-reer
How old is your daughter?
¿Cuántos años tiene su hija?
kwan-tos an-yos tee-e-nay soo ee-ha
My daughter is seven years old
Mi hija tiene siete años
mee ee-ha tee-e-nay see-e-tay an-yos
My son is ten years old
Mi hijo tiene diez años
mee ee-ho tee-e-nay dee-eth an-yos
She goes to bed at nine
o'clock
Se acuesta a las nueve
say a-kwe-sta a las nwe-bay

We will be back in two
hours
Volveremos dentro de dos
horas
bol-bair-ay-mos den-tro day dos o-ras
Where can I buy some
disposable diapers?
¿Dónde puedo comprar
pañales desechables?
don-day pwe-do kom-prar pan-ya-les des-e-cha-bles
Where can I change the
baby?
¿Dónde puedo cambiar al
bebé?
don-day pwe-do kam-byar al be-bay
Where can I feed my baby?
¿Dónde puedo dar de comer al
bebé?
don-day pwe-do dar day ko-mair al be-bay

Other Accommodation

Renting a house

We have rented this house
Hemos alquilado esta casa
ay-mos al-kee-la-do es-tay ca-sa
Here is our booking form
Aquí tiene nuestra reserva
a-kee tee-e-nay nwes-tra re-sair-ba
We need two sets of keys
Necesitamos dos juegos de
llaves
*ne-the-see-ta-mos dos hway-gos
day ya-bes*
**Can I contact you on this
number?**
¿Puedo contactarle en este
teléfono?
*pwe-do kon-tak-tar-lay en es-tay
te-le-fo-no*
Where is the bathroom?
¿Dónde está el baño?
don-day es-ta el ban-yo
How does this work?
¿Cómo funciona ésto?
ko-mo foon-thyo-na es-to
I cannot open the shutters
No puedo abrir los postigos
no pwe-do a-breer los po-stee-gos

Can you send a repairman?
¿Puede enviar alguien a
reparar?
*pwe-day en-byar al-gee-en a re-
pa-rar*
Is the water heater working?
¿Funciona el calentador de
agua?
*foon-thyo-na el ka-len-ta-dor
day a-gwa*
Is the water safe to drink?
¿El agua es potable?
el a-gwa es po-ta-blay
Is there any spare bedding?
¿Hay ropa de cama de más?
eye ro-pa day ka-ma day mas
The cooker does not work
No funciona la cocina
no foon-thyo-na la ko-thee-na
**The refrigerator does not
work**
No funciona el frigorífico
*no foon-thyo-na el free-go-ree-
fee-ko*

The toilet is blocked
El inodoro está atascado
el een-o-do-ro es-ta a-ta-ska-do
There is a leak
Hay un escape
eye oon es-ka-pay
We do not have any water
No tenemos agua
no te-nay-mos a-gwa
**When does the cleaner
come?**
¿Cuándo vienen a limpiar?
kwan-do bee-e-nen a leem-pyar
Where is the fuse box?
¿Dónde están los plomos?
don-day es-tan los plo-mos
¿Dónde está la caja de tacos?
**Where is the key for this
door?**
¿Dónde está la llave de esta
puerta?
*don-day es-ta la ya-bay day es-
ta pwair-ta*

Around the house

bath	**corkscrew**	**mirror**	**spoon**
baño	sacacorchos	espejo	cuchara
ban-yo	*sa-ka-kor-chos*	*es-pe-ho*	*coo-cha-ra*
bathroom	**cup**	**pan**	**stove**
cuarto de baño	taza	sartén	estufa
kwar-to day ban-yo	*ta-tha*	*sar-ten*	*es-too-fa*
bed	**fork**	**plate**	**table**
cama	tenedor	plato	mesa
ka-ma	*te-ne-dor*	*pla-to*	*may-sa*
brush	**glass**	**refrigerator**	**faucet**
cepillo	vaso	frigorífico	grifo
the-pee-yo	*ba-so*	*free-go-ree-fee-ko*	*gree-fo*
can opener	**inventory**	**rubbish**	**toilet**
abrelatas	inventario	basura	inodoro
a-bray-la-tas	*een-ven-ta-ryo*	*ba-soo-ra*	*een-o-do-ro*
chair	**kitchen**	**sheet**	**vacuum cleaner**
silla	cocina	sábana	aspirador
see-ya	*ko-thee-na*	*sa-ba-na*	*as-pee-ra-dor*
cooker	**knife**	**sink**	**washbasin**
cocina	cuchillo	fregadero	lavabo
ko-thee-na	*koo-chee-yo*	*fre-ga-dair-o*	*la-ba-bo*

Getting Around

Asking for directions

Where is — the art gallery?
¿Dónde está — el museo de arte?
don-day es-ta — el moo-say-o day ar-tay
— the post office?
— el correo?
— el ko-ray-os
— the Tourist Information Service?
— la Oficina de Turismo?
— la o-fee-thee-na day too-reez-mo
Can you tell me the way to the bus station?
¿Puede indicarme el camino a la estación de autobuses?
pwe-day een-dee-kar-may el ka-mee-no a la e- sta-thyon day ow-to-boo-ses
I am lost
Estoy perdido/perdida
es-toy pair-dee-do / pair-dee-da
I am lost. How do I get to the … Hotel?
Estoy perdido/perdida. ¿Cómo se llega al Hotel…?
es-toy pair-dee-do / pair-dee-da. Ko-mo say ye-ga al o-tel …

Can you show me on the map?
¿Puede indicarme en el mapa?
pwe-day een-dee-kar-may en el ma-pa
May I borrow your map?
¿Puede prestarme el mapa?
pwe-day pre-star-may el ma-pa
We are looking for a restaurant
Estamos buscando un restaurante
es-ta-mos boo-skan-do oon re-sto-ran-tay
Where are the bathrooms?
¿Dónde están los servicios?
don-day es-tan los sair-bee-thee-os
I am looking for the Tourist Information Office
Estoy buscando la Oficina de Turismo
es-toy boo-skan-do la o-fee-thee-na day too- reez-mo
I am trying to get to the market
Quiero ir al mercado
kee-e-ro eer al mair-ka-do

Can you walk there?
¿Se puede ir andando hasta allí?
say pwe-day eer an-dan-do a-sta a-yee
Is it far?
¿Está lejos?
es-ta lay-hos
I want to go to the theater
Quiero ir al teatro
kee-e-ro eer al tay-a-tro
Is there a bus that goes there?
¿Hay algún autobús que vaya allí?
a-ee al-goon ow-to-boos kay ba-ya a-yee
Where do I get a bus for the city center?
¿Dónde puedo coger el autobús al centro de la ciudad?
don-day pwe-do ko-hair el ow-to-boos al then-tro day la thee-oo-dad
Is there a train that goes there?
¿Hay algún tren que vaya allí?
eye al-goon tren kay ba-ya a-yee

Directions – by road

Where does this road go to?
¿Adónde va esta carretera?
a-don-day ba es-ta ka-re-tair-a
Do I turn here for…?
¿Tengo que girar aquí para…?
ten-go kay hee-rar a-kee pa-ra…
How do I get onto the highway?
¿Por dónde se entra a la autopista?
por don-day say en-tra a la ow-to-pee-sta
How far is it to…?
¿Qué distancia hay a…?
kay dee-stan-thee-a eye a…

How long will it take to get there?
¿Cuánto se tarda en ir allí?
kwan-to say tar-da en eer a-yee
I am looking for the next exit
Busco la siguiente salida
boos-ko la see-gee-en-tay sa-lee-da
Is there a service station near here?
¿Hay una gasolinera aquí cerca?
a-ee oo-na ga-so-lee-nair-a a-kee thair-ka
Is this the right way to the supermarket?
¿Es éste el camino al supermercado?
es es-tay el ka-mee-no al soo-pair-mair-ka-do

Which is the best route to…?
¿Cuál es la mejor carretera para…?
kwal es la me-hor ka-re-tair-a pa-ra…
Which is the fastest route?
¿Cuál es la carretera más rapida?
kwal es la ka-re-tair-a mas ra-pee-da
Which road do I take to…?
¿Qué carretera debo coger para…?
kay ka-re-tair-a de-bo ko-hair pa-ra…

Directions – what you may hear

Vaya — hasta...
by-a —a-sta...
You go — as far as...
— a la izquierda
— a la eeth-kyair-da
— left
— a la derecha
— a la de-ray-cha
— right
Vaya hacia...
by-a a-thya...
You go towards...
Está — en el cruce
es-ta — en el croo-thay
It is — at the crossroads
— a la vuelta de la esquina
— a la bwel-ta day la es-kee-na
— around the corner
— bajo el puente
— ba-ho el pwen-tay
— under the bridge
— después del semáforo
— des-pwes del se-ma-fo-ro
— after the traffic lights
— junto al cine
— hoon-to al thee-nay
— next to the movie theater

— en el siguiente piso
— en el see-gee-en-tay pee-so
— on the next floor
— frente a la estación de
ferrocarril
*— fren-tay a la es-ta-thyon day
fe-ro-ka- reel*
— opposite the railway station
— allí
— a-yee
— over there
Atraviese la calle
a-tra-bee-ay-say la ka-yay
Cross the street
Siga las señales a...
see-ga las sen-ya-les a...
Follow the signs for...
— el próximo cruce
— el prok-see-mo croo-thay
— the next junction
— la autopista
— la ow-to-pee-sta
— the highway, expressway
— la plaza
— la pla-tha
— the square

Siga todo recto
see-ga to-do rek-to
Keep going straight ahead
Gire a la izquierda
hee-ray a la eeth-kyair-da
Turn left
Gire a la derecha
hee-ray a la de-ray-cha
Turn right
Tiene que dar la vuelta
tee-e-nay kay dar la bwel-ta
You have to go back
Coja la primera carretera a
la derecha
*ko-ha la pree-mair-a ka-re-tair-
a a la de-ray-cha*
Take the first road on the right
Coja la carretera de...
ko-ha la ka-re-tair-a day...
Take the road for...
Coja la segunda carretera a
la izquierda
*ko-ha la se-goon-da ka-re-tair-a
a la eeth-kyair-da*
Take the second road on the
left

Hiring an automobile

I want to hire an automobile
Quiero alquilar un coche
kee-e-ro al-kee-lar oon ko-chay
I need it for two weeks
Lo quiero para dos semanas
lo kee-e-ro pa-ra dos se-ma-nas
Can I hire an automobile?
¿Es posible alquilar un coche?
*es po-see-blay al-kee-lar oon ko-
chay*
Can I hire an automobile
with an automatic gearbox?
¿Puedo alquilar un coche con
cambio automático?
*pwe-do al-kee-lar oon ko-chay
kon kam-byo ow-to-ma-tee-ko*
Please explain the docu-
ments
Por favor, explíqueme los
documentos
*por fa-bor, eks-plee-kay-may los
do-koo-men-tos*
We will both be driving
Conduciremos los dos
kon-doo-thee-ray-mos los dos

Do you have — a large
automobile?
¿Tiene — un coche grande?
tee-e-nay — oon ko-chay gran-da
— a smaller automobile?
— un coche más pequeño?
— oon ko-chay mas pe-ken-yo
— an automatic?
— un coche con cambio
automático?
*— oon ko-chay kon kam-byo ow-
to-ma-tee-ko*
— a station wagon?
— una furgoneta?
— oo-na foor-go-nay-ta
I want to leave the
automobile at the airport
Quiero dejar el coche en el
aeropuerto
*kee-e-ro de-har el ko-chay en el
a-air-o-pwair-to*
Is there a charge per
kilometer?
¿Se cobra el kilometraje?
say ko-bra el kee-lo-me-tra-hay

I would like to leave the
automobile at the airport
Me gustaría dejar el coche en
el aeropuerto
*may goo-sta-ree-a de-har el ko-
chay en el a-air- o-pwair-to*
Must I return the automo-
bile here?
¿Tengo que devolver el coche
aquí?
*ten-go kay de-bol-bair el ko-chay
a-kee*
Can I pay for insurance?
¿Puedo pagar un seguro?
pwe-do pa-gar oon se-goo-ro
Do I have to pay a deposit?
¿Tengo que pagar algún
depósito?
*ten-go kay pa-gar oon de-po-zee-
to*
How does the steering lock
work?
¿Cómo funciona el antirrobo?
*ko-mo foon-thyo-na el an-tee-ro-
bo*

Please show me how to operate the lights
Por favor, enséñeme cómo manejar las luces
por fa-bor, en-sen-yay-may ko-mo ma-ne-har las loo-thes
I would like a spare set of keys
Me gustaría tener un juego de llaves de repuesto
may goo-sta-ree-a te-nair oon hway-go day ya-bes day re-pwes-to

Where is reverse gear?
¿Dónde está la marcha atrás?
don-day es-ta la mar-cha a-tras
Where is the tool kit?
¿Dónde está la caja de herramientas?
don-day es-ta la ka-ha day e-ra-myen-tas

Please show me how to operate the windshield wipers
Por favor, enséñeme cómo manejar los limpiaparabrisas
por fa-bor, en-sen-yay-may ko-mo ma-ne-har los leem-pya-pa-ra-bree-sas

By taxi

Where can I get a taxi?
¿Dónde puedo tomar un taxi?
don-day pwe-do to-mar oon tak-see
Take me to the airport, please
Lléveme al aeropuerto, por favor
ye-bay-may al a-air-o-pwair-to, por fa-bor
The bus station, please
La estación de autobuses, por favor
la es-ta-thyon day ow-to-boo-ses, por fa-bor
Please show us around the town
Por favor, enséñenos la ciudad
por fa-bor, en-sen-yay-nos la thee-oo-dad
Please take me to this address
Por favor, lléveme a esta dirección
por fa-bor, ye-bay-may a es-ta dee-rek-thyon
Could you put the bags in the trunk, please?
Puede meter las bolsas en el maletero, por favor
pwe-day me-tair las bol-sas en el ma-le-te-ro, por fa-bor

Turn left, please
Gire a la izquierda, por favor
hee-ray a la eeth-kyair-da, por fa-bor
Turn right, please
Gire a la derecha, por favor
hee-ray a la de-ray-cha, por fa-bor
Wait for me, please
Espéreme, por favor
es-pe-ray-may, por fa-bor
Can you come back in one hour?
¿Puede volver dentro de una hora?
pwe-day bol-bair den-tro day oo-na o-ra
Please wait here for a few minutes
Por favor, espere aquí unos minutos
por fa-bor, es-pe-ray a-kee oo-nos mee-noo-tos
Please stop at the corner
Por favor, pare en la esquina
por fa-bor, pa-ray en la es-kee-na

Please wait here
Espere aquí, por favor
es-pe-ray a-kee, por fa-bor
I am in a hurry
Tengo prisa
ten-go pree-sa
Please hurry, I am late
Dése prisa por favor, se me ha hecho tarde
day-say pree-sa por fa-bor, say may a e-cho tar-day
How much is it per kilometer?
¿Cuánto cuesta por kilómetro?
kwan-to kwes-ta por kee-lo-me-tro
How much is that, please?
¿Cuánto es eso, por favor?
kwan-to es e-so, por fa-bor
Keep the change
Quédese con el cambio
kay-day-say kon el kam-byo

By bus

Does this bus go to the center of town?
¿Este autobús va al centro de la ciudad?
es-tay ow-to-boos ba al ka-stee-yo
How frequent is the service?
¿Con qué frecuencia es el servicio?
kon kay fre-kwen-thee-a es el sair-bee-thee-o
What is the fare to the city center?
¿Cuánto es al centro de la ciudad?
kwan-to es al then-tro day la thee-oo-dad

Where should I change?
¿Dónde tengo que cambiar?
don day ten-go kay kam-byar
Where do I get the bus for the airport?
¿Dónde puedo coger el autobús para el aeropuerto?
don-day pwe-do ko-hair el ow-to-boos pa-ra el a-air-o-pwair-to

Will you tell me when to get off the bus?
¿Por favor me avisa cuándo bajarme del autobus?
may dee-ra kwan-do ba-har-may del ow-to- boos
When is the last bus?
¿Á que hora pasa el último autobús?
a kay o-ra es el ool-tee-mo ow-to-boos

By train

Can I buy a return ticket?
¿Puedo comprar un billete de
ida y vuelta?
*pwe-do kom-prar oon bee-ye-tay
day ee-da ee bwel-ta*

**A return (round-trip ticket)
to Barcelona, please**
Un billete de ida y vuelta a
Barcelona, por favor
*oon bee-ye-tay day ee-da ee bwel-
ta a bar-the-lo-na, por fa-bor*

A return to Paris, first class
Un billete de ida y vuelta a
París, en primera clase
*oon bee-ye-tay day ee-da ee bwel-
ta a pa-rees, en pree-mair-a kla-say*

**A single (one-way ticket) to
Lisbon.**
Un billete de ida a Lisboa.
*oon bee-ye-tay day ee-da a leez-
bo-a, por fa-bor*

A smoking car, first class
Compartimento de fumadores,
primera clase
*kom-par-tee-men-to day foo-ma-
do-res, pree-mair-a kla-say*

A non-smoking car, please
Compartimento de no
fumadores, por favor
*kom-par-tee-men-to day no foo-
ma-do-res, por fa-bor*

**Second class. A window
seat, please**
En segunda. Asiento de
ventana, por favor
*en se-goon-da. a-syen-to day
ben-ta-na, por fa- bor*

Can I take my bicycle?
¿Puedo llevar mi bicicleta?
pwe-do ye-bar mee bee-thee-klay-ta

**Is this the platform for
Zaragoza?**
¿Es éste el andén para
Zaragoza?
*es es-te el an-den pa-ra tha-ra-
go-tha*

**What are the times of the
trains to Paris?**
¿Cuál es el horario de trenes
para París?
*kwal es el o-ra-ree-o day tre-nes
pa-ra pa-rees*

**How long do I have before
my next train leaves?**
¿Cuánto tiempo tengo antes
de mi próximo tren?
*kwan-to tee-em-po ten-go an-tes
day mee prok-see-mo tren*

Where can I buy a ticket?
¿Dónde puedo comprar un
billete?
*don-day pwe-do kom-prar oon
bee-ye-tay*

Where do I have to change?
¿Dónde tengo que cambiar?
don-day ten-go kay kam-byar

**Where do I pick up my
bags?**
¿Dónde se recogen los
equipajes?
*don-day say re-ko-hen los e-kee-
pa-hays*

Can I check in my bags?
¿Puedo facturar el equipaje?
*pwe-do fak-too-rar el e-kee-pa-
hay*

**I want to leave these bags in
the checkroom**
Quiero dejar estas bolsas en la
consigna
*kee-e-ro de-har es-tas bol-sas en
la kon-seeg-na*

How much is it per bag?
¿Cuánto es por cada bolsa?
kwan-to es por ka-da bol-sa

**I shall pick them up this
evening**
Las recogeré esta tarde
las re-ko-hair-ay es-ta tar-day

**I want to book a place on
the sleeper to Paris**
Quiero reservar una plaza en
coche-cama a París
*kee-e-ro re-sair-bar oo-na pla-tha
en ko-chay- ka-ma a pa-rees*

Is there — a checkroom?
¿Hay — consigna de
equipajes?
eye — kon-seeg-na day e-kee-pa-hes
— club car?
— coche bar?
— ko-chay bar
— a restaurant car?
— vagón restaurante?
— ba-gon re-sto-ran-tay

**Where is the departure
listing?**
¿Dónde está el tablón de
salidas?
*don-day es-ta el ta-blon day sa-
lee-das*

What time does the train leave?
¿A qué hora sale el tren?
a kay o-ra sa-lay el tren

**Do I have time to go
shopping?**
¿Tengo tiempo para ir de
compras?
*ten-go tee-em-po pa-ra eer day
kom-pras*

What time is the last train?
¿A qué hora sale el último tren?
a kay o-ra es el ool-tee-mo tren

**When is the next train to
Seville?**
¿Cuándo sale el siguiente tren
para Sevilla?
*kwan-do sa-lay el see-gee-en-tay
tren pa-ra se- bee-ya*

Which platform do I go to?
¿A qué andén tengo que ir?
a kay an-den ten-go kay eer

Is this a through train?
¿Es éste un tren directo?
es es-tay oon tren dee-rek-to

Is this the Madrid train?
¿Es éste el tren de Madrid?
es es-tay el tren day ma-dreed

Do we stop at Vigo?
¿Paramos en Vigo?
pa-ra-mos en bee-go

**What time do we get to
Burgos?**
¿A qué hora llegamos a
Burgos?
a kay o-ra ye-ga-mos a boor-gos

Are we at Durango yet?
¿Hemos llegado a Durango?
ay-mos ye-ga-do a doo-ran-go

Are we on time?
¿Llegaremos a la hora prevista?
ye-ga-ray-mos a la o-ra pray-bee-sta

**Can you help me with my
bags?**
Puede ayudarme con el
equipaje?
*pwe-day a-yoo-dar-may kon el e-
kee-pa-hay*

Is this seat taken?
¿Está ocupado este asiento?
es-ta o-koo-pa-do es-tay a-syen-to
May I open the window?
¿Le importa si abro la ventana?
lay eem-por-ta see a-bro la ben-ta-na
My wife has my ticket
Mi esposa tiene mi billete
mee es-po-sa tee-e-nay mee bee-ye-tay

I have lost my ticket
He perdido el billete
ay pair-dee-do el bee-ye-tay
This is a non-smoking car
Éste es un compartimento de no fumadores
es-tay es oon kom-par-tee-men-to day no foo- ma-do-res

This is my seat
Éste es mi asiento
es-tay es mee a-syen-to
Where is the bathroom?
¿Dónde está el servicio?
don-day es-ta el sair-bee-thee-o
Why have we stopped?
¿Por qué hemos parado?
por kay ay-mos pa-ra-do

Driving

Traffic and weather conditions

Are there any delays?
¿Hay atascos?
eye a-tas-kos
Is the traffic heavy?
¿Hay mucho tráfico?
eye moo-cho tra-fee-ko
Is the traffic one-way?
¿Es sentido único?
es sen-tee-do oo-nee-ko
Is there a different way to the stadium?
¿Hay otro camino al estadio?
eye o-tro ka-mee-no al es-ta-dee-o
Is there a toll on this expressway?
¿Esta autopista es de peaje?
es-ta ow-to-pee-sta es day pay-a-hay

What is causing this traffic jam?
¿Qué está causando este embotellamiento?
kay es-ta kow-san-do es-tay em-bo-te-ya- myen-to
What is the speed limit?
¿Cuál es el límite de velocidad?
kwal es el lee-mee-tay day be-lo-thee-dad
What time does the parking lot close?
¿Cuándo se cierra el parking?
kwan-do say thee-e-ra el par-keen
When is the rush hour?
¿Cuándo es la hora punta?
kwan-do es la o-ra poon-ta

Is the pass open?
¿Está el paso abierto?
es-ta el pa-so a-bee-air-to
Do I need snow chains?
¿Necesito cadenas para la nieve?
ne-the-see-to ka-day-nas pa-ra la nee-e-bay
Is the road to Segovia snowed up?
¿Está nevada la carretera a Segovia?
es-ta ne-ba-da la ka-re-tair-a a se-go-bee-a
When will the road be clear?
¿Cuándo estará la carretera despejada?
kwan-do es-ta-ra la ka-re-tair-a des-pe-ha-da

At the service station

Do you take credit cards?
¿Acepta tarjetas de crédito?
a-thep-ta tar-hay-tas day kre-dee-to
Can you clean the windshield?
¿Puede limpiar el parabrisas?
pwe-day leem-pyar el pa-ra-bree-sas
Fill the tank, please
Llene el depósito, por favor
ye-nay el de-po-zee-to, por fa-bor
25 liters of — unleaded petrol
Veinticinco litros de — gasolina sin plomo
bain-tee-theen-ko lee-tros day — ga-so-lee-na seen plo-mo

— 2 star
— normal
— normal
— nor-mal
— 4 star
— súper
— soo-pair
— diesel
— gas-oil
—ga-zoil
I need some distilled water
Necesito agua destilada
ne-the-see-to a-gwa de-stee-la-da
Check the tire pressure, please
Revise la presión de los neumáticos, por favor
re-bee-say la pre-syon day los nay-oo-ma-tee-kos, por fa-bor

The pressure should be 2.3 at the front and 2.5 at the rear
La presión debería estar en dos coma tres en los delanteros y dos coma cinco en los traseros
la pre-syon de-be-ree-a es-tar en dos ko-ma tres en los de-lan-tair-os ee dos ko-ma theen- ko en los tra-sair-os
Check — the oil
Revise — el aceite
re-bee-say — el a-thay-ee-tay
— the water
— el agua
— el a-gwa

Parking

Is it safe to park here?
¿Es seguro aparcar aquí?
es se-goo-ro a-par-kar a-kee
Can I park here?
¿Puedo aparcar aquí?
pwe-do a-par-kar a-kee
Do I need a parking disc?
¿Necesito ficha de
aparcamiento?
*ne-the-see-to fee-cha day a-par-
ka-myen-to*
Where do I pay?
¿Dónde tengo que pagar?
don-day ten-go kay pa-gar

**Where is there a parking
lot?**
¿Dónde hay un aparcamiento?
*don-day a-ee oon a-par-ka-
myen-to*
How long can I stay here?
¿Cuánto tiempo puedo
permanecer aquí?
*kwan-to tee-em-po pwe-do pair-
ma-ne-thair a-kee*

**Do I need — coins for the
meter?**
¿Necesito — monedas para el
parquímetro?
*ne-the-see-to — mo-nay-das pa-
ra el par-kee- me-tro*
— parking lights?
— luces de posición?
— loo-thes day po-zee-thyon
Where can I get a parking disc?
¿Dónde puedo obtener una
ficha de aparcamiento?
*don-day pwe-do ob-te-nair oo-
na fee-cha day a-par-ka-myen-to*

Breakdowns and repairs

Can you give me — a push?
¿Puede — empujarme?
pwe-day — em-poo-har-may
— a tow?
— remolcarme?
— re-mol-kar-may
Can you send a recovery truck?
¿Puede enviar un camión grúa?
pwe-day en-byar oon ka-myon groo-a
**Can you find out what the
trouble is?**
¿Puede encontrar el problema?
pwe-day en-kon-trar el pro-blay-ma
**Can you take me to the
nearest garage?**
¿Puede llevarme al garage más
cercano?
*pwe-day ye-bar-may al ga-ra-
hay mas thair- ka-no*
Is there a telephone nearby?
¿Hay algún teléfono cercano?
a-ee al-goon te-le-fo-no thair-ka-no
**Can you give me a can of
petrol, please?**
¿Me da un bidón de gasolina,
por favor?
*may da oon bee-don day ga-so-
lee-na, por fa- bor*
Can you repair a flat tire?
¿Puede reparar una rueda
desinflada?
*pwe-day re-pa-rar oo-na roo-ay-
da des-een- fla-da*
**Can you repair it for the
time being?**
¿Puede repararlo provisionalmente?
*pwe-day re-pa-rar-lo pro-bees-yo-
nal-men-tay*

**Can you replace the
windshield wiper blades?**
¿Puede cambiar las paletas del
limpiaparabrisas?
*pwe-day kam-byar las pa-lay-tas
del leem- pya-pa-ra-bree-sas*
My car has broken down
Mi coche se ha averiado
mee ko-chay say a a-be-ree-a-do
My car will not start
Mi coche no arranca
mee ko-chay no a-ran-ka
**Do you have an emergency
fan belt?**
Tiene una correa de ventilador
de emergencia?
*tee-e-nay oo-na ko-ray-a day
ben-tee-la-dor day e-mair-hen-
thee-a*
Do you have the spare parts?
¿Tiene los repuestos?
tee-e-nay los re-pwe-stos
I have a flat tire
Tengo un pinchazo
ten-go oon peen-cha-tho
I have blown a fuse
Se me ha quemado un fusible
*say may a ke-ma-do oon foo-see-
blay*
**I have locked myself out of
the car**
He cerrado el coche con las
llaves dentro
*ay the-ra-do el ko-chay kon las
ya-bes den-tro*

**I have locked the ignition
key inside the car**
He dejado la llave de contacto
dentro del coche
*ay de-ha-do la ya-bay day kon-
tak-to den-tro del ko-chay*
I have run out of gas
Me he quedado sin gasolina
may ay ke-da-do seen ga-so-lee-na
I need a new fan belt
Necesito una nueva correa de
ventilador
*ne-the-see-to oo-na nway-ba ko-
ray-a day ben-tee-la-dor*
**I think there is a bad
connection**
Creo que hay una mala conexión
*kray-o kay eye oo-na ma-la ko-
nek-syon*
Is there a mechanic here?
¿Hay algún mecánico aquí?
eye al-goon me-ka-nee-ko a-kee
The engine has broken down
Se ha averiado el motor
say a a-be-ree-a-do el mo-tor
There is something wrong
Hay algún problema
eye al-goon pro-blay-ma
**There is something wrong
with the car**
Algo va mal en el coche
al-go ba mal en el ko-chay
Will it take long to repair it?
¿Tardará mucho en repararlo?
tar-da-ra moo-cho en re-pa-rar-lo
Is it serious?
¿Es grave?
es gra-bay

My windshield has cracked
Se me ha rajado el parabrisas
say may a ra-ha-do el pa-ra-bree-sas

The air-conditioning does not work
No funciona el aire acondicionado
no foon-thyo-na el a-ee-ray a-kon-dee-thyo-na-do

The battery is flat
La batería está descargada
la ba-te-ree-a es-ta des-kar-ga-da

The engine is overheating
El motor se recalienta
el mo-tor say re-ka-lyen-ta

The exhaust pipe has fallen off
Se ha caído el tubo de escape
say a ka-ee-do el too-bo day es-ka-pay

There is a leak in the radiator
Hay una fuga en el radiador
eye oo-na foo-ga en el ra-dee-a-dor

Do you have jump leads?
¿Tiene cables puente de batería?
tee-e-nay ka-bles pwen-tay day ba-te-ree-a

Accidents and the police

There has been an accident
Ha habido un accidente
a a-bee-do oon ak-thee-den-tay

We must call an ambulance
Tenemos que llamar a una ambulancia
te-nay-mos kay ya-mar a oo-na am-boo-lan-thee-a

We must call the police
Tenemos que llamar a la policía
te-nay-mos kay ya-mar a la po-lee-thee-a

What is your name and address?
¿Cuál es su nombre y dirección?
kwal es soo nom-bray ee dee-rek-thyon

You must not move
No debe moverse
no de-bay mo-bair-say

Do you want my passport?
¿Quiere mi pasaporte?
kee-e-ray mee pa-sa-por-tay

He did not stop
Él no paró
el no pa-ro

He is a witness
Éste es testigo
es-tay es te-stee-go

He overtook on a bend
Él adelantó en una curva
el a-de-lan-to en la coor-ba

He ran into the back of my car
Él chocó con la parte trasera de mi coche
el cho-ko kon la par-tay tra-sair-a day mee ko- chay

He stopped suddenly
Él se paró de repente
el say pa-ro day re-pen-tay

He was moving too fast
Él iba demasiado rápido
el ee-ba de-ma-sya-a-do ra-pee-do

Here are my insurance documents
Aquí está la documentación del seguro
a-kee es-ta la do-koo-men-ta-thyon del se-goo- ro

Here is my driving license
Aquí está mi permiso de conducir
a-kee es-ta mee pair-mee-so day kon-doo- theer

I could not stop in time
No he podido parar a tiempo
no ay po-dee-do pa-rar a tee-em-po

I did not see the bicycle
No vi la bicicleta
no bee la bee-thee-klay-ta

I did not see the sign
No vi la señal
no bee la sen-yal

I did not understand the sign
No entendí la señal
no en-ten-dee la sen-yal

I am very sorry. I am a visitor
Lo siento mucho. Soy turista
lo syen-to moo-cho. Soy too-ree-sta

I did not know about the speed limit
No sabía lo del límite de velocidad
no sa-bee-a lo del lee-mee-tay day be-lo-thee- dad

How much is the fine?
¿Cuánto es la multa?
kwan-to es la mool-ta

I have not got enough money. Can I pay at the police station?
No tengo suficiente dinero
¿Puedo pagar en la comisaría de policía?
no ten-go soo-fee-thee-en-tay dee-ne-ro. Pwe- do pa-gar en la ko-mee-sa-ree-a day po-lee- thee-a

I have not had anything to drink
No he bebido nada
no ay be-bee-do na-da

I was only driving at 50 km/h
Sólo iba a cincuenta por hora
so-lo ee-ba a theen-kwen-ta por o-ra

I was overtaking
Estaba adelantando
es-ta-ba a-de-lan-tan-do

I was parking
Estaba aparcando
es-ta-ba a-par-kan-do

My car has been towed away
La grúa se ha llevado mi coche
la groo-a say a ye-ba-do mee ko-chay

That car was too close
Ese coche venía demasiado cerca
e-say ko-chay be-nee-a de-ma-sya-do thair-ka

The brakes failed
Los frenos fallaron
los fray-nos fa-ya-ron

The car's license plate number was...
La matrícula del coche era...
la ma-tree-koo-la del ko-chay ay-ra...

The car skidded
El coche derrapó
el ko-chay de-ra-po

The car swerved
El coche giró bruscamente
el ko-chay hee-ro broo-ska-men-tay

The car turned right without signaling
El coche giró a la derecha sin señalizar
el ko-chay hee-ro a la de-ray-cha seen sen-ya- lee-thar

The road was icy
La carretera estaba congelada
la ka-re-tair-a es-ta-ba kon-he-la-da

The tire burst
El neumático reventó
el nay-oo-ma-tee-ko re-ben-to

Car parts

aerial
antena
an-tay-na

alternator
alternador
al-tair-na-dor

antifreeze
anticongelante
an-tee-kon-he-lan-tay

axle
eje
e-hay

battery
batería
ba-te-ree-a

brake fluid
líquido de frenos
lee-kee-do day fray-nos

brakes
frenos
fray-nos

carburettor
carburador
kar-boo-ra-dor

child seat
silla de niño
see-ya day neen-yo

choke
estárter
e-star-tair

clutch
embrague
em-bra-gay

cylinder
cilindro
thee-leen-dro

disc brake
freno de disco
fray-no day dee-sko

distributor
distribuidor
dees-tree-boo-ee-dor

dynamo
dinamo
dee-na-mo

electrical system
sistema eléctrico
see-stay-ma e-lek-tree-ko

engine
motor
mo-tor

exhaust system
sistema de escape
see-stay-ma day e-ska-pay

fan belt
correa del ventilador
ko-ray-a del ben-tee-la-dor

fender
parachoques
pa-ra-cho-kes

fuse
fusible
foo-see-blay

fuel pump
bomba de carburante
bom-ba day kar-boo-ran-tay

fuel gage
indicador de carburante
een-dee-ka-dor day kar-boo-ran-tay

gas
gasolina
ga-so-lee-na

gear box
caja de cambios
ka-ha day kam-bee-os

gearshift
palanca de cambios
pa-lan-ka day kam-bee-os

hand brake
freno de mano
fray-no day ma-no

hazard lights
luces de emergencia
loo-thes day e-mair-hen-thee-a

headlights
faros
fa-ros

hood
capó
ka-po

horn
bocina
bo-thee-na

ignition
contacto
kon-tak-to

ignition key
llave de contacto
ya-bay day kon-tak-to

indicator
intermitente
een-tair-mee-ten-tay

jack
gato
ga-to

lights
luces
loo-thes

oil
aceite
a-thay-ee-tay

oil filter
filtro de aceite
feel-tro day a-thay-ee-tay

oil pressure
presión de aceite
pre-syon day a-thay-ee-tay

points
platinos
pla-tee-nos

pump
bomba
bom-ba

radiator
radiador
ra-dee-a-dor

rear-view mirror
espejo retrovisor
es-pe-ho re-tro-bee-sor

reflectors
reflectantes
re-flek-tan-tes

reversing light
luz de marcha atrás
looth day mar-cha a-tras

seat
asiento
a-syen-to

seat belt
cinturón de seguridad
then-too-ron day se-goo-ree-dad

shock absorber
amortiguador
a-mor-tee-gwa-dor

silencer
silenciador
see-len-thee-a-dor

spare part
repuesto
re-pwe-sto

spark plug
bujía
boo-hee-a

speedometer
velocímetro
be-lo-thee-me-tro

speed pedal
acelerador
a-the-le-ra-dor

starter motor
motor de arranque
mo-tor day a-ran-kay

steering wheel
volante
bo-lan-tay

suspension
suspensión
soo-spen-syon

tools
herramientas
e-ra-myen-tas

towbar
barra de remolque
ba-ra day re-mol-kay

transmission
transmisión
trans-mee-syon

trunk
maletero
ma-le-te-ro

tire
neumático
nay-oo-ma-tee-ko

warning light
luz de advertencia
looth day ad-bair-ten-thee-a

wheel
rueda
roo-ay-da

windshield
parabrisas
pa-ra-bree-sas

windshield wipers
limpiaparabrisas
leem-pya-pa-ra-bree-sas

Road signs

Alto
al-to
Stop
Aparcamiento sólo para residentes
a-par-ka-myen-to so-lo pa-ra re-see-den-tes
Parking for residents only
Camino particular
ka-mee-no par-tee-koo-lar
Private road
Ceda el paso
thay-da el pa-so
Give way
Centro ciudad
then-tro thee-oo-dad
Town center

Circule por la derecha
theer-koo-lay por la de-ray-cha
Keep to the right
Deslizamientos
des-lee-tha-myen-tos
Icy roads
Despacio
des-pa-thee-o
Drive slowly
Desviación
des-bee-a-thyon
Diversion
Desvío
des-bee-o
Diversion

Dirección única
dee-rek-thyon oo-nee-ka
One way
Estacionamiento de automóviles
es-ta-thyo-na-myen-to day ow-to-mo-bee-lays
Parking lot
Peaje
pay-a-hay
Toll
Estacionamiento prohibido
es-ta-thyo-na-myen-to pro-ee-bee-do
No parking permitted

Obras
o-bras
Roadworks
Paso prohibido
pa-so pro-ee-bee-do
No through road
Peligro
pay-lee-gro
Danger
Prohibido el paso
pro-ee-bee-do el pa-so
No thoroughfare
No entrar
no en-trar
No entry

Eating Out

Reservations

Should we reserve a table?
¿Debo reservar mesa?
de-be-ree-a-mos re-sair-bar may-sa
Can I book a table for four at eight o'clock?
¿Puedo reservar una mesa para cuatro para las ocho?
po-dree-a re-sair-bar oo-na may-sa pa-ra kwa-tro pa-ra las o-cho

Can we have a table for four?
Una mesa para cuatro, por favor
oo-na may-sa pa-ra kwa-tro, por fa-bor
I am a vegetarian
Soy vegetariano/vegeteriana
soy be-he-ta-ree-a-no / be-he-ta-ree-a-na

We would like a table — by the window
Nos gustaría una mesa — junto a la ventana
nos goo-sta-ree-a oo-na may-sa — hoon-to a la ben-ta-na
— on the terrace
— en la terraza
— en la te-ra-tha

Useful questions

Are vegetables included?
¿Se incluye verdura?
say een-kloo-yay bair-doo-ra
Do you have a local speciality?
¿Tienen alguna especialidad local?
tee-e-nen al-goo-na es-peth-ya-lee-dad lo-kal
Do you have a set menu?
¿Tiene un menú del día?
tee-e-nay oon me-noo del dee-a
What do you recommend?
¿Qué me recomienda?
kay may re-ko-myen-da
What is the dish of the day?
¿Cuál es el plato del día?
kwal es el pla-to del dee-a

What is the soup of the day?
¿Cuál es la sopa del día?
kwal es la so-pa del dee-a
What is this called?
¿Cómo se llama esto?
ko-mo say ya-ma es-to
What is this dish like?
¿Cómo es este plato?
ko-mo es es-tay pla-to
What is this?
¿Qué es esto?
kay es es-to
Is this good?
¿Está bueno esto?
es-ta bway-no es-to

Do you have fruit?
¿Tiene fruta?
tee-e-nay froo-ta
Which local wine do you recommend?
¿Qué vino local recomienda?
kay bee-no lo-kal re-ko-myen-da
How do I eat this?
¿Cómo se come esto?
ko-mo say ko-may es-to
Is the local wine good?
¿Es bueno el vino local?
es bway-no el bee-no lo-kal
Is this cheese very strong?
¿Es muy fuerte este queso?
es mwee fwair-tay es-tay ke-so

Ordering a meal

The menu, please
El menú, por favor
el me-noo, por fa-bor

I will take the set menu
Tomaré el menú del día
to-ma-ray el me-noo del dee-a

Can we start with soup?
¿Podemos empezar con sopa?
po-day-mos em-pe-thar kon so-pa

I like my steak — very rare
Me gusta — muy poco hecho
may goo-sta — mwee po-ko e-cho

— rare
— poco hecho
— po-ko e-cho

— medium rare

— medianamente hecho
— me-dee-a-na-men-tay e-cho

— well done
— bien hecho
— bee-en e-cho

I will have salad
Yo tomaré ensalada
yo to-ma-ray en-sa-la-da

Could we have some butter?
¿Puede traernos mantequilla, por favor?
pwe-day try-air-nos man-te-kee-ya, por fa-bor

We need some bread, please
Nos hace falta pan, por favor
nos a-thay fal-ta pan, por fa-bor

I will take that
Tomaré eso
to-ma-ray e-so

Could we have some more bread?
¿Puede traernos más pan?
pwe-day try-air-nos mas pan

Can I see the menu again, please?
¿Puedo volver a ver el menú, por favor?
pwe-do bol-bair a bair el me-noo, por fa-bor

That is for me
Eso es para mí
e-so es pa-ra mee

Ordering drinks

The wine list, please
La lista de vinos, por favor
la lee-sta day bee-nos, por fa-bor

We will take the Rioja
Tomaremos el Rioja
to-ma-ray-mos el ree-o-ha

Another glass, please
Otro vaso, por favor
o-tro ba-so, por fa-bor

A bottle of house red wine, please
Una botella de vino tinto de la casa, por favor
oo-na bo-te-ya day bee-no teen-to day la ka-sa, por fa-bor

A glass of dry white wine, please
Un vaso de vino blanco seco, por favor
oon ba-so day bee-no blan-ko se-ko, por fa-bor

Another bottle of red wine, please
Otra botella de vino tinto, por favor
o-tra bo-te-ya day bee-no teen-to, por fa-bor

Black coffee, please
Café solo, por favor
ka-fay so-lo, por fa-bor

Can we have some (still/sparkling) mineral water?
¿Nos puede traer agua mineral (sin gas/con gas)?
nos pwe-day try-air a-gwa mee-ne-ral (seen gas / con gas)

Coffee with milk, please
Café con leche, por favor
ka-fay kon le-chay, por fa-bor

Some plain water, please
Agua natural, por favor
a-gwa na-too-ral, por fa-bor

Two beers, please
Dos cervezas, por favor
dos thair-bay-thas, por fa-bor

Paying

Can we have the check?
¿Puede traernos la cuenta?
pwe-day try-air-nos la kwen-ta

Is service included?
¿Está el servicio incluido?
es-ta el sair-bee-thee-o een-kloo-ee-do

Is there any extra charge?
¿Hay algún cargo adicional?
a-ee al-goon kar-go a-deeth-yo-nal

Is tax included?
¿Están los impuestos incluidos?
es-tan los eem-pwe-stos een-kloo-ee-dos

I haven't enough money
No tengo suficiente dinero
no ten-go soo-feeth-yen-tay dee-ne-ro

This is not correct
Esto no es correcto
es-to no es ko-rek-to

This is not my check
Ésta no es mi cuenta
es-ta no es mee kwen-ta

Complaints and compliments

This is not what I ordered
Esto no es lo que he pedido
es-to no es lo kay ay pe-dee-do

This is cold
Esto está frío
es-to es-ta free-o

Can I have the recipe?
¿Puede darme la receta?
pwe-day dar-may la re-thay-ta

This is excellent
Esto está buenísimo
es-to es-ta bwe-nee-see-mo

The meal was excellent
La comida estaba excelente
la ko-mee-da es-ta-ba eks-the-len-tay

Menu reader

aceite
a-thay-tay
oil

aceitunas
a-thay-too-nas
olives

acelga
a-thel-ga
chard

aguacate
a-gwa-ka-tay
avocado

ajo
a-ho
garlic

albahaca
al-ba-a-ka
basil

albaricoques
al-ba-ree-ko-kes
apricots

albondigas
al-bon-dee-gas
meatballs

alcachofa
al-ka-cho-fa
artichoke

almejas
al-may-has
clams

apio
a-pee-o
celery

arroz con leche
a-roth kon le-chay
rice pudding

asado/asada la parrilla
a-sa-do / a-sa-da la pa-ree-ya
grilled

atún
a-toon
tuna

berenjena
be-ren-hay-na
aubergine

berro
be-ro
watercress

berza
ber-tha
cabbage

bizcocho
beeth-ko-cho
sponge cake

bocadillo
bo-ka-dee-yo
sandwich (with French-style bread)

bogavante a la marinera
bo-ga-ban-tay a la ma-ree-nair-a
lobster cooked in Galician style

bollos de pan
bo-yos day pan
bread rolls

budín
boo-deen
pudding

buñuelos
boon-yoo-ay-los
donuts

caballa
ka-ba-ya
mackerel

caballa en escabeche
ka-ba-ya en es-ka-be-chay
marinated mackerel

cabezas de cordero al horno
ka-bay-thas day kor-dair-o al or-no
roast head of lamb (Aragon)

calabacín
ka-la-ba-theen
courgette

calabaza
ka-la-ba-tha
squash

calamares
ka-la-ma-res
squid

caldo
kal-do
broth

caldo de pollo
kal-do day po-yo
chicken broth

caldo de vaca
kal-do day ba-ka
beef broth

callos
ka-yos
tripe

cangrejo de río
kan-gre-ho day ree-o
crayfish

carne
kar-nay
meat

carne asada
kar-nay a-sa-da
grilled meat

carne de vaca en asador
kar-nay day ba-ka en a-sa-dor
braised beef

castañas asadas
kas-tan-yas a-sa-das
roast chestnuts

cebollas
the-bo-yas
onions

cebollinos
the-bo-yee-nos
chives

cerdo asado
thair-do a-sa-do
pork roast

cerezas
the-ray-thas
cherries

chalotes
cha-lo-tes
shallots

champiñones
cham-peen-yo-nes
mushrooms

champiñones al ajillo
cham-peen-yo-nes al a-hee-yo
mushrooms with garlic

champiñones en salsa
cham-peen-yo-nes en sal-sa
mushrooms in sauce

chirivía
chee-ree-bee-a
parsnip

chorizo
cho-ree-tho
hard pork sausage

chuleta de cerdo
choo-lay-ta day thair-do
pork chop

chuleta de cordero
choo-lay-ta day kor-dair-o
lamb chop

chuleta de ternera
choo-lay-ta day tair-nair-a
veal cutlet

churros
choo-ros
fritters

ciruelas
thee-roo-ay-las
plums

cochinillo asado
ko-chee-nee-yo a-sa-do
roast suckling pig (Castile)

cocido de alubias
ko-thee-do day a-loo-byas
bean stew

cocido madrileño
ko-thee-do ma-dree-len-yo
meat stew with vegetables

coles de Bruselas
ko-les day broo-say-las
Brussels sprouts

coliflor
ko-lee-flor
cauliflower

compota de manzana
kom-po-ta day man-tha-na
apple compote

conejo con caracoles
ko-ne-ho kon ka-ra-ko-les
rabbit with snails

conejo estofado
ko-ne-ho e-sto-fa-do
stuffed rabbit

cordero en asador
kor-dair-o en a-sa-dor
mutton on the spit

dátiles
da-tee-les
dates

ensalada
en-sa-la-da
salad

ensalada de maíz
en-sa-la-da day my-eeth
corn salad

ensalada de patata
en-sa-la-da day pa-ta-ta
potato salad

ensalada de pepino
en-sa-la-da day pe-pee-nee-yo
cucumber salad

ensalada de tomate
en-sa-la-da day to-ma-tay
tomato salad

ensalada mixta
en-sa-la-da meek-sta
mixed salad

ensaladilla rusa
en-sa-la-dee-ya roo-sa
Russian salad

...**en salsa**
...*en sal-sa*
...in sauce

escarola
e-ska-ro-la
chicory

espaguetis
es-pa-ge-tees
spaghetti

espárragos
es-pa-ra-gos
asparagus

espinacas
es-pee-na-kas
spinach

estragón
es-tra-gon
tarragorn

fabada
fa-ba-da
bean and pork stew
(Asturias)

faisán
fy-ee-san
pheasant

filete
fee-le-tay
fillet steak

filete de merluza
fee-le-tay day mair-loo-tha
hake fillet

filete de vaca
fee-le-tay day ba-ka
beefsteak

flan
flan
crème caramel

frambuesas
fram-bway-sas
raspberries

fresas
fray-sas

strawberries

fresas con nata
fray-sas kon na-ta
strawberries and
cream

**fruta con nata mon
tada**
froo-ta kon na-ta mon-ta-da
fruit with whipped
cream

gazpacho
gath-pa-cho
cold soup with
cucumber, tomato,
garlic etc

granada
gra-na-da
pomegranate

grosellas negras
gro-se-yas ne-gras
blackcurrants

guisado de carne
gee-sa-do day kar-nay
beef stew

guisado de pollo
gee-sa-do day po-yo
chicken stew

guisantes
gee-san-tes
peas

habas
a-bas
broad beans

helado
e-la-do
ice cream

hierbabuena
yair-ba-bway-na
mint

hoja de laurel
o-ha day low-rel
bayleaf

**huevo pasado por
agua**
way-bo pa-sa-do por a-gwa
soft boiled egg

huevos con jamón
way-bos kon ha-mon
eggs with ham

huevos con tocino
way-bos kon to-thee-no
eggs with bacon

huevos fritos
way-bos free-tos
fried eggs

huevos revueltos
way-bos re-bwel-tos
scrambled eggs

jamón serrano
ha-mon se-ra-no
cured ham

judías verdes
hoo-dee-as bair-des
French beans

langosta
lan-go-sta
lobster

**langostinos
rebozados**
lan-go-stee-nos re-bo-tha-dos
scampi

lechón en asador
le-chon en a-sa-dor
suckling pig on the
spit

lechuga
le-choo-ga
lettuce

lengua
len-gwa
tongue

limón
lee-mon
lemon

macedonia de frutas
ma-the-do-nee-a day froo-tas
fruit salad

maíz
my-eeth
sweet corn

mantequilla
man-te-kee-ya
butter

manzana asada
man-tha-na a-sa-da
roast apple

manzanas
man-tha-nas
apples

mejillones
me-hee-yo-nes
mussels

melocotón
me-lo-ko-ton
peach

melón
me-lon
melon

**merluza en salsa
verde**
*mair-loo-tha en sal-sa
bair-day*
hake in parsley sauce

mermelada
mair-me-la-da
jam

morcilla
mor-thee-ya
black pudding/blood
sausage

mousse de chocolate
moos day cho-ko-la-tay
chocolate mousse

nabo
na-bo
turnip

naranjas
na-ran-has
oranges

natillas
nu-tee-yas
custard

oca
o-ka
goose

ostras
o-stras
oysters

ostras fritas
o-stras free-tas
fried oysters (Galicia)

paella
py-e-ya
paella

pasta
pa-sta
pasta

patas de rana fritas
pa-tas day ra-na free-tas
fried frog legs

patatas a la riojana
pa-ta-tas a la ree-o-ha-na
potatoes, tomatoes,
and haricot beans
(Rioja)

patatas asadas
pa-ta-tas a-sa-das
roast potatoes

patatas bravas
pa-ta-tas bra-bas
spicy fried potatoes

patatas fritas
pa-ta-tas free-tas
French fries

patatas troceadas y
verdura con
mayonesa
pa-ta-tas tro-thay-a-das y bair-doo-ra kon my-o nay-sa
potatoes and
vegetables with
mayonnaise

pato
pa-to
duck

pato relleno con
manzanas
pa-to re-yay-no kon man-tha-nas
roast duck with apples

pavo
pa-bo
turkey

pepinillo
pe-pee-nee-yo
gherkin

pepino
pe-pee-no
cucumber

pera
pay-ra
pear

perdiz en chocolate
pair-deeth en cho-ko-la-tay
partridge with a
chocolate sauce
(Navarra)

perejil
pe-re-heel
parsley

perifollo
pe-ree-fo-yo
chervil

perrito caliente
pe-ree-to kal-lee-en-tay
hot dog

pescado
pes-ka-do
fish

pescado en escabeche
pes-ka-do en es-ka-be-chay
marinated fish

pierna (de cordero
etc)
pee-air-na (day kor-dair-o etc)
shank (of lamb etc)

pimiento rojo
pee-myen-to ro-ho
red pepper

pimiento verde
pee-myen-to bair-day
green pepper

pimientos rellenos
pee-myen-tos re-yay-nos
stuffed peppers

piña
peen-ya
pineapple

plátano
pla-ta-no
banana

pollo cocido/asado
po-yo ko-thee-do / a-sa-do
baked/roasted chicken

pollo frito/rebozado
po-yo free-to/re-bo-tha-do
fried/breaded chicken

pomelo
po-me-lo
grapefruit

puerros
pwe-ros
leeks

puré de patatas
poo-ray day pa-ta-tas
mashed potatoes

queso
ke-so
cheese

queso manchego
ke-so man-chay-go
la Mancha cheese

rábanos
ra-ba-nos
radishes

remolacha
re-mo-la-cha
beetroot

riñones guisados
reen-yo-nes gee-sa-dos
stewed kidney

romero
ro-mair-o
rosemary

salchicha
sal-chee-cha
sausage

salmonete
sal-mo-ne-tay
mullet

salsa de cebolla
sal-sa day the-bo-ya
onion sauce

salsa de manzana
sal-sa day man-tha-na
apple sauce

salsa de pimiento
verde
sal-sa day pee-myen-to
green pepper sauce

salsa de tomate
sal-sa day to-ma-tay
tomato sauce

salsa de vino
sal-sa day bee-no
wine sauce

salvia
sal-bee-a
sage

sandía
san-dee-a
watermelon

sandwich de jamón
san-weech day ha-mon
ham sandwich

sardinas
sar-dee-nas
sardines

sepia
se-pee-a
cuttlefish

sopa de ajo
so-pa day a-ho
garlic soup

sopa de crema de
champiñones
so-pa day kray-ma day cham-peen-yo-nes
cream of mushroom
soup

sopa de fideos
so-pa day fee-day-os
noodle soup

sopa de frijoles
so-pa day free-ho-les
kidney-bean soup

sopa de guisantes
so-pa day gee-san-tes
pea soup

sopa de pollo
so-pa day po-yo
chicken soup

sopa de puerros
so-pa day pwe-ros
leek soup

sopa de tomate
so-pa day to-ma-tay
tomato soup

tallarines de huevo
ta-ya-ree-nes day way-bo
egg noodles

tarta
tar-ta
cake/pie

tarta de almendra
tar-ta day al-men-dra
almond cake

tarta de limón
tar-ta day lee-mon
lemon meringue pie

tarta de manzana
tar-ta day man-tha-na
apple cake

tomates
to-ma-tes
tomatoes

tomillo
to-mee-yo
thyme

tortas
tor-tas
thin pancakes

— con chocolate
— kon cho-ko-la-tay
— with chocolate

— con mermelada
— kon mair-me-la-da
— with jam

tortilla española
tor-tee-ya es-pan-yo-la
Spanish omelet

trucha
troo-cha
trout

trucha cocida
troo-cha ko-thee-da
boiled trout

trucha frita
troo-cha free-ta
fried trout

uvas
oo-bas
grapes

verduras
bair-doo-ras
vegetables

vinagre
bee-na-gray
vinegar

yogur
yo-goor
yogurt

zanahoria
tha-na-o-ree-a
carrot

Wine label reader

abrocado
a-bro-ka-do
medium sweet

almacenista
al-ma-the-nee-sta
unblended sherry with
distinctive flavors

amontillado
a-mon-tee-ya-do
aged

amontillado fino
a-mon-tee-ya-do fee-no
aged and still very dry
but darker, deeper

blanco
blan-ko
white

bodega
bo-day-ga
wine cellar (wherever
wine is made, stored,
or sold)

brut
broot
dry

cava
ka-ba
wine made by the
Champagne method

clarete
kla-re-tay
light red

**criado y embotellado
por**
*kree-a-do ee em-bo-te-
ya-do por...*
grown and bottled
by...

(de) crianza
(day) kree-an-tha
aged in wood

dulce
dool-thay
sweet

**embotellado de
origen**
*em-bo-te-ya-do day o-
ree-hen*
estate-bottled

espumoso
es-poo-mo-so
sparkling wine

fino
fee-no
pale, very dry sherry
made from the
lightest wines, to be
drunk cool and young

generoso
he-ne-ro-so
aperitif or dessert
wine

gran reserva
gran re-sair-ba
top quality Rioja wine

manzanilla
man-tha-nee-ya
form of fino

nuevo
nway-bo
young wine

oloroso
o-lo-ro-so
dark sherry made
from richer wines and
more heavily fortified
but still dry

reserva
re-sair-ba
selected Rioja wine
from a good vintage

rosado
ro-sa-do
rosé

seco
say-ko
dry

semi-seco
se-mee-say-ko
medium dry

sin crianza
seen kree-an-tha
not aged in wood

tinto
teen-to
red

Other drinks

agua mineral
a-gwa mee-ne-ral
mineral water

aguardiente
a-gwar-dee-en-tay
brandy

**aguardiente de
cerezas**
*a-gwar-dee-en-tay day
the-ray-thas*
cherry brandy

**aguardiente de
manzanas**
*a-gwar-dee-en-tay day
man-tha-nas*
apple brandy

anís
a-nees
anis

café
ka-fay
coffee

café americano
ka-fay a-me-ree-ka-no
large black coffee

café con hielo
ka-fay kon ye-lo
iced coffee

café con leche
ka-fay kon le-chay
white coffee

café escocés
ka-fay es-ko-thes
coffee with whisky
and ice cream

café instantáneo
ka-fay een-stan-ta-nay-o
instant coffee

café irlandés
ka-fay eer-lan-des
Irish coffee

café sólo
ka-fay so-lo
small black coffee

una caña
oo-na kan-ya
a small glass of
draught beer

carajillo
ka-ra-hee-yo
coffee with a dash of
brandy

capuchino
ka-poo-chee-no
cappuccino

cerveza
thair-bay-tha
beer

cerveza embotellada
*thair-bay-tha em-bo-te-
ya-da*
bottled beer

cerveza enlatada
*thair-bay-tha en-la-ta-
da*
canned beer

una cerveza grande
*oo-na thair-bay-tha
gran-day*
a large beer

cerveza negra
thair-bay-tha ne-gra
stout (beer)

champán
cham-pan
champagne

coca-cola
ko-ka-ko-la
Coke™

un coñac
oon kon-yak
a brandy

cortado
kor-ta-do
coffee with a dash of
milk

descafeinado
des-ka-fay-na-do
decaffeinated coffee

horchata
or-cha-ta
tiger nut milk

licor
lee-kor
liqueur

limonada
lee-mo-na-da
lemonade

manzanilla
man-tha-nee-ya
chamomile tea

naranjada
na-ran-ha-da
orange drink

pacharán	té	un vaso de vino	**zumo de manzana**
pa-cha-ran	*tay*	tinto	*thoo-mo day man-tha-na*
a type of sloe gin	tea	*oon ba-so day bee-no*	apple juice
ron	**té con leche**	*teen-to*	**zumo de melocotón**
ron	*tay kon le-chay*	a glass of red wine	*thoo-mo day me-lo-ko-ton*
rum	tea with milk	**vermut**	peach juice
sangría	**té con limón**	*bair-moot*	**zumo de naranja**
san-gree-a	*tay kon lee-mon*	vermouth	*thoo-mo day na-ran-ha*
fruit cup with wine	lemon tea	**vino rosado**	orange juice
sidra	**tónica**	*bee-no ro-sa-do*	**zumo de uva**
see-dra	*to-nee-ka*	rosé wine	*thoo-mo day oo-ba*
cider	tonic water	**zumo de albaricoque**	grape juice
soda	**un vaso de vino blanco**	*thoo-mo day al-ba-ree-*	
so-da	*oon ba-so day bee-no blan-ko*	*ko-kay*	
soda water	a glass of white wine	apricot juice	

Out and About

The weather

Is it going to get any warmer?
¿Va a hacer más calor?
ba a a-thair mas ka-lor
Is it going to stay like this?
¿Va a continuar así?
ba a kon-tee-nwar a-see
Is there going to be a thunderstorm?
¿Va a haber tormenta?
ba a a-bair tor-men-ta
Isn't it a lovely day?
¿No es éste un día maravilloso?
no es es-tay oon dee-a ma-ra-bee-yo-so
It has stopped snowing
Ha parado de nevar
a pa-ra-do day ne-bar
It is a very clear night
Hace una noche muy despejada
a-thay oo-na no-chay mwee des-pe-ha-da

It is far too hot
Hace demasiado calor
a-thay de-ma-sya-do ka-lor
It is foggy
Hay niebla
eye nee-e-bla
It is raining again
Está lloviendo de nuevo
es-ta yo-byen-do day nway-bo
It is very cold
Hace mucho frío
a-thay moo-cho free-o
It is very windy
Hace mucho viento
a-thay moo-cho bee-en-to
There is a cool breeze
Hay una brisa fresca
eye oo-na bree-sa fre-ska
What is the temperature?
¿Qué temperatura hace?
kay tem-pe-ra-too-ra a-thay

It is going — to be fine
Va — a hacer bueno
ba — a a-thair bway-no
— to be windy
— a hacer viento
— a a-thair bee-en-to
— to rain
— a llover
— a yo-bair
— to snow
— a nevar
— a ne-bar
Will it be cold tonight?
¿Hará frío esta noche?
a-ra free-o es-ta no-chay
Will the weather improve?
¿Va a mejorar el tiempo?
ba a me-ho-rar el tee-em-po
Will the wind die down?
¿Va a amainar el viento?
ba a a-my-nar el bee-en-to

On the beach

Can we change here?
¿Podemos cambiarnos aquí?
po-day-mos kam-byar-nos a-kee
Can you recommend a quiet beach?
¿Puede sugerir una playa tranquila?
pwe-day soo-he-reer oo-na ply-a tran-kee-la

Is it safe to swim here?
¿Es seguro nadar aquí?
es se-goo-ro na-dar a-kee
Is the current strong?
¿Hay mucha corriente?
eye moo-cha ko-ree-en-tay
Is the sea calm?
¿Está la mar tranquila?
es-ta la mar tran-kee-la

Can I rent — a sailing boat?
¿Puedo alquilar — un barco de vela?
pwe-do al-kee-lar— oon bar-ko day bay-la
— a rowing boat?
— un bote de remos?
— oon bo-tay day re-mo

Is it possible to go — sailing?
¿Es posible — salir a navegar?
es po-see-blay — sa-leer a na-be-gar
— surfing?
— hacer surf?
— a-thair soorf
— water skiing?
— hacer esquí acuático?
— a-thair e-skee a-kwa-tee-ko
— wind surfing?
— hacer windsurf?
— a-thair ween-soorf

Is the water warm?
¿Está el agua templada?
es-ta el a-gwa tem-pla-da
Is there a heated swimming pool?
¿Hay alguna piscina climatizada?
eye al-goo-na pees-thee-na klee-ma-tee-tha-da
Is there a lifeguard here?
¿Hay algún salvavidas aquí?
eye al-goon sal-ba-bee-das a-kee

Is this beach private?
¿Es privada esta playa?
es pree-ba-da es-ta ply-a
When is high tide?
¿Cuándo toca marea alta?
kwan-do to-ka ma-ray-a al-ta
When is low tide?
¿Cuándo toca marea baja?
kwan-do to-ka ma-ray-a ba-ha

Sport and recreation

Can I rent the equipment?
¿Puedo alquilar el material?
pwe-do al-kee-lar el ma-te-ree-al
Can we go horse riding?
¿Podemos ir a montar a caballo?
po-day-mos eer a mon-tar a ka-ba-yo

Can we — play tennis?
¿Podemos — jugar al tenis?
po-day-mos — hoo-gar al te-nees
— play golf?
— jugar al golf?
— hoo-gar al golf

— play volleyball?
— jugar al voleibol?
— hoo-gar al bo-lee-bol
Where can we fish?
¿Dónde podemos pescar?
don-day po-day-mos pe-skar

Entertainment

How much is it for a child?
¿Cuánto cuesta para un niño?
kwan-to kwe-sta pa-ra oon neen-yo
How much is it per person?
¿Cuánto cuesta por persona?
kwan-to kwe-sta por pair-so-na
How much is it to get in?
¿Cuánto cuesta la entrada?
kwan-to kwe-sta la en-tra-da

Is there — a disco?
¿Hay— alguna discoteca?
eye — al-goo-na dee-sko-tay-ka
— a good nightclub?
— algún buen club?
— al-goon bwen kloob
— a theater?
— teatro?
— tay-a-tro

Are there any films in English?
¿Hay alguna película en inglés?
eye al-goo-na pe-lee-koo-la en een-gles
Two tickets, please
Dos entradas, por favor
dos en-tra-das, por fa-bor
Is there a reduction for children?
¿Hay descuento para niños?
eye des-kwen-to pa-ra neen-yos

Sightseeing

Are there any boat trips on the river?
¿Hay excursiones en barco por el río?
eye ek-skoor-syo-nes en bar-ko por el ree-o
Are there any guided tours?
¿Hay visitas con guía?
eye bee-see-tas kon gee-a
What is there to see here?
¿Qué hay para ver aquí?
kay eye pa-ra bair a-kee
What is this building?
¿Qué es este edificio?
kay es es-tay e-dee-fee-thee-o
Is it open to the public?
¿Está abierto al público?
es-ta a-bee-air-to al poo-blee-ko

What is the admission charge?
¿Cuánto cuesta la entrada?
kwan-to kwes-ta la en-tra-da
Can we go in?
¿Podemos entrar?
po-day-mos en-trar
Can I take photos?
¿Puedo hacer fotos?
pwe-do a-thair fo-tos
Can I use flash?
¿Puedo utilizar flash?
pwe-do oo-tee-lee-thar flas
How long does the tour take?
¿Cuánto dura la excursión?
kwan-to doo-ra la ek-skoor-syon
Is there a guide book?
¿Hay alguna guía turística?
eye al-goo-na gee-a too-ree-stee-ka

Is there a tour of the cathedral?
¿Hay visita a la catedral?
eye bee-see-ta a la ka-te-dral
Is there an English-speaking guide?
¿Hay algún guía que hable inglés?
eye al-goon gee-a kay a-blay een-gles
Is this the best view?
¿Es ésta la mejor vista?
es es-ta la me-hor bee-sta
What time does the gallery open?
¿A qué hora abre la galería?
a kay o-ra a-bray la ga-le-ree-a
When is the bus tour?
¿Cuándo es la visita en autobús?
kwan-do es la bee-see-ta en ow-to-boos

Souvenirs

Have you got an English guidebook?
¿Tiene alguna guía turística en inglés?
tee-e-nay al-goo-na gee-a too-ree-stee-ka en een-gles

Where can I buy postcards?
¿Dónde puedo comprar postales?
don-day pwe-do kom-prar po-sta-les

Where can we buy souvenirs?
¿Dónde podemos comprar recuerdos?
don-day po-day-mos kom-prar re-kwair-dos

Going to church

Where is the — Catholic church?
¿Dónde está la — iglesia Católica?
don-day es-ta la — ee-glay-see-a ka-to-lee-ka
— Baptist church?
— la iglesia Bautista?
— la ee-glay-see-a bow-tee-sta
— mosque?
— la mezquita?
— la meth-kee-ta

— Protestant church?
— iglesia Protestante?
— ee-glay-see-a pro-te-stan-tay
— synagogue?
— la sinagoga?
— la see-na-go-ga
What time is mass?
¿A qué hora es la misa?
a kay o-ra es la mee-sa

I would like to see — a priest
Me gustaría hablar con — un sacerdote
may goo-sta-ree-a a-blar kon — oon sa-thair-do-tay
— a minister
— un pastor
— oon pa-stor
— a rabbi
— un rabino
— oon ra-bee-no

Shopping

General phrases and requests

How much does that cost?
¿Cuánto cuesta eso?
kwan-to kwes-ta e-so
How much is it — per kilo?
¿Cuánto cuesta — por kilo?
kwan-to kwes-ta — por kee-lo
— per meter?
— por metro?
— por me-tro
How much is this?
¿Cuánto es esto?
kwan-to es es-to
Have you got anything cheaper?
¿Tiene algo más barato?
tee-e-nay al-go mas ba-ra-to
Can I see that umbrella?
¿Puedo ver ese paraguas?
pwe-do bair e-say pa-ra-gwas
No, the other one
No, el otro
no, el o-tro
Can you deliver to my hotel?
¿Puede entregármelo al hotel?
pwe-day en-tre-gar-may-lo al o-tel

I do not like it
No me gusta
no may goo-sta
I like this one
Me gusta éste
may goo-sta es-tay
I will take — this one
Tomaré — éste
to-ma-ray — es-tay
— that one
— ése
— e-say
— the other one
— el otro
— el o-tro
— that one over there
— aquél de allí
— a-kel day a-ye
Where can I buy some clothes?
¿Dónde puedo comprar ropa?
don-day pwe-do kom-prar ro-pa
Where can I buy tapes for my camcorder?

¿Dónde puedo comprar cintas para el camcórder?
don-day pwe-do kom-prar theen-tas pa-ra el kam-kor-dair
Where can I get my camcorder repaired?
¿A dónde puedo llevar a reparar el camcórder?
a don-day pwe-do ye-bar a re-pa-rar el kam-kor-dair
Where is — the children's department?
¿Dónde está — el departamento infantil?
don-day es-ta — el de-par-ta-men-to een-fan-teel
— the food department?
— el departamento de comestibles?
— el de-par-ta-men-to day ko-me-stee-blays
I am looking for a souvenir
Estoy buscando un recuerdo
es-toy boo-skan-do oon re-kwair-do

Do you sell sunglasses?
¿Venden gafas de sol?
ben-den ga-fas day sol
Can I have — a carrier bag?
¿Puede darme — una bolsa?
pwe-day dar-may — oo-na bol-sa
— a receipt?
— un recibo?
— oon re-thee-bo
— an itemised bill?
— una cuenta detallada?
— oo-na kwen-ta de-ta-ya-da
Can I pay for air insurance?
¿Puedo pagar un seguro aéreo?
pwe-do pa-gar oon se-goo-ro a-air-ay-o
What is the total?
¿Cuánto es el total?
kwan-to es el to-tal

Do you accept traveler's checks?
¿Acepta cheques de viaje?
a-thep-ta che-kays day bee-a-hay
I do not have enough currency
No tengo suficiente cambio
no ten-go soo-fee-thyen-tay kam-bee-o
I do not have enough money
No tengo suficiente dinero
no ten-go soo-fee-thyen-tay dee-ne-ro
I would like to pay with my credit card
Me gustaría pagar con tarjeta de crédito
may goo-sta-ree-a pa-gar kon tar-hay-ta day kre-dee-to

Please forward a receipt to this address
Por favor, envíe un recibo a esta dirección
por fa-bor, en-bee-ay oon re-thee-bo a es-ta dee-rek-thyon
Please wrap it up for me
Por favor, envuélvamelo
por fa-bor, en-bwel-ba-may-lo
There is no need to wrap it
No hace falta envolverlo
no a-thay fal-ta en-bol-bair-lo
Please pack this for shipment
Por favor, envuelva esto para envío
por fa-bor, en-bwel-ba es-to pa-ra en-bee-o
Will you send it by air freight?
¿Lo enviará por avión?
lo en-bee-a-ra por a-byon

Buying groceries

We need to buy some food
Tenemos que comprar comida
te-nay-mos kay kom-prar ko-mee-da
I would like — a kilo of potatoes
Me da — un kilo de patatas
may da — oon kee-lo day pa-ta-tas
— a bar of chocolate
— una barra de chocolate
— oo-na ba-ra day cho-ko-la-tay
— 100 grams of ground coffee
— cien gramos de café molido
— thee-en gra-mos day ka-fay mo- lee-do
— two steaks
— dos filetes
— dos fee-le-tes

— five slices of ham
— cinco lonchas de jamón
— theen-ko lon-chas day ha-mon
— half a dozen eggs
— media docena de huevos
— me-dee-a do-thay-na day way-bos
— half a kilo of butter
— medio kilo de mantequilla
— me-dee-o kee-lo day man-te-kee-ya
Can I have — some sugar, please?
¿Puede darme — azúcar, por favor?
pwe-day dar-may — a-thoo-kar, por fa-bor

— a bottle of wine, please?
— una botella de vino, por favor?
— oo-na bo-te-ya day bee-no, por fa-bor
— a kilo of sausages, please?
— un kilo de salchichas, por favor?
— oon kee-lo day sal-chee-chas, por fa-bor
— a leg of lamb, please?
— una pierna de cordero, por favor?
— oo-na pee-air-na day kor-dair-o, por fa-bor
— a liter of milk, please?
— un litro de leche, por favor?
— oon lee-tro day le-chay, por fa-bor

Groceries

baby food	**coffee**	**margarine**	**rice**
comida para bebés	café	margarina	arroz
ko-mee-da pa-ra be-bes	*ka-fay*	*mar-ga-ree-na*	*a-roth*
biscuits	**cream**	**milk**	**salt**
galletas	nata	leche	sal
ga-yay-tas	*na-ta*	*le-chay*	*sal*
bread	**eggs**	**mustard**	**soup**
pan	huevos	mostaza	sopa
pan	*way-bos*	*mo-sta-tha*	*so-pa*
butter	**flour**	**oil**	**sugar**
mantequilla	harina	aceite	azúcar
man-te-kee-ya	*a-ree-na*	*a-thay-tay*	*a-thoo-kar*
cheese	**jam**	**pepper**	**tea**
queso	mermelada	pimienta	té
ke-so	*mair-me-la-da*	*pee-myen-ta*	*tay*

vinegar	yogurt
vinagre	yogur
*bee-**na**-gray*	*yo-**goor***

Meat and fish

beef	ham	liver	pork
carne de vaca	jamón	hígado	cerdo
kar-nay day ba-ka	*ha-**mon***	*ee-ga-do*	*thair-do*
chicken	herring	meat	sole
pollo	arenque	carne	lenguado
po-yo	*a-ren-kay*	*kar-nay*	*len-**gwa**-do*
cod	kidneys	mussels	veal
bacalao	riñones	mejillones	ternera
*ba-ka-**la**-o*	*reen-yo-nes*	*me-hee-yo-nes*	*tair-**nair**-a*
fish	lamb		
pescado	cordero		
*pe-**ska**-do*	*kor-**dair**-o*		

At the newsagent's

Do you sell — English paperbacks?
¿Vende — libros de bolsillo en inglés?
ben-day — lee-bros day bol-see-yo en een-gles
— postcards?
— postales?
*— po-**sta**-les*
— a local map?
— un plano de la localidad?
*— oon **pla**-no day la lo-ka-lee-dad*
— a road map?
— un mapa de carreteras?
*— oon **ma**-pa day ka-re-**tair**-as*
— colored pencils?
— lápices de color?
*— **la**-pee-thes day ko-lor*

— drawing paper?
— papel de dibujo?
*— pa-**pel** day dee-boo-ho*
— felt-tip pens?
— rotuladores?
*— ro-too-la-**do**-res*
— street maps?
— planos de ciudad?
*— **pla**-nos day thee-oo-**dad***
I would like some postage stamps
Me da sellos de correos
*may da se-yos day ko-**ray**-os*
Do you have — books in English?
¿Tiene — libros en inglés?
tee-e-nay — lee-bros en een-gles

— newspapers in English?
— periódicos en inglés?
— pe-ree-o-dee-kos en een-gles
I need — some writing paper
Necesito — papel de cartas
*ne-the-see-to — pa-**pel** day **kar**-tas*
— a pen
— un bolígrafo
— oon bo-lee-gra-fo
— a pencil
— un lápiz
*— oon **la**-peeth*
— some Sellotape™
— cinta adhesiva
*— **theen**-ta a-de-see-ba*
— some envelopes
— sobres
*— **so**-bres*

At the tobacconist's

Do you have — cigarette papers?
¿Tiene — papel de fumar?
*tee-e-nay — pa-**pel** day foo-**mar***
— a box of matches
— una caja de cerillas
*— **oo**-na **ka**-ha day the-**ree**-yas*
— a cigar
— un cigarro
*— oon thee-**ga**-ro*
— a cigarette lighter
— un mechero
*— oon me-**chair**-o*
— a gas (butane) refill
— una carga de gas
*— **oo**-na **kar**-ga day gas*

— a pipe
— una pipa
*— **oo**-na **pee**-pa*
— a pouch of pipe tobacco
— una petaca de tabaco de pipa
*— **oo**-na pe-**ta**-ka day ta-**ba**-ko day pee-pa*
— some pipe cleaners
— unos limpiapipas
*— **oo**-nos leem-pya-**pee**-pas*
Have you got — any American brands?
¿Tiene — marcas americanas?
*tee-e-nay — **mar**-kas a-me-ree-ka-nas*

— any English brands?
— marcas inglesas?
*— **mar**-kas een-**glay**-sas*
— rolling tobacco?
— tabaco de liar?
*— ta-**ba**-ko day lee-**ar***
A packet of..., please
Un paquete de..., por favor
*oon pa-ke-tay day ... por fa-**bor***
— with filter tips
— con filtro
*— kon **feel**-tro*
— without filters
— sin filtro
*— seen **feel**-tro*

At the chemist's

Do you have toothpaste?
¿Tiene pasta de dientes?
tee-e-nay pa-sta day dee-en-tes
I need some high-protection suntan cream
Necesito una crema solar de alta protección
ne-the-see-to oo-na kray-ma so-lar day al-ta pro-tek-thyon
Can you give me something for — a headache?
¿Puede darme algo para — el dolor de cabeza?
pwe-day dar-may — el do-lor day al-go pa-ra ka-bay-tha
— insect bites
— las picaduras de insectos?
— las pee-ka-doo-ras day een-sek-tos
— a cold
— un catarro
— oon ka-ta-ro

— a cough
— tos
— tos
— a sore throat
— dolor de garganta
— do-lor day gar-gan-ta
— an upset stomach
— mal del estómago
— mal del e-sto-ma-go
— toothache
— dolor de muelas
— do-lor day mway-las
— hay fever
— fiebre del heno
— fee-e-bray del ay-no
— sunburn
— quemadura de sol
— ke-ma-doo-ra day sol

Do I need a prescription?
¿Necesito una receta?
ne-the-see-to oo-na re-thay-ta
How many do I take?
¿Cuántas tengo que tomar?
kwan-tas ten-go kay to-mar
How often do I take them?
¿Con qué frecuencia tengo que tomarlas?
kon kay fre-kwen-thee-a ten-go kay to-mar-las
Are they safe for children to take?
¿Los niños pueden tomarlas sin riesgo?
los neen-yos pwe-den to-mar-las seen ree-ez- go

Medicines and toiletries

antihistamine
antihistamínico
an-tee-ee-sta-mee-nee-ko
antiseptic
antiséptico
an-tee-sep-tee-ko
aspirin
aspirina
a-spee-ree-na
bandage
vendaje
ben-da-hay
bubble bath
espuma de baño
e-spoo-ma day ban-yo
cleansing milk
leche limpiadora
le-chay leem-pya-do-ra
conditioner
suavizante
swa-bee-than-tay
condom
preservativo
pray-sair-ba-tee-bo
contraceptive
anticonceptivo
an-tee-kon-thep-tee-bo
cotton wool
algodón hidrófilo
al-go-don ee-dro-fee-lo

deodorant
desodorante
des-o-do-ran-tay
disinfectant
desinfectante
des-een-fek-tan-tay
eau de Cologne
agua de colonia
a-gwa day ko-lon-ya
eye shadow
sombra de ojos
som-bra day o-hos
face powder
polvos
pol-bos
hair spray
laca para el cabello
la-ka pa-ra el ka-be-yo
hand cream
crema de manos
kray-ma day ma-nos
insect repellent
repelente de insectos
ray-pe-len-tay day een-sek-tos
laxative
laxante
lak-san-tay
lipstick
barra de labios
ba-ra day la-bee-os

mascara
rímel
ree-mel
moisturizer
loción hidratante
lo-thyon ee-dra-tan-tay
mouthwash
antiséptico bucal
an-tee-sep-tee-ko boo-kal
nail file
lima de uñas
lee-ma day oon-yas
nail varnish
esmalte de uñas
es-mal-tay day oon-yas
nail varnish remover
quitaesmalte
kee-ta-es-mal-tay
perfume
perfume
pair-foo-may
plasters
tiritas
tee-ree-tas
razor blades
hojas de afeitar
o-has day a-fay-tar
sanitary napkins
compresas
kom-pray-sas

shampoo
champú
cham-poo
shaving cream
espuma de afeitar
es-poo-ma day a-fay-tar
soap
jabón
ha-bon
suntan lotion
bronceador
bron-thay-a-dor
talc
talco
tal-ko
tampons
tampones
tam-po-nays
tissues
Kleenex™
klee-neks
toilet water
colonia
ko-lon-ya
toothpaste
pasta de dientes
pa-sta day dee-en-tes

Shopping for clothes

I am just looking, thank you
Sólo estoy mirando, gracias
so-lo es-toy mee-ran-do, gra-thee-as

I do not like it
No me gusta
no may goo-sta

I like it
Me gusta
may goo-sta

I will take it
Lo llevaré
lo ye-ba-ray

I like — this one
Me gusta — éste
may goo-sta — es-tay

— that one there
— aquél
— a-kel

— the one in the window
— el que está en el escaparate
— el kay es-ta en el e-ska-pa-ra-tay

I would like — this suit
Quiero comprar — este traje
kee-e-ro kom-prar — es-tay tra-hay

— this hat
— este sombrero
— es-tay som-brair-o

I would like one — with a zip
Quisiera uno — con cremallera
ke-see-air-a oo-no — kon kre-ma-yair-a

— without a belt
— sin cinturón
— seen then-too-ron

Can you please measure me?
¿Puede medirme, por favor?
pwe-day me-deer-may, por fa-bor

Can I change it if it does not fit?
¿Puedo cambiarlo si no me vale?
pwe-do kam-byar-lo see no may ba-lay

Have you got this in other colors?
¿Tiene éste en otros colores?
tee-e-nay es-tay en o-tros ko-lo-res

I take a large shoe size
Uso una talla de zapato grande
oo-so oo-na ta-ya day tha-pa-to gran-day

Is it too long?
¿Es demasiado largo?
es de-ma-sya-do lar-go

Is it too short?
¿Es demasiado corto?
es de-ma-sya-do kor-to

Is there a full-length mirror?
¿Hay algún espejo de cuerpo entero?
eye al-goon es-pe-ho day kwair-po en-tair-o

Is this all you have?
¿Es esto todo lo que tiene?
es es-to to-do lo kay tee-e-nay

It does not fit
No me vale
no may ba-lay

It does not suit me
No me queda bien
no may kay-da byen

May I see it in daylight?
¿Puedo verlo a la luz del día?
pwe-do bair-lo a la looth del dee-a

Where are the dressing rooms?
¿Dónde están los probadores?
don-day es-tan los pro-ba-do-res

Where can I try it on?
¿Dónde puedo probármelo?
don-day pwe-do pro-bar-may-lo

Have you got — a large size?
¿Tiene — una talla grande?
tee-e-nay — oo-na ta-ya gran-day

— a small size?
— una talla pequeña?
— oo-na ta-ya pe-ken-ya

What is it made of?
¿De qué material es?
day kay ma-te-ree-al es

Is it guaranteed?
¿Tiene garantía?
tee-e-nay ga-ran-tee-a

Will it shrink?
¿Encogerá?
en-ko-hair-a

Is it dry-clean only?
¿Es de limpiar en seco sólamente?
es day leem-pyar en se-ko so-la-men-tay

Is it machine washable?
¿Es lavable a máquina?
es la-ba-blay a ma-kee-na

Clothes and accessories

acrylic	**bracelet**	**corduroy**	**earrings**
acrílico	pulsera	pana	pendientes
a-kree-lee-ko	*pool-say-ra*	*pa-na*	*pen-dee-en-tes*
belt	**brooch**	**cotton**	**espadrilles**
cinturón	broche	algodón	alpargatas
theen-too-ron	*bro-chay*	*al-go-don*	*al-par-ga-tas*
billfold	**button**	**denim**	**fur**
cartera	botón	tela vaquera	piel
kar-tair-a	*bo-ton*	*tay-la ba-kair-a*	*pyel*
blouse	**cardigan**	**dress**	**gloves**
blusa	chaqueta de punto	vestido	guantes
bloo-sa	*cha-kay-ta day poon-to*	*be-stee-do*	*gwan-tes*
bra	**coat**	**dungarees**	**handkerchief**
sujetador	abrigo	pantalón de peto	pañuelo
soo-he-ta-dor	*a-bree-go*	*pan-ta-lon day pay-to*	*pan-yoo-ay-lo*

hat	**petticoat**	**skirt**	**tie**
sombrero	combinación	falda	corbata
som-brair-o	*kom-bee-na-thyon*	*fal-da*	*kor-ba-ta*
jacket	**polyester**	**slip**	**tights**
chaqueta	poliéster	enagua	medias
cha-kay-ta	*po-lee-e-stair*	*e-na-gwa*	*me-dee-as*
jeans	**pullover**	**socks**	**towel**
vaqueros	pulóver	calcetines	toalla
ba-kair-os	*poo-lo-bair*	*kal-the-tee-nes*	*to-a-ya*
jersey	**purse**	**stockings**	**trousers**
jersey	bolso; monedero	medias	pantalón
hair-say	*bol-so; mo-ne-dair-o*	*me-dee-as*	*pan-ta-lon*
lace	**raincoat**	**suede**	**umbrella**
encaje	impermeable	ante	paraguas
en-ka-hay	*eem-pair-may-a-blay*	*an-tay*	*pa-ra-gwas*
leather	**ring**	**suit (men's)**	**underpants, shorts**
cuero	anillo	traje	**(men's)**
kwair-o	*a-nee-yo*	*tra-hay*	calzoncillos
linen	**sandals**	**suit (women's)**	*kal-thon-thee-yos*
lino	sandalias	traje de chaqueta	**velvet**
lee-no	*san-da-lee-as*	*tra-hay day cha-kay-ta*	terciopelo
necklace	**scarf**	**sweater**	*tair-thee-o-pe-lo*
collar	bufanda	suéter	**undershirt**
ko-yar	*boo-fan-da*	*swe-tair*	camiseta
nightdress	**shirt**	**swimming trunks**	*ka-mee-say-ta*
camisón	camisa	bañador	**watch**
ka-mee-son	*ka-mee-sa*	*ban-ya-dor*	reloj
nylon	**shoes**	**swimsuit**	*re-loh*
nylon	zapatos	traje de baño	**wool**
nee-lon	*tha-pa-tos*	*tra-hay day ban-yo*	lana
pajamas	**shorts**	**T-shirt**	*la-na*
pijama	pantalón corto	camiseta	**zip**
pee-ha-ma	*pan-ta-lon kor-to*	*ka-mee-say-ta*	cremallera
panties	**silk**		*kre-ma-yair-a*
bragas	seda		
bra-gas	*say-da*		

Photography

I need a film — for this camera	**Can you develop this film, please?**	**When will the photos be ready?**	**— a color slide film**
Quiero una película	¿Puede revelar esta	¿Cuándo estarán las	— una película de
— para esta cámara	película, por favor?	fotos?	diapositivas en color
kee-e-ro oo-na pe-lee-koo-la — pa-ra es-ta ka-ma-ra	*pwe-day re-be-lar es-ta pe-lee-koo-la, por fa-bor*	*kwan-do es-ta-ran las fo-tos*	*— oo-na pe-lee-koo-la day dee-a-po-zee- tee-bas en ko-lor*
— for this camcorder	**I would like this photo enlarged**	**I want — a black and white film**	**— batteries for the flash**
— para este camcórder	Quiero que amplíen esta foto	Quiero — una película en blanco y	— pilas para el flash
— pa-ra es-tay kam-kor-dair	*kee-e-ro kay am-plee-en es-ta fo-to*	negro	*— pee-las pa-ra el flas*
— for this video camera	**I would like two prints of this one**	*kee-e-ro — oo-na pe-lee-koo-la en blan-ko ee ne-gro*	
— para este videocámara	Quiero dos copias de ésta	**— a color print film**	
— pa-ra es-tay bee-day-o-ka-ma-ra	*kee-e-ro dos ko-pyas day es-ta*	— una película en color	
		— oo-na pe-lee-koo-la en ko-lor	

Camera parts

accessory	**flash**	**out of focus**	**shutter speed**
accesorio	flash	desenfocado	velocidad de
ak-the-so-ree-o	*flas*	*des-en-fo-ka-do*	obturación
blue filter	**flash bulb**	**over-exposed**	*be-lo-thee-**dad** day ob-*
filtro azul	bombilla de flash	sobreexpuesto	*too-ra-**thyon***
feel-tro a-thool	*bom-**bee**-ya day flas*	*so-bray-eks-**pwes**-to*	**slide**
camcorder	**focal distance**	**picture**	diapositiva
camcórder	distancia focal	fotografía	*dee-a-po-zee-tee-ba*
kam-kor-dair	*dee-**stan**-thee-a fo-**kal***	*fo-to-gra-**fee**-a*	**transparency**
cartridge	**focus**	**print**	transparencia
carrete	foco	copia	*trans-pa-ren-thee-a*
ka-re-tay	*fo-ko*	*ko-pya*	**tripod**
cassette	**image**	**red filter**	trípode
cassette	imagen	filtro rojo	*tree-po-day*
ka-se-tay	*ee-**ma**-hen*	*feel-tro ro-ho*	**viewfinder**
distance	**in focus**	**reel**	visor
distancia	enfocado	rollo	*bee-sor*
*dee-**stan**-thee-a*	*en-fo-**ka**-do*	*ro-yo*	**wide-angle lens**
enlargement	**lens cover**	**shade**	granangular
ampliación	tapa de objetivo	sombra	*gra-nan-goo-lar*
*am-plee-a-**thyon***	*ta-pa day ob-he-tee-bo*	*som-bra*	**yellow filter**
exposure	**lens**	**shutter**	filtro amarillo
exposición	objetivo	obturador	*feel-tro a-ma-ree-yo*
*ek-spo-zee-**thyon***	*ob-he-**tee**-bo*	*ob-too-ra-**dor***	
exposure meter	**negative**		
fotómetro	negativo		
*fo-**to**-me-tro*	*ne-ga-**tee**-bo*		

At the hairdresser's

I would like to make an appointment
Quisiera reservar hora
*kee-see-**air**-a re-sair-**bar** o-ra*
I want — a haircut
Quiero — cortarme el pelo
*kee-e-ro — kor-**tar**-may el pe-lo*
— a trim
— cortarme las puntas
*— kor-**tar**-may las **poon**-tas*
Not too much off
No quite demasiado
*no **kee**-tay de-ma-**sya**-do*
Take a little more off the back
Quite un poco más por detrás
kee-tay oon po-ko mas por de-tras
Please cut my hair — short
Por favor, córteme el pelo —
corto
*por fa-**bor**, kor-tay-may el pe-lo*
— kor-to

— fairly short
— bastante corto
*— ba-**stan**-tay kor-to*
— with a fringe
— con flequillo
*— kon fle-**kee**-yo*
That is fine, thank you
Está bien, gracias
*es-ta byen, **gra**-thee-as*
I would like — a perm
Quisiera — una permanente
*kee-see-**air**-ra — **oo**-na pair-ma-*
nen-tay
— a blow-dry
— secar con secador
*— se-**kar** kon se-ka-**dor***
— my hair dyed
— teñirme el pelo
*— ten-**yeer**-may el pe-lo*
— my hair streaked
— mechas en el pelo
*— **may**-chas en el pe-lo*

— a shampoo and cut
— lavar y cortar
*— la-**bar** ee kor-tar*
— a shampoo and set
— lavar y marcar
*— la-**bar** ee mar-kar*
— a conditioner
— un suavizante
*— oon swa-bee-**than**-ta*
— hair spray
— laca de pelo
*— **la**-ka day pe-lo*
The dryer is too hot
El secador está demasiado
caliente
*el se-ka-**dor** es-**ta** de-ma-**sya**-do*
ka-lee-en-tay
The water is too hot
El agua está demasiado
caliente
*el **a**-gwa es-**ta** de-ma-**sya**-do ka-*
lee-en-tay

Laundry

Is there a Laundromat™ nearby?
¿Hay alguna lavandería cercana?
eye al-goo-na la-ban-de-ree-a thair-ka-na

How does the washing machine work?
¿Cómo funciona la lavadora?
ko-mo foon-thyo-na la la-ba-do-ra

How long will it take?
¿Cuánto tardará?
kwan-to tar-da-ra

Can you — clean this skirt?
¿Me puede — limpiar esta falda?
may pwe-day — leem-pyar es-ta fal-da

— clean and press these shirts?
— limpiar y planchar estas camisas?
— leem-pyar ee plan-char es-tas ka-mee-sas

— wash these clothes?
— lavar esta ropa?
— la-bar es-ta ro-pa

This stain is — oil
Esta mancha es — de aceite
es-ta man-cha es — day a-thay-ee-tay

— blood
— de sangre
— day san-gray

— coffee
— de café
— day ka-fay

— ink
— de tinta
— day teen-ta

This fabric is delicate
Esta tela es delicada
es-ta tay-la es de-lee-ka-da

I have lost my dry cleaning ticket
He perdido el resguardo de la tintorería
ay pair-dee-do el rez-gwar-do day la teen-to-re-ree-a

Please send it to this address
Por favor, envíelo a esta dirección
por fa-bor, en-bee-ay-lo a es-ta dee-rek-thyon

When will I come back?
¿Cuándo puedo volver?
kwan-do pwe-do bol-bair

When will my clothes be ready?
¿Cuándo estará mi ropa lista?
kwan-do es-ta-ra mee ro-pa lee-sta

I will come back — later
Volveré — más tarde
bol-bair-ay — mas tar-day

— in an hour
— dentro de una hora
— den-tro day oo-na o-ra

General repairs

This is — broken
Esto está — roto
es-to es-ta — ro-to

— damaged
— averiado
— a-be-ree-a-do

— torn
—estropeado
— e-stro-pay-a-do

Can you repair it?
¿Puede repararlo?
pwe-day re-pa-rar-lo

Can you do it quickly?
¿Puede hacerlo rápidamente?
pwe-day a-thair-lo ra-pee-da-men-tay

Have you got a spare part for this?
¿Tiene alguna pieza de repuesto para esto?
tee-e-nay al-goo-na pee-ay-tha day re-pwe-sto pa-ra es-to

Would you have a look at this, please?
¿Puede mirar esto, por favor?
pwe-day mee-rar es-to, por fa-bor

Here is the guarantee
Aquí está la garantía
a-kee es-ta la ga-ran-tee-a

At the post office

Twelve stamps, please
Doce sellos, por favor
do-thay se-yos, por fa-bor

I need to send this by courier
Necesito enviar esto por servicio de mensajero
ne-the-see-to en-byar es-to por sair-bee-thee-o day men-sa-hair-o

I want to send a telegram
Quiero enviar este telegrama
kee-e-ro en-byar es-tay te-le-gra-ma

I want to send this by registered mail
Quiero enviar esto por correo certificado
kee-e-ro en-byar es-to por ko-ray-o thair-tee- fee-ka-do

I want to send this parcel
Quiero enviar este paquete
kee-e-ro en-byar es-tay pa-ke-tay

When will it arrive?
¿Cuándo llegará?
kwan-do ye-ga-ra

How much is a letter — to Britain?
¿Cuánto cuesta una carta — a Gran Bretaña?
kwan-to kwes-ta oo-na kar-ta — a gran bre-tan-ya

— to the United States?
— a los Estados Unidos?
— a los e-sta-dos oo-nee-dos

Can I have six stamps for
postcards to the US?
Me da seis sellos para postales
a los Estados Unidos
may da says se-yos pa-ra po-sta-
les a los e-sta-dos oo-nee-dos

Can I have a telegram form,
please?
¿Puede darme un impreso de
telegrama, por favor?
pwe-day dar-may oon eem-pray-
so day te-le-gra-ma, por fa-bor

Using the telephone

Can I use the telephone, please?
¿Puedo utilizar el teléfono, por
favor?
pwe-do oo-tee-lee-thar el te-le-fo-
no, por fa-bor
Can I dial direct?
¿Puedo marcar directamente?
pwe-do mar-kar dee-rek-ta-
men-tay
Can you connect me with
the international operator?
¿Puede conectarme con la
operadora internacional?
pwe-day ko-nek-tar-may kon la o-
pe-ra-do-ra een-tair-na-thyo-nal
Have you got any change?
¿Tiene cambio?
tee-e-nay kam-bee-o
How do I use the telephone?
¿Cómo se utiliza el teléfono?
ko-mo say oo-tee-lee-tha el te-le-
fo-no

How much is it to phone to
London?
¿Cuánto cuesta llamar a Londres?
kwan-to kwes-ta ya-mar a lon-dres
I must make a phone call to
America
Tengo que llamar a los
Estados Unidos
ten-go kay ya-mar a los e-sta-dos
oo-nee-dos
I need to make a phone call
Tengo que hacer una llamada
ten-go kay a-thair oo-na ya-ma-da
What is the code for the UK?
¿Cuál es el código del Reino
Unido?
kwal es el ko-dee-go del ray-no
oo-nee-do

I would like to make a
reversed charge call
Deseo hacer una llamada a
cobro revertido
de-say-o a-thair oo-na ya-ma-
da a ko-bro re- bair-tee-do
The number I need is...
El número que necesito es...
el noo-me-o kay ne-the-see-to es...
What is the charge?
¿Cuánto es?
kwan-to es
Please call me back
Por favor, devuelva mi llamada
por fa-bor, de-bwel-ba mee ya-
ma-da
I am sorry. We were cut off
Lo siento. Se ha cortado
lo syen-to. Say a kor-ta-do

What you may hear

El número no funciona
el noo-me-ro no foon-thyo-na
The number is out of order
Está comunicando
es-ta ko-moo-nee-kan-do
The line is busy (engaged)
Estoy intentando conectarle
es-toy een-ten-tan-do ko-nek-
tar-lay
I am trying to connect you

Hable, por favor
a-blay, por fa-bor
Please go ahead
Hola, soy el director
o-la, soy el dee-rek-tor
Hello, this is the manager
Le voy a pasar con el señor...
lay boy a pa-sar kon el sen-yor...
I am putting you through to
Mr...

No puedo obtener este
número
no pwe-do ob-te-nair es-tay noo-
me-ro
I cannot obtain this number

Changing money

Can I contact my bank to
arrange for a transfer?
¿Puedo contactar a mi banco
para pedir una transferencia?
pwe-do kon-tak-tar a mee ban-
ko pa-ra pe-deer oo-na trans-fe-
ren-thee-a
Has my cash arrived?
¿Ha llegado mi dinero?
a ye-ga-do mee dee-ne-ro
I would like to obtain a cash

advance with my credit card
Quisiera un anticipo en
efectivo con mi tarjeta de
crédito
kee-see-air-ra oon an-tee-thee-po
en me-ta-lee-ko kon mee tar-
hay-ta day kre-dee-to
This is the name and address
of my bank
Éste es el nombre y la
dirección de mi banco

es-tay es el nom-bray ee la dee-
rek-thyon day mee ban-ko
Can I change — these
traveler's checks?
¿Puedo cambiar — estos
cheques de viajero?
pwe-do kam-byar — es-tos che-
kays day bee-a-hay
— these bills?
— estos billetes?
— es-tos bee-ye-tes

Here is my passport
Aquí tiene mi pasaporte
a-kee tee-e-nay mee pa-sa-por-tay
What is the rate of
exchange?
¿A cuánto está el cambio?
a kwan-to es-ta el kam-bee-o

What is the rate for — dollars?
¿A cuánto está el cambio —
del dólar?
*a kwan-to es-ta el kam-bee-o —
del do-lar*

— sterling?
— de la libra esterlina?
— day la lee-bra es-tair-lee-na
What is your commission?
¿Cuánto es la comisión?
kwan-to es la ko-mee-syon

Health

What's wrong?

I need a doctor
Necesito un médico
ne-the-see-to oon me-dee-ko
Can I see a doctor?
¿Puedo ver a un médico?
pwe-do bair a oon me-dee-ko
He/she is hurt
Está herido/herida
es-ta e-ree-do / e-ree-da
He/she has been badly
injured
Está malherido/malherida
es-ta mal-e-ree-do / mal-e-ree-da
He/she has burnt him/herself
Se ha quemado
say a ke-ma-do
He/she has dislocated his/
her shoulder
Se ha dislocado el hombro
say a dees-lo-ka-do el om-bro
He/she is unconscious
Está inconsciente
es-ta een-kons-thee-en-tay
He/she has a temperature
Tiene fiebre
tee-e-nay fee-e-bray
He/she has been bitten
Tiene una mordedura
tee-e-nay oo-na mor-de-doo-ra
My son has cut himself
Mi hijo se ha cortado
mee ee-ho say a e-cho kor-ta-do
My son is ill
Mi hijo está enfermo
mee ee-ho es-ta en-fair-mo
I am ill
Estoy enfermo/enferma
es-toy en-fair-mo / en-fair-ma
I am a diabetic
Soy diabético/diabética
soy dee-a-be-tee-ko / dee-a-be-tee-ka

I am allergic to penicillin
Soy alérgico/alérgica a la
penicilina
*soy a-lair-hee-ko / a-lair-hee-ka
a la pe-nee-thee-lee-na*
I am badly sunburnt
Tengo fuertes quemaduras de
sol
ten-go ke-ma-doo-ras day sol
I am constipated
Estoy estreñido/estreñida
es-toy es-tren-yee-do / es-tren-yee-da
I cannot sleep
No puedo dormir
no pwe-do dor-meer
I feel dizzy
Estoy mareado/mareada
es-toy ma-ray-a-do / ma-ray-a-da
I feel faint
Me siento mareado/mareada
may syen-to ma-ray-a-do / ma-ray-a-da
I feel nauseous
Siento náuseas
syen-to now-say-as
I fell
Me he caído
may ay ka-ee-do
I have a pain here
Me duele aquí
may dwe-lay a-kee
I have a rash here
Tengo un sarpullido aquí
ten-go oon sar-poo-yee-do a-kee
I have been sick
He estado vomitando
ay es-ta-do bo-mee-tan-do
I have been stung
Tengo una picadura
ten-go oo-na pee-ka-doo-ra

I have cut myself
Me he cortado
may ay kor-ta-do
I have diarrhea
Tengo diarrea
ten-go dee-a-ray-a
I have pulled a muscle
Tengo un tirón en un músculo
ten-go oon tee-ron en oon moo-skoo-lo
I have sunstroke
Tengo insolación
ten-go een-so-la-thyon
I suffer from high blood
pressure
Tengo la tensión alta
ten-go la ten-syon al-ta
I think I have food
poisoning
Creo que tengo una
intoxicación de alimentos
kray-o kay ten-go oo-na een-tok-see-ka-thyon day a-lee-men-tos
It is inflamed here
Esto está inflamado
es-to es-ta een-fla-ma-do
My arm is broken
Me he roto el brazo
may ay ro-to el bra-tho
My stomach is upset
Tengo mal de estómago
ten-go mal day e-sto-ma-go
My tongue is coated
Tengo la lengua sucia
ten-go la len-gwa soo-thya
There is a swelling here
Tengo hinchazón aquí
ten-go een-cha-thon a-kee
I have hurt — my arm
Me he hecho daño en — el brazo
may ay e-cho dan-yo en — el bra-tho

— my leg
— la pierna
— la pee-air-na
It is painful — to walk
Me duele al — caminar
may dwe-lay al — ka-mee-nar
— to breathe
— respirar
— re-spee-rar
— to swallow
— tragar
— tra-gar
I have — a headache
Tengo — dolor de cabeza
ten-go — do-lor day ka-bay-tha
— a sore throat
— dolor de garganta
— do-lor day gar-gan-ta
— an earache
— dolor de oído
— do-lor day o-ee-do

I am taking these drugs
Estoy tomando estos
medicamentos
es-toy to-man-do es-tos me-dee-ka-men-tos
Can you give me a
prescription for them?
¿Puede hacerme una receta
para ellos?
pwe-day dar-may oo-na re-thay-ta pa-ra e-yos
I am on the pill
Estoy tomando la píldora
es-toy to-man-do la peel-do-ra
I am pregnant
Estoy embarazada
es-toy em-ba-ra-tha-da
My blood group is...
Mi grupo sanguíneo es
mee groo-po san-gee-nay-o es ...

I do not know my blood group
No sé el grupo sanguíneo que
tengo
no say el groo-po san-gee-nay-o kay ten-go
I need some antibiotics
Necesito antibióticos
ne-the-see-to an-tee-bee-o-tee-kos
Do I have to go into
hospital?
¿Tengo que ir al hospital?
ten-go kay eer al o-spee-tal
Do I need an operation?
¿Tengo que operarme?
ten-go kay o-pe-rar-may

At the hospital

How do I get reimbursed?
¿Cómo me van a reembolsar?
ko-mo may ban a ray-em-bol-sar
Must I stay in bed?
¿Tengo que estar en la cama?
ten-go kay es-tar en la ka-ma

When will I be able to
travel?
¿Cuándo podré viajar?
kwan-do po-dray bee-a-har

Will I be able to go out
tomorrow?
¿Podré salir mañana?
po-dray sa-leer man-ya-na

Parts of the body

ankle	ear	heart	muscle
tobillo	oreja	corazón	músculo
to-bee-yo	*o-ray-ha*	*ko-ra-thon*	*moos-koo-lo*
arm	elbow	kidney	neck
brazo	codo	riñon	cuello
bra-tho	*ko-do*	*reen-yon*	*kwe-yo*
back	eye	knee	nose
espalda	ojo	rodilla	nariz
es-pal-da	*o-ho*	*ro-dee-ya*	*na-reeth*
bone	face	leg	skin
hueso	cara	pierna	piel
we-so	*ka-ra*	*pee-air-na*	*pyel*
breast	finger	liver	stomach
pecho	dedo	hígado	estómago
pe-cho	*de-do*	*ee-ga-do*	*e-sto-ma-go*
cheek	foot	lungs	throat
mejilla	pie	pulmones	garganta
me-hee-ya	*pee-ay*	*pool-mo-nes*	*gar-gan-ta*
chest	hand	mouth	wrist
pecho	mano	boca	muñeca
pe-cho	*ma-no*	*bo-ka*	*moon-yay-ka*

At the dentist's

I have to see the dentist
Tengo que ir al dentista
ten-go kay eer al den-tee-sta
I have a toothache
Tengo dolor de muelas
ten-go do-lor day mway-las
Are you going to fill it?
¿Va a empastarme?
ba a em-pa-star-may
I have broken a tooth
Me ha roto una muela
may a ro-to oo-na mway-la
Se me partió una muela (*Lat Am*)

Will you have to take it out?
¿Tendrá que sacármela?
ten-dra kay sa-kar-may-la
My false teeth are broken
Se me han roto los dientes
postizos
say may an ro-to los dee-en-tes po-stee-thos
Can you repair them?
¿Puede reparármelos?
pwe-day re-pa-rar-may-los
My gums are sore
Me duelen las encías
may dwe-len las en-thee-as

Please give me an injection
Póngame una inyección, por
favor
pon-ga-may oo-na een-yek-thyon, por fa-bor
That hurts
Eso duele
e-so dwe-lay
The filling has come out
Se me ha caído el empaste
say may a ka-ee-do el em-pas-tay
This one hurts
Me duele ésta
may dwe-lay es-ta

For Your Information

Days

Sunday	Tuesday	Thursday	Saturday
domingo	martes	jueves	sábado
do-meen-go	*mar-tes*	*hwe-bes*	*sa-ba-do*
Monday	**Wednesday**	**Friday**	
lunes	miércoles	viernes	
loo-nes	*mee-air-ko-les*	*bee-air-nes*	

Dates

on Friday	yesterday	in June	next week
el viernes	ayer	en junio	la semana que viene
el bee-air-nes	*a-yair*	*en hoo-nee-o*	*la se-ma-na kay bee-e-nay*
next Tuesday	**today**	**July 7th**	**last month**
el martes próximo	hoy	el siete de julio	el mes pasado
el mar-tes prok-see-mo	*oy*	*el see-e-tay day hoo-lee-o*	*el mes pa-sa-do*
last Tuesday	**tomorrow**		
el martes pasado	mañana		
el mar-tes pa-sa-do	*man-ya-na*		

The seasons

spring	summer	autumn	winter
primavera	verano	otoño	invierno
pree-ma-bair-a	*be-ra-no*	*o-ton-yo*	*een-byair-no*

Times of the year

in spring	in summer	in autumn	in winter
en la primavera	en el verano	en el otoño	en el invierno
en la pree- ma-bair-a	*en el be-ra-no*	*en el o-ton-yo*	*en el een- byair-no*

Months

January	April	July	October
enero	abril	julio	octubre
e-nair-o	*a-breel*	*hoo-lee-o*	*ok-too-bray*
February	May	August	November
febrero	mayo	agosto	noviembre
fe-brair-o	*my-o*	*a-go-sto*	*nob-yem-bray*
March	June	September	December
marzo	junio	setiembre	diciembre
mar-tho	*hoo-nee-o*	*se-tee-em-bray*	*deeth-yem-bray*

Spanish public holidays

January 1, New Year's Day	24 June, St John's Day	15 August, Assumption	6 December, Constitution Day
Año Nuevo	Día de San Juan	Asunción	Día de la
an-yo nway-bo	Batista	*a-soon-thyon*	Constitución
January 6, Epiphany	*dee-a day san hwan ba-tee-sta*	12 October, Columbus Day	*dee-a day la kon-stee-too-thyon*
Día de Reyes		Día de la Hispanidad	8 December,
dee-a day ray-es	Corpus Christi Day	*dee-a day la ee-spa-nee-dad*	Immaculate
Maundy Thursday	(2nd Thursday after		Conception
Jueves Santo	Pentecost — late May	1 November, All Saints Day	Inmaculada
hwe-bes san-to	or early June)	Todos los Santos	Concepción
Good Friday	Corpus Christi	*to-dos los san-tos*	*een-ma-koo-la-da kon-thep-thyon*
Viernes Santo	*kor-poos-kree-stee*		
bee-air-nes san-to	25 July, St James's Day		25 December,
May 1, May Day, Labour Day	Día de Santiago		Christmas Day
Día del Trabajo	Apóstol		Navidad
dee-a del tra-ba-ho	*dee-a day san-tya-go a-po-stol*		*na-bee-dad*

Colors

black	fawn	orange	silver
negro	beis	naranja	plateado
ne-gro	*bays*	*na-ran-ha*	*pla-tay-a-do*
blue	gold	pink	tan
azul	dorado	rosa	color canela
a-thool	*do-ra-do*	*ro-sa*	*ko-lor ka-nay-la*
brown	green	purple	white
marrón	verde	morado	blanco
ma-ron	*bair-day*	*mo-ra-do*	*blan-ko*
cream	gray	red	yellow
crema	gris	rojo	amarillo
kray-ma	*grees*	*ro-ho*	*a-ma-ree-yo*

Common adjectives

bad	big	cold	difficult
malo	grande	frío	dificil
ma-lo	*gran-day*	*free-o*	*dee-fee-theel*
beautiful	cheap	expensive	easy
hermoso	barato	caro	fácil
air-mo-so	*ba-ra-to*	*ka-ro*	*fa-theel*

fast	hot	new	slow
rápido	caliente	nuevo	lento
ra-pee-do	*ka-lee-en-tay*	*nway-bo*	*len-to*
good	**little**	**old**	**small**
bueno	poco	viejo	pequeño
bway-no	*po-ko*	*bee-ay-ho*	*pe-ken-yo*
high	**long**	**short**	**ugly**
alto	largo	corto	feo
al-to	*lar-go*	*kor-to*	*fay-o*

Signs and notices

Abierto
a-bee-air-to
Open

Aduana
a-dwa-n
Customs

Agencia de viajes
a-hen-thee-a day bee-a-hes
Travel agency

Agotado
a-go-ta-do
Sold out

Agua potable
a-gwa po-ta-blay
Drinking water

Alarma de incendios
a-lar-ma day een-then-dee-os
Fire alarm

Ambulancia
am-boo-lan-thee-a
Ambulance

Aparcamiento sólo para residentes
a-par-ka-myen-to so-lo pa-ra re-see-den-tes
Parking for residents only

Area de fumadores
a-ray-a day foo-ma-do-res
Smoking area

Ascensor
as-then-sor
Elevator

Banco
ban-ko
Bank

Bienvenido
byen-be-nee-do
Welcome

Bomberos
bom-bair-os
Fire Brigade

Caballeros
ka-ba-yair-os
Gentlemen (public bathrooms)

Cajero
ka-hair-o
Cashier

Caliente
ka-lee-en-tay
Hot

Camino particular
ka-mee-no par-tee-koo-lar
Private road

Carril de bicicleta
ka-reel day bee-thee-klay-ta
Cycle path

Cerrado
the-ra-do
Closed

Cerrado por la tarde
the-ra-do por la tar-day
Closed in the afternoon

Circule por la derecha
theer-koo-lay por la de-ray-cha
Keep to the right

Colegio
co-le-hee-o
School

Compartimento de fumadores
kom-par-tee-men-to day foo-ma-do-res
Smoking car

Cuidado
kwee-da-do
Caution

Cuidado con el perro
kwee-da-do kon el pe-ro
Beware of the dog

Desviación
des-bee-a-thyon
Diversion

Emergencia
e-mair-hen-thee-a
Emergency

Empujar
em-poo-har
Push

Entrada
en-tra-da
Entrance

Entrada gratuita
en-tra-da gra-twee-ta
No admission charge

Entre sin llamar
en-tray seen ya-mar
Enter without knocking

Equipaje
e-kee-pa-hay
Baggage

Está prohibido hablar con el conductor mientras circula
es-ta pro-ee-bee-do a-blar kon el kon-dook-tor myen-tras theer-koo-la
It is forbidden to speak to the driver while the bus is moving

Frío
free-o
Cold

Horario
o-ra-ree-o
Timetable

Hospital
os-pee-tal
Hospital

Información
een-for-ma-thyon
Information

Libre
lee-bray
Vacant

Lista de precios
lee-sta day pre-thee-os
Price list

Llame
ya-may
Ring

Llame por favor
ya-may por fa-bor
Please ring

Llegadas
ye-ga-das
Arrivals

No entrar
no en-trar
No entry

No pisar el césped
no pee-sar el thes-ped
Keep off the grass

No tocar
no to-kar
Do not touch

Ocupado
o-koo-pa-do
Occupied

Oferta especial
o-fair-ta es-peth-yal
Special offer

Oficina de objetos perdidos
o-fee-thee-na day ob-he-tos pair-dee-dos
Lost property office

Papelera
pa-pe-lair-a
Litter bin

Peligro
pe-lee-gro
Danger

Peligro de incendio
pe-lee-gro day een-then-dee-o
Danger of fire

Peligro de muerte
pe-lee-gro day mwair-tay
Danger of death

Permitido sólo para...
pair-mee-tee-do so-lo pa-ra...
Allowed only for...

Policía
po-lee-thee-a
Police

Prohibida la entrada
pro-ee-bee-da la en-tra-da
No entry

Prohibido asomarse
pro-ee-bee-do a-so-mar-say
No leaning out

Prohibido el paso
pro-ee-bee-do el pa-so
No thoroughfare

Prohibido fumar
pro-ee-bee-do foo-ma
No smoking

Prohibido hacer fotos
pro-ee-bee-do a-thair fo-tos
It is forbidden to take photographs

Rebajas
re-ba-has
Sale

Recuerdos
re-kwair-dos
Souvenirs

Reservado
re-sair-ba-do
Reserved

Salida
sa-lee-da
Exit

Salida de emergencia
sa-lee-da day e-mair-hen-thee-a
Emergency exit

Salidas
sa-lee-das
Departures

Se alquila
say al-kee-la
To let/For hire

Se vende
say ben-day
For sale

Señoras
sen-yo-ras
Ladies (public bathroom)

Sólo empleados
so-lo em-play-a-dos
Employees only

Sólo para uso

externo
so-lo pa-ra oo-so ek-stair-no
For external use only

Teléfono
te-le-fo-no
Telephone

Timbre de alarma
teem-bray day a-lar-ma
Communication cord

Tirar
tee-rar
Pull

Veneno
be-nay-no
Poison

Venta de liquidación
ben-ta day lee-kee-da-thyon
Closing down sale

In an Emergency

What to do

Call — the fire department
Llame — a los bomberos
ya-may — a los bom-bair-os
— the police
— a la policía
— a la po-lee-thee-a
— an ambulance
— a una ambulancia
— a oo-na am-boo-lan-thee-a

Get a doctor
Busque a un médico
boos-kay a oon me-dee-ko
There is a fire
Hay un incendio
eye oon en-then-dee-o

Where is — the American consulate?
¿Dónde está — el consulado americano?
don-day es-ta — el kon-soo-la-do a-me-ree-ka-no
— the police station?
— la comisaría de policía?
— la ko-mee-sa-ree-a day po-lee-thee-a

SPANISH VOCABULARY

The body — El cuerpo

1	
head	la cabeza
hair	los cabellos, el pelo
dark	moreno
fair	rubio
bald	calvo
brown (hair)	castaño
smooth	liso
curly	rizado
gray hair	las canas
scalp	el cuero cabelludo

2	
face	la cara
features	los rasgos
forehead	la frente
cheek	la mejilla
wrinkle	la arruga
dimple	el hoyuelo
chin	la barbilla
beautiful	hermoso
handsome	guapo
pretty	bonito

3	
ugly	feo
ugliness	la fealdad
beauty	la hermosura
beauty spot	el lunar
freckle	la peca
freckled	pecoso
ear	la oreja
hearing	el oído
to hear	oír
to listen	escuchar

4	
listener	el oyente
earlobe	el lóbulo de la oreja
deaf	sordo
mute	mudo
deaf-mute	el sordomudo *m*, la sordomuda *f*
deafness	la sordera
to deafen	ensordecer
deafening	ensordecedor
eardrum	el tímpano
sound	el sonido

5	
noise	el ruido
eye	el ojo
sense	el sentido
eyesight	la vista

tear	la lágrima
eyebrow	la ceja
to frown	**fruncir las cejas,** fruncir el ceño
eyelid	el párpado
eyelash	la pestaña
pupil	la pupila

6	
retina	la retina
iris	el iris
glance	la vislumbre, la mirada
to see	ver
to look	mirar
look	la mirada
visible	visible
invisible	invisible
blind	ciego
blindness	la ceguera

7	
to blind	cegar
blind spot	el punto ciego
one-eyed	tuerto
cross-eyed	bizco
to observe	observar
to notice	reparar
expression	la expresión
to smile	sonreír
smile	la sonrisa
to laugh	reír

8	
laugh	la risa
laughing *adj*	risueño
mouth	la boca
tongue	la lengua
lip	el labio
tooth	el diente
eyetooth	el colmillo
gum	la encía
palate	el paladar
to say	decir

9	
saying	el dicho
to speak	hablar
to shout	gritar
to be quiet	callarse
touch	el tacto
to touch	tocar
to feel	sentir
tactile	táctil
nose	la nariz
nostril	la ventana de la nariz, la fosa nasal

10

bridge (nose)	el caballete
smell (sense)	el olfato
smell	el olor
to smell (of)	oler (a)
to taste (of)	saber (a)
to taste	probar
taste (sense)	el gusto
taste bud	la papila gustativa
tasty	sabroso
tasting	la degustación

11

mustache	el bigote
beard	la barba
facial hair	el vello facial
sideburns	las patillas
dandruff	la caspa
plait	la trenza
curl	el rizo
to shave	afeitarse
to grow a beard	dejar crecer la barba
bearded	barbudo

12

clean-shaven	rasurado
jaw	la mandíbula
throat	la garganta
neck	el cuello
shoulder	el hombro
back	la espalda
chest	el pecho
breast	el seno
to breathe	respirar
breath	el aliento

13

breathing	la respiración
lung	el pulmón
windpipe	la tráquea
heart	el corazón
heartbeat	el latido (del corazón)
rib	la costilla
side	el costado
limb	el miembro
leg	la pierna
lame	cojo

14

to limp	cojear
thigh	el muslo
calf	la pantorilla
tendon	el tendón
groin	la ingle
muscle	el músculo
knee	la rodilla
kneecap	la rótula

to kneel	arrodillarse
foot	el pie

15

heel	el talón
toe	el dedo del pie
sole	la planta del pie
ankle	el tobillo
instep	el empeine
arm	el brazo
forearm	el antebrazo
right-handed	diestro
left-handed	zurdo
right	la derecha

16

left	la izquierda
hand	la mano
to handle	manejar
handshake	el apretón (de manos)
handful	el puñado
finger	el dedo
index finger	el (dedo) índice
thumb	el pulgar
palm	la palma
nail	la uña

17

wrist	la muñeca
elbow	el codo
fist	el puño
knuckle	el nudillo
bone	el hueso
spine	la espina dorsal
skeleton	el esqueleto
skull	el cráneo
blood	la sangre
vein	la vena

18

artery	la arteria
capillary	el capilar
liver	el hígado
skin	la piel
pore	el poro
sweat	el sudor
to sweat	sudar
scar	la cicatriz
wart	la verruga
complexion	la tez

19

brain	el cerebro
kidney	el riñón
bladder	la vejiga
spleen	el bazo
gland	la glándula
larynx	la laringe

ligament	el ligamento	to stand	estar de pie
cartilage	el cartílago	to stand up	levantarse
womb	la matriz, el útero	to raise	levantar
ovary	el ovario	to lie down	acostarse
		to sleep	dormir
20		sleep	el sueño
height	la talla	to be sleepy	tener sueño
big	grande	to dream	soñar
small	pequeño		
tall	alto	**22**	
short	bajo, corto		
fat	gordo	to doze	dormitar
thin	delgado	to fall asleep	dormirse
strong	fuerte	asleep	dormido
strength	la fuerza	to be awake	estar despierto
weak	débil	to wake up	despertarse
		drowsy	somnoliento
21		dream	el sueño
		nightmare	la pesadilla
knock-kneed	patizambo	conscious	consciente
bow-legged	estevado,	unconscious	inconsciente
	cascorbo (*Lat Am*)		

Clothes — La ropa

		tie	la corbata
23		handkerchief	el pañuelo
jacket	la chaqueta	suit	el traje
trousers	el pantalón		
jeans	los vaqueros	**26**	
dungarees	el peto	waistcoat	el chaleco
coveralls, overalls	el mono,	skirt	la falda
	el overol (*Lat Am*)	miniskirt	la minifalda
braces	los tirantes,	blouse	la blusa
	las tirantas (*Lat Am*)	stockings	las medias
sweater	el suéter	veil	el velo
sock	el calcetín	beret	la boina
to darn	remendar	collar	el cuello
raincoat	el impermeable	gloves	las guantes
		belt	el cinturón
24			
overcoat	el abrigo	**27**	
to shelter	abrigar	scarf	la bufanda
to protect	proteger	handkerchief	el pañuelo
hat	el sombrero	button	el botón
shadow	la sombra	to button	abrochar
brim	las alas (de un sombrero)	to unbutton	desabrochar
cap	la gorra	new	nuevo
glasses	las gafas	second-hand	de segunda mano
earmuffs	las orejeras	graceful	gracioso
walking stick	el bastón	narrow	estrecho
		broad	ancho
25			
umbrella	la paraguas	**28**	
cloth	la tela, el paño	ready-made	hecho
fine	fino	to make	hacer
thick	espeso, grueso	to get made	mandar hacer
coarse	basto	to wear	llevar
shirt	la camisa	to use	usar
T-shirt	la camiseta	worn out	usado

useful	útil
useless	inútil
practical	práctico

29

housecoat	la bata
nightdress	el camisón
pajamas	el pijama
underpants	los calzoncillos
panties	las bragas, los pantis (*Lat Am*)
petticoat	la enagua
slip	la combinación
bra	el sostén, el sujetador
leotard	la malla

30

coat hanger	la percha
zip	la cremallera
wristband	la muñequera, manilla (*Lat Am*)
sweatshirt	la sudadera
shorts	el pantalón corto
tracksuit	el chándal
dress	el vestido
to dress	vestir
to dress oneself	vestirse
to take off	quitarse

31

to remove	quitar
to undress	desnudarse
naked	desnudo
to put	poner
to put on	ponerse
sash	la faja
apron	el delantal
shawl	la manta
sleeve	la manga
to sew	coser

32

seam	la costura
seamstress	la costurera
thread	el hilo
needle	la aguja
hole	el agujero
scissors	las tijeras
ribbon	la cinta
linen	el lino

| lace | el encaje |
| velcro | el velcro |

33

fur	la piel
furry	afelpado
silk	la seda
silky	sedoso
velvet	el terciopelo
cotton	el algodón
nylon	el nailón
fan	el abanico
in fashion	de moda
out of fashion	pasado de moda

34

dressmaker	la modista
pocket	el bolsillo
bag	la bolsa
pin	el alfiler
to tie	atar
to untie	desatar
to loosen	soltar
sandal	la sandalia
slipper	la pantufla, la zapatilla
pair	el par

35

lace	el lazo
shoe	el zapato
sole	la suela
heel	el tacón
to polish	pulir
shoe polish	el betún
shoehorn	el calzador
boot	la bota
leather	el cuero
rubber	el caucho

36

suede	el ante, la gamuza
barefoot	descalzado
to put on one's shoes	calzarse
to take off one's shoes	descalzarse
footwear	el calzado
shoemaker	el zapatero
ring	el anillo
diamond	el diamante
necklace	el collar
bracelet	el brazalete

Family and relationships — La familia y las relaciones

37		son-in-law	el yerno	
		daughter-in-law	la nuera	
father	el padre	brother-in-law	el cuñado	
mother	la madre	sister-in-law	la cuñada	
parents	los padres	orphan	el huérfano *m*,	
son	el hijo		la huérfana *f*	
daughter	la hija			
children	los hijos	**42**		
brother	el hermano			
sister	la hermana	stepfather	el padrastro	
brotherhood	la hermandad	stepmother	la madrastra	
brotherly	fraternal	stepson	el hijastro	
		stepdaughter	la hijastra	
38		stepbrother	el hermanastro	
		stepsister	la hermanastra	
elder	mayor	bachelor	el soltero	
younger	menor	spinster	la soltera	
husband	el marido	widower	el viudo	
wife	la esposa	widow	la viuda	
uncle	el tío			
aunt	la tía	**43**		
nephew	el sobrino			
niece	la sobrina	ancestor	el antepasado	
grandfather	el abuelo	descendant	el descendiente	
grandmother	la abuela	boyfriend	el novio	
		girlfriend	la novia	
39		couple	la pareja	
		love	el amor	
grandparents	los abuelos	to fall in love	enamorarse	
grandson	el nieto	to marry	casarse con	
granddaughter	la nieta	wedding	la boda	
boy	el chico, el muchacho	honeymoon	la luna de miel	
girl	la chica, la muchacha			
cousin	el primo *m*, la prima *f*	**44**		
twin	el gemelo			
baby	el bebé	maternity	la maternidad	
child	el niño *m*, la niña *f*	paternity	la paternidad	
to be born	nacer	to be pregnant	estar embarazada	
		to give birth	parir	
40		childbirth	el parto	
		nurse	la nodriza	
to grow up	crecer	child minder	la niñera	
name	el nombre	to baby-sit	hacer de niñero	
surname	el apellido	baby-sitter	la cuidaniños, la niñera	
birthday	el cumpleaños	godmother	la madrina	
age	la edad			
old	viejo	**45**		
to get old	envejecer			
old man	el viejo	godfather	el padrino	
old woman	la vieja	baptism	el bautismo	
youth	la juventud	to baptize	bautizar	
		crèche	la guardería	
41		to breast-feed	dar de pecho, dar seno	
		infancy	la primera infancia	
young	joven	to spoil (child)	mimar	
young man	el joven	spoiled	mimado	
young woman	la joven	divorce	el divorcio	
father-in-law	el suegro	separation	la separación	
mother-in-law	la suegra			

46

family planning	la planificación familiar
contraception	la contracepción,
	la anticoncepción
contraceptive	el contraconceptivo,
	el anticonceptivo
contraceptive pill	la píldora anticonceptiva
condom	el preservativo,
	el condón (Lat Am)
abortion	el aborto
to have an abortion	abortar
period	la regla, el período
to menstruate	menstruar
to conceive	concebir

47

middle-aged	de mediana edad
menopause	la menopausia
to retire	jubilarse, retirarse
pensioner	el pensionista m,
	la pensionista f,
	el pensionado m,
	la pensionada f (Lat Am)
the aging process	el envejecimiento
old age	la vejez
death	la muerte
to die	morir

dying	moribundo
deathbed	el lecho de muerte

48

dead man	el muerto
dead woman	la muerta
death certificate	el certificado de defunción
mourning	el duelo
burial	el entierro
to bury	enterrar
grave	la tumba, la sepultura
cemetery	el cementerio,
	el campo santo
wake	el velorio
coffin	el ataúd

49

deceased, late	difunto
to console	consolar
to weep	llorar
to wear mourning	llevar luto
to survive	sobrevivir
survivor	el sobreviviente
crematorium	el crematorio
cremation	la cremación
to cremate	cremar
ashes	las cenizas

Health — La salud

50

sickness	la enfermedad
nurse	el enfermero m,
	la enfermera f
infirmary	la enfermería
sick	enfermo
hospital	el hospital
patient	el paciente
cough	la tos
to cough	toser
to injure	herir
injury	la herida

51

cramp	el calambre
to cut oneself	cortarse
to dislocate	dislocarse
to faint	desmayarse
to be ill	estar enfermo,
	estar malo
to become ill	ponerse enfermo,
	enfermarse
to look after	cuidar
care	el cuidado
careful	cuidadoso

52

carelessness	el descuido
careless	descuidado
negligent	negligente
doctor	el médico m, la médica f
medicine	la medicina
prescription	la receta
pharmacist	el farmacéutico m,
	la farmacéutica f,
	el/la farmaceuta (Lat Am)
drugstore	la farmacia
cure	la cura
curable	curable

53

incurable	incurable
to cure	curar
healer	el curador m, la curadora f;
	el sanador m, la sanadora f
to get well	sanar
healthy	sano
unhealthy	malsano
to recover	restablecerse
pain	el dolor
painful	doloroso
to suffer	padecer

54

diet	el régimen
obesity	la obesidad
obese	obeso
anorexic	anoréxico
anorexia	la anorexia
obsession	la obsesión
to get fat	engordar
headache	el dolor de cabeza
aspirin	la aspirina
migraine	la jaqueca

55

toothache	el dolor de muelas
stomach upset	el trastorno estomacal
indigestion	la indigestión
food poisoning	la intoxicación alimenticia
sore throat	el dolor de garganta
hoarse	ronco
pale	pálido
to turn pale	palidecer
to faint	desmayarse
cold (illness)	el catarro, el resfriado

56

to catch a cold	resfriarse
wound	la herida
surgeon	el cirujano
to heat	calentar
hot	caliente
temperature	la calentura
perspiration	la transpiración
sweaty	sudoroso
fever	la fiebre
germ	el germen

57

microbe	el microbio
contagious	contagioso
vaccine	la vacuna
to shiver	temblar
madness	la locura
mad	loco
drug	la droga
pill	la píldora
to scar	cicatrizarse
stitches	los puntos

58

to relieve	aliviar
swollen	hinchado
boil	el divieso, el forúnculo (Lat Am)
to bleed	sangrar
to clot	coagularse
blood cell	la célula sanguínea
blood group	el grupo sanguíneo

blood pressure	la presión sanguínea
blood test	el análisis de sangre, el exámen de sangre
check up	el chequeo

59

epidemic	la epidemia
plague	la plaga
allergy	la alergía
allergic	alérgico
angina	la angina
tonsillitis	la amigdalitis
fracture	la fractura
cast	la escayola, el yeso (Lat Am)
crutch	la muleta
wheelchair	la silla de ruedas

60

hemophiliac	el hemofílico m, la hemofílica f
hemophilia	la hemofilia
cholesterol	el colesterol
vitamin	la vitamina
calorie	la caloría
handicapped person	el minusválido
handicap	la minusvalía
pneumonia	la pulmonia, la neumonía
heart attack	el infarto
bypass operation	la operación de bypass

61

heart surgery	la cirugía cardíaca
microsurgery	la microcirugía
pacemaker	el marcapasos
heart transplant	el trasplante del corazón
smallpox	la viruela
stroke	la apoplejía
tumour	el tumor
HIV-positive	VIH-positivo, seropositivo
AIDS	el SIDA
cancer	el cáncer

62

breast cancer	el cáncer de mama
chemotherapy	la quimioterapia
screening	la exploración
diagnosis	el diagnóstico
antibody	el anticuerpo
antibiotic	el antibiótico
depression	la depresión
depressed	deprimido
to depress	deprimir
to undergo an operation	operarse

63

painkiller	el analgésico

treatment	el tratamiento
anesthetic	la anestesia
anesthetist	el anestesista *m*,
	la anestesista *f*
donor	el donante *m*,
	la donante *f*
genetic engineering	la ingeniera genética
test-tube baby	el bebé probeta
infertile	estéril
hormone	la hormona

64

psychologist	el psicólogo *m*,
	la psicóloga *f*
psychology	la psicología
psychoanalyst	el psicoanalista *m*,
	la psicoanalista *f*
psychoanalysis	el psicoanálisis
psychosomatic	psicosomático
hypochondriac	el hypocondríaco *m*,
	la hypocondríaca *f*
plastic surgery	la cirugía estética
face-lift	el estiramiento facial
implant	el implante
self-esteem	la autoestima

65

to smoke	fumar
passive smoking	el fumar pasivo
to inhale	inhalar
withdrawal syndrome	el síndrome de abstinencia
alcohol	el alcohol
hangover	la Resaca,
	el guayabo (*Lat Am*)
alcoholic	el alcohólico *m*,
	la alcohólica *f*
drug addict	el toxicómano
drug addiction	la toxicomanía
drugs traffic	el narcotráfico

66

heroin	la heroína
cocaine	la cocaína
drugs trafficker	el narcotraficante
to launder money	blanquear el dinero,
	lavar dinero
syringe	la jeringuilla
to inject	inyectar
to take drugs	drogarse
clinic	la clínica
outpatient	el paciente externo
therapy	la terapia

Nature — La naturaleza

67

world	el mundo
natural	natural
creation	la creación
the Big Bang theory	la teoría de la gran
	explosión
supernatural	sobrenatural
to create	crear
sky	el cielo
galaxy	la galaxia
the Milky Way	la Vía Láctea
the Big Dipper	el carro, la Osa Mayor

68

astronomer	el astrónomo *m*,
	la astrónoma *f*
astronomy	la astronomía
telescope	el telescopio
UFO	OVNI (objeto volante
	no identificado)
light year	el año luz
asteroid	el asteroide
meteor	el meteorito
comet	el cometa
star	la estrella
starry	estrellado

69

to twinkle	centellear
to shine	resplandecer
planet	el planeta
earth	la Tierra
Mercury	el Mercurio
Venus	el Venus
Mars	el Marte
Jupiter	el Júpiter
Saturn	el Saturno
Neptune	el Neptuno

70

Uranus	el Urano
Pluto	el Plutón
orbit	la órbita
to orbit	orbitar
gravity	la gravedad
satellite	el satélite
moon	la luna
eclipse	el eclipse
sun	el sol
sunspot	la mancha solar

71

| ray | el rayo |
| to radiate | radiar |

radiant	radioso
to shine	brillar
shining	brillante
brilliancy	el brillo
sunrise	la salida del sol
to rise	salir
sunset	la puesta del sol
to set (sun)	ponerse

72

dawn	el amanecer
to dawn	amanecer
dusk	el crepúsculo
to grow dark	anochecer
earthquake	el terremoto
volcano	el volcán
eruption	la erupción
deserted	desierto
desert	el desierto
plain	la llanura, la planicie

73

flat	llano, plano
level	el nivel
valley	el valle
hill	la colina
mountain	el monte, la montaña
mountainous	montañoso
peak	el pico
summit	la cumbre, la cima
range of mountains	la cordillera
crag	el peñasco

74

rock	la roca
steep	empinado
slope	la cuesta
coast	la costa
coastal	costero
shore	la orilla
beach	la playa
cliff	el acantilado
sea	el/la mar
tide	la marea

75

high tide	la pleamar
low tide	la bajamar
ebb tide	el reflujo
flood tide	el flujo
wave	la ola
foam	la espuma
tempest	la tempestad
hurricane	el huracán
gulf	el golfo
bay	la bahía

76

cape	el cabo
straits	el estrecho
island	la isla
spring	la fuente
fountain	el surtidor, la fuente
waterfall	la cascada
stream	el arroyo
river	el río
current	la corriente
draft	la corriente de aire

77

glacier	el glaciar
iceberg	el iceberg
ice cap	el casquete de hielo
icefloe	el témpano de hielo
to flood	inundar
flood	la inundación
border	el borde
lake	el lago
pond	el estanque
marsh	el pantano

78

deep	hondo, profundo
depth	la profundidad
weather	el tiempo
fine, fair	ameno, bueno
climate	el clima
barometer	el barómetro
thermometer	el termómetro
degree	el grado
air	el aire
breeze	la brisa

79

cool, fresh	fresco
wind	el viento
windy	ventoso
dampness	la humedad
damp	húmedo
to wet	mojar
wet	mojado
storm	la tormenta, la borrasca
stormy	borrascoso, tormentoso
dry	seco

80

drought	la sequía
to dry	secar
rainbow	el arco iris
rain	la lluvia
rainy	lluvioso
to rain	llover
drop	la gota
shower	el chaparrón, el aguacero

cloud	la nube	foggy	brumoso
cloudy	nublado	misty	nebuloso
		snow	la nieve
81		to snow	nevar
to cloud over	nublarse	snowstorm	la ventisca
to clear up	despejar	snowfall	la nevada
lightning	el relámpago	hailstone	el granizo
lightning conductor	el pararrayos		
to flash (lightning)	relampaguear	**83**	
sheet lightning	el relámpago fucilazo	to hail	granizar
fork lightning	el relámpago en zigzag	to freeze	helar
harmful	dañoso	frozen	helado
to harm	hacer daño	icicle	el carámbano
thunder	el trueno	frost	la escarcha
		to thaw	deshelarse
82		ice	el hielo
to thunder	tronar	thaw	el deshielo
fog	la bruma	heatwave	la ola de calor
mist	la niebla	sultry	bochornoso

Minerals — Los minerales

		to alloy	alear
84		alloy	la aleación
metal	el metal		
mine	la mina	**87**	
mineral	el mineral	stone	la piedra
forge	la fragua	stony	pedregoso
to forge	fraguar, forjar	quarry	la cantera
steel	el acero	granite	el granito
iron	el hierro	to polish	pulir
iron	ferreo	polished	pulido
bronze	el bronze	smooth	liso
brass	el latón	marble	el mármol
		lime	la cal
85		chalk	la creta, la tiza (*Lat Am*)
copper	el cobre		
tin	el estaño	**88**	
lead	el plomo	clay	la arcilla
zinc	el zinc	sulfur	el azufre
nickel	el níquel	jewel	la joya
aluminum	el aluminio	pearl	la perla
silver	la plata	diamond	el diamante
gold	el oro	ruby	el rubí
platinum	el platino	emerald	la esmeralda
mold	el molde	mother-of-pearl	el nácar
		enamel	el esmalte
86		sapphire	el zafiro
to extract	extraer		
to exploit	explotar	**89**	
miner	el minero	agate	el ágata
to melt, smelt	fundir	opal	el ópalo
to mold	moldear	lapis-lazuli	el lapislázuli
rust	la herrumbre,	obsidian	la obsidiana
	el óxido (*Lat Am*)	garnet	el granate
rusty	herrumbroso,	alkali	el álcali
	oxidado (*Lat Am*)	acid	el ácido
to solder	soldar	acidity	la acidez

| plutonium | el plutonio | radium | el radio |

Animals and plants — Los animales y las plantas

		heifer	la novilla
90		lamb	el cordero
domestic	doméstico	**sheep**	la oveja
tame	manso	**ram**	el carnero
cat	el gato	**ewe**	la oveja
kitten	el gatito	**goat**	la cabra
to mew	maullar	**hog, pig**	el cerdo, el puerco,
feline	felino		el marrano (*Lat Am*)
claw	la garra		
dog	el perro	**95**	
bitch	la perra		
puppy	el cachorro	**to grunt**	gruñir
		to fatten	cebar
91		**wild, savage**	salvaje
		carnivorous	carnicero, carnívoro
to bark	ladrar	**herbivorous**	herbívoro
canine	canino	**omnivorous**	omnívoro
watchful	vigilante	**quadruped**	el cuádrupedo
watchdog	el perro guardián	**biped**	el bípedo
pet	el animal doméstico	**mammal**	el mamífero
breed	la raza	**warm-blooded**	de sangre caliente
greyhound	el galgo		
alsatian	el pastor alemán	**96**	
terrapin	la tortuga de agua dulce	**predator**	el depredador
hamster	el hámster	**prey**	la presa
		lion	el león
92		**lioness**	la leona
aquarium	el acuario	**lion cub**	el cachorro de león
aquatic	acuático	**to roar**	bramar, rugir
horse	el caballo	**mane**	la melena
to neigh	relinchar	**tiger**	el tigre
stallion	el semental	**tigress**	la tigresa
mare	la yegua	**cheetah**	el leopardo cazador
colt	el potro		
donkey	el asno, el burro	**97**	
to bray	rebuznar	**leopard**	el leopardo
mule	el mulo	**lynx**	el lince
		mountain lion	el puma
93		**panther**	la pantera
male	el macho	**wolverine**	el carcayú
female	la hembra	**hyena**	la hiena
livestock	el ganado	**jackal**	el chacal
horn	el cuerno, el asta,	**carrion**	la carroña
	el cacho (*Lat Am*)	**jaguar**	el jaguar
paw	la pata	**tapir**	el tapir
hoof	la pezuña		
tail	el rabo, la cola	**98**	
flock	el rebaño	**buffalo**	el búfalo
cow	la vaca	**mongoose**	la mangosta
ox	el buey	**porcupine**	el puerco espín
		armadillo	el armadillo
94		**skunk**	la mofeta,
to low	mugir		el zorrillo (*Lat Am*)
bull	el toro	**sloth**	el perezoso
calf	el ternero	**rhinoceros**	el rinoceronte

hippopotamus	el hipopótamo	gorilla	el gorila
wolf	el lobo	monkey	el mono
pack	la manada	orang-utan	el orangután
		baboon	el mandril
99		chimpanzee	el chimpancé
bear	el oso		
to hibernate	invernar	**104**	
zebra	la cebra	gibbon	el gibón
bison	el bisonte	marsupial	el marsupial
to graze	apacentar	kangaroo	el canguro
pasture	el pasto	koala	la coala
wild boar	el jabalí	giant panda	el panda gigante
ferocious	feroz	invertebrate	el invertebrado
bristle	la cerda	exoskeleton	el dermatoesqueleto,
elephant	el elefante		el exoesqueleto
		insect	el insecto
100		to hum	zumbar
tusk	el comillo	humming	el zumbido
trunk	la trompa		
camel	el camello	**105**	
hump	la giba	antenna	la antena
dromedary	el dromedario	worm	el gusano
llama	la llama	to worm	serpentear
deer	el ciervo	earthworm	la lombriz
doe	la gama	tapeworm	la lombriz intestinal,
stag	el ciervo		tenia, solitaria
elk	el alce	parasite	el parásito
		beetle	el escarabajo
101		stag beetle	el ciervo volante
moose	el alce de Amérca	silkworm	el gusano de seda
antler	la cuerna, las astas	caterpillar	la oruga
fox	el zorro		
cunning	astuto	**106**	
craft, cunning	la astucia	chrysalis	la crisálida
hare	la liebre	metamorphosis	la metamorfosis
badger	el tejón	to metamorphose	metamorfosear
otter	la nutria	butterfly	la mariposa
dormouse	el lirón	moth	la mariposa nocturna,
shrew	la musaraña		polilla
		fly	la mosca
102		bluebottle	la moscarda
hedgehog	el erizo	spider	la araña
weasel	la comadreja	web	la telaraña
mink	el visón	to spin	devanar, hilar
beaver	el castor		
dam	la presa	**107**	
mole	el topo	wasp	la avispa
molehill	la topera	hornet	el avispón
mouse	el ratón	to sting	picar
mousetrap	la ratonera	sting	la picadura
		bee	la abeja
103		worker (bee, ant)	la obrera
rabbit	el conejo	bumblebee	el abejorro
hutch	la conejera	queen bee	la abeja madre
rat	la rata	beehive	la colmena
bat	el murciélago	apiary	el abejar
nocturnal	nocturno		
primate	el primate		

		antidote	el antídoto
108		poisonous	venenoso

108

apiarist	el apicultor
drone	el zángano
honey	la miel
honeycomb	el panal
grasshopper	el saltamontes
locust	la langosta
to infest	infestar
cricket	el grillo
glow-worm	la luciérnaga
ant	la hormiga

113

bird	el pájaro
aviary	la avería, la pajarera
ostrich	el avestruz
beak, bill	el pico
wing	el ala
to fly	volar
flight	el vuelo
flightless	incapaz de volar
to lay (eggs)	poner (huevos)
to nest	anidar

109

anthill	el hormiguero
colony	la colonia
to itch	hormiguear
itch	el hormigueo
termite	la termita
troublesome	molesto
to molest	molestar
mosquito	el mosquito
mosquito net	el mosquitero
malaria	la malaria

114

canary	el canario
robin redbreast	el petirrojo
chaffinch	el pinzón
nightingale	el ruiseñor
sparrow	el gorrión
swallow	la golondrina
lark	la alondra
cuckoo	el cuclillo
magpie	la urraca

110

flea	la pulga
earwig	la tijereta
praying mantis	la mantis religiosa
scorpion	el escorpión
snail	el caracol
slug	el limaco, la babosa
louse	el piojo
lousy	piojoso
centipede	el ciempiés
millipede	el milpiés

115

blackbird	el mirlo
crow	el cuervo
to caw	graznar
seagull	la gaviota
albatross	el albatros
cormorant	el cormorán
partridge	la perdiz
pheasant	el faisán
stork	la cigüeña
owl	el buho

111

reptile	el reptil
cold-blooded	de sangre fría
tortoise	la tortuga
turtle	la tortuga marina
crocodile	el cocodrilo
alligator	el caimán
serpent	la serpiente
snake	la culebra
slowworm	el lución
harmless	inofensivo

116

rooster	el gallo
cockcrow	el canto del gallo
to crow	cacarear
cock-a-doodle-do	quiquiriquí
hen	la gallina
feather	la pluma
to pluck	desplumar
chicken	el pollo
to brood	empollar
to breed	criar

112

crawl	arrastrarse
viper	la víbora
fang	el colmillo
python	el pitón
anaconda	la anaconda
rattlesnake	la serpiente de cascabel
cobra	la cobra
poison	el veneno

117

pigeon	la paloma
duck	el pato
goose	el ganso
swan	el cisne
parrot	el loro
toucan	el tucán
turkey	el pavo

peacock	el pavo real	shell	la concha
hummingbird	el colibrí	scale	la escama
bird of paradise	la ave del paraíso	squid	el calamar
		octopus	el pulpo
118		tentacle	el tentáculo
rapacious	rapaz	cuttlefish	la sepia
bird of prey	el ave de rapiña	crayfish	el ástaco
eagle	el águila f		
vulture	el buitre	**123**	
peregrine falcon	el halcón peregrino	lobster	la langosta
to swoop	abatirse	sea urchin	el erizo de mar
falcon	el halcón	sea horse	el caballito de mar
falconer	el halconero	starfish	la estrella de mar
falconry	la halconería	shellfish	el molusco
condor	el cóndor	oyster	la ostra
hawk	el halcón	shark	el tiburón
to hover (hawk)	cernerse	whale	la ballena
		killer whale	la orca
119		dolphin	el delfín
amphibious	anfibio		
amphibian	el anfibio	**124**	
frog	la rana	seal	la foca
bullfrog	la rana toro	sea lion	el león marino
tadpole	el renacuajo	walrus	la morsa
toad	el sapo	natural selection	la selección natural
salamander	la salamandra	survival of the fittest	la supervivencia de los
crustacean	el crustáceo		más aptos
crab	el cangrejo	evolution	la evolución
prawn	la gamba	to evolve	evolucionar
		zoology	la zoología
120		zoologist	el zoólogo m,
fish	el pez		la zoóloga f
goldfish	el pez de colores	zoo	el zoo
piranha	la piraña		
voracious	voraz	**125**	
carp	la carpa	habitat	el habitat
sturgeon	el esturión	extinct	extinto
caviar	el caviar	dinosaur	el dinosaurio
trout	la trucha	mammoth	el mamut
hake	la merluza	dodo	el dodó
herring	el arenque	yeti	el yeti
		mythical	mitíco
121		myth	el mito
sardine	la sardina	unicorn	el unicornio
skate	la raya	dragon	el dragón
cod	el bacalao		
eel	la anguila	**126**	
electric eel	la anguila eléctrica	to plant	plantar
elver	la angula	to transplant	trasplantar
salmon	el salmón	root	la raíz
school (fish)	el cardumen, el banco	stem	el vástago
coral	el coral	to take root	arraigar
coral reef	el arrecife de coral	to uproot	desarraigar
		radical	radical
122		tendril	el zarcillo
flipper	la aleta	stalk	el tallo
fin	la aleta	sap	la savia
gills	las agallas		

127

foliage	el follaje
leaf	la hoja
leafy	frondoso
to shed leaves	deshojarse
deciduous	de hoja caduca
evergreen	de hoja perenne
perennial	perenne
thorn	la espina
thorn tree	el espino
thorny	espinoso

128

weed	la mala hierba
to weed	desherbar
to thin	entresacar
thistle	el cardo
nettle	la ortiga
briar	la zarza
hemlock	la cicuta
deadly nightshade	la belladona
Venus flytrap	la atrapamoscas
rush	el junco

129

reed	la caña
epiphyte	el epifito
moss	el musgo
spider plant	la malambre
bud	el brote, el capullo
to bud	brotar
flower	la flor
to flower	florecer
blooming	florido
petal	el pétalo

130

to wither	marchitarse
withered	marchito
garland	la guirnalda
scent	la fragancia
garden	el jardín
gardener	el jardinero
landscape gardener	el jardinero paisajista
to water	regar
watering can	la regadera
irrigation	el riego

131

herb	la hierba (fina)
thyme	el tomillo
rosemary	el romero
sage	la salvia
parsley	el perejil
mint	la menta
tarragon	el dragoncillo, el tarragón, el estragón

coriander	el culantro
dill	el eneldo
watercress	el berro

132

balsam	el bálsamo
chicory	la escarola, achicoria
chive	el cebollino
mustard	la mostaza
basil	la albahaca
clover	el trébol
grass	la hierba
shrub	el arbusto
myrtle	el mirto
gorse	la aulaga, la árgoma

133

flowerbed	el arriate, la era
pansy	el pensamiento
primrose	la prímula
daisy	la margarita
anemone	la anemona
tulip	el tulipán
hyacinth	el jacinto
lily	el lirio
lily of the valley	el muguete
mignonette	la reseda

134

snowdrop	la campanilla blanca
crocus	el azafrán
carnation	el clavel
bluebell	la campanula
poppy	la amapola
cornflower	el alciano
buttercup	el botón de oro
daffodil	el narciso
forget-me-not	la no me olvides

135

foxglove	la dedalera
sunflower	el girasol
dandelion	el diente de león
snapdragon	la boca de dragón
marigold	la caléndula
orchid	la orquídea
bush	el arbusto
magnolia	la magnolia
fuchsia	la fucsia
rhododendron	el rododendro

136

rock plant	la planta rupestre
heather	el brezo
undergrowth	la maleza
scrub	el monte bajo
broom	la hiniesta
mallow	la malva

laurel	el laurel
privet	el ligustro
hedge	el seto
to enclose	cercar

137

vegetables	las hortalizas
kitchen garden	el huerto
mushroom	la seta
fungus	el hongo
harmful	nocivo
leek	el puerro
radish	el rábano
lettuce	la lechuga
celery	el apio
rhubarb	el ruibarbo

138

chard	la acelga
spinach	la espinaca
turnip	el nabo
potato	la patata
to peel	pelar
to scrape	raspar
husk	la vaina
to husk	desvainar
cabbage	la berza, la col
hedge	el seto

139

fruit	la fruta
fruit tree	el árbol frutal
to graft	injertar
graft	el injerto
to shake	sacudir
to prune	podar
pear tree	el peral
pear	la pera
apple tree	el manzano
cherry tree	el cerezo

140

cherry	la cereza
plum	la ciruela
plum tree	el ciruelo
prune	la ciruela seca
stone	el hueso
to stone	deshuesar
almond	la almendra
almond tree	el almendro
peach	el melocotón
peach tree	el melocotonero

141

apricot	el albaricoque
apricot tree	el albaricoquero
walnut	la nuez
walnut tree	el nogal

chestnut	la castaña
chestnut tree	el castaño
hazelnut	la avellana
hazelnut tree	el avellano
lemon	el limón
lemon tree	el limonero

142

orange	la naranja
orange tree	el naranjo
olive	la aceituna
olive tree	el olivo
date	el dátil
palm tree	la palmera, la palma
pomegranate	la granada
pomegranate tree	el granado
banana plant	el plátano
pineapple	el ananá, la piña (Lat Am)

143

coconut	el coco
coconut tree	el cocotero
sugar cane	la caña de azúcar
yam	la batata, el ñame
lychee	el lichi
kiwi	el kiwi
ripe	maduro
to ripen	madurar
juicy	suculento
strawberry	la fresa

144

strawberry plant	el fresal
medlar	la níspola
medlar tree	el níspero
raspberry	la frambuesa
raspberry bush	el frambueso
blackcurrant	la grosella
currant bush	el grosellero
gooseberry	la uva espina
grape	la uva
raisin	la pasa

145

vine	la vid
vineyard	la viña, el viñedo
vintner	el viñero
grape harvest	la vendimia
to gather grapes	vendimiar
press	la prensa
to press	prensar
forest trees	los árboles de bosque
wood	el bosque
jungle	la selva

146

woody	silvoso
wild, uncultivated	silvestre

ivy	la hiedra	pine	el pino
to climb	trepar	hop	el lúpulo
creeping	trepador	monkey puzzle	la araucaria
wisteria	la glicina	sycamore	el sicomoro
mistletoe	el muérdago	maple	el arce
berry	la baya	holly	el acebo
rosewood	el palosanto	alder	el aliso
juniper	el enebro	bamboo	el bambú
fern	el helecho	eucalyptus	el eucalipto

147

150

tree	el árbol	acacia	la acacia
bark	la corteza	rubber tree	el caucho
branch	la rama	mahogany	la caoba
twig	la ramita	ebony	el ébano
knot	el nudo	cedar	el cedro
tree ring	el anillo de árbol	cactus	el cactus
trunk	el tronco	cacao tree	el cacao
oak	el roble	giant sequoia	la secuoya gigante
acorn	la bellota	bonsai	el bonsai
holm oak	la encina	yew	el tejo

148

151

beech	el haya	weeping willow	el sauce llorón
ash	el fresno	azalea	la azalea
elm	el olmo	catkin	el amento
poplar	el álamo	spore	la espora
aspen	el álamo temblón	pollination	la polinización
lime	el tilo	to pollinate	polinizar
birch	el abedul	pollen	el polen
fir	el abeto	to fertilize	fecundar
conifer	la conífera	stock (species)	el alhelí
coniferous	conífero	hybrid	el híbrido

149

| cone | el cono |

The environment — El medio ambiente

152

		industrial waste	los residuos industriales
		toxic	tóxico
environmental	medioambiental	pollutant	el contaminante
environmentalist	el ambientalista *m*,	to pollute	contaminar
	la ambientalista *f*	consumerism	el consumismo
environmentalism	el ambientalismo	consumerist	consumista
pollution	la contaminación		
conserve	conservar	**154**	
conservation	la conservación	to consume	consumir
waste	el despilfarro	solar panel	el placa solar
to waste	despilfarrar	windmill	el molino
rubbish	la basura	wind energy	la energía eólica
rubbish tip	el vertedero	wave energy	la energía de las olas
		wildlife	la fauna
153		harmful	nocivo
sewage	las aguas residuales	atmosphere	la atmósfera
spill	el vertido	smog	la niebla tóxica, el smog
poisonous	venenoso	unleaded gas	la gasolina sin plomo
to poison	envenenar		

155

ecosystem	el ecosistema
ecology	la ecología
ecologist	el ecologista
acid rain	la lluvia ácida
deforestation	la deforestación
to deforest	deforestar
rainforest	la selva
underdeveloped	subdesarrollado
industrialized	industrializado
ozone layer	la capa de ozono

156

oil slick	la marea negra
oil spill	la fuga de petróleo
greenhouse effect	el efecto invernadero
to recycle	reciclar

recycling	el reciclaje
renewable	renovable
fossil fuels	los combustibles fósiles
resource	el recurso
landfill	el vertedero de basuras
to waste	despilfarrar

157

decibel	el decibel
to soundproof	insonorizar
radiation	la radiación
radioactive	radioactivo
nuclear energy	la energía nuclear
fallout	el polvillo radiactivo
reactor	el reactor
fission	la fisión
fusion	la fusión
leak	la fuga

The home — La casa

158

house	la casa
apartment block	el edificio de pisos, el edificio de apartamentos
to let	alquilar
tenant	el inquilino
housing	el alojamiento
to change	mudar
to move house	mudarse
landlord, owner	el dueño, el propietario
own	propio
ownership	la propiedad

159

country house	la casa de campo
farmhouse	el caserío, la quinta, la granja
villa	el chalet
cottage	la casita, la choza, la cabaña
chalet	el chalet
town house	la casa adosada
semidetached house	la casa pareada
country house	la casa solariega
mansion	la mansión
palace	el palacio

160

castle	el castillo
igloo	el iglú
teepee	el tipi
log cabin	la cabina de troncos, la cabaña de troncos
houseboat	el bote-vivienda
hut	la casilla
house trailer	la casa rodante

penthouse	la casa de azotea
lighthouse	el faro
shack	la casucha

161

building	el edificio, la construcción
to build	edificar, construir
building site	la obra
building contractor	el contratista
repair	reparar
solid	sólido
to destroy	destruir
to demolish	derribar, demoler
garage	el garaje
shed	el cobertizo

162

door	la puerta
doorknocker	la aldaba
to knock at the door	llamar a la puerta
doormat	el felpudo
doorbell	el timbre
threshold	el umbral
bolt	el cerrojo
plan	el plan
foundations	las fundaciones
to found	fundar

163

cement	el cemento
concrete	el hormigón
stone	la piedra
cornerstone	la piedra angular
antiquated	antiguo
modern	moderno
luxurious	lujoso
roomy	espacioso

whitewashed	blanqueado	staircase	la escalera
neglected	descuidado	upstairs	escalera arriba
		downstairs	escalera abajo
164		landing	el rellano
worm-eaten	carcomido		
moth-eaten	apollillado	**169**	
shanty	la chabola, la choza	ladder	la escala,
shantytown	la barriada		la escalera (*Lat Am*)
brick	el ladrillo	banisters	la barandilla
sand	la arena	elevator	el ascensor
slate	la pizarra	to go up	subir
gutter	la canaleta	to ascend	ascender
drainpipe	el caño de desagüe	ascent	la subida
step	el peldaño	to go down	bajar
		descent	la bajada
165		low	bajo
plaster	el yeso	storeys	los pisos
baseboard	el zócalo		
floor	el suelo	**170**	
wall	el muro	ground floor	el piso bajo, el sótano
partition wall	la pared	first floor	el primer piso
wood	la madera	cellar	la bodega
board	la tabla	tile	la teja
beam	la viga	roof	el tejado, el techo
to sustain	sostener	ceiling	el techo
to contain	contener	floor	el suelo
		to turn	girar
166		to return	volver
facade	la fachada	return	la vuelta
outside	el exterior		
inside	el interior	**171**	
window	la ventana	to give back	devolver
windowsill	el alféizar	chimney	la chimenea
venetian blind	la celosía	hearth	el hogar
shutter	la persiana	fire	el fuego
balcony	el balcón	spark	la chispa
windowpanes	los cristales	to sparkle	chispear
glass	el vidrio	flame	la llama
		ashes	las cenizas
167		stove	la estufa
veranda	la veranda, mirador	smoke	el humo
door	la puerta		
hinge	el gozne	**172**	
front door	el portal	to smoke (of fire)	humear
doorkeeper	el portero	to burn	quemar
to open	abrir	to blaze	arder
opening	la abertura	ardent	ardiente
entrance	la entrada	coal	el carbón
to enter	entrar (en)	charcoal	el carbón de leña
to go out	salir	embers	el rescoldo
		to scorch	abrasar
168		to glow	resplandecer
way out	la salida	firewood	la leña
lock	la cerradura		
to shut	cerrar	**173**	
key	la llave	woodcutter	el leñador
to lock	cerrar con llave	shovel	la pala
padlock	el candado	poker	el hurgón, el atizador

to poke	atizar
matches	los fósforos, las cerillas
wax	la cera
to light	encender
box	la caja
drawer	el cajón
chest of drawers	la cómoda

174

comfortable	cómodo
uncomfortable	incómodo
lighting	el alumbrado
dazzle, splendor	la lumbre
to light up	alumbrar
to put out, extinguish	apagar
light	la luz
lamp	la lámpara
lampshade	la pantalla
wick	la torcida, la mecha

175

candle	la candela
candlestick	el candelero
room	el cuarto, la habitación
to inhabit	habitar
inhabitant	el habitante
to reside	morar
residence	la morada
hall (as in church hall)	la sala
furniture	los muebles
a piece of furniture	un mueble

176

furnished	amueblado
corridor	el pasillo
hall, lobby	el vestíbulo
hall tree	el perchero
sitting room	la sala de estar
lounge	el salón
to serve	servir
guest	el invitado, el convidado
to invite	invitar
table	la mesa

177

seat	el asiento
to sit down	sentarse
to be sitting	estar sentado
cushion	el cojín
stool	el taburete
chair	la silla
armchair	el sillón, la butaca
rocking chair	la mecedora
sofa	el sofá
couch	el canapé
bench	el banco

178

bookcase	la estantería
bookshelf	el estante
book rest, lectern	el atril
library	la biblioteca
office, study	el despacho
writing desk	el escritorio, el bufete
to write	escribir
handwriting	la escritura
paper	el papel

179

tape recorder	el magnetófon, la grabadora (Lat Am)
compact disc (CD)	el disco compacto
hi-fi	la alta fidelidad
television	la televisión
video recorder	el aparato de video
radiator	el radiador
radio	la radio
ornament	un adorno
clock	el reloj
grandfather clock	el reloj de pie

180

tapestry	la tapicería
a tapestry	un tapiz
to hang	colgar
to take down	descolgar
wallpaper	el papel pintado
to wallpaper	empapelar
tile (decorative)	el azulejo
floor tile	la baldosa
tiling	el embaldosado
picture	el cuadro

181

frame	el marco
portrait	el retrato
photograph	la fotografía
photograph album	el álbum fotográfico
dining room	el comedor
to eat, dine	comer
meals	las comidas
breakfast	el desayuno
to breakfast	desayunar
lunch	el almuerzo

182

dinner	la comida
to lunch	almorzar
supper	la cena
to have supper	cenar
sideboard	el aparador
larder	la alacena
pantry	la despensa
shelf	el anaquel, la balda, la repisa

cup	la taza	to cover	cubrir
draining board	el escurridero	discover	descubrir
		spoon	la cuchara
183		teaspoon	la cucharita
		spoonful	la cucharada
sugar bowl	el azucarero		
coffeepot	la cafetera	**188**	
teapot	la tetera		
tray	la bandeja	fork	el tenedor
table service	el servicio de mesa	cutlery	la cuchillería
tablecloth	el mantel	set of cutlery	los cubiertos
napkin	la servilleta	knife	el cuchillo
plate	el plato	to carve (meat)	trinchar
saucer	el platillo	to cut	cortar
serving dish	la fuente	sharp	cortante
		bottle	la botella
184		cork	el corcho
microwave	el microondas	corkscrew	el sacacorchos
to microwave	calentar en microondas		
food mixer	el robot de cocina,	**189**	
	procesador de alminentos	to pull out	sacar
refrigerator	el refrigerador	to drink	beber
grater	el rallador	beverage, drink	la bebida
flowerpot	el florero	to toast (health)	brindar
glass (drinking)	el vaso, la copa	oven	el horno
glassware	la cristalería	utensils	los utensilios
to cook	cocinar	saucepan	la cacerola
to boil	cocer, hervir	frying pan	la sartén
		pot	el puchero, la olla
185		pitcher	el cántaro
gas cooker	la cocina de gas		
electric cooker	la cocina éléctrica	**190**	
grill	el grill, la parrilla	bucket	el cubo, el valde (*Lat Am*)
barbecue grill	la parrilla	to pour out	verter
saucepan	la cacerola	basket	el cesto
refuse, rubbish	la basura	to fill	llenar
washing machine	la lavadora	full	lleno
sewing machine	la máquina de coser	empty	vacío
washing powder	el detergente	to empty	vaciar
vacuum cleaner	la aspiradora	broom	la escoba
		to sweep	barrer
186		to rub, scrub	frotar
electricity	la electricidad		
fusebox	la caja de fusibles	**191**	
central heating	la calefacción central	to wash (dishes)	fregar, lavar (platos)
light bulb	la bombilla	bedroom	el dormitorio, la alcoba
switch	el interruptor	to go to bed	acostarse
to switch on	encender	bed	la cama
to switch off	apagar	bedspread	la cubrecama
plug	el enchufe	bunk bed	la litera
socket	la toma de corriente	cot	la cuna
air conditioning	el aire acondicionado	mattress	el colchón
		sheets	las sábanas
187		electric blanket	la manta eléctrica
lid, cover	la tapa		
to cover	tapar	**192**	
to uncover	destapar	bolster	el cabezal
to uncork	descorchar	pillow	la almohada
crockery	la vajilla	carpet	la alfombra

rug, mat	el tapete	nail clippers	el cortauñas
to wake	despertar	nail varnish	el esmalte de uñas
to awake	despertarse		
to get up early	madrugar	**197**	
the early hours	la madrugada	hairpin	la horquilla
drape	la cortina	hairdryer	el secador
attic	la buhardilla, el ático	hairspray	el fijador
		hairslide	el pasador
193		hairpiece	el postizo
alarm clock	el despertador	hairnet	la redecilla
hot-water bottle	la bolsa de agua caliente	to wipe	enjugar
nightcap	el gorro de dormir	to clean	limpiar
to sleepwalk	pasearse dormido,	clean	limpio
	caminar dormido	dirty	sucio
sleepwalker	el sonámbulo m,		
	la sonámbua f	**198**	
sleepwalking	el sonambulismo	mirror	el espejo
wardrobe	el guardaropa	basin	la palangana, la jofaina
to keep, preserve	guardar	jug	el jarro
dressing table	el tocador	razor (straight)	la navaja
screen	el biombo	smoke detector	el detector de humo
		razor blade	la hoja de afeitar
194		electric razor	la máquina de afeitar
bathroom	el cuarto de baño	shaving foam	la espuma de afeitar
bath	el baño	comb	el peine,
bathtub	la bañera		la peinilla (Lat Am)
to bathe	bañarse	to comb	peinarse
to wash	lavar		
to wash oneself	lavarse	**199**	
towel	la toalla	tools	las herramientas
washbasin	el lavabo	saw	la sierra
shower	la ducha	to saw	aserrar
to take a shower	ducharse	drill	el taladro
		drill bit	la broca
195		sawdust	el serrín,
faucet	el grifo		el aserrín (Lat Am)
to turn on (faucet)	abrir (el grifo)	hammer	el martillo
to turn off (faucet)	cerrar (el grifo)	nail	el clavo,
sponge	la esponja		la puntilla (Lat Am)
facecloth	el paño	to nail	clavar
toothbrush	el cepillo de dientes	spade	la pala
toothpaste	el dentífrico	pickax	el pico, la pica
toothpick	el palillo		
toilet paper	el papel higiénico	**200**	
toilet bowl	el inodoro	screw	el tornillo
		screwdriver	el destornillador
196		ax	la hacha
soap	el jabón	paint	la pintura
shampoo	el champú	paintbrush	la brocha
makeup	el maquillaje	to paint	pintar
face cream	la crema de belleza	glue	la cola
face pack	la mascarilla	to glue, stick	pegar
compact	la polvera	sander	la lijadora, la lija
lipstick	la barra de labios	sandpaper	el papel de lija
nail file	la lima de uñas		

Society — La sociedad

201

street	la calle
walk, promenade	el paseo
to go for a walk	pasear
passerby	el transeúnte
avenue	la avenida
kiosk	el quiosco
native of	natural de, oriundo de
compatriot	el compatriota
sidewalk	la acera
gutter	la cuneta

202

road	el camino
high road	la carretera
street lamp	el farol
traffic	la circulación
frequented	frecuentado
to frequent	frecuentar
pedestrian	el peatón
pedestrian area	la zona peatonal
square	la plaza
park	el parque

203

crossroads	el cruce
corner	la esquina, el rincón
alley	el callejón
quarter (of town)	el barrio
slum	el barrio bajo
outskirts	los alrededores
around	alrededor de
residential area	la ciudad dormitoria, la zona residencial (*Lat Am*)
premises	el local
warehouse	el almacén

204

cul-de-sac	el callejón sin salida
one-way	único sentido
traffic jam	el embotellamiento
rush hour	la hora punta, la hora pico (*Lat Am*)
crosswalk	el paso de cebra
shop window	el escaparate
poster	el cartel
bus stop	la parada de autobús
to queue	hacer cola
routine	la rutina

205

shop, store	la tienda
shopkeeper	el tendero
counter	el mostrador
to show	mostrar
inn	la posada, la fonda
innkeeper	el posadero
to stay	quedarse
lodging house	la pensión
guest	el huésped
board and lodgings	comida y alojamiento

206

profession	la profesión
trade	el oficio
mechanic	el mecánico
engineer	el ingeniero
spinner	el hilandero
workman	el obrero
operative	el operario
apprentice	el aprendiz
apprenticeship	el aprendizaje
day laborer	el jornalero

207

fireman	el bombero
fire station	la estación de bomberos
fire hydrant	la boca de riego
shop assistant	el dependiente
fishmonger	el pescadero
fish shop	la pescadería
street sweeper	el barrendero
library	la biblioteca
librarian	el bibliotecario
notary	el notario

208

police officer	el policía
police (force)	la policía
police station	la comisaría
secretary	el secretario
plumber	el plomero
jeweler	el joyero
stonecutter	el picapedrero
hatter	el sombrerero
hatter's shop	la sombrerería

209

carpenter	el carpintero
hardware dealer	el quincallero, el ferretero (*Lat Am*)
miller	el molinero
mill	el molino
to grind	moler
baker	el panadero
to knead	amasar
bakery	la panadería
barber	el peluquero
barber shop	la peluquería

210

tobacconist	el estanquero
tobacconist's	el estanco
junkman	el trapero
tailor	el sastre
tailor's	la sastrería
butcher	el carnicero
butcher's	la carnicería
milkman	el lechero
dairy	la lechería
glazier	el vidriero

211

bricklayer	el albañil
stationer	el papelero
stationery shop	la papelería
upholsterer	el tapicero
photographer	el fotógrafo
blacksmith	el herrero
horseshoe	la herradura
to shoe (horses)	herrar
shepherd	el pastor
cowboy	el vaquero

212

farm	la finca, la granja
to lease	arrendar
country estate	la hacienda
courtyard	el patio
well	el pozo
stable	la cuadra, el establo
hayfork	la horca
straw	la paja
hay	el heno
grain	el grano

213

agriculture	la agricultura
agricultural	agrícola
rustic	campestre
countryside	el campo
peasant	el campesino
farmer	el agricultor, el granjero
to cultivate	cultivar
cultivation	el cultivo
tillage	la labranza
to plow	arar

214

plow	el arado
furrow	el surco
fertilizer	el abono
to fertilize (crop)	abonar
fertile	fértil
barren	estéril
dry	árido
to sow	sembrar

seed	la semilla, la simiente
sowing	la siembra

215

to scatter	esparcir
to germinate	germinar
to mow	segar
reaper	el segador
combine harvester	la cosechadora
sickle	la hoz
scythe	la guadaña
to harvest	cosechar
harvest	la cosecha

216

rake	el rastrillo
to rake	rastrillar
spade	la pala
to dig	cavar
hoe	la azada, el azadón (Lat Am)
meadow	el prado
silage	el ensilaje
wheat	el trigo
oats	la avena
barley	la cebada
ear (of wheat)	la espiga

217

maize	la maíz
rice	el arroz
alfalfa, lucerne	la alfalfa
pile	el montón, la pila
to pile up	amontonar, apilar
tractor	el tractor
harrow	la rastra
baler	la empacadora
rotovator	el motocultor
milking machine	la ordeñadora

218

to milk	ordeñar
stockbreeder	el ganadero
stockbreeding	la ganadería
fodder, feed	el pienso, el forraje
to irrigate	regar
greenhouse	el invernadero
subsidy	el subsidio
grape harvest	la vendimia
grape picker	el vendimiador

219

commerce	el comercio
firm	la firma, la casa de comercio
branch	la sucursal
export	la exportación
import	la importación

company	la sociedad, la compañía	unemployed	desempleado, parado
partner	el socio	chief	el jefe
to associate	asociar	word processor	el procesador de palabras
businessman	el comerciante, el negociante	typist	el mecanógrafo m, la mecanógrafa f
business	el negocio	typing	la mecanografía
		shorthand	la taquigrafía

220

		shorthand typist	el taquimecanógrafo m, la taquimecanógrafa f
subject	el asunto		
to offer	ofrecer	audiotypist	el audiomecanógrafo m, la audiomecanógrafa f
offer	la oferta		
demand	la demanda		
account	la cuenta		

225

checking account	la cuenta corriente	director	el director
to settle	arreglar	managing director	el director gerente
order	el pedido	board of directors	la junta directiva
to cancel	anular	dividend	el dividendo
on credit	a crédito	takeover	la adquisición
		to list (shares)	cotizar

221

		asset	el activo
by installments	a plazos	liability	el pasivo
for cash	al contado	contract	el contrato
market	el mercado		
deposit	el depósito		

226

goods	la mercancía, los géneros	purchase	la compra
bargain	la ganga	to buy	comprar
second-hand	de ocasión, de segunda mano	to sell	vender
		sale	la venta
cheap	barato	buyer	el comprador
expensive	caro	seller	el vendedor
to bargain, haggle	regatear	wholesale	(al) por mayor
		retail	(al) por menor

222

		auction	la subasta
packaging	el embalaje	to bid	pujar
to pack up	embalar		
to unpack	desembalar		

227

to wrap	envolver	to auction	subastar
to unwrap	desenvolver	client	el cliente
transport	el transporte	clientele	la clientela
to transport	transportar	catalog	el catálogo
carriage	el porte	price	el precio
portable	portátil	quantity	la cantidad
delivery	la entrega	gross	bruto
		net	neto

223

		to cost	costar
to deliver	entregar	cost	el coste, el costo
to dispatch	despachar		
office	la oficina		

228

manager	el gerente m, la gerente f	free of charge	gratuito
accountant	el contable	to pay	pagar
clerk	el dependiente	wages	el sueldo, la paga
to employ	emplear	salary	el salario
employee	el empleado	payment	el pago
employment	el empleo	in advance	adelantado
		invoice	la factura

224

		checkout	la caja
employer	el empleador	cashier	el cajero m, la cajera f
unemployment	el desempleo, el paro	accounts	la contabilidad

229

balance sheet	el balance general
income	los ingresos
expenditure	los gastos
to spend	gastar
to acknowledge receipt	acusar recibo
to receive	recibir
reception	el recibimiento
profit	la ganancia, el beneficio
loss	la pérdida
loan	el préstamo

230

to borrow	pedir prestado
to lend	prestar
to prepare	preparar, aprestar
to obtain	lograr
creditor	el acreedor
debt	la deuda
debtor	el deudor
to get into debt	endeudarse
to be in debt	estar en deuda
bankruptcy	la quiebra

231

to go bankrupt	quebrar
banking	la banca
bank	el banco
bank bill	el billete de banco
banker	el banquero
bankbook	la libreta de ahorros
credit card	la tarjeta de crédito
bank account	la cuenta bancaria
savings bank	la caja de ahorros

232

to save (money)	economizar, ahorrar
capital	el capital
interest	el interés
income	la renta
stock exchange	la bolsa
share	la acción
shareholder	el accionista
exchange	el cambio
rate	el tipo
to exchange	cambiar

233

to be worth	valer
value	el valor
to value	valuar
discount	el descuento
to deduct	rebajar
to cash a check	cobrar un cheque
payable on sight	pagadero a la vista
signature	la firma
to sign	firmar

draft	el giro

234

postal order	el giro postal
to fall due	vencer
due	vencido
date	la fecha
to date	fechar
to inform	avisar
warning	el aviso
coin	la moneda
money	el dinero
mint	la casa de la moneda

235

post office	el correos
mail	el correo
by return of post	a vuelta de correo
postcard	la tarjeta (postal)
letter	la carta
postman	el cartero
mailbox	el buzón
collection	la recogida
to collect	recoger
delivery	el reparto

236

to distribute	distribuir
envelope	el sobre
postage	el franqueo, el porte
to frank	franquear
to seal	sellar
stamp	el sello, la estampilla
postmark	el matasellos
to stamp	timbrar
to pack	empaquetar
to unpack	desempaquetar

237

to register	certificar
to forward	expedir
sender	el remitente
addressee	el destinario
unknown	desconocido
to send	enviar
price list	la tarifa
courier	el mensajero
airmail	el correo aéreo
by airmail	por avión

238

pound sterling	la libra esterlina
franc	el franco
mark	el marco
dollar	el dólar
euro	el euro
shilling	el chelín
ingot	el lingote

foreign currencies	las divisas
speculation	la especulación
speculator	el especulador

239

wealthy	adinerado
wealth	la riqueza, el caudal
rich	rico
to get rich	enriquecerse
to acquire	adquirir
to possess	poseer
fortune	la fortuna
fortunate	afortunado
poverty	la pobreza
poor	pobre
necessity	la necesidad, el
menester	

240

to need	necesitar
misery	la miseria
miserable	miserable
beggar	el mendigo
to beg	mendigar
homeless	sin techo
squatter	el ocupa *m*, la ocupa *f*
eviction	el desalojo
malnourished	desnutrido
disadvantaged	desfavorecido

241

industry	la industria
industrialist	el industrial
manufacture	la manufactura, la fabricación
to manufacture	fabricar
factory	la fábrica
manufacturer	el fabricante
trademark	la marca (de fábrica)
machine	la máquina
machinery	la maquinaria
to undertake	emprender

242

enterprise	la empresa
expert	el perito
skill	la pericia
skillful	diestro, hábil
ability	la habilidad
clumsy	torpe
to keep busy	occuparse
busy	ocupado
lazy	perezoso
strike	la huelga

243

| striker | el huelguista |
| lock-out | el cierre patronal |

blackleg	el rompehuelgas, el esquirol
picket	el piquete
to go on strike	hacer huelga
labor union	el sindicato
labor unionist	el sindicalista *m*, la sindicalista *f*
labor/trades unionism	el sindicalismo
minimum wage	el salario mínimo
market economy	la economía de mercado

244

government	el gobierno
to govern	gobernar
politics	la política
political	político
politician	el político
fascist	facista
socialist	socialista
conservative	conservador
communist	comunista
democratic	democrático

245

monarchy	la monarquía
monarch	el monarca
king	el rey
queen	la reina
viceroy	el virrey
to reign	reinar
royal	real
crown	la corona
to crown	coronar
throne	el trono

246

court	la corte
courtier	el cortesano
chancellor	el canciller
rank	el rango
prince	el príncipe
princess	la princesa
title	el título
subject	el súbdito
emperor	el emperador
empress	la emperatriz

247

revolution	la revolución
guillotine	la guillotina
to guillotine	guillotinar
counterrevolution	la contrarrevolución
aristocracy	la aristocracia
aristocrat	el aristócrata *m*, la aristócrata *f*
confiscate	confiscar
confiscation	la confiscación
secular	secular

secularization	la secularización	law	la ley
		legal	legal
248		illegal	ilegal
republic	la república	to bequeath	legar
republican	republicano	beneficiary	el beneficiario
president	el presidente		
embassy	la embajada	**253**	
ambassador	el embajador	to make a will	testar
consul	el cónsul	will	el testamento
consulate	el consulado	heir	el heredero
state	el estado	heiress	la heredera
city state	la ciudad estado	to inherit	heredar
councillor	el consejero	inheritance	la herencia
		tribunal	el tribunal
249		to summons	citar, emplazar
council	el consejo	summons	la citación
to advise	aconsejar	appointment	la cita
to administer	administrar		
minister	el ministro	**254**	
ministry	el ministerio	trial	el proceso
cabinet	el gabinete	lawsuit	el pleito
deputy	el diputado	lawyer	el abogado
parliament	el parlamento,	to advocate	abogar
	las cortes (Spain)	to swear	jurar
senate	el senado	oath	el juramento
senator	el senador	witness	un testigo
		to bear witness	atestiguar
250		testimony	el testimonio
session	la sesión	evidence	las pruebas
to deliberate	deliberar		
dialog	el diálogo	**255**	
discuss	discutir	to infringe	infringir, transgredir
adopt	adoptar	indictment	la acusación
decree	el decreto	to plead	alegar
to decree	decretar	to accuse	acusar
to proclaim	proclamar	accused	el acusado, el reo
election	la elección	plaintiff	el demandante
referendum	el referéndum	defendant	el demandado
		to sue	demandar
251		fault	la culpa
to elect	elegir	jury	el jurado
to vote	votar		
vote	el voto	**256**	
town council	el ayuntamiento,	crime	el crimen
	el concejo (Lat Am)	murderer	el asesino
mayor	el alcalde	to murder	asesinar
bailiff	el alguacil	murder	el asesinato
justice	la justicia	to kill	matar
just	justo	suicide	el suicidio (act),
unjust	injusto		el suicida (person)
judge	el juez	to commit	cometer
		offense	el delito
252		thief	el ladrón
to judge	juzgar	bandit	el bandido
court	el juzgado		
judgement	el juicio	**257**	
injury	el perjuicio	theft	el robo
to protect	proteger	to steal	robar

traitor	el traidor	sergeant	el sargento
treason	la traición	corporal	el cabo
fraud	el fraude	rank	el grado
bigamy	la bigamía	general	el general
bigamist	el bígamo	colonel	el coronel
assault	la agresión, el asalto	captain	el capitán
blackmail	el chantaje	lieutenant	el teniente
to blackmail	chantajear	discipline	la disciplina
		order	la orden

258

263

rape	la violación	disorder	el desorden
rapist	el violador	infantry	la infantería
guilty	culpable	cavalry	la caballería
innocent	inocente	artillery	la artillería
defense	la defensa	cannon	el cañón
to defend	defender	grenade	la granada
to prohibit	prohibir	to explode	estallar
acquittal	la absolución	gunpowder	la pólvora
to acquit	absolver	ammunition	las municiones
		bomb	la bomba

259

264

sentence	el dictamen, la sentencia		
to sentence	sentenciar, fallar	to shell	bombardear
verdict	el fallo	bombardment	el bombardeo
fine	la multa	guard, watch	la guardia
conviction	la condena	sentry	el centinela
to condemn	condenar	garrison	la guarnición
prison	la cárcel, la prisión	barracks	el cuartel
to imprison	encarcelar	regiment	el regimiento
prisoner	el preso, el prisionero	detachment	el destacamento
to arrest	detener	reinforcement	el refuerzo
		battalion	el batallón

260

265

capital punishment	la pena de muerte	to equip	equipar
executioner	el verdugo	equipment	el equipaje
gallows	la horca	uniform	el uniforme
firing squad	el pelotón de fusilamiento	flak jacket	el chaleco antibala
electric chair	la silla eléctrica	firearm	el arma de fuego f
pardon	el indulto	to arm	armar
remission	la remisión	to disarm	desarmar
parole	la libertad condicional	to load	cargar
false imprisonment	la detención ilegal	to unload	descargar
self-defense	la defensa propia	to shoot	fusilar

261

266

army	el ejército	shot	el disparo
to drill	ejercitar	bullet	la bala
military	militar	bulletproof	antibalas
soldier	el soldado	cartridge	el cartucho
conscription	la conscripción	revolver	el revólver
conscript	el quinto	bayonet	la bayoneta
conscientious objector	el objetor de conciencia	dagger	el puñal
recruit	el recluta	tank	el tanque
flag	la bandera	armored car	el coche blindado, el carro blindado (Lat Am)
troops	la tropa		

262

officer	el oficial	barbed wire	el alambre de púas

267

cold war	la guerra fría
superpower	la superpotencia
rocket	el cohete
nuclear warhead	la ojiva nuclear
blockade	el bloqueo
holocaust	el holocausto
friendly fire	el fuego amigo
ceasefire	el alto el fuego
disarmament	el desarme
pacifism	el pacifismo

268

war	la guerra
warlike	guerrero
warrior	el guerrero
guerrilla	el guerrillero
guerrilla warfare	la guerrilla
campaign	la campaña
siege	el sitio
to besiege	sitiar
fort	el fuerte
spy	el espía

269

attack	el ataque
to attack	atacar
assault	asaltar
ambush	la emboscada
to surrender	rendirse
surrender	la rendición
encounter	el encuentro
to meet	encontrar
fight	el combate
to fight	combatir, pelear

270

combatant	el combatiente
exploit	la hazaña
battlefield	el campo de batalla
trench	la trinchera
to repel	rechazar
retreat	la retirada
flight	la fuga, la huida
to flee	huir
defeat	la derrota
to defeat	derrotar

271

to pursue	perseguir
pursuit	el perseguimiento
to conquer	vencer
victor	el vencedor
vanquished	el vencido
armistice	el armisticio
treaty	el tratado
peace	la paz

captivity	el cautiverio
to escape	escaparse, fugarse

272

to encamp	acampar
encampment	el campamento
to maneuvre	maniobrar
maneuvre	la maniobra
wounded	herido
hero	el héroe
heroine	la heroína
medal	la medalla
pension	la pensión
war memorial	el monumento a los caídos

273

navy	la marina
sailor	el marino, el marinero
admiral	el almirante
squadron	la escuadra
fleet	la flota, la armada
to float	flotar
to sail	navegar
navigator	el navegante
warship	el buque de guerra
battleship	el acorazado

274

aircraft carrier	el portaaviones
fighter plane	el avión de caza, el caza
destroyer	el destructor
minesweeper	el dragaminas
submarine	el submarino
airdrome	el aeródromo
spotter plane	el avión observador
air raid	el ataque aéreo
to bomb	bombardear
parachute	el paracaídas

275

parachutist	el paracaidista
surface-to-air missile	el misil tierra-aire
helicopter	el helicóptero
to bring down	derribar
anti-aircraft gun	el cañón antiaéreo
bomb shelter	el refugio antiaéreo
bomb disposal	la neutralización de bombas
bomber (plane)	el bombardero
to explode	explotar
explosion	la explosión

276

religion	la religión
religious	religioso
God	Dios
god	el dios
goddess	la diosa

monk	el fraile
nun	la monja
divine	divino
omnipotent	omnipotente
savior	el salvador

277

safe	salvo
pagan	pagano
Christianity	el cristianismo
Christian	cristiano
catholic	católico
Catholicism	el catolicismo
Protestantism	el protestantismo
protestant	protestante
Calvinism	el calvinismo
Calvinist	calvinista

278

Presbyterian	presbiteriano
Mormonism	el mormonismo
Mormon	mormón
Bible	la biblia
Koran	el Corán
Islam	el Islam
Muslim	mahometano
Hindu	hindú
Hinduism	el hinduismo
Buddhist	budista

279

Buddhism	el budismo
Jewish	judío
Judaism	el judaísmo
Rastafarian	rastafariano
scientology	la cientología
scientologist	cientólogo
to convert	convertir
sect	la secta
animism	el animismo
voodoo	el vudú

280

witch doctor	el hechicero
atheist	ateo
atheism	el ateísmo
agnostic	agnóstico
agnosticism	el agnosticismo
heretic	el hereje
heresy	la herejía
fundamentalist	fundamentalista
fundamentalism	el fundamentalismo
to believe	creer

281

believer	el creyente
belief	la creencia

faith	la fe
church	la iglesia
chapel	la capilla
chalice	el cáliz
altar	el altar
mass	la misa
blessing	la bendición
to bless	bendecir

282

to curse	maldecir
clergy	el clero
clergyman	el clérigo
to preach	predicar
preacher	el predicador
sermon	el sermón
apostle	el apóstol
angel	el ángel
holy	santo
saint	el santo *m*, la santa *f*

283

blessed	beato
sacred	sagrado
devil	el diablo
devilish	diabólico
cult	el culto
solemn	solemne
prayer	el rezo
to pray	rezar
devout	devoto
fervent	fervoroso

284

sin	el pecado
to sin	pecar
sinner	el pecador
repentant	penitente
to baptize	bautizar
pope	el papa
cardinal	el cardenal
bishop	el obispo
archbishop	el arzobispo
priest	el cura, el sacerdote

285

parish	la parroquia
abbot	el abad
abbess	la abadesa
abbey	la abadía
convent	el convento
monastery	el monasterio
minister	el pastor
pilgrim	el peregrino
pilgrimage	la peregrinación
to celebrate	celebrar

The intellect and emotions — El intelecto y las emociones

286

mind	la mente, el ánimo
thought	el pensamiento
to think of	pensar en
to meditate	meditar
to remember	acordarse de
to agree with	acordarse con, estar de acuerdo con
agreement	el acuerdo
soul	el alma f
to occur, come to mind	ocurrirse
recollection	el recuerdo

287

renown	la buena fama
to perceive	percibir
to understand	entender
understanding	el entendimiento
intelligence	la inteligencia
intelligent	inteligente
clever	listo
stupid	estúpido
stupidity	la estúpidez
worthy	digno

288

unworthy	indigno
reason	la razón
reasonable	razonable
unreasonable	desrazonable, irracional
to reason	razonar
to discuss	discutir
to convince	convencer
opinion	la opinión
to affirm	afirmar
to deny	negar

289

certainty	la certeza, la certidumbre
certain	cierto
uncertain	incierto
sure	seguro
unsure	inseguro
security	la seguridad
to risk	arriesgar
doubt	la duda
doubtful	dudoso
mistake	la equivocación

290

to make a mistake	equivocarse
suspicion	la sospecha
to suspect	sospechar
suspicious	sospechoso

desire	el deseo
to desire	desear
to grant	conceder
will	la voluntad
to decide	decidir
undecided	indeciso

291

to hesitate	vacilar
capable	capaz
incapable	incapaz
capability	la capacidad
talent	el talento
disposition, temper	el genio
character	el carácter
to rejoice	alegrarse
cheerfulness	la alegría
happiness	la felicidad

292

cheerful	alegre
sad	triste
sadness	la tristeza
to grieve	afligir
enjoyment	el goce
happy	feliz, dichoso
unhappy	infeliz
unfortunate	desdichado
contented	contento
discontented	descontento

293

discontent	el disgusto
displeased	disgustado
pleasure	el placer
to please	agradar
to displease	desagradar
pain	la pena
painful	penoso
sigh	el suspiro
to sigh	suspirar
to complain	quejarse

294

complaint	la queja
to protest	protestar
depressed	abatido, deprimido
to despair	desesperar
despair	la desesperación
hope	la esperanza
to hope	esperar, aguardar
expectation	la espera
consolation	el consuelo
to comfort	confortar

295

consoling	consolador
calm	la calma
calm	calmoso
restless	inquieto
anxiety	la inquietud
fear	el miedo
to fear	temer
to be afraid	tener miedo
to frighten	asustar
to be frightened	asustarse

296

terror	el terror
to terrify	aterrar, aterrorizar
frightful	espantoso
to astonish	asombrar
astonishment	el asombro
to encourage	animar
to discourage	desanimar
conscience	la conciencia
scruple	el escrúpulo
remorse	el remordimiento

297

repentance	el arrepentimiento
to repent	arrepentirse
to regret, feel	sentir
sentiment	el sentimiento
consent	el consentimiento
to consent	consentir
mercy	la misericordia
charitable	caritativo
pity	la lástima
piety	la piedad

298

impiety	la impiedad
friendly	simpático
unfriendly	antipático
favor	el favor
to favor	favorecer
favorable	favorable
unfavorable	desfavorable
confidence	la confianza
trustful	confiado
mistrustful	desconfiado

299

to trust	confiar (en)
friendship	la amistad
friendly	amistoso
kind	amable
friend	el amigo
enemy	el enemigo
hatred	el odio
to hate	odiar

hateful	odioso
contempt	el desdén, el desprecio

300

to despise	despreciar
to get angry	enfadarse, molestarse
quarrel	la riña, la pelea
to quarrel	reñir, pelear
to reconcile	reconciliar
quality	la cualidad
virtue	la virtud
virtuous	virtuoso
vice	el vicio
vicious	vicioso

301

addicted	adicto
defect	el defecto
fault	la falta
to lack, to fail	faltar
custom	la costumbre
to be necessary	hacer falta
to become accustomed	acostumbrarse
habit	el hábito
to boast about	jactarse de
moderate	moderado

302

goodness	la bondad
kind	bondadoso
wickedness	la maldad
gratitude	el agradecimiento
ungrateful	ingrato
ingratitude	la ingratitud
grateful	agradecido
ungrateful	desagradecido
to thank	agradecer
thanks, thank you	gracias

303

honesty	la honradez
honorable	honrado, honorable
to honor	honrar
to dishonor	deshonrar
honor	la honra, el honor
dishonor	la deshonra, el deshonor
honest	honesto
dishonest	deshonesto

304

modesty	el pudor
shame	la vergüenza
shameful	vergonzoso
to be ashamed	avergonzarse
audacity	la audacia
audacious	audaz
daring	atrevido
boldness	el atrevimiento

fearless	intrépido	offense	la ofensa
to dare	osar, atreverse		

309

305

reckless	temerario	to offend	ofender, agraviar
timid	tímido	to insult	insultar, injuriar
timidity	la timidez	excuse	la excusa
rude	grosero	to excuse	excusar
rudeness	la grosería	humble	humilde
courtesy	la cortesía	humility	la humildad
polite	cortés	pride	el orgullo
impolite	descortés	proud	orgulloso
villain	el pícaro	vain	vanidoso
envy	la envidia	to be obstinate	obstinarse

310

306

loyal	leal	obstinacy	la obstinación
disloyal	desleal	whim	el capricho
generous	generoso	sober	sobrio
generosity	la generosidad	sobriety	la sobriedad
selfishness	el egoísmo	sensual	sensual
selfish	egoísta	sensuality	la sensualidad
egoist	el egoísta	hedonistic	hedonista
greed	la avaricia	lust	la lujuria
stingy	avaro, tacaño	revenge	la venganza
miser	el avaro	to revenge	vengar

311

307

truth	la verdad	vindictive	vengativo
true	verdadero	jealous	celoso
to lie	mentir	temperamental	temperamental
liar	el mentiroso	affectionate	cariñoso
lie	la mentira, el embuste	imaginative	imaginativo
hypocritical	hipócrita	extrovert	extrovertido
hypocrite	el hipócrita	introvert	introvertido
frank	franco	demanding	exigente
frankness	la franqueza	sincere	sincero
accuracy	la exactitud	sincerity	la sinceridad

312

308

inaccuracy	la inexactitud	optimistic	optimista
punctuality	la puntualidad	optimist	el optimista
faithfulness	la fidelidad	pessimistic	pesimista
unfaithfulness	la infidelidad	pessimist	el pesimista
faithful	fiel	perceptive	perceptivo
unfaithful	infiel	cautious	cauteloso
coward	el cobarde	sensitive	sensible
cowardice	la cobardía	sensitivity	la sensibilidad
anger	la ira, la cólera	sensible	sensato
		common sense	el sentido común

Education and learning — La educación y los conocimientos

313

to educate	educar
educational	educacional
educationalist	el educador *m*, la educadora *f*
adult education	la educación de adultos
mixed education	la educación mixta
grade school	la escuela primaria
to teach	enseñar
teacher	el profesor
tutor	el preceptor, el tutor
college	el instituto, el colegio

314

university	la universidad
class	la clase
pupil	el alumno
boarder	el interno
day pupil	el externo
to study	estudiar
student	el estudiante
grant	la beca
scholarship holder	el becario
desk	el pupitre

315

chalkboard	la pizarra
chalk	la tiza
pencil	el lápiz
ink	la tinta
pen	el bolígrafo, la pluma
ruler	la regla
line	la línea
exercise book	el cuaderno
to bind (books)	encuadernar
page	la página

316

to fold	plegar, doblar
sheet of paper	la hoja de papel
cover (book)	la cubierta
work	el trabajo
to work	trabajar
hard-working	trabajador
studious	aplicado
lesson	la lección
to learn	aprender
to forget	olvidar

317

forgetful	olvidadizo
forgetfulness	el olvido
absentminded	distraído
course	el curso

attention	la atención
to be attentive	atender
attentive	atento
inattentive	desatento
to explain	explicar
explanation	la explicación

318

task	la tarea
theme	el tema
thematic	temático
exercise	el ejercicio
to exercise	ejercitarse, hacer ejercicios
practice	la práctica
to practice	practicar
easy	fácil
easiness	la facilidad
difficult	difícil

319

difficulty	la dificultad
progress	el progreso
homework	los deberes, las tareas (*Lat Am*)
must	deber
to owe	deber
examination	el examen
to sit an examination	presentarse a un examen
to pass an examination	aprobar un examen
to copy	copiar
to swot	empollar, estudiar duro

320

to examine	examinar
examiner	el examinador
proof	la prueba, el examen (*Lat Am*)
to try	probar
to blame	reprobar
blame	la reprobación
approve	aprobar
disapprove	desaprobar
mark	la nota
to note	anotar

321

annotation	la anotación
remarkable	notable
prize	el premio
to reward	premiar
to praise	elogiar
praise	el elogio, la alabanza
vacation	las vacaciones
vacancy	la vacante

conduct	la conducta	fixed	fijo
to behave	comportarse	to fix	fijar
		to join	juntar
322		together	junto con
effort	el esfuerzo	join	la juntura, la articulación
to endeavor	esforzarse		
to try	procurar, intentar	**327**	
obedience	la obediencia	to correspond	corresponder
disobedience	la desobediencia	correspondence	la correspondencia
obedient	obediente	sentence	la frase
disobedient	desobediente	language	el idioma
to obey	obedecer	idiomatic	idiomático
to disobey	desobedecer	idiom	el modismo
laziness	la pereza	speech	el habla
		talkative	hablador
323		voice	la voz
strict	severo	word	la palabra
severity	la severidad		
threat	la amenaza	**328**	
to threaten	amenazar	to express	expresar
punishment	el castigo	expressive	expresivo
to punish	castigar	vocabulary	el vocabulario
to deserve	merecer	dictionary	el diccionario
grammar	la gramática	letter	la letra, la carta
to indicate	indicar	speech	el discurso
indication	la indicación	lecture	la conferencia
		lecturer	el conferenciante, el conferencista
324		orator	el orador
to point out	señalar	eloquence	la elocuencia
spelling	la ortografía		
to spell	deletrear	**329**	
period	el punto	eloquent	elocuente
colon	los dos puntos	elocution	la elocución
semicolon	el punto y coma	to converse	conversar
comma	la coma	conversation	la conversación
question mark	el signo de interrogación	to understand	comprender
exclamation point	el signo de admiración	to pronounce	pronunciar
to note down	apuntar	to correct	corregir
		example	el ejemplo
325		meaning	la significación
to ask (question)	preguntar	to mean	significar, querer decir
to ask for	pedir		
to answer	contestar, responder	**330**	
answer	la contestación, la respuesta	translation	la traducción
to admire	admirar	to translate	traducir
admiration	la admiración	translator	el traductor
to exclaim	exclamar	interpreter	el intérprete
article	el artículo	to interpret	interpretar
noun	el sustantivo	interpretative	interpretativo
to name	nombrar	interpretation	la interpretación
		to imagine	imaginar
326		imagination	la imaginación
appointment	el nombramiento		
to call	llamar	**331**	
to be called	llamarse	idea	la idea
reference	la referencia	essay	el ensayo, la composición
to relate to	referirse a	essayist	el ensayista

thesis	la tesis
doctorate	el doctorado
to develop	desarrollar
to roll up	arrollar, enrollar
roll	el rollo
object	el objeto
describe	describir

332

description	la descripción
fable	la fábula
drama	el drama
comedy	la comedia
comical	cómico
chapter	el capítulo
to interest	interesar
interesting	interesante
attractive	atractivo
to attract	atraer

333

to publish	publicar, editar
to print	imprimir
printer	el impresor
printing	la impresión
newspaper	el periódico, el diario
journalist	el periodista
magazine	la revista
news	las noticias
to announce	anunciar
advertisement	el anuncio, el aviso (*Lat Am*)

334

history	la historia
historian	el historiador
the Stone Age	la Edad de Piedra
the Bronze Age	la Edad de Bronce
the Iron Age	la Edad de Hierro
the Dark Ages	las Edades Bárbaras, el Oscurantismo
the Middle Ages	la Edad Media
archeology	la arqueología
archeologist	el arqueólogo
to excavate	excavar

335

carbon dating	la datación por la carbono catorce
event	el suceso
to happen	suceder, acontecer
to civilize	civilizar
civilization	la civilización
knight	el caballero
chivalry	la caballerosidad
explorer	el explorador
to explore	explorar
discovery	el descubrimiento

336

to discover	descubrir
pirate	el pirata
piracy	la piratería
treasure	el tesoro
conquest	la conquista
conqueror	el conquistador
to conquer	conquistar
empire	el imperio
imperial	imperial
slave	el esclavo

337

emancipation	la emancipación
to emancipate	emancipar
destiny	el destino
to destine	destinar
power	el poder, la potencia
powerful	poderoso
to be able, can	poder
slavery	la esclavitud
to free	liberar
reformation	la reforma

338

liberator	el libertador
nationalism	el nacionalismo
nationalist	el nacionalista
alliance	la alianza
to ally	aliar
ally	el aliado
to enlarge	ampliar
increase	el aumento
to increase	aumentar
to diminish	disminuir

339

decline	la decadencia
to decay	decaer
to decline	declinar
renowned	célebre
to disturb	turbar
to emigrate	emigrar
emigrant	el emigrante
rebel	el rebelde
rebellion	la rebelión
rising	la sublevación
independence	la independencia

340

geography	la geografía
map	el mapa
North Pole	el Polo Norte
South Pole	el Polo Sur
north	el norte
south	el sur
east	el este

west	el oeste	country	el país
compass	la brújula	compatriot	el paisano
magnetic north	el polo magnético, el norte magnético	**342**	
		citizen	el ciudadano
341		city	la ciudad
distant	lejano, distante	population	la población
distance	la distancia	to people	poblar
near	cercano	populous	poblado
to approach	acercarse	village	el pueblo, la aldea
neighbor	el vecino	people	la gente; el pueblo
to determine	determinar	province	la provincia
limit	el límite	provincial	provincial, provinciano
region	la región, la comarca	place	el lugar

Places — Los lugares

		Swiss	suizo
343		Holland	Holanda
Africa	el África	Dutch	holandés
African	africano	Portugal	Portugal
North America	la América del Norte	Portuguese	portugués
North American	norteamericano	Belgium	Bélgica
South America	Sudamérica, la América del Sur	Belgian	belga
		Great Britain	la Gran Bretaña
South American	sudamericano	British Isles	las Islas Británicas
Central America	Centroamérica, la América Central	**347**	
Central American	centroamericano	United Kingdom	el Reino Unido
Australia	Australia	British	británico
Australian	australiano	England	Inglaterra
		English	inglés
344		Scotland	Escocia
Europe	Europa	Scottish	escocés
European	europeo	Wales	Gales
Arctic	el Ártico	Welsh	galés
Antarctica	la Antártida	Northern Ireland	Irlanda del Norte
Oceania	la Oceanía	Northern Irish	norirlandés
Oceanian	oceánico		
Asia	Asia	**348**	
Asian	asiático	Ireland	Irlanda
New Zealand	Nueva Zelanda	Irish	irlandés
New Zealander	neozelandés	France	Francia
		French	francés
345		Austria	Austria
Spain	España	Austrian	austriaco
Spanish	español	Scandinavia	Escandinavia
Germany	Alemania	Scandinavian	escandinavo
German	alemán	Iceland	Islandia
Italy	Italia	Icelandic	islandés
Italian	italiano		
Greece	Grecia	**349**	
Greek	griego	Greenland	Groenlandia
Russia	Rusia	Greenlander	groenlandés
Russian	ruso	Sweden	Suecia
		Swedish	sueco
346		Norway	Noruega
Switzerland	Suiza	Norwegian	noruego

Finland	Finlandia
Finnish	finlandés
Denmark	Dinamarca
Danish	danés

350

Bavaria	Baviera
Bavarian	bávaro
Saxony	Sajonia
Saxon	sajón
Alsace	Alsacia
Alsatian	alsaciano
Lorraine	Lorena
Dordogne	Dordoña
Auvergne	Auvernia
Provence	Provenza

351

(Adjectival forms given with the city names below describe both the city and its inhabitants, e.g. *el londinense – the Londoner.*)

London	Londres
London adj	londinense
Paris	París
Parisian adj	parisiense, parisino
Madrid	Madrid
Madrid adj	madrileño
Edinburgh	Edinburgo
The Hague	La Haya

352

Toulouse	Tolosa
Milan	Milano
Lisbon	Lisboa
Lisbon adj	lisbonense
Bordeaux	Burdeos
Bordeaux adj	bordelés
Lyons	Lión
Lyons adj	lionés
Marseilles	Marsella
Marseilles adj	marsellés

353

Rome	Roma
Roman adj	romano
Venice	Venecia
Venetian adj	veneciano
Naples	Nápoles
Neapolitan adj	napolitano
Florence	Florencia
Florentine adj	florentino
Turin	Turín
Cologne	Colonia

354

Hamburg	Hamburgo
Hanover	Hanovre
Basle	Basilea

Vienna	Viena
Viennese	vienés
Antwerp	Amberes
Berlin	Berlín
Berlin adj	berlinés
Geneva	Ginebra
Geneva adj	ginebrino

355

Athens	Atenas
Brussels	Bruselas
Strasbourg	Estrasburgo
Bruges	Brujas
Moscow	Moscú
Muscovite adj	moscovita
St Petersburg	San Petersburgo
Warsaw	Varsovia
Prague	Praga
Budapest	Budapest

356

Stockholm	Estocolmo
Oslo	Oslo
Copenhagen	Copenhague
New York	Nueva York
New York adj	neoyorquino
Havana	La Habana
Cairo	el Cairo
Cape Town	Ciudad del Cabo
Beijing	Pekín
Mexico City	Ciudad de México

357

Poland	Polonia
Polish adj	polaco
Czech Republic	la República Checa
Czech adj	checo
Slovakia	Eslovaquia
Slovak adj	eslovaco
Slovenia	Eslovenia
Slovene adj	esloveno
Croatia	Croacia
Croatian adj	croata

358

Hungary	Hungría
Hungarian adj	húngaro
Bosnia	Bosnia
Bosnian adj	bosnio
Serbia	Serbia
Serbian adj	serbio
Albania	Albania
Albanian adj	albanés
Romania	Rumania
Romanian adj	rumano

359

Bulgaria	Bulgaria

Bulgarian *adj*	búlgaro
Macedonia	Macedonia
Macedonian *adj*	macedónico
Moldova	Moldavia
Moldovan *adj*	moldavo
Belarus	Bielorrusia
Belorussian *adj*	bielorruso
Ukraine	Ucrania
Ukrainian *adj*	ucranio

360

Estonia	Estonia
Estonian *adj*	estonio
Latvia	Latvia
Latvian *adj*	latvio
Lithuania	Lituania
Lithuanian *adj*	lituano
Armenia	Armenia
Armenian *adj*	armenio
Azerbaijan	Azerbaiyán
Azerbaijani *adj*	Azerbaiyaní

361

Afghanistan	Afganistán
Afghan *adj*	afgano
Georgia	Georgia
Georgian *adj*	georgiano
Siberia	Siberia
Siberian *adj*	siberiano
Turkey	Turquía
Turkish *adj*	turco
Arabia	Arabia
Arab *adj*	árabe

362

Iran	Irán
Iranian *adj*	iraní
Iraq	Irak
Iraqui *adj*	iraquí
Morocco	Marruecos
Moroccan *adj*	marroquí
Egypt	Egipto
Egyptian *adj*	egipcio
China	China
Chinese *adj*	chino

363

India	la India
Indian *adj*	indio
Paksistan	Pakistán
Pakistani *adj*	pakistaní
Japan	el Japón
Japanese *adj*	japonés
Ghana	Ghana
Ghanaian *adj*	ghaneano
Nigeria	Nigeria
Nigerian *adj*	nigeriano

364

Algeria	Argelia
Algerian *adj*	argelino
Tunisia	Túnez
Tunisian *adj*	tunecino
South Africa	Sudáfrica
South African *adj*	sudafricano
Israel	Israel
Israeli *adj*	israelí
Palestine	Palestina
Palestinian *adj*	palestino

365

Castile	Castilla
Castilian *adj*	castellano
Andalusia	Andalucía
Andalusian *adj*	andaluz
Catalonia	Cataluña
Catalan *adj*	catalán
Galicia	Galicia
Galician *adj*	gallego
Basque Country	el País Vasco
Basque *adj*	vasco

366

United States	(Los) Estados Unidos
North American *adj*	estadounidense
Canada	el Canadá
Canadian *adj*	canadiense
Mexico	México
Mexican *adj*	mexicano
Colombia	Colombia
Colombian *adj*	colombiano
Peru	el Perú
Peruvian *adj*	peruano

367

Brazil	el Brasil
Brazilian *adj*	brasileño
Chile	Chile
Chilean *adj*	chileno
Argentina	Argentina
Argentinian *adj*	argentino
Uruguay	el Uruguay
Uruguayan *adj*	uruguayo
Bolivia	Bolivia
Bolivian *adj*	boliviano

368

Pyrenees	los Pirineos
Alps	los Alpes
Atlas Mountains	los Atlas
Dolomites	las Dolomitas
Carpathians	los Montes Cárpatos
Andes	los Andes
Himalayas	el Himalaya
Mont Blanc	el Monte Blanco

| Table Mountain | el Monte de la Mesa | Caribbean | el Mar Caribe |
| Everest | el Everest | | |

371

369

		Baltic Sea	el Mar Báltico
Amazon	el Amazonas	English Channel	la Mancha
Nile	el Nilo	Bay of Biscay	el Golfo de Vizcaya
Rhine	el Rin	West Indies	las Antillas
Rhône	el Ródano	Canaries	las Canarias
Tagus	el Tajo	The Philippines	las Filipinas
Danube	el Danubio	Balearic Islands	las Islas Baleares
Thames	el Támesis	Sicily	Sicilia
Seine	el Sena	Sardinia	Cerdeña
Loire	el Loira	Corsica	Córcega
Ebro	el Ebro		

372

370

		Corsican adj	corso
Atlantic	el Atlántico	Rhodes	Rodas
Pacific	el Pacífico	Crete	Creta
Arctic Ocean	el Océano Glacial Ártico	Cretan adj	cretense
Indian Ocean	el Océano Índico	Cyprus	Chipre
Antarctic Ocean	el Océano Antártico	Cypriot adj	chipriota
Mediterranean	el Mediterráneo	Dardanelles	los Dardanelos
North Sea	el Mar del Norte	Bosphorus	el Bósforo
Black Sea	el Mar Negro	Scilly Isles	las Sorlingas
Red Sea	el Mar Rojo	Falkland Islands	las Malvinas

Science — La ciencia

		mile	la milla
373		arithmetic	la aritmética
weights	las pesas	mathematics	la matemática
weight	el peso	to calculate	calcular
to weigh	pesar	to count	contar
heavy	pesado	number	el número
light	ligero		
scales	la balanza	**376**	
to measure	medir	figure	la cifra
measure	la medida	zero	el cero
to compare	comparar	addition	la adición
comparison	la comparación	to add	adicionar, sumar
		subtraction	la sustracción
374		remainder	la resta
to contain	contener	equal	igual
contents	el contenido	equality	la igualdad
metric system	el sistema métrico	to multiply	multiplicar
meter	el metro	product	el producto
centimeter	el centímetro		
millimeter	el milímetro	**377**	
gram	el gramo	to produce	producir
kilogram	el kilogramo	producer	el productor
liter	el litro	to divide	dividir, partir
hectare	la hectárea	part	la parte
		fraction	la fracción
375		half	la mitad
kilometer	el kilómetro	third	el tercio
ton	la tonelada	quarter	el cuarto
inch	la pulgada	dozen	la docena
foot	el pie	double	doble

378

triple	triple
geometry	la geometría
algebra	el álgebra
space	el espacio
spacious	espacioso
parallel	paralelo
perpendicular	perpendicular
horizontal	horizontal
horizon	el horizonte
right angle	el ángulo recto

379

triangle	el triángulo
square	el cuadrado
curved	curvo
straight	recto
circumference	la circunferencia
circle	el círculo
center	el centro
diameter	el diámetro
problem	el problema
correct	correcto

380

incorrect	incorrecto
wrong	falso
simple	sencillo
to complicate	complicar
to demonstrate	demostrar
to solve	resolver
result	el resultado
to result	resultar
physics	la física
physical	físico

381

matter	la materia
pressure	la presión
phenomenon	el fenómeno
strange	extraño
movement	el movimiento
to move	moverse
mobile	móvil
immobile	inmóvil
electric	eléctrico
electricity	la electricidad

382

mechanics	la mecánica
invent	inventar
optics	la óptica
optical	óptico
microscope	el microscopio
lens	el lente
to reflect	reflejar
reflection	la reflexión
chemistry	la química
chemical	químico

383

biology	la biología
biological	biológico
biologist	el biólogo
to research	investigar
researcher	el investigador
element	el elemento
oxygen	el oxígeno
hydrogen	el hidrógeno
atom	el átomo
nucleus	el núcleo

384

laboratory	el laboratorio
experiment	el experimento
mixture	la mezcla
mixed	mezclado, mezclado
to decompose	descomponer
to compose	componer
compound	compuesto
rare	raro
science	la ciencia
scientific	científico

385

scientist	el científico m, la científica f
knowledge	el conocimiento, el saber
to know (something)	saber
to know (person)	conocer
wisdom	la sabiduría
wise	sabio
sage	el sabio
to be ignorant of	ignorar
experience	la experiencia
inexperience	la inexperiencia

Communications — Las communicaciones

386

telegraph	el telégrafo
telegram	el telegrama
to telegraph	telegrafiar
telex	el télex
telephone	el teléfono
to telephone	telefonear
telephonist	el telefonista *m*, la telefonista *f*
call	la llamada
receiver	el auricular
mouthpiece	el micrófono

387

telephone booth	la cabina telefónica
telephone exchange	la central telefónica
telephone directory	la guía telefónica, el directorio telefónico
telephone subscriber	el abonado
answerphone	el contestador (automático)
to hang up	colgar
engaged	comunicando
to dial	marcar
radiotelephone	el radioteléfono
videophone	el videófono

388

fax	el fax, el telefax
to fax	faxear, mandar por fax
modem	el módem
electronic mail	el correo electrónico
information technology	la informática
microelectronics	la microelectrónica
screen	la pantalla
keyboard	el teclado
key	la tecla
mouse	el ratón

389

computer	la computadora, el ordenador
computer language	el lenguaje de ordenador, el lenguaje de computador
computer literate	competente en informática
computer scientist	el informático *m*, la informática *f*
computer game	el vídeojuego

computer animation	la animación por ordenador
computer-aided design	el diseño asistido por ordenador
computerese	la jerga infórmatica
to computerize	computerizar, informatizar
computerization	la computerización

390

to program	programar
programer	el programador
systems analyst	el analista de sistemas
word processor	el procesador de textos
memory	la memoria
disk drive	la unidad de disco, la disquetera
software	el software
hardware	el hardware
compact disc (CD)	el disco compacto
cursor	el cursor

391

menu	el menú
to store	almacenar
file	el archivo
to file	archivar
data	los datos
database	la base de datos
desktop publishing	la edición electrónica
to lay out	componer
silicon	el silicio
silicon chip	la pastilla de silicio

392

user-friendly	fácil de usar
laser printer	la impresora láser
ink jet printer	la impresora de chorro de tinta
scanner	el analizador de léxico, el escaner (*Lat Am*)
circuit	el circuito
fiberoptics	la transmisión por fibra óptica
machine translation	la traducción automática
to network	interconectar
networking	la interconexión
information superhighway	la autopista informática

The arts and entertainment — Las artes y la diversión

393

painting	la pintura
painter	el pintor
to paint	pintar
picturesque	pintoresco
artist	el artista
museum	el museo
engraving	el grabado
to engrave	grabar
print	la estampa
background	el fondo

394

foreground	el primer plano
still life	el bodegón
drawing	el dibujo
to draw	dibujar
draftsman	el dibujante
outline	el contorno
to imitate	imitar
imitation	la imitación
abstract	abstracto
innovative	innovativo

395

innovation	la innovación
resemblance	la semejanza
similar	semejante, parecido
forgery	la falsificación
forger	el falsificador *m*, la falsificadora *f*
auction	la subasta
to bid	pujar
lot	el lote
reserve price	el precio mínimo
exhibition	la exposición

396

antique	la antigüedad
antique dealer	el anticuario
art dealer	un marchante de arte
palette	la paleta
brush	el pincel
easel	el caballete
color	el color
to color	colorear
colored	colorado
dull	mate

397

multicolored	multicolor
contrast	el contraste
to contrast	contrastar
white	blanco
black	negro

light blue	azul claro
dark green	verde oscuro
yellow	amarillo
brown	moreno
chestnut	castaño

398

pink	rosado
red	rojo
violet	violeta
mauve	morado
purple	purpúreo
gilt	dorado
to gild	dorar
gray	gris
patron	el mecenas
patronage	el mecenazgo

399

patronize	fomentar, patrocinar
oils	el óleo
watercolor	la acuarela
fresco	el fresco
triptych	el tríptico
cartoon	el cartón
the Renaissance	el Renacimiento
Renaissance art	el arte renacentista
crayon	el creyón
canvas	el lienzo

400

gallery	la galería
tone	el matiz
landscape	el paisaje
portrait	el retrato
portraitist	el retratista
miniature	la miniatura
miniaturist	el miniaturista
landscape painter	el paisajista
impressionism	el impresionismo
impressionist	el impresionista

401

surrealism	el surrealismo
surrealist	surrealista
cubism	el cubismo
cubist	cubista
symbol	el símbolo
to symbolize	simbolizar
symbolic	simbólico
sculpture	la escultura
sculptor	el escultor
workshop	el taller

402	
to carve	tallar
model	el modelo
statue	la estatua
bust	el busto
group	el grupo
chisel	el cincel
cast	el vaciado
shape	la forma
to shape	formar
architecture	la arquitectura
403	
architect	el arquitecto
vault	la bóveda
dome	la cúpula
pillar	el pilar
arch	el arco
tower	la torre
scaffolding	el andamio
arch	el arco
column	la columna
plinth	el zócalo
404	
nave	la nave
cathedral	la catedral
cathedral city	la ciudad catedralicia
apse	el ábside
stained glass	el cristal de colores
transept	el crucero
flying buttress	el arbotante
font	la pila
crypt	la cripta
basilica	la basílica
405	
Gothic	gótico
Romanesque	románico
Baroque	barroco
mosque	la mezquita
minaret	el alminar
synagogue	la sinagoga
pagoda	la pagoda
mausoleum	el mausoleo
pyramid	la pirámide
Sphinx	la esfinge
406	
temple	el templo
Corinthian	corintio
Ionian	jónico
Doric	dórico
forum	el foro
amphitheater	el anfiteatro
aqueduct	el acueducto
dolmen	el dolmen

menhir	el menhir
cave painting	la pintura rupestre
407	
illiterate	analfabeto
literate	alfabetizado
oral culture	la cultura oral
ballad	el romance
saga	la saga
tradition	la tradición
story	la historia
storyteller	el cuentista
narrative	la narración
to learn by heart	aprender de memoria
408	
literature	la literatura
papyrus	el papiro
parchment	el pergamino
alphabet	el alfabeto
character	el carácter
author	el autor
writer	el escritor
editor	el editor
edition	la edición
copyright	los derechos de reproducción
409	
style	el estilo
reader	el lector *m*, la lectora *f*
biography	la biografía
biographer	el biógrafo *m*, la biógrafa *f*
biographical	biográfico
autobiography	la autobiografía
autobiographical	autobiográfico
fiction	la ficción
fictional	ficticio
science fiction	la ciencia-ficción
410	
novel	la novela
novelist	el novelista
publisher	la editorial
royalties	los derechos del autor
bookshop	la librería
bookseller	el librero
encyclopedia	la enciclopedia
encyclopedic	enciclopédico
paperback	el libro de bolsillo
poetry	la poesía
411	
poet	el poeta *m*, la poeta *f*
poetic	poético
rhyme	la rima
to rhyme	rimar
meter	el metro

stanza	la estrofa
sonnet	el soneto
assonance	la asonancia
syllable	la sílaba
nursery rhyme	la canción infantil

412

fairy tale	el cuento de hadas
Cinderella	Cenicienta
Red Riding Hood	Caperucita Roja
Snow White	Blancanieves
dwarf	el enano
goblin	el duende
gnome	el gnomo
elf	el geniecillo, el elfo
Sleeping Beauty	la Bella Durmiente
Snow Queen	Reina de las nieves

413

Puss in Boots	el gato con botas
Bluebeard	Barba Azul
witch	la bruja
wizard	el brujo
spell	el hechizo
to cast a spell	hechizar
magician	el mago
magic	la magia
magical	mágico
mermaid	la sirena

414

mythology	la mitologia
Homer	Homero
Homeric	homérico
Iliad	la Ilíada
Odyssey	la Odisea
Odysseus	Odiseo
Trojan	troyano
Trojan horse	el caballo de Troya
Achilles	Aquiles
Achilles' heel	el talón de Aquiles

415

Cyclops	el cíclope
Atlantis	la Atlántida
Romulus	Rómulo
Hercules	Hércules
Herculean	hercúleo
The Arabian Nights	Las mil y una noches
Armageddon	el Armagedón
Valhalla	el Valhala
Thor	Tor
rune	la runa

416

masterpiece	la obra maestra
music	la música
musician	el músico

to play (an instrument)	tocar, interpretar (un instrumento)
composer	el compositor
orchestra	la orquesta
symphony	la sinfonía
aria	la aria
overture	la obertura
march	la marcha

417

soft	suave
stringed instrument	el instrumento de cuerda
wind instrument	el instrumento de viento
brass instrument	el instrumento de metal
piano	el piano
pianist	el pianista
organ	el órgano
organist	el organista
harmony	la harmonía
flute	la flauta

418

to blow	soplar
bagpipes	la gaita
cornet	la corneta
violin	el violín
auditorium	el auditorio
score	la partitura
opera	la ópera
tenor	el tenor
soprano	el soprano m, la soprano f
baritone	el barítono

419

bass	bajo
conductor	el director
instrumentalist	el instrumentista m, la instrumentista f
rehearsal	el ensayo
violin	el violín
viola	la viola
violinist	el violinista
cello	el violonchelo
bow	el arco
guitar	la guitarra

420

to strum	tañer
harp	el harpa
flute	la flauta
oboe	el oboe
clarinet	el clarinete
bassoon	el fagot
trumpet	la trompeta
trombone	el trombón
French horn	la trompa de llaves
tuba	la tuba

421

songbook	el cancionero
singing	el canto
to sing	cantar
to enchant	encantar
enchanting, delightful	encantador
spell, charm	el encanto
singer	el cantante *m*,
	la cantante *f*
choir	el coro
to accompany	acompañar
accompaniment	el acompañamiento

422

song	la canción, la copla
refrain	el estribillo
concert	el concierto
to syncopate	sincopar
jazz	el jazz
beat	el ritmo
saxophone	el saxofón
rock music	la música rock
rock star	la estrella de rock
drums	la batería

423

synthesizer	el sinetizador
folk music	la música folklórica
mandolin	la mandolina
ocarina	la ocarina
drum	el tambor
accordion	el acordeón
xylophone	el xilófono
tambourine	la pandereta
zither	la cítara
concertina	la concertina

424

dance, dancing	la danza
to dance	danzar, bailar
ball (dance)	el baile
dancer	el bailarín *m*,
	la bailarina *f*
theater	el teatro
theatrical	teatral
mask	la máscara
box office	la taquilla
seat, place	la localidad
stalls	las butacas
box (theater)	el palco

425

pit	el patio, la platea
stage	el escenario
scene	la escena
act	el acto
interval	el entreacto

scenery	las decoraciones,
	la escenografía
curtain	el telón
play	la obra (de teatro)
playwright	el dramaturgo
character	el personaje

426

tragedy	la tragedia
comedy	la comedia
actor	el actor
actress	la actriz
to play a role	desempeñar un papel
to be word-perfect	saber perfectamente su
	papel
costume	el vestuario
lighting	la iluminación
dénouement	el desenlace
to stage, represent	representar

427

performance	la función,
	la representación
flop	el fracaso
to flop	fracasar
debut	el estreno
trap door	el escotillón
to be a success	tener éxito
audience	el auditorio
spectator	el espectador
applause	los aplausos
whistling, hissing	el silbo, la rechifla

428

cinema	el cine
screen	la pantalla
to dub	doblar
to subtitle	subtitular
subtitle	el subtítulo
sequel	la continuación
director	el director
producer	el productor
to censor	censurar
censorship	la censura

429

to whistle, hiss	silbar
amusements	los recreos
playground	el patio de recreo
to enjoy oneself	divertirse, recrearse
entertaining	divertido
amusing	ameno
pastime	el pasatiempo
rest	el descanso
to rest	descansar
weariness	el cansancio

430

to get tired	cansarse
tired	cansado
to get bored	aburrirse
boring	aburrido
fair	la feria
festival	la verbena, la fiesta
crowd	la muchedumbre
to assemble	concurrir
circus	el circo
trapeze	el trapecio

431

trapeze artist	el trapecista m, la trapecista f
tightrope	la cuerda floja
tightrope walker	el funámbulo m, la funámbula f
acrobat	el acróbata m, la acróbata f
acrobatic	acrobático
acrobatics	la acrobacia
clown	el payaso
joke	la broma
lottery	la lotería
to be lucky	tener suerte

432

luck	la suerte
swing	el columpio
to swing (oneself)	columpiarse
seesaw	el balancín
merry-go-round	el tiovivo, la rueda
game	el juego
to play	jugar
player	el jugador
toy	el juguete
match	el partido

433

to win	ganar
to lose	perder
to draw	empatar
to cheat	engañar
deceit	el engaño
deceitful	engañoso
meeting	la reunión
to meet	reunirse
to join	unirse
party	la tertulia, el guateque, la fiesta

434

to visit	visitar
visit	la visita
playing cards	los naipes
to deal	repartir
to shuffle	barajar
suit	el palo
billiards	el billar
cue	el taco
cannon	la carambola
spin	el efecto

435

chess	el ajedrez
piece	la pieza
pawn	el peón
rook	la torre
bishop	el alfil
knight	el caballo
chessboard	el tablero (de ajedrez)
drafts	las damas
dice	los dados
jigsaw	el rompecabezas, el puzzle

Sport — El deporte

436

sport	el deporte
swimming	la natación
to swim	nadar
swimmer	el nadador m, la nadadora f
breaststroke	la braza de pecho, el estilo pecho
crawl	el crol, el estilo libre
backstroke	la braza de espalda, el estilo espalda
butterfly	la braza de mariposa, el estilo mariposa
lifeguard	el salvavidas
to dive	zambullirse, clavarse

437

high diving	el salto de palanca, clavados
to row	remar
rower	el remero
oar	el remo
canoe	la piragua, la canoa
canoeing	el piragüismo, el canoismo
canoeist	el piragüista, el canoista
paddle	el canalete
water polo	el polo acuático, el water polo
skate	el patín

438

to skate	patinar
figure skating	el patinaje artístico
rollerskates	los patines de ruedas
skateboard	el monopatín
amateur	el aficionado
fan	el hincha
bet	la apuesta
to bet	apostar
odds	las ventajas
ball	la pelota

439

football (sport)	el fútbol
football	el balón
footballer	el futbolista
referee	el arbitro
to score	marcar
to shoot	chutar, tirar
goal (objective)	la meta, la portería
goal (score)	el gol
goalscorer	el goleador
team	el equipo

440

league	la liga
trophy	el trofeo
knockout competition	el concurso eliminatorio
rugby	el rugby
to tackle	placar
scrum	la melé
scrum-half	el medio de melé
fly-half	la apertura
prop	el pilar
fullback	el zaguero

441

American football	el fútbol americano
tennis	el tenis
lawn tennis	el tenis sobre hierba
tennis player	el tenista m, la tenista f
set	el set
volley	el voleo
to serve	sacar
table tennis	el tenis de mesa, el ping-pong
racket	la raqueta
boxing	el boxeo

442

boxer	el boxeador
wrestling	la lucha
champion	el campeón
fencing	la esgrima
fencer	el esgrimidor
foil	el florete
gymnast	el gimnasta

gymnastics	la gimnasia
somersault	el salto mortal
cycling	el ciclismo

443

cyclist	el ciclista
mountain bicycle	la bicicleta de montaña
time trial	la cronometrada, la prueba contra-reloj (Lat Am)
stage	la etapa
yellow jersey	el maillot amarillo, la camiseta amarilla (Lat Am)
horseriding	la equitación
showjumping	el concurso de saltos
dressage	la doma clásica
polo	el polo
horseman	el jinete

444

grandstand	la tribuna
racecourse	la pista
race	la carrera
to run	correr
bullfight	la corrida (de toros)
bull fighter	el torero
motor racing	el automovilismo deportivo
scrambling	el motocross
hockey	el hockey
bowls	el juego de las bochas

445

stadium	el estadio
high jump	el salto de altura, el salto alto
record	el récord
long jump	el salto de longitud, el salto largo
triple jump	el triple salto
pole vault	el salto con pértiga
long distance runner	el corredor de fondo
lap	la vuelta
marathon	el maratón
training	el entrenamiento

446

athletics	el atletismo
athlete	el atleta m, la atleta f
sprinter	el esprínter
sprint	el esprint
to sprint	esprintar
track	la pista
starting blocks	los tacos de salida
hurdle	la valla
javelin	la jabalina
shotput	el lanzamiento de peso

447

discus	el disco
hammer	el martillo
relay race	la carrera de relevos
baton	el testigo
Olympic Games	los Juegos Olímpicos
triathlon	el triatlón
triathlete	el triatleta
decathlon	el decatlón
decathlete	el decatleta
pentathlon	el pentatlón

448

pentathlete	el pentatleta
mountaineering	el montañismo
mountaineer	el montañista, el alpinista
rock climbing	la escalada en rocas
rock climber	el escalador (de rocas)
ice-ax	el piolet
skiing	el esquí
to ski	esquiar
ski	el esquí
cross-country skiing	el esquí nórdico

449

ski-lift	el telesquí
skier	el esquiador
ski-stick	el bastón de esquiar
ski-jumping	el salto de esquí
snowshoe	la raqueta (de nieve)
sled	el trineo
ice hockey	el hockey sobre hielo
puck	el puck
water skiing	el esquí acuático
outboard motor	el motor fuera de borda

450

slalom	el slalom
to abseil	descender en rappel
to fish	pescar
angling	la pesca (con caña)
fishing rod	la caña
reel	el carrete
bait	el cebo
to bait	cebar
hook	el anzuelo
fly fishing	la pesca a mosca

Food and drink — La comida y la bebida

451

food	el alimento
provisions	las provisiones
to nourish	alimentar
appetite	el apetito
snack	la merienda
to have a snack	merendar
hunger	el hambre
hungry	hambriento
thirst	la sed
thirsty	sediento

452

to be hungry	tener hambre
to be thirsty	tener sed
sweet	dulce
to have a sweet tooth	ser goloso
sugar	el azúcar
sugary	azucarado
tasteless	soso, desabrido
bitter	amargo
milk	la leche
to pasteurize	pasteurizar

453

skimmed milk	la leche desnatada, la leche descremada
whole milk	la leche sin desnatar, la leche entera
cream	la nata, la crema
butter	la mantequilla
buttermilk	el suero de leche
cheese	el queso
egg	el huevo
egg yolk	la yema (de huevo)
egg white	la clara (de huevo)
shell	la cáscara

454

soft boiled egg	el huevo pasado por agua, el huevo tibio (Lat Am)
scrambled eggs	los huevos revueltos
omelet	la tortilla
bread	el pan
brown bread	el pan moreno
sliced bread	el pan de molde
loaf	el pan
roll	el panecillo, el bollo, el rollo
crumb	la miga
crust	la corteza

455

health foods	los alimentos naturales
organically grown	cultivado biológicamente
vegetarian	el vegeteriano m, la vegeteriana f
fiber	la fibra
wholemeal bread	el pan integral

rye bread	el pan de centeno
to slim	adelgazar
lentil	la lenteja
margarine	la margarina
polyunsaturated	poliinsaturado

456

fast food	el fast-food
hamburger	la hamburguesa
hot dog	el perrito caliente,
	el perro caliente
pizza	la pizza
fat	la grasa
fatty food	la comida grasosa
frozen food	el alimento congelado
french fries	las patatas fritas
chips	las papas fritas
confectionery	las golosinas

457

vegetable	el legumbre, la verdura
carrot	la zanahoria
broccoli	el bróculi, el brócoli
onion	la cebolla
celery	el apio
radish	el rábano
spinach	la espinaca
asparagus	el espárrago
cucumber	el pepino
gherkin	el pepinillo

458

lettuce	la lechuga
tomato	el tomate
pea	el guisante,
	la alverja (Lat Am)
chickpea	el garbanzo
bean	el haba
French bean	la judía, la habichuela
haricot bean	la judía blanca
cauliflower	la coliflor
Brussels sprout	la col de Bruselas
aubergine	la berenjena

459

salad	la ensalada
corn	el maíz
beetroot	la remolacha
green pepper	el pimiento verde,
	el pimentón verde (Lat Am)
mashed potato	el puré de patatas,
	el puré de papas (Lat Am)
garlic	el ajo
courgette	la calabacita
marrow	el calabacín
mushroom	el champiñón
pumpkin	la calabaza

460

condiment	el condimento
spice	la especia
ginger	el jengibre
mustard	la mostaza
nutmeg	la nuez moscada
cinnamon	la canela
turmeric	la cúrcuma
saffron	el azafrán
cumin	el comino
clove	el clavo de especia

461

soup	la sopa
soup tureen	la sopera
broth	el caldo
beef	la carne de vaca
veal	la ternera
steak	el filete
rare	poco hecho,
	poco cocido (Lat Am)
well done	bien hecho,
	bien cocido (Lat Am)
sauce	la salsa
gravy	el jugo de carne

462

cutlet	la chuleta
ham	el jamón
bacon	el tocino
sausage	la salchicha
pepperoni	el salchichón
blood sausage	la morcilla
raw	crudo
soft	tierno, blando
hard	duro
stew	el cocido

463

tripe	los callos
cooking	la cocina
cook	el cocinero
to cook	cocer
to roast	asar
roast	el asado
to stew	guisar
to slice	tajar
slice	la tajada
to fry	freír, fritar

464

fried	frito
chicken	el pollo
breast	la pechuga
leg	la pata, el pernil (Lat Am)
ham	el jamón
to cure	curar

to smoke (food)	ahumar	chocolate	el chocolate
lamb	el cordero	chocolate mousse	el mousse de chocolate
pork	el cerdo	fritters	las frituras, los churros,
veal	la ternera		los buñuelos
		sponge cake	el bizcocho
465		fruit salad	la macedonia de frutas,
to grill	hacer al grill,		la ensalada de frutas
	asar en la parrilla		(*Lat Am*)
to barbecue	asar a la parrilla	whipped cream	la nata montada,
barbecue	la parrillada		la crema batida
to bake	hornear	cheesecake	la tarta de queso,
breaded	empanado		la torta de queso
scampi	los langostinos rebozados	lemon meringue	el merengue de limón
to stuff	estofar		
spit	el espetón	**470**	
suckling pig	el lechón	pudding	el budín
lamb shank	la pierna de cordero	cookie	el bizcocho, la galleta
		baby food	la comida para bebés
466		flour	la harina
fish	el pescado	self-raising flour	la harina de fuerza,
haddock	el abadejo		la harina fortificada
mussel	los mejillón	yeast	la levadura
mullet	el salmonete	baking soda	el bicarbonato de soda
mackerel	la caballa	lard	la manteca
clam	la almeja	oil	el aceite
sole	el lenguado	sunflower oil	el aceite de girasol
tuna	el atún		
salad	la ensalada	**471**	
oil	el aceite	olive oil	el aceite de oliva
		rice	el arroz
467		yogurt	el yogur
vinegar	el vinagre	do-nut	el buñuelo
sour	agrio	apple compote	la compota de manzana
cruet-stand	las vinagreras	sandwich	el sandwich,
salt	la sal		el bocadillo,
saltcellar	el salero		el emparedado
to salt	salar	spaghetti	los espaguetis
pepper	la pimienta	cake	la tarta, la torta (*Lat Am*)
pepperpot	el pimentero	noodles	el tallarín, la pasta
mustard	la mostaza	frog legs	las patas de rana,
mayonnaise	la mayonesa		las zancas de rana (*Lat Am*)
468		**472**	
jam	la confitura, la mermelada	restaurant	el restaurante
marmalade	la mermelada de naranjas	menu	el menú
cake	el pastel	starter	el entremés, el abrebocas
pastry-cook	el pastelero	first course	el primer plato
dough	la pasta, la masa	waitress	la camarera
dessert	el postre	waiter	el camarero
pancake	la torta	drink	la bebida
rice pudding	el arroz con leche	to drink	beber
custard	las natillas	to sip	sorber
roast apple	la manzana asada	to gulp	tragar
469		**473**	
cream caramel,	el flan	to empty	vaciar
crème caramel		empty	vacío
ice cream	el helado	nonalcoholic drink	la bebida sin alcohol

wine	el vino	tea	el té
red wine	el vino tinto	chamomile tea	la manzanilla
rosé wine	el vino rosado		
vintage	añejo	**476**	
beer	la cerveza	lemon tea	el té con limón
water	el agua	coffee	el café
drinkable	potable	coffee with milk	el café con leche
		decaffeinated coffee	el descafeinado
474		iced coffee	el cafe con hielo
milkshake	el batido	instant coffee	el cafe instantáneo
tonic water	la tónica	soda	la soda
juice	el jugo	whisky	el whisky
soft drink	el refresco	canned beer	la cerveza enlatada,
sherry	el jerez		la cerveza en lata
dry	seco	bottled beer	la cerveza embotellada,
sherbet	el sorbete		la cerveza en botella
lemonade	la limonada		
fizzy	gaseoso	**477**	
to uncork	descorchar	cider	la sidra
		champagne	el champán
475		vermouth	el vermut
corkscrew	el sacacorchos	vodka	el vodka
liqueur	el licor	rum	el ron
spirits	los licores	Irish coffee	el cafe irlandés
cognac	el coñac	anise	el anís
bottle	la botella	brandy	el aguardiente, el brandy
orange drink	la naranjada	cherry brandy	el aguardiente de cerezas,
mineral water	el agua mineral		el brandy de cerezas
cappuccino	el capuchino	applejack	el aguardiente de manzanas

Travel and tourism — Los viajes y el turismo

478		**480**	
to travel	viajar	camping	el cámping
traveler	el viajero	campsite	el campamento
travel agency	la agencia de viajes	to go camping	hacer cámping,
travel agent	el agente de viajes		acampar
package holiday	las vacaciones todo pagado	camp-chair	la silla plegadiza,
tourist	el turista		la silla plegable
tourist season	la temporada turística	camper van	la camioneta-casa
hotel	el hotel	air mattress	la colchoneta hinchable,
hotelier	el hotelero		la colchoneta inflable
reception	la recepción	bottle opener	el abrebotellas,
			el destapador (*Lat Am*)
479		camp bed	la cama plegable
information desk	la conserjería	tin opener	el abrelatas
lobby	el vestíbulo		
service	el servicio	**481**	
to book in advance	reservar por adelantado	campfire	la hoguera de
vacant	libre		campamento, la fogata
check	la cuenta	flashlight	la linterna
tip	la propina	fly sheet	el toldo impermeable
hostel	el albergue	ground	el suelo
youth hostel	el albergue de juventud,	ground sheet	el suelo impermeable
	el albergue juvenil	guy line	el viento
boarding house	la pensión	mallet	el mazo
		shelter	el abrigo

to take shelter	abrigarse
to get wet	mojarse

482

sleeping bag	el saco de dormir
to sleep out	dormir al aire libre
tent	la tienda
tent peg	la clavija
tent pole	el mástil de tienda
Thermos™ flask	el termo
trailer	la caravana
to go caravanning	viajar en caravana
to live rough	vivir sin comodidades
hobo	el vagabundo

483

self-catering apartment	el piso sin pensión
day-tripper	el excursionista
trip	la excursión
railway	el ferrocarril
platform	el andén
to derail	descarrillar
derailment	el descarrillamiento
to collide	chocar
collision	el choque
accident	el accidente

484

timetable	el horario
guidebook	la guía
train	el tren
express train	el expreso
through train	el tren directo
to arrive	llegar
arrival	llegada
to leave	salir
departure	la salida
departure listings	el tablón de salidas, la cartelera de salidas

485

subway, underground railway	el metro
diesel	el diesel
steam	el vapor
corridor	el pasillo, el corredor
to alight	apearse, bajarse
halt	el apeadero, la parada (Lat Am)
car, compartment	el departamento
tunnel	el túnel
viaduct	el viaducto
cutting	el desmonte

486

railway network	la red ferroviaria
railhead	la estación terminal
railtrack	la vía férrea

railworker	el ferroviario
stationmaster	el jefe de la estación
waiting room	la sala de espera
single ticket	el billete sencillo, el tiquete sencillo
return ticket	el billete de ida y vuelta, el tiquete ida y vuelta
to examine	revisar
ticket inspector	el revisador

487

guard	el jefe de tren
engine driver	el maquinista
signalman	el guardavía
locomotive	la locomotora
car, carriage	el vagón
sleeping car	el coche cama
dining/restaurant car	el vagón restaurante
baggage	el equipaje
to check in	facturar
checkroom	la consigna, el guarda-maletas

488

trunk (baggage)	el baúl
case	la maleta
rucksack	la mochila
stop	la parada
to stop	pararse
stay	la estancia
customs	la aduana
customs officer	el aduanero
examination	el registro
to examine	registrar

489

duty	el derecho
tax	el impuesto
to tax	tasar
to declare	declarar
duty-free	libre de impuestos
passport	el pasaporte
identity card	el carné, la cédula de identidad, la cédula de ciudadanía
bus	el autobús, el bus
taxi	el taxi
taxi driver	el taxista

490

driving license	el permiso de conducir, la licencia de conducción, el pase (Lat Am)
to drive	conducir, manejar
automobile	el coche, el automóvil, el carro
motoring	el automovilismo
motorist	el automovilista

to hire	alquilar
trailer	el remolque
to give someone a lift	llevar a alguien
hitch-hiker	el autostopista
to hitch-hike	hacer autostop, hacer dedo

491

hitch-hiking	el autostopismo
sharp bend	la curva cerrada
to skid	resbalar
door (vehicle)	la portezuela, la puerta
window (vehicle)	la ventanilla
to park	aparcar, parquear (*Lat Am*)
to slow down	moderar la marcha, reducir la velocidad
to accelerate	acelerar
to start up	arrancar
to overtake	adelantar

492

aerial	la antena
air filter	el filtro de aire
alternator	el alternador
antifreeze	el anti-congelante
gearbox	la caja de cambios
axle	el eje
battery	la batería
flat	descargado
bonnet	el capó
trunk	el maletero, el baul

493

brake fluid	el líquido de frenos
brake	el freno
to brake	frenar
fender	los parachoques
carburetor	el carburador
child seat	la silla de niño
choke	el estárter
clutch	el embrague, el clutch
cylinder	el cilindro
horsepower	el caballo (de fuerza)

494

disc brake	el freno de disco
distributor	el distribuidor
dynamo	el dinamo
dynamic	dinámico
engine	el motor
exhaust	el tubo de escape, el exosto (*Lat Am*)
fan belt	la correa de ventilador
fuel gage	el indicador de carburante, el indicador de gasolina (*Lat Am*)

fuel pump	la bomba de carburante, la bomba de gasolina
fuse	el fusible

495

stick lift	la palanca de cambios
generator	el generador
to generate	generar
alternating current	la corriente alterna
handbrake	el freno de mano
hazard lights	las luces de emergencia
horn	la bocina
ignition	el contacto, el encendido
ignition key	la llave de contacto, la llave de encendido
indicator	el intermitente

496

jack	el gato
silencer	el silenciador
license plate	la matrícula, la placa
oil filter	el filtro de aceite
points	los platinos
rear view mirror	el espejo retrovisor
reflector	el reflectante, el reflector
reverse light	la luz de marcha atrás
roof rack	el portaequipajes
seat	el asiento

497

seat belt	el cinturón de seguridad
shock absorber	el amortiguador
socket set	el juego de llaves de tubo
spanner	la llave inglesa
spare part	el repuesto
spark plug	la bujía
speedometer	el velocímetro
starter motor	el motor de arranque
steering wheel	el volante
sun roof	el techo solar

498

suspension	la suspensión
towbar	la barra de remolque
transmission	la transmisión
tire	el neumático
wheel	la rueda
windshield	el parabrisas
wipers	las limpiaparabrisas
wrench	la llave inglesa
air bag	la bolsa de aire
four-wheel drive	la tracción de cuatro por cuatro

499

motorbike	la motocicleta
helmet	el casco
bicycle	la bicicleta

racing cycle	la bicicleta de carreras	port	el babor
pedal	el pedal	keel	la quilla
to pedal	pedalear	hold	la bodega
tube	la cámara	figurehead	el figurón de proa
to puncture	pincharse	funnel	la chimenea
chain	la cadena	rigging	la jarcia
pannier bag	la cartera	sail	la vela

500

505

ship	el buque	raft	el embalse
boat	el barco, la barca	galley	la galera
sail	la vela	clinker-built	de tingladillo
to embark	embarcarse	galleon	el galeón
to disembark	desembarcar	clipper	el clíper
on board	a bordo	schooner	la goleta
disembarkment	el desembarco	whaler	el ballenero
to tow	remolcar	trawler	el arrastrero
tug	el remolcador	to trawl	rastrear
crossing	la travesía	factory ship	el buque factoría

501

506

to cross	atravesar	hydrofoil	la hidroala
passage	el pasaje	powerboat	el motorbote
passenger	el pasajero	rubber dinghy	la lancha neumática
cabin	el camarote	pontoon	el pontón
deck	el puente	life raft	la balsa salvavidas
mast	el mástil	aqualung	la escafandra autónoma
pilot	el piloto	diver	el buceador
rudder	el timón	navigation	la navegación
crew	la tripulación	to navigate	navegar
anchor	el ancla f	to weigh anchor	zarpar

502

507

to cast anchor	fondear	balloon	el globo
anchorage	el ancladero	airship	el dirigible
cargo	la carga, el cargamento	aviation	la aviación
to sink	hundirse	airplane	el avión
sinking	el hundimiento	hydroplane, seaplane	el hidroavión
shipwreck	el naufragio	airport	el aeropuerto
signal	la señal	air terminal	la terminal aérea
to signal	señalar	passenger	el pasajero
lighthouse	el faro	business class	la clase de negociante
port	el puerto	tourist class	la clase turística

503

508

quay	el muelle	farewell	la despedida
oil tanker	el petrolero	air stewardess	la azafata
to launch	arriar al agua	to land	aterrizar
salvage	el salvamento	forced landing	el aterrizaje forzoso
to salvage	salvar	to take off	despegar
free on board	franco a bordo	take-off	el despegue
waybill	la carta de porte	seatbelt	el cinturón
hovercraft	el hidrodeslizador	to fly	volar
		propeller	la hélice

504

| | | pilot | el piloto |

stern	la popa		
prow	la proa	**509**	
starboard	el estribor	autopilot	el piloto automático

black box	la caja negra	to crash	estrellarse
runway	la pista de aterrizaje	glider	el planeador
undercarriage	el tren de aterizaje	to glide	planear
sound barrier	la barrera sonora,	hang-glider	el ala delta
	la barrera del sonido	autogyro	el autogiro

Numbers — Los números

1	uno, una	1st	primero
2	dos	2nd	segundo
3	tres	3rd	tercero
4	cuatro	4th	cuarto
5	cinco	5th	quinto
6	seis	6th	sexto
7	siete	7th	séptimo
8	ocho	8th	octavo
9	nueve	9th	noveno
10	diez	10th	décimo
11	once	11th	undécimo
12	doce	12th	duodécimo
13	trece	13th	decimotercero
14	catorce	14th	decimocuarto
15	quince	15th	decimoquinto
16	dieciséis	16th	decimosexto
17	diecisiete	17th	decimoséptimo
18	dieciocho	18th	decimoctavo
19	diecinueve	19th	decimonoveno
20	veinte	20th	vigésimo
21	veintiuno	21st	vigésimo primero
22	veintidós	30th	trigésimo
23	veintitrés	31st	trigésimo primero
24	veinticuatro	40th	cuadragésimo
25	veinticinco	50th	quincuagésimo
26	veintiséis	60th	sexagésimo
27	veintisiete	70th	septuagésimo
28	veintiocho	80th	octogésimo
29	veintinueve	90th	nonagésimo
30	treinta	100th	centésimo
40	cuarenta	200th	ducentésimo
50	cincuenta	300th	trecentésimo
60	sesenta	400th	quadringentésimo
70	setenta	500th	quingentésimo
80	ochenta	600th	sexcentésimo
90	noventa	700th	septingentésimo
100	ciento or cien (before a noun)	800th	octingentésimo
200	doscientos	900th	noningentésimo
300	trescientos	1,000th	milésimo
400	cuatrocientos	2,000th	dos milésimo
500	quinientos	a millionth	millonésimo
600	seiscientos	two millionth	dos millonésimo
700	setecientos		
800	ochocientos		
900	novecientos		
1,000	mil		
2,000	dos mil		
1,000000	un millón		

Proverbs and idioms — Los proverbios y los modismos

to be homesick
tener morriña, tener nostalgia
to have pins and needles
tener hormigueo
don't mention it
no hay de qué
it's none of your business
no tiene nada que ver contigo, no es asunto tuyo
it's all the same
me da igual
as deaf as a post
sordo como una tapia
to sleep like a log
dormir como un lirón
as drunk as a lord
más borracho que una cuba
a bird in the hand is worth two in the bush
más vale pájaro en mano que ciento volando
to kill two birds with one stone
matar dos pájaros de un tiro
at full speed
a todo correr
a mil, a millón (*Lat Am*)
no sooner said than done
dicho y hecho
birds of a feather flock together
dios los cría y ellos se juntan

every cloud has a silver lining
no hay mal que por bien no venga
a chip off the old block
del tal palo tal astilla
out of sight, out of mind
ojos que no ven, corazón que no siente
practice makes perfect
la práctica hace maestro
many hands make light work
muchas manos facilitan el trabajo
better late than never
más vale tarde que nunca
at first sight
a primera vista
in the short term
a corto plazo
in the long run
a la larga
on the other hand
por otra parte, de otro lado
in my opinion
a mi juicio, en mi opinión
in fact
de hecho
in other words
dicho de otro modo, en otras palabras

First names — Nombres de pila

Boys		**Girls**	
Alexander	Alejandro	Alice	Alicia
Andrew	Andrés	Anne	Ana
Anthony	Antonio	Catherine	Catalina
Bernard	Bernardo	Charlotte	Carlota
Charles	Carlos	Deborah	Débora
Christopher	Cristóbal	Eleanor	Leonor
Edward	Eduardo	Elizabeth	Isabel
Francis	Francisco	Ellen	Elena
George	Jorge	Emily	Emilia
Henry	Enrique	Esther	Ester
James	Jaime	Frances	Francisca
John	Juan	Josephine	Josefina
Joseph	José	Louise	Luisa
Lawrence	Lorenzo	Margaret	Margarita
Louis	Luis	Mary	María
Martin	Martín	Matilda	Matilde
Michael	Miguel	Ophelia	Ofelia
Nicholas	Nicolás	Patricia	Patricai
Paul	Pablo	Pauline	Paula
Peter	Pedro	Rachel	Raquel
Philip	Felipe	Rose	Rosa
Raymond	Ramón	Susan	Susana
Thomas	Tomás	Sylvia	Silvia
Vincent	Vicente	Veronica	Verónica

Signs of the zodiac – Los signos del zodiaco

Aquarius	el Acuario	Leo	el Leo
Pisces	el Piscis	Virgo	la Virgo
Aries	el Aries	Libra	la Libra
Taurus	el Tauro	Scorpio	el Escorpión
Gemini	el Géminis	Sagittarius	el Sagitario
Cancer	el Cáncer	Capricorn	el Capricornio

Prepositions, adverbs and conjunctions — Las preposiciones, los adverbios y las conjunciones

English	Spanish	English	Spanish
against	contra	then	entonces
at	en	never	nunca
between	entre	always	siempre
for	para, por	at once	en seguida
from	de	soon	pronto
in	en, dentro de	still	todavía
of	de	already	ya
on	en, sobre	like	como
to	a	how	cómo
with	con	neither ... nor...	ni ... ni...
without	sin	either ... or...	o ... o...
above	arriba	and	y
down	abajo	but	pero
under	debajo de	why	por qué
in front of	delante de	because	porque
opposite	enfrente	if	si
forward	adelante	yes	sí
behind	detrás de	no	no
backwards	atrás	well	bien
close to	junto a	badly	mal
near	cerca de	quickly	de prisa
far from	lejos de	slowly	despacio
before	antes de	enough	bastante
after	después, tras	when	cuando
here	aquí	too	demasiado
there	allí	more	más
inside	dentro	less	menos
within	adentro	much	mucho
outside	fuera	nothing	nada
where	donde	nobody	nadie
during	durante	never	nunca
except	excepto	perhaps	quizás, acaso
towards	hacia	once	una vez
until	hasta	instead of	en vez de
according to	según	often	a menudo
now	ahora	at times	a veces
often	a menudo		

SPANISH VERBS
AND ENGLISH
IRREGULAR VERBS

Verb Forms

Auxiliary: auxiliary verbs are used to form compound tenses of verbs, e.g. *have* in *I have seen*. The auxiliary verb in Spanish is *haber*.

Compound: compound tenses are verb tenses consisting of more than one element. In Spanish, compound tenses are formed by the auxiliary verb and the past participle, e.g. *ha escrito – he has written*.

Conditional: the conditional is introduced in English by the auxiliary *would*, e.g. *I would come if I had the time*. In Spanish, this is rendered by a single verb form, e.g. *vendría*.

Gerund: this is a noun formed from a verb, denoting a state or action. In English, the gerund, like the present participle, ends in *-ing*, e.g. *singing – cantando*.

Imperative: the imperative is used for giving orders, e.g. *estáte formal – be good*, or making suggestions, e.g. *vámonos – let's go*.

Imperfect indicative: in Spanish, this tense describes habitual or continuous action in the past, e.g. *hablábamos*.

Indicative: the normal form of a verb, as in *hablo – I speak*, *ha venido – he has come*, *estoy probando – I am trying*.

Perfect indicative: this is one of the two tenses (the other is the preterite) used to describe completed past action in Spanish. It comprises the auxiliary *haber* and the past participle, e.g. *he visto – I have seen*.

Pluperfect indicative: in Spanish and English, this tense is used to describe an action occurring in the past before another past action, e.g. *había ido antes de que llegué – he had gone before I arrived*. In Spanish, the pluperfect indicative is formed by the imperfect indicative of *haber* and the past participle, e.g. *habían comenzado – they had started*.

Preterite: this tense is used to describe completed past action, e.g. *llegó ayer – he arrived yesterday*.

Past participle: this is the form used after the auxiliary *have* in English and after *haber* in Spanish, e.g. *comido – eaten* in *he comido – I have eaten*.

Present participle: this is the form which ends in *-ing* in English, e.g. *singing – cantando*.

Subjunctive: the subjunctive exists in English but goes almost unnoticed as it almost always takes the same form as the indicative. One exception is *if I were you*. It is, however, widely used in Spanish.

Spanish Verbs

abrir *to open*

Gerund *abriendo*

Past participle *abierto*

Present indicative	Present subjunctive
abro	abra
abres	abras
abre	abra
abrimos	abramos
abrís	abráis
abren	abran

Imperfect indicative	Imperfect subjunctive
abría	abriera
abrías	abrieras
abría	abriera
abríamos	abriéramos
abríais	abrierais
abrían	abrieran

Preterite	Future
abrí	abriré
abriste	abrirás
abrió	abrirá
abrimos	abriremos
abristeis	abriréis
abrieron	abrirán

Perfect indicative	Conditional
he abierto	abriría
has abierto	abrirías
ha abierto	abriría
hemos abierto	abriríamos
habéis abierto	abriríais
han abierto	abrirían

Pluperfect indicative	Imperative
había abierto	–
habías abierto	abre
había abierto	abra
habíamos abierto	abramos
habíais abierto	abrid
habían abierto	abran

aburrir *to bore, annoy*

Gerund *aburriendo*

Past participle *aburrido*

Present indicative	Present subjunctive
aburro	aburra
aburres	aburras
aburre	aburra
aburrimos	aburramos
aburrís	aburráis
aburren	aburran

Imperfect indicative	Imperfect subjunctive
aburría	aburriera
aburrías	aburrieras
aburría	aburriera
aburríamos	aburriéramos
aburríais	aburrierais
aburrían	aburrieran

Preterite	Future
aburrí	aburriré
aburriste	aburrirás
aburrió	aburrirá
aburrimos	aburriremos
aburristeis	aburriréis
aburrieron	aburrirán

Perfect indicative	Conditional
he aburrido	aburriría
has aburrido	aburrirías
ha aburrido	aburriría
hemos aburrido	aburriríamos
habéis aburrido	aburriríais
han aburrido	aburrirían

Pluperfect indicative	Imperative
había aburrido	–
habías aburrido	aburre
había aburrido	aburra
habíamos aburrido	aburramos
habíais aburrido	aburrid
habían aburrido	aburran

acabar *to finish*

Gerund *acabando*

Past participle *acabado*

Present indicative	Present subjunctive
acabo	acabe
acabas	acabes
acaba	acabe
acabamos	acabemos
acabáis	acabéis
acaban	acaben

Imperfect indicative	Imperfect subjunctive
acababa	acabara
acababas	acabaras
acababa	acabara
acabábamos	acabáramos
acababais	acabarais
acababan	acabaran

Preterite	Future
acabé	acabaré
acabaste	acabarás
acabó	acabará
acabamos	acabaremos
acabasteis	acabaréis
acabaron	acabarán

Perfect indicative	Conditional
he acabado	acabaría
has acabado	acabarías
ha acabado	acabaría
hemos acabado	acabaríamos
habéis acabado	acabaríais
han acabado	acabarían

Pluperfect indicative	Imperative
había acabado	–
habías acabado	acaba
había acabado	acabe
habíamos acabado	acabemos
habíais acabado	acabad
habían acabado	acaben

aceptar *to accept*

Gerund *aceptando*

Past participle *aceptado*

Present indicative	Present subjunctive
acepto	acepte
aceptas	aceptes
acepta	acepte
aceptamos	aceptemos
aceptáis	aceptéis
aceptan	acepten

Imperfect indicative	Imperfect subjunctive
aceptaba	aceptara
aceptabas	aceptaras
aceptaba	aceptara
aceptábamos	aceptáramos
aceptabais	aceptarais
aceptaban	aceptaran

Preterite	Future
acepté	aceptaré
aceptaste	aceptarás
aceptó	aceptará
aceptamos	aceptaremos
aceptasteis	aceptaréis
aceptaron	aceptarán

Perfect indicative	Conditional
he aceptado	aceptaría
has aceptado	aceptarías
ha aceptado	aceptaría
hemos aceptado	aceptaríamos
habéis aceptado	aceptaríais
han aceptado	aceptarían

Pluperfect indicative	Imperative
había aceptado	–
habías aceptado	acepta
había aceptado	acepte
habíamos aceptado	aceptemos
habíais aceptado	aceptad
habían aceptado	acepten

aconsejar *to advise*

Gerund *aconsejando*

Past participle *aconsejado*

Present indicative	**Present subjunctive**
aconsejo	aconseje
aconsejas	aconsejes
aconseja	aconseje
aconsejamos	aconsejemos
aconsejáis	aconsejéis
aconsejan	aconsejen

Imperfect indicative	**Imperfect subjunctive**
aconsejaba	aconsejara
aconsejabas	aconsejaras
aconsejaba	aconsejara
aconsejábamos	aconsejáramos
aconsejabais	aconsejarais
aconsejaban	aconsejaran

Preterite	**Future**
aconsejé	aconsejaré
aconsejaste	aconsejarás
aconsejó	aconsejará
aconsejamos	aconsejaremos
aconsejasteis	aconsejaréis
aconsejaron	aconsejarán

Perfect indicative	**Conditional**
he aconsejado	aconsejaría
has aconsejado	aconsejarías
ha aconsejado	aconsejaría
hemos aconsejado	aconsejaríamos
habéis aconsejado	aconsejaríais
han aconsejado	aconsejarían

Pluperfect indicative	**Imperative**
había aconsejado	–
habías aconsejado	aconseja
había aconsejado	aconseje
habíamos aconsejado	aconsejemos
habíais aconsejado	aconsejad
habían aconsejado	aconsejen

acordarse *to remember*

Gerund *acordándose*

Past participle *acordado*

Present indicative	**Present subjunctive**
me acuerdo	me acuerde
te acuerdas	te acuerdes
se acuerda	se acuerde
nos acordamos	nos acordemos
os acordáis	os acordéis
se acuerdan	se acuerden

Imperfect indicative	**Imperfect subjunctive**
me acordaba	me acordara
te acordabas	te acordaras
se acordaba	se acordara
nos acordábamos	nos acordáramos
os acordabais	os acordarais
se acordaban	se acordaran

Preterite	**Future**
me acordé	me acordaré
te acordaste	te acordarás
se acordó	se acordará
nos acordamos	nos acordaremos
os acordasteis	os acordaréis
se acordaron	se acordarán

Perfect indicative	**Conditional**
me he acordado	me acordaría
te has acordado	te acordarías
se ha acordado	se acordaría
nos hemos acordado	nos acordaríamos
os habéis acordado	os acordaríais
se han acordado	se acordarían

Pluperfect indicative	**Imperative**
me había acordado	–
te habías acordado	acuérdate
se había acordado	acuérdese
nos habíamos acordado	acordémonos
os habíais acordado	acordaos
se habían acordado	acuérdense

acostarse *to go to bed*

Gerund *acostándose*

Past participle *acostado*

Present indicative	Present subjunctive
me acuesto	me acueste
te acuestas	te acuestes
se acuesta	se acueste
nos acostamos	nos acostemos
os acostáis	os acostéis
se acuestan	se acuesten

Imperfect indicative	Imperfect subjunctive
me acostaba	me acostara
te acostabas	te acostaras
se acostaba	se acostara
nos acostábamos	nos acostáramos
os acostabais	os acostarais
se acostaban	se acostaran

Preterite	Future
me acosté	me acostaré
te acostaste	te acostarás
se acostó	se acostará
nos acostamos	nos acostaremos
os acostasteis	os acostaréis
se acostaron	se acostarán

Perfect indicative	Conditional
me he acostado	me acostaría
te has acostado	te acostarías
se ha acostado	se acostaría
nos hemos acostado	nos acostaríamos
os habéis acostado	os acostaríais
se han acostado	se acostarían

Pluperfect indicative	Imperative
me había acostado	–
te habías acostado	acuéstate
se había acostado	acuéstese
nos habíamos acostado	acostémonos
os habíais acostado	acostaos
se habían acostado	acuéstense

agradecer *to thank*

Gerund *agradeciendo*

Past participle *agradecido*

Present indicative	Present subjunctive
agradezco	agradezca
agradeces	agradezcas
agradece	agradezca
agradecemos	agradezcamos
agradecéis	agradezcáis
agradecen	agradezcan

Imperfect indicative	Imperfect subjunctive
agradecía	agradeciera
agradecías	agradecieras
agradecía	agradeciera
agradecíamos	agradeciéramos
agradecíais	agradecierais
agradecían	agradecieran

Preterite	Future
agradecí	agradeceré
agradeciste	agradecerás
agradeció	agradecerá
agradecimos	agradeceremos
agradecisteis	agradeceréis
agradecieron	agradecerán

Perfect indicative	Conditional
he agradecido	agradecería
has agradecido	agradecerías
ha agradecido	agradecería
hemos agradecido	agradeceríamos
habéis agradecido	agradeceríais
han agradecido	agradecerían

Pluperfect indicative	Imperative
había agradecido	–
habías agradecido	agradece
había agradecido	agradezca
habíamos agradecido	agradezcamos
habíais agradecido	agradeced
habían agradecido	agradezcan

alcanzar *to reach*

Gerund *alcanzando*

Past participle *alcanzado*

Present indicative	Present subjunctive
alcanzo	alcance
alcanzas	alcances
alcanza	alcance
alcanzamos	alcancemos
alcanzáis	alcancéis
alcanzan	alcancen

Imperfect indicative	Imperfect subjunctive
alcanzaba	alcanzara
alcanzabas	alcanzaras
alcanzaba	alcanzara
alcanzábamos	alcanzáramos
alcanzabais	alcanzarais
alcanzaban	alcanzaran

Preterite	Future
alcancé	alcanzaré
alcanzaste	alcanzarás
alcanzó	alcanzará
alcanzamos	alcanzaremos
alcanzasteis	alcanzaréis
alcanzaron	alcanzarán

Perfect indicative	Conditional
he alcanzado	alcanzaría
has alcanzado	alcanzarías
ha alcanzado	alcanzaría
hemos alcanzado	alcanzaríamos
habéis alcanzado	alcanzaríais
han alcanzado	alcanzarían

Pluperfect indicative	Imperative
había alcanzado	–
habías alcanzado	alcanza
había alcanzado	alcance
habíamos alcanzado	alcancemos
habíais alcanzado	alcanzad
habían alcanzado	alcancen

almorzar *to have lunch*

Gerund *almorzando*

Past participle *almorzado*

Present indicative	Present subjunctive
almuerzo	almuerce
almuerzas	almuerces
almuerza	almuerce
almorzamos	almorcemos
almorzáis	almorcéis
almuerzan	almuercen

Imperfect indicative	Imperfect subjunctive
almorzaba	almorzara
almorzabas	almorzaras
almorzaba	almorzara
almorzábamos	almorzáramos
almorzabais	almorzarais
almorzaban	almorzaran

Preterite	Future
almorcé	almorzaré
almorzaste	almorzarás
almorzó	almorzará
almorzamos	almorzaremos
almorzasteis	almorzaréis
almorzaron	almorzarán

Perfect indicative	Conditional
he almorzado	almorzaría
has almorzado	almorzarías
ha almorzado	almorzaría
hemos almorzado	almorzaríamos
habéis almorzado	almorzaríais
han almorzado	almorzarían

Pluperfect indicative	Imperative
había almorzado	–
habías almorzado	almuerza
había almorzado	almuerce
habíamos almorzado	almorcemos
habíais almorzado	almorzad
habían almorzado	almuercen

amar *to love*

Gerund *amando*

Past participle *amado*

Present indicative	Present subjunctive
amo	ame
amas	ames
ama	ame
amamos	amemos
amáis	améis
aman	amen

Imperfect indicative	Imperfect subjunctive
amaba	amara
amabas	amaras
amaba	amara
amábamos	amáramos
amabais	amarais
amaban	amaran

Preterite	Future
amé	amaré
amaste	amarás
amó	amará
amamos	amaremos
amasteis	amaréis
amaron	amarán

Perfect indicative	Conditional
he amado	amaría
has amado	amarías
ha amado	amaría
hemos amado	amaríamos
habéis amado	amaríais
han amado	amarían

Pluperfect indicative	Imperative
había amado	–
habías amado	ama
había amado	ame
habíamos amado	amemos
habíais amado	amad
habían amado	amen

andar *to walk*

Gerund *andando*

Past participle *andado*

Present indicative	Present subjunctive
ando	ande
andas	andes
anda	ande
andamos	andemos
andáis	andéis
andan	anden

Imperfect indicative	Imperfect subjunctive
andaba	anduviera
andabas	anduvieras
andaba	anduviera
andábamos	anduviéramos
andabais	anduvierais
andaban	anduvieran

Preterite	Future
anduve	andaré
anduviste	andarás
anduvo	andará
anduvimos	andaremos
anduvisteis	andaréis
anduvieron	andarán

Perfect indicative	Conditional
he andado	andaría
has andado	andarías
ha andado	andaría
hemos andado	andaríamos
habéis andado	andaríais
han andado	andarían

Pluperfect indicative	Imperative
había andado	–
habías andado	anda
había andado	ande
habíamos andado	andemos
habíais andado	andad
habían andado	anden

aparecer *to appear*

Gerund *apareciendo*

Past participle *aparecido*

Present indicative	Present subjunctive
aparezco	
apareces	aparezca
aparece	aparezcas
aparecemos	aparezca
aparecéis	aparezcamos
aparecen	aparezcáis
	aparezcan

Imperfect indicative	Imperfect subjunctive
aparecía	
aparecías	apareciera
aparecía	aparecieras
aparecíamos	apareciera
aparecíais	apareciéramos
aparecían	aparecierais
	aparecieran

Preterite	Future
aparecí	
apareciste	apareceré
apareció	aparecerás
aparecimos	aparecerá
aparecisteis	apareceremos
aparecieron	apareceréis
	aparecerán

Perfect indicative	Conditional
he aparecido	
has aparecido	aparecería
ha aparecido	aparecerías
hemos aparecido	aparecería
habéis aparecido	apareceríamos
han aparecido	apareceríais
	aparecerían

Pluperfect indicative	Imperative
había aparecido	–
habías aparecido	aparece
había aparecido	aparezca
habíamos aparecido	aparezcamos
habíais aparecido	apareced
habían aparecido	aparezcan

aprender *to learn*

Gerund *aprendiendo*

Past participle *aprendido*

Present indicative	Present subjunctive
aprendo	
aprendes	aprenda
aprende	aprendas
aprendemos	aprenda
aprendéis	aprendamos
aprenden	aprendáis
	aprendan

Imperfect indicative	Imperfect subjunctive
aprendía	
aprendías	aprendiera
aprendía	aprendieras
aprendíamos	aprendiera
aprendíais	aprendiéramos
aprendían	aprendierais
	aprendieran

Preterite	Future
aprendí	
aprendiste	aprenderé
aprendió	aprenderás
aprendimos	aprenderá
aprendisteis	aprenderemos
aprendieron	aprenderéis
	aprenderán

Perfect indicative	Conditional
he aprendido	
has aprendido	aprendería
ha aprendido	aprenderías
hemos aprendido	aprendería
habéis aprendido	aprenderíamos
han aprendido	aprenderíais
	aprenderían

Pluperfect indicative	Imperative
había aprendido	–
habías aprendido	aprende
había aprendido	aprenda
habíamos aprendido	aprendamos
habíais aprendido	aprended
habían aprendido	aprendan

aprobar *to approve*

Gerund *aprobando*

Past participle *aprobado*

Present indicative	Present subjunctive
apruebo	apruebe
apruebas	apruebes
aprueba	apruebe
aprobamos	aprobemos
aprobáis	aprobéis
aprueban	aprueben

Imperfect indicative	Imperfect subjunctive
aprobaba	aprobara
aprobabas	aprobaras
aprobaba	aprobara
aprobábamos	aprobáramos
aprobabais	aprobarais
aprobaban	aprobaran

Preterite	Future
aprobé	aprobaré
aprobaste	aprobarás
aprobó	aprobará
aprobamos	aprobaremos
aprobasteis	aprobaréis
aprobaron	aprobarán

Perfect indicative	Conditional
he aprobado	aprobaría
has aprobado	aprobarías
ha aprobado	aprobaría
hemos aprobado	aprobaríamos
habéis aprobado	aprobaríais
han aprobado	aprobarían

Pluperfect indicative	Imperative
había aprobado	–
habías aprobado	aprueba
había aprobado	apruebe
habíamos aprobado	aprobemos
habíais aprobado	aprobad
habían aprobado	aprueben

argüir *to argue*

Gerund *arguyendo*

Past participle *argüido*

Present indicative	Present subjunctive
arguyo	arguya
arguyes	arguyas
arguye	arguya
argüimos	arguyamos
argüís	arguyáis
arguyen	arguyan

Imperfect indicative	Imperfect subjunctive
argüía	arguyera
argüías	arguyeras
argüía	arguyera
argüíamos	arguyéramos
argüíais	arguyerais
argüían	arguyeran

Preterite	Future
argüí	argüiré
argüiste	argüirás
arguyó	argüirá
argüimos	argüiremos
argüisteis	argüiréis
arguyeron	argüirán

Perfect indicative	Conditional
he argüido	argüiría
has argüido	argüirías
ha argüido	argüiría
hemos argüido	argüiríamos
habéis argüido	argüiríais
han argüido	argüirían

Pluperfect indicative	Imperative
había argüido	–
habías argüido	arguye
había argüido	arguya
habíamos argüido	arguyamos
habíais argüido	argüid
habían argüido	arguyan

arreglar *to arrange*

Gerund *arreglando*

Past participle *arreglado*

Present indicative	Present subjunctive
arreglo	arregle
arreglas	arregles
arregla	arregle
arreglamos	arreglemos
arregláis	arregléis
arreglan	arreglen

Imperfect indicative	Imperfect subjunctive
arreglaba	arreglara
arreglabas	arreglaras
arreglaba	arreglara
arreglábamos	arregláramos
arreglabais	arreglarais
arreglaban	arreglaran

Preterite	Future
arreglé	arreglaré
arreglaste	arreglarás
arregló	arreglará
arreglamos	arreglaremos
arreglasteis	arreglaréis
arreglaron	arreglarán

Perfect indicative	Conditional
he arreglado	arreglaría
has arreglado	arreglarías
ha arreglado	arreglaría
hemos arreglado	arreglaríamos
habéis arreglado	arreglaríais
han arreglado	arreglarían

Pluperfect indicative	Imperative
había arreglado	–
habías arreglado	arregla
había arreglado	arregle
habíamos arreglado	arreglemos
habíais arreglado	arreglad
habían arreglado	arreglen

atravesar *to cross*

Gerund *atravesando*

Past participle *atravesado*

Present indicative	Present subjunctive
atravieso	atraviese
atraviesas	atravieses
atraviesa	atraviese
atravesamos	atravesemos
atravesáis	atraveséis
atraviesan	atraviesen

Imperfect indicative	Imperfect subjunctive
atravesaba	atravesara
atravesabas	atravesaras
atravesaba	atravesara
atravesábamos	atravesáramos
atravesabais	atravesarais
atravesaban	atravesaran

Preterite	Future
atravesé	atravesaré
atravesaste	atravesarás
atravesó	atravesará
atravesamos	atravesaremos
atravesasteis	atravesaréis
atravesaron	atravesarán

Perfect indicative	Conditional
he atravesado	atravesaría
has atravesado	atravesarías
ha atravesado	atravesaría
hemos atravesado	atravesaríamos
habéis atravesado	atravesaríais
han atravesado	atravesarían

Pluperfect indicative	Imperative
había atravesado	–
habías atravesado	atraviesa
había atravesado	atraviese
habíamos atravesado	atravesemos
habíais atravesado	atravesad
habían atravesado	atraviesen

avergonzarse *to be ashamed*

Gerund *avergonzándose*

Past participle *avergonzado*

Present indicative

me avergüenzo
te avergüenzas
se avergüenza
nos avergonzamos
os avergonzáis
se avergüenzan

Imperfect indicative

me avergonzaba
te avergonzabas
se avergonzaba
nos avergonzábamos
os avergonzabais
se avergonzaban

Preterite

me avergoncé
te avergonzaste
se avergonzó
nos avergonzamos
os avergonzasteis
se avergonzaron

Perfect indicative

me he avergonzado
te has avergonzado
se ha avergonzado
nos hemos
  avergonzado
os habéis
  avergonzado
se han avergonzado

Pluperfect indicative

me había
  avergonzado
te habías
  avergonzado
se había avergonzado
nos habíamos
  avergonzado
os habíais
  avergonzado
se habían
  avergonzado

Present subjunctive

me avergüence
te avergüences
se avergüence
nos avergoncemos
os avergoncéis
se avergüencen

Imperfect subjunctive

me avergonzara
te avergonzaras
se avergonzara
nos avergonzáramos
os avergonzarais
se avergonzaran

Future

me avergonzaré
te avergonzarás
se avergonzará
nos avergonzaremos
os avergonzaréis
se avergonzarán

Conditional

me avergonzaría
te avergonzarías
se avergonzaría
nos avergonzaríamos
os avergonzaríais
se avergonzarían

Imperative

–
avergüénzate
avergüéncese
avergoncémonos
avergonzaos
avergüéncense

averiguar *to find out, verify*

Gerund *averiguando*

Past participle *averiguado*

Present indicative

averiguo
averiguas
averigua
averiguamos
averiguáis
averiguan

Imperfect indicative

averiguaba
averiguabas
averiguaba
averiguábamos
averiguabais
averiguaban

Preterite

averigüé
averiguaste
averiguó
averiguamos
averiguasteis
averiguaron

Perfect indicative

he averiguado
has averiguado
ha averiguado
hemos averiguado
habéis averiguado
han averiguado

Pluperfect indicative

había averiguado
habías averiguado
había averiguado
habíamos averiguado
habíais averiguado
habían averiguado

Present subjunctive

averigüe
averigües
averigüe
averigüemos
averigüéis
averigüen

Imperfect subjunctive

averiguara
averiguaras
averiguara
averiguáramos
averiguarais
averiguaran

Future

averiguaré
averiguarás
averiguará
averiguaremos
averiguaréis
averiguarán

Conditional

averiguaría
averiguarías
averiguaría
averiguaríamos
averiguaríais
averiguarían

Imperative

–
averigua
averigüe
averigüemos
averiguad
averigüen

bajar *to go down*

Gerund *bajando*

Past participle *bajado*

Present indicative	Present subjunctive
bajo	baje
bajas	bajes
baja	baje
bajamos	bajemos
bajáis	bajéis
bajan	bajen

Imperfect indicative	Imperfect subjunctive
bajaba	bajara
bajabas	bajaras
bajaba	bajara
bajábamos	bajáramos
bajabais	bajarais
bajaban	bajaran

Preterite	Future
bajé	bajaré
bajaste	bajarás
bajó	bajará
bajamos	bajaremos
bajasteis	bajaréis
bajaron	bajarán

Perfect indicative	Conditional
he bajado	bajaría
has bajado	bajarías
ha bajado	bajaría
hemos bajado	bajaríamos
habéis bajado	bajaríais
han bajado	bajarían

Pluperfect indicative	Imperative
había bajado	–
habías bajado	baja
había bajado	baje
habíamos bajado	bajemos
habíais bajado	bajad
habían bajado	bajen

bañarse *to bathe, have a bath*

Gerund *bañándose*

Past participle *bañado*

Present indicative	Present subjunctive
me baño	me bañe
te bañas	te bañes
se baña	se bañe
nos bañamos	nos bañemos
os bañáis	os bañéis
se bañan	se bañen

Imperfect indicative	Imperfect subjunctive
me bañaba	me bañara
te bañabas	te bañaras
se bañaba	se bañara
nos bañábamos	nos bañáramos
os bañabais	os bañarais
se bañaban	se bañaran

Preterite	Future
me bañé	me bañaré
te bañaste	te bañarás
se bañó	se bañará
nos bañamos	nos bañaremos
os bañasteis	os bañaréis
se bañaron	se bañarán

Perfect indicative	Conditional
me he bañado	me bañaría
te has bañado	te bañarías
se ha bañado	se bañaría
nos hemos bañado	nos bañaríamos
os habéis bañado	os bañaríais
se han bañado	se bañarían

Pluperfect indicative	Imperative
me había bañado	–
te habías bañado	báñate
se había bañado	báñese
nos habíamos bañado	bañémonos
os habíais bañado	bañaos
se habían bañado	báñense

beber *to drink*

Gerund *bebiendo*

Past participle *bebido*

Present indicative	Present subjunctive
bebo	beba
bebes	bebas
bebe	beba
bebemos	bebamos
bebéis	bebáis
beben	beban

Imperfect indicative	Imperfect subjunctive
bebía	bebiera
bebías	bebieras
bebía	bebiera
bebíamos	bebiéramos
bebíais	bebierais
bebían	bebieran

Preterite	Future
bebí	beberé
bebiste	beberás
bebió	beberá
bebimos	beberemos
bebisteis	beberéis
bebieron	beberán

Perfect indicative	Conditional
he bebido	bebería
has bebido	beberías
ha bebido	bebería
hemos bebido	beberíamos
habéis bebido	beberíais
han bebido	beberían

Pluperfect indicative	Imperative
había bebido	–
habías bebido	bebe
había bebido	beba
habíamos bebido	bebamos
habíais bebido	bebed
habían bebido	beban

buscar *to look for*

Gerund *buscando*

Past participle *buscado*

Present indicative	Present subjunctive
busco	busque
buscas	busques
busca	busque
buscamos	busquemos
buscáis	busquéis
buscan	busquen

Imperfect indicative	Imperfect subjunctive
buscaba	buscara
buscabas	buscaras
buscaba	buscara
buscábamos	buscáramos
buscabais	buscarais
buscaban	buscaran

Preterite	Future
busqué	buscaré
buscaste	buscarás
buscó	buscará
buscamos	buscaremos
buscasteis	buscaréis
buscaron	buscarán

Perfect indicative	Conditional
he buscado	buscaría
has buscado	buscarías
ha buscado	buscaría
hemos buscado	buscaríamos
habéis buscado	buscaríais
han buscado	buscarían

Pluperfect indicative	Imperative
había buscado	–
habías buscado	busca
había buscado	busque
habíamos buscado	busquemos
habíais buscado	buscad
habían buscado	busquen

caber *to fit*

Gerund *cabiendo*

Past participle *cabido*

Present indicative	Present subjunctive
quepo	quepa
cabes	quepas
cabe	quepa
cabemos	quepamos
cabéis	quepáis
caben	quepan

Imperfect indicative	Imperfect subjunctive
cabía	cupiera
cabías	cupieras
cabía	cupiera
cabíamos	cupiéramos
cabíais	cupierais
cabían	cupieran

Preterite	Future
cupe	cabré
cupiste	cabrás
cupo	cabrá
cupimos	cabremos
cupisteis	cabréis
cupieron	cabrán

Perfect indicative	Conditional
he cabido	cabría
has cabido	cabrías
ha cabido	cabría
hemos cabido	cabríamos
habéis cabido	cabríais
han cabido	cabrían

Pluperfect indicative	Imperative
había cabido	–
habías cabido	cabe
había cabido	quepa
habíamos cabido	quepamos
habíais cabido	cabed
habían cabido	quepan

caer *to fall*

Gerund *cayendo*

Past participle *caído*

Present indicative	Present subjunctive
caigo	caiga
caes	caigas
cae	caiga
caemos	caigamos
caéis	caigáis
caen	caigan

Imperfect indicative	Imperfect subjunctive
caía	cayera
caías	cayeras
caía	cayera
caíamos	cayéramos
caíais	cayerais
caían	cayeran

Preterite	Future
caí	caeré
caíste	caerás
cayó	caerá
caímos	caeremos
caísteis	caeréis
cayeron	caerán

Perfect indicative	Conditional
he caído	caería
has caído	caerías
ha caído	caería
hemos caído	caeríamos
habéis caído	caeríais
han caído	caerían

Pluperfect indicative	Imperative
había caído	–
habías caído	cae
había caído	caiga
habíamos caído	caigamos
habíais caído	caed
habían caído	caigan

cambiar *to change*

Gerund *cambiando*

Past participle *cambiado*

Present indicative	Present subjunctive
cambio	
cambias	cambie
cambia	cambies
cambiamos	cambie
cambiáis	cambiemos
cambian	cambiéis
	cambien

Imperfect indicative	Imperfect subjunctive
cambiaba	
cambiabas	cambiara
cambiaba	cambiaras
cambiábamos	cambiara
cambiabais	cambiáramos
cambiaban	cambiarais
	cambiaran

Preterite	Future
cambié	
cambiaste	cambiaré
cambió	cambiarás
cambiamos	cambiará
cambiasteis	cambiaremos
cambiaron	cambiaréis
	cambiarán

Perfect indicative	Conditional
he cambiado	
has cambiado	cambiaría
ha cambiado	cambiarías
hemos cambiado	cambiaría
habéis cambiado	cambiaríamos
han cambiado	cambiaríais
	cambiarían

Pluperfect indicative	Imperative
había cambiado	–
habías cambiado	cambia
había cambiado	cambie
habíamos cambiado	cambiemos
habíais cambiado	cambiad
habían cambiado	cambien

cantar *to sing*

Gerund *cantando*

Past participle *cantado*

Present indicative	Present subjunctive
canto	
cantas	cante
canta	cantes
cantamos	cante
cantáis	cantemos
cantan	cantéis
	canten

Imperfect indicative	Imperfect subjunctive
cantaba	
cantabas	cantara
cantaba	cantaras
cantábamos	cantara
cantabais	cantáramos
cantaban	cantarais
	cantaran

Preterite	Future
canté	
cantaste	cantaré
cantó	cantarás
cantamos	cantará
cantasteis	cantaremos
cantaron	cantaréis
	cantarán

Perfect indicative	Conditional
he cantado	
has cantado	cantaría
ha cantado	cantarías
hemos cantado	cantaría
habéis cantado	cantaríamos
han cantado	cantaríais
	cantarían

Pluperfect indicative	Imperative
había cantado	–
habías cantado	canta
había cantado	cante
habíamos cantado	cantemos
habíais cantado	cantad
habían cantado	canten

cargar *to load*

Gerund *cargando*

Past participle *cargado*

Present indicative	Present subjunctive
cargo	cargue
cargas	cargues
carga	cargue
cargamos	carguemos
cargáis	carguéis
cargan	carguen

Imperfect indicative	Imperfect subjunctive
cargaba	cargara
cargabas	cargaras
cargaba	cargara
cargábamos	cargáramos
cargabais	cargarais
cargaban	cargaran

Preterite	Future
cargué	cargaré
cargaste	cargarás
cargó	cargará
cargamos	cargaremos
cargasteis	cargaréis
cargaron	cargarán

Perfect indicative	Conditional
he cargado	cargaría
has cargado	cargarías
ha cargado	cargaría
hemos cargado	cargaríamos
habéis cargado	cargaríais
han cargado	cargarían

Pluperfect indicative	Imperative
había cargado	–
habías cargado	carga
había cargado	cargue
habíamos cargado	carguemos
habíais cargado	cargad
habían cargado	carguen

casarse *to get married*

Gerund *casándose*

Past participle *casado*

Present indicative	Present subjunctive
me caso	me case
te casas	te cases
se casa	se case
nos casamos	nos casemos
os casáis	os caséis
se casan	se casen

Imperfect indicative	Imperfect subjunctive
me casaba	me casara
te casabas	te casaras
se casaba	se casara
nos casábamos	nos casáramos
os casabais	os casarais
se casaban	se casaran

Preterite	Future
me casé	me casaré
te casaste	te casarás
se casó	se casará
nos casamos	nos casaremos
os casasteis	os casaréis
se casaron	se casarán

Perfect indicative	Conditional
me he casado	me casaría
te has casado	te casarías
se ha casado	se casaría
nos hemos casado	nos casaríamos
os habéis casado	os casaríais
se han casado	se casarían

Pluperfect indicative	Imperative
me había casado	–
te habías casado	cásate
se había casado	cásese
nos habíamos casado	casémonos
os habíais casado	casaos
se habían casado	cásense

cenar *to have supper*

Gerund *cenando*

Past participle *cenado*

Present indicative	Present subjunctive
ceno	
cenas	cene
cena	cenes
cenamos	cene
cenáis	cenemos
cenan	cenéis
	cenen

Imperfect indicative	Imperfect subjunctive
cenaba	
cenabas	cenara
cenaba	cenaras
cenábamos	cenara
cenabais	cenáramos
cenaban	cenarais
	cenaran

Preterite	Future
cené	
cenaste	cenaré
cenó	cenarás
cenamos	cenará
cenasteis	cenaremos
cenaron	cenaréis
	cenarán

Perfect indicative	Conditional
he cenado	
has cenado	cenaría
ha cenado	cenarías
hemos cenado	cenaría
habéis cenado	cenaríamos
han cenado	cenaríais
	cenarían

Pluperfect indicative	Imperative
había cenado	–
habías cenado	cena
había cenado	cene
habíamos cenado	cenemos
habíais cenado	cenad
habían cenado	cenen

cerrar *to close*

Gerund *cerrando*

Past participle *cerrado*

Present indicative	Present subjunctive
cierro	
cierras	cierre
cierra	cierres
cerramos	cierre
cerráis	cerremos
cierran	cerréis
	cierren

Imperfect indicative	Imperfect subjunctive
cerraba	
cerrabas	cerrara
cerraba	cerraras
cerrábamos	cerrara
cerrabais	cerráramos
cerraban	cerrarais
	cerraran

Preterite	Future
cerré	
cerraste	cerraré
cerró	cerrarás
cerramos	cerrará
cerrasteis	cerraremos
cerraron	cerraréis
	cerrarán

Perfect indicative	Conditional
he cerrado	
has cerrado	cerraría
ha cerrado	cerrarías
hemos cerrado	cerraría
habéis cerrado	cerraríamos
han cerrado	cerraríais
	cerrarían

Pluperfect indicative	Imperative
había cerrado	–
habías cerrado	cierra
había cerrado	cierre
habíamos cerrado	cerremos
habíais cerrado	cerrad
habían cerrado	cierren

cocer *to boil*

Gerund *cociendo*

Past participle *cocido*

Present indicative	Present subjunctive
cuezo	cueza
cueces	cuezas
cuece	cueza
cocemos	cozamos
cocéis	cozáis
cuecen	cuezan

Imperfect indicative	Imperfect subjunctive
cocía	cociera
cocías	cocieras
cocía	cociera
cocíamos	cociéramos
cocíais	cocierais
cocían	cocieran

Preterite	Future
cocí	coceré
cociste	cocerás
coció	cocerá
cocimos	coceremos
cocisteis	coceréis
cocieron	cocerán

Perfect indicative	Conditional
he cocido	cocería
has cocido	cocerías
ha cocido	cocería
hemos cocido	coceríamos
habéis cocido	coceríais
han cocido	cocerían

Pluperfect indicative	Imperative
había cocido	–
habías cocido	cuece
había cocido	cueza
habíamos cocido	cozamos
habíais cocido	coced
habían cocido	cuezan

coger *to catch*

Gerund *cogiendo*

Past participle *cogido*

Present indicative	Present subjunctive
cojo	coja
coges	cojas
coge	coja
cogemos	cojamos
cogéis	cojáis
cogen	cojan

Imperfect indicative	Imperfect subjunctive
cogía	cogiera
cogías	cogieras
cogía	cogiera
cogíamos	cogiéramos
cogíais	cogierais
cogían	cogieran

Preterite	Future
cogí	cogeré
cogiste	cogerás
cogió	cogerá
cogimos	cogeremos
cogisteis	cogeréis
cogieron	cogerán

Perfect indicative	Conditional
he cogido	cogería
has cogido	cogerías
ha cogido	cogería
hemos cogido	cogeríamos
habéis cogido	cogeríais
han cogido	cogerían

Pluperfect indicative	Imperative
había cogido	–
habías cogido	coge
había cogido	coja
habíamos cogido	cojamos
habíais cogido	coged
habían cogido	cojan

colgar *to hang*

Gerund *colgando*

Past participle *colgado*

Present indicative	Present subjunctive
cuelgo	cuelgue
cuelgas	cuelgues
cuelga	cuelgue
colgamos	colguemos
colgáis	colguéis
cuelgan	cuelguen

Imperfect indicative	Imperfect subjunctive
colgaba	colgara
colgabas	colgaras
colgaba	colgara
colgábamos	colgáramos
colgabais	colgarais
colgaban	colgaran

Preterite	Future
colgué	colgaré
colgaste	colgarás
colgó	colgará
colgamos	colgaremos
colgasteis	colgaréis
colgaron	colgarán

Perfect indicative	Conditional
he colgado	colgaría
has colgado	colgarías
ha colgado	colgaría
hemos colgado	colgaríamos
habéis colgado	colgaríais
han colgado	colgarían

Pluperfect indicative	Imperative
había colgado	–
habías colgado	cuelga
había colgado	cuelgue
habíamos colgado	colguemos
habíais colgado	colgad
habían colgado	cuelguen

comenzar *to start*

Gerund *comenzando*

Past participle *comenzado*

Present indicative	Present subjunctive
comienzo	comience
comienzas	comiences
comienza	comience
comenzamos	comencemos
comenzáis	comencéis
comienzan	comiencen

Imperfect indicative	Imperfect subjunctive
comenzaba	comenzara
comenzabas	comenzaras
comenzaba	comenzara
comenzábamos	comenzáramos
comenzabais	comenzarais
comenzaban	comenzaran

Preterite	Future
comencé	comenzaré
comenzaste	comenzarás
comenzó	comenzará
comenzamos	comenzaremos
comenzasteis	comenzaréis
comenzaron	comenzarán

Perfect indicative	Conditional
he comenzado	comenzaría
has comenzado	comenzarías
ha comenzado	comenzaría
hemos comenzado	comenzaríamos
habéis comenzado	comenzaríais
han comenzado	comenzarían

Pluperfect indicative	Imperative
había comenzado	–
habías comenzado	comienza
había comenzado	comience
habíamos comenzado	comencemos
habíais comenzado	comenzad
habían comenzado	comiencen

comer *to eat*

Gerund *comiendo*

Past participle *comido*

Present indicative	Present subjunctive
como	coma
comes	comas
come	coma
comemos	comamos
coméis	comáis
comen	coman

Imperfect indicative	Imperfect subjunctive
comía	comiera
comías	comieras
comía	comiera
comíamos	comiéramos
comíais	comierais
comían	comieran

Preterite	Future
comí	comeré
comiste	comerás
comió	comerá
comimos	comeremos
comisteis	comeréis
comieron	comerán

Perfect indicative	Conditional
he comido	comería
has comido	comerías
ha comido	comería
hemos comido	comeríamos
habéis comido	comeríais
han comido	comerían

Pluperfect indicative	Imperative
había comido	–
habías comido	come
había comido	coma
habíamos comido	comamos
habíais comido	comed
habían comido	coman

comprar *to buy*

Gerund *comprando*

Past participle *comprado*

Present indicative	Present subjunctive
compro	compre
compras	compres
compra	compre
compramos	compremos
compráis	compréis
compran	compren

Imperfect indicative	Imperfect subjunctive
compraba	comprara
comprabas	compraras
compraba	comprara
comprábamos	compráramos
comprabais	comprarais
compraban	compraran

Preterite	Future
compré	compraré
compraste	comprarás
compró	comprará
compramos	compraremos
comprasteis	compraréis
compraron	comprarán

Perfect indicative	Conditional
he comprado	compraría
has comprado	comprarías
ha comprado	compraría
hemos comprado	compraríamos
habéis comprado	compraríais
han comprado	comprarían

Pluperfect indicative	Imperative
había comprado	–
habías comprado	compra
había comprado	compre
habíamos comprado	compremos
habíais comprado	comprad
habían comprado	compren

conducir *to drive, lead*

Gerund *conduciendo*

Past participle *conducido*

Present indicative	Present subjunctive
conduzco	conduzca
conduces	conduzcas
conduce	conduzca
conducimos	conduzcamos
conducís	conduzcáis
conducen	conduzcan

Imperfect indicative	Imperfect subjunctive
conducía	condujera
conducías	condujeras
conducía	condujera
conducíamos	condujéramos
conducíais	condujerais
conducían	condujeran

Preterite	Future
conduje	conduciré
condujiste	conducirás
condujo	conducirá
condujimos	conduciremos
condujisteis	conduciréis
condujeron	conducirán

Perfect indicative	Conditional
he conducido	conduciría
has conducido	conducirías
ha conducido	conduciría
hemos-conducido	conduciríamos
habéis conducido	conduciríais
han conducido	conducirían

Pluperfect indicative	Imperative
había conducido	–
habías conducido	conduce
había conducido	conduzca
habíamos conducido	conduzcamos
habíais conducido	conducid
habían conducido	conduzcan

conocer *to know*

Gerund *conociendo*

Past participle *conocido*

Present indicative	Present subjunctive
conozco	conozca
conoces	conozcas
conoce	conozca
conocemos	conozcamos
conocéis	conozcáis
conocen	conozcan

Imperfect indicative	Imperfect subjunctive
conocía	conociera
conocías	conocieras
conocía	conociera
conocíamos	conociéramos
conocíais	conocierais
conocían	conocieran

Preterite	Future
conocí	conoceré
conociste	conocerás
conoció	conocerá
conocimos	conoceremos
conocisteis	conoceréis
conocieron	conocerán

Perfect indicative	Conditional
he conocido	conocería
has conocido	conocerías
ha conocido	conocería
hemos conocido	conoceríamos
habéis conocido	conoceríais
han conocido	conocerían

Pluperfect indicative	Imperative
había conocido	–
habías conocido	conoce
había conocido	conozca
habíamos conocido	conozcamos
habíais conocido	conoced
habían conocido	conozcan

conseguir *to succeed, manage*

Gerund *consiguiendo*

Past participle *conseguido*

Present indicative	Present subjunctive
consigo	consiga
consigues	consigas
consigue	consiga
conseguimos	consigamos
conseguís	consigáis
consiguen	consigan

Imperfect indicative	Imperfect subjunctive
conseguía	consiguiera
conseguías	consiguieras
conseguía	consiguiera
conseguíamos	consiguiéramos
conseguíais	consiguierais
conseguían	consiguieran

Preterite	Future
conseguí	conseguiré
conseguiste	conseguirás
consiguió	conseguirá
conseguimos	conseguiremos
conseguisteis	conseguiréis
consiguieron	conseguirán

Perfect indicative	Conditional
he conseguido	conseguiría
has conseguido	conseguirías
ha conseguido	conseguiría
hemos conseguido	conseguiríamos
habéis conseguido	conseguiríais
han conseguido	conseguirían

Pluperfect indicative	Imperative
había conseguido	–
habías conseguido	consigue
había conseguido	consiga
habíamos conseguido	consigamos
habíais conseguido	conseguid
habían conseguido	consigan

construir *to build*

Gerund *construyendo*

Past participle *construido*

Present indicative	Present subjunctive
construyo	construya
construyes	construyas
construye	construya
construimos	construyamos
construís	construyáis
construyen	construyan

Imperfect indicative	Imperfect subjunctive
construía	construyera
construías	construyeras
construía	construyera
construíamos	construyéramos
construíais	construyerais
construían	construyeran

Preterite	Future
construí	construiré
construiste	construirás
construyó	construirá
construimos	construiremos
construisteis	construiréis
construyeron	construirán

Perfect indicative	Conditional
he construido	construiría
has construido	construirías
ha construido	construiría
hemos construido	construiríamos
habéis construido	construiríais
han construido	construirían

Pluperfect indicative	Imperative
había construido	–
habías construido	construye
había construido	construya
habíamos construido	construyamos
habíais construido	construid
habían construido	construyan

contar *to tell, to count*

Gerund *contando*

Past participle *contado*

Present indicative	Present subjunctive
cuento	cuente
cuentas	cuentes
cuenta	cuente
contamos	contemos
contáis	contéis
cuentan	cuenten

Imperfect indicative	Imperfect subjunctive
contaba	contara
contabas	contaras
contaba	contara
contábamos	contáramos
contabais	contarais
contaban	contaran

Preterite	Future
conté	contaré
contaste	contarás
contó	contará
contamos	contaremos
contasteis	contaréis
contaron	contarán

Perfect indicative	Conditional
he contado	contaría
has contado	contarías
ha contado	contaría
hemos contado	contaríamos
habéis contado	contaríais
han contado	contarían

Pluperfect indicative	Imperative
había contado	–
habías contado	cuenta
había contado	cuente
habíamos contado	contemos
habíais contado	contad
habían contado	cuenten

contestar *to answer*

Gerund *contestando*

Past participle *contestado*

Present indicative	Present subjunctive
contesto	conteste
contestas	contestes
contesta	conteste
contestamos	contestemos
contestáis	contestéis
contestan	contesten

Imperfect indicative	Imperfect subjunctive
contestaba	contestara
contestabas	contestaras
contestaba	contestara
contestábamos	contestáramos
contestabais	contestarais
contestaban	contestaran

Preterite	Future
contesté	contestaré
contestaste	contestarás
contestó	contestará
contestamos	contestaremos
contestasteis	contestaréis
contestaron	contestarán

Perfect indicative	Conditional
he contestado	contestaría
has contestado	contestarías
ha contestado	contestaría
hemos contestado	contestaríamos
habéis contestado	contestaríais
han contestado	contestarían

Pluperfect indicative	Imperative
había contestado	–
habías contestado	contesta
había contestado	conteste
habíamos contestado	contestemos
habíais contestado	contestad
habían contestado	contesten

continuar *to continue*

Gerund *continuando*
Past participle *continuado*

Present indicative	Present subjunctive
continúo	continúe
continúas	continúes
continúa	continúe
continuamos	continuemos
continuáis	continuéis
continúan	continúen

Imperfect indicative	Imperfect subjunctive
continuaba	continuara
continuabas	continuaras
continuaba	continuara
continuábamos	continuáramos
continuabais	continuarais
continuaban	continuaran

Preterite	Future
continué	continuaré
continuaste	continuarás
continuó	continuará
continuamos	continuaremos
continuasteis	continuaréis
continuaron	continuarán

Perfect indicative	Conditional
he continuado	continuaría
has continuado	continuarías
ha continuado	continuaría
hemos continuado	continuaríamos
habéis continuado	continuaríais
han continuado	continuarían

Pluperfect indicative	Imperative
había continuado	–
habías continuado	continúa
había continuado	continúe
habíamos continuado	continuemos
habíais continuado	continuad
habían continuado	continúen

correr *to run*

Gerund *corriendo*
Past participle *corrido*

Present indicative	Present subjunctive
corro	corra
corres	corras
corre	corra
corremos	corramos
corréis	corráis
corren	corran

Imperfect indicative	Imperfect subjunctive
corría	corriera
corrías	corrieras
corría	corriera
corríamos	corriéramos
corríais	corrierais
corrían	corrieran

Preterite	Future
corrí	correré
corriste	correrás
corrió	correrá
corrimos	correremos
corristeis	correréis
corrieron	correrán

Perfect indicative	Conditional
he corrido	correría
has corrido	correrías
ha corrido	correría
hemos corrido	correríamos
habéis corrido	correríais
han corrido	correrían

Pluperfect indicative	Imperative
había corrido	–
habías corrido	corre
había corrido	corra
habíamos corrido	corramos
habíais corrido	corred
habían corrido	corran

cortar *to cut*

Gerund *cortando*

Past participle *cortado*

Present indicative	Present subjunctive
corto	corte
cortas	cortes
corta	corte
cortamos	cortemos
cortáis	cortéis
cortan	corten

Imperfect indicative	Imperfect subjunctive
cortaba	cortara
cortabas	cortaras
cortaba	cortara
cortábamos	cortáramos
cortabais	cortarais
cortaban	cortaran

Preterite	Future
corté	cortaré
cortaste	cortarás
cortó	cortará
cortamos	cortaremos
cortasteis	cortaréis
cortaron	cortarán

Perfect indicative	Conditional
he cortado	cortaría
has cortado	cortarías
ha cortado	cortaría
hemos cortado	cortaríamos
habéis cortado	cortaríais
han cortado	cortarían

Pluperfect indicative	Imperative
había cortado	–
habías cortado	corta
había cortado	corte
habíamos cortado	cortemos
habíais cortado	cortad
habían cortado	corten

costar *to cost*

Gerund *costando*

Past participle *costado*

Present indicative	Present subjunctive
cuesto	cueste
cuestas	cuestes
cuesta	cueste
costamos	costemos
costáis	costéis
cuestan	cuesten

Imperfect indicative	Imperfect subjunctive
costaba	costara
costabas	costaras
costaba	costara
costábamos	costáramos
costabais	costarais
costaban	costaran

Preterite	Future
costé	costaré
costaste	costarás
costó	costará
costamos	costaremos
costasteis	costaréis
costaron	costarán

Perfect indicative	Conditional
he costado	costaría
has costado	costarías
ha costado	costaría
hemos costado	costaríamos
habéis costado	costaríais
han costado	costarían

Pluperfect indicative	Imperative
había costado	–
habías costado	cuesta
había costado	cueste
habíamos costado	costemos
habíais costado	costad
habían costado	cuesten

crecer *to grow, increase*

Gerund *creciendo*

Past participle *crecido*

Present indicative	Present subjunctive
crezco	crezca
creces	crezcas
crece	crezca
crecemos	crezcamos
crecéis	crezcáis
crecen	crezcan

Imperfect indicative	Imperfect subjunctive
crecía	creciera
crecías	crecieras
crecía	creciera
crecíamos	creciéramos
crecíais	crecierais
crecían	crecieran

Preterite	Future
crecí	creceré
creciste	crecerás
creció	crecerá
crecimos	creceremos
crecisteis	creceréis
crecieron	crecerán

Perfect indicative	Conditional
he crecido	crecería
has crecido	crecerías
ha crecido	crecería
hemos crecido	creceríamos
habéis crecido	creceríais
han crecido	crecerían

Pluperfect indicative	Imperative
había crecido	–
habías crecido	crece
había crecido	crezca
habíamos crecido	crezcamos
habíais crecido	creced
habían crecido	crezcan

creer *to believe*

Gerund *creyendo*

Past participle *creído*

Present indicative	Present subjunctive
creo	crea
crees	creas
cree	crea
creemos	creamos
creéis	creáis
creen	crean

Imperfect indicative	Imperfect subjunctive
creía	creyera
creías	creyeras
creía	creyera
creíamos	creyéramos
creíais	creyerais
creían	creyeran

Preterite	Future
creí	creeré
creíste	creerás
creyó	creerá
creímos	creeremos
creísteis	creeréis
creyeron	creerán

Perfect indicative	Conditional
he creído	creería
has creído	creerías
ha creído	creería
hemos creído	creeríamos
habéis creído	creeríais
han creído	creerían

Pluperfect indicative	Imperative
había creído	–
habías creído	cree
había creído	crea
habíamos creído	creamos
habíais creído	creed
habían creído	crean

cubrir *to cover*

Gerund *cubriendo*

Past participle *cubierto*

Present indicative	Present subjunctive
cubro	cubra
cubres	cubras
cubre	cubra
cubrimos	cubramos
cubrís	cubráis
cubren	cubran

Imperfect indicative	Imperfect subjunctive
cubría	cubriera
cubrías	cubrieras
cubría	cubriera
cubríamos	cubriéramos
cubríais	cubrierais
cubrían	cubrieran

Preterite	Future
cubrí	cubriré
cubriste	cubrirás
cubrió	cubrirá
cubrimos	cubriremos
cubristeis	cubriréis
cubrieron	cubrirán

Perfect indicative	Conditional
he cubierto	cubriría
has cubierto	cubrirías
ha cubierto	cubriría
hemos cubierto	cubriríamos
habéis cubierto	cubriríais
han cubierto	cubrirían

Pluperfect indicative	Imperative
había cubierto	–
habías cubierto	cubre
había cubierto	cubra
habíamos cubierto	cubramos
habíais cubierto	cubrid
habían cubierto	cubran

dar *to give*

Gerund *dando*

Past participle *dado*

Present indicative	Present subjunctive
doy	dé
das	des
da	dé
damos	demos
dais	deis
dan	den

Imperfect indicative	Imperfect subjunctive
daba	diera
dabas	dieras
daba	diera
dábamos	diéramos
dabais	dierais
daban	dieran

Preterite	Future
di	daré
diste	darás
dio	dará
dimos	daremos
disteis	daréis
dieron	darán

Perfect indicative	Conditional
he dado	daría
has dado	darías
ha dado	daría
hemos dado	daríamos
habéis dado	daríais
han dado	darían

Pluperfect indicative	Imperative
había dado	–
habías dado	da
había dado	dé
habíamos dado	demos
habíais dado	dad
habían dado	den

deber *to have to, owe*

Gerund *debiendo*

Past participle *debido*

Present indicative	Present subjunctive
debo	
debes	deba
debe	debas
debemos	deba
debéis	debamos
deben	debáis
	deban

Imperfect indicative	Imperfect subjunctive
debía	
debías	debiera
debía	debieras
debíamos	debiera
debíais	debiéramos
debían	debierais
	debieran

Preterite	Future
debí	
debiste	deberé
debió	deberás
debimos	deberá
debisteis	deberemos
debieron	deberéis
	deberán

Perfect indicative	Conditional
he debido	
has debido	debería
ha debido	deberías
hemos debido	debería
habéis debido	deberíamos
han debido	deberíais
	deberían

Pluperfect indicative	Imperative
había debido	–
habías debido	debe
había debido	deba
habíamos debido	debamos
habíais debido	debed
habían debido	deban

decidir *to decide*

Gerund *decidiendo*

Past participle *decidido*

Present indicative	Present subjunctive
decido	
decides	decida
decide	decidas
decidimos	decida
decidís	decidamos
deciden	decidáis
	decidan

Imperfect indicative	Imperfect subjunctive
decidía	
decidías	decidiera
decidía	decidieras
decidíamos	decidiera
decidíais	decidiéramos
decidían	decidierais
	decidieran

Preterite	Future
decidí	
decidiste	decidiré
decidió	decidirás
decidimos	decidirá
decidisteis	decidiremos
decidieron	decidiréis
	decidirán

Perfect indicative	Conditional
he decidido	
has decidido	decidiría
ha decidido	decidirías
hemos decidido	decidiría
habéis decidido	decidiríamos
han decidido	decidiríais
	decidirían

Pluperfect indicative	Imperative
había decidido	–
habías decidido	decide
había decidido	decida
habíamos decidido	decidamos
habíais decidido	decidid
habían decidido	decidan

decir *to say*

Gerund *diciendo*

Past participle *dicho*

Present indicative	Present subjunctive
digo	diga
dices	digas
dice	diga
decimos	digamos
decís	digáis
dicen	digan

Imperfect indicative	Imperfect subjunctive
decía	dijera
decías	dijeras
decía	dijera
decíamos	dijéramos
decíais	dijerais
decían	dijeran

Preterite	Future
dije	diré
dijiste	dirás
dijo	dirá
dijimos	diremos
dijisteis	diréis
dijeron	dirán

Perfect indicative	Conditional
he dicho	diría
has dicho	dirías
ha dicho	diría
hemos dicho	diríamos
habéis dicho	diríais
han dicho	dirían

Pluperfect indicative	Imperative
había dicho	–
habías dicho	di
había dicho	diga
habíamos dicho	digamos
habíais dicho	decid
habían dicho	digan

dejar *to leave, let*

Gerund *dejando*

Past participle *dejado*

Present indicative	Present subjunctive
dejo	deje
dejas	dejes
deja	deje
dejamos	dejemos
dejáis	dejéis
dejan	dejen

Imperfect indicative	Imperfect subjunctive
dejaba	dejara
dejabas	dejaras
dejaba	dejara
dejábamos	dejáramos
dejabais	dejarais
dejaban	dejaran

Preterite	Future
dejé	dejaré
dejaste	dejarás
dejó	dejará
dejamos	dejaremos
dejasteis	dejaréis
dejaron	dejarán

Perfect indicative	Conditional
he dejado	dejaría
has dejado	dejarías
ha dejado	dejaría
hemos dejado	dejaríamos
habéis dejado	dejaríais
han dejado	dejarían

Pluperfect indicative	Imperative
había dejado	–
habías dejado	deja
había dejado	deje
habíamos dejado	dejemos
habíais dejado	dejad
habían dejado	dejen

descender *to go down*

Gerund *descendiendo*

Past participle *descendido*

Present indicative	Present subjunctive
desciendo	descienda
desciendes	desciendas
desciende	descienda
descendemos	descendamos
descendéis	descendáis
descienden	desciendan

Imperfect indicative	Imperfect subjunctive
descendía	descendiera
descendías	descendieras
descendía	descendiera
descendíamos	descendiéramos
descendíais	descendierais
descendían	descendieran

Preterite	Future
descendí	descenderé
descendiste	descenderás
descendió	descenderá
descendimos	descenderemos
descendisteis	descenderéis
descendieron	descenderán

Perfect indicative	Conditional
he descendido	descendería
has descendido	descenderías
ha descendido	descendería
hemos descendido	descenderíamos
habéis descendido	descenderíais
han descendido	descenderían

Pluperfect indicative	Imperative
había descendido	–
habías descendido	desciende
había descendido	descienda
habíamos descendido	descendamos
habíais descendido	descended
habían descendido	desciendan

describir *to describe*

Gerund *describiendo*

Past participle *descrito*

Present indicative	Present subjunctive
describo	describa
describes	describas
describe	describa
describimos	describamos
describís	describáis
describen	describan

Imperfect indicative	Imperfect subjunctive
describía	describiera
describías	describieras
describía	describiera
describíamos	describiéramos
describíais	describierais
describían	describieran

Preterite	Future
describí	describiré
describiste	describirás
describió	describirá
describimos	describiremos
describisteis	describiréis
describieron	describirán

Perfect indicative	Conditional
he descrito	describiría
has descrito	describirías
ha descrito	describiría
hemos descrito	describiríamos
habéis descrito	describiríais
han descrito	describirían

Pluperfect indicative	Imperative
había descrito	–
habías descrito	describe
había descrito	describa
habíamos descrito	describamos
habíais descrito	describid
habían descrito	describan

descubrir *to discover*

Gerund *descubriendo*

Past participle *descubierto*

Present indicative

descubro
descubres
descubre
descubrimos
descubrís
descubren

Present subjunctive

descubra
descubras
descubra
descubramos
descubráis
descubran

Imperfect indicative

descubría
descubrías
descubría
descubríamos
descubríais
descubrían

Imperfect subjunctive

descubriera
descubrieras
descubriera
descubriéramos
descubrierais
descubrieran

Preterite

descubrí
descubriste
descubrió
descubrimos
descubristeis
descubrieron

Future

descubriré
descubrirás
descubrirá
descubriremos
descubriréis
descubrirán

Perfect indicative

he descubierto
has descubierto
ha descubierto
hemos descubierto
habéis descubierto
han descubierto

Conditional

descubriría
descubrirías
descubriría
descubriríamos
descubriríais
descubrirían

Pluperfect indicative

había descubierto
habías descubierto
había descubierto
habíamos descubierto
habíais descubierto
habían descubierto

Imperative

–
descubre
descubra
descubramos
descubrid
descubran

despertarse *to wake up*

Gerund *despertándose*

Past participle *despertado*

Present indicative

me despierto
te despiertas
se despierta
nos despertamos
os despertáis
se despiertan

Present subjunctive

me despierte
te despiertes
se despierte
nos despertemos
os despertéis
se despierten

Imperfect indicative

me despertaba
te despertabas
se despertaba
nos despertábamos
os despertabais
se despertaban

Imperfect subjunctive

me despertara
te despertaras
se despertara
nos despertáramos
os despertarais
se despertaran

Preterite

me desperté
te despertaste
se despertó
nos despertamos
os despertasteis
se despertaron

Future

me despertaré
te despertarás
se despertará
nos despertaremos
os despertaréis
se despertarán

Perfect indicative

me he despertado
te has despertado
se ha despertado
nos hemos despertado
os habéis despertado
se han despertado

Conditional

me despertaría
te despertarías
se despertaría
nos despertaríamos
os despertaríais
se despertarían

Pluperfect indicative

me había despertado
te habías despertado
se había despertado
nos habíamos despertado
os habíais despertado
se habían despertado

Imperative

despiértate
despiértese
despertémonos
despertaos
despiértense

destruir *to destroy*

Gerund *destruyendo*

Past participle *destruido*

Present indicative	Present subjunctive
destruyo	destruya
destruyes	destruyas
destruye	destruya
destruimos	destruyamos
destruís	destruyáis
destruyen	destruyan

Imperfect indicative	Imperfect subjunctive
destruía	destruyera
destruías	destruyeras
destruía	destruyera
destruíamos	destruyéramos
destruíais	destruyerais
destruían	destruyeran

Preterite	Future
destruí	destruiré
destruiste	destruirás
destruyó	destruirá
destruimos	destruiremos
destruisteis	destruiréis
destruyeron	destruirán

Perfect indicative	Conditional
he destruido	destruiría
has destruido	destruirías
ha destruido	destruiría
hemos destruido	destruiríamos
habéis destruido	destruiríais
han destruido	destruirían

Pluperfect indicative	Imperative
había destruido	–
habías destruido	destruye
había destruido	destruya
habíamos destruido	destruyamos
habíais destruido	destruid
habían destruido	destruyan

dirigir *to direct*

Gerund *dirigiendo*

Past participle *dirigido*

Present indicative	Present subjunctive
dirijo	dirija
diriges	dirijas
dirige	dirija
dirigimos	dirijamos
dirigís	dirijáis
dirigen	dirijan

Imperfect indicative	Imperfect subjunctive
dirigía	dirigiera
dirigías	dirigieras
dirigía	dirigiera
dirigíamos	dirigiéramos
dirigíais	dirigierais
dirigían	dirigieran

Preterite	Future
dirigí	dirigiré
dirigiste	dirigirás
dirigió	dirigirá
dirigimos	dirigiremos
dirigisteis	dirigiréis
dirigieron	dirigirán

Perfect indicative	Conditional
he dirigido	dirigiría
has dirigido	dirigirías
ha dirigido	dirigiría
hemos dirigido	dirigiríamos
habéis dirigido	dirigiríais
han dirigido	dirigirían

Pluperfect indicative	Imperative
había dirigido	–
habías dirigido	dirige
había dirigido	dirija
habíamos dirigido	dirijamos
habíais dirigido	dirigid
habían dirigido	dirijan

distinguir *to distinguish*

Gerund *distinguiendo*

Past participle *distinguido*

Present indicative

distingo
distingues
distingue
distinguimos
distinguís
distinguen

Present subjunctive

distinga
distingas
distinga
distingamos
distingáis
distingan

Imperfect indicative

distinguía
distinguías
distinguía
distinguíamos
distinguíais
distinguían

Imperfect subjunctive

distinguiera
distinguieras
distinguiera
distinguiéramos
distinguierais
distinguieran

Preterite

distinguí
distinguiste
distinguió
distinguimos
distinguisteis
distinguieron

Future

distinguiré
distinguirás
distinguirá
distinguiremos
distinguiréis
distinguirán

Perfect indicative

he distinguido
has distinguido
ha distinguido
hemos distinguido
habéis distinguido
han distinguido

Conditional

distinguiría
distinguirías
distinguiría
distinguiríamos
distinguiríais
distinguirían

Pluperfect indicative

había distinguido
habías distinguido
había distinguido
habíamos distinguido
habíais distinguido
habían distinguido

Imperative

–
distingue
distinga
distingamos
distinguid
distingan

divertirse *to enjoy oneself*

Gerund *divertiéndose*

Past participle *divertido*

Present indicative

me divierto
te diviertes
se divierte
nos divertimos
os divertís
se divierten

Present subjunctive

me divierta
te diviertas
se divierta
nos divirtamos
os divirtáis
se diviertan

Imperfect indicative

me divertía
te divertías
se divertía
nos divertíamos
os divertíais
se divertían

Imperfect subjunctive

me divirtiera
te divirtieras
se divirtiera
nos divirtiéramos
os divirtierais
se divirtieran

Preterite

me divertí
te divertiste
se divirtió
nos divertimos
os divertisteis
se divirtieron

Future

me divertiré
te divertirás
se divertirá
nos divertiremos
os divertiréis
se divertirán

Perfect indicative

me he divertido
te has divertido
se ha divertido
nos hemos divertido
os habéis divertido
se han divertido

Conditional

me divertiría
te divertirías
se divertiría
nos divertiríamos
os divertiríais
se divertirían

Pluperfect indicative

me había divertido
te habías divertido
se había divertido
nos habíamos
  divertido
os habíais divertido
se habían divertido

Imperative

–
diviértete
diviértase
divirtámonos
divertíos
diviértanse

dormir *to sleep*

Gerund *durmiendo*

Past participle *dormido*

Present indicative	Present subjunctive
duermo	duerma
duermes	duermas
duerme	duerma
dormimos	durmamos
dormís	durmáis
duermen	durman

Imperfect indicative	Imperfect subjunctive
dormía	durmiera
dormías	durmieras
dormía	durmiera
dormíamos	durmiéramos
dormíais	durmierais
dormían	durmieran

Preterite	Future
dormí	dormiré
dormiste	dormirás
durmió	dormirá
dormimos	dormiremos
dormisteis	dormiréis
durmieron	dormirán

Perfect indicative	Conditional
he dormido	dormiría
has dormido	dormirías
ha dormido	dormiría
hemos dormido	dormiríamos
habéis dormido	dormiríais
han dormido	dormirían

Pluperfect indicative	Imperative
había dormido	–
habías dormido	duerme
había dormido	duerma
habíamos dormido	durmamos
habíais dormido	dormid
habían dormido	duerman

embarcar *to embark*

Gerund *embarcando*

Past participle *embarcado*

Present indicative	Present subjunctive
embarco	embarque
embarcas	embarques
embarca	embarque
embarcamos	embarquemos
embarcáis	embarquéis
embarcan	embarquen

Imperfect indicative	Imperfect subjunctive
embarcaba	embarcara
embarcabas	embarcaras
embarcaba	embarcara
embarcábamos	embarcáramos
embarcabais	embarcarais
embarcaban	embarcaran

Preterite	Future
embarqué	embarcaré
embarcaste	embarcarás
embarcó	embarcará
embarcamos	embarcaremos
embarcasteis	embarcaréis
embarcaron	embarcarán

Perfect indicative	Conditional
he embarcado	embarcaría
has embarcado	embarcarías
ha embarcado	embarcaría
hemos embarcado	embarcaríamos
habéis embarcado	embarcaríais
han embarcado	embarcarían

Pluperfect indicative	Imperative
había embarcado	–
habías embarcado	embarca
había embarcado	embarque
habíamos embarcado	embarquemos
habíais embarcado	embarcad
habían embarcado	embarquen

empezar *to begin*

Gerund *empezando*

Past participle *empezado*

Present indicative	Present subjunctive
empiezo	empiece
empiezas	empieces
empieza	empiece
empezamos	empecemos
empezáis	empecéis
empiezan	empiecen

Imperfect indicative	Imperfect subjunctive
empezaba	empezara
empezabas	empezaras
empezaba	empezara
empezábamos	empezáramos
empezabais	empezarais
empezaban	empezaran

Preterite	Future
empecé	empezaré
empezaste	empezarás
empezó	empezará
empezamos	empezaremos
empezasteis	empezaréis
empezaron	empezarán

Perfect indicative	Conditional
he empezado	empezaría
has empezado	empezarías
ha empezado	empezaría
hemos empezado	empezaríamos
habéis empezado	empezaríais
han empezado	empezarían

Pluperfect indicative	Imperative
había empezado	–
habías empezado	empieza
había empezado	empiece
habíamos empezado	empecemos
habíais empezado	empezad
habían empezado	empiecen

empujar *to push*

Gerund *empujando*

Past participle *empujado*

Present indicative	Present subjunctive
empujo	empuje
empujas	empujes
empuja	empuje
empujamos	empujemos
empujáis	empujéis
empujan	empujen

Imperfect indicative	Imperfect subjunctive
empujaba	empujara
empujabas	empujaras
empujaba	empujara
empujábamos	empujáramos
empujabais	empujarais
empujaban	empujaran

Preterite	Future
empujé	empujaré
empujaste	empujarás
empujó	empujará
empujamos	empujaremos
empujasteis	empujaréis
empujaron	empujarán

Perfect indicative	Conditional
he empujado	empujaría
has empujado	empujarías
ha empujado	empujaría
hemos empujado	empujaríamos
habéis empujado	empujaríais
han empujado	empujarían

Pluperfect indicative	Imperative
había empujado	–
habías empujado	empuja
había empujado	empuje
habíamos empujado	empujemos
habíais empujado	empujad
habían empujado	empujen

encender *to light, turn on*

Gerund *encendiendo*

Past participle *encendido*

Present indicative	Present subjunctive
enciendo	enciende
enciendes	enciendas
enciende	encienda
encendemos	encendamos
encendéis	encendáis
encienden	enciendan

Imperfect indicative	Imperfect subjunctive
encendía	encendiera
encendías	encendieras
encendía	encendiera
encendíamos	encendiéramos
encendíais	encendierais
encendían	encendieran

Preterite	Future
encendí	encenderé
encendiste	encenderás
encendió	encenderá
encendimos	encenderemos
encendisteis	encenderéis
encendieron	encenderán

Perfect indicative	Conditional
he encendido	encendería
has encendido	encenderías
ha encendido	encendería
hemos encendido	encenderíamos
habéis encendido	encenderíais
han encendido	encenderían

Pluperfect indicative	Imperative
había encendido	–
habías encendido	enciende
había encendido	encienda
habíamos encendido	encendamos
habíais encendido	encended
habían encendido	enciendan

encontrar *to find*

Gerund *encontrando*

Past participle *encontrado*

Present indicative	Present subjunctive
encuentro	encuentre
encuentras	encuentres
encuentra	encuentre
encontramos	encontremos
encontráis	encontréis
encuentran	encuentren

Imperfect indicative	Imperfect subjunctive
encontraba	encontrara
encontrabas	encontraras
encontraba	encontrara
encontrábamos	encontráramos
encontrabais	encontrarais
encontraban	encontraran

Preterite	Future
encontré	encontraré
encontraste	encontrarás
encontró	encontrará
encontramos	encontraremos
encontrasteis	encontraréis
encontraron	encontrarán

Perfect indicative	Conditional
he encontrado	encontraría
has encontrado	encontrarías
ha encontrado	encontraría
hemos encontrado	encontraríamos
habéis encontrado	encontraríais
han encontrado	encontrarían

Pluperfect indicative	Imperative
había encontrado	–
habías encontrado	encuentra
había encontrado	encuentre
habíamos encontrado	encontremos
habíais encontrado	encontrad
habían encontrado	encuentren

entender *to understand*

Gerund *entendiendo*

Past participle *entendido*

Present indicative	Present subjunctive
entiendo	entienda
entiendes	entiendas
entiende	entienda
entendemos	entendamos
entendéis	entendáis
entienden	entiendan

Imperfect indicative	Imperfect subjunctive
entendía	entendiera
entendías	entendieras
entendía	entendiera
entendíamos	entendiéramos
entendíais	entendierais
entendían	entendieran

Preterite	Future
entendí	entenderé
entendiste	entenderás
entendió	entenderá
entendimos	entenderemos
entendisteis	entenderéis
entendieron	entenderán

Perfect indicative	Conditional
he entendido	entendería
has entendido	entenderías
ha entendido	entendería
hemos entendido	entenderíamos
habéis entendido	entenderíais
han entendido	entenderían

Pluperfect indicative	Imperative
había entendido	–
habías entendido	entiende
había entendido	entienda
habíamos entendido	entendamos
habíais entendido	entended
habían entendido	entiendan

entrar *to enter, go in*

Gerund *entrando*

Past participle *entrado*

Present indicative	Present subjunctive
entro	entre
entras	entres
entra	entre
entramos	entremos
entráis	entréis
entran	entren

Imperfect indicative	Imperfect subjunctive
entraba	entrara
entrabas	entraras
entraba	entrara
entrábamos	entráramos
entrabais	entrarais
entraban	entraran

Preterite	Future
entré	entraré
entraste	entrarás
entró	entrará
entramos	entraremos
entrasteis	entraréis
entraron	entrarán

Perfect indicative	Conditional
he entrado	entraría
has entrado	entrarías
ha entrado	entraría
hemos entrado	entraríamos
habéis entrado	entraríais
han entrado	entrarían

Pluperfect indicative	Imperative
había entrado	–
habías entrado	entra
había entrado	entre
habíamos entrado	entremos
habíais entrado	entrad
habían entrado	entren

enviar *to send*

Gerund *enviando*

Past participle *enviado*

Present indicative	Present subjunctive
envío	envíe
envías	envíes
envía	envíe
enviamos	enviemos
enviáis	enviéis
envían	envíen

Imperfect indicative	Imperfect subjunctive
enviaba	enviara
enviabas	enviaras
enviaba	enviara
enviábamos	enviáramos
enviabais	enviarais
enviaban	enviaran

Preterite	Future
envié	enviaré
enviaste	enviarás
envió	enviará
enviamos	enviaremos
enviasteis	enviaréis
enviaron	enviarán

Perfect indicative	Conditional
he enviado	enviaría
has enviado	enviarías
ha enviado	enviaría
hemos enviado	enviaríamos
habéis enviado	enviaríais
han enviado	enviarían

Pluperfect indicative	Imperative
había enviado	–
habías enviado	envía
había enviado	envíe
habíamos enviado	enviemos
habíais enviado	enviad
habían enviado	envíen

equivocarse *to make a mistake*

Gerund *equivocándose*

Past participle *equivocado*

Present indicative	Present subjunctive
me equivoco	me equivoque
te equivocas	te equivoques
se equivoca	se equivoque
nos equivocamos	nos equivoquemos
os equivocáis	os equivoquéis
se equivocan	se equivoquen

Imperfect indicative	Imperfect subjunctive
me equivocaba	me equivocara
te equivocabas	te equivocaras
se equivocaba	se equivocara
nos equivocábamos	nos equivocáramos
os equivocabais	os equivocarais
se equivocaban	se equivocaran

Preterite	Future
me equivoqué	me equivocaré
te equivocaste	te equivocarás
se equivocó	se equivocará
nos equivocamos	nos equivocaremos
os equivocasteis	os equivocaréis
se equivocaron	se equivocarán

Perfect indicative	Conditional
me he equivocado	me equivocaría
te has equivocado	te equivocarías
se ha equivocado	se equivocaría
nos hemos equivocado	nos equivocaríamos
os habéis equivocado	os equivocaríais
se han equivocado	se equivocarían

Pluperfect indicative	Imperative
me había equivocado	–
te habías equivocado	equivócate
se había equivocado	equivóquese
nos habíamos equivocado	equivocémonos
os habíais equivocado	equivocaos
se habían equivocado	equivóquense

errar *to err, wander*

Gerund *errando*

Past participle *errado*

Present indicative	Present subjunctive
yerro	yerre
yerras	yerres
yerra	yerre
erramos	erremos
erráis	erréis
yerran	yerren

Imperfect indicative	Imperfect subjunctive
erraba	errara
errabas	erraras
erraba	errara
errábamos	erráramos
errabais	errarais
erraban	erraran

Preterite	Future
erré	erraré
erraste	errarás
erró	errará
erramos	erraremos
errasteis	erraréis
erraron	errarán

Perfect indicative	Conditional
he errado	erraría
has errado	errarías
ha errado	erraría
hemos errado	erraríamos
habéis errado	erraríais
han errado	errarían

Pluperfect indicative	Imperative
había errado	–
habías errado	yerra
había errado	yerre
habíamos errado	erremos
habíais errado	errad
habían errado	yerren

escoger *to choose*

Gerund *escogiendo*

Past participle *escogido*

Present indicative	Present subjunctive
escojo	escoja
escoges	escojas
escoge	escoja
escogemos	escojamos
escogéis	escojáis
escogen	escojan

Imperfect indicative	Imperfect subjunctive
escogía	escogiera
escogías	escogieras
escogía	escogiera
escogíamos	escogiéramos
escogíais	escogierais
escogían	escogieran

Preterite	Future
escogí	escogeré
escogiste	escogerás
escogió	escogerá
escogimos	escogeremos
escogisteis	escogeréis
escogieron	escogerán

Perfect indicative	Conditional
he escogido	escogería
has escogido	escogerías
ha escogido	escogería
hemos escogido	escogeríamos
habéis escogido	escogeríais
han escogido	escogerían

Pluperfect indicative	Imperative
había escogido	–
habías escogido	escoge
había escogido	escoja
habíamos escogido	escojamos
habíais escogido	escoged
habían escogido	escojan

escribir *to write*

Gerund *escribiendo*

Past participle *escrito*

Present indicative	Present subjunctive
escribo	escriba
escribes	escribas
escribe	escriba
escribimos	escribamos
escribís	escribáis
escriben	escriban

Imperfect indicative	Imperfect subjunctive
escribía	escribiera
escribías	escribieras
escribía	escribiera
escribíamos	escribiéramos
escribíais	escribierais
escribían	escribieran

Preterite	Future
escribí	escribiré
escribiste	escribirás
escribió	escribirá
escribimos	escribiremos
escribisteis	escribiréis
escribieron	escribirán

Perfect indicative	Conditional
he escrito	escribiría
has escrito	escribirías
ha escrito	escribiría
hemos escrito	escribiríamos
habéis escrito	escribiríais
han escrito	escribirían

Pluperfect indicative	Imperative
había escrito	–
habías escrito	escribe
había escrito	escriba
habíamos escrito	escribamos
habíais escrito	escribid
habían escrito	escriban

escuchar *to listen*

Gerund *escuchando*

Past participle *escuchado*

Present indicative	Present subjunctive
escucho	escuche
escuchas	escuches
escucha	escuche
escuchamos	escuchemos
escucháis	escuchéis
escuchan	escuchen

Imperfect indicative	Imperfect subjunctive
escuchaba	escuchara
escuchabas	escucharas
escuchaba	escuchara
escuchábamos	escucháramos
escuchabais	escucharais
escuchaban	escucharan

Preterite	Future
escuché	escucharé
escuchaste	escucharás
escuchó	escuchará
escuchamos	escucharemos
escuchasteis	escucharéis
escucharon	escucharán

Perfect indicative	Conditional
he escuchado	escucharía
has escuchado	escucharías
ha escuchado	escucharía
hemos escuchado	escucharíamos
habéis escuchado	escucharíais
han escuchado	escucharían

Pluperfect indicative	Imperative
había escuchado	–
habías escuchado	escucha
había escuchado	escuche
habíamos escuchado	escuchemos
habíais escuchado	escuchad
habían escuchado	escuchen

esforzarse *to make an effort*

Gerund *esforzándose*

Past participle *esforzado*

Present indicative	Present subjunctive
me esfuerzo	me esfuerce
te esfuerzas	te esfuerces
se esfuerza	se esfuerce
nos esforzamos	nos esforcemos
os esforzáis	os esforcéis
se esfuerzan	se esfuercen

Imperfect indicative	Imperfect subjunctive
me esforzaba	me esforzara
te esforzabas	te esforzaras
se esforzaba	se esforzara
nos esforzábamos	nos esforzáramos
os esforzabais	os esforzarais
se esforzaban	se esforzaran

Preterite	Future
me esforcé	me esforzaré
te esforzaste	te esforzarás
se esforzó	se esforzará
nos esforzamos	nos esforzaremos
os esforzasteis	os esforzaréis
se esforzaron	se esforzarán

Perfect indicative	Conditional
me he esforzado	me esforzaría
te has esforzado	te esforzarías
se ha esforzado	se esforzaría
nos hemos esforzado	nos esforzaríamos
os habéis esforzado	os esforzaríais
se han esforzado	se esforzarían

Pluperfect indicative	Imperative
me había esforzado	–
te habías esforzado	esfuérzate
se había esforzado	esfuércese
nos habíamos esforzado	esforcémonos
os habíais esforzado	esforzaos
se habían esforzado	esfuércense

esperar *to hope, wait*

Gerund *esperando*

Past participle *esperado*

Present indicative	Present subjunctive
espero	espere
esperas	esperes
espera	espere
esperamos	esperemos
esperáis	esperéis
esperan	esperen

Imperfect indicative	Imperfect subjunctive
esperaba	esperara
esperabas	esperaras
esperaba	esperara
esperábamos	esperáramos
esperabais	esperarais
esperaban	esperaran

Preterite	Future
esperé	esperaré
esperaste	esperarás
esperó	esperará
esperamos	esperaremos
esperasteis	esperaréis
esperaron	esperarán

Perfect indicative	Conditional
he esperado	esperaría
has esperado	esperarías
ha esperado	esperaría
hemos esperado	esperaríamos
habéis esperado	esperaríais
han esperado	esperarían

Pluperfect indicative	Imperative
había esperado	–
habías esperado	espera
había esperado	espere
habíamos esperado	esperemos
habíais esperado	esperad
habían esperado	esperen

estar *to be*

Gerund *estando*

Past participle *estado*

Present indicative	Present subjunctive
estoy	esté
estás	estés
está	esté
estamos	estemos
estáis	estéis
están	estén

Imperfect indicative	Imperfect subjunctive
estaba	estuviera
estabas	estuvieras
estaba	estuviera
estábamos	estuviéramos
estabais	estuvierais
estaban	estuvieran

Preterite	Future
estuve	estaré
estuviste	estarás
estuvo	estará
estuvimos	estaremos
estuvisteis	estaréis
estuvieron	estarán

Perfect indicative	Conditional
he estado	estaría
has estado	estarías
ha estado	estaría
hemos estado	estaríamos
habéis estado	estaríais
han estado	estarían

Pluperfect indicative	Imperative
había estado	–
habías estado	está
había estado	esté
habíamos estado	estemos
habíais estado	estad
habían estado	estén

estudiar *to study*

Gerund *estudiando*

Past participle *estudiado*

Present indicative	Present subjunctive
estudio	estudie
estudias	estudies
estudia	estudie
estudiamos	estudiemos
estudiáis	estudiéis
estudian	estudien

Imperfect indicative	Imperfect subjunctive
estudiaba	estudiara
estudiabas	estudiaras
estudiaba	estudiara
estudiábamos	estudiáramos
estudiabais	estudiarais
estudiaban	estudiaran

Preterite	Future
estudié	estudiaré
estudiaste	estudiarás
estudió	estudiará
estudiamos	estudiaremos
estudiasteis	estudiaréis
estudiaron	estudiarán

Perfect indicative	Conditional
he estudiado	estudiaría
has estudiado	estudiarías
ha estudiado	estudiaría
hemos estudiado	estudiaríamos
habéis estudiado	estudiaríais
han estudiado	estudiarían

Pluperfect indicative	Imperative
había estudiado	–
habías estudiado	estudia
había estudiado	estudie
habíamos estudiado	estudiemos
habíais estudiado	estudiad
habían estudiado	estudien

exigir *to demand*

Gerund *exigiendo*

Past participle *exigido*

Present indicative	Present subjunctive
exijo	exija
exiges	exijas
exige	exija
exigimos	exijamos
exigís	exijáis
exigen	exijan

Imperfect indicative	Imperfect subjunctive
exigía	exigiera
exigías	exigieras
exigía	exigiera
exigíamos	exigiéramos
exigíais	exigierais
exigían	exigieran

Preterite	Future
exigí	exigiré
exigiste	exigirás
exigió	exigirá
exigimos	exigiremos
exigisteis	exigiréis
exigieron	exigirán

Perfect indicative	Conditional
he exigido	exigiría
has exigido	exigirías
ha exigido	exigiría
hemos exigido	exigiríamos
habéis exigido	exigiríais
han exigido	exigirían

Pluperfect indicative	Imperative
había exigido	–
habías exigido	exige
había exigido	exija
habíamos exigido	exijamos
habíais exigido	exigid
habían exigido	exijan

explicar *to explain*

Gerund *explicando*

Past participle *explicado*

Present indicative	Present subjunctive
explico	explique
explicas	expliques
explica	explique
explicamos	expliquemos
explicáis	expliquéis
explican	expliquen

Imperfect indicative	Imperfect subjunctive
explicaba	explicara
explicabas	explicaras
explicaba	explicara
explicábamos	explicáramos
explicabais	explicarais
explicaban	explicaran

Preterite	Future
expliqué	explicaré
explicaste	explicarás
explicó	explicará
explicamos	explicaremos
explicasteis	explicaréis
explicaron	explicarán

Perfect indicative	Conditional
he explicado	explicaría
has explicado	explicarías
ha explicado	explicaría
hemos explicado	explicaríamos
habéis explicado	explicaríais
han explicado	explicarían

Pluperfect indicative	Imperative
había explicado	–
habías explicado	explica
había explicado	explique
habíamos explicado	expliquemos
habíais explicado	explicad
habían explicado	expliquen

fregar *to wash up*

Gerund *fregando*

Past participle *fregado*

Present indicative	**Present subjunctive**
friego	friegue
friegas	friegues
friega	friegue
fregamos	freguemos
fregáis	freguéis
friegan	frieguen

Imperfect indicative	**Imperfect subjunctive**
fregaba	fregara
fregabas	fregaras
fregaba	fregara
fregábamos	fregáramos
fregabais	fregarais
fregaban	fregaran

Preterite	**Future**
fregué	fregaré
fregaste	fregarás
fregó	fregará
fregamos	fregaremos
fregasteis	fregaréis
fregaron	fregarán

Perfect indicative	**Conditional**
he fregado	fregaría
has fregado	fregarías
ha fregado	fregaría
hemos fregado	fregaríamos
habéis fregado	fregaríais
han fregado	fregarían

Pluperfect indicative	**Imperative**
había fregado	–
habías fregado	friega
había fregado	friegue
habíamos fregado	freguemos
habíais fregado	fregad
habían fregado	frieguen

freír *to fry*

Gerund *friendo*

Past participle *frito*

Present indicative	**Present subjunctive**
frío	fría
fríes	frías
fríe	fría
freímos	friamos
freís	friáis
fríen	frían

Imperfect indicative	**Imperfect subjunctive**
freía	friera
freías	frieras
freía	friera
freíamos	friéramos
freíais	frierais
freían	frieran

Preterite	**Future**
freí	freiré
freíste	freirás
frió	freirá
freímos	freiremos
freísteis	freiréis
frieron	freirán

Perfect indicative	**Conditional**
he frito	freiría
has frito	freirías
ha frito	freiría
hemos frito	freiríamos
habéis frito	freiríais
han frito	freirían

Pluperfect indicative	**Imperative**
había frito	–
habías frito	fríe
había frito	fría
habíamos frito	friamos
habíais frito	freíd
habían frito	frían

gemir *to groan, roar*

Gerund *gimiendo*

Past participle *gemido*

Present indicative	Present subjunctive
gimo	gima
gimes	gimas
gime	gima
gemimos	gimamos
gemís	gimáis
gimen	giman

Imperfect indicative	Imperfect subjunctive
gemía	gimiera
gemías	gimieras
gemía	gimiera
gemíamos	gimiéramos
gemíais	gimierais
gemían	gimieran

Preterite	Future
gemí	gemiré
gemiste	gemirás
gimió	gemirá
gemimos	gemiremos
gemisteis	gemiréis
gimieron	gemirán

Perfect indicative	Conditional
he gemido	gemiría
has gemido	gemirías
ha gemido	gemiría
hemos gemido	gemiríamos
habéis gemido	gemiríais
han gemido	gemirían

Pluperfect indicative	Imperative
había gemido	–
habías gemido	gime
había gemido	gima
habíamos gemido	gimamos
habíais gemido	gemid
habían gemido	giman

guiar *to guide*

Gerund *guiando*

Past participle *guiado*

Present indicative	Present subjunctive
guío	guíe
guías	guíes
guía	guíe
guiamos	guiemos
guiáis	guiéis
guían	guíen

Imperfect indicative	Imperfect subjunctive
guiaba	guiara
guiabas	guiaras
guiaba	guiara
guiábamos	guiáramos
guiabais	guiarais
guiaban	guiaran

Preterite	Future
guié	guiaré
guiaste	guiarás
guió	guiará
guiamos	guiaremos
guiasteis	guiaréis
guiaron	guiarán

Perfect indicative	Conditional
he guiado	guiaría
has guiado	guiarías
ha guiado	guiaría
hemos guiado	guiaríamos
habéis guiado	guiaríais
han guiado	guiarían

Pluperfect indicative	Imperative
había guiado	–
habías guiado	guía
había guiado	guíe
habíamos guiado	guiemos
habíais guiado	guiad
habían guiado	guíen

gustar *to please*

Gerund *gustando*

Past participle *gustado*

Present indicative	Present subjunctive
gusto	guste
gustas	gustes
gusta	guste
gustamos	gustemos
gustáis	gustéis
gustan	gusten

Imperfect indicative	Imperfect subjunctive
gustaba	gustara
gustabas	gustaras
gustaba	gustara
gustábamos	gustáramos
gustabais	gustarais
gustaban	gustaran

Preterite	Future
gusté	gustaré
gustaste	gustarás
gustó	gustará
gustamos	gustaremos
gustasteis	gustaréis
gustaron	gustarán

Perfect indicative	Conditional
he gustado	gustaría
has gustado	gustarías
ha gustado	gustaría
hemos gustado	gustaríamos
habéis gustado	gustaríais
han gustado	gustarían

Pluperfect indicative	Imperative
había gustado	–
habías gustado	gusta
había gustado	guste
habíamos gustado	gustemos
habíais gustado	gustad
habían gustado	gusten

haber *to have*

Gerund *habiendo*

Past participle *habido*

Present indicative	Present subjunctive
he	haya
has	hayas
ha	haya
hemos	hayamos
habéis	hayáis
han	hayan

Imperfect indicative	Imperfect subjunctive
había	hubiera
habías	hubieras
había	hubiera
habíamos	hubiéramos
habíais	hubierais
habían	hubieran

Preterite	Future
hube	habré
hubiste	habrás
hubo	habrá
hubimos	habremos
hubisteis	habréis
hubieron	habrán

Perfect indicative	Conditional
he habido	habría
has habido	habrías
ha habido	habría
hemos habido	habríamos
habéis habido	habríais
han habido	habrían

Pluperfect indicative	Imperative
había habido	–
habías habido	he
había habido	haya
habíamos habido	hayamos
habíais habido	habed
habían habido	hayan

hablar *to talk, speak*

Gerund *hablando*

Past participle *hablado*

Present indicative	Present subjunctive
hablo	hable
hablas	hables
habla	hable
hablamos	hablemos
habláis	habléis
hablan	hablen

Imperfect indicative	Imperfect subjunctive
hablaba	hablara
hablabas	hablaras
hablaba	hablara
hablábamos	habláramos
hablabais	hablarais
hablaban	hablaran

Preterite	Future
hablé	hablaré
hablaste	hablarás
habló	hablará
hablamos	hablaremos
hablasteis	hablaréis
hablaron	hablarán

Perfect indicative	Conditional
he hablado	hablaría
has hablado	hablarías
ha hablado	hablaría
hemos hablado	hablaríamos
habéis hablado	hablaríais
han hablado	hablarían

Pluperfect indicative	Imperative
había hablado	–
habías hablado	habla
había hablado	hable
habíamos hablado	hablemos
habíais hablado	hablad
habían hablado	hablen

hacer *to do, make*

Gerund *haciendo*

Past participle *hecho*

Present indicative	Present subjunctive
hago	haga
haces	hagas
hace	haga
hacemos	hagamos
hacéis	hagáis
hacen	hagan

Imperfect indicative	Imperfect subjunctive
hacía	hiciera
hacías	hicieras
hacía	hiciera
hacíamos	hiciéramos
hacíais	hicierais
hacían	hicieran

Preterite	Future
hice	haré
hiciste	harás
hizo	hará
hicimos	haremos
hicisteis	haréis
hicieron	harán

Perfect indicative	Conditional
he hecho	haría
has hecho	harías
ha hecho	haría
hemos hecho	haríamos
habéis hecho	haríais
han hecho	harían

Pluperfect indicative	Imperative
había hecho	–
habías hecho	haz
había hecho	haga
habíamos hecho	hagamos
habíais hecho	haced
habían hecho	hagan

herir *to hurt*

Gerund *hiriendo*

Past participle *herido*

Present indicative	Present subjunctive
hiero	hiera
hieres	hieras
hiere	hiera
herimos	hiramos
herís	hiráis
hieren	hieran

Imperfect indicative	Imperfect subjunctive
hería	hiriera
herías	hirieras
hería	hiriera
heríamos	hiriéramos
heríais	hirierais
herían	hirieran

Preterite	Future
herí	heriré
heriste	herirás
hirió	herirá
herimos	heriremos
heristeis	heriréis
hirieron	herirán

Perfect indicative	Conditional
he herido	heriría
has herido	herirías
ha herido	heriría
hemos herido	heriríamos
habéis herido	heriríais
han herido	herirían

Pluperfect indicative	Imperative
había herido	–
habías herido	hiere
había herido	hiera
habíamos herido	hiramos
habíais herido	herid
habían herido	hieran

huir *to run away*

Gerund *huyendo*

Past participle *huido*

Present indicative	Present subjunctive
huyo	huya
huyes	huyas
huye	huya
huimos	huyamos
huís	huyáis
huyen	huyan

Imperfect indicative	Imperfect subjunctive
huía	huyera
huías	huyeras
huía	huyera
huíamos	huyéramos
huíais	huyerais
huían	huyeran

Preterite	Future
huí	huiré
huiste	huirás
huyó	huirá
huimos	huiremos
huisteis	huiréis
huyeron	huirán

Perfect indicative	Conditional
he huido	huiría
has huido	huirías
ha huido	huiría
hemos huido	huiríamos
habéis huido	huiríais
han huido	huirían

Pluperfect indicative	Imperative
había huido	–
habías huido	huye
había huido	huya
habíamos huido	huyamos
habíais huido	huid
habían huido	huyan

intentar *to try*

Gerund *intentando*

Past participle *intentado*

Present indicative	Present subjunctive
intento	intente
intentas	intentes
intenta	intente
intentamos	intentemos
intentáis	intentéis
intentan	intenten

Imperfect indicative	Imperfect subjunctive
intentaba	intentara
intentabas	intentaras
intentaba	intentara
intentábamos	intentáramos
intentabais	intentarais
intentaban	intentaran

Preterite	Future
intenté	intentaré
intentaste	intentarás
intentó	intentará
intentamos	intentaremos
intentasteis	intentaréis
intentaron	intentarán

Perfect indicative	Conditional
he intentado	intentaría
has intentado	intentarías
ha intentado	intentaría
hemos intentado	intentaríamos
habéis intentado	intentaríais
han intentado	intentarían

Pluperfect indicative	Imperative
había intentado	–
habías intentado	intenta
había intentado	intente
habíamos intentado	intentemos
habíais intentado	intentad
habían intentado	intenten

introducir *to introduce*

Gerund *introduciendo*

Past participle *introducido*

Present indicative	Present subjunctive
introduzco	introduzca
introduces	introduzcas
introduce	introduzca
introducimos	introduzcamos
introducís	introduzcáis
introducen	introduzcan

Imperfect indicative	Imperfect subjunctive
introducía	introdujera
introducías	introdujeras
introducía	introdujera
introducíamos	introdujéramos
introducíais	introdujerais
introducían	introdujeran

Preterite	Future
introduje	introduciré
introdujiste	introducirás
introdujo	introducirá
introdujimos	introduciremos
introdujisteis	introduciréis
introdujeron	introducirán

Perfect indicative	Conditional
he introducido	introduciría
has introducido	introducirías
ha introducido	introduciría
hemos introducido	introduciríamos
habéis introducido	introduciríais
han introducido	introducirían

Pluperfect indicative	Imperative
había introducido	–
habías introducido	introduce
había introducido	introduzca
habíamos introducido	introduzcamos
habíais introducido	introducid
habían introducido	introduzcan

ir *to go*

Gerund *yendo*

Past participle *ido*

Present indicative	Present subjunctive
voy	vaya
vas	vayas
va	vaya
vamos	vayamos
vais	vayáis
van	vayan

Imperfect indicative	Imperfect subjunctive
iba	fuera
ibas	fueras
iba	fuera
íbamos	fuéramos
ibais	fuerais
iban	fueran

Preterite	Future
fui	iré
fuiste	irás
fue	irá
fuimos	iremos
fuisteis	iréis
fueron	irán

Perfect indicative	Conditional
he ido	iría
has ido	irías
ha ido	iría
hemos ido	iríamos
habéis ido	iríais
han ido	irían

Pluperfect indicative	Imperative
había ido	–
habías ido	ve
había ido	vaya
habíamos ido	vayamos
habíais ido	id
habían ido	vayan

jugar *to play*

Gerund *jugando*

Past participle *jugado*

Present indicative	Present subjunctive
juego	juegue
juegas	juegues
juega	juegue
jugamos	juguemos
jugáis	juguéis
juegan	jueguen

Imperfect indicative	Imperfect subjunctive
jugaba	jugara
jugabas	jugaras
jugaba	jugara
jugábamos	jugáramos
jugabais	jugarais
jugaban	jugaran

Preterite	Future
jugué	jugaré
jugaste	jugarás
jugó	jugará
jugamos	jugaremos
jugasteis	jugaréis
jugaron	jugarán

Perfect indicative	Conditional
he jugado	jugaría
has jugado	jugarías
ha jugado	jugaría
hemos jugado	jugaríamos
habéis jugado	jugaríais
han jugado	jugarían

Pluperfect indicative	Imperative
había jugado	–
habías jugado	juega
había jugado	juegue
habíamos jugado	juguemos
habíais jugado	jugad
habían jugado	jueguen

juzgar *to judge*

Gerund *juzgando*

Past participle *juzgado*

Present indicative	Present subjunctive
juzgo	juzgue
juzgas	juzgues
juzga	juzgue
juzgamos	juzguemos
juzgáis	juzguéis
juzgan	juzguen

Imperfect indicative	Imperfect subjunctive
juzgaba	juzgara
juzgabas	juzgaras
juzgaba	juzgara
juzgábamos	juzgáramos
juzgabais	juzgarais
juzgaban	juzgaran

Preterite	Future
juzgué	juzgaré
juzgaste	juzgarás
juzgó	juzgará
juzgamos	juzgaremos
juzgasteis	juzgaréis
juzgaron	juzgarán

Perfect indicative	Conditional
he juzgado	juzgaría
has juzgado	juzgarías
ha juzgado	juzgaría
hemos juzgado	juzgaríamos
habéis juzgado	juzgaríais
han juzgado	juzgarían

Pluperfect indicative	Imperative
había juzgado	–
habías juzgado	juzga
había juzgado	juzgue
habíamos juzgado	juzguemos
habíais juzgado	juzgad
habían juzgado	juzguen

lavar *to wash*

Gerund *lavando*

Past participle *lavado*

Present indicative	Present subjunctive
lavo	lave
lavas	laves
lava	lave
lavamos	lavemos
laváis	lavéis
lavan	laven

Imperfect indicative	Imperfect subjunctive
lavaba	lavara
lavabas	lavaras
lavaba	lavara
lavábamos	laváramos
lavabais	lavarais
lavaban	lavaran

Preterite	Future
lavé	lavaré
lavaste	lavarás
lavó	lavará
lavamos	lavaremos
lavasteis	lavaréis
lavaron	lavarán

Perfect indicative	Conditional
he lavado	lavaría
has lavado	lavarías
ha lavado	lavaría
hemos lavado	lavaríamos
habéis lavado	lavaríais
han lavado	lavarían

Pluperfect indicative	Imperative
había lavado	–
habías lavado	lava
había lavado	lave
habíamos lavado	lavemos
habíais lavado	lavad
habían lavado	laven

leer *to read*

Gerund *leyendo*

Past participle *leído*

Present indicative	Present subjunctive
leo	lea
lees	leas
lee	lea
leemos	leamos
leéis	leáis
leen	lean

Imperfect indicative	Imperfect subjunctive
leía	leyera
leías	leyeras
leía	leyera
leíamos	leyéramos
leíais	leyerais
leían	leyeran

Preterite	Future
leí	leeré
leíste	leerás
leyó	leerá
leímos	leeremos
leísteis	leeréis
leyeron	leerán

Perfect indicative	Conditional
he leído	leería
has leído	leerías
ha leído	leería
hemos leído	leeríamos
habéis leído	leeríais
han leído	leerían

Pluperfect indicative	Imperative
había leído	–
habías leído	lee
había leído	lea
habíamos leído	leamos
habíais leído	leed
habían leído	lean

levantarse *to get up*

Gerund *levantándose*

Past participle *levantado*

Present indicative	Present subjunctive
me levanto	me levante
te levantas	te levantes
se levanta	se levante
nos levantamos	nos levantemos
os levantáis	os levantéis
se levantan	se levanten

Imperfect indicative	Imperfect subjunctive
me levantaba	me levantara
te levantabas	te levantaras
se levantaba	se levantara
nos levantábamos	nos levantáramos
os levantabais	os levantarais
se levantaban	se levantaran

Preterite	Future
me levanté	me levantaré
te levantaste	te levantarás
se levantó	se levantará
nos levantamos	nos levantaremos
os levantasteis	os levantaréis
se levantaron	se levantarán

Perfect indicative	Conditional
me he levantado	me levantaría
te has levantado	te levantarías
se ha levantado	se levantaría
nos hemos levantado	nos levantaríamos
os habéis levantado	os levantaríais
se han levantado	se levantarían

Pluperfect indicative	Imperative
me había levantado	–
te habías levantado	levántate
se había levantado	levántese
nos habíamos levantado	levantémonos
os habíais levantado	levantaos
se habían levantado	levántense

llamar *to call*

Gerund *llamando*

Past participle *llamado*

Present indicative	Present subjunctive
llamo	
llamas	llame
llama	llames
llamamos	llame
llamáis	llamemos
llaman	llaméis
	llamen

Imperfect indicative	Imperfect subjunctive
llamaba	
llamabas	llamara
llamaba	llamaras
llamábamos	llamara
llamabais	llamáramos
llamaban	llamarais
	llamaran

Preterite	Future
llamé	
llamaste	llamaré
llamó	llamarás
llamamos	llamará
llamasteis	llamaremos
llamaron	llamaréis
	llamarán

Perfect indicative	Conditional
he llamado	
has llamado	llamaría
ha llamado	llamarías
hemos llamado	llamaría
habéis llamado	llamaríamos
han llamado	llamaríais
	llamarían

Pluperfect indicative	Imperative
había llamado	–
habías llamado	llama
había llamado	llame
habíamos llamado	llamemos
habíais llamado	llamad
habían llamado	llamen

llegar *to arrive*

Gerund *llegando*

Past participle *llegado*

Present indicative	Present subjunctive
llego	
llegas	llegue
llega	llegues
llegamos	llegue
llegáis	lleguemos
llegan	lleguéis
	lleguen

Imperfect indicative	Imperfect subjunctive
llegaba	
llegabas	llegara
llegaba	llegaras
llegábamos	llegara
llegabais	llegáramos
llegaban	llegarais
	llegaran

Preterite	Future
llegué	
llegaste	llegaré
llegó	llegarás
llegamos	llegará
llegasteis	llegaremos
llegaron	llegaréis
	llegarán

Perfect indicative	Conditional
he llegado	
has llegado	llegaría
ha llegado	llegarías
hemos llegado	llegaría
habéis llegado	llegaríamos
han llegado	llegaríais
	llegarían

Pluperfect indicative	Imperative
había llegado	–
habías llegado	llega
había llegado	llegue
habíamos llegado	lleguemos
habíais llegado	llegad
habían llegado	lleguen

llenar *to fill*

Gerund *llenando*

Past participle *llenado*

Present indicative	Present subjunctive
lleno	
llenas	llene
llena	llenes
llenamos	llene
llenáis	llenemos
llenan	llenéis
	llenen

Imperfect indicative	Imperfect subjunctive
llenaba	
llenabas	llenara
llenaba	llenaras
llenábamos	llenara
llenabais	llenáramos
llenaban	llenarais
	llenaran

Preterite	Future
llené	
llenaste	llenaré
llenó	llenarás
llenamos	llenará
llenasteis	llenaremos
llenaron	llenaréis
	llenarán

Perfect indicative	Conditional
he llenado	
has llenado	llenaría
ha llenado	llenarías
hemos llenado	llenaría
habéis llenado	llenaríamos
han llenado	llenaríais
	llenarían

Pluperfect indicative	Imperative
había llenado	–
habías llenado	llena
había llenado	llene
habíamos llenado	llenemos
habíais llenado	llenad
habían llenado	llenen

matar *to kill*

Gerund *matando*

Past participle *matado*

Present indicative	Present subjunctive
mato	
matas	mate
mata	mates
matamos	mate
matáis	matemos
matan	matéis
	maten

Imperfect indicative	Imperfect subjunctive
mataba	
matabas	matara
mataba	mataras
matábamos	matara
matabais	matáramos
mataban	matarais
	mataran

Preterite	Future
maté	
mataste	mataré
mató	matarás
matamos	matará
matasteis	mataremos
mataron	mataréis
	matarán

Perfect indicative	Conditional
he matado	
has matado	mataría
ha matado	matarías
hemos matado	mataría
habéis matado	mataríamos
han matado	mataríais
	matarían

Pluperfect indicative	Imperative
había matado	–
habías matado	mata
había matado	mate
habíamos matado	matemos
habíais matado	matad
habían matado	maten

mentir to (tell a) lie

Gerund *mintiendo*

Past participle *mentido*

Present indicative	Present subjunctive
miento	mienta
mientes	mientas
miente	mienta
mentimos	mintamos
mentís	mintáis
mienten	mientan

Imperfect indicative	Imperfect subjunctive
mentía	mintiera
mentías	mintieras
mentía	mintiera
mentíamos	mintiéramos
mentíais	mintierais
mentían	mintieran

Preterite	Future
mentí	mentiré
mentiste	mentirás
mintió	mentirá
mentimos	mentiremos
mentisteis	mentiréis
mintieron	mentirán

Perfect indicative	Conditional
he mentido	mentiría
has mentido	mentirías
ha mentido	mentiría
hemos mentido	mentiríamos
habéis mentido	mentiríais
han mentido	mentirían

Pluperfect indicative	Imperative
había mentido	–
habías mentido	miente
había mentido	mienta
habíamos mentido	mintamos
habíais mentido	mentid
habían mentido	mientan

merecer to deserve

Gerund *mereciendo*

Past participle *merecido*

Present indicative	Present subjunctive
merezco	merezca
mereces	merezcas
merece	merezca
merecemos	merezcamos
merecéis	merezcáis
merecen	merezcan

Imperfect indicative	Imperfect subjunctive
merecía	mereciera
merecías	merecieras
merecía	mereciera
merecíamos	mereciéramos
merecíais	merecierais
merecían	merecieran

Preterite	Future
merecí	mereceré
mereciste	merecerás
mereció	merecerá
merecimos	mereceremos
merecisteis	mereceréis
merecieron	merecerán

Perfect indicative	Conditional
he merecido	merecería
has merecido	merecerías
ha merecido	merecería
hemos merecido	mereceríamos
habéis merecido	mereceríais
han merecido	merecerían

Pluperfect indicative	Imperative
había merecido	–
habías merecido	merece
había merecido	merezca
habíamos merecido	merezcamos
habíais merecido	mereced
habían merecido	merezcan

morder *to bite*

Gerund *mordiendo*

Past participle *mordido*

Present indicative	Present subjunctive
muerdo	muerda
muerdes	muerdas
muerde	muerda
mordemos	mordamos
mordéis	mordáis
muerden	muerdan

Imperfect indicative	Imperfect subjunctive
mordía	mordiera
mordías	mordieras
mordía	mordiera
mordíamos	mordiéramos
mordíais	mordierais
mordían	mordieran

Preterite	Future
mordí	morderé
mordiste	morderás
mordió	morderá
mordimos	morderemos
mordisteis	morderéis
mordieron	morderán

Perfect indicative	Conditional
he mordido	mordería
has mordido	morderías
ha mordido	mordería
hemos mordido	morderíamos
habéis mordido	morderíais
han mordido	morderían

Pluperfect indicative	Imperative
había mordido	–
habías mordido	muerde
había mordido	muerda
habíamos mordido	mordamos
habíais mordido	morded
habían mordido	muerdan

morir *to die*

Gerund *muriendo*

Past participle *muerto*

Present indicative	Present subjunctive
muero	muera
mueres	mueras
muere	muera
morimos	muramos
morís	muráis
mueren	mueran

Imperfect indicative	Imperfect subjunctive
moría	muriera
morías	murieras
moría	muriera
moríamos	muriéramos
moríais	murierais
morían	murieran

Preterite	Future
morí	moriré
moriste	morirás
murió	morirá
morimos	moriremos
moristeis	moriréis
murieron	morirán

Perfect indicative	Conditional
he muerto	moriría
has muerto	morirías
ha muerto	moriría
hemos muerto	moriríamos
habéis muerto	moriríais
han muerto	morirían

Pluperfect indicative	Imperative
había muerto	–
habías muerto	muere
había muerto	muera
habíamos muerto	muramos
habíais muerto	morid
habían muerto	mueran

mover *to move*

Gerund *moviendo*

Past participle *movido*

Present indicative	Present subjunctive
muevo	mueva
mueves	muevas
mueve	mueva
movemos	movamos
movéis	ováis
mueven	muevan

Imperfect indicative	Imperfect subjunctive
movía	moviera
movías	movieras
movía	moviera
movíamos	moviéramos
movíais	movierais
movían	movieran

Preterite	Future
moví	moveré
moviste	moverás
movió	moverá
movimos	moveremos
movisteis	moveréis
movieron	moverán

Perfect indicative	Conditional
he movido	movería
has movido	moverías
ha movido	movería
hemos movido	moveríamos
habéis movido	moveríais
han movido	moverían

Pluperfect indicative	Imperative
había movido	–
habías movido	mueve
había movido	mueva
habíamos movido	movamos
habíais movido	moved
habían movido	muevan

nacer *to be born*

Gerund *naciendo*

Past participle *nacido*

Present indicative	Present subjunctive
nazco	nazca
naces	nazcas
nace	nazca
nacemos	nazcamos
nacéis	nazcáis
nacen	nazcan

Imperfect indicative	Imperfect subjunctive
nacía	naciera
nacías	nacieras
nacía	naciera
nacíamos	naciéramos
nacíais	nacierais
nacían	nacieran

Preterite	Future
nací	naceré
naciste	nacerás
nació	nacerá
nacimos	naceremos
nacisteis	naceréis
nacieron	nacerán

Perfect indicative	Conditional
he nacido	nacería
has nacido	nacerías
ha nacido	nacería
hemos nacido	naceríamos
habéis nacido	naceríais
han nacido	nacerían

Pluperfect indicative	Imperative
había nacido	–
habías nacido	nace
había nacido	nazca
habíamos nacido	nazcamos
habíais nacido	naced
habían nacido	nazcan

nadar *to swim*

Gerund *nadando*

Past participle *nadado*

Present indicative	Present subjunctive
nado	nade
nadas	nades
nada	nade
nadamos	nademos
nadáis	nadéis
nadan	naden

Imperfect indicative	Imperfect subjunctive
nadaba	nadara
nadabas	nadaras
nadaba	nadara
nadábamos	nadáramos
nadabais	nadarais
nadaban	nadaran

Preterite	Future
nadé	nadaré
nadaste	nadarás
nadó	nadará
nadamos	nadaremos
nadasteis	nadaréis
nadaron	nadarán

Perfect indicative	Conditional
he nadado	nadaría
has nadado	nadarías
ha nadado	nadaría
hemos nadado	nadaríamos
habéis nadado	nadaríais
han nadado	nadarían

Pluperfect indicative	Imperative
había nadado	–
habías nadado	nada
había nadado	nade
habíamos nadado	nademos
habíais nadado	nadad
habían nadado	naden

necesitar *to need*

Gerund *necesitando*

Past participle *necesitado*

Present indicative	Present subjunctive
necesito	necesite
necesitas	necesites
necesita	necesite
necesitamos	necesitemos
necesitáis	necesitéis
necesitan	necesiten

Imperfect indicative	Imperfect subjunctive
necesitaba	necesitara
necesitabas	necesitaras
necesitaba	necesitara
necesitábamos	necesitáramos
necesitabais	necesitarais
necesitaban	necesitaran

Preterite	Future
necesité	necesitaré
necesitaste	necesitarás
necesitó	necesitará
necesitamos	necesitaremos
necesitasteis	necesitaréis
necesitaron	necesitarán

Perfect indicative	Conditional
he necesitado	necesitaría
has necesitado	necesitarías
ha necesitado	necesitaría
hemos necesitado	necesitaríamos
habéis necesitado	necesitaríais
han necesitado	necesitarían

Pluperfect indicative	Imperative
había necesitado	–
habías necesitado	necesita
había necesitado	necesite
habíamos necesitado	necesitemos
habíais necesitado	necesitad
habían necesitado	necesiten

negar *to deny*

Gerund *negando*

Past participle *negado*

Present indicative	Present subjunctive
niego	
niegas	niegue
niega	niegues
negamos	niegue
negáis	neguemos
niegan	neguéis
	nieguen

Imperfect indicative	Imperfect subjunctive
negaba	
negabas	negara
negaba	negaras
negábamos	negara
negabais	negáramos
negaban	negarais
	negaran

Preterite	Future
negué	
negaste	negaré
negó	negarás
negamos	negará
negasteis	negaremos
negaron	negaréis
	negarán

Perfect indicative	Conditional
he negado	
has negado	negaría
ha negado	negarías
hemos negado	negaría
habéis negado	negaríamos
han negado	negaríais
	negarían

Pluperfect indicative	Imperative
había negado	–
habías negado	niega
había negado	niegue
habíamos negado	neguemos
habíais negado	negad
habían negado	nieguen

obedecer *to obey*

Gerund *obedeciendo*

Past participle *obedecido*

Present indicative	Present subjunctive
obedezco	
obedeces	obedezca
obedece	obedezcas
obedecemos	obedezca
obedecéis	obedezcamos
obedecen	obedezcáis
	obedezcan

Imperfect indicative	Imperfect subjunctive
obedecía	
obedecías	obedeciera
obedecía	obedecieras
obedecíamos	obedeciera
obedecíais	obedeciéramos
obedecían	obedecierais
	obedecieran

Preterite	Future
obedecí	
obedeciste	obedeceré
obedeció	obedecerás
obedecimos	obedecerá
obedecisteis	obedeceremos
obedecieron	obedeceréis
	obedecerán

Perfect indicative	Conditional
he obedecido	
has obedecido	obedecería
ha obedecido	obedecerías
hemos obedecido	obedecería
habéis obedecido	obedeceríamos
han obedecido	obedeceríais
	obedecerían

Pluperfect indicative	Imperative
había obedecido	–
habías obedecido	obedece
había obedecido	obedezca
habíamos obedecido	obedezcamos
habíais obedecido	obedeced
habían obedecido	obedezcan

obligar *to oblige, compel*

Gerund *obligando*

Past participle *obligado*

Present indicative	Present subjunctive
obligo	obligue
obligas	obligues
obliga	obligue
obligamos	obliguemos
obligáis	obliguéis
obligan	obliguen

Imperfect indicative	Imperfect subjunctive
obligaba	obligara
obligabas	obligaras
obligaba	obligara
obligábamos	obligáramos
obligabais	obligarais
obligaban	obligaran

Preterite	Future
obligué	obligaré
obligaste	obligarás
obligó	obligará
obligamos	obligaremos
obligasteis	obligaréis
obligaron	obligarán

Perfect indicative	Conditional
he obligado	obligaría
has obligado	obligarías
ha obligado	obligaría
hemos obligado	obligaríamos
habéis obligado	obligaríais
han obligado	obligarían

Pluperfect indicative	Imperative
había obligado	–
habías obligado	obliga
había obligado	obligue
habíamos obligado	obliguemos
habíais obligado	obligad
habían obligado	obliguen

ofrecer *to offer*

Gerund *ofreciendo*

Past participle *ofrecido*

Present indicative	Present subjunctive
ofrezco	ofrezca
ofreces	ofrezcas
ofrece	ofrezca
ofrecemos	ofrezcamos
ofrecéis	ofrezcáis
ofrecen	ofrezcan

Imperfect indicative	Imperfect subjunctive
ofrecía	ofreciera
ofrecías	ofrecieras
ofrecía	ofreciera
ofrecíamos	ofreciéramos
ofrecíais	ofrecierais
ofrecían	ofrecieran

Preterite	Future
ofrecí	ofreceré
ofreciste	ofrecerás
ofreció	ofrecerá
ofrecimos	ofreceremos
ofrecisteis	ofreceréis
ofrecieron	ofrecerán

Perfect indicative	Conditional
he ofrecido	ofrecería
has ofrecido	ofrecerías
ha ofrecido	ofrecería
hemos ofrecido	ofreceríamos
habéis ofrecido	ofreceríais
han ofrecido	ofrecerían

Pluperfect indicative	Imperative
había ofrecido	–
habías ofrecido	ofrece
había ofrecido	ofrezca
habíamos ofrecido	ofrezcamos
habíais ofrecido	ofreced
habían ofrecido	ofrezcan

oír *to hear*

Gerund *oyendo*

Past participle *oído*

Present indicative	Present subjunctive
oigo	oiga
oyes	oigas
oye	oiga
oímos	oigamos
oís	oigáis
oyen	oigan

Imperfect indicative	Imperfect subjunctive
oía	oyera
oías	oyeras
oía	oyera
oíamos	oyéramos
oíais	oyerais
oían	oyeran

Preterite	Future
oí	oiré
oíste	oirás
oyó	oirá
oímos	oiremos
oísteis	oiréis
oyeron	oirán

Perfect indicative	Conditional
he oído	oiría
has oído	oirías
ha oído	oiría
hemos oído	oiríamos
habéis oído	oiríais
han oído	oirían

Pluperfect indicative	Imperative
había oído	–
habías oído	oye
había oído	oiga
habíamos oído	oigamos
habíais oído	oíd
habían oído	oigan

oler *to smell*

Gerund *oliendo*

Past participle *olido*

Present indicative	Present subjunctive
huelo	huela
hueles	huelas
huele	huela
olemos	olamos
oléis	oláis
huelen	huelan

Imperfect indicative	Imperfect subjunctive
olía	oliera
olías	olieras
olía	oliera
olíamos	oliéramos
olíais	olierais
olían	olieran

Preterite	Future
olí	oleré
oliste	olerás
olió	olerá
olimos	oleremos
olisteis	oleréis
olieron	olerán

Perfect indicative	Conditional
he olido	olería
has olido	olerías
ha olido	olería
hemos olido	oleríamos
habéis olido	oleríais
han olido	olerían

Pluperfect indicative	Imperative
había olido	–
habías olido	huele
había olido	huela
habíamos olido	olamos
habíais olido	oled
habían olido	huelan

pagar *to pay*

Gerund *pagando*

Past participle *pagado*

Present indicative	Present subjunctive
pago	
pagas	pague
paga	pagues
pagamos	pague
pagáis	paguemos
pagan	paguéis
	paguen

Imperfect indicative	Imperfect subjunctive
pagaba	
pagabas	pagara
pagaba	pagaras
pagábamos	pagara
pagabais	pagáramos
pagaban	pagarais
	pagaran

Preterite	Future
pagué	
pagaste	pagaré
pagó	pagarás
pagamos	pagará
pagasteis	pagaremos
pagaron	pagaréis
	pagarán

Perfect indicative	Conditional
he pagado	
has pagado	pagaría
ha pagado	pagarías
hemos pagado	pagaría
habéis pagado	pagaríamos
han pagado	pagaríais
	pagarían

Pluperfect indicative	Imperative
había pagado	–
habías pagado	paga
había pagado	pague
habíamos pagado	paguemos
habíais pagado	pagad
habían pagado	paguen

parecer *to seem*

Gerund *pareciendo*

Past participle *parecido*

Present indicative	Present subjunctive
parezco	
pareces	parezca
parece	parezcas
parecemos	parezca
parecéis	parezcamos
parecen	parezcáis
	parezcan

Imperfect indicative	Imperfect subjunctive
parecía	
parecías	pareciera
parecía	parecieras
parecíamos	pareciera
parecíais	pareciéramos
parecían	parecierais
	parecieran

Preterite	Future
parecí	
pareciste	pareceré
pareció	parecerás
parecimos	parecerá
parecisteis	pareceremos
parecieron	pareceréis
	parecerán

Perfect indicative	Conditional
he parecido	
has parecido	parecería
ha parecido	parecerías
hemos parecido	parecería
habéis parecido	pareceríamos
han parecido	pareceríais
	parecerían

Pluperfect indicative	Imperative
había parecido	–
habías parecido	parece
había parecido	parezca
habíamos parecido	parezcamos
habíais parecido	pareced
habían parecido	parezcan

pasear *to walk*

Gerund *paseando*

Past participle *paseado*

Present indicative	Present subjunctive
paseo	pasee
paseas	pasees
pasea	pasee
paseamos	paseemos
paseáis	paseéis
pasean	paseen

Imperfect indicative	Imperfect subjunctive
paseaba	paseara
paseabas	pasearas
paseaba	paseara
paseábamos	paseáramos
paseabais	pasearais
paseaban	pasearan

Preterite	Future
paseé	pasearé
paseaste	pasearás
paseó	paseará
paseamos	pasearemos
paseasteis	pasearéis
pasearon	pasearán

Perfect indicative	Conditional
he paseado	pasearía
has paseado	pasearías
ha paseado	pasearía
hemos paseado	pasearíamos
habéis paseado	pasearíais
han paseado	pasearían

Pluperfect indicative	Imperative
había paseado	–
habías paseado	pasea
había paseado	pasee
habíamos paseado	paseemos
habíais paseado	pasead
habían paseado	paseen

pedir *to ask for*

Gerund *pidiendo*

Past participle *pedido*

Present indicative	Present subjunctive
pido	pida
pides	pidas
pide	pida
pedimos	pidamos
pedís	pidáis
piden	pidan

Imperfect indicative	Imperfect subjunctive
pedía	pidiera
pedías	pidieras
pedía	pidiera
pedíamos	pidiéramos
pedíais	pidierais
pedían	pidieran

Preterite	Future
pedí	pediré
pediste	pedirás
pidió	pedirá
pedimos	pediremos
pedisteis	pediréis
pidieron	pedirán

Perfect indicative	Conditional
he pedido	pediría
has pedido	pedirías
ha pedido	pediría
hemos pedido	pediríamos
habéis pedido	pediríais
han pedido	pedirían

Pluperfect indicative	Imperative
había pedido	–
habías pedido	pide
había pedido	pida
habíamos pedido	pidamos
habíais pedido	pedid
habían pedido	pidan

pensar *to think*

Gerund *pensando*

Past participle *pensado*

Present indicative	Present subjunctive
pienso	
piensas	piense
piensa	pienses
pensamos	piense
pensáis	pensemos
piensan	penséis
	piensen

Imperfect indicative	Imperfect subjunctive
pensaba	
pensabas	pensara
pensaba	pensaras
pensábamos	pensara
pensabais	pensáramos
pensaban	pensarais
	pensaran

Preterite	Future
pensé	
pensaste	pensaré
pensó	pensarás
pensamos	pensará
pensasteis	pensaremos
pensaron	pensaréis
	pensarán

Perfect indicative	Conditional
he pensado	
has pensado	pensaría
ha pensado	pensarías
hemos pensado	pensaría
habéis pensado	pensaríamos
han pensado	pensaríais
	pensarían

Pluperfect indicative	Imperative
había pensado	–
habías pensado	piensa
había pensado	piense
habíamos pensado	pensemos
habíais pensado	pensad
habían pensado	piensen

perder *to lose*

Gerund *perdiendo*

Past participle *perdido*

Present indicative	Present subjunctive
pierdo	
pierdes	pierda
pierde	pierdas
perdemos	pierda
perdéis	perdamos
pierden	perdáis
	pierdan

Imperfect indicative	Imperfect subjunctive
perdía	
perdías	perdiera
perdía	perdieras
perdíamos	perdiera
perdíais	perdiéramos
perdían	perdierais
	perdieran

Preterite	Future
perdí	
perdiste	perderé
perdió	perderás
perdimos	perderá
perdisteis	perderemos
perdieron	perderéis
	perderán

Perfect indicative	Conditional
he perdido	
has perdido	perdería
ha perdido	perderías
hemos perdido	perdería
habéis perdido	perderíamos
han perdido	perderíais
	perderían

Pluperfect indicative	Imperative
había perdido	–
habías perdido	pierde
había perdido	pierda
habíamos perdido	perdamos
habíais perdido	perded
habían perdido	pierdan

pertenecer *to belong*

Gerund *perteneciendo*

Past participle *pertenecido*

Present indicative	**Present subjunctive**
pertenezco	pertenezca
perteneces	pertenezcas
pertenece	pertenezca
pertenecemos	pertenezcamos
pertenecéis	pertenezcáis
pertenecen	pertenezcan

Imperfect indicative	**Imperfect subjunctive**
pertenecía	perteneciera
pertenecías	pertenecieras
pertenecía	perteneciera
pertenecíamos	perteneciéramos
pertenecíais	pertenecierais
pertenecían	pertenecieran

Preterite	**Future**
pertenecí	perteneceré
perteneciste	pertenecerás
perteneció	pertenecerá
pertenecimos	perteneceremos
pertenecisteis	perteneceréis
pertenecieron	pertenecerán

Perfect indicative	**Conditional**
he pertenecido	pertenecería
has pertenecido	pertenecerías
ha pertenecido	pertenecería
hemos pertenecido	perteneceríamos
habéis pertenecido	perteneceríais
han pertenecido	pertenecerían

Pluperfect indicative	**Imperative**
había pertenecido	–
habías pertenecido	pertenece
había pertenecido	pertenezca
habíamos pertenecido	pertenezcamos
habíais pertenecido	perteneced
habían pertenecido	pertenezcan

poder *to be able to (can)*

Gerund *pudiendo*

Past participle *podido*

Present indicative	**Present subjunctive**
puedo	pueda
puedes	puedas
puede	pueda
podemos	podamos
podéis	podáis
pueden	puedan

Imperfect indicative	**Imperfect subjunctive**
podía	pudiera
podías	pudieras
podía	pudiera
podíamos	pudiéramos
podíais	pudierais
podían	pudieran

Preterite	**Future**
pude	podré
pudiste	podrás
pudo	podrá
pudimos	podremos
pudisteis	podréis
pudieron	podrán

Perfect indicative	**Conditional**
he podido	podría
has podido	podrías
ha podido	podría
hemos podido	podríamos
habéis podido	podríais
han podido	podrían

Pluperfect indicative	**Imperative**
había podido	–
habías podido	puede
había podido	pueda
habíamos podido	podamos
habíais podido	poded
habían podido	puedan

poner *to put*

Gerund *poniendo*

Past participle *puesto*

Present indicative	Present subjunctive
pongo	
pones	ponga
pone	pongas
ponemos	ponga
ponéis	pongamos
ponen	pongáis
	pongan

Imperfect indicative	Imperfect subjunctive
ponía	
ponías	pusiera
ponía	pusieras
poníamos	pusiera
poníais	pusiéramos
ponían	pusierais
	pusieran

Preterite	Future
puse	
pusiste	pondré
puso	pondrás
pusimos	pondrá
pusisteis	pondremos
pusieron	pondréis
	pondrán

Perfect indicative	Conditional
he puesto	
has puesto	pondría
ha puesto	pondrías
hemos puesto	pondría
habéis puesto	pondríamos
han puesto	pondríais
	pondrían

Pluperfect indicative	Imperative
había puesto	–
habías puesto	pon
había puesto	ponga
habíamos puesto	pongamos
habíais puesto	poned
habían puesto	pongan

preferir *to prefer*

Gerund *prefiriendo*

Past participle *preferido*

Present indicative	Preprefect subjunctive
prefiero	
prefieres	prefiera
prefiere	prefieras
preferimos	prefiera
preferís	prefiramos
prefieren	prefiráis
	prefieran

Imperfect indicative	Imperfect subjunctive
prefería	
preferías	prefiriera
prefería	prefirieras
preferíamos	prefiriera
preferíais	prefiriéramos
preferían	prefirierais
	prefirieran

Preterite	Future
preferí	
preferiste	preferiré
prefirió	preferirás
preferimos	preferirá
preferisteis	preferiremos
prefirieron	preferiréis
	preferirán

Perfect indicative	Conditional
he preferido	
has preferido	preferiría
ha preferido	preferirías
hemos preferido	preferiría
habéis preferido	preferiríamos
han preferido	preferiríais
	preferirían

Pluperfect indicative	Imperative
había preferido	–
habías preferido	prefiere
había preferido	prefiera
habíamos preferido	prefiramos
habíais preferido	preferid
habían preferido	prefieran

probar *to taste, try*

Gerund *probando*

Past participle *probado*

Present indicative	Present subjunctive
pruebo	pruebe
pruebas	pruebes
prueba	pruebe
probamos	probemos
probáis	probéis
prueban	prueben

Imperfect indicative	Imperfect subjunctive
probaba	probara
probabas	probaras
probaba	probara
probábamos	probáramos
probabais	probarais
probaban	probaran

Preterite	Future
probé	probaré
probaste	probarás
probó	probará
probamos	probaremos
probasteis	probaréis
probaron	probarán

Perfect indicative	Conditional
he probado	probaría
has probado	probarías
ha probado	probaría
hemos probado	probaríamos
habéis probado	probaríais
han probado	probarían

Pluperfect indicative	Imperative
había probado	–
habías probado	prueba
había probado	pruebe
habíamos probado	probemos
habíais probado	probad
habían probado	prueben

prohibir *to forbid*

Gerund *prohibiendo*

Past participle *prohibido*

Present indicative	Present subjunctive
prohíbo	prohíba
prohíbes	prohíbas
prohíbe	prohíba
prohibimos	prohibamos
prohibís	prohibáis
prohíben	prohíban

Imperfect indicative	Imperfect subjunctive
prohibía	prohibiera
prohibías	prohibieras
prohibía	prohibiera
prohibíamos	prohibiéramos
prohibíais	prohibierais
prohibían	prohibieran

Preterite	Future
prohibí	prohibiré
prohibiste	prohibirás
prohibió	prohibirá
prohibimos	prohibiremos
prohibisteis	prohibiréis
prohibieron	prohibirán

Perfect indicative	Conditional
he prohibido	prohibiría
has prohibido	prohibirías
ha prohibido	prohibiría
hemos prohibido	prohibiríamos
habéis prohibido	prohibiríais
han prohibido	prohibirían

Pluperfect indicative	Imperative
había prohibido	–
habías prohibido	prohíbe
había prohibido	prohíba
habíamos prohibido	prohibamos
habíais prohibido	prohibid
habían prohibido	prohíban

querer *to want, love*

Gerund *queriendo*

Past participle *querido*

Present indicative	Present subjunctive
quiero	quiera
quieres	quieras
quiere	quiera
queremos	queramos
queréis	queráis
quieren	quieran

Imperfect indicative	Imperfect subjunctive
quería	quisiera
querías	quisieras
quería	quisiera
queríamos	quisiéramos
queríais	quisierais
querían	quisieran

Preterite	Future
quise	querré
quisiste	querrás
quiso	querrá
quisimos	querremos
quisisteis	querréis
quisieron	querrán

Perfect indicative	Conditional
he querido	querría
has querido	querrías
ha querido	querría
hemos querido	querríamos
habéis querido	querríais
han querido	querrían

Pluperfect indicative	Imperative
había querido	–
habías querido	quiere
había querido	quiera
habíamos querido	queramos
habíais querido	quered
habían querido	quieran

recibir *to receive*

Gerund *recibiendo*

Past participle *recibido*

Present indicative	Present subjunctive
recibo	reciba
recibes	recibas
recibe	reciba
recibimos	recibamos
recibís	recibáis
reciben	reciban

Imperfect indicative	Imperfect subjunctive
recibía	recibiera
recibías	recibieras
recibía	recibiera
recibíamos	recibiéramos
recibíais	recibierais
recibían	recibieran

Preterite	Future
recibí	recibiré
recibiste	recibirás
recibió	recibirá
recibimos	recibiremos
recibisteis	recibiréis
recibieron	recibirán

Perfect indicative	Conditional
he recibido	recibiría
has recibido	recibirías
ha recibido	recibiría
hemos recibido	recibiríamos
habéis recibido	recibiríais
han recibido	recibirían

Pluperfect indicative	Imperative
había recibido	–
habías recibido	recibe
había recibido	reciba
habíamos recibido	recibamos
habíais recibido	recibid
habían recibido	reciban

recordar *to remember*

Gerund *recordando*

Past participle *recordado*

Present indicative	Present subjunctive
recuerdo	recuerde
recuerdas	recuerdes
recuerda	recuerde
recordamos	recordemos
recordáis	recordéis
recuerdan	recuerden

Imperfect indicative	Imperfect subjunctive
recordaba	recordara
recordabas	recordaras
recordaba	recordara
recordábamos	recordáramos
recordabais	recordarais
recordaban	recordaran

Preterite	Future
recordé	recordaré
recordaste	recordarás
recordó	recordará
recordamos	recordaremos
recordasteis	recordaréis
recordaron	recordarán

Perfect indicative	Conditional
he recordado	recordaría
has recordado	recordarías
ha recordado	recordaría
hemos recordado	recordaríamos
habéis recordado	recordaríais
han recordado	recordarían

Pluperfect indicative	Imperative
había recordado	–
habías recordado	recuerda
había recordado	recuerde
habíamos recordado	recordemos
habíais recordado	recordad
habían recordado	recuerden

reducir *to reduce*

Gerund *reduciendo*

Past participle *reducido*

Present indicative	Present subjunctive
reduzco	reduzca
reduces	reduzcas
reduce	reduzca
reducimos	reduzcamos
reducís	reduzcáis
reducen	reduzcan

Imperfect indicative	Imperfect subjunctive
reducía	redujera
reducías	redujeras
reducía	redujera
reducíamos	redujéramos
reducíais	redujerais
reducían	redujeran

Preterite	Future
reduje	reduciré
redujiste	reducirás
redujo	reducirá
redujimos	reduciremos
redujisteis	reduciréis
redujeron	reducirán

Perfect indicative	Conditional
he reducido	reduciría
has reducido	reducirías
ha reducido	reduciría
hemos reducido	reduciríamos
habéis reducido	reduciríais
han reducido	reducirían

Pluperfect indicative	Imperative
había reducido	–
habías reducido	reduce
había reducido	reduzca
habíamos reducido	reduzcamos
habíais reducido	reducid
habían reducido	reduzcan

rehusar *to refuse*

Gerund *rehusando*

Past participle *rehusado*

Present indicative	Present subjunctive
rehúso	rehúse
rehúsas	rehúses
rehúsa	rehúse
rehusamos	rehusemos
rehusáis	rehuséis
rehúsan	rehúsen

Imperfect indicative	Imperfect subjunctive
rehusaba	rehusara
rehusabas	rehusaras
rehusaba	rehusara
rehusábamos	
rehusabais	rehusarais
rehusaban	rehusaran

Preterite	Future
rehusé	rehusaré
rehusaste	rehusarás
rehusó	rehusará
rehusamos	rehusaremos
rehusasteis	rehusaréis
rehusaron	rehusarán

Perfect indicative	Conditional
he rehusado	
has rehusado	rehusaría
ha rehusado	rehusarías
hemos rehusado	rehusaría
habéis rehusado	rehusaríamos
han rehusado	rehusaríais
	rehusarían

Pluperfect indicative	Imperative
había rehusado	–
habías rehusado	rehúsa
había rehusado	rehúse
habíamos rehusado	rehusemos
habíais rehusado	rehusad
habían rehusado	rehúsen

reír *to laugh*

Gerund *riendo*

Past participle *reído*

Present indicative	Present subjunctive
río	ría
ríes	rías
ríe	ría
reímos	riamos
reís	riáis
ríen	rían

Imperfect indicative	Imperfect subjunctive
reía	riera
reías	rieras
reía	riera
reíamos	riéramos
reíais	rierais
reían	rieran

Preterite	Future
reí	reiré
reíste	reirás
rió	reirá
reímos	reiremos
reísteis	reiréis
rieron	reirán

Perfect indicative	Conditional
he reído	
has reído	reiría
ha reído	reirías
hemos reído	reiría
habéis reído	reiríamos
han reído	reiríais
	reirían

Pluperfect indicative	Imperative
había reído	–
habías reído	ríe
había reído	ría
habíamos reído	riamos
habíais reído	reíd
habían reído	rían

reñir *to quarrel*

Gerund *riñendo*

Past participle *reñido*

Present indicative	Present subjunctive
riño	riña
riñes	riñas
riñe	riña
reñimos	riñamos
reñís	riñáis
riñen	riñan

Imperfect indicative	Imperfect subjunctive
reñía	riñera
reñías	riñeras
reñía	riñera
reñíamos	riñéramos
reñíais	riñerais
reñían	riñeran

Preterite	Future
reñí	reñiré
reñiste	reñirás
riñó	reñirá
reñimos	reñiremos
reñisteis	reñiréis
riñeron	reñirán

Perfect indicative	Conditional
he reñido	reñiría
has reñido	reñirías
ha reñido	reñiría
hemos reñido	reñiríamos
habéis reñido	reñiríais
han reñido	reñirían

Pluperfect indicative	Imperative
había reñido	–
habías reñido	riñe
había reñido	riña
habíamos reñido	riñamos
habíais reñido	reñid
habían reñido	riñan

repetir *to repeat*

Gerund *repitiendo*

Past participle *repetido*

Present indicative	Present subjunctive
repito	repita
repites	repitas
repite	repita
repetimos	repitamos
repetís	repitáis
repiten	repitan

Imperfect indicative	Imperfect subjunctive
repetía	repitiera
repetías	repitieras
repetía	repitiera
repetíamos	repitiéramos
repetíais	repitierais
repetían	repitieran

Preterite	Future
repetí	repetiré
repetiste	repetirás
repitió	repetirá
repetimos	repetiremos
repetisteis	repetiréis
repitieron	repetirán

Perfect indicative	Conditional
he repetido	repetiría
has repetido	repetirías
ha repetido	repetiría
hemos repetido	repetiríamos
habéis repetido	repetiríais
han repetido	repetirían

Pluperfect indicative	Imperative
había repetido	–
habías repetido	repite
había repetido	repita
habíamos repetido	repitamos
habíais repetido	repetid
habían repetido	repitan

rogar *to plead, beg*

Gerund *rogando*

Past participle *rogado*

Present indicative	Present subjunctive
ruego	ruegue
ruegas	ruegues
ruega	ruegue
rogamos	roguemos
rogáis	roguéis
ruegan	rueguen

Imperfect indicative	Imperfect subjunctive
rogaba	rogara
rogabas	rogaras
rogaba	rogara
rogábamos	rogáramos
rogabais	rogarais
rogaban	rogaran

Preterite	Future
rogué	rogaré
rogaste	rogarás
rogó	rogará
rogamos	rogaremos
rogasteis	rogaréis
rogaron	rogarán

Perfect indicative	Conditional
he rogado	rogaría
has rogado	rogarías
ha rogado	rogaría
hemos rogado	rogaríamos
habéis rogado	rogaríais
han rogado	rogarían

Pluperfect indicative	Imperative
había rogado	–
habías rogado	ruega
había rogado	ruegue
habíamos rogado	roguemos
habíais rogado	rogad
habían rogado	rueguen

romper *to break*

Gerund *rompiendo*

Past participle *roto*

Present indicative	Present subjunctive
rompo	rompa
rompes	rompas
rompe	rompa
rompemos	rompamos
rompéis	rompáis
rompen	rompan

Imperfect indicative	Imperfect subjunctive
rompía	rompiera
rompías	rompieras
rompía	rompiera
rompíamos	rompiéramos
rompíais	rompierais
rompían	rompieran

Preterite	Future
rompí	romperé
rompiste	romperás
rompió	romperá
rompimos	romperemos
rompisteis	romperéis
rompieron	romperán

Perfect indicative	Conditional
he roto	rompería
has roto	romperías
ha roto	rompería
hemos roto	romperíamos
habéis roto	romperíais
han roto	romperían

Pluperfect indicative	Imperative
había roto	–
habías roto	rompe
había roto	rompa
habíamos roto	rompamos
habíais roto	romped
habían roto	rompan

saber *to know*

Gerund *sabiendo*

Past participle *sabido*

Present indicative	Present subjunctive
sé	sepa
sabes	sepas
sabe	sepa
sabemos	sepamos
sabéis	sepáis
saben	sepan

Imperfect indicative	Imperfect subjunctive
sabía	supiera
sabías	supieras
sabía	supiera
sabíamos	supiéramos
sabíais	supierais
sabían	supieran

Preterite	Future
supe	sabré
supiste	sabrás
supo	sabrá
supimos	sabremos
supisteis	sabréis
supieron	sabrán

Perfect indicative	Conditional
he sabido	sabría
has sabido	sabrías
ha sabido	sabría
hemos sabido	sabríamos
habéis sabido	sabríais
han sabido	sabrían

Pluperfect indicative	Imperative
había sabido	–
habías sabido	sabe
había sabido	sepa
habíamos sabido	sepamos
habíais sabido	sabed
habían sabido	sepan

sacar *to take out*

Gerund *sacando*

Past participle *sacado*

Present indicative	Present subjunctive
saco	saque
sacas	saques
saca	saque
sacamos	saquemos
sacáis	saquéis
sacan	saquen

Imperfect indicative	Imperfect subjunctive
sacaba	sacara
sacabas	sacaras
sacaba	sacara
sacábamos	sacáramos
sacabais	sacarais
sacaban	sacaran

Preterite	Future
saqué	sacaré
sacaste	sacarás
sacó	sacará
sacamos	sacaremos
sacasteis	sacaréis
sacaron	sacarán

Perfect indicative	Conditional
he sacado	sacaría
has sacado	sacarías
ha sacado	sacaría
hemos sacado	sacaríamos
habéis sacado	sacaríais
han sacado	sacarían

Pluperfect indicative	Imperative
había sacado	–
habías sacado	saca
había sacado	saque
habíamos sacado	saquemos
habíais sacado	sacad
habían sacado	saquen

salir *to go out*

Gerund *saliendo*

Past participle *salido*

Present indicative	Present subjunctive
salgo	
sales	salga
sale	salgas
salimos	salga
salís	salgamos
salen	salgáis
	salgan

Imperfect Indicative	Imperfect subjunctive
salía	
salías	saliera
salía	salieras
salíamos	saliera
salíais	saliéramos
salían	salierais
	salieran

Preterite	Future
salí	
saliste	saldré
salió	saldrás
salimos	saldrá
salisteis	saldremos
salieron	saldréis
	saldrán

Perfect indicative	Conditional
he salido	
has salido	saldría
ha salido	saldrías
hemos salido	saldría
habéis salido	saldríamos
han salido	saldríais
	saldrían

Pluperfect indicative	Imperative
había salido	–
habías salido	sal
había salido	salga
habíamos salido	salgamos
habíais salido	salid
habían salido	salgan

satisfacer *to satisfy*

Gerund *satisfaciendo*

Past participle *satisfecho*

Present indicative	Present subjunctive
satisfago	
satisfaces	satisfaga
satisface	satisfagas
satisfacemos	satisfaga
satisfacéis	satisfagamos
satisfacen	satisfagáis
	satisfagan

Imperfect Indicative	Imperfect subjunctive
satisfacía	
satisfacías	satisficiera
satisfacía	satisficieras
satisfacíamos	satisficiera
satisfacíais	satisficiéramos
satisfacían	satisficierais
	satisficieran

Preterite	Future
satisfice	
satisficiste	satisfaré
satisfizo	satisfarás
satisficimos	satisfará
satisficisteis	satisfaremos
satisficieron	satisfaréis
	satisfarán

Perfect indicative	Conditional
he satisfecho	
has satisfecho	satisfaría
ha satisfecho	satisfarías
hemos satisfecho	satisfaría
habéis satisfecho	satisfaríamos
han satisfecho	satisfaríais
	satisfarían

Pluperfect indicative	Imperative
había satisfecho	–
habías satisfecho	satisfaz; satisface
había satisfecho	satisfaga
habíamos satisfecho	satisfagamos
habíais satisfecho	satisfaced
habían satisfecho	satisfagan

secar *to dry*

Gerund *secando*

Past participle *secado*

Present indicative	Present subjunctive
seco	seque
secas	seques
seca	seque
secamos	sequemos
secáis	sequéis
secan	sequen

Imperfect indicative	Imperfect subjunctive
secaba	secara
secabas	secaras
secaba	secara
secábamos	secáramos
secabais	secarais
secaban	secaran

Preterite	Future
sequé	secaré
secaste	secarás
secó	secará
secamos	secaremos
secasteis	secaréis
secaron	secarán

Perfect indicative	Conditional
he secado	
has secado	secaría
ha secado	secarías
hemos secado	secaría
habéis secado	secaríamos
han secado	secaríais
	secarían

Pluperfect indicative	Imperative
había secado	—
habías secado	seca
había secado	seque
habíamos secado	sequemos
habíais secado	secad
habían secado	sequen

seguir *to follow*

Gerund *siguiendo*

Past participle *seguido*

Present indicative	Present subjunctive
sigo	siga
sigues	sigas
sigue	siga
seguimos	sigamos
seguís	sigáis
siguen	sigan

Imperfect indicative	Imperfect subjunctive
seguía	siguiera
seguías	siguieras
seguía	siguiera
seguíamos	siguiéramos
seguíais	siguierais
seguían	siguieran

Preterite	Future
seguí	seguiré
seguiste	seguirás
siguió	seguirá
seguimos	seguiremos
seguisteis	seguiréis
siguieron	seguirán

Perfect indicative	Conditional
he seguido	
has seguido	seguiría
ha seguido	seguirías
hemos seguido	seguiría
habéis seguido	seguiríamos
han seguido	seguiríais
	seguirían

Pluperfect indicative	Imperative
había seguido	—
habías seguido	sigue
había seguido	siga
habíamos seguido	sigamos
habíais seguido	seguid
habían seguido	sigan

sentarse *to sit down*

Gerund *sentándose*

Past participle *sentado*

Present indicative	**Present subjunctive**
me siento	me siente
te sientas	te sientes
se sienta	se siente
nos sentamos	nos sentemos
os sentáis	os sentéis
se sientan	se sienten

Imperfect indicative	**Imperfect subjunctive**
me sentaba	me sentara
te sentabas	te sentaras
se sentaba	se sentara
nos sentábamos	nos sentáramos
os sentabais	os sentarais
se sentaban	se sentaran

Preterite	**Future**
me senté	me sentaré
te sentaste	te sentarás
se sentó	se sentará
nos sentamos	nos sentaremos
os sentasteis	os sentaréis
se sentaron	se sentarán

Perfect indicative	**Conditional**
me he sentado	me sentaría
te has sentado	te sentarías
se ha sentado	se sentaría
nos hemos sentado	nos sentaríamos
os habéis sentado	os sentaríais
se han sentado	se sentarían

Pluperfect indicative	**Imperative**
me había sentado	–
te habías sentado	siéntate
se había sentado	siéntese
nos habíamos sentado	sentémonos
os habíais sentado	sentaos
se habían sentado	siéntense

sentir *to feel*

Gerund *sintiendo*

Past participle *sentido*

Present indicative	**Present subjunctive**
siento	sienta
sientes	sientas
siente	sienta
sentimos	sintamos
sentís	sintáis
sienten	sientan

Imperfect indicative	**Imperfect subjunctive**
sentía	sintiera
sentías	sintieras
sentía	sintiera
sentíamos	sintiéramos
sentíais	sintierais
sentían	sintieran

Preterite	**Future**
sentí	sentiré
sentiste	sentirás
sintió	sentirá
sentimos	sentiremos
sentisteis	sentiréis
sintieron	sentirán

Perfect indicative	**Conditional**
he sentido	sentiría
has sentido	sentirías
ha sentido	sentiría
hemos sentido	sentiríamos
habéis sentido	sentiríais
han sentido	sentirían

Pluperfect indicative	**Imperative**
había sentido	–
habías sentido	siente
había sentido	sienta
habíamos sentido	sintamos
habíais sentido	sentid
habían sentido	sientan

ser *to be*

Gerund *siendo*

Past participle *sido*

Present indicative	Present subjunctive
soy	sea
eres	seas
es	sea
somos	seamos
sois	seáis
son	sean

Imperfect indicative	Imperfect subjunctive
era	fuera
eras	fueras
era	fuera
éramos	fuéramos
erais	fuerais
eran	fueran

Preterite	Future
fui	
fuiste	seré
fue	serás
fuimos	será
fuisteis	seremos
fueron	seréis
	serán

Perfect indicative	Conditional
he sido	
has sido	sería
ha sido	serías
hemos sido	sería
habéis sido	seríamos
han sido	seríais
	serían

Pluperfect indicative	Imperative
había sido	–
habías sido	sé
había sido	sea
habíamos sido	seamos
habíais sido	sed
habían sido	sean

servir *to serve*

Gerund *sirviendo*

Past participle *servido*

Present indicative	Present subjunctive
sirvo	sirva
sirves	sirvas
sirve	sirva
servimos	sirvamos
servís	sirváis
sirven	sirvan

Imperfect indicative	Imperfect subjunctive
servía	sirviera
servías	sirvieras
servía	sirviera
servíamos	sirviéramos
servíais	sirvierais
servían	sirvieran

Preterite	Future
serví	
serviste	serviré
sirvió	servirás
servimos	servirá
servisteis	serviremos
sirvieron	serviréis
	servirán

Perfect indicative	Conditional
he servido	
has servido	serviría
ha servido	servirías
hemos servido	serviría
habéis servido	serviríamos
han servido	serviríais
	servirían

Pluperfect indicative	Imperative
había servido	–
habías servido	sirve
había servido	sirva
habíamos servido	sirvamos
habíais servido	servid
habían servido	sirvan

situar *to situate*

Gerund *situando*

Past participle *situado*

Present indicative	Present subjunctive
sitúo	
sitúas	sitúe
sitúa	sitúes
situamos	sitúe
situáis	situemos
sitúan	situéis
	sitúen

Imperfect indicative	Imperfect subjunctive
situaba	
situabas	situara
situaba	situaras
situábamos	situara
situabais	situáramos
situaban	situarais
	situaran

Preterite	Future
situé	
situaste	situaré
situó	situarás
situamos	situará
situasteis	situaremos
situaron	situaréis
	situarán

Perfect indicative	Conditional
he situado	
has situado	situaría
ha situado	situarías
hemos situado	situaría
habéis situado	situaríamos
han situado	situaríais
	situarían

Pluperfect indicative	Imperative
había situado	–
habías situado	sitúa
había situado	sitúe
habíamos situado	situemos
habíais situado	situad
habían situado	sitúen

soler *to be accustomed to*

Gerund *soliendo*

Past participle *solido*

Present indicative	Present subjunctive
suelo	
sueles	suela
suele	suelas
solemos	suela
soléis	solamos
suelen	soláis
	suelan

Imperfect indicative	Imperfect subjunctive
solía	
solías	soliera
solía	solieras
solíamos	soliera
solíais	soliéramos
solían	solierais
	solieran

Preterite	Future
solí	
soliste	–
solió	–
solimos	–
solisteis	–
solieron	–
	–

Perfect indicative	Conditional
–	
–	–
–	–
–	–
–	–
–	–
	–

Pluperfect indicative	Imperative
–	–
–	–
–	–
–	–
–	–
–	–

soñar to dream

Gerund soñando

Past participle soñado

Present indicative	Present subjunctive
sueño	sueñe
sueñas	sueñes
sueña	sueñe
soñamos	soñemos
soñáis	soñéis
sueñan	sueñen

Imperfect indicative	Imperfect subjunctive
soñaba	soñara
soñabas	soñaras
soñaba	soñara
soñábamos	soñáramos
soñabais	soñarais
soñaban	soñaran

Preterite	Future
soñé	soñaré
soñaste	soñarás
soñó	soñará
soñamos	soñaremos
soñasteis	soñaréis
soñaron	soñarán

Perfect indicative	Conditional
he soñado	
has soñado	soñaría
ha soñado	soñarías
hemos soñado	soñaría
habéis soñado	soñaríamos
han soñado	soñaríais
	soñarían

Pluperfect indicative	Imperative
había soñado	–
habías soñado	sueña
había soñado	sueñe
habíamos soñado	soñemos
habíais soñado	soñad
habían soñado	sueñen

sonreír to smile

Gerund sonriendo

Past participle sonreído

Present indicative	Present subjunctive
sonrío	sonría
sonríes	sonrías
sonríe	sonría
sonreímos	sonriamos
sonreís	sonriáis
sonríen	sonrían

Imperfect indicative	Imperfect subjunctive
sonreía	sonriera
sonreías	sonrieras
sonreía	sonriera
sonreíamos	sonriéramos
sonreíais	sonrierais
sonreían	sonrieran

Preterite	Future
sonreí	sonreiré
sonreíste	sonreirás
sonrió	sonreirá
sonreímos	sonreiremos
sonreísteis	sonreiréis
sonrieron	sonreirán

Perfect indicative	Conditional
he sonreído	
has sonreído	sonreiría
ha sonreído	sonreirías
hemos sonreído	sonreiría
habéis sonreído	sonreiríamos
han sonreído	sonreiríais
	sonreirían

Pluperfect indicative	Imperative
había sonreído	–
habías sonreído	sonríe
había sonreído	sonría
habíamos sonreído	sonriamos
habíais sonreído	sonreíd
habían sonreído	sonrían

subir *to go up*

Gerund *subiendo*

Past participle *subido*

Present indicative	Present subjunctive
subo	
subes	suba
sube	subas
subimos	suba
subís	subamos
suben	subáis
	suban

Imperfect indicative	Imperfect subjunctive
subía	
subías	subiera
subía	subieras
subíamos	subiera
subíais	subiéramos
subían	subierais
	subieran

Preterite	Future
subí	
subiste	subiré
subió	subirás
subimos	subirá
subisteis	subiremos
subieron	subiréis
	subirán

Perfect indicative	Conditional
he subido	
has subido	subiría
ha subido	subirías
hemos subido	subiría
habéis subido	subiríamos
han subido	subiríais
	subirían

Pluperfect indicative	Imperative
había subido	–
habías subido	sube
había subido	suba
habíamos subido	subamos
habíais subido	subid
habían subido	suban

sugerir *to suggest*

Gerund *sugiriendo*

Past participle *sugerido*

Present indicative	Present subjunctive
sugiero	
sugieres	sugiera
sugiere	sugieras
sugerimos	sugiera
sugerís	sugiramos
sugieren	sugiráis
	sugieran

Imperfect indicative	Imperfect subjunctive
sugería	
sugerías	sugiriera
sugería	sugirieras
sugeríamos	sugiriera
sugeríais	sugiriéramos
sugerían	sugirierais
	sugirieran

Preterite	Future
sugerí	
sugeriste	sugeriré
sugirió	sugerirás
sugerimos	sugerirá
sugeristeis	sugeriremos
sugirieron	sugeriréis
	sugerirán

Perfect indicative	Conditional
he sugerido	
has sugerido	sugeriría
ha sugerido	sugerirías
hemos sugerido	sugeriría
habéis sugerido	sugeriríamos
han sugerido	sugeriríais
	sugerirían

Pluperfect indicative	Imperative
había sugerido	–
habías sugerido	sugiere
había sugerido	sugiera
habíamos sugerido	sugiramos
habíais sugerido	sugerid
habían sugerido	sugieran

tener *to have*

Gerund *teniendo*

Past participle *tenido*

Present indicative	Present subjunctive
tengo	
tienes	tenga
tiene	tengas
tenemos	tenga
tenéis	tengamos
tienen	tengáis
	tengan

Imperfect indicative	Imperfect subjunctive
tenía	
tenías	tuviera
tenía	tuvieras
teníamos	tuviera
teníais	tuviéramos
tenían	tuvierais
	tuvieran

Preterite	Future
tuve	tendré
tuviste	tendrás
tuvo	tendrá
tuvimos	tendremos
tuvisteis	tendréis
tuvieron	tendrán

Perfect indicative	Conditional
he tenido	
has tenido	tendría
ha tenido	tendrías
hemos tenido	tendría
habéis tenido	tendríamos
han tenido	tendríais
	tendrían

Pluperfect indicative	Imperative
había tenido	–
habías tenido	ten
había tenido	tenga
habíamos tenido	tengamos
habíais tenido	tened
habían tenido	tengan

terminar *to finish*

Gerund *terminando*

Past participle *terminado*

Present indicative	Present subjunctive
termino	
terminas	termine
termina	termines
terminamos	termine
termináis	terminemos
terminan	terminéis
	terminen

Imperfect indicative	Imperfect subjunctive
terminaba	
terminabas	terminara
terminaba	terminaras
terminábamos	terminara
terminabais	termináramos
terminaban	terminarais
	terminaran

Preterite	Future
terminé	terminaré
terminaste	terminarás
terminó	terminará
terminamos	terminaremos
terminasteis	terminaréis
terminaron	terminarán

Perfect indicative	Conditional
he terminado	
has terminado	terminaría
ha terminado	terminarías
hemos terminado	terminaría
habéis terminado	terminaríamos
han terminado	terminaríais
	terminarían

Pluperfect indicative	Imperative
había terminado	–
habías terminado	termina
había terminado	termine
habíamos terminado	terminemos
habíais terminado	terminad
habían terminado	terminen

tocar *to touch*

Gerund *tocando*

Past participle *tocado*

Present indicative	Present subjunctive
toco	toque
tocas	toques
toca	toque
tocamos	toquemos
tocáis	toquéis
tocan	toquen

Imperfect indicative	Imperfect subjunctive
tocaba	tocara
tocabas	tocaras
tocaba	tocara
tocábamos	tocáramos
tocabais	tocarais
tocaban	tocaran

Preterite	Future
toqué	tocaré
tocaste	tocarás
tocó	tocará
tocamos	tocaremos
tocasteis	tocaréis
tocaron	tocarán

Perfect indicative	Conditional
he tocado	
has tocado	tocaría
ha tocado	tocarías
hemos tocado	tocaría
habéis tocado	tocaríamos
han tocado	tocaríais
	tocarían

Pluperfect indicative	Imperative
había tocado	–
habías tocado	toca
había tocado	toque
habíamos tocado	toquemos
habíais tocado	tocad
habían tocado	toquen

tomar *to take*

Gerund *tomando*

Past participle *tomado*

Present indicative	Present subjunctive
tomo	tome
tomas	tomes
toma	tome
tomamos	tomemos
tomáis	toméis
toman	tomen

Imperfect indicative	Imperfect subjunctive
tomaba	tomara
tomabas	tomaras
tomaba	tomara
tomábamos	tomáramos
tomabais	tomarais
tomaban	tomaran

Preterite	Future
tomé	tomaré
tomaste	tomarás
tomó	tomará
tomamos	tomaremos
tomasteis	tomaréis
tomaron	tomarán

Perfect indicative	Conditional
he tomado	
has tomado	tomaría
ha tomado	tomarías
hemos tomado	tomaría
habéis tomado	tomaríamos
han tomado	tomaríais
	tomarían

Pluperfect indicative	Imperative
había tomado	–
habías tomado	toma
había tomado	tome
habíamos tomado	tomemos
habíais tomado	tomad
habían tomado	tomen

torcer *to twist*

Gerund *torciendo*

Past participle *torcido*

Present indicative	Present subjunctive
tuerzo	tuerza
tuerces	tuerzas
tuerce	tuerza
torcemos	torzamos
torcéis	torzáis
tuercen	tuerzan

Imperfect indicative	Imperfect subjunctive
torcía	torciera
torcías	torcieras
torcía	torciera
torcíamos	torciéramos
torcíais	torcierais
torcían	torcieran

Preterite	Future
torcí	torceré
torciste	torcerás
torció	torcerá
torcimos	torceremos
torcisteis	torceréis
torcieron	torcerán

Perfect indicative	Conditional
he torcido	torcería
has torcido	torcerías
ha torcido	torcería
hemos torcido	torceríamos
habéis torcido	torceríais
han torcido	torcerían

Pluperfect indicative	Imperative
había torcido	–
habías torcido	tuerce
había torcido	tuerza
habíamos torcido	torzamos
habíais torcido	torced
habían torcido	tuerzan

toser *to cough*

Gerund *tosiendo*

Past participle *tosido*

Present indicative	Present subjunctive
toso	tosa
toses	tosas
tose	tosa
tosemos	tosamos
toséis	tosáis
tosen	tosan

Imperfect indicative	Imperfect subjunctive
tosía	tosiera
tosías	tosieras
tosía	tosiera
tosíamos	tosiéramos
tosíais	tosierais
tosían	tosieran

Preterite	Future
tosí	toseré
tosiste	toserás
tosió	toserá
tosimos	toseremos
tosisteis	toseréis
tosieron	toserán

Perfect indicative	Conditional
he tosido	tosería
has tosido	toserías
ha tosido	tosería
hemos tosido	toseríamos
habéis tosido	toseríais
han tosido	toserían

Pluperfect indicative	Imperative
había tosido	–
habías tosido	tose
había tosido	tosa
habíamos tosido	tosamos
habíais tosido	tosed
habían tosido	tosan

trabajar *to work*

Gerund *trabajando*

Past participle *trabajado*

Present indicative	Present subjunctive
trabajo	trabaje
trabajas	trabajes
trabaja	trabaje
trabajamos	trabajemos
trabajáis	trabajéis
trabajan	trabajen

Imperfect indicative	Imperfect subjunctive
trabajaba	trabajara
trabajabas	trabajaras
trabajaba	trabajara
trabajábamos	trabajáramos
trabajabais	trabajarais
trabajaban	trabajaran

Preterite	Future
trabajé	trabajaré
trabajaste	trabajarás
trabajó	trabajará
trabajamos	trabajaremos
trabajasteis	trabajaréis
trabajaron	trabajarán

Perfect indicative	Conditional
he trabajado	trabajaría
has trabajado	trabajarías
ha trabajado	trabajaría
hemos trabajado	trabajaríamos
habéis trabajado	trabajaríais
han trabajado	trabajarían

Pluperfect indicative	Imperative
había trabajado	–
habías trabajado	trabaja
había trabajado	trabaje
habíamos trabajado	trabajemos
habíais trabajado	trabajad
habían trabajado	trabajen

traducir *to translate*

Gerund *traduciendo*

Past participle *traducido*

Present indicative	Present subjunctive
traduzco	traduzca
traduces	traduzcas
traduce	traduzca
traducimos	traduzcamos
traducís	traduzcáis
traducen	traduzcan

Imperfect indicative	Imperfect subjunctive
traducía	tradujera
traducías	tradujeras
traducía	tradujera
traducíamos	tradujéramos
traducíais	tradujerais
traducían	tradujeran

Preterite	Future
traduje	traduciré
tradujiste	traducirás
tradujo	traducirá
tradujimos	traduciremos
tradujisteis	traduciréis
tradujeron	traducirán

Perfect indicative	Conditional
he traducido	traduciría
has traducido	traducirías
ha traducido	traduciría
hemos traducido	traduciríamos
habéis traducido	traduciríais
han traducido	traducirían

Pluperfect indicative	Imperative
había traducido	–
habías traducido	traduce
había traducido	traduzca
habíamos traducido	traduzcamos
habíais traducido	traducid
habían traducido	traduzcan

traer *to bring*

Gerund *trayendo*

Past participle *traído*

Present indicative	Present subjunctive
traigo	traiga
traes	traigas
trae	traiga
traemos	traigamos
traéis	traigáis
traen	traigan

Imperfect indicative	Imperfect subjunctive
traía	trajera
traías	trajeras
traía	trajera
traíamos	trajéramos
traíais	trajerais
traían	trajeran

Preterite	Future
traje	traeré
trajiste	traerás
trajo	traerá
trajimos	traeremos
trajisteis	traeréis
trajeron	traerán

Perfect indicative	Conditional
he traído	traería
has traído	traerías
ha traído	traería
hemos traído	traeríamos
habéis traído	traeríais
han traído	traerían

Pluperfect indicative	Imperative
había traído	–
habías traído	trae
había traído	traiga
habíamos traído	traigamos
habíais traído	traed
habían traído	traigan

tropezar *to stumble*

Gerund *tropezando*

Past participle *tropezado*

Present indicative	Present subjunctive
tropiezo	tropiece
tropiezas	tropieces
tropieza	tropiece
tropezamos	tropecemos
tropezáis	tropecéis
tropiezan	tropiecen

Imperfect indicative	Imperfect subjunctive
tropezaba	tropezara
tropezabas	tropezaras
tropezaba	tropezara
tropezábamos	tropezáramos
tropezabais	tropezarais
tropezaban	tropezaran

Preterite	Future
tropecé	tropezaré
tropezaste	tropezarás
tropezó	tropezará
tropezamos	tropezaremos
tropezasteis	tropezaréis
tropezaron	tropezarán

Perfect indicative	Conditional
he tropezado	tropezaría
has tropezado	tropezarías
ha tropezado	tropezaría
hemos tropezado	tropezaríamos
habéis tropezado	tropezaríais
han tropezado	tropezarían

Pluperfect indicative	Imperative
había tropezado	–
habías tropezado	tropieza
había tropezado	tropiece
habíamos tropezado	tropecemos
habíais tropezado	tropezad
habían tropezado	tropiecen

vaciar *to empty*

Gerund *vaciando*

Past participle *vaciado*

Present indicative	Present subjunctive
vacío	
vacías	vacíe
vacía	vacíes
vaciamos	vacíe
vaciáis	vaciemos
vacían	vaciéis
	vacíen

Imperfect indicative	Imperfect subjunctive
vaciaba	
vaciabas	vaciara
vaciaba	vaciaras
vaciábamos	vaciara
vaciabais	vaciáramos
vaciaban	vaciarais
	vaciaran

Preterite	Future
vacié	
vaciaste	vaciaré
vació	vaciarás
vaciamos	vaciará
vaciasteis	vaciaremos
vaciaron	vaciaréis
	vaciarán

Perfect indicative	Conditional
he vaciado	
has vaciado	vaciaría
ha vaciado	vaciarías
hemos vaciado	vaciaría
habéis vaciado	vaciaríamos
han vaciado	vaciaríais
	vaciarían

Pluperfect indicative	Imperative
había vaciado	–
habías vaciado	vacía
había vaciado	vacíe
habíamos vaciado	vaciemos
habíais vaciado	vaciad
habían vaciado	vacíen

valer *to be worth*

Gerund *valiendo*

Past participle *valido*

Present indicative	Present subjunctive
valgo	
vales	valga
vale	valgas
valemos	valga
valéis	valgamos
valen	valgáis
	valgan

Imperfect indicative	Imperfect subjunctive
valía	
valías	valiera
valía	valieras
valíamos	valiera
valíais	valiéramos
valían	valierais
	valieran

Preterite	Future
valí	
valiste	valdré
valió	valdrás
valimos	valdrá
valisteis	valdremos
valieron	valdréis
	valdrán

Perfect indicative	Conditional
he valido	
has valido	valdría
ha valido	valdrías
hemos valido	valdría
habéis valido	valdríamos
han valido	valdríais
	valdrían

Pluperfect indicative	Imperative
había valido	–
habías valido	vale
había valido	valga
habíamos valido	valgamos
habíais valido	valed
habían valido	valgan

vencer *to win*

Gerund *venciendo*

Past participle *vencido*

Present indicative	Present subjunctive
venzo	venza
vences	venzas
vence	venza
vencemos	venzamos
vencéis	venzáis
vencen	venzan

Imperfect indicative	Imperfect subjunctive
vencía	venciera
vencías	vencieras
vencía	venciera
vencíamos	venciéramos
vencíais	vencierais
vencían	vencieran

Preterite	Future
vencí	venceré
venciste	vencerás
venció	vencerá
vencimos	venceremos
vencisteis	venceréis
vencieron	vencerán

Perfect indicative	Conditional
he vencido	vencería
has vencido	vencerías
ha vencido	vencería
hemos vencido	venceríamos
habéis vencido	venceríais
han vencido	vencerían

Pluperfect indicative	Imperative
había vencido	–
habías vencido	vence
había vencido	venza
habíamos vencido	venzamos
habíais vencido	venced
habían vencido	venzan

vender *to sell*

Gerund *vendiendo*

Past participle *vendido*

Present indicative	Present subjunctive
vendo	venda
vendes	vendas
vende	venda
vendemos	vendamos
vendéis	vendáis
venden	vendan

Imperfect indicative	Imperfect subjunctive
vendía	vendiera
vendías	vendieras
vendía	vendiera
vendíamos	vendiéramos
vendíais	vendierais
vendían	vendieran

Preterite	Future
vendí	venderé
vendiste	venderás
vendió	venderá
vendimos	venderemos
vendisteis	venderéis
vendieron	venderán

Perfect indicative	Conditional
he vendido	vendería
has vendido	venderías
ha vendido	vendería
hemos vendido	venderíamos
habéis vendido	venderíais
han vendido	venderían

Pluperfect indicative	Imperative
había vendido	–
habías vendido	vende
había vendido	venda
habíamos vendido	vendamos
habíais vendido	vended
habían vendido	vendan

venir *to come*

Gerund *viniendo*

Past participle *venido*

Present indicative	**Present subjunctive**
vengo	venga
vienes	vengas
viene	venga
venimos	vengamos
venís	vengáis
vienen	vengan

Imperfect indicative	**Imperfect subjunctive**
venía	viniera
venías	vinieras
venía	viniera
veníamos	viniéramos
veníais	vinierais
venían	vinieran

Preterite	**Future**
vine	vendré
viniste	vendrás
vino	vendrá
vinimos	vendremos
vinisteis	vendréis
vinieron	vendrán

Perfect indicative	**Conditional**
he venido	vendría
has venido	vendrías
ha venido	vendría
hemos venido	vendríamos
habéis venido	vendríais
han venido	vendrían

Pluperfect indicative	**Imperative**
había venido	–
habías venido	ven
había venido	venga
habíamos venido	vengamos
habíais venido	venid
habían venido	vengan

ver *to see*

Gerund *viendo*

Past participle *visto*

Present indicative	**Present subjunctive**
veo	vea
ves	veas
ve	vea
vemos	veamos
veis	veáis
ven	vean

Imperfect indicative	**Imperfect subjunctive**
veía	viera
veías	vieras
veía	viera
veíamos	viéramos
veíais	vierais
veían	vieran

Preterite	**Future**
vi	veré
viste	verás
vio	verá
vimos	veremos
visteis	veréis
vieron	verán

Perfect indicative	**Conditional**
he visto	vería
has visto	verías
ha visto	vería
hemos visto	veríamos
habéis visto	veríais
han visto	verían

Pluperfect indicative	**Imperative**
había visto	–
habías visto	ve
había visto	vea
habíamos visto	veamos
habíais visto	ved
habían visto	vean

vestirse *to get dressed*

Gerund *vistiéndose*

Past participle *vestido*

Present indicative	Present subjunctive
me visto	me vista
te vistes	te vistas
se viste	se vista
nos vestimos	nos vistamos
os vestís	os vistáis
se visten	se vistan

Imperfect indicative	Imperfect subjunctive
me vestía	me vistiera
te vestías	te vistieras
se vestía	se vistiera
nos vestíamos	nos vistiéramos
os vestíais	os vistierais
se vestían	se vistieran

Preterite	Future
me vestí	me vestiré
te vestiste	te vestirás
se vistió	se vestirá
nos vestimos	nos vestiremos
os vestisteis	os vestiréis
se vistieron	se vestirán

Perfect indicative	Conditional
me he vestido	me vestiría
te has vestido	te vestirías
se ha vestido	se vestiría
nos hemos vestido	nos vestiríamos
os habéis vestido	os vestiríais
se han vestido	se vestirían

Pluperfect indicative	Imperative
me había vestido	–
te habías vestido	vístete
se había vestido	vístase
nos habíamos vestido	vistámonos
os habíais vestido	vestíos
se habían vestido	vístanse

viajar *to travel*

Gerund *viajando*

Past participle *viajado*

Present indicative	Present subjunctive
viajo	viaje
viajas	viajes
viaja	viaje
viajamos	viajemos
viajáis	viajéis
viajan	viajen

Imperfect indicative	Imperfect subjunctive
viajaba	viajara
viajabas	viajaras
viajaba	viajara
viajábamos	viajáramos
viajabais	viajarais
viajaban	viajaran

Preterite	Future
viajé	viajaré
viajaste	viajarás
viajó	viajará
viajamos	viajaremos
viajasteis	viajaréis
viajaron	viajarán

Perfect indicative	Conditional
he viajado	viajaría
has viajado	viajarías
ha viajado	viajaría
hemos viajado	viajaríamos
habéis viajado	viajaríais
han viajado	viajarían

Pluperfect indicative	Imperative
había viajado	–
habías viajado	viaja
había viajado	viaje
habíamos viajado	viajemos
habíais viajado	viajad
habían viajado	viajen

vivir *to live*

Gerund *viviendo*

Past participle *vivido*

Present indicative	Present subjunctive
vivo	viva
vives	vivas
vive	viva
vivimos	vivamos
vivís	viváis
viven	vivan

Imperfect indicative	Imperfect subjunctive
vivía	viviera
vivías	vivieras
vivía	viviera
vivíamos	viviéramos
vivíais	vivierais
vivían	vivieran

Preterite	Future
viví	viviré
viviste	vivirás
vivió	vivirá
vivimos	viviremos
vivisteis	viviréis
vivieron	vivirán

Perfect indicative	Conditional
he vivido	viviría
has vivido	vivirías
ha vivido	viviría
hemos vivido	viviríamos
habéis vivido	viviríais
han vivido	vivirían

Pluperfect indicative	Imperative
había vivido	–
habías vivido	vive
había vivido	viva
habíamos vivido	vivamos
habíais vivido	vivid
habían vivido	vivan

volar *to fly*

Gerund *volando*

Past participle *volado*

Present indicative	Present subjunctive
vuelo	vuele
vuelas	vueles
vuela	vuele
volamos	volemos
voláis	voléis
vuelan	vuelen

Imperfect indicative	Imperfect subjunctive
volaba	volara
volabas	volaras
volaba	volara
volábamos	voláramos
volabais	volarais
volaban	volaran

Preterite	Future
volé	volaré
volaste	volarás
voló	volará
volamos	volaremos
volasteis	volaréis
volaron	volarán

Perfect indicative	Conditional
he volado	volaría
has volado	volarías
ha volado	volaría
hemos volado	volaríamos
habéis volado	volaríais
han volado	volarían

Pluperfect indicative	Imperative
había volado	–
habías volado	vuela
había volado	vuele
habíamos volado	volemos
habíais volado	volad
habían volado	vuelen

volver *to return*

Gerund *volviendo*

Past participle *vuelto*

Present indicative	Present subjunctive
vvuelvo	vuelva
vuelves	vuelvas
vuelve	vuelva
volvemos	volvamos
volvéis	volváis
vuelven	vuelvan

Imperfect indicative	Imperfect subjunctive
volvía	volviera
volvías	volvieras
volvía	volviera
volvíamos	volviéramos
volvíais	volvierais
volvían	volvieran

Preterite	Future
volví	volveré
volviste	volverás
volvió	volverá
volvimos	volveremos
volvisteis	volveréis
volvieron	volverán

Perfect indicative	Conditional
he vuelto	volvería
has vuelto	volverías
ha vuelto	volvería
hemos vuelto	volveríamos
habéis vuelto	volveríais
han vuelto	volverían

Pluperfect indicative	Imperative
había vuelto	–
habías vuelto	vuelve
había vuelto	vuelva
habíamos vuelto	volvamos
habíais vuelto	volved
habían vuelto	vuelvan

yacer *to lie*

Gerund *yaciendo*

Past participle *yacido*

Present indicative	Present subjunctive
yaczco; yazgo; yago	yazca; yazga; yaga
yaces	yazcas; yazgas; yagas
yace	yazca; yazga; yaga
yacemos	yazcamos; yazgamos; yagamos
yacéis	yazcáis; yazgáis; yagáis
yacen	yazcan; yazgan; yagan

Imperfect indicative	Imperfect subjunctive
yacía	yaciera
yacías	yacieras
yacía	yaciera
yacíamos	yaciéramos
yacíais	yacierais
yacían	yacieran

Preterite	Future
yací	yaceré
yaciste	yacerás
yació	yacerá
yacimos	yaceremos
yacisteis	yaceréis
yacieron	yacerán

Perfect indicative	Conditional
he yacido	yacería
has yacido	yacerías
ha yacido	yacería
hemos yacido	yaceríamos
habéis yacido	yaceríais
han yacido	yacerían

Pluperfect indicative	Imperative
había yacido	–
habías yacido	yace; yaz
había yacido	yazca; yazga; yaga
habíamos yacido	yazcamos; yazgamos; yagamos
habíais yacido	yaced
habían yacido	yazcan; yazgan; yagan

Irregular English verbs

Present tense	Past tense	Past participle	Present tense	Past tense	Past participle
arise	arose	arisen	eat	ate	eaten
awake	awoke	awaked, awoke	fall	fell	fallen
be [I am, you/			feed	fed	fed
we/they are,			feel	felt	felt
he/she/it is,			fight	fought	fought
gerund being]	was, were	been	find	found	found
bear	bore	borne	flee	fled	fled
beat	beat	beaten	fling	flung	flung
become	became	become	fly [he/she/		
begin	began	begun	it flies]	flew	flown
behold	beheld	beheld	forbid	forbade	forbidden
bend	bent	bent	forecast	forecast	forecast
beseech	besought,	besought,	forget	forgot	forgotten
	beseeched	beseeched	forgive	forgave	forgiven
beset	beset	beset	forsake	forsook	forsaken
bet	bet, betted	bet, betted	forsee	foresaw	foreseen
bid	bade, bid	bid, bidden	freeze	froze	frozen
bite	bit	bitten	get	got	got, (US)
bleed	bled	bled			gotten
bless	blessed, blest	blessed, blest	give	gave	given
blow	blew	blown	go [he/she/		
break	broke	broken	it goes]	went	gone
breed	bred	bred	grind	ground	ground
bring	brought	brought	grow	grew	grown
build	built	built	hang	hung, hanged	hung, hanged
burn	burnt,	burnt, burned	have [I/you/we/		
	burned		they have, he/		
burst	burst	burst	she/it has,		
buy	bought	bought	gerund having]	had	had
can	could	(been able)	hear	heard	heard
cast	cast	cast	hide	hid	hidden
catch	caught	caught	hit	hit	hit
choose	chose	chosen	hold	held	held
cling	clung	clung	hurt	hurt	hurt
come	came	come	keep	kept	kept
cost	cost	cost	kneel	knelt	knelt
creep	crept	crept	know	knew	known
cut	cut	cut	lay	laid	laid
deal	dealt	dealt	lead	led	led
dig	dug	dug	lean	leant, leaned	leant, leaned
do [he/she/			leap	leapt, leaped	leapt, leaped
it does]	did	done	learn	learnt, learned	learnt, learned
draw	drew	drawn	leave	left	left
dream	dreamed,	dreamed,	lend	lent	lent
	dreamt	dreamt	let	let	let
drink	drank	drunk	lie [gerund lying]	lay	lain
drive	drove	driven	light	lighted, lit	lighted, lit
dwell	dwelt,	dwelt, dwelled	lose	lost	lost
	dwelled		make	made	made

Present tense	Past tense	Past participle	Present tense	Past tense	Past participle
may	might	—	spend	spent	spent
mean	meant	meant	spill	spilt, spilled	spilt, spilled
meet	met	met	spin	spun	spun
mistake	mistook	mistaken	spit	spat	spat
mow	mowed	mowed, mown	split	split	split
must	(had to)	(had to)	spoil	spoilt	spoilt
overcome	overcame	overcome	spread	spread	spread
pay	paid	paid	spring	sprang	sprung
put	put	put	stand	stood	stood
quit	quit, quitted	quit, quitted	steal	stole	stolen
read	read	read	stick	stuck	stuck
rid	rid	rid	sting	stung	stung
ride	rode	ridden	stink	stank	stunk
ring	rang	rung	stride	strode	stridden
rise	rose	risen	strike	struck	struck
run	ran	run	strive	strove	striven
saw	sawed	sawn, sawed	swear	swore	sworn
say	said	said	sweep	swept	swept
see	saw	seen	swell	swelled	swelled,
seek	sought	sought			swollen
sell	sold	sold	swim	swam	swum
send	sent	sent	swing	swung	swung
set	set	set	take	took	taken
sew	sewed	sewn, sewed	teach	taught	taught
shake	shook	shaken	tear	tore	torn
shall	should	—	tell	told	told
shear	sheared	sheared, shorn	think	thought	thought
shed	shed	shed	throw	threw	thrown
shine	shone	shone	thrust	thrust	thrust
shoot	shot	shot	tread	trod	trodden, trod
show	showed	shown, showed	understand	understood	understood
shrink	shrank	shrunk	upset	upset	upset
shut	shut	shut	wake	woke	woken
sing	sang	sung	wear	wore	worn
sink	sank	sunk	weave	wove,	wove, woven
sit	sat	sat	wed	wedded	wed, wedded
slay	slew	slain	weep	wept	wept
sleep	slept	slept	win	won	won
slide	slid	slid	wind	wound	wound
sling	slung	slung	withdraw	withdrew	withdrawn
smell	smelt, smelled	smelt, smelled	withhold	withheld	withheld
sow	sowed	sown, sowed	withstand	withstood	withstood
speak	spoke	spoken	wring	wrung	wrung
speed	sped, speeded	sped, speeded	write	wrote	written
spell	spelt, spelled	spelt, spelled			